FEMINISM IN LITERATURE

A Gale Critical Companion

FEMINISM IN LITERATURE

A Gale Critical Companion

Volume 2: 19th Century, Topics & Authors (A-B)

Foreword by *Amy Hudock, Ph.D.*
University of South Carolina

Jessica Bomarito, Jeffrey W. Hunter, Project Editors

Detroit • New York • San Francisco • San Diego • New Haven, Conn. • Waterville, Maine • London • Munich

Feminism in Literature, Vol. 2

Project Editors
Jessica Bomarito, Jeffrey W. Hunter

Editorial
Tom Burns, Jenny Cromie, Kathy D. Darrow, Michelle Kazensky, Jelena O. Krstović, Michael L. LaBlanc, Julie Landelius, Michelle Lee, Allison McClintic Marion, Ellen McGeagh, Joseph Palmisano, Linda Pavlovski, James E. Person Jr., Thomas J. Schoenberg, Marie Toft, Lawrence J. Trudeau, Russel Whitaker

Indexing Services
Synapse, the Knowledge Link Corporation

Permissions
Emma Hull, Lori Hines, Shalice Shah-Caldwell

Imaging and Multimedia
Lezlie Light, Daniel Newell, Kelly A. Quin

Product Design
Michael Logusz, Pamela Galbreath

Composition and Electronic Capture
Carolyn Roney

Manufacturing
Rhonda Williams

Product Manager
Janet Witalec

For more information, contact
Thomson Gale
27500 Drake Rd.
Farmington Hills, MI 48331-3535
Or you can visit our internet site at
http://www.gale.com

LIBRARY OF CONGRESS CATALOGING-IN-PUBLICATION DATA

Feminism in literature : a Gale critical companion / foreword by Amy Hudock ; Jessica Bomarito, project editor, Jeffrey W. Hunter, project editor.
p. cm. -- (Gale critical companion collection)
Includes bibliographical references and index.
ISBN 0-7876-7573-3 (set hardcover : alk. paper) -- ISBN 0-7876-7574-1 (vol 1) -- ISBN 0-7876-7575-X (vol 2) -- ISBN 0-7876-7576-8 (vol 3) -- ISBN 0-7876-9115-1 (vol 4) -- ISBN 0-7876-9116-X (vol 5) -- ISBN 0-7876-9065-1 (vol 6)
1. Literature--Women authors--History and criticism. 2. Women authors--Biography. 3. Women--History. I. Bomarito, Jessica, 1975- II. Hunter, Jeffrey W., 1966- III. Series.
PN471.F43 2005
809'.89287--dc22
2004017989

Printed in the United States of America
10 9 8 7 6 5 4 3 2

CONTENTS

VOLUME 2

VOLUME 3

VOLUME 4

VOLUME 5

VOLUME 6

FOREWORD

When I was a girl, I would go to the library with my class, and all the girls would run to the Nancy Drew books, while the boys would head toward the Hardy Boys books—each group drawn to heroes that resembled themselves. Yet, when I entered formal literary studies in high school and college, I was told that I should not read so much in the girls' section any more, that the boys' section held books that were more literary, more universal, and more valuable. Teachers and professors told me this in such seemingly objective language that I never questioned it. At the time, the literary canon was built on a model of scarcity that claimed that only a few literary works could attain "greatness"—defined according to a supposed objective set of aesthetic criteria that more often than not excluded women authors. New Criticism, a way of reading texts that focuses on a poem, short story, or novel as an autonomous artistic production without connections to the historical and social conditions out of which it came, ruled my classrooms, making the author's gender ostensibly irrelevant. Masculine experience was coded as universal, while women's experience was particular. Overall, I had no reason to question the values I had been taught, until I encountered feminism.

Feminism, sometimes put in the plural *feminisms*, is a loose confederation of social, political, spiritual, and intellectual movements that places women and gender at the center of inquiry with the goal of social justice. When people in the United States speak of feminism, they are often referring to the mainstream liberal feminism that grew out of the relationship between grassroots civil rights movements of the 1960s and 1970s and these movements' entrance into the academy through the creation of Women's Studies as an interdisciplinary program of study in many colleges and universities. Mainstream liberal feminism helped many women achieve more equity in pay and access to a wider range of careers while it also transformed many academic disciplines to reflect women's achievements. However, liberal feminism quickly came under attack as largely a movement of white, heterosexual, university-educated, middle-class women who were simply trying to gain access to the same privileges that white, middle-class men enjoyed, and who assumed their experiences were the norm for a mythical universal "woman." Liberal feminists have also been critiqued for echoing the patriarchal devaluation of traditional women's nurturing work in their efforts to encourage women to pursue traditional men's work, for creating a false opposition between work and home, and for creating the superwoman stereotype that can cause women to believe they have failed if they do not achieve the perfect balance of work and home lives. Other feminisms developed representing other women and other modes of thought: Marxist, psychoanalytic, social/radical, lesbian, trans- and bi-sexual, black womanist, first nations, chicana, nonwestern, postcolonial, and approaches that even question the use of "woman" as a unifying signifier in the first place. As Women's Studies and these many feminims gained power and credibility in the academy, their presence forced the literary establishment to question its methodology, definitions, structures, philosophies, aesthetics, and visions as well at to alter the curriculum to reflect women's achievements.

Once I learned from Women's Studies that women mattered in the academy, I began exploring women in my own field of literary studies. Since male-authored texts were often the only works taught in my classes, I began to explore the images of women as constructed by male authors. Many other women writers also began their critique of women's place in society studying similar sites of representation. Mary Wollstonecraft's *A Vindication of the Rights of Women* (1792), Margaret Fuller's *Woman in the Nineteenth Century* (1845), Simone de Beauvoir's *The Second Sex* (1949), and Kate Millet's *Sexual Politics* (1969) explored how published images of women can serve as a means of social manipulation and control—a type of gender propaganda.

However, I began to find, as did others, that looking at women largely through male eyes did not do enough to reclaim women's voices and did not recognize women's agency in creating images of themselves. In *Sexual/Textual Politics* (1985), Toril Moi further questioned the limited natures of these early critical readings, even when including both male and female authors. She argued that reading literature for the accuracy of images of women led critics into assuming their own sense of reality as universal: "If the women in the book feel real to me, then the book is good." This kind of criticism never develops or changes, she argued, because it looks for the same elements repetitively, just in new texts. Also, she was disturbed by its focus on content rather than on how the text is written—the form, language, and literary elements. Moi and others argued for the development of new feminist critical methods.

However, examination of images of women over time has been fruitful. It has shown us that representation of women changes as historical forces change, that we must examine the historical influences on the creators of literary texts to understand the images they manufacture, and that we cannot assume that these images of women are universal and somehow separate from political and culture forces. These early explorations of woman as image also led to discussions of femininity as image, not biologically but culturally defined, thus allowing analysis of the feminine ideal as separate from real women. This separation of biological sex and socially constructed gender laid the foundation for the later work of Judith Butler in *Gender Trouble: Feminism and the Subversion of Identity* (1990) and Marjorie Garber's *Vested Interests: Cross Dressing and Cultural Anxiety* (1992) in questioning what IS this thing we call "woman." These critics argued that gender is a social construct, a performance that can be learned by people who are biologically male, female, or transgendered, and therefore should not be used as the only essential connecting element in feminist studies. The study of woman and gender as image then has contributed much to feminist literary studies.

Tired of reading almost exclusively texts by men and a small emerging canon of women writers, I wanted to expand my understanding of writing by women. As a new Ph. D. student at the University of South Carolina in 1989, I walked up the stairs into the Women's Studies program and asked the first person I saw one question: were there any nineteenth-century American women writers who are worth reading? I had recently been told there were not, but I was no longer satisfied with this answer. And I found I was right to be skeptical. The woman I met at the top of those stairs handed me a thick book and said, "Go home and read this. Then you tell me if there were any nineteenth-century American women writers who are worth reading." So, I did. The book was the *Norton Anthology of Literature by Women* (1985), and once I had read it, I came back to the office at the top of the stairs and asked, "What more do you have?" My search for literary women began here, and this journey into new terrain parallels the development of the relationship between western feminism and literary studies.

In *A Room of Her Own* (1929), Virginia Woolf asks the same questions. She sits, looking at her bookshelves, thinking about the women writers who are there, and the ones who are not, and she calls for a reclaiming and celebrating of lost women artists. Other writers answered her call. Patricia Meyer Spacks's *The Female Imagination: A Literary and Psychological Investigation of Women's Writing* (1972), Ellen Moers's *Literary Women: The Great Writers* (1976), Elaine Showalter's *A Literature of Their Own: British Women Novelists from Brontë to Lessing* (1977), and Sandra Gilbert and Susan Gubar's *The Madwoman in the Attic* (1979) are a few of the early critical studies that explored the possibility of a tradition in women's literature.

While each of these influential and important books has different goals, methods, and theories, they share the attempt to establish a tradition in women's literature, a vital means through which marginalized groups establish a community identity and move from invisibility to visibility. These literary scholars and others worked to republish and reclaim women authors, expanding the number and types of women-authored texts available to readers, students, and scholars.

Yet, I began to notice that tradition formation presented some problems. As Marjorie Stone pointed out in her essay "The Search for a Lost Atlantis" (2003), the search for women's traditions in language and literature has been envisioned as the quest for a lost continent, a mythical motherland, similar to the lost but hopefully recoverable Atlantis. Such a quest tends to search for similarities among writers to attempt to prove the tradition existed, but this can sometimes obscure the differences among women writers. Looking to establish a tradition can also shape what is actually "found": only texts that fit that tradition. Traditions are defined by what is left in and what is left out, and the grand narratives of tradition formation as constructed in the early phases of feminist literary criticism inadvertently mirrored the exclusionary structures of the canon they were revising.

Some critics began discussing a women's tradition, a lost motherland of language, in not only what was written but also how it was written: in a female language or *ecriture feminine*. Feminist thinkers writing in France such as Hélène Cixous, Julia Kristeva, and Luce Irigaray argued that gender shapes language and that language shapes gender. Basing their ideas on those of psychoanalyst Jacques Lacan, they argued that pre-oedipal language—the original mother language—was lost when the law and language of the fathers asserted itself. While each of these writers explored this language differently, they all rewrote and revisioned how we might talk about literature, thus offering us new models for scholarship. However, as Alicia Ostriker argued in her essay, "Notes on 'Listen'" (2003), for the most part, women teach children language at home and at school. So, she questioned, is language really male and the "the language of the father," or is it the formal discourse of the academy that is male? Ostriker and others question the primacy of the father as the main social/language influence in these discussions. Other critics attacked what came to be known as "French Feminism" for its ahistorical, essentializing approach to finding a women's tradition in language. Despite its problems, it offered much to the general understanding of gender and language and helped us imagine new possible forms for scholarship.

The idea that language might be gendered itself raised questions about how aesthetic judgement, defined in language, might also be gendered. Problems with how to judge what is "good" literature also arose, and feminist literary critics were accused of imposing a limited standard because much of what was being recovered looked the same in form as the traditional male canon, only written by women. Early recovered texts tended to highlight women in opposition to family, holding more modern liberal political views, and living nontraditional lives. If a text was "feminist" enough, it was included. Often times, this approach valued content over form, and the forms that were included did not differ much from the canon they were reacting against. These critics were still using the model of scarcity with a similar set of critical lens through which to judge texts worthy of inclusion. However, because later scholars started creating different critical lenses through which to view texts does not mean we need to perceive difference as inequality. Rather, texts that differ greatly began to be valued equally for different reasons. In order to do this, critics had to forfeit their tendency to place literary forms on a hierarchical model that allows only one at the apex. Instead, they exchanged the structure of value from one pyramid with a few writers at the apex for one with multiple high points, a model which celebrates a diversity of voices, styles, and forms. The model functioning in many past critical dialogues allowed for little diversity, privileging one type of literature—western, male, linear, logical, structured according to an accepted formula—over others—created by women and men who fail to fit the formula, and, thus, are judged not worthy. Creating hierarchies of value which privilege one discourse, predominantly Anglo male, over another, largely female, non-Anglo, and nonwestern undermines the supposed "impartiality" of critical standards. Breaking down the structure of canon formation that looks for the "great men" and "great women" of literature and instead studies what was actually written, then judging it on its own terms, has the potential for less bias. Challenging the existence of the canon itself allows more writers to be read and heard; perhaps we can base our understanding of literature not on a model of scarcity where only a few great ones are allowed at the top of the one peak, but where there are multiple peaks.

Another problem is that the tradition that was being recovered tended to look most like the critics who were establishing it. Barbara Smith's essay "Toward a Black Feminist Criticism" (1977) and bell hooks's *Ain't I a Woman? Black Women and Feminism* (1981) argued that academic feminism focused on the lives, conditions, histories, and texts of white, middle-class, educated women. Such writers revealed how the same methods of canon formation that excluded women were now being used by white feminists to exclude women of color. They also highlighted the silencing of black women by white women through the assumption that white womanhood was the norm. These writers and others changed the quest for one lost Atlantis to a quest for many lost continents as anthologies of African American, Chicana, Native American, Asian, Jewish, lesbian, mothers, and many more women writers grouped together by identity began to emerge. *This Bridge Called My Back: Writings by Radical Women of Color* (1981), edited by Ana Castillo and Cherríe Moraga, is one such collection. Yet, while these and other writers looked for new traditions of women's writing by the identity politics of the 1980s and 1990s, they were still imposing the same structures of tradition formation on new groups of women writers, still looking for the lost Atlantis.

Western feminist critics also began looking for the lost Atlantis on a global scale. Critiques from non-western critics and writers about their exclusion from feminist literary histories that claimed to represent world feminisms is bringing about the same pattern of starting with an exploration of image, moving to recovery of writers and traditions, then a questioning of recovery efforts that we have seen before. Now, however, all these stages are occurring at the once. For example, American feminist critics are still attempting to make global primary texts available in English so they can be studied and included at the same time they are being critiqued for doing so. Chandra Talpade Mohanty in "Under Western Eyes: Feminist Scholarship and Colonial Discourses" (1991) argues that systems of oppression do not affect us all equally, and to isolate gender as the primary source of oppression ignores the differing and complex webs of oppressions non-western women face. Western tendencies to view non-western women as suffering from a totalizing and undifferentiated oppression similar to their own "universal" female oppression cause feminist literary critics to impose structures of meaning onto non-western texts that fail to reflect the actual cultures and experiences of the writers. Therefore, to simply add the women from non-western literary traditions into existing western timelines, categories, and periodizations may not fully reflect the complexity of non-western writing. In fact, critics such as Gayatri Chakravorty Spivak, Ann DuCille, and Teresa Ebert argue post-colonial and transnational critics have created yet another master narrative that must be challenged. Yet, before the westernness of this new, transnational narrative can be addressed, critics need to be able read, discuss, and share the global texts that are now being translated and published before we can do anything else; therefore, this reclaiming and celebration of a global women's tradition is a necessary step in the process of transforming the very foundations of western feminist literary criticism. But it is only an early step in the continual speak, react, revise pattern of feminist scholarship.

Some critics argue that the ultimate goal of feminist literary history should be to move beyond using gender as the central, essential criteria—to give up looking for only a woman's isolated traditions and to examine gender as one of many elements. In that way, we could better examine female-authored texts in relationship with male-authored texts, and, thus, end the tendency to examine texts by women as either in opposition to the dominant discourse or as co-opted by it. As Kathryn R. King argues in her essay "Cowley Among the Women; or, Poetry in the Contact Zone" (2003), women writers, like male writers, did not write in a vacuum or only in relationship to other women writers. King argues for a more complex method of examining literary influence, and she holds up Mary Louise Pratt's discussion of the contact zone in *Imperial Eyes: Travel Writing and Transculturation* (1992) as a potential model for exploring the web of textual relationships that influence women writers. Pratt argues that the relationship between the colonized and the colonizer, though inflected by unequal power, often creates influence that works both ways (the contact zone). Using Pratt's idea of mutual influence and cultural hybridity allows, King argues, women's literary history to be better grounded in social, historical, philosophical, and religious traditions that influenced the texts of women writers.

So, what has feminism taught me about literary studies? That it is not "artistic value" or "universal themes" that keeps authors' works alive. Professors decide which authors and themes are going to "count" by teaching them, writing scholarly books and articles on them, and by making sure they appear in dictionaries of literary biography, bibliographies, and in the grand narratives of literary history. Reviewers decide who gets attention by reviewing them. Editors and publishers decide who gets read by keeping them in print. And librarians decide what books to buy and to keep on the shelves. Like the ancient storytellers who passed on the tribes' history from generation to generation, these groups keep our cultural memory. Therefore, we gatekeepers, who are biased humans living in and shaped by the intellectual, cultural, and aesthetic paradigms of an actual historical period must constantly reassess our methods, theories, and techniques, continually examining how our own ethnicities, classes, genders, nationalities, and sexualities mold our critical judgements.

What has literary studies taught me about feminism? That being gendered is a text that can be read, interpreted, manipulated, and altered. That feminisms themselves are texts written by real people in actual historical situations, and that feminists, too, must always recognize our own biases, and let others recognize them. That feminism is forever growing and changing and reinventing itself in a continual cycle of statement, reaction, and revision. As the definitions and goals of feminisms change before my eyes, I have learned that feminism is a process, its meaning constantly deferred.

—Amy Hudock, Ph.D.
University of South Carolina

The Gale Critical Companion Collection

In response to a growing demand for relevant criticism and interpretation of perennial topics and important literary movements throughout history, the Gale Critical Companion Collection (GCCC) was designed to meet the research needs of upper high school and undergraduate students. Each edition of GCCC focuses on a different literary movement or topic of broad interest to students of literature, history, multicultural studies, humanities, foreign language studies, and other subject areas. Topics covered are based on feedback from a standing advisory board consisting of reference librarians and subject specialists from public, academic, and school library systems.

The GCCC is designed to complement Gale's existing Literary Criticism Series (LCS) , which includes such award-winning and distinguished titles as *Nineteenth-Century Literature Criticism* (*NCLC*), *Twentieth-Century Literary Criticism* (*TCLC*), and *Contemporary Literary Criticism* (*CLC*). Like the LCS titles, the GCCC editions provide selected reprinted essays that offer an inclusive range of critical and scholarly response to authors and topics widely studied in high school and undergraduate classes; however, the GCCC also includes primary source documents, chronologies, sidebars, supplemental photographs, and other material not included in the LCS products. The graphic and supplemental material is designed to extend the usefulness of the critical essays and provide students with historical and cultural context on a topic or author's work. GCCC titles will benefit larger institutions with ongoing subscriptions to Gale's LCS products as well as smaller libraries and school systems with less extensive reference collections. Each edition of the GCCC is created as a stand-alone set providing a wealth of information on the topic or movement. Importantly, the overlap between the GCCC and LCS titles is 15% or less, ensuring that LCS subscribers will not duplicate resources in their collection.

Editions within the GCCC are either single-volume or multi-volume sets, depending on the nature and scope of the topic being covered. Topic entries and author entries are treated separately, with entries on related topics appearing first, followed by author entries in an A-Z arrangement. Each volume is approximately 500 pages in length and includes approximately 50 images and sidebar graphics. These sidebars include summaries of important historical events, newspaper clippings, brief biographies of important figures, complete poems or passages of fiction written by the author, descriptions of events in the related arts (music, visual arts, and dance), and so on.

The reprinted essays in each GCCC edition explicate the major themes and literary techniques of the authors and literary works. It is important to note that approximately 85% of the essays reprinted in GCCC editions are full-text, meaning that they are reprinted in their entirety, including footnotes and lists of abbreviations. Essays are selected based on their coverage of the seminal works and themes of an author, and based on the importance of those essays to an appreciation of the author's contribution to the movement and to literature in general. Gale's editors select those essays of most value to upper high school and undergraduate students, avoiding narrow and highly pedantic interpretations of individual works or of an author's canon.

Scope of Feminism in Literature

Feminism in Literature, the third set in the Gale Critical Companion Collection, consists of six volumes. Each volume includes a detailed table of contents, a foreword on the subject of feminism in literature written by noted scholar Amy Hudock, and a descriptive chronology of key events throughout the history of women's writing. Volume 1 focuses on feminism in literature from antiquity through the 18th century. It consists of three topic entries, including Women and Women's Writings from Classical Antiquity through the Middle Ages, and seven author entries on such women writers from this time period as Christine de Pizan, Sappho, and Mary Wollstonecraft. Volumes 2 and 3 focus on the 19th century. Volume 2 includes such topic entries as United States Women's Suffrage Movement in the 19th Century, as well as author entries on Jane Austen, Charlotte Brontë, and Elizabeth Barrett Browning. Volume 3 contains additional author entries on figures of the 19th century, including such notables as Kate Chopin, Emily Dickinson, and Harriet Beecher Stowe. Volumes 4, 5, and 6 focus on the 20th century to the present day; volume 4 includes coverage of topics relevant to feminism in literature during the 20th century and early 21st century, including the Feminist Movement, and volumes 5 and 6 include author entries on such figures as Margaret Atwood, Charlotte Perkins Gilman, Sylvia Plath, and Virginia Woolf.

Organization of Feminism in Literature

A *Feminism in Literature* topic entry consists of the following elements:

- The **Introduction** defines the subject of the entry and provides social and historical information important to understanding the criticism.
- The list of **Representative Works** identifies writings and works by authors and figures associated with the subject. The list is divided into alphabetical sections by name; works listed under each name appear in chronological order. The genre and publication date of each work is given. Unless otherwise indicated, dramas are dated by first performance, not first publication.
- Entries generally begin with a section of **Primary Sources**, which includes essays, speeches, social history, newspaper accounts and other materials that were produced during the time covered.
- Reprinted **Criticism** in topic entries is arranged thematically. Topic entries commonly begin with general surveys of the subject or essays providing historical or background information, followed by essays that develop particular aspects of the topic. Each section has a separate title heading and is identified with a page number in the table of contents. The critic's name and the date of composition or publication of the critical work are given at the beginning of each piece of criticism. Unsigned criticism is preceded by the title of the source in which it appeared. Footnotes are reprinted at the end of each essay or excerpt. In the case of excerpted criticism, only those footnotes that pertain to the excerpted texts are included.
- A complete **Bibliographical Citation** of the original essay or book precedes each piece of criticism.
- Critical essays are prefaced by brief **Annotations** explicating each piece. Unless the descriptor "excerpt" is used in the annotation, the essay is being reprinted in its entirety.
- An annotated bibliography of **Further Reading** appears at the end of each entry and suggests resources for additional study. In some cases, significant essays for which the editors could not obtain reprint rights are included here.

A *Feminism in Literature* author entry consists of the following elements:

- The **Author Heading** cites the name under which the author most commonly wrote, followed by birth and death dates. Also located here are any name variations under which an author wrote. If the author wrote consistently under a pseudonym, the pseudonym will be listed in the author heading and the author's actual name given in parentheses on the first line of the biographical and critical information. Uncertain birth or death dates are indicated by question marks.
- A **Portrait of the Author** is included when available.
- The **Introduction** contains background infor-

mation that introduces the reader to the author that is the subject of the entry.

- The list of **Principal Works** is ordered chronologically by date of first publication and lists the most important works by the author. The genre and publication date of each work is given. Unless otherwise indicated, dramas are dated by first performance, not first publication.
- Author entries are arranged into three sections: **Primary Sources, General Commentary,** and **Title Commentary.** The Primary Sources section includes letters, poems, short stories, journal entries, novel excerpts, and essays written by the featured author. General Commentary includes overviews of the author's career and general studies; Title Commentary includes in-depth analyses of seminal works by the author. Within the Title Commentary section, the reprinted criticism is further organized by title, then by date of publication. The critic's name and the date of composition or publication of the critical work are given at the beginning of each piece of criticism. Unsigned criticism is preceded by the title of the source in which it appeared. All titles by the author featured in the text are printed in boldface type. However, not all boldfaced titles are included in the author and subject indexes; only substantial discussions of works are indexed. Footnotes are reprinted at the end of each essay or excerpt. In the case of excerpted criticism, only those footnotes that pertain to the excerpted texts are included.
- A complete **Bibliographical Citation** of the original essay or book precedes each piece of criticism.
- Critical essays are prefaced by brief **Annotations** explicating each piece. Unless the descriptor "excerpt" is used in the annotation, the essay is being reprinted in its entirety.
- An annotated bibliography of **Further Reading** appears at the end of each entry and suggests resources for additional study. In some cases, significant essays for which the editors could not obtain reprint rights are included here. A list of **Other Sources from Gale** follows the further reading section and provides references to other biographical and critical sources on the author in series published by Gale.

Indexes

The **Author Index** lists all of the authors featured in the *Feminism in Literature* set, with references to the main author entries in volumes 1, 2, 3, 5, and 6 as well as commentary on the featured author in other author entries and in the topic volumes. Page references to substantial discussions of the authors appear in boldface. The Author Index also includes birth and death dates and cross references between pseudonyms and actual names, and cross references to other Gale series in which the authors have appeared. A complete list of these sources is found facing the first page of the Author Index.

The **Title Index** alphabetically lists the titles of works written by the authors featured in volumes 1 through 6 and provides page numbers or page ranges where commentary on these titles can be found. Page references to substantial discussions of the titles appear in boldface. English translations of foreign titles and variations of titles are cross-referenced to the title under which a work was originally published. Titles of novels, dramas, nonfiction books, films, and poetry, short story, or essay collections are printed in italics, while individual poems, short stories, and essays are printed in roman type within quotation marks.

The **Subject Index** includes the authors and titles that appear in the Author Index and the Title Index as well as the names of other authors and figures that are discussed in the set, including those covered in sidebars. The Subject Index also lists hundreds of literary terms and topics covered in the criticism. The index provides page numbers or page ranges where subjects are discussed and is fully cross referenced.

Citing Feminism in Literature

When writing papers, students who quote directly from the *FL* set may use the following general format to footnote reprinted criticism. The first example pertains to material drawn from periodicals, the second to material reprinted from books.

Bloom, Harold. " Feminism as the Love of Reading," *Raritan* 14, no. 2 (fall 1994): 29-42; reprinted in *Feminism in Literature: A Gale Critical Companion,* vol. 6, eds. Jessica Bomarito and Jeffrey W. Hunter (Farmington Hills, Mich: Thomson Gale, 2004), 29-42.

Coole, Diana H. "The Origin of Western Thought and the Birth of Misogyny," in *Women in Political Theory: From Ancient Misogyny to Contemporary Feminism* (Brighton, Sussex: Wheatsheaf Books, 1988), 10-28; reprinted in *Feminism in Literature: A Gale Critical Companion,* vol. 1, eds. Jessica Bomarito and Jeffrey W. Hunter (Farmington Hills, Mich: Thomson Gale, 2004), 15-25.

Feminism in Literature *Advisory Board*

The members of the *Feminism in Literature* Advisory Board—reference librarians and subject specialists from public, academic, and school library systems—offered a variety of informed perspectives on both the presentation and content of the *Feminism in Literature* set. Advisory board members assessed and defined such quality issues as the relevance, currency, and usefulness of the author coverage, critical content, and topics included in our product; evaluated the layout, presentation, and general quality of our product; provided feedback on the criteria used for selecting authors and topics covered in our product; identified any gaps in our coverage of authors or topics, recommending authors or topics for inclusion; and analyzed the appropriateness of our content and presentation for various user audiences, such as high school students, undergraduates, graduate students, librarians, and educators. We wish to thank the advisors for their advice during the development of *Feminism in Literature*.

Suggestions are Welcome

Readers who wish to suggest new features, topics, or authors to appear in future volumes of the Gale Critical Companion Collection, or who have other suggestions or comments are cordially invited to call, write, or fax the Product Manager.

Product Manager, Gale Critical Companion Collection
Thomson Gale
27500 Drake Road
Farmington Hills, MI 48331-3535
1-800-347-4253 (GALE)
Fax: 248-699-8054

ACKNOWLEDGMENTS

The editors wish to thank the copyright holders of the excerpted criticism included in this volume and the permissions managers of many book and magazine publishing companies for assisting us in securing reproduction rights. We are also grateful to the staffs of the Detroit Public Library, the Library of Congress, the University of Detroit Mercy Library, Wayne State University Purdy/Kresge Library Complex, and the University of Michigan Libraries for making their resources available to us. Following is a list of the copyright holders who have granted us permission to reproduce material in this edition of *Feminism in Literature*. Every effort has been made to trace copyright, but if omissions have been made, please let us know.

Copyrighted material in Feminism in Literature *was reproduced from the following periodicals:*

African American Review, v. 35, winter, 2001 for "'The Porch Couldn't Talk for Looking': Voice and Vision in *Their Eyes Were Watching God*" by Deborah Clarke; v. 36, 2002 for "Phillis Wheatley's Construction of Otherness and the Rhetoric of Performed Ideology" by Mary McAleer Balkun. Copyright © 2001, 2002 by the respective authors. Both reproduced by permission of the respective authors.—***Agora: An Online Graduate Journal,*** v. 1, fall, 2002 for "Virgin Territory: Murasaki Shikibu's Ôigimi Resists the Male" by Valerie Henitiuk. Copyright © 2001-2002 Maximiliaan van Woudenberg. All rights reserved. Reproduced by permission of the author.—***American Literary History,*** v. 1, winter, 1989 for "Bio-Political Resistance in Domestic Ideology and *Uncle Tom's Cabin*" by Lora Romero. Copyright © 1989 by Oxford University Press. Reproduced by permission of the publisher and the author.—***American Literature,*** v. 53, January, 1982. Copyright © 1982, by Duke University Press. Reproduced by permission.—***The American Scholar,*** v. 44, spring, 1975. Copyright © 1975 by the United Chapters of Phi Beta Kappa. Reproduced by permission of Curtis Brown Ltd.—***The Antioch Review,*** v. 32, 1973. Copyright © 1973 by the Antioch Review Inc. Reproduced by permission of the Editors.—***Ariel: A Review of International English Literature,*** v. 21, January, 1990 for "Female Sexuality in Willa Cather's *O Pioneers!* and the Era of Scientific Sexology: A Dialogue between Frontiers" by C. Susan Wiesenthal; v. 22, October, 1991 for "Margaret Atwood's *Cat's Eye*: Re-Viewing Women in a Postmodern World" by Earl G. Ingersoll. Copyright © 1990, 1991 The Board of Governors, The University of Calgary. Both reproduced by permission of the publisher and the author.—***Atlantis: A Women's Studies Journal,*** v. 9, fall, 1983. Copyright © 1983 by *Atlantis*. Reproduced by permission.—***Black American Literature Forum,*** v. 24, summer, 1990 for "Singing the Black Mother: Maya Angelou and Autobiographical Continuity" by Mary Jane Lupton. Copyright © 1990 by the author. Reproduced by permission of the author.—***The Book Collector,*** v. 31, spring, 1982. Reproduced by permission.—***The CEA Critic,*** v. 56, spring/summer, 1994 for "Feminism and Children's Literature: Fitting *Little Women* into the American Literary Canon" by Jill P. May. Copyright © 1994 by the College English Association, Inc. Reproduced by permission of the publisher and the author.—***The Centennial Review,*** v. xxix, spring, 1985 for "'An Order of Constancy': Notes on Brooks and the Feminine" by Hortense J. Spillers. Michigan State University Press. Copyright © 1985 by *The Centennial Review.* Reproduced by permission of the publisher.—***Chaucer Review,*** v. 37, 2003. Copyright © 2003 by The Pennsylvania State University. All rights reserved. Reproduced by permission.—***Christianity and Literature,*** v. 51, spring, 2002. Copyright © 2002 by the Conference on Christianity and Literature. Reproduced by permission.—***CLA Journal,*** v. XXXIX, March, 1996. Copyright © 1966 by The College Language Association. Used by permission of The College Language Association.—***Classical Quarterly,*** v. 31, 1981 for "Spartan Wives: Liberation or Licence?" by Paul Cartledge. Copyright © 1981 The Classical Association. Reproduced by permission of Oxford University Press and the author.—***Colby Library Quarterly,*** v. 21, March, 1986. Reproduced by permission.—***Colby Quarterly,*** v. XXVI, September 1990; v. XXXIV, June, 1998. Both reproduced by permission.—***College English,*** v. 36, March, 1975 for "Who Buried H. D.?: A Poet, Her Critics, and Her Place in 'The Literary Tradition'" by Susan Friedman. Copyright © 1975 by the National Council of Teachers of English. Reproduced by permission of the publisher and the author.—***Connotations,*** v. 5, 1995-96. Copyright © Waxmann Verlag GmbH, Munster/New York 1996. Reproduced by permission.—***Contemporary Literature,*** v. 34, winter, 1993. Copyright © 1993 by University of Wisconsin Press. Reproduced by permission.—***Critical Quarterly,*** v. 14, autumn, 1972; v. 27, spring, 1985. Copyright © 1972, 1985 by Manchester University Press. Both reproduced by permission of Blackwell Publishers.—***Critical Survey,*** v. 14, January, 2002. Copyright © 2002 Berghahn Books, Inc. Reproduced by permission.—***Critique: Studies in Modern Fiction,*** v. XV, 1973. Copyright © by *Critique,* 1973. Copyright © 1973 by Helen Dwight Reid Educational Foundation. Reproduced with permission of the Helen Dwight Reid Educational Foundation, published by Heldref Publications, 1319 18th Street, NW, Washington, DC 20036-1802.—***Cultural Critique,*** v. 32, winter, 1995-96. Copyright © 1996 by *Cultural Critique.* All rights reserved. Reproduced by permission.—***Denver Quarterly,*** v. 18, winter, 1984 for "Becoming Anne Sexton" by Diane Middlebrook. Copyright © 1994 by Diane Middlebrook. Reproduced by permission of Georges Borchardt, Inc. for the author.—***Dissent,*** summer, 1987. Copyright © 1987, by Dissent Publishing Corporation. Reproduced by permission.—***The Eighteenth Century,*** v. 43, spring, 2002. Copyright © 2002 by Texas Tech University Press. Reproduced by permission.—***Eighteenth-Century Fiction,*** v. 3, July, 1991. Copyright © McMaster University 1991. Reproduced by permission.—***Emily Dickinson Journal,*** v. 10, 2000. Copyright © 2000 by The Johns Hopkins University Press for the Emily Dickinson International Society. All rights reserved. Reproduced by permission.—***The Emporia State Research Studies,*** v. 24, winter, 1976. Reproduced by permission.—***Essays and Studies,*** 2002. Copyright © 2002 Boydell & Brewer Inc. Reproduced by permission.—***Essays in Literature,*** v. 12, fall, 1985. Copyright © 1985 Western Illinois University. Reproduced by permission.—***Feminist Studies,*** v. 6, summer, 1980; v. 25, fall, 1999. Copyright © 1980, 1999 by *Feminist Studies.* Both reproduced by permission of Feminist Studies, Inc., Department of Women's Studies, University of Maryland, College Park, MD 20724.—***French Studies,*** v. XLVIII, April, 1994; v. LII, April, 1998. Copyright © 1994, 1998 by The Society for French Studies. Reproduced by permission.—***Frontiers,*** v. IX, 1987; v. XIV, 1994. Copyright © The University of Nebraska Press 1987, 1994. Both reproduced by permission.—***Glamour,*** v. 88, November 1990 for "Only Daughter" by Sandra Cisneros. Copyright © 1996 by Wendy Martin. All rights reserved. Reproduced by permission of Susan Bergholz Literary Services, New York.—***Harper's Magazine,*** for "Women's Work" by Louise Erdrich. Copyright © 1995 by *Harper's Magazine.* All rights reserved. Reproduced from the May edition by special permission.—***History Today,*** v. 50, October, 2000; v. 51, November, 2001. Copyright © 2000, 2001 by The H. W. Wilson Company. All rights reserved. Reproduced by permission.—***The Hudson Review,*** v. XXXVI, summer, 1983. Copyright © 1983 by The Hudson Review, Inc. Reproduced by permission.—***Hypatia,*** v. 5, summer, 1990 for "Is There a Feminist Aesthetic?" by Marilyn French. Copyright by Marilyn French. Reproduced by permission.—***International Fiction Review,*** v. 29, 2002. Copyright © 2002. International Fiction Association. Reproduced by permission.—***Irish Studies Review,*** spring, 1996 from "History, Gender and the Colonial Movement: Castle Rackrent" by Colin Graham. Reproduced by permission of Taylor & Francis and the author.—***Journal of Evolutionary Psychology,*** v. 7, August, 1986. Reproduced by permission.—***Journal of the Midwest Modern Language Association,*** v. 35, 2002 for "The Gospel According to Jane Eyre: The Suttee and the Seraglio" by Maryanne C. Ward. Copyright © 2002 by The Midwest Modern Language Association. Reproduced by permission of the publisher and the author.—***Journal of the Short Story in English,*** autumn, 2002. Copyright © Université d'Angers, 2002. Reproduced by permission.—***Keats-Shelley Journal,*** v. XLVI, 1997. Reproduced by permission.—***Legacy,*** v. 6, fall, 1989. Copyright © The University of Nebraska Press 1989. Reproduced by permission.—***The Massachusetts Review,*** v. 27, summer, 1986. Reproduced from *The Massachusetts Review,* The Massachusetts Review, Inc. by permission.—***Meanjin,*** v. 38, 1979 for "The Liberated Heroine: New Varieties of Defeat?" by Amanda Lohrey. Copyright © 1979 by *Meanjin.* Reproduced by permission of the author.—***MELUS,*** v. 7, fall, 1980; v. 12, fall, 1985; v.18, fall, 1993. Copyright © MELUS: The Society for the Study of Multi-Ethnic Literature of the United States, 1980, 1985, 1993. Reproduced by permission.—***Modern Drama,*** v. 21, September, 1978. Copyright © 1978 by the University of Toronto, Graduate Centre for Study of Drama. Reproduced by permission.—***Modern Language Studies,*** v. 24, spring, 1994 for "Jewett's Unspeakable Unspoken: Retracing the Female Body Through *The Country of the Pointed Firs*" by George Smith. Copyright © Northeast Modern Language Association 1990. Reproduced by permission of the publisher and author.—***Mosaic,*** v. 23, summer, 1990; v. 35, 2002. Copyright © 1990, 2002 by *Mosaic.* All rights reserved. Acknowledgment of previous publication is herewith made.—***Ms.,*** v. II, July, 1973 for "Visionary Anger" by Erica Mann Jong; June 1988 for "Changing My Mind About Andrea Dworkin" by Erica Jong. Copyright © 1973, 1988. Both reproduced by permission of the author.—***New Directions for Women,*** September-October, 1987 for "Dworkin Critiques Relations Between the Sexes" by Joanne Glasgow. Copyright © 1987 New Directions for Women, Inc., 25 West Fairview Ave., Dover, NJ 07801-3417. Reproduced by permission of the author.—***The New Yorker,*** 1978 for "Girl" by Jamaica Kincaid. Copyright © 1979 by Jamaica Kinkaid. All rights reserved. Reproduced by permission of the Wylie Agency; v. 73, February 17, 1997 for "A Society of One: Zora Neal Hurston, American Contrarian" by Claudia Roth Pierpont. Copyright © 1997 by The New Yorker Magazine, Inc. All rights reserved. Reproduced by permission of the author.—***Nineteenth-Century Feminisms,*** v. 2, spring-summer, 2000. Reproduced by permission.—***Nineteenth-Century French Studies,*** v. 25, spring-summer, 1997. Copyright © 1977 by *Nineteenth-Century French Studies.* Reproduced by permission.—***Novel,*** v. 34, spring, 2001. Copyright © NOVEL Corp. 2001. Reproduced with permission.—***Oxford Literary Review,*** v. 13, 1991. Copyright © 1991 the *Oxford Literary Review.* All rights reserved. Reproduced by permission.—***P. N. Review,*** v. 18, January/February, 1992. Reproduced by permission of Carcanet Press Ltd.—***Papers on Language & Literature,*** v. 5, winter, 1969. Copyright © 1969 by The Board of Trustees, Southern Illinois University at Edwardsville. Reproduced by permission.—***Parnassus,*** v. 12, fall-winter, 1985 for "Throwing the Scarecrows from the Garden" by Tess Gallagher; v. 12-13, 1985 for "Adrienne Rich and Lesbian/Feminist Poetry" by Catharine Stimpson. Copyright © 1985, 1986 by Poetry in Review Foundation. Both reproduced by permission of the publisher and the respective authors.—***Philological Papers,*** v. 38, 1992. Copyright © 1992 by *Philological Papers.* Reproduced by permission.—***Philological Quarterly,*** v. 79, winter, 2000. Copyright © 2001 by the University of Iowa. Reproduced by permission.—***Quadrant,*** v. 46, November, 2002 for "The Mirror of Honour and Love: A Woman's View of Chivalry" by Sophie Masson. Copyright © 2002 Quadrant Magazine Company, Inc. Reproduced by permission of the publisher and the author.—***Raritan,*** v. 14, fall, 1994. Copyright © 1994 by *Raritan: A Quarterly Review.* Reproduced by permission.—***Resources for American Literary Study,*** v. 22, 1996. Copyright © 1996 by The Pennsylvania State University. Reproduced by permission of The Pennsylvania State University Press.—***Revista Hispánica Moderna,*** v. 47, June, 1994. Copyright © 1994 by Hispanic Institute, Columbia University. Reproduced by permission.—***Rhetoric Society Quarterly,*** v. 32, winter, 2002. Reproduced by permission of the publisher, conveyed through the Copyright Clearance Center.—***Romanic Review,*** v. 79, 1988. Copyright © 1988 by The Trustees of Columbia University in the City of New York. Reproduced by permission.—***The Russian Review,*** v. 57, April, 1998. Copyright © 1998 *The Russian Review.* Reproduced by permission of Blackwell Publishers.—***San Jose Studies,*** v. VIII, spring, 1982 for "Dea, Awakening: A Reading of H. D.'s *Trilogy*" by Joyce Lorraine Beck. Copyright © 1982 by Trustees of the San Jose State University Foundation. Reproduced by permission of the publisher and the author.—***South Atlantic Review,*** v. 66, winter, 2001. Copyright © 2001 by the South Atlantic Modern Language Association. Reproduced by permission.—***Southern Humanities Review,*** v. xxii, summer, 1988. Copyright © 1988 by Auburn University. Reproduced by permission.—***The Southern Quarterly,*** v. 35, spring, 1997; v. 37, spring-summer, 1999. Copyright © 1997, 1999 by the University of Southern Mississippi. Both reproduced by permission.—***Southern Review,*** v. 18, for "Hilda in Egypt" by Albert Gelpi. Reproduced by permission of the author.—***Soviet Literature,*** v. 6, June, 1989. Reproduced by permission of FTM Agency Ltd.—***Studies in American Fiction,*** v. 9, autumn, 1981. Copyright © 1981 Northeastern University. Reproduced by permission.—***Studies in American Humor,*** v. 3, 1994. Copyright © 1994 American Humor Studies Association. Reproduced by permission.—***Studies in the Humanities,*** v. 19, December, 1992. Copyright © 1992 by Indiana University Press of Pennsylvania. Reproduced by permission.—***Studies in the Novel,*** v. 31, fall 1999; v. 35, spring, 2003. Copyright © 1999, 2003 by North Texas State University. Reproduced by permission.—***Textual Practice,*** v. 13, 1999 for "Speaking Un-likeness: The Double Text in Christina Rossetti's 'After Death' and 'Remember'" by Margaret Reynolds. Copyright © 1999 Routledge. Reproduced by permission of the publisher and the author.—***The Threepenny Review,*** 1990 for "Mother Tongue" by Amy Tan. Reproduced by permission.—***Transactions of the American Philological Association,*** v. 128, 1998. Copyright © 1998 American Philological Association. Reproduced by permission of The Johns Hopkins University Press.—***Tulsa Studies in Women's Literature,*** v. 6, fall, 1987 for "Revolutionary Women" by Betsy Erkkila. Copyright © 1987, The University of Tulsa. All rights reserved. Reproduced by permission of the publisher and the author.—***The Victorian Newsletter,*** v. 82, fall, 1992 for "Revisionist Mythmaking in Christina Rossetti's 'Goblin Market': Eve's Apple and Other Questions" by Sylvia Bailey Shurbutt; v. 92, fall, 1997 for "The Poet and the Bible: Christina Rossetti's Feminist Hermeneutics" by Lynda Palazzo; spring, 1998 for "'No Sorrow I Have Thought More About': The Tragic Failure of George Eliot's St. Theresa" by June Skye Szirotny. All reproduced by permission of The Victorian Newsletter and the author.—***Victorians Institute Journal,*** v. 13, 1985. Copyright © Victorians Institute Journal 1985. Reproduced by permission.—***Women: A Cultural Review,*** v. 10, winter, 1999 from "Consorting with Angels: Anne Sexton and the Art of Confession" by Deryn Rees-Jones. Copyright © 1999, by Taylor & Francis Ltd. Reproduced by permission of the publisher and the author. (http://www.tandf.co.uk/journals).—***Women and Language,*** v. 13, March 31, 1995; v. 19, fall, 1996. Copyright © 1995, 1996 by Communication Department at George Mason University. Reproduced by permission of the publisher.—***Women's Studies: An Interdisciplinary Journal,*** v. 3, 1975; v. 4, 1976; v. 17, 1990; v. 18, 1990; v. 23, September, 1994; v. 30, 2001. Copyright © 1975, 1976, 1990, 1994, 2001 Gordon and Breach Science Publishers S.A. Reproduced by permission.—***Women's Studies in Communication,*** v. 24, spring, 2001. Reproduced by permission.—***Women's Writing,*** v. 3, June, 1996. Reproduced by permission of the publisher; v. 4, 1997 for "(Female) Philosophy in the Bedroom: Mary Wollstonecraft and Female Sexuality" by Gary Kelly. Copyright © Triangle Journals Ltd, 1997. All rights reserved. Reproduced by permission of the publisher and the author.—***World & I,*** v. 18, March, 2003. Copyright © 2003 News World Communications, Inc. Reproduced by permission.—***World Literature Today,*** v. 73, spring, 1999. Copyright © 1999 by the University of Oklahoma Press. Reprinted by permission of the publisher.—***World Literature Written in English,*** v. 15, November, 1976 for "Doris Lessing's Feminist Plays" by Agate Nesaule Krouse. Copyright © 1976 by WLWE. Reproduced by permission of the publisher and the author.

Copyrighted material in Feminism in Literature *was reproduced from the following books:*

Acocella, Joan. From ***Willa Cather and the Politics of Criticism.*** University of Nebraska Press, 2000. Copyright © 2000, by Joan Acocella. All rights reserved. Reproduced by permission.—Aimone, Joseph. From "Millay's Big Book, or the Feminist Formalist as Modern," in ***Unmanning Modernism: Gendered Re-Readings.*** Edited by Elizabeth Jane Harrison and Shirley Peterson. University of Tennessee Press, 1997. Copyright © 1997 by The University of Tennessee Press. All rights reserved. Reproduced by permission of The University of Tennessee Press.—Allende, Isabel. From "Writing as an Act of Hope," in ***Paths of Resistance: The Art and Craft of the Political Novel.*** Edited by William Zinsser. Houghton Mifflin Company, 1989. Copyright © 1989 Isabel Allende. Reproduced by permission of the author.—Angelou, Maya. From ***And Still I Rise.*** Random House, 1978. Copyright © 1978 by Maya Angelou. Reproduced by permission of Random House, Inc. and Time Warner Books UK.—Arenal, Electa. From "The Convent as Catalyst for Autonomy: Two Hispanic Nuns of the Seventeenth Century," in ***Women in Hispanic Literature.*** Edited by Beth Kurti Miller. University of California Press, 1983. Copyright © 1983 by The Regents of the University of California. Reproduced by permission of the publisher and the author.—Arndt, Walter. From "Introduction: I The Akhmatova Phenomenon and II Rendering the Whole Poem," in ***Anna Akhmatova: Selected Poems.*** Edited and translated by Walter Arndt. Ardis, 1976. Reproduced by permission.—Atwood, Margaret. From ***Second Words.*** Anansi Press Limited, 1982. Copyright © 1982, by O. W. Toad Limited. All rights reserved. Reproduced by permission of the author.—Baker, Deborah Lesko. From "Memory, Love, and Inaccessibility in *Hiroshima mon amour,*" in ***Marguerite***

Duras Lives On. Edited by Janine Ricouart. University Press of America, 1998. Copyright © 1998 University Press of America, Inc. All rights reserved. Reproduced by permission.—Barlow, Judith E. From "Into the Foxhole: Feminism, Realism, and Lillian Hellman," in ***Realism and the American Dramatic Tradition.*** Edited by William W. Demastes. University of Alabama Press, 1996. Copyright © 1996, The University of Alabama Press. Reproduced by permission.—Barratt, Alexandra. From ***Women's Writing in Middle English.*** Edited by Alexandra Barratt. Longman Group UK Limited, 1992. Copyright © Longman Group UK Limited 1992. Reproduced by permission.—Barrett Browning, Elizabeth. From "A Letter to Mary Russell Mitford, September 18, 1846," in ***Women of Letters: Selected Letters of Elizabeth Barrett Browning and Mary Russell Mitford.*** Edited by Meredith B. Raymond and Mary Rose Sullivan. Twayne Publishers, 1987. Reproduced by permission of The Gale Group.—Barrett Browning, Elizabeth. From "Glimpses into My Own Life and Literary Character," in ***The Brownings' Correspondence,*** Vol. 1. Edited by Phillip Kelley and Ronald Hudson. Wedgestone Press, 1984. All rights reserved. Reproduced by permission of Eton College.—Bassard, Katherine Clay. From ***Spiritual Interrogations: Culture, Gender, and Community in Early African American Women's Writing.*** Princeton University Press, 1999. Copyright © 1999 by Katherine Clay Bassard. Reproduced by permission of Princeton University Press.—Beauvoir, Simone de. From "The Independent Woman," in ***The Second Sex.*** Translated by H. M. Parshley. Alfred A. Knopf, Inc., 1952. Copyright © 1952, renewed 1980 by Alfred A. Knopf, Inc. All rights reserved. Reproduced by permission of Alfred A. Knopf, Inc., a division of Random House, Inc. and The Random House Group.—Behrendt, Stephen. From "Mary Shelley, Frankenstein, and the Woman Writer's Fate," in ***Romantic Women Writers: Voices and Countervoices.*** Edited by Paula R. Feldman and Theresa M. Kelley. University Press of New England, 1995. Copyright © 1995 by University Press of New England. All rights reserved. Reproduced by permission.—Bell, Barbara Currier and Carol Ohmann. From "Virginia Woolf's Criticism: A Polemical Preface," in ***Feminist Literary Criticism: Explorations in Theory.*** Edited by Josephine Donovan. The University Press of Kentucky, 1989. Copyright © 1975, 1989 by The University Press of Kentucky. Reproduced by permission of The University Press of Kentucky.—Berry, Mary Frances. From ***Why ERA Failed: Politics, Women's Rights, and the Amending Process of the Constitution.*** Indiana University Press, 1986. Copyright © 1986 by Mary Frances Berry. All rights reserved. Reproduced by permission.—Birgitta of Sweden. From ***Life and Selected Revelations.*** Edited with a preface by Marguerite Tjader Harris, translation and notes by Albert Ryle Kezel, introduction by Tore Nyberg from ***The Classics of Western Spirituality.*** Paulist Press, 1990. Copyright © 1990 by the Order of St. Birgitte, Rome. Translation, notes and Foreword copyright © 1990 by Albert Ryle Kezel, New York/Mahwah, NJ. Reproduced by permission of Paulist Press. www.paulistpress.com.—Blundell, Sue. From ***Women in Ancient Greece.*** British Museum Press, 1995. Copyright © 1995 Sue Blundell. Reproduced by permission of the author.—Bogan, Louise. From ***The Blue Estuaries: Poems 1923-1968.*** Farrar, Straus & Giroux, Inc., 1968. Copyright © 1968 by Louise Bogan. Copyright renewed 1996 by Ruth Limmer. All rights reserved. Reproduced by permission of Farrar, Straus and Giroux, LLC.—Booth, Alison. From "Not All Men Are Selfish and Cruel," in ***Greatness Engendered: George Eliot and Virginia Woolf.*** Cornell University Press, 1992. Copyright © 1992 by Cornell University Press. Reproduced by permission of the publisher, Cornell University Press.—Brammer, Leila R. From ***Excluded from Suffrage History: Matilda Joslyn Gage, Nineteenth-Century American Feminist.*** Greenwood Press, 2000. Copyright © by Leila R. Brammer. All rights reserved. Reproduced by permission of Greenwood Publishing Group, Inc., Westport, CT.—Britzolakis, Christina. From ***Sylvia Plath and the Theatre of Mourning.*** Oxford at the Clarendon Press, 1999. Copyright © 1999 by Christina Britzolakis. All rights reserved. Reproduced by permission of Oxford University Press.—Broe, Mary Lynn. From "Bohemia Bumps into Calvin: The Deception of Passivity in Lillian Hellman's Drama," in ***Critical Essays on Lillian Hellman.*** Edited by Mark W. Estrin. G. K. Hall, 1989. Copyright © 1989 by Mark W. Estrin. All rights reserved. Reproduced by permission of The Gale Group.—Brontë, Charlotte. From "Caroline Vernon," in ***Legends of Angria: Compiled from The Early Writings of Charlotte Brontë.*** Edited by Fannie E. Ratchford. Yale University Press, 1933. Copyright © 1933 by Yale University Press. Renewed 1961 by Fannit Ratchford. Reproduced by permission.—Brooks, Gwendolyn. From ***Blacks.*** The David Company, 1987. Copyright © 1945, 1949, 1953, 1960, 1963, 1968, 1969, 1970, 1971, 1975, 1981, 1986 by Gwendolyn Brooks Blakely. All rights reserved. Reproduced by consent of Brooks Permissions.—Brown-Grant, Rosalind. From "Christine de Pizan: Feminist Linguist Avant la Lettre?," in ***Christine de Pizan 2000: Studies on Christine de Pizan in Honour of Angus J. Kennedy.*** Edited by John Campbell and Nadia Margolis. Rodopi, 2000. Copyright © Editions Rodopi B. Reproduced by permission.—Brownmiller,

Susan. From ***In Our Time: Memoir of a Revolution.*** The Dial Press, 1999. Copyright © 1999, by Susan Brownmiller. All rights reserved. Reproduced by permission of The Dial Press/Dell Publishing, a division of Random House, Inc.—Brügmann, Margret. From "Between the Lines: On the Essayistic Experiments of Hélène Cixous in 'The Laugh of the Medusa'," translated by Debbi Long in ***The Politics of the Essay: Feminist Perspectives.*** Edited by Ruth-Ellen Boetcher Joeres and Elizabeth Mittman. Indiana University Press, 1993. Copyright © 1993 by Indiana University Press. All rights reserved. Reproduced by permission.—Bunch, Charlotte. From "Women's Human Rights: The Challenges of Global Feminism and Diversity," in ***Feminist Locations: Global and Local, Theory and Practice.*** Edited by Marianne DeKoven. Rutgers University Press, 2001. Copyright © 2001 by Rutgers, the State University. All rights reserved. Reproduced by permission.—Burke, Sally. From ***American Feminist Playwrights: A Critical History.*** Twayne, 1996. Copyright © 1996 by Twayne Publishers. All rights reserved. Reproduced by permission of The Gale Group.—Butler-Evans, Elliott. From ***Race, Gender, and Desire: Narrative Strategies in the Works of Toni Cade Bambara, Toni Morrison, and Alice Walker.*** Temple University Press, 1989. Copyright © 1989, by Temple University. All rights reserved. Reproduced by permission.—Byerman, Keith. From "Gender and Justice: Alice Walker and the Sexual Politics of Civil Rights," in ***The World is Our Home: Society and Culture in Contemporary Southern Writing.*** Edited by Jeffrey J. Folks and Nancy Summers Folks. The University Press of Kentucky, 2000. Copyright © 2000 by The University Press of Kentucky. Reproduced by permission.—Callaghan, Dympna C. From "The Ideology of Romantic Love," in ***The Weyward Sisters: Shakespeare and Feminist Politics.*** Edited by Dympna C. Callaghan, Lorraine Helms, and Jyotsna Singh. Blackwell Publishers, 1994. Copyright © Dympna C. Callaghan, Lorraine Helms and Jyotsna Singh 1994. Reproduced by permission of Blackwell Publishers.—Carmody, Denise Lardner. From ***Biblical Woman: Contemporary Reflections on Scriptural Texts.*** Crossroad Publishing Company, 1988. Copyright © 1988 by Denise Lardner Carmody. All rights reserved. Reproduced by permission of the author.—Castro, Ginette. From ***American Feminism: A Contemporary History.*** Translated by Elizabeth Loverde-Bagwell. New York University Press, 1990. Copyright © Presses de la Foundation Nationale des Sciences Politiques, Paris, 1990. All rights reserved. Reproduced by permission of New Directions Publishing Corporation and in the UK by Pollinger Limited and the proprietor.—Chadwick, Whitney. From ***Women, Art, and Society.*** Thames and Hudson, 1990. Copyright © 1990 Thames and Hudson Ltd, London. All rights reserved. Reproduced by permission.—Chafe, William H. From "World War II as a Pivotal Experience for American Women," in ***Women and War: The Changing Status of American Women from the 1930s to the 1940s.*** Edited by Maria Diedrich and Dorothea Fischer-Horning. Berg, 1990. Copyright © 1990, by Maria Diedrich and Dorothea Fischer-Hornung. All rights reserved Reproduced by permission.—Chesler, Ellen. From ***Woman of Valor: Margaret Sanger and the Birth Control Movement in America.*** Anchor Books, 1992. Copyright © 1992 by Ellen Chesler. All rights reserved. Reproduced by permission of International Creative Management, Inc.—Cholmeley, Katherine. From ***Margery Kempe, Genius and Mystic.*** Longmans, Green and Co., 1947. Reproduced by permission.—Christian, Barbara T. From an introduction to ***"Everyday Use": Alice Walker.*** Edited by Barbara T. Christian. Rutgers University Press, 1994. Copyright © 1994 by Rutgers, The State University. Reproduced by permission of Rutgers, The State University.—Christine de Pizan. From ***The Writings of Christine de Pizan.*** Translated by Charity Cannon Willard. Persea Books, 1994. Copyright © 1994 by Persea Books, Inc. Reproduced by permission.—Cixous, Hélène. From "The Laugh of the Medusa," in ***New French Feminisms: An Anthology.*** Edited by Elaine Marks and Isabelle de Courtivron. Essay translated by Keith and Paula Cohen. *Signs,* 1975. All rights reserved. Reproduced by permission of University of Chicago Press and the author.—Conley, Verana Andermatt. From ***Hélène Cixous: Writing the Feminine.*** University of Nebraska Press, 1984. Copyright © 1984 by University of Nebraska Press. All rights reserved. Reproduced by permission.—Coole, Diana H. From ***Women in Political Theory: From Ancient Misogyny to Contemporary Feminism.*** Wheatsheaf Books Ltd, 1988. Copyright © Diana Coole, 1988. All rights reserved. Reproduced by permission of the author.—Cooper, Michaela Bruckner. From "Textual Wandering and Anxiety in Margaret Fuller's *Summer on the Lakes,*" in ***Margaret Fuller's Cultural Critique: Her Age and Legacy.*** Edited by Fritz Fleischmann. Peter Lang, 2000. Copyright © 2000 Peter Lang Publishing. All rights reserved. Reproduced by permission.—Cott, Nancy. From "Historical Perspectives: The Equal Rights Amendment Conflict in 1920s," in ***Conflicts in Feminism.*** Edited by Marianne Hirsch and Evelyn Fox Keller. Routledge, 1990. Copyright © 1990 by Routledge, Chapman and Hall, Inc. All rights reserved. Reproduced by permission of Routledge/Taylor & Francis Books and the author.—Cotton, Nancy. From "Women Playwrights in England," in ***Read-***

ings in Renaissance Women's Drama: Criticism, History, and Performance 1594-1998. Edited by S. P. Cerasano and Marion Wynee-Davies. Bucknell University Press 1981. Reproduced by permission of Associated University Presses and the author.—Coultrap-McQuin, Susan. From ***Doing Literary Business: American Women Writers in the Nineteenth Century.*** The University of North Carolina Press, 1990. Copyright © 1990 Susan Coultrap-McQuin. All rights reserved. Used by permission of the University of North Carolina Press.—Daly, Brenda. From ***Lavish Self-Divisions: The Novels of Joyce Carol Oates.*** University Press of Mississippi, 1996. Copyright © 1996 by the University Press of Mississippi. All rights reserved. Reproduced by permission.—Davis, Cynthia J. "What 'Speaks in Us': Margaret Fuller, Woman's Rights, and Human Nature," in ***Margaret Fuller's Cultural Critique: Her Age and Legacy.*** Edited by Fritz Fleischmann. Peter Lang, 2000. Copyright © 2000 Peter Lang Publishing. All rights reserved. Reproduced by permission.—de Gouges, Olympe. From "The Rights of Women," in ***Women in Revolutionary Paris 1789-1795: Selected Documents.*** Edited and translated by Daline Gay Levy, Harriet Branson Applewhite, and Mary Durham Johnson. University of Illinois, 1979. Reproduced by permission.—Depla, Annette. From "Women in Ancient Egyptian Wisdom Literature," in ***Women in Ancient Societies: An Illusion of the Night.*** Edited by Léonie J. Archer, Susan Fischler, and Maria Wyke. Macmillan Press Ltd, 1994. Copyright © The Macmillan Press Ltd 1994. Reproduced with permission of Palgrave Macmillan and Routledge/Taylor & Francis Books, Inc.—Deutsch, Sarah Jane. From "From Ballots to Breadlines: 1920-1940," in ***No Small Courage: A History of Women in the United States.*** Edited by Nancy F. Cott. Oxford University Press, 2000. Copyright © 2000, by Sarah Jane Deutsch. All rights reserved. Used by permission of Oxford University Press.—Dever, Carolyn. From "Obstructive Behavior: Dykes in the Mainstream of Feminist Theory," in ***Cross-Purposes: Lesbians, Feminists, and the Limits of Alliance.*** Indiana University Press, 1997. Copyright © 1997, by Indiana University Press. All rights reserved. Reproduced by permission.—Donawerth, Jane. From "Women's Poetry and the Tudor-Stuart System of Gift Exchange," in ***Women, Writing, and the Reproduction of Culture in Tudor and Stuart Britain.*** Edited by Mary E. Burke, Jane Donawerth, Linda L. Dove, and Karen Nelson. Syracuse University Press, 2002. Reproduced by permission.—Doolittle, Hilda. From ***HERmione.*** New Directions Publishing, 1981. Copyright © 1981 by the Estate of Hilda Doolittle. Reproduced by permission of New Directions Publishing Corp.—Douglas, Ann. From ***The Feminization of American Culture.*** Anchor Press/Doubleday, 1988. Copyright © 1977 by Ann Douglas. Used by permission of Alfred A. Knopf, a division of Random House, Inc.—Driver, Dorothy. From "Reconstructing the Past, Shaping the Future: Bessie Head and the Question of Feminism in a New South Africa," in ***Black Women's Writings.*** Edited by Gina Wisker. St. Martin's Press, 1993. Copyright © 1993, by Editorial Board, Lumière (Co-operative) Press Ltd. All rights reserved. Reprinted by permission of Palgrave Macmillan.—DuBois, Ellen Carol. From ***Remembering Seneca Falls: Honoring the Women Who Paved the Way: An Essay.*** Reproduced by permission of the author.—DuBois, Ellen Carol. From "Taking the Law Into Our Own Hands: Bradwell, Minor and Suffrage Militance in the 1870s," in ***One Woman, One Vote: Rediscovering the Woman Suffrage Movement.*** Edited by Marjorie Spruill Wheeler. NewSage Press, 1995. Copyright © 1995 by NewSage Press and Educational Film Company. All rights reserved. Reproduced by permission.—DuBois, Ellen Carol. From the introduction to ***Feminism and Suffrage: The Emergence of An Independent Women's Movement in America.*** Cornell University Press, 1978. Copyright © 1978 by Cornell University. All rights reserved. Used by permission of Cornell University Press.—DuBois, Ellen Carol. From "The Limitations of Sisterhood: Elizabeth Cady Stanton and the Division of the American Suffrage Movement, 1875-1902" in ***Women and the Structure of Society.*** Duke University Press, 1984. Copyright © 1984 by Duke University Press, Durham, NC. All rights reserved. Used by permission.—DuBois, Ellen Carol. From ***Woman Suffrage and Women's Rights.*** New York University Press, 1998. Copyright © 1998 by New York University. All rights reserved. Reproduced by permission of the publisher and the author.—DuBois, Ellen Carol. From "Woman Suffrage Around the World: Three Phases of Suffragist Internationalism," in ***Suffrage and Beyond: International Feminist Perspectives.*** Edited by Caroline Daley and Melanie Nolan. Auckland University Press, 1994. Copyright © by Auckland University Press 1994. All rights reserved. Reproduced by permission of the publisher and the author.—Ducrest, Stéphanie-Félicité. From "The Influence of Women on French Literature," in ***Women Critics: 1660-1820: An Anthology.*** Indiana University Press, 1995. Copyright © 1995 by Indiana University Press. All rights reserved. Reproduced by permission.—Dworkin, Andrea. From ***Letters from a War Zone: Writings 1976-1989.*** E. P. Dutton, 1988. Copyright © 1988 by Andrea Dworkin. Reproduced by permission of Elaine Markson Literary Agency.—Echols, Alice.

From ***The Sixties: From Memory to History.*** Edited by David R. Farber. University of North Carolina Press, 1994. Copyright © 1994 by the University of North Carolina Press. Used by permission of the Publisher.—Ehrenreich, Barbara and Deirdre English. From ***For Her Own Good: 150 Years of the Experts' Advice to Women.*** Anchor Books/Doubleday, 1978. Copyright © 1978 by Barbara Ehrenreich and Deirdre English. All rights reserved. Used by permission of Doubleday, a division of Random House.—Elbert, Sarah. From ***A Hunger for Home: Louisa May Alcott and*** **Little Women.** Temple University Press, 1984. Copyright © 1984 by Temple University. All rights reserved. Reproduced by permission of the author.—Emecheta, Buchi. From "Feminism with a Small 'f'!," in ***Criticism and Ideology: Second African Writers' Conference.*** Edited by Kirsten Holst Petersen. Scandinavian Institute of African Studies, 1988. Copyright © 1988 by Scandinavian Institute of African Studies. All rights reserved. Reproduced by permission of Nordic Africa Institute.—Ensler, Eve. From ***The Vagina Monologues: The V-Day Edition.*** Villard, 2001. Copyright © 1998, 2001 by Eve Ensler. All rights reserved. Reproduced by permission of Villard Books, a division of Random House, Inc.—Enstad, Nan. From ***Ladies of Labor, Girls of Adventure: Working Women, Popular Culture, and Labor Politics at the Turn of the Twentieth Century.*** Columbia University Press, 1999. Copyright © 1999 Columbia University Press, New York. All rights reserved. Republished with permission of the Columbia University Press, 61 W. 62nd St., New York, NY 10023.—Ezell, Margaret J. M. From "Women and Writing," in ***A Companion to Early Modern Women's Writing.*** Edited by Anita Pacheco. Blackwell Publishing Ltd, 2002. Copyright © 2002 by Blackwell Publishers Ltd. Reproduced by permission of Blackwell Publishers.—Fallaize, Elizabeth. From "Resisting Romance: Simone de Beauvoir, *The Woman Destroyed* and the Romance Script," in ***Contemporary French Fiction by Women: Feminist Perspectives.*** Edited by Margaret Atack and Phil Powrie. Manchester University Press, 1990. Reproduced by permission of the author.—Feng, Pin-chia. From ***The Female Bildungsroman*** by Toni Morrison and Maxine Hong Kingston: A Postmodern Reading. Peter Lang, 1998. Copyright © 1988 Peter Lang Publishing, Inc. All rights reserved. Reproduced by permission.—Ferree, Myra Marx and Beth B. Hess. From ***Controversy and Coalition: The New Feminist Movement across Three Decades of Change.*** Twayne Publishers, 1994. Copyright © 1994 by Twayne Publishers. All rights reserved. Reproduced by permission of The Gale Group.—Fishkin, Shelley Fisher. From an interview with Maxine Hong Kingston, in ***Conversations with Maxine Hong Kingston.*** Edited by Paul Skenazy and Tera Martin. University Press of Mississippi, 1998. Copyright © 1998 by University Press of Mississippi. All rights reserved. Reproduced by permission of the author.—Fishkin, Shelley Fisher. From "Reading Gilman in the Twenty-First Century," in ***The Mixed Legacy of Charlotte Perkins Gilman.*** Edited by Catherine J. Golden and Joanna Schneider Zangrando. University of Delaware Press, 2000. Copyright © 2000 by Associated University Press. Reproduced by permission.—Fleischmann, Fritz. From "Margaret Fuller, the Eternal Feminine, and the 'Liberties of the Republic'," in ***Women's Studies and Literature.*** Edited by Fritz Fleischmann and Deborah Lucas Schneider. Palm & Enke, 1987. Reproduced by permission.—Foster, M. Marie Booth. From "Voice, Mind, Self: Mother-Daughter Relationships in Amy Tan's *The Joy Luck Club* and *The Kitchen God's Wife*," in ***Women of Color: Mother-Daughter Relationships in 20th-Century Literature.*** Edited by Elizabeth Brown-Guillory. University of Texas Press, 1996. Copyright © 1996 by the University of Texas Press. All rights reserved. Reproduced by permission.—Fowler, Robert Booth. From ***Carrie Catt: Feminist Politician.*** Northeastern University Press, 1986. Copyright © 1986 by R. B. Fowler. All rights reserved. Reproduced by permission.—Fraiman, Susan. From "The Humiliation of Elizabeth Bennett," in ***Refiguring the Father: New Feminist Readings of Patriarchy.*** Edited by Patricia Yaeger and Beth Kowaleski-Wallace. Southern Illinois University Press, 1989. Copyright © 1989 by the Board of Trustees, Southern Illinois University. All rights reserved. Reproduced by permission.—Francis, Emma. From "Is Emily Brontë a Woman?: Femininity, Feminism, and the Paranoid Critical Subject," in ***Subjectivity and Literature from the Romantics to the Present Day.*** Edited by Philip Shaw and Peter Stockwell. Pinter, 1991. Copyright © Emma Francis. All rights reserved. Reproduced by permission of the author.—Freedman, Estelle B. and Erna Olafson Hellerstein. From an introduction to ***Victorian Women: A Documentary Account of Women's Lives in Nineteenth-Century England, France, and the United States.*** Edited by Erna Olafson Hellerstein, Leslie Parker Hume, and Karen M. Offen. Stanford University Press, 1981. Copyright © 1981 by the Board of Trustees of Leland Stanford Junior University. Reproduced with permission of Stanford University Press, www.sup.org.—Frenk, Susan. From "The Wandering Text: Situating the Narratives of Isabel Allende," in ***Latin American Women's Writing: Feminist Readings in Theory and Crisis.*** Edited by Anny Brooksbank Jones and Catherine Davies. Oxford at the Clarendon Press, 1996. Copyright © 1996 by Anny Brooksbank Jones and Catherine Davies. All rights reserved. Reproduced by permission of Oxford University Press.—From ***Victorian Women: A Documentary Account of Women's Lives in Nineteenth-Century England, France, and the United States.*** Edited by Erna Olafson Hellerstein, Leslie Parker Hume, and Karen M. Offen. Stanford University Press, 1981. Copyright © 1981 by the Board of Trustees of Leland Stanford Junior University. Reproduced with permission of Stanford University Press, www.sup.org.—Galvin, Mary E. From ***Queer Poetics: Five Modernist Women Writers.*** Praeger, 1999. Copyright © 1999 by Mary E. Galvin. All rights reserved. Reproduced by permission.—Garner, Shirley Nelson. From "Constructing the Mother: Contemporary Psychoanalytic Theorists and Women Autobiographers," in ***Narrating Mother: Theorizing Maternal Subjectivities.*** Edited by Brenda O. Daly and Maureen T. Reddy. University of Tennessee Press, 1991. Copyright © 1991 by The University of Tennessee Press. Reproduced by permission of the publisher.—Ghymn, Esther Mikyung. From an introduction to ***Images of Asian American Women by Asian American Women Writers.*** Peter Lang, 1995. Copyright © 1995, by Esther Mikyung Ghymn. All rights reserved. Reproduced by permission.—Gilbert, Sandra M. and Gubar, Susan. From "Charred Skirts and Deathmask: World War II and the Blitz on Women," in ***No Man's Land: The Place of the Woman Writer in the Twentieth Century, Volume 3: Letters from the Front.*** Yale University Press, 1994. Copyright © 1994, by Sandra M. Gilbert and Susan Gubar. All rights reserved. Reproduced by permission.—Gilbert, Sandra M. and Susan Gubar. From "The Battle of the Sexes: The Men's Case," in ***No Man's Land: The Place of the Woman Writer in the Twentieth Century, Volume 1: The War of the Words.*** Yale University Press, 1988. Copyright © 1988, by Yale University Press, All rights reserved. Reproduced by permission.—Gilbert, Sandra M., and Susan Gubar. From "The Second Coming of Aphrodite: Kate Chopin's Fantasy of Desire," in ***No Man's Land: The Place of the Woman Writer in the Twentieth Century.*** Yale University Press, 1989. Copyright © 1989 by Yale University. Copyright © 1984 by Sandra M. Gilbert and Susan Gubar. All rights reserved. Reproduced by permission.—Gilbert, Susan M., and Susan Gubar. From ***The Madwoman in the Attic: The Woman Writer and the Nineteenth-Century Literary Imagination.*** Yale University Press, 1979. Copyright © 1979 by Yale University. All rights reserved. Reproduced by permission.—Gleadle, Kathryn. From an introduction to ***The Early Feminists: Radical Unitarians and the Emergence of The Women's Rights Movement, 1831-51.*** Macmillan Press Ltd., 1995. Copyright © Kathryn Gleadle 1995. All rights reserved. Reproduced by permission of Palgrave Macmillan.—Golden, Catherine. From "One Hundred Years of Reading 'The Yellow Wallpaper'," in ***The Captive Imagination: A Casebook on "The Yellow Wallpaper."*** Edited by Catherine Golden. The Feminist Press at the City University of New York, 1992. Copyright © 1992 by Catherine Golden. All rights reserved. Reproduced by permission.—Gorsky, Susan Rubinow. From ***Femininity to Feminism: Women and Literature in the Nineteenth Century.*** Twayne Publishers, 1992. Copyright © 1992 by Twayne Publishers. All rights reserved. Reproduced by permission of The Gale Group.—Greer, Germaine. From ***The Madwoman's Underclothes: Essays and Occasional Writings.*** The Atlantic Monthly Press, 1986. Copyright © 1970, 1986, by Germaine Greer. All rights reserved. Reproduced by permission.—Grewal, Gurleen. From ***Circles of Sorrow, Lines of Struggle: The Novels of Toni Morrison.*** Louisiana State University Press, 1998. Copyright © 1998 by Louisiana State University Press. All rights reserved. Reproduced by permission.—Griffin, Alice and Geraldine Thorsten. From ***Understanding Lillian Hellman.*** University of South Carolina Press, 1999. Copyright © 1999 University of South Carolina. Reproduced by permission.—Griffin, Susan E. From "Resistance and Reinvention in Sandra Cisneros' *Woman Hollering Creek,*" in ***Ethnicity and the American Short Story.*** Edited by Julie Brown. Garland Publishing, Inc., 1997. Copyright © 1997 by Julie Brown. All rights reserved. Reproduced by permission of the publisher and the author.—Grogan, Susan K. From an introduction to ***French Socialism and Sexual Difference: Women and the New Society, 1803-44.*** St. Martin's Press, 1992. Copyright © Susan K. Grogan 1992. All rights reserved. Reprinted by permission of Palgrave Macmillan.—Grössinger, Christa. From ***Picturing Women in Late Medieval and Renaissance Art.*** Manchester University Press, 1997. Copyright © Christa Grössinger 1997. Reproduced by permission.—Grubbs, Judith Evans. From ***Women and the Law in the Roman Empire: A Sourcebook on Marriage, Divorce and Widowhood.*** Routledge, 2002. Reproduced by permission of the publisher.—Grundy, Isobel. From "(Re)discovering Women's Texts," in ***Women and Literature in Britain 1700-1800.*** Edited by Vivien Jones. Cambridge University Press, 2000. Copyright © 2000 by Cambridge University Press. Reproduced by permission of Cambridge University Press.—Gubar, Susan. From "Feminist Misogyny: Mary Wollstonecraft and the Paradox of 'It Takes One to Know One'," in ***Feminism Beside Itself.*** Edited by Diane Elam and Robyn Wiegman. Routledge, 1995. Copyright © 1995 by Routledge.

All rights reserved. Reproduced by permission of Routledge/Taylor & Francis and the author.—Gubar, Susan. From "Sapphistries," in ***Re-reading Sappho: Reception and Transmission.*** Edited by Ellen Greene. University of California Press, 1996. Copyright © 1996 by The Regents of The University of California. Reproduced by permission of the publisher and the author.—Gunther-Canada, Wendy. From ***Rebel Writer: Mary Wollstonecraft and Enlightenment Politics.*** Northern Illinois University Press, 2001. Copyright © 2001 by Northern Illinois University Press. All rights reserved. Reproduced by permission.—Hagen, Lyman B. From ***Heart of a Woman, Mind of a Writer, and Soul of a Poet: A Critical Analysis of the Writings of Maya Angelou.*** University Press of America, 1997. Copyright © 1997 by University Press of America. All rights reserved. Reproduced by permission.—Hallett, Judith From "The Role of Women in Roman Elegy: Counter-Cultural Feminism," in ***Women in the Ancient World: The Arethusa Papers.*** Edited by John Peradotto and J. Sullivan. State University of New York Press, 1984. Reproduced by permission of the State University of New York Press.—Hansberry, Lorraine. From ***A Raisin in the Sun.*** Modern Library, 1995. Copyright © 1958, 1986 by Robert Nemiroff, as an unpublished work. Copyright © 1959, 1966, 1984, 1987, 1988 by Robert Nemiroff. All rights reserved. Reproduced by permission of Random House, Inc., Jewell Gresham-Nemiroff and Methuen Publishing Ltd.—Harris, Susan K. From "'But is it any good?' Evaluating Nineteenth-Century American Women's Fiction," in ***The (Other) American Traditions: Nineteenth-Century Women Writers.*** Edited by Joyce W. Warren. Rutgers University Press, 1993. Copyright © 1993 by Rutgers University Press. All rights reserved. Reproduced by permission of the author.—Head, Bessie. From "Despite Broken Bondage, Botswana Women Are Still Unloved," in ***A Woman Alone: Autobiographical Writings.*** Selected and edited by Craig MacKenzie. Heinemann, 1990. Copyright © 1990, by The Estate of Bessie Head. Reproduced by permission of Johnson & Alcock.—Head, Bessie. From "The Woman from America," in ***A Woman Alone: Autobiographical Writings.*** Selected and edited by Craig MacKenzie. Heinemann, 1990. Copyright © 1990, by The Estate of Bessie Head. Reproduced by permission of Johnson & Alcock.—Hellerstein, Erna, Leslie Parker Hume and Karen M. Offen from an introduction to ***Victorian Women: A Documentary Account of Women's Lives in Nineteenth-Century England, France, and the United States.*** Edited by Erna Olafson Hellerstein, Leslie Parker Hume, and Karen M. Offen. Stanford University Press, 1981. Copyright © 1981 by the Board of Trustees of the Leland Stanford Junior University. Reproduced with permission of Stanford University Press, www.sup.org.—Henderson, Bruce. From ***Images of the Self as Female: The Achievement of Women Artists in Re-envisioning Feminine Identity.*** Edited by Kathryn N. Benzel and Lauren Pringle De La Vars. The Edwin Mellen Press, 1992. Copyright © 1992 by Kathryn N. Benzel and Lauren Pringle De La Vars. All rights reserved. Reproduced by permission.—Hill, Mary A. From "Charlotte Perkins Gilman: A Feminist's Struggle with Womanhood," in ***Charlotte Perkins Gilman: The Woman and Her Work.*** Edited by Sheryl L. Meyering. UMI Research Press, 1989. Copyright © 1989 by Sheryl L. Meyering. All rights reserved. Reproduced by permission of Boydell & Brewer, Inc.—Hobby, Elaine. From ***Virtue of Necessity: English Women's Writing 1649-88.*** The University of Michigan Press, 1989. Copyright © 1988 by Elaine Hobby. All rights reserved. Reproduced by permission of the author.—Hoffert, Sylvia D. From an introduction to ***When Hens Crow: The Woman's Rights Movement in Antebellum America.*** Indiana University Press, 1995. Copyright © 1995 by Sylvia D. Hoffert. All rights reserved. Reproduced by permission.—Hurston, Zora Neale. From ***Their Eyes Were Watching God.*** Perennial Library, 1990. Copyright © 1937 by Harper & Row, Publishers, Inc. Renewed 1965 by John C. Hurston and Joel Hurston. Reproduced by permission of Time Warner Books UK. In North America by HarperCollins Publishers Inc.—James, Adeola. From "Bessie Head's Perspectives on Women," in ***Black Women Writers across Cultures.*** Edited by Valentine Udoh James, James S. Etim, Melanie Marshall James, and Ambe J. Njoh. International Scholars Publications, 2000. Copyright © 2000, by International Scholars Publications. All rights reserved. Reproduced by permission.—Jardine, Alice A. From an interview with Marguerite Duras, translated by Katherine Ann Jensen, in ***Shifting Scenes: Interviews on Women, Writing, and Politics in Post-68 France.*** Edited by Alice A. Jardine and Anne M. Menke. Columbia University Press, 1991. Copyright © 1991 Columbia University Press, New York. All rights reserved. Reprinted with the permission of the publisher.—Jelinek, Estelle C. From "The Paradox and Success of Elizabeth Cady Stanton," in ***Women's Autobiography: Essays in Criticism.*** Edited by Estelle C. Jelinek. Indiana University Press, 1980. Copyright © Estelle C. Jelinek. Reproduced by permission of the author.—Juhasz, Suzanne. From "Maxine Hong Kingston: Narrative Technique & Female Identity," in ***Contemporary American Women Writers: Narrative Strategies.*** Edited by Catherine Rainwater and William J. Scheik. The University Press of Kentucky, 1985. Copyright © 1985 by The University Press of

Kentucky. Reproduced by permission.—Kaminer, Wendy. From "Feminism's Identity Crisis," in ***Public Women, Public Words: A Documentary History of American Feminism.*** Edited by Dawn Keetley and John Pettegrew. First published in *The Atlantic.* Reproduced by permission of the author.—Kaplan, Cora. From "Pandora's Box: Subjectivity, Class and Sexuality in Socialist Feminist Criticism," in ***Making a Difference: Feminist Literary Criticism.*** Edited by Gayle Greene and Coppélia Kahn. Methuen & Co., 1985. Copyright © 1985 Gayle Greene and Coppélia Kahn. All rights reserved. Reproduced by permission of Routledge and the author.—Keetley, Dawn and John Pettegrew. From "Identities through Adversity," in ***Public Women, Public Words: A Documentary History of American Feminism.*** Edited by Dawn Keetley and John Pettegrew. Madison House Publishers, Inc., 1997. Copyright © 1997 by Madison House Publisher, Inc. All rights reserved. Reproduced by permission.—Kelly, Gary. From ***Revolutionary Feminism: The Mind and Career of Mary Wollstonecraft.*** St. Martin's Press, 1996. Copyright © 1996 by Gary Kelly. All rights reserved. Reproduced by permission of Palgrave Macmillan.—Kempe, Margery. From "Margery Kempe's Visit to Julian of Norwich," in ***The Shewings of Julian Norwich.*** Edited by Georgia Ronan Crampton. Medieval Publishing Institute, 1994. Reproduced by permission.—Kempe, Margery. From ***The Book of Margery Kempe.*** Translated by B. A. Windeatt. Penguin, 1985. Copyright © B. A. Windeatt, 1985. All rights reserved. Reproduced by permission.—Kirkham, Margaret. From ***Jane Austen, Feminism, and Fiction.*** Harvester Press Limited, 1983. Copyright © Margaret Kirkham, 1983. All rights reserved. Reproduced by permission.—Klemans, Patricia A. From "'Being Born a Woman': A New Look at Edna St. Vincent Millay," in ***Critical Essays on Edna St. Vincent Millay.*** Edited by William B. Thesing. G. K. Hall, 1993. Copyright © by 1993 by William B. Thesing. All rights reserved. Reproduced by permission of The Gale Group.—Knapp, Bettina L. From ***Gertrude Stein.*** Continuum, 1990. Copyright © 1990 by Bettina L. Knapp. All rights reserved. Reproduced by permission.—Kolodny, Annette. From "Dancing Through the Minefield: Some Observations on the Theory, Practice, and Politics of a Feminist Literary Criticism," originally published in ***Feminist Studies,*** 1980. Copyright © 1980 by Annette Kolodny. All rights reserved. Reproduced by permission of the author.—Kumin, Maxine. From "How It Was," in ***The Complete Poems: Anne Sexton.*** Houghton Mifflin Company, 1981. Copyright © 1981, by Maxine Kumin. All rights reserved. Reproduced by permission of Houghton Mifflin and The Anderson Literary Agency.—Lamonica, Drew. From ***We Are Three Sisters: Self and Family in the Writing of the Brontës.*** University of Missouri Press, 2003. Copyright © 2003 by The Curators of the University of Missouri. All rights reserved. Reproduced by permission.—Larsen, Jeanne. From "Lowell, Teasdale, Wylie, Millay, and Bogan," in ***The Columbia History of American Poetry.*** Edited by Jay Parini. Columbia University Press, 1993. Copyright © 1993 Columbia University Press, New York. All rights reserved. Reprinted with permission of the publisher.—Lascelles, Mary. From ***Jane Austen and Her Art.*** Oxford University Press, 1939. Reproduced by permission of Oxford University Press.—Lavezzo, Kathy. From "Sobs and Sighs Between Women: The Homoerotics of Compassion in *The Book of Margery Kempe,*" in ***Premodern Sexualities.*** Edited by Louise Fradenburg and Carla Freccero. Routledge, 1996. Copyright © 1996 by Routledge. All rights reserved. Reproduced by permission of Routledge/Taylor & Francis and the author.—Lessing, Doris. From a preface to *The Golden Notebook* in ***A Small Personal Voice.*** Edited by Paul Schleuter. Alfred A. Knopf, Inc., 1974. Copyright © 1974 by Doris Lessing. All rights reserved. Reproduced by permission of Jonathan Clowes, Ltd.—Levertov, Denise. From ***Poems, 1960-67.*** New Directions, 1966. Copyright © 1967, by Denise Levertov. All rights reserved. Reproduced by permission of New Directions Publishing Corporation and in the UK by Pollinger Limited and the proprietor.—Logan, Shirley Wilson. From ***"We are Coming": The Persuasive Discourse of Nineteenth-Century Black Women.*** Southern Illinois University Press, 1999. Copyright © 1999 by the Board of Trustees, Southern Illinois University. All rights reserved. Reproduced by permission of Southern Illinois University Press and the University of South Carolina Press.—Lorde, Audre. From ***The Black Unicorn.*** Norton, 1978. Copyright © 1978, by Audre Lorde. All rights reserved. Reproduced by permission of W. W. Norton & Company and Charlotte Sheedy Literary Agency.—Lumsden, Linda J. From ***Rampant Women: Suffragists and the Right of Assembly.*** The University of Tennessee Press, 1997. Copyright © 1997 by The University of Tennessee Press. Reproduced by permission of The University of Tennessee Press.—Lunardini, Christine A. ***From Equal Suffrage to Equal Rights: Alice Paul and the National Women's Party, 1910-1928.*** New York University Press, 1986. Copyright © 1986 by New York University. All rights reserved. Reproduced by permission of the author.—Madsen, Deborah L. From "Sandra Cisneros," in ***Understanding Contemporary Chicana Literature.*** Edited by Matthew J. Bruccoli. University of South Carolina Press, 2000. Copyright © 2000 by University of South Carolina. Reproduced by permission.—Marder, Herbert. From ***Feminism & Art: A Study of Virginia Woolf.*** University of Chicago Press, 1968. Copyright © 1968 by the University of Chicago. All rights reserved. Reproduced by permission of the publisher and the author.—Marilley, Suzanne M. From ***Woman Suffrage and the Origins of Liberal Feminism in the United States.*** Harvard University Press, 1996. Copyright © 1996 by the President and Fellows of Harvard College. All rights reserved. Reproduced by permission Harvard University Press.—Marsh-Lockett, Carol P. From "What Ever Happened to Jochebed? Motherhood as Marginality in Zora Neale Hurston's *Seraph on the Suwanee,*" in ***Southern Mothers: Facts and Fictions in Southern Women's Writing.*** Edited by Nagueyalti Warren and Sally Wolff. Louisiana State University, 1999. Reproduced by permission.—Mason, Nicholas. From "Class, Gender, and Domesticity in Maria Edgeworth's *Belinda,*" in ***The Eighteenth-Century Novel,*** Vol. 1. Edited by Susan Spencer. AMS Press, 2001. Reproduced by permission.—Massardier-Kenney, Françoise. From ***Gender in the Fiction of George Sand.*** Rodopi, 1985. Copyright © Editions Rodopi B. V. Reproduced by permission.—McCracken, Ellen. From "Sandra Cisneros' *The House on Mango Street*: Community-Oriented Introspection and the Demystification of Patriarchal Violence," in ***Breaking Boundaries: Latina Writing and Critical Readings.*** Edited by Asunción Horno-Delgado, Eliana Ortega, Nina M. Scott, and Nancy Saporta Sternbach. University of Massachusetts Press, 1989. Copyright © 1989 by The University of Massachusetts Press. All rights reserved. Reproduced by permission.—McNamara, Jo Ann. From "Women and Power through the Family Revisited," in ***Gendering the Master Narrative: Women and Power in the Middle Ages.*** Edited by Mary C. Erler and Maryanne Kowaleski. Cornell University Press, 2003. Copyright © 2003 by Cornell University Press. Used by permission of Cornell University Press.—Meisenhelder, Susan. From "Ethnic and Gender Identity in Zora Neale Hurston's *Their Eyes Were Watching God,*" in ***Teaching American Ethnic Literatures: Nineteen Essays.*** Edited by John R. Maitino and David R. Peck. University of New Mexico Press, 1996. Copyright © 1996, by the University of New Mexico Press. All rights reserved. Reproduced by permission.—Mellor, Anne K. From "Possessing Nature: The Female in Frankenstein," in ***Romanticism and Feminism.*** Edited by Anne K. Mellor. Indiana University Press, 1988. Copyright © 1988 by Indiana University Press. All rights reserved. Reproduced by permission.—Mermin, Dorothy. From ***Godiva's Ride: Women of Letters in England, 1830-1880.*** Indiana University Press, 1993. Copyright © 1993 by Dorothy Mermin. All rights reserved. Reproduced by permission.—Millay, Edna St. Vincent. From "Sonnet III of Fatal Interview," in ***Collected Sonnets of Edna St. Vincent Millay.*** HarperCollins, 1952. Copyright © 1931, 1958 by Edna St. Vincent Millay and Norma Millay Ellis. All rights reserved. Reproduced by permission of Elizabeth Barnett, Literary Executor.—Millay, Edna St. Vincent. From "First Fig," in ***Collected Poems of Edna St. Vincent Millay.*** HarperCollins, 1952. Copyright © 1922, 1950 by Edna St. Vincent Millay. Reproduced by permission of Elizabeth Barnett, Literary Executor.—Millay, Edna St. Vincent. From "I, Being Born a Woman and Distressed," in ***Collected Poems of Edna St. Vincent Millay.*** HarperCollins, 1952. Copyright © 1923, 1951 by Edna St.Vincent Millay and Norma Millay Ellis. All rights reserved. Reproduced by permission of Elizabeth Barnett, Literary Executor.—Millett, Kate. From "How Many Lives Are Here...," in ***The Feminist Memoir Project.*** Edited by Rachel DuPlessis and Ann Snitow. Three Rivers Press, 1998. Copyright © 1998 by Rachel DuPlessis and Ann Snitow. All rights reserved. Used by permission of Crown Publishers, a division of Random House, Inc. and Sanford J. Greenburger Associates.—Moi, Toril. From "Who's Afraid of Virginia Woolf? Feminist Readings of Woolf," in ***New Casebooks: 'Mrs. Dalloway' and 'To the Lighthouse.'*** Edited by Su Reid. St. Martin's Press, 1993. Copyright © Su Reid 1993. All rights reserved. Reproduced by permission of Palgrave Macmillan.—Moore, Marianne. From ***The Selected Letters of Marianne Moore.*** Edited by Bonnie Costello. Alfred A. Knopf, 1997. Copyright © 1997 by the Estate of Marianne Moore. Introduction, annotations and additional editorial material copyright 1997 by Bonnie Costello. All rights reserved. Reproduced by permission of Alfred A. Knopf, Inc., a division of Random House, Inc.—Morgan, Winifred. From "Alice Walker: *The Color Purple* as Allegory," in ***Southern Writers at Century's End.*** Edited by Jeffrey J. Folks and James A. Perkins. The University Press of Kentucky, 1997. Copyright © 1997 by The University Press of Kentucky. All rights reserved. Reproduced by permission.—Morrison, Toni. From ***Race-ing Justice, En-Gendering Power.*** Pantheon Books, 1992. Copyright © 1992 by Toni Morrison. All rights reserved. Used by permission International Creative Management, Inc.—Morrison, Toni. From "What the Black Woman Thinks About Women's Lib," in ***Public Women, Public Words: A Documentary History of American Feminism.*** Edited by Dawn Keetley and John Pettegrew. Madison House, 1997. Copyright © 1997 by Toni Morrison. Reproduced by permission of International Creative Management, Inc.—Mortimer, Armine Kotin. From "Male and Female Plots in Staël's *Corinne,*" in ***Correspondences:***

Studies in Literature, History, and the Arts in Nineteenth-Century France: Selected Proceedings of the Sixteenth Colloquium in Nineteenth-Century French Studies, The University of Oklahoma-Norman, October 11th-13th, 1990. Edited by Keith Busby. Rodopi, 1992. Copyright © Editions Rodopi B. V. Reproduced by permission.—Motard-Noar, Martine. From "From Persephone to Demeter: A Feminist Experience in Cixous's Fiction," in ***Images of Persephone: Feminist Readings in Western Literature.*** Edited by Elizabeth T. Hayes. University Press of Florida, 1994. Copyright © 1994 by Board of Regents of the State of Florida. All rights reserved. Reproduced with the permission of the University Press of Florida.—Mukherjee, Bharati. From ***The Middleman and Other Stories.*** Viking, 1988. Copyright © 1988, by Bharati Mukherjee. All rights reserved. Reprinted by permission of Penguin Group Canada and the author.—Mumford, Marilyn R. From "A Feminist Prolegomenon for the Study of Hildegard of Bingen," in ***Gender, Culture, and the Arts: Women, the Arts, and Society.*** Edited by Ronald Dotterer and Susan Bowers. Associated University Presses, 1993. Copyright © 1993 by Associated University Presses.—Oates, Joyce Carol. From ***Where I've Been, and Where I'm Going.*** Plume, 1999. Copyright © The Ontario Review, 1999. All rights reserved. Reproduced by permission of Plume, an imprint of Penguin Putnam Inc. In the United Kingdom by John Hawkins & Associates, Inc.—Okely, Judith. From "Re-reading The Second Sex," in ***Simone de Beauvoir: A Re-Reading.*** Virago, 1986. Reproduced by permission of the author.—Ovid. From "Sappho to Phaon," in ***The Sappho Companion.*** Edited by Margaret Reynolds. Chatto and Windus, 2000. Copyright © Margaret Reynolds 2000. Reproduced by permission of the editor.—Pan Chao. From ***Pan Chao: Foremost Woman Scholar of China.*** Edited by Nancy Lee Swann. University of Michigan Center for Chinese Studies, 1932. Copyright © The East Asian Library and the Gest Collection, Princeton University. Reproduced by permission.—Parks, Sheri. From "In My Mother's House: Black Feminist Aesthetics, Television, and *A Raisin in the Sun,*" in ***Theatre and Feminist Aesthetics.*** Edited by Karen Laughlin and Catherine Schuler. Farleigh Dickinson University Press, 1995. Copyright © 1995 by Associated University Presses. All rights reserved. Reproduced by permission.—Paul, Alice. From ***Party Papers: 1913-1974.*** Microfilming Corporation of America, 1978. Reproduced by permission of Sewall-Belmont House and Museum.—Paz, Octavio. From "The Response," in ***Sor Juana or, The Traps of Faith.*** Translated by Margaret Sayers Peden. Cambridge, Mass.: The Belknap Press of Harvard University Press, 1988. Copyright © 1988 by the President and Fellows of Harvard College. All rights reserved. Reproduced by permission.—Perkins, Annie. From "The Poetry of Gwendolyn Brooks (1970s-1980s)," in ***Women Making Art: Women in the Visual, Literary, and Performing Arts Since 1960.*** Edited by Deborah Johnson and Wendy Oliver. Peter Lang, 2001. Copyright © 2001 Peter Lang Publishing, Inc., New York. Reproduced by permission.—Pierpont, Claudia Roth. From ***Passionate Minds: Women Rewriting the World.*** Alfred A. Knopf, 2000. Copyright © 2000 by Claudia Roth Piepont. All rights reserved. Reproduced by permission of Alfred A. Knopf, Inc., a division of Random House, Inc.—Plath, Sylvia. From ***The Bell Jar.*** Faber & Faber, 1966; Harper & Row, 1971. Copyright © 1971 by Harper & Row, Publishers, Inc. Reproduced by permission Faber & Faber Ltd. In the United States by HarperCollins Publishers Inc.—Pryse, Marjorie. From "Origins of American Literary Regionalism: Gender in Irving, Stowe, and Longstreet," in ***Breaking Boundaries: New Perspectives on Women's Regional Writing.*** Edited by Sherrie A. Inness and Diana Royer. University of Iowa Press, 1997. Copyright © 1997 by the University of Iowa Press. All rights reserved. Reproduced by permission.—Radice, Betty. From an introduction to ***The Letters of Abelard and Heloise.*** Translated by Betty Radice. Penguin Books, 1974. Copyright © Betty Radice, 1974. Reproduced by permission of Penguin Books, a division of Penguin Putnam Inc.—Rendall, Jane. From an introduction to ***The Origins of Modern Feminism: Women in Britain, France and the United States 1780-1860.*** Macmillan, 1985. Copyright © Jane Rendall 1985. All rights reserved. Reproduced by permission of Palgrave Macmillan.—Rich, Adrienne. From "Vesuvius at Home: The Power of Emily Dickinson," in ***On Lies, Secrets, and Silence: Selected Prose 1966-1978.*** W. W. Norton & Company, Inc., 1979. Copyright © 1979 by W. W. Norton & Company, Inc. Reproduced by permission of the author and W. W. Norton & Company, Inc.—Rich, Adrienne. From "When We Dead Awaken: Writing as Re-Vision," in ***Arts of the Possible: Essays and Conversations.*** W. W. Norton & Company, Inc., 2001. Copyright © 2001 by Adrienne Rich. Reproduced by permission of the publisher and the author.—Richmond, M. A. From ***Bid the Vassal Soar: Essays on the Life and Poetry of Phillis Wheatley and George Moses Horton.*** Howard University Press, 1974. All rights reserved. Copyright © 1974 by Merle A. Richmond. Reproduced by permission.—Risjord, Norman K. From ***Representative Americans: The Colonists.*** Second Edition. Rowman & Littlefield Publishers, Inc., 2001. Copyright © 2001 by Rowman & Littlefield Publishers, Inc. All rights reserved. Reproduced by permission.—Robbins,

Ruth. From ***Transitions: Literary Feminisms.*** St. Martin's Press, 2000. Reproduced with permission of Palgrave Macmillan.—Rohrbach, Erika. From H. D. and Sappho: 'A Precious Inch of Palimpsest'," in ***Re-Reading Sappho: Reception and Transmission.*** Edited by Ellen Greene. University of California Press, 1996. Copyright © 1996 by The Regents of the University of California. Reproduced by permission.—Rosenman, Ellen Bayuk. From ***"A Room of One's Own": Women Writers and the Politics of Creativity.*** Twayne, 1995. Copyright © 1995 by Twayne Publishers. All rights reserved. Reproduced by permission of The Gale Group.—Rosslyn, Wendy. From "Don Juan Feminised," in ***Symbolism and After: Essays on Russian Poetry in Honour of Georgette Donchin.*** Edited by Arnold McMillin. Bristol Classical Press, 1992. Copyright © 1992 by Gerald Duckworth & Co. Ltd. All rights reserved. Reproduced by permission of The School of Slavonic Studies in the University of London.—Sanders, Valerie. From "Women, Fiction and the Marketplace," in ***Women and Literature in Britain: 1800-1900.*** Edited by Joanne Shattock. Cambridge University Press, 2001. Copyright © Cambridge University Press 2001. Reproduced by permission of Cambridge University Press.—Sandler, Martin W. From ***Against the Odds: Women Pioneers in the First Hundred Years of Photography.*** Rizzoli International Publications, Inc., 2002. Copyright © 2002, by Martin W. Sandler. All rights reserved. Reproduced by permission of the author.—Saunders, Corinne. From ***Rape and Ravishment in the Literature of Medieval England.*** D. S. Brewer, 2001. Copyright © Corinne J. Saunders 2001. All rights reserved. Reproduced by permission.—Scheick, William J. From ***Authority and Female Authorship in Colonial America.*** The University Press of Kentucky, 1998. Copyright © 1998 by The University Press of Kentucky. Reproduced by permission of The University Press of Kentucky.—Schroeder, Patricia R. From "Remembering the Disremembered: Feminist Realists of the Harlem Renaissance," in ***Realism and the American Dramatic Tradition.*** Edited by William W. Demastes. University of Alabama Press, 1996. Copyright © 1996, by the University of Alabama Press. All rights reserved. Reproduced by permission.—Selous, Trista. From ***The Other Woman: Feminism and Femininity in the Work of Marguerite Duras.*** Yale University Press, 1988. Copyright © 1988 by Yale University. All rights reserved. Reproduced by permission.—Sexton, Anne. From "All God's Children Need Radios," in ***No Evil Star: Selected Essays, Interviews, and Prose of Anne Sexton.*** Edited by Steven E. Colburn. The University of Michigan Press, 1985. Copyright © Anne Sexton. Reproduced by permission of SLL/Sterling Lord Literistic.—Shaw, Harry B. From "*Maud Martha*: The War with Beauty," in ***A Life Distilled: Gwendolyn Brooks, Her Poetry and Fiction.*** Edited by Maria K. Mootry and Gary Smith. University of Illinois Press, 1987. Copyright © 1987 by the Board of Trustees of the University of Illinois. Reproduced by permission.—Shiach, Morag. From an introduction to ***Hélène Cixous: A Politics of Writing.*** Routledge, 1991. Copyright © 1991 by Morag Shiach. All rights reserved. Reproduced by permission of the publisher and the author.—Showalter, Elaine. From ***A Literature of Their Own: British Women Novelists from Brontë to Lessing.*** Princeton University Press, 1977. Copyright © 1977 by Princeton University Press. Renewed 2005 Princeton University Press, 1999 exp. Paperback edition. Reproduced by permission of Princeton University Press.—Showalter, Elaine. From ***Sister's Choice: Tradition and Change in American Women's Writing.*** Oxford at the Clarendon Press, 1991. Copyright © 1991, by Elaine Showalter. All rights reserved. Reproduced by permission of Oxford University Press.—Sigerman, Harriet. From "Laborers for Liberty," in ***No Small Courage: A History of Women in the United States.*** Edited by Nancy F. Cott. Oxford University Press, 2000. Copyright © 2000 by Oxford University Press, Inc. Copyright © 1994, 2000 by Harriet Sigerman. All rights reserved. Used by permission of Oxford University Press.—Signori, Lisa F. From ***The Feminization of Surrealism: The Road to Surreal Silence in Selected Works of Marguerite Duras.*** Peter Lang, 2001. Copyright © 2001 Peter Lang Publishing, Inc., New York. All rights reserved. Reproduced by permission.—Silko, Leslie Marmon. From ***Storyteller.*** Seaver Books, 1981. Copyright © 1981, by Leslie Marmon Silko. All rights reserved. Reproduced by permission.—Simson, Rennie. From "Afro-American Poets of the Nineteenth Century," in ***Nineteenth-Century Women Writers of the English-Speaking World.*** Edited by Rhoda B. Nathan. Greenwood Press, 1986. Copyright © 1986 by Hofstra University. All rights reserved. Reproduced by permission of Greenwood Publishing Group, Inc., Westport, CT.—Sizer, Lyde Cullen. From ***The Political Work of Northern Women Writers and the Civil War, 1850-1872.*** The University of North Carolina Press, 2000. Copyright © 2000 The University of North Carolina Press. All rights reserved. Reproduced by permission.—Smith, Hilda L. From "Introduction: Women, Intellect, and Politics: Their Intersection in Seventeenth-Century England," in ***Women Writers and the Early Modern British Political Tradition.*** Edited by Hilda L. Smith. Cambridge University Press, 1998. Copyright © Cambridge University Press 1998. Reproduced with the permission of Cambridge University Press.—Smith,

Johanna M. From "'Cooped Up': Feminine Domesticity in *Frankenstein,*" in ***Case Studies in Contemporary Criticism: Mary Shelley's* Frankenstein.** Edited by Johanna M. Smith. St. Martin's Press, 1992. Copyright © 1992 by Bedford Books of St. Martin's Press. All rights reserved. Reproduced by permission.—Smith, Sidonie. From "Resisting the Gaze of Embodiment: Women's Autobiography in the Nineteenth Century," in ***American Women's Autobiography: Fea(s)ts of Memory.*** Edited by Margo Culley. University of Wisconsin University Press, 1992. Copyright © 1992 The Board of Regents of the University of Wisconsin System. All rights reserved. Reproduced by permission.—Smith, Sidonie. From ***Where I'm Bound: Patterns of Slavery and Freedom in Black American Autobiography.*** Greenwood Press, 1974. Copyright © 1974 by Sidonie Smith. All rights reserved. Reproduced by permission of Greenwood Publishing Group, Inc., Westport, CT.—Snyder, Jane McIntosh. From ***The Woman and the Lyre: Women Writers in Classical Greece and Rome.*** Southern Illinois University Press, 1989. Copyright © 1989 by the Board of Trustees, Southern Illinois University. All rights reserved. Reproduced by permission.—Sor Juana Ines de la Cruz. From ***The Answer = La respuesta.*** Edited by Electa Arenal and Amanda Powell. The Feminist Press, 1994. Copyright © 1994 by Electa Arenal and Amanda Powell. All rights reserved. Reproduced by permission of The Feminist Press at the City University of New York. www.feministpress.org.—Spender, Dale. From "Introduction: A Vindication of the Writing Woman," in ***Living by the Pen: Early British Women Writers.*** Edited by Dale Spender. Teachers College Press, 1992. Copyright © 1992 by Teachers College. All rights reserved. Reproduced by permission.—Staley, Lynn. From ***Margery Kempe's Dissenting Fictions.*** Pennsylvania State University Press, 1994. Copyright © 1994 The Pennsylvania State University. All rights reserved. Reproduced by permission.—Stehle, Eva. From ***Performance and Gender in Ancient Greece: Nondramatic Poetry in Its Setting.*** Princeton University Press, 1997. Copyright © 1997 by Princeton University Press. All rights reserved. Reproduced by permission of Princeton University Press.—Stein, Gertrude. From "Degeneration in American Women," in ***Sister Brother: Gertrude and Leo Stein.*** Edited by Brenda Wineapple. G. Putnam's Sons, 1996. Copyright © 1996 by Brenda Wineapple. All rights reserved. Used by permission of G. Putnam's Sons, a division of Penguin Group (USA) Inc. and Bloomsbury Publishing Plc.—Stott, Rebecca. From ***Elizabeth Barrett Browning.*** Pearson Education Limited, 2003. Copyright © Pearson Educated Limited 2003. All rights reserved. Reproduced by permission.—Straub, Kristina. From ***Divided Fictions: Fanny Burney and Feminine Strategy.*** University Press of Kentucky, 1987. Copyright © 1987 by the University Press of Kentucky. Reproduced by permission.—Swann, Nancy Lee. From ***Pan Chao: Foremost Woman Scholar of China.*** Russell & Russell, 1968. Copyright © The East Asian Library and the Gest Collection, Princeton University. Reproduced by permission.—Tanner, Laura E. From ***Intimate Violence: Reading Rape and Torture in Twentieth-Century Fiction.*** Indiana University Press, 1994. Copyright © 1994, by Laura E. Tanner. All rights reserved. Reproduced by permission.—Terborg-Penn, Rosalyn. From ***African American Women in the Struggle for the Vote, 1850-1920.*** Indiana University Press, 1998. Reproduced by permission.—Tharp, Julie. From "Women's Community and Survival in the Novels of Louise Erdrich," in ***Communication and Women's Friendships: Parallels and Intersections in Literature and Life.*** Edited by Janet Doubler Ward and JoAnna Stephens Mink. Bowling Green State University Popular Press, 1993. Copyright © 1993 by Bowling Green State University Popular Press. Reproduced by permission of the University of Wisconsin Press.—Trilling, Lionel. From "Emma and the Legend of Jane Austen," in ***Beyond Culture: Essays on Literature and Learning.*** Harcourt Brace Jovanovich, 1965. Copyright © 1965 by Lionel Trilling. All rights reserved. Reproduced by permission of the Wylie Agency, Inc.—Turner, Katherine S. H. From "From Classical to Imperial: Changing Visions of Turkey in the Eighteenth Century," in ***Travel Writing and Empire: Postcolonial Theory in Transit.*** Edited by Steve Clark. Zed Books, 1999. Copyright © Katherine S. H. Turner. Reproduced by permission.—Van Dyke, Annette. From "Of Vision Quests and Spirit Guardians: Female Power in the Novels of Louise Erdrich," in ***The Chippewa Landscape of Louise Erdrich.*** Edited by Allan Chavkin. The University of Alabama Press, 1999. Copyright © 1999, by The University of Alabama Press. Copyright © 1999. All rights reserved. Reproduced by permission.—Waelti-Waters, Jennifer and Steven C. Hause. From an introduction to ***Feminisms of the Belle Époque: A Historical and Literary Anthology.*** Edited by Jennifer Waelti-Waters and Steven C. Hause. University of Nebraska Press, 1994. Copyright © The University of Nebraska Press, 1994. All rights reserved. Reproduced by permission.—Wagner-Martin, Linda. From "Panoramic, Unpredictable, and Human: Joyce Carol Oates' Recent Novels," in ***Traditions, Voices, and Dreams: The American Novel since the 1960s.*** Edited by Melvin J. Friedman and Ben Siegel. University of Delaware Press, 1995. Copyright © 1995 by Associated University Presses, Inc. Reproduced by permission.—Wagner-Martin, Linda. From ***Sylvia Plath: A Literary Life.***

St. Martin's Press, 1999. Copyright © 1999 by Linda Wagner-Martin. All rights reserved. Reproduced by permission of Palgrave Macmillan.—Walker, Alice. From ***Revolutionary Petunias & Other Poems.*** Harcourt Brace Jovanovich, 1971. Copyright © 1970, 1971, 1972, 1973, renewed 1998 by Alice Walker. All right reserved. Reproduced by permission of Harcourt Inc. In the British Commonwealth by David Higham Associates.—Watts, Linda S. From ***Rapture Untold: Gender, Mysticism, and the 'Moment of Recognition' in Works by Gertrude Stein.*** Peter Lang, 1996. Copyright © 1996 Peter Lang Publishing, Inc., New York. All rights reserved. Reproduced by permission.—Weatherford, Doris. From ***A History of the American Suffragist Movement.*** ABC-CLIO, 1998. Copyright © 1998 by The Moschovitis Group, Inc. Reproduced by permission of Moschovitis Group, Inc.—Weeton, Nellie. From "The Trials of an English Governess: Nelly Weeton Stock," originally published in ***Miss Weeton: Journal of a Governess.*** Edited by Edward Hall. Oxford University Press (London), H. Milford, 1936-39. Reproduced by permission of Oxford University Press.—Weston, Ruth D. From "Who Touches This Touches a Woman," in ***Critical Essays on Alice Walker.*** Edited by Ikenna Dieke. Greenwood Press 1999. Reproduced by permission of Greenwood Publishing Group, Inc., Westport, CT.—Wheeler, Marjorie Spruill. From an introduction to ***One Woman, One Vote: Rediscovering the Woman Suffrage Movement.*** Edited by Marjorie Spruill Wheeler. NewSage Press, 1995. Copyright © 1995 by NewSage Press and Educational Film Company. All rights reserved. Reproduced by permission.—Willard, Charity Cannon. From ***Christine de Pizan: Her Life and Works.*** Persea Books, 1984. Copyright © 1984 by Charity Cannon Willard. Reproduced by permission.—Willis, Sharon A. From "Staging Sexual Difference: Reading, Recitation, and Repetition in Duras' *Malady of Death,*" in ***Feminine Focus: The New Women Playwrights.*** Edited by Enoch Brater. Oxford University Press, 1989. Copyright © 1989 by Oxford University Press, Inc. Reproduced by permission of Oxford University Press.—Winter, Kate H. From ***Marietta Holley: Life with "Josiah Allen's Wife."*** Syracuse University Press, 1984. Copyright © 1984 by Syracuse University Press. All rights reserved. Reproduced by permission.—Woolf, Virginia. From "George Eliot," in ***The Common Reader,*** Harcourt, Brace & Company, 1925, L. & V. Woolf, 1925. Copyright 1925 by Harcourt Brace & Company. Renewed 1953 by Leonard Woolf. Reprinted by permission of Harcourt, Brace & Company and The Society of Authors.—Wynne-Davies, Marion. From an introduction to ***Women Poets of the Renaissance.*** Edited by Marion Wynne-Davies. Routledge, 1999. Reprint. Copyright © 1998 by J. M. Dent. All rights reserved. Reproduced by permission of Routledge/Taylor & Francis and the author—Yalom, Marilyn. From "Toward a History of Female Adolescence: The Contribution of George Sand," in ***George Sand: Collected Essays.*** Edited by Janis Glasgow. The Whitson Publishing Company, 1985. Reproduced by permission of the author.—Yu Xuanji. From "Joining Somebody's Mourning and Three Beautiful Sisters, Orphaned Young," in ***The Clouds Float North: The Complete Poems of Yu Xuanji.*** Translated by David Young and Jiann I. Lin. Wesleyan University Press, 1998. Copyright © 1998 by David Young and Jiann I. Lin. All rights reserved. Reproduced by permission.

Photographs and Illustrations in Feminism in Literature *were received from the following sources:*

16th century men and women wearing fashionable clothing, ca. 1565 engraving. Hulton/Archive.—A lay sister preparing medicine as shown on the cover of *The Book of Margery Kempe,* photograph. MS. Royal 15 D 1, British Library, London.—Akhmatova, Anna, photograph. Archive Photos, Inc./Express Newspaper.—Alcott, Louisa May, drawing. The Granger Collection, New York.—Alcott, Louisa May, photograph. Archive Photos, Inc.—Allen, Joan, Joanne Camp, Anne Lange, and Cynthia Nixon, in a scene from the play "The Heidi Chronicles," photograph. Time Life Pictures/Getty Images.—Allende, Isabelle, photograph. Getty Images.—An estimated 5,000 people march outside the Minnesota Capitol Building in protest to the January 22, 1973 Supreme Court ruling on abortion as a result of the "Roe vs. Wade" case, photograph. AP/Wide World Photos.—Angelou, Maya, photograph. AP/Wide World Photos.—Anthony, Susan B., Frances Willard, and other members of the International Council of Women, photograph. Copyright © Corbis.—Atwood, Margaret, photograph by Jerry Bauer. Copyright © Jerry Bauer.—Autographed manuscript of Phillis Weatley's poem "To the University of Cambridge." The Granger Collection, New York.—Beller, Kathleen as Kate in the 1980 film version of Margaret Atwood's novel, *Surfacing,* photograph. Kobal Collection/Surfacing Film.—Blackshear, Thomas, illustrator. From a cover of *The Bluest Eye,* written by Toni Morrison. Plume, 1994. Reproduced by permission of Plume, a division of Penguin USA.—Broadside published by the National American Woman Suffrage Association, featuring "Why Women Want to Vote." The Library of Congress.—Brontë, Anne, Emily and Charlotte, painting by Patrick Branwell Brontë, located at the National Portrait Gallery,

1939, photograph. Copyright © Corbis-Bettmann.—Brontë, Charlotte, painting. Archive Photos.—Brooks, Gwendolyn, holding a copy of *The World of Gwendolyn Brooks,* photograph. AP/Wide World Photos.—Brown, John Mason (right) talking to National Book Award winners Marianne Moore, James Jones, and Rachel Carson, in New York City, NY, 1952, photograph. AP/Wide World Photos.—Brown, Rita Mae, photograph. AP/Wide World Photos.—Browning, Elizabeth Barret, 1848, illustration. Copyright © Corbis-Bettmann.—Burney, Fanny, engraving. Archive Photos, Inc.—Carter, Angela, photograph by Jerry Bauer. Copyright © Jerry Bauer.—Cather, Willa, photograph. AP/Wide World Photos.—Catherine the Great, illustration. Copyright © Archivo Iconografico, S.A./Corbis.—Catt, Carrie Chapman, photograph. The Library of Congress.—Cavendish, Margaret Lucas, engraving. Mary Evans Picture Library.—Child, Lydia Maria, photograph. The Library of Congress.—Childress, Alice, photograph by Jerry Bauer. Copyright © Jerry Bauer.—Chin, Tsai and Tamlyn Tomita in the 1993 film production of Amy Tan's *The Joy Luck Club.* Buena Vista/Hollywood/The Kobal Collection.—Chopin, Kate, photograph. The Library of Congress.—Cisneros, Sandra, 1991, photograph by Dana Tynan. AP/Wide World Photos.—Cixous, Hélène, photograph. Copyright © Bassouls Sophie/Corbis Sygma.—Class on a field trip to Library of Congress, photograph by Frances Benjamin Johnston. Copyright © Corbis.—Cleopatra VII, illustration. The Library of Congress.—Cyanotype by Frances Benjamin Johnson, ca. 1899, of girls and a teacher in a high school cooking class, photograph. Copyright © Corbis.—de la Cruz, Juana Inez, painting. Copyright © Philadelphia Museum of Art/Corbis-Bettmann.—de Pizan, Christine, writing in her study, photograph. MS. Harley 4431, f.4R. British Library, London.—Dickinson, Emily, photograph of a painting. The Library of Congress.—Doolittle, Hilda, 1949, photograph. AP/Wide World Photos.—Duras, Marguerite, photograph. AP/Wide World Photos.—Dworkin, Andrea, 1986, photograph. AP/Wide World Photos.—Edgeworth, Maria, engraving. The Library of Congress.—Eliot, George, photograph. Copyright © The Bettman Archive.—Emecheta, Buchi, photograph by Jerry Bauer. Copyright © Jerry Bauer.—Emily Dickinson Homestead in Amherst, Massachusetts, photograph. Copyright © James Marshall/Corbis.—Erdrich, Louise, photograph by Eric Miller. AP/Wide World Photos.—French, Marilyn, photograph by Jerry Bauer. Copyright © Jerry Bauer.—Friedan, Betty, president of the National Organization for Women, and other feminists march in New York City, photograph. Copyright © JP Laffont/Sygma/Corbis.—Friedan, Betty, with Yoko Ono, photograph. Copyright © Bettmann/Corbis.—Frontpiece and title page from *Poems on Various Subjects, Religious and Moral,* written by Phillis Wheatley. Copyright © The Pierpont Morgan Library/Art Resource, NY.—Fuller, Margaret, painting by John Plumbe. The Library of Congress.—Gandhi, Indira, photograph. Copyright © Corbis-Bettmann.—Garrison, William Lloyd, (bottom right), with the Pennsylvania Abolition Society, photograph. National Portrait Gallery.—Gilman, Charlotte Perkins, cover photograph. Copyright © Corbis.—Gilman, Charlotte P., photograph. Copyright © Corbis-Bettmann.—Godwin, Mary Wollstonecraft, illustration. Copyright © Corbis-Bettmann.—Hansberry, Lorraine, photograph by David Attie. AP/Wide World Photos.—Head, Bessie, photograph. Reproduced by the kind permission of the Estate of Bessie Head.—"Head of Medusa," marble sculpture by Gianlorenzo Bernini. Copyright © Araldo de Luca/Corbis.—Hellman, Lillian, photograph. AP/Wide World Photos.—Hurston, Zora Neale looking at "American Stuff," at the *New York Times* book fair, photograph. The Library of Congress.—Hurston, Zora Neale, photograph by Carl Van Vechten. The Carl Van Vechten Trust.—Hypatia, conte crayon drawing. Copyright © Corbis-Bettmann.—Illustration depicting a woman's body being the subject of political and social conflict, photograph. Barbara Kruger/Mary Boone Gallery.—Jolie, Angelina (right), and unidentified person, in the film *Foxfire,* photograph by Jane O'Neal. The Kobal Collection/O'Neal, Jane.—Karloff, Boris, in movie *Frankenstein*; 1935, photograph. The Kobal Collection.—Kingston, Maxine Hong, photograph by Jerry Bauer. Copyright © Jerry Bauer.—"La Temptation," depicting Adam and Eve in the Garden of Paradise. The Library of Congress.—Lessing, Doris, photograph by Jerry Bauer. Copyright © Jerry Bauer.—Luce, Clare Booth, portrait. Copyright © UPI/Bettmann Archive.—Manuscript page from *The Book of Ladies,* by Christine de Pizan. Bibliotheque Nationale de France.—Manuscript page of *Vieyra Impugnado,* written by Sor Margarita Ignacia and translated to Spanish by Inigo Rosende. Madrid: Antonio Sanz, 1731. The Special Collections Library, University of Michigan.—Martineau, Harriet, engraving. The Library of Congress.—Migrant mother with child huddled on either shoulder, Nipomo, California, 1936, photograph by Dorothea Lange. The Library of Congress.—Millay, Edna St. Vincent, photograph. AP/Wide World Photos.—Montagu, Lady Mary Wortley, engraving. Archive Photos, Inc.—Moore, Marianne, photograph by Jerry Bauer. Copyright © Jerry Bauer.—Morrison, Toni, 1993, photograph. AP/Wide World Photos.—Murasaki, Lady, looking out from the veranda of a monastery, illustration from *Tale of Genji.* Copyright © Asian Art Archaeology, Inc./Corbis.—National League of Women Voters' Headquarters, photograph. Copyright © Corbis-Bettmann.—National Women's Suffrage Association (NWSA), during a political convention in Chicago, Illinois, photograph. Copyright © Bettmann/Corbis.—Naylor, Gloria, photograph. Marion Ettlinger/AP/Wide World Photos.—Oates, Joyce Carol, 1991, photograph. AP/Wide World Photos.—October 15, 1913 publication of the early feminist periodical, *The New Freewoman,* photograph. McFarlin Library, Department of Special Collections, The University of Tulsa.—Paul, Alice (second from right), standing with five other suffragettes, photograph. AP/Wide World Photos.—Pfeiffer, Michelle, and Daniel Day-Lewis, in the film *The Age of Innocence,* 1993, photograph by Phillip Caruso. The Kobal Collection.—Plath, Sylvia, photograph. AP/Wide World Photos.—Poster advertising *Uncle Tom's Cabin,* by Harriet Beecher Stowe, "The Greatest Book of the Age," photograph. Copyright © Bettmann/Corbis.—Rich, Adrienne, holding certificate of poetry award, Chicago, Illinois, 1986, photograph. AP/Wide World Photos.—Rossetti, Christina, 1863, photograph by Lewis Carroll. Copyright © UPI/Bettmann.—Russell, Rosalind and Joan Crawford in the 1939 movie *The Women,* written by Clare Boothe Luce, photograph. MGM/The Kobal Collection.—Salem Witch Trial, lithograph by George H. Walker. Copyright © Bettmann/Corbis.—Sand, George, illustration. Copyright © Leonard de Selva/Corbis.—Sand, George, photograph. The Library of Congress.—Sanger, Margaret, Miss Clara Louise Rowe, and Mrs. Anne Kennedy, arranging the first American Birth Control Conference, photograph. Copyright © Underwood and Underwood/Corbis.—Sappho, bronze sculpture. The Library of Congress.—Sappho, illustration. The Library of Congress.—Sappho performing outdoors, illustration. The Library of Congress.—"Sara in a Green Bonnet," painting by Mary Cassatt, c. 1901. National Museum of American Art, Smithsonian Institution, Washington, DC, U.S.A.—Scene from the film *Mill on the Floss,* by George Eliot, engraving. Hulton Archive/Getty Images.—Segwick, Catherine Maria, slide. Archive Photos, Inc.—Sexton, Anne, photograph. Copyright © Bettmann/Corbis.—Sexton, Anne, with her daughters Joy and Linda, photograph. Time Life Pictures/Getty Images.—Shelley, Mary Wollstonecraft, painting by Samuel John Stump. Copyright © Corbis-Bettmann.—Stael, Madame de, color lithograph. Archive Photos, Inc.—Stanton, Elizabeth Cady, illustration. Copyright © Bettmann/Corbis.—Stanton, Elizabeth Cady, photograph. AP/Wide World Photos.—Stein, Gertrude (left), arriving in New York aboard the S. S. Champlain with her secretary and companion Alice B. Toklas, photograph. AP/Wide World Photos.—Stein, Gertrude, photograph by Carl Van Vechten. The Estate of Carl Van Vechten.—Steinem, Gloria, photograph. AP/Wide World Photos.—Stowe, Harriet Beecher, photograph. Copyright © Bettmann/Corbis.—Suffrage parade in New York, New York, October 15, 1915, photograph. The Library of Congress.—Supporters of the Equal Rights Amendment carry a banner down Pennsylvania Avenue, Washington, DC, photograph. AP/Wide World Photos.—Sur la Falaise aux Petites Dalles, 1873. Painting by Berthe Morisot. Copyright © Francis G. Mayer/Corbis.—Tan, Amy, 1993, photograph. AP/Wide World Photos.—*Time,* cover of Kate Millett, from August 31, 1970. Time Life Pictures/Stringer/Getty Images.—Title page of *A Vindication of the Rights of Woman: With Strictures on Political and Moral Subjects,* written by Mary Wollstonecraft. William L. Clements Library, University of Michigan.—Title page of *Adam Bede,* written by George Eliot. Edinburgh & London: Blackwood, 1859, Volume 1, New York: Harper, 1859. The Graduate Library, University of Michigan.—Title page from *De L'influence des Passions sur le Bonheur des Individus et des Nations,* (A Treatise on the Influence of the Passions upon the Happiness of Individuals and of Nations), written by Stael de Holstein, photograph. The Special Collections Library, University of Michigan.—Title page from *Evelina,* written by Fanny Burney, photograph. The Special Collections Library, University of Michigan.—Title page from *Mansfield Park,* written by Jane Austen. The Special Collections Library, University of Michigan.—Title page of *Mary, A Fiction,* written by Mary Wollstonecraft.—Title page from *Youth and the Bright Medusa,* written by Willa Cather. New York, Alfred A Knopf. The Special Collections Library, University of Michigan.—Title page of *A New-England Tale,* written by Catharine Maria Sedgewick. New York: E. Bliss and E. White, 1822. The Special Collections Library, University of Michigan.—Title page of *Aurora Leigh,* written by Elizabeth Barrett Browning. New York, Boston: C. S. Francis and Co., 1857. The Special Collections Library, University of Michigan.—Title page of *Mrs. Dalloway,* written by Virginia Woolf. London: Hogarth Press, 1925. The Special Collections Library, University of Michigan.—Title page of *The Dial: A Magazine for Literature, Philosophy, and Religion.* Boston. Weeks, Jordan and Company (etc.); London, Wiley and Putnam (etc.). Volume 1. The Special Collections Library, University of Michigan.—Title page of *The House of Mirth,* written by Edith Wharton. New York: C. Scribner's Sons, 1905. The Special Collections Library, University of Michigan.—Title page of *The Little Review,*

March 1916. The Purdy/Kresge Library, Wayne State University.—Title page of *Woman in the Nineteenth Century,* written by Sarah Margaret Fuller. New York, Greeley and McElrath. 1845. The Special Collections Library, University of Michigan.—Title page of *Wuthering Heights,* written by Emily Brontë. New York: Harper and Brothers. 1848. The Special Collections Library, University of Michigan.—Truth, Sojourner, photograph. Archive Photos, Inc.—Tubman, Harriet, photograph. The Library of Congress.—Victoria, Queen of England, illustration. The Library of Congress.—Walker, Alice, 1989, photograph. AP/Wide World Photos.—Welles, Orson, as Edward Rochester, with Joan Fontaine as Jane Eyre, in the film *Jane Eyre,* photograph. The Kobal Collection.—Wharton, Edith, photograph. AP/Wide World Photos.—Wheatley, Phillis, photograph. Copyright © The Bettman Archive.—Winfrey, Oprah, as Celie and Danny Glover as Albert with baby in scene from the film *The Color Purple,* written by Alice Walker, directed by Steven Spielberg, photograph. The Kobal Collection.—Women in French Revolution, invade assembly, demanding death penalty for members of the aristocracy, Woodcut. Copyright © Bettmann/Corbis.—Women workers in a shoe factory in Lynn, Massachusetts, photograph. Copyright © Corbis.—Woodhull, Victoria, reading statement before House Committee, drawing. The Library of Congress.—Woolf, Virginia, photograph. AP/Wide World Photos.—Woolson, Constance Fenimore, engraving. Archive Photos.

● = historical event

■ = literary event

1570 B.C.

● Queen Ahmose Nefertari, sister and principal wife of King Ahmose, rules as "god's wife," in a new position created by a law enacted by the King.

C. 1490 B.C.

● Queen Hatshepsut rules as pharaoh, several years after the death of her husband, King Thutmose II.

C. 1360 B.C.

● Queen Nefertiti rules Egypt alongside her husband, pharaoh Akhenaten.

C. 620 B.C.

● Sappho is born on the Isle of Lesbos, Greece.

C. 600 B.C.

■ Sappho organizes and operates a *thiasos,* an academy for young, unmarried Greek women.

● Spartan women are the most independent women in the world, and are able to own property, pursue an education, and participate in athletics.

C. 550 B.C.

● Sappho dies on the Isle of Lesbos.

C. 100 B.C.

● Roman laws allow a husband: to kill his wife if she is found in the act of adultery, to determine the amount of money his wife is owed in the event of divorce, and to claim his children as property.

69 B.C.

● Cleopatra VII Philopator is born in Egypt.

36 B.C.

● Marriage of Antony and Cleopatra.

C. 30 B.C.

● Cleopatra VII Philopator commits suicide in Egypt.

18

● Emperor Augustus decrees the *Lex Julia,* which penalizes childless Roman citizens, adulterers, and those who marry outside of their social rank or status.

C. 370

- Hypatia is born in Alexandria, Egypt.

415

- Hypatia is murdered in Alexandria, Egypt.

C. 500

- Salians (Germanic Franks living in Gaul) issue a code of laws which prohibit women from inheriting land; the law is used for centuries to prevent women from ruling in France.

592

- Empress Suiko (554-628) becomes the first woman sovereign of Japan.

C. 690

- Wu Zetian (624-705) becomes the only female emperor of Imperial China.

C. 700

- Japanese legal code specifies that in law, ceremony, and practice, Japanese men can be polygamous—having first wives and an unlimited number of "second wives" or concubines—, but women cannot.

877

- Lady Ise, Japanese court lady, is born. She is considered one of the most accomplished poets of her time and her poems are widely anthologized.

935

- Hrotsvitha (also Hrotsvit or Roswitha), considered the first German woman poet, is born.

940

- Lady Ise dies.

950

- Publication of the *Kagero Nikki* (*The Gossamer Years*), a diary written by an anonymous Japanese courtesan. The realism and confessional quality of the work influence the works of later court diarists.

C. 960

- Japanese poet Izumi Shikibu, known for her expression of erotic and Buddhist themes, is born. Her body of work includes more than 1,500 *waka* (31-syllable poems).

C. 1002

- Sei Shonagon, Japanese court lady, writes *Makura no Soshi* (*The Pillow Book*), considered a classic of Japanese literature and the originator of the genre known as *zuihitsu* ("to follow the brush") that employs a stream-of-consciousness literary style.

C. 1008

- Murasaki Shikibu writes *Genji Monogatari* (*The Tale of Genji*), considered a masterpiece of classical prose literature in Japan.

C. 1030

- Izumi Shikibu dies.

1098

- Hildegard von Bingen is born in Bermersheim, Germany.

C. 1100

- Twenty women troubadours—aristocratic poet-composers who write songs dealing with love—write popular love songs in France. About twenty-four of their songs survive, including four written by the famous female troubadour known as the Countess of Dia, or Beatrix.

1122

- Eleanor of Aquitaine is born in Aquitaine, France. Her unconventional life is chronicled for centuries in books and dramatic works.

C. 1150

- Sometime in the twelfth century (some sources say 1122), Marie de France, the earliest known female French writer and author of *lais,* a collection of twelve verse tales written in octosyllabic rhyming couplets, flourished. She is thought to be the originator of the *lay* as a poetic form.

C. 1170

- Marie of Champagne (1145-1198), daughter of King Louis VII of France and Eleanor of Aquitaine, cosponsors "courts of love" to debate points on the proper conduct of knights toward their ladies. Marie encourages Chrétien de Troyes to write *Lancelot,* and Andreas Capellanus to write *The Art of Courtly Love.*

1179

- Hildegard von Bingen dies in Disibodenberg, Germany.

C. 1200

- Women shirabyoshi performances are a part of Japanese court and Buddhist temple festivities. In their songs and dances, women performers dress in white, male attire which includes fans, court caps, and swords. This form of traditional dance plays an important role in the development of classical Japanese noh drama.

1204

- Eleanor of Aquitaine dies on 1 April.

C. 1275

- Japanese poet and court lady Abutsu Ni (1222?-1283) writes her poetic travel diary, *Izayoi Nikki* (*Diary of the Waning Moon*) on the occasion of her travel to Kyoto to seek inheritance rights for herself and her children.

C. 1328

- The French cite the Salic Law, which was promulgated in the early medieval period and prohibits women from inheriting land, as the authority for denying the crown of France to anyone—man or woman—whose descent from a French king can be traced only through the female line.

1346

- Famous mystic St. Birgitta of Sweden (c.1303-1373) founds the Roman Catholic Order of St. Saviour, whose members are called the Brigittines. She authors *Revelations,* an account of her supernatural visions.

1347

- Caterina Benincasa (later St. Catherine of Siena) is born on 25 March in Siena, Italy.

C. 1365

- Christine de Pizan is born in Venice, Italy.

C. 1373

- Margery Kempe is born in King's Lynn (now known as Lynn), in Norfolk, England.

1380

- St. Catherine of Siena dies on 29 April in Rome, Italy.

C. 1393

- Julian of Norwich (1342?-1416?), the most famous of all the medieval recluses in England, writes *Revelations of Divine Love,* expounding on the idea of Christ as mother.

1399

- Christine de Pizan writes the long poem "Letter to the God of Love," which marks the beginning of the *querelle des femmes* (debate on women). This attack on misogyny in medieval literature triggers a lively exchange of letters among the foremost French scholars of the day, and the *querelle* is continued by various European literary scholars for centuries.

1429

- Joan of Arc (1412-1431)—in support of Charles I, who is prevented by the English from assuming his rightful place as King of France—leads liberation forces to victory in Orléans.

1431

- Joan of Arc is burned at the stake as a heretic by the English on 30 May. She is acquitted of heresy by another church court in 1456 and proclaimed a saint in 1920.

C. 1431

- Christine de Pizan dies in France.

C. 1440

- Margery Kempe dies in England.

1451

- Isabella of Castile, future Queen of Spain, is born. She succeeds her brother in 1474 and rules jointly with her husband, Ferdinand of Aragon, from 1479.

1465

- Cassandra Fedele, who becomes the most famous woman scholar in Italy, is born in Venice.

1469

- Laura Cereta, outspoken feminist and humanist scholar, is born in Brescia, Italy.

1485

- Veronica Gambara is born in Italy. Her court becomes an important center of the Italian Renaissance, and Gambara earns distinction as an author of Petrarchan sonnets as well as for her patronage of the artist Corregio.

1486

- *Malleus Maleficarum* (*The Hammer of Witches*), an encyclopedia of contemporary knowledge about witches and methods of investigating the crime of witchcraft, is published in Europe. The volume details numerous justifications for women's greater susceptibility to evil, and contributes to the almost universal European persecution of women as witches that reaches its height between 1580 and 1660 and makes its way to Salem, Massachusetts in 1692.

1492

- Marguerite de Navarre is born on 11 April in France.

1499

- Laura Cereta dies in Brescia, Italy.

C. 1512

- Catherine Parr is born in England.

1515

- Teresa de Alhumadawas (later St. Teresa de Ávila) is born on 28 March in Gotarrendura, Spain.

1524

- Courtesan Gaspara Stampa, widely regarded as the greatest woman poet of the Renaissance, is born in Padua, Italy.

1533

- Queen Elizabeth I is born on 7 September in Greenwich, England, the daughter of King Henry VIII and his second wife, Anne Boleyn.

1536

- King Henry VIII of England beheads his second wife, Anne Boleyn, on 19 May. Boleyn is convicted of infidelity and treason after she fails to produce the desired male heir.

1538

- Vittoria Colonna (1492-1547), an influential woman in Renaissance Italy, achieves distinction as a poet with the publication of her first book of poetry.

1548

- Catherine Parr dies in England.

1549

- Marguerite de Navarre dies in France.

1550

- Veronica Gambara dies in Italy.

1554

- Gaspara Stampa dies on 23 April in Venice, Italy.

1555

- Moderata Fonte (pseudonym of Modesta Pozzo) is born in Venice, Italy.

1558

- Elizabeth I assumes the throne of England and presides over a period of peace and prosperity known as the Elizabethan Age.

- Cassadra Fedele dies in Venice. She is honored with a state funeral.

1559

- Marguerite de Navarre completes her *L'Heptaméron des Nouvelles* (the *Heptameron*), a series of stories primarily concerned with the themes of love and spirituality.

1561

- Mary Sidney, noted English literary patron, is born in England. She is the sister of poet Sir Philip Sidney, whose poems she edits and publishes after his death in 1586, and whose English translation of the Psalms she completes.

1565

- French scholar Marie de Gournay is born on 6 October in Paris. Known as the French "Minerva" (a woman of great wisdom or learning), she is a financial success as a writer of treatises on various subjects, including *Equality of Men and Women* (1622) and *Complaint of Ladies* (1626), which demand better education for women.

1582

- St. Teresa de Avila dies on 4 October in Alba.

1592

- Moderata Fonte (pseudonym of Modesta Pozzo) dies in Venice, Italy.

C. 1600

- Catherine de Vivonne (c. 1588-1665), Madame de Rambouillet, inaugurates and then presides over salon society in Paris, in which hostesses hold receptions in their salons or drawing rooms for the purpose of intellectual conversation. Salon society flourishes in the seventeenth and eighteenth centuries, and stimulates scholarly and literary development in France and England.
- Geisha (female artists and entertainers) and prostitutes are licensed by the Japanese government to work in the pleasure quarters of major cities in Japan.

1603

- Queen Elizabeth I dies on 24 March in Surrey, England.
- Izumo no Okuni is believed to originate kabuki, the combination of dance, drama, and music which dominates Japanese theater throughout the Tokugawa period (1600-1868).

1607

- Madeleine de Scudéry, one of the best-known and most influential writers of romance tales in seventeeth-century Europe, is born on 15 November in Le Havre, France.

C. 1612

- American poet Anne Bradstreet is born in Northampton, England.

1614

- Margaret Askew Fell, who helps establish the Society of Friends, or Quakers, and becomes known as the "mother of Quakerism," is born in Lancashire, England. Quakers give women unusual freedom in religious life. An impassioned advocate of the right of women to preach, Fell publishes the tract *Women's Speaking Justified, Proved and Allowed of by the Scriptures* in 1666.

1621

- Mary Sidney dies in England.

C. 1623

- Margaret Lucas Cavendish, later Duchess of Newcastle, is born in England. She authors fourteen volumes of works, including scientific treatises, poems, and plays, and her autobiography *The True Relation of My Birth, Breeding and Life* (1656).

1631

- Katherine Phillips (1631-1664), who writes poetry under the pseudonym "Orinda," is born. She is the founder of a London literary salon called the Society of Friendship that includes such luminaries as Jeremy Taylor and Henry Vaughn.

C. 1640

- Aphra Behn is born.

C. 1645

- Deborah Moody (c. 1580-c. 1659) becomes the first woman to receive a land grant in colonial America when she is given the title to land in Kings County (now Brooklyn), New York. She is also the first colonial woman to vote.

C. 1646

- Glückel of Hameln, who records her life as a Jewish merchant in Germany in her memoirs, is born in Hamburg.

1651

- Juana Ramírez de Asbaje (later known as Sor Juana Inés de la Cruz) is born on 12 November on a small farm called San Miguel de Nepantla in New Spain (now Mexico).

1670

- Aphra Behn becomes the first professional woman writer in England when her first play *The Forced Marriage; or, The Jealous Bridegroom,* is performed in London.

1672

- Anne Bradstreet dies on 16 September in Andover, Massachusetts.

C. 1673

- Francois Poulain de la Barre publishes *The Equality of the Sexes,* in which he supports the idea that women have intellectual powers equal to those of men. His work stimulates the betterment of women's education in succeeding centuries.

1673

- Margaret Lucas Cavendish, Duchess of Newcastle, dies in England.

1676

- After being captured and then released by Wampanaoag Indians, Puritan settler Mary White Rowlandson (1636-1678) writes what becomes a famous account of her captivity.

1689

- Mary Pierrpont (later Lady Mary Wortley Montagu) is born on 26 May in London, England.
- Aphra Behn dies on 16 April and is buried in the cloisters at Westminster Abbey.

1692

- The Salem, Massachusetts, witch hysteria begins in February, and eventually leads to the execution of eighteen women convicted of witchcraft in the infamous Salem Witchcraft Trials (1692-1693).

C. 1694

- Mary Astell (1666-1731) publishes the treatise *A Serious Proposal to the Ladies* in two volumes (1694-1697). In the work, Astell calls for the establishment of private institutions where single women live together for a time and receive quality education.

1695

- Sor Juana Inés de la Cruz dies on 17 April at the Convent of St. Jerome in Mexico.

1701

- Madeleine de Scudéry dies on 2 June in Paris, France.

C. 1704

- Sarah Kemble Knight (1666-1727), a Puritan author, records her arduous journey from Boston to New York to settle the estate of her cousin.

C. 1713

- Anne Kingsmill Finch (1661-1720) writes many poems dealing with the injustices suffered by women of the aristocratic class to which she belonged. As Countess of Winchilsea, she becomes the center of a literary circle at her husband's estate in Eastwell, England.

1728

- Mercy Otis Warren is born on 14 September in Barnstable, Massachusetts.

1729

- Catherine the Great is born on 2 May in Germany as Sophia Friederica Augusta.

1744

- Abigail Adams is born Abigail Smith on 11 November in Weymouth, Massachusetts.

1748

- Olympe de Gouges, French Revolutionary feminist, is born Olympe Gouze in Montauban, France. She plays an active role in the French Revolution, demanding equal rights for women in the new French Republic.

1752

- Frances "Fanny" Burney is born on 13 June in England.

C. 1753

- Phillis Wheatley is born in Africa.

1759

- Mary Wollstonecraft is born on 27 April in England.

1762

- Lady Mary Wortley Montagu dies on 21 August in London, England.
- Catherine the Great becomes Empress of Russia.

1766

- Germaine Necker (later Madame de Staël) is born on 22 April in Paris, France.

1768

- Maria Edgeworth is born on 1 January at Black Bourton in Oxfordshire, England.

1774

- Clementina Rind (1740-1774) is appointed publisher of the *Virginia Gazette* by the House of Burgesses in Virginia.

1775

- Jane Austen is born on 16 December at Steventon Rectory, Hampshire, England.

1776

- Men and women who hold property worth over 50 pounds are granted suffrage in New Jersey.

C. 1780

- Madame Roland (1754-1793), formerly Marie Philppon, hosts an important salon where revolutionary politicians and thinkers debate during the French Revolution. An outspoken feminist, she presses for women's political and social rights.

1784

- Hannah Adams (1758-1831) becomes the first American woman author to support herself with money earned from writing, with the publication of her first book, *View of Religions* (later *Dictionary of Religions*).
- Phillis Wheatley dies on 5 December in Boston, Massachusetts.

1787

- Catherine Sawbridge Macaulay publishes *Letters on Education,* an appeal for better education of women.
- Mary Wollstonecraft's *Thoughts on the Education of Daughters: With Reflections on Female Conduct, in the More Important Duties of Life* is published by J. Johnson.

1789

- Catharine Maria Sedgwick is born on 28 December in Stockbridge, Massachusetts.
- Olympe de Gouges writes *The Declaration of the Rights of Women and Citizen,* a 17-point document demanding the recognition of women as political, civil, and legal equals of men, and including a sample marriage contract that emphasizes free will and equality in marriage.

1792

- Sarah Moore Grimké is born on 26 November in Charleston, South Carolina.

- Mary Wollstonecraft's *A Vindication of the Rights of Woman, with Strictures on Political and Moral Subjects* is published by J. Johnson.

1793

- Lucretia Coffin Mott is born on 3 January in Nantucket, Massachusetts.
- Olympe de Gouges is executed by guillotine for treason on 3 November.
- Madame Roland is executed in November, ostensibly for treason, but actually because the Jacobins want to suppress feminist elements in the French Revolution.

1796

- Catherine the Great dies following a stroke on 6 November in Russia.

1797

- Mary Wollstonecraft Shelley is born on 30 August, in London, England.
- Mary Wollstonecraft dies on 10 September in London, England, from complications following childbirth.
- Sojourner Truth is born Isabella Bomefree in Ulster County, New York.

1799

- Mary Wollstonecraft's *Maria; or, The Wrongs of Woman: A Posthumous Fragment* is published by James Carey.

1801

- Caroline M. (Stansbury) Kirkland is born on 11 January in New York City.

1802

- Lydia Maria Child is born on 11 February in Medford, Massachusetts.

1804

- George Sand (pseudonym of Armandine Aurore Lucille Dupin) is born on 1 July in Paris, France.
- The Napoleonic Code is established in France under Napoleon I, and makes women legally subordinate to men. The code requires women to be obedient to their husbands, bars women from voting, sitting on juries, serving as legal witnesses, or sitting on chambers of commerce or boards of trade.

1805

- Angelina Emily Grimké is born on 20 February in Charleston, South Carolina.

1806

- Elizabeth Barrett Browning is born on 6 March in Coxhoe Hall, Durham, England.

1807

- Germaine de Staël's *Corinne, ou l'Italie* (*Corinne, or Italy*) is published by Nicolle.
- Suffrage in New Jersey is limited to "white male citizens."

1808

- Caroline Sheridan Norton is born on 22 March in England.

1810

- (Sarah) Margaret Fuller is born on 23 May in Cambridgeport, Massachusetts.
- Elizabeth Cleghorn Gaskell is born on 29 September in London, England.

1811

- Harriet Beecher Stowe is born on 14 June in Litchfield, Connecticut.
- Jane Austen's *Sense and Sensibility* is published by T. Egerton.

1813

- Harriet A. Jacobs is born in North Carolina.
- Jane Austen's *Pride and Prejudice* is published by T. Egerton.

1814

- Mercy Otis Warren dies on 19 October in Plymouth, Massachusetts.

1815

- Elizabeth Cady Stanton is born on 12 November in Johnstown, New York.
- King Louis XVIII of France outlaws divorce.

1816

- Charlotte Brontë is born on 21 April in Thornton, Yorkshire, England.
- Jane Austen's *Emma* is published by M. Carey.

1817

- Madame Germaine de Staël dies on 14 July in Paris, France.
- Jane Austen dies on 18 July in Winchester, Hampshire, England.

1818

- Emily Brontë is born on 30 July in Thornton, Yorkshire, England.
- Lucy Stone is born on 13 August near West Brookfield, Massachusetts.
- Abigail Adams dies on 28 October in Quincy, Massachusetts.
- Jane Austen's *Northanger Abbey and Persuasion* is published by John Murray.
- Educator Emma Hart Willard's *A Plan for Improving Female Education* is published by Middlebury College.
- Mary Wollstonecraft Shelley's *Frankenstein; or, The Modern Prometheus* is published by Lackington, Hughes, Harding, Mavor & Jones.

1819

- Julia Ward Howe is born on 27 May in New York City.
- George Eliot (pseudonym of Mary Ann Evans) is born on 22 November in Arbury, Warwickshire, England.

1820

- Susan B. Anthony is born on 15 February in Adams, Massachusetts.

1821

- Emma Hart Willard establishes the Troy Female Seminary in Troy, New York.

1822

- Frances Power Cobbe is born on 4 December in Dublin, Ireland.

1823

- Charlotte Yonge is born 11 August in Otterbourne, Hampshire, England.

1825

- Frances Ellen Watkins Harper is born on 24 September in Baltimore, Maryland.

1826

- Matilda Joslyn Gage is born on 24 March in Cicero, New York.

1830

- Christina Rossetti is born on 5 December in London, England.
- Emily Dickinson is born on 10 December in Amherst, Massachusetts.
- *Godey's Lady's Book*—the first American women's magazine—is founded by Louis Antoine Godey and edited by Sarah Josepha Hale (1788-1879).

1832

- Louisa May Alcott is born on 29 November in Germantown, Pennsylvania.
- George Sand's *Indiana* is published by Roret et Dupuy.

1833

- Oberlin Collegiate Institute—the first coeducational institution of higher learning— is established in Oberlin, Ohio.

1836

- Marietta Holley is born on 16 July near Adams, New York.

1837

- Mt. Holyoke College—the first college for women—is founded by Mary Lyon in South Hadley, Massachusetts.

- Alexandria Victoria (1819-1901) becomes Queen Victoria at the age of eighteen. Her reign lasts for 63 years, the longest reign of any British monarch.

1838

- Victoria Woodhull is born on 23 September in Homer, Ohio.
- Sarah Moore Grimké's *Letters on the Equality of the Sexes, and the Condition of Woman* is published by I. Knapp.

1840

- Frances "Fanny" Burney dies on 6 January in London, England.
- Ernestine Rose (1810-1892) writes the petition for what will become the Married Woman's Property Law (1848).

C. 1844

- Sarah Winnemucca is born on Paiute land near Humboldt Lake in what is now Nevada.

1845

- Margaret Fuller's *Woman in the Nineteenth Century* is published by Greeley & McElrath.

1847

- Charlotte Brontë's *Jane Eyre* is published by Smith, Elder.
- Emily Brontë's *Wuthering Heights* is published by T. C. Newby.

1848

- The first women's rights convention is called by Lucretia Coffin Mott and Elizabeth Cady Stanton on 19 July and is held in Seneca Falls, New York on 20 July.
- Emily Brontë dies on 19 December in Haworth, Yorkshire, England.
- New York State Legislature passes the Married Woman's Property Law, granting women the right to retain possession of property they owned prior to marriage.

1849

- Maria Edgeworth dies on 22 May in Edgeworthstown, her family's estate in Ireland.
- Sarah Orne Jewett is born on 3 September in South Berwick, Maine.
- Amelia Bloomer publishes the first issue of her Seneca Falls newspaper *The Lily,* which provides a forum for both temperance and women's rights reformers.
- The first state constitution of California extends property rights to women in their own name.

1850

- Margaret Fuller drowns—along with her husband and son—on 19 July in a shipwreck off of Fire Island, New York.
- The first National Woman's Rights Convention, planned by Lucy Stone and Lucretia Mott, is attended by over one thousand women on 23 and 24 October in Worcester, Massachusetts.
- Elizabeth Barrett Browning's *Poems,* containing her *Sonnets from the Portuguese,* is published by Chapman & Hall.
- *The Narrative of Sojourner Truth,* transcribed by Olive Gilbert, is published in the Boston periodical, the *Liberator.*

1851

- Mary Wollstonecraft Shelley dies on 1 February in Bournemouth, England.
- Kate Chopin is born on 8 February in St. Louis, Missouri.
- Sojourner Truth delivers her "A'n't I a Woman?" speech at the Women's Rights Convention on 29 May in Akron, Ohio.

1852

- Harriet Beecher Stowe's *Uncle Tom's Cabin; or, Life among the Lowly* is published by Jewett, Proctor & Worthington.
- Susan B. Anthony founds The Women's Temperance Society, the first temperance organization in the United States.

1853

- Charlotte Brontë's *Villette* is published by Smith, Elder.
- Paulina Kellogg Wright Davis (1813-1876) edits and publishes *Una,* the first newspaper of the women's rights movement.

1854

- Margaret Oliphant's *A Brief Summary in Plain Language of the Most Important Laws Concerning Women,* a pamphlet explaining the unfair laws concerning women and exposing the need for reform, is published in London.

1855

- Charlotte Brontë dies on 31 March in Haworth, Yorkshire, England.
- Elizabeth Cady Stanton, speaking in favor of expanding the Married Woman's Property Law, becomes the first woman to appear before the New York State Legislature.

1856

- Harriot Eaton Stanton Blatch is born on 20 January in Seneca Falls, New York.

1857

- Elizabeth Barrett Browning's *Aurora Leigh* is published by Chapman & Hall.

1858

- Emmeline Pankhurst is born on 4 July in Manchester, England.
- Anna Julia Haywood Cooper is born on 10 August in Raleigh, North Carolina.

1859

- Carrie Chapman Catt is born on 9 January in Ripon, Wisconsin.

1860

- Charlotte Perkins Gilman is born on 3 July in Hartford, Connecticut.
- Jane Addams is born on 6 September in Cedarville, Illinois.

1861

- Victoria Earle Matthews is born on 27 May in Fort Valley, Georgia.
- Elizabeth Barrett Browning dies on 29 June in Florence, Italy.
- Harriet Jacobs's *Incidents in the Life of a Slave Girl, Written by Herself,* edited by Lydia Maria Child, is published in Boston.

1862

- Edith Wharton is born on 24 January in New York City.
- Ida B. Wells-Barnett is born on 16 July in Holly Springs, Mississippi.
- Julia Ward Howe's "The Battle Hymn of the Republic" is published in the *Atlantic Monthly.*

1864

- Caroline M. (Stansbury) Kirkland dies of a stroke on 6 April in New York City.

1865

- Elizabeth Cleghorn Gaskell dies on 12 November in Holybourne, Hampshire, England.

1866

- The American Equal Rights Association—dedicated to winning suffrage for African American men and for women of all colors—is founded by Susan B. Anthony and Elizabeth Cady Stanton on 1 May. Lucretia Coffin Mott is elected as the group's president.
- Elizabeth Cady Stanton runs for Congress as an independent; she receives 24 of 12,000 votes cast.

1867

- Catharine Maria Sedgwick dies on 31 July in Boston, Massachusetts.

1868

- Susan B. Anthony and Elizabeth Cady Stanton found the New York-based weekly newspaper, *The Revolution,* with the motto: "The true republic—men, their rights and nothing more; women, their rights and nothing less," in January.
- Julia Ward Howe founds the New England Woman Suffrage Association and the New England Women's Club.
- Louisa May Alcott's *Little Women; or, Meg, Jo, Beth, and Amy* (2 vols., 1868-69) is published by Roberts Brothers.

1869

- John Stuart Mill's treatise in support of women's suffrage, *The Subjection of Women,* is published in London.

- Emma Goldman is born on 27 June in Kovno, Lithuania.
- Louisa May Alcott's *Hospital Sketches and Camp and Fireside Stories* is published by Roberts Brothers.
- Women are granted full and equal suffrage and are permitted to hold office within the territory of Wyoming.
- The National Woman Suffrage Association is founded by Elizabeth Cady Stanton and Susan B. Anthony in May in New York City.
- The American Woman Suffrage Association is founded by Lucy Stone, Julia Ward Howe, and others in November in Boston, Massachusetts.

1870

- *The Woman's Journal,* edited by Lucy Stone, Henry Blackwell, and Mary Livermore, begins publication on 8 January.
- Victoria Woodhull and Tennessee Claflin publish the first issue of their controversial New York weekly newspaper, *Woodhull and Claflin's Weekly.*

1871

- Women are granted full and equal suffrage in the territory of Utah. Their rights are revoked in 1887 and restored in 1896.
- Victoria Woodhull presents her views on women's rights in a passionate speech to the House Judiciary Committee, marking the first personal appearance before such a high congressional committee by a woman.
- Wives of many prominent U. S. politicians, military officers, and businessmen found the Anti-Suffrage party to fight against women's suffrage.

1872

- Victoria Woodhull, as a member of the Equal Rights Party (or National Radical Reform Party), becomes the first woman candidate for the office of U.S. President. Her running mate is Frederick Douglass.
- Susan B. Anthony and 15 other women attempt to cast their votes in Rochester, New York, in the presidential election. Anthony is arrested and fined $100, which she refuses to pay.
- Sojourner Truth attempts to cast her vote in Grand Rapids, Michigan in the presidential election but is denied a ballot.

1873

- Colette is born on 28 January in Burgundy, France.
- Maria Mitchell (1818-1889), astronomer and faculty member at Vassar College, establishes the Association of the Advancement of Women.
- Willa Cather is born on 7 December in Back Creek Valley, Virginia.
- Sarah Moore Grimké dies on 23 December in Hyde Park, Massachusetts.
- Louisa May Alcott's *Work: A Story of Experience* is published by Roberts Brothers.

1874

- Gertrude Stein is born on 3 February in Allegheny, Pennsylvania.
- Amy Lowell is born on 9 February in Brookline, Massachusetts.

1876

- George Sand dies on 9 June in Nohant, France.
- Susan Glaspell is born on 1 July (some sources say 1882) in Davenport, Iowa.

1877

- Caroline Sheridan Norton dies on 15 June in England.

1878

- Passage of the Matrimonial Causes Act in England enables abused wives to obtain separation orders to keep their husbands away from them.
- The "Susan B. Anthony Amendment," which will extend suffrage to women in the United States, is first proposed in Congress by Senator A. A. Sargent.

1879

- Margaret Sanger is born on 14 September in Corning, New York.
- Angelina Emily Grimké dies on 26 October in Hyde Park, Massachusetts.

1880

- Christabel Pankhurst is born on 22 September in Manchester, England.
- Lydia Maria Child dies on 20 October in Wayland, Massachusetts.
- Lucretia Coffin Mott dies on 11 November in Philadelphia, Pennsylvania.
- George Eliot (pseudonym of Mary Ann Evans) dies on 22 December in London, England.

1881

- Hubertine Auclert founds *La Citoyenne* (*The Citizen*), a newspaper dedicated to female suffrage.
- The first volume of *A History of Woman Suffrage* (Vols. 1-3, 1881-1888; Vol. 4, 1903), edited and compiled by Susan B. Anthony, Elizabeth Cady Stanton, Ida Harper Husted, and Matilda Joslyn Gage, is published by Fowler & Welles.

1882

- Virginia Woolf is born on 25 January in London, England.
- Sylvia Pankhurst is born on 5 May in Manchester, England.
- Aletta Jacobs (1854-1929), the first woman doctor in Holland, opens the first birth control clinic in Europe.

1883

- Sojourner Truth dies on 26 November in Battle Creek, Michigan.
- Olive Schreiner's *The Story of an African Farm* is published by Chapman & Hall.

1884

- Eleanor Roosevelt is born on 11 October in New York City.

1885

- Alice Paul is born on 11 January in Moorestown, New Jersey.
- Isak Dinesen is born Karen Christentze Dinesen on 17 April in Rungsted, Denmark.

1886

- Emily Dickinson dies on 15 May in Amherst, Massachusetts.
- H. D. (Hilda Doolittle) is born on 10 September in Bethlehem, Pennsylvania.

1887

- Marianne Moore is born on 15 November in Kirkwood, Missouri.
- Article five of the Peace Preservation Law in Japan prohibits women and minors from joining political organizations and attending meetings where political speeches are given, and from engaging in academic studies of political subjects.

1888

- Louisa May Alcott dies on 6 March in Boston, Massachusetts, and is buried in Sleepy Hollow Cemetery in Concord, Massachusetts.
- Susan B. Anthony organizes the International Council of Women with representatives from 48 countries.
- Louisa Lawson (1848-1920) founds Australia's first feminist newspaper, *The Dawn.*
- The National Council of Women in the United States is formed to promote the advancement of women in society. The group also serves as a clearinghouse for various women's organizations.

1889

- Anna Akhmatova is born Anna Adreyevna Gorenko on 23 June in Bolshoy Fontan, Russia.

1890

- The National American Woman Suffrage Association (NAWSA) is formed by the merging of the American Woman Suffrage Assocation and the National Woman Suffrage Association. Elizabeth Cady Stanton is the NAWSA's first president; she is succeeded by Susan B. Anthony in 1892.

1891

- Zora Neale Hurston is born on 15 (some sources say 7) January in Nostasulga, Alabama. (Some sources cite birth year as c. 1901 or 1903, and birth place as Eatonville, Florida).

- Sarah Winnemucca dies on 16 October in Monida, Montana.

1892

- Edna St. Vincent Millay is born on 22 February in Rockland, Maine.
- Djuna Barnes is born on 12 June in Cornwall on Hudson, New York.
- Rebecca West (pseudonym of Cicily Isabel Fairfield) is born on 21 December in County Kerry, Ireland.
- Charlotte Perkins Gilman's *The Yellow Wallpaper* is published in *New England Magazine.*
- Frances E. W. Harper's *Iola Leroy; or, Shadows Uplifted* is published by Garrigues Bros.
- Olympia Brown (1835-1926), first woman ordained minister in the United States, founds the Federal Suffrage Association to campaign for women's suffrage.
- Ida Wells-Barnett's *Southern Horrors. Lynch Law in All its Phases* is published by Donohue and Henneberry.

1893

- Lucy Stone dies on 18 October in Dorchester, Massachusetts.
- The National Council of Women of Canada is founded by Lady Aberdeen.
- Suffrage is granted to women in Colorado.
- New Zealand becomes the first nation to grant women the vote.

1894

- Christina Rossetti dies on 29 December in London, England.

1895

- The first volume of Elizabeth Cady Stanton's *The Woman's Bible* (3 vols., 1895-1898) is published by European Publishing Company.

1896

- Harriet Beecher Stowe dies on 1 July in Hartford, Connecticut.
- Idaho grants women the right to vote.
- The National Assocation of Colored Women's Clubs is founded in Washington, D.C.

1897

- Harriet A. Jacobs dies on 7 March in Cambridge, Massachusetts.

1898

- Matilda Joslyn Gage dies on 18 March in Chicago, Illinois.
- Charlotte Perkins Gilman's *Women and Economics* is published by Small Maynard.
- The Meiji Civil Law Code, the law of the Japanese nation state, makes the patriarchal family, rather than the individual, the legally recognized entity.

1899

- Elizabeth Bowen is born on 7 June in Dublin, Ireland.
- Kate Chopin's *The Awakening* is published by Herbert S. Stone.

1900

- Colette's *Claudine a l'ecole* (*Claudine at School,* 1930) is published by Ollendorf.
- Carrie Chapman Catt succeeds Susan B. Anthony as president of the NAWSA.

1901

- Charlotte Yonge dies of bronchitis and pneumonia on 24 March in Elderfield, England.

1902

- Elizabeth Cady Stanton dies on 26 October in New York City.
- Women of European descent gain suffrage in Australia.

1903

- The Women's Social and Political Union, led by suffragists Emmeline and Christabel Pankhurst, stage demonstrations in Hyde Park in London, England.

1904

- Frances Power Cobbe dies on 5 April.
- Kate Chopin dies following a cerebral hemorrhage on 22 August in St. Louis, Missouri.

- Susan B. Anthony establishes the International Woman Suffrage Alliance in Berlin, Germany.

C. 1905

- Lillian Hellman is born on 20 June in New Orleans, Louisiana.

1905

- Austrian activist and novelist Bertha von Suttner (1843-1914) receives the Nobel Peace Prize.

1906

- Susan B. Anthony dies on 13 March in Rochester, New York.
- Finnish women gain suffrage and the right to be elected to public office.

1907

- Victoria Earle Matthews dies of tuberculosis on 10 March in New York City.
- Mary Edwards Walker, M.D.'s pamphlet on women's suffrage, "Crowning Constitutional Argument," is published.
- Harriot Stanton Blatch founds the Equality League of Self-Supporting Women, later called the Women's Political Union.

1908

- Simone de Beauvoir is born on 9 January in Paris, France.
- Julia Ward Howe becomes the first woman to be elected to the American Academy of Arts and Letters.

1909

- Sarah Orne Jewett dies on 24 June in South Berwick, Maine.
- Swedish author Selma Lagerlöf (1858-1940) becomes the first woman to receive the Nobel Prize for Literature.
- "The Uprising of the 20,000" grows from one local to a general strike against several shirtwaist factories in New York City. Over 700 women and girls are arrested, and 19 receive workhouse sentences. The strike is called off on 15 February 1910. Over 300 shops settle with the union, and workers achieve the terms demanded.
- Jeanne-Elisabeth Archer Schmahl (1846-1915) founds the French Union for Woman Suffrage.

1910

- Julia Ward Howe dies of pneumonia on 17 October in Newport, Rhode Island.
- The Women' Political Union holds the first large suffrage parade in New York City.
- Suffrage is granted to women in Washington State.
- Jane Addams's *Twenty Years at Hull House* is published by Macmillan.

1911

- Frances Ellen Watkins Harper dies on 22 February in Philadelphia, Pennsylvania.
- A fire at the Triangle Shirtwaist Factory in New York City on 25 March claims the lives of 146 factory workers, 133 of them women. Public outrage over the fire leads to reforms in labor laws and improvement in working conditions.
- Suffrage is granted to women in California.
- Edith Wharton's *Ethan Frome* is published by Scribner.

1912

- Suffrage is granted to women in Arizona, Kansas, and Oregon.
- A parade in support of women's suffrage is held in New York City and draws 20,000 participants and half a million onlookers.

1913

- Muriel Rukeyser is born on 15 December in New York City.
- Willa Cather's *O Pioneers!* is published by Houghton.
- Ida Wells-Barnett founds the Alpha Suffrage Club in Chicago.
- Suffrage is granted to women in Alaska.
- The Congressional Union is founded by Alice Paul and Lucy Burns.

1914

- Marguerite Duras is born on 4 April in Gia Dinh, Indochina (now Vietnam).
- The National Federation of Women's Clubs, which includes over two million white women and women of color, formally endorses the campaign for women's suffrage.
- Suffrage is granted to women in Montana and Nevada.
- Margaret Sanger begins publication of her controversial monthly newsletter *The Woman Rebel,* which is banned as obscene literature.

1915

- Charlotte Perkins Gilman's *Herland* is published in the journal *Forerunner.*
- *Woman's Work in Municipalities,* by American suffragist and historian Mary Ritter Beard (1876-1958), is published by Appleton.
- Icelandic women who are age 40 or older gain suffrage.
- Members of the NAWSA from across the United States hold a large parade in New York city.
- Most Danish women over age 25 gain suffrage.

1916

- Ardent suffragist and pacifist Jeannette Pickering Rankin (1880-1973) of Montana becomes the first woman elected to the U. S. House of Representatives. She later votes against U. S. involvement in both World Wars.
- The Congressional Union becomes the National Women's Party, led by Alice Paul and Lucy Burns.
- NAWSA president Carrie Chapman Catt unveils her "Winning Plan" for American women's suffrage at a convention held in Atlantic City, New Jersey.
- Suffrage is granted to women in Alberta, Manitoba, and Saskatchewan, Canada.
- Margaret Sanger opens the first U. S. birth-control clinic in Brooklyn, New York. The clinic is shut down 10 days after it opens and Sanger is arrested.
- Margaret Sanger's *What Every Mother Should Know; or, How Six Little Children were Taught the Truth* is published by M. N. Maisel.

1917

- Gwendolyn Brooks is born on 7 June in Topeka, Kansas.
- The National Women's Party becomes the first group in U.S. history to picket in front of the White House. Picketers are arrested and incarcerated; during their incarceration, Alice Paul leads them in a hunger strike. Many of the imprisoned suffragists are brutally force-fed, including Paul. The suffragettes' mistreatment is published in newspapers, the White House bows to public pressure, and they are released.
- White women in Arkansas are granted partial suffrage; they are able to vote in primary, but not general, elections.
- Suffrage is granted to women in New York.
- Suffrage is granted to women in Estonia, Latvia, and Lithuania.
- Women in Ontario and British Columbia, Canada, gain suffrage.
- Suffragists and members of the NAWSA, led by president Carrie Chapman Catt, march in a parade in New York City.
- Margaret Sanger founds and edits *The Birth Control Review,* the first scientific journal devoted to the subject of birth control.

1918

- Willa Cather's *My Antonia* is published by Houghton.
- Suffrage is granted to women in Michigan, Oklahoma, and South Dakota; women in Texas gain suffrage for primary elections only.
- President Woodrow Wilson issues a statement in support of a federal constitutional amendment granting full suffrage to American women.
- A resolution to amend the U.S. constitution to ensure that the voting rights of U.S. citizens cannot "be denied or abridged by the United States or any state on account of sex" passes in the House of Representatives.
- President Wilson urges the Senate to support the 19th amendment, but fails to win the two-thirds majority necessary for passage.
- Women in the United Kingdom who are married, own property, or are college graduates over the age of 30, are granted suffrage.
- Women in Austria, Czechoslovakia, Germany, Luxembourg, and Poland gain suffrage.

- Women in New Brunswick and Nova Scotia, Canada, gain suffrage. Canadian women of British or French heritage gain voting rights in Federal elections.
- Marie Stopes's *Married Love* and *Wise Parenthood* are published by A. C. Fifield.
- Harriot Stanton Blatch's *Mobilizing Woman-Power,* with a foreword by Theodore Roosevelt, is published by The Womans Press.

1919

- Women in the Netherlands, Rhodesia, and Sweden gain suffrage.
- Doris Lessing is born on 22 October in Kermanshah, Persia (now Iran).
- The "Susan B. Anthony Amendment," also known as the 19th Amendment to the U. S. Constitution, after it is defeated twice in the Senate, passes in both houses of Congress. The amendment is sent to states for ratification.

1920

- The 19th Amendment to the U.S. Constitution is ratified by the necessary two-thirds of states and American women are guaranteed suffrage on 26 August when Secretary of State Bainbridge Colby signs the amendment into law.
- The NAWSA is reorganized as the National League of Women Voters and elects Maud Wood Park as its first president.
- Bella Abzug is born on 24 July in New York City.
- Icelandic women gain full suffrage.
- Edith Wharton's *The Age of Innocence* is published by Meredith.
- Colette's *Cheri* is published by Fayard.

1921

- Betty Friedan is born on 4 February in Peoria, Illinois.
- Edith Wharton receives the Pulitzer Prize for fiction for *The Age of Innocence.*
- Margaret Sanger organizes the first American Conference on Birth Control in New York City.

1922

- Irish women gain full suffrage.
- Grace Paley is born on 11 December in New York City.
- Edna St. Vincent Millay's *The Ballad of the Harp-Weaver* is published by F. Shay.

1923

- Edna St. Vincent Millay receives the Pulitzer Prize for Poetry for *The Ballad of the Harp-Weaver.*
- Margaret Sanger opens the Birth Control Clinical Research Bureau in New York to dispense contraceptives to women under the supervision of a licensed physician and to study the effect of contraception upon women's health.
- Margaret Sanger founds the American Birth Control League.
- The Equal Rights Amendment (ERA), written by Alice Paul, is introduced in Congress for the first time in December.

1924

- Phyllis Schlafly is born on 15 August in St. Louis, Missouri.
- Shirley Chisolm is born on 30 November in Brooklyn, New York.

1925

- Amy Lowell dies on 12 May in Brookline, Massachusetts.
- *Collected Poems of H.D.* is published by Boni & Liveright.
- Virginia Woolf's *Mrs. Dalloway* is published by Harcourt.

1926

- Marietta Holley dies on 1 March near Adams, New York.
- Marianne Moore becomes the first woman editor of *The Dial* in New York City, a post she holds until 1929.
- Carrie Chapman Catt and Nettie Rogers Schuler's *Woman Suffrage and Politics; the Inner Story of the Suffrage Movement* is published by Charles Scribner's Sons.
- Grazia Deledda receives the Nobel Prize in Literature.

1927

- Victoria Woodhull dies on 10 June in Norton Park, England.
- Virginia Woolf's *To the Lighthouse* is published by Harcourt.

1928

- Maya Angelou is born Marguerite Johnson on 4 April in St. Louis, Missouri.
- Emmeline Pankhurst dies on 14 June in London, England.
- Anne Sexton is born on 9 November in Newton, Massachusetts.
- Virginia Woolf's *Orlando* is published by Crosby Gaige.
- Women are granted full suffrage in Great Britain.
- Gertrude Stein's *Useful Knowledge* is published by Payson & Clarke.
- Sigrid Undset receives the Nobel Prize in Literature.

1929

- Adrienne Rich is born on 16 May in Baltimore, Maryland.
- Marilyn French is born on 21 November in New York City.
- While Arthur M. Schlesinger Sr. reads her speech for her, Margaret Sanger appears in a gag on a stage in Boston where she has been prevented from speaking.
- Virginia Woolf's *A Room of One's Own* is published by Harcourt.

1930

- Lorraine Hansberry is born on 19 May in Chicago, Illinois.
- Cairine Wilson is appointed the first woman senator in Canada.

1931

- Jane Addams receives the Nobel Peace Prize.
- Toni Morrison is born Chloe Anthony Wofford on 18 February in Lorain, Ohio.
- Ida B. Wells-Barnett dies on 25 March in Chicago, Illinois.

1932

- Sylvia Plath is born on 27 October in Boston, Massachusetts.

1933

- Gertrude Stein's *The Autobiography of Alice B. Toklas* is published by Harcourt.
- Frances Perkins (1882-1965) is appointed Secretary of Labor by President Franklin D. Roosevelt, and becomes the first female cabinet member in the United States.

1934

- Gloria Steinem is born on 25 March in Toledo, Ohio.
- Kate Millett is born on 14 September in St. Paul, Minnesota.
- Lillian Hellman's *The Children's Hour* debuts on 20 November at Maxine Elliot's Theatre in New York City.

1935

- Jane Addams dies of cancer on 21 May in Chicago, Illinois.
- Charlotte Perkins Gilman commits suicide on 17 August in Pasadena, California.
- The National Council of Negro Women is founded by Mary McLeod Bethune (1875-1955).

1936

- First lady Eleanor Roosevelt begins writing a daily syndicated newspaper column, "My Day."
- Margaret Mitchell's *Gone with the Wind* is published by Macmillan.

1937

- Hélène Cixous is born on 5 June in Oran, Algeria.
- Bessie Head is born on 6 July in Pietermaritzburg, South Africa.
- Edith Wharton dies on 11 August in St. Brice-sous-Foret, France.
- Zora Neale Hurston's *Their Eyes Were Watching God* is published by Lippincott.

- Margaret Mitchell (1900-1949) receives the Pulitzer Prize in Letters & Drama for novel for *Gone with the Wind.*
- Anne O'Hare McCormick becomes the first woman to receive the Pulitzer Prize in Journalism, which she is given for distinguished correspondence for her international reporting on the rise of Italian Fascism in the *New York Times.*

1938

- Joyce Carol Oates is born on 16 June in Lockport, New York.
- Pearl Buck receives the Nobel Prize in Literature.

1939

- Germaine Greer is born on 29 January near Melbourne, Australia.
- Lillian Hellman's *The Little Foxes* debuts on 15 February at National Theatre in New York City.
- Margaret Atwood is born on 18 November in Ottawa, Ontario, Canada.
- Paula Gunn Allen is born in Cubero, New Mexico.
- French physician Madeleine Pelletier (1874-1939) is arrested for performing abortions in Paris, France; she dies later the same year. Throughout her medical career, Pelletier advocated women's rights to birth control and abortion, and founded her own journal, *La Suffragist.*

1940

- Emma Goldman dies on 14 May in Toronto, Ontario, Canada.
- Maxine Hong Kingston is born on 27 October in Stockton, California.
- Harriot Eaton Stanton Blatch dies on 20 November in Greenwich, Connecticut.

1941

- Virginia Woolf commits suicide on 28 March in Lewes, Sussex, England.

1942

- Erica Jong is born on 26 March in New York City.
- Isabel Allende is born on 2 August in Lima, Peru.
- Ellen Glasgow (1873-1945) receives the Pulitzer Prize for her novel *In This Our Life.*
- Margaret Walker (1915-1998) becomes the first African American to receive the Yale Series of Young Poets Award for her collection *For My People.*

1944

- Alice Walker is born on 9 February in Eatonton, Georgia.
- Martha Gellhorn (1908-1998) is the only woman journalist to go ashore with Allied troops during the D-Day invasion of Normandy, France in June.
- Buchi Emecheta is born on 21 July in Yaba, Lagos, Nigeria.
- Rita Mae Brown is born on 28 November in Hanover, Pennsylvania.
- Women are granted suffrage in France and Jamaica.

1945

- Eleanor Roosevelt becomes the first person to represent the U. S. at the United Nations. She serves until 1951, is reappointed in 1961, and serves until her death in 1962.
- Gabriela Mistral receives the Nobel Prize in Literature.
- Louise Bogan is named U. S. Poet Laureate.

1946

- Gertrude Stein dies of cancer on 27 July in Neuilly-sur-Seine, France.
- Andrea Dworkin is born on 26 September in Camden, New Jersey.
- Mary Ritter Beard's *Woman as a Force in History: A Study in Traditions and Realities* is published by Macmillan.
- Eleanor Roosevelt becomes chair of the United Nations Human Rights Commission. She remains chair until 1951.

1947

- Carrie Chapman Catt dies on 9 March in New Rochelle, New York.

- Willa Cather dies on 24 April in New York City.
- Dorothy Fuldheim, a newscaster in Cleveland, Ohio, becomes the first female television news anchor at WEWS-TV.

1948

- Susan Glaspell dies on 27 July in Provincetown, Massachusetts.
- Ntozake Shange is born Paulette Linda Williams on 18 October in Trenton, New Jersey.
- Leonie Adams is named U. S. Poet Laureate.

1949

- Simone de Beauvoir's *Le deuxième sexe* (*The Second Sex,* H. M. Parshley, translator: Knopf, 1953) is published by Gallimard.
- Elizabeth Bishop is named U. S. Poet Laureate.
- Gwendolyn Brooks's *Annie Allen* is published by Harper.

1950

- Gloria Naylor is born on 25 January in New York City.
- Edna St. Vincent Millay dies of a heart attack on 19 October at Steepletop, Austerlitz, New York.
- Gwendolyn Brooks receives the Pulitzer Prize for poetry for *Annie Allen.*

1951

- Marianne Moore's *Collected Poems* is published by Macmillan.
- Marguerite Higgins (1920-1960) receives the Pulitzer Prize for Journalism in overseas reporting for her account of the battle at Inchon, Korea in September, 1950.

1952

- Amy Tan is born on 19 February in Oakland, California.
- Rita Dove is born on 28 August in Akron, Ohio.
- bell hooks is born Gloria Jean Watkins on 25 September in Hopkinsville, Kentucky.
- Marianne Moore receives the National Book Critics Circle award for poetry and the Pulitzer Prize for poetry for *Collected Poems.*

1953

- *A Writer's Diary: Being Extracts from the Diary of Virigina Woolf,* edited by Leonard Woolf, is published by Hogarth.
- The International Planned Parenthood Federation is founded by Margaret Sanger, who serves as the organization's first president.
- Women are granted suffrage in Mexico.

1954

- Louise Erdrich is born on 7 June in Little Falls, Minnesota.
- Colette dies on 3 August in Paris, France.
- Sandra Cisneros is born on 20 December in Chicago, Illinois.

1955

- On 1 December American civil rights activist Rosa Parks (1913-) refuses to move from her seat for a white passenger on a Montgomery, Alabama bus and is arrested.

1956

- The Anti-Prostitution Act, written and campaigned for by Kamichika Ichiko, makes prostitution illegal in Japan.

1958

- Christabel Pankhurst dies on 13 February in Los Angeles, California.

1959

- Susan Faludi is born on 18 April in New York City.
- Lorraine Hansberry's *A Raisin in the Sun* debuts in March at the Ethel Barrymore Theatre in New York City.
- Lorraine Hansberry becomes the youngest woman and first black artist to receive a New York Drama Critics Circle Award for best American play for *A Raisin in the Sun.*

1960

- Zora Neale Hurston dies on 28 January in Fort Pierce, Florida.
- Sylvia Pankhurst dies on 27 September in Addis Ababa, Ethiopia.

- The U.S. Food and Drug Administration approves the first oral contraceptive for distribution to consumers in May.
- Harper Lee's *To Kill a Mockingbird* is published by Lippincott.

1961

- H. D. (Hilda Doolittle) dies on 27 September in Zurich, Switzerland.
- Harper Lee receives the Pulitzer Prize for the novel for *To Kill a Mockingbird.*
- President John F. Kennedy establishes the President's Commission on the Status of Women on 14 December and appoints Eleanor Roosevelt as head of the commission.

1962

- Isak Dinesen dies on 7 September in Rungsted Kyst, Denmark.
- Eleanor Roosevelt dies on 7 November in New York City.
- Naomi Wolf is born on 12 November in San Francisco, California.
- Doris Lessing's *The Golden Notebook* is published by Simon & Schuster.

1963

- Betty Friedan's *The Feminine Mystique* is published by Norton and becomes a bestseller.
- Sylvia Plath's *The Bell Jar* is published under the pseudonym Victoria Lucas by Heinemann.
- Sylvia Plath commits suicide on 11 February in London, England.
- Barbara Wertheim Tuchman (1912-1989) becomes the first woman to receive the Pulitzer Prize for general nonfiction for *The Guns of August.*
- The Equal Pay Act is passed by the U.S. Congress on 28 May. It is the first federal law requiring equal compensation for men and women in federal jobs.
- Entitled *American Women,* the report issued by the President's Commission on the Status of Women documents sex discrimination in nearly all corners of American society, and urges the U.S. Supreme Court to clarify legal status of women under the U.S. Constitution.

1964

- Anna Julia Haywood Cooper dies on 27 February in Washington, DC.

1965

- Lorraine Hansberry dies of cancer on 12 January in New York City.
- Women are granted suffrage in Afghanistan.

1966

- Anna Akhmatova dies on 6 March in Russia.
- Margaret Sanger dies on 6 September in Tucson, Arizona.
- National Organization for Women (NOW) is founded on 29 June by Betty Friedan and 27 other founding members. NOW is dedicated to promoting full participation in society for women and advocates for adequate child care for working mothers, reproductive rights, and the Equal Rights Amendment to the U.S. Constitution.
- Anne Sexton's *Live or Die* is published by Houghton.
- Nelly Sachs (1891-1970) receives the Nobel Prize in Literature, which she shares with Shmuel Yosef Agnon.

1967

- Anne Sexton receives the Pulitzer Prize for poetry for *Live or Die.*
- Senator Eugene McCarthy, with 37 cosponsors, introduces the Equal Rights Amendment in the U.S. Senate.

1968

- Audre Lorde's *The First Cities* is published by Poets Press.

1969

- Joyce Carol Oates's *them* is published by Vanguard Press.
- Shirley Chisolm becomes the first African American woman elected to Congress when she takes her seat in the U.S. House of Representatives on 3 January.
- Golda Meir (1898-1978) becomes the fourth Prime Minister of Israel on 17 March.

- California adopts the nation's first "no fault" divorce law, allowing divorce by mutual consent.

1970

- Toni Morrison's *The Bluest Eye* is published by Holt.
- Germaine Greer's *The Female Eunuch* is published by MacGibbon & Kee.
- Maya Angelou's *I Know Why the Caged Bird Sings* is published by Random House.
- Kate Millett's *Sexual Politics* is published by Doubleday and becomes a bestseller.
- Joyce Carol Oates receives the National Book Award for fiction for *them.*
- The Equal Rights Amendment passes in the U.S. House of Representatives by a vote of 350 to 15 on 10 August.
- Bella Abzug is elected to the U.S. House of Representatives on 3 November.
- The Feminist Press is founded at the City University of New York.
- *Off Our Backs: A Women's News Journal* is founded in Washington, D.C.
- *The Women's Rights Law Reporter* is founded in Newark, New Jersey.

1971

- Josephine Jacobsen is named U. S. Poet Laureate.

1972

- Marianne Moore dies on 5 February in New York City.
- *Ms.* magazine is founded; Gloria Steinem serves as editor of *Ms.* until 1987. The 300,000 copy print run of the first issue of *Ms.* magazine sells out within a week of its release in January.
- Shirley Chisolm becomes the first African American woman to seek the presidential nomination of a major political party, although her bid for the Democratic Party nomination is unsuccessful.
- The Equal Rights Amendment is passed by both houses of the U.S. Congress and is signed by President Richard M. Nixon. The amendment expires in 1982, without being ratified by the required two-thirds of the states; it is three states short of full ratification.
- President Nixon signs into law Title IX of the Higher Education Act banning sex bias in athletics and other activities at all educational institutions receiving federal assistance.
- Women's Press is established in Canada.

1973

- The U.S. Supreme Court, in their decision handed down on 21 January in *Roe v. Wade,* decides that in the first trimester of pregnancy women have the right to choose an abortion.
- Elizabeth Bowen dies of lung cancer on 22 February in London, England.
- Rita Mae Brown's *Rubyfruit Jungle* is published by Daughters, Inc.
- Erica Jong's *Fear of Flying* is published by Holt and becomes a bestseller.
- Alice Walker's *In Love and Trouble: Stories of Black Women* is published by Harcourt.
- The Boston Women's Health Book Collective's *Our Bodies, Ourselves: A Book By and For Women* is published by Simon and Schuster.

1974

- Andrea Dworkin's *Women Hating* is published by Dutton.
- Adrienne Rich receives the National Book Award for *Diving into the Wreck: Poems, 1971-1972.*
- Anne Sexton commits suicide on 4 October in Weston, Massachusetts.
- Katharine Graham (1917-2001), publisher of the *Washington Post,* becomes the first woman member of the board of the Associated Press.

1975

- Paula Gunn Allen' essay "The Sacred Hoop: A Contemporary Indian Perspective on American Indian Literature" appears in *Literature of the American Indian: Views and Interpretations,* edited by Abraham Chapman and published by New American Library.
- Hélène Cixous and Catherine Clement's *La Jeune nee* (*The Newly Born Woman,* University of Minnesota Press, 1986) is published by Union Generale.

- Margaret Thatcher is elected leader of the Conservative Party and becomes the first woman to head a major party in Great Britain.
- Susan Brownmiller's *Against our Will: Men, Women, and Rape* is published by Simon and Schuster.

1976

- Andrea Dworkin's *Our Blood: Prophecies and Discourses on Sexual Politics* is published by Harper.
- Maxine Hong Kingston's *The Woman Warrior: Memoirs of a Girlhood among Ghosts* is published by Knopf.
- Maxine Hong Kingston's receives the National Book Critics Circle award for general nonfiction for *The Woman Warrior.*
- Barbara Walters (1931-) becomes the first female network television news anchorwoman when she joins Harry Reasoner as coanchor of the *ABC Evening News.*
- Shere Hite's *The Hite Report: A Nationwide Study of Female Sexuality* is published by Macmillan.

1977

- Alice Paul dies on 9 July in Moorestown, New Jersey.
- Marilyn French's *The Women's Room* is published by Summit.
- Toni Morrison's *Song of Solomon* is published by Knopf.
- Toni Morrison receives the National Book Critics Circle Award for fiction for *Song of Solomon.*
- Labor organizer Barbara Mayer Wertheimer's *We Were There: The Story of Working Women in America* is published by Pantheon.
- Women's Press is established in Great Britain.

1978

- The Pregnancy Discrimination Act bans employment discrimination against pregnant women.
- Tillie Olsen's *Silences* is published by Delcorte Press/Seymour Lawrence.

1979

- Margaret Thatcher becomes the first woman prime minister of Great Britain. She serves until her resignation in 1990, marking the longest term of any twentieth-century prime minister.
- Barbara Wertheim Tuchman becomes the first woman elected president of the American Academy and Institute of Arts and Letters.
- Mother Teresa (1910-1997) receives the Nobel Peace Prize.
- Sandra M. Gilbert and Susan Gubar's *The Madwoman in the Attic: The Woman Writer and the Nineteenth-Century Imagination* is published by Yale University Press.

1980

- Muriel Rukeyser dies on 12 February in New York City.
- Adrienne Rich's essay "Compulsory Heterosexuality and Lesbian Experience" is published in *Signs: Journal of Women in Culture and Society.*

1981

- bell hooks's *Ain't I a Woman: Black Women and Feminism* is published by South End Press.
- Sylvia Plath's *Collected Poems,* edited by Ted Hughes, is published by Harper.
- Sandra Day O'Connor (1930-) becomes the first woman Justice of the U.S. Supreme Court, after being nominated by President Ronald Reagan and sworn in on 25 September.
- Women of Color Press is founded in Albany, New York by Barbara Smith.
- Cleis Press is established in Pittsburgh, Pennsylvania, and San Francisco, California.
- *This Bridge Called My Back: Writings by Radical Women of Color,* edited by Cherríe Moraga and Gloria Anzaldúa, is published by Persephone Press.
- Maxine Kumin is named U. S. Poet Laureate.

1982

- Djuna Barnes dies on 19 June in New York City.
- Sylvia Plath is posthumously awarded the Pulitzer Prize in poetry for *Collected Poems.*
- Alice Walker's *The Color Purple* is published by Harcourt.
- Carol Gilligan's *In a Different Voice: Psychological Theory and Women's Development* is published by Harvard University Press.

1983

- Rebecca West dies on 15 March in London, England.
- Gloria Steinem's *Outrageous Acts and Everyday Rebellions* is published by Holt.

1984

- Sandra Cisneros's *The House on Mango Street* is published by Arte Publico.
- Lillian Hellman dies on 30 June in Martha's Vineyard, Massachusetts.
- Geraldine Ferraro (1935-) becomes the first woman to win the Vice-Presidential nomination and runs unsuccessfully for office with Democratic Presidential candidate Walter Mondale.
- Firebrand Books, publisher of feminist and lesbian literature, is established in Ann Arbor, Michigan.
- bell hooks's *Feminist Theory: From Margin to Center* is published by South End Press.

1985

- Margaret Atwood's *The Handmaid's Tale* is published by McClelland & Stewart.
- Wilma P. Mankiller is sworn in as the first woman tribal chief of the Cherokee nation. She serves until 1994.
- Gwendolyn Brooks is named U. S. Poet Laureate.

1986

- Simone de Beauvoir dies on 14 April in Paris, France.
- Bessie Head dies on 17 April in Botswana.
- Rita Dove's *Thomas and Beulah* is published by Carnegie-Mellon University Press.
- Sylvia Ann Hewlett's *A Lesser Life: The Myth of Women's Liberation in America* is published by Morrow.

1987

- Toni Morrison's *Beloved* is published by Knopf.
- Rita Dove receives the Pulitzer Prize for poetry for *Thomas and Beulah.*

1988

- Toni Morrison receives the Pulitzer Prize for fiction for *Beloved.*
- *The War of the Words,* Volume 1 of Sandra M. Gilbert and Susan Gubar's *No Man's Land: The Place of the Woman Writer in the Twentieth Century,* is published by Yale University Press.

1989

- Amy Tan's *The Joy Luck Club* is published by Putnam.

1990

- Naomi Wolf's *The Beauty Myth: How Images of Beauty Are Used against Women* is published by Chatto & Windus.
- The Norplant contraceptive is approved by the FDA on 10 December.
- Camille Paglia's *Sexual Personae: Art and Decadence from Nefertiti to Emily Dickinson* is published by Yale University Press.
- Wendy Kaminer's *A Fearful Freedom: Women's Flight from Equality* is published by Addison-Wesley.
- Laurel Thatcher Ulrich's *A Midwife's Tale: The Life of Martha Ballard, Based on Her Diary, 1785-1812* is published by Knopf.
- Judith Butler's *Gender Trouble: Feminism and the Subversion of Identity* is published by Routledge.

1991

- Susan Faludi's *Backlash: The Undeclared War Against American Women* is published by Crown.
- Antonia Novello (1944-) is appointed by President George H.W. Bush and becomes the first woman and first person of Hispanic descent to serve as U. S. Surgeon General.
- Bernadine Healy, M.D. (1944-) is appointed by President George H.W. Bush and becomes the first woman to head the National Institutes of Health.
- Suzanne Gordon's *Prisoners of Men's Dreams: Striking Out for a New Feminine Future* is published by Little, Brown.
- Laurel Thatcher Ulrich receives the Pulitzer Prize for history for *A Midwife's Tale: The Life of Martha Ballard, Based on Her Diary, 1785-1812.*

1992

- Carol Elizabeth Moseley Braun (1947-) becomes the first African American woman elected to the U. S. Senate on 3 November.
- Carolyne Larrington's *The Feminist Companion to Mythology* is published by Pandora.
- Marilyn French's *The War against Women* is published by Summit.
- Clarissa Pinkola Estes's *Women Who Run with the Wolves: Myths and Stories of the Wild Woman Archetype* is published by Ballantine.
- Naomi Wolf's *Fire with Fire: The New Female Power and How It Will Change the Twenty-first Century* is published by Random House.
- Mona Van Duyn is named U. S. Poet Laureate.

1993

- Appointed by President Bill Clinton, Janet Reno (1938-) becomes the first woman U.S. Attorney General when she is sworn in on 12 March.
- Toni Morrison receives the Nobel Prize in Literature.
- Toni Morrison receives the Elizabeth Cady Stanton Award from the National Organization for Women.
- Canada's Progressive Conservative party votes on 13 June to make Defense Minister Kim Campbell the nation's first woman prime minister. Canadian voters oust the Conservative party in elections on 25 October as recession continues; Liberal leader Jean Chrétien becomes prime minister.
- On 1 October Rita Dove becomes the youngest person and the first African American to be named U. S. Poet Laureate.
- Faye Myenne Ng's *Bone* is published by Hyperion.

1994

- The Violence Against Women Act tightens federal penalties for sex offenders, funds services for victims of rape and domestic violence, and provides funds for special training for police officers in domestic violence and rape cases.
- Mary Pipher's *Reviving Ophelia: Saving the Selves of Adolescent Girls* is published by Putnam.

1995

- Ireland's electorate votes by a narrow margin in November to end the nation's ban on divorce (no other European country has such a ban), but only after 4 years' legal separation.

1996

- Marguerite Duras dies on 3 March in Paris, France.
- Hillary Rodham Clinton's *It Takes a Village, and Other Lessons Children Teach Us* is published by Simon and Schuster.

1998

- Bella Abzug dies on 31 March in New York City.
- Drucilla Cornell's *At the Heart of Freedom: Feminism, Sex, and Equality* is published by Princeton University Press.

1999

- Susan Brownmiller's *In Our Time: Memoir of a Revolution* is published by Dial Press.
- Gwendolyn Mink's *Welfare's End* is published by Cornell University Press.
- Martha C. Nussbaum's *Sex and Social Justice* is published by Oxford University Press.

2000

- Gwendolyn Brooks dies on 3 December in Chicago, Illinois.
- Patricia Hill Collins's *Black Feminist Thought: Knowledge, Consciousness, and the Politics of Empowerment* is published by Routledge.
- Jennifer Baumgardner and Amy Richards's *Manifesta: Young Women, Feminism, and the Future* is published by Farrar, Straus, and Giroux.

2002

- Estelle B. Freedman's *No Turning Back: The History of Feminism and the Future of Women* is published by Ballantine.
- *Colonize This! Young Women of Color on Today's Feminism*, edited by Daisy Hernandez and Bushra Rehman, is published by Seal Press.

2003

- Iranian feminist and human rights activist Shirin Ebadi (1947-) receives the Nobel Peace Prize.
- Louise Glück is named U. S. Poet Laureate.
- *Catching a Wave: Reclaiming Feminism for the 21st Century,* edited by Rory Cooke Dicker and Alison Piepmeier, is published by Northeastern University Press.

2004

- The FDA approves the contraceptive mifepristone, following a 16-year struggle by reproductive rights activists to have the abortion drug approved. Opponents made repeated efforts to prevent approval and distribution of mifepristone.
- *The Fire This Time: Young Activists and the New Feminism,* edited by Vivien Labaton and Dawn Lundy Martin, is published by Anchor Books.
- *The Future of Women's Rights: Global Visions and Strategies,* edited by Joanna Kerr, Ellen Sprenger, and Alison Symington, is published by ZED Books and Palgrave Macmillan.

WOMEN IN THE 19TH CENTURY: AN OVERVIEW

European and American women in the nineteenth century lived in an age characterized by gender inequality. At the beginning of the century, women enjoyed few of the legal, social, or political rights that are now taken for granted in western countries: they could not vote, could not sue or be sued, could not testify in court, had extremely limited control over personal property after marriage, were rarely granted legal custody of their children in cases of divorce, and were barred from institutions of higher education. Women were expected to remain subservient to their fathers and husbands. Their occupational choices were also extremely limited. Middle- and upper-class women generally remained home, caring for their children and running the household. Lower-class women often did work outside the home, but usually as poorly-paid domestic servants or laborers in factories and mills.

The onset of industrialization, urbanization, as well as the growth of the market economy, the middle class, and life expectancies transformed European and American societies and family life. For most of the eighteenth century through the first few decades of the nineteenth century, families worked together, dividing farming duties or work in small-scale family-owned businesses to support themselves. With the rapid mercantile growth, big business, and migration to larger cities after 1830, however, the family home as the center of economic production was gradually replaced with workers who earned their living outside the home. In most instances, men were the primary "breadwinners" and women were expected to stay at home to raise children, to clean, to cook, and to provide a haven for returning husbands. Most scholars agree that the Victorian Age was a time of escalating gender polarization as women were expected to adhere to a rigidly defined sphere of domestic and moral duties, restrictions that women increasingly resisted in the last two-thirds of the century.

Scholarly analysis of nineteenth-century women has included examination of gender roles and resistance on either side of the Atlantic, most often focusing on differences and similarities between the lives of women in the United States, England, and France. While the majority of these studies have concentrated on how white, middle-class women reacted to their assigned domestic or private sphere in the nineteenth century, there has also been interest in the dynamics of gender roles and societal expectations in minority and lower-class communities. Although these studies can be complementary, they also highlight the difficulty of making generalizations about the lives of women from different cultural, racial, economic, and religious backgrounds in a century of steady change.

Where generalizations can be made, however, "the woman question," as it was called in debates of the time, has been seen as a tendency to define the role of women in terms of private domesticity. Most often, depictions of the lives of nineteenth-century women, whether European or American, rich or poor, are portrayed in negative terms, concentrating on their limited sphere of influence compared to that of men from similar backgrounds. In some cases, however, the private sphere of nineteenth-century women had arguably more positive images, defining woman as the more morally refined of the two sexes and therefore the guardian of morality and social cohesion. Women were able to use this more positive image as a means for demanding access to public arenas long denied them, by publicly emphasizing and asserting the need for and benefits of a more "civilized" and "genteel" influence in politics, art, and education.

The same societal transformations that were largely responsible for women's status being defined in terms of domesticity and morality also worked to provoke gender consciousness and reform as the roles assigned women became increasingly at odds with social reality. Women on both sides of the Atlantic, including Angelina and Sarah Grimké, Sarah Josepha Hale, Charlotte Brontë, George Eliot, Elizabeth Gaskell, and Frances Power Cobbe, both expressed and influenced the age's expectations for women. Through their novels, letters, essays, articles, pamphlets, and speeches these and other nineteenth-century women portrayed the often conflicting expectations imposed on them by society. These women, along with others, expressed sentiments of countless women who were unable to speak, and brought attention and support to their concerns. Modern critical analyses often focus on the methods used by women to advance their cause while still maintaining their delicate balance of propriety and feminine appeal by not "threatening" men, or the family unit.

REPRESENTATIVE WORKS

Lydia Becker
Woman's Suffrage Journal [editor] (journal) 1870s

Barbara Leigh-Smith Bodichon
"A Brief Summary in Plain Language of the Most Important Laws Concerning Women, Together with a Few Observations" (essay) 1854

Charlotte Brontë
Jane Eyre (novel) 1847

Villette (novel) 1853

Emily Brontë
Wuthering Heights (novel) 1847

Anna Julia Haywood Cooper
"Womanhood a Vital Element in the Regeneration and Progress of a Race" (essay) 1886

Frederick Douglass
"Why I Became a Woman's Rights Man" (essay) 1881

George Eliot
Adam Bede (novel) 1859

Charles Fourier
"Degradation of Women in Civilization" (essay) 1808

Margaret Fuller
Woman in the Nineteenth Century (nonfiction) 1845

Elizabeth Gaskell
Mary Barton (novel) 1848

Cranford (novel) 1853

Ruth (novel) 1853

Frances Ellen Watkins Harper
"Women's Political Future" (essay) 1893

Victoria Earle Matthews
"The Awakening of the Afro-American Woman" (essay) 1897

John Stuart Mill
The Subjection of Women (philosophy) 1869

Caroline Norton
The Natural Right of A Mother to the Custody of her Child (essay) 1837

Emma Peterson
Women's Union Journal [editor] (journal) 1870s

Elizabeth Cady Stanton
"1848 Seneca Falls Women's Rights Convention Speech" (speech) 1848

"Solitude of Self" (speech) 1892

Harriet Beecher Stowe
Uncle Tom's Cabin (novel) 1852

William Thompson and Anna Wheeler
Appeal of One Half the Human Race, Women, Against the Pretensions of the other Half, Men, To Retain them in Political and Thence in Civil and Domestic Slavery (pamphlet) 1825

Sojourner Truth
"Colored Men Will Be Masters Over the Women" (speech) 1867

Charlotte Yonge
Heir of Redclyffe (novel) 1853

English Woman's Journal [*Englishwoman's Review*] (journal) 1857

PRIMARY SOURCES

CHARLES FOURIER (ESSAY DATE 1808)

SOURCE: Fourier, Charles. "Degradation of Women in Civilization." *Theorie des Quatre Mouvements et des Destinees Generales,* pp. 131-33. Paris, France: n.p., 1841-48.

In the following excerpt, originally published in 1808, Fourier argues that French and English women are treated little better than slaves and that social progress in both countries depends on granting women greater freedoms and rights.

Is there a shadow of justice to be seen in the fate that has befallen women? Is not a young woman a mere piece of merchandise displayed for sale to the highest bidder as exclusive property? Is not the consent she gives to the conjugal bond derisory and forced on her by the tyranny of the prejudices that obsess her from childhood on? People try to persuade her that her chains are woven only of flowers; but can she really have any doubt about her degradation, even in those regions that are bloated by philosophy such as England, where a man has the right to take his wife to market with a rope around her neck, and sell her like a beast of burden to anyone who will pay his asking price? Is our public opinion on this point much more advanced than in that crude era when the Council of Mâcon, a true council of vandals, debated whether or not women had a soul and decided in the affirmative by a margin of only three votes? English legislation, which the moralists praise so highly, grants men various rights that are no less degrading for the sex [women], such as the right of a husband to sue his wife's recognized lover for monetary indemnification. The French forms are less gross, but at bottom the slavery is always the same. Here as everywhere you can see young women languishing, falling ill and dying for want of a union that is imperiously dictated by nature but forbidden by prejudice, under penalty of being branded, before they have been legally sold. Such incidents, though rare, are still frequent enough to attest to the slavery of the weaker sex, scorn for the urgings of nature, and the absence of all justice with respect to women.

Among the signs that promise the happy results to come from the extension of women's privileges, we must cite the experience of other countries. We have seen that the best nations are always those that accord women the greatest amount of liberty; this can be seen as much among the Barbarians and Savages as among the Civilized. The Japanese, who are the most industrious, the bravest, and the most honorable of the Barbarians, are also the least jealous and the most indulgent toward women; this is so true that the Magots of China travel to Japan to deliver themselves up to the love that is forbidden them by their own hypocritical customs.

Likewise the Tahitans were the best among the Savages; given their relative lack of natural resources, no other people have developed their industry to such an extent. Among the Civilized, the French, who are the least inclined to persecute women, are the best in that they are the most flexible nation, the one from which a skillful ruler can get the best results in any sort of task. Despite a few defects such as frivolity, individual presumptuousness, and uncleanliness, however, the French are the foremost civilized nation owing to this single fact of adaptability, the trait most alien to the barbarian character.

Likewise it can be seen that the most corrupt nations have always been those in which women were most completely subjugated . . .

As a general thesis: *Social progress and historic changes occur by virtue of the progress of women toward liberty, and decadence of the social order occurs as the result of a decrease in the liberty of women.*

Other events influence these political changes, but there is no cause that produces social progress or decline as rapidly as change in the condition of women. I have already said that the mere adoption of closed harems would speedily turn us into Barbarians, and the mere opening of the harems would suffice to transport the Barbarians into Civilization. In summary, *the extension of women's privileges is the general principle for all social progress.*

NELLIE WEETON (JOURNAL/LETTER DATES 26 JANUARY 1810 AND 15 SEPTEMBER 1810)

SOURCE: Weeton, Nellie. "The Trials of an English Governess." In *Victorian Women: A Documentary Account of Women's Lives in Nineteenth-Century England,*

France, and the United States, edited by Erna Olafson Hellerstein, Leslie Parker Hume, and Karen M. Offen, p. 343. Stanford, Calif.: Stanford University Press, 1981.

In the following journal entry and letter, written in 1810 and originally published in Journal of a Governess *in 1936, Weeton recounts several incidents during her tenure as a governess.*

[Nellie Weeton's journal entry for Jan. 26, 1810]

The comforts of which I have deprived myself in coming here, and the vexations that occur sometimes during the hours of instruction with a child of such strange temper to instruct, would almost induce me to give up my present situation, did not the consideration which brought me here, still retain me. O Brother! sometime thou wilt know perhaps the deprivations I have undergone for thy sake, and that thy attentions have not been such as to compensate them. For thy sake I have wanted food and fire, and have gone about in rags; have spent the flower of my youth in obscurity, deserted, and neglected; and now, when God has blessed me with a competence, have given up its comforts to promote thy interest in the world. Should I fail in this desire, should I not succeed!—what will recompense me?—God perhaps will bless me for the thought that was in my heart; and if I am rewarded in heaven—I am rewarded indeed! I will be patient—I will be resigned, and—with the help of the Power around me, I will persevere.

[Nellie Weeton to her brother, Sept. 15, 1810. Mr. Pedder's child was killed in a fire, but Weeton was asked to stay on as companion to Mrs. Pedder. The situation soon became intolerable, owing to Mr. Pedder's ungovernable temper.]

I am scarcely permitted either to speak or stir in his presence; nor ever to maintain any opinion different to his own. When in a violent passion (which is but too frequent), on the most trifling occasions he will sometimes beat and turn his wife out of doors. Twice she has run away to her father's—oh! brother, and then, such a house! Mr. P. roaring drunk and swearing horridly, and making all the men about the house drunk. I have thought at such times, I really could not bear to stay any longer, particularly when he has been in his violent passions with me, which has occurred six or seven times. As he at one time found fault with almost everything I did, I have ceased to do anything I am not asked to do. The consequence is, I have almost all my time to myself, as I do little else than sew for Mr. and Mrs. P. Mr. P. will have Mrs. P. take such an active part in the house, that she has little time for my instruction; and as my assistance in domestic concerns has not been required for 3 or 4 months back, I sit a great deal alone, chiefly employed at my needle. Whether Mr. P. means to keep me thus idle, or to dismiss me, I know not. Mrs. P's gentle and kind treatment of me makes me very comfortable, for in general, I see little of Mr. P. except at dinner.

EMMA WILLARD (ADDRESS DATE 1819)

SOURCE: Willard, Emma. "An Address to the Public, Proposing a Plan for Improving Female Education." *An Address to the Public; Particularly to the Members of the Legislature of New York, Proposing a Plan for Improving Female Education.* Middlebury, Conn.: J. W. Copeland, 1819.

In the following address, Willard notes the benefits of improved education for women.

The object of this Address, is to convince the public, that a reform, with respect to female education, is necessary; that it cannot be effected by individual exertion, but that it requires the aid of the legislature; and further, by shewing the justice, the policy, and the magnamity of such an undertaking, to persuade the body to endow a seminary for females, as the commencement of such reformation.

The idea of a college for males will naturally be associated with that of a seminary, instituted and endowed by the public; and the absurdity of sending ladies to college, may, at first thought, strike every one to whom this subject shall be proposed. I therefore hasten to observe, that the seminary here recommended, will be as different from those appropriated to the other sex, as the female character and duties are from the male. The business of the husbandman is not to waste his endeavours, in seeking to make his orchard attain the strength and majesty of his forest, but to rear each, to the perfection of its nature.

That the improvement of female education will be considered by our enlightened citizens as a subject of importance, the liberality with which they part with their property to educate their daughters, is a sufficient evidence; and why should they not, when assembled in the legislature, act in concert to effect a noble object, which, though dear to them individually, can not be accomplished by their unconnected exertions.

If the improvements of the American female character, and that alone, could be effected by public liberality, employed in giving better means of instruction; such improvement of one half of society, and that half, which barbarous and despotic nations have ever degraded, would of itself be an object, worthy of the most liberal government on earth; but if the female character be raised, it must inevitably raise that of the other sex: and thus does the plan proposed, offer, as the object of legislative bounty, to elevate the whole character of the community.

As evidence that this statement does not exaggerate the female influence in society, our sex need but be considered, in the single relation of mothers. In this character, we have the charge of the whole mass of individuals, who are to compose the succeeding generation; during that period of youth, when the pliant mind takes any direction, to which it is steadily guided by a forming hand. How important power is given by this charge! yet, little do too many of my sex know how, either to appreciate or improve it. Unprovided with the means of acquiring that knowledge, which flows liberally to the other sex—having our time of education devoted to frivolous acquirements, how should we understand the nature of the mind, so as to be aware of the importance of those early impressions, which we make upon the minds of our children?—or how should we be able to form enlarged and correct views, either of the character, to which we ought to mould them, or of the means most proper to form them aright?

Considered in this point of view, were the interests of male education alone to be consulted, that of females becomes of sufficient importance to engage the public attention. Would we rear the human plant to its perfection, we must first fertilize the soil which produces it. If it acquire its first bent and texture upon a barren plain, it will avail comparatively little, should it be afterwards transplanted to a garden. . . .

Civilized nations have long since been convinced that education, as it respects males, will not, like trade, regulate itself; and hence, they have made it a prime object to provide that sex with everything requisite to facilitate their progress in learning: but female education has been left to the mercy of private adventurers; and the consequence has been to our sex, the same, as it would have been to the other, had legislatures left their accommodations, and means of instruction, to chance also.

Education cannot prosper in any community, unless, from the ordinary motives which actuate the human mind, the best and most cultivated talents of that community, can be brought into exercise in that way. Male education flourishes, because, from the guardian care of legislatures, the presidencies and professorships of our colleges are some of the highest objects to which the eye of ambition is directed. Not so with female institutions. Preceptresses of these, are dependent on their pupils for support, and are consequently liable to become the victims of their caprice. In such situation, it is not more desirable to be a preceptress, than it would be, to be a parent, invested with the care of children, and responsible for their behaviour, but yet, depending on them for subsistence, and destitute of power to enforce their obedience. . . .

It is impossible that in these schools such systems should be adopted and enforced, as are requisite for properly classing the pupils. Institutions for young gentlemen are founded by public authority, and are permanent; they are endowed with funds, and their instructors and overseers, are invested with authority to make such laws, as they shall deem most salutary. From their permanency, their laws and rules are well known. With their funds they procure libraries, philosophical apparatus, and other advantages, superior to what can elsewhere be found; and to enjoy these, individuals are placed under their discipline, who would not else be subjected to it. Hence the directors of these institutions can enforce, among other regulations, those which enable them to make a perfect classification of their students. They regulate their qualifications for entrance, the kind and order of their studies, and the period of their remaining at the seminary. Female schools present the reverse of this. Wanting permanency, and dependent on individual patronage, had they the wisdom to make salutary regulations, they could neither enforce nor purchase compliance. The pupils are irregular in their times of entering and leaving school; and they are of various and dissimilar acquirements.

Each scholar, of mature age, thinks she has a right to judge for herself respecting what she is to be taught; and the parents of those, who are not, consider that they have the same right to judge for them. Under such disadvantages, a school cannot be classed, except in a very imperfect manner. . . .

Another errour [in female education] is, that it has been made the first object in educating our sex, to prepare them to please the other. But reason and religion teach that we too are primary existences; that it is for us to move, in the orbit of our duty, around the Holy Centre of perfection, the companions not the satellites of men; else, instead of shedding around us an influence, that

ON THE SUBJECT OF...

LUCY STONE (1818-1893)

Lucy Stone gave her first lecture on women's rights in 1847, and soon also became an orator for the Antislavery Society. In 1855 Stone married noted abolitionist Henry B. Blackwell, and their joint protest against the legal disabilities of women was given wide publicity. Stone became the first of many feminists to retain her birth name after marriage. She was a leader in the American Equal Rights Association, and in 1867 became president of the New Jersey Woman Suffrage Association, which she had helped organize. In 1868 Stone and Blackwell helped organize the New England Woman Suffrage Association. In 1869 a major schism occurred in the woman's movement. Susan B. Anthony and Elizabeth Cady Stanton, formerly allies of Stone, wanted the cause to embrace many social and political issues, from the marriage question to labor unions. Stone, along with Julia Ward Howe and other New England feminists, favored concentrating on a single issue, the franchise for women, and felt that other reforms would follow from the vote. Stanton and Anthony formed the National Woman Suffrage Association in May, 1869; Stone and Howe formed the American Woman Suffrage Association in November, 1869. Stone then launched the *Woman's Journal* in 1870, a publication supported by the written contributions of woman's rights advocates from all over the United States, as well as France and England, and in which Stone and Blackwell published editorials that discussed the relationship between contemporary political issues and women's rights as well as analyses of legal proceedings and political events.

JULIA WARD HOWE (1819-1910)

Julia Ward Howe, a prominent abolitionist and women's rights activist, is best known for her patriotic antislavery poem, "The Battle Hymn of the Republic," published in 1862. The poem was later put to music and, among other things, became an anthem for civil rights activists in the 1960s. Howe used the wide popular attention, acclaim, and notoriety she received for her poem to greatly advance the cause of enfranchisement of women and African Americans. Howe was a vice president of the Association of American Authors, and in 1908 became the first woman elected to the American Academy of Arts and Letters.

may help to keep them in their proper course, we must accompany them in their wildest deviations.

I would not be understood to insinuate, that we are not, in particular situation, to yield obedience to the other sex. Submission and obedience belong to every being in the universe, except the great Master of the whole. Nor is it a degrading particularity to our sex, to be under human authority. Whenever one class of human beings, derive from another the benefits of support and protection, they must pay its equivalent, obedience. . . .

The inquiry, to which these remarks have conducted us is this—What is offered by the plan of female education, here proposed, which may teach, or preserve, among females of wealthy families, that purity of manners, which is allowed, to be so essential to national prosperity, and so necessary, to the existence of a republican government. . . .

By being enlightened in moral philosophy, and in that, which teaches the operations of the mind, females would be enabled to perceive the nature and extent, of that influence, which they possess over their children, and the obligation, which this lays them under, to watch the formation of their characters with unceasing vigilance, to become their instructors, to devise plans for their improvement, to weed out the vices from their minds, and to implant and foster the virtues. . . .

Thus, laudable objects and employments, would be furnished for the great body of females, who are not kept by poverty from excesses. But among these, among the other sex, will be found master spirits, who must have pre-eminence, at whatever price they acquire it. Domestic life cannot hold these, because they prefer to be infamous, rather than obscure. To leave such, without any virtuous road to eminence, is unsafe to community; for not unfrequently, are the secret springs of revolution, set in motion by their intrigues. Such aspiring minds, we will regulate, by education, we will remove obstructions to the course of literature, which has heretofore been their only honorable way to distinction; and we offer them a new object, worthy of their ambition; to govern, and improve the seminaries for their sex.

PARISIAN GARMENT WORKERS (PETITION DATE AUGUST 1848)

SOURCE: Parisian Garment Workers. "The Adult Woman: Work." In *Victorian Women: A Documentary Account of Women's Lives in Nineteenth-Century England,*

France, and the United States, edited by Erna Olafson Hellerstein, Leslie Parker Hume, and Karen M. Offen, p. 330. Stanford, Calif.: Stanford University Press, 1981.

In the following petition, written to the Parisian government in 1848, women workers who were losing work to contractors outside of France appeal to lawmakers to intercede on their behalf.

Gentlemen:

Please consider the request of some poor working women. The convents and the prisons take all our work away from us; they do it for such a low price that we can't compete with them. Almost all of us are mothers of families. We have our keep, our nourishment and our lodgings to pay for and we are not able to make enough money to cover these expenses. The employers also wrong us by sending their garment-making orders out of Paris; thus we can find no work and are nearly reduced to begging. Therefore, gentlemen, we urge you to put an end to these injustices. All we want is work.

We hope, Gentlemen, that you will be good enough to consider our request. We salute you with respect.

[Signed by seven women, with their addresses]

ELIZABETH CADY STANTON (SPEECH DATE 1848)

SOURCE: Cady Stanton, Elizabeth. "Elizabeth Cady Stanton's 1848 Seneca Falls Woman's Rights Convention Speech (abridged)." In *Returning to Seneca Falls: The First Woman's Rights Convention & Its Meaning for Men & Women Today,* edited by Bradford Miller, pp. 172-77. Hudson, N.Y.: Lindisfarne Press, 1995.

In the following speech, delivered at the 1848 Seneca Falls Convention, Cady Stanton argues that there is no biblical or natural justification for the subjugation of women, and that women must organize to overturn unjust laws and customs that leave them without legal rights or political representation.

I should feel exceedingly diffident to appear before you at this time, having never before spoken in public, were I not nerved by a sense of right and duty, did I not feel the time had fully come for the question of woman's wrongs to be laid before the public, did I not believe that woman herself must do this work; for woman alone can understand the height, the depth, the length, and the breadth of her own degradation. Man can not speak for her. . . .

Among the many important questions which have been brought before the public, there is none that more vitally affects the whole human family than that which is technically called Woman's Rights. Every allusion to the degraded and inferior position occupied by women all over the world has been met by scorn and abuse. From the man of highest mental cultivation to the most degraded wretch who staggers in the streets do we meet ridicule, and coarse jests, freely bestowed upon those who dare assert that woman stands by the side of man, his equal, placed here by her God, to enjoy with him the beautiful earth, which is her home as it is his, having the same sense of right and wrong, and looking to the same Being for guidance and support. So long has man exercised tyranny over her, injurious to himself and numbing to his faculties, that few can nerve themselves to meet the storm; and so long has the chain been about her that she knows not there is a remedy. . . .

. . . In every country and clime does man assume the responsibility of marking out the path for her to tread. In every country does he regard her as a being inferior to himself, and one whom he is to guide and control. From the Arabian Kerek, whose wife is obliged to steal from her husband to supply the necessities of life; from the Mahometan who forbids pigs, dogs, women and other impure animals, to enter a Mosque, and does not allow a fool, madman or woman to proclaim the hour of prayer; from the German who complacently smokes his meerschaum, while his wife, yoked with the ox, draws the plough through its furrow; from the delectable carpet-knight, who thinks an inferior style of conversation adapted to woman; to the legislator, who considers her incapable of saying what laws shall govern her, is the same feeling manifested. . . .

Let us consider . . . man's superiority, intellectually, morally, physically.

Man's intellectual superiority cannot be a question until woman has had a fair trial. When we shall have had our freedom to find out our sphere, when we shall have had our colleges, our professions, our trades, for a century, a comparison then may be justly instituted. When woman, instead of being taxed to endow colleges where she is forbidden to enter—instead of forming sewing societies to educate 'poor, but pious,' young men, shall first educate herself, when she shall be just to herself before she is generous to others; improving the talents God has given her, and leaving her neighbor to do the same for himself, we shall not hear so much about this boasted superiority. . . .

In consideration of man's moral superiority, glance now at our theological seminaries, our divinity students, the long line of descendents from our Apostolic fathers, the immaculate priesthood, and what do we find there? Perfect moral rectitude in every relation of life, a devoted spirit of self-sacrifice, a perfect union of thought, opinion, and feeling among those who profess to worship God, and whose laws they feel themselves called upon to declare to a fallen race? Far from it. . . . Is the moral and religious life of this class what we might expect from minds said to be fixed on mighty themes? By no means. . . . The lamentable want of principle among our lawyers, generally, is too well known to need comment. The everlasting backbiting and bickering of our physicians is proverbial. The disgraceful riots at our polls, where man, in performing the highest duty of citizenship, ought surely to be sober-minded, the perfect rowdyism that now characterizes the debates in our national Congress,—all these are great facts which rise up against man's claim for moral superiority. In my opinion, he is infinitely woman's inferior in every moral quality, not by nature, but made so by a false education. . . .

. . . God's commands rest upon man as well as woman. It is as much his duty to be kind, self-denying and full of good works, as it is hers. As much his duty to absent himself from scenes of violence as it is hers. A place or position that would require the sacrifice of the delicacy and refinement of woman's nature is unfit for man, for these virtues should be as carefully guarded in him as in her. . . . I would not have woman less pure, but I would have men more so. I would have the same code of morals for both. . . .

Let us now consider man's claim to physical superiority. Methinks I hear some say, surely, you will not contend for equality here. Yes, we must not give an inch, lest you take an ell. We cannot accord to man even this much, and he has no right to claim it until the fact has been fully demonstrated. . . . We cannot say what the woman might be physically, if the girl were allowed all the freedom of the boy in romping, climbing, swimming, playing whoop and ball.

Among some of the Tartar tribes of the present day, women manage a horse, hurl a javelin, hunt wild animals and fight an enemy as well as a man. The Indian women endure fatigues and carry burdens that some of our fair-faced, soft-handed, moustached young gentlemen would consider quite impossible for them to sustain. . . .

But there is a class of objectors who say they do not claim superiority, they merely assert a difference. But you will find by following them up closely, that they soon run this difference into the old groove of superiority. . . .

We have met here today to discuss our rights and wrongs, civil and political, and not, as some have supposed, go into the detail of social life alone. We do not propose to petition the legislature to make our husbands just, generous and courteous, to seat every man at the head of a cradle, and to clothe every woman in male attire. . . .

We are assembled to protest against a form of government, existing without the consent of the governed—to declare our right to be free as man is free, to be represented in the government which we are taxed to support, to have such disgraceful laws as give man the power to chastise and imprison his wife, to take the wages which she earns, the property which she inherits, and, in the case of separation, the children of her love; laws which make her the mere dependent on his bounty. It is to protest against such unjust laws as these that we are assembled today, and to have them, if possible, forever erased from our statute-books, deeming them a shame and a disgrace to a Christian republic in the nineteenth century. . . .

And, strange as it may seem to many, we now demand our right to vote according to the declaration of the government under which we live. . . . We have no objection to discuss the question of equality, for we feel that the weight of argument lies wholly with us, but we wish the question of equality kept distinct from the question of rights, for the proof of the one does not determine the truth of the other. All white men in this country have the same rights, however they may differ in mind, body or estate. The right is ours. The question now is, how shall we get possession of what rightfully belongs to us. . . . To have drunkards, idiots, horse-racing, rumselling rowdies, ignorant foreigners, and silly boys fully recognized, while we ourselves are thrust out from all the rights that belong to citizens, it is too grossly insulting to the dignity of woman to be longer quietly submitted to. The right is ours. Have it we must. Use it we will. The pens, the tongues, the fortunes, the indomitable wills of many women are already pledged to secure this right. The great truth, that no just government can be formed without the consent of the governed, we shall echo and re-echo in the ears of the unjust judge until by continual coming we shall weary him. . . .

When women know the laws and constitutions on which they live, they will not publish their degradation by declaring themselves satisfied, nor their ignorance, by declaring they have all the rights they want. . . .

Let woman live as she should. Let her feel her accountability to her Maker. Let her know her spirit is fitted for as high a sphere as man's, and that her soul requires food as pure and exalted as his. Let her live first for God, and she will not make imperfect man an object of reverence and awe. Teach her responsibility as a being of conscience and reason, that all earthly support is weak and unstable, and that her only safe dependence is the arm of omnipotence, and that true happiness springs from duty accomplished. Thus will she learn the lesson of individual responsibility for time and eternity. That neither father, husband, brother, or son, however willing they may be, can discharge her high duties of life, or stand in her stead when called into the presence of the great searcher of Hearts at the last day. . . .

One common objection to this movement is, that if the principles of freedom and equality which we advocate were put into practice, it would destroy all harmony in the domestic circle. Here let me ask, how many truly harmonious households have we now? . . . The only happy households we now see are those in which husband and wife share equally in counsel and government. There can be no true dignity or independence where there is subordination to the absolute will of another, no happiness without freedom. Let us then have no fears that the movement will disturb what is seldom found, a truly united and happy family. . . .

There seems now to be a kind of moral stagnation in our midst. Philanthropists have done their utmost to rouse the nation to a sense of its aims. . . . Our churches are multiplying on all sides, our missionary societies, Sunday schools, and prayer meetings and innumerable charitable and reform organizations are all in operation, but still the tide of vice is swelling, and threatens the destruction of everything. . . . Verily, the world waits the coming of some new element, some purifying power, some spirit of mercy and love. The voice of woman has been silenced in the state, the church, and the home, but man cannot fulfill his destiny alone, he cannot redeem his race unaided. . . . The world has never seen a truly great and virtuous nation, because in the degradation of woman the very fountains of life are poisoned at their source. It is vain to look for silver and gold from mines of copper and lead. It is the wise mother that has the wise son. So long as your women are slaves you may throw your colleges and churches to the winds. . . . Truly are the sins of the fathers visited upon the children to the third and fourth generation. God, in his wisdom, has so linked the whole human family together that any violence done at one end of the chain is felt throughout its length, and here, too, is the law of restoration, as in woman all have fallen, so in her elevation shall the race be recreated.

. . . We do not expect our path to be strewn with flowers of popular applause, but over the thorns of bigotry and prejudice will be our way, and on our banners will beat the dark storm-clouds of opposition from those who have entrenched themselves behind the stormy bulwarks of custom and authority, and who have fortified their position by every means, holy and unholy. . . .

THE SIBYL (LETTER DATE FEBRUARY 1857)

SOURCE: *The Sibyl.* "Short Hair and Short Dresses." In *Public Women, Public Words: A Documentary History of American Feminism,* edited by Dawn Keetley and John Pettegrew, p. 145. Madison, Wis.: Madison House, 1997.

In the following letter, published in The Sibyl *in February 1857, the unknown writer, E. E. S, champions* The Sibyl *for supporting the wearing of short hair and dresses. The editor offers a response that admonishes outdated fashions and traditions.*

Waynesville, Ill., Jan. 26, 1857.

Dear Madam.—Enclosed I sent you $2, for which please send numbers of THE SIBYL to those I mention below. By accident I came across two numbers of your invaluable paper, for which I was very thankful, for it gave me the privilege of subscribing and getting subscribers.

I have worn the short dress for several years, and think it far superior to the long and heavy skirts that fashion demands. I have borne the insults of the people, and the salutes of the passers by, but have never felt my determination shaken. I feel that I am right, and mean to go ahead. I am the only one who wears the Reform Dress in this vicinity; so you can judge of the pleasure it was to me to meet with your paper. It seems like an old and tried friend; and with it to help me, I think that, with never-tiring zeal, I can accomplish something. I often meet with ladies who say that they 'glory in my spunk,' but they dare not come out and face public opinion.

I was glad to learn that I am not alone in wearing short hair, as I had supposed; I am very much opposed to long hair, but never could get any one to agree with me on that point. I have been told that I committed an unpardonable sin by wearing my hair short, because the Bible says that 'long hair is an ornament to woman;' but I believe in consulting nature as well as the Bible. Every one knows that when bathing the head, we have to suffer the inconvenience of letting the hair hang around the shoulders till dry, or twist it up wet, and let it sour and mould before it can dry thoroughly; and then, with the help of a half dozen hair pins to rust the hair, it is in a fine fix. I think there is a great need of reform in hair dressing. Wishing you success, I am yours,

E. E. S.

Remarks

Daily are we in receipt of such letters. All agree in the opinion that THE SIBYL fills a niche in journalism vacant before its advent. . . .

. . . With respect to short hair, we cut ours off in the first place because it was rather thin, and troublesome to comb, brush and braid, as well as a painful annoyance—causing our head to ache with twisting and braiding, supported by combs and pins, none of which we intend ever to trouble ourselves with again, for the ease, lightness and relief we experience suits us much better than long hair. As to the Bible argument, it is an utter absurdity, being, like all other silly things said to be denounced in that book, merely distorted to suit the imagination of fanatics, who have no better occupation than to search for denunciations from its pages. The whole spirit of the Bible tends to uphold simplicity and neatness, while the braiding and plaiting of the hair, and the wearing of silly ornaments, now so common, are most strongly disapproved. Besides this, such arguments generally originate from minds having no real deference for truths anywhere found, save as they can present them as bugbears to frighten the weak and timid, among whom we are not one. And if those who pander to the silly and blighting fashions and falseness of the times, would only scan their own walk, and shape it more to the letter and spirit of the Bible, they would find need of a different walk and conversation from that they now indulge in, causing them to pause and reflect whether their course was one which tended toward the celestial city.—*Ed.*

LOUISA BASTIAN, MARY HAMELTON, AND ANNA LONG (PETITION DATE JULY 1862)

SOURCE: Bastian, Louisa, Mary Hamelton, and Anna Long. "The Adult Woman: Work." In *Victorian Women: A Documentary Account of Women's Lives in Nineteenth-Century England, France, and the United States,* edited by Erna Olafson Hellerstein, Leslie Parker Hume, and Karen M. Offen, p. 330. Stanford, Calif.: Stanford University Press, 1981.

In the following petition, sent to lawmakers during the American Civil War, seamstresses ask the government to intervene against unfair labor practices.

We the undersigned formerly doing sewing for the United States Arsenal at Philadelphia most respectfully remonstrate against the action of Col. Crossman in taking the work from us and giving it to contractors who will not pay wages in which we can live—many of us have husbands, fathers, sons & brothers now in the army and from whom we derived our support. Deprived of that as we are our only mode of living was by sewing and we were able by unceasing exertions to barely live at the prices paid by the Arsenal. The Contractors who are speculators offer about fifty per cent of the prices paid heretofore by the arsenal—we respectfully ask your attention to our case. We have all given satisfaction in the work we have done. Then why should the government money be taken from the families of the poor to enrich the wealthy speculator without any gain to the government.

Very Resp Yours &C
Anna Long Widow 5 children 121 Mois St.
Louisa Bastian 124 Mirris St.
Mary Hamelton 1673 Front St. Husband at war

HARRIET H. ROBINSON (REPORT DATE 1883)

SOURCE: Robinson, Harriet H. "Early Factory Labor in New England." In *Massachusetts Bureau of Statistics of Labor, Fourteenth Annual Report,* pp. 380-92. Boston: Wright & Potter, 1883.

In the following report, Robinson describes the experiences of women factory workers in Lowell, Massachusetts.

In what follows, I shall confine myself to a description of factory life in Lowell, Massachusetts, from 1832 to 1848, since, with that phase of Early Factory Labor in New England, I am the most familiar—because I was a part of it. In 1832, Lowell was little more than a factory village. Five "corporations" were started, and the cotton mills belonging to them were building. Help was in great demand and stories were told all over the country of the new factory place, and the high wages that were offered to all classes of work-people; stories that reached the ears of mechanics' and farmers' sons and gave new life to lonely and dependent women in distant towns and farmhouses. . . . Troops of young girls came from different parts of New England, and from Canada,

Photograph showing women laborers in a factory in Lynn, Massachusetts, c. 1895.

and men were employed to collect them at so much a head and deliver them at the factories. . . .

At the time the Lowell cotton mills were started the caste of the factory girl was the lowest among the employments of women. In England and in France, particularly, a great injustice had been done to her real character. She was represented as subjected to influences that must destroy her purity and self-respect. In the eyes of her overseer she was but a brute, a slave, to be beaten, pinched and pushed about. It was to overcome this prejudice that such high wages and been offered to women that they might be induced to become mill-girls, in spite of the opprobrium that still clung to this degrading occupation. . . .

The early mill-girls were of different ages. Some were not over ten years old; a few were in middle life, but the majority were between the ages of sixteen and twenty-five. The very young girls were called "doffers." They "doffed," or took off, the full bobbins from the spinning-frames, and replaced them with empty ones. These mites worked about fifteen minutes every hour and the rest of the time was their own. When the overseer was kind they were allowed to read, knit or go outside the mill-yard to play. They were paid two dollars a week. The working hours of all the girls extended from five o'clock in the morning until seven in the evening, with one half-hour each, for breakfast and dinner. Even the doffers were forced to be on duty nearly fourteen hours a day. This was the greatest hardship in the lives of these children. Several years later a ten-hour law was passed, but not until long after some of these little doffers were old enough to appear before the legislative committee on the subject, and plead, by their presence, for a reductions of the hours of labor. Those of the mill-girls who had homes generally worked from eight to ten months in the year; the rest of the time was spent with parents or friends. A few taught school during the summer months. Their life in the factory was made pleasant to them. In those days there was no need of advocating the doctrine of the proper relation between employer and employed. Help was too valuable to be ill-treated. . . .

The most prevailing incentive to labor was to secure the means of education for some male member in the family. To make a gentleman of a brother or a son, to give him a college education, was the dominant thought in the minds of a great many of the better class of mill-girls. I have known more than one to give every cent of her wages, month after month, to her brother, that he might get the education necessary to enter some profession. I have known a mother to work years in this way for her boy. I have known women to educate young men by their earnings, who were not sons or relatives. There were many men now living who were helped to an education by the wages of the early mill-girls. It is well to digress here a little, and speak of the influence the possession of money had on the characters of some of these women. We can hardly realize what a change the cotton factory made in the status of the working women. Hitherto woman had always been a money saving rather than a money earning, member of the community. Her labor could command but small return. If she worked out as servant, or "help," her wages were from 50 cents to $1.00 a week; or, if she went from house to house by the day to spin and weave, or do tailoress work, she could get but 75 cents a week and her meals. As teacher, her services were not in demand, and the arts, the professions, and even the trades and industries, were nearly all closed to her.

As late as 1840 there were only seven vocations outside the home into which the women of New England had entered. At this time woman had no property rights. A widow could be left without her share of her husband's (or the family) property, an "incumbrance" to his estate. A father could make his will without reference to his daughter's share of the inheritance. He usually left her a home on the farm as long as she remained single. A woman was not supposed to be capable of spending her own, or of using other people's money. In Massachusetts, before 1840, a woman could not, legally, be treasurer of her own sewing society, unless some man were responsible for her. The law took no cognizance of woman as a money-spender. She was a ward, an appendage, a relict. Thus it happened that if a woman did not choose to marry, or, when left a widow, to remarry, she had no choice but to enter one of the few employments open to her, or to become a burden on the charity of some relative. . . .

One of the first strikes that ever took place in this country was in Lowell in 1836. When it was announced that the wages were to be cut down, great indignation was felt, and it was decided to strike or "turn out" en masse. This was done. The mills were shut down, and the girls went from their several corporations in procession to the grove on Chapel Hill, and listened to incendiary speeches from some early labor reformers. One of the girls stood on a pump and gave vent to the feelings of her companions in a neat speech, declaring that it was their duty to resist all attempts at cutting down the wages. This was the first time a woman had spoken in public in Lowell, and the event caused surprise and consternation among her audience. It is hardly necessary to say that, so far as practical results are concerned, this strike did no good. The corporation would not come to terms. The girls were soon tired of holding out, and they went back to their work at the reduced rate of wages. The ill-success of this early attempt at resistance on the part of the wage element seems to have made a precedent for the issue of many succeeding strikes.

FRANCES ELLEN WATKINS HARPER (ESSAY DATE 1893)

SOURCE: Watkins Harper, Frances Ellen. "Woman's Political Future." In *With Pen and Voice: A Critical Anthology of Nineteenth-Century African-American Women,* edited by Shirley Wilson Logan, pp. 43-46. Carbondale, Ill.: Southern Illinois University Press, 1995.

In the following excerpt, originally published in 1893, Harper argues that the influence of women in American political life is necessary to bring an end to the many injustices that plague the nation.

If before sin had cast its deepest shadows or sorrow had distilled its bitterest tears, it was true that it was not good for man to be alone, it is no less true, since the shadows have deepened and life's sorrows have increased, that the world has need of all the spiritual aid that woman can give for the social advancement and moral development of the human race. The tendency of the present age, with its restlessness, religious upheavals, failures, blunders, and crimes, is toward broader freedom, an increase of knowledge, the emancipation of thought, and a recognition of the brotherhood of man; in this movement woman, as the companion of man, must be a sharer. So close is the bond between man and woman that you can not raise one without lifting the other. The world can not move without

ON THE SUBJECT OF...

FRANCES ELLEN WATKINS HARPER (1825-1911)

Born to free parents in Baltimore, Maryland Frances Ellen Watkins Harper was orphaned when she was three years old, and was subsequently raised by an aunt and an uncle who was an ardent abolitionist and who ran the school for free children that Harper attended as a child. During her teen years Harper composed poems with religious and moral themes, some of which were reprinted in newspapers and in a now-lost volume called *Autumn Leaves* or *Forest Leaves.* Harper moved to Ohio—a free state—in the early 1850s, where she taught domestic science at Columbus Union Seminary. Harper later taught at an elementary school in Little York, Pennsylvania, and it was there that she first witnessed the passage of runaway slaves along the Underground Railroad. Harper sought ways to actively participate in the antislavery movement. Boston abolitionists encouraged her to become an elocutionist, and she soon became a sought-after lecturer on the East coast.

Following the conclusion of the Civil War and the enforcement of the Emancipation Proclamation, Harper began emphasizing in her speeches he divisive effects of racism as well as the need for temperance, domestic morality, and education for African Americans. Harper's written works, popular in her time with both black and white audiences, mediate between the subject matter and viewpoints of pre- and post-Civil War African American writers: while she wrote against slavery, she also broke away from the purely propagandistic mode of the antislavery poet and became one of the first African American writers to focus on national and universal problems. In her novel *Iola Leroy; or, Shadows Uplifted* (1892), Harper countered the negative stereotypes of African Americans that pervaded contemporary fiction with educated, highly principled black protagonists who foreshadowed the characters created by twentieth-century writers.

woman's sharing in the movement, and to help give a right impetus to that movement is woman's highest privilege.

If the fifteenth century discovered America to the Old World, the nineteenth is discovering woman to herself. Little did Columbus imagine, when the New World broke upon his vision like a lovely gem in the coronet of the universe, the glorious possibilities of a land where the sun should be our engraver, the winged lightning our messenger, and steam our beast of burden. But as mind is more than matter, and the highest ideal always the true real, so to woman comes the opportunity to strive for richer and grander discoveries than ever gladdened the eye of the Genoese mariner.

Not the opportunity of discovering new worlds, but that of filling this old world with fairer and higher aims than the greed of gold and the lust of power, is hers. Through weary, wasting years men have destroyed, dashed in pieces, and overthrown, but to-day we stand on the threshold of woman's era, and woman's work is grandly constructive. In her hand are possibilities whose use or abuse must tell upon the political life of the nation, and send their influence for good or evil across the track of unborn ages.

As the saffron tints and crimson flushes of morn herald the coming day, so the social and political advancement which woman has already gained bears the promise of the rising of the full-orbed sun of emancipation. The result will be not to make home less happy, but society more holy; yet I do not think the mere extension of the ballot a panacea for all the ills of our national life. What we need to-day is not simply more voters, but better voters. To-day there are red-handed men in our republic, who walk unwhipped of justice, who richly deserve to exchange the ballot of the freeman for the wristlets of the felon; brutal and cowardly men, who torture, burn, and lynch their fellow-men, men whose defenselessness should be their best defense and their weakness an ensign of protection. More than the changing of institutions we need the development of a national conscience, and the upbuilding of national character. Men may boast of the aristocracy of blood, may glory in the aristocracy of talent, and be proud of the aristocracy of wealth, but there is one aristocracy which must ever outrank them all, and that is the aristocracy of character; and it is the women of a country who help to mold its character, and to influence if not determine its destiny; and in the political future of our nation woman will not have done what she could if she does not endeavor to have our republic stand foremost among the nations of the earth, wearing sobriety as a crown and righteousness as a garment and a girdle. In coming into her political estate woman will find a mass of illiteracy to be dispelled. If knowledge is power, ignorance is also power. The power that educates wickedness may manipulate and dash against the pillars of any state when they are undermined and honeycombed by injustice.

I envy neither the heart nor the head of any legislator who has been born to an inheritance of privileges, who has behind him ages of education, dominion, civilization, and Christianity, if he stands opposed to the passage of a national education bill, whose purpose is to secure education to the children of those who were born under the shadow of institutions which made it a crime to read.

To-day women hold in their hands influence and opportunity, and with these they have already opened doors which have been closed to others. By opening doors of labor woman has become a rival claimant for at least some of the wealth monopolized by her stronger brother. In the home she is the priestess, in society the queen, in literature she is a power, in legislative halls lawmakers have responded to her appeals, and for her sake have humanized and liberalized their laws. The press has felt the impress of her hand. In the pews of the church she constitutes the majority; the pulpit has welcomed her, and in the school she has the blessed privilege of teaching children and youth. To her is apparently coming the added responsibility of political power; and what she now possesses should only be the means of preparing her to use the coming power for the glory of God and the good of mankind; for power without righteousness is one of the most dangerous forces in the world.

Political life in our country has plowed in muddy channels, and needs the infusion of clearer and cleaner waters. I am not sure that women are naturally so much better than men that they will clear the stream by the virtue of their womanhood; it is not through sex but through character that the best influence of women upon the life of the nation must be exerted.

I do not believe in unrestricted and universal suffrage for either men or women. I believe in moral and educational tests. I do not believe that the most ignorant and brutal man is better prepared to add value to the strength and durability of the government than the most cultured, upright, and intelligent woman. I do not think that willful ignorance should swamp earnest intelligence at the ballot-box, nor that educated wickedness, violence, and fraud should cancel the votes of honest men. The unsteady hands of a drunkard can not cast the ballot of a freeman. The hands of lynchers are too red with blood to determine the political character of the government for even four short years. The ballot in the hands of woman means power added to influence. How well she will use that power I can not foretell. Great evils stare us in the face that need to be throttled by the combined power of an upright manhood and an enlightened womanhood; and I know that no nation can gain its full measure of enlightenment and happiness if one-half of it is free and the other half is fettered. China compressed the feet of her women and thereby retarded the steps of her men. The elements of a nation's weakness must ever be found at the hearthstone.

More than the increase of wealth, the power of armies, and the strength of fleets is the need of good homes, of good fathers, and good mothers.

The life of a Roman citizen was in danger in ancient Palestine, and men had bound themselves with a vow that they would eat nothing until they had killed the Apostle Paul. Pagan Rome threw around that imperiled life a bulwark of living clay consisting of four hundred and seventy human hearts, and Paul was saved. Surely the life of the humblest American citizen should be as well protected in America as that of a Roman citizen was in heathen Rome. A wrong done to the weak should be an insult to the strong. Woman coming into her kingdom will find enthroned three great evils, for whose overthrow she should be as strong in a love of justice and humanity as the warrior is in his might. She will find intemperance sending its flood of shame, and death, and sorrow to the homes of men, a fretting leprosy in our politics, and a blighting curse in our social life; the social evil sending to our streets women whose laughter is sadder than their tears, who slide from the paths of sin and shame to the friendly shelter of the grave; and lawlessness enacting in our republic deeds over which angels might weep, if heaven knows sympathy.

How can any woman send petitions to Russia against the horrors of Siberian prisons if, ages after the Inquisition has ceased to devise its tortures, she has not done all she could by influence, tongue, and pen to keep men from making bonfires of the bodies of real or supposed criminals?

O women of America! into your hands God has pressed one of the sublimest opportunities that ever came into the hands of the women of any race or people. It is yours to create a healthy public sentiment; to demand justice, simple justice, as the right of every race; to brand with everlasting infamy the lawless and brutal cowardice that lynches, burns, and tortures your own countrymen.

To grapple with the evils which threaten to undermine the strength of the nation and to lay magazines of powder under the cribs of future generations is no child's play.

Let the hearts of the women of the world respond to the song of the herald angels of peace on earth and good will to men. Let them throb as one heart unified by the grand and holy purpose of uplifting the human race, and humanity will breathe freer, and the world grow brighter. With such a purpose Eden would spring up in our path, and Paradise be around our way.

OVERVIEWS

ERNA OLAFSON HELLERSTEIN, LESLIE PARKER HUME, AND KAREN M. OFFEN (ESSAY DATE 1981)

SOURCE: Olafson Hellerstein, Erna, Leslie Parker Hume and Karen M. Offen. "General Introduction." In *Victorian Women: A Documentary Account of Women's Lives in Nineteenth-Century England, France, and the United States,* edited by Erna Olafson Hellerstein, Leslie Parker Hume, and Karen M. Offen, pp. 1-3. Stanford, Calif.: Stanford University Press, 1981.

In the following excerpt, Hellerstein, Hume, and Offen argue that the social roles and expectations of French, English, and American women living during the Victorian era underwent fundamental and often contradictory transformations due to changes in the market economy, life expectancy, democratic institutions, state regulations, and gender polarization.

In the ferment about sex roles and the family that characterizes our own time, men and women still define themselves in terms of the Victorians, either living out ideas and defending institutions that came to fruition in the nineteenth century or reacting against these ideas and institutions and against Victorian "repression." Modern "objective" social science, born during the Victorian period, both incorporated and legitimized Victorian prejudices about gender, the family, work, and the division between public and private spheres. These inherited categories still influence the way we organize our information, not only about ourselves, but about cultures different from our own. For women especially, the Victorian heritage continues to affect their lives and their self-conceptions. Because of this, the Victorian woman has attracted both scholarly and popular attention.

The term Victorian was used in the late nineteenth century to refer to English life during the reign of Queen Victoria (1837-1901). In this book, following Carl Degler, Michel Foucault, and others, we extend its coverage to France and the United States as well. For all their differences, the three countries formed an Atlantic community, a transatlantic culture that tells us more about Victorian attitudes and institutions than we could learn from a single nation. Our transatlantic focus underscores the fact that in the nineteenth century, England and France were a much greater part of the American consciousness than now. Whether defining themselves against the Old World or trying to imitate it, Americans were deeply influenced by European ideas and culture, as the many American reprints of European publications suggest. In turn, the English and the French, whether intrigued or repelled, were keenly aware of the new civilization across the Atlantic.

In addition to the commonalities England, France, and the United States shared as members of the Atlantic community, these countries underwent similar changes in the nineteenth century. In fact, the tempo of change in all areas of life, from politics to household management, accelerated throughout the century. Industrialization transformed agriculture and manufacturing in England, and to a lesser extent, in America and France, by mechanizing production and concentrating the labor force. As the market economy penetrated the countryside, more people came into the cash economy wherein more goods were available. These twin processes resulted in a vast increase in material wealth, although at the cost of the proletarianization of artisans and peasants and an increase in class conflict, social dislocation, and social fear. For women, industrialization, by separating the home from the workplace, began to force an unprecedented choice between home and children on the one hand, and the continued possibility of earning a cash wage, however meager, on the other. This development tended to create a dichotomy between woman as homemaker and woman as worker, a dichotomy that survives in the twentieth century as perhaps the most enduring legacy of the Victorian period.

Demographic changes also profoundly affected women's lives. Life expectancy, especially for women, rose significantly between 1800 and 1900. For example, French women born in 1801 could expect to live only about thirty-five years; those born a hundred years later could look forward to forty-nine years of life. As population increased, the pressure of people on the land became more intense, contributing to two other demographic changes: a gradual decline in the birthrate, first in France and later in the United States and England; and European outmigration, a vast movement of Old World peoples to the Americas and other parts of the globe. This transoceanic mobility was accompanied by internal mobility, as hundreds of thousands of men and women left the countryside to settle in the cities.

The growth of democratic institutions from which women were excluded paradoxically helped to politicize women. Egalitarian and democratic ideas spread to both men and women of all social classes, a diffusion that was aided by rising literacy rates, improved communications, and demographic and social mobility. But although women were touched by these ideas, they were left out of the political process and denied the vote. Similarly, among the working classes, men organized themselves into unions and political parties, from which women were as a rule barred. English, French, and American women responded by founding feminist organizations to protect their rights and promote their interests.

In all three countries political instability and the concomitant fear of social anarchy contributed to the growth of state power and the attempt to use the agency of the state to impose social order and homogeneity on its citizenry. These developments, too, profoundly affected the lives of women. The Victorians witnessed the explosive expansion of state bureaucracies and the enactment of legislation aimed at regularizing and standardizing both public and private activities: governments made education compulsory, criminalized abortion, established or strengthened municipal police forces to control city populations, and passed laws that subjected both industry and labor to a host of regulations. State power and a corresponding secular view of reality grew at the expense of family institutions and village traditions, as well as of church, charity, and workers' associations. With the help of the school and the railroad, the state intruded increasingly on the lives of its citizens.

An obsession with surveillance and regulation characterized not only the activities of the state, but also those of the private citizen. Household manuals and books on child-rearing proliferated as Victorian authors strove to create ideal mothers and perfect household managers. Men in the professions of law and medicine banded together and adopted codes that governed admission to their ranks and regulated the behavior of their members; these codes, like protective labor legislation, had the effect of barring women from public activities in which they had formerly engaged. The Victorian compulsion to regulate, and the professional invasion of both the public and the private sphere, subjected women to a host of new strictures, both legal and prescriptive; not surprisingly, women often resisted and resented these demands.

An extreme polarization of sex roles accompanied the imposition of the ordering vision: this was probably the change that had the most impact on the lives of Victorian women. In both practice and prescription the male and female spheres became increasingly separated, and the roles of men and women became ever more frozen. Social scientists by and large sanctified the separation of spheres and consigned women to the domestic, private sphere. In France the maverick socialist Pierre-Joseph Proudhon relegated women to domestic drudgery; because of their inferiority, he argued, women should be subject to male authority. His compatriot Auguste Comte subscribed to a more elevated vision of women and eulogized their civilizing mission; yet, like Proudhon, he believed that women, because of their weak brains and bodies, belonged in the home. Across the Channel social anthropologists, armed with the evolutionary theories of Charles Darwin, gave patriarchy scientific underpinnings by declaring that both history and evolution sanctioned the subordination of women to men. Herbert Spencer, undoubtedly the most famous of the social Darwinists, argued that evolution had placed women in the home, and that the dictates of social survival necessitated rigidly defined sex roles and male domination. Patriarchy was now equated not only with nature, but with the forces of progress and civilization as well.

Novelists, moralists, and journalists—both male and female—agreed for the most part with the social scientists. Both Charles Dickens and Honoré de Balzac, in their extremely influential works, took women's special domestic mission for granted and applied to their female characters very different standards from those used for males. Authors of popular children's books like Hannah More and the Comtesse de Ségur taught young girls the virtues of passivity and obedience. Similarly, the arbiters of etiquette and writers of manuals, from Sarah Stickney Ellis to Catharine Beecher, decreed that woman's mission was very different from man's, and that her natural sphere was the home. Of course, the image conveyed by the literature diverged dramatically from the reality of women's lives: these exalted domestic angels bore scant resemblance to Georgia slaves, Lancashire mill workers, or even Parisian bourgeoises. Although the idea of separate spheres was not new to the nineteenth century, the obsessive manner in which all three cultures insisted on this separation seems peculiarly novel. As one nineteenth-century reviewer of Charlotte Brontë's *Jane Eyre* indicated, and as many female writers and activists were to discover, any woman who, however tangentially, rejected the role that Victorian culture thrust on her, seemed as noxious and threatening to her contemporaries as the political revolutionary or the social anarchist.[1]

Jane Eyre, refusing to be Rochester's mistress, asks herself, as he tries to break her will, "Who in the world cares for *you,*" and finds this answer, "*I* care for myself. The more solitary, the more friendless, the more unsustained I am, the more I will respect myself." Victorians might have applauded her rejection of adultery, but some could—and did—feel more than a little uneasy at its rationale.[2] In an era that saw selfless submission as woman's essential posture—whether in acceptance of family or marital status, or in acquiescence to established religious belief, or in attendance on children—Jane's assertion of a personal significance unrelated to any social function or relation was alarming. It brought the threat of some radical inconvenience to the smooth running of a world ordered along completely different lines.

Yet if the doctrine Charlotte Brontë puts into the mouth of her heroine seems to question or even defy the right of privileged men to control societies in which women serve as functionaries, it also, however paradoxically, is an expression of the nineteenth century's very spirit and idea—for women as well as for men. For the concept of personal significance, mysterious and complex as a factor in Western history, appears to be linked to cultural change, and such change characterizes England, France, and America throughout the century. Thus women of that time, while being urged to think of themselves only relationally, were also, by the very nature of the metamorphosing societies in which they lived, being challenged to the creation of themselves as persons with separate and interesting destinies.[3] These two virtually antithetical impulses shaped the early years of the Victorian girl.

Birth of a Girl

The first problem encountered, even if unconsciously, by the girl who wished to believe in her own significance was the reaction to her birth. To be sure, the comments gathered to illustrate this reaction (Doc. 1) contain some samples of what appears to be unfeigned pleasure at the news that the baby is a girl; but in their general negativity they reflect the dominant feeling in all three countries virtually throughout the century: the appropriate reaction to a boy's arrival was joyous congratulation, to a girl's something closer to condolence. Priscilla Robertson, writing of England and of Europe, states, "At every stage, in every country, however subtly, boys continued to be favored over girls."[4] Lest we think of such attitudes as maddening but of no real significance coming so early in a baby's life, we should keep in mind the conclusions arrived at by both Lloyd de Mause and Sheila Johansson in their examination of statistics on infant mortality. De Mause, noting the suspicious preponderance of boys over girls throughout Europe until the seventeenth century, when the proportions became nearly equal, suggests that until that time a girl child, even a legitimate one, was in more danger of filicide than a boy. Since we now know that the human female has the biological advantage over the male in possessing a greater hardiness through all stages of life, even the fact that the infant mortality rates of the sexes were equal appears somewhat suspicious. Johansson points out as well that in England throughout the nineteenth century girls between the ages of five and nine had a higher death rate than boys, a strong hint that a girl received with less enthusiasm may also have been fed less adequately (Doc. 2) and nursed in illness less carefully.[5] It is worth noting, however, that in America the reaction to the birth of a girl was not as uniformly negative as in France and England.

Clothing

On arrival, the infant, if French, would in all likelihood have been bound up in swaddling bands (Doc. 5); she or he may have been swaddled in England or America as well (Doc. 51), for the age-old custom persisted in both countries, but diapers were more commonly used. The Biblical associations of the word swaddling may make the process sound rather charming to modern ears, but actually the bands, constricting as they did a baby's legs and sometimes its arms as well, were cruel. Yet in some situations swaddling may have been a safety device: women in predominantly agricultural France, for instance, who carried their infants with them while they labored at field work, needed a way of keeping the baby "put." Whatever the reason for their use, swaddling bands were without question a positioning device and as such may have had a psychological effect on the child's sense of its social place. The adoption of diapers in England and America toward the end of the eighteenth century may well coincide with the growing concern there for personal experience and meaning. At the same time, we should remember that.

Because of the contradictory demands placed on women by changes in the structure and style of personal interaction in all spheres of life, their role in family and society was, at best, fraught with ambivalence. Women confronted these changes most immediately within the family. Among many families in the middle and upper classes, the nineteenth century witnessed a transition from what has been called the positional family to the personal family.[6] In the positional family the child was controlled by the "continual building up of a sense of social pattern," that is, behavior was governed by reference to relative position, such as placement by sex, age, or hierarchy. On the other hand, the more modern personal family that emerged during the Victorian period emphasized the unique and autonomous quality of each individual. In contrast to the positional family, the personal family did not stress status, position, and fixed or ritual patterns of action in its child training. Instead, parents controlled their children's behavior in a manipulative and flexible manner and justified their authority by verbal explanation adjusted to individual circumstance.

The changeover from the positional to the personal family style, complicated enough in the case of boys, was particularly complex for girls, for throughout the century in all three countries the dominant culture decreed that women had a static position in society; they were viewed as instruments. Thus familial treatment of women tended to take a positional tone. But, paradoxically, the fulfillment of that position—dutiful yet companionable wife, communicative and loving mother—demanded that they become more personally oriented. That is, in their interaction with family members, women necessarily became more aware of themselves as persons, and they transmitted their sense of autonomy to their children, both male and female. Thus, with each generation women's sense of their own intrinsic significance grew, even as they fulfilled an instrumental role within a dominantly male culture.

Notes

1. See footnote 1, p. 8.
2. Charlotte Brontë, *Jane Eyre,* chapter 27. Elizabeth Rigby, reviewing the book in 1848, sounded the alarm in these terms:

   > "Altogether the autobiography of Jane Eyre is pre-eminently an anti-Christian composition. There is throughout it a murmuring against the comforts of the rich and the privations of the poor, which, as far as each individual is concerned, is a murmuring against God's appointment—there is a proud and perpetual assertion of the rights of man, for which we find no authority either in God's word or in God's providence. . . . We do not hesitate to say that the tone of mind and thought which has overthrown authority and violated every code human and divine abroad, and fostered Chartism and rebellion at home, is the same which has written *Jane Eyre.*"
   >
   > *Quarterly Review,* 84.167 (Dec.): 173-74.

3. On the differences between a relational or, to use Mary Douglas's term, a "positional" orientation and a personal one, see the editors' discussion in the General Introduction, p. 4.
4. Robertson 1974: 409.
5. De Mause 1976: 6; Johansson 1977: 171.
6. Douglas 1973. We are grateful to Barbara Charlesworth Gelpi for calling our attention to this theory and suggesting its applicability to women in the nineteenth century.

Works Cited

de Mause, Lloyd. 1974. "The Evolution of Childhood," *History of Childhood Quarterly,* 1.4 (Spring): 503-75.

Douglas, Mary. 1973. *Natural Symbols: Explorations in Cosmology.* London.

Johansson, Sheila Ryan. 1977. "Sex and Death in Victorian England." In Martha Vicinus, ed., *A Widening Sphere: Changing Roles in Victorian Women.* Bloomington, Ind.

Robertson, Priscilla. 1974. "Home As a Nest: Middle-Class Childhood in Nineteenth-Century Europe," in Lloyd de Mause, ed., *The History of Childhood.* New York.

ESTELLE B. FREEDMAN AND ERNA OLAFSON HELLERSTEIN (ESSAY DATE 1981)

SOURCE: Freedman, Estelle B. and Erna Olafson Hellerstein. Introduction to *Victorian Women: A Documentary Account of Women's Lives in Nineteenth-Century England, France, and the United States,* pp. 118-33. Stanford, Calif.: Stanford University Press, 1981.

In the following essay, Freedman and Hellerstein examine the domestic, sexual, and mothering duties of Victorian women in France, England, and the United States, citing first-hand accounts to show that women responded in a variety of ways to the often contradictory nature of their idealized and actual roles in private life.

The doctrine of the separate spheres, as elaborated in literature, law, medicine, and religion, prescribed that women's personal lives center around home, husband, and children. The traditional separation between the male public sphere and the female private sphere took on new meaning in the nineteenth century as the distance between these worlds grew and as ever fewer jobs were performed in and around the household. Women at home became, ideally, specialists in emotional and spiritual life, protecting tradition and providing a stable refuge from the harsh, impersonal public sphere that men now entered in increasing numbers. Tennyson captured the ordering vision behind this sexual polarization in the words spoken by the old king in *The Princess:*[1]

> Man for the field and woman for the hearth:
> Man for the sword and for the needle she:
> Man with the head and woman with the heart:
> Man to command and woman to obey;
> All else confusion.

Not only in the middle classes, where the ideal predominated, but throughout each society, the dream of the "angel in the house" lent stability to a rapidly changing world.

The domestic ideal should not, however, be confused with the personal experiences of women, whether at home or in the workplace. Despite the rhetoric about the wife's "domestic empire" or the home as refuge, a woman's daily world was likely to be a single, poorly ventilated room in which an entire family ate and slept, and all too often worked as well. French peasants frequently shared dirt-floored hovels with their livestock, women slaves in America, even those who worked in their master's comfortable household during the day, returned at night to care for their families in cramped and dark cabins and the many women—and occasionally still entire families—who worked at home in the textile cottage industries had to eat and sleep amid the unwieldy looms, lint, and other detritus of their assorted trades.[2]

There were other obstacles to the achievement of the domestic ideal as well. Whatever the physical condition of their homes, women factory, field, and sweatshop workers had to spend as many as sixteen hours a day away from their households. Single working women who lived in urban boarding houses and domestic servants in narrow attic or basement rooms could do little to create cozy nests for themselves. And certainly the women who migrated to the uncertain conditions on the American frontier had to fight heroically just to preserve the idea of the home in an alien land.[3] Mary Abell, a Kansas homesteader who lived one winter in a prairie sod hut, wrote about this struggle in a letter to her sister back in comfortable New York State:

> Do you wonder that I get nervous shut up so week after week with the children in a room 10 x 11 for that is every inch of room we have. Em talks about being crowded, but let her try keeping house in the further bedroom with four small children. . . . I have to cook and do everything right here. Get milk—make butter, eat, sleep, etc. etc. The vessel under the bed a few feet from the stove does not thaw out week in and week out.
>
> (Doc. 66)

Even for the middle and upper classes, the private sphere over which women allegedly ruled slowly lost its isolation and autonomy as professionals like doctors and educators became the authorities on private matters such as childbirth, sexuality, and the raising of children. As the century wore on, more and more experts from the public world of the professions influenced home life with their standardized, printed advice, gradually displacing the traditional lore and rituals of female culture that women had customarily transmitted to each other orally and informally.[4]

These contradictions within the angelic domestic ideal and between this ideal and the real circumstances of women's lives are vividly revealed in the first-hand accounts of family life that follow. Not only do they illustrate the conflicts experienced by women, but they illustrate as well the ways different women responded to these tensions. In deciding whether and whom to marry, in living with husbands and children, and in friendships with their own sex, women of the Victorian era demonstrated both an awareness of the dilemmas they faced and an impressive resiliency in confronting them.

The Decision to Marry or Remain Single

In 1833 Stéphanie Jullien, a Parisian bourgeoise, wrote to her brother about a marriage proposal she had received: "*Mon Dieu*! Such indecision! Such perplexity! What should I do! I almost wish I were not so free, that I were restrained or controlled, so that I would not have the responsibility for my future unhappiness or happiness. Because the more I think about it, the more confused I become, the more I hesitate". Jullien, who almost seemed to long for a return to arranged marriages, was not alone in her anxiety, as the troubled musings in the courtship documents reveal. The decision about marrying took on new weight in the nineteenth century as both the patterns and the meaning of marriage changed. In England and France the percentage of people who married gradually rose, while the average age at first marriage slowly fell, and life expectancy increased. The life expectancy of a French woman, for example, was only thirty years in 1800, compared with nearly fifty years in 1900. Americans had experienced a pattern of early marriage in the colonial period, but women's age at first marriage stabilized at twenty to twenty-three during the nineteenth century. At the same time, white American women shared in the increase in life expectancy that could lead to longer marriages. With marriages beginning earlier, and life spans getting longer, women in the Atlantic world could expect to spend more of their lives married than in the past.[5]

Victorian women may well have looked for greater emotional satisfaction from these lengthy marriages than their ancestors had, for a new emphasis on romantic love as a basis for union raised expectations for marital happiness.[6] Jullien wrote that she would never marry merely to give herself "a lot in life," and felt that she must love and desire her future husband for his sake as well as for hers. Helen Bourn, a young Englishwoman, warned her suitor about the importance of sincerity in love. Moreover, Victorian women embarked on courtship knowing that a bad marriage could become a hell from which there was no exit. Indeed, divorce was not legally possible in France from 1816 to 1884; and law and custom continued to make even separation extremely rare in England and America.

In addition, as Jullien complained, the choices on which women's future happiness depended now lay with them. Despite much regional and class variation, women in all three countries generally had more personal freedom in courtship and marriage than their grandmothers or even their mothers had. In the traditional "European marriage pattern," couples had characteristically waited until they could be certain of a house and some land before marrying, so that the average peasant woman had been almost thirty years old at marriage. Even these mature premodern brides had chosen their mates within the tight controls of kin and community. Although some remnants of this control survived into the Victorian period, the ex-peasants among the growing classes of industrial and wage laborers now courted more independently, with less participation by parents and community, and now founded and supported families on their own wages while relatively young.[7] Among the aristocracy and the bourgeoisie, arranged marriages were also becoming relics of the past; and though French demoiselles were still watched and chaperoned as in the past, young American women moved about quite freely, joked about courtship with their friends, and wrote love letters to their suitors.[8]

The weakening of external controls on courtship was in fact a mixed blessing for women. To the extent that it lessened the surveillance over their romantic and sexual behavior, it brought greater personal autonomy; but at the same time it left them unprotected as they ventured into a larger world. Increases in illegitimacy rates in Europe suggest a new sexual vulnerability, particularly among migrants to the cities. Many of these illegitimate births resulted from coerced sexual relations by co-workers or neighbors, which would have been followed, in traditional societies, by marriage—village sanctions would have seen to that.[9] Now, however, men could take sexual advantage of women with impunity. Other evidence from the United States and Europe shows that rapes or seductions were often by social superiors: Lucy Brewer of Plymouth, Massachusetts, was seduced and abandoned by a respectable neighbor boy; Suzanne Voilquin, a Parisian seamstress, had been raped by a "courting" medical student, only to be similarly abandoned; Olive Ashe, a Vermont servant, was made pregnant by the farmer for whom she worked and died after a botched abortion.

Women's sexual and economic vulnerability, their desire for respectability and security, and their longing (in many cases) for children combined with the growing ideal of romantic love to place great pressure on them to marry. Spinsterhood was, in fact, rare in the nineteenth century—by the end of the century, more than 90 percent of all American women married, as did 85-88 percent of the women in England and France.[10]

The consequences of remaining single could vary greatly, depending on a woman's race, class, and nationality. The decision not to marry, for instance, might mean independence for white, middle-class women like Catharine Beecher, Louisa May Alcott, and Harriet Martineau; such women could move about unchaperoned and become teachers, writers, lecturers, or social reformers.[11] And many single women found emotional support by living with family or friends. Eugénie de Guérin, who lived on her father's southern French estate, was insulated from worry by her comfortable economic position and had a tender relationship with her sister Mimi. But most spinsters, without family means and social status, faced economic hardship and social marginality. Frances Marion Eddy, who gave up her dreams of college and a career in order to support her widowed mother, was more typical; for her spinsterhood meant hard work and considerable self-sacrifice.

The consequences of marrying also varied widely among women. For a white woman in antebellum America or in Europe, marriage meant a loss of civil rights, including the rights to property, wages, and the custody of children. Under English law, as one critic, Barbara Bodichon, put it, her existence was entirely absorbed in that of her husband; and in the United States, a women's rights conference described married women as "civilly dead".[12] In contrast, the slave woman in the American South had no civil rights from birth. Furthermore, her marriage, although it may have been performed according to complex Afro-American ritual, was not recognized by the state and entailed no transition in legal status.[13] In all three countries, marriage might come to mean primarily an economic partnership; however, for some, as we have seen in the Jullien case, marriage had to include the prospect of emotional and sexual satisfaction, in addition to financial security.

Marriage

Once married, nineteenth-century women found their personal lives beset with contradictions. On the one hand, the idea of the "angel in the house" called for a selfless, dependent creature who pleased and fascinated her husband and devoted herself to him without reserve. On the other hand, the realities of coping with a household, very likely with a job as well, and almost certainly with children, required sustained strength, skill, and creativity. To add further confusion, the marriage vows, reflecting the ideal of romantic love, evoked the image of loving partnership and mutual trust, yet the woman entered a "partnership" in which she had none of the legal and economic rights enjoyed by her spouse. How could she be an active, loving partner, yet remain a dependent angel?

It is possible that for many women such questions never arose. An angel rarely presided in the farm, factory, or slave family where marriage—indeed, where survival—clearly required a partnership in unremitting work. Middle-class women, too, although culturally and even physically constrained by the angelic ideal, were seldom idle, for all but the very rich had to work, if only in the home, tending the young, mending clothes, or nursing the sick.[14]

Despite all these difficulties, many women found personal happiness in marriage. For some simply fulfilling their marital duties and helping their families survive brought satisfaction. Married couples did attain loving partnerships in each country, especially in families where the "separate" spheres overlapped. Mémé Santerre reported that her father, a linen weaver who worked at home with his family, "adored" her mother; the aristocratic British Amberleys, engaged in a nursery battle to get their first-born son to breast-feed properly, were also clearly a loving couple who shared their trials. Even in the United States, with its more rigid separation of sexual spheres, the New England wife Persis Sibley Andrews found her husband a "sympathising partner," although she often expressed frustration at her inability to share his political life more fully; and the letters of Mary Ellen Castle Rankin, an American bride, shine with happiness.

But even happy marriages did not satisfy all of women's needs, and many women turned outside of marriage for friendship and support. In the United States a strong female culture, which included both single and married women, could ease some of the strains of married life.[15] Through visits and letters married women found personal support from close female friends and relatives, especially when they faced life crises such as childbirth. Despite a devoted husband who brought her breakfast in bed during her first pregnancy, the California pioneer Georgiana Bruce Kirby wrote of her longing for the company of other women and the pleasure of her rare visits with distant neighbors. The lifelong correspondence of the girlhood friends Mary Hallock Foote and Helena de Kay Gilder, whose marriages separated them by thousands of miles, brought great comfort at times of birth and death.

For every one of the examples indicating the possibility for marital adjustment, another can be found to indicate how conflict in marriage could erupt, in all social classes, into extreme discord and even violence. The relative powerlessness of women in marriage left them vulnerable to physical and sexual abuse, as contemporary accounts of domestic violence, incest, and adultery illustrate.[16] Frédéric Le Play in his studies of European workers, for instance, recorded cases of wife-beating, drunkenness, and abandonment—and the case of at least one beaten French wife who regularly fought back. Temperance advocates decried the effect of alcohol on family life, and claimed that drunken husbands neglected and abused their wives and children, though court and prison records show that women, too, could resort to alcohol and violence under economic and personal stress.[17]

Women's efforts to resist the power imbalances within the family and to control the world around them took both individual and social forms. French women had a reputation as wielders of power within the home through their responsibility for the family budget, and many middle-class women in England employed the same managerial leverage where they could. Some were able to impose their will on those around them by sheer force of personality, if not by manipulative charm, then by plain meanness or even sickness; in fact, invalided or hysterical women could wield formidable power. Some American historians have suggested that women gained power in the home by refusing marital sex so that they might exercise control over their own fertility. Such individual efforts had parallels in the social causes led by Anglo-American middle-class women in the last third of the century. Women's Christian Temperance Union members, voluntary motherhood advocates, and social purity reformers sought to convert men to the female ideals of temperance and chastity, standards that they believed to be in the interests of all women.[18] A direct call for egalitarian marriage appeared at mid-century in each country when the early women's rights advocates campaigned publicly to reform marriage and divorce laws, hoping to end the subjection of women in marriage.

Queen Victoria (1837-1901).

Finally, some women simply took refuge from their husbands in adultery. The French doctor Auguste Debay, in a vastly popular marriage manual, counseled husbands to please their wives so as to keep them faithful. And as the confessional letters of Louise Abber to the novelist Honoré de Balzac show, if adultery did not always make a woman calm and happy, it could at least provide her with some excitement and a sense of her own importance.

Sexuality

Marriage entailed the right—and the duty—of mutual sexual access. The marriage ceremony of the Church of England required the groom to say to his bride, "With my body I thee worship". Indeed, Church and State recognized sex as of the essence of marriage, and counted the inability or the refusal to perform as among the few grounds for the annulment of the marriage contract. Nevertheless, Victorian sexual ideology was replete with anxious and conflicting advice. Bestselling manuals about conjugal health and happiness warned that insanity, disease, and even death could result from either sexual excess or sexual abstinence. The most blatant stereotypes of prudish Victorian attitudes, as epitomized by Queen Victoria's wedding-night advice to her daughter, "Lie still, and think of the Empire," have been modified by recent historical scholarship. The question of how women experienced their own sexuality remains, all the same, a controversial one.[19]

The sex manuals offered no monolithic advice for women. Although the view of women's passionlessness held by the English physician William Acton strongly influenced Anglo-American thinking, the works of some of his fellow English writers, as well as of such other doctors as Auguste Debay in France and Elizabeth Blackwell in America, place Acton's ideas within a larger context. These sexual theorists all believed that female sexuality differed from male sexuality; yet each granted different properties to the female sex. Blackwell, arguing from a feminist perspective, criticized the limited, phallic definition of sexual passion employed by men and favored a more universal standard that took spirituality and female sensuality into account. The French, in art, literature, and medical advice, seemed generally more cognizant of women's erotic potential; Debay nevertheless resembled the English doctor Acton in advising women to defer to their husband's sexual interests. Debay's recommendation that women should simulate orgasm for the sake of marital stability indicates that the relatively greater interest of the French in female sexual satisfaction should not automatically be interpreted as liberating for women.

The passionless woman, then, was neither a simple nor a dominant cultural model in the nineteenth century, nor was it a model that necessarily extended to women outside the middle and upper classes. Indeed, Victorian moralists and social scientists alike often projected onto lower-class, slave, or foreign women the sexual drives they denied the bourgeois wife. Most respectable Victorians distinguished their own social classes from the rest of society on the basis of female virtue and purity, while at the same time leaving poorer women—whether servants, slaves, or prostitutes—vulnerable to sexual exploitation.[20] The French socialist Flora Tristan and the American union organizer Leonora Barry, among others, pointed with indignation to this double standard for rich and poor women.

Although the range of sexual norms may have been wider than some historians have suggested, the agents of sexual regulation nevertheless grew stricter over the course of the century. The French case is instructive. Secular prescriptive literature in France deemed sex not only desirable, but almost compulsory; anticlerical republicans, in alliance with the increasingly influential medical profession, argued that good marital sexual hygiene fostered stable families, and these in turn fostered a stable State. A similar drive for professional authority characterized the regulation of sexuality in England and America, where male doctors strove for greater status by exercising control over women's health. American doctors, for instance, began to condemn abortion in the 1860's as part of their quest for authority over public policy. By preventing women's access to contraception and criminalizing abortion, they restricted the married woman's ability either to avoid or to terminate her pregnancies, thus bolstering the ideology of motherhood as the goal of sexual experience.[21]

In the face of this drive to channel female sexuality into marital service, women's struggle for sexual autonomy sometimes took the form of avoiding sexual intercourse. In so doing, women were also protecting their physical health and well-being. As Blackwell explained, the results of sex could permanently harm a woman's health. Sexual intercourse evoked the fear of pregnancy and childbirth, and in the nineteenth century childbearing could cause tearing, uterine prolapse, and ulcerations. These and other "female troubles," such as anemia, vaginal infections, and venereal diseases, weakened women and could make intercourse unpleasant. Pregnancy and childbirth could also mean death; toxemia, hemorrhage, and puerperal fever were notorious killers. It is thus no wonder that some women avoided the marriage bed, and that others shared the secrets of contraception with their friends. Physicians—and some women—claimed, moreover, that a woman's passion simply could not be gratified in intercourse with a man who was indifferent to female sexuality; and that likewise when a man relied on *coitus interruptus* for birth control a woman might well be left unsatisfied. Indeed, one French physician published case studies to show that women who were repeatedly interrupted while approaching or experiencing orgasm became nervous and even ill.[22]

Despite these deterrents to sexual expression, Victorian women sought sexual pleasure both inside and outside of marriage, and in many cases found it. Writers like Debay obviously knew that women experienced clitoral orgasms. A late-nineteenth-century survey of American women's sexual practices showed that a sizable proportion of educated, middle-class women enjoyed their sex lives and regularly achieved orgasm.[23] The Frenchwomen Stéphanie Jullien and Louise Abber clearly saw sexual desire and sexual fulfillment as essential to their happiness in marriage; Abber complained that her husband was too brutal in his passions, and she wrote vibrantly about the intense joys of adulterous sex.

Other women experienced sexual pleasure through masturbation or lesbian relationships. According to one American survey, nearly 70 percent of the female respondents who were adolescents in the late nineteenth century reported masturbating to orgasm, and about 20 percent of the educated, middle-class women of the same era had had lesbian experiences at some time in their lives.[24]

Women's relationships with each other took various forms, ranging from intimate friendship, to homoerotic attraction, to explicitly lesbian partnerships. The passionate letters women friends exchanged and the crises precipitated by their marriages provide clues to the erotic content of these relationships. It is impossible to know how many women friends who shared beds also shared their physical passions; but the intimacy of the letters and the self-reported homosexual experiences of some suggest that far more Victorian women than has been previously acknowledged knew the pleasures of lesbian sexuality. Some women who recognized their attraction to their own sex adopted men's attire in an effort to "pass" as the husbands of their lovers. But openly lesbian relationships rarely had public approval; indeed, the marriage of Annie Hindle and Annie Ryan was an exception within the marginal world of the American theater. By the end of the century doctors and psychologists had begun to label lesbianism as a pathological form of sexual deviance, thus making it more difficult for all women—whether lesbian or not—to express their loving feelings for each other openly.[25]

Motherhood

Even more than sexuality, motherhood was central to the identities of most nineteenth-century women. Indeed, as the personal experiences in the documents reveal, the bearing and raising of children dominated women's adult lives, and their experiences as mothers provided their greatest joys and deepest tragedies.

Yet for all this, women bore relatively fewer children as the century progressed. Although the population exploded in all three countries, marital fertility rates declined as more and more couples began to employ a variety of contraceptive techniques. The French were the first to use contraception on a population-wide basis; statistics reveal that the practice spread rapidly after about 1790. In the United States adult white women bore fewer children in each generation after 1800, and the total fertility rate dropped from 7.04 per adult woman in 1800 to 5.42 in 1850 to 3.56 in 1900. The British began limiting births on a statistically significant scale only after 1870.[26]

The evidence does not permit us to say precisely how and for what reasons couples in different social groups made the decision to limit family size.[27] A falling birthrate does not, of itself, signify that women controlled their reproductive lives; the most common form of prevention was probably coitus interruptus, a technique that depends absolutely on male cooperation, and that can of course be performed without female consent. In some cases women may even have been deprived of babies they desired.

Many women, however, clearly resisted childbearing: by sharing contraceptive information, by cooperating with their sexual partners in preventive measures, by abortion, by infanticide, and by deliberate neglect of the infant. Such women had pressing reasons to avoid motherhood. Many working women knew that they could not support another child, and that their own labors in factories and fields would leave them little time for the joys of motherhood. Mothers of illegitimate babies faced dishonor and economic hardship; in England many could support themselves only as live-in wet nurses, so that their own babies often died of malnutrition and disease.[28] But even an economically secure married woman sometimes decided to avoid or terminate pregnancy when her own health was at risk or when another child would be inconvenient. When these women got "caught," they resigned themselves to bearing their babies, voicing their complaints about the misfortune in letters to friends and relatives.

In America the birthrate remained higher in the black population than in the white throughout the century, for a number of reasons.[29] For one thing, black women generally began childbearing younger than white women. Although slave families feared the sale of their children, and mothers knew that pregnancy would not reduce their tasks in the master's house or in the fields, slave owners encouraged breeding in order to increase their valuable human property. It is possible, too, that slaves themselves desired more children because their families could offer them personal meaning in contrast with their institutionalized exploitation. After slavery ended, the majority of blacks remained agricultural workers for whom children were an economic asset. Since poverty and inadequate health care kept the black infant mortality rates extremely high, black women continued to bear many children to ensure the survival of their families.

For women in all three countries the experience of motherhood was profoundly affected by pervasive nineteenth-century changes—migration, professionalization, and the growth of the state. It appears that in the course of the century the typical family—whether rural or urban—went through a transitional stage of self-reliance as the older institutions that had traditionally buttressed the family were gradually replaced by new ones. Migration to cities, to the frontier, or to a new country meant the loss of supportive village networks and rituals, so that women, isolated from familiar settings, had to rely on themselves, on letters from distant friends and families, or on their husbands, during pregnancies and while raising children. Although new or expanded services for the family, such as family physicians, advice manuals, and public schools, gradually replaced the traditional networks, in the interim, mothers (and to some extent, fathers) struggled alone. Parents improvised childbirth arrangements and taught, trained, and doctored their children in the time they could spare from wage labor and household work.

To be sure, many families were almost untouched by these changes, even by the end of the century. Even a good number of those who migrated managed to take kin and custom with them. The Kentucky-born Eleanor Brittain, for example, widowed in California and left with three children to support, was able to call for help on a cousin of her mother's who had migrated to a nearby town. The transitional self-reliant family was, then, an important but not a universal nineteenth-century family type.

Another factor also profoundly affected the experience of bearing and raising children: in England, France, and the United States alike, motherhood was celebrated with unprecedented intensity in the nineteenth century. Although the cult of motherhood and the idea of the child-centered family had taken shape through centuries of European development, in the Victorian era bureaucrats and politicians fostered the ideal of the personal family and stressed the social responsibilities of the "Republican Mother," breeder of citizens. The good mother, like the submissive and sexually pleasing wife, had her role to play in this new ideology by seeing to it that the family remained strong and intact, a bastion against social upheaval as well as a pillar of the state. Influential women writers, too, seeking a worthy role for women in a changing world, celebrated motherhood, as did Catholic and Evangelical authorities. Mother-educators did in fact play a critical role in all three countries until public education was equal to the task of turning out the desired literate, patriotic, and uniform citizenry.[30] No doubt this elevation of motherhood gave some women a tool for exerting moral influence. But it may be that, as with sexuality, women in the end lost a degree of autonomy as the standardizing influence of professional experts increased.

The gradual professionalization of medical care had its greatest impact on women during pregnancy and childbirth, but by no means all women were affected by it. Although physicians came to dominate in the birth chamber, developing in the process a new technology that included anesthetics, corrective surgery, and safer cesarean sections, many rural or migrant women continued to give birth and to learn about the care of their babies within traditional female cultures and rituals. Ironically, "modern" medicine reached the urban poor first, for they alone gave birth in hospitals, where they often served as teaching subjects and where the unhygienic practices that resulted from the contemporary ignorance of the germ theory of disease made deliveries too often fatal for both mother and child. Women of modest means typically continued to give birth at home or at maternity hospitals with the assistance of lay or licensed midwives, although physicians eventually succeeded in ousting most midwives from the birth chamber. Well-to-do women like Caroline Clive and Kate Amberley struck a balance between old and new, giving birth at home with trusted doctors in attendance, while continuing to observe some traditional childbirth rituals. The direction of change, then, was away from female culture and ritual and toward the male professional birth attendant, but the change took place unevenly and with much regional variation.[31]

In raising children during this transitional period of familial self-reliance, mothers functioned as doctors and teachers to their children, provided emotional nurturance, and taught them a variety of skills. Rural or migrant mothers "broke up" their children's diseases with homemade or patent medicines and often taught them at home to read, write, and cipher. For religious families, whether Catholic or Protestant, training for salvation was a prime parental duty: the American Quaker Lucy Lovell worried that maternal softness might foster depravity in her daughter, unlike the prosperous Catholic woman of Lille who saw herself as her children's "visible angel" and believed that the teaching of religious precepts was her most important duty as a mother. In artisan and farm families, parents transmitted economic skills to their children: Santerre's parents taught her to weave, and the family spent long hours together at their looms. Most mothers, even among the prosperous, taught their daughters household skills: Athénaïs Michelet was given her baby brother to care for, while her older sister learned to spin, cook, and manage the house; Nettie Abell, the daughter of indulgent "modern" American parents, had nonetheless been so thoroughly trained in cooking, sewing, and child care by age eight that when her mother died she could virtually take over the management of the household.

Mothers in the burgeoning urban working classes could rarely offer their children much in the way of tradition, teaching, or affection. The French socialist Flora Tristan made bitter reference to the angelic ideal, pointing to the wretched conditions in the life of the French working class that made its achievement impossible. Proletarianization had robbed working-class families of religious affiliation and of pride in traditional domestic or artisanal skills; and the press of factory and sweatshop labor left them little time or inclination for domestic grace and tender family life. The dream of domesticity nevertheless spread gradually to the lower classes, and in the 1860's, in one of the oddest contradictions of this contradictory century, many union and socialist spokesmen began to call for women's right to return to the home just as middle-class women in all three countries were beginning their organized campaigns to free themselves from the stifling constraints of angelic domesticity and maternity.[32]

As the documents show, women often longed for children and were delighted with their babies. Victorine B—, a Parisian working woman, described the joys of caring for her baby and noted each minute change in his development; she wrote that her experiences as a mother were the happiest of her life. But just as the emotional experience of mothering differed from individual to individual, so the style of mothering varied from class to class and country to country. In general French and American middle-class women enjoyed a more intimate and tender family life than their counterparts in England, where a stable servant class provided a full supply of nannies and wet nurses. The English-style isolated nursery was an impossibility for the French because of their relatively lower living standard; all but the very rich lived in small apartments or modest houses and had to find ways to get along with each other in cramped quarters. And because the United States, apart from the South, did not have a servant class, most American middle-class women spent a good deal of time with their children, too. Except for a few months when she had a hired girl, Mary Abell tended her five children—affectionately and steadily, although she often complained about their noise and mess—helped only intermittently by her busy husband.

Many other women, in all three countries, were separated from their children because they had to work. English working women often had to leave their babies in the care of older children, who might well does them with opiates to quiet their hungry squalling. French working women often put their babies out to nurse in the country, a situation from which a tragically high number of them did not return.[33] American slave mothers were forced to leave their babies with children or old women in the quarters, often so as to be free to care for white babies. Not surprisingly, the infant mortality rates in such cases ran exceedingly high. Slaves and the poorest women, especially, were thus forced by circumstance to continue childcare practices that middle- and upper-class women, influenced by a growing sentiment of tenderness toward children, had foregone by the nineteenth century. As the bitter slave lullaby and the urgent letter from a Parisian working mother attest, their dilemma grieved and embittered such mothers.

In fact, no account of nineteenth-century motherhood could be complete without mentioning the death of babies and young children. Death stalked the nursery, and such infectious diseases as diptheria and infant diarrhea could strike at any time. Accidents, too, especially where children were left alone or where mothers did wage labor at home, were tragically common. Infant death rates remained high throughout the century, and the fear of losing a child made decisions about feeding, wet nurses, medicines, and other aspects of child care urgent and anxiety-ridden for women in every social class. Some found that their bereavements tested their faith in God; others took comfort that their families would one day be unbroken and reunited in Paradise.

The End of Marriage

Under pressure for marital reform, divorce became somewhat more accessible to women toward the end of the century, although the divorced woman continued to suffer from a greater social stigma than her ex-husband. Nevertheless, divorce remained largely a privilege of the upper classes; it also remained almost entirely a male prerogative.[34]

The campaign to make divorce accessible took place within conflicting demographic and ideological trends. At the beginning of the century one marriage partner or the other was likely to have died before all the children had left home. But as men and women began to live longer and to have smaller families, more and more marriages continued long past the child-rearing years. With death parting fewer couples, the possibility of legal dissolution became a pressing issue. Divorce, however, conflicted with the domestic ideal and the cult of motherhood so heavily promoted by both religious institutions and the state. Thus, those who campaigned for the reform of divorce legislation now argued that divorce could actually help to ensure that homes were happy; on the whole, divorce reformers did not base their arguments on the woman's right to independence. The angel was to remain intact, even in the divorce court. Furthermore, reformers argued that the threat of divorce could shore up the marriage relationship by controlling both male and female behavior. The man who beat his wife, the woman who denied her husband his conjugal rights, would now face the sanction of public censure in the courts.

For all the gains in life expectancy, however, death rather than divorce still ended most marriages, in many cases when the marriage partners were still relatively young. When women died and left children behind them, their bereaved husbands were likely to be inexperienced in domesticity and child care, and many found it a struggle to keep their children with them and to care for them properly. Some were fortunate in having friends and relatives to help out. Robert Abell, for example, turned his four little boys and his household over to his eight-year-old daughter, and Warren Cranston fell back on parents who lived close by and took in his daughters.

But because of women's limited job opportunities and low wages, the widow's struggle could be (as the widower's almost never was) a struggle for survival. Men in all social classes who knew they were leaving young wives alone to economic hardship expressed concern. "What can you do to make a living?" David Brittain asked his wife from his deathbed; Leander—, a New York clerk dying of consumption, expressed a similar worry to his young wife. Both men were troubled that their wives, left to support themselves, would have to endure not only poverty, but also the social disgrace of low-status jobs. Thus David asked Eleanor not to take in washing after his death, and Leander begged Almira, a sweatshop worker, not to degrade herself by becoming a domestic servant. David went so far as to wish he could take his "angel wife" with him, for he feared that in frontier America a woman and her children, left without a man's protection, might be vulnerable to bad men or adventurers. In fact, a year after his death, Eleanor had to horsewhip a man who tried to carry off her fifteen-year-old daughter.

Eleanor Brittain, an "angel wife" on the frontier who defended her home with a whip, embodies the contradictions between the Victorian domestic ideal for women and the realities of women's lives in the nineteenth century. Her life also gives some idea of the great range of the angelic myth, which surfaced not only in a deathbed declaration in the American West, but also in the rhetoric of the French working classes, in the speeches of English and American union organizers, and in the dreams of black female reformers. As the documents make abundantly clear, the domestic dream spread and grew even among women who could not possibly attain it, while the women who already lived within its confines of dress and decorum struggled to free themselves from the parlor and get out into the world.

Notes

1. *The Princess* (1849): part V, lines 427-31. Although this passage has often been quoted as epitomizing Victorian attitudes about the separate spheres, Tennyson himself did not defend these sentiments. In the poem, he made the king who uttered them a harsh, crude, and old-fashioned curmudgeon who, in the same speech, suggested that men should break women like horses. For a further discussion of this poem and of the angelic ideal in literature, see Christ 1977. F. Basch 1974 discusses the ideal of domesticity and Victorian criticisms of it in novels, poetry, and protest literature. Two classic studies of Victorian domestic ideology still worth reading are Houghton 1957 and Welter 1966.

2. On the living conditions for English working-class families, see Gauldie 1974. On the overlap of work and home and a review of literature on the subject, see Pleck 1976.

3. On boarding, servants, and frontier women, see, respectively, Modell & Haveren 1973; McBride 1976; and Faragher & Stansell 1975.

4. On the impact of the professions on women, see Wertz & Wertz 1977; and Ehrenreich & English 1978.

5. For a concise summary of European demographic changes, see Tilly & Scott 1978: chap. 5. On America, see Wells 1979: 20, 22. See also Coale & Zelnik 1963; Wrigley 1969; Van de Walle 1974; and Johansson 1977. Consult as well the Part IV essay by Marilyn Yalom.

6. Classic literary statements of this theme are presented in Taylor 1953; and Watt 1957. Such evidence is probably unrepresentative of the great numbers of peasants, slaves, and sweatshop workers who lacked the literacy and the time to read romantic novels and marriage manuals. Edward Shorter, in one of his more careful articles (1974), tries to show such a change among ordinary people.

7. Hajnal 1965. On early modern family life and family strategies in France, see N. Z. Davis 1977, which includes a very thorough bibliography. On 19th-century patterns, see D. S. Smith 1978: 94-96; and Tilly & Scott 1978: 93-98. See also Anderson 1971.
8. For a comparison of European and American single women in the 1830's, see Alexis de Tocqueville's *Democracy in America,* vol. 2, 3d book, chap. 9.
9. See Shorter 1975; and the criticisms of that work in Scott & Tilly 1975. See also Tilly, Scott, & Cohen 1976. In the U.S., however, illegitimacy rates were higher in the late 18th century and declined during the 19th. Smith & Hindus 1975.
10. D. S. Smith 1974: 121; Tilly & Scott 1978: 92.
11. The constraints on the activism of single women are discussed in Chambers-Schiller 1978. See also Schupf 1974.
12. N. Basch 1979.
13. On Afro-American marriage, see Genovese 1976: 475-81; Gutman 1977; and Burnham 1978.
14. Branca 1974 and 1975. On the domestic tasks in the U.S., see, for instance, Kleinberg 1976.
15. Smith-Rosenberg 1975.
16. Pleck 1979.
17. On women's violent crimes, see Hartman 1977; and on women prisoners, Freedman 1981: chap. 5.
18. O'Neill 1971: 40-42; Smith-Rosenberg 1972; Gordon 1974: 61-62; D. S. Smith 1974: 131-33.
19. On Victorian sexual ideology, see, for the U.S., Barker-Benfield 1973; Degler 1974; Haller & Haller 1974; Walters 1974; and Cott 1978. For England, see Cominos 1963 and 1973; Marcus 1966 (which should be approached cautiously); and F. B. Smith 1977; and for France, McLaren 1974, and his more speculative 1975 article; and Hellerstein 1980, chaps. 4, 5 (on French sexual morality). For a lighthearted study, see Aron & Kempf 1978. See also Foucault's controversial 1978 work.
20. On the sexualization of servants, see Davidoff 1979. On the distinction between respectable and impoverished women, see Cominos 1963 and 1973; Marcus 1966; Pearsall 1969; and F. Basch 1974: chap. 3.
21. McLaren 1974, 1975; Branca 1975; Mohr 1978; Hellerstein 1980: chaps. 2, 4.
22. Zeldin 1973: 87-115; Gordon 1974: 60-63; Knibiehler 1976a and 1976b; Stage 1979.
23. Degler 1974. For a different interpretation of this survey, which was conducted by Dr. Clelia Mosher, see Smith-Rosenberg 1976.
24. Figures based on the answers of respondents over age 40 (in the 1920's), presented in K. B. Davis 1929: 101, 257, 307. The percentages were still higher for younger women.
25. Klaich 1974: 55-67; Smith-Rosenberg 1975; Katz 1976; Sahli 1979; Schwarz 1979.
26. D. S. Smith 1974: 123; Tilly & Scott 1978: 89-103.
27. Demographic and historical analyses of family limitation appear in Banks 1954; Berguès 1960; Bourgeois-Pichat 1965; Biraben 1966; Noonan 1966, part 4; D. S. Smith 1974; Langer 1975; and Gordon 1976.
28. Roberts 1976.
29. For data on black women's higher rate of childbearing, see Grabell, Kiser, & Whelpton 1973: 390. On the importance of family life under slavery, see A. Davis 1972. See also Loewenberg & Bogin 1976; and Gutman 1977.
30. Ariès 1962; Sklar 1973: 158-63; Ryan 1975: chap. 4; Kerber 1976; Pope 1976. For other literature about mothers and children, see the Part I essay by Barbara C. Gelpi.
31. Wertz & Wertz 1977; Ehrenreich & English 1978: 84-88. Traditional childbirth rituals among Native Americans are described in Niethammer 1977: 1-21. On the struggle between doctors and midwives, see the Part III essay by Leslie Hume and Karen Offen.
32. Perrot 1976.
33. Sussman 1975; Wohl 1978.
34. McGregor 1957; O'Neill 1973; Wells 1979: 21. For a guide to the reform literature about divorce in 19th-century France, see Offen 1977.

Works Cited

Anderson, Michael. 1971. *Family Structure in Nineteeth-Century Lancashire.* Cambridge, Eng.

Aron, Jean-Paul, and Roger Kempf. 1978 *Le Pénis et la démoralisation de l'occident.* Paris.

Basch, Françoise. 1974. *Relative Creatures: Victorian Women in Society and the Novel.* Tr. Anthony Rudolf. New York.

Basch, Norma. 1979. "Invisible Women: The Legal Fiction of Marital Unity in Nineteenth-Century America," *Feminist Studies,* 5.2 (Summer): 346-66.

Biraben, Jean-Noël. 1966. "Communication ur l'évolution de la fécondité en Europe occidentale," *Official Documents of the European Population Conference,* vol. 1. Strasbourg.

Bourgeois-Pichat, Jean. 1965. "The General Development of the Population of France Since the Eighteenth Century," in D. V. Glass and D. E. C. Eversley, eds., *Population in History: Essays in Historical Demography.* Chicago.

Branca, Patricia. 1974. "Image and Reality: The Myth of the Idle Victorian Woman," in Mary S. Hartman and Lois Banner eds., *Clio's Consciousness Raised: New Perspectives on the History of Women.* New York.

———. 1975. *Silent Sisterhood: Middle-Class Women in the Victorian Home.* Pittsburgh.

———. 1975. "A New Perspective on Women's Work: A Comparative Typology," *Journal of Social History,* 9.2 (Winter): 129-53.

Burnham, Dorothy. 1978. "The Life of the Afro-American Woman in Slavery." *International Journal of Woman Studies,* 1.4 (July-Aug): 363-77.

Chambers-Schiller, Lee. 1978. "The Single Woman Reformer: Conflict Between Family and Vocation, 1830-1860." *Frontiers,* 3 (Fall): 41-48.

Christ, Carol. 1977. "Victorian Masculinity and the Angel in the House," in Martha Vicinus, ed., *A Widening Sphere: Changing Roles of Victorian Women.* Bloomington: Ind.

Coale, Ansley J., and Melvin Zelnik. 1963. *New Estimates of Fertility and Population in the United States*. Princeton, N.J.

Cominos, Peter T. 1963. "Late Victorian Sexual Respectability and the Social System." *International Review of Social History*, (2 parts), 8.1: 18-48; 8.2: 216-50.

———. 1973. "Innocent Femina Sensualis in Unconscious Conflict," in Martha Vicinus, ed., *Suffer and Be Still: Women in the Victorian Age*. Bloomington, Ind.

Cott, Nancy F. 1977. *The Bonds of Womanhood: "Woman's Sphere" in New England, 1780-1835*. New Haven, Conn.

———. 1978. "Passionless: An Interpretation of Victorian Sexual Ideology, 1790-1850," *Signs*, 4.2 (Winter): 219-36.

Davidoff, Lenore. 1979. "Class and Gender in Victorian England: The Diaries of Arthur J. Munby and Hannah Cullwick," *Feminist Studies*, 5.1 (Spring): 87-141.

Davis, Angela, 1972. "Reflections on the Black Woman's Role in the Community of Slaves," *Massachusetts Review*, 13.1-2 (Winter-Spring): 81-100.

Davis, Katharine Bement. 1929. *Factors in the Sex Life of Twenty-Two Hundred Women*. New York. 1972 reprint edition available.

Davis, Natalie Zemon. 1977. "Ghosts, Kin, and Progeny: Some Features of Family Life in Early Modern France," *Daedalus*, 106 (Spring): 87-114.

Degler, Carl N. 1974. "What Ought to Be and What Was: Women's Sexuality in the Nineteenth Century," *American Historical Review*, 79.5 (Dec.): 1467-90.

Ehrenreich, Barbara, and Deirdre English. 1978. *For Her Own Good: 150 Years of the Experts' Advice to Women*. Garden City, N.Y.

Faragher, Johnny, and Christine Stanswell. 1975. "Women and Their Families on the Overland Trail, 1842-1867," *Feminist Studies*, 2.2-3: 150-66.

Foucalt, Michel. 1978. *The History of Sexuality*, vol. 1: *An Introduction*. Tr. Robert Hurley. New York.

Freedman, Estelle B. 1981. *Their Sisters' Keepers: Women's Prison Reform in America, 1830-1930*. Ann Arbor, Mich.

Gauldie, Enid. 1974. *Cruel Habitations: A History of Working-Class Housing, 1780-1918*. London.

Genovese, Eugene D. 1976. *Roll, Jordan, Roll: The World the Slaves Made*. New York.

Gordon, Linda. 1974. "Voluntary Motherhood: The Beginnings of Feminist Birth Control Ideas in the United States," in Mary S. Hartman and Lois Banner, eds., *Clio's Consciousness Raised: New Perspectives on the History of Women*. New York.

Grabell, Wilson H., Clyde V. Kiser, and Pascal K. Whelpton. 1973. "A Long View," in Michael Gordon, ed., *The American Family in Social-Historical Perspective*. 1st ed. New York.

Gutman, Herbert G. 1976. *Work, Culture, and Society in Industrializing America: Essays in American Working Class and Social History*. New York.

———. 1977. *The Black Family in Slavery and Freedom, 1750-1925*. New York. Reprint of 1976 edition.

Hajnal, John. 1965. "European Marriage Patterns in Perspective," in D. V. Glass and D. E. C. Eversley, eds. *Population in History: Essays in Historical Demography*. Chicago.

Haller, John S., Jr., and Robin M. Haller. 1974. *The Physician and Sexuality in Victorian America*, Urbana, Ill.

Hartman, Mary S. 1977. *Victorian Murderesses: A True History of Thirteen Respectable French and English Women Accused of Unspeakable Crimes*. New York.

Hellerstein, Erna Olafson. 1980. "Women, Social Order, and the City: Rules for French Ladies, 1830-1870." Ph.D. dissertation, University of California, Berkeley.

Houghton, Walter E. 1957. *The Victorian Frame of Mind, 1830-70*. New Haven, Conn.

Johansson, Sheila Ryan. 1977. "Sex and Death in Victorian England." In Martha Vicinus, ed., *A Widening Sphere: Changing Roles in Victorian Women*. Bloomington, Ind.

Katz, Jonathan. 1976. "Passing Women: 1782-1920," in Katz, ed., *Gay American History: Lesbians and Gay Men in the U.S.A., A Documentary*. New York.

Kerber, Linda. 1976. "The Republican Mother: Women and the Enlightenment—An American Perspective," *American Quarterly*, 28.2 (Summer): 187-205

Klaich, Dolores. 1974. *Woman Plus Woman: Attitudes Toward Lesbianism*. New York.

Kleinberg, Susan J. 1976. "Technology and Women's Work: The Lives of Working Class Women in Pittsburgh, 1870-1900," *Labor History*, 17.1 (Winter): 58-72.

Knibiehler, Yvonne. 1976a. "Le Discours médical sur la femme," *Romantisme: Revue du Dix-Neuvième Siècle*, 13-14: 41-55.

———. 1976b. "Les Médecins et al 'nature féminine' au temps du Code Civil," *Annales: Economies, Sociétés, Civilisations*, 31.4: 824-45.

Langer, William L. 1975. "Origins of the Birth Control Movement in England in the Early Nineteenth Century," *Journal of Interdisciplinary History*, 5.4 (Spring): 669-86.

Loewenberg, Bert J., and Ruth Bogins, eds. 1976. *Black Women in Nineteenth-Century American Life: Their Words, Their Thoughts, Their Feelings*. College Park, Pa.

McBride, Theresa M. 1976. *The Domestic Revolution: The Modernization of Household Service in England and France, 1820-1920*. New York.

McGregor, Oliver Ross. 1957. *Divorce in England, a Centenary Study*. London.

McLaren, Angus. 1974. "Some Secular Attitudes Toward Sexual Behavior in France, 1760-1860," *French Historical Studies*, 8.4 (Fall): 604-25.

———. 1975. "Doctor in the House: Medicine and Private Morality in France, 1800-1850," *Feminist Studies*, 2.2-3: 39-54.

Marcus, Steven. 1966. *The Other Victorians: A Study of Sexuality and Pornography in Mid-Nineteenth Century England*. New York.

Modell, John and Tamara K. Hareven. 1973. "Urbanization and the Malleable Household: An Examination of Boarding and Lodging in American Families," *Journal of Marriage and Family*, 35.3 (Aug): 467-79.

Mohr, James C. 1978. *Abortion in America: The Origins and Evolution of National Policy*. New York.

Neithammer, Carolyn. 1977. *Daughters of the Earth: The Lives and Legends of American Indian Women*. New York.

Offen, Karen M. 1977. "The 'Woman Question' as a Social Issue in Nineteenth-Century France: A Bibliographical Essay," *Third Republic/Troisième République,* 3-4 (Fall): 238-99.

O'Neill, William. 1971. *The Woman Movement: Feminism in the United States and England.* Chicago.

Pearsall, Ronald. 1969. *The Worm in the Bud: The World of Victorian Sexuality.* New York.

Perrot, Michelle. 1976. "L'Eloge de la ménagère dans le discours des ouvriers français au XIXe siècle," *Romantisme: Revue du Dix-Neuvième Siècle,* 13-14: 105-21.

Pleck, Elizabeth H. 1976. "Two Worlds in One: Work and Family," *Journal of Social History,* 10.2 (Winter): 178-95.

———. 1979. "Wife-Beating in Nineteeth-Century America," *Victimology,* 4.1: 60-74.

Pope, Barbara Corrado. 1976. "Maternal Education in France, 1815-1848," *Proceedings of the Western Society for French History,* 3: 368-77.

Roberts, Ann. 1976. "Mothers and Babies: The Wetnurse and Her Employer in Mid-Nineteenth Century England," *Women's Studies,* 3.3: 279-93.

Ryan, Mary P. 1975. *Womanhood in America: From Colonial Times to the Present.* New York.

Schupf, Harriet Warm. 1974. "Single Women and Social Reform in Mid-Nineteenth Century England: The Case of Mary Carpenter," *Victorian Studies,* 17.3 (March): 301-17.

Schwarz, Judith. 1979. "Yellow-Clover: Katharine Lee Bates and Katharine Coman," *Frontiers,* 4.3 (Spring): 59-67.

Scott, Joan W. and Louise A. Tilly. 1975. "Woman's Work and the Family in Nineteenth-Century Europe," *Comparative Studies in Society in Society and History,* 17.1 (Jan.): 36-64.

Shorter, Edward. 1974. "Différences de classe et sentiment depuis 1750: l'exemple de las France," *Annales Economies, Sociétés, Civilisations,* 29.4 (July-Aug.): 1034-57.

Sklar, Kathryn Kish. 1973. *Catharine Beecher: A Study in American Domesticity.* New Haven, Conn.

Smith, Daniel Scott. 1974. "Family Limitation, Sexual Control, and Domestic Feminism in the United States," in Mary S. Hartman and Lois Banner, eds. *Clio's Consciousness Raised: New Perspectives on the History of Women.* New York.

———. 1978. "Parental Power and Marriage Patterns: An Analysis of Histrical Trends in Hingham, Massachusetts," in Michael Gordon, ed., *The American Family in Social-Historical Perpective.* Rev. ed. New York.

Smith, Daniel Scott, and Michael S. Hindus. 1975. "Premarital Pregnancy in America, 1640-1971: An Overview Interpretation," *Journal of Interdisciplinary History,* 5.5 (Spring): 537-70.

Smith, F. Barry. 1977. "Sexuality in Britain, 1800-1900: Some Suggested Revisions," in Martha Vicinus, ed., *A Widening Sphere: Changing Roles in Victorian Women.* Bloomington, Ind.

Smith-Rosenberg, Carroll. 1972. "The Hysterical Woman: Some Reflections on Sex Roles and Role Conflict in Nineteenth Century America," *Social Research,* 39.1 (Winter): 652-78.

———. 1974. "Puberty to Menopause: The Cycle of Femininity in Nineteenth-Century America" in Mary S. Hartman and Lois Banner, eds., *Clios's Consciousness Raised: New Perspectives on the History of Women.* New York.

———. 1975. "The Female World of Love and Ritual: Relations Between Women in Nineteenth-Century America," *Signs,* 1.1 (Autumn): 1-29.

Stage, Sarah. 1979. *Female Complaints: Lydia Pinkham and the Business of Women's Medicine.* New York.

Sussman, George D. 1975. "The Wet-Nursing Business in Nineteenth-Century France," *French Historical Studies,* 9.2 (Fall): 304-28.

Taylor, Gordon Rattray. 1953. *Sex in History: The Story of Society's Changing Attitudes to Sex Throughout the Ages.* London. 1973 reprint edition available.

Tilly, Louise A., and Joan W. Scott. 1978. *Women, Work, and Family.* New York.

Tilly, Louise A, Joan W. Scott, and Miriam Cohen. 1976. "Women's Work and European Fertility Patterns," *Journal of Interdisciplinary History,* 6.3 (Winter): 447-76.

Van de Walle, Etienne. 1974. *The Female Population of France in the Nineteenth Century.* Princeton, N.J.

Walters, Ronald E. 1974. *Primers for Prudery: Sexual Advice to Victorian America.* Englewood Cliffs, N.J.

Watt, Ian. 1957. *The Rise of the Novel: Studies in Defoe, Richardson, and Fielding.* London.

Wells, Robert V. 1979. "Women's Lives Transformed: Demographic and Family Patterns in America, 1600-1970," in Carol Ruth Berkin and Mary Beth Norton, eds., *Women of America: A History.* Boston.

Welter, Barbara. 1966. "The Cult of True Womanhood, 1820-1860," *American Quarterly,* 18.2 (Summer): 151-74.

Wertz, Richard W., and Dorothy C. Wertz. 1977. *Lying-In: A History of Childbirth in America.* New York.

Wohl, Anthony, ed. 1978. *The Victorian Family: Structure and Stresses.* New York.

Wrigley, E. A. 1969. *Population and History.* New York.

Zeldin, Theodore. 1973. *France, 1848-1945,* vol. 1: *Ambition, Love, and Politics.* New York.

JANE RENDALL (ESSAY DATE 1985)

SOURCE: Rendall, Jane. Introduction to *The Origins of Modern Feminism: Women in Britain, France and the United States 1780-1860,* pp. 1-6. London, England: Macmillan, 1985.

In the following essay, Rendall argues that a comparison between the rise of feminist sentiment in England, France, and the United States helps in understanding the domestic life and social aspirations of women between 1780 and 1860.

In a sense the title of this book is anachronistic. The English word 'feminism' was not in use within this period. The French word *féminisme* was coined by the Utopian socialist, Charles Fourier, and used only by him. The first recorded use of the term in English, derived from the French, was in 1894, according to the 1933 *Supplement* to the *Oxford English Dictionary*. The relevant volume of the *Dictionary* itself was written from 1894 to 1897 and does not contain the accepted modern meaning of the term.[1] Twentieth-century historians have found the word an essential tool for analysis, and it is a term which may have many nuances of meaning. Gerda Lerner has distinguished between movements for 'woman's rights', in the sense of civil and political equality, and 'woman's emancipation', in the sense of a broader striving for 'freedom from oppressive restrictions imposed by sex; self-determination; autonomy'.[2] I have here used the latter description, using the word 'feminist' to describe women who claimed for themselves the right to define their own place in society, and a few men who sympathised with that claim. Yet it should be stressed that the women described here did not necessarily believe that implied an equality of roles between men and women. They lived and wrote before the impact of Karl Marx was felt, and they interpreted the word 'equality' in terms of moral and rational worth, not in terms of an equality of labour. Such aspirations, of course, were not entirely new; they are to be found, for instance, among seventeenth-century feminists, as well as in the fifteenth-century writer, Christine de Pisan.

I have therefore used the term 'modern feminism' to describe the way in which women came, in the period from the late eighteenth to the mid-nineteenth century, to associate together, perhaps at first for different reasons, and then to recognise and to assert their common interests as women. There has, in the historical literature, been much concentration on the lives and writings of individual feminists, male and female. Though this is vital, so too are the conditions of feminist practice and the social context in which such practice becomes possible. By such practice, I mean the association of women together for a feminist purpose: the ability of women to address other women, and men, in public: and the organisation of a range of activities, campaigns and writing, around the claims of women to determine different areas of their lives. Here I have tried to concentrate less on the careers of individual women, so that there is relatively little, for instance, on Frances Wright, on Anna Wheeler, or even on Florence Nightingale, and more on the historical context which allowed some, often very few, women to come together and assert in their lives and in their actions the values of self-determination and autonomy.

In looking at this context I have chosen to begin this account in the age of the American and French Revolutions, since the 1790s mark a very clear increase in feminist thinking, which must be viewed against the background of the Enlightenment. In ending around 1860, I have taken a point when, in Britain, the *English Woman's Journal* and its associated societies were already launched, and when John Stuart Mill was drafting his *Subjection of Women*. In the United States, the end of the ante-bellum period is a useful moment at which to consider the character and achievements of the feminist movement before the outbreak of the Civil War. In France, the first decade of the Second Empire reveals the weakness of a movement defeated after 1848, and the continuing debate between feminists and their male opponents which takes place from 1858 to 1860 usefully indicates the degree of hostility which French feminists had to counter. Overall by the end of the period, there did exist both a public awareness of the question of women's rights and women's future role and, it will be argued, some sense of the emergence of an international movement among feminists themselves. Yet it still has to be stressed that the numbers of women involved were very small, and their ideas still regarded as extreme and isolated.

There are, however, problems to be encountered in understanding the nineteenth-century world of women, and its relationship to the origins of feminism. In what sense is it possible to describe that world, to enter into a 'woman's culture' which may of its nature seem conservative, moralistic, even itself authoritarian? How far can we relate the firmly held commitment of, say, 'conservative' women like Hannah More or Catherine Beecher, to improve women's condition, to the emergence of a feminist movement concerned to challenge male power? It is not, I think, possible to evaluate the work of nineteenth-century feminists without entering sympathetically into such language and such writing. It is very difficult to discard twentieth-century assumptions about equality, and to understand that the assertion of an 'equality in difference' could mean a radical step forward, a claim to the political rights from which women had been automatically excluded for so long. Stress on the latent moral superiority of women could bring with it the basis for a new confidence, a new energy, a new assertion of women's potential power. Belief in the equality and, at the same time, the complementarity of

ON THE SUBJECT OF...

JOHN STUART MILL'S DEFENSE OF WOMEN'S RIGHTS

The object of this essay to is to explain as clearly as I am able, the grounds of an opinion which I have held from the very earliest period when I had formed any opinions at all on social or political matters, and which, instead of being weakened or modified, has been constantly growing stronger by the progress of reflection and the experience of life. That the principle which regulates the existing social relations between the two sexes "the legal subordination of one sex to the other" is wrong in itself, and now one of the chief hindrances to human improvement; and that it ought to be replaced by a principle of perfect equality, admitting no power or privilege on the one side, nor disability on the other.

Mill, John Stuart. Excerpt from *The Subjection of Women,* London: Longmans, Green and Co., 1869.

the different qualities of men and women, could provide the means for a radical assertion of feminist practice, as the French feminists of 1848 were to show. Increasingly, the worlds of men and women were separated in the nineteenth century, a separation based on the growing division between the home and the place of work. Within that primarily domestic world, women could and did create a culture which was not entirely an imposed one, which contained within it the possibilities of assertion. Here, I am concerned with the ways in which that assertion could become the assertion of autonomy. It will be suggested that from discussion of such themes as the need to improve women's education, the demand for the expansion of women's employment, the case for the reform of the marriage laws, came statements and actions which went beyond the limits of their separate world, into a different debate.

At the same time it is important to remember that the only model available to women to state their public demands was the political language of men. We can only understand the importance of the demand for citizenship if we remember that long tradition of European thought, based on the classical education from which women were firmly excluded, which entrenched the notion of the classical republic and the virtuous citizen at the heart of political debate. These themes offer the key to the claims made by women in the 1790s. They had to challenge the view that citizenship was possible only for male heads of households, excluding the dependent of all kinds. The means for that challenge, came, eventually, from two sources: from the republican notion of the increasing and moralising domestic power of motherhood, and from the feminised language of evangelicalism. As political conflicts shifted their ground, so too did the language of feminism, though not as rapidly as is often thought. The case made by socialist feminists in the 1830s was to draw upon and to secularise the theme of the moral and regenerating power of woman. The liberal case of the 1850s was to hark back to the republican ideal of virtue through citizenship. Feminist arguments had to combine both the demands that arose from the perceived needs of women, and the contemporary language of the male political world.

The starting point for women lay in the assumption that their lives and their future had to be seen in the context of their family roles. For them, in reality, there was no future outside the confines either of the family into which they were born or the one which they might themselves create, or, in default of either, the household which they might serve, as servant or governess. Demographers today accept that throughout most of western Europe and the United States, the 'conjugal' family group, of husband, wife and four or five children, with servants, lodgers or apprentices where appropriate, represented the normal and conventional framework of life, at least from the sixteenth century onwards.[3] There were some exceptions to this in a few areas of southern France where the co-residence of households of the same generation still existed at the beginning of this period. In material terms, there was virtually no employment for middle-class women outside marriage—with the exception of poorly paid teaching and, for a few, writing. For the working-class woman, there was little prospect of a 'living wage' for an adult single woman, outside domestic service in another househould. A demographic pattern of late marriage, at the age of 24 or 25 for women, meant a long period of waiting. That time might be spent, for working women, partly in aiding the parental family, partly in saving for a future household of their own. Middle-class women might need to wait until capital, or training, or experience, was acquired, on which a future household could be based. High rates of fertility, and a short life expectancy, could mean that much of a woman's twenties, thirties and forties might be dominated by bearing children and caring for them. In an age where mechanical means of contraception were lacking, though family limitation was by no means unknown, the possibilities of choice were indeed limited.

In legal terms, women's very existence depended on their family roles. In Britain, single women over the age of 21 were legal persons. Married women, however, under the provisions of the common law, had no civil existence: they owned no personal property, they could neither sue nor be sued, they could not divorce their husbands, or claim any rights over their children. Wealthy women might have their property protected by a legal trust: but in the interests of their parental family, rather than their own. In colonial America, legal patterns largely followed English practice, though there is evidence, especially in New England, of some moderation of the harshness of the common law. In pre-revolutionary France, there were wide variations in the law and custom of marriage, and the status of women. In the area governed by customary law, broadly the north and centre of France, there was a similar pattern of the community of goods held by husband and wife, with the husband exercising the rights of ownership. In the Midi, where the inheritance of Roman law was still fundamentally important, a wife might have some rights over her property, both the dowry brought to marriage, and her personal belongings. The rights of both husband and wife over the property brought to the marriage - including, particularly, the wife's dowry—were normally established before marriage by means of the marriage contract.[4] Marriage, for all classes, in all three societies, remained an economic institution, for the mutual support, even survival, of all members of the family.

There is, of course, a continuing debate about changing expectations of family life, and about the extent to which the eighteenth century, or indeed earlier periods, saw the growth of 'affective individualism', or a 'romantic revolution'.[5] One aspect of this, it has been suggested, is the growth of the ideal of the 'companionate marriage', with consequences that are relevant to the position of women. My own view is that among sections of the middle and upper classes there may indeed have been some cultural shifts, which stressed the emotional bonds of family members, and more intense expectations of the rewards of family life. But this is in no way intended to suggest any absence of affection between husbands and wives, parents and children, in different classes or in earlier periods. It may indeed rather reflect the time that material security afforded to explore the pleasures of domestic life, and the wider diffusion of literature of all kinds in the eighteenth century. But what is important is that the character of family life was determined by a variety of material considerations, as well as by such elusive cultural shifts: the extent to which marriages were chosen, not arranged; the extent to which family property arrangements might dictate marriage; the nature and the sources of the family income to be relied upon; the kind of domestic labour, paid and unpaid, undertaken on behalf of the household by women. All these could profoundly affect the shape of the family and the situation of women within it: and the possibility of expanding their lives beyond domestic horizons. Twentieth-century assumptions about the separation of home from work may blind us to factors determining the relative strength or weakness of women within domestic life, and the interaction of domestic and public concerns.

My aim here has been to look at the origins of association among women in a comparative way, drawing on the experience of three western societies which shared many common roots, but which, at the same time, experienced urban and industrial changes in the course of the first half of the nineteenth century in very different ways. Religious and cultural contrasts helped to shape the character of women's movements in these three societies. I am aware that this is an ambitious project, even a premature one. Yet it is important that the demands which women made in the mid-nineteenth century should be understood against the background of the political, social and economic life of that world, if we are to understand more clearly the roots of women's continuing subordination in the late twentieth century. So I have tried to offer a comparative discussion, relying primarily on secondary literature rather than on original research. It will be obvious how much I have relied upon the work of a number of distinguished scholars in the field of women's history. It would be invidious to name authors. But I have been prompted to a comparative view partly by the excellence and sophistication of approach of a number of American historians of American women's lives in this period, and I have been helped by several works of considerable distinction published over the last few years on women in Britain. I have also benefited greatly from the questions raised about the character of French feminism by both French- and English-speaking historians of the nineteenth- and early twentieth-century movements. I am sure that they will be able to recognise this dependence and I hope that they will accept this inadequate acknowledgement.

Notes

1. The *Supplement* to the *Oxford English Dictionary* gives as the first usage of the word: '*Daily News,* 12 October 1894 "What our Paris correspondent describes as a 'Feminist' group is being formed in the French Chamber of Deputies"'; for the French use of the word, see *Trésor de la langue française*, vol. 8, Paris, 1980.
2. See Gerda Lerner's contribution to Ellen DuBois, Mari Jo Buhle, Temma Kaplan, Gerda Lerner and Carroll Smith-Rosenberg, 'Politics and culture in women's history: a symposium', *Feminist Studies,* 6 (Spring 1980), 26-63; see also, among many items, G. Lerner, *The Majority Finds its Past. Placing Women in History* (New York, 1979); B. A. Carroll (ed.), *Liberating Women's History* (Urbana, Illinois, 1976), especially the essays in Part I; Juliet Mitchell, 'Women and equality' in A. Oakley and Juliet Mitchell, (eds), *The Rights and Wrongs of Women* (London, 1976).
3. The best starting point on this issue remains M. Anderson, *Approaches to the History of the Western Family 1500-1914* (London, 1980); see also M. W. Flinn, *The European Demographic System, 1500-1820* (Brighton, 1981); J. L. Flandrin, *Families in Former Times Kinship, Household and Sexuality* (Cambridge, 1979); Louise Tilly and Joan Scott, *Women, Work and Family* (New York, 1978).
4. On the legal situation of women see Lee Holcombe, *Wives and Property. Reform of the Married Women's Property Law in Nineteenth Century England* (Oxford, 1983), Chs 2-3; R. B. Morris, 'Women's rights in early American law', in *Studies in the History of American Law* (1958; reprinted New York, 1974); L. Abensour, *La femme et le féminisme avant la révolution* (Paris, 1923), Ch. 1.
5. See Lawrence Stone, *The Family, Sex and Marriage in England, 1500-1800* (London, 1977); E. Shorter, *The Making of the Modern Family* (New York, 1975).

SUSAN K. GROGAN (ESSAY DATE 1992)

SOURCE: Grogan, Susan K. Introduction to *French Socialism and Sexual Difference: Women and the New Society, 1803-44,* pp. 1-19. New York: St. Martin's Press, 1992.

In the following excerpt, Grogan discusses how the idealized roles and proper lifestyles of French women were debated by the French clergy, philosophers, and doctors during the nineteenth century in an effort to maintain domestic and national stability.

The place of woman in early nineteenth-century French society was fraught with contradictions. She was worshipped as 'Muse and Madonna' of the society,[1] but was legally a non-person. She was the symbol of Truth and Justice, of Liberty and the Republic, yet she was simultaneously exploited and despised. In fact, the idealisation of 'Woman' as abstract entity contrasted dramatically with the subordinate position of real women in the economic, political and civil structures of their society. Since men dominated those structures and created the images, the contradictions between them illustrated men's ambivalence towards women. However, the ambiguities in women's position also reflected the uncertainties of a society which had undergone (and continued to experience) major political upheavals, and which faced the disruptions of incipient industrialisation. New patterns of economic and political life required and created new patterns of identity; new ways of relating to others in the society. For conservatives seeking 'order', liberals seeking 'progress', and socialists seeking a radical restructuring of society, defining women's place in society, and constructing models of femininity which justified it, were crucial undertakings.

Charles Fourier, the Saint-Simonians and Flora Tristan—amongst the most important figures in French socialism in the first half of the nineteenth century—all shared the belief that the subordination of women was unjust, and a hindrance to the construction of a more perfect society. They argued for immediate changes in the status and treatment of women, and assigned them specific roles in transforming the social system. The socialists' theories on women were based in part on their observation of women's inferior position in their own society, but they also made assumptions about women's nature which were widely shared at that time. These assumptions about female 'otherness' shaped their speculations about ideal female roles in the future. Socialists deliberately strengthened and extended the concept of sexual complementarity, employing this concept as the basis for a new social order, and in particular, for the liberty of women. Their theories aimed to turn all women into free and productive members of the new society, in order to achieve the social and moral benefits which this would produce.

Women's Lifestyles: Workers and Bourgeoisie at the Turn of the Nineteenth Century

Socialist calls for women's liberty reflected their critiques of the lifestyles of women in early nineteenth-century French society. Women dependent on wages lived very different lives from women of the wealthy classes, but the exploitation of both groups demonstrated to socialists the injustices and inefficiencies of the existing order. The working woman, subject of concern to socialists and conservatives alike at this time, faced contracting earning opportunities. The processes which restricted women's employment in craft production had accelerated during the eighteenth century, as legislation and pressure from male workers gradually excluded them from lucrative areas of work and skilled occupations.[2] Women in the old commercial and craft centres, including Paris, were increasingly confined within a narrow range of jobs in textile production, garment-making and street-trading, although they were represented in all industrial sectors. Midwifery and domestic service also remained important female occupations.[3]

The growth and mechanisation of the textiles industry at this time drew heavily on a pool of under-employed rural women, offering them domestic outwork or drawing them into the mills in emergent spinning towns. Their appeal to employers lay, above all, in their cheapness, since they were paid little more than children and rarely more than half the male wage. Outwork allowed costs to be minimised because the worker bore most overheads herself, although many women with children found this the best way of combining their domestic and wage-earning duties. Women's maternal responsibilities were invoked to justify the payment of a supplementary wage (rather than a living wage, or a wage commensurate with output), and to force the acceptance of intermittent work. However, women's reproductive role did not protect them in the factories, where they laboured in dangerous and debilitating conditions.[4]

The inadequacy of women's wages and earning capacity was dramatically illustrated by the upsurge in prostitution in the early nineteenth century, particularly in the capital. The hardships caused by revolution, war and economic crisis led to an explosion in the numbers of prostitutes in Paris, and a system of supervision and registration was introduced in 1802 in an effort to contain them. By mid-century there were 34 000 registered prostitutes in Paris, working in about 200 official brothels. However, the registration system accounted for only a small proportion of working prostitutes, whose real numbers were much higher than the official figure.[5]

Prostitution was the subject of considerable public debate in French society at that time. Many were offended by the public scandal which it occasioned, while socialists regarded it as the ultimate indictment of the contemporary social order. The publication in 1836 of Doctor Parent-

ON THE SUBJECT OF...

CAROLINE SHERIDAN NORTON (1808-1877)

Caroline Sheridan Norton was born into the widely respected Sheridan family; she was a granddaughter of the English dramatist Richard Brinsley Sheridan. She married George Norton in 1827 and together the couple had three sons. The marriage proved to be troubled, and Norton turned to writing poetry as a creative outlet. She published *The Sorrows of Rosalie: A Tale with Other Poems* in 1829 and *The Undying One and Other Poems* one year later. Norton was viewed as an accomplished poet and novelist by her contemporaries. Critics favorably compared her to Elizabeth Barrett and compared her to Lord Byron due to the intense emotion characteristic of her work. Norton drew extensively on her personal life in poetry and novels; this has typically informed criticism of her literary works. For example, reviewers of *The Dream and Other Poems* (1840) discussed both its artistic merits and its suggestions of Norton's unhappy life.

In 1836 Norton and her husband separated, and according to English law of the time, she was denied custody of her children. For the next five years, she sought to influence Parliament to grant separated women rights to their children. In 1837 she wrote a pamphlet entitled *Separation of Mother and Child by the Laws of Custody of Infants Considered.* By 1839, a bill was passed that slightly reformed infant custody laws. Throughout this period, Norton continued to publish poetry, as well as several novels. In 1842 her youngest son died while in his father's care, and the two older boys were returned to their mother. Subsequently Norton wrote the pamphlet *English Laws for Women in the Nineteenth Century* (1854) and *Letter to the Queen* (1855), influencing an 1857 bill reforming marriage and divorce laws.

Duchâtelet's study, *De la Prostitution dans la Ville de Paris,* highlighted the economic causes of prostitution. It demonstrated that most Parisian prostitutes lacked education and were normally employed in the lower levels of the garment trades.[6] Many had come to Paris from nearby areas in search of employment, and they resorted to prostitution as a result of 'lack of work and misery, the inevitable result of insufficient salaries'. 'One can only reproach them', Parent-Duchâtelet argued, 'for not having had the courage to die of hunger.'[7]

'Insufficient salaries' affected the entire working class in the early nineteenth century. Wages declined in all trades by an average of 22% by 1830, while the cost of consumer goods rose about 60%.[8] Increasing numbers of families required aid in order to survive. During this period the 'dangerous classes', the 'barbarians in the midst' of the civilised bourgeoisie, were born.[9] This was not a time when working women could have adopted the domestic ideal offered to bourgeois women, had they desired to do so. As Groppi has remarked of the popular classes, the woman at home, unless engaged in some form of domestic production or outwork, was an unemployed woman.[10] Housework was quickly completed where families had few possessions and lived in one or two rooms. Besides, many tasks could not be done at home because the facilities were lacking. Clothes were washed in public laundries or in a nearby river; a communal well provided water, limiting both cooking and cleaning; in the towns bread was purchased, not baked at home, where a large pot over an open fire provided the only cooking facilities. Daily chores were therefore communal chores for women of the popular classes. They were performed in a social context incompatible with bourgeois notions of private household management.[11] Nevertheless, the domestic ideal could provide a focus of aspiration, since it was associated with a degree of domestic comfort. Working-class leaders adopted the model as the century progressed, and it sometimes appealed to working women because it promised an end to laborious, exhausting and poorly remunerated employment. Still, working women's support for the domestic ideal was by no means universal.[12]

Domesticity was more influential amongst bourgeois women, in many cases shaping both the ideal and the reality of their lives. To the early socialists, bourgeois women's lifestyles illustrated some of the worst abuses of contemporary society. These women were criticised as idle consumers, and their status as merchandise on the marriage market was also condemned. Bourgeois marriage was first and foremost an alliance between families, although the likely happiness of the couple was not necessarily ignored.[13] Young women were carefully chaperoned to introduce them only to suitable men, thus minimising the risk of a *mésalliance.* The argument that they were not well-equipped to judge the suitability of a partner was justified given the sheltered conditions in which girls were raised, and the considerable age gap between brides and grooms suggests that men were in a stronger position than women to play a decisive part in the selection of their partners.[14]

The appropriate role of the bourgeois wife was laid out in the large number of books which explored this issue in the early nineteenth century. Many of these were written by women of aristocratic or bourgeois background, and attempted to define an honourable role for women of the wealthy classes in a changing society. They praised domesticity, arguing that the role of 'wife-companion' gave women dignity and significant moral influence over their husbands.[15] It offered them a degree of independence and social status which the spinster never attained.[16] However, the domestic ideal also stressed effacement, dependence and public invisibility for women, and accepted that domestic harmony required patriarchal authority within the home. The Civil Code of 1804 legitimised male power. It denied women equal legal status with men, and ensured their economic dependence by restricting women's property rights. Bourgeois women did not share the political power increasingly concentrated in the hands of bourgeois men during the nineteenth century.[17]

The role of the *bourgeoise* was defined as familial, but women's participation in the family business was often crucial amongst shopkeeping and industrial families on the way up. This direct and public involvement was uncommon amongst women of the *haute bourgeoisie,* and female withdrawal from active participation in business generally accompanied the family's rise up the social scale.[18] Conformity to the domestic ideal was thus more pronounced amongst the wealthier sectors of the bourgeoisie, and in the professional sector where women lacked the education to share their husbands' work.

The domestic ideal placed special emphasis on motherhood. This role was praised and respected, although mothers had few guaranteed parental rights. Bourgeois women generally had only one or two children in the early nineteenth century, limiting the size of their families in order

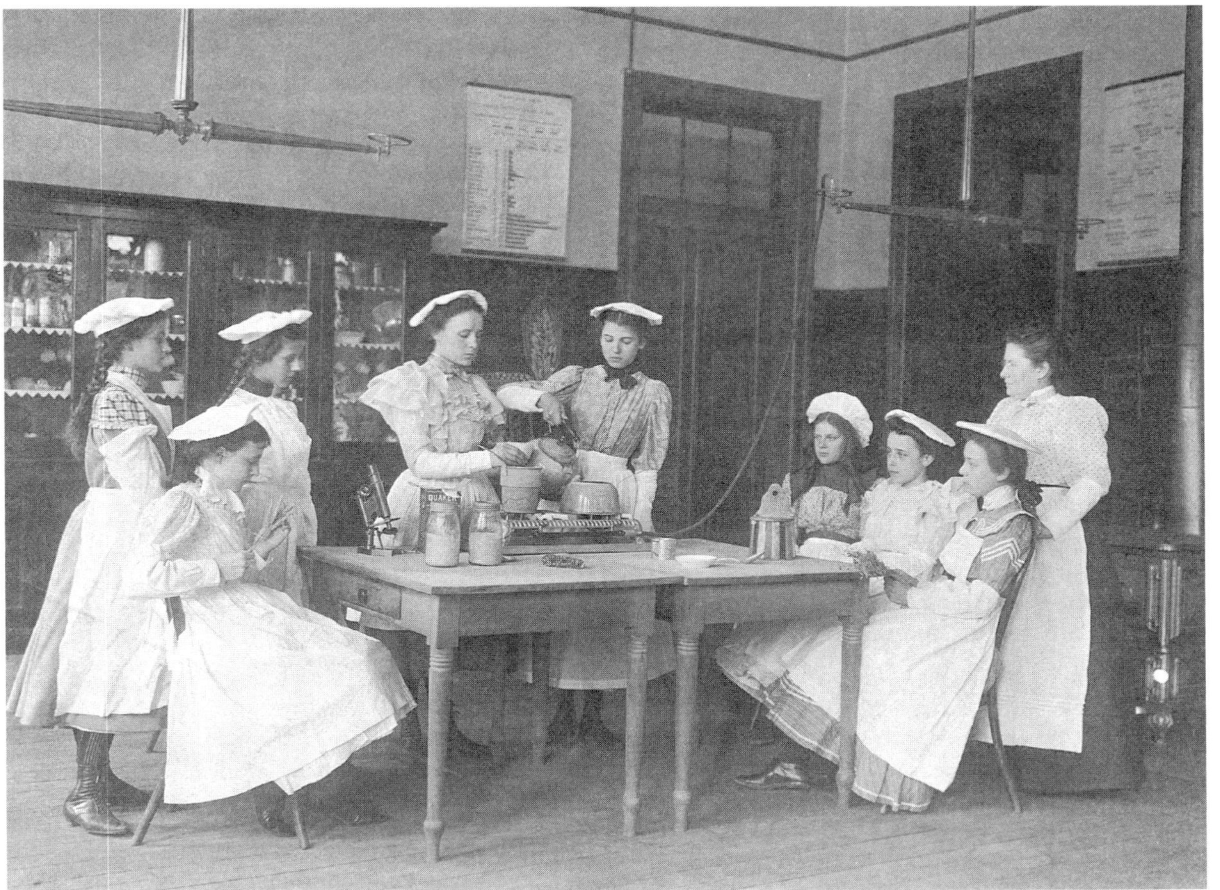

Cyanotype by Frances Benjamin Johnson of a typical high school cooking class c. 1899.

to provide abundant attention and substantial inheritances to each of their offspring. In wealthier families, where the fragmentation of inheritance was not a cause for concern, larger numbers of children were more common.[19] Children were generally lavished with love and affection, but bourgeois mothers offset this by a zealous inculcation of the virtues of self-discipline, thrift and hard work.[20] The mother-educator had responsibility for her sons' instruction only for the first six or seven years, but girls' education often rested entirely in the hands of their mothers. They strove to instill in their daughters the simplicity, self-discipline and devotion to others which were regarded as the most desirable qualities for a well brought-up woman. These qualities, supplemented by some general knowledge, the polite accomplishments, and practice in household management, would produce a marriageable daughter. The mother's task was then complete.[21]

The family was idealised by the bourgeoisie as a place of emotional and psychological refuge. In France, this was essentially a reaction to the traumatic experience of the French Revolution.[22] From the perspective of the bourgeoisie, the popular revolution had almost destroyed the social fabric, and the re-establishment of a stable society required particular attention to the family, the nucleus of society. The role assigned to the bourgeois woman was valued, therefore, and it was primarily a moral one. She instilled accepted values in her children and exercised moral influence over her husband. She also created a world of order and regularity within the home, in contrast with the disordered world of the masses.[23] The middle-class mother thus established a model of family life to be imitated by, or imposed upon, the lower classes.

Family relations amongst the urban working classes diverged from the bourgeois pattern in a number of ways, and the bourgeois model was not easily enforced. Workers usually chose their own partners, but financial considerations were often important for them too. Women's inadequate wages made partnership with a male worker a matter of survival, yet a competent tradeswoman was also a desirable partner for a working man. In theory, greater equality was possible in workers' relationships, because partners were freely chosen and closer in age than was usual amongst the bourgeoisie. Socialists often praised the moral superiority of working-class marriages on these grounds. However, workers' memoirs indicate that the patriarchal family model survived at this level of society as well.[24] Workers' family lives were diverse, like those of the bourgeoisie, and for many unskilled, migrant and casual workers family life was an unaffordable luxury.[25] The attitudes of working men towards their wives and children were influenced by the codes of behaviour of the various trades and occupations. Carpenters, for instance, had a reputation as good family men and considerate husbands, whereas tailors and ragdealers were contemptuous of their wives and preferred the company of their workmates. There were exceptions, but the peer group exerted pressure on men to conform to its norms.[26]

Women frequently held a significant level of power within working-class families. They were often partners in decision-making as well as in business, and in many cases controlled the family finances.[27] Bourgeois moralists and social critics sought to reinforce this power, envisaging women as purveyors of bourgeois moral order amongst the working classes. The image of the clean-living, thrifty and teetotal worker, taking home his wages to a domestic wife, socialising at home rather than at the *cabaret,* was the model they sought to enforce. As agents of social control within the working-class home, wives would subdue their husbands and keep them out of the public places: the places where grievances were aired and discontent festered, and hence where strikes and revolution were born.[28]

During the July Monarchy the bourgeoisie became increasingly concerned that workers were living in common-law unions rather than legal marriages. These unions were often stable and long-term partnerships, which were not formalised because of the complexities and expense of meeting the legal requirements for marriage.[29] However, to the middle-class mind, workers' failure to marry illustrated both the sexual depravity and disorder of the masses, and the decline of the family.[30] The failure of working-class mothers was singled out for attention. The increase in illegitimacy rates was viewed with alarm, since it was feared that mothers who gave birth to such children lacked the moral capacity to instil in them the appropriate social virtues. Illegitimate births had been increasing since the mid-eighteenth century, partly due to the rising proportion of common-law unions. In large cities such as Paris and Lyon, between a third and a half of all children were illegitimate in the early nineteenth century.[31] Furthermore, about 33 000 foundlings a year came into State custody in France in the 1815-30 period.[32] To bourgeois observers, these figures illustrated an absence of parental (and especially maternal) feelings amongst the workers. They denounced the *mère dénaturée* whose abandonment of her child flouted the laws of nature, although the laws of economics, so revered by the bourgeoisie, generally lay at the heart of a woman's decision to surrender her infant.[33] Bourgeois social policy in the early nineteenth century therefore focused on enforcing familial sentiment amongst the masses by offering limited home assistance to needy mothers. This, they hoped, would '. . . reawaken . . . in the breasts of mothers who wished to abandon [their children] a maternal feeling that had been cooled . . .'.[34]

There were vast discrepancies between the lives of the majority of women in early nineteenth-century France, therefore, and the idealised roles of wife and mother deemed proper for them. Women's lifestyles were thus the subject of major debate. Their roles were seen as crucial, not only to men's comfort and happiness, but to the survival and welfare of the nation. The construction of normative models of femininity assumed increasing importance in order to justify and enforce the allotted gender division. Religion, philosophy and science were called upon for this purpose.

Defining 'Woman': Ideology and Imagery

Images of 'woman' played an important part in the negotiation of power between the sexes, at a time when traditional forms of authority were under attack, and a new social order was being created. Patterns of domestic life were deeply affected by the late eighteenth-century challenge to religious and monarchical power in France, and the attempts over succeeding years to base political relations on a social contract between theoretically equal citizens. Since the hierarchical family had provided a model for relations in the State, patriarchal authority in the home was threatened by its condemnation in the political sphere. The redefining of political bonds thus entailed a redefinition of sexual relations, and this in turn required a reconsideration of the nature of each sex, and a reinterpretation of the differences between them.[35]

The eighteenth century marked a turning point in the perception of womanhood. 'Woman's place' was no longer defined (in theory, at least) solely by the teachings of Catholicism. The insights of Nature and Reason were also brought to bear on this subject and science, in particular, made possible the 'unveiling' of woman.[36] As a result the earlier model of woman as imperfect man was replaced by a concept of the specificity of female nature. Woman was defined as 'other' than man in every respect, and in her 'otherness' theorists observed the unmistakeable signs of her destiny and social role. However, the newfound uniqueness and perfection of woman were not seen as justifying her social equality with man. Rather, the notion of 'incommensurability' was used to deny the application of 'natural rights' to woman.[37] By defining woman as 'other', therefore, late eighteenth- and early nineteenth-century theorists found a new justification for preserving hierarchy in sexual relations, and for excluding women from public life. Their images of 'woman' provided the intellectual context in which socialist theories on women were framed.

Images of Woman in the Catholic Tradition

The Catholic religion had long maintained a polarised view of women, which emphasised their potential as agents of evil and as models of Christian virtue.[38] The first tradition derived from the Genesis account of woman's secondary creation, her role in the Fall, and her subsequent punishment by God. All women bore the stigma of Eve the temptress. Furthermore, women were defined as representatives of 'the flesh' and sexuality, which were despised and mistrusted. This view therefore emphasised women's natural and Divinely-ordained subordination to men.[39] A selective reading of the Scriptures and a heavy reliance on the Church Fathers justified the Church's defence of female subordination, and alternative egalitarian accounts of gender relations in both the Old and New Testaments were ignored.[40]

The view of woman as a physical and moral threat to man was alive and well in the first half of the nineteenth century. Influential figures in the French Church expressed their suspicion of women, and their preference for a way of life from which women were excluded. Frédéric Ozanam, founder of the Saint Vincent de Paul Society, advocated virginity or late marriage, arguing that '. . . man surrenders much of his dignity the day he chains himself to the arms of woman'.[41] Abbé Jean-Joseph Gaume, writer and key advocate of devotion to Mary, was more hostile. He described woman as 'corrupt and corrupting', and demanded the revival of the ancient practice of ritual purification after childbirth.[42] His condemnation of woman as 'a foul spider [who] spreads her seductive power over the whole expanse of the earth like a vast web' was designed to justify female subordination, as well as suggesting that male hostility to women had deep psychological causes.[43]

The mistrust of woman exhibited in Catholic teaching, and in the attitudes of some clergymen, contrasted with the significant position assigned to Mary in the Catholic tradition. Michaud suggests that the cult of Mary performed an exorcistic function, countering the sexual and moral threat which real women posed. It was therefore compatible with repressive attitudes to women.[44] The early nineteenth century witnessed a dramatic upsurge in devotion to Mary, especially after 1830. This was the age of apparitions, the Virgin appearing to Catherine Labouré in Paris in 1830; to the children of La Salette in 1846; and later to Bernadette Soubirous at Lourdes in 1858.[45] The Miraculous Medal, supposedly requested of Labouré by the Virgin herself, had twenty million wearers by 1837. Confraternities dedicated to Mary expanded rapidly; pilgrimages to sites of the Virgin's appearances and to churches dedicated to Mary were popular; and religious orders under her protection multiplied.[46]

Mary was the model presented to women for imitation, because her submission to the Divine will had enabled her to play a role in redemption and to counter the sin of Eve. The idealisation of Mary thus made possible the idealisation of women who modelled themselves on her image. Like Mary, woman became an angelic and saving figure in the life of man. Chateaubriand, a leading figure in the nineteenth-century Catholic revival, made this connection in his *Génie du Christianisme*. Mary was portrayed as the archetypal woman, the epitome of beauty and innocence, exhibiting 'the sweet virtue of her sex'. Above all she was virgin and mother, 'the two most divine states of womanhood'.[47]

The potential benefit to women of a feminised Catholicism lay, therefore, in its glorification of the Christian wife and mother. Chateaubriand wrote fervently:

> The Christian wife is not a mere mortal: she is an extraordinary, mysterious, angelic being . . .

> Without woman, [man] would be primitive, uncouth and alone . . . woman adorns him with the flowers of life, as the vines of the forest adorn the trunk of the oak tree with their perfumed garlands.[48]

However, Chateaubriand also emphasised woman's innate physical and moral weakness and her capacity to transmit her failings to others. Being 'born of woman', rather than created by God as Adam had been, was man's true 'fall'.[49] His attitude to women, therefore, conformed with that of another conservative Catholic theorist, Joseph de Maistre. In de Maistre's opinion, the weakening of the power of the Church and the advocacy of women's liberty promised 'shameful licence', 'universal corruption' and the collapse of the State.[50] Apart from religious celibacy, women's only valid roles were those of wives and mothers, subject to the control of their husbands. Despite women's 'mysterious' and 'angelic' qualities, therefore, male authority within the family was regarded as essential for social order. The early nineteenth-century Church proved reluctant to accept change, rejecting the ideas and learning of the new age, and supporting the Restoration and its values.[51] Similarly, by condemning women to subservience and domesticity, the Church attempted to maintain the hierarchical gender order of the past without any amendment.

'Enlightened' Views of Woman

The systematic study of human nature by eighteenth-century 'Enlightenment' philosophers provided an alternative source for ideas on women's nature and social roles. Several influential texts on women were produced by the *philosophes.* Montesquieu's *Persian Letters* was widely read throughout Europe; while Rousseau's *Emile* was 'devoured' by women readers in the period before the Revolution.[52] Diderot wrote an essay *On Women,* although it was not published in his lifetime; and the question of woman's nature and place in society was also discussed by such writers as Laclos, Helvétius, D'Holbach and Condorcet.[53]

Enlightenment writers generally emphasised the natural differences between the sexes, and the more powerful determinism of biology in the lives of women. Sexual difference was regarded as a total distinction, extending from the physical to the intellectual and moral spheres. According to Rousseau, the original reproductive differences between the sexes had assumed new dimensions as society progressed. Perfectly adapted for her reproductive role, woman had not needed to develop the faculties which denoted 'civilised' man: reason, memory and imagination. As a consequence woman had become increasingly different from man over time, rather than closer to him.[54]

Femininity was frequently portrayed as a less perfect condition than masculinity by the *philosophes.* Diderot believed that woman's physical 'limitations' made her a prey to her biology and a permanent invalid, and Montesquieu held a similar view. Rousseau claimed to defend the particularity rather than the inferiority of woman. The sexes were separate and distinct states of being, and comparison between them was meaningless.[55] However, he also stressed the limiting impact of women's physiology on their social roles.[56] This essentialist perspective was rejected by other *philosophes,* such as Helvétius, d'Alembert and Condorcet, who attributed sexual difference largely to environment and education. According to this view, both women and men could be shaped and improved, though not necessarily made equal.[57] Condorcet's insistence on woman's potential for rational development ran counter to the dominant emphasis on difference and complementarity.[58] According to most of the *philosophes,* the great social danger lay in sexual confusion and inversion.[59]

In defining woman's difference from man, Rousseau identified her as the representative of Nature, locating her outside history and outside the processes of social development.[60] The concept of woman as 'Nature' served a variety of purposes in Enlightenment writings, and was not incompatible with an alternative view of woman as 'Culture'. In the latter role, woman was portrayed as a civilising influence within the home and society. She oversaw the moral education of her children and tamed the lower instincts of 'natural' man.[61] The definition of woman as 'Nature', however, had both positive and negative ramifications. As 'Nature', woman embodied the virtues of simplicity, spontaneity and innocence. She thus symbolised the new morality which emphasised innate human goodness, and whose legitimacy was independent of religion. The 'natural' woman, defined in opposition to the superficial and false society woman, became a model of virtue and a source of moral regeneration for society. However, woman's closeness to Nature also had a negative sense. Woman as 'Nature' represented the uncontrolled and disorderly. She was the embodiment of ignorance and superstition, the defender of tradition, the creature of instinct. 'Nature' was therefore a tool of social criticism, open to a variety of meanings, and its association with women served the broader political purposes of its wielders.[62]

The question of whether women were capable of developing their reason, and whether it was socially desirable that they do so, was addressed at length by the *philosophes,* as they sought to establish appropriate roles for women in society. As Lloyd points out, possession of reason forms one of the basic criteria for personhood in the Western philosophical tradition.[63] The argument of several *philosophes* that women lacked full rational power therefore justified their status as dependent beings who belonged in the care of men. Diderot regarded women as pre-rational, and contrasted female 'mystery' with male logic.[64] Although Rousseau had argued against drawing comparisons between the sexes, he maintained that women's reason was of a lower order than that of men. They possessed a 'practical' rather than 'theoretical' reason; one adapted to means not ends; one incapable of original thought. Education would never make women men's intellectual equals, therefore, though it would threaten women's natural qualities and deter them from fulfilling their duties.[65] The intellectual realm thus remained safely the preserve of men and women's exclusion from intellectual pursuits was justified.

The *philosophes* emphasised that woman's whole being was designed for maternity.[66] Extrapolating from a potential function to an obligatory social role, they argued that motherhood was women's moral destiny, and that their rejection of this role carried serious personal and social consequences.[67] Rousseau was the most celebrated advocate of the maternal role, and his writings featured amongst the most influential works on women in this period. Contemporaries attributed the fashionable return to breastfeeding in the 1770s largely to his advocacy, though Diderot also emphasised its desirability on both medical and moral grounds.[68] The role of motherhood was defined in positive terms, and Rousseau emphasised its nurturing and educative aspects. Mothers formed citizens, instilling the appropriate social virtues. The importance of their role thus stemmed from its moral component, since the basis of society and of its virtues lay in the family.[69] However, by confining women entirely to the maternal role, the theories of Rousseau, and other *philosophes,* offered no place to women outside a nuclear family structure. Rousseau was unambiguous on this point, defining a woman without a husband and children as sexless, with no reason for existence.[70] Woman did not exist for herself as an independent being, as man did, but only in relation to man. Although Rousseau sought to idealise woman as 'mother', and to insist on the incommensurability of the two sexes, his concept of female nature assumed its inferiority to male nature, which was inherently self-sufficient.

With the exception of Condorcet, the *philosophes* defended the subordination of women to men. Female weakness and the physical constraints imposed by motherhood prevented their full participation in communal life, according to the *philosophes.* Women were naturally dependent on men, and hence necessarily submissive.[71] Rousseau located the transition to sexual hierarchy at the dawn of history, when woman supposedly proved less adaptable than man to the demands of an increasingly complex social life, and chose to focus on her childrearing role. The hierarchical family unit, in which woman was subordinate to man, was therefore natural and just. However, despite the 'naturalness' of the female condition, both Rousseau and Montesquieu highlighted the need to shape girls for submission and dependence from childhood.[72]

Enlightenment arguments about the 'naturalness' of female dependence were accompanied by the claim that their subordination was necessary for the security of the State. For Montesquieu, woman represented the anarchic forces of sensuality. Her confinement signified and achieved the control of the passions, and the public good justified the restriction of liberty which this entailed.[73] For Rousseau, even women's virtues became vices if transported into the political sphere. The exclusive quality of maternal love, for instance, was incompatible with the social ties of citizenship.[74] Female domestic subordination was therefore a precondition for the healthy functioning of the male public sphere. Its separation from the domestic world, defined as feminine, allowed the 'spirit of virile discipline', which characterised the State, to flourish.[75] Women's exclusion from public life thus freed men for the role of citizenship undistracted by sensual and familial temptations.

The submission of women to their husbands was also a symbol of the just hierarchy which was necessary in the State. The submissive wife, representation of domestic order, provided a model for the acceptance of the rule of law, and the subordination of self-interest to the general good. Montesquieu argued that this hierarchy was not inconsistent with the 'true equality' desirable in a Republic, which allowed for authority to be exercised between equals. Woman's formal equality was thus reconciled with the power to be exercised by man 'as magistrate, as senator, as judge, as father, as husband, as master'.[76] The concept of women's free consent to male authority disguised their subordination in Enlightenment visions of society. It suggested women's acceptance that their subordination was just. 'Freely-consenting' women, rather than despotic men, thus became responsible for female subordination.[77] Male authority was defended in these theories by a variety of strategies, therefore, and in this respect Enlightenment thought demonstrated its continuity with the Catholic view of woman's place.

Medical Experts Examine Women

Doctors provided another source of authority on the nature and social roles of women in the late eighteenth and early nineteenth centuries. They relied mainly on authorities such as Rousseau for their ideas about women, and produced a 'medical philosophy' rather than an empirical science.[78] However, where learned examiners of female physiology had formerly seen only beings similar to men, they now noticed fundamental differences which permeated every fibre of woman's being. Doctors thus reinforced the philosophers' pronouncements on the uniqueness of woman, who was no longer a lesser, inadequate man but a radically different embodiment of the human species. As 'experts' in the study of bodies and their healthy functioning, doctors were ideally suited to reveal and interpret the significance of sexual differences. Their proclamations about women thus extended beyond physiology to the social and moral realms.[79]

The expanding science of anatomy aided the exploration of sex differences from the eighteenth century.[80] Skeleton, muscles, tissues, nerves and fibres were all subjected to scrutiny, and confirmed physicians' views of the specificity of the female. Doctors emphasised two physiological characteristics of women: their weakness and *sensibilité*. 'Weakness' was never clearly defined, let alone measured, but it referred to a general lack of muscular development in women, and to a perception that the female body was soft, delicate and fragile.[81] In both respects, a normative (and idealised) male physiology was the point of reference, as physicians attempted to construct a female image which contrasted with it.[82] Women's *sensibilité* was more carefully delineated by physicians, although their findings reflected conviction rather than clinical observation. Women's superior *sensibilité* described an acute responsiveness to sensory inputs, so that women were dominated, even overwhelmed, by sensory 'messages'. Doctor Cabanis explained:

> The speed and the liveliness of activity in the nervous system are the measures of the general sensibility of the subject . . . Woman is more sensitive and more unstable because the structure of all her organs is softer and weaker . . . The greater the sensibility and the freer and more rapid the messages, the more too this influence must produce sudden, varied, extraordinary phenomena.[83]

According to this theory, women's brains were subjected to an incessant battery of sensations. They were less able to process all the messages received and translate them into concepts. Despite the fact that a sensationalist theory of knowledge was predominant in the late eighteenth century, then, women's sensory superiority was not interpreted as a sign of superior rational potential. Instead, women's sensibility defined them as intuitive rather than rational; lacking in concentration; incapable of the higher intellectual functions of reflection, analysis and synthesis; incapable, finally, of creativity and genius.[84]

The allocation of sensibility rather than rationality to women indicated their destiny within society, and established the basis of their relationship with men. According to the physicians, sensibility gave women a superior capacity for tenderness and compassion which, in the view of doctors like Roussel and Virey, indicated their destiny of motherhood.[85] In reaching this conclusion the doctors were influenced by their understanding of women's sexual and reproductive biology. The uterus remained the female organ *par excellence,* although it was gradually displaced by the ovaries after the discovery of ovulation in 1827, and more especially, after the discovery of spontaneous ovulation in some mammals in 1843.[86] Doctors argued that the female body was totally sexualised by nature in order to ensure and facilitate the reproductive function. The uterus, ovaries and breasts, and also woman's natural delicacy and dependence, marked her out for motherhood. Maternity was not only a biological imperative, then, but a social and moral imperative for women. Doctors ignored the fact that family limitation was increasingly being exercised by French couples, as the falling birthrate attests.[87] They omitted birth-control from their treatises and described abortion as an entirely accidental phenomenon, probably to avoid becoming a source of information on such practices. At a time when the demands of maternity showed some potential for reduction, therefore, doctors were keen to lock women securely into that 'predestined' role.[88]

The focus on the breast in the eighteenth-century medical literature reflected doctors' admiration for the maternal role, and symbolised the links they established between the biological, social and moral realms. The breast represented physical motherhood, and doctors such as Roussel made breastfeeding a physical and moral duty for women:

> The care of infants is the destiny of women; it is a task which nature has assigned to them . . . If reasons concerning the organisation and natural sequence of her functions oblige every woman who is not too ill to breastfeed, the moral reasons which appear to compel this are no less significant. . . .[89]

There was some truth in the claim that infants not fed by their own mothers were in jeopardy. However, medical arguments emphasised the moral rather than the physical benefits of maternal breastfeeding: infants would absorb moral principles with their mothers' milk.[90] For this very reason, however, other doctors were reluctant to make maternal suckling an infallible law, since it could also become a vehicle for transmitting undesirable passions and vices to the child.[91]

In denoting the nurturant role of woman, the breast also defined the female role as a private and familial one.[92] The configuration of women's bodies thus marked out the social spaces they were to occupy, just as the physiological features of male sexuality indicated to doctors men's destined social prominence:

> Since man's whole being seeks to expand, to extend, since the heat and vigour of his sex impose this law of expansion on him physically as well as morally, everything, in woman, must somehow unite to contain, to gather her affections, her thoughts and actions in the home for the reproduction and education of the family. It is not our institutions, it is nature which proclaims this truth, that a wife is only in her element, in the place which is most respectable, even most happy for her, when she is where her essential duties call her . . . If she abandons it, her virtues, lacking their purpose, become vices which are rarely forgiven.[93]

Doctors stressed the pitfalls for women who evaded their sacred duty in the home and sought fulfilment in other realms. In particular, they warned against intellectual pursuits for women. The cultivation of reason would necessarily entail the weakening of sentiment, argued Cabanis, and hence destroy the grace and charm which constituted femininity. Woman's beauty would fade, and since (as he argued) 'women's happiness will always depend on the impression they make on men', unhappiness would surely follow.[94] Cabanis and Roussel agreed that women who rejected their 'maternal' role or protested against it were depraved.[95]

Like Cabanis, Virey argued that women's subordination to men was natural and inescapable:

> [Woman] does not live for herself, but for the multiplication of the species, in conjunction with man; that is the only goal which Nature, society and morality allow. It follows that woman is a being naturally subordinate to man by her needs, her duties, and especially by her physical constitution . . . If woman is weak in her very constitution, Nature has thus sought to make her submissive and dependent in the sexual union . . . she must therefore bear the yoke of constraint without complaining, to preserve peace in the family by her submission and her example.[96]

He criticised women for resisting dependence, and 'seeing in even the most deserved submission only the shackles of slavery'.[97] Women lacked the rational strength to recognise their own legitimate subordination, he claimed, but of course if they had possessed that level of rationality their subordination would no longer have been warranted. For the leading French doctors of the early nineteenth century, however, the construction of a particular model of femininity which stressed female specificity and biological determinism, served to justify a patriarchal family structure. The veneer of 'science' reinforced restrictive views about women's place in society. Like theology and philosophy, science emphasised women's 'special' nature, and defined as 'natural' women's confinement to the home and their subordination to men.

French socialists shared some of the assumptions made in the religious, philosophical and medical discourses on women in this period. It is significant, for instance, that pre-1848 socialist writings on ideal female roles did not appeal to the models of the French Revolution, which would have provided a precedent for redefining women's place.[98] No doubt the early socialists wished to avoid raising the spectre of female disorder and social chaos, which many of their contemporaries associated with women's entry into the public sphere during those years. The silence of the socialists on the activities of Revolutionary women was also consistent with their attempts to define a set of 'female' roles which were essentially different from those of men, and thus a reflection of women's different nature.

While the weight of religious, philosophical and medical opinion on female nature justified a restricted domestic role for women, however, a number of French socialists employed the concept of women's special nature in order to advocate a non-domestic role for women. Charles Fourier, the Saint-Simonians and Flora Tristan were strong defenders of this position, making it central to their visions of a new social order. Women would take their places alongside men in all areas of life. Both public and private life would be transformed and the barriers between them lowered. They rejected the widespread insistence on separate spheres, although they generally accepted the distinctiveness of male and female natures. Their understanding of sexual difference and its social significance, therefore, provides a counterweight to the dominant ideology of their day. For these socialists, sexual difference pointed the way to a new society which avoided the repressive features of the emergent world of separate spheres. Their attempts to transform sexual difference into a concept of liberation for women and for society, and the theoretical and practical difficulties this posed, are considered in the following chapters.

Notes

1. This Expression of Baudlaire's recently became the title of a study by Stéphane Michaud: *Muse et Madone. Visage de la Femme de la Révolution française aux Apparitions de Lourdes* (Paris, 1985).
2. Angela Groppi, 'Le Travail des Femmes à Paris à l' époque de la Révolution française', *Bulletin d'Histoire Economique et Sociale de la Révolution française* (1979), pp. 30-7.
3. Louise A. Tilly, 'Three faces of capitalism: women and work in French cities', in John Merriman (ed.), *French Cities in the Nineteenth Century* (London, 1982), pp. 168-70; Tony Judt, *Marxism and the French Left. Studies on Labor and Politics in France 1830-1981* (Oxford, 1986), chap. 2.
4. M. Guilbert, *Les Fonctions des Femmes dans l'Industrie* (Paris and the Hague, 1966), pp. 28-33; A. Groppi, 'Travail des Femmers', pp. 42-4; T. Judt, *Marxism,* pp. 48-51.
5. T. Zeldin, *France 1848-1945,* 2 vols. (Oxford, 1973-7), I, p. 307; G. de Bertier de Sauvigny, *The Bourbon Restoration,* transl. L. M. Case (Philadelphia, 1967), p. 243.
6. Jill Harsin, *Policing Prostitution in Nineteenth Century Paris* (Princeton, 1985), pp. 114-16.
7. J. -B. Parent-Duchâtelet, *De la Prostitution dans la Ville de Paris,* 2 vols. (Paris, 1836), I, pp. 103-4; II, pp. 116-17, quoted in J. Harsin, *Policing Prostitution,* pp. 121, 130.
8. G. de Bertier de Sauvigny, *The Bourbon Restoration,* pp. 254-5.
9. See Louis Chevalier, *Labouring Classes and Dangerous Classes in Paris During the First Half of the Nineteenth Century,* transl. Frank Jellinek (London, 1973). Eugène Sue was responsible for the claim that 'the barbarians are in our midst' (G. de Bertier de Sauvigny, *The Bourbon Restoration,* p. 259).
10. A. Groppi, 'Travail des Femmes', p. 39.
11. *Ibid.,* p. 40; Arlette Farge, ''L'Histoire ébruitée des femmes dans la société pré-révolutionnaire parisienné', in Christiane Dufrancatel *et al.* (eds), *L'Histoire Sans Qualités* (Paris, 1979), pp. 23-31; Michelle Perrot, 'La Femme populaire rebelle', in *ibid.,* pp. 130-49; Jane Rendall, *The Origins of Modern Feminism: Women in Britain, France and the United States, 1780-1860* (London, 1985), pp. 191-3.
12. See Joan W. Scott. 'Men and Women in the Parisian Garment Trades: Discussions of Family and Work in the 1830s and 1840s', in Roderick Floud, Geoffrey Crossick and Patricia Thane (eds), *The Power of the Past: Essays in Honour of Eric Hobsbawm* (Cambridge, 1984), pp. 67-93; M. Rebérioux, 'L'Ouvrière', in J. -P. Aron (ed), *Misérable et Glorieuse la Femme du XIXe Siècle* (Paris 1980), pp. 59-78, and below, chap. 5.
13. T. Zeldin, *France,* I, p. 287; Bonnie G. Smith, *Ladies of the Leisure Class. The Bourgeoises of Northern France in the Nineteenth Century* (Princeton, N.J., 1981), pp. 57-8; A. Daumard, *La Bourgeoisie Parisienne de 1815 à 1848* (Paris, 1963), pp. 328-31.
14. B. Smith, *Ladies of the Leisure Class,* pp. 57-58; A. Daumard, *La Bougeois, Parisienne,* pp. 328, 375.
15. Barbara Corrado Pope, 'Maternal Education in France, 1815-1848', *Proceedings of the Third Annual Meeting of the Western Society for French History, December 1975* (Texas, 1976), p. 366; 'Revolution and Retreat: Upper-Class French Women After 1789', in Carol M. Berkin and Clara M. Lovett (eds), *Women, War and Revolution* (New York, 1980), p. 223. For a similar interpretation of the role of the bourgeois wife in mid-nineteenth century England see J. F. C. Harrison, *The Early Victorians 1823-51* (New York, 1971), chap. 4.
16. Claire Goldberg Moses, *French Feminism in the Nineteenth Century* (New York, 1984), p. 35; A. Daumard, *La Bourgeoisie Parisienne,* pp. 357-8.
17. B. C. Pope, 'Revolution and Retreat', pp. 216-20. See Patrick K. Bidelman, *Pariahs Stand Up! The Founding of the Liberal Feminist Movement in France, 1858-1889* (Westport, Conn., 1982), pp, 3-32 for an outline of the legal position of French women in the early nineteenth century.
18. B. Smith, *Ladies of the Leisure Class,* chap. 3; A. Daumard, *La Bourgeoise Parisienne,* pp. 361-70.
19. A. Daumard, *La Bourgeoise Parisienne,* pp. 336-40; B. Smith, *Ladies of the Leisure Class,* pp. 336-9.
20. David Landes, 'Religion and Enterprise: The Case of the French Textile Industry', in Edward C. Carpenter II, Robert Foster and John N. Moody (eds), *Enterprise and Entrepreneurs in Nineteenth and Twentieth Century France* (Baltimore and London, 1976), pp. 55-63.
21. L. Strumingher, 'L'Ange de la Maison. Mothers and Daughters in Nineteenth Century France', *International Journal of Women's Studies,* 2 (1979) 54-9.
22. B. C. Pope, 'Maternal Education', pp. 366-7; A. Daumard, *La Bourgeoise Parisienne,* p. 325.

23. A. Daumard, *La Bourgeoise Parisienne,* pp. 366-8; Erna Olafson Hellerstein, 'Women, Social Order and the City: Rules for French Ladies, 1830-1870', unpub. Ph.D. thesis, Uni. of California, Berkeley, 1980, chap. 2.

24. G. de Bertier de Sauvigny, *The Bourbon Restoration,* p. 244.

25. On the diversity of family life amongst the working population see Roger Price, *A Social History of Nineteenth Century France* (London, 1987), pp. 221-8; K. Lynch, *Family, Class, and Ideology in Early Industrial France. Social Policy and the Working Class Family 1825-1848* (Madison, Wisc., 1988), chap. 3.

26. Austin Gough, 'French Workers and their Wives in the Mid-Nineteenth Century', *Labour History,* 42 (May 1982) 78-9.

27. *Ibid.,* 79-82; David Garrioch, *Neighbourhood and Community in Paris, 1740-1790* (Cambridge, 1986), pp. 79-83.

28. L. Strumingher, 'L'Ange de las Maison', pp. 51-6; K. Lynch, *Family, Class,* pp. 159, 166-7; J. Rendall, *Origins,* pp. 122-5. Michelle Perrot argues strongly that this strategy was unsuccessful. See La Femme populaire rebelle', pp. 123-56.

29. These complexities are outlined in K. Lynch, *Family, Class,* pp. 88-100.

30. *Ibid.,* p. 114

31. C. G. Moses, *French Feminism,* p. 24.

32. G. de Bertier de Sauvigny, *The Bourbon Restoration,* p. 243; K. Lynch, *Family, Class,* p. 121.

33. K. Lynch, *Family, Class,* pp. 140-2; 160-5.

34. Report on the Prefect of Police to the Minister for the Interior, 1838, quoted in *ibid.,* p. 159.

35. Geneviève Fraisse, *Muse de la raison. La démocratie exclusive et la différence des sexes* (Paris, 1989); Linda Schiebinger, 'Skeletons in the Closet: The First Illustrations of the Female Skeleton in Eighteenth Century Anatomy', in Catherine Gallagher and Thomas Laqueur (eds), *The Making of the Modern Sexuality and Society in the Nineteenth Century* (California, 1987), pp. 42-82; Thomas Laqueur, 'Orgasm, Generation, and the Politics of Reproductive Biology', in *ibid.,* pp. 1-41.

36. Ludmilla, Jordanova has pointed out the importance in eighteenth century medical discourse of the notion of women's 'unveiling' by science. See 'Natural Facts: a historical perspective on science and sexuality', in Carol MacCormack and Marilyn Strathern (eds), *Nature, Culture and Gender* (Cambridge, 1980), pp. 42-69.

37. T. Laqueur, 'Orgasm,' p. 3; G. Fraisse, *Muse de la Raison,* p. 9.

38. For a detailed study of the Catholic Church's attitudes to women, see Jean-Marie Aubert, *La Femme. Antiféminisme et christianisme* (Paris, 1975).

39. *Ibid.,* pp. 52-60.

40. *Ibid.,* pp. 99-100.

41. Letter to François Lallier, 22 February 1839, quotes in S. Michaud, *Muse et Madone,* p. 46.

42. S. Michaud, *Muse et Madone,* p. 32.

43. J. -J. Gaume, *Histoire de la Société domestique,* 2 vols. (Paris, 1841), I, pp. 169-70, quotes in *ibid.,* p. 45.

44. S. Michaud, *Muse et Modone,* p. 32.

45. *Ibid.,* pp. 39, 40, 69.

46. *Ibid.,* pp. 39-49.

47. *Ibid.,* p. 30.

48. M. le Vicomte de Chateaubriand, *Génie dy Christianisme* (Paris, 1838), p. 44. This work was first published in 1802.

49. S. Michaud, *Muse et Madone,* pp. 31-32.

50. Joseph de Maistre, *Traité sur les Sacrifices* (1831), quotes in Stéphane Michaud 'Science, droit, religion: Trois contes cur les deux natures', *Romantisme,* 13-14 (1976) 31.

51. S. Michaud, *Muse et Madone,* p. 42; J. -M. Aubert, *La Femme,* pp. 65-8, 107-8, 130-1.

52. Arthur M. Wilson, '"Treated Like Imbecile Children" (Diderot): The Enlightenment and the Status of Women', in Paul Fritz and Richard Morton (eds), *Woman in the Eighteenth Century and Other Essays* (Toronto and Sarasota, 1976), pp. 89-90; Ruth Graham, 'Rousseau's Sexism Revolutionised', in *ibid.,* p. 12.

53. Arthur M. Wilson, '"Treated Like Imbecile Children"', p. 98; Jean H. Bloch, 'Women and the Reform of the Nation', in Eva Jacobs *et al.* (eds), *Women and Society in Eighteenth Century Fracne. Essays in Honour of John Stephenson Spink* (London, 1979), pp. 3-18; Elizabth Gardner, 'The *Philosophes* and Women: Sensationalism and Sentiment', in *ibid.,* pp. 19-27.

54. Paul Hoffman, *La Femme dans la Pensée des Lumières* (Paris, 1977), pp. 378, 381.

55. *Ibid.,* p. 424; L. Schiebinger, 'Skeletons in the Closet', p. 67.

56. P. Hoffman, *La Femme,* pp. 337, 377-8, 532; E. Gardner, 'The *Philosophes* and Women', pp. 23-4.

57. T. Moreau, *Le Sang de l'Histoire. Michelet, l'Histoire et l'Idée de la Femme au XIXe Siécle* (Paris, 1982), pp. 46-8.

58. E. Gardner, 'The *Philosophes* and Women', pp. 19-27.

59. G. Fraisse, *Muse de la Raison,* p. 25.

60. P. Hoffman, *La Femme,* p. 359.

61. Sylvana Tomaselli, 'The Enlightenment Debate on Women', *History Workshop Journal,* 20 (1985) 105-9, 119-21.

62. L. J. Jordanova, 'Natural Facts', pp. 43-53, 66-7; M. Bloch and J. H. Bloch, 'Women and the Dialectics of Nature in Eighteenth Century French Thought', in *Nature, Culture and Gender,* ed. C. MacCormack & M. Strathern, pp. 27-31; Genevieve Lloyd, *The Man of Reason. 'Male' and 'Female' in Western Philosophy* (London, 1984), pp. 61-64.

63. G. Lloyd, *The Man of Reason,* p. ix.

64. Laura W. Fleder, 'Female physiology and psychology in the works of Diderot and the medical writers of his day,' unpublished Ph. D. thesis, Columbia University, 1978, pp. 151-5, 231-9; Arthur M. Wilson, '"Treated like Imbecile Children"', pp. 100-1.

65. P. Hoffman, *La Femme,* pp. 30, 390-1, 400, 424; G. Fraisse, *Muse de la Raison,* p. 152.
66. P. Hoffman, *La Femme,* pp. 342, 388-9; 'L'Héritage des lumières: mythes et modèles de la féminité au XIXe siècle, *Romantisme,* 13-14 (1976) 17-18.
67. G. Fraisse, *Muse de la Raison,* pp. 84-8.
68. Jean H. Bloch. 'Women and the Reform of the Nation', pp. 8, 16-17; L. Fleder, 'Female physiology', pp. 88-123.
69. P Hoffman, *La Femme,* p. 380; L. J. Jordanova, 'Natural Facts', pp. 58-9.
70. P. Hoffman, *La Femme,* pp. 445-6.
71. *Ibid.,* pp. 331, 380-1.
72. *Ibid.,* pp. 344, 394-5.
73. *Ibid.,* pp. 332-5, 341.
74. G. Lloyd, *The Man of Reason,* p. 77
75. P. Hoffman, *La Femme,* pp. 341, 374-5.
76. *De L'Esprit des Lois,* VIII, p. 3, quoted in P. Hoffman, *La Femme,* p. 340.
77. See G. Fraisse, *Muse de la Raison,* p. 100; P. Hoffman, *La Femme,* p. 342.
78. Yvonne Knibiehler, 'Led médecins et la "nature féminine" au temps du Code civil', *Annales E. S. C.,* 31, no. 4 (July-Aug. 1976) 824-45.
79. *Ibid.,* pp. 827-8.
80. L. Schiebinger, 'Skeletons in the Closet', p. 51.
81. P. Hoffman, *La Femme,* p. 143.
82. P. Hoffman, 'L'Héritage des Lumières', p. 7.
83. P. J. G. Cabanis, 'De l'influence des sexes sur le caractère des idées et des affections morales', quoted in P. Hoffman, *La Femme,* p. 163, n. 39. Dr. Roussel reached a similar conclusion. See *ibid.,* p. 143.
84. *Ibid.,* pp. 143-4, 165; Y. Knibiehler, 'Les médecins', 836.
85. Y. Knibiehler, *ibid.*; P. Hoffman, *La Femme,* p. 144.
86. T. Laqueur, 'Orgasm, Generation', p. 27; Y. Knibiehler, 'Les médecins', 832.
87. Louis Henry, 'The Population of France in the Eighteenth Century', in D. V. Glass and D. E. C. Eversley (eds), *Population in History* (London, 1965), pp. 451-2; Etienne Van de Walle, 'Motivations and Technology in the Decline of French Fertility,' in R. Wheaton and T. K. Hareven (eds), *Family and Sexuality in French History* (Philadelphia, 1980), pp. 135-78.
88. Y. Knibiehler, 'Les médecins', 830, 834.
89. Quoted in P. Hoffman, *La Femme,* p. 146.
90. *Ibid.,* p. 144.
91. Rachel G. Fuchs, *Abandoned Children. Foundlings and Child Welfare in Nineteenth Century France* (Albany, N.Y., 1984), p. 44.
92. L. J. Jordanova, 'Natural Facts', pp. 49-50.
93. J. J. Virey, *De la Femme sous ses rapports physiologique, moral et littéraire,* 2nd ed. (Paris, 1825), pp. 228-9. J. J. Virey was a disciple of Roussel. He published three major works on women between 1801 and 1823, as well as a number of articles. See P. Hoffman, *La Femme,* p. 165.
94. Quoted in P. Hoffman, *La Femme,* p. 165.
95. *Ibid.,* pp. 144, 165.
96. J. J. Virey, *De l' Education* (1802), quoted in Y. Knibiehler, 'Les médecins', 836-7.
97. Y. Knibiehler, 'Les médecins', 836.
98. Flora Tristan's reference to the 'heroic' action of Charlotte Corday, who killed Marat in 1793, is the exception. See *Les Pérégrinations d'une Paria 1833-1834* (Paris 1979), p. 34. On the roles of women in the Revolution see Paule-Marie Duhet, *Les Femmes et la Révolution 1789-1794* (Paris, 1971); Olwen Hufton, 'Women in Revolution 1789-1796', *Past and Present,* 53 (1971) 43-62; D. G. Levy and H. B. Applewhite, 'Women of the Popular Classes in Revolutionary Paris, 1789-95 in *Women, War and Revolution,* ed. C. M. Berkin & C. M. Lovett, pp. 9-35.

SHIRLEY WILSON LOGAN (ESSAY DATE 1999)

SOURCE: Logan, Shirley Wilson. "Black Women on the Speaker's Platform, 1832-1900." *"We are Coming": The Persuasive Discourse of Nineteenth-Century Black Women,* pp. 1-22. Carbondale, Ill.: Southern Illinois University Press, 1999.

In the following excerpt, Logan provides evidence for the important place that women lecturers held in both the abolitionist and feminist movements.

> *Our progress depends in the united strength of both men and women—the women alone nor the men alone cannot do the work. We have so fully realized that fact by witnessing the work of our men with the women in the rear. This is indeed the women's era, and we are coming.*
>
> —Rosetta Douglass-Sprague, July 20, 1896

Nineteenth-century African American women were full participants in the verbal warfare for human dignity. Describing the women and the times, Rosetta Douglass-Sprague, daughter of Anna Murray Douglass and Frederick Douglass, proclaimed at the First Annual Convention of the National Federation of Afro-American Women, July 20-22, 1896, "This is indeed the women's era, and we are coming" (*History* 37). During the three-day conference, the footsteps of advancing black women resonated in the speeches and remarks of such forward-thinking intellectuals as Ida B. Wells, Victoria Earle Matthews, Alice Ruth Moore, and Frances Ellen Watkins Harper. They echoed, as well, in the poem "We Are Coming," which "little Margaret Tate" recited at the closing session (*History* 57).[1] The participants at this convention, held at the Nineteenth Street Baptist Church in Washington, D.C., united with the other national black women's organization, the National League of Colored Women, to form the National Association of Colored Women (NACW).[2] Representing a milestone rather than a beginning, the merger provided a larger forum for public expression. Black women addressed women's organizations, church groups, antislavery associations, and temperance unions. They spoke in all sections of the United States, in Canada, and in the British Isles. They spoke to black audiences, white audiences, and mixed audiences on the panoply of issues challenging peoples of African descent throughout America at the time. In addition to the oppressive defining issue of slavery, these concerns included employment, civil rights, women's rights, emigration, and self-improvement. After the Civil War, mob violence, racial uplift, and support for the Southern black woman were added to the list.

Not limiting themselves to being mere participants in public forums, black women also created, organized, and publicized a large number of them. Maria W. Stewart, the first American woman to speak publicly to a mixed group of women and men to leave extant texts, was such a woman. She delivered her first address in 1832, six years before Angelina Grimeké's appearance at Pennsylvania Hall, and her speeches were published in Garrison's *Liberator.* Mary Ann Shadd Cary, after considerable discussion, was reluctantly seated at the 1855 Colored National Convention in Philadelphia, becoming the first woman to address that body by a vote of 38 yeas and 23 nays (*Minutes 10*). An article in the October 26, 1855, edition of *Frederick Douglass' Paper* describes that performance:

> She at first had ten minutes granted her as had the other members. At their expiration, ten more were granted, and by this time came the hour of adjournment; but so interested was the House, that it granted additional time to her to finish, at the commencement of the afternoon session; and the House was crowded and breathless in its attention to her masterly exposition of our present condition, and the advantages open to colored men of enterprise.
>
> (Sterling, *Sisters* 171)

Frances Harper was employed as a lecturer for the Maine Anti-Slavery Society in 1854, becoming possibly the first black woman to earn a living as a traveling lecturer. She was certainly the most prolific. The black women's club movement was also a site extensive issue-oriented public discussion, as any edition of the *Woman's Era* demonstrated. The pages of the periodical, published by the Woman's Era Club of Boston, from 1894 to 1897, were filled with reports from the various black women's clubs around the country relating their public presence in current affairs. For example, the April 1895 issue carried an article by Mary Church Terrell, editor of the Washington, D.C., column, in which she condemned T. Thomas Fortune, editor of the *New York Age,* for criticizing "the race with which he is identified for whining" (3). Fortune had complained that blacks needed to become more self-sufficient and to stifle their demands for rights. In the same issue, the column from Georgia, edited by Alice Woodby McKane, reports on the club's interest in the emigration of two hundred blacks to Liberia. In the June 1, 1894 issue, Ednah Cheney, white Boston reformer, commends the *Woman's Era* for its involvement in opening the medical profession to women. Later issues teem with support for a national gathering of women, which did not occur in 1895, providing another opportunity for black women to address publicly urgent race concerns. Although this volume develops around the rhetorical accomplishments of individual nineteenth-century black women, in this overview chapter, I consider those rhetors within the larger sociohistorical context. This context was shaped by the following broad and necessarily overlapping issues: the abolition of slavery, women's rights, mob violence, and racial uplift.

Abolition of Slavery

It should be clear that abolition of slavery dominated discourse among black women during the first half of the century. Of the 750,000 blacks living in the United States at the time of the census of 1790, approximately 92 percent or 691,000 were enslaved, and most lived in the South Atlantic states. In 1808, legislation finally made the African slave trade illegal, although it continued underground for many years. In the 1790 census, Boston was the only city that listed no slaves, with approximately 27,000 free blacks living in the North and 32,000 blacks in South (Franklin and Moss 80-81).

One can best appreciate the range of black women's abolitionist rhetoric by considering the careers of three speakers who migrated to new locales, delivering their antislavery messages to audiences in England, Canada, and across the United States. Sarah Parker Remond, a member of a prominent abolitionist family in Massachusetts, lectured in England and Scotland. Mary Ann Shadd Cary, whose father was a leader in the Underground Railroad movement in Delaware, fled with her family to Canada to avoid the consequences of the Fugitive Slave Act of 1850 and developed into an outspoken presence in the antislavery movement there. Frances Harper, whose uncle William Watkins was active in the abolitionist movement, left Baltimore about 1850, also in response to the Fugitive Slave Act, eventually traveling across the country with her antislavery message.

Although slavery was abolished in the British Empire in 1833, antislavery activities against its American version continued throughout the first half of the century, when a number of black abolitionists, including Sarah Remond (1815-1894), traveled to the British Isles to generate support for their cause. Sarah Remond's family was part of the abolitionist society of Salem, Massachusetts. In 1856 Remond was appointed agent for the American Anti-Slavery Society and, as an affiliate of William Lloyd Garrison, became one of the first black women to lecture regularly before antislavery audiences. Initially a reluctant speaker, Remond toured throughout New England, New York, and Ohio between 1856 and 1858 and developed into an accomplished orator. From 1859 to 1861, she delivered more than forty-five lectures in eighteen cities in England, three cities in Scotland, and four cities in Ireland (Wesley 974). She was received enthusiastically wherever she spoke. In 1866 she returned to the United States and applied her oratorical skills to the task of racial uplift, in the manner of her brother Charles Remond and of Frederick Douglass. In 1867 she traveled again to England and subsequently in Florence, Italy, to practice medicine. It was said that she spoke in a "well-toned"and "pleasing style" and "demonstrated an unerring sensitivity to the political and social concerns of her listeners—particularly women reform activists" (Ripley, vol. 1, 441).

Unlike most male lecturers, Remond did not hesitate to speak about the exploitation of enslaved black women. In an hour-and-fifteen-minute lecture delivered to an overflow crowd at the Music Hall in Warrington, England, January 24, 1859, Remond relentlessly detailed the treatment of the enslaved black woman, using as a case in point the story of Kentucky slave mother Margaret Garner. Garner, who "had suffered in her own person the degradation that a woman could not mention," escaped with her husband and four children across the Ohio River into Cincinnati in 1856. Under the fugitive Slave Law of 1850, escapees could be recaptured in free states and returned to captivity. To prevent this, when Garner realized that they would be overcome by a large posse, she killed her three-year-old daughter but was prevented from killing the others.[3] Remond stated that "above all sufferers in America, American women who were slaves lived in the most pitiable condition. They could not protect themselves from the licentiousness which met them on every hand—they could not protect their honour from the tyrant" (Remond, "Music Hall" 437). She also criticized the Dred Scott Decision of 1857, denying blacks the right to citizenship, and the heinous Fugitive Slave Act, which sent may blacks fleeing to abolitionist communities within northern states, Canada, and the British Isles.

Remond drew support for her arguments from contemporary events. She chronicled current and widely publicized incidents with significant impact on American slavery, showing how such events, like the trial of Margaret Garner and the Dred Scott Decision, mirror the sad conditions of a slave society. Stressing the hypocrisy of the Christian church, in this same speech Remond cited the shooting of a black man for insubordination by a clergyman in Louisiana and the dismissal of a minister in Philadelphia after he preached an antislavery sermon. From her English audiences she wanted public outcry. In a September 14, 1859, speech delivered at the Athenaeum in Manchester, England, she asked them to exert their influence to abolish slavery in America:

> Give us the power of your public opinion, it has great weight in America. Words spoken here are read there as no words written in America are read. . . . I ask you, raise the moral public opinion until its voice reaches the American shores. Aid us thus until the shackles of the American slave melt like dew before the morning sun.
>
> (Remond, "Athenaeum" 459)

Mary Ann Shadd Cary (1823-1893), the first black female newspaper editor, published the *Provincial Freeman,* a weekly Canadian newspaper for fugitive slaves and others who had fled to Canada in the wake of the Fugitive Salve Act during the 1850s. From 1852 to 1853, she was the only black missionary in the field for the American Missionary Association (AMA), the largest abolitionist organization in America (DeBoer xi). Cary taught fugitive slaves recently arrived, who, in her view, lacked motivation and self-discipline. Along with Samuel Ward and Alexander McArthur, Cary established the *Provincial Freeman* in March of 1853, after the AMA informed her that it would no longer support her school. The *Freeman* soon became Cary's vehicle for promoting industry among former slaves and exposing the misconduct of unscrupulous antislavery agents. In her historic 1855 address to the Colored National Convention, mentioned above, she advocated for the emigration of blacks to Canada and for their total integration into Canadian society. Cary's intense speaking style left its impression, as noted by the eye witness quoted above and here:

> Miss Shadd's eyes are small and penetrating and fairly flush when she is speaking. Her ideas seem to flow so fast that she, at times hesitates for words; yet she overcomes any apparent imperfections in her speaking by the earnestness of her manner and the quality of her thoughts. She is a superior woman; and it is useless to deny it; however much we may differ with her on the subject of emigration.
>
> (Sterling, *Sisters* 170-71).

All accounts of the works and days of the strong-willed Cary suggest that she rarely held her tongue or backed down from a position. Offering Cary as an example of the many mid-century "literary and professional colored men and women," Martin R. Delany, in his book titled *The Condition, Elevation, Emigration, and Destiny of the Colored People of the United States,* described her as "intelligent" and "peculiarly eccentric" (131).[4] She opposed the growing popularity of evangelical, better-life-in-the-afterworld preachers who neglected contemporary issues, with "their gross ignorance and insolent bearing, together with their sanctimonious garb," who "hang tenaciously to exploded customs," giving some impression that "money, and not the good of the people" motivates them (Letter 32-33). One biographer describes her style as follows:

> By nineteenth-century norms, Cary's caustic, jolting language seemed ill-suited to a woman. She used phrases such as "gall and wormwood," "moral pest," "petty despot," "superannuated minister," "nest of unclean birds," "moral monsters," and "priest-ridden people," in order to keep her ideas before the public.
>
> (Calloway-Thomas 225)

Most of Cary's extant writings are letters and scathing editorials from the pages of *Provincial Freeman* railing against intemperance, those who have "addled the brains of our young people," and any number of other displeasing states of affairs (DeBoer 175). Texts of her speeches are scarce, but the following excerpt, reprinted with limited editorial intervention, comes from a sermon "apparently delivered before a Chatham [Canada West] audience on 6 April 1858" (Ripley 2: 388) and suggest the fervor of her biblically based on feminist antislavery rhetoric:

> We cannot successfully Evade duty because the Suffering fellow . . . is only a woman! She too is a neighbor. The good Samaritan of this generation must not take for their Exemplars the priest and the Levite when a fellow woman is among thieves—neither will they find excuse in the custom as barbarous and anti-Christian as any promulgated by pious Brahmin that . . . they may be only females. The spirit of true philanthropy knows no sex.
>
> (Cary, Sermon 389)

As William Still's history of the Underground Railroad documents, Frances Ellen Watkins Harper (1825-1911) joined the abolitionist movement largely because of an incident that occurred in the slave state of Maryland, her home state. In 1853 a law was passed prohibiting free blacks from entering Maryland. When a man unintentionally violated that law, he was arrested and sent to Georgia as a slave. He escaped but was recaptured and soon died. Hearing of this sequence of events, Harper remarked, "Upon that grave I pledge myself to the Anti-Slavery cause" (Still 758). In 1854, Harper, gave up teaching to become a lecturer for the Maine Anti-Slavery Society.

Harper delivered what was probably her first antislavery speech at a meeting in New Bedford, Massachusetts, in 1854, possibly titled the "Education and Elevation of the Colored Race" (Still 758). She continued to speak out against slavery and its consequences, traveling throughout New England, southern Canada, and west to Michigan and Ohio. During one six-week period in 1854, she gave at least thirty-three lectures in twenty-one New England towns (Foster, *Brighter* 13).

Because of her articulate and reserved manner, many who heard her found it difficult to believe that she was of African descent. Grace Greenwood, a journalist, labeled her "the bronze muse," bemoaning the fact that a woman of such stature could possibly have been a slave, as if to suggest that slavery was more acceptable for the unwashed. For such observers, she was considered a fascinating aberration, as this account by a Maine abolitionist suggest: "Miss W.[atkins] is slightly tinged with African blood, but the color only serves to add a charm to the occasion which nothing else could give, while at the same time it disarms the fastidious of that so common prejudice which denies to white ladies the right to give public lectures" (Sterling, *Sisters* 161). This commentary also highlights the perception that white women were different and that while they were yet denied the right to give public lectures, anomalous black women were not always frowned upon in this role.

Harper frequently focused on the economic aspects of slavery and the irony of owning "property that can walk." In a lecture, "Could We Trace the Record of Every Human Heart," delivered during the 1857 meeting of the New York City Anti-

Slavery Society, she argued that slavery's financial benefits would make its abolishment more difficult:

> A hundred thousand new-born babes are annually added to the victims of slavery; twenty-thousand lives are annually sacrificed on the plantations of the South. Such a sight should send a thrill of horror through the nerves of civilization and impel the heart of humanity to lofty deeds. So it might, if men had not found a fearful alchemy by which this blood can be transformed into gold. Instead of listening to the cry of agony, they listen to the ring of dollars and stoop down to pick up the coin.
> (n. pag.)

Notes

1. Margaret Tate had also recited at the Congress of Colored Women of the United States, held in Atlanta, Georgia, in conjunction with the December 1895 Cotton States and International Exposition. Many of the same women, among them Frances Harper, Fannie Barrier Williams, and Victoria Matthews, attended this gathering leading to the formation of the National Association of Colored Women. Elizabeth Davis records that Tate, "a mere child," had been "voted honorary member of the Congress because of her excellence in recitation" (26).
2. I refer throughout this volume to various configurations of black women's associations that are identified in relationship to one another and relationship to the black women intellectuals who were instrumental in their development. The national club movement, most active in Washington, D.C., New York, and Boston, ultimately evolved into the National Association of Colored Women (NACW) in 1896 with Mary Church Terrell as the first president. For an overview of the black women's club movement, see "National Association of Colored Women" (842-51) and B. Jones.
3. In her fictionalized revision of Margaret Garner's story, *Beloved* (1987), Toni Morrison focuses on the psychological impact of a bondage that drives one to infanticide.
4. Martin Robison Delany (1812-1885) was, among other occupations, a physician, lecturer, novelist, and journalist, who published his own newspaper and edited the *North Star* with Frederick Douglass. *The Condition, Elevation, Emigration, and Destiny of the Colored People of the United States* (1852) proposed a range of solutions to the problems of blacks in pre-Civil War America, including their emigration to predominantly black areas of the world, instead of to Canada (as Shadd Cary would propose in *A Plea for Emigration,* or *Notes of Canada West* [1852]). In this same sketch, Delany mentioned having read a pre-publication version of Shadd Cary's 1849 pamphlet titled *Condition of Colored People.*

Works Cited

Cary, Mary Ann Shadd. "Trades for Our Boys." Letter. New National Era (21 Mar. 1872). *The Black Worker. During the Era of the National Labor Union.* Ed. Philip S. Foner and Ronald L. Lewis. Philadelphia: Temple UP, 1978. 177-78.

———. Sermon. 6 Apr. 1858. *The Black Abolitionist Papers.* Vol. 2. Canada, 1830-1865. Ed C. Peter Ripley. Chapel Hill: U of North Carolina P, 1986. 388-91.

———. Letter to Frederick Douglass. 25 Jan. 1849. *The Black Abolitionist Papers.* Vol. 4. The United States, 1847-1858. Ed. C. Peter Ripley. Chapel Hill: U of North Carolina P, 1991. 31-34.

Davis, Elizabeth Lindsay. *Lifting as They Climb.* New York: G. K. Hall, 1996.

Delany, Martin Robison. *The Condition, Elevation, Emigration, and Destiny of the Colored People of the United States.* 1852. New York: Arno, 1968.

Jones, Beverly Washington. *Quest for Equality: The Life and Writings of Mary Eliza Church Terrell, 1863-1954.* Brooklyn: Carlson, 1990.

"National Association of Colored Women." *Black Women in America: An Historical Encyclopedia.* Bloomington: Indiana UP, 1993. 842-51.

EARLY FEMINISTS

JENNIFER WAELTI-WALTERS AND STEVEN C. HAUSE (ESSAY DATE 1994)

SOURCE: Waelti-Walters, Jennifer and Steven C. Hause. Introduction to *Feminisms of the Belle Epoque: A Historical and Literary Anthology,* edited by Jennifer Waelti-Walters and Steven C. Hause, pp. 1-13. Lincoln, Neb.: University of Nebraska Press, 1994.

In the following excerpt, Waelti-Walters and Hause argue that France made important contributions to modern feminism even though social and legal obstacles in that country made nineteenth-century reform towards achieving women's rights slower than in England or the United States.

Many of the roots of modern feminism lie in France. This may surprise readers who are more familiar with feminism than they are with France. After all, the philosophic masterworks of early feminism, from Mary Wollstonecraft's *Vindication of the Rights of Woman* (1792) to John Stuart Mill's *Subjection of Women* (1869), appeared chiefly in the English language. The first large organizations dedicated to seeking women's rights emerged in Britain and the United States, and the first great feminist reforms, the Married Women's Property Acts, were won across America (1839-50) and in Britain (1882) long before France adopted the Schmahl Law of 1907. In the global struggle to win women's suffrage, Australia, New Zealand, and Scandinavia often led in the adoption of feminist reforms, whereas French women did not even win the vote until 1945.

Such facts show that modern feminism reached its first maturity chiefly in Protestant states, where doctrines of individualism flourished. This pattern, however, should not obscure the roots of feminism in late eighteenth- and early nineteenth-century France. Parisian salons, organized and directed by women such as Madame Geoffrin, involved women in the greatest debates of a lively age. The more enlightened philosophers who assembled there, such as the Marquis de Condorcet, advocated women's rights as early as the 1780s. Subsequently, the French Revolution, despite its record of hostility to women's issues, stimulated the growth of feminism by forcing a long European reconsideration of human rights. It produced an eloquent manifesto calling for women's rights in Olympe de Gouges's *Declaration of the Rights of Women* (1791), and it saw the birth of women's political clubs, the precursors of nineteenth-century feminist societies. Indeed, the revolution of 1789 was a profound stimulus to Wollstonecraft, who participated in a radical discussion circle in London and then moved to Paris in 1792, staying in France until 1794. When a European conservative reaction triumphed over French revolutionary ideas in the early nineteenth century, the roots of modern feminism were still to be found in France. French utopian socialism provided an important forum for the continuing discussion of equality and began a tradition of socialist support for women's rights.[1]

Even the word "feminism" came to the English-speaking world with French roots. The first appearance in any language of the word "feminism" (and its cognates) occurred in French, as "*féminisme*" and "*féministe,*" in the late nineteenth century. Some scholars have suggested that the words were first used by French utopian socialists in the 1830s (when parallel "-ism" words, such as "liberalism" and "conservatism," were being coined), but no trace of this has been found in print.[2] The words did appear in France in the 1870s and 1880s, championed by one of the women included in this anthology (see part 5). By the 1890s, both terms were widely used there.[3] The *Oxford English Dictionary* locates the first English usage in 1895; American advocates of women's rights took even longer to adopt the term.[4]

The struggle for women's equality was slow and difficult in France, however; French religious, legal, and political structures created impediments to a women's rights movement more severe than those in Britain and America.[5] Feminism grew more readily in Protestant countries, where individualism and the acceptance of individual rights grew naturally from a religious tradition that emphasized direct, individual access to the Bible, individual interpretation and investigation, and individual conscience as a guide to action. Because 97 percent of its population was nominally Catholic, France lacked the stimulus of such traditions; rather, its religious tradition stressed the importance of obedience to authority.

The French legal system also created severe obstacles. Legal structures were a problem for women in all countries, but they were an unusually formidable impediment in France. Two millenia of Roman legal tradition had reduced all women to the status of being permanent minors, without direct rights of their own. Napoleon's codification of French civil law in 1804 reiterated this status and even worsened it. Married women were reduced to a form of servitude: Article 213 of the Napoleonic Code legally required wives to obey their husbands. Other portions of the code made women powerless to control their public or private lives, their bodies, or their offspring.[6] French laws inhibited the birth of a movement to protest such inequality by limiting the rights of association, assembly, and the press.

The political structure of nineteenth-century France also caused that nation's women's rights movement to lag behind Britain's and America's. The conservative Catholic monarchy of the Bourbon Restoration (1815-30) and Napoleon III's authoritarian Second Empire (1852-70), were less responsive to social innovation, fundamental reform, or the extension of individual rights than were republican America or liberal England. Even when the French finally created an enduring and democratic state, the Third Republic (1871-1940), French politics limited progress toward women's rights. Many of the republican feminists (who dominated the movement in the late nineteenth century) limited their demands and restricted their behavior for fear of adding to the instability of an apparently shaky regime. Many of the democratic men who founded the Third Republic hesitated to give full rights to women for fear that they would use those rights to aid the conservative enemies of the republic. The republican slogan—"Liberty! Equality! Fraternity!"—meant exactly what it says, gender specificity included.

As the nineteenth century passed, French women did win some minor advances, such as the Pelet Law of June 1836, which facilitated the creation of elementary schools for girls and led to a significant increase in the literacy rate among women. What little was achieved, however, had to be won within the misogynistic atmosphere of a society where even a progressive thinker (the anarchist-socialist Pierre-Joseph Proudhon) could insist that women were suited to be only "housewives or harlots," providing for the comfort or pleasure of men.[7] The model of the socially acceptable choice in this dichotomy was the passive and self-sacrificing bourgeois wife; the ideal woman was held by the cultural norm, as well as the law, to be subservient to men.[8] This polarized view of women persisted throughout the century and found many cultural expressions. As feminism grew, for example, artists increasingly depicted women as sinners and temptresses who led men to perdition. Woman was either the "idol of perversity" or the "new woman," both of which were a threat to men's happiness, or even to their very survival.[9] Indeed, according to the male-dominated press of that era, the "new women" were man-hating, man-imitating, cigarette-smoking shrews who refused their "natural" roles while fighting for rights that no real woman either wanted or needed.

Thus, during the belle époque at the end of the nineteenth century, French men could celebrate the centennial of the revolution that had established their basic human rights. French women could not. Victor Hugo predicted that whereas the eighteenth century had proclaimed the Rights of Man, the nineteenth would proclaim the Rights of Woman, but this did not prove true.[10] Instead, French women of the belle époque were still developing their first large feminist organizations and just beginning to educate the French nation about feminist grievances. Indeed, even today, two hundred years after the French Revolution, many of the issues raised by the feminists in this anthology are still at the heart of debates.

The feminist movement of the belle époque was not a homogeneous, monolithic phenomenon: then, as today, there were many varieties of feminism, many feminisms.[11] More than a dozen associations for political action were active by the turn of the century, and they represented a wide range of opinion. The older organizations (dating from the 1870s and 1880s) were strongly republican in their political philosophy, reflecting the French struggle to create the Third Republic during the 1870s. Their leadership, and most of their membership, came from the educated, urban (overwhelmingly Parisian) middle classes. Groups such as Léon Richer's *Ligue française pour le droit des femmes* (the LFDF: the French League for Women's Rights), Maria Deraismes's *Société pour l'amélioration du sort de la femme* (Society for the Improvement of Woman's Condition), and Hubertine Auclert's *Droit des femmes* (Women's Rights) and *Suffrage des femmes* (Women's Suffrage) supported republican France and sought to win the civil and political equality of women within it. They disagreed on priorities, such as seeking the vote, but they typically cooperated well.[12]

Notes

1. The bibliography for this volume lists only works published during the belle époque and later works about that period. The footnotes will add brief introductions to the woman question in earlier periods. A good starting place for such background is Claire G. Moses, *French Feminism,* or Maité Albistur and Daniel Armogathe, *Histoire du féminisme français.*

2. For example, in the essay on women in his Oxford history of modern France, Theodore Zeldin stated that "Fourier invented the word" (*France, 1848-1945,* 2 vols. [Oxford, 1973-77], 1:345) but gave no citation. Karen Offen has undertaken a careful study of this claim and found it in some French dictionaries and even in the writings of French feminists in the 1890s, but none of these claims has provided a verifiable usage in the writings of Fourier; see Offen's "Sur l'origine des mots 'féminisme' et 'féministe'"; "On the Origins of the Word 'Feminist' and 'Feminism'"; and "Defining Feminism: a Comparative Historical Approach." *Signs.* Claire Moses has also concluded that Fourier did not coin the terms; see her article "Debating the Present."

3. See Offen's study of this evolution and the claims made by Hubertine Auclert in part 5. For Auclert's role in popularizing the terms, see Steven C. Hause, *Hubertine Auclert.*

4. The supplement to the first edition of the OED acknowledges the French origin of "feminism" and cites *Athenaeum* magazine, April 27, 1895, as the earliest English usage. For American usage of the terms, see Nancy F. Cott, *The Grounding of Modern Feminism* (New Haven, 1987).

5. For a fuller discussion of these impediments, see Steven C. Hause with Anne R. Kenney, *Women's Suffrage,* 18-27 and esp. 254-81.

6. The legal treatment of French women as inferiors can be found throughout the original text of the Napoleonic Code, but it is most clear in the eight chapters of Title Five, "On Marriage" (Articles 144-228). The original text of Article 213, promulgated on March 17, 1803, stated simply: "The husband owes protection to his wife, the woman obedience to her husband." That text remained unchanged until Léon Blum's Popular Front government began reconsideration in the mid-1930s, resulting in the law of February 18, 1938. The expanded Article 213 of 1938 still identified the husband as "head of the family" and gave him specific powers, such as the choice of the family residence. The Vichy government of Marshal Pétain rewrote Article 213 in the law of September 22, 1942, asserting a traditional vision of the family in which the father was empowered to act "in the common interest." That text remained the law in France until the new feminist movement won a revision in the law of June 4, 1970 (currently in force), stating that "The spouses together assure the moral and material direction of the family."

7. Proudhon (1809-65) was one of the most important founders of anarchist thought and a leading influence on the shape of socialism in France. He was vehemently opposed to the emancipation of women, as he

showed in this oft-quoted line from his electoral program of 1848. For further translations of Proudhon's pronouncements on the woman question, see Susan Groag Bell and Karen M. Offen, eds., *Women, the Family, and Freedom,* 1:190-92 and 1:280-81; see also the comments of Hélène Brion in part 3. For further discussion of Proudhon, see Moses, *French Feminism,* and the works of Marilyn J. Boxer on socialism and feminism.

8. For an introduction to such cultural attitudes in the mid-nineteenth century, see Anne Martin-Fugier, *La Bourgeoise* (Paris, 1983).

9. For a discussion of women as "idols of perversity" in the arts, see Bram Dijkstra, *Idols of Perversity: Fantasies of Feminine Evil in Fin-de-siècle Culture* (Oxford, 1986). For a discussion of the "new women" in literature, see Jennifer Waelti-Walters, *Feminist Novelists of the Belle Epoque.*

10. Hugo (1802-85) supported the feminist movement. In 1853 he delivered a eulogy for Louise Julien that included the following: "Friends, in future times, in that beautiful and peaceful fraternal and social republic of the future, the role of women will be great. . . . The eighteenth century proclaimed the rights of man; the nineteenth century will proclaim the rights of woman" (*Oeuvres complètes* [Paris, 1968], 7:872); see Nelly Roussel's discussion of Hugo in part 1. For more on Hugo and feminism, see Moses, *French Feminism,* esp. 149; Patrick Bidelman, *Pariahs Stand Up!,* 10; and Hause, *Hubertine Auclert,* esp. 19-20.

11. The plural form, "feminisms," was used in a variety of ways during the belle époque. It appears, for example, in the title of one contemporary essay found in our bibliography, Jeanne Laloe's "Les Deux féminismes"; it is discussed, as the title shows, in Jean Rabaut's *Histoire des féminismes français* (Paris, 1978); and it survives in the title of an anthology from present-day France, Marks and Courtivron's *New French Feminisms: An Anthology* (Amhearst, 1980). For current usage of the plural form, see Jane Jensen, "*Ce n'est pas un hasard*: The Varieties of French Feminism," in Jolyon Howorth and George Ross, eds., *Contemporary France: A Review of Interdisciplinary Studies* 3 (1989): 114-43.

12. For an introduction to the range of the women's movement at the turn of the century, see Hause with Kenney, *Women's Suffrage*; Moses, *French Feminism;* Bidelman, *Pariahs Stand Up!*; Albistur and Armogathe, *Histoire du féminisme français*; and Laurence Klejman and Florence Rochefort, *L'Egalité en marche.*

Works Cited

Albistur, Maïté, and Daniel Armogathe. *Histoire du féminisme français.* 2 vols. Paris: Editions des femmes, 1977.

Bell, Susan Groag, and Karen M. Offen, eds. *Women, the Family and Freedom: The Debate in Documents, 1750-1950.* 2 vols. Stanford: Stanford UP, 1983.

Bidelman, Patrick. *Pariahs Stand Up! The Founding of the Liberal Feminist Movement in France, 1858-1889.* Westport, CT: Greenwood, 1982.

Boxer, Marilyn J. "French Socialism, Feminism, and the Family." *Third Republic/Troisième République,* 3-4 (1977): 128-67.

———. "Socialism Faces Feminism: The Failure of Synthesis in France, 1879-1914." In Marilyn J. Boxer and Jean H. Quataert, eds., *Socialist Women,* 75-111. New York: Greenwood, 1978.

———. "Socialism Faces Feminism in France, 1879-1913." Diss. Univ. of California-Riverside, 1975.

———. "When Radical and Socialist Women Were Joined: The Extraordinary Failure of Madeleine Pelletier." In Jane Slaughter and Robert Kern, eds., *European Women on the Left: Socialism, Feminism, and the Problems Faced by Political Women,* 57-74. Westport, CT: Greenwood, 1981.

Hause, Steven C. *Hubertine Auclert: The French Suffragette.* New Haven, Yale University Press, 1987.

Hause, Steven C., with Anne R. Kenney. *Women's Suffrage and Social Politics in the French Third Republic.* Princeton UP, 1984.

Klejman, Laurence, and Florence Rochefort. *L'Egalité en marche: le féminisme sous la Troisième République.* Paris: Editions des femmes, 1989.

Moses, Claire G. *French Feminism in the 19th Century.* Albany: SUNY P, 1984.

———. "Debating the Present, Writing the Past: 'Feminism' in French History and Historiography." *Radical History Review* 52 (1992): 79-94.

———. "Defining Feminism: A Comparative Historical Approach." *Signs* 14 (1988): 119-57.

———. "On the Origins of the Words 'Feminist' and 'Feminism.'" *Feminist Issues* 8 (1988).

———. "Sur l'origine des mots 'féminisme et féministe.'" *Revue d'histoire moderne et contemporaine* 34 (1987): 492-96.

Waelti-Walters, Jennifer. *Feminist Novelists of the Belle Epoque: Love as a Lifestyle.* Bloomington: Indiana UP, 1990.

KATHRYN GLEADLE (ESSAY DATE 1995)

SOURCE: Gleadle, Kathryn. Introduction to *The Early Feminists: Radical Unitarians and the Emergence of The Women's Rights Movement, 1831-51,* pp. 1-7. New York: St. Martin's Press, 1995.

In the following excerpt, Gleadle argues that the roots of the women's rights movement preceded the Seneca Falls Convention by at least two decades, and that its principles were initially articulated and embraced by feminist activity inspired by radical unitarianism.

The nineteenth-century woman has been subject to exhaustive historical scrutiny over the past two decades. The dichotomy between the realities of her iniquitous legal and social standing on the one hand, and the cultural worship of the womanly nature by contemporaries on the other, has made her a fascinating object of study. Moreover, it was during that century that women first began to organise themselves into campaigns to demand reforms in their status. Indeed, historians have now delved beyond the suffragettes' battles to argue that from the 1850s onwards, a small, but vocal group of middle-class women started to agitate for better education, improved legal rights (especially within marriage), employment opportunities and the right to vote.[1]

This book seeks to highlight the weaknesses of the existing historiography of early Victorian feminism, by addressing itself to the origins of these campaigns. In particular, it questions the historical assumption that the women's rights movement began in the 1850s. The study of a particular group of reforming activists, whom I have termed the 'radical unitarians', demonstrates that it was during the 1830s and 1840s that the essential ideologies and personnel networks which were to determine the feminist movement of the succeeding decades were laid.

The existence of a feminist tradition dating back to the early 1830s has been woefully overlooked by previous histories of the women's rights movement. While the work of some of the more famous of these radicals is often alluded to, their vital role as the direct precursors of the women's rights movement has not been subject to analysis.[2] Biographies of some of the more prominent figures, such as Mary Howitt, W. J. Fox and W. J. Linton point to the existence of such a feminist circle, but fail to expand upon its nature or significance.[3] Jane Rendall's work on the origins of modern feminism has performed a great service in articulating the cultural forces shaping progressive debates on the woman question (she points in particular to the contribution of Evangelical and republican discourses). Moreover, Olive Banks has considered the role of Evangelical, Enlightenment and socialist influences on the development of feminist thought during the early stages of the movement.[4] While she refers to the radicalism of those such as W. J. Fox (a figure central to this work), neither of these valuable studies explores the existence of a widespread, nascent women's rights movement in the 1830s and 1840s.

A number of historians, pointing to the prevalence of literary figures in the early days of the organised campaigns, have noted the existence of a 'literary feminism'. The activity of writing, it is suggested, enables 'power, self-assertion, active shaping rather than passive acceptance',[5] and thus provided an appropriate route to feminist awareness. This study relies heavily upon the activity and work of literary circles and accepts the important role which writing might play in the formation of a feminist consciousness. It also acknowledges the comparative unconventionality of literary coteries, which doubtless provided their female adherents with a freedom and opportunity for self-expression often denied them elsewhere. However, it is contended that an ignorance of the comprehensive reforming activity and ideological creeds of such groups has prohibited a full understanding of the role of the literary intelligentsia in the early women's rights movements.

Many other historians have tended to assume that between the great declamations of Mary Wollstonecraft in the 1790s and the beginnings of the organised campaign in the 1850s, feminism fell into something of a wasteland. Indeed, many histories present feminism during this period as little more than a series of isolated protests, by such figures as Sydney Smith or Lady Morgan.[6] This book argues that a specific feminist movement emerged during this period, based upon a network of writers and reformers, who supported and relied upon each others' work. It is to this precise group of activists, who were part of a self-conscious movement, that we must turn in order to understand the development of the Victorian feminist movement.

The notable exceptions to the portrayal of early feminist activity as isolated phenomena are the studies of communitarian and Owenite feminism during the 1830s and 1840s.[7] However, a concentration on this aspect of early feminism has exacerbated a tendency to consider feminism during these years as an extreme and minority movement. As such it is considered to have had little in common with the women's rights movement proper, which is thought to have begun many years later, at the instigation of a group of comfortably well-off women, many of whom came from the great dissenting Unitarian families. However, as will become apparent during the course of this book, the campaigners of the 1850s were the direct heirs of a particular feminist tradition, which was built upon an amalgamation of communitarian and Unitarian philosophies.

The essentially intellectual nature of this early feminism points to the second way in which this book dissents from much of the customary historiography. In searching for the roots of feminist activity, many historians have tended to focus upon the existence of collective female political action and the development of a specific female consciousness. In recent years such an approach has been exemplified by the work of feminist historians such as C. Smith-Rosenberg and L. Faderman who have evaluated the importance of friendship and sisterhood in women's experience.[8] These models have greatly influenced historians' conception of the nineteenth-century women's rights movement. This is clearly seen in the work of Jane Rendall, who adopts such a framework in her study of the two great Victorian feminists, Barbara Leigh Smith Bodichon and Bessie Raynor Parkes. Philippa Levine's *Victorian Feminism 1850-1900* is similarly informed by such an approach. This excellent monograph is very much concerned with the growth of female support networks as a vital accompaniment to the development of the women's rights movement.[9] Many other studies have pointed to the importance of female participation in such movements as the anti-Corn Law agitation and the anti-slavery campaign as a crucial precursor to feminist activity. This is especially true of those studies which emerged in the wake of the suffragette movement. Many feminist historians from this period tended to look back to a tradition of direct female political action in order to make sense of their own campaigns, rather than seeking to understand the intellectual origins of the movement.[10]

Certainly many of the women who were to become important figures in the Victorian feminist movement, such as Emilie Venturi and Priscilla Bright, appear to have played an active role in both these movements.[11] However, as this work will seek to demonstrate, such an approach is not always the most fruitful or accurate means of understanding the development of a specific feminist tradition. As Kenneth Corfield has shown, the relationship between anti-slavery campaigning and British feminism has often been greatly exaggerated. Certainly when the American feminist-abolitionist, Lucretia Mott, visited Britain in 1840, she was greatly disappointed by the female anti-slavery campaigners, complaining that they had 'little confidence in women's action either separately or co-jointly with men, except as drudges'.[12] However, Mott and the other American activists found their feminist sympathies did strike chords with the particular radical intelligentsia with which this study is concerned and with whom they formed strong and lasting bonds.[13] Therefore, to understand the close relationship between the anti-slavery movement and feminism what we need to focus upon is not necessarily collective female action, but the existence of a particular reforming outlook - shared by men and women alike.

Analysing this progressive circle is vital in understanding the beginnings of Victorian feminism. However, in tracing the origins of the women's rights movement back to a specific group of radical reformers - the 'radical unitarians', this book also seeks to re-examine the traditional historiography concerning the relationship between the Unitarian and feminist movements. It is a connection which has often been commented upon by historians.[14] Although, as Olive Banks and Philippa Levine have shown, the majority of 'first wave' feminists hailed from an Anglican background,[15] Unitarian women did make a huge contribution to the women's rights movement. This fact is particularly striking as the Unitarian movement was numerically very small. Yet, despite this, it managed to produce many of the leading names in Victorian feminism, as well as a host of lesser-known activists. Barbara Leigh Smith, Bessie Parkes, Elizabeth Malleson, Elizabeth Reid, Eleanor Rathbone, Emmeline Pethick-Lawrence, the Biggs sisters, Emilie Venturi and Caroline Stansfeld, Eliza Fox, Helen Taylor and Clementia Taylor, all came from Unitarian backgrounds. The reasons why this should have been so are clearly vital in appreciating the nature of Victorian feminism.

The conventional historiography explains the widespread participation of Unitarian women in the campaign in terms of the superior education and liberal backgrounds which their Unitarian heritage bequeathed to them. Such is the approach pursued by Sheila Herstein in her biography of Barbara Leigh Smith, for example.[16] Nevertheless, recent studies of Unitarianism, such as those by Ruth Watts and John Seed have noted that Unitarians were often extremely conservative socially, persisting in patriarchal attitudes and relationships towards female members.[17] It is this paradox that needs to be investigated fully in order to truly understand the appeal of early Victorian feminism to many Unitarian women.

However, of even greater importance in tracing the origins of the women's rights movement, is the need to distinguish between Unitarianism proper, and the offshoot of progressive thinkers from the main body of the movement—the 'radical unitarians'.

The term 'radical unitarian', as it is used in the following chapters, should be seen as a fluid category. It is argued that it may be applied to the adherents of certain reforming circles who came to develop a distinctive ideological perspective. These writers and reformers entertained close links with the socialist, secularist, Unitarian and utilitarian movements of the day—to whose publications they often contributed. While the feminist slant of a couple of these journals, such as the *Monthly Repository* and the *New Moral World* has been acknowledged,[18] the feminism of the majority has not been explored. A handful of these publications, such as the *Star in the East* or the *Reasoner* have been studied in the context of the cooperative, secularist or Owenite movements of the day, but their progressive angle on the woman question has been neglected.[19] This is not least because of an ignorance of the network of radical unitarian feminist journalists who wrote for such papers. By the 1840s, these same journalists were playing a leading role in such publications as *Douglas Jerrold's Weekly Newspaper,* the *Howitt's Journal* and the *People's Journal,* the feminist aspect of which has been greatly overlooked. Catering for a wide audience, these journals did not always follow a feminist line. Their significance is that they offered a mouthpiece to the growing network of feminist writers to air their ideas. Indeed, by the late 1840s, these journals acted as a central forum for the developing feminist movement.

Certainly, all radical unitarians appear to have advocated progressive views on women and most (despite the anachronism of the term), were of 'feminist' views.[20] This work uses the terms 'feminism' and 'feminists' to apply to those who not only wished to improve women's position, but also had a cogent awareness of women's subordination in relation to men, and wished this anomaly to be revoked. The radical unitarians formulated just such an insight in their critiques of contemporary society.

The radical unitarian coterie was born from the Unitarian ministry of William Johnson Fox at South Place Chapel in Finsbury, London. As Olive Banks explains briefly in *Faces of Feminism,* Fox's extreme views on female suffrage, marriage and divorce, combined with his own personal problems, alienated him from the mainstream Unitarian body and caused him to resign from the Unitarian church.[21] In this book it is suggested that this breach was instrumental in precipitating the formation of the feminist movement. The willingness of the majority of the congregation to remain loyal to Fox effectively gave him a sanction to continue his feminist activities and unconventional lifestyle. From this point onwards, South Place Chapel became the breeding-ground for feminist ideas and discussions, with the *Monthly Repository* acting as a much-needed platform.

The origins of radical unitarianism thus lay within the mainstream Unitarian movement and radical unitarian circles continued to enjoy direct input from individuals who were either of direct Unitarian descent, or who were frequenters of Unitarian churches. Nevertheless, many of its adherents were not connected to Unitarianism itself. Indeed many do not appear to have ever made formal contact with the Unitarian denomination. Radical unitarian groups appear to have attracted those seeking a religion which sought to capture the heart of Christian ethics. Indeed it appealed to many from the liberal wing of the Anglican church, who exhibited a disillusionment with what they perceived as the ceremony, formality and pomp of establishment religion. Yet, despite this loose relationship with Unitarianism, the radical unitarians continued to be vitally informed by Unitarian thought. They shared, or took to greater extremes, many of its central premises—such as the emphasis on education and the need to search for truth; political radicalism; a tremendous faith in science and support for technology; a fascination with German Romanticism; and also the close relationship which Unitarians fostered with literary circles.

By the late 1840s, the radical unitarians had developed a powerful social, political and cultural critique of modern society, and women's role within it. Their proclivity to consider new modes of social organisation, and their willingness to use the imaginative arts to penetrate to both the truths and potential of society meant that the barriers to conventional ways of thinking about women might be lifted. This, combined with the environmentalist ideas they inherited from both the Owenite and Unitarian movements, made for a very comprehensive perception of women's oppression. Mary Leman Grimstone deftly encapsulated the need for such a broad approach to women's liberation in her declamation that, 'much has to be put from the literature, institutions, laws, customs, and manners to redeem man from the degrading marks of his own ignorant pride, as well as to raise her from her miserable vassalage'.[22]

The wide agenda for female emancipation which the early feminists thus formulated created an awareness that women might only be freed through a radical evolution in the existing culture. They perceived that true liberation would be achieved not merely by short-term measures, such as the abrogation of unjust laws. What was equally required was a far more profound revolution—one in which people were re-educated about their ideas concerning women; in which cultural representations and literary myths about women were replaced by the 'truth'; in which ancient conventions of behaviour were overturned; and in which women themselves learnt to adopt new modes of behaviour to break free of their 'slave' characters.

Such goals could not be achieved overnight. They would have to be won by a long-term evolution in the country's culture.

This analysis of female emancipation was a product of the radical unitarian confidence that society was undergoing a gradual process of liberalisation, leading towards a state of perfect civilisation. The *Monthly Repository* spoke of 'a period like the present of mental activity and improving reason, when every ancient opinion is brought to the crucible'. The early feminists placed women's emancipation in precisely this context. Hence, *Eliza Cook's Journal* claimed that a march of civilisation was under way, in which religious disabilities had been removed; the serfs had been emancipated; and the condition of the working classes was improving. The liberation of women, it was claimed, would in time also be effected by this great movement.[23] Whereas later suffragettes were to stake their feminist claims upon a belief that female rights had been gradually eroded during the nineteenth century,[24] most of the early feminists were confident that they had already begun to detect signs of improvement in women's condition within this universal trend. 'Women are better off dear Barbara than they were', proclaimed the young Bessie Raynor Parkes in 1847.[25] Such declarations chimed in with the self-perception of the radical unitarians. They believed themselves to be at the forefront of modern improvement. Their ideas were not eccentric or fantastical propositions, but reflected, they opined, real developments at the cutting edge of cultural progress.

Originally a small and frequently maligned coterie, by the 1840s many radical unitarians were beginning to assume a more prominent position within contemporary culture. Their visionary agenda had led them to embark upon a number of specific campaigns to elevate women's position—including the reform of women's legal position; an attempt to secure female suffrage on the Chartist programme; efforts to tackle the problem of prostitution; and the launching of a unique experiment in adult education. It is these early feminists who were the pioneers of the Victorian women's rights movement.

It is my personal view that these neglected reformers developed a feminist vision which it is important for us to recapture today. Their thought and work remains a vital part of our women's rights heritage—and one that should be embraced. It may well be that the insights they developed have enduring significance for our situation, for the path modern feminism has taken remains alien to the lives and values of many women.

The radical unitarians articulated a feminism in which, although women's rights to equal treatment with men was essential, this was only half the battle. Indeed, they did not promote women purely in those areas where they might achieve like men, but were also keen to herald the particular contribution women might make to society in their capacity as mothers. Indeed, they celebrated the importance of the domestic situation, encouraging men to also embrace the caring values of the home and to reconsider their role within it. They wished women to advance in society not purely on men's terms, but hoped that the emancipation of women would form part of a wider cultural revolution, in which new values and priorities might triumph. Today, when society is increasingly geared to a work culture, in which the needs of children and working parents are often sacrificed, the early feminists' wish to truly abolish the dichotomy of separate-spheres ideology remains a valuable lesson. Indeed, to place feminism within a wider cultural focus, to see it not merely as securing the rights of women, but as advancing the wider needs of society and the health and happiness of the next generation; this is the early feminists' bequest.

SYLVIA D. HOFFERT (ESSAY DATE 1995)

SOURCE: Hoffert, Sylvia D. Introduction to *When Hens Crow: The Woman's Right Movement in Antebellum America,* pp. 1-14. Bloomington, Ind.: Indiana University Press, 1995.

In the following essay, Hoffert argues that American women who demanded a voice in national and domestic affairs in the first half of the nineteenth century created a philosophy that escaped the narrow confines of the ideology of Republican Motherhood, enabling women of future generations to enter public life.

Let me begin with a fable. "There once lived in a Farm Yard a great many Roosters and Hens, and it chanced one morning that a young Hen with a very fine voice began to crow. Thereupon all the Roosters hurried together and solemnly declared that there was nothing so dreadful as a Crowing Hen! Now there was in the Yard a Rooster who had always been feeble and could only cackle, but when the Hen mentioned this, the Roosters shook their heads and said, 'Females do not understand Logic.'" The moral to the story: "There is a great deal of difference between a Cackling Rooster and a Crowing Hen."[1]

ON THE SUBJECT OF...

SARAH WINNEMUCCA (1844?-1891)

Sarah Winnemucca was born in approximately 1844 on Paiute land near Humboldt Lake in what is now Nevada. In 1866 she traveled to Fort McDermit to persuade the United States military to put an end to white aggression against her tribe. Shortly thereafter, a segment of the Paiute were resettled to a reservation at Malheur, Oregon. In the ensuing years, Winnemucca was frequently engaged as a military interpreter and liaison to the Paiute, a capacity in which she served when hostilities between U. S. armed forces and the Paiute, Bannock, and Shoshoni people erupted in the Bannock War of 1878. The conflict ended with the indefinite relocation of Paiute prisoners to the Yakima reservation in Washington State. Winnemucca, meanwhile, spoke out publicly in a number of lectures designed to raise awareness of inhumane practices demonstrated by government agents and missionaries on the reservation.

In 1883, Winnemucca began a lengthy lecture tour of New England, denouncing U. S. government policy toward Native Americans, and while speaking in Boston she formed a friendship with Elizabeth Palmer Peabody, an educator, and her sister Mary Mann. Both women encouraged Winnemucca in her political activities, and provided her with the financial and editorial assistance to write her autobiography, *Life Among the Piutes: Their Wrongs and Claims* (1883). In *Life Among the Piutes* Winnemucca recounts, in stark detail, the violence, injustices, and devastation inflicted upon the Paiutes between 1844 and 1883.

Winnemucca is noted for her endeavors to overturn negative stereotypes of Native Americans through her lectures, stage appearances, and autobiography, and her espousal of the peaceful coexistence of whites and Native Americans. She has come to represent the struggles of Native American women in the nineteenth century, and her autobiography is studied as an important cultural document.

This fable is instructive on a number of levels. It testifies to the control that men traditionally have had over public discourse and by extension public life (the right to "crow"). It suggests that "crowing" (male language) is not only different from but better than "cackling" (female language). It attests to the ability of some women to appropriate male language and express themselves with a clarity and eloquence that is unexpected and to the ease and predictability with which that appropriation evokes a strong response. It stands as witness to the cohesiveness of the male community and its determination to protect the prerogatives of men against the incursions of presumptuous women. It testifies to man's need to know that, whatever his inadequacies, he is different from woman. And it stands as witness to the wish on the part of some to silence women's public voices, as well as to their unwillingness to participate in public debate with women. It was from within this sort of cultural context that a group of articulate male and female reformers in the mid-nineteenth century collectively began to challenge the ideas that men and women were inherently different and that American public life and the discourse that characterized and accompanied it should be a male preserve.

The American woman's rights movement represents one of the most notable and dramatic examples of an attempt, in this case by a small cadre of both male and female activists, to organize efforts to improve the legal, economic, political, and social status of women. Thus, it is not surprising that as widespread interest in the history of women emerged in the 1970s, scholars turned their attention to the movement. The result was that the story of the Seneca Falls convention became well known, the significance of reform influences in general and abolitionism in particular to the development of the woman's rights movement were generally acknowledged, the movement's goals were identified, and the names of its most prominent leaders, while they may not have become household words, became at least familiar to the well-informed.

Despite their predictable interest in woman's rights activism, however, pioneers in the field of women's history tended to concentrate on something other than the woman's rights movement during the antebellum period. In her survey of the movement, Eleanor Flexner, for example, devoted only a few pages in two short chapters to its organization between 1848 and 1860. Keith Melder, looking back to the early nineteenth century, concerned himself with those factors that contributed to the development of the movement rather than with the movement itself. And Ellen Carol DuBois used the antebellum movement as the starting point from which to trace the subsequent development of organized feminist activism.[2] Others who followed focused on the philosophy and activities of the movement from the point of view of individuals like Elizabeth Cady Stanton, Susan B. Anthony, and Lucy Stone.[3]

This book looks at the leaders of the antebellum woman's rights movement as a group and is concerned with broadening our understanding of the ideology of the early woman's rights movement, the way that the woman's rights vanguard expressed that ideology, the strategies that they devised to attract attention to their message, and the response that their message elicited from some of those who were exposed to it. It argues that they accomplished a good deal during the first twelve years of the movement's existence. First, those who led the movement developed an ideology and a public language or idiom that helped women move beyond the limits placed on them by the domestic ideal and Republican Motherhood. They also developed strategies guaranteed to elicit responses to their demands which created a political culture that could no longer ignore the participation of women.

Throughout the ages, communication for women, most of whom were excluded from public life and thus from public discourse because of their gender, was largely confined to the private sphere. Certainly, there were exceptions. Queens and noblewomen, by virtue of their rank, both spoke and wrote for a public audience. Women with an intellectual bent published books of poetry and prose, sometimes under their own names and sometimes under the names of others. Women testified in court, participated in public demonstrations, led armies, lobbied legislators, and circulated petitions. They did so as individuals and sometimes in groups.

But women never had the opportunity to contribute to public language, to debate public issues, or to participate in public affairs to the same degree that was possible for most men. The degree of their exclusion and their consciousness of it varied depending on time, circumstance, and place. That is what makes the meeting that took place on Sunday, July 16, 1848, so significant. On that day Elizabeth Cady Stanton, Jane Hunt, Martha Coffin Wright, and her sister Lucretia Mott sat around a mahogany table in Mary Ann McClintock's parlor in Waterloo, New York, quite conscious of their exclusion and quite determined to create a collective public language for all American women, thus building on the efforts of those individuals who had spoken out before on behalf of the female sex. They were equally determined to force American men not only to listen to their message but to acknowledge their political competency and the legitimacy of their message by responding to it.

They spent that day writing a series of documents that they intended to present to the first woman's rights convention scheduled to be held three days later in the Wesleyan Chapel in Seneca Falls, three miles away. By Wednesday they had completed their task, and they presented to the audience of the convention a Declaration of Sentiments, modeled after Jefferson's Declaration of Independence, which specified the disabilities that women suffered in American society. In that document they asserted that "men and women are created equal," that women had the same "inalienable rights" as men, and that women had the right to withdraw their "allegiance" from any government that denied them their rights and to demand the institution of a new government which would protect their rights. They blamed men for denying women such things as the vote, the right to control their own property, guardianship of their children, and equal opportunities in education and employment. Those who participated in the convention responded by passing a series of twelve resolutions asserting women's right to redress of their grievances. Those resolutions set forth five quite specific goals. They demanded that any statute or legal precedent that placed women in a position of inequality with men be invalidated, they insisted that men be held to the same standards of moral behavior as women, they claimed for women equal access to education and economic opportunity, they demanded that women be granted the right to vote, and they asserted women's right to speak in public from both podium and pulpit in order to pursue their goals.[4] The Declaration of Sentiments called for changes in law and social custom as well as in the attitudes upon which both were based.

The speeches and documents presented at the Seneca Falls convention in 1848 set forth the goals of what was eventually to become the organized feminist movement in the United States.[5] The Declaration of Sentiments was a document born of frustration and indignation as well as of optimism and hope. Most of the ideas it expressed had been articulated before, sometimes privately (as in Abigail Adams's 1776 plea to her husband to "remember the ladies") and sometimes in public (as in Mary Wollstonecraft's *A Vindication of the Rights of Woman* [1792]).

Public protest about the inferior status of women in the English-speaking world can be traced back to the seventeenth century. Early British feminists established a construct that defined women as a sociological group and argued that the condition of woman was a product of social convention rather than nature. But those early protesters apparently had little if any direct influence on the generations that followed them.[6]

The same cannot be said for those in the eighteenth century who critiqued the condition of women. Eighteenth-century British feminists, responding to the continued subordination of women, not only demanded that educational opportunities for women be improved but also exploited the increasing respectability of sentiment to undergird their demands that women be granted more rights.[7] Their protests were continued in nineteenth-century America by such notables as Frances Wright, Sarah and Angelina Grimké, and Ernestine Rose, who spoke out eloquently in public against the subjugation of women. Their appropriation of the right to lecture from podium and platform caused a great uproar among the clergy and among others who understood, whether consciously or not, that women's right to speak established the foundation of their right to extend their participation in public affairs. It was this controversy combined with the legislative debate over the right of New York women to control their own property and the experience of women who had confronted gender discrimination from within the abolitionist and other reform movements that provided the impetus for the Seneca Falls convention in particular and feminist protest in general during the antebellum period.[8]

The Declaration of Sentiments and the speeches given in support of its resolutions struck a responsive chord in those who attended the convention and brought derision from some but not all of the representatives of the popular press.[9] In an age when for all practical purposes American women's claim on public rhetoric was tentative at best, the presentation of the Declaration of Sentiments can best be described as the first organized attempt to build on previous individual efforts by women like the Grimké sisters to create an idiom through which women could express themselves politically as a group and articulate an ideology which would help to extend their right to participate in public life.

The ideas of the early feminists and the way in which they chose to express those ideas were of primary importance in directing the early public debate on the subject of woman's rights. But some aspects of the ideology that they developed and the language that they used to express their discontent have only begun to receive the attention that they deserve. That is unfortunate because, as I will argue, both verbal and nonverbal language and the ideas that they expressed were the single most important weapons of the early woman's rights movement. They represented the desire and determination on the part of woman's rights advocates to identify themselves, to describe the female experience, and to trace their history as well as to renegotiate gender relations in all aspects of American life. In the absence of a national organization, they served as the organizing principles which held the movement together before the Civil War. Moreover, the transformation of society that woman's rights activists envisioned was expressed in words long before it began to take place in fact. Their ideology and the way they chose to express it was dissonant, provocative, and compelling enough to elicit a response from those who were exposed to it. It was the resulting discourse that established the basis for the pursuit of gender equality in the United States and full participation for women in economic and political life. For these reasons, the ideology and language of the early woman's rights movement and the response that it evoked merit closer attention by historians.

. . . The degree to which boys and girls were socialized to occupy separate spheres before the Civil War influenced the way they were taught to express themselves. Because the public political roles for women were limited before the Civil War, there was no reason to teach female children to express themselves in that milieu.[10] Therefore, the language of most women did not have the same political dimension as did the language of most men. That being the case, women could not effectively articulate their grievances and demand redress until they had legitimized their right either to use the same political language that men used or to create a political idiom of their own.

Because it was exclusive, political language was both a resource and a symbol of identity for men. It represented a source of power that was gender-specific.[11] The fact that men discussed politics in public—and the *way* that they discussed the subject—linguistically connected them to political power in the same way that fraternal, athletic, and military language connected them with their clubs, teams, and regiments. It provided them with what sociolinguists would call "competency," an asset derived by one member of a group from being able to communicate with other members of a group using an idiom specific to that group.[12] Political language, therefore, carried with it political competency and served as an instrument which helped men to establish and maintain their masculinity.

When a small cadre of women, supported by sympathetic male supporters, laid claim to the right to use political language, they both challenged male political and social hegemony and exposed the tenuousness of the mid-nineteenth-century definitions of maleness. By rejecting domestic metaphors as a way of expressing their demands, woman's rights advocates laid claim to an enhanced place for women in the public world rather than confirming their traditional place in the home. In essence, they asserted the right to express themselves in a language to which, because of their previous exclusion, they had no claim and in so doing forced their audiences to reassess the meaning of gender in America. The debate that followed was, therefore, as much a debate over what it meant to be a man and a woman as it was over whether or not women should be granted more rights.

Feminist historians have added yet another dimension to the study of discourse. Scholars such as Carroll Smith-Rosenberg have argued that women avoid the oppression of language by modifying and changing its meaning in order to fulfill their own needs, express themselves in their own way, and achieve their own ends. By directing attention toward images and metaphors, this model encourages us to try to understand the ways in which "words both reflect and alter the world in which they are spoken."[13]

Smith-Rosenberg and others have also enhanced our understanding of the cultural context from which the movement for woman's rights arose. They describe a context characterized by a complex interaction of a number of factors which together set the stage for public political protest on the part of women and the men who supported their demand for equal rights. Among the most important of those factors were the rise of commercial capitalism, the beginnings of industrialization, and the growth of towns and cities. These developments affected the lives of women in a number of ways. First they began the process of removing economic production from the home and thus changing women's domestic roles. This process relieved middle- and upper-class women of some kinds of productive labor. They paid at least two prices for that relief. One was that, as Jeanne Boydston has pointed out, the work they continued to do in the home was marginalized—if not in reality, at least in terms of public perception. The second was that they became increasingly dependent upon those male breadwinners willing to support them and their children. Popular authors also subjected them to a set of prescriptions, described by Barbara Welter as the "cult of true womanhood," that designated the domestic sphere as woman's proper place and demanded that middle-class women, black as well as white, also exhibit such characteristics as piety, purity, and submission to male authority.[14] Nancy Cott and others have suggested, however, that the female culture that developed from gender segregation may have contributed to a refined sense of gender identity among women from which the demand for equal rights could evolve.[15] For less privileged women, the rise of commercial capitalism and industrialization meant that they often found it necessary to seek employment outside the home. While they too established a distinctive female culture, that culture was significantly different from that of women in the middle and upper classes.[16] Economic development also brought about changes in the law which affected women. States like New York led the way in attempts to make regulations involving debt, bankruptcy, and liability more responsive to changing economic conditions. One of the results was the passage of laws granting married women the right to more control over their property.[17]

The growth of towns and cities began the process of concentrating and making more visible social problems such as poverty and drunkenness, thus making them hard to ignore. At the same time it brought together large numbers of women with the sense of moral superiority and disinterested social responsibility, time, and energy to organize benevolent societies in order to deal with those problems.[18] That propensity was encouraged by the social activism of religious groups like the Quakers as well as by the religious revivals of the Second Great Awakening and the spread of evangelical Protestantism, whose millennial vision demanded that true Christians, men and women alike, work to improve the world.[19] The reform movements which resulted welcomed women's participation even while they typically segregated them. In many cases, it was their experiences within those reform movements that forced activists to confront and respond to discrimination based on gender. Indeed, among the most important precipitating events leading to the Seneca Falls convention were the 1840 split in the American Anti-Slavery Society over the participation of women in the organization and the exclusion of female delegates from the World Anti-Slavery Convention in London that same year.[20] Despite this problem, however, benevolent societies and reform movements responding to the effects of social and economic change provided women with an unprecedented opportunity to develop their leadership, fundraising, and public speaking skills and made them aware of the limitations of relying on moral suasion to achieve their goals.[21]

The existing political culture also set the stage for the rise of the woman's rights movement. As Linda Kerber has pointed out, the political culture created after the American Revolution encouraged women to carry out their political roles within the home as Republican Mothers by training future republican citizens. But while Republican Motherhood limited women's political role, it also encouraged an improvement in women's educational opportunities, opportunities that would eventually lead women to take an interest in issues not directly related to either housekeeping or child rearing.[22]

The early nineteenth century was also characterized by an increase in the numbers of white men who could vote.[23] As long as there were restrictions on the numbers of men allowed to participate in political activities, the exclusion of women did not seem quite so egregious. But with the advent of universal, white, adult, manhood suffrage, the exclusion of women from voting and holding office was magnified since it placed them on a par with children, slaves, Native-Americans, convicts, and the mentally incompetent as the only groups left who were denied the vote.

All of these factors combined to produce the kind of climate necessary to encourage some women to develop a consciousness of the inequities to which they were being subjected. Personal circumstances determined which aspects of gender discrimination triggered feminist consciousness and brought individual women into the woman's rights movement. For Elizabeth Cady Stanton it was the restrictiveness of life as a housewife in Seneca Falls combined with her earlier resentment of laws which oppressed women, social custom that denied them access to higher education, and the lack of opportunity for women like Lucretia Mott to participate as equals with men in the World Anti-Slavery Convention.[24] For Susan B. Anthony it was experiences like the public humiliation of being refused the right to speak from the floor of a Sons of Temperance meeting.[25] For Lucretia Mott it was things like the realization that in her Quaker school male teachers earned twice as much as female teachers.[26] And for Lucy Stone it was her anger at being denied the right to vote as a member in the affairs of her church and the attitude of Congregational ministers toward women who wished to speak in public.[27]

The experience of the men who participated in the woman's rights movement was somewhat different. For men like Gerrit Smith, Samuel May, and Wendell Phillips, sensitivity toward gender discrimination came from their association with female friends and family members, their reform activities in abolition and temperance, and their outraged sense of justice when faced with the consequences of the belief that women were not the equals of men.[28] But for men and women alike, it was the anger that resulted from their personal sensitivity to discrimination based on gender that encouraged them collectively to seek social, economic, and political change by participating in the early woman's rights movement.

Early woman's rights activists, working within this context, depended upon ideas expressed both verbally and nonverbally rather than on institutions and organizations to try to change their world. These so-called strong-minded women and their male supporters appropriated an inherently sexist political philosophy and a political language created by men to serve their own ends. After identifying the leaders of this reform movement and discussing their relationships to one another and how they attempted to maintain those relationships, we will turn to an examination of aspects of the ideological origins of their demand for equal rights, the metaphors they used to express their ideas, the composition of their audience and how it was cultivated, and how some of those in that audience interpreted the message and responded to it.

Using woman's rights speeches, convention proceedings, tracts, pamphlets, newspaper reports and editorials, and articles from reform periodicals as well as the personal papers of such leaders as Lucretia Mott, Elizabeth Cady Stanton, and Susan B. Anthony, we will address a number of issues. The first concerns the role of both verbal and nonverbal forms of communication in cementing the casual network of friendship and reform sympathies that served as the basis for group identity and solidarity among the early leaders of the woman's rights movement. The second is an attempt to explain how early woman's rights advocates were able to move beyond the ideology and rhetoric of Republican Motherhood to demand an enhanced public political role. That ideology erected two barriers to expanding woman's political life. First, it defined her political role as private and therefore thwarted the efforts of women to expand their political activities into the public sphere. It also defined her political role in terms of her relationship with others. I will argue that in order for women to move beyond the ideology of Republican Motherhood, they had to embrace a different philosophy, one filtered through the natural rights doctrine of John Locke, early utilitarianism, and common sense philosophy of the Scottish Enlightenment. The resulting hybrid ideology provided those who became woman's rights advocates with a way of conceptualizing a political role for women that was not dependent upon domestic relationships or woman's work in benevolence, and allowed women to separate themselves from men, children, home, and church, and to claim the rights of citizenship based on the principles of individualism and self-interest rather than on the principles of self-sacrifice.

Many studies of the woman's rights movement are more concerned with its goals and tactics than they are with an in-depth analysis of its ideology.[29] Those scholars who do address the issue of its ideology argue convincingly that a number of influences such as evangelical Protestantism, Romanticism, Transcendentalism, and abolitionism combined with Enlightenment ideas and the principles of natural rights to bring about the early woman's rights movement.[30] But those who acknowledge feminist indebtedness to Enlightenment philosophers do not elaborate enough either to identify explicitly which of their ideas were the most significant or to explain in detail how those ideas were used by those who spoke out for the cause of woman's rights before the Civil War. Some even conclude that the Enlightenment provided women with little guidance in their attempts to establish for themselves a political persona in the new republic or argue that its legacy was "an extraordinarily confusing one."[31] More recently, Rosemarie Zagarri has challenged these assessments by illustrating how Scottish Enlightenment philosophers like Adam Smith and David Hume contributed to the concept of Republican Motherhood, but she does not carry her analysis beyond the early national period.[32] It is my intention, therefore, to try to enhance our understanding of how Enlightenment philosophy, particularly ideas derived from early utilitarianism and the Scottish Common Sense School, read both in the original and in diluted popularized versions, helped woman's rights activists justify their claim to equal social and political rights and economic opportunity.

Those who were most active in speaking out for the cause of woman's rights before the Civil War rejected metaphors most closely associated with woman's traditional sphere of home and benevolence in favor of the metaphors of nature, combined with those referring to the oppression of slavery, architectural renovation, machines, the millennium, and war, to express their discontent and articulate their reform ideology. This combination of metaphors provided them with a language which bound them together as a group and provided them with an especially effective way to promote their cause by rhetorically placing women in contexts that had traditionally been controlled and dominated by men. It also helped them to establish their political competency and provoked those in their audience to reassess their ideas about gender roles and relations.

Finally, I will focus on the way early woman's rights advocates cultivated their audience and the response they elicited when they made their demands public. The audience that was most publicly articulate in its response to the demands of these reformers and, therefore, the one that can be most systematically studied was composed of journalists representing two different kinds of periodicals: the newspapers of the penny press and reform journals. Newspapers had traditionally been an important weapon in the political arsenal of men. They became even more important in the mid-nineteenth century when, because of the development of paper and printing technology, new marketing techniques, and the rise of literacy, newspapers could be published and sold quickly and cheaply. Political in focus but not necessarily partisan, they increasingly contained human-interest stories as well as political and commercial information.[33]

Historians of the woman's rights movement have observed in passing that before the Civil War the popular press was generally contemptuous of woman's rights advocates and did little or nothing to help their cause.[34] But a systematic study of the matter using primary sources indicates that this assessment is not entirely accurate. The attention of newspaper editors was critical for the promotion of woman's rights demands. Silence on the part of the press would have condemned the movement, which had no official press of its own, to obscurity if not virtual invisibility as far as the general public was concerned. The leaders of the woman's rights movement intuitively understood that fact and quite consciously developed strategies designed to assure that newspaper editors reported their activities and responded to their demands. By manipulating the penny press and its male editors, woman's rights activists succeeded in directing toward themselves and their message the kind of attention that was crucial to the advancement of their interests and made male newspaper editors, both sympathetic and unsympathetic, unwitting and sometimes unwilling accomplices in the effort to gain more rights for women.

Careful analysis of the amount and kind of newspaper coverage directed towards the woman's movement in the Northeast and middle sections of the country before, during, and shortly after the convocation of woman's rights conventions in the antebellum period indicates that descriptions of and editorial comments upon woman's rights activities were extensive and that the editorial policies of daily newspapers in cities like New York, Philadelphia, Boston, St. Louis, Chicago, and Cleveland represented a broad range of opinion concerning the issue of more rights for women.[35] Some papers like the *New York Daily Herald* were indeed contemptuous. But others like the *New York Daily Times* reported the activities of woman's rights advocates straightforwardly. And still others like the *Philadelphia Public Ledger and Daily Transcript,* the *New York Tribune,* and the *Chicago Daily Tribune* were generally supportive. The important point is that papers all over the northern half of the country reported and commented upon those activities. The result was that the penny press in those sections played a significant role in diffusing information about the status of women and the demand for more rights. By doing so, it served the movement as its most important conduit to the general public and helped to legitimize the claims of women for enhanced social, economic, and political opportunities by promoting discussion of them.

Woman's rights advocates had to exert less effort to attract the attention of the editors of reform journals like *The Lily, The Sibyl, The Una, Frederick Douglass's Paper,* and *The Liberator.* And, not surprisingly, historians have emphasized the importance of these journals to the early woman's rights movement.[36] Periodicals like these could be counted on to support any number of reforms. *The Lily* edited by Amelia Bloomer, for example, promoted dress reform and temperance as well as woman's rights. The purpose of *The Liberator* was to advance the cause of abolition, but its editor William Lloyd Garrison also supported equal rights for women. Reform editors gave space to the cause of woman's rights when they could. But I will argue that their willingness to promote the cause was not as significant as the attention that the issue of woman's rights received in the penny press. The editors of journals like *The Lily* and *The Una* were faced with low budgets and limited circulation and were to some degree dependent upon stories printed in the penny press for information about the movement. Penny press newspapers had daily, biweekly or triweekly, and weekly editions. They were hawked on the street as well as sent through the mail to subscribers. Reform journals, unlike large circulation dailies, were normally published weekly, bimonthly, or monthly and were sold primarily through subscription. They also differed from the large circulation newspapers in that they tended to speak primarily to those already predisposed to support the demands of woman's rights advocates. Their major contribution to the cause, therefore, was limited primarily to cultivating those already interested in reform and to preserving the loyalty of the committed.

This study is confined to the period before the Civil War because in the very beginning there was among those who led the woman's rights movement comparatively little public disagreement about their goals and strategy. At no other time in their history did the most active woman's rights advocates speak so much with one voice. This does not mean that they always agreed with one another. Disagreements were to be expected given the fact that the point of reference from which they approached the cause of woman's rights sometimes differed. Some, like Elizabeth Cady Stanton, approached feminist issues from a singularly secular point of view. Others, as we shall see, placed the movement in the context of the coming millennium. Some were determined to try to establish the fact that men and women were the same as a basis for claiming equality of rights. Others found it difficult to give up the idea that men and women were different and insisted that women should be given more rights because they were morally superior to men. Some were willing to combine the struggle for political rights with dress reform and temperance. Others objected to that kind of inclusiveness. The early woman's rights movement was also characterized by the kind of squabbling and pettiness that sometimes erupts in groups whose members work closely together and feel passionately about what they are doing. But despite their differences, the leaders of the movement only occasionally criticized each other in public. And when they did, those criticisms tended to reflect their commitment to the spirit of debate or their need to clarify the issues rather than any really deeply felt antagonism. In the beginning, their desire to gain as much support as possible required a degree of tolerance that would not characterize the movement after the war. The differences that would eventually divide them lay just below the surface.

Indications that their ability to maintain tolerance for difference was limited became clear at the 1860 national convention when Elizabeth Cady Stanton, despite warnings from some of her friends, raised the issue of divorce. But in 1861 woman's rights advocates were as distracted by disunion and the possibility of war as the rest of the nation, and they agreed among themselves to cancel their annual convention. During the war, voices raised for the cause of equality for women were largely silent or focused on the more immediate problem of supporting the war effort and working for the abolition of slavery. And after the war, the movement split between the National Woman's Suffrage Association and the American Woman's Suffrage Association, organizations that would spend most of the rest of the century competing rather than cooperating with each other.[37]

Before the war and the split in the movement that followed, women gained more control over their property, took advantage of increased educational and economic opportunities, and claimed their right to speak out on their own behalf. They did not achieve equality before the law. They also failed to gain the right to vote. But they were able to engage influential men in widely disseminated public political discourse on the subject of woman's right to full participation in all aspects of American life. It was their success in maintaining that discourse that established a political competency for women that went beyond the one which had been granted to them by the ideology of Republican Motherhood. That discourse was a prerequisite for any significant improvement in woman's political, economic, and social status. Because of it, woman's interests could not be disregarded. Along with the kind of petitioning and lobbying long associated with women's work in the area of benevolence and reform, it served as a bridge that linked the private political role assigned to women after the American Revolution to the increasingly public one they would eventually assume in the twentieth century.

Notes

1. Attributed to Lillie Devereux Blake, "Women's Rights Fables" (n.p.: n.p., n.d. [nineteenth century]) by Cheris Kramarae and Mercilee M. Jenkins, "Women Take Back Talk," in *Women and Language in Transition*, ed. Joyce Penfield (Albany: State University of New York Press, 1987), 147-48.
2. Eleanor Flexner, *Century of Struggle: The Woman's Rights Movement in the United States* (New York: Atheneum, 1972), 71-101; Keith E. Melder, *Beginnings of Sisterhood: The American Woman's Rights Movement: 1800-1850* (New York: Schocken, 1977), 143-59; Ellen Carol DuBois, *Feminism and Suffrage: The Emergence of an Independent Women's Movement in America, 1848-1869* (Ithaca: Cornell University Press, 1978), 21-52.
3. Elisabeth Griffith, *In Her Own Right: The Life of Elizabeth Cady Stanton* (New York: Oxford University Press, 1984); Lois Banner, *Elizabeth Cady Stanton: A Radical for Women's Rights* (Boston: Little, Brown, 1980), 69-89; Kathleen Barry, *Susan B. Anthony: A Biography of a Singular Feminist* (New York: New York University Press, 1988); Andrea Moore Kerr, *Lucy Stone: Speaking Out for Equality* (New Brunswick, N.J.: Rutgers University Press, 1992).
4. Elizabeth Cady Stanton, Susan B. Anthony, and Matilda Joslyn Gage, eds. *History of Woman Suffrage,* 2 vols. (New York: Fowler and Wells, 1881), 1: 67-74; Griffith, 51-59.
5. As a number of scholars have pointed out, those who struggled to improve the status of women in the nineteenth century called themselves and were known as woman's rights advocates. They did not call themselves *feminists. Feminism* is a twentieth-century term. See Nancy F. Cott, *The Grounding of Modern Feminism* (New Haven: Yale University Press, 1987), 3. When I occasionally use the term, I use it to mean anyone who advocates the kind of changes necessary to bring about social, economic, and political equality between men and women.
6. Hilda L. Smith, *Reason's Disciples: Seventeenth-Century English Feminists* (Urbana: University of Illinois Press, 1982), xiv, 4, 9, 15, 207.
7. Katharine M. Rogers, *Feminism in Eighteenth-Century England* (Urbana: University of Illinois Press, 1982), 81, 143.
8. Stanton, Anthony, and Gage, eds., 1: 51-52; see also Norma Basch, "Equity vs. Equality: Emerging Concepts of Women's Political Status in the Age of Jackson," *Journal of the Early Republic* 3 (Fall 1983), 297-318.
9. Stanton, Anthony, Gage, eds., 1: 73-75.
10. As Anne Boylan has pointed out, while women could not vote in the early nineteenth century, they did participate in politics through such activities as boycotts, petitions, and lobbying. See Anne M. Boylan, "Women and Politics in the Era Before Seneca Falls," *Journal of the Early Republic* 10 (Fall 1990), 363-82.
11. Sankoff, [*The Social Life of Language* (Philadelphia: University of Pennsylvania Press, 1980)] 13-14; see also McConnell-Ginet, Borker, and Furman, eds., [*Women and Language in Literature and Society* (New York: Praeger, 1980)] 55.
12. See Ward H. Goodenough, *Culture, Language, and Society* (Menlo Park, Calif.: Benjamin/Cummings Publisher, 1981), 30-36.

13. Carroll Smith-Rosenberg, "Hearing Women's Words: A Feminist Reconstruction of History," in *Disorderly Conduct: Visions of Gender in Victorian America* (New York: Oxford University Press, 1985), 11-52, esp. 26-47, quotation on page 42.

14. The Literature which discusses these issues is vast. What follows are suggestions as to where to begin. Barbara Welter was the first to discuss the cult of domesticity in "The Cult of the True Womanhood: 1820-1860," *American Quarterly* 18 (Summer 1966), 151-74. Shirley J. Yee suggests in *Black Women Abolitionists: A Study of Activism, 1828-1860* (Knoxville: University of Tennessee Press, 1992), 40-59, that black journalists, teachers, and ministers subjected women in their communities to many of the same expectations. For a discussion of changing attitudes toward housework, see Jeanne Boydston, *Home and Work: Housework, Wages, and the Ideology of Labor in the Early Republic* (New York: Oxford University Press, 1990). For commentary on the cult of domesticity and the degree to which women were isolated in a sphere separate from men, see Linda K. Kerber, "Separate Spheres, Female Worlds, Woman's Place: The Rhetoric of Women's History," *Journal of American History* 75 (June 1988), 9-39.

15. For descriptions of women's domestic culture in the North, see Nancy F. Cott, *The Bonds of Womanhood: "Woman's Sphere" in New England, 1780-1835* (New Haven: Yale University Press, 1977); Carroll Smith-Rosenberg, "The Female World of Love and Ritual: Relations between Women in Nineteenth-Century America," *Signs* 1 (Autumn 1975), 1-29. For discussions of Southern women's culture, see Suzanne Lebsock, *The Free Women of Petersburg: Status and Culture in a Southern Town, 1784-1860* (New York: Norton, 1985) and Elizabeth Fox-Genovese, *Within the Plantation Household: Black and White Women of the Old South* (Chapel Hill: University of North Carolina Press, 1988).

16. Gerda Lerner discusses the ways that industrialization affected women in different classes in "The Lady and the Mill Girl: Changes in the Status of Women in the Age of Jackson," *Midcontinent American Studies Journal* 10 (Spring 1969), 5-15. Christine Stansell describes the world of working-class women in New York City. See Christine Stansell, *City of Women: Sex and Class in New York, 1789-1860* (Urbana: University of Illinois Press, 1987).

17. For discussions of the New York Married Women's Property Act, see Norma Basch, *In the Eyes of the Law: Women, Marriage, and Property in Nineteenth-Century New York* (Ithaca: Cornell University Press, 1982) and Peggy A. Rabkin, *Fathers to Daughters: The Legal Foundations of Female Emancipation* (Westport, Conn.: Greenwood, 1980).

18. Barbara J. Berg argues that urbanization was a necessary precondition for the rise of American feminism in *The Remembered Gate: Origins of American Feminism: The Woman and the City, 1800-1860* (New York: Oxford University Press, 1978). See Cott, *Bonds*, 70-71, for a discussion of disinterestedness as the basis for woman's reputation as a morally superior being. For discussions of women and benevolence, see Lori D. Ginzberg, *Women and the Work of Benevolence: Morality, Politics, and Class in the Nineteenth-Century United States* (New Haven: Yale University Press, 1990); Nancy A. Hewitt, *Women's Activism and Social Change: Rochester, New York, 1822-1872* (Ithaca: Cornell University Press, 1984); Anne Firor Scott, *Natural Allies: Women's Associations in American History* (Urbana: University of Illinois Press, 1992).

19. Many of the early woman's rights activists were Quakers. For background on the influence of the principle egalitarianism on Quaker women, their lives, and their social activism, see Mary Maples Dunn, "Saints and Sisters: Congregational and Quaker Women in the Early Colonial Period," *American Quarterly* 30 (Winter 1978), 582-601; Jean R. Soderland "Women's Authority in Pennsylvania and New Jersey Quaker Meetings, 1680-1760," *William and Mary Quarterly* 44 (October 1987), 722-49; Nancy A. Hewitt, "Feminist Friends: Agararian Quakers and the Emergence of Woman's Rights in America," *Feminist Studies* 12 (Spring 1986), 27-79; Joan M. Jensen, *Loosening the Bonds: Mid-Atlantic Farm Women, 1750-1850* (New Haven: Yale University Press, 1986). For one discussion of the influence of religious revivals on women, see Mary P. Ryan, *Cradle of the Middle Class: The Family in Oneida County, New York, 1790-1865* (New York: Cambridge University Press, 1981).

20. Blanche Glassman Hersh, *The Slavery of Sex: Feminist-Abolitionists in America* (Urbana: University of Illinois Press, 1978), 20-28; for another discussion of the connection between abolitionism and the rise of woman's rights movement, see DuBois, *Feminism and Suffrage.*

21. Ginzberg, 98-132.

22. Linda Kerber, *Women of the Republic: Intellect and Ideology in Revolutionary America* (Chapel Hill: University of North Carolina Press, 1980), 269-88; Linda Kerber, "Daughters of Columbia: Educating Women for the Republic, 1787-1805," in *The Hofstadter Aegis: A Memorial,* eds. Stanley Elkins and Eric McKitrick (New York: Knopf, 1974), 36-59; Kathryn Kish Sklar, *Catharine Beecher: A Study in American Domesticity* (New Haven: Yale University Press, 1973).

23. For discussions of political culture and the rise of male suffrage, see Chilton Williamson, *American Suffrage: From Property to Democracy, 1760-1860* (Princeton: Princeton University Press, 1960).

24. Griffith, 9, 11, 49-50.

25. Katharine Anthony, *Susan B. Anthony: Her Personal History and Her Era* (Garden City, N.Y.: Doubleday, 1954), 102.

26. Otelia Cromwell, *Lucretia Mott* (Cambridge: Harvard University Press, 1958), 18-19.

27. Alice Stone Blackwell, *Lucy Stone: A Pioneer of Woman's Rights* (Boston: Little, Brown, 1930), 22-23, 25.

28. Hersh, 220-29.

29. See, for example, Flexner, *Century of Struggle*; William L. O'Neill, ed. *The Woman Movement: Feminism in the United States and England* (Chicago: Quadrangle, 1969); Anne F. Scott and Andrew M. Scott, *One Half the People: The Fight for Woman Suffrage* (Philadelphia: J. B. Lippincott, 1975); Ross Evans Paulson, *Women's Suffrage and Prohibition: A Comparative Study of Equality and Social Control* (Gelnview, Ill.: Scott, Foresman, 1973); and William O'Neill *Everyone Was Brave: The Rise and Fall of Feminism in America* (Chicago: Quadrangle, 1969).

30. See, for example, Robert E. Riegel, *American Feminists* (Lawrence: University of Kansas Press, 1963), preface;

Hersh, 41, 191, 193; Olive Banks, *Faces of Feminism: A Study of Feminism as a Social Movement* (New York: St. Martin's Press, 1981), 7-8; James L. Cooper and Sheila McIsaac Cooper, *The Roots of American Feminist Thought* (Boston: Allyn and Bacon, 1973), 6-7; Cott, *Grounding,* 16-17; Josephine Donovan, *Feminist Theory: The Intellectual Traditions of American Feminism* (New York: Frederick Ungar, 1985), 1-36.

31. Kerber, *Women of the Republic,* 15-32; Jane Rendall, *The Origins of Modern Feminism: Women in Britain, France, and the United States, 1780-1860* (London: Macmillan, 1985), 7-32, quotation on page 7.

32. Rosemarie Zagarri, "Morals, Manners, and the Republican Mother," *American Quarterly* 44 (June 1992), 192-215.

33. For general discussions of journalism in this period, see Frank Luther Mott, *American Journalism, A History: 1690-1960* (New York: Macmillan, 1962); Donald Lewis Shaw, "At the Crossroads: Change and Continuity in American Press News, 1820-1860," *Journalism History* 8 (Summer 1981), 38-50; John C. Nerone, "The Mythology of the Penny Press," *Critical Studies in Mass Communications* 4 (December 1987), 376-404.

34. See, for example, Flexner, 81-82.; Melder, 148, 151; E. Claire Jerry, "The Role of Newspapers in the Nineteenth-Century Woman's Movement," in *A Voice of Their Own: The Woman's Suffrage Press, 1840-1910,* ed. Martha M. Solomon (Tuscaloosa: University of Alabama Press, 1991), 19; Lynne Masel-Walters, "To Hustle with the Rowdies: The Organization and Functions of the American Woman Suffrage Press,"*Journal of American Culture* 3 (Spring 1980), 168.

35. I began my analysis of penny press response to the issue of woman's rights by determining which papers had the largest circulation, the assumption being that those papers with the largest circulation probably had the most influence nationally. The *New York Daily Herald,* the *New York Tribune,* and the *New York Daily Times* had the largest circulations during the period in question. For circulation figures, see Douglas Fermer, *James Gordon Bennett and the* New York Herald *: A Study of Editorial Opinion in the Civil War Era, 1854-1867* (New York: St. Martin's Press, 1986), 323-27. I read daily issues of each of these three papers for one month preceding and two weeks after every known state and national convention held between 1848 and 1860. In order to assess the degree to which these three newspapers contributed to the diffusion of information about the movement and to survey the attitude of editors in other parts of the country to woman's rights, I read each issue of the *Chicago Tribune,* the *Boston Daily Advertiser,* and the *St. Louis Daily Republican Ledger and Daily Transcript* for one week before and two weeks after the convention that they hosted and from the first day of other national conventions to up to ten days after.

36. See, for example, Ann Russo and Cheris Kramarae, *The Radical Women's Press of the 1850s* (New York: Routledge, 1991), 1-17; Bertha-Monica Stearns, "Reform Periodicals and Female Reformers, 1830-1860," *American Historical Review* 37 (July 1932), 678-99; Martha M. Solomon, "The Role of the Suffrage Press in the Woman's Rights Movement," in *A Voice of Their Own,* 1-16.

37. For a general discussion of these developments, see DuBois, *Feminism and Suffrage;* Wendy Hamand Venet, *Neither Ballots nor Bullets: Women Abolitionists and the Civil War* (Charlottesville: University Press of Virginia, 1991).

REPRESENTATIONS OF WOMEN IN LITERATURE AND ART IN THE 19TH CENTURY

BARBARA EHRENREICH AND DEIRDRE ENGLISH (ESSAY DATE 1978)

SOURCE: Ehrenreich, Barbara and Deirdre English. "The Sexual Politics of Sickness." In *For Her Own Good: 150 Years of the Experts' Advice to Women,* pp. 101-09. New York: Anchor Books/Doubleday, 1978.

In the following excerpt, Ehrenreich and English argue that many of the illnesses routinely affecting women during the nineteenth century were most likely manifestations of their gender subjugation, their feelings of powerlessness, and their unrealistic domestic roles.

When Charlotte Perkins Gilman collapsed with a "nervous disorder," the physician she sought out for help was Dr. S. Weir Mitchell, "the greatest nerve specialist in the country." It was Dr. Mitchell—female specialist, part-time novelist, and member of Philadelphia's high society—who had once screened Osler for a faculty position, and, finding him appropriately discreet in the disposal of cherry-pie pits, admitted the young doctor to medicine's inner circles. When Gilman met him, in the eighteen eighties, he was at the height of his career, earning over $60,000 per year (the equivalent of over $300,000 in today's dollars). His reknown for the treatment of female nervous disorders had by this time led to a marked alteration of character. According to an otherwise fond biographer, his vanity "had become colossal. It was fed by torrents of adulation, incessant and exaggerated, every day, almost every hour. . . ."[1]

Gilman approached the great man with "utmost confidence." A friend of her mother's lent her one hundred dollars for the trip to Philadelphia and Mitchell's treatment. In preparation, Gilman methodically wrote out a complete history of her case. She had observed, for example, that her sickness vanished when she was away from her home, her husband, and her child, and returned as soon as she came back to them. But Dr. Mitchell dismissed her prepared history as evidence of "self-conceit." He did not want information from his patients; he wanted "complete obedience." Gilman quotes his prescription for her:

> "Live as domestic a life as possible. Have your child with you all the time." (Be it remarked that if I did but dress the baby it left me shaking and crying—certainly far from a healthy companionship for her, to say nothing of the effect on me.) "Lie down an hour after each meal. Have but two hours intellectual life a day. And never touch pen, brush or pencil as long as you live."[2]

Gilman dutifully returned home and for some months attempted to follow Dr. Mitchell's orders to the letter. The result, in her words, was—

> . . . [I] came perilously close to losing my mind. The mental agony grew so unbearable that I would sit blankly moving my head from side to side . . . I would crawl into remote closets and under beds—to hide from the grinding pressure of that distress. . . .[3]

Finally, in a "moment of clear vision" Gilman understood the source of her illness: she did not want to be a *wife*; she wanted to be a writer and an activist. So, discarding S. Weir Mitchell's prescription and divorcing her husband, she took off for California with her baby, her pen, her brush and pencil. But she never forgot Mitchell and his near-lethal "cure." Three years after her recovery she wrote *The Yellow Wallpaper*[4] a fictionalized account of her own illness and descent into madness. If that story had any influence on S. Weir Mitchell's method of treatment, she wrote after a long life of accomplishments, "I have not lived in vain."[5]

Charlotte Perkins Gilman was fortunate enough to have had a "moment of clear vision" in which she understood what was happening to her. Thousands of other women, like Gilman, were finding themselves in a new position of dependency on the male medical profession—and with no alternative sources of information or counsel. The medical profession was consolidating its monopoly over healing, and now the woman who felt sick, or tired or simply depressed would no longer seek help from a friend or female healer, but from a male physician. The general theory which guided the doctors' practice as well as their public pronouncements was that women were, by nature, weak, dependent, and diseased. Thus would the doctors attempt to secure their victory over the female healer: with the "scientific" evidence that woman's essential nature was not to be a strong, competent help-giver, but to be a *patient.*

A Mysterious Epidemic

In fact at the time there were reasons to think that the doctors' theory was not so farfetched. Women were decidedly sickly, though not for the reasons the doctors advanced. In the mid- and late nineteenth century a curious epidemic seemed to be sweeping through the middle- and upper-class female population both in the United States and England. Diaries and journals from the time give us hundreds of examples of women slipping into hopeless invalidism. For example, when Catherine Beecher, the educator, finished a tour in 1871 which included visits to dozens of relatives, friends and former students, she reported "a terrible decay of female health all over the land," which was "increasing in a most alarming ratio." The notes from her travels go like this:

> Milwaukee, Wis. Mrs. A. frequent sick headaches. Mrs. B. very feeble. Mrs. S. well, except chills. Mrs. L. poor health constantly. Mrs. D. subject to frequent headaches. Mrs. B. very poor health . . .
>
> Mrs. H. pelvic disorders and a cough. Mrs. B. always sick. Do not know one perfectly healthy woman in the place. . . .[6]

Doctors found a variety of diagnostic labels for the wave of invalidism gripping the female population: "neurasthenia," "nervous prostration," "hyperesthesia," "cardiac inadequacy," "dyspepsia," "rheumatism," and "hysteria." The symptoms included headache, muscular aches, weakness, depression, menstrual difficulties, indigestion, etc., and usually a general debility requiring constant rest. S. Weir Mitchell described it as follows:

> The woman grows pale and thin, eats little, or if she eats does not profit by it. Everything wearies her,—to sew, to write, to read, to walk,—and by and by the sofa or the bed is her only comfort. Every effort is paid for dearly, and she describes herself as aching and sore, as sleeping ill, and as needing constant stimulus and endless tonics. . . . If such a person is emotional she does not fail to become more so, and even the firmest women lose self-control at last under incessant feebleness.[7]

The syndrome was never fatal, but neither was it curable in most cases, the victims sometimes patiently outliving both husbands and physicians.

Women who recovered to lead full and active lives—like Charlotte Perkins Gilman and Jane Addams—were the exceptions. Ann Greene Phillips—a feminist and abolitionist in the eighteen thirties—first took ill during her courtship. Five years after her marriage, she retired to bed, more or less permanently. S. Weir Mitchell's unmarried sister fell prey to an unspecified "great pain" shortly after taking over housekeeping for her brother (whose first wife had just died), and embarked on a life of invalidism. Alice James began her career of invalidism at the age of nineteen, always amazing her older brothers, Henry (the novelist) and William (the psychologist), with the stubborn intractability of her condition: "Oh, woe, woe is me!" she wrote in her diary:

> . . . all hopes of peace and rest are vanishing—nothing but the dreary snail-like climb up a little way, so as to be able to run down again! And then these doctors tell you that you will die or *recover*! But you *don't* recover. I have been at these alterations since I was nineteen and I am neither dead nor recovered. As I am now forty-two, there has surely been time for either process.[8]

The sufferings of these women were real enough. Ann Phillips wrote, ". . . life is a burden to me, I do not know what to do. I am tired of suffering. I have no faith in anything."[9] Some thought that if the illness wouldn't kill them, they would do the job themselves. Alice James discussed suicide with her father, and rejoiced, at the age of forty-three, when informed she had developed breast cancer and would die within months: "I count it the greatest good fortune to have these few months so full of interest and instruction in the knowledge of my approaching death."[10] Mary Galloway shot herself in the head while being attended in her apartment by a physician and a nurse. She was thirty-one years old, the daughter of a bank and utility company president. According to the New York *Times* account (April 10, 1905), "She had been a chronic dyspeptic since 1895, and that is the only reason known for her suicide."[11]

Marriage: The Sexual Economic Relation

In the second half of the nineteenth century the vague syndrome gripping middle- and upper-class women had become so widespread as to represent not so much a disease in the medical sense as a way of life. More precisely, the way this type of woman was expected to live predisposed her to sickness, and sickness in turn predisposed her to continue to live as she was expected to. The delicate, affluent lady, who was completely dependent on her husband, set the sexual romanticist ideal of femininity for women of all classes.

Clear-headed feminists like Charlotte Perkins Gilman and Olive Schreiner saw a link between female invalidism and the economic situation of women in the upper classes. As they observed, poor women did not suffer from the syndrome. The problem in the middle to upper classes was that marriage had become a "sexuo-economic relation" in which women performed sexual and reproductive duties for financial support. It was a relationship which Olive Schreiner bluntly called "female parasitism."

To Gilman's pragmatic mind, the affluent wife appeared to be a sort of tragic evolutionary anomaly, something like the dodo. She did not work: that is, there was no serious, productive work to do in the home, and the tasks which were left—keeping house, cooking and minding the children—she left as much as possible to the domestic help. She was, biologically speaking, specialized for one function and one alone—sex. Hence the elaborate costume—bustles, false fronts, wasp waists—which caricatured the natural female form. Her job was to bear the heirs of the businessman, lawyer, or professor she had married, which is what gave her a claim to any share of his income. When Gilman, in her depression, turned away from her own baby, it was because she already understood, in a half-conscious way, that the baby was living proof of her economic dependence—and as it seemed to her, sexual degradation.

A "lady" had one other important function, as Veblen pointed out with acerbity in the *Theory of the Leisure Class*. And that was to do precisely nothing, that is nothing of any economic or social consequence.[12] A successful man could have no better social ornament than an idle wife. Her delicacy, her culture, her childlike ignorance of the male world gave a man the "class" which money alone could not buy. A virtuous wife spent a hushed and peaceful life indoors, sewing, sketching, planning menus, and supervising the servants and children. The more adventurous might fill their leisure with shopping excursions, luncheons, balls, and novels. A "lady" could be charming, but never brilliant; interested, but not intense. Dr. Mitchell's second wife, Mary Cadwalader, was perhaps a model of her type: she "made no pretense at brilliancy; her first thought was to be a foil to her husband. . . ."[13] By no means was such a lady to concern herself with politics, business, international affairs, or the aching injustices of the industrial work world.

But not even the most sheltered woman lived on an island detached from the "real" world of men. Schreiner described the larger context:

> Behind the phenomenon of female parasitism has always lain another and yet larger social phenomenon . . . the subjugation of large bodies of other human creatures, either as slaves, subject races, or classes; and as a result of the excessive labors of those classes there has always been an accumulation of unearned wealth in the hands of the dominant class or race. *It has invariably been by*

> *feeding on this wealth, the result of forced or ill-paid labor,* that the female of the dominant race or class has in the past lost her activity and has come to exist purely through the passive performance of her sexual functions.[14]
>
> [Emphasis in original]

The leisured lady, whether she knew it or not and whether she cared or not, inhabited the same social universe as dirt-poor black sharecroppers, six-year-old children working fourteen-hour days for subsubsistence wages, young men mutilated by unsafe machinery or mine explosions, girls forced into prostitution by the threat of starvation. At no time in American history was the contradiction between ostentatious wealth and unrelenting poverty, between idleness and exhaustion, starker than it was then in the second half of the nineteenth century. There were riots in the cities, insurrections in the mines, rumors of subversion and assassination. Even the secure business or professional man could not be sure that he too would not be struck down by an economic downturn, a wily competitor, or (as seemed likely at times) a social revolution.

The genteel lady of leisure was as much a part of the industrial social order as her husband or his employees. As Schreiner pointed out, it was ultimately the wealth extracted in the world of work that enabled a man to afford a more or less ornamental wife. And it was the very harshness of that outside world that led men to see the home as a refuge—"a sacred place, a vestal temple," a "tent pitch'd in a world not right," presided over by a gentle, ethereal wife. A popular home health guide advised that

> . . . [man's] feelings are frequently lacerated to the utmost point of endurance, by collisions, irritations, and disappointments. To recover his equanimity and composure, home must be a place of repose, of peace, of cheerfulness, of comfort; then his soul renews its strength, and will go forth, with fresh vigor, to encounter the labor and troubles of the world.[15]

No doubt the suffocating atmosphere of sexual romanticism bred a kind of nervous hypochondria. We will never know, for example, if Alice James's lifelong illness had a "real" organic basis. But we know that, unlike her brothers, she was never encouraged to go to college or to develop her gift for writing. She was high-strung and imaginative, but *she* could not be brilliant or productive. Illness was perhaps the only honorable retreat from a world of achievement which (it seemed at the time) nature had not equipped her to enter.

For many other women, to various degrees, sickness became a part of life, even a way of filling time. The sexuo-economic relation confined women to the life of the body, so it was to the body that they directed their energies and intellect. Rich women frequented resortlike health spas and the offices of elegant specialists like S. Weir Mitchell. A magazine cartoon from the eighteen seventies shows two "ladies of fashion"meeting in an ornately appointed waiting room. "What, *you*-here, Lizzie? Why, ain't you well?" asks the first patient. "Perfectly thanks!" answers the second. "But what's the matter with *you*, dear?" "Oh, nothing whatever! I'm as right as possible dear."[16] For less well-off women there were patent medicines, family doctors, and, starting in the eighteen fifties, a steady stream of popular advice books, written by doctors, on the subject of female health. It was acceptable, even stylish, to retire to bed with "sick headaches," "nerves" and various unmentionable "female troubles," and that indefinable nervous disorder "neurasthenia" was considered, in some circles, to be a mark of intellect and sensitivity. Dr. Mary Putnam Jacobi, a female regular physician, observed impatiently in 1895:

> . . . it is considered natural and almost laudable to break down under all conceivable varieties of strain—a winter dissipation, a houseful of servants, a quarrel with a female friend, not to speak of more legitimate reasons.. . . Women who expect to go to bed every menstrual period expect to collapse if by chance they find themselves on their feet for a few hours during such a crisis. Constantly considering their nerves, urged to consider them by well-intentioned but short-sighted advisors, they pretty soon become nothing but a bundle of nerves.[17]

But if sickness was a reaction, on women's part, to a difficult situation, it was not a way out. If you have to be idle, you might as well be sick, and sickness, in turn, legitimates idleness. From the romantic perspective, the sick woman was not that far off from the ideal woman anyway. A morbid aesthetic developed, in which sickness was seen as a source of female beauty, and, beauty—in thehigh-fashion sense—was in fact a source of sickness. Over and over, nineteenth-century romantic paintings feature the beautiful invalid, sensuously drooping on her cushions, eyes fixed tremulously at her husband or physician, or already gazing into the Beyond. Literature aimed at female readers lingered on the romantic pathos of illness and death; popular women's magazines featured such stories as "The Grave of My Friend" and "Song of Dying." Society ladies cultivated a sickly countenance by drinking vinegar in quantity or, more effectively, arsenic.[18] The Lovliest of heroines were those who died young, like Beth in *Little Women*, too good and too pure for life in this world.

Meanwhile, the requirements of fashion insured that the well-dressed woman would actually be as frail and ornamental as she looked. The style of wearing tight-laced corsets, which was *de rigeur*throughout the last half of the century, has to be ranked somewhere close to the old Chinese practice of foot-binding for its crippling effects on the female body. A fashionable woman's corsets exerted, on the average, twenty-one pounds of pressure on her internal organs, and extremes of up to eighty-eight pounds had been measured.[19] (Add this to the fact that a well-dressed woman wore an average of thirty-seven pounds of street clothing in the winter months, of which nineteen pounds were suspended from from her tortured waist. [20]) Some of the short-term results of tight lacing were shortness of breath, constipation, weakness, and a tendency to violent indigestion. Amoung the long-term effects were bent or fractured ribs, displacement of the liver, and uterine prolapse (in some cases, the uterus would be gradualy forced, by the pressure of the corset, out through the vagina).

The morbidity of nineteenth-century tastes in female beauty reveals the hostility which never lies to far below the surface of sexual romanticism. To be sure, the romantic spirit puts woman on a pedestal and ascribes to her every tender virtue absent from the Market. But carried to an extreme the demand that a woman be a *negation*of man's world left almost nothing for women to actually *be*: if men are busy, she is idle; if men are rough, she is gentle; if men are strong, she is frail; if men are rational, she is irrational; and so on. The logic which insists that femininity is negative masculinity necessarily romanticizes the moribund woman and encourages a kind of paternalistic necrophilia. In the nineteenth century this tendency becomes overt, and the romantic spirit holds up as its ideal—the *sick*woman, the invalid who lives at the edge of death.

Notes

1. Anna Robeson Burr, *Weir Mitchell: His Life and Letters* (New York: Duffield and Co., 1929), p. 289.
2. Charlotte Perkins Gilman, *The Living of Charlotte Perkins Gilman: An Autobiography* (New York: Harper Colophon Books, 1975), p. 96.
3. Gilman, loc. cit.
4. Charlotte Perkins Gilman, *The Yellow Wallpaper* (Old Westbury, New York: The Feminist Press, 1973).
5. Gilman, *Autobiography*, p. 121.
6. Catherine Beecher, "Statistics of Female Health," in Gail Parker (ed.), *The Oven Birds: American Women on Womanhood 1820-1920* (Garden City, New York: Doubleday/Anchor, 1972), p. 165.
7. Ilza Veith, *Hysteria: The History of a Disease* (Chicago and London: The University of Chicago Press, 1965), p. 216.
8. Quoted in F. O. Matthiessen, *The James Family* (New York: Alfred A. Knopf, 1961), p. 272.
9. Quoted in Irving H. Bartlett, *Wendell Phillips: Brahmin Radical* (Boston: Beacon Press, 1961), p. 78.
10. Quoted in Leon Edel (ed.), *The Diary of Alice James* (New York: Dodd, Mead, 1964), p. 14.
11. We thank medical historian Rick Brown for sharing this story with us.
12. Thorstein Veblen, *Theory of the Leisure Class* (New York: Modern Library, 1934).
13. Burr, op. cit., p. 176.
14. Olive Schreiner, *Woman and Labor* (New York: Frederick A. Stokes, 1911), p. 98.
15. John C. Gunn, M.D., *Gunn's New Family Physician* (New York: Saalfield Publishing, 1924), p. 120.
16. New York Public Library Picture Collection, no source given.
17. Dr. Mary Putnam Jacobi, "On Female Invalidism," in Nancy F. Cott (ed.), *Root of Bitterness: Documents of the Social History of American Women* (New York: E. P. Dutton, 1972), p. 307.
18. John S. Haller, Jr., and Robin M. Haller, *The Physician and Sexuality in Victorian America* (Urbana, Illinois: University of Illinois Press, 1974), pp. 143-44.
19. Ibid., p. 168.
20. Ibid., p. 31.

ANN DOUGLAS (ESSAY DATE 1988)

SOURCE: Douglas, Ann. "The Legacy of American Victorianism." In *The Feminization of American Culture*, pp. 7-13. New York: Anchor Press/Doubleday, 1988.

In the following excerpt, Douglas argues that in the nineteenth century, the vacuum left by the demise of Calvinist theology in America was filled by a feminizing sentiment that did little to empower women.

. . . Between 1820 and 1875,[1] in the midst of the transformation of the American economy into the most powerfully aggressive capitalist system in the world, American culture seemed bent on establishing a perpetual Mother's Day. As the secular activities of American life were demonstrating their utter supremacy, religion became the message of America's official and conventional cultural life. This religion was hardly the Calvinism of the founders of the Bay Colony or that of New England's great eighteenth-century divines.

It was a far cry, moreover, from the faith which at least imaginatively still engaged serious authors like Melville and Hawthorne.

Under "Calvinism" we can place much of what rigorous theology Protestant Americans have ever officially accepted. Until roughly 1820, this theological tradition was a chief, perhaps the chief, vehicle of intellectual and cultural activity in American life. The Calvinist tradition culminated in the Edwardsean school:[2] most notably, Jonathan Edwards (1703-58) and his friends and followers, Samuel Hopkins (1721-1803), Joseph Bellamy (1719-90), and Nathaniel Emmons (1745-1840). The Edwardsean school has often been mythologized, but, whatever its very real faults, it undoubtedly constituted the most persuasive example of independent yet institutionalized thought to which our society has even temporarily given credence. Its members studied together; they trained, questioned, and defended one another. They exhibited with some consistency the intellectual rigor and imaginative precision difficult to achieve without collective effort, and certainly rare in more recent American annals.

For some time, roughly between 1740 and 1820, the rigor exhibited by the Edwardsean ministers seemed representative of the wider culture or at least welcomed by it. Edwardsean theology, however, outlived its popular support. In the eighteenth and nineteenth centuries, as in the twentieth, the vast majority of American Christians identified themselves as members of one of the various Protestant groups.[3] Yet the differences between the Protestants of, say, 1800 and their descendants of 1875 and after are greater than the similarities. The everyday Protestant of 1800 subscribed to a rather complicated and rigidly defined body of dogma; attendance at a certain church had a markedly theological function. By 1875, American Protestants were much more likely to define their faith in terms of family morals, civic responsibility, and above all, in terms of the social function of churchgoing. Their actual creed was usually a liberal, even a sentimental one for which Edwards and his contemporaries would have felt scorn and horror. In an analogous way, Protestant churches over the same period shifted their emphasis from a primary concern with the doctrinal beliefs of their members to a preoccupation with numbers. In ecclesiastical and religious circles, attendance came to count for more than genuine adherence. Nothing could show better the late nineteenth-century Protestant Church's altered identity as an eager participant in the emerging consumer society than its obsession with popularity and its increasing disregard of intellectual issues.

The vitiation and near-disappearance of the Calvinist tradition have been sufficiently lamented, and perhaps insufficiently understood. The numerous historians and theologians of the last four decades who have recorded and mourned its loss themselves constitute an unofficial school which can loosely be termed "Neo-orthodox."[4] In analyzing Calvinism's decline, however, they have not examined all the evidence at their disposal. They have provided important studies of the effects of the democratic experiment in a new and unsettled land, effects all tending to a liberal creed in theology as in politics: immigration on a scale unparalleled in the modern world, huge labor resources facilitating rapid urbanization and industrialization, amalgamation of diverse cultural heritages often at the level of their lowest common denominator. Yet they have neglected what might be called the social history of Calvinist theology. They have given scant consideration to the changing nature of the ministry as a profession or to the men who entered its ranks during the critical decades between 1820 and 1875. And they have overlooked another group central to the rituals of that Victorian sentimentalism that did so much to gut Calvinist orthodoxy: Little Eva's most ardent admirers, the active middle-class Protestant women whose supposedly limited intelligences liberal piety was in part designed to flatter. As if in fear of contamination, historians have ignored the claims of what Harriet Beecher Stowe astutely called "Pink and White Tyranny":[5] the drive of nineteenth-century American women to gain power through the exploitation of their feminine identity as their society defined it.

These women did not hold offices or own businesses. They had little formal status in their culture, nor apparently did they seek it. They were not usually declared feminists or radical reformers. Increasingly exempt from the responsibilities of domestic industry, they were in a state of sociological transition. They comprised the bulk of educated churchgoers and the vast majority of the dependable reading public; in ever greater numbers, they edited magazines and wrote books for other women like themselves. They were becoming the prime consumers of American culture. As such they exerted an enormous influence on the chief male purveyors of that culture, the liberal, literate ministers and popular writers who were being read while Melville and Thoreau were ignored. These masculine groups, ministers and authors, occupied a precarious position in society. Writers had never received public support; ministers ceased to do so after 1833 when the "disestablishment" of the Protestant Church became officially complete in the United States. In very real ways, authors and clergymen were on the market; they could hardly afford to ignore their feminine customers and competitors.

What bound the minister and the lady together with the popular writer was their shared preoccupation with the lighter productions of the press; they wrote poetry, fiction, memoirs, sermons, and magazine pieces of every kind. What distinguished them from the writer, and made them uniquely central agents in the process of sentimentalization this book undertakes to explore, is the fact that their consuming interest in literature was relatively new. At the turn of the nineteenth century, the prominent Edwardsean minister, Nathaniel Emmons, returned a novel by Sir Walter Scott lent him by a friend with protestations of genuine horror. A scant fifty years later, serious ministers and orthodox professors of theology were making secular literature a concern and even an occupation. During the same period, women writers gradually flooded the market with their efforts. While a female author at the beginning of the nineteenth century was considered by definition an aberration from her sex, by its close she occupied an established if not a respected place. The Victorian lady and minister were joining, and changing, the literary scene.

Northeastern clergymen and middle-class literary women lacked power of any crudely tangible kind, and they were careful not to lay claim to it. Instead they wished to exert "influence," which they eulogized as a religious force.[6] They were asking for nothing more than offhand attention, and not even much of that: "influence" was to be discreetly omnipresent and omnipotent. This was the suasion of moral and psychic nurture, and it had a good deal less to do with the faith of the past and a good deal more to do with the advertising industry of the future than its proponents would have liked to believe. They exerted their "influence" chiefly through literature which was just in the process of becoming a mass medium. The press offered them the chance they were seeking to be unobtrusive and everywhere at the same time. They inevitably confused theology with religiosity, religiosity with literature, and literature with self-justification. They understandably attempted to stabilize and advertise in their work the values that cast their recessive position in the most favorable light. Even as they took full advantage of the new commercial possibilities technological revolutions in printing had made possible, they exercised an enormously conservative influence on their society.

On a thematic level, they specialized in the domestic and religious concerns considered appropriate for members of their profession or sex. But content was not the most important aspect of their work, nor of its conservative impulse. Ministerial and feminine authors were as involved with the method of consumption as with the article consumed. Despite their often prolific output, they were in a curious sense more interested in the business of reading than in that of writing. Indeed, this book, while focused upon written sources, might be described in one sense as a study of readers and of those who shared and shaped their taste. Of course involvement and identification between authors and their readers was characteristically and broadly Victorian. Henry James could rebuke Anthony Trollope for his constant asides to the reader, for his casual admissions that he was making up a story to please an audience,[7] but Trollope was in the majority. To ask a Victorian author, American or British, not to address his readers was a bit like asking a modern-day telecaster to ignore his viewers. Literature then, like television now, was in the early phase of intense self-consciousness characteristic of a new mass medium: the transactions between cultural buyer and seller, producer and consumer shaped both the content and the form. The American groups I am discussing, however, showed an extraordinary degree, even by Victorian standards, of market-oriented alertness to their customers. They had a great deal in common with them.

The well-educated intellectual minister of the eighteenth century read omnivorously, but the dense argumentative tracts he tackled forced him to think, not to "read" in our modern sense; metaphorically speaking, he was producing, not consuming. His mid-nineteenth-century descendant was likely to show a love of fiction and poetry and a distaste for polemical theology; he preferred "light" to "heavy" reading. By the same token, numerous observers remarked on the fact that countless young Victorian women spent much of their middle-class girlhoods prostrate on chaise longues with their heads buried in "worthless" novels. Their grandmothers, the critics insinuated, had spent their time studying the Bible and performing useful household chores. "Reading" in its new form was many things; among them it was an occupation for the unemployed, narcissistic self-education for those excluded from the harsh school of practical competition. Literary men of the cloth and middle-class women writers of the Victorian period knew from firsthand evidence that literature was functioning more and more as a form of leisure, a complicated mass dream-life in the busiest, most wide-awake society in the world. They could not be altogether ignorant that literature was revealing and supporting a special class, a class defined less by what its members produced than by what they consumed. When the minister and the lady put pen to paper, they had ever in their minds their reading counterparts; the small scale, the intimate scenes, the chatty tone of many of their works complement the presumably comfortable posture and domestic backdrop of their readers. They wrote not just to win adherents to their views, but to make converts to literature, to sustain and encourage the habit of reading itself.[8] Inevitably more serious writers like Melville attempted alternately to re-educate, defy, and ignore a public addicted to the absorption of sentimental fare.

To suggest that problems of professional class or sexual status played a part in the creation and character of nineteenth- and twentieth-century American culture is not, hopefully, to suggest a conspiracy view of history. The ministers and women I am considering were intent on claiming culture as their peculiar property, one conferring on them a special duty and prerogative. They were rightly insecure about their position in the broader society; they sought to gain indirect and compensatory control. Yet they were not insincere, ill-intentioned, or simple-minded. It must be remembered how these people saw themselves, and with what reason: they were Christians reinterpreting their faith as best they could in terms of the needs of their society. Their conscious motives were good—even praiseworthy; their effects were not altogether bad. Under the sanction of sentimentalism, lady and clergyman were able to cross the cruel lines laid down by sexual stereotyping in ways that were clearly historically important and undoubtedly personally fulfilling. She could become aggressive, even angry, in the name of various holy causes; he could become gentle, even nurturing, for the sake of moral overseeing. Whatever their ambiguities of motivation, both believed they had a genuine redemptive mission in their society: to propagate the potentially matriarchal virtues of nurture, generosity, and acceptance; to create the "culture of the feelings" that John Stuart Mill was to find during the same period in Wordsworth.[9] It is hardly altogether their fault that their efforts intensified sentimental rather than matriarchal values.

Moreover, whatever the errors of the sentimentalists, they paid for them. The losses sustained by the ministers and the women involved, as well as by the culture which was their arena, were enormous. The case of the ministers is clear-cut; they lost status and respect. The case of the women is equally painful, but more difficult to discuss, especially in the atmosphere of controversy that attends feminist argument today. I must add a personal note here. As I researched and wrote this book, I experienced a confusion which perhaps other women scholars have felt in recent years. I expected to find my fathers and my mothers; instead I discovered my fathers and my sisters. The best of the men had access to solutions, and occasionally inspiring ones, which I appropriate only with the anxiety and effort that attend genuine aspiration. The problems of the women correspond to mine with a frightening accuracy that seems to set us outside the processes of history; the answers of even the finest of them were often mine, and sometimes largely unacceptable to me. I am tempted to account my response socialization, if not treachery. Siding with the enemy. But I think that is wrong.

I have a respect for so-called "toughness," not as a good in itself, not isolated and reified as it so often is in male-dominated cultures, but as the necessary preservative for all virtues, even those of gentleness and generosity. My respect is deeply ingrained; my commitment to feminism requires that I explore it, not that I abjure it. Much more important, it does no good to shirk the fact that nineteenth-century American society tried to damage women like Harriet Beecher Stowe—and succeeded. It is undeniable that the oppressed preserved, and were intended to preserve, crucial values threatened in the larger culture. But it is equally true that no one would protest oppression with fervor or justification if it did not in part accomplish its object: the curtailment of the possibilities of growth for significant portions of a given community. Nineteenth-century American women were oppressed, and damaged; inevitably, the influence they exerted in turn on their society was not altogether beneficial. The cruelest aspect of the process of oppression is the logic by which it forces its objects to be oppressive in turn, to do the dirty work of their society in several senses. Melville put the matter well: weakness, or even "depravity in the oppressed is no apology for the oppressor; but rather an additional stigma to him, as being, in a large degree, the effect and not the cause of oppression."[10] To view the victims of oppression simply as martyrs and heroes, however, undeniably heroic and martyred as they often were, is only to perpetuate the sentimental heresy I am attempting to study here.

I have been more interested in the effects than in the conscious motives of the women and ministers under consideration, for there is no better indication of their dilemma than the often wide and tragic divergence between the two. In the process of sentimentalization which they aided, many women and ministers espoused at least in theory to so-called passive virtues, admirable in themselves, and sorely needed in American life. They could not see to what alien uses their espousal might be put. Sentimentalism is a complex phenomenon. It asserts that the values a society's activity denies are precisely the ones it cherishes; it attempts to deal with the phenomenon of cultural bifurcation by the manipulation of nostalgia. Sentimentalism provides a way to protest a power to which one has already in part capitulated. It is a form of dragging one's heels. It always borders on dishonesty but it is a dishonesty for which there is no known substitute in a capitalist country. Many nineteenth-century Americans in the Northeast acted every day as if they believed that economic expansion, urbanization, and industrialization represented the greatest good. It is to their credit that they indirectly acknowledged that the pursuit of these "masculine" goals meant damaging, perhaps losing, another good, one they increasingly included under the "feminine" ideal. Yet the fact remains that their regret was calculated not to interfere with their actions. We remember that Little Eva's beautiful death, which Stowe presents as part of a protest against slavery, in no way hinders the working of that system. The minister and the lady were appointed by their society as the champions of sensibility. They were in the position of contestants in a fixed fight: they had agreed to put on a convincing show, and to lose. The fakery involved was finally crippling for all concerned.

The sentimentalization of theological and secular culture was an inevitable part of the self-evasion of a society both committed to laissez-faire industrial expansion and disturbed by its consequences. America, impelled by economic and social developments of international scope, abandoned its theological modes of thought at the same time its European counterparts abandoned theirs; it lacked, however, the means they possessed to create substitutes. American culture, younger and less formed than that of any European country, had not yet developed sufficiently rich and diversified secular traditions to serve as carriers for its ongoing intellectual life. The pressures for self-rationalization of the crudest kind were overpowering in a country propelled so rapidly toward industrial capitalism with so little cultural context to slow or complicate its course; sentimentalism provided the inevitable rationalization of the economic order.

In the modernization of American culture that began in the Victorian period, some basic law of dialectical motion was disrupted, unfulfilled, perhaps disproved. Calvinism was a great faith, with great limitations: it was repressive, authoritarian, dogmatic, patriarchal to an extreme. Its demise was inevitable, and in some real sense, welcome. Yet it deserved, and elsewhere and at other times found, great opponents. One could argue that the logical antagonist of Calvinism was a fully humanistic, historically minded romanticism. Exponents of such romanticism appeared in mid-nineteenth-century America—one thinks particularly of Margaret Fuller and Herman Melville—but they were rare. In America, for economic and social reasons, Calvinism was largely defeated by an anti-intellectual sentimentalism purveyed by men and women whose victory did not achieve their finest goals; America lost its male-dominated theological tradition without gaining a comprehensive feminism or an adequately modernized religious sensibility. It is crucial that I be as clear here as I can. The tragedy of nineteenth-century northeastern society is not the demise of Calvinist patriarchal structures, but rather the failure of a viable, sexually diversified culture to replace them. "Feminization" inevitably guaranteed, not simply the loss of the finest values contained in Calvinism, but the continuation of male hegemony in different guises. The triumph of the "feminizing," sentimental forces that would generate mass culture redefined and perhaps limited the possibilities for change in American society. Sentimentalism, with its tendency to obfuscate the visible dynamics of development, heralded the cultural sprawl that has increasingly characterized post-Victorian life.

Notes

1. I hope the reasons I have chosen this period (1820-75) as the crucial one for the development of Victorian sentimentalism in the Northeast will become clear in the course of this book. Recent historical opinion has minimized the importance of the Civil War as a crucial dividing line for American culture. I will make just a few further points here. First, the period 1820-1875 includes the initial commercialization of culture, most notably the revolution in printing and the rise of

nationally circulated magazines. Second, the most important work of the leading figures in the sentimentalization process seems to appear and, more significantly, to receive its highest valuation during these years. Elizabeth Stuart Phelps, for example, who was born late in the period (1844), produces her most characteristic work, *The Gates Ajar,* in 1868; thereafter, she repeats herself and receives steadily less critical attention and praise until her death in 1911. Third, the period marks the time when the majority of Protestants in the Northeast changed from a strict to a "liberal" creed and when the Protestant Church forged its relationship with the newly commercialized culture: both changes are still in force today. In Chapter Three, I try to break the period into smaller, defined units. In Chapter Seven, I discuss its culmination in the early 1870s with the late work of Henry Ward Beecher and Harriet Beecher Stowe.

2. In discussing what I am calling Calvinism, the older Protestant tradition of the Northeast, I am focusing throughout this study on its eighteenth- rather than its seventeenth-century New England exponents not because the former were greater than the latter but because it was the word the ministerial and feminine groups I am studying most commonly employed to describe the older, sterner creed of their forebears.

3. Martin Marty, in the "Foreword" to *Righteous Empire: The Protestant Experience in America* (New York, 1970), notes: "today seven out of ten citizens identify themselves as Protestants" (n.p.).

4. For an excellent introduction to Neo-orthodoxy, see Sydney E. Ahlstrom, *A Religious History of American People* (New Haven and London, 1972), pp. 932-48, and Martin E. Marty, *op. cit.,* pp. 233-43. For the most astute Neo-orthodox analysis of the American religious tradition, see Francis Miller, Wilhelm Pauck, and H. Richard Niebuhr, *The Church Against the World* (Chicago, 1935), and H. Richard Niebuhr, *The Social Sources of Demonationalism* (New York, 1929). Scholars like Perry Miller, who might be seen as the head of "Neo-Orthodox" historiography, did not necessarily share the religious beliefs of those they studied, or of the Neo-orthodox theologians (the Niebuhr brothers, Paul Tillich, and others) who began to write in the 1920s. But they are "Neo-orthodox" in the sense that they admire the Calvinist tradition and regret its passing.

5. This is the title of a novel published by Stowe in 1871.

6. My understanding of "influence" and how it functioned foe the clerical and feminine groups under discussion was shaped by the work of Sigmund Freud and Heinz Kohut on narcissism as well as by the theories of a number of sociologists. I came to feel that, while Protestant ministers had been part of an elite group, they were increasingly joining middle-class women and becoming part of a special subculture. Such subculture groups, past and present, evince certain inherent patterns. Most simply, one might say that society forces members of a subculture at any moment of intersection with the larger culture into a constant, simplified, and often demeaning process of self-identification. The minister between 1820 and 1875 was beginning to experience the enforced self-simplification women had long known. In 1820 the statement "I am a minister" had a series of possible precise connotations, theological and political. By 1875, the statement meant what it does today: it connotes vague church-bound efforts at "goodness." "I am a housewife," millions of American women have been explaining implicitly and explicitly for the last hundred and fifty years; yet, the term "housewife" is imprecise and obfuscating to an extreme. Surely that was (and is) as much difference between tending a childless urban apartment and running a fully populated farm household as there was between practicing law and selling merchandise. Yet just at the period when women were increasingly adopting a punitively generalized mode of self-description, men were labeling themselves in ever more specialized terms. The all-inclusive designation "lady" slowly gave way over the nineteenth century to the equally blank-check appellation "housewife." In contrast, the polite term "gentleman" had no real successor; it fragmented into a thousand parts, personal, political, and professional. Why have not men identified themselves by an equally adequate, or inadequate, catchall phrase such as "breadwinner"? Quite obviously, because society expresses its greater esteem for masculine occupations by honoring them with a highly differentiated nomenclature.

   Naturally, those belonging to a subculture will themselves be preoccupied with who they are, often in equally simplistic terms. They will struggle obsessively, repetitiously, and monotonously to deal with the burden of self-dislike implied and imposed by their society apparently low evaluation of them. In a sense, they will be forced into some version of narcissism, by which I mean to suggest not only a psychological process but a sociological and even a political one. Narcissism is best defined not as exaggerated self-esteem but as a refusal to judge the self by alien, objective means, a willed inability to allow the world to play its customary role in the business of self-evaluation. Heinz Kohut has explained lucidly the causes for development of narcissism: "Being threatened in the maintenance of a cohesive self because in early life . . . [the narcissist is] lacking in adequate confirming responses . . . from the environment, [he] turns to self-stimulation in order to retain [his] . . . precarious cohesion." The narcissist must always by definition be self-taught, because the world's lessons are inevitably unacceptable to his ego. He is committed not only to an underestimation of the facts, but, in Freud's words, to an "over-estimation of the power of wishes and mental processes . . . a belief in the magical virtue of words and a method of dealing with the outer world—the art of magic." Narcissism can necessitate the replacement of society by the self, reality by literature. See Heinz Kohut, "Thoughts on Narcissism and Narcissistic Rage," a paper delivered as the A. A. Brill Lecture of the New York Psychoanalytic Society on November 30, 1971; Sigmund Freud, "On Narcissism: An Introduction" in *A General Selection from the Works of Sigmund Freud,* ed. John Rickman, M. D. (New York, 1957), p. 106. For a definition of minority groups, see Helen Mayer Hacker, "Women as a Minority Group," Bobbs-Merrill Reprint Series in the Social Sciences, 5-108. The ministry had constituted in the past what Suzanne Keller calls a "strategic elite"; see Suzanne Keller, *Beyond the Ruling Elite: Strategic Elites in Modern Society* (New York, 1963).

7. See Henry James, "Anthony Trollope," in *The Future of the Novel: Essays on the Art of Fiction,* ed. Leon Edel (New York, 1956), pp. 247-8.

8. There are many interesting studies of this aspect of the reading phenomenon. Works that particularly

stimulated my thinking are the "Introduction" in *The Oven Birds: American Women on Womanhood 1820-1920,* ed. Gail Parker (New York, 1972), pp. 1-56; Roland Barthes, *The Pleasures of the Text,* trans. Richard Miller (New York, 1975); and Raymond Williams, "Base and Superstructure in Marxists Cultural Theory," *New Left Review* 82 (1973), especially 12-16.

9. I am indebted for my understanding of the positive side of sentimentalism to the superb study by Elaine Showalter, *The Female Tradition in the English Novel: From Charlotte Brontë to Doris Lessing* (Princeton, 1976). For the J. S. Mill reference, see *The Autobiography of John Stuart Mill* (New York, n.d.), pp. 103-17.

10. Herman Melville, *White-Jacket, or the World in a Man-of-War* (New York, 1967), p. 141.

WHITNEY CHADWICK (ESSAY DATE 1990)

SOURCE: Chadwick, Whitney. "Separate But Unequal: Woman's Sphere and the New Art." In *Women, Art, and Society,* pp. 210-35. London, England: Thames and Hudson, 1990.

In the following essay, Chadwick describes how late-nineteenth century art by American women, often influenced by French art and society, reflected changes in women's perceptions of how their social roles should be defined.

The Philadelphia Centennial Exposition of 1876 represented a milestone in women's struggles to achieve public visibility in American cultural life. Approximately one tenth of the works of art in the United States section were by women, more than in any other country's display. Emily Sartain of Philadelphia received a Centennial gold medal, the only one awarded to a woman, for a painting called *The Reproof* (now lost). Sartain's painting was displayed in the United States section, but the exhibition also boasted a Women's Pavilion with over 40,000 square feet of exhibition space devoted to the work of almost 1500 women from at least 13 countries.

Presided over by Elizabeth Duane Gillespie, Benjamin Franklin's great-grand-daughter and an experienced community leader, the Women's Centennial Executive Committee had raised over $150,000 amid considerable controversy. The building's existence as a segregated display area had been contested from the beginning. "It would, in my opinion," wrote the Director of Grounds, "be in every respect better for *them* to occupy a building exclusively their own and devoted to women's work alone." To others, the presence of a separate exhibition facility for women at the Exposition signaled an institutionalizing of women's productions in isolation from those of men. Sensitive to the implications of exhibiting women's art only in relation to other areas of feminine creative activity, and angered because no attention was given to women's wages and working conditions, radical feminists refused to participate. "The Pavilion was not a true exhibit of women's art," declared Elizabeth Cady Stanton, because it did not include samples of objects made by women in factories owned by men. Ironically, the building became both the most powerful and conspicuous symbol of the women's movement for equal rights and the most visible indication of woman's separate status.

The Pavilion's eclectic and controversial exhibits included furniture, weaving, laundry appliances, embroideries, educational and scientific exhibitions, and sculpture, painting, and photography, as well as engravings. Jenny Brownscombe, a graduate of Cooper Union and one of the first members of the Art Students' League of New York sent examples of the genre subjects she drew for *Harper's* Weekly. Among the many paintings by women were the landscapes of Mary Kollock, Sophia Ann Towne Darrah, and Annie C. Shaw; the still-lifes of Fidelia Bridges and Virginia and Henrietta Granberry; drawings of old New York by Eliza Greatorex; historical subjects by Ida Waugh and Elizabeth C. Gardner; and portraits by Anna Lea Merritt. The Philadelphia sculptor Blanche Nevins sent plaster casts of an *Eve* and a *Cinderella;* Florence Freeman offered a small bust. Foley and Whitney sent bas-reliefs and statuettes, and Whitney also provided a bronze cast of the *Roma,* a bronze head of an old peasant woman asleep, and a fountain for the center of the Horticulture Hall.

The lumping together of fine arts, industrial arts, and handicrafts, and of the work of professional and amateur artists implicitly equated the work of all women on the basis of gender alone. Critics were quick to challenge the displays for their lack of "quality" and women once again found themselves confronting universalizing definitions of "women's" production in a gender-segregated world.

In 1876 Louisa May Alcott, using the proceeds from her writing to pay for her sister's European art education, sent May to Paris for further study. May Alcott's copies of Turner's paintings had won Ruskin's praise in London and she was determined to succeed as an artist. Her letters home describe a comfortable lifestyle with a supportive group of female art students sharing meals and encouraging each other's ambitions. The woman they most admired in Paris was Mary Cassatt, who with

ON THE SUBJECT OF...

ANNA JULIA HAYWOOD COOPER (1858-1964)

Anna Julia Haywood Cooper, born into slavery, overcame the political, social, and economic obstacles imposed upon her because of her gender, race, and economic circumstances, and became a pioneering—and often controversial—figure in the struggle for African American rights in the late nineteenth century. A longtime educator, Cooper earned a doctorate at the Sorbonne in Paris in 1925. She expressed the personal beliefs reflected in her political and social activism and in her dedication as an educator in her well-known collection of essays, *A Voice from the South* (1892). In this work, which received both critical and popular acclaim upon its publication, Cooper examines the chronic American afflictions of racism and sexism, carefully delineating the African American woman's situation in the 1890s.

In "Womanhood: A Vital Element in the Regeneration and Progress of a Race" Cooper argues that African American people will not be able to overcome the burden of slavery until black men acknowledge their connection with black women. She argues that women provide a unique sensibility to social and political circles, despite being barred from those arenas. Cooper claims that the sense of duty and community felt in American society stems directly from female influence, and by not acknowledging these traits and debts men limit how far that society can progress. As an active participant in the feminist movement in the 1900s, Cooper took issue with the racism rampant within the movement, and in her essay "Woman Versus the Indian" Cooper points out that feminist ideals and missions for changing the situation for women would not be complete until fundamental rights and opportunities had been extended to all women—regardless of race, religion, or creed. She was one of the first writers to argue for this more "global" feminist perspective.

several other women painters became the first women to align themselves with a stylistically radical movement.

Cassatt (1844-1926), daughter of a wealthy Pennsylvania businessman, became a student at the Pennsylvania Academy in 1861, taking her place among a number of dedicated women students which eventually included Alice Barber Stephens, Catherine A. Drinker, Susan MacDowell Eakins, Anna Sellers, Cecilia Beaux, and Anna Klumpke. By 1866, she was settled in Paris where she was soon joined by the rest of her family. Her teas were a mecca for younger women, she was generous with introductions and advice, and her professional commitment was an inspiration to the young students. "Miss Cassatt was charming as usual in two shades of brown satin and rep," wrote May Alcott to her family in Concord, "being very lively and a woman of real genius, she will be a first-class light as soon as her pictures get a little circulated and known, for they are handled in a masterly way, with a touch of strength one seldom finds coming from a woman's fingers."

Alcott's comments reveal the conflicts still facing the woman artist caught within an ideology of sexual difference which gave the privilege to male expression and often forced women to choose between marriage and a career. These conflicts make up Louisa May Alcott's short novella *Diana and Persis* (written in 1879 but only recently published). The novel's female characters were modeled on herself and her sister, and on their friends among the White Marmorean Flock. One chapter is titled "Puck" in reference to Hosmer's successful piece. Alcott explores the connections between art, politics, spinsterhood, and the female community. Persis, a young painter funded by her family to study abroad, wins minor recognition in the Paris art world (where May Alcott had a still-life accepted in the Salon of 1877). Devotion to her art and devotion to home and family are her consuming passions, but after first choosing art, Persis discovers that as a True Woman she cannot deny her feelings and her desire for domestic life. May/Persis demanded the right both to marital happiness and artistic success, but her expectations ran counter to the structures of patriarchal nineteenth-century society. She loudly proclaims her allegiance to an earlier, heroic generation of female artists like Rosa Bonheur, but in the end her choice of marriage limits her options as an artist.

During the years when Cassatt, May Alcott, and other young women flocked to Paris for study, the city itself was undergoing dramatic changes.

The rebuilding of Paris by Baron Haussmann and Napoleon III in the 1850s and 1860s physically transformed the city. T. J. Clark, Eunice Lipton, Griselda Pollock, and others have ably demonstrated the evolution of a new social matrix as artists and writers, prostitutes and the new bourgeoisie were drawn into the streets and parks, the cafés and restaurants. Baudelaire's call for an art of modern life emphasizing the fleeting and transitory moment, and the fugitive sensation was embodied in the contemporary focus and realist approach of Degas's and Manet's paintings, in the broken brushstrokes and fleeting gestures of Impressionism, and in the poetic imagery of the flâneur, that exclusively masculine figure who moved about the new public arenas of the city relishing its spectacles.

The collapse of the Second Empire in 1870 and the establishment of the Third Republic in 1875 produced an increasingly democratized middle-class culture. By the 1870s, an active consuming public thronged the boulevards, department stores, and international expositions. The painters later known as the Impressionists—Claude Monet, Camille Pissarro, Berthe Morisot, Pierre-Auguste Renoir, Edouard Manet, Edgar Degas, Alfred Sisley, Mary Cassatt, and others—produced their own version of modernity, but their stylistic innovations and their new subject-matter must be seen in the larger context of a restructuring of public and private spheres.

In "Modernity and the Spaces of Femininity," Pollock maps the new spaces of masculinity and femininity and articulates the differences "socially, economically, subjectively" between being a woman and being a man in Paris at the end of the century. Some women were drawn to Impressionism precisely because the new painting legitimized the subject-matter of domestic social life of which women had intimate knowledge, even as they were excluded from imagery of the bourgeois social sphere of the boulevard, café, and dance hall. Recent feminist scholarship has focused on the fact that, as upper-class women, Morisot and Cassatt did not have access to the easy exchange of ideas about painting which took place among male artists in the studio and the café. Yet despite Morisot's inability to join her male colleagues at the Café Guerbois, the Morisots were regulars at Manet's Thursday evening soirées, where they met and talked with other painters and critics. Likewise, Cassatt and Degas regularly exchanged ideas about painting. And there is considerable evidence to suggest that Impressionism was equally an

"Sara in Green Bonnet," by Mary Cassett, 1901.

expression of the bourgeois family as a defense against the threat of rapid urbanization and rapid industrialization: domestic interiors, private gardens, seaside resorts. Although Morisot's access to public sites was limited, critics of the time appear not to have ranked the subject-matter of her work in any way differently from that of her male colleagues, though most of them agreed that her presentation of it was more "agreeable."

Work now being done on the social meanings produced by Impressionist paintings suggests a complex relationship between the new painting and the new middle-class family (to which most of the Impressionists belonged). Moreover, the decision to work *en plein air* and to forego the historical subjects, with the complex studio setups and multiple models they required, transformed the relationship between the painter's daily life and his or her studio life; this aspect of Impressionism deserves more study for it profoundly shaped women's relationship to the movement.

During the earlier nineteenth century, academic painters in France often maintained studios in, or near, their homes, but it was the decision to paint scenes of everyday life that moved the easel into the drawing room. Visiting Mme. Manet, Morisot's mother is able to offer a commentary on Manet's painting-in-progress of Eva Gonzales,

"Sur la Falaise aux Petites Dalles," by Berthe Morisot, 1873.

as the women sit in the studio while Manet works. When Degas sketches in the Morisot garden after lunch, Mme. Morisot provides her own critique; "Monsieur Degas has made a sketch of Yves, that I find indifferent; he chatted all the time he was doing it. . . ." "Your life must be charming at this moment," Edmé Morisot wrote enviously to her sister in 1869, "to talk with Monsieur Degas while watching him draw, to laugh with Manet, to philosophize with Puvis."

Recent publications by Pollock, Tamar Garb, Kathleen Adler, and other feminist art historians have exhaustively documented the work of women Impressionists in relationship to the new painting. Tracing the constraints placed on women like Cassatt, Morisot, Gonzales, and Marie Bracquemond by the social ideologies of bourgeois culture, they have explored the development of their work and isolated their specific contributions to the imagery of Impressionism.

Berthe Morisot numbered Manet, Renoir, Degas, Pissarro, and Monet among her friends. Written about by Emile Zola and Stéphane Mallarmé, among others, she was described in 1877 by the critic for *Le Temps* as the "one real Impressionist in this group." Yet until the appearance of revisionist art histories, and the first major retrospective of her work in 1987, art historians almost exclusively framed her work within the structures of her associations with male painters. There is no evidence that Morisot, or Cassatt, were patronized by their painter friends. Yet they moved in an artistic circle in which the threat of women was never entirely silenced. "I consider women writers, lawyers, and politicians (such as George Sand, Mme. Adam and other bores) as monsters and nothing but five-legged calves," declared Renoir. "The woman artist is merely ridiculous, but I am in favor of the female singer and dancer." Renoir's comment divides women by class and occupation. Working-class women are admired for entertaining men; professional women with public roles are seen as usurpers of male authority or destroyers of domestic harmony, as they were earlier pictured in Honoré Daumier's lithograph *The Blue Stockings* (1844). The modern feminist movement in France, launched in 1866 by Maria Deraismes and Léon Richer, organized the first international congress on women's rights in 1878, at the height of Impressionism, but Impressionist painting records no traces of this aspect of contemporary life. Nor does it acknowledge the increasing numbers of middle-class women who were seeking training and employment outside the home (in 1866, there were 2,768,000 women employed in non-agricultural jobs in France) for Impressionism presents us with few images of women at work outside the domestic environment.

Morisot and Cassatt's ability to sustain professional lives and negotiate relationships of some parity with their male colleagues was class specific. Morisot's marriage to Manet's brother Eugène, and her family's wealth and continuing support were factors in her success; Cassatt's role as an unmarried daughter carried with it time-consuming domestic responsibilities, but it also provided the secure network of relationships from which she drew her art. Bracquemond (1841-1916), on the other hand, did not come from a prosperous, cultured family and enjoyed no such support. Marriage to the engraver Félix Bracquemond in 1869 provided an introduction into artistic circles, but his jealousy of her work inhibited her development and today she is the least well-known of the women Impressionists.

The Paris of the Third Republic offered a variety of artists' societies and exhibition venues from the official Salon to the Union des Femmes Artistes which, shaped by Rosa Bonheur's example, conducted an annual Salon des Femmes. Women Impressionists related to these exhibitions in varying ways. Gonzales, a friend and pupil of Manet's who had studied at the Chaplin atelier, exhibited only at the official salons. Her *Little Soldier* (1870), influenced by the straightforward realism of Manet's *The Fifer* (1866), was exhibited at the Salon of 1870. Bracquemond and Cassatt exhibited with the Impressionists from 1876. Morisot, on the other hand, was one of the original members of the group, exhibited with them in 1874, and continued to participate in every exhibition save the one held in 1878, the year her daughter was born. She was also included in the group's auction at the Hôtel Drouot in 1875, where her painting, *Interior* (now called *Young Woman With a Mirror,* c. 1875), brought 480 francs, the highest price paid for any painting.

Born in 1841, the youngest of three daughters of a wealthy French civil servant, Morisot and her sister Edme displayed an early talent for drawing. Their second teacher, Joseph Guichard, was moved to warn Mme. Morisot of the implications of such precocious talent; "Considering the characters of your daughters, my teaching will not endow them with minor drawing room accomplishments, they will become painters. Do you realize what this means? In the upper-class milieu to which you belong, this will be revolutionary, I might say almost catastrophic." Further instruction by Corot and Oudinot strengthened the naturalism of their work and the two sisters exhibited together in four successive salons beginning in 1864. Edmé's marriage to a naval officer in 1869 ended her professional life, a fact she lamented in letters to her sister. Despite the support of her family, and that of her husband Eugène Manet, whom she married in 1874, Morisot's letters frequently express her own hesitations and doubts about her work. "This painting, this work that you mourn for," she wrote to Edmé in 1869 shortly after the latter's wedding, "is the cause of many griefs and many troubles."

Morisot's subjects, like those of Gonzales, Cassatt, Bracquemond, and their male colleagues, were drawn from everyday life. The casual immediacy, lack of sentimentality, and feathery brushstrokes of paintings like *Catching Butterflies* (1873), *Summer's Day* (1879), and *Mother and Sister of the Artist* (1870) meld contemporary subjects with the Impressionist desire to capture the transitory effects of life. Gonzales's *Pink Morning,* a pastel of 1874, is typical of her many interiors with women, while Marie Bracquemond sited many of her works in the family garden, perhaps a secure spot in her troubled life.

Morisot and Cassatt met around 1878, probably through Degas who encouraged Cassatt to exhibit with the Impressionists after the painting she submitted to the Salon was rejected. "At last I could work with complete independence without concerning myself with the eventual judgment of a jury," she later said. "I already knew who were my true masters. I admired Manet, Courbet, and Degas. I hated conventional art. I began to live." Cassatt had been exhibiting for more than ten years when she joined the Impressionist group. Like Morisot, her subjects evolved within the boundaries of her sex and class. Prevented from asking men other than family members to pose, limited in their access to the public life of the café and boulevard, both women concentrated on aspects of modern domestic life. Pollock has ably demonstrated how Morisot's and Cassatt's paintings demarcate the spaces of masculinity and femininity through their spatial compressions and their juxtapositions of differing spatial systems. Long considered a painter of unproblematic depictions of mothers and children, Cassatt in fact brought an incisive eye to bear on the rituals and gestures through which femininity is constructed and signified: crocheting, embroidering, knitting, attending children, visiting, taking tea.

The intellectual concentration and self-contained focus of Cassatt's depiction of her mother in *Reading "Le Figaro"* (1883) is now understood as relating more directly to representations of the intellectual life of men like Cézanne's *Portrait of Louis-Auguste Cézanne Reading L'Evènement* (1866) than to the history of representations of women. Her painting of her sister Lydia driving a trap, *Woman and Child Driving* (1879), may be unique in late nineteenth-century French painting in depicting a woman doing the driving while a coachman sits idly by; and her many paintings of women and children, though influenced by Correggio's madonnas and children which she greatly admired, are less universalized depictions of maternity than responses to the specific ways that social class is reproduced through the family.

Paintings like Morisot's *Psyche* (1876) and Cassatt's *Mother and Child* (c. 1905) return to the conventional association of women and mirrors. The private daily rituals of women at their toilette were a popular subject for painters in the 1870s and 1880s. Morisot's *Psyche,* with its double-play on the mythological tale of Venus's son Cupid who fell in love with a mortal and on the French term for mirror, or *psyché,* turns on the adolescent woman's contemplation of her own image. Garb and Adler have pointed out that, as there are no representations of men bathing and dressing, we must assume that although symbolic associations with Venus and Vanitas are abandoned, such paintings nevertheless perpetuate notions of vanity as "natural" to women. Yet Morisot's painting is a deeply sympathetic representation of self-awareness and awakening sexuality, while Cassatt's painting emphasizes the role of the mirror in inculcating an idea of femininity as something mediated through observation.

The complex and gendered organization of a subject is brilliantly articulated in Cassatt's *Woman in Black at the Opera* (1880). The subject of the ball, concert, or opera was a popular one among the Impressionists and one in which event and audience could be collapsed into the same spectacle. Cassatt, however, suppresses details of the event in order to concentrate on the figure of a young woman in black. Intent on the opera, she focuses her glass on the stage. But in this public world, she herself has become part of the spectacle, and the object of the gaze of a man in the balcony who turns his glasses on her.

Issues of public and private space, and amateur and professional production, also reshaped the design fields during the second half of the nineteenth century. The new focus on the middle-class home, and the self-sufficient world which it signified, is central to the reform of the decorative arts in England and America. Here also, women played a considerable, if complicated role.

There were markedly more women in the design fields by the 1860s as a result of institutionalized arts education for women. By 1870, Hannah Barlow, trained at the Lambeth School of Art and Design in London and one of the first and most important art pottery decorators, was producing freelance designs for Doulton Pottery. The surge of interest in art pottery was sparked by the efforts of the two most famous ceramic firms in Britain—Minton and Doulton—to produce handcrafted ware on a large commercial scale for middle-class homes. Commercial production, however, was organized around traditional divisions of labor. While male designers received credit for their designs for china surfaces, the painters, usually female and often working and artisan class, remained anonymous. At the same time, the popularity of china painting as a hobby for upper-class women grew rapidly, becoming an amateur craze after 1870.

A similar situation prevailed in the production of professional secular embroidery. The Royal School of Art Needlework was founded in 1872 to provide suitable employment for gentlewomen and to revive the craft of ornamental needlework. By 1875, with Queen Victoria as its patron and Lady Marion Alford its vice-president, the school's embroidery department was producing crewel work from designs by leaders in the Arts and Crafts Movement like Edward Burne-Jones, William Morris, and Walter Crane.

The first major exhibition of work from the Royal School of Art Needlework took place at the Philadelphia Centennial Exposition in 1876 where its success launched the craft revival in America. Between 1876 and 1891, when new facilities opened at Jane Addams's Hull House in Chicago with an exhibition borrowed from Toynbee Hall—London's center for the application of Arts and Crafts theory to improving the lives of the urban poor—large numbers of women contributed to the reform of design.

At the heart of the Arts and Crafts Movement, as it came to be known in Britain and America, was a pre-industrial medieval ideal of a fusion of the designer and the maker. Revolting against the anonymous authorship and shoddy craftsmanship of industrially produced goods, William Morris dreamed of a socialist utopia in which individuals were not alienated from their labor. The origins of the Movement in Britain lay in nineteenth-century medieval revivals like Gothic, but the spirit of rural craft collaboratives which Morris envisioned belonged to the nineteenth century's idealization of a rural way of life fast giving way to industrialization and urbanization. Wishing to make art available to everyone, and to unite artists, designers, and craftworkers around the ideals of craftsmanship, good design, and the renewed dignity of labor, Morris dreamed of setting up small workshops and countrywide organizations which could revive dying traditions like lacemaking and crewel embroidery.

Morris anticipated a day when the sexual division of labor within the arts would vanish and even domestic life would be equably shared by the sexes. Anthea Callen's *Women Artists of the Arts and Crafts Movement* (1979) elaborates another reality—the gradual evolution of an entirely traditional sexual division of labor within the Movement itself, with women staffing the embroidery workshops and men conducting the business and serving as named designers. Above all, Callen emphasizes, it was men who evolved the Movement's philosophy, articulated its goals, and organized the major aspects of its production.

Women, primarily family or friends of Morris and his colleagues, were involved in the Morris firm itself from the beginning. In the 1850s, Morris and his wife Jane had revived the lost art of crewel embroidery by studying and "unpicking" old examples (an undertaking which has generally been credited to Morris alone). Morris then left the production of embroideries in medieval techniques to his wife and her sister Elizabeth. In 1885, Morris placed his daughter May in charge of the embroidery workshop. Georgiana Burne-Jones, the wife of Edward Burne-Jones, was also soon involved in embroidery and wood engraving while Charles Faulkner's sisters, Kate and Lucy, painted tiles, executed embroidery and, Kate at least, designed wallpaper. Apart from the embroidery section, however, the Morris firm employed few women in its workshops and the general involvement of women was heavily weighted in the direction of traditionally "feminine" undertakings like lace and needlework.

In addition to embroidery designed by Morris, Burne-Jones, and Crane and executed at the Royal School of Art Needlework, the decorative arts displayed at the Philadelphia Centennial Exposition in 1876 included Doulton pottery, Ernest Chaplet's "Limoges" glazes, and Japanese-influenced proto-Art Nouveau ceramics. Ceramics and embroidery had the greatest impact on American women.

The American Arts and Crafts Movement was more stylistic than ideological (with the exception of Gustav Stickley and Elbert Hubbard's ideal of a return to the simple, community life of preindustrial America). Yet it provided many middle-class women with a socially respectable and humanitarian outlet for their artistic productions. Candace Wheeler, a wealthy and progressive New Yorker, was impressed by the embroideries of Morris and Company. Struck by the fact that needlework could have financial value, "for it meant the conversion of the common and inalienable heritage of feminine skill in the use of the needle into a means of art expression and pecuniary profit," she envisioned a society similar to the Royal Society of Art Needlework which would organize the sale of needlework, china painting, and other crafts, by women who needed income. Between 1877 and 1883, Wheeler organized the Society of Decorative Art of New York City and worked with Tiffany in setting up a company called Associated Artists, in which she was in charge of textiles, embroidery, tapestry, and needlework, while Tiffany took charge of glass design. By 1883, she was running an enormously successful textile company composed entirely of women and producing printed silks and large-scale tapestries.

The display of china painting by members of the Cincinnati Pottery Club at the Philadelphia Centennial Exposition represented the vanguard of a surprising number of American women who went on to professional careers in the field of art pottery, despite the fact that women's involvement in the Arts and Crafts Movement began with socially prominent women wishing to perfect their skills as an accomplishment.

Among the many visitors to the ceramics display was Mary Louise McLaughlin (1847-1939) of Cincinnati, whose experiments with reproducing the underglaze slip decoration on Haviland faience pieces became the prototype for art pottery decoration in the United States for the next quarter century. Women, many of whom began as amateur china painters, were behind the formation of the Newcomb, Pauline, Robineau, and other American art potteries. McLaughlin's rival was Maria Longworth Nichols (later Storer, 1849-1932), who had also begun experimenting with underglaze techniques at the Dallas Pottery in Cincinnati after the Philadelphia Exposition. In 1879, Nicholas Longworth offered his daughter premises of her own and the Rookwood Pottery was founded in the Spring of 1880.

Her family's wealth, her father's long history of artistic patronage, and her own social standing in Cincinnati made possible Nichols's increasing professionalism. Her work was viewed as both morally and artistically charitable for she "follows the traditions of her family in devotion to the wellbeing and advancement of her native place." She herself summarized her objective as "my own gratification" rather than the employment of needy women; perhaps not surprisingly, most of the early Rookwood pieces were produced by amateurs. In 1881, Nichols began the Rookwood School of Pottery Decoration. Two years later, she employed her old friend, William Watts Taylor, to take over the administration and organization of the pottery. Taylor, who had little sympathy for lady amateurs, soon closed the school as a pretext for evicting the amateurs, who were then largely replaced by men.

Despite its labor practices, which included a division between designer and decorator that became the model for most art potteries, the Rookwood Pottery played a formative role in the development of art pottery in America, winning a gold medal at the Paris Exposition Universelle of 1889. The full history of women's involvement in the art pottery movement, including the Cincinnati women's training centers and art clubs, remains to be written. What little we know of the careers of Mary McLaughlin, Mary Sheerer, the Overbeck sisters, Pauline Jacobus, and Adelaide Robineau offers tantalizing evidence of a female presence in the American Arts and Crafts Movement which extended to other areas of production as well. Intimately connected with women's roles as domestic and social reformers, the art pottery movement also represented a move by American middle-class women to professionalize the decorative arts.

By the time the World's Columbian Exposition (or World's Fair) opened in Chicago in 1893, American women had evolved a new sense of identity and purpose. Goals and strategies varied widely among feminists, and there were still many women not involved in the struggle for equal rights and the vote, but representatives of all groups came together to organize a woman's building intended to prove that women's achievements were equal to those of men. "The World's Columbian Exposition has afforded woman an unprecedented opportunity to present to the world a justification of her claim to be placed on complete equality with man," stated the preface to the official edition of *Art and Handicraft in the Woman's Building,* edited by Maud Howe Elliott.

The direction of the Woman's Building was in the hands of Mrs. Palmer Potter, a wealthy Chicago art collector, and her 117-member Board of Lady Managers. Palmer herself did not advocate equal rights for women, but her belief in women's potential was characteristic of mainstream middle-class feminism at the time. Although women had made great strides in education, art training, and social organizing, they still lacked the vote. And they remained caught between the demands of careers and motherhood, struggling continually against the limitations placed on them by the social category of femininity, against the trivializing of their work in relation to that of men, and against the mythologizing of its "otherness."

Elliott's description of the Woman's Building, designed by Sophia G. Hayden, a young graduate of the Massachusetts Institute of Technology architecture and design program, expressed her own acceptance of the ideology of separate spheres; "At that time [the first half of the nineteenth century] the highest praise that could be given to any woman's work was the criticism that it might be easily mistaken for a man's. Today we recognize that the more womanly a woman's work is the stronger it is. In Mr. Henry Van Brunt's appreciative account of Miss Hayden's work, the writer points out that it is essentially feminine in quality, as it should be. If sweetness and light were ever expressed in architecture, we find them in Miss Hayden's building." Sweetness and light are not, however, the criteria generally applied to architecture and Hayden's building, in fact, was admirably suited to the Neoclassical Beaux-Arts style which dominated the Fair's buildings.

The tensions underlying Elliott's and Van Brunt's comments were felt throughout the exposition, nowhere more keenly than in the Woman's Building. In 1889, tension was already evident between the Woman's Department, which had as one of its goals the building of a women's exhibition space, and the Queen Isabella Society, a suffragist group which did not want a segregated women's exhibition. The divisions between the various factions involved in the Woman's Building make a complex chapter in the history of late nineteenth-century American feminism. Nevertheless, women's creative presence was more powerfully felt in Chicago in 1893 than at any other time in the country's history.

The Board of Lady Managers had solicited historical and contemporary artifacts from around the world with the intention of demonstrating that women "were the originators of most of the industrial arts," having been the original makers of household goods, baskets, and clothing. Ethnographic displays sent by the Smithsonian Institution documented women's work in the form of embroidery, textiles, and basketry from American Indian, Eskimo, Polynesian, and African tribes. Women's contributions to industries from sheepshearing and raising silkworms to patents for household aids were included and the Women's Library, organized by the women of New York, included seven thousand volumes written by women around the world. Frederick Keppel, a well-known print dealer, provided 138 prints by women etchers and engravers from the late Renaissance to the present, including Diana Ghisi, Elisabetta Sirani, Geertruid Roghman, Maria Cosway, Marie de Medici, Angelica Kauffmann, Caroline Watson, Marie Bracquemond, Rosa Bonheur, Anna Lea Merritt, and Mary Cassatt. Visitors to the Woman's Building passed beneath murals of *Primitive Woman* and *Modern Woman* executed by Mary McMonnies and Cassatt.

Some professional women continued to resist exhibiting alongside amateurs in a building that included everything from household goods to embroidery, and others wished to exhibit with men in the Fine Arts Building. The result of the segregation and the wide range of amateur and professional production, wrote one critic, was a "gorgeous wealth of mediocrity." Although the Metropolitan Museum declined a request to send Bonheur's *Horse Fair,* the fine arts exhibition in the Woman's Building included works by respected artists like Cecilia Beaux, Vinnie Ream Hoxie, and Edmonia Lewis, as well as cat paintings by a seventy-two-year old Belgian artist named Henrietta Ronner and two paintings of dogs by Queen Victoria. Elizabeth Thompson's *Quatre Bras* and Anna Klumpke's *Portrait of Miss M.D.* were displayed, along with busts by Anne Whitney and Adelaide McFayden Johnson of prominent women in the suffrage, women's, and temperance movements. The largest exhibitions at the Fair were from women's craft associations in Britain. Rookwood Pottery and the Cincinnati Pottery Club were also well represented.

In the end, despite the unevenness of its displays and the critics' argument that mediocrity was the only possible result when "femininity was the first requisite and merit a secondary consideration," the Woman's Building overwhelmed visitors by the sheer magnitude and ambition of its displays. The building summed up women's past achievements, and made visible the multiple ways they had renegotiated the ideology of separate spheres, but the future belonged to a new generation and a new century. Mrs. Palmer's speech at the opening of the building did not ignore the fact that, by 1893, radical American women perceived the ideology of separate spheres as a male invention and a male response to feared competition in the work place.

By 1893, a new female heroine had emerged in the popular literary imagination, though her presence is barely recorded in painting. The novels of Grant Allen, Thomas Hardy, and George Gissing present female heroines who were in direct conflict with the traditional values of conservative society. Flaunting convention, the New Woman drinks, smokes, reads books, and leads a healthy athletic life. The photographer Frances Benjamin Johnson (1864-1952) burlesqued her delightfully in a self-portrait photograph and she is the subject of Albert Morrow's 1897 poster, *The New Woman,* for *Punch.* Also in 1897, the *Ladies Home Journal* serialized six illustrations by Alice Barber Stephens which collectively outlined the facets of new womanhood. Along with *The Woman in Religion, The Woman in the Home,* and *The Beauty of Motherhood,* they included *The Woman in Business, The Woman in Society,* and *The American Girl in Summer.* By 1900, feminists were demanding not just voting rights for women, but their right to higher education and the right to earn an income, and the modern woman had appeared.

Works Cited

The Philadelphia Centennial Exposition: Wanda M. Corn, "Women Building History," in *American Women Artists: 1830-1930,* pp. 26-34; Judith Paine, "The Women's Pavilion of 1876," *Feminist Art Journal* (Winter 1975-1976), pp. 5-12; Elizabeth Cady Stanton's response is quoted on p. 11.

The Pennsylvania Academy of the Fine Arts: *The Pennsylvania Academy and Its Women 1850-1920* (exh. cat., Pennsylvania Academy of the Fine Arts, Philadelphia, 1973), essay by Christine Jones Huber.

Susan MacDowell Eakins: *Thomas Eakins, Susan MacDowell Eakins, Elizabeth MacDowell Kenton* (exh. cat., North Cross School, Roanoke, Virginia, 1977); Louise Lippincott "Thomas Eakins in the Academy," *In This Academy* (Washington, D.C., 1976); *Susan MacDowell Eakins: 1851-1938* (exh. cat., The Pennsylvania Academy of the Fine Arts, Philadelphia, 1973), essays by Seymour Adelman and Susan Casteras.

May Alcott: Caroline Ticknor, *May Alcott: A Memoir* (Boston, 1927); Alcott's description of Cassatt is on p. 152; see also Sarah Elbert, *A Hunger for Home: Louisa May Alcott and Little Women*

(Philadelphia, 1984); Nina Auerbach, *Communities of Women: An Idea in Fiction* (Cambridge, Mass., 1978).

Women and Impressionism: Eunice Lipton, *Looking Into Degas: Uneasy Images of Women and Modern Life* (Berkeley, Los Angeles, and London, 1986); Tamar Garb, *Women Impressionists* (Oxford, 1986); Charles Moffett et al., *The New Painting: Impressionism 1874-1886* (Oxford, 1986); John Rewald, *The History of Impressionism* (New York, 1973); Theresa Ann Gronberg, "Femmes de Brasserie," *Art History* (vol. 7, September 1984), pp. 329-44; Norma Broude, "Degas's 'Misogyny'" in Broude and Garrard, *Feminism and Art History,* pp. 247-69; Griselda Pollock, "Modernity and the Spaces of Femininity," *Vision and Difference,* pp. 50-90.

Mary Cassatt: Griselda Pollock, *Mary Cassatt* (New York, 1980); Adelyn Breeskin, *The Graphic Work of Mary Cassatt: A Catalogue Raisonné* (New York, 1948); Breeskin, *Mary Cassatt: A Catalogue Raisonné of Paintings, Watercolors and Drawings* (Washington, D.C. 1970); Nancy Hale, *Mary Cassatt* (New York, 1975); John D. Kysela, "Mary Cassatt's Mystery Mural and the World's Fair of 1893," *Art Quarterly* (vol. 19, 1966), pp. 129-45; F. Sweet, *Miss Mary Cassatt: Impressionist from Pennsylvania* (Norman, Ok., 1966); Susan Fillin-Yeh, "Mary Cassatt's Images of Women," *Art Journal* (vol. 35, Summer 1976), pp. 359-63; Cassatt's remarks about painting are quoted in Pollock, *Mary Cassatt,* p. 9.

Berthe Morisot: *Berthe Morisot: Impressionist* (exh. cat., The National Gallery of Art, Washington, D.C., 1987), essays by Charles F. Stuckey and William P. Scott; Kathleen Adler and Tamar Garb, *Berthe Morisot* (Ithaca, N.Y., 1987); Mme. Morisot and Edmé are quoted in Denis Rouart, ed., *The Correspondence of Berthe Morisot* (New York, 1957), p. 35; M. L. Bataille and G. Wildenstein, *Berthe Morisot: Catalogue des peintures, pastels et aquarelles* (Paris, 1961); Leila Kinney, "Genre: A Social Contract?," *Art Journal* (vol. 46, Winter 1987), pp. 267-77; Linda Nochlin, "Morisot's *Wet Nurse*: The Construction of Work and Leisure in Impressionist Painting," *Women, Art, and Power,* pp. 37-56; Renoir's remarks about professional women are in *Renoir* (exh. cat., The Museum of Fine Arts, Boston, 1987), p. 15.

Eva Gonzales: François Mathey, *Six femme peintres* (Paris, 1931); *Salons de la Vie Moderne: Catalogue des peintures et pastels de Eva Gonzales* (Paris, 1885).

The Arts and Crafts Movement: Anthea Callen, *Women Artists of the Arts and Crafts Movement 1870-1914* (New York, 1979); Isabelle Anscombe, *A Woman's Touch: Women in Design from 1860 to the Present* (London, 1984); Anscombe and Charlotte Gere, *Arts and Crafts in Britain and America* (New York, 1978); *The Subversive Stitch*; Candace Wheeler is quoted in *A Woman's Touch,* p. 36.

Art pottery: Paul Evans, *Art Pottery of the United States: An Encyclopedia of Producers and Their Marks* (New York, 1974).

World's Columbian Exposition: Jeanne Madeline Weimann, *The Fair Women: The Story of the Woman's Building, World's Columbian Exposition, Chicago 1893* (Chicago, 1981).

FURTHER READING

Barry, David. *Women and Political Insurgency: France in the Mid-Nineteenth Century.* Basingstoke, England: Macmillan Press, Ltd., 1996, 213 p.

Recounts the participation of French women in political and social rebellions from the 1789 Revolution through the 1870s.

Browne, Stephen Howard. *Angelina Grimké.* East Lansing, Mich.: Michigan State University Press, 1999, 201 p.

Studies the social activism of Angelina Grimké, one of the first American women to publicly contest the institution of slavery and the social limitations placed on women.

Chadwick, Whitney. "Toward Utopia: Moral Reform and American Art in the Nineteenth Century." In *Women, Art, and Society,* pp. 191-209. London, England: Thames and Hudson, 1990.

Describes how American women in the first half of the nineteenth century increasingly used art as a means to show their support for social reform.

Clinton, Catherine. *The Other Civil War: American Women in the Nineteenth Century.* New York: Hill and Wang, 1984, 212 p.

Provides a chronological study of the increasingly organized struggles American women fought in the nineteenth century to challenge traditional roles assigned to them and to gain access to a number of social and political rights.

———. *The Columbia Guide to American Women in the Nineteenth Century.* New York: Columbia University Press, 1999, 364 p.

Examines the social activism of American women in the nineteenth century, concentrating on their efforts to secure domestic, educational, religious, legal, commercial, sexual, and political reforms.

Cole, Stephanie, and Alison M. Parker, eds. *Women and the Unstable State in Nineteenth-Century America.* College Station: Texas A & M University, 2000, 164 p.

Offers a collection of essays focusing on gender, political instability, and the centrality of marriage in the United States during the Civil War era.

Creese, Mary R. S. with contributions by Thomas M. Creese. *Ladies in the Laboratory? American and British Women in Science, 1800-1900: A Survey of Their Contributions to Research.* Lanham, Md.: The Scarecrow Press, Inc., 1998, 452 p.

Surveys the scientific achievements of nineteenth-century women in Britain and the United States.

Delamont, Sara and Lorna Duffin, eds. *The Nineteenth-Century Woman: Her Cultural and Physical World.* London, England: Croom Helm, 1978, 213 p.

Provides a collection of seven essays that explore the historical context which defined the role and status of nineteenth-century women in the United States and Britain, especially in the areas of education, medicine, and social science.

Dorsey, Bruce. *Reforming Men and Women: Gender in the Antebellum City.* Ithaca, N.Y.: Cornell University Press, 2002, 299 p.

Presents a comparative analysis of the language and ideas of nineteenth-century reformers in order to offer a fresh interpretation of gender history in the United States.

Douglass, Frederick. *Frederick Douglass on Women's Rights,* edited by Philip S. Foner. New York: Da Capo Press, 1976, 190 p.

First collection of the writings and speeches of a "woman's rights man."

Epstein, Barbara Leslie. *The Politics of Domesticity: Women, Evangelism and Temperance in Nineteenth-Century America.* Middletown, Conn.: Wesleyan University Press, 1981, 188 p.

Studies the ways nineteenth-century women used religion and evangelism and the temperance movement to become aware of and express their increasing antagonism toward men.

Freeman, Jo. *A Room at a Time: How Women Entered Party Politics.* Lanham, Md.: Rowman & Littlefield Publishers, Inc., 2000, 353 p.

Studies the political lives of American women, presenting two chapters dealing with the suffrage movement and other nineteenth-century reform organizations advocating women's rights.

Gilbert, Sandra M. and Susan Gubar. *The Madwoman in the Attic: The Woman Writer and the Nineteenth-Century Literary Imagination.* New Haven, Conn.: Yale University Press, 1979, 770 p.

Concentrates on nineteenth-century representations of women in the works of women authors, including Jane Austen, Emily and Charlotte Brontë, George Eliot, and Emily Dickinson.

———. Introduction to *No Man's Land: The Place of the Woman Writer in the Twentieth Century, Volume I: The War of the Words,* pp. 3-64. New Haven, Conn.: Yale University Press, 1988.

Sets the stage for a discussion of twentieth-century gender debates in literature by detailing the roots of gender debates in the nineteenth century.

Ginzberg, Lori D. *Women and the Work of Benevolence: Morality, Politics, and Class in the Nineteenth-Century United States.* New Haven, Conn.: Yale University Press, 1990, 230 p.

Study of the ideology of the superiority of female moral benevolence which underpinned most nineteenth-century reform movements led by middle-class American women.

Green, Harvey with the assistance of Mary-Ellen Perry. *The Light of the Home: An Intimate View of the Lives of Women in Victorian America.* New York: Pantheon Books, 1983, 204 p.

Examines the material possessions of women living in the late nineteenth and early twentieth centuries, discussing what the belongings reveal about women's domestic lives and concerns.

Greer, Germaine. "The Nineteenth Century." In *The Obstacle Race: The Fortunes of Women Painters and Their Work,* pp. 310-27. New York: Farrar, Straus, and Giroux, 1979.

Discusses the obstacles and condescension faced by female artists in the second half of the nineteenth century.

Groneman, Carol and Mary Beth Norton, eds. *"To Toil the Livelong Day": America's Women At Work, 1780-1980.* Ithaca, N.Y.: Cornell University Press, 1987, 313 p.

Includes six essays on issues related to the entrance of women into paid labor positions in the nineteenth century.

Hall, Catherine. "'The Butcher, the Baker, the Candlestick-maker': the shop and the family in the Industrial Revolution." In *White, Male and Middle-Class: Explorations in Feminism and History,* pp. 108-23. Oxford, England: Polity Press, 1992.

Describes how changes brought on by the industrial revolution transformed the domestic and working lives of urban, middle-class women and their families between 1780 and 1850.

Hellerstein, Erna Olafson, Leslie Parker Hume, and Karen M. Offen, eds. *Victorian Women: A Documentary Account of Women's Lives in Nineteenth-Century England, France, and the United States.* Stanford, Calif.: Stanford University Press, 1981, 534 p.

Documentary collection of letters, diary entries, and newsprint articles by nineteenth-century women in England, France, and the United States that shed light on a broad range of issues and conditions faced by women in the 1800s.

Helsinger, Elizabeth K. and Robin Lauterbach Sheets and William Veeder. *The Woman Question: Society and Literature in Britain and America, 1837-1883,* 3 Vols. New York: Garland Publishing, Inc., 1983.

Examines the status of the Victorian woman in England and the United States; Volume I studies the Victorian ideal and idealization of woman; Volume II discusses legal, scientific, religious and workplace arguments about the nature, rights, and duties of women; Volume III focuses on the value and influence of literary works by women and the depiction of women in writings by women and men.

Jose, Jim. "Contesting Patrilineal Descent in Political Theory: James Mill and Nineteenth-Century Feminism." *Hypatia* 15, no. 1 (winter 2000): 151-74.

Argues against the claim that James Mill was an early feminist, saying this false interpretation does not help explain the source of the feminist sympathies of his noted son, the political philosopher John Stuart Mill.

Keetley, Dawn and John Pettegrew, eds. *Public Women, Public Words: A Documentary History of American Feminism.* Madison, Wis.: Madison House, 1997, 377 p.

Offers a collection of speeches, essays, and other writings by American women since the colonial period identifying gender inequities as social problems to be reformed.

Kleinberg, S. J. *Women in the United States, 1830-1945.* Basingstoke, England: Macmillan Press Ltd., 1999, 368 p.

Includes chapters discussing the economic activity, education, and domestic and religious life of white, black, and Indian women in the United States in the nineteenth century.

Leach, William. *True Love and Perfect Union: The Feminist Reform of Sex and Society.* Middletown, Conn.: Wesleyan University Press, 1980, 449 p.

Argues that the 1860s and 1870s were the apex of American feminism, decades in which women's rights advocates organized and rallied for an astonishingly broad range of private, public, and civic reforms.

Lerner, Gerda. *The Feminist Thought of Sarah Grimké.* Oxford, England: Oxford University Press, 1998, 208 p.

Studies Sarah Grimké, an American pioneer against slavery and supporter of the empowerment of women.

Levine, Philippa. *Feminist Lives in Victorian England: Private Roles and Public Commitment.* Oxford, England: Basil Blackwell, Ltd., 1990, 241 p.

Analyzes the emergence of feminist discontent with private and public roles assigned to women in nineteenth-century England.

Logan, Shirley Wilson. *With Pen and Voice: A Critical Anthology of Nineteenth-Century African-American Women,* edited by Shirley Wilson Logan. Carbondale, Ill.: Southern Illinois University Press, 1995, 169 p.

Offers a collection of speeches and essays by African-American women detailing and seeking reform of the many customs and laws that denied them basic rights.

Matthews, Glenna. *"Just a Housewife": The Rise and Fall of Domesticity in America.* Oxford, England: Oxford University Press, 1987, 281 p.

Focuses on the evolving domestic roles of women in the nineteenth century.

McFadden, Margaret H. *Golden Cables of Sympathy: The Transatlantic Sources of Nineteenth-Century Feminism.* Lexington, Ky.: The University Press of Kentucky, 1999, 270 p.

Argues that transatlantic connections between American and European women existed much earlier in the nineteenth century than is generally assumed.

Mendus, Susan, and Jane Rendall, eds. *Sexuality and Subordination: Interdisciplinary Studies of Gender in the Nineteenth Century.* New York: Routledge, 1989, 260 p.

Provides a collection of essays that deal with the literary representations and sexual subordination of British and French women during the nineteenth century.

Pilato, Denise E. *The Retrieval of a Legacy: Nineteenth-Century American Women Inventors.* Westport, Conn.: Praeger Publishers, 2000, 232 p.

Showcases female inventors in the nineteenth century, concentrating on the cultural assumptions they had to overcome as women.

Roberts, Giselle. *The Confederate Belle.* Columbia, Missouri: University of Missouri Press, 2003, 245 p.

Studies the domestic and social lives of southern slave-holding women during the Civil War era.

Rosenblum, Naomi. *A History of Women Photographers.* New York: Abbeville Press, 1994, 400 p.

Early chapters concentrate on the contributions by women to the new artistic medium of photography during the nineteenth century.

Sandler, Martin W. *Against the Odds: Women Pioneers in The First Hundred Years of Photography.* New York: Rizzoli International Publications, Inc., 2002, 188 p.

Details the enormous cultural obstacles that female photographers in the nineteenth century had to overcome to pursue their art.

Shepard, Suzanne V. *The Patchwork Quilt: Ideas of Community in Nineteenth-Century American Women's Fiction.* New York: Peter Lang, 2001, 171 p.

Examines the ways in which nineteenth-century American women authors conceived of community.

Shiman, Lilian Lewis. *Women and Leadership in Nineteenth-Century England.* New York: St. Martin's Press, 1992, 263 p.

Studies the religious and social reform movements of English women during the nineteenth century, which culminated in their demand for political equality through enfranchisement.

WOMEN'S LITERATURE IN THE 19TH CENTURY

Modern critical analysis of nineteenth-century women's literature seeks, in part, to understand the underlying reasons that women authors, especially in America, Britain, and France, were able to gain such widespread exposure and prominence in an age known for its patriarchal and often dismissive attitude toward the intellectual abilities of women. In addition, scholars have examined the broad thematic concerns that characterize much of the literary output of nineteenth-century women writers, many arguing that it was in the nineteenth century that gender-consciousness and feminist attitudes first came to the forefront of the literary imagination, changing forever how the works of female authors would be written and regarded.

The number of published women authors was greater in the nineteenth century than in any preceding century. Women's access to higher education increased exponentially during the century, providing them with skills that they could use to develop their art. The growth of market economies, cities, and life expectancies changed how women in Europe and the United States were expected to conform to new societal pressures, and made many women more conscious of their imposed social, legal, and political inequality. Finally, the many social reform movements led by nineteenth-century women, such as religious revivalism, abolitionism, temperance, and suffrage, gave women writers a context, an audience, and a forum in which they could express their views. While most scholars agree that many women writers expressly or tacitly accepted the separate sphere of domesticity that the age assumed of them, they also argue that as the century progressed, an increasing number of women began to express, in their writing, their dissatisfaction with gender relations and the plight of women in general. Throughout the Victorian era, the "woman question" regarding woman's true place in art and society was a subject that was hotly debated, spurred in large part by the rapid rise in literature by and for women.

At the beginning of the nineteenth century, women writers were largely confined to the genres of children's literature and poetry. The emotionalism of poetry, particularly poetry in which depth of feeling and sentiment, morality, and intuition were expressed and celebrated, was considered a "feminine genre," suitable for women writers. As nineteenth-century women increasingly began to write fiction, however, critical reviews of the age often derided the inferior talents of women novelists, faulting what they perceived as women's lack of worldly experience, critical judgment, and rationality—traits thought to characterize men—and dismissing their works as little better than pulp designed to appeal to the unrefined tastes of an ever-expanding female readership. Many of the century's greatest novelists, including Charlotte Brontë, George Eliot, Mary Shelley, and George

Sand, never completely escaped the condescension of critics whose negative assessments of their works were often based on the author's gender. Scholars argue that the legacy of this sexism has been a historic dismissal of the work of many of the age's most popular, gifted, and influential women writers, consistently judged as unworthy of academic study.

Some modern critics have continued to disregard the contributions of nineteenth-century women authors, while others have noted that by the end of the century, women novelists were more prevalent, and often more popular, than male novelists. Others have focused on representations of women in literature written both by men and women to illuminate the full spectrum of expectations of and perspectives on women and their perceived roles in society. Commentators have also compared the thematic concerns of women writers in England, France, and the United States, recognizing in these three cultures intersecting movements toward creative and feminist literary expression. In recent decades, critics have examined the contributions of African American and Native American women authors, as well as the influence of the nineteenth-century periodical press, analyzing the increasing radicalism of journals and essays edited and written by feminist pioneers such as Frances Power Cobbe and Sarah Josepha Hale.

Toward the end of the century, nineteenth-century women writers expanded their subject matter, moving beyond highlighting the lives and hardships suffered by women locked in domestic prisons. Instead, they increasingly expressed their individualism and demanded more equal partnerships—in marriage, public life, law, and politics—with men.

REPRESENTATIVE WORKS

Jane Austen
Northanger Abbey: And Persuasion (novels) 1818

Miss Marjoribanks (novel) 1866

Charlotte Brontë
Jane Eyre (novel) 1847

Villette (novel) 1853

Elizabeth Barrett Browning
Aurora Leigh (poetry) 1857

Josephine Butler
The Education and Employment of Women (nonfiction) 1868

Kate Chopin
The Awakening (novel) 1898

Frances Power Cobbe
Essays in the Pursuit of Women (essays) 1863

The Life of Frances Power Cobbe: By Herself (autobiography) 1894

Dinah Craik
Olive (novel) 1850

George Eliot
Romola (novel) 1863

Middlemarch (novel) 1871-72

Fanny Fern
Ruth Hall (novel) 1855

Margaret Fuller
Woman in the Nineteenth Century (nonfiction) 1845

Elizabeth Gaskell
Ruth (novel) 1853

Adam Bede (novel) 1859

Charlotte Perkins Gilman
The Yellow Wallpaper (novella) 1892

Women and Economics (nonfiction) 1898

Sarah Grimké
Letters on the Equality of the Sexes and the Condition of Women (letters and essays) 1834

Frances Ellen Watkins Harper
"The Two Offers" (short story) 1859

Sketches of Southern Life (folklore poetry) 1872

Nathaniel Hawthorne
The Scarlet Letter (novel) 1859

Marietta Holley
My Opinions and Betsey Bobbet's (short stories) 1873

Sarah Orne Jewett
A White Heron and other Stories (short stories) 1886

A Country Doctor (novel) 1884

"Tom's Husband" (short story) 1886

The Country of the Pointed Firs (short stories) 1896

Anna Cora Mowatt
Fashion; or, Life in New York (play) 1854

Caroline Sheridan Norton
English Laws for Women (essay) 1854

Elizabeth Cady Stanton
The Woman's Bible (prose) 1895

Harriet Beecher Stowe
"Uncle Lot" (short story) 1834

Uncle Tom's Cabin (novel) 1852

The Pearl of Orr's Island (novel) 1862

Susan Warner
The Wide, Wide World (novel) 1851

PRIMARY SOURCES

STÉPHANIE-FÉLICITÉ DUCREST, COMTESSE DE GENLIS (ESSAY DATE 1811)

SOURCE: Ducrest, Stéphanie-Félicité. "Preliminary Reflections." In *The Influence of Women on French Literature,* translated by Matthew Bray and Amy Simowitz, pp. 208-11. Paris: Maradan, 1811.

In the following essay, Ducrest relates the importance of women writers to French literature.

Men of letters have over women authors a superiority of achievement that, assuredly, one cannot fail to recognize or contest. All of the works of women taken together are not worth a few choice pages from Bossuet or Pascal, or a few scenes from Corneille, Racine, or Molière. But it is not necessary to infer from this that women's natural ability is inferior to that of men. Genius composes itself out of all those qualities which we know that women possess, often to the highest degree: imagination, sensibility, and elevation of spirit. Lack of study and education having in all ages cut off women from a literary vocation, they have displayed their grandeur of spirit not through tracing historic deeds, nor in presenting ingenious fictions, but rather through genuine, material actions. They have done more than write: they have often, by their conduct, furnished models of sublime heroism. It may be true that not one woman has, in her writing, painted the great spirit of Cornelia, but what does this matter, seeing that Cornelia herself is not an imaginary being? And have we not seen, in our days, during the revolutionary tempests, some women equal the male heroes by the vigor of their courage and grandeur of their spirit? "Great thoughts come from the heart," and similar effects should spring (when nothing is there to obstruct them) from the same source.

In order to establish woman's inferiority, men repeat that not one woman has penned good tragedy or epic poetry. An innumerable multitude of men of letters have written tragedies, yet when we count only four great French tragic poems, it is thought a great number, considering that no other nation can count as many. On the other hand, we have just one French epic poem, and we must admit that it is extremely inferior to *Paradise Lost* or *Jerusalem Delivered.* Only five women among us have tried their hand at tragedy. Not only were none of these women exposed, as some authors are, to the vexation of shameful failure, but all of their tragedies experienced great success on opening night.

Young men at college, nourished by reading Greek and Latin, are almost all poets. If they have a little talent, they form the ambitious desire of working for the theatre. We ought to acknowledge that this idea does not naturally occur to a convent student or a young woman who has just entered the world. Can we say that none our of our kings, great captains, or men of state have possessed genius, merely because not one of them has written a tragedy, even though several have been poets? Can we say of the Swiss, the Danes, the Russians, the Poles, and the Dutch—people so lively and so civilized—that their mental capacity is inferior to that of the French, the English, the Italians, the Spanish, and the Germans just because they have not produced great dramatic poetry? We can only excel in a particular art when that art is generally cultivated in our nation, and by the class into which we are born. The Romans, the most celebrated people in history, did not have good tragic poets. Millions of street porters, thousands of nuns or mothers—any of these people could have, with a different education and in different circumstances, composed excellent tragedies. The ability to feel and admire that which is good and which is beautiful, and the power to love, are the same for men and women. Therefore, they are morally equal.

But if too few women (for want of study and sheer audacity) have written tragedies in order to prove that they could equal men in this regard, they have often surpassed men in another genre. Not a single man has left behind a collection of personal letters which can hold a candle to the letters of Madame de Sévigné or Madame de Maintenon. *La Princesse de Clèves,* the *Lettres Péruviennes,* the letters of Madame Riccoboni, and the two most recent novels of Madame Cotin are infinitely superior to the entire output of the male romancers. I am not excepting the works of Marivaux from this evaluation or worse still, the boring and voluminous works of l'Abbé Prevot. And *Gilblas* is another sort of work; it is a picture of vice, of the ridiculous products of ambition, vanity and cupidity, and not the development of the natural sentiments of the heart—love, friendship, jealousy, filial piety, and so on. The author, spirited and often quite profound in his witticisms, had only studied subaltern intrigues and the absurdities of pride. When he lays down his satiric pencil, he becomes common; all the episodes of *Gilblas* intended to be interesting and touching are instead poorly written and dull.

Madame Deshoulières had no equal for the genre of poetry in which she left such charming models. The men who assign ranks in literature—dispensing honors and distributing places to authors, always excluding women—often give celebrity to talents which are quite mediocre. For example, if d'Alembert were neither a geometrician, nor a member of the French Academy—despite his relentless hatred of religion and his contempt for France and her king—his writing, so cold, so devoid of substance, grace and naturalness, would be forgotten already. A woman, if she had the unhappiness of having composed the majority of his academic eulogies. would be dismissed by the public as a *"précieuse ridicule."* And yet the Academy received d'Alembert as a most distinguished writer. The author of *Ariane* and *Comte d'Essex,* brother to the creator of French tragedy and comedy, was elected only after the death of the great Corneille; the marquis of Saint-Aulaire, however, was welcomed for a madrigal. The son of the great Racine, himself author of a beautiful poem, was never admitted! This same Academy issue a most unjust critique of *The Cid,* the first masterpiece to grace the French stage, yet went into mourning for the death of Voiture! . . . If there existed an academy of women, one ventures to guess that it could, without trouble, better conduct itself and judge more sanely.

It is difficult to reconcile the various judgments made of women; they are either contradictory or devoid of sense. Women are said to possess an extreme sensibility, beyond that of men, and a lack of energy. But what is an extreme sensibility without energy? It is a sensibility incapable of making all the sacrifices of a great devotion. And what is energy, or else this strength of spirit, this power of the will which, well or poorly employed, provides unshakable constancy in order to arrive at its mark and braves everything—all obstacles, peril and death—for the object of a dominant passion? Women's tenacity of will for all that they ardently desire has passed into proverb. Therefore, one does not contest that they possess the type of energy which requires an extreme perserverance. Who could not fail to recognize in women the energy which an heroic courage demands? Does she lack it, that unfortunate princess who has just hurled herself into flames to find her daughter? And among so many noble victims of the faith, so many martyrs who persisted in their belief with an energy so sublime, and despite the horror of shocking torments, do you count as many women as men? We maintain that women are endowed with a delicacy that men can not possess. This favorable judgment does not appear to me better founded than all of the others which are to the disadvantage of women. Several works by men of letters prove that this quality is by no means an exclusively female trait, but it is true that it is one of the distinctive characteristics of almost all their works.

That must be because education and propriety impose upon them the law of restraint—of concentrating almost all of their feelings, of always softening their expressions by delicate turns of phrase. This delicacy tries to convey what they cannot venture to explain. This is not dissimulation; this art, in general, is not hiding what one feels. Its perfection, to the contrary, is making known without explaining, without using the words that one could cite as a positive confession. Love especially renders this delicacy ingenious. In such a case, it grants women a touching and mysterious language that, because it is made only for the heart and the imagination, has something heavenly in it. Spoken words are nothing; the secret sense is all, and is fully understood only by the lover to whom it is addressed.

Apart from all the principles which render modesty and discretion so indispensable in a woman, what contrasts are provided by timidity on the one hand and audacity and ardor on the other! Grace exists in a young woman when she is that which she must be: all of her is in accord: the delicacy of her traits and of her discourse, the modesty of her bearing, of her long garments, and the sweetness of her voice and character. She does not disguise herself, but she always conceals herself. Her expressions of affection are all the more touching because she does not exaggerate; rather she must understate her feeling. Her sensibility is more profound than that of men because she is more constrained. She discloses herself, but not completely. In order to know and understand her, it is necessary to conjecture about her. She appeals as much by the attraction of piqued curiosity as by genuine charms. What poor taste it is to unveil all of this mystery, to destroy all these graces, by presenting the heroine of a novel or play without modesty, and having her express the most impetuous outbursts of love! Yet this is what we have seen for some years now. In thus transforming women, we believed we were giving them energy, but we deceived ourselves. Not only were we unable to strip them of their natural graces without removing all their dignity, but this vehement and passionate language strips them also of all they might possess of what is truly stirring and moving.

ELIZABETH OAKES SMITH (ESSAY DATE 1851)

SOURCE: Smith, Elizabeth Oakes. *Woman and Her Needs*, pp. 10-29. New York: Fowlers and Wells, 1851.

In the following excerpt, Smith underscores the importance of "Woman thought."

Whatever difference of opinion may exist amongst us as to the *propriety* of the recent Conventions held in our Country, called "Woman's Rights," the fact stands by itself, a handwriting on the wall, proclaiming a sense of wrong, a sense of something demanding redress, and this is fact enough to *justify the movement* to all candid eyes. Indeed enough to render it praiseworthy. For one, I am glad to see that our Republic has produced a class of women, who, feeling the Need of a larger sphere and a better recognition, have that clearness of intellect and strength of purpose by which they go to work resolutely to solve the difficulty. They might stay at home and fret and dawdle; be miserable themselves and make all within their sphere miserable likewise; but instead of this, they meet and talk the matter over, devise plans, explain difficulties, rehearse social oppressions and political disabilities, in the hope of evolving something permanently good.

All this is well, and grows naturally from the progress of institutions like our own, in which opinions are fearlessly discussed, and all thought traced home to its source. It isn't in the nature of things that any class in our midst should be long indifferent to topics of general interest; far less that such should feel the pressure of evils without inquiring into the best means of abatement. When our Fathers planted themselves upon the firm base of human freedom, claimed the inalienable rights of life, liberty, and the pursuit of happiness, they might have foreseen that at some day their daughters would sift thoroughly their opinions and their consequences, and daringly challenge the same rights.

For myself, I may not sympathize with a Convention—I may not feel *that* the best mode of arriving at truth to my own mind—I may feel that its singleness of import would be lost to me while standing in the solid phalanx of associated inquiry; but these objections do not apply to the majority of minds, and I reverence their search in their own way, the many converging lights of many minds all bent upon the same point, even although I myself peer about with my solitary lantern. . . .

The world needs the action of Woman thought in its destinies. The indefinite influence springing from the private circle is not enough; this is shaded away into the graceful lights of feminine subserviency and household endearment; blessing the individual husband, or ennobling the one group at the family altar, but the world goes on with its manifold wrongs, and woman has nothing but tears to bestow—the outrages that may wring either her own heart or that of others, are perpetrated before her eyes, and she can only wring helpless hands, or plead with ideal remonstrance, while her lord and master tells her these things are quite beyond her comprehension; she can not see how unavoidable it is, but it is not the less unavoidable, and she must shut her eyes and ears, and "mind her spinning." Or, if blessed with a large share of manly arrogance, he will tell her, as did the captain of a militia company of a country town, who, in practising in the court of his house those martial evolutions that were to electrify the village upon parade, accidentally stepped down the trap-door of the cellar. His wife rushed out to succor her liege lord, when she was met with, "Go in, woman; what do you know about war?"

Sure enough, what does she? But this directness of sympathy, this promptitude to relieve, makes her fruitful in resource in small matters, and why should it not in large? If an evil come under her own inspection, she at once casts about for redress, and good comes of it. There is no reason why she should not enlarge her sphere in this way, and no fear of her being the less feminine or endearing by the process. . . .

I have said the world needs the admixture of Woman thought in its affairs; a deep, free, woman-souled utterance *is needed*. It is the disseverance of the sexes, the condemning of the one to *in-door* thought only, to the degradation of in-door toil, far more limiting in its nature than that of the out-door kind, beneath the invigorations of air and sky, that has done so much in our country to narrow and paralyze the energies of the sex. Excessive maternity, the cares and the labors consequent upon large families, with inadequate support (when we consider the amount of general intelligence amongst us) have conspired to induce the belief that the most entire domestic seclusion is the only sphere for a woman. Our republic has hitherto developed something akin to a savage lordliness in the other sex, in which he is to usurp all the privileges of freedom, and she is to take as much as she can get, after he is served.

Now, a woman may or may not be adapted to an in-door life exclusively. There is as much difference in us in that respect as there is in men. The expanse of earth and sky have unquestionably worked enlargement upon the mind of the other sex; and, in our own, have developed for the poor serving girl of the Inn of Domremy, inured to the toils of the stable, the chivalric and enthusiastic Joan of Arc. It is the making woman a creature of luxury—an object of sensuality—a vehicle for reproduction—or a thing of toil, each one, or all of these—that has caused half the miseries of the world. She, as a soul, has never been recognized. As a human being, to sin and to suffer, she has had more than an acknowledgment. As a human being, to obey her God, to think, to enjoy, men have been blind to her utmost needs.

She has been treated always as subservient; and yet all and the most entire responsibility has been exacted of her. She has had no voice in the law, and yet has been subjected to the heaviest penalties of the law. She has been denied the ability to make or enforce public opinion, and yet has been outraged, abandoned, given over to degradation, misery, and the thousand ills worse than a thousand deaths, by its terrible action. Even her affections—those arbitrary endowments imparted by the Most High for her own safeguard, and for the best being of society—have been warped and crushed by the action of masculine thought upon their manifestations, till their unadulterated play is well nigh lost.

Men have written for us, thought for us, legislated for us; and they have constructed from their own consciousness an effigy of a woman, to which were are expected to conform. It is not a Woman that they see; God forbid that it should be; it is one of those monsters of neither sex, that sometimes outrage the pangs of maternity, but which expire at the birth: whereas the distorted image to which men wish us to conform, lives to bewilder, to mislead, and to cause discord and belittlement where the Creator designed the highest dignity, the most complete harmony. Men have said we should be thus and thus, and we have tried to be in accordance, because we are told it is womanly. . . .

Let woman learn to take a woman's view of life. Let her feel the need of a woman's thought. Let her search into her own needs—say, not what has the world hitherto thought in regard to this or that, but what is the *true* view of it from the nature of things. Let her not say, what does my husband, my brother, my father think—wise and good and trustworthy though they be—but let her evolve her own thoughts, recognize her own needs, and judge of her own acts by the best lights of her own mind.

Let her feel and understand that there is a difference in the soul as in the bodies of the sexes—a difference designed to produce the most beautiful harmony. But let her not, in admitting this, admit of inferiority. While the *form* of a man is as it were more arbitrary, more of a fact in creation, more distinct and uniform, a sort of completeness of the material, and his mind also more of a fixture, better adapted to the exactitudes of science, and those protracted labors needful to the hardier developments of the understanding, let her bear in mind that this fixedness, this patience of labor, this steadiness of the understanding, are in conformity with his position as *Lord of the material Universe,* to which God has appointed him; whereas she was an after-creation, with something nearer allied to the heavenly. In her shape there is a flexibility, a variety, more graceful, ethereal, and beautiful, appealing more intimately to that something within the soul of man, that goes onward to the future and eternal—a softening down of the material to the illusions of the unseen—her mind, also, when unstinted and unadulterated, has in it more of aspiration, more of the subtle and intuitive character, that links it to the spiritual; she is impatient of labor, because her wings are nearly freed of the shell of the chrysalis, and prompt to a better element; she cares less for the deductions of reason, because she has an element in herself nearer to the truth than reason can ever reach, by which she *feels* the approaches of the true and the beautiful, without the manly wrestlings all night of the Patriarch to which the other sex are subjected. She does not need the ladder of Bethel, the step by step of the slow logician, because her feet are already upon the first rung of that mystic pass-way; this is why she is bid by the arrogance of apostolic injunction to veil her head in public, "because of the Angels."

She is a step nearer them than her *material* lord and master. The angels recognize her as of nearer affinity. . . .

Would that women should learn to recognize their own individuality—their own singleness of thought. Let them not feel disparaged at the difference which I have recognized; it is a difference that crowns them with a new glory. We give the material Universe to men, and to those of our own sex who, from whatever cause, approximate to their standard; to such let us yield ungrudgingly the way; but it is no less certain that there is a woman-thought, a woman-perception, a woman-intuition, altogether distinct from the same things in the other sex; and to learn what these are, and to act from these, is what women must learn, and when they have so learned and impressed themselves thus through these upon the world, it will be regenerated and disenthralled. . . .

Women must recognize their unlikeness, and then understanding what needs grow out of this unlikeness, some great truth must be evolved. Now they busy themselves with methods of thought, springing, it is true, from their own sense of something needed, but suggested altogether by the masculine intellect. Let us first shake ourselves of this pupilage of mind by which our faculties are dwarfed, and courageously judge for ourselves. In doing this, I see no need of Amazonian strides or disfigurements, or a stentorian lungs. The more deeply and earnestly a woman feels the laws of her own existence, the more solemn, reverent, and harmonious is her bearing. She sees what nature designed in her creation, and her whole being falls gracefully into its allotted sphere. If she be a simple, genial, household divinity, she will bind garlands around the altar of the Penates, and worship in content. If more largely endowed, I see no reason why she should not be received cordially into the school of Arts, or Science, or Politics, or Theology, in the same manner as the individual capacities of the other sex are recognized. They do not all square themselves to one standard, and why should we? They have a very large number engaged in sewing, cooking, spinning, and writing very small articles for very small works, designed for very small minds.

The majority are far from being Platos, or Bayards, or Napoleons. When so very large a portion of the other sex are engaged in what is regarded as unmanly, I see no reason why those of ours who have a fancy to tinker a constitution, canvass a county, or preach the Gospel, should not be permitted to do so, provided they feel this to be the best use of their faculties. I do not say this is the best thing for them to do; but I see no reason, if their best intelligence finds its best expression in any such channel, why they should not be indulged.

Our right to individuality is what I would most assert. Men seem resolved to have but one type in our sex. They recognize the prerogative of the matter-of-fact Biddy to raise a great clamor, quite to the annoyance of a neighborhood, but where's the use of Nightingale? The laws of stubborn utilitarianism must govern us, while they may be as fantastic as they please. They tell much about a "woman's sphere"—can they define this? As the phrase is used, I confess it has a most shallow and indefinite sense. The most I can gather from it is, the consciousness of the speaker, which means something like the philosophy of Mr. Murderousness firmness; it is sphere by which every woman creature, of whatever age, appending to himself, shall circle very much within his own—see and hear through his senses, and believe according to his dogmas, with a sort of general proviso, that if need be for his growth, glorification, or well-being, in any way, they will instantly and uncompromisingly become extinct.

There is a Woman's sphere—harmonious, who have been developed by labor or accident, with some of your puny metropolitans who have never seen the sun rise or set. Theory may say that if man and woman from the beginning were educated precisely alike, man would still be the larger, the stronger. When the experiment is fully made, it will be time enough to admit the assumption. But suppose we admit that man is physically larger than woman, what do you gain by the admission? Among men the athletic, the muscular, the brawny, are by no means the great men in the best sense of that word, neither are they the strongest physically. The sight of a small man whipping a large one is not uncommon. The force of will has much more to do with strength than the size of the frame, the impelling organs of the brain than the size of the arm and chest. By far the greater proportion of distinguished men, of generals, statesmen, and philosophers, have been small men of fine nervous organization and exquisite sensibilities. Look at Napolean, Lord Nelson, Guizot, Hamilton, Burr, Adams, Channing, Emerson and Seward. So, should we grant man the superiority of the ox, we should but prove him an inferior order of being.

Men and women are not so unlike in person either, but by skilful dressing the one may pass for the other. George Sand, the assumed name of the distinguished Madame Dudevant, has travelled incognito in man's attire through many countries and observed society in all its phases in Parisian life. There are many instances of men escaping from prison in women's attire, undiscovered, and of women disguised as soldiers fighting in the hottest of the battle, side by side with those they loved. In children's plays, boys and girls are constantly seen wrestling, running, climbing, comparing their strength and swiftness. I never heard it hinted in the playground or the schoolroom, that boys and girls were not legitimate subjects of comparison. When a girl, I have gone many a time from our Academy gate to the belfry, snowball in hand, to punish a boy for washing my face. The girls in my native village not only tried strength with boys in the play-ground, but we measured lances with them, in the sciences, languages, and mathematics. In studying Algebra and Geometry, in reading Virgil or the Greek Testament, I never found out the difference in the male and female mind. In those days there was no feminine way of extracting the cube root of x, y, z; no masculine way of going through all the moods and tenses of the verbs Amo and Tupto. We have had so much sentimental talk in all our woman's conventions, by the friends of the cause, about the male and female element, and by outsiders, on women's sphere, her mission, her peculiar duties, &c., that I should like to have all this mysterious twaddle thoroughly explored; all these nice shades of difference fully revealed. It is not enough to assert that there always has been, is, and always will be a difference. The question is, What is it?

JOSEPHINE BUTLER (ESSAY DATE 1868)

SOURCE: Butler, Josephine. "The Education and Employment of Women." In *Women's Writing of the Victorian Period 1837-1901: An Anthology,* edited by Harriet Devine Jump, pp. 162-65. Edinburgh, Scotland: Edinburgh University Press, 1999.

In the following excerpt, originally published in The Education and Employment of Women *in 1868, Butler describes two separate rationales for women's rights to equal education, concluding that educated women would prove to be a benefit to gender relations and society as a whole.*

There are two classes of advocates of the improvement of the education and condition of women The one class urge everything from the domestic point of view. They argue in favour of all which is likely to make women better mothers, or better companions for men, but they seem incapable of judging of a woman as a human being by herself, and superstitiously afraid of anything which might strengthen her to stand alone, prepared, single-handed, to serve her God and her country. When it is urged upon them that the women who do and must stand alone are counted by millions, they are perplexed, but only fall back on expressions of a fear lest a masculine race of women should be produced, if we admit any theories respecting them apart from conjugal and maternal relationships.

On the other hand, there are advocates who speak with some slight contempt of maternity; in whose advocacy there appears to me little evidence of depth of thought, or tenderness, or wisdom, and which bespeaks a dry, hard, unimaginative conception of human life. They appear to have no higher ideal for a woman than that of a *man* who has been "tripos'ed," and is going to "get on in the world," either in the way of making money or acquiring fame. They speak of women as if it were a compliment to them, or in any way true, to say that they are like men. Now it appears to me that both these sets of advocates have failed to see something which is very true, and that their ears are deaf to some of the subtle harmonies which exist in God's creation—harmonies sometimes evolved from discords—and which we are much hindered from hearing by the noise of the world, and by our own discordant utterances.

The first class of advocates do not know how strong Nature is, how true she is for the most part, and how deeply the maternal character is rooted in almost all women, married or unmarried: they are not, therefore, likely to see that when a better education is secured to women, when permission is granted them not only to win bread for themselves, but to use for the good of society, every gift bestowed on them by God, we may expect to find, (as certainly we shall find,) that they will become the *more* and not the *less* womanly. Every good quality, every virtue which we regard as distinctively feminine, will, under conditions of greater freedom, develop more freely, like plants brought out into the light from a cellar in which they languished, dwarfed and blanched, without sun or air. The woman is strong in almost every woman; and it may be called an infidelity against God and against the truth of nature to suppose that the removal of unjust restrictions, and room given to breathe freely, and to do her work in life without depression and without bitterness, will cause her to cast off her nature. It will always be in her nature to foster, to cherish, to take the part of the weak, to train, to guide, to have a care for individuals, to discern the small seeds of a great future, to warm and cherish those seeds into fulness of life. "I serve," will always be one of her favourite mottos, even should the utmost freedom be accorded her in the choice of vocation; for she, more readily perhaps than men do, recognises the wisdom and majesty of Him who said—"I am among you as he that serveth."

The second kind of advocacy of the rights of women, of which I spoke, may be said to be simply a reaction against the first. It is chiefly held by a few women of superior intellect who feel keenly the disadvantages of their class, their feebleness, through want of education, against public opinion, which is taken advantage of by base people, their inability, through want of representation, to defend their weaker members, and the dwarfing of the faculties of the ablest and best among them. These women have associated little with men, or at best, know very little of their inner life, and do not therefore see as clearly as they see their own loss, the equal loss that it is to men, and the injury it involves to their characters, to live dissociated from women: they therefore look forth from their isolation with something of an excusable envy on the freer and happier lot, which includes, they believe, a greater power to do good, and imagine that the only hope for themselves is to push into the ranks of men, to demand the same education, the same opportunities, in order that they may compete with them on their own ground. They have lost the conception of the noblest development possible for both men and women, for assuredly that which men, for the most part, aim at, is not the noblest, and yet that is what such women appear to wish to imitate; they have lost sight of the truth, too, that men and women were made equal indeed, but not alike, and were meant to supplement one another, and that in so doing,—each supplying force which the other lacks,—they are attracted with a far greater amount of impulse to a common centre. . . .

The above misconception, like many other errors, results from men and women living so dissociated as they do in our country; hence comes also all that reserve, and incapacity for understanding each other which has existed between the sexes for so many generations, those false notions about women which are entertained in society, and great injury to the work, and happiness, and dignity of man and woman alike: for it may be truly said that many of the most serious evils in England are but the bitter and various fruit of the sacrilegious disjoining of the which God had joined together, the disunion of men and women, theoretically and practically, in all the graver work of life.

To conclude this part of my subject, although I grant that too much stress cannot be laid upon the improvement of the education of women who will be actually the mothers of a future generation, yet I wish, on the one hand, that persons who only look at it from this point of view would take more into account the valuable service our country might command if it but understood the truth about the condition and feelings of its unmarried women, and that a more generous trust were felt in the strength of woman's nature, and the probable direction of its development when granted more expansion, while on the other hand I should like to see a truer conception of the highest possibilities for women than is implied in the attempt to imitate men, and a deeper reverence for the God of nature, whose wisdom is more manifested in variety than in uniformity. It cannot be denied that a just cause has sometimes been advocated by women in a spirit of bitterness. Energy impeded in one direction, will burst forth in another; hence the defiant and sometimes grotesque expression which the lives and acts of some few women have been of the injustice done to them by society. This will cease, and while it lasts, it ought to excite our pity rather than our anger. It must be remembered that it is but a symptom of a long endured servitude, a protest against a state of things which we hope will give place to a better. It is folly to regard it as the natural fruit of that of which we have scarcely seen the beginning. Acts of violence on the part of a long oppressed nation are not the offspring of dawning liberties, but of a doomed tyranny. Again, no important reform can be carried without a measure of attendant confusion. Evil agencies are the most vigilant for destruction at the beginning of a great and good work, and many lives have to be consumed in its inauguration. Any evils which may at first attend a social reform ought not to alarm us: they are transient; they are but the breakers on the bar which must be crossed before we launch into deep waters, but the "noise and dust of the wagon which brings the harvest home."

FRANCES POWER COBBE (POEM DATE 1871)

SOURCE: Cobbe, Frances Power. "To Elizabeth Garrett Anderson." In *Women's Writing of the Victorian Period 1837-1901: An Anthology,* edited by Harriet Devine Jump, pp. 181-82. Edinburgh, Scotland: Edinburgh University Press, 1999.

In the following poem, originally published in 1871, Cobbe details many of the institutions that the women's rights movement needed to overcome.

ON THE SUBJECT OF...

FRANCES POWER COBBE (1822-1904)

Frances Power Cobbe combined a radical demand for suffrage with a moderate view of woman as being the equivalent rather than the equal of man. Although she emphasized gender differences, and was convinced that women had particular duties associated with their sex, she was also adamant that they have equal access to the public sphere. She held that because God had created women as morally autonomous individuals, they were as capable as men of deciding what was best for themselves, of living up to their potential, and of determining the direction their lives would take. In 1862 Cobbe drafted her conservative argument defending a woman's right—as long as she was either single or a childless wife without family responsibilities—to an education and a useful and remunerative life.

Cobbe's feminist consciousness developed further when she moved to South Kensington with her companion, Welsh sculptor Mary Lloyd, in 1864, and met other women's rights activists, including Lydia Becker, Bessie Rayner Parkes, and Barbara Bodichon. In 1866 Cobbe signed the petition for women's suffrage that was presented to Parliament by John Stuart Mill. In her 1868 essay, "Criminals, Idiots, Women, and Minors: Is the Classification Sound?" she attacked the inequitable social and legal systems that reduced women—rational free agents created by God in His image—to the quasi-legal status of "Criminal, Idiot, Minor." She was particularly critical of marriage and the common law that victimized women, destroying their individuality and potential while consolidating male power in the private and public sphere. Cobbe sat on the committee that formed in 1868 to secure property rights for wives and from the mid-1870s publicized cases of wife abuse; this latter activity was instrumental in passing the 1878 Matrimonial Causes Act.

TO ELIZABETH GARRETT ANDERSON

The Woman's cause was rising fast
When to the Surgeons' College past
A maid who bore in fingers nice
A banner with the new device
Excelsior!

"Try not to pass!" the Dons exclaim,
"M.D. shall grace no woman's name"—
"Bosh!" cried the maid, in accents free,
"To France I'll go for my degree."
Excelsior!

The School-Board seat came next in sight,
"Beware the foes of woman's right!"
"Beware the awful husting's fight!"
Such was the moan of many a soul—
A voice replied from top of poll—
Excelsior!

In patients' homes she saw the light
Of household fires beam warm and bright;
Lectures on Bones grew wondrous dry,
But still she murmured with a sigh
Excelsior!

"Oh, stay!"—a lover cried,—"Oh, rest
Thy much-learned head upon this breast;
Give up ambition! Be my bride!"
—Alas! *no* clarion voice replied
Excelsior!

At end of day, when all is done,
And woman's battle fought and won,
Honour will aye be paid to one
Who erst called foremost in the van
Excelsior!

But not for her that crown so bright,
Which her's had been, of surest right,
Had she still cried,—serene and blest—
"The Virgin throned by the West."
Excelsior!

MARY ELIZABETH COLERIDGE (POEM DATE 1892)

SOURCE: Coleridge, Mary Elizabeth. "The Witch." In *The Norton Anthology of Literature by Women,* Second Edition, edited by Sandra M. Gilbert and Susan Gubar, p. 1147. New York: W. W. Norton, 1996.

In the following poem, originally published in 1892, Coleridge characterizes marriage as being akin to death for women.

THE WITCH

I have walked a great while over the snow,
And I am not tall nor strong.
My clothes are wet, and my teeth are set,
And the way was hard and long.
I have wandered over the fruitful earth,
But I never came here before.
Oh, lift me over the threshold, and let me in at
the door!

The cutting wind is a cruel foe.
I dare not stand in the blast.
My hands are stone, and my voice a groan,
And the worst of death is past.

I am but a little maiden still,
My little white feet are sore.
Oh, lift me over the threshold, and let me in at
the door!

Her voice was the voice that women have,
Who plead for their heart's desire.
She came—she came—and the quivering flame
Sank and died in the fire.
It never was lit again on my hearth
Since I hurried across the floor,
To lift her over the threshold, and let her in at
the door.

OVERVIEWS

ELAINE SHOWALTER (ESSAY DATE 1977)

SOURCE: Showalter, Elaine. "The Female Tradition." In *A Literature of Their Own: British Women Novelists From Brontë to Lessing*, pp. 3-36. Princeton, N.J. Princeton University Press, 1977.

In the following excerpt, Showalter discusses the implications of identifying female sensibilities in the literary output of nineteenth-century female authors, identifying three distinct phases in the development of themes and gender battles as addressed in women's writing in the nineteenth century.

The advent of female literature promises woman's view of life, woman's experience: in other words, a new element. Make what distinctions you please in the social world, it still remains true that men and women have different organizations, consequently different experiences. . . . But hitherto . . . the literature of women has fallen short of its functions owing to a very natural and a very explicable weakness—it has been too much a literature of imitation. To write as men write is the aim and besetting sin of women; to write as women is the real task they have to perform.

—G. H. Lewes, *"The Lady Novelists,"* 1852

English women writers have never suffered from the lack of a reading audience, nor have they wanted for attention from scholars and critics. Yet we have never been sure what unites them as women, or, indeed, whether they share a common heritage connected to their womanhood at all. Writing about female creativity in *The Subjection of Women* (1869), John Stuart Mill argued that women would have a hard struggle to overcome the influence of male literary tradition, and to create an original, primary, and independent art. "If women lived in a different country from men," Mill thought, "and had never read any of their writings, they would have a literature of their own." Instead, he reasoned, they would always be imitators and never innovators. Paradoxically, Mill would never have raised this point had women not already claimed a very important literary place. To many of his contemporaries (and to many of ours), it seemed that the nineteenth century was the Age of the Female Novelist. With such stellar examples as Jane Austen, Charlotte Brontë, and George Eliot, the question of women's aptitude for fiction, at any rate, had been answered. But a larger question was whether women, excluded by custom and education from achieving distinction in poetry, history, or drama, had, in defining their literary culture in the novel, simply appropriated another masculine genre. Both George Henry Lewes and Mill, spokesmen for women's rights and Victorian liberalism in general, felt that, like the Romans in the shadow of Greece, women were overshadowed by male cultural imperialism: "If women's literature is destined to have a different collective character from that of men," wrote Mill, "much longer time is necessary than has yet elapsed before it can emancipate itself from the influence of accepted models, and guide itself by its own impulses."[1]

There is clearly a difference between books that happen to have been written by women, and a "female literature," as Lewes tried to define it, which purposefully and collectively concerns itself with the articulation of women's experience, and which guides itself "by its own impulses" to autonomous self-expression. As novelists, women have always been self-conscious, but only rarely self-defining. While they have been deeply and perennially aware of their individual identities and experiences, women writers have very infrequently considered whether these experiences might transcend the personal and local, assume a collective form in art, and reveal a history. During the intensely feminist period from 1880 to 1910, both British and American women writers explored the theme of an Amazon utopia, a country entirely populated by women and completely isolated from the male world. Yet even in these fantasies of autonomous female communities, there is no theory of female art. Feminist utopias were not visions of primary womanhood, free to define its own nature and culture, but flights from the male world to a culture defined in opposition to the male tradition. Typically the feminist utopias are pastoral sanctuaries, where a population of prelapsarian Eves cultivate their organic gardens, cure water pollution, and run exemplary child care centers, but do not write books.

In contradiction to Mill, and in the absence, until very recently, of any feminist literary manifestoes, many readers of the novel over the past two centuries have nonetheless had the indistinct but persistent impression of a unifying voice in women's literature. In *The History of the English*

Novel, Ernest Baker devotes a separate chapter to the women novelists, commenting that "the woman of letters has peculiarities that mark her off from the other sex as distinctly as peculiarities of race or of ancestral traditions. Whatever variety of talent, outlook or personal disposition may be discernible among any dozen women writers taken at random, it will be matched and probably outweighed by resemblances distinctively feminine."[2] Baker wisely does not attempt to present a taxonomy of these feminine "peculiarities"; most critics who have attempted to do so have quickly found themselves expressing their own cultural biases rather than explicating sexual structures. In 1852, Lewes thought he could identify the feminine literary traits as Sentiment and Observation; in 1904, William L. Courtney found that "the female author is at once self-conscious and didactic"; in 1965, Bernard Bergonzi explained that "women novelists . . . like to keep their focus narrow."[3] Women reading each other's books have also had difficulties in explaining their potential for what George Eliot called a "precious speciality, lying quite apart from masculine aptitudes and experience." Eliot herself tried to locate the female speciality in the maternal affections.[4]

Statements about the personal and psychological qualities of the woman novelist have also flourished, and have been equally impressionistic and unreliable. The "lady novelist" is a composite of many stereotypes: to J. M. Ludlow, she is a creature with ink halfway up her fingers, dirty shawls, and frowsy hair; and to W. S. Gilbert, a "singular anomaly" who never would be missed.[5] To critics of the twentieth century, she is childless and, by implication, neurotic: "We remind ourselves," writes Carolyn Heilbrun, "that of the great women writers, most have been unmarried, and those who have written in the state of wedlock have done so in peaceful kingdoms guarded by devoted husbands. Few have had children."[6] Nancy Milford asks whether there were any women "who married in their youth and bore children and continued to write . . . think of the women who have written: the unmarried, the married and childless, the very few with a single child and that one observed as if it were a rock to be stubbed against."[7]

There are many reasons why discussion of women writers has been so inaccurate, fragmented, and partisan. First, women's literary history has suffered from an extreme form of what John Gross calls "residual Great Traditionalism,"[8] which has reduced and condensed the extraordinary range and diversity of English women novelists to a tiny band of the "great," and derived all theories from them. In practice, the concept of greatness for women novelists often turns out to mean four or five writers—Jane Austen, the Brontës, George Eliot, and Virginia Woolf—and even theoretical studies of "the woman novelist" turn out to be endless recyclings and recombinations of insights about "indispensable Jane and George."[9] Criticism of women novelists, while focusing on these happy few, has ignored those who are not "great," and left them out of anthologies, histories, textbooks, and theories. Having lost sight of the minor novelists, who were the links in the chain that bound one generation to the next, we have not had a very clear understanding of the continuities in women's writing, nor any reliable information about the relationships between the writers' lives and the changes in the legal, economic, and social status of women.

Second, it has been difficult for critics to consider women novelists and women's literature theoretically because of their tendency to project and expand their own culture-bound stereotypes of femininity, and to see in women's writing an eternal opposition of biological and aesthetic creativity. The Victorians expected women's novels to reflect the feminine values they exalted, although obviously the woman novelist herself had outgrown the constraining feminine role. "Come what will," Charlotte Brontë wrote to Lewes, "I cannot, when I write, think always of myself and what is elegant and charming in femininity; it is not on these terms, or with such ideas, that I ever took pen in hand."[10] Even if we ignore the excesses of what Mary Ellmann calls "phallic criticism" and what Cynthia Ozick calls the "ovarian theory of literature," much contemporary criticism of women writers is still prescriptive and circumscribed.[11] Given the difficulties of steering a precarious course between the Scylla of insufficient information and the Charybdis of abundant prejudice, it is not surprising that formalist-structuralist critics have evaded the issue of sexual identity entirely, or dismissed it as irrelevant and subjective. Finding it difficult to think intelligently about women writers, academic criticism has often overcompensated by desexing them.

Yet since the 1960s, and especially since the reemergence of a Women's Liberation Movement in England and in America around 1968, there has been renewed enthusiasm for the idea that "a special female self-awareness emerges through literature in every period."[12] The interest in establishing a more reliable critical vocabulary and a more accurate and systematic literary history for women writers is part of a larger interdisciplinary effort by psychologists, sociologists, social historians, and art historians to reconstruct the political, social, and cultural experience of women.

Scholarship generated by the contemporary feminist movement has increased our sensitivity to the problems of sexual bias or projection in literary history, and has also begun to provide us with the information we need to understand the evolution of a female literary tradition. One of the most significant contributions has been the unearthing and reinterpretation of "lost" works by women writers, and the documentation of their lives and careers.

In the past, investigations have been distorted by the emphasis on an elite group, not only because it has excluded from our attention great stretches of literary activity between, for example, George Eliot and Virginia Woolf, but also because it has rendered invisible the daily lives, the physical experiences, the personal strategies and conflicts of ordinary women. If we want to define the ways in which "female self-awareness" has expressed itself in the English novel, we need to see the woman novelist against the backdrop of the women of her time, as well as in relation to other writers in history. Virginia Woolf recognized that need:

> The extraordinary woman depends on the ordinary woman. It is only when we know what were the conditions of the average woman's life—the number of her children, whether she had money of her own, if she had a room to herself, whether she had help in bringing up her family, if she had servants, whether part of the housework was her task—it is only when we can measure the way of life and the experience of life made possible to the ordinary woman that we can account for the success or failure of the extraordinary woman as writer.[13]

As scholars have been persuaded that women's experience is important, they have begun to see it for the first time. With a new perceptual framework, material hitherto assumed to be nonexistent has suddenly leaped into focus. Interdisciplinary studies of Victorian women have opened up new areas of investigation in medicine, psychology, economics, political science, labor history, and art.[14] Questions of the "female imagination" have taken on intellectual weight in the contexts of theories of Karen Horney about feminine psychology, Erik Erikson about womanhood and the inner space, and R. D. Laing about the divided self. Investigation of female iconography and imagery has been stimulated by the work of art historians like Linda Nochlin, Lise Vogel, and Helene Roberts.[15]

As the works of dozens of women writers have been rescued from what E. P. Thompson calls "the enormous condescension of posterity,"[16] and considered in relation to each other, the lost continent of the female tradition has risen like Atlantis from the sea of English literature. It is now becoming clear that, contrary to Mill's theory, women have had a literature of their own all along. The woman novelist, according to Vineta Colby, was "really neither single nor anomalous," but she was also more than a "register and a spokesman for her age."[17] She was part of a tradition that had its origins before her age, and has carried on through our own.

Many literary historians have begun to reinterpret and revise the study of women writers. Ellen Moers sees women's literature as an international movement, "apart from, but hardly subordinate to the mainstream: an undercurrent, rapid and powerful. This 'movement' began in the late eighteenth century, was multinational, and produced some of the greatest literary works of two centuries, as well as most of the lucrative potboilers."[18] Patricia Meyer Spacks, in *The Female Imagination,* finds that "for readily discernible historical reasons women have characteristically concerned themselves with matters more or less peripheral to male concerns, or at least slightly skewed from them. The differences between traditional female preoccupations and roles and male ones make a difference in female writing."[19] Many other critics are beginning to agree that when we look at women writers collectively we can see an imaginative continuum, the recurrence of certain patterns, themes, problems, and images from generation to generation.

This book is an effort to describe the female literary tradition in the English novel from the generation of the Brontës to the present day, and to show how the development of this tradition is similar to the development of any literary subculture. Women have generally been regarded as "sociological chameleons," taking on the class, lifestyle, and culture of their male relatives. It can, however, be argued that women themselves have constituted a subculture within the framework of a larger society, and have been unified by values, conventions, experiences, and behaviors impinging on each individual. It is important to see the female literary tradition in these broad terms, in relation to the wider evolution of women's self-awareness and to the ways in which any minority group finds its direction of self-expression relative to a dominant society, because we cannot show a pattern of deliberate progress and accumulation. It is true, as Ellen Moers writes, that "women studied with a special closeness the works written by their own sex";[20] in terms of influences, borrowings, and affinities, the tradition is strongly marked. But it is also full of holes and hiatuses, because of what Germaine Greer calls the "phenomenon of the transcience of female literary fame"; "almost uninterruptedly since the Interregnum, a small group of women have enjoyed dazzling literary prestige during their own lifetimes, only to vanish without trace from the records of posterity."[21] Thus each generation of women writers has found itself, in a sense, without a history, forced to rediscover the past anew, forging again and again the consciousness of their sex. Given this perpetual disruption, and also the self-hatred that has alienated women writers from a sense of collective identity, it does not seem possible to speak of a "movement."

I am also uncomfortable with the notion of a "female imagination." The theory of a female sensibility revealing itself in an imagery and form specific to women always runs dangerously close to reiterating the familiar stereotypes. It also suggests permanence, a deep, basic, and inevitable difference between male and female ways of perceiving the world. I think that, instead, the female literary tradition comes from the still-evolving relationships between women writers and their society. Moreover, the "female imagination" cannot be treated by literary historians as a romantic or Freudian abstraction. It is the product of a delicate network of influences operating in time, and it must be analyzed as it expresses itself, in language and in a fixed arrangement of words on a page, a form that itself is subject to a network of influences and conventions, including the operations of the marketplace. In this investigation of the English novel, I am intentionally looking, not at an innate sexual attitude, but at the ways in which the self-awareness of the woman writer has translated itself into a literary form in a specific place and time-span, how this self-awareness has changed and developed, and where it might lead.

I am therefore concerned with the professional writer who wants pay and publication, not with the diarist or letter-writer. This emphasis has required careful consideration of the novelists, as well as the novels, chosen for discussion. When we turn from the overview of the literary tradition to look at the individuals who composed it, a different but interrelated set of motives, drives, and sources becomes prominent. I have needed to ask why women began to write for money and how they negotiated the activity of writing within their families. What was their professional self-image? How was their work received, and what effects did criticism have upon them? What were their experiences as women, and how were these reflected in their books? What was their understanding of womanhood? What were their relationships to other women, to men, and to their readers? How did changes in women's status affect their lives and careers? And how did the vocation of writing itself change the women who committed themselves to it? In looking at literary subcultures, such as black, Jewish, Canadian, Anglo-Indian, or even American, we can see that they all go through three major phases. First, there is a prolonged phase of *imitation* of the prevailing modes of the dominant tradition, and *internalization* of its standards of art and its views on social roles. Second, there is a phase of *protest* against these standards and values, and *advocacy* of minority rights and values, including a demand for autonomy. Finally, there is a phase of *self-discovery,* a turning inward freed from some of the dependency of opposition, a search for identity.[22] An appropriate terminology for women writers is to call these stages *Feminine, Feminist,* and *Female.* These are obviously not rigid categories, distinctly separable in time, to which individual writers can be assigned with perfect assurance. The phases overlap; there are feminist elements in feminine writing, and vice versa. One might also find all three phases in the career of a single novelist. Nonetheless, it seems useful to point to periods of crisis when a shift of literary values occurred. In this book I identify the Feminine phase as the period from the appearance of the male pseudonym in the 1840s to the death of George Eliot in 1880; the Feminist phase as 1880 to 1920, or the winning of the vote; and the Female phase as 1920 to the present, but entering a new stage of self-awareness about 1960.

It is important to understand the female subculture not only as what Cynthia Ozick calls "custodial"[23]—a set of opinions, prejudices, tastes, and values prescribed for a subordinate group to perpetuate its subordination—but also as a thriving and positive entity. Most discussions of women as a subculture have come from historians describing Jacksonian America, but they apply equally well to the situation of early Victorian England. According to Nancy Cott, "we can view women's group consciousness as a subculture uniquely divided against itself by ties to the dominant culture. While the ties to the dominant culture are the informing and restricting ones, they provoke within the subculture certain strengths as well as weaknesses, enduring values as well as accommodations."[24] The middle-class ideology of the proper sphere of womanhood, which developed in post-industrial England and America, prescribed a woman who would be a Perfect Lady, an Angel in the House, contentedly submissive to men, but strong in her inner purity and religiosity, queen in her own realm of the Home.[25] Many observers have pointed out that the first professional activities of Victorian women, as social reformers, nurses, governesses, and novelists, either were based in the home or were extensions of the feminine role as teacher, helper, and mother of mankind. In describing the American situation, two historians have seen a subculture emerging from the doctrine of sexual spheres:

> By "subculture" we mean simply "a habit of living" . . . of a minority group which is self-consciously distinct from the dominant activities, expectations, and values of a society. Historians have seen female church groups, reform associations, and philanthropic activity as expressions of this subculture in actual behavior, while a large and rich body of writing by and for women articulated the subculture impulses on the ideational level. Both behavior and thought point to child-rearing, religious activity, education, home life, associationism, and female communality as components of women's subculture. Female friendships, strikingly intimate and deep in this period, formed the actual bonds.[26]

For women in England, the female subculture came first through a shared and increasingly secretive and ritualized physical experience. Puberty, menstruation, sexual initiation, pregnancy, childbirth, and menopause—the entire female sexual life cycle—constituted a habit of living that had to be concealed. Although these episodes could not be openly discussed or acknowledged, they were accompanied by elaborate rituals and lore, by external codes of fashion and etiquette, and by intense feelings of female solidarity.[27] Women writers were united by their roles as daughters, wives, and mothers; by the internalized doctrines of evangelicalism, with its suspicion of the imagination and its emphasis on duty; and by legal and economic constraints on their mobility. Sometimes they were united in a more immediate way, around a political cause. On the whole these are the implied unities of culture, rather than the active unities of consciousness.

From the beginning, however, women novelists' awareness of each other and of their female audience showed a kind of covert solidarity that sometimes amounted to a genteel conspiracy. Advocating sisterhood, Sarah Ellis, one of the most conservative writers of the first Victorian generation, asked: "What should we think of a community of slaves, who betrayed each other's interests? of a little band of shipwrecked mariners upon a friendless shore who were false to each other? of the inhabitants of a defenceless nation, who would not unite together in earnestness and good faith against a common enemy?"[28] Mrs. Ellis felt the binding force of the minority experience for women strongly enough to hint, in the prefaces to her widely read treatises on English womanhood, that her female audience would both read the messages between her lines and refrain from betraying what they deciphered. As another conservative novelist, Dinah Mulock Craik, wrote, "The intricacies of female nature are incomprehensible except to a woman; and any biographer of real womanly feeling, if ever she discovered, would never dream of publishing them."[29] Few English women writers openly advocated the use of fiction as revenge against a patriarchal society (as did the American novelist Fanny Fern, for example), but many confessed to sentiments of "maternal feeling, sisterly affection, *esprit de corps*"[30] for their readers. Thus the clergyman's daughter, going to Mudie's for her three-decker novel by another clergyman's daughter, participated in a cultural exchange that had a special personal significance.

It is impossible to say when women began to write fiction. From about 1750 on, English women made steady inroads into the literary marketplace, mainly as novelists. As early as 1773, the *Monthly Review* noticed that "that branch of the literary trade" seemed "almost entirely engrossed by the ladies." J. M. S. Tompkins finds that most eighteenth-century epistolary novels were written by women; the Minerva Press published twice as many novels by women as by men; and Ian Watt simply says that the majority of all eighteenth-century novels came from the female pen.[31] At the same time, men were able to imitate, and even usurp, female experience. Oliver Goldsmith suspected that men were writing sentimental novels under female pseudonyms, and men did write books on childcare, midwifery, housekeeping, and cooking.[32]

Early women writers' relationship to their professional role was uneasy. Eighteenth-century women novelists exploited a stereotype of helpless femininity to win chivalrous protection from male reviewers and to minimize their unwomanly

ON THE SUBJECT OF...

ELIZABETH CLEGHORN GASKELL (1810-1865)

A figure of the "golden age" of nineteenth-century English literature, Gaskell is best known for her novels of social reform and psychological realism, notably *Ruth* (1853) and *North and South* (1854). Her treatment of issues ranging from prostitution to mother-daughter relations both captured the public imagination and generated controversy during Gaskell's own lifetime. Critics have emphasized the tensions—between the working and middle classes, between traditional authority and young women, and between the responsibilities of the public and the responsibilities of the individual—that animate Gaskell's novels and foreshadow major social reforms. Gaskell's refined and compassionate portrayals of her central characters—often young, unmarried women who suffer misfortune—and her skillful use of detail have established an enduring popularity for and interest in her work.

Born in London, Gaskell developed her life-long love of reading at an early age. She married William Gaskell, a young Unitarian clergyman, in 1832 and lived in Manchester. Of her six children, five survived infancy; it was in response to the death of her second child, William, from scarlet fever in 1845 that her husband suggested Gaskell begin writing as a form of distraction from mourning. The resulting novel, *Mary Barton* (1848), reflected Gaskell's interest in the plight of families, and particularly of women, affected by the industrialization of England. Gaskell was active in charitable endeavors, and developed friendships with a number of prominent persons of literary or charitable circles, including George Eliot, Mary Howitt, Charlotte Brontë, and Florence Nightingale. After the popular success of *Mary Barton* Gaskell produced a prolific number of short stories and novels over the remaining years of her life, many of which appeared in *Household Words,* a popular journal edited by Charles Dickens.

self-assertion. In 1791 Elizabeth Inchbald prefaced *A Simple Story* with the lie that she was a poor invalid who had written a novel despite "the utmost detestation to the fatigue of inventing."[33] At the turn of the century, women evaded the issue of professional identity by publishing anonymously. In 1810 Mary Brunton explained in a letter to a friend why she preferred anonymity to taking credit for her novels:

> I would rather, as you well know, glide through the world unknown, than have (I will not call it *enjoy*) fame, however brilliant, to be pointed at,—to be noticed and commented upon—to be suspected of literary airs—to be shunned, as literary women are, by the more unpretending of my own sex; and abhorred as literary women are, by the pretending of the other!—my dear, I would sooner exhibit as a rope-dancer.[34]

Here again we need to remember the distinction between the novel as a form, and the professional role of the novelist. Many of the most consistent themes and images of the feminine novel, from the mysterious interiors of Gothic romance to the balancing of duty and self-fulfillment in domestic fiction, can be traced back to the late eighteenth century. Certainly nineteenth-century women novelists had some familiarity with Burney, Edgeworth, Radcliffe, and Austen, as well as with scores of lesser writers such as Inchbald and Hofland. But almost no sense of communality and self-awareness is apparent among women writers before the 1840s, which Kathleen Tillotson sees as the decade in which the novel became the dominant form. Tillotson points out that, despite the respectful attention paid by mid-Victorian critics to Jane Austen (attention that had some negative impact on Victorian women novelists), there appears to have been relatively little direct influence by Austen on Mrs. Gaskell, Harriet Martineau, the Brontës, and several minor writers.[35] Even George Eliot's debt to Austen has been much exaggerated by the concept of the Great Tradition.[36] The works of Mary Wollstonecraft were not widely read by the Victorians due to the scandals surrounding her life.

More important than the question of direct literary influence, however, is the difference between the social and professional worlds inhabited by the eighteenth- and nineteenth-century women. The early women writers refused to deal with a professional role, or had a negative orientation toward it. "What is my life?" lamented the poet Laetitia Landon. "One day of drudgery after another; difficulties incurred for others, which have ever pressed upon me beyond health, which every year, in one severe illness after another, is taxed beyond its strength; envy, malice, and all uncharitableness—these are the fruits of a successful literary career for a woman."[37] These women may have been less than sincere in their insistence that literary success brought them only suffering, but they were not able to see themselves as involved in a vocation that brought responsibilities as well as conflicts, and opportunities as well as burdens. Moreover, they did not see their writing as an aspect of their female experience, or as an expression of it.

Thus, in talking about the situation of the feminine novelists, I have begun with the women born after 1800, who began to publish fiction during the 1840s when the job of the novelist was becoming a recognizable profession. One of the many indications that this generation saw the will to write as a vocation in direct conflict with their status as women is the appearance of the male pseudonym. Like Eve's fig leaf, the male pseudonym signals the loss of innocence. In its radical understanding of the role-playing required by women's effort to participate in the mainstream of literary culture, the pseudonym is a strong marker of the historical shift.

There were three generations of nineteenth-century feminine novelists. The first, born between 1800 and 1820, included all the women who are identified with the Golden Age of the Victorian authoress: the Brontës, Mrs. Gaskell, Elizabeth Barrett Browning, Harriet Martineau, and George Eliot. The members of this group, whose coevals were Florence Nightingale, Mary Carpenter, Angela Burdett, and other pioneer professionals, were what sociologists call "female role innovators"; they were breaking new ground and creating new possibilities. The second generation, born between 1820 and 1840, included Charlotte Yonge, Dinah Mulock Craik, Margaret Oliphant, and Elizabeth Lynn Linton; these women followed in the footsteps of the great, consolidating their gains, but were less dedicated and original. The third generation, born between 1840 and 1860, included sensation novelists and children's book writers. They seemed to cope effortlessly with the double roles of woman and professional, and to enjoy sexual fulfillment as well as literary success. Businesslike, unconventional, efficient, and productive, they moved into editorial and publishing positions as well as writing.

By the time the women of the first generation had entered upon their careers, there was already a sense of what the "feminine" novel meant in terms of genres. By the 1840s women writers had adopted a variety of popular genres, and were specializing in novels of fashionable life, education, religion, and community, which Vineta Colby subsumes under the heading "domestic realism." In all these novels, according to Inga-Stina Ewbank, "the central preoccupation . . . is with the woman as an influence on others within her domestic and social circle. It was in this preoccupation that the typical woman novelist of the 1840s found her proper sphere: in using the novel to demonstrate (by assumption rather than exploration of standards of womanliness) *woman's* proper sphere."[38] A double standard of literary criticism had also developed with a special set of terms and requirements for fiction by women.

There was a place for such fiction, but even the most conservative and devout women novelists, such as Charlotte Yonge and Dinah Craik, were aware that the "feminine" novel also stood for feebleness, ignorance, prudery, refinement, propriety, and sentimentality, while the feminine novelist was portrayed as vain, publicity-seeking, and self-assertive. At the same time that Victorian reviewers assumed that women readers and women writers were dictating the content of fiction, they deplored the pettiness and narrowness implied by a feminine value system. "Surely it is very questionable," wrote Fitzjames Stephen, "whether it is desirable that no novels should be written except those fit for young ladies to read."[39]

Victorian feminine novelists thus found themselves in a double bind. They felt humiliated by the condescension of male critics and spoke intensely of their desire to avoid special treatment and achieve genuine excellence, but they were deeply anxious about the possibility of appearing unwomanly. Part of the conflict came from the fact that, rather than confronting the values of their society, these women novelists were competing for its rewards. For women, as for other subcultures, literature became a symbol of achievement.

In the face of this dilemma, women novelists developed several strategies, both personal and artistic. Among the personal reactions was a persistent self-deprecation of themselves as women, sometimes expressed as humility, sometimes as coy assurance-seeking, and sometimes as the purest self-hatred. In a letter to John Blackwood, Mrs. Oliphant expressed doubt about "whether in your most manly and masculine of magazines a womanish story-teller like myself may not become wearisome."[40] The novelists publicly proclaimed, and sincerely believed, their antifeminism. By working in the home, by preaching submission and self-sacrifice, and by denouncing female self-assertiveness, they worked to atone for their own will to write.

Vocation—the will to write—nonetheless required a genuine transcendence of female identity. Victorian women were not accustomed to *choosing* a vocation; womanhood was a vocation in itself. The evangelically inspired creed of work did affect women, even though it had not been primarily directed toward them. Like men, women were urged to "bear their part in the *work* of life."[41] Yet for men, the gospel of work satisfied both self-interest and the public interest. In pursing their ambitions, they fulfilled social expectations.

For women, however, work meant labor for *others*. Work, in the sense of self-development, was in direct conflict with the subordination and repression inherent in the feminine ideal. The self-centeredness implicit in the act of writing made this career an especially threatening one; it required an engagement with feeling and a cultivation of the ego rather than its negation. The widely circulated treatises of Hannah More and Sarah Ellis translated the abstractions of "women's mission" into concrete programs of activity, which made writing appear selfish, unwomanly, and unchristian. "'What shall I do to gratify myself—to be admired—or to vary the tenor of my existence?'" are not, according to Mrs. Ellis, "questions which a woman of right feelings asks on first awakening to the avocations of the day." Instead she recommends visiting the sick, fixing breakfast for anyone setting on a journey in order to spare the servant, or general "devotion to the good of the whole family." "Who can believe," she asks fervently, "that days, months, and years spent in a continual course of thought and action similar to this, will not produce a powerful effect upon the character?"[42] Of course it did; one notices first of all that feminine writers like Elizabeth Barrett, "Charlotte Elizabeth," Elizabeth M. Sewell, and Mrs. Ellis herself had to overcome deep-seated guilt about authorship. Many found it necessary to justify their work by recourse to some external stimulus or ideology. In their novels, the heroine's aspirations for a full, independent life are undermined, punished, or replaced by marriage.

Elizabeth Barrett Browning's *Aurora Leigh* (1857) is one of the few autobiographical discussions of feminine role conflict. Aurora's struggle to become an artist is complicated by the self-hatred in which she has been educated, by her internalized convictions of her weakness and narcissism, and by the gentle scorn of her suitor Romney. She defies him, however, and invokes divine authority to reject his proposal that she become his helpmeet:

> You misconceive the question like a man
> Who sees the woman as the complement
> Of his sex merely. You forget too much
> That every creature, female as the male,
> Stands single in responsible act and thought . . .
> I too have my vocation,—work to do,
> The heavens and earth have set me.
>
> (Book II, 460-466)

Aurora succeeds as a poet. But she marries Romney in the end, having learned that as a woman she cannot cope with the guilt of self-centered ambition. It is significant that Romney has been blinded in an accident before she marries him, not only because he has thereby received firsthand knowledge of being handicapped and can empathize with her, but also because he then needs her help and can provide her with suitably feminine work. When Aurora tells Romney that "No perfect artist is developed here / From any imperfect woman" (Book IX, 648-649) she means more than the perfection of love and motherhood; she means also the perfection of self-sacrifice. This conflict remains a significant one for English novelists up to the present; it is a major theme for women novelists from Charlotte Brontë to Penelope Mortimer. Male novelists like Thackeray, who came from an elite class, also felt uncomfortable with the aggressive self-promotion of the novelist's career. As Donald Stone points out:

> Thackeray's ambivalent feelings towards Becky Sharp indicate the degree to which he attempted to suppress or make light of his own literary talents. The energies which make her (for a time) a social success are akin to those which made him a creative artist. In the hands of a major woman novelist, like Jane Austen or George Eliot, the destructive moral and social implications of Becky's behavior would have been defined more clearly and more urgently. Jane Austen's dissection of Lydia Bennet, and George Eliot's demolition of Rosamond Vincy, for example, indicate both how and why the defense of the status quo—insofar as women of the nineteenth century were concerned—was most earnestly and elaborately performed by women writers. Their heroines are hardly concerned with self-fulfillment in the modern sense of the term, and if they have severely limited possibilities in life it is because their authors saw great danger in, plus a higher alternative to, the practice of self-assertiveness.[43]

The dilemma is stated by George Eliot in *Romola* as the question of where "the duty of obedience ends and the duty of resistance begins."[44] Yet this was the question any Victorian woman with the will to write would have had to ask herself: what did God intend her to do with her life? Where did obedience to her father and husband end, and the responsibility of self-fulfillment become paramount? The problem of obedience and resistance that women had to solve in their own lives before they could begin to write crops up in their novels as the heroine's moral crisis. The forms that the crisis takes in feminine fiction are realistically mundane—should Margaret, in Mrs. Gaskell's *North and South,* lie to protect her brother? should Ethel May, in Charlotte Younge's *Daisy Chain,* give up studying Greek to nurse her father?—but the sources were profound, and were connected to the women novelists' sense of epic life. At the same time that they recognized the modesty of their own struggles, women writers recognized their heroism. "A new Theresa will hardly have the opportunity of reforming a conventual life," wrote George Eliot in *Middlemarch,* "any more than a new Antigone will spend her heroic piety in daring all for a brother's burial: the medium in which their ardent deeds took shape is forever gone. But we insignificant people with our daily words and acts are preparing the lives of many Dorotheas, some of which may present a far sadder sacrifice than that of the Dorothea whose story we know."[45]

The training of Victorian girls in repression, concealment, and self-censorship was deeply inhibiting, especially for those who wanted to write. As one novelist commented in 1860, "Women are greater dissemblers than men when they wish to conceal their own emotions. By habit, moral training, and modern education, they are obliged to do so. The very first lessons of infancy teach them to repress their feelings, control their very thoughts."[46] The verbal range permitted to English gentlewomen amounted almost to a special language. The verbal inhibitions that were part of the upbringing of a lady were reinforced by the critics' vigilance. "It is an immense loss," lamented Alice James, "to have all robust and sustaining expletives refined away from one."[47] "Coarseness" was the term Victorian readers used to rebuke unconventional language in women's literature. It could refer to the "damns" in *Jane Eyre,* the dialect in *Wuthering Heights,* the slang of Rhoda Broughton's heroines, the colloquialisms in *Aurora Leigh,* or more generally to the moral tone of a work, such as the "vein of perilous voluptuousness" one alert critic detected in *Adam Bede.*[48] John Keble censored Charlotte Yonge's fiction, taking the greatest care "that no hint of 'coarseness' should sully the purity of Charlotte's writings. Thus he would not allow Theodora in *Heartsease* to say that 'really she had a heart, though some people thought it was only a machine for pumping blood.' He also transformed the 'circle' of the setting sun into an 'orb' and a 'coxcomb' into a 'jackanapes'."[49] While verbal force, wit, and originality in women was criticized, a bland and gelatinous prose won applause. "She writes as an English gentlewoman should write," the *North British Review* complimented Anne Marsh in 1849; "her pages are absolutely like green pastures."[50] Reduced to a pastoral flatness, deprived of a language in which to describe their bodies or the events of their bodies, denied the expression of pain as well as the expression of pleasure, women writers appeared deficient in passion.

It is easy to understand why many readers took the absence of expression for the absence of feeling. In "The False Morality of Lady Novelists," W. R. Greg argued that woman's sexual innocence would prevent her ever writing a great novel:

> Many of the saddest and deepest truths in the strange science of sexual affection are to her mysteriously and mercifully veiled and can only be purchased at such a fearful cost that we cannot wish it otherwise. The inevitable consequence however is that in treating of that science she labours under all the disadvantages of partial study and superficial insight. She is describing a country of which she knows only the more frequented and the safer roads, with a few of the sweeter scenes and the prettier by-paths and more picturesque detours which be not far from the broad and beaten thoroughfares; while the rockier and loftier mountains, and more rugged tracts, the more sombre valleys, and the darker and more dangerous chasms, are never trodden by her feet, and scarcely ever dreamed of by her fancy.[51]

The results of restrictive education and intensive conditioning were taken as innate evidence of natural preference. In an ironic twist, many reviewers who had paternally barred the way to the sombre valleys, the darker chasms, and the more rugged tracts also blamed women for the emasculation of male prose, finding, like the *Prospective Review,* that the "writing of men is in danger of being marked" by "the delicacy and even fastidiousness of expression which is *natural* to educated women" [my italics].[52] When G. H. Lewes complained in 1852 that the literature of women was "too much a literature of imitation" and demanded that women should express "what they have really known, felt and suffered,"[53] he was asking for something that Victorian society had made impossible. Feminine novelists had been deprived of the language and the consciousness for such an enterprise, and obviously their deprivation extended beyond Victoria's reign and into the twentieth century. The delicacy and verbal fastidiousness of Virginia Woolf is an extension of this feminized language.

Florence Nightingale thought the effort of repression itself drained off women's creative energy. "Give us back our suffering," she demanded in *Cassandra* (1852), "for out of nothing comes nothing. But out of suffering may come the cure. Better have pain than paralysis."[54] It does sometimes seem as if feminine writers are metaphorically paralyzed, as Alice James was literally paralyzed, by refinement and restraint, but the repression in which the feminine novel was situated also forced women to find innovative and covert ways to dramatize the inner life, and led to a fiction that was intense, compact, symbolic, and profound. There is Charlotte Brontë's extraordinary subversion of the Gothic in *Jane Eyre,* in which the mad wife locked in the attic symbolizes the passionate and sexual side of Jane's personality, an alter ego that her upbringing, her religion, and her society have commanded her to incarcerate. There is the crippled artist heroine of Dinah Craik's *Olive* (1850), who identifies with Byron, and whose deformity represents her very womanhood. There are the murderous little wives of Mary Braddon's sensation novels, golden-haired killers whose actions are a sardonic commentary on the real feelings of the Angel in the House.

Many of the fantasies of feminine novels are related to money, mobility, and power. Although feminine novelists punished assertive heroines, they dealt with personal ambition by projecting the ideology of success onto male characters, whose initiative, thrift, industry, and perseverance came straight from the woman author's experience. The "woman's man," discussed in Chapter iv, was often a more effective outlet for the "deviant" aspects of the author's personality than were her heroines, and thus male role-playing extended beyond the pseudonym to imaginative content.

Protest fiction represented another projection of female experience onto another group; it translated the felt pain and oppression of women into the championship of mill-workers, child laborers, prostitutes, and slaves. Women were aware that protest fiction converted anger and frustration into an acceptable form of feminine and Christian expression. In the social novels of the 1840s and 1850s, and the problem novels of the 1860s and 1870s, women writers were pushing back the boundaries of their sphere, and presenting their profession as one that required not only freedom of language and thought, but also mobility and activity in the world. The sensation novelists of the 1870s, including Mary Braddon, Rhoda Broughton, and Florence Marryat, used this new freedom in a transitional literature that explored genuinely radical female protest against marriage and women's economic oppression, although still in the framework of feminine conventions that demanded the erring heroine's destruction.

From Jane Austen to George Eliot, the woman's novel had moved, despite its restrictions, in the direction of an all-inclusive female realism, a broad, socially informed exploration of the daily lives and values of women within the family and the community. By 1880, the three-decker had become flexible enough to accommodate many of the formerly unprintable aspects of female experience. Yet with the death of George Eliot and the appearance of a new generation of writers, the woman's novel moved into a Feminist phase, a confrontation with male society that elevated Victorian sexual stereotypes into a cult. The feminists challenged many of the restrictions on women's self-expression, denounced the gospel of self-sacrifice, attacked patriarchal religion, and constructed a theoretical model of female oppression, but their anger with society and their need for self-justification often led them away from realism into oversimplification, emotionalism, and fantasy. Making their fiction the vehicle for a dramatization of wronged womanhood, they demanded changes in the social and political systems that would grant women male privileges and require chastity and fidelity from men. The profound sense of injustice that the feminine novelists had represented as class struggle in their novels of factory life becomes an all-out war of the sexes in the novels of the feminists. Even their pseudonyms show their sense of feminist pride and of matriarchal mission to their sisters; one representative feminist called herself "Sarah Grand." In its extreme form, feminist literature advocated the sexual separatism of Amazon utopias and suffragette sisterhoods.

In the lives of the feminists, the bonds of the female subculture were particularly strong. The feminists were intensely devoted to each other and needed the support of close, emotional friendships with other women as well as the loving adulation of a female audience. In this generation, which mainly comprises women born between 1860 and 1880, one finds sympathetically attuned women writing in teams; Edith Somerville and Violet Martin were even said to have continued the collaboration beyond the grave.[55] Although they preached individualism, their need for association led to a staggering number of clubs, activities, and causes, culminating in the militant groups and the almost terrifying collectivity of the suffrage movement. They glorified and idealized the womanly values of chastity and maternal love, and believed that those values must be forced upon a degenerate male society.

In their lives and in their books, most feminist writers expressed both an awareness of, and a revulsion from, sexuality. Like the feminine novelists, they projected many of their own experiences onto male characters, creating, for example, the Scarlet Pimpernels, "effeminate" fops by day and fearless heroes by night, semi-androgynous symbols of a generation in uneasy transition. To some degree these tactics were typical of the period in which they wrote; male novelists were creating "masculine" independent women who, as Donald Stone puts it, "could be used as a cover for those men who, for one reason or another, were anxious to proclaim their own standards and follow their own instincts."[56]

As the feminists themselves often seem neurotic and divided in their roles, less productive than earlier generations, and subject to paralyzing psychosomatic illnesses, so their fiction seems to break down in its form. In the 1890s the three-decker novel abruptly disappeared due to changes in its marketability, and women turned to short stories and fragments, which they called "dreams," "keynotes," and "fantasias." At the turn of the century came the purest examples of feminist literature, the novels, poems, and plays written as suffragette propaganda and distributed by the efficient and well-financed suffrage presses.

The feminist writers were not important artists. Yet in their insistence on exploring and defining womanhood, in their rejection of self-sacrifice, and even in their outspoken hostility to men, the feminist writers represented an important stage, a declaration of independence, in the female tradition. They did produce some interesting and original work, and they opened new subjects for other novelists. Sarah Grand's powerful studies of female psychology, George Egerton's bitter short stories, and Olive Schreiner's existential socialism were all best-sellers in their own day and still hold attention. Through political campaigns for prostitutes and working women, and in the suffrage crusades, the feminists insisted on their right to use the male sexual vocabulary, and to use it forcefully and openly. The feminists also challenged the monopoly of male publishers and rebelled against the dictatorship of the male establishment. Men—John Chapman, John Blackwood, Henry Blackett, George Smith—had published the works of feminine novelists and had exerted direct and enormous power over their contents. Sarah Grand parodied the masculine critical hegemony by describing a literary journal she called the *Patriarch,* and feminist journalists, writing in their own magazines, argued against the judgments of the men of letters. In the 1860s the sensation novelists had begun to retain their copyrights, work with printers on a commission basis, and edit their own magazines. The feminists continued to expand this economic control of publishing outlets. Virginia Woolf, printing her own novels at the Hogarth Press, owed much of her independence to the feminists' insistence on the need for women writers to be free of patriarchal commercialism.

. . . Feminine, feminist, or female, the woman's novel has always had to struggle against the cultural and historical forces that relegated women's experience to the second rank. In trying to outline the female tradition, I have looked beyond the famous novelists who have been found worthy, to the lives and works of many women who have long been excluded from literary history. I have tried to discover how they felt about themselves and their books, what choices and sacrifices they made, and how their relationship to their profession and their tradition evolved. "What is commonly called literary history," writes Louise Bernikow, "is actually a record of choices. Which writers have survived their time and which have not depends upon who noticed them and chose to record the notice.[57] If some of the writers I notice seem to us to be Teresas and Antigones, struggling with their overwhelming sense of vocation and repression, many more will seem only Dorotheas, prim, mistaken, irreparably minor. And yet it is only by considering them all—Millicent Grogan as well as Virginia Woolf—that we can begin to record new choices in a new literary history, and to understand why, despite prejudice, despite guilt, despite inhibition, women began to write.

Notes

1. "The Subjection of Women," in John Stuart Mill and Harriet Taylor Mill, *Essays on Sex Equality,* ed. Alice S. Rossi, Chicago, 1970, ch. III, p. 207.
2. "Some Women Novelists," *History of the English Novel,* X, London, 1939, p. 194.

3. G. H. Lewes, "The Lady Novelists," *Westminster Review*, n.s. II (1852): 137; W. L. Courtney, *The Feminine Note in Fiction*, London, 1904, p. xiii; Bernard Bergonzi, *New York Review of Books*, June 3, 1965. In a review of Beryl Bainbridge's *The Bottle Factory Outing*, Anatole Broyard comments "that quite a few extremely attractive women write rather despairing books" (*New York Times*, May 26, 1975, p. 13).

4. "Silly Novels by Lady Novelists," *Westminster Review* LXVI (1856); reprinted in *Essays of George Eliot*, ed. Thomas Pinney, London, 1963, p. 324.

5. "Ruth," *North British Review* XIX (1853): 90-91; and "Ko-Ko's Song" in *The Mikado*. The stereotype of the woman novelist that emerges in the early nineteenth century conflates the popular images of the old maid and the bluestocking; see Vineta Colby, *Yesterday's Woman: Domestic Realism in the English Novel*, Princeton, 1974, pp. 115-116, and Katharine M. Rogers, *The Troublesome Helpmate: A History of Misogyny in Literature*, London, 1966, pp. 201-207.

6. Introduction to May Sarton, *Mrs. Stevens Hears the Mermaids Singing*, New York, 1974, p. xvi.

7. "This Woman's Movement" in *Adrienne Rich's Poetry*, ed. Barbara Charlesworth Gelpi and Albert Gelpi, New York, 1975, p. 189.

8. *The Rise and Fall of the Man of Letters*, London, 1969, p. 304.

9. Cynthia Ozick, "Women and Creativity," in *Woman in Sexist Society*, ed. Vivian Gornick and Barbara K. Moran, New York, 1971, p. 436.

10. Letter of November 1849, in Clement Shorter, *The Brontës: Life and Letters*, II, London, 1908, p. 80.

11. Mary Ellmann, *Thinking About Women*, London, 1979, pp. 28-54; and Ozick, "Women and Creativity," p. 436.

12. Patricia Meyer Spacks, *The Female Imagination*, London, 1976, p. 3.

13. "Women and Fiction," *Collected Essays*, London 1976, p. 142.

14. See, for example, Sheila Rowbotham, *Hidden from History*, London, 1973; Martha Vicinus, ed., *Suffer and Be Still: Women in the Victorian Age*, London 1980; Mary S. Hartman and Lois N. Banner, eds., *Clio's Consciousness Raised: New Perspectives on the History of Women*, New York, 1974, and Françoise Basch, *Relative Creatures: Victorian Women in Society and the Novel*, London, 1974.

15. Linda Nochlin, "Why Are There No Great Women Artists?" in *Woman in Sexist Society*; Lise Vogel, "Fine Arts and Feminism: The Awakening Consciousness," *Feminist Studies* II (1974): 3-37; Helene Roberts, "The Inside, the Surface, the Mass: Some Recurring Images of Women," *Women's Studies* II (1974): 289-308.

16. *The Making of the English Working Class*, London, 1968, p. 13.

17. Vineta Colby, *The Singular Anomaly: Women Novelists of the Nineteenth Century*, New York, 1970, p. 11.

18. "Women's Lit: Profession and Tradition," *Columbia Forum* I (Fall 1972): 27.

19. Spacks, p. 7.

20. Moers, "Women's Lit," p. 28.

21. "Flying Pigs and Double Standards," *Times Literary Supplement*, (July 26, 1974): 784.

22. For helpful studies of literary subcultures, see Robert A. Bone, *The Negro Novel in America*, New York, 1958; and Northrop Frye, "Conclusion to *A Literary History of Canada*," in *The Stubborn Structure: Essays on Criticism and Society*, London, 1970, pp. 278-312.

23. "Women and Creativity," p. 442.

24. Nancy F. Cott, introduction to *Root of Bitterness*, New York, 1972, pp. 3-4.

25. For the best discussions of the Victorian feminine ideal, see Françoise Basch, "Contemporary Ideologies," in *Relative Creatures*, pp. 3-15; Walter E. Houghton, *The Victorian Frame of Mind*, London, 1957, pp. 341-343; and Alexander Welsh's theory of the Angel in the House in *The City of Dickens*, London, 1971, pp. 164-195.

26. Christine Stansell and Johnny Faragher, "Women and Their Families on the Overland Trail, 1842-1867," *Feminist Studies* II (1975): 152-153. For an overview of recent historical scholarship on the "two cultures," see Barbara Sicherman, "Review: American History," *Signs: Journal of Women in Culture and Society* I (Winter 1975): 470-484.

27. For a sociological account of patterns of behavior for Victorian women, see Leonore Davidoff, *The Best Circles: Society, Etiquette and the Season*, London, 1973, esp. pp. 48-58, 85-100.

28. Sarah Ellis, *The Daughters of England*, London, 1845, ch. IX, p. 338.

29. Dinah M. Craik, "Literary Ghouls," *Studies from Life*, New York, 1861, p. 13.

30. Letter of October 6, 1851, in *Letters of E. Jewsbury to Jane Welsh Carlyle*, ed. Mrs. Alex Ireland, London, 1892, p. 426. For Fanny Fern, see Ann Douglas Wood, "The 'Scribbling Women' and Fanny Fern: Why Women Wrote," *American Quarterly* XXIII (Spring 1971): 1-24.

31. J. M. S. Tompkins, *The Popular Novel in England 1770-1800*, London, 1932, pp. 119-121; Dorothy Blakey, *The Minerva Press 1790-1820*, London, 1939; and Ian Watt, *The Rise of the Novel*, London, 1963, pp. 298-299.

32. Myra Reynolds, *The Learned Lady in England 1650-1760*, New York, 1920, pp. 89-91.

33. William McKee, *Elizabeth Inchbald, Novelist*, Washington, D.C., 1935, p. 20.

34. "Memoirs of the Life of Mrs. Mary Brunton by Her Husband," preface to *Emmeline*, Edinburgh, 1819, p. xxxvi.

35. Kathleen Tillotson, *Novels of the Eighteen-Forties*, London, 1956, pp. 142-145.

36. For a refutation of Leavis's view of Austen and Eliot, see Gross, *Rise and Fall of the Man of Letters*, pp. 302-303.

37. Quoted in S. C. Hall, *A Book of Memories of Great Men and Women of the Age*, London, 1877, p. 266.

38. Inga-Stina Ewbank, *Their Proper Sphere: A Study of the Brontë Sisters as Early-Victorian Female Novelists*, London, 1966, p. 41.

39. *Saturday Review* IV (July 11, 1857): 40-41. See also David Masson, *British Novelists and Their Styles,* Cambridge, 1859, p. 134.

40. *Autobiography and Letters of Mrs. M.O.W. Oliphant,* ed., Mrs. Harry Coghill, London, 1899, p. 160.

41. "An Enquiry into the State of Girls' Fashionable Schools," *Fraser's* XXXI (1845): 703.

42. Sarah Ellis, *The Women of England,* London, 1838, ch. U, p. 35.

43. "Victorian Feminism and the Nineteenth-Century Novel," *Women's Studies* I (1972): 69.

44. *Romola,* London, 1863, II, ch. XXIII.

45. *Middlemarch,* ed., W. J. Harvey, London, 1965, "Finale," p. 896.

46. Jane Vaughan Pinckney, *Tacita Tacit,* II, p. 276; quoted in Myron Brightfield, *Victorian England in Its Novels,* IV, Los Angeles, 1968, p. 27.

47. *The Diary of Alice James,* ed. Leon Edel, London, 1965, p. 66.

48. *British Quarterly Review* XLV (1867): 164. On the term "coarseness," see Ewbank, *Their Proper Sphere,* pp. 46-47.

49. Margaret Mare and Alicia C. Percival, *Victorian Best-Seller: The World of Charlotte Yonge,* London, 1947, p. 133.

50. James Lorimer, "Noteworthy Novels," XI (1849): 257.

51. "The False Morality of Lady Novelists," *National Review* VII, (1859): 149.

52. "Puseyite Novels," VI (1850): 498.

53. "The Lady Novelists," p. 132.

54. "Cassandra," in *The Cause,* ed. Ray Strachey, London, 1978, p. 398.

55. See Maurice Collis, *Somerville and Ross,* London, 1968, for an account of the careers of Edith Somerville and Violet Martin. After Martin's death in 1915, the "collaboration" continued through psychic communications. Katherine Bradley and Edith Cooper wrote under the name of "Michael Field"; the sisters Emily and Dorothea Gerard used the name "E. D. Gerard" for such joint efforts as *Beggar My Neighbor* (1882).

56. "Victorian Feminism and the Nineteenth-Century Novel," p. 79.

57. *The World Split Open: Four Centuries of Women Poets in England and America, 1552-1950,* New York, 1979, p. 3.

Works Cited

Books on women and the novel, Victorian women, the women's movement, individual novelists.

Baker, Ernest A. *The History of the English Novel.* 10 vols. London: Witherby, 1924-1939.

Basch, Françoise. *Relative Creatures: Victorian Women in Society and The Novel.* London: Allen Lane, 1974.

Brightfield, Myron. *Victorian England in its Novels.* 4 vols. Los Angeles: U.C.L.A., 1968.

Coghill, Mrs. Harry, ed. *Autobiography and Letters of Mrs. M. O. W. Oliphant.* London: Blackwood, 1899.

Colby, Vineta. *The Singular Anomaly: Women Novelists of the Nineteenth Century.* New York: New York U. Press, 1970.

———. *Yesterday's Women: Domestic Realism in the English Novel.* Princeton: Princeton U. Press, 1974.

Cott, Nancy F. *Root of Bitterness.* New York: E. P. Dutton, 1972.

Courtney, William L. *The Feminine Note in Fiction.* London: Chapman & Hall, 1904.

Davidoff, Leonore. *The Best Circles: Society, Etiquette and the Season.* London: Croom Helm, 1973.

Edel, Leon, ed. *The Diary of Alice James.* London: Hart-Davis, 1965.

Ellmann, Mary. *Thinking About Women.* London: Virago, 1979.

Ewbank, Inga-Stina. *Their Proper Sphere: A Study of the Brontë Sisters as Early-Victorian Novelists.* London: Edward Arnold, 1966.

Gornick, Vivian and Barbara K. Moran, eds. *Woman in Sexist Society.* New York: Basic Books, 1971.

Hartman, Mary S. and Lois Banner, eds. *Clio's Consciousness Raised: New Perspectives on the History of Women.* New York: Harper & Row, 1974.

Ireland, Mrs. Alex, ed. *Letters of Geraldine Jewsbury to Jane Welsh Carlyle.* London: Longmans, Green, 1892.

Mill, John Stuart and Harriet Taylor Mill. *Essays on Sex Equality.* Ed. Alice S. Rossi. Chicago: U. of Chicago Press, 1970.

Moers, Ellen. *Literary Women.* London: The Women's Press, 1978.

Moore, Doris Langley. *E. Nesbit: A Biography.* London: Benn, 1967.

Pinney, Thomas, ed. *Essays of George Eliot.* London: Routledge, 1963.

Rogers, Katherine M. *The Troublesome Helpmate: A History of Misogyny in Literature.* Seattle and London: U. of Washington Press, 1966.

Rowbotham, Sheila. *Hidden From History.* London: Pluto Press, 1973.

Shorter, Clement. *The Brontës: Life and Letters.* 2 vols. London: Hodder and Stoughton, 1908.

Spacks, Patricia Meyer. *The Female Imagination.* London: Allen and Unwin, 1976.

Stone, Donald. *Novelists in a Changing World.* Cambridge, Mass.: Harvard U. Press, 1972.

Strachey, Ray. *The Cause.* London: Virago, 1978.

Thomson, Patricia. *The Victorian Heroine: A Changing Ideal.* London: Oxford U. Press, 1956.

Tillotson, Kathleen. *Novels of the Eighteen-Forties.* London: Oxford U. Press, 1954.

Tompkins, J. M. S. *The Popular Novel in England 1770-1800.* London: Methuen, 1932.

Vicinus, Martha, ed. *Suffer and Be Still: Women in the Victorian Age*. London: Methuen University Paperbacks, 1980.

Welsh, Alexander. *The City of Dickens*. London: Oxford U. Press, 1971.

Woolf, Virginia. *Collected Essays*. II. Ed. Leonard Woolf. London: Chatto & Windus, 1967.

Articles in nineteenth-century periodicals, listed chronologically.

[Lorimer, James]. "Noteworthy Novels," *North British Review*, XI (1849), 255-265.

"Puseyite Novels," *Prospective Review*, VI (1850), 512-534.

[Lewes, G. H.]. "The Lady Novelists," *Westminster Review*, n.s. II (1852), 129-141.

[Greg, W. R.]. "The False Morality of Lady Novelists," *National Review*, VII (1859), 144-167.

"Romola," *British Quarterly Review*, XXXVIII (1863), 448-465.

"George Eliot," *British Quarterly Review*, XLV (1867), 141-178.

Wood, Ann Douglas. "The 'Scribbling Women' and Fanny Fern: Why Women Wrote," *American Quarterly*, XXIII (Spring 1971), 1-24.

SUSAN RUBINOW GORSKY (ESSAY DATE 1992)

SOURCE: Gorsky, Susan Rubinow. "Introduction: Literature and Society." In *Femininity to Feminism: Women and Literature in the Nineteenth Century*, pp. 1-15. New York: Twayne Publishers, 1992.

In the following essay, Gorsky describes women's dominating role in development of the realistic novel in the nineteenth century, arguing that a century filled with profound change was heavily influenced by female authors and readers.

> Toward the end of the eighteenth century a change came about which, if I were rewriting history, I should describe more fully and think of greater importance than the Crusades or the War of the Roses. The middle-class woman began to write.
>
> —Virginia Woolf, *A Room of One's Own*[1]

Exploring the role of women during the nineteenth century means considering the evolution of feminism, a loaded word that implies a variety of ideas and arouses conflicting reactions. Feminism suggests a practical determination to alter unjust laws, whether about divorce, property, or voting rights. But it also implies a philosophical questioning of traditional values and ideas, from women's intellectual and emotional capacities to male-female relationships to the ways women and men think, act, and feel. A lot happened to women's roles and the women's movement during this period of ferment. The greatest visible changes occurred in family life, education, and jobs, areas that affect all aspects of human existence.

England and America share a heritage of culture, assumptions, laws, and beliefs. American law has its origins in British common law, American literature has often imitated England's and America's dominant religions came over with the pilgrims. Until the nineteenth century, philosophical and artistic movements tended to cross the Atlantic from east to west. In the 1800s, however, America found that unique political, economic, and social realities in the New World required new attitudes, laws, and literature. Through war and economic expansion, the American territory spread from sea to sea and beyond. Westward pioneers pursued dreams of land, freedom, and wealth, and the creation of canals and roads suggested that the vast land could become one nation. Sectional differences threatened the fragile alliance, painfully reasserted through the Civil War. An earlier war separated the American colonies from England, but by the nineteenth century the British Empire stretched from Africa to Asia, from the Indian Ocean to the Caribbean. It included more than fifty colonies—areas as diverse as today's New Zealand, Sierra Leone, India, and Jamaica.

The nineteenth century is often seen as a time of relative stability, when people shared the values of family, progress, patriotism, and God; but it was truly an era of change. Cities and industries erupted in the countryside. Social reform, new educational opportunities and jobs, and writings like Darwin's *Origin of Species* challenged the established order of the universe and the position of humankind. Romanticism legitimized individuality, imaginative expression, and freedom, fostering an atmosphere in which to explore feminist ideas. In this era of search, change, and retreat, familiar patterns seemed sometimes a comforting sanctuary, sometimes a trap to destroy. Accepted values and behaviors sanctified by lip service could mask a reality quite different from the myth. The impact of change is especially obvious in women's lives.

Women's position at the end of the eighteenth century was little changed from the Middle Ages. According to British common law and thus American law, women were essentially men's property: before marriage, a woman's life was determined by her father; after marriage, by her husband; the unmarried woman was considered somehow unnatural. A woman's social status and economic well-being depended on the man in her life, and, to a very large degree, her happiness depended on his goodwill. She had almost no opportunity for education, no chance to develop special interests or choose a career other than wife and mother.

In establishing its constitution, the United States made it clear that neither slaves nor women deserved the full rights of citizenship. A few years after emancipation, male former slaves were granted the right to vote, but it took another half century for women of any color, born slave or not, to earn the same right in the United States and in England. Symbolically and actually, women were seen as less than fully human.

The roots of this attitude lie deep in Western culture. Laws codified attitudes dating back at least to the Old Testament, reinforced by Christian writings. The Book of Genesis states that the first woman was created from man, thus establishing a hierarchy that persists in church doctrine and practice to this day. Anne Bradstreet underscores the positions of God, man, and woman in her poem "To My Dear and Loving Husband" (1678): "Thy love is such I can no way repay / The heavens reward thee manifold I pray."

The Bible defines woman as saint *and* sinner, mother of the human race, source of suffering and source of salvation. Eve, tempted by the devil, in turn tempts Adam to sin, and thus sorrow and death enter the world. Mary, untouched by sexuality, gives birth to the son of God and thereby offers a path out of sin and suffering. The Old Testament God is a patriarch; the New Testament offers God the Father *and* God the Son. The most significant women in the Judeo-Christian tradition appear only in relationship to male figures, as wife or mother. So women were defined for centuries.

Women who maintain socially acceptable relationships with men are "good" women; those who defy the norms are "bad." The archetypal good woman starts as a virtuous, obedient daughter and ends as a submissive wife and nurturing mother. If, through fate or accident, she remains unmarried, she can become a saint, devoting her life to religion, good works, her parents, or perhaps her orphaned nieces and nephews. The archetypal bad woman undercuts the role and power of men: if married, she becomes a shrew or nag; if unmarried, she might be seductive, perhaps bearing a child out of wedlock, or mannish, perhaps seeking an education or career. Even her unintentional defiance of the norm disturbs society's equanimity.

In time the social norm, inherently destructive of women's individuality and rights, had to change. Recognizing the opportunity provided by the new nation's birth, Abigail Adams warned her husband: "remember the ladies and be more generous and favorable to them than your ancestors. Do not put such unlimited power into the hands of the husbands. Remember, all men would be tyrants if they could. If particular care and attention is not paid to the ladies, we are determined to foment a rebellion, and will not hold ourselves bound by any laws in which we have no voice or representation."[2] While John Adams responded, "I cannot but laugh," women—and some men—soon took such ideas quite seriously.

The early feminist movement, from late in the eighteenth century through the first decades of the twentieth, addressed both practical and theoretical issues. Feminists sought to change marriage laws, control their own property, and obtain jobs and education. They wanted political power, the "voice or representation" to make laws themselves. But they also attempted to change their second-class status in another sense, desiring recognition as independent people defined by their actions and valued in and for themselves. These philosophical issues lay beneath the surface of pragmatic actions and goals. By the early twentieth century, feminists made many practical gains, but women's position did not yet equal men's. The nineteenth-century feminists left a legacy of change, but also a legacy of work yet to be done: they sought—as today's feminists still seek—true equality.

Literature in a Time of Change

Literature both influences and reflects the times in which it is written, sometimes prefiguring events in society and sometimes supporting an earlier reality by suggesting that it still exists. In the nineteenth century, poetry tended to be stylized, formal, and often dissociated from social reality; an exception is Elizabeth Barrett Browning's poem about child labor, "Cry of the Children" (1844). In part because of Victorian censorship, the theater largely degenerated into imitations and revivals of eighteenth-century comedies, presentations of Shakespeare's plays suitably purged to fit new sensibilities, and banal or melodramatic contemporary works: Mark Twain's "Royal Nonesuch" parody is more apt and less exaggerated than many modern readers of *Huckleberry Finn* (1844) realize.

Fiction dominated the literary scene. The chosen vehicle for many great writers, the novel reached the widest and most varied audience and most directly revealed social change. Because it was women who most often read and wrote novels, changing attitudes toward women's roles are most reflected in and perhaps influenced by fiction. Finally, as Virginia Woolf suggests in the words heading this chapter, many women wrote about and for themselves. Thus, the best literary source for considering women's changing roles is fiction, especially the realistic novel.

But how real is the realistic novel? Some historians use fiction as a source, arguing that since history tends to ignore women, novels provide more useful information about their lives; theorists may even challenge the objectivity of history itself, suggesting that it, too, is fiction. Further complicating matters, some literary critics argue that the author is also a kind of fiction. Yet clearly literature has an author, a human being influenced by the beliefs and events of the time and whose writings are likewise colored; clearly, regardless of bias, historians use facts differently from novelists.

Novels use details of external reality to establish a character, describe a setting, or suggest a theme. They use social data not necessarily to provide an accurate picture of society at a given time and place but to enhance some element of fiction. Given that purpose, they distort fact, whether consciously or unconsciously. To expect fiction to serve as a literal source of history is to ignore what makes it art. Yet, while not social documents, novels are closer to reality than most other genres.

The fictional use of realistic detail derives from and affirms an aesthetic theory and philosophical stance with these premises: the world "out there" is objectively definable; it is separate from the perceiver; it is "real" and significant in itself, not just in relation to the perceiver. When these ideas lost their widespread acceptance around 1900, the nature of the novel began to change.

Nineteenth-century fiction presents a fairly consistent picture of daily life: Husband and wife live comfortably with one or two children and at least one servant in a fairly large private house. Each day except Sunday, the man goes to work in one of the professions or in business. The woman spends her days close to home, visiting neighbors, performing charitable acts, sewing, reading, or subtly forwarding her daughters' chances of marriage. The boys attend school and perhaps college, while the girls receive little education but acquire a few graceful arts. Marriages almost never end in divorce, men are nearly always faithful, and women virtually never work outside the home. But social reality did not always match this picture, for a variety of reasons.

Because even the most realistic novel is still art, it reflects literary convention as much as social reality. Understanding how writers define women's changing roles and the evolution of feminist thought requires recognizing the interrelationship between literature and reality and knowing something about literary heritage.

The Realistic Novel

Early in the eighteenth century, the novel developed both the parameters that loosely demarcate the genre and the constant bending of those parameters that gives the genre its characteristic flexibility. Defoe explored the boundaries between fiction and nonfiction; Richardson tried various modes of narration; Fielding struggled tongue-in-cheek to connect the new genre to the old ones, suggesting that *Joseph Andrews* (1774) might be either a biography or a "comic epic-poem in prose" (7). As early as 1767, Laurence Sterne could challenge the barely established conventions with the outrageous, great, and experimental *Tristram Shandy*. The genre's versatility appears not only in the work of these masters but also in a proliferation of variants. Sterne's exploration of psychological theory and human nature found followers; Walpole, Radcliffe, and others introduced the Gothic novel; Fanny Burney's *Evelina* (1778) prefigured Jane Austen's more important novels of manners, and all of these authors had uncounted imitators.

By the early nineteenth century, the novel was established as the genre that most directly represented real life. True, Sir Walter Scott's historical romance, designed to reflect the imagination of the author more than the reality of ordinary life, had many followers who met the universal need to escape from the ordinary and to savor the enchantment of other worlds. Romanticism dominated America's extraordinary midcentury literary flowering, but even Melville and Hawthorne adhered to the fundamental rule of allowing their audience to identify with their characters and situations. England's "penny dreadfuls" and America's "dime novels" spawned a plethora of adventure tales with contemporary references, bloodshed, and violence; Dickens adapted this popular genre to his purposes. Gothic fiction also remained, to find major exponents such as Edgar Allan Poe and Mary Shelley, to sneak into the works of Scott and the Brontës, and to be satirized in Austen's *Northanger Abbey* (1803). But every variant of the novel has some realistic portrayal of human nature if not of ordinary human life; literature would hold little interest if it lacked connection with its readers' real concerns.

The dominant form in the nineteenth century had a far more direct connection with the real world: through variations such as the novel of manners, the problem novel, and the psychological novel, the genre consistently attempts to portray reality in fiction—to use ordinary language to show ordinary people doing ordinary things. Regional fiction, such as the short-story collections *A New England Nun* (1891) by Mary E. Wilkins Freeman and *The Country of the Pointed Firs* (1896) by Sarah Orne Jewett, set its characters' situations in the context of a specific culture—thus revealing social history, especially women's daily lives. Among these local colorists were other poets and novelists of the American south and west: Kate Chopin, Mary Murfree, Grace Elizabeth King, and Constance Fenimore Woolson, sometimes described as the first realistic writer. The romantic love story of Jackson's *Ramona* (1884) depends upon the actual struggle for land and power among Indians, Mexicans, and whites in California. So, too, propagandistic fiction like Stowe's *Uncle Tom's Cabin* (1852) or historical romances like Hawthorne's *The Scarlet Letter* (1859) let us ask what the Victorians considered "the question of supreme interest in art, the question upon which depends our whole interest in art": namely, "what are its relations to life?"[3]

Mimesis—the notion that art imitates the world outside itself—is an ancient aesthetic theory. Devoted to truthful representation, realistic novels are designed to reflect the authors' understanding of the world immediately around them, a world whose attributes can be determined through direct experience, and in which the consequences of actions can be discerned. Authors deal not with absolute truths but with relative ones, not an ideal sought through transcendence but a reality found in experience. Such a theory of art pretty much demands a representational mode: thus, realists strive to present a world very much like the one they perceive, and they struggle to make their perception widely accepted rather than esoteric.

Most practitioners of the realistic novel tend to see themselves partly as teachers or moral guides. Realistic novels display an unusual degree of social consciousness, attempting to address the conscience and redress the ignorance of their readers. The most trivial plot may work toward this end. Decrying the sentimentality and escapism they see in romantic fiction, and usually avoiding overt moralizing, realists present a picture of ordinary life designed to inculcate in the reader an understanding of some truth, to enhance a sense of morality or reveal essential human bonds. Moralizing or propagandizing novels necessarily assert a fairly direct relationship between art and life: if art did not imitate life, it could not hope to influence it. Early-nineteenth-century novelists, more comfortable with the assumptions of their age, tend to speak for them, whereas later writers tend, however subtly, to criticize their society, as is obvious when they deal with the transformation of women's roles.

Constance Fenimore Woolson (1840-1894).

Concerned with presenting an immediately significant world with which their readers can sympathize, realists focus on character, the external and psychological effects of action, the outcome of moral decisions or ethical positions, and, above all, the everyday details of normal life in ordinary middle-class society. Because of the realistic novel's social setting and educational or moral purpose, its plot often revolves around a social problem. The heroic adventures and misadventures of the romance and the distancing effect of the historical novel give way to the mundane events and issues relevant to men and women supposedly very much like the men and women reading about them. The point is verisimilitude, though not simply for its own sake. The small truths should lead to greater ones.

Victorian novelists and critics questioned how imagination affects writing and how a novel relates to the world it reflects. Defending *Oliver Twist* (1841) as realistic, Dickens, in his preface, claimed to present degraded figures "as they really are," without the "allurements and fascinations" used by less realistic writers, because truthfulness is artistically and morally justified (ix). Many authors insist on the veracity of the most romantic tales: Hawthorne may call *The Scarlet Letter* a "romance," distinguishing it from a "novel"; yet even in the pretense of finding tantalizing historical records in the "Custom House" introduction, he symbolically reminds us of what Thackeray, in the "Preface" to *Pendennis* (1850) calls "the advantage of a certain truth and honesty." Charlotte Brontë argues that a book in which "Nature and Truth" are the sole guides would probably lack an audience and would wrongly ignore that "strong, restless faculty," the imagination.[4] Bored by popular realistic fiction, one critic proclaimed, "We may hope that the next fashion in fiction will take us to something more exciting and poetical than the domestic sorrows of brewers' wives."[5] Some argue against restrictions of topic or language, others say realism limits the place of ideas in fiction. George Eliot is not alone in objecting that those writers who claim to be most realistic are often the least, for they base their characters on convention rather than life. Literature is not life: literature selects, organizes, unifies, and transforms what exists outside it. Still, the predominant form of prose fiction, most popular at midcentury but flourishing to the end, had at least a pretense of realism, for both literary and philosophical reasons.

The forms and devices of eighteenth-century fiction, like the values and beliefs of the Enlightenment, lingered only briefly into the new century. Novels with tighter structures replaced the episodic picaresque. *David Copperfield* (1850), *Ruth* (1853), *Adam Bede* (1859), and even *The Adventures of Huckleberry Finn,* though literary descendants of *Tom Jones* (1749) and *Moll Flanders* (1722), bring the adventures nearer to home and present characters with more ordinary lives, interests, and problems. Character and realism take center stage. While Dickens and Twain may echo the "comic epic-poem" in their hyperbole and symbolic stock figures, they more honestly merit *Joseph Andrews*'s name of "biography" than does the original.

Dickens and Twain use aspects of melodrama and low comedy; Eliot, Gaskell, and Hawthorne, psychological fiction and symbolism; Alcott, sentimentality; the Brontës, Gothic romance. Yet all of their novels are more or less faithful to the society they describe, more or less designed to call attention to human nature as revealed through social interaction. Prison reform, slavery, sexual double standards, the poor laws, contemporary religious practice, jobs for women, education, or class distinctions—the most popular novels confront such issues directly and with thematic purpose.

The realistic novel may or may not be propagandistic or well formed; it may or may not make use of symbolism, melodrama, mythic patterns, or traditional plots. This variety makes it more difficult to determine whether a realistic novel accurately reflects society or skews its analysis of a given social issue, either intentionally or unintentionally. To complicate matters, society underwent fundamental redefinition on both sides of the Atlantic during these years.

The Society Reflected in Literature

Nineteenth-century life in England and America was extremely diverse. To identify the "typical" reader or character, one must consider a variety of issues, including place, time, and social class.

As America grew from a strip of land along the Atlantic Ocean to a nation stretching beyond continental bounds, *where* one lived implied differences in citizenship (state or territory?), economics, and life-style (factory owner or mill-hand? plantation owner or slave?). While social distinctions outweighed regional ones in England, agriculture dominated the south, factories the midlands and the north. A London home could be a slum tenement, a fine urban residence, or a house in a garden suburb. Each variation profoundly affected daily life, from religion to education to attitudes about women.

The extent of change in social reality and in attitudes in the nineteenth century was so great that it is very difficult to determine *when* our typical person lived. The first years of the century were a time of optimism during which many people believed that science and technology could resolve all of society's problems. In contrast, by the end of the century, the overall picture was one of agricultural depression, labor unrest, and increasing political, economic, and ideologic tensions. Thus life in 1895 barely resembled life in 1855 or 1805.

Much of the new hope derived from technological and attitudinal changes. In 1825, the new Erie Canal symbolized America's growth, and in

1832 the First Reform Bill ushered in an era of English social reform. In these early decades, Manifest Destiny seemed natural, economic prosperity and expansion seemed assured. In 1851, American literature flourished, and England celebrated the Great Exhibition of the Works of Industry of All Nations, better known as the Crystal Palace. From 1851 to 1881, Britain's gross national product doubled; Britain became the world's wealthiest country, London the greatest city. Cities and railroads multiplied, the middle class expanded and moved upward, and the working classes also reaped some financial rewards.

Yet the seeds of disillusion were always present: from the beginning of the period, reformers pointed to miserable conditions in slums and factories, even worse on plantations. By mid-century, events ranging from the publication of Darwin's *Origin of Species* to the Crimean War had rocked the Western world. The United States experienced a bloody, demoralizing Civil War; the closing of the frontier by the 1890s further undercut the American dream. As the English argued over new laws like the Second Reform Bill (1857) which gave town workers the vote and suggested that political and social power might slip from traditional aristocratic leaders to the "masses," similar fears emerged in the postwar American South when freed black slaves sometimes outnumbered former masters. And in England, Prince Albert's death led Queen Victoria into a period of seclusion suggesting to many the end of the monarchy.

Still, the Queen's Jubilee in 1887 showed that Victoria was both alive and beloved, whatever the state of the monarchy. She outlived the period that bears her name, dying long after the halcyon era of progress and certainty gave way to the incipient doubts inherent in the transition to modernism. The derogatory sense of the term "Victorianism," used since the 1890s, aptly suggests a conservative tendency in manners and mores. Victorianism remains a complex and loaded term, increasing the difficulty of defining a "typically" Victorian time period.

Once we have identified *when* and *where,* we still need to decide *who* best represents nineteenth-century life. Despite stunning diversity in society and culture, two significant and related features are the rise of the middle class and the rise of the realistic novel, which was written largely about and for that middle class.

In *Sybil* (1845), Disraeli made popular the idea of England as "two nations . . . the rich and the poor . . . between whom there is no intercourse and no sympathy; who are as ignorant of each other's habits, thoughts, and feelings, as if they were dwellers in different zones, or inhabitants of different planets; who are formed by a different breeding, are fed by a different food, are ordered by different manners, and are not governed by the same laws" (74). Was it two nations, as Disraeli says (a sufficiently startling idea), or three—the traditional "upper," "middle," and "lower" (or "working") classes—or five, or ten, or more classes, each distinguishable by some economist or social historian? Important distinctions existed, based on objective factors such as income, housing, occupation, and education, and unquantifiable factors such as the status and power traditionally associated with a particular occupation or school, a set of manners or beliefs. Despite professions of egalitarianism, America shared some of England's emphasis on class.

Believing in the rightness of a preordained social hierarchy, the English also felt that worthy individuals could rise "above their station," an idea intrinsic to the American dream. Yet antagonism between classes and jockeying for position within a given class characterized both nations, and often appear as literary themes, with special relevance for women.

The once-stable British society became frankly pluralistic. Urban laborers differed from farm laborers; both opposed mill operators; all three differed from aristocrats, some of whom maintained a traditional feudal relationship with tenant farmers while others, discovering coal on their land, became great mine owners. In the United States, such distinctions were most obvious in the South, where white plantation owners outranked rural "poor whites," who maintained a sense of superiority by forming the backbone of the Ku Klux Klan to harass and terrorize former slaves. Slaves and American Indians stood outside the social stratification defined by property, education, religion, and background. Yet as a nation of immigrants, America more easily defined people through individual achievement rather than group identity.

In England, where birth normally establishes status, the hereditary nobility remained far more than a titled and leisured class. They were the nation's acknowledged leaders, whose attitudes and values had profound influence. While others struggled to acquire the attributes of gentility, birth and training gave the aristocrat style, grace, courage, and nobility of manners. When aristocrats bought up much of the "commons" (commonly used meadowlands) early in the century, they increased their tangible power along with their acreage. Feudal landlords on immense holdings, they might invite tenants to agricultural fairs or coming-of-age feasts or evict them from modest family homes; tenants were wooed for their votes—and the secret ballot was unknown until 1872.

Next came the gentry, the country families, younger sons of peers, the baronets, squires, and "gentlemen." Law and tradition gave them power in local government and society. Land conferred status, financial clout, and the right to play landlord, sportsman, or country host. The impact of both the gentry and the aristocracy spread as the middle class tried to emulate if not enter higher social circles.

The burgeoning middle class (or classes) came next, defined by jobs, living conditions, and attitudes. According to the *Oxford English Dictionary,* the term *middle class* was first used as early as 1812. The Industrial Revolution added commercial men and manufacturers to the original shopkeepers and professionals. As they gained wealth, acumen, and polish, the new members increased their upward mobility. Each level imitated the manners and mores of the group immediately above, with tremendous impact on women.

The desire for gentility supported the traditional social hierarchy. The title of "gentleman" might accrue to a village shopkeeper, doctor, or small landowner. The size, location, stock, and clientele of a shop determined the status of the owner and his wife. Manufacturers and industrialists purchased land and sent their sons to the right schools in order to approximate membership in the gentry. Through his efforts, a man could become a gentleman; a woman could become a lady by marrying a gentleman.

Theoretically, anyone could obtain the moral ideal of respectability, honor, industry, courage, and self-control, and in that sense be genteel. Respectability, the most important of these qualities, reflected the power of absolutes derived more or less directly from the Bible, variously interpreted by different religious groups. The implication that individuals could redeem themselves through faith and good works supported the idea of labor as ennobling and the value of deferring immediate gratification in favor of higher but ultimately attainable goals. Yet this same theory led to restrictive codes of behavior, censorship, unwavering assertions of moral propriety, and the fervor to convert a whole populace, which in turn contributed to both hypocrisy and psychological confusion.

While opinions varied about the propriety of card-playing or dancing, respectability always connoted decorous dress and manners, honesty, chastity, a serious attitude toward family and work, cleanliness, tidiness, and an earnest avoidance of mere frivolity. Although interpretation of the rules might be more or less liberal or sanctimonious, it was always sufficiently strict to support the status quo. True, some people flaunted their rebellion by gambling, maintaining a mistress, or succumbing to a bohemian artist's life. Against such behavior, the middle class strove through example and preaching to make real an image half borrowed from the gentry and half derived from its own sense of moral and social propriety. From this, and against it, developed the realistic and social-problem novels. Though not always representative, the "respectable" were vocal, and they read realistic fiction.

In all social classes and almost without exception, women earned their status from their fathers and husbands. Middle-class men demonstrated financial success by giving wives and daughters lives of leisure, and genteel ladies did not work outside the home or for pay. These families had to ensure women an idle respectability in which feminine pursuits replaced useful activity unless related to charity or family life. The devaluation of women's jobs from pre-Industrial times to the middle of the century, a devaluation based largely on economics, was handily supported by the fundamental belief that women were men's physical, moral, and mental inferiors. In turn, the belief in women's innate inferiority fostered the view of women's work as socially undesirable. This vicious circle caused profound differences in education, expectations, responsibilities, and opportunities for girls and boys.

In contrast, lower-class men and women worked together in fields and factories, and women were exploited rather than sheltered. As the middle class became increasingly aware of the poor people crowded into mews and alleys just behind the fashionable city streets, reform movements grew. The objects of attention included farmers, semiskilled or unskilled workers, servants, slaves, craftsmen dispossessed by machines, and country laborers dispossessed as small farms merged into large ones. The urge for reform fit middle-class ideas of social and moral responsibility, but it also resulted from labor agitation and publicity exposing the workers' plight. Fearing that slums bred not just physical but moral disease, reformers looked first at the obvious misery of factory workers and slum dwellers. The smoke rising from new factories became symptom and symbol of the Industrial Revolution.

Artisans might aspire to rise in status by emulating middle-class virtues, but most laborers merely sought to survive the long hours and poor conditions of mines or factories, if they even found work. By 1900, reform efforts eradicated the worst conditions—five-year-olds working in mines, fifty-hour work weeks for nine-year-olds in the cotton industry, pregnant women (cheaper than horses) strapped to coal carts, mining towns without water, urban slums with one privy for half a dozen families.

Literature about slum life and industrialization became popular, especially during times of agitation for reform. Yet even that literature was directed at the middle class, who might do something to help. Throughout the century, the middle class formed both subject and audience of the most important literature.

The Novel and the Middle Class

The phenomenon of a mass reading public began in the nineteenth century.[6] Poems appeared in magazines and in slim books that might grace a parlor table. But the most popular reading material was fiction, whether published in one volume or three, serialized in newspapers or magazines, bought or borrowed from libraries. As inexpensive editions of popular works proliferated to meet the new literacy and interest of the middle and working classes, the ability to own books spread downward. Still, most middle-class readers subscribed to circulating libraries or patronized "free" libraries designed to give workers access to books.

Opening a package from the circulating library was a family occasion. Like advertising today, a subscription library such as Charles Edward Mudie's "Select Circulating Library" in England could determine a book's success through large orders and a seal of approval. Circulating libraries, assuming they knew the public's taste and morals, supported the prevalent censorship. Moral rather than literary merit often determined a book's availability and popularity.

For the upper classes, reading was not a new interest or skill. Although workers' literacy increased, reading for pleasure differs greatly from signing your name or deciphering a job application. Poor lighting, crowded living conditions, and exhaustion made theaters, parks, railway excursions, and other forms of cheap entertainment more popular than reading. Still, workers whiled away long train rides with books, sought advancement through tracts and moral tales from public reading rooms and libraries, or relaxed over a penny dreadful or dime novel, an easy-to-read adventure tale or sentimental story, a newspaper or tabloid, a broadside featuring grisly or sensational stories, or even a condensed Shakespeare play or Scott novel.

The middle class had more money, time, and literacy than the lower classes, and more interest in education and advancement than the upper classes. Even in recreation, they sought the useful and uplifting as well as the entertaining. They connected moral and social improvement, ideas fostered by the American Puritan heritage and the English Evangelicals and Utilitarians. If reading for fun might injure rising and righteous members of the middle class, wholesome literature with a moral purpose could benefit them. Reading became the dominant form of entertainment as well as a way to enforce morality and family unity: each evening, families would gather into the famous reading circle with the latest newspapers, magazines, or novels.

That image influenced publishers, libraries, and writers, and censorship was a fact of literary production. In 1818, Thomas Bowdler published *The Family Shakespeare,* containing oddly expurgated versions of the plays, changing words and altering scenes to protect the innocence of daughters in the reading circle. Bowdler gives his name as well as his practice to many "bowdlerized" books. With the innocent young girl as touchstone, editors cut and altered words in contemporary and earlier works. First to go were unorthodox opinions and hints of sexuality—references to the body, passion, or pregnancy. The editors' purpose and defense lay overtly in the desire to uphold the contemporary moral ideal and covertly in the desire to avoid offending readers.

One observer, evaluating the books found in miners' houses, suggests laborers are "backward to attempt anything that requires steady thinking": miners "had rather read any popular work, such as The Christian Philosopher, the Pilgrim's Progress, or Walter Scott's novels, choosing fiction, history, geography, and books about British warfare rather than logic, mathematics, economics, and grammar."[7] Modern readers hardly judge the selection as frivolous, but Victorians read sermons, biographies, essays, scientific texts, religious tracts, inspiring tales with overt morals, and self-help books. Weeklies and monthlies carrying serious literature, art criticism, debates on social, moral, and religious issues matched papers devoted to sports, humor, adventurous exploits, and household hints. And always there was a market for fiction.

Determining the popularity of a given book would require knowing both sales and library circulation figures. Even that information falls short, for a dozen people might hear a book in the family circle, and a whole neighborhood might share a single newspaper. Inflated advertisements and manipulated sales figures create further inaccuracies. Attempts to outline the story of nineteenth-century readership rely on such data plus trade rumors and comments in private diaries or letters.

We cannot know for sure which novels were most popular, or which best represent contemporary life. Given the sheer volume of literature produced and the fact that some is unavailable, we cannot read exactly what Victorians read. But we know that fiction was the most popular genre, and within that genre, the most popular was the realistic novel dealing with and read by the middle class. We also know that a fair representation must include novels that, though now unread, were once popular enough to leave a mark on literature and society. Remembering Woolf's words at the head of the chapter, we know that women were central, as both writers and readers. Women both influenced and were influenced by social change, and they both influenced and were influenced by literature. Novels written by, about, and for the middle class reveal a great deal about women's roles, people's reactions to those roles, and the evolution of feminism.

Notes

1. Virginia Woolf, *A Room of One's own* (New York: Harcourt Brace Jovanovich, 1929), 68.
2. Abigail Adams to John Adams, 31 March 1777, *Familiar Letters of John Adams and His Wife Abigail Adams, During the Revolution,* ed. Charles Francis Adams (Boston: Houghton, Mifflin, & Co., 1875), 149.
3. Eneas Sweetland Dallas, *The Gay Science* (London, 1866), 2:287, quotes in Richard Stang, *The Theory of the Novel in England, 1850-1870* (New York: Columbia University Press, 1969), xi.
4. Currer Bell [Charlotte Brontë] to G. H. Lewes, 6 November1847, quoted in *Nineteenth-Century British Novelists on the Novel,* ed. George L. Barnett (New York: Meredith Corporation, 1971), 136.
5. *Saturday Review* (24 October 1863), 555, quoted in Stang, *Theory,* 181.
6. On the general issue of social class, see Richard Faber, *Proper Stations: Class in Victorian Fiction* (London: Faber and Faber, 1971). Good sources on the reading public and the marketplace include: Margaret Dalziel, *Popular Fiction One Hundred Years Ago: An Un-explored Tract of Literary History* (London: Cohen and West, 1957); and Richard Altick, *The English Common Reader: A Social History of the Mass Reading Public 1800-1900* (Chicago and London: University of Chicago Press, 1957). Also useful are: Stang, *Theory* 3-88; Guinevere L. Griest, *Mudie's Circulating Library and the Victorian Novel* (Bloomington: Indiana University Press, 1970); Amy Cruse, *The Victorian and Their Books* (London: Allen and Unwin, 1935); J. A. Sutherland, *Victorian Novelists and Publishers* (Chicago: University of Chicago Press, 1976); Richard Altick, *Victorian People and Ideas* (New York: W. W. Norton & Co., 1973); and Frank Luther Mott, *Golden Multitudes: The Story of Best-sellers in the United States* (New York: Macmillan, 1947).
7. Seymour Tremenheere, *Report on the Mining Districts* (1850), Parliamentary Papers 1850, 23: 53-54; cited in E. Royston Pike, *"Golden Times": Human Documents of the Victorian Age* (New York and Washington: Frederick A. Praeger, 1967), 254-55.

SUSAN K. HARRIS (ESSAY DATE 1993)

SOURCE: Harris, Susan K. "'But is it any good?' Evaluating Nineteenth-Century American Women's Fiction." In *The (Other) American Traditions: Nineteenth-Century Women Writers,* edited by Joyce W. Warren, pp. 263-79. Brunswick, N.J.: Rutgers University Press, 1993.

In the following essay, Harris attempts to define specific methodologies to help evaluate the literary merits of nineteenth-century women's fiction.

The revival of interest in nineteenth-century American women's literature is less than fifteen years old.[1] Since Nina Baym published *Woman's Fiction* in 1978, it has become academically respectable to acknowledge interest in works like Susan Warner's *The Wide, Wide World* or Fanny Fern's *Ruth Hall,* and they are slowly becoming features of the academic terrain. Mary Kelley's *Private Woman, Public Stage,*[2] Alfred Habegger's *Gender, Fantasy, and Realism,*[3] Jane Tompkins's *Sensational Designs,*[4] the articles in *Legacy: A Journal of Nineteenth-Century American Women's Writing,* and articles in *Signs, American Quarterly, ESQ,* and others are all signposts to the new territories. But with the notable exception of Tompkins, few scholars have ventured to construct appropriate evaluative criteria. Rather, there appears to be an unspoken agreement not to submit nineteenth-century American women's novels to extended analytical evaluation, largely, I think, because the evaluative modes most of us were taught devalue this literature a priori.

I propose that we initiate an ongoing dialogue that will enable us to talk fruitfully about pre-twentieth-century American women's literature in terms of "good" and "bad," that we begin creating methodologies that will ramify the implications of Tompkins's *Sensational Designs*. One avenue is to learn how to describe noncanonical American women's literature in terms of *process*—that is, to see it within the shifting currents of nineteenth-century American ideologies. Acknowledging that imaginative literature is both reactive and creative, we can examine the ways that it springs from, reacts against, or responds to the plots, themes, languages in the discoursive arena that engendered it at the same time that it creates new possibilities for that arena by reshaping old words into new ones. For Richard Rorty, this happens through the creation of new metaphors that evolve over time into new ideas; "truth," he claims, is neither "out there" nor "in here"; rather it is compounded of a set of linguistic contingencies. What we know, believe, is dependent on our ability to speak it, and our ability to speak it depends on the slow historical conjunction of ideas, images, and metaphors that evolve into the languages available to us.[5] For Hans Robert Jauss, literary works continuously interact with their readers to create, over time, new moral and aesthetic perceptions: "The relationship between literature and reader can actualize itself in the sensorial realm as an incitement to aesthetic perception as well as in the ethical realm as a summons to moral reflections."[6]

If we accept these fluid accounts of the relationship between language, consciousness, and social change as the bases for reshaping our ways of perceiving what imaginative literature is, what it does, and how it "works," we will have a tool that will help us create criteria for evaluating noncanonical literatures of the past and, equally important, for acknowledging our own motives for doing so and the implications of our own critical acts. Our first step is to acknowledge the ideological basis of our endeavor. What teleological shape the literature we are examining has is imposed on it by us, retrospectively; it is not inherent in the material itself. We are doing so, first, because we see ourselves positively, if not as end points then at least as significant markers; second, because we are drawn to nineteenth-century women's texts despite their apparently antithetical values and want to find some way of talking about them; and, third, because we are searching for antecedents to ourselves and the future we envision that we have not found in canonical texts and canonical ways of reading them.

I am not suggesting that we read these texts ahistorically. Rather, historical contextualization is a vital aspect of what I am calling process analysis. I *am* suggesting, however, that we clarify our own motives. Acknowledging why we are doing what we do will enable us, once we have understood the books' relationships with their own time, to reach back and see how they contribute to ours. If we look at them as both reactive and creative rather than asking them to self-consciously embody "timeless truths," we can understand their aesthetic, moral, and political values, both for their contemporaries and for us. While traditional criticism tends to examine literary works either historically, rhetorically, or ideologically, the method I am calling process analysis investigates all three axes in its contemplation of any given work. Consequently, although specific analytical tasks may look the same as they have always looked (pursuing metaphors, for instance), the final mosaic produced by process analysis looks very different because it has shifted the hermeneutic and evaluative projects into a far more complex socio-temporal scheme. And unlike traditional Anglo-American criticism, process analysis foregrounds the relationship of the literary-critical task to the critic's stance in her own time.

In order to show, within the scope of an essay, how this can work, I am going to focus on sentimental novels written by American women primarily between 1840 and 1870. We have begun to create a literary history for nineteenth-century American women's novels, a "remapping" of hitherto unknown terrain.[7] Within this history, enough research has been conducted among the novels that used to be classed as "literary sentimentality" to enable us to make some generalizations about the group, and this in turn should help us formulate critical questions about individual texts. For instance, critics have long noted—mostly with distaste—that the large majority of nineteenth-century American women's novels have "happy endings" in which their heroines marry and give up any idea of autonomy.[8] Recent critics, however, have pointed out that a closer view shows that the novels also question that inscription, even when their structures submit to it.[9] Despite following a fairly consistent pattern culminating in the protagonist's marriage to a dominating man, most sentimental novels also challenge the idea of female subordination, either through their plots, their narrators' addresses to the reader, or their patterns of rhetoric. In other words, their themes and structures tend to work at cross-purposes. Once dismissed as confused, such texts are now described as dialogic. This is not simply a cynical relabeling for young jargonists. Rather, it is evidence of a critical paradigm shift that gives us much more access to the novels than we ever had before. Attuned, on the one hand, to shifts in structural approaches to fiction, and, on the other, to reader-response criticism, we are now able to recognize that the dialogic patterning inherent in the novels' structures facilitates readers' participation in the novels' ideological debates. In other words, attention to structure is central to contextual placement. Prior to evaluating any given nineteenth-century sentimental novel, then, it is important to establish the terms of the debate(s) in which the text participates, the positions it takes, and how these positions are embodied in its textual structure.

There are many ways of going about situating a text within a historical debate. As groundwork for evaluating sentimental novels by American women, however, it seems especially important to investigate the impact of public ideologies on market strategies because these directly influence the novels' structures. Nineteenth-century America was characterized by strident—although often contradictory—*public* pronouncements about what constituted the nature of the two sexes (any others were not mentioned). I stress public because it is clear that, privately, there was considerable agonizing over the subject, just as there was over the subject of different races and their intrinsic "natures" and "characteristics." The differences between what reviewers saw happening in the texts and what we see happening when we factor in the existence of more than one linguistic construct of gender is a fascinating illustration of ideologically based reading strategies. By and large, reviewers and publicists subscribed to an essentialist definition of female nature, while the texts attempt to persuade women that they can re-create themselves. Given the nature of the public discourse and the power it had in the marketplace, writers aiming for a popular audience had to observe, at least superficially, essentialist rules for inscribing female protagonists and for their narrators' attitudes toward their heroines' adventures.

The conflict between public and textual definitions of female possibilities may well be the primary cause of the tensions between structure and theme that the novels display. One of the areas opened up by the study of noncanonical literature has been the examination of "the marketplace" as a condition of production. (Perhaps no surer proof exists of the influence of the New Critics than the fact that this is a "discovery.") By "conditions of production" I mean less the biographical circumstances of the individual author—which is Mary Kelley's focus in *Private Woman, Public Stage*—than the demands of the booksellers, reviewers, and buyers for whom the book is intended and that women authors could not—at least if they wanted to publish—ignore. With Kelley's study, Ann Douglas's *The Feminization of American Culture,*[10] Baym's *Novels, Readers, and Reviewers,*[11] and Cathy N. Davidson's *Revolution and the Word*[12] give us information about the values held by eighteenth and nineteenth-century arbiters of literary taste. For instance, Baym speculates:

> Apart from the question whether novelists were or were not radical in the particularities of their social, sexual, or personal world views . . . lies the possibility that the form of the novel assumes discontent as the psychological ground from which it springs. The essence of plot . . . is that something is wrong; there is a disturbance that needs correcting. Because women and youths mostly read novels, it was thought, their discontents in particular would be ministered to and hence exacerbated. The conviction of many contemporary students of popular culture that popular forms sedate discontent was not held by this earlier group of critics. If, as many feminist critics have argued, the "better novel" appears regularly to be instinct with misogyny, this may not be an accident. Novels putting women in their place may well have been selected by reviewers as better than—more true to nature than—novels that legitimated their discontents.[13]

Of course what this meant for authors was that any challenges to the public definition of "women's place" had to be covert if they wanted to sell. The contradictions between structure and theme provide one way of doing that: the emotional and cognitive discrepancies aroused by the texts permit readers alternative modes of processing them. One mode, written to conform to "public" values, privileges female subordination through structural closure; the other, appealing to "private" values, privileges female independence through structural open-endedness. Processing these novels, then, depends on the reader's choice of interpretive modes. Challenges to the public definition of women's place are embedded in texts' structures and accessible only to readers who are predisposed to grasp them.

Evidence suggests that nineteenth-century readers were quite capable of reading texts in more than one mode. One of the most illuminating examples that I have discovered of this multi-leveled reading process was recorded in 1848 by the author Lydia Maria Child in a letter to a close friend:

> I had read Jane Eyre before you had the kindness to send a copy. I was perfectly carried away with it. I sat up all night long to finish it. I do not at all agree with the critics who pronounce Rochester unloveable. *I* could have loved him with my whole heart. His very imperfections brought him more within the range of warm human sympathies. *Ought Jane* to have left him at that dreadful crisis? She was all alone in the world, and could do no harm to mother, sister, child, or friend, by taking her freedom. The tyrannical law, which bound him to a mad and wicked wife, seems such a mere figment! I wanted much, however, to make *one* change in the story. I liked Rochester all the better for the impetuous feeling and passion which carried him away; but I wanted conscience to come in and check him, like a fiery horse reined in at full gallop. At the *last* moment, when they were ready to go to church to be married, I wish he had thrown himself on her generosity. I wish he had said, "Jane, I *cannot* deceive you!" and so told her the painful story he afterward revealed. There might have been the same struggle, and the same result; and it would have saved the nobleness of Rochester's love for Jane, which has only this one blot of deception. I am glad the book represents Jane as refusing to trust him; for in the present disorderly state of the world, it would not be well for public morality to represent it otherwise. But my *private* opinion is, that a real living Jane Eyre, placed in similar circumstances, would have obeyed an *inward* law, higher and better than outward conventional scruples.[14]

Here Child demonstrates both awareness and approval of social constraints—the sense that public morality was fragmenting and that literature's function was to teach readers moral conduct—and applauds the text's resulting definition of female nature (Jane flees from the horror of bigamy because in order to be a heroine she has to be instinctively virtuous). At the same time, however, Child reveals her private reading, which recognizes that a character as independent as Jane would have pursued her own desires rather than complying with social fictions. The sexual and social tensions inherent in the text itself stimulate the modes in which it will be processed. In Child's "public" reading, social mandates are foremost. In her "private" reading, autonomy and sexual desire are privileged over social mandates. The possibilities for autonomy inherent in each "reading" of female nature are embodied in the radically different episodes of the novel. Child processes both, in full consciousness of what she is doing.

Child's enthusiastic response to *Jane Eyre* was typical; Charlotte Brontë was one of the most powerful direct influences on American women writers, and their novels reflect the energy with which she inscribed Victorian conflicts about gender and autonomy. Moreover, in the American

Lydia Maria Child (1802-1880).

texts the energy produced fuels new possibilities for female self-creation. The contradictory structures of sentimental American texts highlight rather than obscure these possibilities. If a heroine creates an autonomous self and succeeds in impressing it on her society and her reader for six hundred pages, she has left convincing evidence that it can be done. The fact that she gives it all up upon marriage in the last twenty-five pages should have less of an impact on readers—especially readers themselves entertaining dreams of autonomy—than the fact that she succeeded. (Or less long-term impact. My personal theory is that the renunciation of autonomy in the face of the marriage proposal has its strongest impact when these books are first read—probably because it involves sex[15]—but that over time readers tend to remember protagonists' extended quests for autonomy rather than their sudden, and fairly formulaic, renunciations.) The standardized conclusions may even have annoyed nineteenth-century readers as much as they do twentieth, thus undermining their "message."

Moreover, the "middles" of sentimental novels—the long narratives of the heroine's self-creation and social success—may well explain why such very different texts emerged later in the century. There is a fairly sharp ideological dissimilarity between the apparently conservative sentimental women's novels of the 1840s-1860s and the fairly radical ones of the 1870s-1890s. Examining the earlier novels as process enables us to see that rather than springing forth unheralded, the later novels evolve from the quests for autonomy explored in their predecessors and articulated so frequently that, despite their failures, the "traces" they left came to be "real." For Herman Melville, referring to his own work, such traces were accessible to the "eagle-eyed reader," who grasped truths "covertly, and by snatches." Melville contrasts this perceptive reader to the "superficial skimmer of pages,"[16] the same reader whose reading behavior Augusta Evans Wilson (author of *St. Elmo*) castigates as the "hasty, careless, novelistic glance."[17] Both writers acknowledge the subversive capacities of written texts, the fact that some, at least, were deliberately written to pass muster with a careless or conservative readership and to appeal to discerning readers. In regard to mid-century women's novels, perceptive readers would recognize that these texts argued against essentialist definitions of the feminine. In Jauss's terms, these early texts articulate new possibilities for female aspiration and behavior that are later realized both in subsequent fiction and in the social and political realms.[18]

To understand thoroughly what the readers as well as the reviewers saw in these texts we would have to do an exhaustive reader-response search, a project I have attempted and found exceedingly difficult, largely because, then as now, few ordinary readers recorded their responses to books they read. Those who did seemed to share our predilection for dividing their reading into high and low cultures; they recorded responses to "serious" literature (biographies, essays, sermons) far more often than for "light" novels. But this division is also part of the social construction of literary values,[19] an aspect of the linguistic revolution with which we are concerned. What may be more important than diary and letter records of actual reading is the fact that the same writers also indicated in other contexts a variety of concerns that the novels address. For example, many expressed a wish to improve their educations—their classical, not their domestic, educations—to learn Greek, Latin, and the higher mathematics. As Gerald Graff has recently reminded us, these were the cornerstones of the most esteemed educational apparatus, enabling those who mastered them to enter the ministry and law.[20] Despite the disaster most classical educations may have been in fact, in theory men so educated had mastered society's highest wisdom. Women's desire to achieve similar educational levels suggests that they, too, sought wisdom—in a culture that publicly and medically denied women the ability to think beyond their ovaries.

When, then, a woman protagonist in a novel masters abstruse languages, philosophy, world history, and mythology (as does the heroine of *St. Elmo*), she presents a model of female achievement for readers already predisposed to valorize educated women. What Wilson presents is a quest for autonomy and power that succeeds before she forces it to fail; not only does the protagonist become a scholar, she also becomes famous, powerful, and fully conscious of her own imperatives, a heroine who cries out that "I love my work! Ah, I want to live long enough to finish something grand and noble . . . something that will follow me across and beyond the dark, silent valley . . . something that will echo in eternity!"[21] By the time she gives it up to marry her overbearing minister-lover, the text has proved that women can become very powerful intellectuals.

In terms of its plot, *St. Elmo* manages to juggle sexual attraction, intellectual zeal, and public success, all before it surrenders to the requirement that it end by merging its heroine with the male figure who embodies everything she had sought for herself. In terms of its structure, it creates a heroine whose relationship with her self and her public mirrors the relationship Wilson implies exists between *her* text and its readers. Seen within the process framework I am proposing, *St. Elmo* is an excellent novel because it not only textually embodies the heroine's quest but also self-consciously places that quest within the cultural struggle over gender possibilities and then critiques its own project.

In preparing to reevaluate these novels, then, one set of questions we can ask is functional and historical: what needs did they serve for their intended audience? Did they, as imaginative literature, somehow present the "spiritual truth" of women's aspirations as essays and other more forthright genres could not? Did they give hope to readers, let them know that there were other questing souls out there? (In Elizabeth Stuart Phelps's *The Story of Avis,* Avis discovers her life's goal to be an artist while reading *Aurora Leigh.*) What effect does the text's structure have on its theme or themes? What kinds of cognitive or emotional discrepancies exist, and how might contemporary readers have responded to them? What is the power of fascination the texts hold? Is it the same power that holds us (those of us who read them) today? If so, can we describe it? Is it sexual?—moral?—aesthetic?—affective?

Because we have admitted that our endeavor is ideological, we can evaluate the novels in terms of their contribution to the expansion of women's possibilities (i.e., politically), as well as for the degree of power with which they present their subjects. For the novels to be published and favorably reviewed, they had to conform to the strictures articulated above; for them to achieve their "subversive" objects, they had to find a form that would embody these dual, and often contradictory, ideas. There are a number of ways this can be done: as in *St. Elmo,* the plot can outweigh the narrator's interpretive gestures or the dense "flowery" rhetoric can hide heretical phrases and clauses; as in *Ruth Hall,* the narrator can play more than one role (in which case the text risks being labeled "confused"). However this task is accomplished, there must be a point on which the antithetical impulses balance. Another set of evaluative criteria, then, lies in determining how well the texts strike the balance between socially and textually created ideological imperatives.

Creating a methodology for evaluating textual structures and assessing readers' access to subversive propositions is one side of the task. The other is to create one for evaluating the language(s) that constitute the texts' building blocks. Process analysis lets us see how the discoursive modes of nineteenth-century texts both reflect and engage their society's ideological diversity. In a culture shifting from the conception of truth residing "out there," in the objective world, or "in here," in the subjective world, to a conception of truth as linguistically determined (i.e., contingent, in Rorty's use of the term[22]), women were latecomers. The novels that have been labeled "sentimental" embody women's entry into the fray. These display the battle of languages with particular intensity because they focus on the ways that language creates gender and the possibilities for autonomous selfhood. One of the objections often raised about these novels is that their protagonists do not have strongly defined, individual characters—that they are not female American Adams, creating a New Woman for a New World. Here, as Baym did in "Melodramas of Beset Manhood,"[23] we can approach women's texts by looking at criteria used to evaluate American male texts, criteria that tend to thematize the struggle between an autonomous self associated, in some way, with timeless truth, and a corrupt, temporal society (Huck's struggle with his conscience). In these canonical male texts, the traditional critical story informs us, heroes flee from social coercion (mostly defined as female). One of their strategies is to get rid of the women, to exist, as critics from Leslie Fiedler on have suggested, in an essentially and happily single-sexed universe. These are American Romances; their models are Christian texts, and their premise is that truth and selfhood are "real," that they reside within the individual and can and should be discovered. Canonical American male novels value the individual over his society.

In contemporary women's texts, on the other hand, the basic thematic is less self against society than self against self; that is, the women's internal conflicts represent conflicting definitions of womanhood. The characters battle themselves far more often, and with greater intensity, than they engage an openly corrupt society. One of the selves is most usefully seen as Nietzschean, willing itself into power and existence (which is what differentiates it from Huck, whose integral self is discoverable by readers, but not willed into being by the character); the other is the self that is socially determined. Both selves are presented metaphorically: in Richard Rorty's terms, these texts embody a battle for definition that pits two linguistically contingent worldviews against one another. Neither the self struggling to come into being nor the one (usually spoken by the narrator) socially determined has any intrinsically objective reality; rather, the validity of each rests on the reader's capacity for processing it. If the male texts are quintessentially Christian/Romantic quests, demonstrating the value of the True Soul against a corrupting society, the female ones are self-consciously contingent: they concern protagonists willing themselves into existence in an effort to *create* their own society. Never going so far into fantasy as to assume the possibility—or desirability—of living without other people, the women's novels anticipate the *real* problem of the twentieth century: how to nurture and protect a self that has only just become aware of its own possibility and that is trying to work out the parameters of its obligations to others.

Meanwhile, *other* voices continue to insist that women are Platonic essences, that the individual is only a historical accident, and that what really matters is her conformity to the eternal feminine. The clashing of these antithetical constructs provides the aesthetic and moral energy of the texts; moreover, the slow swells, the burgeoning of figures recording protagonists' struggles to create themselves, constitute the linguistic "traces" that enable us, in retrospect, to track the evolution of what would eventually become the figure of the New Woman. When Hagar Churchill, of E.D.E.N. Southworth's *The Deserted Wife,* insists that "*I* have a will! and tastes, and habits, and propensities! and loves and hates! yes, and conscience! that all go to make up the sum total of a separate individuality—a distinct life! for which *I alone* am accountable, and *only* to God!"[24] and then proceeds to create a successful life for herself and her children without male help, she has inscribed a dynamic predecessor to later novels that celebrate independent women. Similarly, Elizabeth Drew Stoddard's *The Morgesons* foregrounds the word "possession" in reference to its iconoclastic protagonist; the figure shifts from its demonic to its self-creating (as in "self-possession") associations as the heroine increasingly understands her own powers. With our consideration of how well the text juggles its thematic and structural obligations, then, we can determine how effectively it embodies the discoursive battles that engender it.

This involves a more thorough investigation into the nature of sentimental language and its values than most twentieth-century academic readers have cared to conduct. In fact, sentimental language is probably the aspect of pre-twentieth-century American women's literature that modern readers resist most. It is often difficult to process because it is so baroque, and it often seems vacantly redundant. But these are precisely the aspects of it that can and should be directly engaged. Certainly one function of sentimental language was to create a sacred space dedicated to women, analogous to the private sphere in which they moved. As Jane Tompkins demonstrates, sentimental language is intertextually related to religious language, both functionally and aesthetically.[25] Religious language functions as part of a ritual intended to draw participants' attention away from their temporal lives and make them focus on their spiritual relationship to the divine. Auditors are encouraged to conceive of their experiences metaphorically, placing them in a universal context, to reenvision themselves as part of a set of universal patterns. Similarly, sentimental language functions ritualistically, having set patterns of imagery and rhythm that strive to reenvision women, to continually project them in terms of universal patterns. Ultimately, what is created is a Platonic image of the feminine that is intensely intertextual. Shot through with allusions to nature, the Bible, classical mythologies, and medieval literature, sentimental language is constantly referring to texts beyond the boundaries of that in which it appears. Sometimes these *are* empty, mindless. Often, they project an image of ideal womanhood whose implications for the individual are painfully repressive. Just as often, however, they serve to place the female protagonists within a world/historical context of female endeavor and, obliquely, female oppression. In fact, the intertextual portions of the individual novels, taken out of the contexts of the works and brought into conjunction with each other, create a dialogue of their own about the nature and status of women that is simultaneously historicized and universalized. It is the locus of the ideological battle about women.

Our devaluation of the language with which this battle has been conducted has prevented us from recognizing it. Once we do so, we also can evaluate its occurrence in individual texts. How effectively does it engage the issues? What is the author's position? How astutely does she analyze her subject? What are the energy exchanges between the way she inscribes women in general and the way she describes her heroine? What, exactly, does her figurative language *do*?

Any analysis and/or evaluation of sentimental discourse must determine how deliberately its figures are employed. The prevailing critical assumption has been that in these novels the baroque metaphors are all rather mindlessly borrowed. Borrowed they are, but very self-consciously; they are used to serve a variety of functions, and, over time, they are revitalized, feminized into figures pregnant with possibility. At least one writer uses them offensively: to attack as well as to explore definitions of female nature. In *Ruth Hall* Fanny Fern alternates between sentimental and acerbic language, all in the interest of defending women's right to be economically independent. The girl whom we meet on her bridal eve meditating on her future and wondering "would love flee affrighted from [her] bent form, and silver locks, and faltering footsteps"[26] finds that love has nothing to do with survival; after her husband's death Ruth painfully learns that the patriarchal society that valorizes clinging, dependent women will also shut its doors if they ask for cash. Before the book ends Ruth has not only become a successful writer, she has also learned to hold her maternal ("sentimental") affections in abeyance while she negotiates long-term publishing contracts. This time meditating not on love but on her choice between immediate money, available by selling her copyright, or a percentage, which would delay her reunion with one child and incur continued privation for the other, Ruth muses that the copyright money is "a temptation; but supposing her book should prove a hit? and bring double, treble, fourfold that sum, to go into her publisher's pockets instead of hers? how provoking!" and she decides, "No, I will not sell my copyright; I will rather deny myself a while longer, and accept the percentage" (*RH* [*Ruth Hall*], 153). Juxtaposed to the figurative language with which Ruth was introduced, this sharp language of commerce challenges the original inscription's premise that true women have to depend on love for survival.

Another way sentimental language is used to change consciousness is as a political tool, as when Frances Harper, in *Iola Leroy,* images her black, enslaved heroine as a fair damsel imprisoned in a dark castle: the narrator refers to "the beautiful but intractable girl who was held in durance vile" and images her rescue as being "taken as a trembling dove from the gory vulture's nest and given a place of security."[27] Here, the language is directed to those who identify with the values of the white community; its figures strenuously attempt to make readers accept Iola as a white ("dove") heroine because that is the only way these readers will identify with her as a "real" woman/human. In other words, the language itself acknowledges white Americans' inability to empathize with black Americans. Harper's language here has a double function: first to project her black protagonist within the parameters of white sympathy, i.e., as white, then to lift her female protagonist to heroic status as a damsel from the heroic ages. Only after having captured the white-oriented reader's sympathy through this idealized image does the text then project its other heroine, the heroine's heroine, Lucille Delany: a physically black woman who Iola claims "is my ideal woman. She is grand, brave, intellectual, and religious" (*IL* [*Iola Leroy*], 242). In other words, the fair damsel the text valorizes has her own agenda; she does not speak in white figures herself, and she looks to black women for role models. Thus the intertextually "white" or "European" references serve both to obscure and to point toward the text's alternative values. Seen retrospectively, the trace record left by Iola's own values makes the novel a precursor to twentieth-century black American women's texts that self-consciously valorize dark-skinned black women.

The oneiric nature of sentimental language also merits examination, for it often signals the existence of a radically feminist shadow text. Stowe's *The Minister's Wooing,* for instance, constantly places its protagonist, Mary Scudder, within a cosmic dream, associating her with shells, nests, and the ocean. With repeated references to the Virgin Mary, with Mary Scudder's friendship with an unhappily married woman named Virginie who insists that her private self, the self capable of happiness, is unmarried; and with the example of independent "spinsters" who arrange life to suit themselves, these references create a countertext within the novel that argues against marriage—the story's plot—and for a state of empowering "virginity." As with the medieval allusiveness of Harper's figures, the oneirism of Stowe's portrayal serves at once to obscure—it can be read as part of Stowe's portrayal of Mary's adolescent sensibility—and to highlight this countertheme. If dreams express our repressed desires, texts that dream (as opposed to texts that feature dreams) have to be evaluated for the contexts, and contents, of their dreams.

Structure and language, then, are the dual focuses of process analysis. Each demands three levels of study: the first, contextual, places the text within its own time; the second, rhetorical, examines narrator/narratee contracts and the ways in which the text may play with cultural significances; the third, retrospective, searches for traces of changing consciousness, building blocks for an ideologically self-conscious literary history. Together, they offer a paradigm that produces evaluative as well as investigative questions.

Some of these questions have arisen in the course of this essay. While continued dialogue will change it, a tentative list might look something like this:

1. What is the author's degree of consciousness about her protagonist's status in a patriarchal society; that is, where does the novel stand in the sociopolitical spectrum of its time? How does the author demonstrate her political stance? What thematic, narrative, and aesthetic choices does she make in order to exhibit its position within her sociopolitical world? Books I would rank high on this list would include Stoddard's *The Morgesons,* Warner's *The Wide, Wide World,* Stowe's *The Pearl of Orr's Island,* and Southworth's *The Deserted Wife.*

2. What modes (thematic, narrative, linguistic) does the author employ to balance the story of her protagonist's self-creation with the socially and/or generically dictated need to deny female selfhood and originality?

3. How does the text embody the *linguistic* debate; that is, what discursive worldviews are brought into conjunction or confrontation?

Though I have only addressed sentimental language in this essay, there are many other modes operating in the texts themselves. Two often discussed in earlier critical works are "realism"—i.e., representational discourse—and the vernacular. With sentimentality, these are probably the most relevant discoursive modes in nineteenth-century sentimental novels by American women. But many other modes operate as well. A fruitful way to approach these might be through a methodology constructed from Mikhail Bakhtin's concept of heteroglossia, which gives us a "poetics" for discussing the fictional representation of multiple discoursive modes and the worldviews they express.[28] For example, even the most genteel women's texts often feature vernacular and/or working-class characters whose voices implicitly (and occasionally explicitly) counter the dominant, essentialist definitions of female nature held by the middle-class protagonists, the narrators, and, often, the authors.

4. What functions do the characters serve and what means has the individual author used to "mark" her characters for her readers? It has always struck me that Susan Warner chose an extraordinarily resonant name for the feisty, independent aunt against whom the sanctimonious heroine of *The Wide, Wide World* struggles. Fortune Emerson, who tries to teach her reluctant charge that only self-reliance will bring self-respect, stands alone in the novel as a fully realized, financially and emotionally independent woman. Disliked by the protagonist, and cast within the frame of the wicked stepmother by the author, she nonetheless exists as an example of the rugged, rural American woman. Readers seeking to read Ralph Waldo Emerson into female possibility can see in Aunt Fortune Emerson one way for women to achieve success in the American landscape.

5. What stylistic devices does the author choose and how skillfully and appropriately does she employ them to embody the issues with which she is concerned? For example, if she employs classical allusions, how does she use them to illustrate her own, or her characters', positions in the ideological debate in which she is engaged? For instance, Susanna Rowson's *Charlotte Temple* (1794) plays with the semantics of the word "content" as she evokes a classical image of female virtue whose "name is *Content.*"[29] This text valorizes passive heroines, but its implication that contented women lack content is a position that later sentimental novels will vigorously refute.

6. What were the marketing conditions under which the novel was produced (including serialization) and how well does the author juggle the marketing demands and her artistic and thematic requirements?

7. What is the intertextual *gestalt* of the novel? From what other texts does it take its premises? How does it transform these premises to fit its own peculiar needs? How appropriate is its "rereading" or its "misprisioning" of the earlier texts? (Louisa May Alcott's *Work: A Story of Experience* is framed by *Pilgrim's Progress.* Yet its Celestial City is temporal, and its holy community distinctly female.)

8. What later ideological or political debate does it anticipate? Reading retrospectively, what textual trace-markers can we detect that could have helped change the shape of later women's novels? How useful is this text as a precursor of that debate? (Does Fortune Emerson become Alexandra Bergson? Does Lucille Delany become Dessa Rose?)

This is of course only a sketchy overview of some of the ways nineteenth-century American women's novels work and some of the questions we can ask about them. As we continue to study them and the culture that produced them, we will be continuously finding new areas to explore. Meanwhile, it is time for us to begin assessing the territories already discovered.

Notes

1. Prior to World War II, American women's literature had a recognized place in literary history, as works by Herbert Ross Brown (*The Sentimental Novel in America, 1789-1860* [Durham, N.C.: Duke University Press, 1940]) and Fred Lewis Pattee demonstrate. Pattee's *The First Century of American Literature, 1770-1870* (1935; reprint, New York: Cooper Square, 1966) is generally measured and fair. Not until his *The Feminine Fifties* (New York: Appleton-Century, 1940) did he set the tone for the intensely misogynist evaluations, and finally silence, that followed. With the exception of Helen Waite Papashvily's *All the Happy Endings: A Study of the Domestic Novel in America, the Women Who Wrote It, the Women Who Read It, in the Nineteenth Century* (New York: Harper, 1956) and parts of Henry Nash Smith's *Virgin Land: The American West as Symbol and Myth* (Cambridge, Mass.: Harvard University Press 1950), little work focusing specifically on nineteenth-century women writers was produced before the "revival" of the 1970s.

2. Mary Kelley, *Private Woman, Public Stage: Literary Domesticity in Nineteenth-Century America* (New York: Oxford University Press, 1984).

3. Alfred Habegger, *Gender, Fantasy, and Realism in American Literature* (New York: Columbia University Press, 1982).

4. Jane Tompkins, *Sensational Designs: The Cultural Work of American Fiction, 1790-1860* (New York: Oxford University Press, 1985).

5. Richard Rorty, "The Contingency of Selfhood," in Rorty, *Contingency, Irony, and Solidarity* (Cambridge and New York: Cambridge University Press, 1989), 27-28.

6. Hans Robert Jauss, "Literary History as Challenge," in Jauss, *Toward an Aesthetic of Reception* (Minneapolis: University of Minnesota Press, 1982), 41.

7. See Annette Kolodny's "A Map for Rereading: Gender and the Interpretation of Literary Texts," *New Literary History* II (1980): 451-468; reprinted in Elaine Showalter, ed., *The New Feminist Criticism: Essays on Women, Literature Theory* (New York: Pantheon Books, 1985), 46-62.

8. Papashvily, *All The Happy Endings.*

9. A good example of this is Joanne Dobson's "The Hidden Hand: Subversion of Cultural Ideology in Three Mid-Nineteenth-Century Women's Novels," *American Quarterly* 38 (Summer 1986): 223-242.

10. Ann Douglas, *The Feminization of American Culture* (New York: Avon Books, 1977).

11. Nina Baym, *Novels, Readers, and Reviewers: Responses to Fiction in Antebellum America* (Ithaca: Cornell University Press, 1984).

12. Cathy N. Davidson, *Revolution and The Word: The Rise of the Novel in America* (New York: Oxford University Press, 1986).

13. Baym, *Novels, Readers, and Reviewers,* 172.

14. Milton Meltzer and Patricia G. Hollands, eds., *Lydia Maria Child: Selected Letters, 1817-1880* (Amherst: University of Massachusetts Press, 1982), 238-239.

15. Habegger's *Gender, Fantasy, and Realism,* especially pages 15-20, probably has the best analysis to date of the sexual appeal of nineteenth-century American women's novels.

16. Quoted by Steven Mailloux in *Rhetorical Power* (Ithaca: Cornell University Press, 1989), 36-37. I am grateful to Professor Mailloux for furnishing me with advance pages of this text and reminding me of Melville's remarks.

17. Augusta Evans Wilson, *St. Elmo* (Chicago: M. A. Donohue & Company, n.d.), 439.

18. "The horizon of expectations of literature distinguishes itself before the horizon of expectations of historical lived praxis in that it not only preserves actual experiences, but also anticipates unrealized possibility, broadens the limited space of social behavior for new desires, claims, and goals, and thereby opens paths of future experience" (Jauss, *Toward an Aesthetic of Reception,* 41).

19. See Baym, *Novels, Readers, and Reviewers,* for an analysis of the Victorian creation of taste and its impact on mid-century American literature.

20. Gerald Graff, *Professing Literature: An Institutional History* (Chicago: University of Chicago Press, 1987), esp. ch. i.

21. Wilson, *St. Elmo,* 371.

22. "[O]nly sentences can be true, and . . . human beings make truths by making languages in which to phrase sentences" (Rorty, "The Contingency of Language," in *Contingency, Irony, and Solidarity,* 9).

23. Nina Baym, "Melodramas of Beset Manhood: How Theories of American Fiction Exclude Women Authors," *American Literature* 33 (Summer 1981): 123-139; reprinted in Showalter, *The New Feminist Criticism,* 63-80.

24. E.D.E.N. Southworth, *The Deserted Wife* (Philadelphia: T. B. Peterson, 1855), 229.

25. Tompkins, "Sentimental Power: *Uncle Tom's Cabin* and the Politics of Literary History," in *Sensational Designs,* 122-146.

26. Fanny Fern, *Ruth Hall and Other Writings,* ed. Joyce W. Warren (New Brunswick, N.J.: Rutgers University Press, 1986), 13. Subsequent references to this text are cited parenthetically as *RH.* In her Introduction to the novel, Warren discusses both the theme of economic independence and the stylistic dualities of Fern's writing.

27. Frances E. W. Harper, *Iola Leroy* (1893; reprint, Boston: Beacon Press, 1987), 38. Subsequent references to this text are cited parenthetically as *IL.*

28. M. M. Bakhtin, *The Dialogic Imagination,* trans. Caryl Emerson and Michael Holquist (Austin: University of Texas Press, 1981). The most pertinent essay is the last, "Discourse in the Novel." A preliminary model for such an analysis is David R. Sewell's *Mark Twain's Languages: Discourse, Dialogue, and Linguistic Variety* (Berkeley: University of California Press, 1987).

29. Susanna Rowson, *Charlotte Temple,* ed. Cathy N. Davidson (New York: Oxford University Press, 1986), 34.

DOROTHY MERMIN (ESSAY DATE 1993)

SOURCE: Mermin, Dorothy. "Entering the Literary Market." In *Godiva's Ride: Women of Letters in England, 1830-1880,* pp. 43-59. Bloomington, Ind.: Indiana University Press, 1993.

In the following essay, Mermin describes the subject matter and other literary elements that defined the novels of nineteenth-century women authors.

The pleasures fame brought women writers show not only the gap between premonitory terror and a realized fact but also changes occurring in the literary world. It has been estimated that half the novels published in England in the eighteenth century were written by women, but the prestige of the genre was low, in large part because of its female associations. In the Victorian period, however, it became the dominant literary form. As the status of the novel rose, the status of women writers rose with it. Of the 878 novelists included in John Sutherland's *Stanford Companion to Victorian Fiction,* 312 are women, who published an average of 21 novels each, while 565 men published on average 17.7. And for the first time in the history of any literary genre women authors were a significant proportion of those most highly esteemed. The low prestige of novel writing allowed women to enter the field; later in the century fiction became defined as high art and women were pushed to the periphery.[1] But in the middle decades of the nineteenth century they flourished.

Women poets had also become more numerous during the eighteenth century, but poetry remained at the apex of the literary hierarchy and was wholly dominated by men. Still, change was beginning here too. The Romantic movement listened for new voices—the poor, the mad, children, women—although such voices found canonical utterance through male poets. In the nineteenth century women's devotional, didactic, and descriptive verse, lyric laments, poems for or about children or the poor, and quasi-novelistic narratives were published in vast quantities and often reviewed favorably if with considerable condescension. Amatory verse, however, especially with audible sexual overtones, was problematic, and anything political, apart from effusions of sympathy, was touchier still: Barrett Browning's sentimental verses about poverty-stricken children were admired, but her fierce incursions into politics provoked outrage. Drama had entered a long decline, so that the paucity of female playwrights did not materially affect the literary landscape. But a plenitude of periodicals and readers eager for edification produced an enormous demand for nonfictional prose, much of which women supplied. About 20 percent of published writers in the nineteenth century, it is estimated, were women.[2]

The shifting status of literary genres and the opening of new literary markets were facilitated by an increase in the reading public, cheaper methods of printing, better transportation and communication, and new modes of distribution. The spread of elementary education made basic literacy more common; Richard Altick estimates that by mid-century perhaps 60 percent of the adult population could read at least minimally, creating for the first time what might be considered a mass literary audience.[3] Cheap newspapers catering to an interest in politics spurred by agitation for Reform, cheap magazines, fiction sold by the penny, and edifying materials distributed by religious and philanthropic groups were available for the newly literate. Harriet Martineau's *Illustrations of Political Economy,* published from 1832 to 1835 in monthly parts at a very low price and designed to teach the working classes practical lessons about such matters as trade, commerce, and banking, sold in 1834 at the rate of 10,000 a month.[4] Books, which were expensive, were available to a higher social class through the circulating libraries for a small annual fee, and also in cheap reprints and in serial publication. The greatest single purchaser of new books was Mudie's Circulating Library, begun in 1842 and surviving in diminished form into the next century, which exercised an influence on what was published that authors and publishers resented but could not effectively resist. Mudie's preference for three-volume novels (since each volume could be loaned out separately) encouraged prolixity; and since his subscribers were mostly families, the books he bought had to meet his standards for family reading. The censorship exercised by Mudie and reinforced by many reviewers helped ensure fiction's social respectability, if not its artistic quality.

There were also periodicals at all levels and for many audiences, intellectual or frivolous: for men, women, children, or particular religious groups; dealing with literature, art, politics, science, religion, travel, and many other subjects; and publishing reviews, essays, poems, stories, and serialized novels. For many women, journalism served as an entrance to a literary career or augmented income from poetry or fiction. All sorts of journals were happy to accept poems from unknown writers, and Elizabeth Barrett and George Eliot first achieved publication in this way—not very prestigious, but encouraging to the young. The most prestigious journals that printed new literary works were edited by men, including Dickens, Thackeray, and Trollope, but women could be editors too, particularly of journals for women and children, or, like Geraldine Jewsbury, exercise similar power as publishers' readers. Mary Howitt's varied, wide-ranging literary career, for instance, included *Howitt's Journal,* a joint venture with her husband, and Eliza Cook, a poet, published *Eliza Cook's Journal* from 1849 to 1854. Anonymous reviewing and the constant demand for fiction and poetry to fill the journals created even more openings for women. Before she became a novelist George Eliot regularly wrote reviews and essays for the *Westminster Review* and served for a while as its de facto editor—secretly, though, letting the publisher and official editor, John Chapman, take the credit, and without pay. It was hard but not impossible to make a living writing nonfiction for periodicals, but at worst it was a kind of participation in the literary world.

In the nineteenth century many women became writers because there was nothing else for them to do. Many began writing in childhood, literary composition being one of the few amusements, like "castle building," as available to girls as to boys. And at mid-century there were very few ways for a middleclass woman to earn a living or enjoy the satisfactions of work outside her home or the unpaid, unprofessional rounds of church and charity. If she were talented and enterprising she might become an actress; but at a time when many people still disapproved even of attending the theater her family would almost certainly disapprove. She could be a governess or a teacher, with low status, few pleasures, and little financial reward. Lower still on the social and economic scale, she could be a seamstress or milliner, but would probably not earn enough to live on and might easily drop into the working class or the moral abyss of prostitution. Florence Nightingale was almost maddened by the uselessness of her life before she made herself a unique career as a hospital administrator and reformer and created nursing as a reputable occupation; but Nightingale's aristocratic family and friends were essential to her success, and she was never constrained by the need to earn money.

Writing, however, required no training or special skills. Georgiana Fullerton and Geraldine Jewsbury achieved print and popularity despite a shaky command even of English grammar. Augusta Webster, pointing out that an astonishingly large number of women with little talent or education wrote "light literature" successfully, suggests that their mental worlds had been so thoroughly formed by novel-reading that they were as much at home in the conventions of the novel as in their actual lives.[5] Writing did not require money or materials beyond the books and paper that would be available in most middle-class homes. Social connections were not necessary either, although having writers or publishers among one's friends and relations certainly helped. The fact that poetry was usually less remunerative than fiction meant that it did not imply humiliating financial need, and its generic prestige could educe family pride and encouraged precocious publication. Elizabeth Barrett's father and Christina Rossetti's grandfather had the girls' poems privately printed when Barrett was fourteen, Rossetti seventeen.

Male writers were afraid that the apparent predominance of women as producers and audience (a predominance much magnified in nervous imaginations) would feminize—that is, degrade—the profession of literature. Their fears were all the stronger because by mid-century literature already seemed to be in some alarming ways intrinsically feminine. Male superiority in poetry remained unchallenged, despite a few partial exceptions of the rule of female incapacity, but writing poetry seemed unpleasantly similar to women's work as the early Victorians, following the Romantics, defined it: apart from and opposed to the public world of business and power, trafficking only in the most delicate feelings and perceptions, speaking from the heart to touch the hearts of others. Critics liked simple, homely poetic themes and language and sincere, spontaneous expressions of feeling: the artless spontaneity Jameson's *Ennuyée* enacts, which was assumed to be natural to women. And insofar as prose fiction examined domestic matters and the inner life, it too was in the feminine domain.[6] The novel did not have a long male tradition, as poetry did, to ward off feminine intrusion. There were more women novelists than women poets, and they took indisputably higher rank and were harder to ignore or explain away.

It was taken for granted by writers, reviewers, and publishers that many, perhaps most, readers of novels were female.[7] Middle-class women, and especially young girls, were likely to be confined to home, with a lot of free time and little to fill it. Fiction concentrated on personal relationships and the minutiae of social life—the material of their own existences—while also allowing them a sense of experiencing a wider world. (French novels, being by English definition wicked and corrupting, were particularly rich in worldly knowledge, but relatively few girls had access to them.) A predominantly young and female audience was thought to require love stories, which almost every novelist duly provided. Whereas (presumably male) reviewers assessed the attractiveness of heroines, female readers were expected to fall in love with the hero, and a common objection to novel-reading was that it fueled erotic daydreams.

Such an audience was naturally the object of satire, especially by men. Within fiction itself the housemaid dreaming of love while reading cheap romances and the idle young lady lounging on a sofa devouring novels and chocolate are objects of contempt left over from the eighteenth century. Jane Austen mocked this habit of derision in *Northanger Abbey* without being able to laugh it away. Poets and their reviewers, in contrast, apparently assumed the existence of a fairly serious and intellectual male audience, with a substratum of sentimental female readers (best ignored) somewhere below. But the identification of poetry's readers with young women and aesthetic young men was becoming established in the general consciousness, comically exemplified by the effete poet and his chorus of female adorers in Gilbert and Sullivan's *Patience.*

The multisided threat of femininization in literature provoked a vigorous satiric counterattack in Thackeray's *Pendennis,* published just at mid-century. Arthur Pendennis (whose nickname, "Pen," is as appropriate as the combined first and last syllables of his surname) becomes a successful novelist after encountering and resisting various feminine corruptions of literature. First he is ensnared by a good-natured provincial actress whose only artistic gift is her ability to follow male direction. Later he attracts the affection of a nice but silly girl, a porter's daughter, who has "heated her little brain with novels, until her whole thoughts are about love and lovers, and she scarcely sees that she treads on a kitchen floor" (142). And he has both an object of infatuation and a parodic opposite in beautiful, wily Blanche Amory. Blanche's sexual corruption is demonstrated if not caused by the fact that she read all the novels of Balzac and George Sand before she was sixteen. She represents everything that is insincere, disreputable, and false about the feminine in literature: she is self-named, full of genteel pretensions but in fact a convict's daughter, given to uttering the highest sentiments for public effect while being unpleasant and spiteful at home. Worst of all, summing it all up, she is a genuinely sentimental poet. She "indeed loved poets and men of letters if she loved anything, and was sincerely an artist in feeling" (429).

Blanche's volume of (unpublished) verses in English and French, entitled "Mes Larmes," foreshadows the sentimental effusions of Mark Twain's Emmeline Graingerford.

> It appeared from these poems that the young creature had indeed suffered prodigiously. She was familiar with the idea of suicide. Death she repeatedly longed for. A faded rose inspired her with such grief that you would have thought she must die in pain of it. It was a wonder how a young creature should have suffered so much—should have found the means of getting at such an ocean of despair and passion (as a runaway boy who *will* get to sea), and having embarked on it, should survive it. What a talent she must have had for weeping to be able to pour out so many of "Mes Larmes"!
>
> (250)

Blanche embodies both the corruption and the absurdity of the feminized notion of poetry: that it should express deep (and mostly painful) feelings, that its greatest virtue is sincerity, and that it should emerge as a kind of involuntary effusion or indeed (her poems are tears, "Mes Larmes") bodily secretion. Thackeray mocks Blanche's writing in precisely the terms women most feared: as an expression of vanity, a manifestation of an ambition that destroys filial affection and parental authority (her intellectual superiority allows her to terrorize her stepfather and bully her good-natured, vulgar mother), and a tool of seduction.

Pen likes Blanche's verses—he "thought them very well for a lady" (250)—and composes his own in reply, but he soon outgrows both poetry and Blanche and becomes a successful novelist. The most admirable man in the book, however, is George Warrington, who is entirely cut off from the feminine element in literature and indeed from women, since after being seduced into an unfortunate early marriage he has lived apart from his wife but cannot remarry. Warrington is a professional writer, but only of nonfiction. He scorns everything that is self-expressive and self-dramatizing in art. "All [modern] poets are humbugs, all literary men are humbugs; directly a man begins to sell his feelings for money he's a humbug" (434), says Warrington, and while he does not give a name to a *woman* who sells her feelings one can guess what it would be. Literary life as *Pendennis* satirically and affectionately depicts it is a masculine world of comradeship, drink, debt, and harmless raffishness, with no women except a few poor desexualized hacks. Miss Bunion, author of "Passion Flowers," is "a large and bony woman in a crumpled satin dress, who came creaking into the room with a step as heavy as a grenadier's" (368). It is not an exalted world, socially or morally, but the growing power and tawdry glamour of the press, along with the income and modest degree of fame it offers to those with no special skills or connections, make it attractive; and it is safe from Blanche Amory.

Anthony Trollope (whose mother's writings supported the family for many years) and Thomas Hardy (whose impoverished background was a barrier as hard to cross as that of gender) treat female aspirants to literature more kindly than Thackeray does, but still as figures of comedy. Trollope's Lady Carbury in *The Way We Live Now* works hard, manipulates the reciprocal-flattery system of reviewing, publishes a feeble work of romanticized history called *Criminal Queens,* and begins a novel. Her literary ambitions are amiably preposterous, based on vague ambition and a desperate need for money to support her profligate son, and when she marries a powerful editor she no longer has to write—indeed, he will not let her. Hardy's heroine in *The Hand of Ethelberta,* a pleasant and highly improbable comedy, is nicer and more sensible than Lady Carbury. She publishes a volume of bold, unsentimental poetry and then sets herself up as a kind of Corinne, telling stories in public performance to make money and catch a husband so that she can provide for her numerous siblings. Like Blanche Amory, Lady Carbury and Ethelberta are decidedly unromantic in the actual conduct of their lives, and their literary efforts, while justified by altruistic familial ends, are in reality little more than husband-hunting—although Ethelberta after ensnaring an elderly, debauched, disagreeable, but very rich nobleman is reported as the novel ends to be composing an epic poem.

Women who did not want to be dismissed as a Blanche Amory or Lady Carbury or even a talented but lowborn husband-hunter like Ethelberta often hid behind anonymous or pseudonymous publication. Female novelists' use of male pseudonyms has been said to characterize the period from the 1840s to 1880.[8] In this as in other ways, women's entrance into literature was facilitated by an established convention which they used with special intensity and an inflection peculiar to themselves. Anonymous reviewing (including long essays only nominally connected to the books ostensibly in question) remained customary throughout the century, allowing women to assume an authoritative tone that a gendered signature would undermine. Most male poets inaugurated their careers without disclosing their identities, testing the waters while following a tradition going back to Renaissance poets' eagerness to define themselves as gentlemanly amateurs; such poets, the venerable convention went, wrote for their own and their friends' amusement, published more or less inadvertently, and were indifferent to reward—a useful pose for women too. Tennyson, Browning, and Arnold, like Elizabeth Barrett and the Brontës, sent their first books forth anonymously. Disguising gender is most difficult in lyric poetry, and was rarely attempted, although the Brontës' first book was *Poems,* by "Currer, Ellis and Acton Bell," and Augusta Webster published her first volume of poetry in 1860 with a name that left the question open, "Cecil Home." (In the last decades of the century the joint compositions of Katherine Bradley and Edith Cooper appeared under the name of "Michael Field" and William Sharp published as "Fiona Macleod.") Novelists had Austen and Scott as precedents for anonymity, the latter of whom guarded his secret with unusual pertinacity, and Dickens and Thackeray used pen names although without any real attempt at concealment. But the Brontës dropped their disguise only when an unscrupulous publisher made it seem absolutely necessary, and Gaskell, who had considered using a male name, published *Mary Barton* anonymously and submitted to be known with real reluctance. Mary Ann Evans is still called George Eliot.

Eliot's persistence in that name is sufficiently accounted for by the fact that she had no "real" one. Her publisher John Blackwood wanted as desperately as she did to preserve the secret, since there seemed no safe way to disclose it. "Mary Ann Evans" was the name of the translator of notoriously heretical books on religion and of a woman living openly with another woman's husband, and in any case she insisted on being called by still another assumed name, "Mrs. Lewes." Eliot's two pseudonyms were not just protective—they represented deliberately chosen identities, and she forced the world to acknowledge them—but they served first of all to cover moral and sexual irregularities. Similarly, the Brontës would have been spared many insults if Currer, Acton, and Ellis Bell had been taken to be men. A man's name could ward off sneers at unladylike writing, as the sensation novelist Mary Braddon explained:

> Did you see what the——————says about *Aurora Floyd* and my philosophy in the matter of beer, brandy, and cigars and tobacco? It is all Mr. Tinsley's fault for advertising me as "Mary Elizabeth." I used to be called *Mr.* Braddon, and provincial critics were wont to regret that my experience of woman had been so bitter as to make me an implacable foe to the fair sex. They thought I had been "cradled into magazines by wrong," and had learned in the Divorce Court what I taught in three-volume novels.[9]

The association of publishing with sexual exposure, added to women's more generalized ambivalence about fame, accounts for the intensity of the distress—quite unlike anything men experienced—that the Brontës, Gaskell, and Eliot felt about having their identities revealed. But there were other reasons to conceal name and gender. Reviews of books known or suspected to be by women were greeted with an exasperating condescension, like Thackeray's, that it was well worth trying to avoid. The assumption that women wrote from their own experience, moreover, was very often true of first novels, both by women and by men, so that prudence as well as timidity might warn a beginner against revealing her name.[10]

But although anonymous and pseudonymous publication were designed to ward off personal scrutiny, they also invited it. Reviewers enjoyed speculating about masked authors, and uncertainty about gender opened the way for particularly wounding insults.[11] The problem was not unique to women, intrusive personal publicity being generally agreed to be one of the disagreeable hallmarks of the age. People who were well-known, or hoped to be, or corresponded with those who were, assumed that someone would want to publish their correspondence, and many of them tried to prevent it. Harriet Martineau demanded that her friends destroy letters from her, and Robert Browning burned a vast correspondence. "I never keep very private letters, but destroy them at once," Geraldine Jewsbury assured Jane Welsh Carlyle, her most intimate correspondent and the wife of a very famous husband, "having the fear of a coroner's inquest before my eyes, and a great horror of all executors who can pry into secrets from a sense of duty!"[12] Others' families protected their posthumous privacy with similar acts of destruction, and either prohibited biographies, wrote them themselves, or chose biographers they hoped to control or trusted to be discreet. Women writers' double-edged concealment of their names reflected in intensified form the ambivalence of the whole literary culture about the loss of privacy that publication entailed.

Rivals and reviewers liked to take for granted that women could not write as well as men, and many women believed this too. Women's brains were too weak, their emotions too uncontrolled, their reproductive systems inimical to and easily damaged by mental exertion, and their experience of life and the world necessarily, given the social constraints that bound them, inadequate. Their undeniable successes in prose fiction only proved their limitations. The eminent critic Richard Holt Hutton, for example, asserted in 1858 that women's imaginations cannot go beyond "the visible surface and form of human existence"[13]—the domain of the novel—into the higher realms of poetry. Impressionable and quick to feel, women were incapable of conceptual profundity, abstract thought, or sustained, shaping creativity. Few women could entirely reject such discouraging views, which literary history apparently confirmed. Many of them were passionately certain, however, that women's inferiority was at least partly the result of education.

Until well into the nineteenth century most girls of the middle and upper classes were educated primarily at home, and some were hardly educated at all. When the major Victorian women writers were growing up, schools for girls offered a smattering of fairly elementary academic instruction and (in varying degrees according to wealth and class) some "accomplishments": music, drawing, dancing, and other activities designed to make them attractive to suitors and agreeable at home. Most schools were small, and a comfortable family atmosphere was an important attraction. The best of them taught French, Italian, and sometimes even Latin, but they did not copy the curriculum, dominated by the classical languages and a little mathematics, that was given to boys. A girl from a reasonably cultivated family could learn as much at home. During the 1840s and 1850s some excellent, highly influential secondary schools for girls came into being, as well as a few nonresidential, non-degree-granting colleges. In the 1860s women were allowed to take examinations given by the University of London, and in 1869 the first university college for women and the first lectures for women began at Cambridge. These developments gradually altered the shape of the arguments about women's abilities, but they came too late to benefit the major Victorian writers. The Brontës, Eliot, and Gaskell attended schools that were reasonably satisfactory by the standards of their day, but Barrett Browning and Rossetti (whose mother had been a governess), as well as Oliphant and many others, were educated entirely at home, and most of those who attended schools did so for only a few years and often with little benefit. Elizabeth Sewell's mother wanted her daughters to be capable of independence and sent them to expensive, well-regarded boarding schools where Sewell was ill-taught and unhappy. Harriet Martineau, more fortunate, attended an excellent day school for boys that had been forced by declining numbers to admit girls, but the school's decline continued and after two years it closed; later she spent some time at a boarding school run by cultivated and intelligent women, her cousins and aunt.

In some respects girls were lucky. Boys' schools were often brutally unpleasant, with narrow curricula, teaching methods ranging from uninspired to sadistic, and uncontrolled bullying and sexual exploitation among the pupils. Some, such as Thomas Arnold's Rugby, were well run and drew students' grateful loyalty; but no woman writer's educationally deprived childhood matches for sheer sustained awfulness Trollope's account of his years at the best schools in England, where he was ostracized, bullied, and beaten, and learned (so he claimed) nothing at all.[14] The Greek and Latin to which schoolboys devoted almost all their

Harriet Martineau (1802-1876).

time were no more useful to most of them (even those who, unlike Trollope, actually learned something) than girls' amateur dabbling in the arts; many boys would have been better off in practical terms studying modern languages, like girls. But the point was not utility. It was access to culture and power, to which the classical languages, and especially Greek with its exotic alphabet, held the magic key. Training in these languages was required for entrance to the universities, where genuine intellectual life and companionship were available to those who wanted them. Boys' studies, being considered more difficult, both demonstrated and developed their intellectual superiority to girls'; and the ability to quote fragments of Greek and Latin that was all most of them retained from years of schooling reinforced class and gender identity by marking them definitively as gentlemen. They naturally wished to keep women out of the club, which was partly defined by precisely that exclusion; and women ambitious for literary accomplishment, just as naturally, yearned to get in.

Such women had mostly to educate themselves. A start might come from a few years at a good school, a well-educated mother, a governess, a brother's tutor willing to let the sister sit in on lessons, or a cultivated father (most often a clergyman) who taught a daughter along with her brother or because he had no son. Boys always came first: Charlotte Yonge's clergyman father eventually taught her Greek and mathematics, but he began teaching her Latin only when her brother, who was five years younger, was ready to study it too, and Elizabeth Barrett's ardent desire to learn Greek had to wait until a tutor arrived to prepare her younger brother for school. Older siblings often taught younger ones, usually neither willingly nor well. Girls in their teens, left to their own educational devices, made resolutions and reading lists, but without substantial encouragement or assistance few could keep their resolves. Time not needed for other pursuits was supposed to be given to sewing (called "work"), a sociable and frequently useful activity carried out in the midst of the family circle. Girls' reading, in contrast, was regarded in many households, especially in the early part of the century, as unsociable, useless, even dangerous: knowledge gleaned from books might be injurious to innocence, erudition would scare off suitors, and mental exertion was blamed for illness and forbidden to those in poor health. Reading and studying were often secretly indulged and attended by guilt. Charlotte Brontë was among the few who persisted, guiltless but unhappy, in formal schooling, but even she felt some guilt at preferring the pen to the needle. She and her sisters stayed as long as they could endure it at schools they intensely disliked in order to qualify themselves to make a living as teachers. For this they needed French and music, not Latin and Greek, so those were the subjects they set themselves to master. Branwell, who was designed but not destined for higher things, stayed home and studied the usual male subjects with his father; but he was none the better for it.

Of the major women writers, only Barrett Browning and Eliot reached (in fact they exceeded) the level of a highly educated man. They had formidable intellectual endowments and immense self-discipline as well as access to books and to men willing to instruct them. After Elizabeth Barrett's brother went to school and his tutor left she read Greek on her own, and after years of successful self-instruction she became the protegée of a blind middle-aged classical scholar who happened to turn up in the neighborhood. She learned Latin, French, Italian, and German, and in her twenties solaced an anxious period with lonely studies in Hebrew. She demonstrated her scholarly credentials by translating Aeschylus' *Prometheus Bound* and publishing a series of essays on some exceedingly obscure Greek Christian writers. Eliot attended a school that offered music, drawing, English, French, history, and arithmetic, and then taught herself Latin, found teachers for Italian and German, and learned Greek, postponing mastery of Hebrew to her late forties.[15] Both women read widely in many subjects, especially history, but their formal instruction and self-instruction, like almost all women's, centered on languages.

When she was in her thirties Barrett Browning decided that learning languages was a waste of time, but by then she had learned them and reaped the benefit. She had acquired exact and extensive firsthand knowledge, in English and other literatures, of the poetic tradition in which she intended to take a place. Her formidable learning deflected critical condescension, although it seemed unnatural, even monstrous, and gave rise to some preposterous exaggerations in the press: that when she was eight years old, for instance, she "read Homer in the original, holding her book in one hand and nursing her doll upon her other arm"; or that she and Browning corresponded in classical Greek.[16] Having established her intellectual equality with men she forgot, perhaps, how crucial her mastery of the classical languages had been to her success.

Women poets who lacked Barrett Browning's linguistic accomplishments rarely ventured beyond the relatively unpretentious forms of verse, lyric and narrative and especially the ballad, for which English alone might seem sufficient. Keats, after all, knew no Greek. But the voice of Tennyson, master lyricist of the age, was drenched in classical verse; Browning was always displaying odd bits of erudition and frequently drew on classical languages and literature; Arnold extolled and overtly imitated classical forms of poetry, and most of his critical manifestos assumed an audience that read and appreciated Greek. Christina Rossetti had the good fortune to grow up in an intensely literary household where Italian was frequently spoken and read and everyone had an intimate knowledge of the great Italian poets. She knew French, German, and a little Latin but did not attempt Greek, which her brothers studied at school and her sister learned at home; her acceptance of the linguistic limitations thought proper for girls is both a sign and a cause of her exclusion from "masculine" realms of poetry. Augusta Webster, the best of the poets whose reputations died with the century, was as learned in languages as Barrett Browning and published translations of Aeschylus' *Prometheus Bound* (as Barrett Browning had done) and Euripedes' *Medea.* Only Emily Brontë wrote powerful verse rooted wholly in English tradition, and her idiosyncratic poems received almost no attention. For poets the lack of a classical education was both a perceived and a genuine disadvantage.

For novelists it mattered much less, the novel not being part of the classical tradition. Thackeray had the usual upper-middle-class education, culminating in an incomplete and unproductive sojourn at Cambridge; but Dickens's intermittent schooling ended at fifteen, and Trollope had to teach himself not only French but also Latin when his useless school years were over. Thackeray drew on Fielding and the tradition of classical satire, but the powerful precursors for women novelists were French and female: Madame de Staël and George Sand. For novelists, unlike poets, a catch-as-catch-can education based on modern languages and backed by a good library may well have been the best of all.

Eliot's novels obliquely acknowledge this in their repeated mockery of classical learning, which is presented as arid and useless except as a key to male power. Maggie Tulliver's frustration at not being taught Latin is largely a matter of ambition and jealousy: she yearns to exercise her quick intelligence, and she wants to demonstrate her superiority to her brother. Romola's father taught her Greek so that she could assist his scholarly labors and help establish his fame, but she herself takes no interest in it, and the bequest of his library and his unfinished labor is a dead weight on her life. Dorothea Brooke in *Middlemarch* is simply mistaken in thinking that Greek and Hebrew hold the keys to happiness; her husband, like Romola's father, bewilders himself with envious ambition and sterile scholarship and tries to bequeath to her the deadly burden of his work. Fred Vincy hasn't learned much at Oxford, but he knows enough Greek to squelch his sister.

> "Tell me [Fred challenges her whether it is slang or poetry to call an ox a *legplaiter.*"
>
> "Of course you can call it poetry if you like."
>
> "Aha, Miss Rosy, you don't know Homer from slang. I shall invent a new game; I shall write bits of slang and poetry on slips, and give them to you to separate."
>
> (*Middlemarch,* 126)

Knowing Greek allows men to establish "poetry" as their exclusive possession and to set the rules of a game women can't win. In Eliot's novels, classical learning functions as a weapon either in the battle of male egos or to intimidate women; the weapon may not be worth much, but those who don't possess it are defenseless against it, and while Eliot scorns the battle, she never lets us forget that she herself is well armed.

It is striking, in fact, that increasing educational opportunities for girls roused women novelists to satirical coolness if not downright disapprobation. It is as if the ethos of women's fiction, which arose outside the realm of male high culture, was intrinsically hostile to women who wanted to move into that antithetical realm. The novelists understood that power and prestige, not knowledge, were really at issue. A learned young woman in a Victorian novel is almost certain to be selfish, unfeminine, and probably a fraud. One expects no better from Charlotte Yonge, who preached women's obligations to home, church, and father, although the punishments that befall women in her books who pride themselves on intelligence and learning may still strike us as extreme; the eponymous heroine of *The Clever Woman of the Family,* for instance, is not only humiliated by having her intellectual pretensions exploded but literally kills where she seeks to benefit. Yonge sympathizes with girls who crave a man's education, but not with those who flatter themselves that they have it, or would be selfish enough really to attain it. But the worldly and independent Mary Braddon is almost as cool as Yonge to "Poor Lucy," who "had been mercilessly well educated; she spoke half a dozen languages, knew all about the natural sciences, had read Gibbon, Niebuhr, and Arnold" (*Aurora Floyd,* 22). Mrs. Oliphant's Phoebe Jr. has studied German, attended lectures at a ladies' college, and read "Virgil at least, if not Sophocles" (*Phoebe, Junior,* 18); but she hides her learning, using it only to write brilliant speeches for her rich and stupid husband once she gets him into Parliament. And of all her heroines Eliot allows classical learning only to Romola, who is neither English nor modern and prefers not to use it.

The debates about female education, abilities, and roles in society went on throughout the century and provided gainful employment for many female pens. There was an apparently inexhaustible market for books and essays on childrearing and education and a growing demand for children's books suited to the changing times. Conduct literature for girls and women, generally of a conservative sort, was an established genre, the most famous Victorian examples being Sarah Ellis's exhortations to the women, wives, mothers, and daughters of England. Elizabeth Sewell's *Principles of Education* and Charlotte Yonge's *Womankind* complement their almost equally didactic fiction and teach the same lessons. "I have no hesitation in declaring my full belief in the inferiority of woman," Yonge asserts, "nor that she brought it upon herself."[17] Christina Rossetti also asserted women's inferiority, taking like Sewell and Yonge a religious ground. "The fact of the Priesthood being exclusively man's," she told Augusta Webster, "leaves me in no doubt that the highest functions are not in this world open to both sexes." In one of her tracts for girls Rossetti teaches "the limit of God's ordinance concerning our sex," but she adds that "one final consolation yet remains to careful and troubled hearts: in Christ there is neither male nor female, for we are all one."[18] Different writers, of course, located "the limits of God's ordinance" in different places. Some, from Anna Jameson and Harriet Martineau early in the period to Augusta Webster at its end, supported the feminist movement. Others, like Eliza Lynn Linton—best known as the author of a notorious attack on female emancipation as manifested in the "Girl of the Period"—entered the fray from whatever viewpoint was most salable at any given moment. Voices were raised on all sides.

Such questions bore both directly and by implication on writers' professional functions, and few women found easy answers. They generally deplored (usually from bitter experience) the scanty and haphazard education given to girls, whether or not they wanted them to have the same opportunities boys did. Many lamented the prejudices against female authors and the lack of satisfactory occupations for women who had to support themselves.[19] Almost all successful writers were ambivalent at best about feminism, even as their own examples helped create a wider view of female life. They were inclined to underestimate the obstacles they had surmounted and to assume that any women who deserved success could attain it. Harriet Martineau wrote in 1855:

> Often as I am appealed to speak, or otherwise assist in the promotion of the cause of Woman, my answer is always the same:—that women, like men, can obtain whatever they show themselves fit for. Let them be educated,—let their powers be cultivated to the extent for which the means are already provided, and all that is wanted or ought to be desired will follow of course. Whatever a woman proves herself able to do, society will be thankful to see her do,—just as if she were a man. . . . I judge by my own case.[20]

They all agreed that it was essential for women to be "womanly"—selfless, loving, and pure—and most were afraid that womanliness was incompatible with work directed outside the house or with agitation for a wider sphere.

Very few, in fact, were interested in opening up careers that could not be carried on at home, or at least in a home-like setting. *Aurora Leigh* offers passionate testimony to a woman's right and sacred obligation to do her own work, but the ideal situation toward which the poem moves is that of a married woman plying her pen within a reformed domestic sphere. And perhaps because being a writer required both a commitment to interiority and a frightening degree of publicity, poets and novelists tended to shun engagement in public affairs. Many were willing to sign a petition in favor of a bill that would allow married women control of their own earnings, but few cared much about the less personally urgent question of the vote. Harriet Martineau thought it absurd that she herself, a property-owning woman with a significant influence on public affairs, was disenfranchised, but the suffrage movement was not high on her agenda, and the two most important political women of the century, Queen Victoria and Florence Nightingale, did not support it at all. Caroline Norton fought for women's rights in regard to divorce and the custody of young children, but her own children, freedom, and money were at stake. The first woman writer of note to hold elective office was Augusta Webster, who worked actively for women's suffrage and in 1879 and 1885 was elected to the London School Board: the welfare of children and the lower classes, including their education, belonging like issues of custody in an extended feminine sphere.

For most women, motherhood was the central defining fact of gender difference, and it was a fact that could tell in different ways. Anna Jameson, who warmly encouraged a younger generation of feminist reformers, took it in a conservative direction:

> The natural and Christian principles of the moral equality and freedom of the two sexes being fully recognised, I insist that the ordering of domestic life is our sacred province indissolubly linked with the privileges, pleasures, and duties of maternity, and that the exclusive management of the executive affairs of the community at large belongs to men as the natural result of their exemption from the infirmities and duties which maternity entails on the female part of the human race.
>
> And by maternity I do not mean the actual state of motherhood—which is not necessary nor universal—but the maternal organisation, common to all women.[21]

Christina Rossetti, despite her belief in the inferiority of women, thought mothers deserved to vote:

> I do think if anything ever does sweep away the barrier of sex, and make the female not a giantess or a heroine but at once and full grown a hero and giant, it is that mighty maternal love which makes little birds and little beasts as well as little women matches for very big adversaries.[22]

In an essay published before she began writing fiction, George Eliot attributes women's special literary contribution to maternal "sensations and emotions," as well as to "the fact of her comparative physical weakness."[23] The enshrinement of maternity was in some ways the least disabling formulation of sexual difference that was current in the period, since it emphasized female power. If the maternal ideal implied self-sacrifice, self-effacement, and domestic seclusion, it also included the power to create, nourish, guide, and teach.

Few of the leading women writers—Gaskell, Wood, Braddon, Oliphant, Webster, and Barrett Browning after the age of forty-three—were mothers, and while Jameson and Martineau took quasi-maternal responsibility for their nieces and Eliot was a devoted stepmother to Lewes's sons, none of these relationships involved caring for young children. Writing itself, however, could be defined in maternal terms, and engagement in public life was acceptable if it seemed to fulfill a maternal role. Queen Victoria was the exemplar of prolific maternity, her ambivalence about childbearing not being generally known. Florence Nightingale, although she was unmarried and childless and her great career was as an administrative reformer, was idealized as a nurse. The traditional models of feminine public engagement were the country squires' and clergymen's wives and daughters who brought soup, clothing, practical advice, a little elementary schooling, and simple spiritual instruction to their poor neighbors. Among the many disappointments of Dorothea Brooke's unfortunate first marriage is a local population that requires no such assistance, while Oliphant's benevolently domineering Miss Marjoribanks's prospects of marital felicity are completed by a delightfully needy village at her gate.

> It gave her the liveliest satisfaction to think of all the disorder and disarray of the Marchbank village. Her fingers itched to be at it—to set all the crooked things straight, and clean away the rubbish, and set everything, as she said, on a sound foundation. . . . The recollection of all the wretched hovels and miserable cottages exhilarated her heart.
>
> (*Miss Marjoribanks,* 488)

The hovels and cottages are extensions of the sphere of home, awaiting her maternalistic intervention.

By 1866, when *Miss Marjoribanks* was published, such opportunities were already declining. The new urban proletariat was less accessible, less easily assisted, and less grateful than the rural poor, as the heroines of Gaskell's *North and South* and Rhoda Broughton's *Not Wisely But Too Well* discover. But new kinds of philanthropy, more elaborately organized, arose instead, bringing groups of like-minded women together and extending maternal and domestic values across barriers of class, moral standing, and even species. Prostitutes and other "fallen women" were particular objects of concern; Catholics and high Anglicans like Georgina Fullerton and Christina Rossetti worked with religious sisterhoods that assisted poor and outcast women, while others organized political action such as the agitation to repeal the "lock laws," which attempted to control venereal disease by forcing women whom the police thought might be prostitutes to undergo medical examination. The antivivisection movement attracted others. And writing served similar functions.

That literature has a moral effect—for good or for ill—was generally agreed, and in the high Victorian period no necessary conflict was seen between art and instruction. George Eliot's entertaining stories and her explications of moral law were woven together in satisfactory if not always seamless wholes, and even at lower levels of art and intellect the nineteenth-century novel was a schooling in morals and manners, especially for girls. Women were said to rule by influence—on their children first of all, although also on their husbands—and writers did the same on a wider scale. All novelists teach, Trollope insisted, whether they know it or not, and most of them knew it. "I have ever thought of myself," said Trollope, "as a preacher of sermons." The first serious review of sensation fiction, in 1863, complained that sensation novelists corrupt society by doing "the preacher's office . . . moulding the minds and forming the habits and tasks of its generation"—but doing it all wrong.[24] Poetry was expected to perform its educational task by cultivating pure feelings and high sentiments, an expectation some male poets, like Swinburne, zestfully defied. Literature was thought to nourish the sympathies that bind people together, an essential function in an increasingly industrialized society that saw social bonds decaying and selfishness enshrining itself in the doctrines of laissez-faire.

Like philanthropists, women writers reached across the iron boundaries of respectability, money, and class to declare sisterhood with sexually disgraced women and arouse maternal and sisterly sympathy in their readers. Barrett Browning's Marian Erle in *Aurora Leigh,* who emerges from the brutalizing depths of poverty and bears an illegitimate child as the result of rape, is in spirit a virgin mother, and Gaskell's Ruth, the pure-hearted victim of a callous seducer, is also sanctified by motherhood. *Mary Barton* offers sympathy between individuals of opposed social classes as the cure for class warfare and the ravages of urban poverty: the rich man and the poor, the crudely materialistic manufacturer and the embittered Chartist who saw his own child die of starvation and murdered the manufacturer's son, come together in their common pain as bereaved fathers. *Mary Barton* is designed to give its middle-class readers an experience like that of its characters: to make them see the essentially domestic virtues and feel the sufferings of people from whom in reality they would be alienated by class and economic status. This may not strike us as much of a solution to the horrors of unregulated industrialism, but to many intelligent people at the time it seemed the only one available. It is a solution that is uniquely in the power of the novelist and the poet; and as a kind of superior philanthropy that educates and binds society together through the affections, offering in effect to solve the most intractable social problems by translating them into the domestic sphere—the sphere to which Southey urged Charlotte Brontë to restrict herself—it is uniquely suited to women. Even in their most conservative forms, that is, the ideas about women's role and nature that made them afraid to write also enabled them to do so.

Notes

1. John Sutherland, *The Stanford Companion to Victorian Fiction* (Stanford: Stanford Univ. Press), Watt, *The Rise of the Novel: Studies in Defoe, Richardson, and Fielding* (Berkeley: Univ. of California Press, 1957), p. 298. Jane Spencer points out that women's association with the novel was emphasized in the eighteenth century, when its prestige was low, and was ignored by later critics who took fiction more seriously; *The Rise of the Woman Novelist: From Aphra Behn to Jane Austen* (Oxford: Basil Blackwell, 1986), p. viii.

2. Richard D. Altick, "The Sociology of Authorship: The Social Origins, Education, and Occupations of 1,100 British Writers, 1800-1935" [1962], in *Writers, Readers,*

and Occasions: Selected Essays on Victorian Literature and Life (Columbus: Ohio State Univ. Press, 1989), p. 97. Included in these figures are "all but the very lowest stratum of hacks" (p. 97).

3. Altick, "The Sociology of Authorship," p. 141. See also Altick's *The English Common Reader: A Social History of the Mass Reading Public, 1800-1900* (Chicago: Univ. of Chicago Press, 1957).

4. Valerie Pichanick, *Harriet Martineau: The Woman and Her Work, 1802-76.* (Ann Arbor: Univ. of Michigan Press, 1980), p. 50.

5. Augusta Webster, *A Housewife's Opinions,* pp. 188, 191-92.

6. Again, this was the continuation of a trend. "The moral utility of literature was an all-pervasive concern of eighteenth-century critics; modesty in the writer and his work was becoming an important term of praise; and simplicity and spontaneity in writing became greatly admired as the century progressed. What was happening, in fact, was that the properly 'feminine' and the properly 'literary' were both being re-defined along the same lines." Spencer, *Rise of the Woman Novelist,* p. 77. On the identification of interiority with the female, see Myra Jehlen, "Archimedes and the Paradox of Feminist Criticism," *Signs* 6 (1981): 596.

7. Terry Lovell notes, however, that male readership seemed to be increasing. "By the 1840s and in 'serious' realist fiction, women were writing novels which addressed men as well as women, and the novel-reading public now included a higher proportion of men"; and this, Lovell suggests, may help account for women's increased success in entering the canon, canonization perhaps depending on the maleness less of the author than of the audience. *Consuming Fiction* (London: Verso, 1987), p. 83.

8. Elizabeth K. Helsinger, Robin Lauterbach Sheets, and William Veeder, *The Woman Question: Society and Literature in Britain and America, 1837-1883,* 3 vols. (New York: Garland, 1983), 3: 65. In America, as Showalter points out, women were more likely to use feminine pseudonyms with pastoral overtones (p. 59). Gaye Tuchman's researches show that in the 1860s and 1870s men who submitted manuscripts to publishers were more likely to use female pseudonyms than women were to use either male or neuter names. *Edging Women Out,* pp. 53-54.

9. *Edmund Yates: His Recollections and Experiences,* 4th ed. (London: Richard Bentley & Son, 1885), pp. 354-55.

10. Showalter lists many of these considerations in *A Literature of Their Own* (pp. 57-60) and suggests that male names reflect childhood fantasies of being male (p. 58). On Eliot and her names, see Alexander Welsh, *George Eliot and Blackmail* (Cambridge, Mass.: Harvard Univ. Press, 1985), pp. 123-28. At first, Welsh points out, she "took advantage of her incognito by drawing more closely on her memory of actual persons and places than prudence afterward allowed" (p. 132). Gillian Beer suggests that Eliot used the male name in order to "slough off the contextuality of her own name and enter a neutral space"; "The 'we' of her text moves," Beer says, "often with deliberate disturbance, askance gender, class, and time." *George Eliot*(Bloomington: Indiana Univ. Press, 1989), pp. 25, 28. In the course of her life Eliot took many names: Mary Ann, Marian, and Marianne Evans, Polly, Pollian (from Apollyon), Clematis (meaning mental beauty, adopted in a youthful correspondence with a friend), Mrs. Lewes, George Eliot, and when she finally married, Mrs. John Cross. Lewes sometimes called her "Madonna" and she was "Mutter" to his sons. Eliot herself remarked that "a nom de plume secures all the advantages without the disagreeables of reputation" (*Letters* 2: 292).

11. "Pseudonymity . . . cannot be regarded as solely a defensive maneuver . . . since it immediately fuels speculation and publicity for a successful book" (Welsh, *George Eliot and Blackmail,* p. 123).

12. *Selections from the Letters of Geraldine Endsor Jewsbury to Jane Welsh Carlyle,* ed. Mrs. Alexander Ireland (London: Longman's, Green; New York, 1892), p. 89; see also pp. 337, 387. The most famous, and regretted, papers destroyed by surviving friends were Byron's.

13. R. H. Hutton, "Novels by the Authoress of 'John Halifax,'" *North British Review* 29 (1858): 467.

14. Trollope, *Autobiography,* pp. 4-19. Closest, perhaps, (besides, of course, the Brontë children's brief but fatal sojourn at "Lowood") is Eliza Lynn Linton's experience as the youngest member of a large motherless family, neglected by her father and tormented by her elder siblings.

15. Gordon S. Haight, *George Eliot: A Biography* (Oxford: Oxford Univ. Press, 1968), pp. 11, 25, 470.

16. The anecdote about reading Homer in childhood is from Alfred H. Miles, ed., *The Poets and the Poetry of the Century,* 10 vols., VII: *Joanna Baillie to Mathilde Blind* (London: Hutchinson, 1891-97), p. 155. The correspondence "in the language of Homer" is reported in "Modern English Poets," *American Whig Review* 14 (1851): 463.

17. *Womankind,* 2 vols. (Leipzig: Tauchnitz, 1878), 1: 1.

18. Mackenzie Bell, *Christina Rossetti: A Biographical and Critical Study,* 4th ed. (1898; New York: Haskell House, 1971), p. 112. *Seek and Find: A Double Series of Short Studies of the Benedicite* (1869; New York: Pott, Young, 1879), p. 32.

19. The argument for providing employment for women was strengthened by a numerical preponderance of women that made it impossible for all of them to marry; Helsinger et al., 2: 135-36. The poet Adelaide Procter, among many others, actively supported expanding employment opportunities for women.

20. *Autobiography,* 1: 302-303.

21. Clara Thomas, *Love and Work Enough: The Life of Anna Jameson* (Toronto: Univ. of Toronto Press, 1967), p. 209, from *Letters of Anna Jameson to Ottilie von Goethe,* ed. G. H. Needler (London: Oxford Univ. Press, 1939), p. 234.

22. Bell, *Christina Rossetti,* p. 112.

23. Eliot, "Woman in France: Madame de Sablé," *Westminster Review* 62 n.s. 6 (1854): 449.

24. Trollope, *Autobiography,* p. 146. [Henry Longueville Manse], "Sensation Novels," *Quarterly Review* 113 (April 1863): 482; quoted in Robert Lee Wolff, *Sensational Victorian: The Life and Fiction of Mary Elizabeth Braddon* (New York: Garland, 1979), p. 190.

AMERICAN WOMEN WRITERS

RENNIE SIMSON (ESSAY DATE 1986)

SOURCE: Simson, Rennie. "Afro-American Poets of the Nineteenth Century." In *Nineteenth-Century Women Writers of the English-Speaking World,* edited by Rhoda B. Nathan, pp. 181-91. Westport, Conn.: Greenwood Press, 1986.

In the following essay, Simson argues that the small amount of literary output available by nineteenth-century African-American women is deserving of scholarly attention.

As long ago as 1893 Dr. L. A. Scruggs in his book *Women of Distinction* (a work discussing noted Afro-American women) made the observation that it was "a painful experience to see how little is known of our great women and their works."[1] This neglect is echoed in the words of contemporary scholars. Bert Lowenberg and Ruth Bogin in their recent work, *Black Women in 19th Century American Life,* commented: "If the black male's words, before the most recent period of ferment, were recorded only spasmodically, those of the black female were still less frequently set down on paper."[2] In their introduction to *Sturdy Black Bridges,* an anthology containing works by and about Afro-American women writers, the editors state:

> Only slight attention has been given to Black women in creative literature, thus evoking grave concerns among female artists and scholars. . . . Recently a number of Black Anthologies and major critical works have been published. It is unfortunate, however, that in most cases, attention accorded Black women writers is sparse.[3]

This condition of neglect is particularly true of the works of nineteenth-century Afro-American women authors. Their autobiographies, poems, short stories, and novels are not only unread today, but they are virtually unheard of. This situation becomes doubly unfortunate and absurd when we consider the rather uniform inclusion in American literature anthologies of such literary luminaries as Mary Rowlandson, Anne Bradstreet, Sarah Kemble Knight, Harriet Beecher Stowe, and Julia Ward Howe. The editors of the fourth edition of the well-known *Norton Anthology of American Literature* concluded their discussion of Anne Bradstreet by stating: "When all has been said, the principal contribution of Anne Bradstreet to posterity is what she revealed, through herself, of the first generation of New Englanders."[4] Based on the obvious omission of nineteenth-century Afro-American women authors from our literary

Sojourner Truth (c. 1797-1883), a leading voice for abolition of slavery and women's rights, known primarily for her skill as an orator.

anthologies, we must assume that the editors of these anthologies have felt that Afro-American women did not make meaningful revelations about American society during the nineteenth-century. Perhaps Addison Gayle was correct when he made the following observation in 1975 to Roseann Bell, an editor of *Sturdy Black Bridges.*

> We can go back to the eighteenth century in English literature when criticism first begins its large impetus and males always wrote condescendingly about women writers. This is historic among Black male critics and, I think, all males have probably done so. I suppose the big chance will come when women begin doing critical work of their own on women writers.[5]

Even though Gerda Lerner, when discussing the "black female literary tradition" in *Black Women in White America,* skips from Phyllis Wheatly to Frances Harper and mentions no other black female poets of the nineteenth-century, black women were making meaningful literary contributions during this period.

It seems safe to say that the earliest works written by nineteenth-century Afro-Americas were not issued primarily to create a body of literature nor to entertain readers, but rather to arouse a sentiment that would work toward the abolition of slavery. In this category can be placed many slave narratives and pre-Civil War novels such as *Clotel, The Heroic Slave, The Garies and Their Friends* and *Blake*. These works were promoted by the abolitionists of the North and thus gained a relatively large white audience. During this period relatively few blacks were educated, and so these early pre-Civil War works were initially read by more whites than blacks. The only black women to achieve widespread recognition during this period were Francis Harper and Harriet Jacobs. While none of the works just mentioned can be classified as great literature, some of them definitely qualify as good literature and are deserving of far more attention than they have received in the past. The works of these writers reflect their dual position as members of a large society as well as of a specific culture within that larger society. This dualism was best expressed by W.E.B. Du Bois in his book *The Souls of Black Folk*. Wrote Du Bois: "One ever feels his twoness—an American, a Negro; two souls, two thoughts, two unreconciled strivings; two warring ideals in one dark body, whose dogged strength alone keeps it from being torn asunder."[6] A second class of writers appeared after the Civil War. Freed from an overwhelming absorption in the institution of slavery, they were free to explore and diversify their literary approaches as well as content. Their topics ranged from humorous folk tales to bitter satires reflecting the racial climate of post-Civil War America. The white audience interested in their works was smaller than in pre-Civil War days. Many whites preferred to read about the lives of black men from the pens of white racist romanticists like Thomas Dixon. The Civil War was over and for many whites the "race issue" was settled, and the concerns expressed in the works of black Americans no longer held any interest for them. Black authors like Charles Chesnutt and Paul Lawrence Dunbar found acceptance both with the general white populace and the critics (such as William Dean Howells) as long as they focused their talents on producing folk tales and dialect verse. However, white readers and critics turned away from them in dismay when their observations about their environment become harsh and bitter. While no Afro-American woman writers of this period achieved recognition comparable to that attained by Chesnutt and Dunbar, many talented black women turned to literature as a means of presenting their views. Most of their works reached a limited audience. They faced not only the handicap of being female writers, a "d———d mob of scribbling women" as Nathaniel Hawthorne called them, but of being black. A number of them felt it expedient to establish their own journals with black women as editors and these journals formed a major outlet for the stories, poems, and essays of a number of nineteenth-century Afro-American women authors. Among some of the more notable journals of that period were *Ringwoods* (Julia Costen, editor), *St. Matthews Lyceum Journal* (M. E. Lambert, editor), *Virginia Lancet* (Lucinda Bragg, editor), *The Boston Courant* (Josephine Ruffin, editor), *Women's Light and Love* (Lidia Lowry and Emma Ransom, editors) and *Waverly's Magazine* (Victoria Earle, editor). A number of books by Afro-American women were published either privately or by small, relatively unknown publishing companies. For the most part neither the journals nor the books enjoyed a long lifespan, so when they went out of print, the works of many black women were unavailable to the general public and existed only (and still exist only) in the rare bookrooms of specialized libraries scattered throughout the country. This very lack of accessibility has helped to perpetuate the myth that black women of the nineteenth century made few if any contributions to American literature. Their works are simply not available for general study and examination.

For the most part the work of nineteenth century Afro-American women poets conforms to the poetic standards of the nineteenth century. In discussing Frances Harper, the most prolific of the nineteenth-century Afro-American poetesses, Benjamin Brawley in the *Negro's Genius* observes that her poetry distinctly shows the influence of Longfellow. But Harper's poetry, as well as that of her contemporary Clara Ann Thompson, also shows the influence of black folklore and folk legend; each poetess wrote dialect verse spoken by a wise old narrator. In general, however, most Afro-American poetesses of the nineteenth-century wrote in a style typical of traditional nineteenth-century verse.

While black poetesses concerned themselves about such issues as religion, intemperance, and women's rights, their overwhelming concern focused on racial issues and it was in this area that their poetry achieved its greatest strength. It is true that some of their poetry dealing with racial matters was either overly sentimental and/or melodramatic, but for the most part it was forceful and direct, evoking empathy rather than sympathy for the position of the nineteenth-century Afro-American. In May 1837, Sarah Forten addressed a poem to the interracial Anti-Slavery Free Women of America Society in which she ap-

ON THE SUBJECT OF...

VICTORIA EARLE MATTHEWS (1861-1907)

Victoria Earle Matthews was one of the most vocal and active African American clubwomen and social reformers of the last decade of the nineteenth century. She co-founded the Woman's Loyal Union and was its first president, served as chair of the executive board of the National Federation of Afro-American Women (NFA-AW), and as chair of the Committee on Union for the Federation leading to its merger with the League of Colored Women. Matthews was national organizer of the newly formed National Association of Colored Women (NACW), and contributed numerous articles to the *Woman's Era,* the official journal of the NACW. She established the White Rose Home and Industrial Association for young working women and, later, the White Rose Traveler's Aid Society.

Matthews was one of only a few women to deliver a formal address at the 1895 Boston Conference of the Colored Women of America. In 1897 she spoke at the San Francisco convention of the Society of Christian Endeavor at a special program attended by prominent race leaders, including Booker T. Washington. In her speech, "The Awakening of the Afro-American Woman," Matthews recalled past horrors of slavery, including the sexual exploitation of slave women. She indicated how remarkable it was that these women had overcome such enormous obstacles to accomplish as much as they had, with little help from anyone but the white women who traveled South after the war to help educate the masses. She closed with a final admonition that much more remained to be done. Matthews contributed articles to the major New York newspapers and leading African American publications. Along with her journalistic writings and speeches, she authored several short stories and edited *Black-Belt Diamonds: Gems from the Speeches, Addresses and Talks to Students of Booker T. Washington* (1898), a collection of excerpts from Washington's speeches.

pealed to her audience's sense of sisterhood to unite blacks and whites in fighting for the abolition of slavery.

> We are thy sisters, God has truly said,
> That of one blood all nations He has made.
> O Christian woman! in a Christian land,
> Canst thou unblushing, read this great com-
> mand,
> Suffer the wrongs which wrong our inmost heart
> To draw one throb of pity on thy part;
> Our skins may differ, but from thee we claim
> A sister's privilege and a sister's name.[7]

The first book of poetry published by a black poetess in the nineteenth-century, Ann Plato's *Essays: Prose and Poetry* (1841), contained a tribute to England for its abolition of slavery in the poem "To the First of August."

> Lift ye that country's banner high,
> And may it nobly wave,
> Until beneath the azure sky
> Man shall be no more a slave.[8]

One of the earliest poems of Frances Harper, "The Dying Fugitive," appeared in 1859 in the *Anglo African Magazine* and is a strong statement in favor of the abolition of slavery. We can share the extreme frustration of a goal unfulfilled, a dream forever deferred.

> He must die, when just before him,
> Lay the long'd for precious prize—
>
> And the hopes that led him onward
> Faded out before his eyes.
>
> For a while a fearful madness,
> Rested on his weary brain;
> And he thought the hateful tyrant,
> Had rebound his galling chain.[9]

It is highly unlikely that any literary critic will argue that these three poems are literary masterpieces, but they are strong testimonials to the sentiments of Afro-Americans in pre-Civil War America and thus are as worthy of our attention as the poems of Anne Bradstreet as reflections on early Puritanism.

Racial injustice continued to be an issue of concern which was reflected in the poetry of Afro-American writers after the conclusion of the Civil War. Harper, in *Sketches of Southern Life* (1872), created a wise old ex-slave, Aunt Chloe, who, as narrator, offers the folk wisdom of generations of slaves. Upon the death of Lincoln, Aunt Chloe speculated upon the presidency of Andrew Johnson:

> Then we had another President—
> What do you call his name?
> Well, if the colored folks forget him
> They wouldn't be much to blame.[10]

Aunt Chloe felt great disgust with any man who sold his vote, and her friends shared her distress at such behavior on the part of their menfolk.

Day after day did Milly Green
Just follow after Joe
And told him if he voted wrong
To take his rags and go.[11]

But Aunt Chloe had only praise for men

Who know their freedom cost too much
Of Blood and pain and treasure
For them to fool away their vote
For profit or for pleasure.[12]

Like Harper, Clara Ann Thompson created an old character, Uncle Rube, who reflected on the society of his day. In the poem "Uncle Rube's Defense" Uncle Rube expressed his disgust with the stereotyping that white Americans directed toward black Americans.

Ev'ry low truk dat te black man's a doing',
'flects right back on de race, as a whole;
But de low co'se dat de white man's pursuin'
Costs not a blot on his good brudder's soul.

Let de black man do somepin wuth mentionin',
White folks ez still and shy ez a fawn;
Let him do somepin dat's mean and belittlin',
Umph! den de whole race has got it an'
gone.[13]

No doubt one of the most outspoken protest poets of the nineteenth century is the little known poetess Josephine Heard, whose single volume of poetry, *Morning Glories,* was published in 1890. In her poem "Black Samson" she made a sweeping indictment of post-Civil War American society in the treatment of its black population. Her bitter words did not show the conciliatory tone of so much of the literature written during "The Age of Washington" as Robert Bone has called the period of late nineteenth-century Afro-American literature. Nor did she seek to camouflage her criticisms in the guise of folk wisdom and folk dialect. Her tone was straightforward and direct, and even the most obtuse reader could scarcely miss her sharp message:

O, what cruelty and torture has he [the Black
Samson] felt?
Could his tears, the heart of his oppressor melt?
In his gore they bathed their hands,
Organized and lawless bands—
And the innocent was left in blood to wilt.[14]

But the Black Samson of Heard was not going to lie sleeping forever; he was not a pitiful victim, but rather a courageous man ready to lose his life, if need be, fighting for what he believed in. He was not Harper's dying fugitive for whom the reader cannot help but shed tears of pity, nor was he Stowe's Uncle Tom stoically ready to die for his principles, but the Black Samson was a fighter:

The Black Samson is awaking,
And the fetters fiercely breaking,
By his mighty arm his rights shall be
obtained![15]

Traditionally whites have had a harder time dealing with black fighters than with black victims, with realistic black figures than with black folk figures, so Aunt Chloe was a lot more popular with nineteenth-century audiences than the Black Samson was.

Heard had great confidence that the Black Samson would be successful and this confidence is reflected in her poem "They are Coming." At the beginning of the poem "they" (her fellow black citizens) are coming "slowly," then "proudly," and finally "boldly." In their ranks

There are Doctors, Lawyers, Preachers;
There are Sculptors, Poets, Teachers—
Men and women, who with honor yet shall
shine.[16]

This joy of pride in accomplishment is also reflected in Cordelia Ray's two poems "In Memoriam: Frederick Douglass" and "In Memoriam: Paul Lawrence Dunbar." Published in her collection *Poems* (1910), both poems possess a sense of triumph in accomplishments achieved in the face of what seemed to be insurmountable odds. Ray's pride in Douglass is clearly evident when she writes:

. . . what matter then
That he in chains was held, what matter when
He could uplift himself to noblest heights![17]

Dunbar's creative genius was an equal cause of celebration of the black race.

Who was this child? The offspring of a race
That erst had toiled 'neath slavery's galling
chains,
And soon he woke to utterance and sang.[18]

It was a long journey from the helpless fugitive of Frances Harper to the glorious talent of Paul Lawrence Dunbar, and that journey has been well documented by the pens of Afro-American poetesses of the nineteenth-century. Surely if we can learn of the Puritans from Anne Bradstreet and of the early Native Americans from Mary Rowlandson, both of whom are routinely included in American Literature anthologies, then we can learn of the early Afro-American from early Afro-American women writers.

As stated earlier Afro-American women wrote of issues other than race. Christianity played an important role in the lives of the nineteenth-century Afro-American, but it must be clearly understood that this was not the version of Christianity promoted by the white man. Throughout the days of slavery and even after, the white man twisted the scriptures to suit his purposes. His abuse of Christianity was initiated to serve three purposes: first, to soothe his own gnawing conscience about the fact that he was enslaving his fellow man; second, to convince the world that his actions were compatible with the will of God; and third, to convince the slaves themselves that they were inferior beings. His purposes succeeded in diminishing order; he did a good job of brainwashing himself, less of a job in brainwashing the rest of the world, and a poor job of brainwashing the slaves. Even after slavery some segments of the white Christian church continued to preach the gospel of black inferiority. But blacks established their own relationship with the Christian faith. Even during the days of slavery, when it was illegal for slaves to read and write, there were those who managed to learn and they read the Bible and informed the others of the distortions that were being perpetrated by the whites. Many blacks followed the example of Frederick Douglass, becoming devout believers in the Christianity of Christ, but rejecting the Christianity preached to them by the whites.

This dual concern, devout belief in an honest Christianity and total rejection of a hypocritical Christianity, is reflected in the works of nineteenth-century Afro-American women. This dualism is perhaps best reflected in Clara Ann Thompson's poem, "His Answer."

> He prayed for patience: Care and sorrow came
> And dwelt with him, grim and unwelcome
> guests;
> He felt their galling presence night and day;
> And wondered if the Lord had heard him pray,
> And why his life was filled with weariness.
>
> He prayed again and now he prayed for light
> The darkness parted and the light shone in;
> And lo! he saw the answer to his prayer—
> His heart had learned, through weariness and
> care,
> The patience that he deemed he'd sought in
> vain.[19]

The true Christian, according to Thompson, finds his spirituality through God directly and not in his relations with his fellow man here on earth. When he prays for relief from the care and misery imposed by others, his prayers appear to go unanswered, but if his prayers are for spiritual enlightenment he will be blessed. He will not perceive Christ through an intermediary, but will do so directly. It is only in such a perception that Christianity is possible, since any form of Christianity that rooted its faith in God as presented by a people who sanctioned slavery was not acceptable to a black person.

Frances Harper's poetry likewise expressed her faith in the Christian religion. Although she expressed skepticism and downright rejection of the white man's Christianity in her novel *Iola LeRoy,* she reflected a deep faith in the Christianity of Christ in her poetry. One of her earliest poems, "Gone to God," published in the *Anglo African Magazine* of 1859, is a eulogy of a woman who has died and whose soul has gone to heaven. Subsequent poems, such as "A Grain of Sane," "Go Work in My Vineyard," "Renewal of Strength," "The Night of Death" and "The Refiner's Gold" all attest to Harper's strong faith in Christianity.

This faith in Christianity is also seen in Josephine Heard's lines on the death of Abraham Lincoln in her poem "Solace":

> The grave no terror hath, and death no sting,
> For him who fully trusts in Christ the King.[20]

Nineteenth-century women were frequently the victims of alcohol abuse. Usually unable to fend for themselves economically, they were dependent on their husbands, fathers, or brothers for support. Temperance thus became a significant issue for a number of nineteenth-century women, including a few Afro-Americans. The only black poetess who devoted a considerable amount of her energies to this cause was Frances Harper. She lectured widely on the evils of intemperance, and several of her poems dealt with that subject. In "The Total Pledge," a reformed alcoholic takes a drink when asked by his bride to make a toast at their wedding; it was not long thereafter that she wept over a drunkard's grave. In "A Little Child Shall Lead Them," Harper depicted the death of a drunkard's child as the only factor which could influence him to reform. In "Save the Boys" she illustrated how it was too late to save a drunkard, but not too late to save his sons, and in "Nothing and Something" she chronicled how people become alcoholics and criminals.

Like many nineteenth-century women, black women were concerned about the position of the female in their society. Their poetry concerned itself not only with love and marriage, but also with women's rights. Frances Harper rejected the double sexual standard of her day which "excuses all in the male and accuses all in the female,"[21] and she elaborated her views in a poem entitled simply "The Double Standard."

Crime has no sex and yet to-day
  I wear the brand of shame
Whilst he amid the gay and proud
  Still bears an honored name.[22]

Can you blame if I've learned to think
  Your hate of vice a sham,
When you so coldly crushed me down
  And then excused the man.

Alice Dunbar Nelson, wife of the famous poet Paul Lawrence Dunbar, in her poem "I Sit and Sew" drew a vivid contrast between the task of sewing, acceptable for a woman, and the task of fighting, acceptable for a man. The narrator of "I Sit and Sew" longs to participate in battle, to live the active life of the male, but her task as a female is to passively sit and sew.

I sit and sew—a useless task it seems,
My hands grown tired, my head weighed down
    with dreams
The panoply of war, the martial tread of men.
Grim faced, stern-eyed, gazing beyond the ken
Of lesser souls, whose eyes have not seen Death,
Nor learned to hold their lives but as a breath—
But I must sit and sew.

I sit and sew—my heart aches with desire—
That pageant terrible, that fiercely pouring fire
On wasted fields, and writhing grotesque things
Once men, My soul in pity flings
Appealing cries, yearning only to go
There in that holocaust of hell, those fields of
    woe—
But I must sit and sew.

The little useless seam, the idle patch;
Why dream I here beneath my homely thatch.
When there they lie in sodden mud and rain.
Pitifully calling me, the quick ones and the
    slain?
You need me, Christ! It is no roseate dream
That beckons me—this pretty futile seam.
It stifles me—God, must I sit and sew?[23]

Lest it be believed that nineteenth-century Afro-American poetesses did not write of themselves as lovers, such is not the case. Frances Harper, Cordelia Ray, and especially Josephine Heard wrote some very fine love lyrics. Heard's "The Parting Kiss" reflects a particular charm.

We were waiting at the station,
  Soon the cars would surely start,
Hearts beat high with love's emotion,
  For we knew we soon must part.
On dark lashes seem to glisten
  Tiny crystal tear drops shine;
To the fond voice glad I listen,
  While teary eyes look into mine.[24]

Black women writers of nineteenth-century America in their works offer us the opportunity to explore a dimension of understanding offered by no other group. As Julia Cooper pointed out in *A Voice From the South* (1892), black women face a special dilemma in American society:

> The colored woman of today occupies, one may say, a unique position in this country. . . . She is confronted by both a woman question and a race problem.[25]

Her unique position cannot be completely comprehended by either her black brother nor her white sister and certainly not by the white male. Thus if we wish to understand her unique position in American society we must study her own words as reflected in her writings. Few critics will claim literary greatness for any of the writers mentioned in this paper, but much of their writing was good if not great, and as long as we study good literature as well as great literature, our study should include Afro-American women authors of the nineteenth century.

Notes

1. L. A. Scruggs, *Women of Distinction* (Raleigh, N.C.: L. A. Scruggs Publisher, 1893), p. vi.
2. Bert Lowenberg and Ruth Bogin, *Black Women in 19th Century Life* (University Park: Pennsylvania State University Press, 1976), p. 5.
3. Roseann Bell, Bettye J. Park, and Beverly Guy-Sheftall, *Sturdy Black Bridges* (New York: Anchor Books, 1979), p. xxviii.
4. Sculley Bradley, Richard Beatty, E. Hudson Long, and George Perkins, *The American Tradition in Literature* (New York: Grosset and Dunlap, 1974), p. 34.
5. Bell, Parker, and Guy-Sheftall, p. xxiv.
6. W.E.B. Du Bois: *The Souls of Black Folk* included in *Three Negro Classics,* ed. John Hope Franklin (New York: Avon Books, 1973), p. 215.
7. Sarah Forten quoted in M. A. Majors, *Noted Negro Women* (Chicago: Donohue and Hennebury, 1893), p. 194.
8. Ann Plato, *Essays: Prose and Poetry* (Hartford: n.p., 1841), p. 115.
9. Frances Harper, "The Dying Fugitive," *The Anglo African Magazine,* vol. I (May, 1859), 253-54.
10. Frances Harper, *Sketches of Southern Life* (Philadelphia: Merrihew and Son, 1872), p. 12.
11. Ibid., p. 15.
12. Ibid., p. 16.
13. Clara Ann Thompson, *Songs From the Wayside* (Ross Mogre, Ohio: n.p., 1904), p. 4.
14. Josephine Heard quoted in M. A. Majors, p. 263.
15. Ibid., p. 264.
16. Ibid., p. 265.
17. Cordelia Ray, *Poems* (New York: The Grafton Press, 1910), p. 161.

18. Ibid., p. 166.

19. Thompson, p. 133.

20. Josephine Heard quoted in M. A. Majors, p. 267.

21. Frances Harper, *The Sparrows Fall and Other Poems* (n.p., n.d.), p. 13.

22. Ibid., p. 13.

23. Alice Dunbar Nelson, quoted in Robert Kerlin: *Negro Poets and Their Poems* (Washington, D.C.: Associated Publishers, 1935), pp. 145-46.

24. Josephine Heard, *Morning Glories* (Philadelphia: n.p., 1890), pp. 13-14.

25. Anna Cooper, *A Voice From the South* (Ohio: The Aldine Printing House, 1892), p. 134.

SUSAN COULTRAP-MCQUIN (ESSAY DATE 1990)

Coultrap-McQuin, Susan. "Why Try a Writing Career?: The Ambiguous Cultural Context for Women Writers of the Mid-Nineteenth Century." In *Doing Literary Business: American Women Writers in the Nineteenth Century,* pp. 2-13. Chapel Hill: The University of North Carolina Press, 1990.

In the following excerpt, Coultrap-McQuin details the second-rate treatment that women writers in the nineteenth century received, detailing one incident involving the Atlantic *where women writers were excluded from a dinner party which celebrated the anniversary of the literary magazine.*

On December 17, 1877, H. O. Houghton and Company, publishers of the prestigious *Atlantic Monthly*, hosted a dinner party to celebrate the twentieth anniversary of their literary magazine and the seventieth birthday of one of its major contributors, the poet John Greenleaf Whittier. Among the sixty guests were such famous writers as Henry Wadsworth Longfellow, Ralph Waldo Emerson, Oliver Wendell Holmes, and Samuel Clemens (Mark Twain). Held in the East Room of the fashionable Hotel Brunswick in Boston, the event included a seven-course dinner, served with various wines and followed by lively speeches marking the historic occasion.[1] But one group of *Atlantic* contributors was missing. Women had not been invited to the celebration, even though they were a considerable percentage of the contributors to the *Atlantic* in the 1870s, had been a significant part of the American literary community since before the 1850s, and were good friends with many of the *Atlantic* writers who attended the party, especially with its guest of honor, John Greenleaf Whittier.

Although absent from this important dinner in literary history, women authors were very popular and prominent in the nineteenth century, particularly during and after the 1850s. Statistics clearly reveal their increasing visibility as the nineteenth century passed. Before 1830 about one-third of those who published fiction in the United States were by women. During the antebellum years, almost 40 percent of the novels reviewed in journals and newspapers were women, which suggests that an equally high percentage were being published. Best-seller lists reveal that by the 1850s women were authors of almost half of the popular literary works. Among them was Susan Warner's *Wide, Wide World* (1851), the first of many books of "women's fiction" with sales that went far beyond 100,000 copies. Another, Harriet Beecher Stowe's *Uncle Tom's Cabin* (1852), surpassed the 300,000 mark within the first year of publication. By 1872 women wrote nearly three-quarters of all of the novels published. In the same year, patrons of the Boston Public Library, called for books by E.D.E.N. Southworth, Mary Jane Holmes, and Caroline Lee Hentz more frequently than any other works, and Mary Jane Holmes received a thousand fan letters a week. Women were hardly invisible as writers.[2]

Among the most successful writers between the 1840s and the 1880s were the five women whose careers are examined in depth in later chapters: E.D.E.N. Southworth, Harriet Beecher Stowe, Mary Abigail Dodge (Gail Hamilton), Helen Hunt Jackson (H. H. and Saxe Holm), and Elizabeth Stuart Phelps (Ward). But there were many other women writers from those years whose careers and writings should not be forgotten. Rose Terry Cooke, for instance, so impressed her peers that she was given the lead story in the premier issue of the *Atlantic* in 1857. Harriet Prescott Spofford, short-story writer and poet, intrigued the nation with her story "In a Cellar," published in the *Atlantic* in 1859, and continued to be prominent in literary circles for the rest of the century. Rebecca Harding Davis has been credited with introducing realism to the *Atlantic* with her "Life in the Iron Mills," in 1861. Outside the pages of the *Atlantic,* women were equally successful. Louisa May Alcott, who had published some early work in the *Atlantic,* earned her popular following with the publication by Roberts Brothers of *Little Women* in 1868. The poetry of Louise Chandler Moulton was considered among the finest in the second half of the century. Sara Payson Parton (Fanny Fern) and Sara Jane Lippincott (Grace Greenwood) had thousands of readers for their essays on social and domestic topics, as did Maria Cummins for her novels. The list of well-known women writers could go on.

The prominence of women writers and their absence from the *Atlantic* dinner reveal a major paradox confronting literary historians of the nineteenth century: How can we explain women's persistence and success as writers in the face of attitudes and behaviors that could render them invisible? What ideas and social circumstances sustained their literary work in spite of the frequent devaluation of it? To answer those questions, we need to examine some cultural beliefs and social circumstances in nineteenth-century America that both created the possibility of *woman writer* and devalued her efforts. By doing so, we will begin to discover some reasons why women pursued literary careers.

At the outset, it is important to recognize that women writers caught in the paradox of their situation were often quite outspoken on their own behalf. Not long after the *Atlantic* dinner, the following "bagatelle" appeared in a western newspaper:

> Mr. Houghton's Mistake
>
> We are glad that the lady contributors to the Atlantic, who did not attend the Whittier dinner were not disappointed. Indeed, they had intended all along not to be present, and they so indicated to Mr. Houghton in letters written the very day before the dinner. "I hear it intimated," writes Mrs. Stowe, "that I am to be selected to sit at the right hand of Mr. Whittier. Now, my dear Mr. Houghton, while I'm deeply grateful for the compliment, I cannot accept. I believe in the largest freedom for everybody, and I am sure the gentlemen who participate in the festivities would not be pleased to have their programme embarrassed by the presence of ladies. He, he! I suppose you, know what I mean. One of these days, perhaps the ladies of the Atlantic will have a dinner, and I think they are selfish enough to desire to be alone."
>
> Mr. Houghton read the letter and said, passing his hand through his hair, "I think I have forgotten something. I detect sarcasm in this."
>
> "I am glad, Mr. Houghton," wrote Harriet Prescott Spofford, "that you have decided not to call the ladies from their sylvan solitude. I am deeply gaged in studying the peculiarities of some rushes that grow upon the banks of the beautiful river that rolls on by my door, crystallized at present, by the way—I mean river—in the mellowest moonlight that ever sifted its gold upon a beautiful world; so I couldn't attend anyhow. Thank you for sending no invitation. It would have embarrassed me greatly.
>
> "Have you heard that Mrs. Stowe is about to give a dinner? Are you aware that there is to be a new ladies' magazine? But I cannot write more. Thank you again, and good-bye."
>
> "I am quite confident," said Mr. Houghton, looking worried, "that there is an inadvertence somewhere. It's very singular I didn't [sic] think of these ladies before." He turned wearily and opened a letter from Gail Hamilton [Mary Abigail Dodge].
>
> "Well, my boy," wrote this lady, "so you're going to give a dinner, are you? To Mr. Whittier, the dearest and best for whom my soul longeth? And without us? I didn't think it of you, Mr. Houghton. I was about to say I didn't think anything of you, but I won't. You can thank your true goodness for that. O, say nothing of that last check. Seriously, however, I don't blame you. If there's anything unpleasant in this world, it is a woman in a wide house—I mean in a banquet hall. I will not stop to argue the wine question; I have no liquid by me to create the necessary inspiration. I suppose it would do no good either—you men are determined to have your own way always, and ours are often as possible. I write to say that I won't come, and to insist that Mr. Whittier and the rest shall not break their hearts over it. Sufficient is it on these occasions to break bread, and, perhaps, also heads. I have just seen a circular in behalf of a new ladies' magazine. Have you seen it? Excuse me now. I have an engagement to spank the Administration at this very moment. Do you know, by the way, that Mrs. Spofford is about to give a grand dinner to the lady contributors of the Atlantic?"
>
> "Alas! for my stupidity!" remarked Mr. Houghton, his face growing pale, and his knees knocking together. "This great moral earthquake will be after me next."
>
> "Oh, Mr. Houghton," wrote H. H. [Helen Hunt Jackson], enthusiastically, "I am so pleased to hear of the honor to grand old Mr. Whittier. My pleasure is only exceeded by my joy that I am not to be there. I should be highly honored by being permitted to be in such company, of course, but I am timid, and I fear that literary men do 'cut up' dreadfully—you will pardon the expression—on these occasions. Do you know, Mr. Houghton, that Gail Hamilton talks of starting a magazine? and they do say that there is to be a grand literary reunion at her house, or rather at the house of Mr. Blaine. I shall not be able to send you anything for some time to come."
>
> "Merciful Heavens!" exclaimed Mr. Houghton, "this must be a conspiracy. They are all of them pleased, and yet they all seem to be contemplating the worst kind of retaliation. I do not understand this!"
>
> He turned with a sigh to a letter from Philadelphia. "You will accept my regrets," said Rebecca Harding Davis. "I cannot possibly be present. I have not received my invitation, but of course it has been delayed in the mail. However, none of that brilliant gathering will feel my absence. I am not so presuming as to suppose that such a slight vacancy in so immense a place will be noticeable. And I do know, Mr. Houghton, that gentlemen delight to be by themselves at times. I hear Helen Hunt and Louisa M. Alcott have put their heads together in behalf of a ladies' magazine and I understand that Rose Terry is to give a dinner to

> several well-known writers of the gentler sex. Such a magazine might be profitable, and I know the dinner would be delightful.
>
> "Now this is the dreadful," said Mr. Houghton, striking the desk with his clenched hand. "I have actually been applying the paper-cutter to my own nose. It is the stupidest thing I ever did in my life. Why, oh! why could I not have seen this result before?" He thought very fast a moment, and then his face brightened and he laughed right out. "I have it!" he exclaimed. "Two months hence there shall be a dinner to the lady contributors of the Atlantic Monthly. It shall be given in honor of Gail Hamilton's seventieth birthday."[3]

Henry O. Houghton's mistake in not inviting "lady contributors" reflected the paradoxical nature of nineteenth-century beliefs about women writers. On the one hand, Houghton often published and paid well for literary works by women that accorded with is Victorian sense of morality, didacticism, and literary excellence; on the other hand, he never considered women's literature to be as important as men's. A rather typical gentleman of his time, he believed in male superiority and the more honorable place of women in the home. No doubt he felt he could relax more with men and wine than with women and water (which he served at a breakfast for Oliver Wendell Holmes in 1880 when he did invite women).[4] In many respects, Henry Houghton exemplified the ambiguous response of nineteenth-century American society to the woman writer.

"Mr. Houghton's Mistake" illustrates the variety of responses women showed to those attitudes. Whether the article was actually written by one or more of the women parodied in it (the humor and style suggest Mary Abigail Dodge), or by another humorist, it demonstrates women's ability to define themselves beyond their culture's most limiting values and expectations. It is absolutely true, of course, that women's lives and careers were controlled by their society's patriarchal perspectives; even after building successful careers, women had to respond to social circumstances, stereotypes, and assumptions about women and women writers that were largely created and perpetuated by men. Nevertheless, women were not uniformly molded by those social expectations; they developed a variety of responses, such as those illustrated in the letters to Houghton—responses that ranged from Spofford's poetic conformity to Dodge's abrasive defiance. Even when faced by cultural prescriptions and social institutions that undervalued women's capabilities and achievements in comparison to men's, women demonstrated remarkable individuality and determination in their pursuit of a literary career. "Mr. Houghton's Mistake" is a good reminder that patriarchal perspectives did not completely define women's options nor their views of themselves in the world. If patriarchal views had been wholly accepted, the article would never have been written.

The article also makes the important point that, by virtue of their connections with one another and their popularity with their audiences, women were not without power in the literary arena. "Mr. Houghton's Mistake" demonstrates, even if through fiction, that there was a network among the women writers that sustained and encouraged each others' efforts. Futhermore, these writers had an audience familiar enough with their works to understand the humorist's allusions to spanking the Administration and meeting in Mr. Blaine's house. (See Chapter 5 on Mary Abigail Dodge.) Collectively at least, and in many cases individually, women writers were important to the economics of the literary marketplace; if they decided to start a new magazine, it would have to be taken seriously. In fact, their threat (or those of the humorist) seem to have had some impact on Houghton himself, although they did not prevent the same sort of discrimination against women writers from happening again and again. Although Houghton never gave dinner for Mary Abigail Dodge, he was careful to include women in his next big celebration, the Holmes breakfast in 1880, and he honored Harriet Beecher Stowe similarly in 1882.[5]

In short, the position of women writers in the mid-nineteenth century—say, from the 1840s to the 1880s—was paradoxical: they had a place in the literary world, yet that world often rendered them invisible. The explanation of the paradox lies, first, in the ambiguous nature of cultural messages to and about women. While the ideology of woman's sphere in the nineteenth century could restrict women's participation in society, other messages about ideal Americans and about authorship sometimes did accommodate women. The changing social circumstances of women, particularly middle-class ones, also provided opportunities for fuller public participation, despite messages that woman's place was in the home. Both cultural prescriptions and social circumstances provided the context within which women writers pursued their careers.

The subjects of this study grew up in antebellum America, a time of great possibilities created by industrial and urban growth, westward expansion, and improved communications. They were aware of voluntary associations, utopian experiments, and reform crusades, including those for abolition and women's rights, that were changing the ways people ordered their private and public lives. And they probably heard much debate about individualism, equality, and self-government, for there was not unanimity on what those ideals meant or to whom they applied.[6] In addition, they, like their brothers, were encouraged to adopt ethical views that historians have come to label "Victorian."

To simplify greatly, we can say that American Victorianism encouraged moral, didactic, and patriarchal approaches to life. Victorians promoted strict sexual codes, social responsibility, and genteel, patriarchal social standards. They stressed hard work, deferred gratification, sobriety, and conscientiousness—qualities that were essential to an industrializing society. They also encouraged competition but warned that too much of it would destroy the rational social order.[7] Victorians urged conformity to genteel social standards as the humane, democratic route to status and success. Sentimentalism and emotional expression, according to them, were inappropriate in the business world but acceptable in literature, the church, and the home—all three areas seen primarily as the province of women.

The ideal American who attempted to conform to these views was said to have "character." A person of character felt a sense of obligation to promote the general welfare of society as well as to improve the self—educationally, culturally, and morally. In their words, Victorians wanted "well-informed minds, pure hearts, and refined manners."[8] With that end in mind, they worked to master their weaknesses through self-discipline and restraint. Character building, a lifelong process, was supposed to begin in the (ideal middle-class) home under the direction of a devoted mother.[9]

Though espoused by the majority of Americans (the dissenters coming particularly but not entirely from outside the white middle class), Victorian ideals were most thoroughly articulated by northern, middle-class, Protestant males and carried the stamp of their class, race, and gender.[10] These men assumed that everyone should adopt their values, and, in fact, their ideas ultimately permeated much of nineteenth-century society. As public education became more common, male and female students across the country learned lessons reflecting Victorian beliefs. In addition, the rapidly expanding publishing industry, as demonstrated in the next chapter, became a mouthpiece for the expression of Victorian values. Orators and community programs took Victorian values to rural hamlets, spreading the worldview still further.

While the values of American Victorianism were derived primarily from the values of white males and were meant to apply primarily to men in society, they were also heard by and had an influence on women. We can see this in the women writers studied in this book. E.D.E.N. Southworth, for example, argued strongly in defense of the moral rectitude of her writings, as did most other Victorians. Mary Abigail Dodge urged women to develop their character more than their looks. Harriet Beecher Stowe felt it appropriate to speak out against Lord Byron's sexual immorality. Other women writers expressed Victorian views when they encouraged genteel manners, hard work, and the social importance of familial ties. To some extent anyway, Victorian perspectives were shared by women and men.

But Victorians also expected men and women to be essentially different and to have separate "spheres" of activity; women, for example, were thought to be more sentimental and emotional and less interested in competitiveness and the public arena than men were. Although the ideology of separate spheres could be restrictive to women, it also gave them an area of authority (the home) and an expertise (domesticity and morality) that some of them eventually used to justify an expanded role in society. Within their separate sphere women developed bonds with other women that nourished a rich female culture and spawned the collective activity of nineteenth-century women in voluntary associations and reform crusades. Nevertheless, the rhetoric of separate spheres usually emphasized women's dependence and subordination.[11]

Like other nineteenth-century values, the belief in separate spheres was both a cause of and a response to what was actually happening to women and men in their lives. As America industrialized, adult activities were more frequently segregated by sex than they had been in earlier times.[12] The separation between home and business meant that the control of economic resources shifted from the home to employed males in the marketplace, leaving women and children in the middle-class or affluent home, who did not have income-producing jobs, in a more subordinate and dependent position. The ideology of separate spheres seems to have arisen to justify these middle-and upper-class circumstances, though the concept was used as an ideal against which to judge people in all classes. Such a prescription was not simply imposed by men to justify the patriarchal social order, although men certainly did argue for separate spheres to that end. Women themselves, seeking to cope with the social changes, often embraced the ideology of separate spheres and argued that their position was one of significance, not subordination. Others in varying degrees chafed against its restrictions and demanded equal rights.

But what exactly was a nineteenth-century woman supposed to be? Actually, there was no single view of womanhood, but a continuum of views ranging from conservative to more liberal perspectives.[13] The conservative view was widespread in the media of antebellum America, which included books on etiquette, sermons, literary gift books, and annuals; those who supported this view insisted that "true women" were naturally domestic, submissive, and morally pure. The more liberal perspective, which was definitely a minority view in antebellum America, although one that increased in popularity as the century passed, was expressed by proponents of women's education, legal rights, suffrage, and career opportunities; this group maintained that "true women" were normally superior to men and valued family relations, but could and should be as self-reliant and competent as men. According to the conservative view, women were emotional and had few rational capabilities; according to the more liberal view, women were capable of affection *and*intelligence. The conservatives believed that women were assigned by God and nature to their separate sphere of activity and should rejoice in that. The liberals felt that the restrictions on woman's sphere, imposed only by social circumstances, should be eliminated, while the values of the sphere—nurturance, love, and morality—should be spread throughout society.

The conservative view has been called the "Cult of True Womanhood" because of what appears from a twentieth-century perspective to be an obsessive, almost ritualistic repetition of very narrow views of women.[14] The liberal view might be called the "Vision of New Womanhood" because it often provided the justification for women's participation in many new areas of society, including the literary marketplace, in the nineteenth century. In between the two poles were various arguments, including those for honoring Domesticity—the role of the mother in the home. What all the views shared in common was a belief in women's morality, spirituality, and nurturance; they can be distinguished by their disagreements over (1) whether those values restricted women to the home or justified their participation throughout society; and (2) whether they made women superior to, subordinate to, or separate but equal to men.

True Womanhood, the conservative view, influenced most writings about nineteenth-century women, especially, but not exclusively, before the Civil War. For example, Mary Jane Holmes's minister described the private life of this best-selling writer in its terms, saying she "possesses in a high degree, those Christian graces and virtues which alone give lustre to mental accomplishment. . . . She prefers the quiet of home life. . . . Her piety is deep, serene and unostentatious." With a similar vision of purity, piety, and domesticity in mind, Harriet Prescott Spofford praised the poet Louise Chandler Moulton as "a being of absolute uprightness, incapable of untruth, faithful to her ideals, ingenuous, confiding, unsuspicious, without guile, caring nothing for place or power, for social rank and position, or for wealth; of childlike nature throughout life,' a triumphant woman, but always a child." Indeed, the image of True Womanhood was so appealing that even advocates of expanding woman's role in society, like Sara Jane Lippincott (Grace Greenwood), sometimes felt compelled to use it, saying, for instance, "true feminine genius is ever timid, doubtful, and clingingly dependent; a perpetual childhood. A true woman shrinks instinctively from greatness."[15]

Despite the fervor of these claims, none of the above descriptions accurately reflect or describe the authors themselves. Holmes was a smart, determined, and ambitious writer; Moulton, a woman capable of using literary friendships to her own advantage in building her career; and Lippincott, a proponent of woman suffrage. Yet so luminous was the ideal of the True Woman that other characteristics of women often fell into deep shadow and were not seen or remarked upon at all. Thus, behaviors demonstrating ambition or assertion or the use of literary influence were often denied or ignored, and, if seen, were criticized resoundingly. In other words, while there is ample evidence that women themselves did not wholly conform to prescriptions of True Womanhood, nevertheless, those prescriptions exerted a strong influence on what was seen, understood, and said about women's lives. True Womanhood was the ideal against which most women's activities, including their literary ones, were judged.

Being woman was the primary fact and being womanly the major glory, according to proponents of True Womanhood. A woman of her time,

Ellen Olney Kirk, called it "the essential need of being womanly" against which other characteristics and motives faded. From this perspective being a True Woman was a vocation in itself, more distinguished than any other. According to its most conservative proponents, therefore, being a True Woman was incompatible with being a woman writer. As one such commentator said, "If women were wise they would understand that they have a mission quite as grand as that of literary authorship. It is the mission of keeping alive for men certain ideas, and ideals too, which would soon pass out of the world." The True Woman's special responsibility was to be guardian of the cultural, religious, and moral values of Victorian society in America. She was to maintain the noncommercial values of love, hope, and charity in a secular age fascinated with business, competition, and endless expansion. With her innocence and charms, woman was to create a home life that was a refuge for men and children from the cruelty and unpredictability of the world.[16]

Literary critics of the period, like most other social commentators, not only accepted but also preached the conservative vision of True Womanhood. While they commended male characters in novels for displaying individuality, they praised female characters who were True Women: pious, pure, domestic, and pleasing to others.[17] For example, a critic in the *Christian Examiner* (September 1852) said of the main character in *The Sunny Side* that she was "the good man's crown" because she was "the cheerer of her husband in despondency, the kind and wise guide of her children in the right way, with modesty prompting the wish to shrink from publicity, but high principle curbing the indulgence of that wish, she appears the true pastor's wife, ready when occasion calls to be the friend and counsellor of those around her, but finding her peculiar sphere of duty in her own home." Like twentieth-century advice columnists, nineteenth-century literary reviewers, both male and female, encouraged female readers to pattern their lives after those heroines who best conformed to the role of True Woman. Reviewers praised most highly those novels that kept women in their sphere, rather than legitimizing their discontent with it. They also created idealized descriptions of literary women, like those quoted above, as models for other women to follow. Finally, they usually argued that "women ought to write not as individuals, but as exemplars of their sex." The conservative message of True Womanhood was widespread.

Despite its popularity, True Womanhood as an ideal was criticized in its own time by liberals espousing a Vision of New Womanhood. The most radical of the critics, like the suffragist Elizabeth Cady Stanton, argued that women were, most importantly, human beings like men with aspirations for achievement and only incidentally wives and mothers with their special responsibilities. Moderate critics like Catharine Beecher saw womanhood as primary but would not concede that this made women weaker or less important than men.[18] Actually, most liberals agreed with conservatives that women were prepared to nurture and care for others because they were morally superior, but liberals also argued that women could and should move beyond the home into volunteer and career opportunities to make society a better place in which to live. Many thought men should imitate women's piety, purity, and gentleness; conversely, women in their sphere or beyond it should be as intelligent, self-reliant, and courageous as men. This Vision of New Womanhood sometimes called for blending masculine and feminine characteristics as the nineteenth century defined them, but it usually did not go so far as to say that women and men could be the same. As Mary Abigail Dodge (Gail Hamilton) wrote, "They make a great mistake, who think a strong, brave, self-poised woman is unwomanly. The stronger she is, the truer she is to her womanly instincts."[19]

Women themselves varied in their attitudes toward their society's prescriptions for womanhood, but whatever their view, the values they were socialized to accept did not make them wholly distinct from their male counterparts. With men they were expected to share Victorian beliefs in, for example, moral purity, self-improvement, hard work, genteel behavior, and, in some cases, self-reliance. When articulating any of the shared values, women might be heard as *women* or as *Victorians* like the men. This is an important point because it begins to explain why women were ambivalently accepted in the literary world and also how they might step beyond the prescriptions of separate spheres. The rhetoric of separate coupled with that of Victorianism helped to create an ambiguous intellectual context for women's participation in society beyond the home: one in which at least middle-class white women were both insiders (Victorians) and outsiders (women), or, as the 1877 *Atlantic* dinner illustrated, both prominent writers and uninvited guests. While this intellectual context made responses to women contradictory, it simultaneously created the possibility that some women would believe they had something to say to the world in regard to either those shared values or their separate sphere.

Notes

1. This event is usually remembered for Clemens's speech about Emerson, Longfellow, and Holmes. See Ballou, *The Building of the House,* 218-19.

2. Statistics in this paragraph can be found in Dexter, *Career Women of America,* 97; Baym, *Novels, Readers, and Reviewers,* 100; Hart, *The Popular Book,* 306-7; Tebbel, *History of Book Publishing,* 2:170; Garrison, "Immoral Fiction," 81; Reynolds, *The Fiction Factory,* 38.

3. Reprinted in Derby, *Fifty Years among Authors,* 283-85. The final joke was that Mary Abigail Dodge (Gail Hamilton) was only fifty-five years old at the time.

4. Scudder, *Henry Oscar Houghton,* 136, 150; Ballou, 268.

5. For an example of continued discrimination, see "Our 'Forty Immortals.'" Houghton, however, had been somewhat sensitized. He defended himself in his opening remarks at the Holmes breakfast, claiming he had been too shy to ask the "ladies" to attend before. Others in attendance also commented on the presence of women. See "The Holmes Breakfast."

6. Bartlett, *The American Mind,* 32-72; Sara M. Evans, *Born for Liberty,* 67-92.

7. Baym, for example, finds that, in the reviews of literary works, individualism was applauded only when expressed on behalf of social stability. Baym, *Novels, Readers, and Reviewers,* 193. On sentimentalism in Victorian culture, see Douglas, *The Feminization of American Culture.*

8. Said by a character in the work of Catharine Sedgwick quoted in Kelley, *Private Woman, Public Stage,* 67. For a fuller discussion of Victorianism, see Howe, "American Victorianism as a Culture," and the special issue of *American Quarterly* in which it appears.

9. See Ryan, "The Empire of the Mother."

10. This phenomenon persisted through the Gilded Age. See Tomsich, *Genteel Endeavor.*

11. See Sara M. Evans, esp. 70-76; Woloch, *Women and the American Experience,* 116; Epstein, *The Politics of Domesticity.*

12. See Kessler-Harris, *Out to Work.*

13. An excellent discussion of the connections between True Womanhood and New Womanhood is found in Hersh, "The 'True Woman.'"

14. Welter, "Cult of True Womanhood."

15. Quotes in this paragraph are from a passage quoted in Derby, 574; from Spofford, Introduction, xviii-xix; and from a passage quoted in Wood, "'Scribbling Women,'" 5.

16. Quotes in this paragraph are from Kirk, "Women Fiction Writers of America," 2003, and "Literary Women," 610. See also Jeffrey, "The Family as Utopian Retreat."

17. Baym, *Novels, Readers, and Reviewers,* 97-107. The quotes that follow in this paragraph are from reviews quoted in Baym, 102, and from Baym, 249. *The Sunny Side* was written by the mother of Elizabeth Stuart Phelps (Ward), who is discussed in Chapter 7. It should be pointed out, as Baym does (p. 104), that reviewers did not understand the subversive implications of some of the nineteenth-century heroines any more than those describing True Women saw the real women behind the expected image. See also Baym, 172.

18. Hersh, 273-74; Sklar, *Catharine Beecher.*

19. Hamilton, "Men and Women," in *Country Living,* 123. Hersh (p. 276) also makes this point.

Works Cited

Ballou, Ellen B. *The Building of the House: Houghton Mifflin's Formative Years.* Boston: Houghton Mifflin, 1970.

Bartlett, Irving H. *The American Mind in the Mid-Nineteenth Century.* New York: Thomas V. Crowell Company, 1967.

Baym, Nina. *Novels, Readers, and Reviewers: Responses to Fiction in Antebellum America.* Ithaca, N.Y.: Cornell University Press, 1984.

Derby, James C. *Fifty Years among Authors, Books, and Publishers.* New York: G. W. Carleton and Co., 1884.

Dexter, Elisabeth Anthony. *Career Women of America, 1776-1840.* Francestown, N.H.: Marshall Jones Company, 1950.

Douglas, Ann. *The Feminization of American Culture.* New York: Avon, 1977.

Epstein, Barbara Leslie. *The Politics of Domesticity: Women, Evangelism, and Temperance in Nineteenth-Century America.* Middletown, Conn.: Wesleyan University Press, 1981.

Evans, Sara M. *Born for Liberty: A History of Women in America.* New York: The Free Press, 1989.

Garrison, Dee. "Immoral Fiction in the Late Victorian Library." *American Quarterly* 28 (September 1976): 71-89.

Hamilton, Gail [Mary Abigail Dodge]. *Country Living and Country Thinking.* Boston: Ticknor and Fields, 1865.

Hart, James D. *The Popular Book: A History of America's Literary Taste.* Berkeley: University of California Press, 1963.

Hersh, Blanche Glassman. "The 'True Woman' and the 'New Woman' in Nineteenth-Century America: Feminist Abolitionists and a New Concept of True Womanhood." In *Woman's Being, Woman's Place: Female Identity and Vocation in American History,* edited by Mary Kelley, 271-82. G. K. Hall and Company, 1979.

"The Holmes Breakfast." *Atlantic Monthly* 45, no. 268 Supplement (February 1880): 1-24.

Howe, Daniel Walker. "American Victorianism as a Culture." *American Quarterly* 27, no. 5 (December 1975): 507-32.

Jeffrey, Kirk. "The Family as Utopian Retreat from the City: The Nineteenth-Century Contribution." *Soundings* (1972): 21-41.

Kelley, Mary. *Private Woman, Public Stage: Literary Domesticity in Nineteenth-Century America.* New York: Oxford University Press, 1984.

Kessler-Harris, Alice. *Out to Work: A History of Wage-Earning Women in the United States.* New York: Oxford University Press, 1982.

Kirk, Ellen Olney. "Women Fiction Writers of America." In *What America Owes Women,* edited by Lydia Hoyt Farmer, 194-204. Buffalo, N.Y.: C. W. Moulton, 1893.

"Literary Women." *The Living Age* (June 25, 1864): 609-10.

"Our 'Forty Immortals.'" *The Critic and Good Literature* 4 (April 12, 1884): 169-70.

Reynolds, Quentin. *The Fiction Factory, or From Pulp Row to Quality Street.* New York: Random House, 1955.

Ryan, Mary P. "The Empire of the Mother: American Writing about Domesticity, 1830-1860." *Women and History* 2, 3 (1982).

Scudder, Horace E. *Henry Oscar Houghton: A Biographical Outline.* Cambridge, Mass.: Riverside Press, 1897.

Sklar, Kathryn Kish. *Catharine Beecher: A Study in American Domesticity.* New Haven: Yale University Press, 1973.

Spofford, Harriet Prescott. Introduction to *The Poems of Louise Chandler Moulton,* by Louise Chandler Moulton, v-xix. Boston: Little, Brown, and Company, 1909.

Tebbel, John. *A History of Book Publishing in the United States.* 4 vols. New York: R. R. Bowker, 1975.

Tomsich, John. *A Genteel Endeavor: American Culture and Politics in the Gilded Age.* Stanford, Calif.: Stanford University Press, 1971.

Welter, Barbara. "The Cult of True Womanhood, 1820-1860." *American Quarterly* 18 (Summer 1966): 151-75.

Woloch, Nancy. *Women and the American Experience.* New York: Alfred A. Knopf, 1984.

Wood, Ann D. " The 'Scribbling Women' and Fanny Fern: Why Women Wrote." *American Quarterly* 23 (Spring 1971): 3-24.

Abbreviations

AAS: American Antiquarian Society, Worcester, Mass.

AHS: Andover Historical Society, Andover, Mass.

BC: Bowdoin College Library, Brunswick, Maine

BPL: Boston Public Library, Boston, Mass.

BYU: Brigham Young University Library, Provo, Utah

CC: Colorado College: Tutt Library, Colorado Springs, Colo.

CHS: Chicago Historical Society, Chicago, Ill.

CrU: Cornell University: John M.Olin Library, Ithaca, N.Y.

CU: Columbia University: Rare Book and Manuscript Library, New York, N.Y.

DU: Duke University: William R. Perkins Library, Durham, N.C.

EI: Essex Institute: James Duncan Phillips Library, Salem, Mass.

HC: Haverford College Library, Haverford, Pa.

HL: Huntington Library, San Marino, Calif.

HSP: Historical Society of Pennsylvania, Philadelphia, Pa.

HU: Harvard University: Houghton Library, Cambridge, Mass.

JL: Jones Library, Amherst, Mass.

LC: Library of Congress, Washington, DC.

LSU: Louisiana State University Libraries, Baton Rouge, La.

MHS: Massachusetts Historical Society, Boston, Mass.

MNH: Minnesota Historical Society, St. Paul, Minn.

NPL: New York Public Library: Rare Books and Manuscripts Division, Astor, Lenox, and Tilden Foundations, New York, N.Y.

PU: Princeton University Library, Princeton, N.J.

RH: Rutherford B. Hayes Presidential Center, Fremont, Ohio

RS: Radcliffe College: Arthur and Elizabeth Schlesinger Library, Cambridge, Mass.

SC: Smith College Library: Sophia Smith Collection, Northampton, Mass.

S-D: Stowe-Day Foundation, Hartford, Conn.

SU: Stanford University Libraries: Department of Special Collections and University Archives, Stanford, Calif.

TC: Trinity College: Watkins Library, Hartford, Conn.

VC: Vassar College Library, Poughkeepsie, N.Y.

UV: University of Virginia: Special Collections Department, Manuscripts Division, Clifton Waller Barrett Library, Charlottesville, Va.

YU: Yale University: Collection of American Literature, Beinecke Rare Book and Manuscript Library, New Haven, Conn.

MARJORIE PRYSE (ESSAY DATE 1997)

SOURCE: Pryse, Marjorie. "Origins of American Literary Regionalism: Gender in Irving, Stowe, and Longstreet." In *Breaking Boundaries: New Perspectives on Women's Regional Writing,* edited by Sherrie A. Inness and Diana Royer, pp. 17-37. Iowa City: University of Iowa Press, 1997.

In the following essay, Pryse argues that Harriet Beecher Stowe helped pioneer the literary genre of regionalism that allowed her and other women to seize greater narrative freedom beyond the traditional space allotted to women.

Any attempt to construct a narrative of the origins of regionalism must begin by acknowledging the problematic status of such an attempt in a critical climate where both "origins" and "regionalism" are themselves contested terms. In a survey of this problem, Amy Kaplan builds her discussion of late-nineteenth-century regionalism on the post-Civil War cultural project of national reunification. For Kaplan, this project involved forgetting a past that included "a contested relation between national and racial identity" as well as "reimagining a distended industrial nation as an extended clan sharing a 'common inheritance' in its imagined rural origins" ("Nation" 242, 251). My own project in this essay takes up the concept of origins from an earlier historical point than does Kaplan. In her first published fiction, "A New England Sketch" (1834) (or "Uncle Lot," as she later retitled it when she included it in *The May-flower* [1843]), Harriet Beecher Stowe associates regionalism with remembering that American literary culture emerged from a contested relation in which men were victorious, that, for Stowe, the values of women's sphere offered a moral ground for the construction of nation, and that any subsequent reinvention of national origins that did not take into account the contest over men's and women's "spheres" of influence would indeed serve as cultural "forgetting."

Philip Fisher complicates our understanding of the term "regionalism" by defining it as a series of "episodes" in American cultural history that have in common a politicized "struggle" within representation," an ongoing cultural civil war that serves as "the counterelement to central myths within American studies" (243, 233). For the nineteenth century, sectional voices split along geographical lines; in the late nineteenth and early twentieth centuries, massive immigration between 1870 and 1914 produced "a regionalism of languages, folk customs, humor, music and beliefs" set against processes of Americanization; "the regionalism of our own times . . . is one of gender and race" (242-43). Suggesting that such a counterelement makes a critical move from myths (of a unified America) to rhetorics (as sites of cultural work), Fisher identifies Harriet Beecher Stowe as one of the "masters" of "collaborative and implicational relations between writer or speaker and culture" (237). For critics interested in how literature accomplishes what Jane Tompkins in *Sensational Designs* described as "cultural work," Stowe appears to have joined the late-twentieth-century conversation over the relationship between literature and culture.

Far from viewing Stowe herself and the particular form of regionalism she took for her fiction as a "diminished thing," a "subordinate order" (to cite James M. Cox's dismissive critical assessment of regionalism in *Columbia Literary History of the United States* [764-65]), we can view her work as engaged in a rhetoric of cultural dislocation, a project of inventing alternatives to national views on slavery, women's education, the profession of literature, and women's roles in nation building. Joan Hedrick observes in the preface to her recent biography of Stowe that the hostility to Stowe's writing that judged her work "to be amateur, unprofessional, and 'bad art'" emerged "in the 1860s between the dominant women writers and the rising literary establishment of men who were determined to displace them" (*Harriet Beecher Stowe* ix). As I shall demonstrate; although Stowe began writing before the Civil War and appears to equate regionalism with a geographical concept—and memory—of New England life in her first published work, she was from the beginning engaged in the kind of rhetorical contestation Philip Fisher associates with "new Americanist" concepts of regionalism. For Stowe, this cultural work involved gender and the role of women in the nation—a rhetorical struggle that remains unresolved.

In writing her first sketch Stowe discovers that the process of conversion, a distant forerunner of what feminists in the 1970s termed "consciousness raising," can provide the narrative intention for a work of fiction, thereby allowing ministers' daughters (both Stowe herself and Grace Griswold in the sketch) to imagine expanding their authority in literary and domestic spheres. My own understanding of conversion in Stowe is similar to that of Jane Tompkins, who writes in her analysis of *Uncle Tom's Cabin* that for Stowe, "historical change takes place only through religious conversion" but that such conversion for Stowe has "revolutionary potential" (133, 145). Tompkins argues that Stowe pushes her beliefs "to an extreme and by insisting that they be applied universally, not just to one segregated corner of civil life, but to the conduct of all human affairs, Stowe means to effect a radical transformation of her society" (145). In "Uncle Lot," conversion becomes a model for narrative form as well as a transformative theme: Stowe is attempting to "convert" her (male) readers to the power of women's narrative authority.

In presenting conversion as both the source of action and the goal of fiction in "Uncle Lot," Stowe anticipates the empathic point of view characteristic of women regionalist writers and their narrators, thus originating the cultural and literary developmental line of the regionalist tradition. If for the Beechers conversion required a "private change of heart" (Sklar 27), the conversion of evolving American literary culture would require a cultural change of heart. And in this way, from her earliest published sketch, Stowe attempted to transform the direction of American fiction with the same passion that her sister Catharine addressed to the transformation of the profession of teaching; for both sisters, teaching and storytelling were forms of preaching, and women were suited to practice all three. By the time Harriet Beecher came to view herself as a writer, she already knew that American women wrote and published their work. Yet creating a legitimate arena within which American women might exert national influence would require for Stowe not the overt confrontation with paternal authority which had characterized her sister's experience of conversion, during which Catharine proved unable or unwilling to achieve conversion on her father, Lyman's, terms (Sklar 31-38), but the subtle, persuasive, affectional process of eliciting inner change. For women to achieve a position in American literary culture, Stowe's early work indicates, men, especially those men like Washington Irving who were already producing an "American" fiction, must also be "converted" to those same qualities that Catharine Beecher had argued "placed women closer to the source of moral authority and hence established their social centrality" (Sklar 83). Such an argument requires fuller elaboration and a more detailed and historicized reading than we have previously granted Stowe's first sketch and its rhetorical strategies. For while literary historians have recognized the contributions of humor of the Old Southwest, another "minor" literary tradition, to the development of American fiction, we have yet to acknowledge regionalism as either a narrative tradition in its own right or one that substantially influenced the direction of American literature.[1]

Although "Uncle Lot" has been ignored by literary historians, critics, and theorists alike, the sketch marks a significant moment in the development of American literature in the nineteenth century, and I read it in the context of this moment. Remaining within a critical regionalism that continues to define itself along the lines of Philip Fisher's "struggle within representation," I trace evidence of both conflict and influence that established Stowe from the beginning, even before the publication of *Uncle Tom's Cabin* in 1852, as a writer for whom civil war was as viable a cultural concept as it became an economic and political one by the 1860s.

"Uncle Lot" locates Stowe's early rhetorical position on the question of women's potential contribution to American authorship, and the position involves cultural battle lines and opposing sides. I suggest that we may view literary regionalism as the emergence of the "Ichabod Crane school" of American narrative, despite Crane's ignominious defeat at the hands of Brom Bones, and that we can identify Stowe's sketch as her attempt to "convert" American readers to the values of what Irving had termed, albeit disparagingly, the "female circle" and the "sleepy region." In the process Stowe creates the possibility of regionalism itself as a literary form capable of conferring literary authority on American women. What we might term the "Brom Bones school" emerges through the work of Augustus Baldwin Longstreet in *Georgia Scenes* (1835) and in the fiction of the Old Southwest humorists of the 1840s and 1850s, who respond to the question of gender either by relegating women characters to the source and object of sexual humor or by omitting women from their tales altogether. Stephen Railton's extensive discussion of southwestern humor and its "national audience of men" (91) makes a clear case for the gendered separation of early-nineteenth-century American fiction, suggesting that "gentlemen" themselves felt "excluded and powerless" in American society but "could find vicarious compensation in the rough world of the humorists, where it is women who do not matter, except as occasional objects of unfrustrated resentment" (103-04). The women writers of domestic and didactic scenes of American life, Catharine Sedgwick, Lydia Huntley Sigourney, and Stowe's sister Catharine Beecher, who influenced both Stowe and later writers in the regionalist tradition, occupied entirely different rhetorical and cultural territory from the humorists. Even the editors who published the works of these writers—William T. Porter and his *Spirit of the Times,* and James T. Hall and the *Western Monthly Magazine*—take up opposing or "separate" positions on the topic of women as cultural subjects. We can view the humor of the Old Southwest and early regionalism as manifestations of two possible but mutually exclusive gender-specific directions for the development of American fiction before the Civil War.

Although "Uncle Lot" announces a departure in American fiction from the sketches of Stowe's male predecessors and contemporaries, her own female successors would more fully delineate the features of regionalism and more explicitly link these features to women's lives in nineteenth-century America than Stowe herself did. Conversion based on "private change of heart" (Sklar 27) in Stowe reemerges as the "collaborative and implicational relations between writer or speaker and culture" (Fisher 237), to extend Fisher's formulation beyond Stowe herself, and becomes a feature of regionalist narrative.

Later in the century, beginning with Alice Cary's *Clovernook* sketches of the early 1850s and including such writers as Rose Terry Cooke, Celia Thaxter, Sarah Orne Jewett, Mary Wilkins Freeman, Zitkala-Śa, Grace King, Kate Chopin, Alice

Dunbar-Nelson, Sui Sin Far, and Mary Austin, American women writers would refine regionalism as an approach to narrative that would develop parallel to but divergent from the techniques and forms of local color fiction. Judith Fetterley and I have made this argument in the introduction to *American Women Regionalists,* our collection of some of the central works in the regionalist tradition, and an analysis of the cultural moment in which "Uncle Lot" first appears provides early evidence that regionalism and "local color," though often conflated, do represent different articulations of and attitudes toward regional subjects.

Without Stowe's own later work, "Uncle Lot" would not assume the significance it does, but Stowe further elaborated the themes of "Uncle Lot" in her most important fiction. *Uncle Tom's Cabin,* as I have indicated, further develops the theme of conversion. *The Pearl of Orr's Island* (1862) establishes women's development and education as a contested site (see Fetterley, "Only a Story"). And in great late works, *Oldtown Folks* (1869) and *Sam Lawson's Old-town Fireside Stories* (1872), Stowe continues to propose regionalism as a direction for American fiction. Sam Lawson, Stowe's narrator in these works, is a more successful and benign version of Rip Van Winkle. Stowe's persistence in developing these themes gives her first published sketch renewed significance in our own century, as we attempt to trace the origins of literary authority for American women writers and attempt, as well, to fairly assess their contribution to nineteenth-century American literature. Writing regional sketches in particular gave Stowe a way of educating her contemporaries. Stowe makes it possible for her readers to take a second look at characters others might find laughable or without literary value, such as Uncle Lot himself, or, later, in *The Pearl of Orr's Island,* Aunts Roxy and Ruey—rural, female, elderly, and otherwise disenfranchised persons. Reading "Uncle Lot" in its various contexts thus opens up, to use Stowe's own language in the sketch, a "chestnut burr" of genre in American fiction; the sketch kept alive for Stowe the possibility that her female successors might experience the authority of authorship, thereby "converting" her own readers to the idea that women's voices and women's values can influence her own postrevolutionary and our own postmodern American culture.

Two conclusions become possible from reexamining Stowe's first sketch within the context of early-nineteenth-century writers' responses to gender: first, that while some women began to make an issue of women's roles and rights after 1835,[2] the question of whether American fiction itself would follow lines confirmed by the cultural ideology of "separate spheres" remained as yet unanswered in the 1830s, so that ultimately our analysis of "Uncle Lot" presents a moment not unlike our own, in which gender as a cultural construct was much more fluid than it would be for at least the next century (or in our case, the previous century); and second, that the very consciousness of gender and its relation to narrative for early-nineteenth-century American writers created an opening for the development of "separate genres" or narrative traditions within which women writers might develop their authority as storytellers. Regionalism has its origins both in this as-yet-indeterminate relationship between gender and genre and at the same time in a consciousness of gender in Stowe's early work and the writing of her male and female contemporaries.

"Uncle Lot" makes for interesting reading in its own right: it is the first published sketch by an important American writer; it coincides with the influential Beecher family's move to Cincinnati and thus presents New England life and values to a western audience; and it is a work which has remained in the archives of American literary history.[3] But it becomes an even more interesting text read as the young Harriet Beecher's awareness of an emerging American fiction and her attempts to redirect that fiction by revising Washington Irving. An analysis of the significance of "Uncle Lot" as a cultural moment therefore begins with a discussion of "Rip Van Winkle" and "The Legend of Sleepy Hollow."

When Rip Van Winkle comes down from the mountain and finds his new place in his postrevolutionary village as a "chronicle of the old times 'before the war'" (40), Washington Irving creates a vocation for the American artist. At the beginning of the tale Rip has "an insuperable aversion to all kinds of profitable labour" (Irving 30), preferring instead to spend his time telling ghost stories to children, but he awakens from his twenty-year sleep to discover that the storyteller in the new republic has an important role to play. In "Rip Van Winkle" Irving avoids prescribing a form for the American story, but he does suggest that it will have a content different from English narrative; like the image of George Washington on the sign in front of the Union Hotel, American fiction may derive from English and European models but is also "singularly metamorphosed" (Irving 37). However, despite Rip's altered perception in the tale, Irving makes it clear that certain things have not changed. George is still a George, not a Dame; Irving allows Rip a "drop of comfort" when he discovers that he has survived two wars at once, the American Revolution and the tyranny of "petticoat government," for Dame Van Winkle is dead. And Irving spares Rip any complicity in her death; she has broken a blood vessel "in a fit of passion at a New-England pedlar" (Irving 39). Angry women do not survive to tell the story of the "old times 'before the war.'" Dame Van Winkle cannot be a candidate for the American artist; such would be a singular metamorphosis indeed.[4] For Irving the American storyteller, like the American hero, must be male.

By granting the postrevolutionary American artist a cultural role with secular rather than divine authority (George Washington replaces King George), Irving asserts the separation of literature from theology as the political ground for an American story. Irving's Knickerbocker tales reveal the gender anxiety that this shift created for early-nineteenth-century male American writers.[5] In their separation from Puritanism as a cultural base, turning away from the writing of sermons and toward the writing of fiction, Irving's male contemporaries split off that anxiety, which Irving figures as the psychocultural castration image of the headless horseman. They projected "headlessness" onto women writers and asserted masculinity itself as evidence of divine authority. Irving's narrator thus fiercely refuses to take women—the already "castrated"—seriously. And just in case his readers remain insufficiently convinced that Dame Van Winkle is dead and worry that she might return to haunt them or pose a threat to Rip's postrevolutionary authority, Irving resurrects her in a literary way as Ichabod Crane in "The Legend of Sleepy Hollow," then frightens "her" out of town, not needing the Freudian and Lacanian theories of our own century to make the point that gender anxiety for men signifies the fear of absence, castration, headlessness.[6]

In "The Legend of Sleepy Hollow," Irving removes the undesirable qualities that characterized Dame Van Winkle from his portraits of the Dutch wives and projects them instead onto the character of Ichabod Crane. During Ichabod's reign over his "little literary realm," the schoolroom, the pedagogue uses "a ferule, that sceptre of despotic power" and "the birch of justice reposed on three nails" to enforce his limited government (Irving 283). Like Dame Van Winkle, Ichabod Crane in the schoolroom becomes someone to escape, and Irving describes the scholars' early dismissal as "emancipation" (284). However, outside the schoolroom, Ichabod undergoes a transformation and becomes the embodiment of Rip rather than Dame. He has a "soft and foolish heart towards the [female] sex" like his counterpart in Irving's earlier tale. He becomes the playmate of his own charges and the congenial companion of their mothers: he would often "sit with a child on one knee, and rock a cradle with his foot, for whole hours together" (Irving 276). He seems initially content to become one of the region's "native inhabitants," deriving pleasure from visiting, "snugly cuddling in the chimney corner," filling the role of "travelling gazette," and expressing his desire for the "comforts of the cupboard" (Irving 273, 278, 276, 275). And within the "female circle," he enjoys the position of "man of letters" (Irving 276). Yet Irving does not grant him Rip's place as American artist; the extracts from Cotton Mather that Ichabod contributes to the storytelling at Van Tassel's castle do not appear to be successful in competing with the ghost stories Brom Bones tells.

Ichabod Crane will not serve as Irving's image of the American artist; neither will he provide a model for the American hero. For Irving reveals him to be a fraud—not a real contender for the love of Katrina Van Tassel but instead a glutton whose desire for Katrina derives from greed and gorging. Most startling of all, Ichabod turns out to be no settler after all but rather to have fantasies of sacking the "sleepy region" in order to invest "in immense tracts of wild land, and shingle palaces in the wilderness," toward which he would set off, Katrina and the children on top of a wagon and "himself bestriding a pacing mare" (Irving 280). Too much a member of the "female circle," as Irving defines women's culture, to bring off this quintessentially masculine vision, Ichabod becomes by the end of the tale merely a debased version of it, an unsuccessful suitor, an "affrighted pedagogue," an "unskilful rider" (Irving 292, 294). Reminding us that women had produced "more than a third of the fiction published in America before 1820," Lloyd Daigrepont suggests that Irving "instilled in Ichabod Crane the characteristics of those writers who dominated the American literary scene" in the early days of the Republic—what he calls a "burgeoning popular taste for the excessive emotionalism of the sentimental tale, the novel of sensibility, and the Gothic romance"—and that in the conclusion of "The Legend of Sleepy Hollow," Irving "symbolically portrayed their defeat" (69-70).

Irving creates Brom Bones instead as Crane's triumphant adversary and as an image of American manhood. "Brom Bones . . . was the hero of the scene," a man who has tamed Daredevil, a man "in fact noted for preferring vicious animals, . . . for he held a tractable well broken horse as unworthy of a lad of spirit" (Irving 287). As Daniel Hoffman observes, Brom Bones "is a Catskill Mike Fink, a Ring-Tailed Roarer from Kinderhook" (89). Brom Bones above all represents masculinity, a quality absent in Irving's characterizations of both Rip Van Winkle and Ichabod Crane, and this masculinity gives him authority over Ichabod. The "burley, roaring, roystering blade" has a "bluff, but not unpleasant countenance," "more mischief than ill-will in his composition," and "with all his overbearing roughness, there was a strong dash of waggish good humour at bottom" (Irving 737). The excesses of the "female circle" may threaten the cultural order with "petticoat government," but the excesses of masculinity merely contribute to our national health—we all have a good laugh at Ichabod Crane's cowardice, incompetence, and basic cultural impotence. "The Legend of Sleepy Hollow" turns the folktale into a tall tale: sobered by the seriousness of his own attempt to reflect American identity in the Republic's fiction, Irving rejects as "sleepy" any literary authority the Dutch wives might claim and establishes the "roaring blade" as the literary descendant of Rip Van Winkle.

Like many other writers in the 1830s, Stowe begins "Uncle Lot" by reworking Irving's "The Legend of Sleepy Hollow." Most of these writers, however, as Hennig Cohen and William B. Dillingham observe, imitated what they term the "ingredients of a typical sketch of Southwest humor: the physically awkward, ugly, and avaricious Ichabod; the good-natured but rowdy Brom Bones and his friends, who love a practical joke; the desirable plum, Katrina Van Tassel." Cohen and Dillingham report that "it would be difficult to estimate the number of Southern tales directly influenced by 'Sleepy Hollow,'" and they cite some examples: Joseph B. Cobb's "The Legend of Black Creek," William Tappan Thompson's "The Runaway Match" and "Adventures of a Sabbath-Breaker," and Francis James Robinson's "The Frightened Serenaders" (xii). Thus Stowe was not alone in modeling a work of fiction on "The Legend of Sleepy Hollow."[7] However, Stowe's text critiques Irving, thereby establishing the context for regionalism, an approach to the representation of rural and regional people and values that involves respect and empathy and grants voice to regional characters in the work, an approach that differs markedly from that of the "humorists," who created such characters as objects of derision rather than subjects of their own agency.

Stowe's text specifically reveals similarities between her village of Newbury, "one of those out-of-the-way places where nobody ever came unless they came on purpose: a green little hollow" ("Uncle Lot" 2), and Irving's "little valley, or rather lap of land among high hills, which is one of the quietest places in the whole world," a "green, sheltered, fertile nook" (272, 279). Stowe notes the "unchangeability" of Newbury, particularly in its "manners, morals, arts, and sciences" ("Uncle Lot" 2); Irving describes the "population, manners, and customs" of his "sleepy region" as "fixed" (274). Both authors introduce their characters as representatives of the larger citizenry. Irving's Ichabod Crane "was a native of Connecticut, a state which supplies the Union with pioneers for the mind as well as for the forest" (274), and Stowe describes James Benton as "one of those whole-hearted, energetic Yankees" who possessed a "characteristic national trait" ("Uncle Lot" 3). Like Ichabod Crane, James Benton is a newcomer to the village of Newbury, he "figured as schoolmaster all the week, and as chorister on Sundays," he makes himself at home "in all the chimney-corners of the region," devouring "doughnuts and pumpkin pies with most flattering appetite," and he generally "kept the sunny side of the old ladies" ("Uncle Lot" 4, 6). James Benton holds what Stowe describes as "an uncommonly comfortable opinion of himself" ("Uncle Lot" 3); Irving characterizes as Ichabod's "vanity" his belief that in his performance as chorister "he completely carried away the palm from the parson" (276). Both tell stories, and both have, as Stowe writes of James Benton, "just the kindly heart that fell in love with everything in feminine shape" ("Uncle Lot" 6).

There is thus a great deal of evidence to suggest that Stowe begins "Uncle Lot" by invoking "The Legend of Sleepy Hollow." However, Stowe imitates in order to revise. For Stowe, there is no threat of castration, nothing to "lose"; what seems revolutionary about "Uncle Lot" is not its explicit content—since unlike Irving's tales, "Uncle Lot" reinforces the values of a theology based on inner feeling and a literature congruent with theology—but rather the demonstration of a woman's authority to be the writer of the tale.[8] Unlike Irving, Stowe identifies women's values not as debased but as central to the "private change of heart" that must precede cultural conversion, a conversion of domestic ideology that would acknowledge women's moral centrality and women's role in creating American culture, and she asserts the centrality of feeling in American culture by transforming Ichabod Crane into James Benton, a hero willing to acknowledge women's authority at least in the domestic sphere.[9] "Uncle Lot" thereby links place—Newbury as invocation and reinvention of Irving's "sleepy region"—with values of domestic ideology, conversion, and women's authority that together lay the foundation for her successors in the regionalist tradition. Regional "place" becomes more or less a feature of the fiction and a sign of preindustrial, even prepatriarchal authority for the women of faculty that move throughout Stowe's own work and the later herbalists, healers, and empathic visitors that populate sketches and stories by later women regionalist writers.

Stowe claims that her "main story" involves a romance between her hero, James Benton, and Uncle Lot Griswold's daughter, Grace. However, like Irving in his portrait of Katrina Van Tassel, Stowe gives her readers only an occasional glimpse of Grace; instead she focuses on the process by which male characters in the sketch become converted or transformed in various ways. Stowe places Uncle Lot at the thematic center of her sketch. She describes him as a "chestnut burr, abounding with briers without and with substantial goodness within" but "'the *settest* crittur in his way that ever you saw'" ("Uncle Lot" 7, 12). Initially Uncle Lot expresses an aversion to the young hero, James Benton, so in order to "win" Grace's favors, James must first elicit Uncle Lot's recognition of what James believes to be Uncle Lot's inner feelings. Thus the "conversion" of Uncle Lot's opinion of James replaces courtship as Stowe's organizing principle in the narrative; James tries to reach Uncle Lot behind the defenses he has created, the overlays of his "chestnut burr," and to convert him into a person capable of expressing feeling, that "substantial goodness within." In addition, James Benton achieves his own spiritual conversion, and conversion to the ministry, by falling in love with Grace's minister brother, George, then, upon young George's untimely death, replacing him within the family as Uncle Lot's "son." Marriage with Grace at the end of the sketch merely ritualizes this "son" relationship. Thus, despite Stowe's claim that Grace figures as her heroine, she pays very little attention to Grace herself.

However, unlike Irving's portrait of Katrina, what characterization Stowe does provide underscores Grace's intellectual capacity and moral superiority, features congruent generally with the ideology of domesticity and specifically with Stowe's sister Catharine's vision of women. Catharine appears to have believed that conversion was a much less strenuous task for women than for men, that women only needed to be educated in the schools she proposed, where they would "learn proper social, religious, and moral principles and then establish their own schools elsewhere on the same principles" (Sklar 95), and that women would then be in a position to assert their influence on the nation. As Katharine Kish Sklar writes, "Catharine Beecher not only wanted to 'save' the nation, she wanted women to save it" and engaged in a campaign to transform teaching from a men's profession to a profession "dominated by—indeed exclusively belonging to—women" (96, 97). Catharine Beecher herself took over much of the care of her younger siblings, including the then-four-year-old Harriet, after their mother, Roxana, died, and it was Catharine who supervised Harriet's education from the time she was about thirteen (Sklar 60).

Given her sister's powerful model, we can view Stowe's portrait of Grace Griswold as suggesting that her sketch does not need to convert Grace, who is the already-converted, and therefore does not need to focus on Grace's development as part of the sketch's "plot." Stowe describes Grace as follows:

> Like most Yankee damsels, she had a longing after the tree of knowledge, and, having exhausted the literary fountains of a district school, she fell to reading whatsoever came in her way. True, she had but little to read; but what she perused she had her own thoughts upon, so that a person of information, in talking with her, would feel a constant wondering pleasure to find that she had so much more to say of this, that, and the other thing than he expected.
>
> ("Uncle Lot" 9)

Grace already represents grace; she possesses the moral character to which the men in Stowe's sketch must aspire in order to demonstrate their own spiritual conversion, which becomes manifested for James in his success at winning over Uncle Lot, then winning a congregation and a wife, and for Uncle Lot in his ability to express his feeling for James Benton. The men in particular must experience that "private change of heart" which characterized conversion for Lyman Beecher (Sklar 27). Within the ideology that asserted women's moral centrality, it does not surprise readers that after speaking very little throughout the sketch, Grace asserts herself in the sketch's final scene, when she tells Uncle Lot, a visitor to her house following her marriage to James, "Come, come, father, I have authority in these days, so no disrespectful speeches" ("Uncle Lot" 31).[10]

Thus conversion, rather than the confrontation and defeat that characterize "The Legend of Sleepy Hollow," gives Stowe's narrative its direction, and conversion figures as an aspect of plot as well as of theme. Stowe gives James Benton the task of trying to "convert" Uncle Lot; conversion, not seduction, becomes her hero's test. In the scene which depicts this "conversion," James Benton arrives for an unannounced visit to Uncle Lot's house with the ostensible goal of winning Uncle Lot's affection. Stowe writes:

> James also had one natural accomplishment, more courtier-like than all the diplomacy in Europe, and that was the gift of feeling a *real* interest for anybody in five minutes; so that, if he began to please in jest, he generally ended in earnest. With great simplicity of mind, he had a natural tact for seeing into others, and watched their motions with the same delight with which a child gazes at the wheels and springs of a watch, to "see what it will do."
>
> ("Uncle Lot" 16)

James wishes to open up the "chestnut burr" that characterizes Uncle Lot's defenses against feeling, and he uses powers of empathy—his "natural tact for seeing into others"—to help Uncle Lot recognize and reveal the "latent kindness" he holds within his "rough exterior" ("Uncle Lot" 16).

Stowe reverses Irving's condemnation of women, suggesting that instead of annihilating what Irving calls "petticoat government" at the end of "Rip Van Winkle," American society might benefit from genuine government, at least in the domestic sphere, by women; and instead of frightening Ichabod Crane out of town, as Irving does in "The Legend of Sleepy Hollow," she creates her own hero in Ichabod Crane's image, then "converts" him from his prankish boyishness into a man of deep feeling, into a man, in Catharine Beecher's sense, who becomes more like a woman as the sketch progresses and ends by submitting to Grace's authority.

In Stowe's world, Dame Van Winkle might exert genuine influence, might even speak, as does Stowe herself in assuming authorship; in "Uncle Lot," Stowe reinforces the nineteenth-century view of women's interest in feeling and moral character, while the masculine behaviors of Brom Bones disappear from the fiction. Thus Dame Van Winkle survives in the work of Harriet Beecher Stowe not as a shrill-voiced termagant but as a woman capable of using her verbal facility in order to assert, in Grace's closing lines, "authority in these days" ("Uncle Lot" 31). Irving has to justify the exclusion of women from the province of storytelling; Stowe wants not to exclude men but to include women in the profession of literature (even though, ironically, she never created a female narrator in her work). Nevertheless, the fact that "Uncle Lot" has remained unremarked for most of this century attests to the apparent victory of Irving's position. At least as literary history has recorded it, Brom Bones inspired an entire "school" of tall tale fiction by the Old Southwest humorists, whereas Ichabod Crane disappeared into the "sleepy region."

In reading "Uncle Lot" to the Semi-Colon Club, Stowe had the good fortune to attract the attention of editor James Hall of the *Western Monthly Magazine*. One of Stowe's biographers, in describing James Hall's influence, writes that he advocated "cheerfulness, morality, and regionalism" as a literary aesthetic, was "a chivalrous admirer of women writers," and encouraged payment for contributors to American periodicals (Adams, *Harriet Beecher Stowe* 35-36).[11] In awarding his fiction prize to Harriet Beecher's first New England sketch, he was also implicitly urging her to counter the portrait of American life that the frontier appeared to encourage—as he knew very well. In *Letters from the West,* Hall had recorded the telling of yarns by an old keelboatman named Pappy, whom he had encountered while traveling down the Ohio on a flatboat (W. Blair 70);[12] and as editor of *The Western Souvenir,* issued in Cincinnati in 1828, "the first of American gift books from beyond the Alleghenies" (Thompson 95-96), Hall achieved the distinction of having been the first editor to publish a lengthy account of the career of the legendary Mike Fink (W. Blair 81-82). Like Washington Irving, Hall appears to have been interested very early in the tall tale; but unlike Irving, he would choose, as editor of the *Western Monthly Magazine,* to encourage his contributors, especially women, to write about other regional material than the portraits of frontier life that would survive in American literary history as humor of the Old Southwest.[13]

Hall contrasts sharply with his contemporary, William T. Porter, whose sporting magazine, the *Spirit of the Times,* first published in 1831, provided gentlemen interested in the leisure pursuits of horse racing, hunting, and listening to tall tales with a way of gratifying their fantasies of upper-class superiority (since much of the humor Porter published derived from "the foibles and follies of the lower classes" [Yates 881]) and of ratifying their belief in masculine values and male dominance. Unlike Hall, whose interest in developing western material inspired his work, Porter was a commercialist, interested more in the culture of the sporting world than in literature. He initially catered "to the wealthy slaveholding sportsmen and their friends and allies, who 'ruled' racing" (Yates 17). With the decline of horse racing by the end of the 1830s, Porter began to include the early local color fiction literary historians term humor of the Old Southwest. As Norris W. Yates observes, "The bulk of [Porter's] later readers belong to a new and larger economic and social class—a class which may have shared the values and interests but not the economic resources of the old" (21). Thus the values and interests of the slave-holding sportsmen and their allies contrast decidedly with the values and interests of the audience for and contributors to Hall's *Western Monthly Magazine*. The readers who allowed the *Spirit of the Times* to flourish for more than thirty years may not have been able to prevent women from speaking out in public meetings, but by excluding morality from the province of humor they attempted to exclude the particular sphere of women's influence in nineteenth-century culture from fiction and effectively defined storytelling as a masculine occupation. The writers who contributed to William T. Porter's sporting magazine continued to develop American literature as a masculine enterprise. To the extent that humor of the Old Southwest establishes Brom Bones as the American hero, this particular literary genre describes a direction for fiction that women writers could not and did not follow.[14]

Augustus Baldwin Longstreet and his colleague on the Augusta *Sentinel,* William Tappan Thompson, both of whom published their sketches in the 1830s, were the only Old Southwest humorist writers who treated female characters in their fiction (W. Blair 74).[15] Of these two, Longstreet in *Georgia Scenes* (1835) had the greater influence.[16] *Georgia Scenes* is an important text to examine in establishing gender consciousness as a feature of early American fiction, for while it reaffirms Irving's perspective and establishes further precedent for the humorists' exclusion of women, it also suggests a lingering fluidity in the relationship between gender and genre in the 1830s. At the same time, *Georgia Scenes* suggests that Old Southwest humor evolved in part from suppressing the possibility of female literary authority. In Longstreet's preface to *Georgia Scenes* he tells us "that when he first wrote and published the sketches which went into the volume, he was 'extremely desirous' of concealing his authorship; and that in order to accomplish his purpose, he had used two pseudonyms. For sketches in which men are the principal actors, he says, he uses the name Hall; for those in which women are the most prominent, he writes under the name Baldwin" (Meriwether 358; Longstreet v).

James Meriwether writes that "the dominant figure of the book is Hall; . . . Baldwin simply serves as a foil to the ultimately much more masculine and successful Lyman Hall" (359). In Baldwin's sketches, the narrator becomes a moralist who stands back from the action, contrasting "country girls" with their urban counterparts and condemning women who become "charming" creatures and lead their husbands to early graves. By contrast, in Hall's sketches, Hall participates in the action, proves himself to be a crack shot, and establishes himself as a man's man. A third character who appears in the sketches, Ned Brace of "A Sage Conversation," establishes storytelling as one of many contests, like gander pulling, horse swapping, or horse racing, in which boys or men can prove their masculinity. Both Ned Brace and Lyman Hall achieve a less ambiguous masculinity than does Baldwin.

In suggesting Baldwin's ultimate ineffectuality, Longstreet, like Irving in his portrait of Ichabod Crane, links Baldwin to the world of women that he simultaneously mocks. The "country girls" of "The Dance" are so "wholly ignorant" of urban fashion that "consequently, they looked, for all the world, like human beings" (14); thus Longstreet manages to make fun of both country and urban "girls" in the same jest. In "The Song," piano player Miss Aurelia Emma Theodosia Augusta Crump has hands that engage in conflict at the keyboard, and "anyone, or rather no one, can imagine what kind of noises the piano gave forth" as a result (Longstreet 70). Longstreet's portraits of women characters, primarily in Baldwin's sketches, led his biographer Kimball King to remark, "It is hard to understand how a man who appears to have had close, satisfying relationships with his wife and daughters, all sensible, intelligent women who led exemplary lives, could portray their sex so unflatteringly, unless his bias were actually a pose, a part of his writer's mask" (80). However, the emerging gender consciousness of the 1830s makes this explicable; Longstreet, like Irving, associates storytelling with masculinity and political power, for Hall ends the volume, in "The Shooting-Match," by proving his marksmanship and thereby earning the potential votes of the country people. The people promise to support him if he "offers" for anything; "Longstreet makes it clear that the judgment of these people is to be respected and if Hall will accept such responsibilities he will be an able and successful public official" (Meriwether 361), such as Longstreet himself later became in his career as a judge, preacher, and college president. Baldwin, on the other hand, clearly lacks the shooting ability to qualify as either effective storyteller or political man; as he demonstrates in his failure to execute the humorous "double cross-hop" step of his first sketch in *Georgia Scenes,* he cannot even dance (Longstreet 21).

In Baldwin's most powerful sketch, "A Sage Conversation," the three aged matrons who relate anecdotes to each other prove Longstreet's point, for they seem unable to understand the meaning of the very anecdotes they are attempting to tell and thus do not succeed in the actively masculine pursuit of contriving and telling stories. Baldwin opens "A Sage Conversation" with the assertion, "I love the aged matrons of our land. As a class, they are the most pious, the most benevolent, the most useful, and the most harmless of the human family" (Longstreet 186). Nevertheless, the women cannot solve the riddle of Ned Brace's story concerning "two most excellent men, who became so attached to each other that they actually got married" (Longstreet 188), and although the women light their pipes and sit around the fire until late in the night, their talking never rises above the level of what one of them calls "an old woman's chat" (Longstreet 196). Although they may look like men, engaging in pipe smoking and late-night conversation, the women are innocents on the subject of cross-dressing, recalling women who "dress'd in men's clothes" and followed their true loves "to the wars," and one of them concludes that "men don't like to marry gals that take on that way" (Longstreet 191). They miss the humorous potential of their own material; they prove themselves incapable of sustaining the line of a narrative longer than a brief comment or two; they suggest that their only expertise lies in the realm of herbal remedies; and throughout, they demonstrate the general inability of women to be storytellers.

James M. Cox suggests, with irony, that in the final "showdown" between Stowe and the frontier humorists, Stowe "wins"; that in *Uncle Tom's Cabin,* she turns the bear hunt characteristic of much of southern and frontier humor into a man hunt; and that she "killed" the humorists by raising the question of serious moral culture. He claims that he does not wish to "put down Mrs. Stowe" but argues that it was ultimately Samuel Clemens who found the form of genius for the materials of native American humor ("Humor" 591-92). It is difficult to imagine how Stowe or any other woman writer of the 1830s and 1840s could have written the kind of American humor Cox refers to here, since in order to do so she would have had to achieve that humor at women's expense and ironically agree to take only masculine culture, with its sport, jests, frolics, and put-downs, seriously.[17] Cox views Clemens as the product of the implicit conflict between Stowe and the Old Southwest humorists, implying that the local color school of American fiction, including Bret Harte and Hamlin Garland, emerged from the same origins as Old Southwest humor.[18] For Cox, Stowe and Longstreet appear to sketch alternative directions in American fiction, and Hall's sketches in *Georgia Scenes* (if not Baldwin's) support this point. Hall's narratives create further variations on the theme of masculine dominance, serve to reify the distinctions between men and women characteristic of "separate spheres," and contribute to dividing early-nineteenth-century American fiction along the lines of humor at others' expense, exemplified by Old Southwest and local color "schools," and empathy for others, in the tradition of literary regionalism, primarily exemplified by women writers.[19]

With the publication of "A New England Sketch" or "Uncle Lot," Stowe joined an emerging group of women who had begun to publish in magazines—Lydia Maria Child, Catharine Sedgwick, Lydia Huntley Sigourney, among others—and who, by their very success as publishing authors, underscored the issue of gender in nineteenth-century literary culture. In her delineation of woman's fiction, however, Nine Baym suggests that Stowe's interests in slavery and religion were "issues transcending gender" and that they "set her apart from the other American women writing fiction in her day" (15). Stowe certainly knew Sedgwick's *A New England Tale* (1822), the novel Baym credits with inaugurating the genre of woman's fiction; Sklar notes that it had created controversy within the Beecher family and that Catharine in particular had attacked Sedgwick, a convert to Unitarianism, as having betrayed her social position and the Calvinist tradition (44-45). It was perhaps in recognition of Sedgwick as well as an attempt to distance herself from the controversy that led Stowe to change the title of "A New

ON THE SUBJECT OF...

CAROLINE M. KIRKLAND (1801-1864)

Best known for her three books that illuminate a distinct phase of American settlement of the West, *A New Home—Who'll Follow? Or, Glimpses of Western Life* (1839), *Forest Life* (1842), and *Western Clearings* (1845), Caroline M. Kirkland established a reputation as an energetic and opinionated exponent of the woman's view of an era dominated by male writers. While most of her fellow women writers of the period were specializing in fiction, Kirkland preferred the realm of literary journalism, contributing numerous articles to periodicals and working as a magazine editor—all during a time when women were rarely involved in the business end of publishing. Though her work, like that of many other antebellum American women writers, was labeled "sentimental" and dismissed by early scholars, her realism as and her simple, frank style earned praise and attention from later scholars.

Kirkland was born Caroline Matilda Stansbury in New York City. She attended a Quaker school and began teaching in Clinton, New York. In the late 1820s, she married William Kirkland, and with him founded a girls' school near Utica, New York. In 1835, the Kirklands moved to Detroit, where together they headed the Detroit Female Seminary. In 1837 they purchased eight hundred acres of land sixty miles west of Detroit, where they founded the village of Pinckney—the village that would serve as the model for Kirkland's town of Montacute in *A New Home.* The Kirklands returned to New York City in 1843, and following William's death in 1846 Kirkland earned money through teaching and writing, serving as editor of the *Union Magazine of Literature and Art* until 1850. Among many other literary achievements, Kirkland compiled three collections of her magazine articles, *The Evening Book* (1852), *A Book for the Home Circle* (1853), and *Autumn Hours* (1854).

England Sketch" to "Uncle Lot." Yet if Stowe chooses not to model herself on Sedgwick, more is at stake than a defense of her family's social standing and theological allegiance; she also chooses not to write in the formal tradition of Sedgwick. Instead, she raises questions of region that Sedgwick, despite the regional flavor of her title, does not address.[20] Stowe's interests in "Uncle Lot" suggest that as early as 1834 there existed the possibility that women would create not a single major tradition but two—women's fiction and regionalism—that would develop independently of each other, yet share some common themes, concerns, and influences. Thus, while Stowe responds to Irving in "Uncle Lot," she also drew her inspiration from her female contemporaries. Critics have identified several works by women with the roots of the regional tradition in American fiction, in particular Lydia Huntley Sigourney, *Sketch of Connecticut. Forty Years Since* (1824), Sarah Josepha Hale, *Northwood: A Tale of New England* (1827), Eliza Buckminster Lee, *Sketches of a New-England Village in the Last Century* (1838), and Caroline Kirkland, *A New Home—Who'll Follow?; or, Glimpses of Western Life* (1839), in addition to Sedgwick's *A New England Tale.*[21]

Stowe herself, in *The Pearl of Orr's Island* (1862), would bring female characters and values into the center of a regional novel. In this book in particular, Stowe demonstrates the influence of Sigourney, who published the memoir *Sketch of Connecticut* in Hartford the same year thirteen-year-old Harriet Beecher moved there to become a student at her sister Catharine's Hartford Female Seminary.[22] In *Sketch of Connecticut,* Madam L. tells Farmer Larkin, a regional character who makes a brief appearance, that she doesn't recollect the names of his children. He replies, "It's no wonder that ye don't Ma'am, there's such a neest on 'em. They're as thick as hops round the fire this winter. There's Roxey and Reuey, they're next to Tim, and look like twins. They pick the wool, and card tow, and wind quills, and knit stockins and mittins for the fokes in the house; and I've brought some down with me to day, to see if they'll buy 'em to the marchants' shops, and let 'em have a couple o' leetle small shawls" (Sigourney 118). This passage provides evidence that Stowe had read *Sketch of Connecticut* before she began *The Pearl of Orr's Island,* for she names her own characters Roxy and Ruey in that novel after the daughters of Farmer Larkin. The model Sigourney created in her New England farmer with his Connecticut speech rhythms also served to influence Stowe's own portrait of Uncle Lot, the one character in her first sketch who speaks in dialect. In her analysis of *Sketch of Connecticut,* Sandra A. Zagarell argues that Sigourney's writing "was quite directly concerned with the foundations and organization of public life," and that both she and Sedgwick (in *Hope Leslie* [1827]) "addressed a major political topic of the day, the nature of the American nation" ("Expanding" 225). Thus Sigourney becomes a model for Stowe in two ways: she offers regional characters for Stowe's later meditation and expansion in "Uncle Lot" and *The Pearl of Orr's Island,* and she also confirms for Stowe that women have an inalienable claim to an evolving American political and cultural vision. Sigourney explores, as Stowe would later do, the possibilities of literary authority for women.

"Uncle Lot," unlike *A New England Tale,* does not inaugurate a genre. Regionalism, in contrast to woman's fiction, begins inchoately, reflecting uncertainty on the part of both male and female writers in the 1830s concerning the ways in which the gender of the author might inscribe the formal concerns of the work. For by the 1830s the direction of critical judgment concerning women writers, though clearly forming, was not yet set. Stowe's vision of Uncle Lot as the "settest crittur you ever saw" and the challenge she sets her hero to convert Uncle Lot to the expression of feeling establishes her perspicacity in implicitly predicting that gender itself would remain a "chestnut burr" within American culture, that is, a briery issue difficult to open but yet containing its own reward. Genre is also a "chestnut burr" in the emerging world of "separate spheres."[23] What Stowe begins to explore in the regionalism of "Uncle Lot" is the possibility that the limits of genre can indeed be transformed or, to use a word more in keeping with the ideology of "woman's sphere," "converted" to the cultural work of developing a form for women's narrative voice.

Notes

1. Numerous scholars and critics are working to define the tradition of regionalism and to explicate its features and significance. Most scholars link regionalism with the development of the fictional sketch in nineteenth-century American literature. See Jeffrey Rubin Dorsky for a discussion of Irving's development of the sketch form. See also Sandra Zagarell, "Narrative of Community: The Identification of a Genre," in which she identifies a "department of literature" she terms "narrative of community" and includes numerous American writers often described as regional in this "department." See also Josephine Donovan, *New England Local Color Literature: A Women's Tradition;* Perry D. Westbrook, *Acres of Flint: Writers of Rural New England, 1870-1900* and *The New England Town in Fact and Fiction;* and introductory essays on regional writers in Elizabeth Ammons, ed., "Introduction"; Judith Fetterley, ed., "Introduction"; and Marjorie Pryse, ed., "Introduction," *Stories from the Country of Lost Borders;* see also critical essays on Cary, Cooke, and Stowe in Fetterley, ed., *Provisions: A Reader from 19th-Century American Women;* see also Pryse, "Introduction," *The Country of the Pointed Firs and Other Stories;* and Pryse, ed., *Selected Stories of Mary E. Wilkins Freeman.* Lawrence Buell notes some disagreement with the tendency of what he calls the "feminist revisionary scholarship" to identify the regionalist tradition as female. In his own work, he examines regional representation in American literature, arguably a broader survey but one which does not locate itself within the boundaries of prose fiction, although he does acknowledge that "the staple of regional prose, however, continued to be the short sketch or tale" (296). In Buell's survey of the field of regional representation, he finds that it "looks considerably more androgynous once we survey the whole panoply . . . So although I agree that the conception of social reality that underlay New England regional poetry and prose lent itself to feminist appropriation and became, in the postwar era, increasingly a woman's construct, . . . provincial literary iconography [is] a project in which writers of the two sexes participated together" (302-03). See Louis Renza for a discussion of the ways "minor literature" (such as regionalism) in Jewett demonstrates pressures to become "major literature," and see Richard Brodhead for "a different account of the regionalist genre from what feminist studies have proposed" (*Cultures* 144).

2. See Nancy Cott. She locates the origins of nineteenth-century American feminism within the decade of the 1830s and asserts that the development of feminism actually depended on the ideology of "woman's sphere."

3. Stowe herself collected "Uncle Lot," originally titled "A New England Sketch," in *The Mayflower, or Sketches of the Descendents of the Pilgrim* (1843), a work with a limited circulation and out of print by 1855. Following the success of *Uncle Tom's Cabin,* the collection was reissued, with additional sketches, and this collection then became part of the Riverside Edition of Stowe's works. However, the sketch has not appeared in anthologies of American literature and remains unknown except by Stowe scholars. John Adams included the sketch in his edition of Stowe's work (see Adams, ed., *Regional Sketches: New England and Florida*), and the sketch appears in Fetterley and Pryse, eds., *American Women Regionalists 1850-1910.*

4. For further explication of the significance of the silencing of Dame Van Winkle, see Fetterley, *The Resisting Reader* 1-11.

5. For a general discussion of gender unease in early-nineteenth-century American culture and the relationship between the minister and culture, see Ann Douglas, *The Feminization of American Culture,* although Douglas's work has been superseded by others. See in particular Jane Tompkins, *Sensational Designs: The Cultural Work of American Fiction 1790-1860.* For an argument that manhood produces its own anxiety for nineteenth-century writers, see David Leverenz, *Manhood and the American Renaissance.*

6. Railton discusses the "psychic underside" of early-nineteenth-century American men's public selves and suggests that "it reveals their instinctual doubts about the sacrifices that the role of gentleman in a democracy exacted of them" (102).

7. See also John Seelye, "Root and Branch: Washington Irving and American Humor." Buell notes that "probably the single most important American prose work in teaching native writers to exploit regional material for literary purposes was Washington Irving's *The Sketch-Book*" (294).

8. Biographical evidence suggests that Harriet Beecher was writing with her father as well as with Washington Irving in mind. Although she initially called her most interesting character in "A New England Sketch" Uncle Timothy Griswold, changing his name when the story reappeared as "Uncle Lot" in *The Mayflower,* there would have been no confusion in the Beecher family that "Uncle Tim" was based on Harriet's father Lyman's Uncle Lot Benton. Lyman Beecher's mother had died two days after his birth, he had been raised by a childless aunt and uncle instead of in his father's household, and he had apparently entertained his own children with numerous tales about his childhood with Uncle Lot (Rugoff 4, 219). Thus James Benton, who becomes the "adopted" son of Lot Griswold in the sketch, serves as Harriet's portrait of her father as a young man. By choosing to write a sketch based on her father's own tales from childhood, to become like Lyman Beecher a storyteller, Harriet implicitly expressed her desire to model herself on her father, but she carefully disclaimed the ambitiousness of this desire, describing her work, in a letter to her brother George, as "a little bit of a love sketch . . . , a contemptible little affair" (Boydston, Kelley, and Margolis 62). Thus we can see her hiding behind the "love sketch" as a story more suitable than others a woman might tell, even though her interest in conversion in the sketch clearly identifies her as the daughter of Lyman Beecher, the Congregational minister known in the early 1800s for his power as a revivalist and the man who produced seven sons, all of whom became ministers.

9. Although the senior Beecher had definite views about gender differences, often lamenting that Harriet, with her intelligence, had not been born a boy and therefore a potential minister, he appears to have made no distinctions between young men's and young women's potential for experiencing conversion, and Lyman Beecher taught both daughters and sons that conversion involved a "private change of heart" rather than merely a social and public acknowledgment of belief (Sklar 27).

10. In collecting "Uncle Lot" for *The Mayflower,* Stowe changed the original wording of Grace's closing lines. In "A New England Sketch," Grace tells her father, "I'm used to authority in these days" (191). The change, with its echo of biblical usage, serves to reinforce Grace's moral authority to speak.

11. Hall appears early in the history of the Beecher family's move to Cincinnati. Prior to the publication of "Uncle Lot," Hall's *Western Monthly Magazine* had published an essay titled "Modern Uses of Language," signed "B," and attributed to Catharine although written by Harriet (Boydston, Kelley, and Margolis 50-51). Sklar notes that Catharine viewed the *Western Monthly Magazine* as a potential outlet for her educational ideas, and that she included its editor James Hall among the trustees for the Western Female Institute, the school she opened in Cincinnati (110). Hall continued as a friend of the Beechers until he engaged in a defense of Roman Catholics in open conflict with Lyman Beecher's position on Catholicism, with the result that the *Western Monthly Magazine* lost its influential supporters and suffered financial failure, and Hall retired into banking (Flanagan 66-67).

12. Hall describes "Pappy" as a "humourist" who "would sit for hours scraping upon his violin, singing catches, or relating merry and marvellous tales" (182).

13. Ironically, in Flanagan's biography of James Hall, he writes that "Hall sketched women infrequently and on the whole rather badly" (143).

14. Caroline Kirkland may have been viewed as an exception; she was one of the few women, if not the only one, whom Porter published in *The Spirit of the Times*; Porter reprinted Kirkland, but she did not contribute original material (Yates 60).

15. William Tappan Thompson collected his Major Jones letters in 1843 as *Major Jones's Courtship,* the same year Stowe collected her own sketches in *The Mayflower.*

16. Alone among the major Southwest humorists, Longstreet did not publish his work in the *Spirit of the Times* (Blair 85).

17. See Blair's discussion of early American humor, especially 18-19.

18. Guttman terms "Sleepy Hollow" "a prefiguration of the tradition of Mark Twain and the frontier humorists" (171).

19. After Augustus Baldwin Longstreet graduated from Yale in 1813, he entered law school in Litchfield, Connecticut, where he attended sermons by the Reverend Lyman Beecher and visited in the Beecher home. "He also found time to visit Miss Pierce's School for Young Ladies, where he frequently regaled the young women with his droll accounts of rural Georgia in his 'country boy' pose. His first practice as a raconteur began during the Connecticut years" (King, *Augustus* 12), with women, and likely the Beecher family, as his audience. The young Harriet would not have directly benefited from hearing Longstreet's stories (she would have been hardly three years old), and yet it is one of the delightful coincidences of literary history that the two writers who would each begin to develop alternative possibilities for the treatment of American materials that Irving sets out in "The Legend of Sleepy Hollow"—Longstreet with his southern humor and male world of sporting stories, Stowe with the "sleepy" regionalism of "Uncle Lot"—would both have "met" in Litchfield, Connecticut.

20. Buell terms *A New-England Tale* "really more an expose than an exposition of provincial village culture, too heavily committed to a Cinderella plot . . . and anti-Calvinist satire . . . to accomplish much by way of regional mimesis" (295).

21. See discussions of Hale and Sedgwick in Nina Baym, *Woman's Fiction: A Guide to Novels by and about Women in America 1820-1870*; see discussions of Sigourney and Sedgwick in Sandra A. Zagarell, "Expanding 'America': Lydia Sigourney's *Sketch of Connecticut,* Catharine Sedgwick's *Hope Leslie.*"

22. John Adams in *Harriet Beecher Stowe* terms *Sketch* "a true forerunner of Mrs. Stowe's work" (31). As an

adolescent, Harriet met, knew, and very likely read Sigourney, her sister's dear friend in Hartford.

23. Tompkins suggests that even Hawthorne, in some of his earliest sketches collected in *Twice-Told Tales* (1837) ("Little Annie's Ramble," "A Rill from the Town Pump," "Sunday at Home," and "Sights from a Steeple"), began as a "sentimental author" long before he would become the genius of the American romance and damn the "scribbling women" (10-18). Buell focuses on the iconographic representation of region rather than the relationship between regional representation and genre; he does observe that "the staple of regional prose, however, continued to be the short sketch or tale" (296).

LYDE CULLEN SIZER (ESSAY DATE 2000)

SOURCE: Sizer, Lyde Cullen. "Introduction: My Sphere Rounds Out: Northern Women and the Written War, 1850-1872." In *The Political Work of Northern Women Writers and the Civil War,* pp. 1-15. Chapel Hill, N.C.: The University of North Carolina Press, 2000.

In the following essay, Sizer argues that controversies leading to and following the American Civil War encouraged many women authors from the North to reject their exclusion from public affairs and to use their writings to influence public opinion.

> And I shall not confine myself to my sphere. I hate my sphere. I like everything that is outside of it,—or, better still, my sphere rounds out into undefined space. I was born into the whole world. I am monarch of all I survey.
>
> —Gail Hamilton (Mary Abigail Dodge), *Skirmishes and Sketches* (1865)

The start of the Civil War found Chicagoan Mary Livermore in Boston tending her sick father. "It was a time of extreme and unconcealed anxiety," she wrote in 1889, when "the daily papers teemed with the dreary records of secession." Nevertheless, she and her father were amazed and heartened at Boston's swift response, and this minister's wife and mother of two joined the swelling tide of activism. "If it be a question of the supremacy of freedom or slavery underlying this war," she remembered thinking, "then I pray God it may be settled now, by us, and not be left to our children. And oh that I may be a hand, a foot, an eye, a voice, an influence, on the side of freedom and my country!"[1] Livermore's memoirs, which chronicled her work in the U.S. Sanitary Commission, testified to the breadth and depth of her contribution to the Union cause.[2] The war, for her, was a life-changing event, impacting on her views, her work, and her subsequent life. Given the dramatic quality of this change, Livermore was not so much representative as suggestive of the war's transformative possibility for writers and actors alike.

Writing of Livermore and others in 1882, the authors of the *History of Woman Suffrage* confidently asserted that the Civil War had "created a revolution in woman herself, as important in its results as the changed condition of the former slaves, and this silent influence is still busy." This revolution occurred after men left for the battlefield, when "new channels of industry were opened to [women], the value and control of money learned, thought upon political questions compelled, and a desire for their own personal, individual liberty intensified." The history of the war, they further argued, "which has never yet been truly written—is full of heroism in which woman is the central figure."[3]

Such celebrations of women's achievements in wartime began with the first shots at Fort Sumter and had become the sentimental norm by the 1880s and 1890s. Among the writers of this alternative history of the war there was agreement: "woman" had offered "a hand, a foot, an eye, a voice, an influence, on the side of freedom and [her] country," and this offering had created "a revolution in woman herself." The majority of the writers on the subject, with some important exceptions, were middle-class white women primarily from the Northeast.[4] The texts, illustrations, and narratives, and through them the explanations of the war's meaning they offered to the public and to posterity, filled popular magazines, pamphlets, autobiographies, and novels throughout the war period to the 1870s, when they almost entirely disappeared until a new flowering returned in the 1880s.

For all the celebration of women's participation and its corresponding emancipatory effect, however, a few women writers described the actual consequences of the war in grim terms. Elizabeth Stuart Phelps, who came of age as a writer during the war, perhaps more accurately captured its meaning when she remembered in her 1897 autobiography a country "dark with sorrowing women."[5] In the North alone 320,000 men were killed, and thousands more were maimed or died later from wounds or illness brought home from the front. It was unlikely that any woman was without a relative, friend, or acquaintance lost to the war.

These were not only emotional costs. The war created widows but few jobs to help them survive. As historian J. Matthew Gallman puts it, this was no "earlier generation of 'Rosie the Riveters' moving into new branches of heavy industry"; those jobs open to women tended to be female defined, low paying and too few, sought by desperate women who were compelled by their circumstances to take lower and lower wages or compensation. Without savings, and even with them, many women had to depend on kin and neighbors to support themselves and their children. The number of children in New York City almshouses alone, Gallman reports, "jumped by 300 percent during the war."[6] Northern wartime newspapers regularly included stories, both actual and fictional, of women who had been found starving and ill, their soldier husbands killed in the war or simply unable to support them.

Many women faced a profoundly difficult postwar life. African American women, if freed from bondage by the war's end, soon were enmeshed in economic peonage in the South and squeezed by the lack of economic opportunity in the North, often limiting them solely to demeaning and low-paying domestic work.[7] Women's suffrage organizers, hopeful that the war would prove a revolution in man as well as woman, hoped in vain. The Fifteenth Amendment, passed by the states in 1870, explicitly included only African American men as new voters despite women's patriotic efforts throughout the war.[8]

The public social conventions of womanhood were not discernibly loosened in the decades that followed; in fact, the reverse may be true. White middle-class women were more likely to teach in high schools, clerk for the government, and nurse in hospitals after the war, but these gains were in many cases won before the war, or represented only a small advance overall for women seeking employment. Greater numbers of women flocked to the factories of the postwar North, but it is likely this would have happened despite any wartime advances. In any case, conditions in many places worsened as Yankee workers were replaced with immigrants.[9]

It is true that some women who had participated in the war went on to create careers for themselves afterward—Mary Livermore, for example, became a lecturer and her family's main source of income, while Clara Barton founded the Red Cross—yet these were the exceptions. The rule remained: women in the mid-nineteenth century had few options for employment or for public or political power. If the war had produced a revolution in "woman's sense of herself," it had produced no immediate corresponding revolution in society or in material conditions. Why, then, the widespread incantations of the war's transformative meaning?

One can begin to understand the gap between public rhetoric and social reality by considering that the Civil War was a time when middle-class women came to believe that they had an acknowledged stake in a national ordeal of overwhelming importance, a personal stake in national politics. By the end of the war, many believed they had a right to a place in the history books, and they continued to believe this even after they became aware that their stories might never be written by the male scholars of the war. Despite economic and social reversals, despite the constricting fabric of conventional society, a personal and cultural vision of possibility evolved and was remembered. Although it was necessarily a limited and constructed vision, it was no less real for that.

The contours of this vision of woman's role in society during wartime emerged early in the newspapers, magazines, and novels of the war period. This written and public women's war became the site for cultural struggle over the meaning of the many divisions in Northern society. Within the dominant ideology of separate spheres, which prescribed appropriate behavior for both women and men, Northern women writers debated, contested, and confirmed their understanding of their role in wartime, as well as in national society, in more general terms. In the literary mass market they actively engaged in what Jane Tompkins calls "cultural" and Mary Poovey calls "ideological" work, finding an appropriate place of power and autonomy despite societal limitations.[10] Here they acted in their own arena of cultural politics, remaking and interpreting societal norms to achieve their own ends.

The work of women writers during the Civil War era was intended to move their readers: to shore up traditional ideas, to rearrange them, or to change them altogether. This idea, that minds can be worked upon by words, stories, and images, was related to the prewar insistence upon the power of moral suasion. It represented the ongoing power of the concept for middle-class women readers in the North, which, given an expanded literate public, was quite an audience. This work was emphatically political—meaning that it participated in the power relations in society—if it was rarely directly partisan: it entered a terrain of national concern, offering an interpretation of the nation's needs and fears.[11]

This effort toward creating a consensus—what I call a rhetoric of unity—was a common aspiration of Northern women writers during the 1850s. It was a claiming of a common purpose as the sections firmly defined themselves against each other: to wage a war successfully they had to see themselves in some sense as fundamentally different. In the early war years, this work was crucial to the Union effort to motivate a fractured populace to concerted effort. This rhetoric of unity, most successful in 1861 and early 1862, was no longer as effective by midwar, given the strains of the conflict. Afterward, women (and men) again adopted it for varying political purposes and in varying ways, using it largely to center the nation around ascendant middle-class capitalist values.

Political Work

Rhetoric, or the art of persuasion through language, only works when it draws upon a powerful common longing; without such longing, it is utterly ineffectual. The war formally began after a decade in which Northern women expressed a growing desire to be respected, understood, and valued by their society for their public as well as their private opinions.[12] This effort toward meaningfulness and a new form of self-respect was also in many cases a drive toward greater class and racial control. It represented an effort to define a universal womanhood that could provide both credibility and power to women, yet it defined women in ways that would most—or only—benefit the middle-class whites for whom such a definition was possible.

The wartime and the postwar period drew special attention to men specifically and to gender arrangements generally. Such a phenomenon was not unique to the Civil War. War, of course, tends to dramatize societal understandings of gender difference.[13] As political scientist Jean Bethke Elshtain argues, "[T]o men's wars, women are backdrop. . . . Women's involvement in war seems to us . . . inferential, located somewhere offstage if war is playing."[14] For women struggling to express a political voice, the war posed immediate and real challenges, even as it created opportunities.

In Civil War stories written by women, it was almost always a woman who played what the authors of *History of Woman Suffrage* later called the "central figure." Instead of accepting their offstage relation to war, they described the war's crucial events as happening where they were located, be it at home well away from the fighting, in a hospital in Washington, D.C., or on the battlefield itself.[15] And as Elshtain argues, "[T]o tell the tale gives power to the teller; he or she is implicated in the narrative and honored as a risk taker, for such one must be to tell this story." Women gained new social power in telling such stories.

Moreover, these stories have particular meaning for the culture, both now and then. In moments of national definition, trauma, and change, the power of the teller increases exponentially. "[S]ocieties are, in some sense, the sum total of their 'war stories': one can't think, for example, of the American story *without* the Civil War, for that war structured identities that are continually reinscribed."[16] If the Civil War was, as Shelby Foote suggested in Ken Burns's documentary film series *The Civil War,* the "crossroads of our being," how did women imagine that crossroads?

The tools of contemporary cultural theory can help the historian reconstruct the diverse meanings that once resided at this imaginative crossroads. The first step in this process is to recognize the complexity, even the ambiguity, of what may now seem to be simple texts. The elegies scattered throughout mainstream newspapers, as sentimental and lachrymose as they tended to be, had political implications, however muddled. As theorist Stuart Hall writes, "Popular culture is one of the sites where . . . [a] struggle for and against a culture of the powerful is engaged; it is also the stake to be won or lost *in* that struggle. It is the arena of consent and resistance."[17] This culture of the powerful was not only capitalism but also the accepted gender conventions of society, and the two were at times in conflict. Women's writings revealed a constant tension between "consent and resistance" to that society.[18]

Within the stories, poems, and narratives of the war, as well as within this rhetoric of unity itself, there was no real political consistency. That this would be true, however, is consistent with much popular or mass culture at that time and since. Writing of another "contested terrain," that of the nineteenth-century dime novels, historian Michael Denning argues that "these stories, which are products of the culture industry—'popular,' 'mass,' or 'commercial' culture—can be understood neither as forms of deception, manipulation, and social control nor as expressions of a genuine people's culture, opposing and resisting the dominant culture. Rather they are best seen as a contested terrain, a field of cultural conflict where signs with wide appeal and resonance take on contradictory disguises and are spoken in contrary accents."[19] In the stories of wartime women, conventional and transgressive messages spar even within the same text, where a yearning for self-expression is coupled with a rhetoric of unity that flattens difference. Rather than opposing the dominant culture and its ideologies of womanhood, writers manipulated those ideologies, first one way and then another, along a spectrum of cultural politics contained within accepted bounds.

These political negotiations took place in a variety of cultural forms, including poems, stories, novels, narratives, essays, and letters to the editor. None of these forms ipso facto established a singular meaning. As historian George Lipsitz persuasively argues, genre implies no inherent message. "Popular culture has no fixed forms," he writes, "individual artifacts of popular culture have no fixed meanings: it is impossible to say whether any one combination of sounds or set of images or grouping of words innately expresses one unified political position."[20] Poems and short stories, domestic and realist novels, narratives and essays all demonstrated ideas in conflict rather than particular visions in themselves.

Lipsitz's work also helps explain the complicated relationship between cultural forms and politics. In some sense, of course, all writing is inherently political: it expresses a set of assumptions, a viewpoint or viewpoints, each of which can be analyzed in terms of political ideology and meaning.[21] "Culture," Lipsitz argues, "can seem like a substitute for politics, a way of posing only imaginary solutions to real problems, but under other circumstances culture can become a rehearsal for politics, trying out values and beliefs permissible in art but forbidden in social life."[22] This concept of cultural expression as political rehearsal is central to understanding what women undertook in writing about the Civil War. In some instances, this approach was practiced explicitly; in other instances, it was practiced covertly.[23] In all these cases, women revealed through their cultural work their political understanding of society. They "tr[ied] out beliefs and values" that would be impermissible in stark unadulterated form—in Congress, for example—with a woman speaker.[24]

What I identify as the political work of women, then, was neither direct, nor purely radical or conservative, nor consistent in its messages, nor specific to a genre. Rarely in the North did any true consensus hold, even in the edited arena of public writing. For all that, however, certain patterns emerged, if only in the breach. Women writers used the opportunity to speak in the pages of literary magazines, political and religious newspapers, novels and stories, to change the way the nation saw the task it was undertaking. They wrote out of a collective longing for a meaningful place in the polity, even if it meant denying a similar place to another woman. This was their political work.

Separate Spheres Ideology

In order for women to write publicly, they had to begin with some obeisance to separate spheres ideology, whether or not that ideology had any material relevance to their lives. Whatever concerns beyond the limits or possibilities of this ideology they might hold—about the conditions of the working class, about the indolence of the rich, about the baleful influence of the Slave Power, about racial stereotypes, or about religious adherence among soldiers far from home—were refracted through an apologia for speaking or writing for the public.

Two ubiquitous themes emerged during the prewar years in the public writing of women, although they were never agreed upon. The first of these was slavery, and, after 1863, race. Throughout the war, an important minority of women writers insisted that the moral meaning of the war could only be the end to slavery, and that women were appropriately called upon to enter politics and to make that happen as the natural arbiters of morality. A few African American women, Charlotte Forten and Frances Ellen Watkins Harper among them, wrote both with and against the grain of gender convention to affirm and interpret their roles as women and as African Americans in white society. Yet the majority of writers on issues of slavery and race at this time were white, and their varying political perspectives shaped their understanding of the meaning and urgency of emancipation.

Secondly, a new recognition of class difference and the limits of gender solidarity emerged during the late 1850s. This strengthened throughout the war, particularly after 1863. Not surprisingly, class issues took on new relevance for middle-class women concerned about national unity as well as eager to establish a vision of universal womanhood. Most ended the war with a stronger sense of the middle-class values they deemed most crucial to the nation's recovery, thereby criticizing both ruling-class and working-class women. For a few major young writers these distinctions were ones to overcome. Class injustices became the defining problem in their writing during and especially after the war, heralding a new movement into the social protest novel of the 1870s and 1880s.[25]

With few exceptions, all of these themes were explored by Northern middle-class women within an overarching framework of separate spheres ideology. Women described the world in terms of complementary arenas of power, some of which were seen as possibly permeable (class and, to varying extents, gender) and others of which were not (race). This ideological construct, which grew in influence with the shifts in economic life in New England and the Northwest in the early years of the century, had solidified as the central social matrix of the emerging Protestant middle class by the 1830s. Within this construct men and women were understood to occupy distinct social spaces.[26] Men were to dominate and control a public "sphere," while women were to supervise and inhabit a private "sphere." Although the ideology implied parity, there was an assumed hierarchy of importance and power: public life was where change happened and was the arena of history. Private life, by contrast, was a timeless arena of domesticity and piety, where women took on a familial rather than individual identity. Men made history; women made families.[27]

By the early 1850s, however, the social arrangements that limited women were under challenge. In 1848 a group of women gathered in Seneca Falls, New York, to protest the legal, political, and societal liabilities of womanhood. Despite public ridicule, they continued to meet, give lectures, and organize petitions throughout the 1850s. Other reformers, some of whom were connected to this movement, published magazines, including the *Una* and *Sibyl,* directed toward reform of conventional social norms.

A few individual writers questioned separate sphere ideology explicitly. "Men and Women," an essay published in the *National Era* in 1859, was an ironic but nonetheless critical piece of this literature. In it, Mary Abigail Dodge, or Gail Hamilton, laughingly scorned the tired "platitudes" concerning "woman's opportunities for self-sacrifice, moral heroism, silent influence, might of love, and all that cut-and-dried woman's-sphere-ism." Give women rubber boots to walk in the rain, take away their constricting clothes (and, by implication, codes), she wrote, and free them from themselves, and you will give them more power than any platitudes. Her mother, it seemed, was shocked by her writing and the criticism it generated. In a private letter, Dodge was anything but conciliatory and remained frank about her purposes as a writer. "I wish you to understand that if I write much I shall probably meet with a great deal of opposition," she wrote, "for I shall express views which run counter to popular conviction, so if you faint now, you will have a catalepsy by and by when worst comes to worst."[28]

As Dodge implied, popular conviction supported separate sphere ideology. In a typical letter to the editor of the *New York Ledger* in 1860, for example, "Gula Meredith" wrote of "Woman's True Position" in no uncertain terms. "Woman can best understand woman's nature," she wrote, "and it is against our nature as against our reason to be seen in the Pulpit, at the Bar or the Polls. Woman's sphere is to elevate, to purify, to teach, and her empire is home."[29] Sarah Josepha Hale, editor of the popular *Godey's Ladies Book,* would surely have agreed.

The ideology of separate spheres was understood and applied in widely divergent ways, however. Dodge said as much in "A Spasm of Sense," an essay published in the *Atlantic Monthly* during the war. "But without any suspicious lunges into that dubious region which lies outside of woman's universally acknowledged 'sphere' (a blight rest upon that word!)," she wrote ironically, "there is within the pale, within the boundary-line which the most conservative never dreamed of questioning, room for a great divergence of ideas."[30] Dodge was right: what any study of the North from the 1850s to the 1870s reveals is a divergence of ideas, yet ideas still limited by boundary lines.

Tangled within separate sphere ideology were assumed ideologies of class and race. As with gender, there was an implied hierarchy of value, even at the same time that middle-class white women proclaimed a universal womanhood. For example, when Gula Meredith argued that women could only work in professions that kept them largely in the home, she excluded many women even while professing to speak for all.

The ideology of separate spheres was intimately connected with its material and economic context. Meant to explain and justify the new lives of women in an industrializing region, separate spheres played a crucial part in middle-class formation.[31] The ideology itself allowed for a standardization of domestic values controlled by the middle class, which Catharine Beecher in her 1841 *Treatise on Domestic Economy* so clearly understood.[32] As historian Christine Stansell argues, "Within the propertied classes, women constituted themselves the moral guardians of their families and their nation, offsetting some of the inherited liabilities of their sex. Laboring women were less fortunate."[33] That middle-class women owed their position to fortune rather than to virtue went unacknowledged by most of the women writers of the period. To acknowledge that notion, of course, would be to undercut their claims to universal moral authority.

By writing on issues of great national concern and by professing to speak for all women, middle-class white women writers were continuing the work of class formation, the political work central to their understanding of the war. Their stories, essays, and narratives constructed an appropriate standard of behavior meant to create and sustain national unity. At the same time, these women were protecting their own claim to legitimacy and respectability despite their stepping, if only with their words, into a public and, by implication, a political arena.

The ideology of separate spheres also assumed whiteness. In their writing, white women rarely if ever extended their assumptions to encompass black women, who were by implication thought literally beyond the pale of respectable womanhood.[34] At the same time, antislavery writers insisted that a natural sense of universal womanhood meant a shared sisterhood, albeit a sisterhood of unequals. As with gender and class, here was an implied and unquestioned hierarchy. White middle-class women were to succor their bereaved and wronged sisters, both African American and white working class, and thereby give themselves power and legitimacy. This rhetoric of unity was not democratic, despite its claim to a kind of democracy.

African American women were well aware of the racial limitations of the ideology of separate spheres. As historian James Horton has shown, the Northern antebellum African American community in Philadelphia found it impossible to accommodate to this ideology on a daily basis. With remunerative labor for African American men severely limited, and that for women generally domestic and thus outside the home, the result was an added yoke of oppression.[35] Literary historian Hazel Carby has argued that African American women explicitly challenged the ideology of separate spheres by reconstructing a new vision of womanhood that affirmed their racial community.[36] African American women exposed the fortune and privilege that allowed white middle-class women their claims of moral authority, and claimed their own moral authority through their experience of injustice.

The political work of Northern women writers, white or African American, rich or poor, was in writing an alternative history and narrative of the war. This story was written through a matrix of gender, class, and racial assumptions. If the white mainstream ideology of separate spheres was not broken by the war, at the end of the war it was severely bent and adjusted; its reimposition in the postwar years, enabled by a celebratory story of patriotic women now eager to return to domesticity, was never complete. The public war dialogue on women, African American slavery, and class demonstrated both the ideology's inherent elasticity and its clear limitations. Yet for many the war served as a transformative moment, a revolution in the *understanding* of woman herself.

In some sense, women—other than those few hundred that historians estimate cross-dressed and fought as men—could never truly understand what Walt Whitman called the "real war."[37] (Nor could he, never having faced combat.) In letters home, North and South, soldiers reiterated again and again how impossible the job of translating the horror and chaos was, even as they kept trying to do just that.[38] The reasons Union soldiers gave to their kin and friends for fighting, despite that horror, were in general not those women offered in letters or—what is under scrutiny here—more public documents. This was not, in general, because of an acknowledged "timorous nature," as historian James M. McPherson finds one post-war novel suggesting; women publicly described their work during wartime as requiring enormous courage, if only the courage to let their loved ones live up to their expressed ideals.[39]

Women, these sources suggest, had a complicated relationship to the ideals of republicanism that both motivated men to fight and sustained men even through the dark endless days of the midwar and the grueling bloodbaths of 1864. In many ways women clearly participated in the value systems expressed by the war-torn North, and they wondered publicly whether the North could sustain the character necessary for republicanism. Their work celebrated sacrifice, and often claimed that such sacrifice was necessary to reestablish virtue in a wavering nation.[40] In a sense, white middle-class women's effort to create a rhetoric of unity was part of a larger national effort toward consensus. As historian Earl J. Hess argues, "Northerners . . . stressed the viability of free government, seeing proof that ideological consensus could unite individualistic people in a common cause, focus their energy on a central purpose, and give them the motivation and strength to endure."[41] Particularly for women like Lydia Maria Child, Jane Swisshelm, Mary Abigail Dodge, and others trained (or self-taught) in the tradition of republicanism and liberalism, these were powerfully motivating ideas.

Other women did not demonstrate the same confidence in the power of republicanism, liberty, or the belief in progress to sustain them. Women's relationship to republicanism was uneasy, given their subordinate status within it: as dependents, at least ideologically, their voices were not meant to be heard in a national public context, just as their political ideas, represented by the vote, were not accepted. Similarly, the ideology of individualism, held in tension with republicanism, was problematic as well. Embraced by some, it was emphatically rejected by others as a kind of dismissal of the connections and responsibilities of family and community. As a result, women had diverging positions on the reigning ideologies supporting the Union war effort, even as they claimed a public space in the discussion of the war's necessity and purpose.

This is not to say that Northern women were not patriotic—many, given their work, sacrifice, and words, decidedly were—but their relationship to war, fought at a distance, claiming family members to whom they were deeply committed, and based on an ideological system within which they fit at times poorly, was distinct from men's. For women there seemed to be no ruling consensus on the meaning of Union, or on the cause of the strife. For many of them—with crucial exceptions—the question was not always how to justify the sacrifice but how to endure it.

That uneasy relationship to the national struggle can help explain women's constant reference to their "place": even to speak in support of the ideological meaning of the war effort was to disturb its internal logic, and yet not to intervene in the crisis consuming the nation seemed to lack virtue as well. Their rhetoric of unity, then, was a kind of offering: women would be a virtuous backbone for the battlefront, stalwart in the face of loss, not quite dependent, if never independent, yet claiming space in the national crisis. The problem was, however, that this ideological offering could not sustain the material and political differences among Northern women: its rhetoric only briefly had resonance for the wider public.

This book explores two separate and related histories of the war in order to illuminate the revolution Northern women writers claimed for their sex. First, this is a history gleaned through literary works designed for public consumption, focusing on political issues in the writing of Northern women from 1850 to 1872. This history

ON THE SUBJECT OF...

LYDIA MARIA CHILD (1802-1880)

Child was a best-selling author of novels, books of advice for homemakers, and literature for children who garnered even more attention for her antislavery literature. Abolitionism was a highly controversial and often unpopular position in the 1830s when Child published her antislavery works, but she was unapologetic about her principles and continued to produce political tracts despite initial damage to her financial success and her reputation. Nevertheless, Child's novels and advice books, generally praised in reviews, sold very well and were reprinted multiple times. Her first novels, *Hobomok: A Tale of Early Times* (1824) and *The Rebels; or, Boston before the Revolution* (1825), depicted Massachusetts in the early colonial period and the revolutionary era, respectively. Child's nonfiction books included a series of advice books, including *The Frugal Housewife* (1829), *The Mother's Book* (1831), and *The Little Girl's Own Book* (1831), as well as collections of biographical sketches of such women as Germaine de Staël, and a compendium of facts titled *The History of the Condition of Women* (1835). Child's *The Juvenile Miscellany* (1826-34), a children's periodical she created and published, was also popular.

In 1828, Child married David Lee Child, a prominent lawyer, member of the Massachusetts Legislature, and a dedicated abolitionist. Child continued to publish books, providing financial security for she and her husband until 1833, when she published *An Appeal in Favor of That Class of Americans Called Africans,* a solid, thorough, and ultimately very influential argument for emancipation. Feminist studies of Child have focused upon the apparently conservative impulses of her advice books as reinforcing women's domestic roles, as well as her life of activism and her antislavery writings as examples of ground-breaking challenges to nineteenth century gender norms.

suggests a gradual and contested shift from sentimental to realistic writing, demonstrated within as well as between texts. Women writers continued to see their work as moral activism throughout the period, periodically changing the objects of their struggles but not their commitment to moral suasion itself. During this period in literary history as well, women writers moved from what literary critic Susan K. Harris calls the exploratory to the later didactic novel, a move that meant a changed understanding of womanhood and social possibility, as well as a discernible lifting of some of the boundaries of woman's sphere, if only fictionally.

Secondly, and equally as important, this work offers an intellectual portrait of nine popular women writers by following them and their work through the war years and afterward. These include Lydia Maria Child, Harriet Beecher Stowe, Fanny Fern, Mrs. E.D.E.N. Southworth, Frances Ellen Watkins Harper, Gail Hamilton (Mary Abigail Dodge), Louisa May Alcott, Rebecca Harding Davis, and Elizabeth Stuart Phelps. Among the dozens of women writers who broached the war topic—some popular and others virtually unknown—these nine seemed both exceptional and representative, covering varied audiences and overlapping generations. An analysis of the lives and writing of these women demonstrates the transformation in thinking and writing that the Civil War meant for working writers. The war moved writers of an older generation to a more active politics while helping to establish the new confident voices of a younger generation coming of age during the late 1850s and early 1860s.

These nine were exceptional, for Northern women, primarily because they were writers, earning their living and often supporting their families on income from published work. They were also exceptional in their politics: it is very unlikely that Northern women as a whole were as committed to the end of slavery as these writers were. Yet they were also, in a sense, representative, or at least resonant for their readers: these were women whose work was sought out and eagerly awaited, reprinted in numerous magazines and newspapers, and referred to in lesser-known novels in an offhand way, as if the readers would immediately see and understand the references. If these were not the politics of the readers, they were at least positions readers wanted to know about and ponder. Their work appeared, also, in the more progressive venues: to publish a woman writer on any issue approaching politics was a kind of political statement by editors and publishers. Given these venues—papers like the *New York Ledger,* magazines like *Atlantic Monthly*—the politics of these nine women were representative.

The Civil War and the sectional issues that preceded it offered women writers the opportunity to enter into debates of national significance. Even if using the back door of cultural documents, women joined a political dialogue. Their heroines, whether autobiographical or fictional, were meant to inspire and influence their readers; even the most sensationalist works had didactic—and political—purposes. These writings demonstrated an ongoing and consistent effort to redefine in an outward motion the limits of women's sphere. As essayist Mary Abigail Dodge wryly wrote in 1865, "I shall not confine myself to my sphere. I hate my sphere. I like everything that is outside of it,—or, better still, my sphere rounds out into undefined space. I was born into the whole world. I am monarch of all I survey."[42] This book explores how the writings of women reached out into public life during this tumultuous time, "round[ing] out into undefined space," and touching their hearts, as Oliver Wendell Holmes put it, "with fire."[43]

1. Livermore, *My Story,* 85, 92.
2. The U.S. Sanitary Commission (USSC) was organized early in the war as a voluntary association designed to help the Army Medical Bureau. Given official sanction in June 1861, it was staffed almost entirely by women, although led largely by men. Among other related tasks, the commission gathered money, food, and supplies of all kinds and distributed them to the soldiers.
3. Stanton, Anthony, and Gage, eds., *History of Woman Suffrage,* 23.
4. The experience of white and black Southern women during and just after the war is the subject of numerous and useful twentieth-century books and articles; see, among others, Bynum, *Unruly Women*; Clinton, *Tara Revisited*; Clinton and Silber, eds., *Divided Houses*; Forbes, *African American Women*; Hodes, *White Women, Black Men*; Hunter, *To 'Joy My Freedom*; Jones, *Labor of Love*; Rable, *Civil Wars*; and Whites, *Civil War.*
5. Phelps, *Chapters from a Life,* 97.
6. Gallman, *North Fights,* 107, 105.
7. See, especially, Forbes, *African American Women*; Jones, *Labor of Love,* and Lebsock, *Free Women.*
8. See Stanton, Anthony, and Gage, eds. *History of Woman Suffrage*; DuBois, *Woman Suffrage* and *Feminism and Suffrage*; Flexner, *Century of Struggle*; and Newman, *White Women's Rights.*
9. See Dublin, *Women at Work,* ch. 9, and Kessler-Harris, *Out to Work,* ch. 4.
10. For the notion of "cultural work" undertaken through literature, I am indebted to Tompkins, *Sensational Designs*; a similar understanding of "ideological work," also tremendously useful, is from Poovey's *Uneven Developments.*

11. My understanding of the parameters of the word "political" has been deeply shaped by Joan Scott. See Scott, *Gender and the Politics.* Rebecca Edwards argues that this expanded understanding of politics does not represent how nineteenth-century Americans thought. During the Civil War and in the decades before and after it, however, middle-class women who were writing for a public audience at times explicitly claimed their work to be political; at others they coyly claimed it not to be while it made demands about the direction of national politics (see, for example, Mrs. Bird in *Uncle Tom's Cabin,* one of the most political of novels). See Edwards, *Angels,* 9. In any case, if the women writers studied here did not consistently claim politics as their domain, they nonetheless participated in political discussions, writing for a public audience about issues of national concern in order to make change.

12. My understanding of rhetoric and its power has come to me through Plato's *Gorgias* and its explication by my colleague in the Philosophy Department at Sarah Lawrence College, Michael Davis.

13. See Elshtain, *Women and War,* and Joan Scott, "Rewriting History," in Higonnet et al., eds., *Behind the Lines,* 26. See also Faust, "Altars of Sacrifice," 1200, as well as Faust, *Mothers of Invention.*

14. Elshtain, *Women and War,* 165.

15. This theme of locating the central story with women rather than men is common to much women's fiction in the mid-nineteenth century. See Baym, *Women's Fiction.*

16. Elshtain, *Women and War,* 22, 166.

17. Hall, "Notes," 76. See also Jameson, "Reification and Utopia."

18. On this point see Baym, *Novels,* 27.

19. Denning, *Mechanic Accents,* 3.

20. Lipsitz, *Time Passages,* 13.

21. As Elshtain says, "Politics is the work of citizens, human beings in their civic capacities" (*Women and War,* 227).

22. Lipsitz, *Time Passages,* 16.

23. Lydia Maria Child's and Harriet Beecher Stowe's "letters to the editor" of the *National Anti-Slavery Standard* and the *Independent,* respectively, are frank expressions of politics; didactic stories funded by religious societies and the earlier mentioned death poetry tended to be more covert.

24. Significantly it was during the Civil War that the first woman *did* speak in the congressional halls. Anna Dickinson, a young and popular political lecturer, spoke to assembled legislators in the House of Representatives in 1864, spontaneously recommending President Abraham Lincoln for reelection during the course of her talk.

25. See Harris, *Nineteenth-Century American Women's Novels.*

26. The literature on this ideology and its relevance to daily social life in the nineteenth century is vast. Of particular note are the following in order of appearance in the historical dialogue: Barbara Welter, "The Cult of True Womanhood: 1800-1860," *American Quarterly* 18 (1966): 151-74; Sklar, *Catharine Beecher;* Cott, *Bonds of Womanhood;* Douglas, *Feminization of American Culture;* Epstein, *Politics of Domesticity;* Smith-Rosenberg, *Disorderly Conduct;* Kerber, "Separate Spheres"; Cogan, *All-American Girl;* and Harris, *Nineteenth-Century American Women's Novels.*

27. The degree to which this ideology applied to lived experience has been challenged by historians. Mary Ryan, for example, in *Women in Public,* makes the argument that women led public lives despite conventional dicta.

28. Dodge, ed., *Gail Hamilton's Life,* I:280.

29. "Meredith," "Woman's True Position," *New York Ledger* 16, no. 37 (Nov. 17, 1860): 4.

30. Gail Hamilton, "A Spasm of Sense," in Hamilton, *Gala-Days,* 271; the essay was first published in the *Atlantic Monthly.*

31. See Blumin, *Emergence of the Middle Class,* ch. 5. My understanding of class formation has also been informed by Stansell, *City of Women,* and Wilentz, *Chants Democratic.* For the impact of domestic ideology on ideas about women and work, see Kessler-Harris, *Out to Work,* 53.

32. See Sklar, *Catharine Beecher,* 165.

33. Stansell, *City of Women,* ix. For the relationship of working women to the ideology of separate spheres, see also Alexander, "We Are Engaged," and Ginzberg, *Women and the Work of Benevolence.*

34. See Newman, *White Women's Rights.*

35. Horton, "Freedom's Yoke." See also Forbes, *African American Writers.*

36. See Carby, *Reconstructing Womanhood.*

37. See Leonard, *All the Daring of a Soldier.*

38. McPherson, *For Cause and Comrades,* 12.

39. Ibid., 77.

40. Hess, Liberty, *Virtue and Progress,* 17, 50.

41. Ibid., 107.

42. Hamilton, *Skirmishes and Sketches,* 432.

43. Quoted in McPherson, *Ordeal by Fire,* 487.

Works Cited

Alexander, Ruth M. "We Are Engaged as a Band of Sisters." *Journal of American History* 75, (Dec. 1988).

Blumin, Stuart. *The Emergence of the Middle Class: Social Experience in the American City, 1760-1900.* Cambridge: Cambridge University Press, 1989.

Bynum, Victoria. *Unruly Women: The Politics of Social and Sexual Control in the Old South.* Chapel Hill: University of North Carolina Press, 1992.

Carby, Hazel. *Reconstructing Womanhood: The Emergence of the Afro-American Woman Novelist.* New York and London: Oxford University Press, 1987.

Child, Lydia Maria. *Correspondence between Lydia Maria Child, and Gov. Wise and Mrs. Mason, of Virginia.* New York: Anti-Slavery Society, 1860.

———. *The Freedman's Book.* Boston: Ticknor and Fields, 1865.

———. *Lydia Maria Child, Selected Letters, 1817-1880.* Edited by Milton Meltzer and Patricia Holland. Amherst: University of Massachusetts Press, 1982.

Clinton, Catherine. *Tara Revisited: Women, War, and the Plantation Legend.* New York: Abbeville Press, 1995.

Clinton, Catherine, and Nina Silber, eds. *Divided Houses: Gender and the Civil War.* New York and London: Oxford University Press, 1992.

Cogan, Frances B. *All-American Girl: The Ideal of Real Womanhood in Mid-Nineteenth-Century America.* Athens: University of Georgia Press, 1989.

Cott, Nancy. *The Bonds of Womanhood: "Woman's Sphere" in New England, 1780-1835.* New Haven: Yale University Press, 1977.

Denning, Michael. *Mechanic Accents: Dime Novels and Working-Class Culture in America.* New York and London: Verso, 1987.

Dodge, H. Augusta, ed. *Gail Hamilton's Life in Letters.* 2 vols. Boston: Lee and Shepard, 1901.

Douglas, Ann. *The Feminization of American Culture.* New York: Knopf, 1977.

Dublin, Thomas. *Women at Work.* New York: Columbia University Press, 1979.

DuBois, Ellen Carol. *Feminism and Suffrage.* Ithaca, N.Y.: Cornell University Press, 1978.

———. *Woman Suffrage and Women's Rights.* New York: New York University Press, 1958.

Edwards, Rebecca. *Angels in the Machinery: Gender in American Party Politics from the Civil War to the Progressive Era.* New York: Oxford University Press, 1997.

Elshtain, Jean Bethke. *Women and War.* New York: Basic Books, 1987.

Epstein, Barbara Leslie. *The Politics of Domesticity: Women, Evangelism, and Temperance in Nineteenth-Century America.* Middletown, Conn.: Wesleyan University Press, 1981.

Faust, Drew Gilpin. "Altars of Sacrifice: Confederate Women and the Narratives of War." *Journal of American History* (Spring 1990): 1200-1228.

———. *Mothers of Invention: Women of the Slaveholding South in the American Civil War.* Chapel Hill: University of North Carolina Press, 1996.

Flexner, Eleanor. *Century of Struggle.* 1957. Cambridge, Mass.: The Belknap Press of Harvard University Press, 1975.

Forbes, Ella. *African American Women during the Civil War.* New York: Garland Publishing, 1998.

Gallman, J. Matthew. *The North Fights the Civil War: The Home Front.* Chicago: Ivan R. Dee Press, 1994.

Ginzburg, Lori. *Women and the Work of Benevolence.* New Haven: Yale University Press, 1990.

Hall, Stuart. "Notes on Deconstructing 'The Popular'." In *People's History and Socialist Theory,* edited by Raphael Samuel, 227–40. London: Routledge and Kegan Paul, 1981.

Hamilton, Gail [Mary Dodge]. *Gala-Days.* Boston: Ticknor and Fields, 1863.

———. *Skirmishes and Sketches.* Boston: Ticknor and Fields, 1865.

Harris, Susan K. *Nineteenth-Century American Women's Novels: Interpretive Strategies.* Cambridge: Cambridge University Press, 1990.

Hess, Earl J. *Liberty, Virtue and Progress: Northerners and Their War for the Union.* New York: Fordham University Press, 1997.

Higonnet, Margaret Randolph, Jane Jenson, Sonya Michel, and Margaret Collins Weitz, eds. *Behind the Lines: Gender and the Two World Wars.* New Haven: Yale University Press, 1987.

Hodes, Martha. *White Women, Black Men: Illicit Sex in the Nineteenth-Century South.* New Haven: Yale University Press, 1997.

Horton, James Oliver. "Freedom's Yoke: Gender Conventions among Antebellum Free Blacks." *Feminist Studies* 12, no. 1 (Spring 1986).

Hunter, Tera. *To 'Joy My Freedom: Southern Black Women's Lives and Labors after the Civil War.* Cambridge, Mass.: Harvard University Press, 1998.

Jameson, Frederic. "Reification and Utopia in Mass Culture." *Social Text* (Winter 1979): 130-48.

Jones, Jacqueline. *Labor of Love, Labor of Sorrow.* New York: Vintage, 1985.

Kerber, Linda K. "Separate Spheres, Female Worlds, Women's Place: The Rhetoric of Women's History." *Journal of American History* 75 (June 1988): 9-39.

Kessler-Harris, Alice. *Out to Work: A History of Wage-Earning Women in the United States.* New York and London: Oxford University Press, 1982.

Lebsock, Susan. *The Free Women of Petersburg: Status and Culture in a Southern Town, 1784-1860.* New York: W. W. Norton and Co., 1984.

Leonard, Elizabeth D. *All the Daring of a Soldier: Women of the Civil War Armies.* New York: W. W. Norton and Co., 1999.

Lipsitz, George. *Time Passages: Collective Memory and American Popular Culture.* Minneapolis: University of Minnesota Press, 1990.

Livermore, Mary. *My Story of the War.* Hartford, Conn.: A. D. Worthington and Company, 1888.

McPherson, James M. *For Cause and Comrades: Why Men Fought in the Civil War.* New York: Oxford University Press, 1997.

———. *Ordeal by Fire: The Civil War and Reconstruction.* 2nd ed. New York: McGraw Hill Inc., 1992.

Newman, Louise. *White Women's Rights: The Racial Origins of Feminism in the United States.* New York: Oxford University Press, 1999.

Poovey, Mary. "A Housewifely Woman: The Social Construction of Florence Nightingale." *Uneven Developments: The Ideological Work of Gender in Mid-Victorian England.* Chicago: University of Chicago Press, 1988.

Rable, George. *Civil Wars: Women and the Crisis of Southern Nationalism.* Urbana: University of Illinois Press, 1989.

Ryan, Mary P. *Women in Public: Between Banners and Ballots, 1825-1880.* Baltimore, Md.: Johns Hopkins University Press, 1989.

Scott, Joan W. *Gender and the Politics of History.* New York: Columbia University Press, 1988.

Sklar, Kathryn Kish. *Catharine Beecher: A Study of American Domesticity.* New York: W. W. Norton and Co., 1973.

Smith-Rosenberg, Carroll. *Disorderly Conduct: Visions of Gender in Victorian America.* New York: Knopf, 1985.

Stansell, Christine. *City of Women: Sex and Class in New York, 1789-1860.* Urbana: University of Illinois Press, 1982.

Stanton, Elizabeth Cady, Susan B. Anthony, and Matilda Joslyn Gage, eds. *History of Woman Suffrage.* Vol. 2. New York: Fowler and Wells, Publishers, 1882.

Stowe, Charles Edward, ed. *Life of Harriet Beecher Stowe, Compiled from Her Letters and Journals.* Boston: Houghton Mifflin, 1889.

Stowe, Harriet Beecher. "Getting Ready for a Gale." *Independent* 13, no. 647 (Apr. 25, 1861): 1.

Tompkins, Jane. *Sensational Designs: The Cultural Work of American Fiction, 1790-1860.* New York and Oxford: Oxford University Press, 1985.

Welter, Barbara. *Dimity Convictions: The American Woman in the Nineteenth Century.* Athens: Ohio University Press, 1976.

Whites, LeeAnn. *The Civil War as a Crisis in Gender: Augusta, Georgia, 1860-1890.* Athens: University of Georgia Press, 1995.

Wilenz, Sean. *Chants Democratic: New York City and the Rise of the American Working Class, 1788-1850.* New York: Oxford University Press, 1984.

BRITISH WOMEN WRITERS

ELAINE SHOWALTER (ESSAY DATE 1977)

SOURCE: Showalter, Elaine. "The Double Critical Standard and the Feminine Novel." In *A Literature of Their Own: British Women Novelists From Brontë to Lessing,* pp. 73-99. Princeton, N. J.: Princeton University Press, 1977.

In the following essay, Showalter describes how women authors in the Victorian age, including George Eliot and Charlotte Brontë, were unable to escape the condescending judgment of critics who refused to believe that women were capable of producing art that was equal to that of men.

To their contemporaries, nineteenth-century women writers were women first, artists second. A woman novelist, unless she disguised herself with a male pseudonym, had to expect critics to focus on her femininity and rank her with the other women writers of her day, no matter how diverse their subjects or styles. The knowledge that their individual achievement would be subsumed under a relatively unfavorable group stereotype acted as a constant irritant to feminine novelists. George Eliot protested against being compared to Dinah Mulock; Charlotte Brontë tried to delay the publication of *Villette* so that it would not be reviewed along with Mrs. Gaskell's *Ruth.* Brontë particularly wanted to prevent the male literary establishment from making women writers into competitors and rivals for the same small space: "It is the nature of writers to be invidious," she wrote to Mrs. Gaskell, but "we shall set them at defiance; they *shall* not make us foes."[1]

We tend to forget how insistently Victorian reviewers made women the targets of *ad feminam* criticism. An error in Gordon Haight's *A Century of George Eliot Criticism* illustrates this common modern oversight; Haight quotes E. S. Dallas as saying of Eliot that no "Englishman" could approach her as a writer of prose. The word Dallas actually used was "English*woman*."[2] To Haight, such a distinction may seem trivial; to George Eliot, it was not. Gentleman reviewers had patronized lady novelists since the beginning of the nineteenth century; in 1834, for example, the reviewer for *Fraser's* had gloated prematurely over what he believed to be the true authorship of *Castle Rackrent* and *The Absentee*: "Ay: it is just as we expected! Miss Edgeworth *never* wrote *the* Edgeworth novels . . . all that, as we have long had a suspicion, was the work of her father."[3] But the intense concentration on the proper sphere of the woman writer did not appear in criticism until the 1840s. Victorian critics strained their ingenuity for terms that would put delicate emphasis on the specialness of women and avoid the professional neutrality of "woman writer": authoress, female pen, lady novelist, and as late as Hurst & Blackett's 1897 commemorative volume, *Women Novelists of Queen Victoria's Reign,* the elegant "lady fictionists," described by "living mistresses of the craft." Through the 1850s and 1860s there was a great increase in theoretical and specific criticism of women novelists. Hardly a journal failed to publish an essay on women's literature; hardly a critic failed to express himself upon its innate and potential qualities.

This situation, similar to the expanded market for literature by and about women in the late 1960s, suggests that the Victorians were responding to what seemed like a revolutionary, and in many ways a very threatening, phenomenon. As the number of important novels by women increased through the 1850s and 1860s, male journalists were forced to acknowledge that women were excelling in the creation of fiction, not just in England, but also in Europe and America. As it became apparent that Jane Austen and Maria

Edgeworth were not aberrations, but the forerunners of female participation in the development of the novel, jokes about dancing dogs no longer seemed an adequate response.

One form of male resistance was to see women novelists as being engaged in a kind of aggressive conspiracy to rob men of their markets, steal their subject matter, and snatch away their young lady readers, to see them as "dominating" because of superior numbers rather than superior abilities. As late as 1851, there were a few hardy souls who continued to deny that women *could* write novels. Coventry Patmore conceded that "there certainly have been cases of women possessed of the properly masculine power of writing books, but these cases are all so truly and obviously exceptional, and must and ought always to remain so, that we may overlook them without the least prejudice to the soundness of our doctrine."[4] Some reviewers found the situation so embarrassing that they had to treat it as an unfortunate accident. In 1853 J. M. Ludlow glumly advised his readers, "We have to notice the fact that at this particular moment of the world's history the very *best* novels in several great countries happen to have been written by women."[5] But by 1855, even before the appearance of George Eliot, the emergence of the woman's novel was so striking that most readers and reviewers would have agreed with Margaret Oliphant in linking it to other symptoms of social progress: "This, which is the age of so many things—of enlightenment, of science, of progress—is quite as distinctly the age of female novelists."[6]

Even those critics who disapproved of changes in the doctrine of the two sexual spheres were far from advocating women's retirement from the literary field. The new questions of women's *place* in literature proved endlessly fascinating, and the Victorians approached them with all the weight of their religious commitments and their interest in the sciences of human nature. Although most periodical criticism, especially between 1847 and 1875, employed a double standard for men's and women's writing and seemed shocked or chagrined by individual women's failures to conform to the stereotypes, a few critics, notably G. H. Lewes, George Eliot, and R. H. Hutton, were beginning to consider what women as a group might contribute to the art of the novel.

Most of the negative criticism tried to justify the assumption that novels by women would be recognizably inferior to those by men. When the Victorians thought of the woman writer, they immediately thought of the female body and its presumed afflictions and liabilities. They did so, first, because the biological creativity of childbirth seemed to them directly to rival the aesthetic creativity of writing. The metaphors of childbirth familiarly invoked to describe the act of writing directed attention toward the possibility of real conflict between these analogous experiences. In an 1862 review of Mrs. Browning, Gerald Massey wrote: "It is very doubtful if the highest and richest nature of woman can ever be unfolded in its home life and wedded relationships, and yet at the same time blossom and bear fruit in art or literature with a similar fulness. What we mean is, that there is so great a draft made upon women by other creative works, so as to make the chance very small that the general energy shall culminate in the greatest musician, for example. The nature of woman demands *that* to perfect it in life which must half-lame it for art. A mother's heart, at its richest, is not likely to get adequate expression in notes and bars, if it were only for the fact that she must be absorbed in other music."[7]

Second, there was a strong belief that the female body was in itself an inferior instrument, small, weak, and, in Geraldine Jewsbury's words, "liable to collapses, eclipses, failures of power . . . unfitting her for the steady stream of ever-recurring work."[8] Victorian physicians and anthropologists supported these ancient prejudices by arguing that women's inferiority could be demonstrated in almost every analysis of the brain and its functions. They maintained that, like the "lower races," women had smaller and less efficient brains, less complex nerve development, and more susceptibility to certain diseases, than did men. Any expenditure of mental energy by women would divert the supply of blood and phosphates from the reproductive system to the brain, leading to dysmenorrhea, "ovarian neuralgia," physical degeneracy, and sterility. Physicians estimated that "maternal functions diverted nearly 20 percent of women's vital energies from potential brain activity."[9]

Female intellectual distinction thus suggested not only a self-destructive imitation of a male skill but also a masculine physical development. Elizabeth Barrett referred in a general way to this widespread association when she apostrophized her heroine, George Sand, as "thou large-brained woman and large-hearted man," but it was often used more snidely in allusions to George Eliot's "large hand" and "large eye"—metaphors of artistic mastery that invariably suggested to the Victorians large noses and large feet.[10] This physical imagery was further popularized by Victorian phrenologists like George Combe, who believed creative traits to be revealed by the shape of the skull. The bizarre theories of the phrenologists and the quacks were reinforced by the expertise of scientists like James Macgrigor Allan, who stated dogmatically to his fellow anthropologists in 1869 that "in intellectual labour, man has surpassed, does now and always will surpass woman, for the obvious reason that nature does not periodically interrupt his thought and application."[11] Advanced thinkers were influenced by these ideas even if they rejected them. George Eliot wondered whether women's lack of originality might be attributable to her brain structure: "The voltaic-pile is not strong enough to produce crystallization."[12] Mill, refuting the brain-weight argument in *The Subjection of Women,* thought it necessary to mention that the heaviest brain on record belonged to a woman.[13]

Although women writers often believed that they did labor under innate handicaps of mind and body, they nonetheless felt pressured to prove both their reliability and their physical endurance. What women must demonstrate, Eliot wrote, is the capability for "accurate thought, severe study, and continuous self-command."[14] As they met deadlines, edited magazines, and coped with the strenuous burdens of part-publication and serialization, women writers expressed more openly their irritation with those sisters who exploited the old stereotypes of weakness and sickliness. In reviewing Harriet Martineau's *Autobiography* in 1877, for example, Mrs. Oliphant could not conceal her annoyance at Martineau's woeful claim that overwork had destroyed her health and would send her to an early grave. Oliphant commented that "many a hard literary worker will smile at these tremendous prognostications."[15] Similarly, women physicians like Alice Putnam Jacobi made a point of debating male doctors on the question of female health and of correcting some of their more peculiar assumptions. Even so, arguments from physiology retained sufficient force in 1929 to lead Virginia Woolf to ignore a century of three-deckers and suggest that women's physical weakness meant that they should write shorter books than men.[16]

Another explanation given in criticism for the inferiority of female literature was women's limited experience. Vast preserves of masculine life—schools, universities, clubs, sports, businesses, government, and the army—were closed to women. Research and industry could not make up for these exclusions, and, as indicated in *Fraser's,* women writers were at a disadvantage: "A man's novel is generally a more finished production than a woman's; his education and experience give him a wider range of thought and a larger choice of character, and he usually groups his personages and incidents more artistically, and writes better English than his rivals."[17] As a form of social realism and a medium for moral and ethical thought, the novel obviously required maturity and mobility in its creators. Further, it required a complete set of emotions. Since the Victorians had defined women as angelic beings who could not feel passion, anger, ambition, or honor, they did not believe that women could express more than half of life. E. S. Dallas proclaimed it "evident that from that inexperience of life, which no amount of imagination, no force of sympathy, can ever compensate, women labour under serious disadvantages in attempting the novel."[18]

Denied participation in public life, women were forced to cultivate their feelings and to overvalue romance. In the novels, emotion rushed in to fill the vacuum of experience, and critics found this intensity, this obsession with personal relationships, unrealistic and even oppressive. The chief fault of Julia Kavanagh's *Daisy Burns,* according to the *Westminster,* was the fatiguingly sustained high pitch of emotion that it shared with other novels by women: "Human nature is not so constituted as to be able to keep a never-failing fountain of tears always at work; deep passion and wild sorrow pass over us—whom do they spare?—but they are not the grand occupation of our lives, still less the chief object of them."[19] The question of *whose* lives were so occupied is neglected here; the reviewer writes from the masculine perspective. Harriet Martineau, George Eliot, Mrs. Oliphant, and Florence Nightingale also criticized the overemphasis on love and passion in feminine fiction, but they understood that lack of education, isolation, and boredom had distorted women's values and channeled creative energy into romantic fantasy and emotional self-dramatization.

The simplistic psychology and naive religious optimism characteristic of some feminine writing reflected a female subculture in which confirmation in the church was often the most dramatic external event between the schoolroom and marriage; church-organized charity work, the only activity outside the home; and piety, the speciality of women and children. Reviewers deplored the immaturity of the fiction but could not bring themselves to do away with or expand the role. Charles Dickens and Wilkie Collins parodied the Puseyite fanaticism of Charlotte Yonge's *Heir of*

Redclyffe in *Household Words;* even Guy's death scene they found "marred or made obscured, either by the writer's want of experience of human nature, or utter uncompatability of abstraction from one narrow circle of ideas."[20] W. R. Greg, although he abhorred the "false morality of lady novelists," their faith in the expedience of self-sacrifice and in the workings of providence, could not see how women's ethical horizons could be much expanded: "If the writer be a young lady, whole spheres of observation, whole branches of character and conduct, are almost inevitably closed to her."[21]

While it was theoretically possible for women novelists to write about female physical experience, including childbirth and maternal psychology, they faced many obstacles to self-expression in their own sphere. Victorian women were taught to keep these experiences to themselves, to record them in very private diaries (such as Mrs. Gaskell's diary about her first child, Marianne), or to share them in intimate friendships with one or two other women. There were strong taboos against sharing them with men. As one historian explains: "From early childhood, girls . . . were taught self-effacement and modesty, were encouraged to feel shame about their bodies, and were advised to try to 'hide' the natural conditions of menstruation and pregnancy. The single woman of the middle-class was forced to deceit if she was to taste any of the freedom of knowledge given her brothers. The married woman of the class was constantly told not to trouble her husband with her own petty problems, to bear the pain of illness in silence, and to prevent knowledge of all indelicate matters from reaching 'innocent' ears."[22] Women educated to perceive themselves, in the popular horticultural imagery of the period, as lilies-of-the-valley or violets seeking the shade were understandably ambivalent about the self-revelation necessary in fiction.[23] The conflict between art and self-exposure, rather than any physical weakness, probably accounts for the stress symptoms of sickness and headache suffered by novelists like Geraldine Jewsbury, who fell ill each time she completed a book and finally gave up writing fiction on her doctor's orders.

Victorian critics agreed that if women were going to write at all they should write novels. Yet this assessment, too, denigrated and resisted feminine achievement. Theories of female aptitude for the novel tended to be patronizing, if not downright insulting. The least difficult, least demanding response to the superior woman novelist was to see the novel as an instrument that transformed feminine weaknesses into narrative strengths. Women were obsessed by sentiment and romance; well, these were the staples of fiction. Women had a natural taste for the trivial; they were sharp-eyed observers of the social scene; they enjoyed getting involved in other people's affairs. All these alleged female traits, it was supposed, would find a happy outlet in the novel. "Women," wrote E. S. Dallas, "have a talent for personal discourse and familiar narrative, which, when properly controlled, is a great gift, although too frequently it degenerates into a social nuisance."[24] Such an approach was particularly attractive because it implied that women's writing was as artless and effortless as birdsong, and therefore not in competition with the more rational male eloquence.

To critics who sentimentalized and trivialized women's interest in psychological motivation, the novel was the inevitable crystallization of femininity. The spectacle of J. M. Ludlow, straining to explain away Mrs. Gaskell and her sister writers without appearing ungentlemanly or making any concessions about female intelligence, is an instructive illustration:

> Now, if we consider the novel to be the picture of human life in a pathetic, or as some might prefer the expression, in a sympathetic form, that is to say, addressed to human feeling, rather than to human taste, judgment, or reason, there seem nothing paradoxical in the view, that women are called to the mastery of this peculiar field of literature. We know, all of us, that if man is the head of humanity, woman is its heart; and as soon as education has rendered her ordinarily capable of expressing feeling in written words, why should we be surprised to find that her words come more home to us than those of men, where feeling is chiefly concerned?[25]

By eliminating from his definition of the novel all the qualities he could not bring himself to see in women, Ludlow could accept even his own response to women's novels without having to modify any of his stereotypes. So intent was he on showing the perfect compatability of the stereotype and the product that he could dismiss the question of "expressing feeling in written words" as the merest trick of the literate. Rather than protesting against such criticism, women writers, as we have seen, reinforced it by playing down the effort behind their writing, and trying to make their work appear as the spontaneous overflow of their womanly emotions. This strategy was partly a way of minimizing the professional and intellectual aspects of the work, and partly a way of describing the powerful drives for self-expression that, especially for feminine novelists like Mrs. Oliphant, made the act of writing initially a possession by the muse: "I have written because it gave me pleasure, because it came natural to me."[26]

The feminine subcultural ideology did, however, have strengths as well as weaknesses. Men like Ludlow and Dallas, and even Hutton, may have regarded fiction as a form of repressive desublimation for women, a safe and suitable channel for energies that might otherwise have been turned to business, politics, religion, and revolutionary action. But feminine novelists, as Lorna Sage brilliantly suggests, came to take their role as the educators of the heart very seriously, so that "while deferring to male knowledge and power, they subtly revise and undermine the world from which they are excluded." Sage describes how Margaret Hale in Mrs. Gaskell's *North and South,* for example, quietly introduces the industrialist Mr. Thornton to the feminine values of domestic duty, familial loyalty, and personal affection, so that gradually his discussions of political economy, collective action, and violent strikes recede into the background. Gaskell transposes the political into "local, individual terms, much as she tames Mr. Thornton and redirects his savage energies into private life."[27] I would add to Sage's observations the fact that the women's victories are economic as well as emotional. Like Jane Eyre and Shirley Helstone, Margaret not only tames Thornton but also, in a final humiliation, endows him with her legacy so that he can pay off his debts and keep his mill. To get a great deal of money and to give it to a man for his work was the feminine heroine's apotheosis, the ultimate in the power of self-sacrifice.

One of the most persistent denigrations of women novelists was the theory that only unhappy and frustrated women wrote books. G. H. Lewes, writing in 1852, was one of the earliest to analyze the "compensatory" nature of female literature:

> If the accidents of her position make her solitary and inactive, or if her thwarted affections shut her somewhat from that sweet domestic and maternal sphere to which her whole being spontaneously moves, she turns to literature as to another sphere. . . . The happy wife and busy mother are only forced into literature by some hereditary organic tendency, stronger even than the domestic.[28]

In 1862, Gerald Massey repeated Lewes' point: "Women who are happy in all home-ties and who amply fill the sphere of their love and life, must, in the nature of things, very seldom become writers."[29] And the same idea, in almost the same words, was still cropping up as late as 1892; Catherine J. Hamilton's introduction to *Women Writers: Their Works and Ways* concurs: "Happy women, whose hearts are satisfied and full, have little need of utterance. Their lives are rounded and complete, they require nothing but the calm recurrence of those peaceful home duties in which domestic women rightly feel that their true vocation lies."

Feminine novelists responded to these innuendos of inferiority, as to others, not by protest but by vigorous demonstration of their domestic felicity. They worked hard to present their writing as an extension of their feminine role, an activity that did not detract from their womanhood, but in some sense augmented it. This generation would not have wanted an office or even "a room of one's own"; it was essential that the writing be carried out in the home, and that it be only one among the numerous and interruptible household tasks of the true woman. Mrs. Gaskell wrote in her dining-room with its four doors opening out to all parts of the house; Mrs. Oliphant half-complained and half-boasted that she had never had a study, but had worked in "the little 2nd drawing room where all the (feminine) life of the house goes on."[30] When interviewers came to visit, Mrs. Linton would display her embroidered cushions, fire-screens, and chair-seats; Mrs. Walford would pour tea; Mrs. Oliphant would pose in black silk and lace. Mrs. Craik modestly described the position of the feminine novelists: "We may . . . write shelvesful of books—the errant children of our brain may be familiar half over the grown world, and yet we ourselves sit as quiet by our chimney-corner, live a life as simple and peaceful as any happy common woman of them all."[31]

This grass-roots approach, this domestication of the profession, was also a trap. Women novelists might have banded together and insisted on their vocation as something that made them superior to the ordinary woman, and perhaps even happier. Instead they adopted defensive positions and committed themselves to conventional roles. If womanliness was defined as something that had to be proved, it had to be proved again and again. The feminine writers' self-abasement backfired and caused the kind of patronizing trivialization of their works found in George Smith's obituary of Mrs. Gaskell: "She was much prouder of ruling her household well . . . than of all she did in those writings."[32]

Even a sophisticated critic like Lewes, who believed that a full knowledge of life was dependent upon the depiction of feminine as well as masculine experience, had difficulties in separating a theory of female literature from his own sexual stereotypes. In his significantly titled pre-George Eliot essay, "The Lady Novelists," Lewes begins with the "abstract heights" of female "nature," rather than with the empirical evidence of female achievement:

> The domestic experience which forms the bulk of woman's knowledge finds an appropriate form in novels; while the very nature of fiction calls for that predominance of Sentiment which we have already attributed to the feminine mind. Love is the staple of fiction, for it "forms the story of a woman's life." The joys and sorrows of affection, the incidents of domestic life, assume typical forms in the novel. Hence we may be prepared to find women succeeding better in *finesse* of detail, in pathos and sentiment, while men generally succeed better in the construction of plots and the delineation of character.[33]

Obviously, being "prepared" to find such a polarization of narrative skills would affect critical judgments. When Lewes turns, in a rather whimsical way, to specific writers, he can only discern the combinations of Sentiment and Observation that he has already decided are feminine traits: the signs of gentility, domesticity, and breeding that the title of his article implies. For Lewes, as for other Victorian critics, women of genius did not require a modification in sexual theory; the apparent exception was readily seen to be charmingly and ineffectually disguising her true womanhood. Thus, Jane Austen's books are first and foremost "novels written by a woman, an Englishwoman, a gentlewoman"; George Sand has vainly "chosen the mask of a man; the features of a woman are everywhere visible"; and Sand's philosophy is "only a reflex of some man whose ideas she has adopted."[34] When he gets to Charlotte Brontë, Lewes has a moment's trouble with his categories, but he reminds the reader that if one is not "blinded" by the masculine force of *Jane Eyre,* one can perceive the "rare powers of observation" that stamp it as feminine.[35]

A much more successful effort to define a theory of female literature was Richard Holt Hutton's "Novels by the Authoress of 'John Halifax,'" which appeared in the *North British Review* in 1858. Hutton, who later became a percipient and responsible critic of George Eliot, used his review of Dinah Mulock to analyze "the main characteristics on which feminine fictions, as distinguished from those of men, are strong or defective." Hutton began his article with practical criticism and moved outward toward the theoretical; although he would obviously have come out with different views with Austen or Brontë, rather than Mulock, as his chief example, his inductive method was a good one, and he was careful to keep his generalizations narrow. Hutton recognized the problems of choosing a representative female author, and explained that Mulock had been selected chiefly because she was not a genius, but a competent writer who might better represent "the kind of faculty which is potential or actual in most clever women."[36]

Hutton agreed with Lewes that "feminine ability has found for itself a far more suitable sphere in novel-writing than in any other branch of literature,"[37] but he attributed the predilection of women's deficiencies in intellectual training and discipline, rather than to any positive correlation between female psychology and narrative realism. For the philosophical modes that he valued most highly, he thought, women substituted documentation, a copious circumstantial descriptiveness. Observation thus could be seen not as an innate feminine gift but as a developed compensatory skill. Hutton theorized that differences in masculine and feminine education and intellectual processes had led to two poles of narrative structure. In men's novels some kind of philosophy, some general idea, dictated the artistic composition of the narrative. The characters were placed in this broad intellectual framework, like Waverley in Scott's contrasts of past and present, or Becky in Thackeray's satire. Women's novels, on the other hand, concentrated on the characters themselves. Reader identification with the characters gave those novels a special intensity, but one that was transitory since it was intellectually limited. By these standards, Hutton defined Dickens as a "feminine" writer, one of the many indications in his article that he was not insisting on rigid biologically sexual terms.

Yet "feminine" is always a pejorative term for Hutton. He found that even in delineating character, their specialty, women were at a serious disadvantage, partly because of changing fashions in the novel:

> In many ways, the natural limitations of feminine power are admirably adapted to the standard of fiction held up as the true model of a feminine novelist in the last century. It was then thought sufficient to present finished sketches of character, just as it appeared under the ordinary restraints of society; while the deeper passions and spiritual impulses, which are the springs of all the higher drama of real life, were, at most, only allowed so far to suffuse the narrative as to tinge it with the excitement necessary for a novel.[38]

In other words, when readers began to look to fiction for a more ambitious realism, for psychological analysis, and for intellectual subtlety, women were handicapped by the social pressures of feminine gentility. Women were expert at rendering the surface, but art now required an exploration of the springs of life.

Like Lewes and Mill, Hutton felt that lack of imagination was the "main deficiency of feminine genius": "It can observe, it can recombine, it can delineate, but it cannot trust itself farther: it cannot leave the world of characteristic traits and expressive manner, so as to imagine and paint successfully the distinguishable, but not easily distinguished, world out of which those characteristics grew."[39] Because they were unable to speculate about motivations, to project themselves into the unseen interiors of their characters, particularly their male characters, women writers, Hutton thought, were increasingly being forced into use of the autobiographical form to give their books superficial unity and a center of imaginative authenticity. Although a vivid central character based on personal experience seemed to be within their abilities, women's concentration on such a character could wreck the novel's aesthetic balance.

Hutton traced this deficiency in imagination to cultural circumstance rather than to nature. Women were at a disadvantage, first, because their direct experience was so limited; and second, because they were poorly educated, especially in the masculine fields of science, economics, and philosophy, which developed the ability to generalize and theorize: "The same mind that has been trained to go apart with laws of matter, and laws of wealth, and laws of intellect, and to elaborate them as if no outer world for the time existed at all, also enables men to go apart with conceptions of character."[40] On the other hand, Hutton thought, "the patient and pliant genius" of women enabled them to deal with the evolution and gradual growth of character; because of this ability to portray growth, writers such as Mulock or Charlotte Yonge could deal with moral and spiritual problems without becoming didactic.

Hutton had to modify some of these views when George Eliot appeared on the scene, and he might have modified them sooner if he had understood *Jane Eyre, Villette,* or *Wuthering Heights.* But literary stereotypes adapted very slowly to any real evidence of feminine achievement. If we break down the categories that are the staple of Victorian periodical reviewing, we find that women writers were acknowledged to possess sentiment, refinement, tact, observation, domestic expertise, high moral tone, and knowledge of female character; and thought to lack originality, intellectual training, abstract intelligence, humor, self-control, and knowledge of male character. Male writers had most of the desirable qualities: power, breadth, distinctness, clarity, learning, abstract intelligence, shrewdness, experience, humor, knowledge of everyone's character, and openmindedness.

This double standard was so widely accepted through about 1875 that critics and readers automatically employed it in the game of literary detection. Approaching an anonymous or pseudonymous novel, reviewers would break it down into its elements, label these masculine or feminine, and add up the total. The predominance of masculine or feminine elements determined the sex of the author. As a critical instrument this practice was not very reliable; considering the odds based on chance alone, the percentage of correct guesses is not impressive. Male writers were occasionally misidentified as women. R. D. Blackmore's first novel, *Clara Vaughan* (1864), had a female narrator; and the *Saturday Review,* convinced they had detected an authoress, used the opportunity for an attack on maidenly ignorance: "Another decided feature by which our lady novelists are wont to betray the secret of their authorship is the characteristic mode in which they unconsciously make sport of the simplest principles of physics, and of the most elementary rules or usages of the law."[41] Blackmore had practiced law in London for five years. But even embarrassing errors such as this could not persuade reviewers that the sexual double standard needed revision.

Jane Eyre was published in 1847; and *Adam Bede,* in 1859. Both novels appeared under pseudonyms, and on both occasions critics were baffled by qualities in the novels that could not be simplistically defined as masculine or feminine. When the authors behind the pseudonyms were revealed to be women, critics were dismayed. The main difference between the two episodes was that Charlotte Brontë had been shocked, dismayed, and hurt to discover that her realism struck others as improper; George Eliot had seen what had happened to Charlotte Brontë, and was prepared.

Early critics of *Jane Eyre* were obsessed with discovering the sex of Currer Bell. "The whole reading-world of England was in a ferment to discover the unknown author. . . . Every little incident mentioned in the book was turned this way and that to answer, if possible, the much-vexed question of sex."[42] Incidents included clothes, domestic details, and conversations. Harriet Martineau, for example, determined on the basis of chapter 16, in which Grace Poole sews curtain rings on Rochester's bed drapings, that the book "could have been written only by a woman or an upholsterer."[43] Circumstantial evidence aside, the presentation of female sexuality and human passion disturbed and amazed readers. If Currer Bell was a woman, they could not imagine what sort of woman she might be. Even while critics acknowledged the presence of genius, they felt stunned by its unconventionality. The *Christian Remembrancer* declared that it would be hard to find "a book more unfeminine, both in its excellencies and its defects . . . in the annals of female authorship." According to Lewes, "a more masculine book in the sense of vigour was never written."[44] Others, like the American E. P. Whipple, were "gallant enough to detect the hand of a gentleman" in composing the "profanity, brutality, and slang."[45] The relationship between Rochester and Jane, and Jane's admission of passion for her married employer, could not be accepted. Thus one sees over and over in the reviews words like "sensual," "gross," and "animal." Tom Winnifrith, who has written a comprehensive study of the reception of *Jane Eyre,* has the impression that the most hostile reviews were written by women.[46]

The appearance of Mrs. Gaskell's *Life of Charlotte Brontë* while the novelist's fame was at its posthumous height convinced critics that Brontë could not have been guilty of immorality, and also provided them with some explanations for her knowledge of passion. The *Saturday Review* was happy to exonerate Charlotte and to blame her education in Brussels for the unfeminine sophistication of the novels:

> Women regarded her novels with that sort of fluttering alarm which is always awakened in unpolluted breasts by the signs of a knowledge greater than their own. Men recognized the truthful touches which these novels contained, but wondered how they came to be there, for the general purity of their tone refuted the notion that they were the symptoms of depravity. . . . We cannot doubt that Miss Brontë derived an instruction which to a less noble, unstained and devotional mind might have been perilous, from her residence in a foreign school, her observation of foreign manners, and her analysis of the thoughts of foreigners.[47]

The *Quarterly Review* looked closer to home, at the influence of Branwell, "thoroughly depraved himself, and tainting the thoughts of all within his sphere."[48] Many readers, including Charlotte Yonge, felt that Branwell's influence on his sisters had been dastardly, but they found it comfortably in accordance with their notions of male and female temperament.

George Eliot, as the editor of the *Westminister Review* and the translator of Strauss and Feuerbach, had already offended conservative factions. As the mistress of Lewes, she had put herself outside the boundaries of Victorian respectability. Thus she risked more critical hostility by revealing herself than Charlotte Brontë did, as she, Lewes, and the publisher Blackwood were well aware. It was the example of *Jane Eyre,* however, that Lewes cited in explaining the pseudonym to Blackwood: "When *Jane Eyre* was finally known to be a woman's book, the tone [of criticism] noticeably changed."[49] Furor about the sex of the author characterized the publication of *Adam Bede,* as it had the publication of Eliot's first, less successful book, *Scenes from Clerical Life.* With a few distinguished exceptions, reviewers believed George Eliot to be a clerical gentleman. The *Saturday Review* later confessed, "to speak the simple truth, without affectation or politeness, it [*Adam Bede*] was thought to be too good for a woman's story."[50]

Barbara Bodichon and Anne Mozley were among those who guessed the truth. Bodichon, a radical feminist, rejoiced in the authorship as a triumph for womanhood: "1. That a woman should write a wise and *humorous* book which should take a place by Thackeray. 2. That YOU *that you* whom they spit at should do it!"[51] Anne Mozley, the reviewer for *Bentley's Quarterly Review,* was certain that the book was a woman's in spite of its felicity, force, and freedom of expression because it was written by an outsider, an observer: "The knowledge of female nature is feminine, not only in its details, which might be borrowed from other eyes, but in its whole tone of feeling . . . the position of the writer towards every point in discussion is a woman's position, that is, from a stand of observation rather than more active participation." Her review went on to cite other evidence of female culture as proof that a woman had written the book: "the knowledge of female nature . . . the full close scrutiny of observation . . . acquaintance with form life in its minute particulars . . . the secure ground . . . in matters of domestic housewifery." Finally, Mozley triumphantly cited, "women are known dearly to love a 'well-directed moral.'"[52] Mozley's analysis was shrewd and perceptive. The brilliant conjectures of the *Westminster Review,* however, were not; the editor, John Chapman, had learned the secret from Herbert Spencer. He nevertheless congratulated himself on his prescience when the pseudonym was revealed to the public in 1860.[53]

Lewes hoped that the pseudonym had won the book a fair reading; to Barbara Bodichon he wrote: "They can't now unsay their admiration." But he was wrong. At least one journal went back for a second look. William Hepworth Dixon, the editor of the *Athenaeum* (who sometimes reviewed his own books under a pseudonym), wrote a vicious notice for the gossip column: "It is time to end this pother about the authorship of 'Adam Bede.' The writer is in no sense a great unknown; the tale, if bright in parts, and such as a clever woman with an observant eye and unschooled moral nature might have written, has no great quality of any kind."[54] With the appearance of *The Mill on the Floss,* criticism of George Eliot noticeably changed and cheapened; it placed her among the "modern female novelists" and judged her by the collective standards. The *Saturday Review* was "not sure that it is quite consistent with feminine delicacy to lay so much stress on the bodily feelings of the other sex."[55] The *Quarterly* went back to its sneers at female ignorance: "There are traces of knowledge which is not usual among women (although some of the classical quotations might at least have been more correctly printed)."[56]

The Brontës, in their radical innocence, confronted all sexually biased criticism head-on. Charlotte constantly had to be restrained by her publishers from attacking critics in the prefaces to her books, and she frequently wrote directly to reviewers and journals in protest. She admonished the critic of the *Economist:* "To you I am neither man nor woman. I come before you as an author only. It is the sole standard by which you have a right to judge me—the sole ground on which I accept your judgment."[57] Anne Brontë prefaced the second edition of *Wildfell Hall* with a defiant declaration of equal literary rights: "I am satisfied that if the book is a good one, it is so whatever the sex of the author may be." George Eliot stopped reading reviews of her books when criticism became personal; all were vetted by Lewes. However, one sees signs of self-censorship both in her shift after 1860 to less autobiographical fiction, and in her careful elimination of possible double entendres in proof.

George Eliot was virtually alone among feminine novelists in speculating about the psychological and moral impact of women's experience on the structure and content of the novel. She found most of the feminine literature of her day inept and derivative, and wondered "how women have the courage to write and publishers the spirit to buy at a high price the false and feeble representations of life and characters that most feminine novels give."[58] She considered some of the literature inauthentic, "an absurd exaggeration of the masculine style, like the swaggering gait of a bad actress in male attire."[59] In "Silly Novels by Lady Novelists," Eliot denounced the covert victories of feminine values, the fantasies of instant intellectual mastery and intuitive spiritual authority. She understood that the habits of the professional were at variance with the indoctrination of women, but, in literature, as in other activities, she wished women to substitute "the hard drudgery of real practice" for feminine fantasy and self-indulgence.[60] Eliot also believed, however, that women writers had a "precious speciality, lying quite apart from masculine aptitudes and experience," a speciality that was grounded in the maternal emotions.[61] Somehow, she thought, the maternal affections would lead to "distinctive forms and combinations" in the novel.[62]

The feminine novelists did share the cultural values of Victorian middle-class women, and they clung to the traditional notion of femininity. They were not, however, simply ordinary women who happened to write books; they were different from the start. Lewes and Massey were partly correct that "happy wives and busy mothers" did not become writers, but they failed to understand that women with strong imaginative drives and achievement needs could not be content with domesticity. Even those women writers who began to work because they needed to earn money soon found themselves changed by the disciplines and rewards of the profession. They were not like "any happy common woman"; they were more organized, more businesslike, more assertive, more adventurous, more flexible, and more in control of their lives.

Being Victorian women, they were concerned about these changes in themselves. Geraldine Jewsbury worried about the psychological transformations of female professionalism both in her letters to Jane Carlyle and in her novels. In the latter, she put her own doubts, ludicrously exaggerated, into the mouths of libertines and rogues: "The intrinsic value of a woman's work out of her own sphere is nothing, and what are the qualities developed to make up for it? . . . The bloom and charm of her innocence is gone; she has gained a dogmatic, harsh, self-sufficing vanity, which she calls principle; she strides and stalks through life, neither one thing nor another."[63]

Critics, too, wondered if the women novelists had removed themselves so far from the sphere of the common woman that they had lost the power to describe it. Richard Simpson pointed out some of the obvious problems in a review of George Eliot:

> Though she ought to be able to draw women in herself, for the simple reason that she is a woman, yet she may be too far separated from the ordinary life of her sex to be a good judge of its relations. The direct power and the celebrity of authorship may obscure and replace the indirect influence and calm happiness of domestic feminine life. For admiration and affection do not easily combine. Celebrity isolates the authoress, and closes her heart; it places her where experience of the ordinary relations of the sex is impossible, and where she is tempted to supply by theory what is lacking in experience. She gives us her view of woman's vocation, and paints things as they ought to be, not as they are. Women work more by influence than by force, by example than reasoning, by silence than speech; the authoress grasps at direct power through reasoning and speech. Having thus taken up the male position, the male ideal becomes hers,—the ideal of power,—which expressed by her feminine heart and intellect, means the supremacy of passion in the affairs of the world.[64]

On the contrary, women novelists had authority to describe the lives of ordinary women, those powerless lives of influence, example, and silence, precisely because they had outgrown them. As critics like Simpson uneasily sensed, they were writing not only to develop direct personal power, but also to change the perceptions and aspirations of their female readers. The strong utilitarian thrust of feminine criticism—what good will this book do us?—was partly the spirit of the age, but it was also a part of the search for new heroines, new role-models, and new lives.

Notes

1. Clement K. Shorter, *The Brontës: Life and Letters,* London, 1908, II, p. 30.
2. *A Century of George Eliot Criticism,* Boston, 1965, p. 37. Dallas's review of *Felix Holt* in the *Times,* June 26, 1866, p. 6, discusses Eliot's place relative to Jane Austen "among our lady novelists," and concludes, "We don't know any Englishwoman who can be placed near her as a writer of prose."
3. "A Dozen of Novels," *Fraser's* IX (1834): 483.
4. "The Social Position of Women," *North British Review* XIV (1851): 281.
5. "Ruth," *North British Review* XIX (1853): 90.
6. "Modern Novelists—Great and Small," *Blackwoods* LXXVII (1855): 555.
7. "Last Poems and Other Works of Mrs. Browning," *North British Review* XXXVI (1862): 271.
8. Introduction to *The Half-Sisters,* London, 3 vols., 1848.
9. John S. Haller and Robin M. Haller, *The Physician and Sexuality in Victorian America,* Urbana, 1974, pp. 65-66.
10. Browning's sonnet, "To George Sand: A Desire" (1844), was frequently cited by critics of women novelists. Gerald Massey writes that Eliot "lay hold of life with a large hand, looked at it with a large eye, and felt it with a large heart" ("Last Poems and Other Works of Mrs. Browning," 271).
11. "On the Real Differences in the Minds of Men and Women," *Journal of the Anthropological Society of London* VII (1869): LXIX For a discussion of Allan's ideas, see Katharine M. Rogers, *The Troublesome Helpmate: A History of Misogyny in Literature,* Seattle, 1966, pp. 219-221.
12. "Woman in France," in *Essays of George Eliot,* ed. Thomas Pinney, New York, 1963, p. 56.
13. "The Subjection of Women," in John Stuart Mill and Harriet Taylor Mill, *Essays on Sex Equality,* ed. Alice S. Rossi, Chicago, 1970, ch. 3, p. 199.
14. "Three Novels," in *Essays of George Eliot,* p. 334.
15. "Harriet Martineau," *Blackwood's* CXXI (1877): 487.
16. *A Room of One's Own,* New York, 1957, p. 134.
17. "Novels of the Day," LXII (1860): 205.
18. "Current Bell," *Blackwood's* LXXXII (1857): 79. See also "The Lady Novelists of Great Britain," *Gentleman's Magazine,* n.s. XL (1853): 18-25.
19. "The Progress of Fiction as an Art," *Westminster Review,* LX (1853): 372.
20. "Doctor Dulcamara, M. P.," in *Charles Dickens' Uncollected Writings from "Household Words," 1850-1859,* II, ed. Harry Stone, Bloomington, 1968, p. 624.
21. "The False Morality of Lady Novelists," *National Review* VII (1859): 148.
22. Mary S. Hartman, introduction to *Victorian Murderesses: A True History of Thirteen Respectable French and English Women Accused of Unspeakable Crimes,* New York, 1976. I am indebted to Mary Hartman for allowing me to read her book in manuscript.
23. See, for example, Miss M. A. Stodart, quoted in Inga-Stina Ewbank, *Their Proper Sphere: A Study of the Brontë Sisters as Early-Victorian Female Novelists,* London, 1966, p. 39: "Publicity can, to woman, never be a native element; she may be forced into it by circumstances, but the secret sigh of every truly feminine heart will be for the retirement of private life. The lily of the valley which shields itself under the huge high leaf, the violet which seeks the covert of the shady hedge, may both be forced from under their retreat, and be compelled to stand in the broad open sunshine, but will not their withered and blighted petals tell us that they are pining for the congenial shade?"
24. "Currer Bell," *Blackwood's* LXXXII (1857): 77.
25. "Ruth," *North British Review,* XIX (1853): 90.
26. Robert Colby and Vineta Colby, *The Equivocal Virtue: Mrs. Oliphant and the Victorian Literary Marketplace,* Hamden, Connecticut, 1966, p. 5.
27. "The Case of the Active Victim," *Times Literary Supplement* (July 26, 1974): 803-804.

28. "The Lady Novelists," *Westminster Review,* n.s. II (1852): 133-134.

29. "Last Poems of Mrs. Browning," 271.

30. *Autobiography,* pp. 23-24. In her interviews with Victorian women novelists, Helen Black frequently notes that all evidence of the woman's profession is absent from the home: "Where are the manuscripts, the 'copy,' the 'proofs' . . . ? There is no indication of her work on the old oak knee-hole writing table" ("Rhoda Broughton," *Notable Women Authors of the Day,* Glasgow, 1893, p. 40).

31. *A Woman's Thoughts About Women,* London, 1858, p. 58.

32. "Mrs. Gaskell and Her Novels," *Cornhill Magazine* XXIX (1874): 192.

33. "The Lady Novelists," 133.

34. Ibid., 135, 136.

35. Ibid., 139.

36. "Novels by the Authoress of *John Halifax,*" *North British Review* XXIX (1858): 254, 255.

37. Ibid., 254.

38. Ibid., 257.

39. Ibid., 258.

40. Ibid., 260.

41. Quoted by Waldo Dunn in *R. D. Blackmore,* New York, 1956, p. 112. See also Kenneth Budd, *The Last Victorian: R. D. Blackmore and His Novels,* London, 1960, p. 33.

42. Elizabeth Gaskell, *The Life of Charlotte Brontë,* London, 1919, p. 271.

43. Harriet Martineau, *Autobiography,* II, London, 1877, p. 324.

44. "Jane Eyre," *Christian Remembrancer* XV (1848); "Currer Bell's *Shirley,*" *Edinburgh Review* XCI (1850): 158.

45. "Novels of the Season," *North American Review* LXVII (1848): 357.

46. *The Brontës and Their Background: Romance and Reality,* London, 1973, p. 125. Mrs. Gaskell noted that "*women* infinitely more than men" disapproved of *Ruth* as well (*Letters,* p. 226).

47. "The Professor," III (1857): 550.

48. James Craigie Robertson, "Eliot's Novels," CVIII (1860): 470.

49. Gordon S. Haight, *George Eliot: A Biography,* New York, 1968, p. 268.

50. "The Mill on the Floss," IX (1860): 470.

51. Letter of April 26, 1859, in *The George Eliot Letters,* III, ed. Gordon S. Haight, New Haven, 1954, p. 56.

52. "Adam Bede and Recent Novels," I (1859): 436-437.

53. See "The Mill on the Floss," *Westminster Review* LXXIV (1860): 24-33.

54. Haight, *George Eliot,* pp. 290-291. For an account of Dixon, see Leslie Marchand, *The Athenaeum: A Mirror of Victorian Culture,* Chapel Hill, 1941, p. 80.

55. "The Mill on the Floss," 471.

56. James Craigie Robertson, "George Eliot's Novels," CVIII (1860): 471. "The parenthetical hint that the 'classical quotations' in my books might be 'more correctly printed' is an amusing example of the genuineness that belongs to review-writing in general, since there happens to be only *one* classical quotation in them all," Eliot wrote John Blackwood (February 20, 1860; *Letters,* III, pp. 356-357).

57. Shorter, *The Brontës,* II, pp. 63-64.

58. Quoted in Ewbank, *Their Proper Sphere,* p. 12.

59. "Woman in France," *Essays of George Eliot,* p. 53.

60. "Three Novels," *Essays of George Eliot,* p. 334.

61. "Silly Novels by Lady Novelists," *Essays of George Eliot,* p. 324.

62. "Woman in France," p. 53.

63. *The Half-Sisters,* II, p. 23.

64. "George Eliot's Novels," *Home and Foreign Review,* III (1863), in David Carroll, ed., *George Eliot: The Critical Heritage,* New York, 1971, p. 241. See also Coventry Patmore, "The Social Position of Women," *North British Review* XIV (1851): 279: "Books are written by literary men and women, a class whose peculiar temperament very often unfits them for the performance of duties, and the enjoyments of the quiet pleasures of domestic life; and this unfitness too frequently betrays itself in erroneous notions concerning the average condition of the family life."

ALBERT C. SEARS (ESSAY DATE SPRING-SUMMER 2000)

SOURCE: Sears, Albert C. "The Politics and Gender of Duty in Frances Power Cobbe's *The Duties of Women.*" *Nineteenth-Century Feminisms* 2 (spring-summer 2000): 67-78.

In the following essay, Sears argues that Frances Power Cobbe viewed the transition of the women's movement into the political sphere not as an abrogation, but rather as an extension of their domestic duties.

In 1880 Frances Power Cobbe delivered her series of lectures, *The Duties of Women,* to audiences in London and Clifton (near Bristol), inciting women to assume political roles in the public world. Later, in 1881, the lectures were published, and they successfully went into several editions in England and America.[1] Only a few years earlier, Cobbe's own activities might be seen as exhibiting the kind of public power to which she called women in these lectures. In 1878, her article "Wife-Torture in England" effected Parliament's amendment to the Matrimonial Causes Act. The article so thoroughly exposed the inadequacy of laws pertaining to domestic violence that Parliament answered her call for legislation by passing a bill within two months.[2] Cobbe's actions illustrated what would be one of her most salient points in her last lecture of *The Duties of Women*: "We are bound to do all we can to promote the virtue and happiness of our fellow-men and women, and therefore we must accept and seize every instrument of power, every vote, every influence which we can obtain, to enable us to promote virtue and happiness" (178-9). This essay seeks to understand why Cobbe reserves this call for political power until the very end of her lecture series, especially when it follows several talks that seem to emphasize women's traditional duties rather than their acquisition of rights. The lectures reformed familiar rhetoric on women's domestic duties so that women could acquire agency within the public and political arena. The emphasis on duties rather than on rights or equality may seem contradictory, particularly coming from such an advocate of women's rights as Cobbe;[3] however, access to the public world for Cobbe is not a right for women, but a responsibility. Her goal is to achieve "the power which makes us, not the *equals* of men (I never care to claim such equality), but their *equivalents*" (168). In other words, Cobbe wants women to retain their gender difference with pride, at the same time that they utilize that difference to achieve the equivalent of men's power in the public arena.

The Duties of Women surveys many of the themes found in Cobbe's other writing: intuitive morality, animal abuse, despotism in marriage, celibacy for women, domestic violence, and women's suffrage. It is primarily the latter, though, that Cobbe especially wants to address in the lectures, even though her remarks on the vote arrive only in the last section. Cobbe, herself, had already been participating in the Central Committee of the National Society for Women's Suffrage, contributing pamphlets to the organisation's goals during the 1870s.[4] While it took until 1918 for women to join in national elections, the Municipal Franchise Act of 1869 did provide unmarried women ratepayers access to municipal elections. Women's participation in school elections soon followed. Local government, then, afforded women the kind of duty Cobbe describes at the end of her lectures: "The possession of votes for municipal elections and the occasional election of women (like the excellent Miss Merrington) as Guardians of the Poor are also vast strides in the direction of public usefulness for women" (176). While Cobbe's discussion of such usefulness primarily profiles the state of married women, rather than that of the single woman like herself, the lectures reveal, even to the housewife, women's potential for public work and politics.[5]

Cobbe hierarchically structures the lectures around the principle that women's public and political duties are a logical and necessary extension of essential and domestic femininity. In her first lecture she classifies duties into three categories: religious, personal, and social. Religious duties clearly are at the top of Cobbe's hierarchy, but she does not lecture on them since "no one . . . has been silly enough to suggest that there is any difference between the Religious Duties of a man and those of a woman" (39).[6] The principal subject of the lectures, then, is the personal and social duties of women, each of which has several detailed subcategories. After she elucidates the moral characteristics of personal duty (chastity, temperance, veracity, courage, and the vindication of rightful liberty) in the second lecture, Cobbe spends the remaining lectures exploring social duty. It is in the social duties (woman as a member of the family, as mistress of the household, as a member of society, and as citizen of the state) that Cobbe transforms woman's private role into a public one. The hierarchy keeps the practitioners of Cobbe's system from moral conflict as they perform these various duties. She states, "the first thing to be done is to determine their relative rank in the hierarchy of moral obligations, so that, if they ever seem to clash (they cannot really do so), we may know at once which of the two possessed the first claim on our obedience" (39). Women must first fulfill and their "private duties" (187) within the home and toward the family in order to enter the public realm of politics. If followed carefully, the exacting hierarchy leads women to political power within the public sphere. Cobbe's code of duty is not intended as a path to personal freedoms; rather, it helps women extend their domestic talents to the public world.

Her discourse on duty conforms to the broad Victorian conception of the term. Walter Houghton connects the notion of Victorian duty to self advancement: doing "the best for yourself was to do the best for society" (Houghton 188). Furthermore, "[s]ocial ambition, driving one to the utmost economic effort, was the blessed means of social progress" (188). In other words, Houghton suggests that duty entailed advancing oneself socially at the same time that one was improving society. Cobbe's sense of duty parallels Houghton's description; as will be seen in the last lecture, Cobbe demonstrates that women have an important role in the betterment of society. However, she drastically downplays the desire for ambition and self advancement that is so important to Houghton's definition. As Jane Lewis and Martha

Vicinus both note, Victorian women connected duty with service to others rather than with fulfilling one's own desires (Lewis 6, 11; Vicinus 16, 30).

Interestingly, a similar work that structures duty hierarchically is Samuel Smiles's *Duty, with Illustrations of Courage, Patience, and Endurance* (1880), published the same year that Cobbe delivered *The Duties of Women*. While Cobbe and Smiles address vastly different audiences in terms of class and gender, their similarities suggest conventional thinking about duty in the second half of the nineteenth century.[7] Like Cobbe, duty for Smiles begins with an "abiding sense of duty to God" (Smiles 13). From there duty stretches outward in concentric circles from the self (11), starting with "duty to one's family" and "duty to our neighbours," and then leads to "duty to the state" (13). Cobbe, like Smiles, begins with duty to God and duties of inner personal morality, and then gradually progresses from the family to duties as citizens of the world. What is critical for both writers is that social and public duties must follow the fulfillment of personal duties.

Such a discourse that espouses power while seeming to limit individual freedom may sound contradictory to the late twentieth-century reader. Cobbe is interested in the ways female gender can be restricted, but she insists that such restriction does not result from following the discipline she advocates. She asserts in her first lecture that women have suffered from a host of "artificial restrictions" (15) that have prevented them from fulfilling their natural duties. Indeed, the nineteenth-century woman's life, Cobbe states, has become a "spectacle of waste" (13), because she has been prevented from achieving her "natural happiness" (13). Happiness for Cobbe can occur only through the completion of one's natural duties, which for women are linked to maternal femininity. The capacity to give birth naturally makes women loving, sympathetic, and nurturing. Cobbe's complaint, then, is that "artificial restrictions," such as "senseless fashions of dress" (15), lack of education, and the encouragement of frivolity and self-indulgence in girls, separate women from their natural femininity and hinder the fulfillment of their natural duties.

Cobbe's affirmation of an essential maternal femininity, which leads not to restriction but to freedom, coincides with her belief that gender is tied to sexual difference. She adapts the essentialist notion of "separate spheres" in such a way that she retains any power that domesticity affords women, while rejecting what she sees as confining. She opposes "the miserable *claustration* of women, their sequestration in their separate portions of the house, their banishment from all social pleasures of the other sex . . ." (20-21). Cobbe's language is important here: she wants to collapse the strict division of the sexes into private and public worlds, by underscoring how women's isolation from the "male" world has been an impairment to the fulfillment of their true duties. Cobbe, however, never rejects woman's propensity toward domesticity; rather, she redefines the concept into "domestic freedom" (22). Domesticity, then, becomes a direct path to power for women. Philippa Levine states: "For many women committed to the fight for women's rights, the most effective weapon was not the total rejection of that ideology but rather a manipulation of its fundamental value. After all, if women's purity made them the natural custodians of religious teachings and values, then their effect in public life could only be uplifting" (13). Barbara Caine similarly notes that "while Cobbe accepted much of what is generally termed Victorian domestic ideology, she rejected the notion that women were designed to serve men" (138). Cobbe's prescription for female power in *The Duties of Women* functions in the way Levine and Caine assert: the lectures revalue the codes of gender that nineteenth-century culture ascribed to women.

Elizabeth Langland has recently interpreted domestic ideology in terms of the power and agency it afforded middle-class women. She criticizes the belief that domesticity made women into passive victims; she carefully shows how the middle-class Victorian woman became a powerful agent through the ideology:

> [M]iddle-class women were produced by domestic discourses even as they reproduced them to consolidate middle-class control. Such a reinterpretation of the subject and agency complicates more traditional analyses of women's roles in Victorian society and forestalls a view of women as victims passively suffering under patriarchal social structures; it equally prevents a picture of them as heroines supporting unproblematic values in the way they deal with society on issues of gender and class.
>
> (11)

Thus, Langland complicates our understanding of domesticity in important ways. Such a reading helps to reveal the complex nuances of Cobbe's representation of women's duty. It is unquestionable that moments in Cobbe's lectures restrict the freedoms that women would gain after she wrote; nonetheless, she thoughtfully reworked her culture's construction of gender to help women reach their potential as agents for social good.

While domestic freedom does not stress self-interest and the acquisition of personal rights, such duty, as Langland shows, did not necessarily make women completely powerless. More importantly, many women at the end of the nineteenth century reshaped the dominant domestic ideology of the period to emphasize women's active duty to make the condition of women better. Among them was Cobbe, who retained a commitment to the betterment of women's lives by redefining the static gender discourses into ones that gave women agency. Cobbe understands the primary threat to women's progress to be the "growth of hardness and of selfishness among women as their lives cease to be a perpetual self-oblation, and they . . . pursue ends of their own" (24). The objective for women is not "a larger and freer life, but of a life of higher self-reverence, broader piety, more tender goodness, purer purity, truer truth" (26). Of course, such directive coming from Cobbe may sound ironic, because by the time she is speaking, her life had been unencumbered for many years within an unconventional domestic arrangement with Mary Lloyd.[8] It is true that Cobbe's freer life did not begin until her mid-thirties, after she had fulfilled her duties as a daughter, caring for her ill and widowed father.[9] Nonetheless, she wants to foreclose the belief that women need more freedom to do whatever they please; consequently, she retains a component of the nineteenth-century gender discourse that defines women's nature as passive and selfless. Here she clearly focuses on the traditional option: woman as pious, moral, and pure. Yet, she ultimately reframes this discourse so that it leads directly to women's power within the public sphere. The challenge to Cobbe's late twentieth-century audience is to understand that the power Cobbe advocates comes out of the nineteenth century's traditional conception of female gender rather than the belief that women need to be relieved of such confining roles.

A comparison between Cobbe and a writer like Sarah Stickney Ellis helps to demarcate how Cobbe is producing a more powerful position for women. Ellis states in *The Women of England* (1837), as Cobbe would later, that the deterioration of women's moral character would render them "less influential, less useful, and less happy" (Ellis 14). Similarly, both writers underscore "disinterested kindness" (48) as one of women's primary virtues. Yet, unlike Cobbe's reformulation of domestic ideology, Ellis maintains that women's duties should be restricted or sequestered, to use Cobbe's terminology, within her private and domestic space. Ellis illustrates her preference for women's private life over public life in the following passage:

> [A] high-minded and intellectual woman is never more truly great than when willingly and judiciously performing kind offices for the sick; and much as may be said, and said justly, in praise of the public virtues of women the voice of nature is so powerful in every human heart, that, could the question of superiourity on these two points be universally proposed, a response would be heard throughout the world, in favour of woman in her private and domestic character.
>
> (Ellis 34-5)

For Ellis, then, public duties are never fundamental to a woman's life, because they are not central to a her nature; essential feminine nature will always overpower the dutiful women's intellect. Thus, a woman remains isolated in her limited sphere. Cobbe, on the other hand, will see the "public virtues" of women more closely related to those she has in the home.[10]

A close look at the second lecture of *The Duties of Women* reveals how Cobbe reworks the earlier vision of gender found in Ellis. In the foundational level of duties, the personal, Cobbe lays out her essentialist ideas about gender. Personal duties concern "inward rather than outward virtue" (38), and consist of such moral qualities as chastity, temperance, truthfulness, courage, and free will. Cobbe genders the first three personal duties (that is, chastity, temperance, and truthfulness) female and the last two (courage and free will) male, naturalizing specific qualities as essential either to women or men. The "potential Motherhood in every true woman's heart" (16) supplies women with precious feelings of love, tenderness, and sympathy. Furthermore, Cobbe notes that men possess a "natural boldness and combativeness" (58) that inclines them toward courage. For women, however, these qualities are not inherent: for women to be courageous and true "is really praiseworthy and honorable" (58), just as it is praiseworthy in a male "to curb his passions and be chaste and temperate" (58).

Despite maintaining biological difference as gender difference, Cobbe does call for some gender fluidity between men and women. For example, "virtue is essentially *the same thing* for every moral being, and, among moral beings, for a man and for a woman. Thus we recognize that, in speaking of the duties of women, we are not concerned with a different *set of virtues* from those of men—heroes and men—saints, but with just the same virtues exercised in a somewhat different field" (34-5). Cobbe claims that "whatever be the aim and end of the creation of a man . . . that same aim and end is ours" (35). All human virtues or personal duties, whether those natural to women or men, lead to the same end. Even though men and women have essential propensities toward certain of these virtues, each sex must adopt the other's to be moral. Cobbe calls for a female identity that is innately maternal and domestic and actively acquired by adopting traditional male virtues. Her discussion of courage illustrates this point. Courage is a natural masculine virtue, yet women should not be excluded from employing it to achieve their duties. Much like her earlier discussion of domestic restriction and freedom, Cobbe here believes that gender should not be restricted by its essential nature: "There is no point wherein the great moral heresy of the different nature of virtue in men and in women has had more miserable consequences than in this matter of courage; and now we who renounce that heresy must make it one of our first cares to develop among us this virtue of courage, hitherto so neglected" (74). Cobbe, then, dichotomizes gender, but she also wants both women and men to inculcate in themselves the personal duties natural to the other sex. Elsewhere she claims that women are "made of some more plastic material" than men, and they are capable of molding their identities ("The Final Cause of Woman" 1). She insists on women's natural domestic identity, but wants room for variation: "The woman, by being *nothing* but a domestic being, has failed to be truly domestic. She has lost the power of ministering to the higher wants of those nearest to her, by over-devotion to the ministry of their lower necessities" (14). In *The Duties* Cobbe illustrates how the plasticity of women and domesticity can be stretched so that women can engage in political work.

Cobbe also manipulates traditional codes of gender when she explains a woman's social duties. As a woman proceeds up the hierarchy of duties, she must maintain her commitment to the personal duties outlined above. These allow her to enter "the vast expanse of *Social Duty* . . . and its ever-widening horizon" (86). Cobbe represents social duty as an endless potential: once a woman proceeds into the realm of social duty, she enters a threshold of social power. Virtue is important above all, but social duty affords women worthwhile labor that betters their fellow creatures. In the third lecture she creates a vital link between personal and social duties: "Our *Personal* Duty is the setting of a little divine kingdom in our own breasts: our *Social* Duty is the extending of that kingdom, first making our homes a *province* of it, then spreading it as best we may, and as our poor powers may permit, in all directions . . ." (87). While this passage is conventional in its call for women to make the home a place of virtue, Cobbe emphasizes that this is the location where future possibility emerges. She transforms the home from woman's private realm into the gateway to public power. It is the place where personal duty gets transformed into social duty, through a woman's power of influence.

Cobbe states clearly that personal duties are at the top of the hierarchy of women's duties: "Do not be shocked or startled if I lay it down as an unquestionable principle that Personal Duties have supreme obligation, and must never be postponed to Social ones" (40). Her claim here is somewhat ironic since she will indeed be most interested in social duties; however, she wants her audience to be clear that personal duties lead to social ones. It may be more useful, then, to think of Cobbe's hierarchy as a ladder that women climb gradually. As they ascend, they increase their public responsibilities while continuing to carry their private ones. Despite their stated importance, personal duties take up only one early lecture in *The Duties of Women*. Women's social duties and duties toward the state seem to have been more important to Cobbe. Indeed, when she later wrote her autobiography she excerpted a substantial portion of only her last lecture on women's duties to the state.[11] So, despite the stated significance of personal duties within Cobbe's hierarchy, they are less important to the lectures as a whole. Through the lectures Cobbe carefully works toward her revolutionary statement about women's duty: the redefinition of women's traditional role for power within the public sphere.

The woman's lower level of social duties is typical: these duties involve her familial relationships, in which her moral status provides the foundation for her duty. For example, in a mother's relationship with her children, Cobbe asserts that "[t]here is, first, the duty of conducing to her child's moral welfare, the highest of all her duties" (100). Cobbe becomes more remarkable, however, when she begins to redefine woman's role as household manager. In her effort to declare women's power within the domestic sphere, she adopts the metaphor of queenliness to describe women's housekeeping of the home and the state.[12] She replicates earlier accounts of domesticity when she claims that "the Englishwoman's home is the Englishwoman's kingdom; and those homes with all their faults and shortcomings, are the glories of our country" (138). John Ruskin, in 1865, also employed this metaphor to define women; in "Of Queen's Gardens" he asks: "What is her queenly office with respect to the State?" (160). While Ruskin does affirm that women have "a public work and duty," this duty "is to assist in the ordering, in the comforting, and in the beautiful adornment of the State" (160). Ruskin's call to women is less a public and political power than it will be for Cobbe. He confines women's public role to the sacred and moral dimensions of women's nature:

> Power to heal, to redeem, to guide, and to guard; power of the sceptre and shield; the power of the royal hand that heals in touching, that binds the fiend, and looses the captive; the throne that is founded on the rock of justice, and descended from only by steps of mercy. Will you not covet such power as this, and seek such throne as this, and be no more housewives, but queens?
>
> (162)

While the implications for women's power in Ruskin's statement might be suggestive, he leaves them abstractly understated. His ethereal language tends to obscure the potential for power that Cobbe wants to reveal, and it skirts the practicality that will be important for Cobbe. Throughout her lectures, Cobbe wants to explain explicitly how a woman should fulfill her duty. She wants women to understand how to "bind the fiend" and "loose the captive," matters that Ruskin leaves unclear.

Cobbe interprets queenliness so that once women rule within the home, they can become powerful and political rulers outside the home. "Out of the English home," she states, "has sprung much of that which is most excellent in the national character" (138). Furthermore, it is women's "peculiar and inalienable right" (139) to make the true English home. Men, in fact, "can no more make a home than a drone can make a hive" (139). Cobbe draws a distinct relationship between the home and the nation; because they are both managed alike, women have a natural place in the affairs of the nation. She states the public role of women's housekeeping duties more concretely than does Ruskin: "If we cannot perform these [duties] well, if we are not orderly enough, clear-headed enough, powerful enough, in short, to fulfil this immemorial function of our sex well and thoroughly, it is somewhat foolish of us to press to be allowed to share in the great housekeeping of the State" (151). Like Ruskin, Cobbe notes women's skill in keeping order within the household; however, keeping order within the state is more than domestic adornment for Cobbe. She claims that "womanly genius for organization applied to the affairs of the nation would be extremely economical and beneficial" (151). Since women are experts at household management, they could skillfully manage the government, curing it from "such wastefulness as Chancellors of the Exchequer keep the State" (151). Just as she bends the essential qualities of masculinity and femininity, so Cobbe here bends the tenets of domesticity so that they become women's path to active political life.

Cobbe sees the risk she takes when she encourages women to become "housekeepers of the State." Even though social duties are at the bottom of her hierarchy (or, if one likes, at the top of the ladder), they are duties with which Cobbe is extremely concerned. She is moving toward justifying a public and political role for women that is central to women's duties. She asks women to complete their lives by taking up causes of philanthropy and reform. She clarifies, however:

> Remember, pray, that I say emphatically "*adding* to . . . private duties," not *subtracting* from them. I should think it a most grievous and deplorable error to neglect any private duties already incurred for the sake of new public duties subsequently adopted. But, in truth, though we read of "Mrs. Jellybys" in novels, I have failed yet to find, in a pretty large experience of real life, a single case in which a woman who exercised public spirit, even to the extent of self-devotion, was not *also* an admirable and conscientious daughter, wife, mother or mistress of a household. This spectre of the female politician, who abandons her family to neglect for the sake of passing bills in Parliament, is just . . . an illusion of the masculine brain. . . .
>
> (187)

Mrs. Jellyby we will recall from Dickens's *Bleak House* as the satirized philanthropist who, as Mr. Kenge states, "'devotes herself entirely to the public'" (Dickens 26) at the expense of running a disgraceful home full of her own dirty and ill-attended children. The effect of Dickens's representation, of course, is the disavowal of any public role for women. Cobbe's incisive criticism of Dickens discloses the restrictive aspect of domestic ideology within the male literary imagination. For Cobbe, public work is the natural extension of all that domesticity embodies. She is aware, nevertheless, that a criticism against public women will be that they are neglecting their household duties, as Mrs. Jellyby does. Cobbe's argument thus hinges on her hierarchy: women can only add to their private duties pertaining to the home and family.

The hierarchy of duties prevents the occurrence of household neglect, because public spirit necessarily entails the fulfillment of private duties.

For Cobbe, it seems that women's duties toward the state were, in fact, most important in her lectures. In her autobiography, Cobbe quotes from a letter she wrote in 1884, several years after the lectures, which points to her concern about women's role in the public sphere: "'If I may presume to offer an old woman's counsel to the younger workers in our cause, it would be that they should adopt the point of view—that it is before all things our duty to obtain the franchise'" (2: 532). This statement seems to contradict what Cobbe claims with her hierarchy of duties; yet, the whole point of the hierarchy is to lead up to this final public and political duty. Indeed, it is the subject of Parliamentary franchise that concludes Cobbe's lectures: "[I]n asking for the Parliamentary franchise we are asking, as I understand it, for the power to influence legislation generally; and in every other kind of franchise, municipal, parochial, or otherwise, for similar power to bring our sense of justice and righteousness to bear on public affairs" (*Duties* 182). What this means for Cobbe and for her audience is adopting a "public spirit" that extends women's "sympathies beyond the narrow bounds of our homes" (182). In short, women should enlarge their natural domestic duties so that public duties become equally essential.

Martha Vicinus suggests that part of Cobbe's success as a public woman was "due to her willingness to work within the traditional definitions women's duties" (16). At the same time, her unmarried and childless status must have enabled Cobbe to participate in a full public life, "untrammelled by husband or children," as she herself had once described the "old maid" ("Celibacy vs. Marriage" 233). She had not the duties she insisted the mothers in her audience must fulfill before taking their domestic skills to the public world. Some years earlier she noted that the single woman "has not fewer duties than other women, only more diffused ones. The 'old maid's' life may be as rich, as blessed, as that of the proudest of mothers with her crown of clustering babes. Nay, she feels that in the power of devoting her *whole* time and energies to some benevolent task, she is enabled to effect perhaps some greater good than would otherwise have been possible" (233). Despite her difference from the women she addressed in the lectures, she could share with her audience her vision of how the power that was inherent within women's traditional domestic roles could help women cultivate public spirit to become "Citizens of the State" (*Duties* 174).

Notes

1. See Cobbe's *Life*: "These lectures when printed went through three editions in England and, I think, eight in America . . ." (2: 549).
2. See Bauer and Ritt.
3. Most of Cobbe's writing concerning women calls for the improvement of their rights. Besides "Wife-Torture in England," see in particular "Criminals, Idiots, Women, and Minors," a piece that argues for married women's rights to their own property.
4. See "Our Policy: An Address to Women Concerning the Suffrage" and "Why Women Desire the Franchise."
5. Cobbe appears to assume her audience to be primarily mothers: "I hope you, my friends, who are mothers, and possess the experience which I shall never know, will pardon my presumption in laying down before you what appears to me the leading outlines of parental duty" (98). For further discussion of Victorian women's struggle to gain political rights, see Levine, *Victorian Feminism*, chapter 3: "The public sphere: politics, local and national."
6. Cobbe does, though, refer her audience to her book *Religious Duty.*
7. Smiles's discussion of women's duties is more rigidly defined by "separate spheres" than Cobbe's, however. See, for example his discussion of Florence Nightingale (236-39).
8. For accounts of this "female marriage" see Caine (128-30) and Raftery (93-4).
9. See Cobbe's *Life* (1: 206-7), Caine (116-17), and Raftery (98-100) for discussions of Cobbe's relationship with her authoritarian and imperious father, Charles Cobbe.
10. See also Caine for differences between Ellis and Cobbe (51,130-31).
11. See *Life of Frances Power Cobbe* (2:550-52).
12. See Langland for additional discussion of this metaphor (65-6).

Works Cited

Bauer, Carol and Lawrence Ritt. "'A Husband is a Beating Animal': Frances Power Cobbe Confronts the Wife-Abuse Problem in Victorian England." *International J of Women's Studies*. 6 (1983): 99-118.

Caine, Barbara. *Victorian Feminists*. NY: Oxford UP, 1992.

Cobbe, Frances Power. "Celibacy v. Marriage." *Fraser's Magazine* 65 (Feb. 1862): 228-35.

———. "Criminals, Idiots, Women, and Minors." *Fraser's Magazine* 78 (Feb. 1868): 777-94.

———. *The Duties of Women*. 1882. Boston: G. H. Ellis, 1978.

———. "The Final Cause of Women." *Woman's Work and Woman's Culture. A Series of Essays*. Ed. Josephine E. Butler. London: Macmillan, 1869. 1-26.

———. *Life of Frances Power Cobbe by Herself.* 2 vols. Boston: Houghton, 1894.

———. "Our Policy: An Address to Women Concerning the Suffrage." London: National Society for Women's Suffrage, 1870. Online. The Victorian Women Writers Project. Indiana University. Internet. http://www.indiana.edu/~letrs/vwwp/cobbe/ourpolicy.html.

———. "Why Women Desire the Franchise." London: National Society for Women's Suffrage, 1870. Online. The Victorian Women Writers Project. Indiana University. Internet. http://www.indiana.edu/~letrs/vwwp/cobbe/cobbewhy.html

———. "Wife-Torture in England" *Contemporary Review* 32 (1878): 56-87.

Dickens, Charles. *Bleak House.* 1853. Ed. Morton Dauwen Zabel. Boston: Houghton, 1956.

Ellis, Sarah Stickney. *The Women of England. Their Social Duties, and Domestic Habits.* 1839. Philadelphia: Herman Hooker, 1841.

Houghton, Walter E. *The Victorian Frame of Mind, 1830-1870.* New Haven: Yale UP, 1957.

Langland, Elizabeth. *Nobody's Angels: Middle-Class Women and Domestic Ideology in Victorian Culture.* Ithaca: Cornell UP, 1995.

Levine, Philippa. *Victorian Feminism, 1850-1900.* Tallahassee: Florida State UP, 1987.

Lewis, Jane. *Women and Social Action in Victorian and Edwardian England.* Stanford, CA: Stanford UP, 1991.

Raftery, Deirdre. "Frances Power Cobbe." *Women, Power and Consciousness in 19th-Century Ireland, Eight Biographical Studies.* Ed. Mary Cullen and Maria Luddy. Dublin: Attic Press, 1995. 89-123.

Ruskin, John. "Of Queen's Gardens." *Sesame and Lilies, The Ethics of Dust.* 1865. Oxford: Oxford UP, 1951. 84-123.

Smiles, Samuel. *Duty with Illustrations of Courage, Patience, and Endurance.* NY: Harper, 1880.

Vicinus, Martha. *Independent Women: Work and Community for Single Women, 1850-1920.* Chicago: U of Chicago P, 1985.

VALERIE SANDERS (ESSAY DATE 2001)

Sanders, Valerie. "Women, Fiction and the Marketplace." In *Women and Literature in Britain 1800-1900,* edited by Joanne Shattock, pp. 142-161. Cambridge: Cambridge University Press, 2001.

In the following essay, Sanders reports the treatment of women writers in the literary marketplace of the nineteenth century.

> I have now so large and eager a public, that if we were to publish the work without a preliminary appearance in the Magazine, the first sale would infallibly be large, and a considerable profit would be gained even though the work might not ultimately impress the public so strongly as 'Adam' has done.[1]

George Eliot, discussing with John Blackwood the best way to publish *The Mill on the Floss,* sounds shrewd and confident. Her comments show an awareness of the business issues involved in selecting the right formula for a relative newcomer on the literary scene, and one whose first appearance had set the public gossiping and speculating. Margaret Oliphant's observation that the nineteenth century, 'which is the age of so many things—of enlightenment, of science, of progress—is quite as distinctly the age of female novelists', has now become a truism.[2] Yet the ways in which professional women writers handled their careers changed significantly from the early 1800s, when Jane Austen was being ignored by publishers and reviewers, to the 1890s, when Mrs. Humphry Ward, riding high on the success of *Robert Elsmere* (1888), was insisting on the early release of a cheap edition of *Marcella* (1894). According to John Sutherland, 'the reprint of *Marcella* was the torpedo that sunk the three-decker and by so doing stripped Mudie of his dictatorial powers'.[3] Women novelists, who had begun the century in apologetic mode, ended it, to a considerable extent, calling the shots. Yet the emergence of these conditions was uneven and complex. Writers that we now regard as 'canonical' struggled for recognition, while those since relegated to minor status seem to have exploited the marketplace on a scale that relatively few novelists achieve even today. Others, who started well, had to rebuild their careers in mid-stream, and begin afresh, perhaps diversifying into other genres. Many found ways of juggling their novel-writing with contributions to the periodical press or literary reviewing. Investigating how the conditions of the marketplace developed, what use women novelists made of them, and how they shaped their careers as they sought acceptance in the male-dominated world of publishing is the main purpose of this chapter.

The nineteenth century saw a major expansion of what might loosely be called the 'literature industry', and in particular a proliferation of new methods of novel publication. For much of the century, however, the expensive three-volume novel was the staple of the book-publishing industry. Selling at thirty-one shillings and sixpence for three volumes, the novel was clearly a luxury item, intended mainly for library stock. Mudie's Select Library, founded in 1843, was the chief bulk purchaser of novels, which meant that publishers had constantly to defer to library tastes. Margaret Oliphant later recalled that it seemed to her 'the patronage of Mudie was a sort of recognition from heaven'.[4] Without substantial orders from Mudie—the insatiable Mudie', 'the magnanimous Mudie', as John Blackwood called him

(*George Eliot Letters,* vol. III, pp. 33, 289)—a novel was unlikely to make much money for either its author or its publishers, and, according to Gaye Tuchman, Charles Mudie's taste was 'that of a religious fundamentalist and patriarchal, Victorian'.[5] While this may be a slight exaggeration, he certainly considered boycotting *The Mill on the Floss* when he discovered that its author was Marian Evans, living unmarried with George Henry Lewes (*George Eliot Letters,* vol. III, p. 209). Mudie also discouraged the issuing of cheap reprints (twelve- or six-shilling editions were the norm) before the three-volume library sets had time to circulate widely: a year was his ideal time-lapse between first publication and first cheap reprint. John Blackwood refers in a letter of 1859 to a two-volume, twelve-shilling edition of *Adam Bede* as being 'intermediate to a people's edition' (*George Eliot Letters,* vol. III, p. 33). As with the difference now between hardback and paperback novels, the longer readers were prepared to wait, the cheaper a book would become, but the nineteenth century was very much an age, when new novels caused a sensation and people were in a hurry to read them.

Publishers therefore looked to additional ways of selling their books to the public: hence the introduction of part serialization—both in separately bound and sold monthly parts (for which there were eighteenth-century precedents, taken up by Dickens for *Pickwick Papers*) and in magazines (which George Eliot accepted for *Scenes of Clerical Life,* but not for the *The Mill on the Floss*). This method had the advantage of whetting the reader's appetite for more, thereby also increasing sales of the magazine, though it could reduce interest in the novel when serialization came to and end.[6] Occasionally, too, a novel serialization proved unpopular, and dragged down magazine sales with it—as happened with Gaskell's *North and South* in Dickens's *Household Words*. Part serialization, by both these methods, was particularly popular from the late 1830s until the 1860s, though magazine serialization quickly gained ascendancy over the monthly part.

Once a novelist had established a readership, there was an additional market for complete sets of novels, especially for cheap reprints at more affordable prices for the private purchaser. This was something that came into vogue in the 1830s, starting with Bentley's Standard Novels (1831), but was especially popular in the second half of the century when some of the greatest novelists had died and complete sets of their works could be issued. The Cabinet Edition of George Eliot's novels stretched to twenty-four volumes from 1878 to 1885, while the Cheap Edition came out in six volumes in 1881, with an additional twelve-volume 'fire-side edition' in New York in 1885. Collections of Elizabeth Gaskell's works (in fifteen volumes) were issued in Leipzig as early as 1849-57 when she was in mid career. Like many other Victorian novelists she was published in Tauchnitz's cheap English reprint series which began in 1837.[7] In 1879-80 Macmillan's brought out their famous sixteen-volume selection of Charlotte Yonge's works in the familiar blue-covered edition which copied the small-print format used by her original publishers, Parker.[8] Writers such as Margaret Oliphant and Eliza Lynn Linton, who were never reissued in a uniform edition, are now very much harder to recover except via odd second-hand copies. Yonge's works had a steady following among those who had grown up with her family sagas, whereas Oliphant and Linton were less consistently popular. Oliphant, moreover, was too prolific a novelist to be readily containable in a 'complete works'.

As John Sutherland has commented, 'high prices, multiple outlets, wide sales and abundant creative genius combined to make 1850-80 one of the richest periods that fiction has known'.[9] The women novelists discussed in this chapter were fortunate in living and working through a period of such productive activity in the fiction industry, but it was also a time when relations between novelists, publishers, libraries and readers were at their most personal and intense. Conditions favoured the arrival of fresh talent, and could turn high quality books into best-sellers, yet the balance of power between all the participants in a novel's launch was often precarious, with the novelist generally the most vulnerable party. As reviewers were only just coming to terms with the high-profile presence of women in the novel-writing market—moreover, women writing because they wanted to write, and not just because they needed the money—stage was set for many turbulent episode, as (mainly male) reviewers judged the work of (mainly female) new novelists, whose work had initially been accepted by male editors, many of them from publishing dynasties, like the Blackwoods.

Women novelists of the eighteenth century had already set an example of how to adapt to a system originally designed for and run by men. The most successful among them had attracted patronage and got up subscriptions when necessary, gradually winning the confidence of publishers and steadily raising their own earning power.

ON THE SUBJECT OF...

CHARLOTTE YONGE (1823-1901)
Yonge was the most popular and prolific novelist associated with the Oxford Movement, also known as the Tractarian Movement or Anglo-Catholic Revival. Led by John Henry (later Cardinal) Newman, this group resisted the trend toward liberalism in the Church of England during the mid-nineteenth century, urging a return to the stricter doctrines and more elaborate rituals derived from Roman Catholicism. Although Yonge wrote nearly two hundred works, including histories, juvenile novels, historical romances, biographies, and essays on religious topics, she is best remembered for novels that portray the tensions, rivalries, and intense affections in middle-class domestic life during the mid-Victorian era.

Yonge was born in the Hampshire village of Otterbourne. Educated at home by her parents, she received instruction in ancient and modern languages, history, literature, and theology. At fifteen, Yonge was prepared for confirmation by the theologian John Keble, the vicar of a nearby church. Keble, whose 1833 sermon on "national apostasy" had led to the establishment of the Oxford Movement, inspired in Yonge an ardent religious fervor. Keble became her literary mentor and, along with her father, edited all her manuscripts until his death in 1866.

Although her family initially disapproved of her desire to become a writer, as it was considered socially improper for a woman to profit from her own labor, they agreed to let Yonge continue writing as long as all proceeds were contributed to missionary activities. In 1851 she founded *The Monthly Packet,* a magazine she edited for nearly half a century and in which many of her novels were serialized. Following the publication of *The Heir of Redclyffe* (1853), a novel presenting traditional Christian ideals of piety, self-sacrifice, and devotion to family, she became a highly popular novelist.

Fanny Burney's career is a case in point. Having started small with £20 from Lowndes for *Evelina* (1778), she earned £2,000 for *Camilla* (1796) and built a cottage on the proceeds.[10] Though her earnings were less spectacular, Ann Radcliffe made an impressive £500 on *The Mysteries of Udolpho* (1794) and £800 on *The Italian* (1797). With Jane Austen, however, the story of women's publishing seems to restart more diffidently. She relied at first on male relatives to approach publishers, but her father failed in 1797 to sell *First Impressions* to Cadell, while her brother Henry's sale of *Susan* in 1803 for £10 to the publishers Crosby in London had produced no results six years later. Austen, calling herself 'Mrs Ashton Dennis' (the initials spelt MAL') was offered little choice but to buy back the manuscript at her own expense, or else wait indefinitely for its publication. When she did succeed in having a novel published, it was 'on commission,' which meant that the author was herself responsible for the printing and advertising costs, while the publisher charged 10 per cent commission on each volume sold. As late as 1815, Austen took over her brother Henry's correspondence with John Murray over *Emma* apparently only because Henry was himself too ill to write, and then she stressed: 'I beg you to understand that I leave the terms on which the Trade should be supplied with the work, entirely to your Judgment'. Unlike her successors, especially Charlotte Brontë, Elizabeth Gaskell and George Eliot, she was never on intimate corresponding terms with her publishers. Her transactions with them remained formal and businesslike to the end. Nevertheless, Austen liked the idea of earning money and becoming a professional writer: 'I have now therefore written myself into £250—which only makes me long for more', she told her brother Frank in 1813.[11] Overall, however, counting all her novels, she seems to have earned less than £700.[12] John Murray, who remaindered what he had left of her works in 1820, subsequently disposed of Austen's copyrights to Richard Bentley's firm.

Concern about earnings was something that affected most of her successors—not just because they needed the money to live on, but also because they wanted to be treated as professionals. Authorship, for men as well as women, had been gaining in dignity and credibility largely because successful novelists were being paid more realistic sums, yet also because they were entering the profession for more than purely economic reasons. Most nineteenth-century women novelists broached the marketplace as outsiders, excluded from the male 'clubland' of editors and publishers. A popular route was through journalism, which allowed the newcomer to establish some degree of confidence and authority in short articles and book reviews, often in magazines with a national, rather than a purely local, circulation, which might, in turn, lead to more extensive literary connections. Harriet Martineau's Unitarian family origins made W. J. Fox's *Monthly Repository* her natural point of entry; Fox's brother Charles ultimately published her hugely successful *Illustrations of Political Economy* (1832-4). Unlike George Eliot, who largely abandoned magazine journalism after the success of *Scenes of Clerical Life* in 1858, Martineau remained an active contributor to a wide range of quality newspapers and journals, most notably the *Edinburgh Review* and *Daily News,* for which she wrote on the progress of the American Civil War. George Eliot herself gained the courage and experience to write fiction partly through her apprenticeship as John Chapman's unofficial editor for the *Westminster Review*; while Elizabeth Gaskell came to writing through her contributions to *Howitt's Journal* in 1847 (though her first publication had been a poem, composed jointly with her husband, in the style of Crabbe, for *Blackwood's* in 1837): her contact with William Howitt, who read the manuscript of *Mary Barton* and passed it to John Forster, reader for Chapman and Hall, led to the publication of her first novel. Margaret Oliphant makes a great deal in her *Autobiography* of introducing Dinah Mulock to the publisher Henry Blackett: 'he, apparently with some business gift or instinct imperceptible to me, having made out that there were elements of special success in her' (p. 101). Hit-and-miss networking of this kind was often a woman's quickest route to finding the right publisher, though the direct approach with an unsolicited manuscript was always an alternative option.

Harriet Martineau's epic battle to find a publisher for her *Illustrations of Political Economy* in 1832 is recounted with considerable drama in the first volume of her *Autobiography.* Determined to publish her tales at whatever cost, Martineau was repeatedly told that the Reform Bill and the cholera epidemic would damage sales and make publication inadvisable. After failing to interest any publishers by letter, Martineau set out for London and began seeing them personally. Even then, the terms she was offered by Charles Fox were so insulting that his brother was embarrassed to press them: the work was to be published by subscription, in the eighteenth-century style, 'and moreover, the subscription must be for five hundred copies before the work began.' She was also to sell 1,000 in the first fortnight, or the series would end after only two numbers. 'As Charles Fox had neither money nor connexion, I felt that the whole risk was thrown up me,' Martineau recalled.[13] As it happened, the series was a huge success, but Martineau remembered sending out circulars to all likely subscribers, including members of her own family who thought she was being rash and conceited. When the suspense was over, she felt permanently relieved from financial insecurity: 'The entire periodical press, daily, weekly, and, as soon as possible, monthly, came out in my favour, and I was overwhelmed with newspapers and letters, containing every sort of flattery' (1, 178). Martineau's narrative reminds us of how unstable and unpredictable the publishing industry was at that difficult time between the deaths of the great Romantic poets and the beginning of the Victorian period when the novel became the most popular genre.

Publishers had pointed ways of making it clear to their clients that they expected their works to fail. Discouraging terms and mean first payments were usually the best a new author could expect; moreover, many first novels by women were either published anonymously (*Frankenstein* and *Mary Barton* are good examples) or under pseudonyms, to protect them from prejudiced judgments by reviewers. For the Brontës, doing everything on their own, and without even the useful contacts that Martineau had made for herself by the time she was thirty, the battle to be noticed by publishers was often demoralizing. When Charlotte Brontë came to review her own and her sisters' fortunes with their novels, she felt they had had an arduous struggle for acceptance: 'The great puzzle lay in the difficulty of getting answers of any kind from the publishers to whom we applied', she recalled in the 'Biographical Notice of Ellis and Acton Bell'.[14] While Anne and Emily were prepared to accept disadvantageous terms from Newby, a notoriously roguish publisher Charlotte found herself being offered nothing at all, as *The Professor* went its weary rounds—famously rewrapped in used paper, the next publisher's address added to the lengthening list each time the novel was rejected. That *Jane Eyre* was finally accepted and published with so much haste and enthusiasm was largely due to the enterprising outlook of one man, George Smith, who became her friend and adviser for the rest of her life.

What makes this period of literary history especially interesting is the peculiar conditions in which aspiring women novelists had to work professionally with equally ambitious young male editors in the best publishing houses. It is important to remember that there were no women editors at the top of Victorian publishing firms: the key publisher of the day were men—and young men at that—a new breed of keen, business-like operators, such as George Smith (1824-1801), John Chapman (1822-94) and John Blackwood (1818-79), who were eager to know their clients personally and, if necessary, help them with their personal problems. The blurring of lines between the professional and personal could be fruitful or it could be awkward. John Blackwood sent George Eliot a pug dog, and thought of the title for *The Mill on the Floss*; Charlotte Brontë asked George Smith for advice on investing the £500 she was paid for the copyright of *Shirley* (1849); he also sent her selections of new books to broaden her horizons, and, having finally persuaded her to visit his family, squired her around the sights of London. She even had a proposal of marriage from one of the firm, James Taylor (whom she rejected). Smith perhaps felt more comfortable with Elizabeth Gaskell, to whom he sent a valentine in 1864, urging her to write more of *Cousin Phillis* (which appeared monthly in the *Cornhill* from 1863 to 1864):

> More, more, he cried, e'er Phillis breathed her last,
> Three Volumes more, I want them quick and fast.
> Trollope's too long: Macdonald slow and tame
> There's only you can raise the Cornhill's fame.[15]

Gaskell, in turn, felt she could be humorous with Smith—so long as they were discussing anything except money. When he sent her an advance copy of *The Mill on the Floss,* she was ecstatic: 'Oh Mr. Smith! your grandfather was a brick, and your grandmother an angel' (*Gaskell Letters,* p. 611).

As John Sutherland has observed, women novelists tended to stay longer than men with the same publishers:[16] hence the close working partnerships of John Blackwood with George Eliot and Margaret Oliphant; George Smith with Charlotte Brontë and Elizabeth Gaskell, later with Mrs. Humphry Ward; Richard Bentley with Eliza Lynn Linton; and W. J. Fox with Harriet Martineau. In 1853, Gaskell declined to be lured away from Chapman and Hall overtures from Richard Bentley via Dinah Mulock, partly because she had 'no complaint to make' against them but also because they had taken 'the risk of Mary Barton, when Mr Moxon refused it as a *gift*' (*Gaskell Letters,* p. 250). Later, when she became disillusioned with them and was publishing with Smith, Elder, she confessed to being tempted by a better offer from Sampson Low, who had a lucrative American outlet: 'But I would much rather have 800£ from you than 1,000£, from them', she loyally told George Smith (p. 558). Not that these partnerships always protected smoothly. Martineau became disgusted with Fox's private life, while Eliot and Brontë struggled with editors who were kind-hearted and supportive, but not always entirely convinced by what their authors were trying to do. Significantly, Eliot continued addressing Blackwood as 'Dear Mr Blackwood', unlike the more relaxed Lewes, who was soon beginning letters, 'My dear Blackwood'. John Blackwood, initially stuck for how to address the author of *Scenes of Clerical Life,* tried 'My Dear Amos' (30 January 1857) after the hero of the first story. Although their relationship gradually warmed, its initial stages were complicated by the secrecy surrounding Eliot's identity, and Blackwood's sensitivity to her position. Like the Brontës, she was never entirely at ease in 'literary circles' (except perhaps in Germany), and at first avoided the full London literary life beyond the point where it had been useful to her during her *Westminster Review* years—though of course her position was greatly exacerbated by her unmarried relationship with Lewes. Towards the end of her life, when the public were more prepared to overlook her controversial history, she became more sociable, and held regular Sunday 'afternoons' at The Priory.

Jane Austen, Charlotte Brontë and Elizabeth Gaskell made little attempt to conceal their newcomer status when writing to their publishers. Austen had to back down over the dedication to the Prince of Wales in *Emma,* which she had instructed John Murray to put in the wrong place: 'it was arising from my ignorance only', she confessed, 'and from my having never noticed the proper place for a dedication' (*Austen Letter,* p. 305). Brontë, with no male intermediaries to act for her, had to ask even publishers who had turned her down for help in approaching others. 'For instance', she asked Aylott and Jones (who had published the 'Bell' brothers' poems) in 1846 'in the present case, where a work of fiction is in question, in what form would a publisher be most likely to accept the M.S-? whether offered as a work of 3 vols or as tales which might be published in numbers or as contributions to a periodical'.[17] In fact Brontë always eschewed any form of publication other than the three-volume novel, but at this stage of her career, she was anxious to learn all the possibilities.

Elizabeth Gaskell sounds just as unsure of herself in her business correspondence with George Smith: 'Can you begin to print before you have the whole of the MS. That is a question I want much to have answered, & I'll tell you why' she explained when she was preparing the *Life of Charlotte Brontë* in 1856: 'I have 100 pages quite ready—only with so many erasures, insertions at the *back* of the leaves &c (owing to the unchronological way in which I obtained information) that I should much like to correct all I can myself.' A week or two later she was confessing: 'I am no judge of type &c—and I find it difficult to say how far the MS will extend; I can scarcely tell what space it will occupy.'[18] It was not only the type that bothered Gaskell: money was another area that made her feel uncomfortable. 'I have a great dislike to bargaining, & I should not like to be (what the Lancashire people call) "having"; but if I must deal frankly with you, as I wish, the terms proposed for the Biography are below what I thought I might reasonably expect'. It is hard to tell with passages like this whether Gaskell was being entirely straight. After all, by 1856, she was an experienced novelist, with *Mary Barton* (1848), *Ruth* (1853) and *North and South* (1855) behind her. Indeed she uses her previous experience to substantiate her claims for more money: 'My way of reckoning was this—For "North and South" I received 600£ (from H[ousehold]. W[ords]. & Mr Chapman together,) retaining the copyright, having the Tauchnitz profit,—and only losing the American profit by my own carelessness in forgetting to answer the note, until some other American publisher had begun to reprint' (*Gaskell Letters,* p. 430). For good measure Gaskell added that the biography had been more arduous and expensive to write than a novel, and was also likely to interest a wider class of readers.

Smith was convinced and she succeeded in having her original offer of £600 for the copyright of the *Life* raised to £800, but her discussion of the issues at stake combines professional terminology and unprofessional disorder in a welter of facts, figures, opinions, and confessions of carelessness.

In her *Autobiography,* Margaret Oliphant insists that she was unable to bargain for the fabulous deals she felt had accrued to Trollope, Dinah Mulock Craik and Mrs. Humphry Ward: 'I never could fight for a higher price or do anything but trust to the honour of those I had to deal with'.[19] In fact, as Elisabeth Jay's biography of Oliphant reveals, this was by no means the case. Oliphant did ask for better deals, and often reminded Blackwood of the going-rate for other novels which she felt were comparable with her own. Sometimes she got what she wanted, and sometimes not. Blackwood, who gave her £1,500 for *The Perpetual Curate* (1864), was less generous over *Miss Majoribanks* (1866). Both had been serialized in *Blackwood's Magazine,* but, according to Elisabeth Jay, Blackwood, 'apparently put off by the harshness of tone of *Miss Majoribanks,* which many subsequent readers have found her most accomplished work, refused to recognize her Carlingford series as the financial equal of Trollope's Barsetshire series'.[20] Though friendly with the whole Blackwood dynasty (she made John Blackwood her son's official guardian, and held a big literary party at Runnymede in 1877 to celebrate her twenty-five years of authorship with the firm), Oliphant was sometimes hurt by his professional firmness. The complete version of her *Autobiography* opens with a painful memory of his rejecting 'paper after paper', whilst she chocked back the tears, 'lest the hard men—who were very kind notwithstanding, and friendly and just—should see I was crying and think it an appeal to their sympathies' (p. 3). Blackwood was indeed 'kind' and 'friendly', doing his best to find Oliphant many and varied opportunities for increasing her salary as a professional author, while recognizing (as she did) that she would never be another George Eliot.

Relationships with editors could swing between cautious negotiation, mild flirtation, anger, disappointment and huffy withdrawal. There is every sign that such relationships were more complicated because the novelists were women negotiating with men: desperate to be taken seriously, but deeply conscious of their 'outsider' status, and unsure what tone to adopt in business negotiations; unsure, too, how to conduct the more personal side of the relationship. Achieving the correct balance between the two was a challenge, especially when the novelist needed to defend her own position. However inexperienced, many of them had firm ideas about what they could and could not manage. The Brontës and Jane Austen avoided serial publication in magazines, though Charlotte Brontë was invited to consider this for *Shirley*: 'I am not yet qualified for the task', she told W. S. Williams of Smith, Elder: 'I have neither gained a sufficiently firm footing with the public, nor do I possess sufficient confidence in myself, nor can I boast those unflagging animal spirits, that even command of the faculty of composition, which, as you say and I am persuaded, most justly, is an indispensable requisite to success in serial literature' (*Brontë Letters,* p. 574). Harriet Martineau went further in seeing serial publication of a novel as 'unprincipled', and 'a false principle of composition'. Her own *Illustrations of Political Economy,* serialized monthly over two years, were presumably exempt from disapproval because they came out as separate tales, complete in themselves; whereas John Murray's offer to publish a serialized novel on conspiratorial terms struck her as improper. 'He said that he could help me to a boundless fortune, and a mighty future fame, if I would adopt his advice', she recalls in the passage of her *Autobiography* (II, p. 116) describing the publication of *Deerbrook* (1839). In the end, Murray withdrew his offer as the humdrum domestic subject displeased him, and Martineau settled for a less spectacular, three-volume deal with Edward Moxon (who would later refuse *Mary Barton* as a gift).

While Martineau did her own negotiating, George Eliot continued using George Henry Lewes as her middle-man in discussions with Blackwood. The terms of each of her novels were laboriously debated as she weighed up what would be best for each book aesthetically and for herself economically. For Eliot, there were always conflicting considerations at stake, largely because, although she wanted to make money from her writing, she did not want to be seen *only* or *mainly* as writing for money. 'I don't want the world to give me anything for my books except money enough to save me from the temptation to write *only* for money', she told John Blackwood in 1859 (*George Eliot Letters,* III, p. 152). Nevertheless her instructions to Blackwood on the judicious timing of cheaper reprints are remarkably exact and anxious. 'I would on no account publish a 6/- edition of the books until the 12/- edition of the Mill has had a fair chance of disappearing from the shelves', she urged him in 1861; 'And pray print the smallest practicable number of Adam at 12/-, for I have a great dread of having my books printed to lie in warehouses' (*George Eliot Letters,* III, p. 392). She had learnt a great deal since the days of *Adam Bede,* when she declined to advise Blackwood on the timing of cheaper reprints, referring him instead to Lewes as 'a more experienced judge' (III, p. 33). From then on Eliot scrutinized every stage of the publication schedules for her novels. She also agonized about attaining the right kind of popularity. She wanted to be appreciated, but mainly by the more discerning kind of reader who would understand her moral earnestness; she wanted to push the more expensive editions of her books until the market was exhausted, but then she shrank from the shame of being remaindered. While Lewes continued proposing new publication arrangements (it was his idea that *Middlemarch* should appear in bimonthly parts), Eliot tended to write more often about the niggling details of new editions. Her terror of bad reviews and habit of fleeing abroad immediately on publication of a new book testify to her continuing self-doubt in the world of mid-Victorian publishing, despite her own apparently unassailable position in it. Gaskell also timed her 1857 holiday so that she would be out of the country when her Brontë biography was published.

If it was difficult enough persuading publishers to believe in a new author, the problems of maintaining a literary career over a period of twenty or thirty years were no less daunting. Eliot herself made some decisions which now look strange, but at the time sounded convincing, as when she temporarily abandoned her best-selling line in Warwickshire rural tragedies, and turned to short tales, poems, and fifteenth-century Florence with *Romola* (1863), briefly also breaking with the Blackwood firm to publish with George Smith.[21] Smith offered Eliot as astounding £10,000 for *Romola;* though he reduced it to £7,000 for serialization in the *Cornhill.* When her next novel, *Felix Holt,* was up for negotiation, Eliot returned humbly to Blackwood, aware that the brief flirtation with Smith had been embarrassing all around.

The sums of money paid for copyright at this time varied, like other payments, according to the publisher's faith in his author; even with a promising first novel, some publishers were cautious until they had tested the market. George Smith, who was to be so generous with George Eliot, offered Charlotte Brontë only £100 for the copyright of *Jane Eyre,* which even she, with all her inexperience, though rather mean: 'One hundred pounds is a small sum for a year's intellectual labour—', she told him despondently (*Brontë Letters,* p. 540)—though this was also what Gaskell was paid for *Mary Barton* the following year by Chapman and Hall. *Ruth* (1853), however, earned £500. Fees tended to rise encouragingly once publishers were confident that their authors were going to be successful. The question of keeping or selling copyrights was another problem new authors had to settle for themselves, without always being sure they were acting for the best. George Eliot clung carefully to hers, as one might expect. Harrison Ainsworth urged Mrs. Henry Wood never to sell any of her copyrights, though she did dispose of *The Channings* to Bentley (Gettmann, *A Victorian Publisher,* p. 111). Gaskell, far less professional than Eliot, parted with the copyright of *Mary Barton,* without fully understanding what she was doing: 'but I was then so unknowing, and so little expected that it would ever come to a second edition, that I did not sufficiently make myself acquainted with the nature of the parchment document sent to me to sign' (*Gaskell Letters,* p. 132). While the selling of copyright brought in instant cash, it was a one-off payment, which might represent much less than a successful novel would eventually earn. Some authors, therefore, sold their copyrights for a fixed period of years, and then reclaimed them. Without literary agents to act for them (which was the case before the 1870s), all inexperienced Victorian novelists—men as well as women—were at risk of making the wrong decisions and losing considerable sums of money. According to Royal Gettmann, the royalty system, as we understand it today, came into play as late as 1885 with Eliza Lynn Linton's *Autobiography of Christopher Kirkland.* This ensured that novelists kept on being paid for successive sales of their work, once a certain number had been cleared.[22]

The market was also unpredictable in terms of taste. Whereas Eliza Lynn Linton was surprisingly successful with her first two historical novels, *Azeth the Egyptian* (1847) and *Amymone* (1848)—the first published at her own expense with Newby, the second by Bentley (who paid her £100)—her third novel, *Realities* (1851), so shocked the public that Linton abandoned novel-writing altogether for the next fourteen years. Faced with the need to redirect her career, she took up newspaper journalism, first with the *Morning Chronicle,* and later with the *Saturday Review,* which carried her notorious 'Girl of the Period' articles (1868). Though she returned to novel-writing with *Grasp Your Nettle* (1865), combining sensationalism with anti-feminism, her novels quickly came to seem old-fashioned and loosely constructed. She was still turning out three-deckers, such as *The One Too Many* (1894), when the new novelists of the next generation were writing shorter, tighter works in the novella style, and forcing Mudie to back down over the three-volume format.

Harriet Martineau, too, took several changes of direction within her long career—driven by her own political interests and declining taste for imaginative writing. Her novel *Deerbrook* (1839) was followed by only one other, *The Hour and the Man* (1841), an historical novel about Toussaint L'Ouverture. She then concentrated on writing up her own experiences of foreign travel, protracted illness, and visits to industrial sites in Birmingham (the last for Dickens's *Household Words*). Her lasting *métier* was as lead writer for the *Daily News* during the period of the American Civil War. Nevertheless, Martineau, in a curious experimental episode in 1851, nearly published a novel called *Oliver Weld,* using a pseudonym, but was persuaded not to go ahead with it by judicious criticism from Charlotte Brontë—a friend whose work Martineau herself criticized two years later when she asked for her opinion of *Villette.* Brontë had actually offered to be her intermediary with George Smith, who hoped for another *Deerbrook.* What he was offered was a book full of religious and political controversy, which Martineau herself quickly suppressed as 'a foolish prank', admitting that her fiction-writing days were over.[23] The episode is perhaps more interesting for showing how quickly Brontë had moved from the role of humble petitioner to would-be patron of an older, more established writer, whose career had been more varied than Brontë's own.

By the middle of the century, women novelists were becoming distinctly more professional in their handling of their careers, and more directly involved in every stage of the publication process. During the 1860s, when many new magazines were started, several women took leading roles in running them. Mary Howitt had already edited, with her husband, *Howitt's Journal,* which had published Gaskell's early stories. Mary Elizabeth Braddon edited *Belgravia* from 1866 to 1876 and the *Belgravia Annual* from 1867 to 1876, quite apart from contributing to the other major literary journals of the day, including *Temple Bar* and *All the Year Round.* Mrs Henry Wood took over the running of Alexander Strahan's magazine, the *Argosy,* in 1867, and wrote much of the material herself, as did Charlotte Yonge for the *Monthly Packet,* which she edited from 1851 to 1890: as her entry in the *Oxford Guide to British Women Writers* (1994) confirms, 'one of the longest-serving editorships of any Victorian periodical'.[24] When Alexander Macmillan in 1865 offered Yonge the chance to edit the *Sunday Library for Household Reading,* she wanted to be sure that she would have total control over the contributions and editorial team as she had with the *Monthly Packet* 'where I have been used to admit nothing that I do not quite go along with'.[25] Whereas Jane

Austen and the Brontës took no part in the wider literary life of their times, it became increasingly common for women novelists to write for several journals simultaneously, review other novels, and work as publishers' readers—the best-known example being Geraldine Jewsbury, who not only reviewed regularly for the *Athenaeum,* but was also reader for Bentley's firm for twenty years, along with Maria Featherstonhalgh, Adeline Sergeant and Lady Dorchester. Not that women readers could be relied on to sympathize with up-and-coming women novelists. Jewsbury strongly opposed publishing Rhoda Broughton's *Not Wisely but Too Well* (1867), claiming: 'It will not do you any credit—indeed people will wonder at a House like yours bringing out a work so *ill* calculated for the reading of decent people' (Gettmann, *A Victorian Publisher,* p. 195). Having lost this round to Jewsbury, Bentley made sure that he published Broughton's next thirteen, besides publishing Mrs. Henry Wood's *East Lynne* (1861), which Jewsbury had recommended, but with strong reservations about her ungrammatical writing. This was, however, a case of a woman reader preferring something that had been rejected by a man: George Meredith, reader for Chapman and Hall. Bentley published it on a half-profit basis, but Wood received no payment for the various adaptations and dramatizations of the novel which were such a huge success.[26]

The connection between magazine serialization and book publication was particularly close in the 1860s, with many novels having their first public exposure in monthly installments. Braddon's best-seller *Lady Audley's Secret* first appeared in the short-lived magazine *Robin Goodfellow* in 1861; when the magazine failed, the novel was rescued and continued in the *Sixpenny Magazine.* Rhoda Broughton's first novel, *Not Wisely but Too Well,* first appeared in the *Dublin University Magazine* in 1867, but established novelists such as Elizabeth Gaskell and George Eliot also continued publishing in magazines well into their careers. Gaskell's *Wives and Daughters* (1864-6), her final novel, was being serialized in the *Cornhill Magazine* when she died suddenly in 1865; Eliot also published *Romola* (1863) in the *Cornhill.* Margaret Oliphant, who mainly stayed loyal to *Blackwood's,* serialized stories in *Macmillan's Magazine, Cornhill,* and *Longman's* among others.

Oliphant is an especially striking example of a woman who was determined on a literary career, and participated fully in all aspects of her profession. Besides reviewing regularly for *Blackwood's,* she wrote a history of their firm, *Annals of a Publishing House* (1897); two literary histories (*Literary History of England in the End of the Eighteenth and Beginning of the Nineteenth Century* [1882]), and *The Victorian Age of English Literature,* (1892); five biographies of her male contemporaries, including Edward Irving (1863) and her distant relative, Laurence Oliphant (1891); and several sets of 'historical sketches'—some from the reign of George II (1868-9), others from the reign of Queen Anne (1894). There was little she was unwilling to write about—whether it was John Stuart Mill's *Subjection of Women* or the latest 'sensation novel'. In 1884, she proposed writing a series of articles to be called 'The Old Saloon', which would allow her to comment on any aspect of current affairs and culture that caught her fancy; 'Short of politics', she suggested, 'I should be inclined to take everything that was going on—theatre, pictures, books, even a taste of gossip when legitimate'.[27] Though some of her literary criticism now seems wrongheaded and limited in outlook, she recognized *Jane Eyre* as 'one of the most remarkable works of modern times' and Brontë herself as 'the most distinguished female writer' of age.[28]

Not that Oliphant herself had a smooth career, and she certainly outlived her own reputation. It was a lasting disappointment to her that she was outperformed by George Eliot, Charlotte Brontë and Anthony Trollope—her own Carlingford series overshadowed by the latter's *Barchester Chronicles.* Oliphant regarded Carlingford as the crucial turning point that saved her career, when in the early 1860s John Blackwood kept rejecting her work: 'I dashed at the first story of the Chronicles of Carlingford and wrote it in two or three days feeling as if it was my last chance', she recalls in her *Autobiography* (p. 3). The series was 'pretty well forgotten now', she admits later, though 'it made a considerable stir at the time, and *almost* made me one of the popularities of literature. *Almost,* never quite, though "Salem Chapel" really went very near it, I believe' (*Autobiography,* p. 91). Reflecting on the difference between Trollope's career and her own, Oliphant decided her position as a 'friendless woman' had disadvantaged her. She always had the sense that other people (George Eliot in particular) did well because they were believed in and fussed over, whereas she had to do everything for herself.

Another writer whose success (to her inexplicable) she contrasted with her own was Mrs. Humphry Ward, Matthew Arnold's niece and author of the surprising best-seller *Robert Elsmere* (1888). Entering her literary career, like so many nineteenth-century women, via journalism (articles on Spanish literature for *Macmillan's Magazine* in 1871-2), Ward's foray into novel-writing was at first unspectacular. Her novel *Miss Bretherton* (1884), published by Macmillan, made a loss of £22, as her editor, George L. Craik, explained to her in terse statistics: 'We printed 2500. We gave away 71. We have sold 1150. We have sent to America 750. We have on hand 521. The book sells at 6s. We gave you £50. We are out of pocket £22' (Sutherland, *Victorian Novelists,* p. 107). 'Quite dismayed at the results of *Miss Bretherton*' (in her own words), Ward neverthess declined Macmillan's offer of £100 for her next book, and took *Robert Elsmere* to Smith Elder—the publisher who, in nineteenth-century literary history, has the best reputation for 'discovering' women novelists disdained by other firms. Even so, the pre-publication history of Ward's novel was laborious and discouraging. At first the text was far too long and had to be rewritten. 'But how patient Mr Smith was over it', she recalls in her *Writer's Recollections* (1918), remembering his loyalty as friend and publisher for the next fourteen years. 'I am certain that he had no belief in the book's success and yet, on the ground of his interest in *Miss Bretherton* he had made liberal terms with me, and all through the long incubation he was always indulgent and sympathetic'.[29] The book's success—even this late in the century—hinged on library sales: according to Ward's own recollection of events, the 'circulating libraries were being fretted to death for copies' (p. 86). She was amused to find herself in a railway carriage with a woman she had just seen on the platform triumphantly waving the first volume of *Elsmere* which she had snatched against the odds from the library: "Of course it was promised to somebody else; but as I was *there,* I laid hands on it, and here it is!"' the woman told Ward without realizing who she was (p. 87). Mudie had in fact taken only a cautious 200 copies of *Elsmere* initially, thus arousing Ward's distrust of the library's stranglehold on the publishing industry. Neither Mudie nor Smith could have predicted that *Elsmere*—the story of a country clergyman's religious doubts and his relationship with an intensely pious wife—would become a best-seller: the one-volume six-shilling version, for instance, ran through seventeen editions in 1888-9. She preferred the American system, which was based on the assumption that people wanted to *buy* books for their own homes, rather than borrow them from a library.

Though Ward remained popular for about a decade, and adapted her work successfully for the new single-volume market (as did Rhoda Broughton), she too lived to see tastes change, and her tales of spoilt beauties in country houses superseded by D. H. Lawrence's novels of working-class life in Eastwood and James Joyce's of Dublin's pubs and brothels. Gaye Tuchman, in *Edging Women Out: Victorian Novelists, Publishers and Social Change,* has argued that, by the end of the nineteenth century, women novelists were receiving less favourable contracts than men, and as the title of her book indicates, being 'edged out' of the literary marketplace. This may have been the case with Macmillan's, the publisher from whose archives Tuchman gained this impression, but a survey of nineteenth-century publishing history as a whole suggests a different picture. Although women writers rose to the heights of their profession in the late eighteenth century, it was not until the nineteenth that they fully established themselves as active participants in the rapidly evolving literature industry. Once there, their presence had to be accepted as a positive influence. Despite the centrality of Dickens, Thackeray and Trollope as popular novelists of the day, women novelists quickly established their right to be discussed on equal terms. It was repeatedly the advent of new *women* writers—Harriet Martineau, the Brontës, George Eliot, Elizabeth Gaskell, Mary Ward—that caused the greatest excitement, the most mystery, or the best Mudie sales, and many of these were lasting successes. Moreover, women novelists became fully involved in shaping their own profession, challenging the dominance of the three-volume novel, holding out for better terms, reviewing their peers, and rejecting modes of publication they found uncongenial. When H. G. Wells surveyed the state of the contemporary novel in 1911, deploring what he called the 'weary giant' attitude to novel reading and writing which he found in men, he exempted women from his criticism. 'Women are more serious, not only about life, but about books', he insisted, identifying in the literature of the 1890s, 'a rebel undertow of earnest and aggressive writing and reading, supported chiefly by women and supplied very largely by women, which gave the lie to the prevailing trivial estimate of fiction'.[30] By the end of the century the right of women novelists to be at the very heart of the marketplace was no longer questioned by any critic who wanted to be taken seriously.

Notes

1. *The George Eliot Letters,* ed. Gordon S. Haight, 9 vols. (Yale University Press, 1954-79), vol. III, p. 151.
2. [Margaret Oliphant], 'Modern Novelists "Great and Small", *Blackwood's Magazine* 77 (May 1855), p. 555.
3. John Sutherland, *Mrs Humphry Ward: Eminent Victorian, Pre-eminent Edwardian* (Oxford: Clarendon Press, 1990), p. 148. It has to be said, however, that there was already mounting pressure against the 'three-decker', most notable from Arthur Mudie (Charles Mudie's son) and George Moore. See Royal A. Gettmann, *A Victorian Publisher: a Study of the Bentley Papers* (Cambridge University Press, 1960), p. 257; and John Feather, *A History of British Publishing* (London and New York: Routledge, 1988), pp. 154-5.
4. Mrs. Oliphant, *Annals of a Publishing House: William Blackwood and His Sons, Their Magazine and Friends,* 2 vols. (Edinburgh and London: Blackwood, 1897), vol. II, p. 458.
5. Gaye Tuchman with Nina E. Fortin, *Edging Women Out: Victorian Novelists, Publishers and Social Change* (London: Routledge, 1989), p. 29.
6. Recognizing this, publishers usually produced the complete volumes simultaneously with the final part of the serial.
7. According to Gordon Haight, Tauchnitz 'had a stranglehold on English reprints on the Continent, many of which found their way into England'. George Eliot was so frustrated with Tauchnitz's terms (he paid her £39 for *Scenes of Clerical Life,* and £100 for *The Mill on the Floss*) that Lewes negotiated new terms for *Middlemarch* with Albert Cohn of Asher and Co., Berlin. 'The competition forced Tauchnitz to raise his offers for subsequent books', Haight notes in *George Eliot: a Biography* (Oxford: Clarendon Press, 1968), pp. 437-8.
8. Like Charles Kingsley, Yonge joined Macmillan when John Parker went out of business in 1863: Charles Morgan, *The House of Macmillan (1843-1943)* (London: Macmillan, 1944), p. 65.
9. John Sutherland, *Victorian Novelists and Publishers* (London: Athlone Press, 1976), p. 39.
10. Cheryl Turner, *Living By the Pen: Women Writers in the Eighteenth Century* (London and New York: Routledge, 1992), p. 114.
11. *Jane Austen's Letters,* ed. Deirdre Le Faye (3rd edn, Oxford University Press, 1995), pp. 304, 217.
12. Jan Fergus, 'The Professional Woman Writer', in Edward Copeland and Juliet McMaster, eds., *The Cambridge Companion to Jane Austen* (Cambridge University Press, 1997): she actually earned 'something over £631' (p. 28).
13. *Harriet Martineau's Autobiography* (1877; rptd ed. Gaby Weiner, 2 vols. London: Virago, 1983), vol. 1, p. 167.
14. The 'Biographical Notice of Ellis and Acton Bell' (1850) is frequently reprinted in editions of *Wuthering Heights*: for example in the Penguin English Library edition, ed. David Daiches (Harmondsworth: Penguin, 1965) or in *Case Studies in Contemporary Criticism: Wuthering Heights,* ed. Linda Peterson (New York: St. Martin's Press, 1992).
15. Jenny Uglow, *Elizabeth Gaskell: a Habit of Stories* (London and Boston: Faber and Faber, 1993), pp. 338-9.
16. Sutherland, *Victorian Novelists and Publishers,* p. 84.
17. *The Letters of Charlotte Brontë,* ed. Margaret Smith, vol. I 1829-1847 (Oxford: Clarendon Press, 1995), p. 462.
18. *The Letters of Mrs Gaskell,* ed. J. A. V. Chapple and Arthur Pollard (Manchester University Press, 1966), pp. 426-7. Gaskell found it difficult to judge space, as shown in her troubled relations with Dickens over the serialization of *North and South* in *Household Words.* Peter Ackroyd comments that Gaskell was 'somewhat difficult' as a contributor, 'particularly in her inability or slowness to cut her text as Dickens desired' (Peter Ackroyd, *Dickens* (London: Minerva, 1991), p. 745).
19. *The Autobiography of Margaret Oliphant: the Complete Text,* ed. Elisabeth Jay (Oxford University Press, 1990), p. 91.
20. Elisabeth Jay, *Mrs Oliphant: a Fiction to Herself: a Literary Life* (Oxford: Clarendon Press, 1995), p. 280.
21. Margaret Harris and Judith Johnson see Eliot's Italian tour of 1860 as a turning point in her career: 'in the shift from the working out of childhood memories-to-more studied work on the past in relation to present, both reading the past in relation to the present and writing it. . . . There is a consciousness in the journal of history being constantly remade' (*The Journals of George Eliot,* ed. Margaret Harris and Judith Johnston (Cambridge University Press, 1998), pp. 333-4).
22. Gettmann, *A Victorian Publisher,* p. 116.
23. *The Brontës: Their Lives, Friendships and Correspondence,* ed. T. J. Wise and J. A. Symington, 4 vols. (Oxford: Shakespeare Head, 1932), vol. III, pp. 320-2.
24. Joanne Shattock, *The Oxford Guide to British Women Writers* (Oxford University Press, 1994), p. 481.
25. *Letters to Macmillan,* ed. Simon Nowell-Smith (London: Macmillan / New York: St Martin's, 1967), p. 88.
26. Shattock, *The Oxford Guide to British Writers,* p. 473.
27. Vineta and Robert A. Colby, *The Equivocal Virtue: Mrs Oliphant and the Victorian Literary Market Place* (New York: Archon Books, 1966), p. 164.
28. 'Modern Novelists—Great and Small', *Blackwood's Magazine* 77 (May 1855), pp. 558, 568.
29. Mrs Humphry Ward, *A Writer's Recollections,* 2 vols. (London: Collins, 1918), vol. II, pp. 65-6.
30. H. G. Wells, 'The Contemporary Novel', *Fortnightly Review* 96 (1 November 1911), p. 861.

FURTHER READING

Ardis, Ann L. "The Controversy over Realism in Fiction, 1885-1895." In *New Women, New Novels: Feminism and Early Modernism,* pp. 29-58. New Brunswick, N.J.: Rutgers University Press, 1990.

Analyzes the condescension that typically marked the critical review of novels written by women authors in the late nineteenth century.

Bauer, Dale M., and Philip Gould, eds. *The Cambridge Companion to Nineteenth-Century American Women's Writing.* Cambridge, England: Cambridge University Press, 2001, 366 p.

Collection of essays on a range of issues related to the literary production of nineteenth-century American women writers, much of it focused on their reformist rhetoric.

Bernstein, Susan David. *Confessional Subjects: Revelations of Gender and Power in Victorian Literature and Culture.* Chapel Hill: University of North Carolina Press, 1997, 206 p.

Study of the thematic concerns of gender and power in confessional literature of the Victorian era.

Bloom, Harold, ed. *British Women Fiction Writers of the Nineteenth Century.* Philadelphia: Chelsea House Publishers, 1999, 160 p.

Collection of nineteenth- and twentieth-century reviews and critical essays on the literary works of eleven nineteenth-century British authors, including the Brontë sisters, Jane Austen, George Eliot, Harriet Martineau, Mary Shelley, and Frances Trollope.

Burke, Sally. *American Feminist Playwrights: A Critical History.* New York: Twayne Publishers, Inc., 1996, 270 p.

Study of early American feminist playwrights, including chapters on nineteenth-century dramatic works that depicted the oppressive nature of patriarchal customs and laws.

Coultrap-McQuin, Susan. *Doing Literary Business: American Women Writers in the Nineteenth Century.* Chapel Hill, N. C.: The University of North Carolina Press, 1990, 253 p.

Examines the literary careers of E.D.E.N Southworth, Harriet Beecher Stowe, Mary Abigail Dodge, Helen Hunt Jackson, and Elizabeth Stuart Phelps as a representative sample of how American women writers forged literary careers from 1840 to 1900, a period of rapidly increasing female authorship.

Finch, Alison. *Women's Writing in Nineteenth-Century France.* Cambridge, England: Cambridge University Press, 2000, 336 p.

Study of French women authors of the nineteenth century; includes chapters on the increasing social and political activism in their writings.

Fleischner, Jennifer. *Mastering Slavery: Memory, Family, and Identity in Women's Slave Narratives.* New York: New York University Press, 1996, 232 p.

Examination of the psychological strategies used by former slave women to represent and remember their lives in their narratives.

Foster, Frances Smith. *Written by Herself: Literary Production by African American Women, 1746-1892.* Bloomington, Ind.: Indiana University Press, 1993, 194 p.

Analysis of the literary output and thematic concerns of African American women writers from 1746 to the end of the nineteenth century.

Gilbert, Sandra M. and Susan Gubar. *The Madwoman in the Attic: The Woman Writer and the Nineteenth-Century Literary Imagination.* New Haven, Conn.: Yale University Press, 1979, 770 p.

Concentrates on representations of women in literature and the feminist response to patriarchal attitudes in the works of Jane Austen, Emily and Charlotte Brontë, Mary Shelley, George Eliot, and Emily Dickinson.

———, eds. *The Norton Anthology of Literature by Women, Second Edition.* New York: W. W. Norton, 1996, 2441 p.

Includes lengthy section on the literature of numerous nineteenth-century women, notably Margaret Fuller, Fanny Fern, Rebecca Harding Davis, Constance Fenimore Woolson, Mary Elizabeth Coleridge, and Mary Austin.

Gorsky, Susan Rubinow. *Femininity to Feminism: Women and Literature in the Nineteenth Century.* New York: Twayne Publishers, 1992, 209 p.

Full-length study of the relationship between women's growing demands for social, economic, and political opportunities during the nineteenth century and the literature they wrote.

Grasso, Linda M. *The Artistry of Anger: Black and White Women's Literature in America, 1820-1860.* Chapel Hill, N.C.: The University of North Carolina Press, 2002, 264 p.

Full-length study of the anger expressed by black and white American women authors that the critic claims was a response to their exclusion from the failed promises of democratic America and their inability to express their outrage overtly.

Hamilton, Susan. "Locating Victorian Feminism: Frances Power Cobbe, Feminist Writing, and the Periodical Press." *Nineteenth-Century Feminisms* 2 (spring-summer 2000): 67-78.

Describes the feminist essays of the British social critic Frances Power Cobbe, who, it is argued, has not received literary recognition as a pioneering feminist because nearly all her work was published in the periodical press.

———. "Making History with Frances Power Cobbe: Victorian Feminism, Domestic Violence, and the Language of Imperialism." *Victorian Studies* 43, no. 3 (spring 2001): 437-60.

Argues that the careful reconsideration of the trope of imperialism that runs throughout Cobbe's 1878 "Wife Torture in England" is helpful in recognizing how Cobbe's feminist periodical connected to mainstream British audiences of her day.

Herndl, Diane Price. "The Threat of Invalidism: Responsibility and Reward in Domestic and Feminist Fiction." In *Invalid Women: Figuring Feminine Illness in American Fiction and Culture, 1840-1940,* pp. 43-74. Chapel Hill, N. C.: University of North Carolina Press, 1993.

Argues that the centrality of sickly women in Harriet Beecher Stowe's Uncle Tom's Cabin, *E.D.E.N. Southworth's* Retribution, *and Laura J. Curtis Bullard's* Christine *show that even these authors were unsure how to reconcile the strength of women that they espoused with the stereotypical image of helpless female invalids common in the literature of the nineteenth century.*

Hoeveler, Diane Long. *Gothic Feminism: The Professionalization of Gender from Charlotte Smith to the Brontës.* University Park, Pa.: Pennsylvania State University Press, 1998, 272 p.

Study of the connection between feminism and Gothic literature in the work of writers such as Charlotte Smith, Ann Radcliffe, Jane Austen, and the Brontë sisters.

Hoffman, Nicole Tonkovich. "Legacy Profile: Sarah Josepha Hale (1788-1874)." *Legacy* 7, no. 2 (fall 1990): 47-54.

Seeks to reestablish the reputation of Sarah Josepha Hale, editor of The Ladies' Magazine *and* Godey's Lady's Book, *as an important advocate for women's rights, especially in the areas of education and property rights.*

Jump, Harriet Devine, ed. *Women's Writing of the Victorian Period 1837-1901: An Anthology.* Edinburgh, Scotland: Edinburgh University Press, 1999, 384 p.

Collection of writings by nineteenth-century British women, many of which express feminist sentiments and advocacy of social, political, and legal reforms.

Kilcup, Karen L., ed. *Nineteenth-Century American Women Writers: A Critical Reader.* Malden, Mass.: Blackwell Publishers, Inc., 1998, 240 p.

Collection of essays about the literary works of numerous American women authors of the nineteenth century.

Knight, Denise D., ed. *Nineteenth-Century American Women Writers: A Bio-Bibliographical Critical Sourcebook.* Westport, Conn.: Greenwood Press, 1997, 251 p.

Offers biographical-critical overviews of 79 American women authors.

Logan, Shirley Wilson. *"We Are Coming": The Persuasive Discourse of Nineteenth-Century Black Women.* Carbondale, Illinois: Southern Illinois University Press, 1999, 255 p.

Studies race and gender concerns of black women authors and reform leaders of the nineteenth century.

Mattingly, Carol. *Well-Tempered Women: Nineteenth-Century Temperance Rhetoric.* Carbondale, Ill.: Southern Illinois University Press, 1998, 256 p.

Studies the historical context and rhetorical language in the second half of the nineteenth century used to advocate temperance.

———. *Appropriate[ing] Dress: Women's Rhetorical Style in Nineteenth-Century America.* Carbondale, Ill.: Southern Illinois University Press, 2002, 192 p.

Analyzes the connections between the restrictive clothing required of nineteenth-century women and how a number of female speakers used their attire to challenge the patriarchal hierarchy.

Michie, Elsie B. *Outside the Pale: Cultural Exclusion, Gender Difference, and the Victorian Woman Writer.* Ithaca, N.Y.: Cornell University Press, 1993, 224 p.

Analysis of the representation of women in nineteenth-century literature and how the works of Mary Shelley, Elizabeth Gaskell, George Eliot, and the Brontës responded to the connection between gender and questions of politics, class, and economics.

Morgan, Thais, E., ed. *Victorian Sages and Cultural Discourse: Renegotiating Gender and Power.* New Brunswick, N.J.: Rutgers University Press, 1990, 330 p.

Collection of essays dealing with various issues related to representations of gender in writing of the Victorian era.

Noble, Marianne. "An Ecstasy of Apprehension: The Gothic Pleasures of Sentimental Fiction." In *American Gothic: New Interventions in a National Narrative,* edited by Robert K. Martin & Eric Savoy, pp. 163-82. Iowa City, Iowa: University of Iowa Press, 1998.

Concentrates on feminist themes of repressive gender construction, nullification of the female body, sexuality, and violence in the sentimental gothic fiction of nineteenth-century women authors.

Shurbutt, Sylvia Bailey. "The Popular Fiction of Caroline Sheridan Norton: The Woman Question and the Theme of Manipulation." *Studies in Popular Culture* 9, no. 2 (1986): 24-40.

Argues that the poetry, short stories, and novels of Caroline Sheridan Norton are worthy of scholarly attention for their thematic treatment of women as objects of property and male manipulation as well as their forward-thinking refusal to portray women as passive and weak.

Showalter, Elaine. *A Literature of Their Own: British Women Novelists From Brontë to Lessing.* Princeton, N.J.: Princeton University Press, 1977, 378 p.

Full-length study of literary hallmarks, thematic concerns, and aesthetic sensibilities of British women novelists in the nineteenth and twentieth centuries.

Simson, Rennie. "Afro-American Poets of the Nineteenth Century." In *Nineteenth-Century Women Writers of the English-Speaking World,* edited by Rhoda B. Nathan, pp. 275. Westport, Conn.: Greenwood Press, 1986.

Collection of essays covering a broad range of issues related to the literary output of English and American women authors of the nineteenth century.

Sizer, Lyde Cullen. *The Political Work of Northern Women Writers and the Civil War.* Chapel Hill, N.C.: The University of North Carolina Press, 2000, 348 p.

Study of the political literature produced by Yankee women related to events leading up to, during, and just after the American Civil War.

UNITED STATES SUFFRAGE MOVEMENT IN THE 19TH CENTURY

For two days in July 1848, a convention of women and a number of male supporters met in Seneca Falls, New York, to publicly address a number of grievances related to the subjugation of women. The culmination of this gathering was the *Declaration of Sentiments and Resolutions,* modeled directly on the language of the 1776 *Declaration of Independence,* and it called for gender equality in relation to marriage, property rights, legal status, contract law, child custody matters, and, most radically, voting rights. Undeterred by the chorus of criticism they received from the press and the public at large, women leaders from the Seneca Falls Convention, among them Elizabeth Cady Stanton, Lucretia Mott, Julia Ward Howe, and Lucy Stone, began a lifetime crusade to win voting rights for American women. Most of these early suffragists, including Susan B. Anthony, and Sojourner Truth, would not live long enough to enjoy the right for which they fought so long. Only in 1920, with the ratification of the Nineteenth Amendment, were women given federal access to the polling booth.

The most common explanation for why the Seneca Falls convention took place has to do with the outrage that American women abolitionists felt when they were denied positions as delegates at the World Anti-Slavery Convention held in London in 1840. They were forced to sit behind a curtain during the official proceedings, silently listening to the arguments of men. Spurred by this event, as well as countless jeers from an audience that overwhelmingly believed it unseemly for a woman to speak in public, nineteenth-century abolitionists vented their anger about their imposed inferiority in their declarations of woman's rights at the 1848 Seneca Falls Convention. There, in the hometown of Elizabeth Cady Stanton, women demanded that they be given rights traditionally enjoyed only by property-owning, white men—especially the right to vote, which Stanton argued was the most important obstacle in the path of true gender equality. The following year, in 1849, the National Woman's Rights Association was formed, its membership firmly committed to winning voting rights for American women.

For the remainder of the century, women's suffrage gradually gained support from an ever-skeptical public that often argued that American social and national stability would be undermined if women were allowed to vote. After the American Civil War ended in 1865, momentum for women's suffrage increased as questions related to whether former slaves should be allowed to vote consumed the nation's attention. While nearly all suffragists had supported the extension of citizenship, civil rights, and liberties to freed blacks in the Fourteenth Amendment, their leadership split over whether to support the Fifteenth Amendment as it was proposed—guaranteeing citizens the right to vote, regardless of their race—or to campaign for the inclusion of gender in the equal protection clause. In 1869 suffragists divided into two organizations over this debate: the American Woman Suffrage Association, led by Howe and Stone, which supported ratification, and the National Woman Suffrage Association, led by Anthony and Stanton, which argued that although black men should be allowed to vote, any constitutional amendment which excluded women could not in good conscience be supported. After passage of the Fifteenth Amendment, the rival suffrage organizations continued their work. In 1869 the National Woman Suffrage Association held its first convention in what would become an annual event for the next fifty years to build grassroots support for a federal amendment to the constitution, granting women voting rights. The American Woman Association increasingly turned its attention to state congresses in hopes of winning female enfranchisement state by state. Their first victory came quickly in 1869 when the Territory of Wyoming became the first place where women were allowed to vote; in 1870 Utah followed suit. Other western states and territories would continue this trend over the next two decades, probably due to social conditions in frontier regions where women often assumed roles that were not available to them in eastern states.

After 1870, women suffragists also became increasingly militant in their tactics to win voting rights. Victoria Woodhull ran for president in 1872 despite the fact that she and the women she hoped to represent could not vote. Also in 1872, Anthony tested voting rights in New York by placing her ballot in a local election. She was promptly arrested for illegal voting, and the following year she was pronounced guilty in a trial in which she was not allowed to testify in her own defense because she was a woman. Anthony's eloquent and forceful denunciation of that verdict after the judge asked her if she had anything to say about her sentence and fine became a lightning rod for fellow suffragists. Over the next decades, numerous women intentionally challenged the law against voting, using their acts of civil disobedience and the guilty verdicts they invariably received to showcase the injustice of unequal voting rights. For the remainder of the nineteenth century, suffragists continued to work for voting rights. In 1890 the American Woman Suffrage Association and the National Woman Suffrage Association merged to form the National American Woman Suffrage Association. As many scholars have noted, their tactics in the last decade of the century were often aimed at gaining popular support for their movement by making the cause seem less radical than it was commonly perceived. This was done in a variety of ways, some women stressing that woman's supposed moral superiority would prove itself a boon for social reform and regeneration through the ballot box. Others argued that women needed the vote to gain power in relationships too often dominated by drunken, abusive husbands.

Scholars continue to study the language, strategies, and influence of the nineteenth-century woman suffrage movement, examining in particular the outspoken articulations of women's increasing demand to be given rights traditionally denied them. These studies have also begun in the past three decades to focus on lesser-known voices for gender equality and woman suffrage, especially from black women who suffered the prejudices of both gender and race, even from white women who often excluded black women from their delegations and conventions either as a result of their own or the perceived prejudices of their audiences.

REPRESENTATIVE WORKS

Susan B. Anthony

"Letter to the Colored Men's State Convention in Utica, New York" (letter) 1868

United States of America v. Susan B. Anthony (court records) 1873

Amelia Barr

"Discontented Women" (essay) 1896

Elizabeth Burrill Curtis

"The Present Crisis" (essay) 1897

Frances D. Gage

"Woman's Natural Rights, Address to the Woman's Rights Convention in Akron" (essay) 1851

Matilda Joslyn Gage

"Woman's Rights Catechism" (speech) 1871

The National Citizen and Ballot Box [editor] (journal) 1878-1881

Angelina Grimké

"An Appeal to the Christian Women of the South" (essay) 1836

"Appeal to the Women of the Nominally Free States" (essay) 1837

Sarah Grimké
"Address to Free Colored Americans" (essay) 1837

Ida Husted Harper
The Life and Work of Susan B. Anthony 2 vols. (biography) 1899

Frances Ellen Watkins Harper
"Dialogue on Woman's Rights" (poem) 1857

Isabella Beecher Hooker
"Two Letters on Women's Suffrage" (essay) 1868

Julia Ward Howe
Reminiscences, 1819-1899 (autobiography) 1899

Anna Garlin Spencer
"The Fitness of Women to Become Citizens from the Standpoint of Moral Development" (essay) 1898

Elizabeth Cady Stanton
"Address to The New York Legislature" (speech) 1854

"Suffrage for All, White and Black, Male and Female" (speech) 1868

"Petitions for a Sixteenth Amendment" (speech) 1876

"An Educational Suffrage Qualification Necessary" (speech) 1897

Eighty Years and More (autobiography) 1898

Elizabeth Cady Stanton, Susan B. Anthony and Matilda Joslyn Gage
History of Women Suffrage 4 vols. [editors] (essays, speeches, letters, nonfiction) 1881-1902

Elizabeth Cady Stanton, Lydia Mott, Ernestine L. Rose, Martha C. Wright, and Susan B. Anthony
"Appeal to the Women of New York" (speech) 1860

Elizabeth Cady Stanton, Lucretia Mott, Martha C. Wright, Mary Ann McClintock, and Jane C. Hunt
Declaration of Sentiments and Resolutions at the First Woman's Rights Convention in Seneca Falls (pamphlet) 1848

Lucy Stone and Julia Ward Howe
The Woman's Journal [editors] (periodical) 1870-90

Charlotte Carmichael Stopes
British Freewoman (nonfiction) 1894

Sojourner Truth
"A'n't I A Woman?" (speech) 1851

"Colored Men Will Be Masters Over the Women" (speech) 1867

Victoria Woodhull
"Declaration of Candidacy" (speech) 1870

"The Argument for Woman's Electoral Rights under Amendment XIV and XV of the Constitution of the United States" (essay) 1887

PRIMARY SOURCES

ELIZABETH CADY STANTON, LUCRETIA MOTT, MARTHA C. WRIGHT, MARY ANN MCCLINTOCK, AND JANE C. HUNT (DOCUMENT DATE 1848)

SOURCE: Cady Stanton, Elizabeth, Lucretia Mott, Martha C. Wright, Mary Ann McClintock, and Jane C. Hunt. "Declaration of Sentiments and Resolutions at the First Woman's Rights Convention in Seneca Falls (1848)." In *Public Women, Public Words: A Documentary History of American Feminism,* edited by Dawn Keetley and John Pettegrew, pp. 190-93. Madison, Wis.: Madison House, 1997.

In the following excerpt, originally published in 1848, early suffragist leaders mimic the tone and sentiments of the American Declaration of Independence to advocate for women's rights, most notably equal voting rights.

Declaration of Sentiments

When, in the course of human events, it becomes necessary for one portion of the family of man to assume among the people of the earth a position different from that which they have hither to occupied, but one to which the laws of nature and of nature's God entitle them, a decent respect to the opinions of mankind requires that they should declare the causes that impel them to such a course.

We hold these truths to be self-evident: that all men and women are created equal; that they are endowed by their Creator with certain inalienable rights, that among these are life, liberty, and the pursuit of happiness; that to secure these rights governments are instituted, deriving their just powers from the consent of the governed. Whenever any form of government becomes destructive of these ends, it is the right of those who suffer from it to refuse allegiance to it, and to insist upon the institution of a new government, laying its foundation on such principles, and organizing its powers in such form as to them shall seem most likely to effect their safety and happiness. Prudence, indeed, will dictate that governments long established should not be changed for light and transient causes; and accordingly, all experience hath shown that mankind are more disposed to suffer, while evils are sufferable, than to right themselves by abolishing the forms to which they were accustomed. But when a long train of abuses and usurpations, pursuing invariably the same object evinces a design to reduce them under absolute despotism, it is their duty to throw off such government, and to provide new guards for their future security. Such has been the patient sufferance of the women under this government, and such is now the necessity which constrains them to demand the equal station to which they are entitled.

The history of mankind is a history of repeated injuries and usurpations on the part of man toward woman, having in direct object the establishment of an absolute tyranny over her. To prove this, let facts be submitted to a candid world.

He has never permitted her to exercise her inalienable right to the elective franchise.

He has compelled her to submit to laws, in the formation of which she had no voice.

He has withheld from her rights which are given to the most ignorant and degraded men—both natives and foreigners.

Having deprived her of this first right of a citizen, the elective franchise, thereby leaving her without representation in the halls of legislation, he has oppressed her on all sides.

He has made her, if married, in the eye of the law, civilly dead.

He has taken from her all right in property, even to the wages she earns.

He has made her, morally, an irresponsible being, as she can commit many crimes with impunity, provided they be done in the presence of her husband. In the covenant of marriage, she is compelled to promise obedience to her husband, he becoming, to all intents and purposes, her master—the law giving him power to deprive her of her liberty, and to administer chastisement.

He has so framed the laws of divorce, as to what shall be the proper causes of divorce; in case of separation, to whom the guardianship of the children shall be given; as to be wholly regardless of the happiness of women—the law, in all cases, going upon a false supposition of the supremacy of man, and giving all power into his hands.

After depriving her of all rights as a married woman, if single and the owner of property, he has taxed her to support a government which recognizes her only when her property can be made profitable to it.

He has monopolized nearly all the profitable employments, and from those she is permitted to follow, she receives but a scanty remuneration.

He closes against her all the avenues to wealth and distinction, which he considers most honorable to himself. As a teacher of theology, medicine, or law, she is not known.

He has denied her the facilities for obtaining a thorough education—all colleges being closed against her.

He allows her in Church, as well as State, but a subordinate position, claiming Apostolic authority for her exclusion from the ministry, and, with some exceptions, from any public participation in the affairs of the Church.

He has created a false public sentiment, by giving to the world a different code of morals for men and women, by which moral delinquencies which exclude women from society, are not only tolerated but deemed of little account in man.

He has usurped the prerogative of Jehovah himself, claiming it as his right to assign for her a sphere of action, when that belongs to her conscience and to her God.

He has endeavored, in every way that he could, to destroy her confidence in her own powers, to lessen her self-respect, and to make her willing to lead a dependent and abject life.

Now, in view of this entire disfranchisement of one-half the people of this country, their social and religious degradation,—in view of the unjust laws above mentioned, and because women do feel themselves aggrieved, oppressed, and fraudulently deprived of their most sacred rights, we insist that they have immediate admission to all the rights and privileges which belong to them as citizens of the United States.

In entering upon the great work before us, we anticipate no small amount of misconception, misrepresentation, and ridicule; but we shall use every instrumentality within our power to effect our object. We shall employ agents, circulate tracts, petition the state and national legislatures, and endeavor to enlist the pulpit and the press in our behalf. We hope this Convention will be followed by a series of Conventions, embracing every part of the country.

Illustration of Elizabeth Cady Stanton speaking at the Seneca Falls Convention in New York on July 19, 1848.

Firmly relying upon the final triumph of the Right and the True, we do this day affix our signatures to this declaration.

Lucretia Mott, Elizabeth Cady Stanton, Eunice Newton Foote, Mary Ann McClintock, Martha C. Wright, Jane C. Hunt, Amy Post, Catharine A. F. Stebbins, Mary H. Hallowell, Charlotte Woodward, Sarah Hallowell.

Richard P. Hunt, Samuel D. Tilman, Elisha Foote, Frederick Douglass, Elias J. Doty, James Mott, Thomas McClintock.

This Declaration was unanimously adopted and signed by 32 men and 68 women.

Resolutions

Whereas the great precept of nature is conceded to be, "that man shall pursue his own true and substantial happiness." Blackstone, in his Commentaries, remarks, that this law of Nature being coeval with mankind, and dictated by God himself, is of course superior in obligation to any other. It is binding over all the globe, in all countries, and at all times; no human laws are of any validity if contrary to this, and such of them as are valid, derive all their force, and all their validity, and all their authority, mediately and immediately, from this original; therefore,

Resolved, That such laws as conflict, in any way, with the true and substantial happiness of woman, are contrary to the great precept of nature, and of no validity; for this is "superior in obligation to any other."

Resolved, That all laws which prevent woman from occupying such a station in society as her conscience shall dictate, or which place her in a position inferior to that of man, are contrary to the great precept of nature, and therefore of no force or authority.

Resolved, That woman is man's equal—was intended to be so by the Creator—and the highest good of the race demands that she should be recognized as such.

Resolved, That the women of this country ought to be enlightened in regard to the laws under which they live, that they may no longer publish their degradation, by declaring themselves satisfied with their present position, nor their ignorance, by asserting that they have all the rights they want.

Resolved, That inasmuch as man, while claiming for himself intellectual superiority, does accord to woman moral superiority, it is preeminently his duty to encourage her to speak, and teach, as she has an opportunity, in all religious assemblies.

Resolved, That the same amount of virtue, delicacy, and refinement of behavior, that is required of woman in the social state, should also be required of man, and the same transgressions should be visited with equal severity on both man and woman.

Resolved, That the objection of indelicacy and impropriety, which is so often brought against woman when she addresses a public audience, comes with a very ill-grace from those who encourage, by their attendance, her appearance on the stage, in the concert, or in feats of the circus.

Resolved, That woman has too long rested satisfied in the circumscribed limits which corrupt customs and a perverted application of the Scriptures have marked out for her, and that it is time she should move in the enlarged sphere which her great Creator has assigned her.

Resolved, That it is the duty of the women of this country to secure to themselves their sacred right to the elective franchise.

Resolved, That the equality of human rights results necessarily from the fact of the identity of the race in capabilities and responsibilities.

Resolved, therefore, That, being invested by the Creator with the same capabilities, and the same consciousness of responsibility for their exercise, it is demonstrably the right and duty of woman, equally with man, to promote every righteous cause, by every righteous means; and especially in regard to the great subjects of morals and religion, it is self-evidently her right to participate with her brother in teaching them, both in private and in public, by writing and by speaking, by any instrumentalities proper to be used, and in any assemblies proper to be held; and this being a self-evident truth, growing out of the divinely implanted principles of human nature, any custom or authority adverse to it, whether modern or wearing the hoary sanction of antiquity, is to be regarded as a self-evident falsehood, and at war with the interests of mankind.

The only resolution which met opposition was the 9th, demanding the right of suffrage which, however, after a prolonged discussion was adopted. All of the meetings throughout the two days were largely attended, but this, like every step in progress, was ridiculed from Maine to Louisiana.

LUCY STONE (ADDRESS DATE 6 MARCH 1867)

SOURCE: Stone, Lucy. *Woman Suffrage in New Jersey: An Address delivered by Lucy Stone at a Hearing Before the New Jersey Legislature,* pp. 3-19. Boston: C. H. Simmons & Co., 1867.

In the following excerpted address, Stone underscores the importance of women's suffrage.

GENTLEMEN OF THE COMMITTEE:—

Grateful for the hearing so promptly accorded, I will proceed without preliminary to state the object of the petition, and to urge its claim.

Woman ask you to submit to the people of New Jersey amendments to the Constitution of the State, striking out respectively the words "white" and "male" from Article 2, Section I, thus enfranchising the women and the colored men, who jointly constitute a majority of our adult citizens. You will thereby establish a republican form of government.

I am to speak to you of Suffrage. In any other country, it would be necessary to show that political power naturally vests in the people. But here the whole ground is granted in advance. When our fathers came out of the war of the Revolution, made wiser by those seven years of suffering, they affirmed these truths to be self-evident: "Governments are instituted among men, deriving their just powers from the consent of the governed." "Taxation without representation is tyranny."

The Declaration of Independence, affirming these self evident truths, was unanimously adopted by the representatives of the thirteen United States. The descendants of those representatives have held these principles in theory ever since. We have called it "The Immortal Declaration." It has been read in every State, on every Fourth of July, since 1776. We have honored its authors and the day that gave it utterance, as we honor no other day and no other men. Not only we, but, the wide world round, men suffering under hoary despotisms, by a quick instinct turn their longing eyes to this country, and know that in the realization of our self-evident truths lies the charm by which their own bonds shall be broken.

New Jersey, in her State Constitution, in the very first Section of the first Article affirms that, "All men are, by nature, free and independent, and have certain natural and unalienable rights, among which are those of enjoying and defending life and liberty, of acquiring, possessing and protecting property, and of pursuing and obtaining safety and happiness." Again in Article 2. That, "All political power is inherent in the people, and they have a right, at all times, to alter, or reform the same, whenever the public good may require it."

Gentlemen will see it is no new claim that women are making. They only ask for the practical application of admitted, self-evident truths. If "all political power is inherent in the people," why have women, who are more than half the entire population of this State, no political existence? Is it because they are not people? Only a madman would say of a congregation of negroes, or of women, that there were no people there. They are counted in the census, and also in the ratio of representation of every State, to increase the political power of white men. Women are even held to be citizens without the full rights of citizenship, but to bear the burden of "taxation without representation," which is "tyranny."

"Governments derive their just powers from the consent of the governed." Not of the governed property-holders, nor of the governed white men, nor of the governed married men, nor of the governed fighting men; but of the governed. Sad to say, this principle, so beautiful in theory, has never been fully applied in practice!

What is Suffrage? It is the prescribed method whereby, at a certain time and place, the will of the citizen is registered. It is the form in which the popular assent or dissent is indicated, in reference to principles, measures and men. The essence of suffrage is rational choice. It follows, therefore, under our theory of government, that every individual capable of independent rational choice is rightfully entitled to vote.

The alien who is temporarily resident among us is excepted. He is still a citizen of his native country, from which he may demand protection and to which he owes allegiance. But if he become a permanent resident and renounce allegiance to foreign potentates and powers, then he is admitted to all the rights of citizenship,—suffrage included.

The minor is excepted. He is held an infant in law. He has not attained mental maturity. He is under guardianship, as being incapable of rational choice. He cannot legally buy, nor sell, nor make a valid contract. But when the white male infant arrives as years of discretion, he may do all these things and vote also.

Idiots and lunatics are excepted, because they are incapable of rational choice and so cannot vote.

None of these cases conflict with the principle. But when a persons disfranchised because he is a negro the principle of rational, individual choice is violated. For the negro possesses every human faculty. Many colored persons are wiser and better than many white voters. During the late war, the negroes were loyal to a man. Neither threats nor bribes could induce them to join their enemies and ours. They freely shared the poverty of their small cabins with our sick and wounded soldiers, tenderly offered the cooling cup to their fevered lips, and, again and again, at great personal peril guided them to our lines. Two hundred thousand colored soldiers wore the blue uniform of the United States and fought bravely in the Union ranks. Their blood was mingled with ours on many a hard-fought field. Yet this class, so loyal and patriotic, have no vote in the loyal State of New Jersey!

So, too, when a woman is disfranchised because she is a woman, the principle is violated. For woman possesses every human faculty. No man would admit, even to himself, that his mother is not capable of rational choice. And if the woman he has chosen for a wife is a fool, that fact lies at least as much against his ability to make a rational choice as against hers, and should accordingly put them both into the class of excepted persons.

The great majority of women are more intelligent, better educated, and far more moral than multitudes of men whose right to vote no man questions.

Woman are loyal and patriotic. During the late war, many a widow not only yielded all her sons to the cause of freedom, but strengthened their failing courage when the last good-bye was said, and kept them in the field by words of lofty cheer and the hope of a country really free.

An only son, crowned with the honors of Harvard University, living in elegance and wealth, with every avenue of distinction open before him, was offered the Colonelcy of a regiment of colored volunteers. His mother, with pulses such as thrilled the proud mother of the Gracchi when she called her sons her jewels, hailed the son's acceptance of the offer of fellowship with the lowliest for his country's sake. And when he fell, murdered at Fort Wagner, and was "buried with his negroes," her grief for his loss was more than equaled by the high satisfaction she felt that young life, so nobly lived, was so nobly given back to Him from whom it came. That mother is classed politically with madmen and fools. By her side stand ten million American woman who are taxed without representation and governed without consent. Women are fined, imprisoned, hanged—and no one of them was ever yet granted a trial by "a jury of her peers."

Every Fourth of July gentlemen invite women to "reserved seats for the ladies," and then read what these women too well knew before, that governments are just only when they obtain the consent of the governed. Strange to say, men do not seem to know that what they read condemns their practice.

But it may be said, "the consent of the governed is only a theory, a 'glittering generality'"—that, in fact, the governed do not consent and never have consented. Yet this theory is the "golden rule" of political justice. The right of the citizen to participate in making the laws is the sole foundation of political morality. As Mr. Lincoln said of slavery—if a government without consent of the governed is not wrong, nothing political is wrong. Deny this and you justify despotism. On the principle of limited suffrage, aristocracy is blameless and republican institutions are impossible. Can you believe that when God established an immutable code of morals for the individual, he left society without a moral code—a mere battle-ground of force and fraud? The men who deny political rights to the negro and the woman can show no title to their own.

Now, as there can be no argument against a self-evident truth, so none has ever been attempted. But ridicule, without stint or measure has been so heaped upon those who claim political equality, that many women have been induced to deny that they desire it, lest "the world's dread laugh," which few can bear, should burst upon them an unsexed viragos, "strong-minded women who wish to drive men to the nursery while take the rostrum." As, in the days of the Revolution, Tory priest sought to weaken the hands of our fathers by the Scripture, iterated and reiterated, "Honor the King," so now the haters of human liberty hurl texts at women and do not know that the golden rule, "Whatsoever ye would that men should do unto you, do ye even so unto them,"—that central truth round which all other divine utterance revolves—would settle this question in favor of women.

We are asked in triumph: "What good would it do women and negroes to vote"? We answer: "What good does it do white men to vote? Why do *you* want to vote, gentlemen? Why did the Revolutionary fathers fight seven years for a vote? Why do the English workingmen want to vote? Why do their friends—John Bright and Thomas Hughes and the liberal party—want the suffrage for them?" Women want to vote, just as men do, because it is the only way in which they can be protected in their rights. To men, suffrage stands for "a fair day's wages for a fair day's work." The workingmen of England do not get that because they have had no vote. Negroes and women in America do not get it, because they have no vote.

In Auburn, New York, the teachers of the public schools, male and female, united last spring in a petition for an increase of salary. So $200 was added to the salary of each man, and only $25 to that of each woman. The women, indignant at the injustice, wrote an ironical letter of thanks to the Board of Education for their very large liberality. Thereupon the Board required them to retract the letter, and coupled the demand with a threat of dismissal if the teachers did not comply. A part, driven by necessity, succumbed. A part, who preferred their own self-respect and a poorer crust, refused. Would those women have been thus treated, either in regard to salary or dismissal, if, as voters, they could have had a voice in the election of the Board for the following year?

It is said that women are now represented by their husbands, fathers, brothers or sons. Would *men* consent to be represented by their wives and sisters? If it were possible for any class to legislate well for another, it might be supposed that those who sustain to each other these tender relations, could do so. But we find, on the contrary, that in every State, the laws affecting woman as wife, mother and widow, are different from and worse than those which men make for themselves as husband, father and widower.

I will quote a few laws to show how women are represented in New Jersey.

A widower is entitled to the life use of all his deceased wife's real estate, but a widow is entitled only to the life use of one-third of her deceased husband's real estate.

A widower succeeds to the whole of his deceased wife's personal property, whether she will, or not, with the right to administer on her estate without giving bonds. But a widow has only one-third of her deceased husband's personal property (or one-half of it if he leaves no children), but none at all if he choose to will it to any one else, and if she administer on his estate she must give bonds.

A mother inherits the whole of her deceased child's estate only when that child leaves no brothers, nor sisters, nor children of brothers and sisters, and no father. But a father inherits the whole property of such a child when all these survive. In this State, where my child was born, a father has the sole custody of the children. The law provides (see Revised Statutes, page 915, Sec. 9,) that "any father, whether he be of age, or not, by a deed executed in his life-time, or by a last will, may dispose of the custody of his child, *born or to be born*—and such disposition shall be good against the child's mother and against every other person. And if the mother, or any other person, shall attempt to acquire the custody of the child, she, or they shall be subject to an action for ravishment, or trespass." Thus, the minor, whom the law holds incompetent to make any valid contract, whose written promise to pay even is worthless, who is not old enough to vote, is empowered by law to come to her side, whose wild strife with death and agony is ushering their child to life, to seize the new-born being and will it from her sight forever. The successful attempt on her part to recover her God-given right, the law calls "ravishment." the only woman in this

State who is legally entitled to her child is the unhonored mother whose baby is a bastard!

By the law of New Jersey the sole definition of an orphan is "a fatherless child." And yet, in contempt, we are asked "why do women want to vote?" There are women, too, who say they "have all the rights they want!"

"When any husband and wife live in a state of separation, and have minor children, the Chancellor, the Supreme Court, or any Justice of said Court, many, if the children are brought before them by habeas corpus, make and order for the access of the mother to her infant child, or children, at such times and under such circumstances as they many direct—and if the child, or children are under seven years of age, shall make an order to deliver them to the mother, until they are seven." And then, still just as much in need of a mother's love, they must go back to the custody of the father. (Statutes page 361.)

Thus she has no legal right to her children, whose breast blessed their baby lips, whose tender care soothed their baby sorrows, whose hand guided their first tottering footsteps, and whose love for those who are "the bone of her bone and the flesh of her flesh" will last when all other love but the love of God shall fail!

"A widow may live forty days in the house of her deceased husband without paying rent, or even longer if her dower has not, within that time, been set off to her." But when the dower is assigned, this home, made by the mutual toil and thrift of husband and wife, this roof under which her children were born and where her husband died, hallowed by associations of their early love and her recent loss, can no longer give her shelter, unless she pay rent. The very crops, which would have been her food if the strong arm on which she leaned were not cold in death, are no longer hers. Appraisers have searched cupboard, closet and drawer, have set a market value upon articles of which no money could pay the price to her;—a sale is made, and this woman is houseless, as well as widowed.

But if death had chosen her for its victim, instead of her husband, the widower could remain in undisturbed possession of house and property, could gather his unmothered children around the still warm hearth-stone, desolate indeed, but not robbed.

A husband can sell his real estate and make a valid deed subject only to the wife's right of dower. But a wife can neither sell her personal property, nor her real estate, nor make a valid deed, without her husband's consent.

A husband can make a will of everything he possesses, except the dower of his wife. But a wife cannot will her personal property at all without her husband's consent indorsed upon the will. And even then if, after her death, the husband recall his consent before the will is admitted to probate, her will is null and void.

The above quotations show how women are now represented. They prove the truth of the old adage, "If you don't want your business done, send another; if you want it done, go yourself."

And still men object: "Women and negroes don't know enough to vote." As though it were possible for us to do worse for ourselves than they have done for us. Do they fear we shall return evil for evil? This objection comes with an ill grave from those who welcome to the polls voters of every degree of ignorance, so only they be white men. When a white man comes of age, it is never asked whether he knows enough to vote. He may not know the first letter of the alphabet. He many be an habitual drunkard, a haunter of gambling houses and brothels. But he belongs to the "white male" aristocracy, and so the way is prepared, without his asking, by which he shall take his place with the self-constituted sovereigns, to whose law-making power women and negroes must bow in silent submission. All such men think that "women don't know enough to vote." Will intelligent men rank their wives politically lower than these?

It is said that "if women vote it will make domestic discord." On the contrary, we always find that those who wish to secure the votes of others are extremely polite to them. Witness any election. "My dear fellow, I rely on your invaluable aid." "In this emergency, America expects every man to do his duty; let me treat you." "Here is a five dollar bill." "How is your good wife? Are the children well?" And straightway the deluded voter goes after him to vote, perhaps against his own interest and that of the State.

But seriously, does any man mean to say that if his wife have a different political opinion from his own and dare to express it, he will quarrel with her? Will he make his own narrowness and ill-temper a reason why his wife should not exercise a God-given right? If so, the argument is against him and not against her. A husband and wife often hold different religious opinions, respect their differences, and go quietly to their respective churches. It will be so in politics among decent men. But the unfortunate woman who has married a brute needs a vote all the more. With or without a vote, he will pound her all the same.

It is said that "it will demoralize women to vote." On the contrary, the presence of women would purify politics. Why is the political meeting which admits women an orderly assemblage, while that which excludes them in boisterous? If the wives and daughters of ignorant and intemperate men are not demoralized by daily association with them, it is scarcely possible that going once or twice a year to vote would do so. Are women demoralized by going to the market, or the post-office? But experience has already proved the contrary. Women now vote in Michigan, Kentucky, and Canada upon school questions. In Holland, women who are property holders vote. In Sweden they do the same. In Austria, women who are Nobles in their own right are members of the Diet.

But we have an example nearer home. In New Jersey, women and negroes voted from 1776 to 1807, a period of thirty-one years. The facts are as follows:

In 1709, a Provincial law confined the privilege of voting to "male freeholders having one hundred acres of land in their own right, or £50 current money of the province in real and personal estate," and during the whole of the Colonial period these qualifications continued unchanged.

But on the 2nd of July, 1776, (two days before the Declaration of Independence) the Provincial Congress of New Jersey, at Burlington, adopted a Constitution, which remained in force until 1844, of which Sec. 4 is as follows: "Qualifications of Electors for members of Legislatures. All inhabitants of the Colony, of full age, who are worth £50 Proclamation money, clear estate, in the same, and have resided within the county, in which they claim a vote, for twelve months immediately preceding the election, shall be entitled to vote for representatives in Council and Assembly, and also for all other public officers that shall be elected by the people of the county at large."

Sec. 7 provides that the Council and Assembly jointly shall elect some fit person within the Colony, to be Governor. This Constitution remained in force until 1844.

Thus, by deliberate change of the terms "male freeholder," to "all inhabitants," suffrage and ability to hold the highest office in the State, were conferred both on women and negroes.

In 1790 a committee of the Legislature reported a bill regulating elections, in which the words "he or she" are applied to voters, thus giving legislative indorsement to the alleged meaning of the Constitution.

In 1797 the Legislature passed an act to regulate elections, containing the following provisions:

"Sec. 9. Every voter shall openly and in full view deliver his or her ballot, which shall be a single written ticket containing the names of the person, or persons, for whom he or she votes," etc.

"Sec. 11. All free inhabitants of full age who are worth £50 Proclamation money, and have resided within the county in which they claim a vote, for twelve months immediately preceding the election, shall be entitled to vote for all public officers which shall be elected by virtue of this act, and no person shall be entitled to vote in any other township, or precinct, [except] that in which he, or she, doth actually reside at the time of the election."

Women voted. Yet no catastrophe, social or political, ensued. Women did not cease to be womanly. They did not neglect their domestic duties. Indeed the noble character and exalted patriotism of the women of New Jersey all through the Revolution have been the subject of historical eulogy. There is no evidence that the women and free negroes abused or neglected their political privileges. It is said that "woman don't want to vote." Yet, in New Jersey, when they were allowed to vote, they manifested a growing interest in public affairs. Mr. Wm. A. Whitehead, of Newark, an opponent of female suffrage, expressly states that as time elapsed "the practice extended," and that "in the Presidential election of 1800, between Adams and Jefferson, females voted very generally throughout the State and such continued to be the case until the passage of the act (1807) excluding them from the polls. At first the law had been so construed as to admit single women only, but, as the practice extended, the construction of the privilege became broader and was made to include females 18 years old, married or single, and even women of color; at a contested election in Hunterdon County, in 1802, the votes of two or three such actually electing a member of the Legislature."

But, unfortunately, New Jersey remained a Salve State. And, like all communities cursed with slavery, she had no efficient system of free schools. Her soil proved less fertile than the newer States of the West, and the more enterprising class of emigrants passed on. The later settlers of New Jersey were far inferior to the original Quaker and Puritan elements which controlled the Constitutional Convention of 1776. Society retrograded. Slavery smothered the spirit of liberty. In the sprint of 1807, a special election was held in Essex County to decide upon the location of a Court House and Jail—Newark and its vicinity struggling to retain the County buildings, Elizabethtown and its neighborhood striving to remove them to "Day's Hill."

The question excited intense interest, as the value of every man's property was thought to be involved. Not only was every legal voter, man or woman, white or black, brought out, but on both sides gross frauds were practised. The property qualification was generally disregarded; aliens and minors participated, and many persons "voted early and voted often." In Acquackanonk Township, thought to contain about 300 legal voters, over 1800 votes were polled, all but seven in the interest of Newark.

It does not appear that either women or negroes were more especially implicated in these frauds than the white men. But the affair caused great scandal and they seem to have been made the scapegoats.

When the Legislature assembled, they set aside the election as fraudulent, yet Newark retained the buildings. Then they passed as act (Nov. 15, 1807), restricting the suffrage to white male about citizens, residents in the county for the twelve months preceding and worth £50 Proclamation money. But they went on, and provided that all such, whose names appeared on the last duplicate of State or county taxes should be considered worth £50; thus virtually abolishing the property qualification.

In 1820 the same provisions were repeated, and were maintained until 1844, when the present State Constitution was substituted.

Thus, in defiance of the letter of the Constitution and of the Statutes and uniform practice of a generation, women and negroes were disfranchised by an arbitrary act of the Legislature, without discussion and almost without comment. Yet the very act which disfranchised voters whose only crime was sex and color, set aside the property qualification and admitted to the polls all white male tax-payers, however ignorant or degraded. Therefore, women come before you here in New Jersey with a peculiar and special claim. We have had this right. We have exercised it. It has been unjustly and illegally taken away, without our consent, without our being allowed to say a word in our own defence. We have been condemned unheard, not by the people, but by the Legislature. To-day, we ask you, after the lapse of more than half a century, to give the people of New Jersey an opportunity of rectifying an act of atrocious political usurpation and injustice. For it was worse in principle than the "coup d'etat" of Louis Napoleon. He, at least, went through the form of submitting the question to the verdict of the people. The Legislature of 1807 did not submit it. Our disfranchisement can only be justified upon the robber's plea that "might makes right."

It is said that "women would vote as their husbands and brothers do." If so, why should men object? These votes, at least, they could get without bribery, and thus double the vote of their party. But does any one believe that the drunkards' wives would vote with the drunkards? I do not.

It is said that "women do not want to vote." Then, let those who do not, stay away from the polls. No one is compelled to vote. Let those who do wish to vote be free to do so.

It is said that "women would sometimes want to hold office." Certainly. Those who bear the burdens of government should share its honors. Why should not a woman be President of the United States? The name of Elizabeth of England, or Catherine of Russia, of Isabella of Spain, or Maria Theresa of Austria—each of these proves woman's capacity to govern. And to-day, no sovereign in the world receives such love and loyalty as Queen Victoria. Are American women alone incompetent for great responsibilities? If so, alas, for free institutions!

It is said that "bad women will vote." True. But so do bad men. In both cases, the bad are a small minority.

It is asked "who will take care of the children while the mothers go to vote?" Who takes care of them now, while the mothers go to church fifty-two times a year? Who takes care of them while the mothers are at parties and balls? If caretakers can be found for the children on all these occasions, it will be easy to find some one to care for them during the half hour it takes the mother to go and vote, that she may have a legal right to take care of them and to share in their guardianship. Hon. Richard O'Gorman made a speech in Cooper Institute, Sunday evening, Feb. 24, in behalf of the destitute poor of the South. He said, "The women now-a-days did not want loyalty, did not want respect for their sex. They demanded liberty and equality." Whereupon there was "great laughter and applause." He said, "Woman would have to talk a great deal, before they could eradicate from the pure heart of man its delicate submission to the weaker, but nobler sex." More applause. Then he drew a picture of a country ravaged by a war of the "nobler sex." showing how very bad affairs would be in such a case, and he received more applause. In conclusion, he had the hardihood to make an especial appeal to the ladies, to help him raise the funds he wanted. By-and-by, when women have the ballot, Mr. O'Gorman will probably ask us to vote for him.

It is said that "women would be insulted and annoyed by contact with rowdies at the polls." A friend in Canada West told me that when the law was first passed, giving women who owned a certain amount of property, or who paid a given rental, a vote, he went trembling to the polls to see the result. This first woman who came was a large property holder in Toronto; with marked respect the crowd gave way as she advanced. She spoke her vote and walked quietly away, sheltered by her womanhood. It was all the protection she needed. But, if it seem best, what can be easier than to have separate polls for women?

These are some of the arguments against woman's demand that she may give her consent to the laws she is required to obey; that the political power which "inheres in the people" may be shared irrespective of sex, or color, by the more than half of the people to whom it is now denied.

Now let me state some of the reasons why women and negroes need to vote.

1. Because it is right. Wendell Phillips once said: "The broadest and most far-sighted intellect is utterly unable to foresee the ultimate consequences of any great social change. Ask yourself on all such occasions if there be any element of right and wrong in the question, any principle of clear, natural justice that turns the scale? If so, take your part with the perfect and abstract right, and trust God to see that it shall prove the expedient.

2. To repeal unjust laws, some of which I have quoted.

3. To enable women and negroes to share all profitable employments, and thus to obtain fair wages of fair work. Colored men can now only be bootblacks, barbers or waiters. It is skilled labor that pays. The skilled labor is monopolized by white men who shut them out. In the South, indeed, where white men think it a disgrace to work, the trades were all in the hand of colored men, before the War. The master pocketed the proceeds, but the negro proved his capacity to excel in every branch of skilled labor. While voters of every grade of intelligence are freely admitted to all industrial pursuits, colored men, who are not voters but in every other respect competent, can get no openings but such as no one else will use. A colored mechanic, a Georgia slave, whose labor as a harness-maker earned his master from three to five dollars a day, ran away to the North. A gentleman who had known his in the South found him a waiter in a hotel at Saratoga. Being asked why he did not work at his trade, he replied that he would gladly do so, but in the North, nobody would employ him. At one harness shop, the proprietor was willing to give him work, but every mechanic in his employ refused to "work with a nigger." Slavery had robbed him of all his earnings while a slave. He had no capital with which to establish himself. And so, this strong, skilful harness-maker, whose skill is his only capital, and who might provide for is family a comfortable home, and add to his country's wealth, can only earn as a waiter the pittance which supplies his daily bread. Give this colored man a vote and the harness shops will no longer exclude him. Yet, in spite of these disadvantages, there is a smaller percentage of drunkards, paupers and criminals among out Northern black population than among our whites. You seldom see a negro beggar.

To women also, who are not voters, and because they are not voters, only the poorest employments are open, except that of teaching. Even as a teacher, while a woman instructs as many pupils, for as many hours, in the same studies, and with equal ability, she gets only from one-third to one-half as much salary as a man gets who does similar work in every respect. This is true of the schools of New Jersey and of every other State. Horace Mann advised the employment of female teachers because, he said "they were better teachers and could be hired at a lower rate."

The last annual report of the Superintendent of Public Schools in New York City stated that the salaries of the male Principals range from $2000 to $3000, those of female Principals from $900 to $1200; of male Assistants from $800 to $1500, those of female Assistants from $500 to $800.

The great mass of women are crowded by the narrow range of female occupations into housework and needle-work. But the law of supply and demand knows no exception, and these employments, always over-stocked, are always underpaid. Rarely, by these occupations, can a woman save anything, either to make a home, or for her old age. Is it strange that multitudes, driven by the hunger-cry for the bread that perishes, should fall into the ranks of abandoned women, whose dreadful trade the New York Legislature is actually petitioned to license? Oh, if legislators could only see that neither "midnight missions" nor licenses can avail to regulate or destroy this unspeakable crime! Let them arm woman with the ballot. Acknowledge her right to protect herself, and when society has had time to adjust itself to the new conditions, this class will disappear. Believe me, when woman can earn her bread in honor, she will not seek it by disgrace.

4. Women and negroes need the ballot to secure equal means of education. The children of all white voters of every means of education. The children of all white voters of every nationality are admitted to the public schools of New Jersey. But the colored children are excluded. In my immediate neighborhood is an aged colored man who owns and built with his own hands the house which he has occupied for more than twenty years. He possesses 2 ½ acres of ground. For twenty-three years, he has paid taxes for the support of school of his district. All white children, native or foreign, go freely to the school, but neither his children, nor his grandchildren have ever been admitted. The colored school in Newark is so far away, that virtually no education is provided for the descendants of this respectable, law-abiding, tax paying colored man. The two disfranchised classes, women and negroes, are the only ones excluded from the highest schools of the State, from the colleges, from the schools of Law, Medicine, and Theology. The avenues to the highest and widest spheres of influence are thus closed to us both.

But, in Boston, colored men are voters. What follows? Their children are in all the schools, doing as well as white children. They are admitted to Harvard College. Two colored men are members of the Legislature, and several others are lawyers in successful practice. Thus it is easy to see how much better it is, as a mere matter of policy, to open to every class the avenues to respectability and usefulness, instead of incurring, by shutting them out, the inevitable results of ignorance and degradation. The vote is a power. With the vote women can protect themselves. In the District of Columbia, previous to the passage of the recent suffrage bill, the colored people had been for years unable to get their share of the public school fund. Within a week after the passage of the bill, $10,000 was voted to them without their asking, by the very men who had hitherto refused the money. At the late election in Georgetown, D.C., the colored men cast a solid vote for a loyal mayor, and elected him. Their quiet and orderly behavior in face of the grossest provocation was worthy of all praise.

Again, Society needs the direct, responsible influence of women to purify politics. Men too often think and speak of politics as "a dirty pool," and ignoble scramble for place and power, a scene of bribery and intrigue. Such is not the American idea of politics. Such will not be the case when women share the political life of the nation. Our legislation now lacks precisely what women can give and what no other class can give—viz., moral tone, a recognition of higher principles than mere force and personal interest. Women will influence legislation by their tastes and character. Being temperate, they will be a power for temperance. Being chaste, they will repress licentiousness. Being peaceful, they will discourage war. Being religious and humane, they will create a religious and humane spirit in legislation.

SOJOURNER TRUTH (SPEECH DATE 1867)

SOURCE: Truth, Sojourner. "Colored Men Will Be Masters Over the Women (1867)." In *Public Women, Public Words: A Documentary History of American Feminism,* edited by Dawn Keetley and John Pettegrew, pp. 237. Madison, Wis.: Madison House, 1997.

In the following speech, originally delivered in 1867 and published in History of Woman Suffrage, Vol. 2, 1861-1876 *in 1886, Truth argues that former slave women deserve the right to vote just as much as black men.*

My friends, I am rejoiced that you are glad, but I don't know how you will feel when I get through. I come from another field—the country of the slave. They have got their liberty—so much good luck to have slavery partly destroyed; not entirely. I want it root and branch destroyed. Then we will all be free indeed. I feel that if I have to answer for the deeds done in my body just as much as a man, I have a right to have just as much as a man. There is a great stir about colored men getting their rights, but not a word about the colored women; and if colored men get their rights, and not colored women theirs, you see the colored men will be masters over the women, and it will be just as bad as it was before. So I am for keeping the thing going while things are stirring;

ON THE SUBJECT OF...

SOJOURNER TRUTH (C. 1797-1883)

Sojourner Truth was a complex and popular figure who established a powerful persona for herself as a woman's suffragist and an African American rights crusader. In addition to *The Narrative of Sojourner Truth: A Northern Slave* (1850), an autobiography that she dictated to Olive Gilbert, Truth is best remembered for her public speeches, the most famous of which was delivered at a women's rights convention in Akron, Ohio, in 1851. Transcribed by contemporary author Frances Dana Gage, Truth's challenge to the assembly—"A'n't I a woman?"—immortalized her speech that demanded equal rights for all women, black and white, who comprised the early suffrage movements in America.

Truth was born into slavery in New York State, sometime around 1797. Named only Isabella, she married Thomas, a fellow slave, in 1814; the couple had five children between 1815 and 1826. In 1827, prior to the emancipation act of 1828 that freed all slaves in New York State, Isabella heard that her master planned to go back on his promise to grant her freedom and found refuge with the Van Wagenens, a Quaker family with whom she lived until 1829, when she moved to New York City. She remained in New York City until 1843, when she left to become a travelling evangelist and formally changed her name to Sojourner Truth to reflect what she believed was her destiny: to wander the earth spreading spiritual truth. Although she never learned to read or write, Truth was widely known and respected for her intelligence and wisdom. In Massachusetts, Truth became acquainted with the Northampton Association, a group of reformers, abolitionists, and women's rights advocates; she embraced the principles of abolitionism and equal rights and refocused her lectures to reflect these newfound beliefs. In 1981, Truth was inducted into the National Women's Hall of Fame.

because if we wait till it is still, it will take a great while to get it going again. White women are a great deal smarter, and know more than colored women, while colored women do not know scarcely anything. They go out washing, which is about as high as a colored woman gets, and their men go about idle, strutting up and down; and when the women come home, they ask for their money and take it all, and then scold because there is no food. I want you to consider on that, chil'n. I call you chil'n; you are somebody's chil'n, and I am old enough to be mother of all that is here. I want women to have their rights. In the courts women have no right, no voice; nobody speaks for them. I wish woman to have her voice there among the pettifoggers. If it is not a fit place for women, it is unfit for men to be there.

I am above eighty years old; it is about time for me to be going. I have been forty years a slave and forty years free, and would be here forty years more to have equal rights for all. I suppose I am kept here because something remains for me to do; I suppose I am yet to help to break the chain. I have done a great deal of work; as much as a man, but did not get so much pay. I used to work in the field and bind grain, keeping up with the cradler; but men doing no more, got twice as much pay; so with the German women. They work in the field and do as much work, but do not get the pay. We do as much, we eat as much, we want as much. I suppose I am about the only colored woman that goes about to speak for the rights of the colored women. I want to keep the thing stirring, now that the ice is cracked. What we want is a little money. You men know that you get as much again as women when you write, or for what you do. When we get our rights we shall not have to come to you for money, for then we shall have money enough in our own pockets; and may be you will ask us for money. But help us now until we get it. It is a good consolation to know that when we have got this battle once fought we shall not be coming to you any more. You have been having our rights so long, that you think, like a slave-holder, that you own us. I know that it is hard for one who has held the reins for so long it give up; it cuts like a knife. It will feel all the better when it closed up again. I have been in Washington about three years, seeing about these colored people. Now colored men have the right to vote. There ought to be equal rights now more than ever, since colored people have got their freedom. I am going to talk several times while I am here; so now I will do a little singing. I have not heard any singing since I came here.

ISABELLA BEECHER HOOKER (ESSAY DATE 1868)

SOURCE: Hooker, Isabella Beecher. "If Women Could Vote." In *Early American Women: A Documentary History, 1600-1900,* edited by Nancy Woloch, pp. 512-15. Belmont, Calif.: Wadsworth Publishing Company, 1992.

In the following excerpt, originally published in Putnam's Magazine *in 1868, Hooker argues that women are in fact better suited for enfranchisement and political office than men.*

———,———, 1868

My Dear Daughter:

You ask me what I think of the modesty and sense of a woman who can insist, in these days, that she is not sufficiently cared for in public and in private, and who wishes to add the duties of a politician to those of a mother and housekeeper.

This is a large question to ask, and a still larger one to answer by letter; but since you have a clear and thoughtful head of your own, and we are widely separated just now and unable to converse together as in times past, I will see what can be said by pen and paper for just the woman you have described.

And let me begin by asking you the meaning of the word *politician.* Having consulted your dictionary, you reply, "One who is versed in the science of government and the art of governing." Very well. Now who is thus versed in the science and art of governing, so far as the family is concerned, more than the mother of it? In this country, certainly, the manners, the habits, the laws of a household, are determined in great part by the mother; so much so, that when we see lying and disobedient children, or coarse, untidy, and ill-mannered ones, we instinctively make our comments on the mother of that brood, and declare her more or less incompetent to her place.

Now let me suppose her to be one of the competent ones who, like your Aunt E., has helped six stout boys and four of their quick-witted sisters all the way from babyhood up to manhood and womanhood, with a wisdom and gentleness and patience that have been the wonder of all beholders—and let us think of her as sitting down now in her half-forsaken nest, calm, thoughtful, and matured, but fresh in her feeling as ever she was, and stretching out by her sympathies in many directions after the younglings who have gone each to a special toil, and what wonder if she finds it hard to realize that she is unfitted either by nature or education for the work of law making, on a broader and larger scale than she has ever yet tried.

Her youngest boy, the privileged, saucy one of the crowd, has just attained his majority, we will say, and declaims in her hearing on the incompetence of women to vote—the superiority of the masculine element in politics, and the danger to society if women are not carefully guarded from contact with its rougher elements—and I seem to see her quiet smile and slightly curling lip, while in memory she runs back to the years when said stripling gathered all he knew of laws, country, home, heaven, and earth, at her knee—"and as for soiling contacts, oh! my son, who taught you to avoid these, and first put it into your curly little head, that evil communications corrupt good manners, and that a man cannot *touch* pitch, except he be defiled."

I have taken the bull by the horns, you perceive, in thus taking our mother from her quiet country home and setting her by imagination among the legislators of the land—but it is just as well, because the practical end of suffrage is, not *eligibility* to office merely, but a larger *use* of this privilege than most women have ever yet dreamed of, much less desired. . . .

And now she is there, we will say, in the legislature of our State—a high-minded, well-bred woman; one who, amid all her cares, has never failed to read the newspapers more or less, and to keep alive her interest in the prosperity of her country, whatever the claims of her numerous family. She is one, too, who has not had the assistance of wealth in doing all this; she is, as you know, straight from the rural districts, a genuine farmer's wife. But she has more leisure now than she once had, and with it there comes a longing for change, for more cultivated society, for recreations and diversions such as her busy hours have seldom afforded her; and just now, by the unanimous vote of her townspeople, she is sent to our glorious old Hub, to spend the winter in considering what the Commonwealth of Massachusetts shall do this year, by legislation, for the public good. . . .

Having secured a home not far from the old State House, she seeks the Assembly Room and meets there gentlemen from all parts of the State—farmers, merchants and mechanics, physicians, teachers and ministers, lawyers and bankers, and they go into debate on such questions as these: Shall our deaf mutes be educated at home, or in the Institution at Hartford, as heretofore? What of the economies of our past practice, and are there better methods of training than those instituted there? State Prison—shall the discipline be penal merely, or reformatory? the institution self-supporting by a system of rigid tasks, or partially supported by the State? What punishment shall be allowed, what religious and moral instruction furnished, and what sanitary regulations enforced? The prohibitory law—has it proved itself adapted to the suppression of intemperance? Are its provisions enforced, and why not? Is a special license law better adapted to the desired end, or is there any thing which human ingenuity can devise that shall arrest the spread of intemperance over the land? The school for juvenile offenders—is that managed judiciously? Here obviously the great aim should be reformation. Is a system of rewards or punishments, or both together, best adapted to that end? Should boys and girls be associated in the same buildings and classes, and for what length of time should they be retained for improvement before sending them out again into society? Endowments for colleges and other educational institutions supported in whole or in part by the State: Shall these be confined to institutions designed exclusively for men, or shall they be applied equally to the education of both sexes? Taxation—how apportioned? What interests can best bear heavy taxation, and is any further legislation needed to secure the right of representation to all who are taxed? Prostitution—shall it be licensed as in the old countries, or left to itself, or subjected to severe penalties? Divorces—by whom granted, and for what cause, and upon what conditions? Common schools, and high schools, and the whole system of State education; insane asylums, poor-houses, jails, and many other institutions of modern civilization—in all these objects, you will perceive, our mother has a deep and intelligent interest, and it is not difficult to imagine the warm, even enthusiastic energy with which she will give herself to the discussion of the questions involved—some of them the highest that can come before a human tribunal.

If you say, There are other State interests with which she is less familiar, I reply, No one legislator understands the detail of all the business that comes before the House, or is expected to; committees are appointed for specialties, as you know, and composed, or they ought to be, of those whose education and training have fitted them for that special investigation.

Our mother will have her hands full if she should serve on the Committee of Charitable Institutions alone; and none can do better service there than such a wise, prudent, affectionate caretaker as she has ever been. . . . She need not necessarily perfect herself in the technicalities of a legal education, though some would like well to do that, no doubt; professional gentlemen are generally called upon now by committees at their need; but she can bring a clear, practical, and experienced head and sound heart to the help of many a vexed question. And as to railroad bills and management—would that she might have a voice there; you may be sure that all charters would contain provisions for the comfort and safety of passengers, and the holding of all officials to a strict responsibility for neglect of duty.

And so in all matters pertaining to merchandise and business, which fairly come under state jurisdiction; it is late in the day to assert that women know nothing of those things, and could not learn if they should try. There are too many honest and successful women-traders, artists, and littérateurs in every city of the land, and too many men dependent in whole or in part upon their earnings, to give a show of color to such assertions. . . .

On the whole, then, my dear, you begin to perceive that my mind receives no shock when I am charged with the crime of desiring to meddle with politics, and to educate my daughters as well as my sons to take an intelligent, and, if need be, an active part in the government of their country; though I begin to fear, since the receipt of your letter, that my efforts in your behalf have not been crowned with the success I had much reason to hope. However, there is a gallant young husband in the case now, and I am very much mistaken if this is not the chief cause of your present difficulty; so I wish to say further, that I owe my young son-in-law no grudge whatever for this counter influence, nor do I abate one jot my confidence in him as a man of intelligence, integrity, and true nobility. The truth is, that one chief reason why your husband, and so many like him, oppose the extension of suffrage is, that their sense of true gallantry, their desire to shield and protect, is violated by *their conception* of the probable result of a woman's going to the polls. This is certainly a misconception. Every woman knows in her own heart that she does not hold her purity and delicacy subject to injury by such cause. We know that we have never entered any precinct, however vile and debased, without carrying something of that God-given power of womanhood—of motherhood—with us, which is a greater protection against insult and contamination than all the shields that man can devise. But we ought not to blame men too severely for their reluctance to relinquish this office of protector and guardian, which custom has so long laid upon them as a high duty and privilege.

In the days when physical forces ruled the world, men might naturally offer, and women receive with thankfulness, the protection of a strong arm, and become greatly dependent upon it, without serious harm to either sex; but in the day of moral forces it is quite otherwise. This day has come upon us, however, so silently, so gradually, that we ourselves have scarcely recognized that we are now near its noon-tide: how then can our fathers, brothers, and husbands be expected to feel its quickening glow and inspiration? It may seem to them a consuming heat though to me it is delicious warmth, pure air, God's own blue sky, and His benignant smile over all.

But I must stop here and wait your reply, since on your acceptance of my views thus far stated will depend the courage and enthusiasm with which I shall proceed to develop further my thought on the whole matter of the relation of the sexes to each other and to government. . . . I am persuaded, contrary to the judgment of many earnest advocates of equal suffrage, that women are quite as much responsible for the present condition of affairs as men, and that they, as a body, will be the last to be convinced of their duty in the matter of good citizenship; so I am seriously anxious to make converts to my faith from the young mothers, rather than from any other class. I know, of course, that the power of regulating suffrage now lies wholly with men; that not a single vote can be given, save by them; but I know as well that the minds of all honest, earnest thinkers among them are turned to this subject, and that they are inclined to give it an impartial hearing; and I am convinced that the indifference, not to say opposition, of their wives, mothers, and sisters, stands in the way of their coming to a right solution of the problem before them, beyond anything or all things else.

I beg you, therefore, to give my argument so far a candid consideration, and let me hear from you in reply.

I am always your affectionate

Mother

NATIONAL WOMAN SUFFRAGE AND EDUCATIONAL COMMITTEE (LETTER DATE 19 APRIL 1871)

National Woman Suffrage and Educational Committee. *An Appeal to the Women of the United States*, pp. 2-4. Hartford: Case, Lockwood & Brainard, 1871.

In the following letter, the committee for woman suffrage and education implores the women of America to ban together in an effort to attain equal rights.

Dear Friends:—

The question of your rights as citizens of the United States, and the grave responsibilities which a recognition of those rights will involve, is becoming the great question of the day in this country, and is the culmination of the great question which has been struggling through the ages for solution, that of the highest freedom and largest personal responsibility of the individual under such necessary and wholesome restraints as are required by the welfare of society. As you shall meet and act upon this question, so shall these great questions of freedom and responsibility sweep on, or be retarded, in their course.

This is pre-eminently the birth day of womanhood. The material has long held in bondage the spiritual; henceforth the two, the material refined by the spiritual, the spiritual energized by the material, are to walk hand in hand for the moral regeneration of mankind. Mothers, for the first time in history, are able to assert, not only their inherit first right to the children they have borne, but their right to be a protective and purifying power in the political society into which those children are to enter. To fulfil, therefore, their whole duty of motherhood, to satisfy their whole capacity in that divine relation, they are called of God to participate, with man, in all the responsibilities of human life, and to share with him every work of brain and of heart, refusing only those physical labors that are inconsistent with the exalted duties and privileges of maternity, and requiring these of men as the equivalent of those heavy yet necessary burdens which women alone can bear.

Under the constitution of the United States justly interpreted, you were entitled to participate in the government of the country, in the same manner as you were held to allegiance and subject to penalty. But in the slow development of the great principles of freedom, you, and all, have failed both to recognize and appreciate this right; but to-day, when the rights and responsibilities of women are attracting the attention of thoughtful minds throughout the whole civilized world, this constitutional right, so long unobserved and unvalued, is becoming one of prime importance, and calls upon all women who love their children and their country to accept and rejoice in it. Thousands of years ago God uttered this mingled command and promise, "Honor thy father and thy mother that thy days may be long upon the land which the Lord thy God giveth thee." May we not hope that in the general recognition of this right and this duty of woman to participate in government, our beloved country may find her days long and prosperous in this beautiful land which the Lord hath given her.

To the women of this country who are wiling to unite with us in securing the full recognition of our rights, and to accept the duties and responsibilities of a full citizenship, we offer for signature the following Declaration and Pledge, in the firm belief that our children's children will with fond veneration recognize in this act our devotion to the great doctrines of liberty in their new and wider and more spiritual application, even as we regard with reverence the prophetic utterances of the Fathers of the Republic in their Declaration of Independence:

> Declaration and Pledge of the Women of the United States concerning their Right to and their Use of the Elective Franchise.
>
> We, the undersigned, believing that the sacred rights and privileges of citizenship in this Republic were guaranteed to us by the original Constitution, and that these rights are confirmed and more clearly established by the Fourteenth and Fifteenth Amendments, so that we can no longer refuse the solemn responsibilities thereof, do hereby pledge ourselves to accept the duties of the franchise in our several States, so soon as all legal restrictions are removed.
>
> And believing that character is the best safe-guard of national liberty, we pledge ourselves to make the personal purity and integrity of candidates for public office of the *first* test of fitness.
>
> And lastly, believing in God, as the Supreme Author of the American Declaration of Independence, we pledge ourselves in the spirit of that memorable Act, to work hand in hand with our fathers, husbands, and sons, for the maintenance of those equal rights on which our Republic was originally founded, to the end that it may have, what is declared to be the first condition of just government, *the consent of the governed.*

You have no new issue to make, no new grievances to set forth. You are taxed without representation, tried by a jury not of your peers, condemned and punished by judges and officers not of your choice, bound by laws you have had no voice in making, many of which are specially burdensome upon you as women; in short, your rights to life, liberty and the pursuit of happiness are daily infringed, simply because you have heretofore been denied the use of the ballot, the one weapon of protection and defence under a republican form of government. Fortunately, however, you are not compelled to resort to force in order to secure the rights of a complete citizenship. These are provided for by the original Constitution, and by the recent amendments you are recognized as citizens of the United States, whose rights, including the fundamental right to vote, may not be denied or abridged by the United States, nor by any State. The obligation is thus laid upon you to accept or reject the duties of citizenship, and to your own consciences and your God you must answer if the future legislation of this country shall fall short of the demands of justice and equality.

The participation of woman in political affairs is not an untried experiment. Woman suffrage has within a few years been fully established in Sweden and Austria, and to a certain extent in Russia. In Great Britain women are re now voting equally with men for all public officers except members of Parliament, and while no desire is expressed in any quarter that the suffrage already given should be withdrawn or restricted, over 126,000 names have been signed to petitions for its extension to parliamentary elections; and Jacob Bright, the leader of the movement in Parliament, and brother of the well known John Bright, says that no well informed person entertains any doubt that a bill for such extension will soon pass.

In this country, which stands so specially on equal representation, it is hardly possible that the same equal suffrage would not be established by law if the matter were to be left merely to the progress of public sentiment and the ordinary course of legislation. But as we confidently believe, and as we have before stated, the right already exists in our national constitution, and especially under the recent amendments. The interpretation of the Constitution which we maintain, we cannot doubt, will be ultimately adopted by the Courts, although, as the assertion of our right encounters a deep and prevailing prejudice, and judges are proverbially cautious and conservative, we must expect to encounter some adverse decisions. In the mean time it is of the highest importance that in every possible way we inform the public mind and educate public opinion on the whole subject of equal rights under a republican government, and that we manifest our desire for and willingness to accept all the rights and responsibilities of citizenship, by asserting our right to be registered as voters and to vote at the Congressional elections. The original Constitution provides in express terms that the representatives in Congress shall be elected by the PEOPLE of the several States &———with no restriction whatever as to the application of that term. This right, thus clearly granted to all the people, is confirmed and placed beyond reasonable question by the fourteenth and fifteenth amendments. The act of May, 1870, the very title of which, *"An Act to enforce the rights of citizens of the United States to vote,"* is a concession of all that we claim, provides that the officers of elections throughout the United States shall give an equal opportunity to all citizens of the United States to become qualified to vote by the registry of their names or other pre-requisite; and that where upon the application of any citizen such pre-requisite is refused, such citizen may vote without performing such pre-requisite; and imposes a penalty upon the officers refusing either the application of the citizen to be qualified or his subsequent application to vote. The Constitution also provides that "each House shall be the judge of the elections, returns, and qualifications of its own members." When therefore the election of any candidate for the lower House is effected or defeated by the admission or rejection of the votes of the women, the question is brought directly before the House, and it is compelled to pass at once upon the question of the right of women to vote under the Constitution. All this may be accomplished without the necessity of bringing suits for the penalty imposed upon public officers by the act referred to: but should it be thought best to institute prosecutions where the application of women to register and to vote if refused, the question would thereby at once be brought into the Courts. If it be thought expedient to adopt the latter course, it is best that some test case be brought upon full consultation with the National Committee, that the ablest counsel may be employed and the expenses paid out of the public fund. Whatever mode of testing the question shall be adopted, we must not be in the slightest degree discouraged by adverse decisions, for the final result in our favor is certain, and we have besides great reason to hope that Congress at an early day will pass a Declaration Act affirming the interpretation of the Constitution which we claim.

The present time is specially favorable for the earnest presentation before the public mind of the question of the political rights of women. There are very positive indications of the approaching disintegration and re-formation of political parties, and new and vital issues are needed by both the great parties of the country. As soon as the conviction possesses the public mind that women are to be voters at an early day, as they certainly are to be, the principles and the action of public parties will be shaping themselves with reference to the demands of this constituency. Particularly in nominations for office will the moral character of candidates become a matter of greater importance.

To carry on this great work a Board of sic women has been established, called "The National Woman Suffrage and Educational Committee," whose office at Washington it is proposed to make the centre of all action upon Congress and the country, and with whom through their Secretary, resident there, it is desired that all associations and individuals interested in the cause of woman suffrage should place themselves in communication. The committee propose to circulate the very able and exhaustive Minority Report of the House Judiciary Committee on the constitutional right of woman suffrage. They also propose ultimately, and as a part of their educational work, to issue a series of tracts on subjects vitally affecting the welfare of the country, that women may become intelligent and thoughtful on such subjects, and the intelligent educators of the next generation of citizens.

The Committee are already receiving urgent appeals from women all over the United States to send them our publications. The little light they have already received concerning their rights under the constitution, and the present threatening political aspect of the country, make them impatient of ignorance on these vital points. A single Tract has often gone the rounds in a neighborhood until worn out, and the call is for thousands and thousands more.

A large printing fund will therefore be needed by the Committee, and we appeal first to the men of this country, who control so large a part of its wealth, to make liberal donations toward this great educational work. We also ask every thoughtful woman to send her name to the Secretary to be inserted in the Pledge Book, and if she is able, one dollar. But as many working women will have nothing to send but their names, we welcome these as a precious gift, and urge those who are able, to send us their fifties and hundreds, which we promise faithfully to use and account for. Where convenient it is better that many names should be sent upon the same paper, and the smallest contributions in money can be put together and sent with them. Every signature and every remittance will be at once acknowledged by the Secretary, and one or more tracts enclosed, with a circular as to the work to be done by individuals.

Isabella Beecher Hooker, President.
Paulina Wright Davis.
Josephine S. Griffing, Secretary.
Ruth Carr Denison.
Mary B. Bowen, Treasurer.
Susan B. Anthony.
Washington, D.C., April 19, 1871.

SUSAN B. ANTHONY (TRANSCRIPT DATE 1873)

SOURCE: Anthony, Susan B. "*United States of America vs. Susan B. Anthony* (1873)." In *Public Women, Public Words: A Documentary History of American Feminism,* edited by Dawn Keetley and John Pettegrew, pp. 244-45. Madison, Wis.: Madison House, 1997.

In the following court transcript, originally published in History of Woman Suffrage, Vol. 2, 1861-1876 *in 1886, Anthony argues that the guilty verdict rendered against her for the crime of voting is unjust because she is denied the fundamental rights of an American taxpaying citizen.*

. . . The Court, after listening to an argument from the District Attorney, denied the motion for a new trial.

THE COURT: The prisoner will stand up. Has the prisoner anything to say why sentence shall not be pronounced?

MISS ANTHONY: Yes, your honor, I have many things to say; for in your ordered verdict of guilty, you have trampled underfoot every vital principle of our government. My natural rights, my civil rights, my political rights, are all alike ignored. Robbed of the fundamental privilege of citizenship, I am degraded from the status of a citizen to that of a subject; and not only myself individually, but all of my sex, are, by your honor's verdict, doomed to political subjection under this so-called Republican government.

JUDGE HUNT: The Court can not listen to a rehearsal of arguments the prisoner's counsel has already consumed three hours in presenting.

MISS ANTHONY: May it please your honor, I am not arguing the question, but simply stating the reasons why sentence can not, in justice, be pronounced against me. Your denial of my citizen's right to vote is the denial of my right of consent as one of the governed, the denial of my right of representation as one of the taxed, the denial of my right to a trial by a jury of my peers as an offender against law, therefore, the denial of my sacred rights to life, liberty, property, and—

JUDGE HUNT: The Court can not allow the prisoner to go on.

MISS ANTHONY: But your honor will not deny me this one and only poor privilege of protest against this high-handed outrage upon my citizen's rights. May it please the Court to remember that since the day of my arrest last November, this is the first time that either myself or any person of my disfranchised class has been allowed a word of defense before judge or jury—

JUDGE HUNT: The prisoner must sit down; the Court can not allow it.

MISS ANTHONY: All my prosecutors, from the 8th Ward corner grocery politician, who entered the complaint, to the United States Marshal, Commissioner, District Attorney, District Judge, your honor on the bench, not one is my peer, but each and all are my political sovereigns; and had your honor submitted my case to the jury, as was clearly your duty, even then I should have had just cause of protest, for not one of those men was my peer; but, native or foreign, white or black, rich or poor, educated or ignorant, awake or asleep, sober or drunk, each and every man of them was my political superior; hence, in no sense, my peer. Even, under such circumstances, a commoner of England, tried before a jury of lords, would have far less cause to complain than should I, a woman, tried before a jury of men. Even my counsel, the Hon. Henry R. Selden, who has argued my cause so ably, so earnestly, so unanswerably before your honor, is my political sovereign. Precisely as no disfranchised person is entitled to sit upon a jury, and no woman is entitled to the franchise, so, none but a regularly admitted lawyer is allowed to practice in the courts, and no woman can gain admission to the bar—hence, jury, judge, counsel, must all be of the superior class.

JUDGE HUNT: The Court must insist—the prisoner has been tried according to the established forms of law.

MISS ANTHONY: Yes, your honor, but by forms of law all made by men, interpreted by men, administered by men, in favor of men, and against women; and hence, your honor's ordered verdict of guilty, against a United States citizen for the exercise of "that citizen's right to vote," simply because that citizen was a woman and not a man. But, yesterday, the same man made forms of law declared it a crime punishable with $1,000 fine and six months' imprisonment, for you, or me, or any of us, to give a cup of cold water, a crust of bread, or a night's shelter to a panting fugitive as he was tracking his way to Canada. And every man or woman in whose veins coursed a drop of human sympathy violated that wicked law, reckless of consequences, and was justified in so doing. As then the slaves who got their freedom must take it over, or under, or through the unjust forms of law, precisely so now must women, to get their right to a voice in this Government, take it; and I have taken mine, and mean to take it at every possible opportunity.

JUDGE HUNT: The Court orders the prisoner to sit down. It will not allow another word.

MISS ANTHONY: When I was brought before your honor for trial, I hoped for a broad and liberal interpretation of the Constitution and its recent amendments, that should declare all United States citizens under its protecting aegis—that should declare equality of rights the national guarantee to all persons born or naturalized in the United States. But failing to get this justice—failing, even, to get a trial by a jury *not* of my peers—I ask not lenience at your hands—but rather the full rigors of the law.

JUDGE HUNT: The Court must insist—(Here the prisoner sat down.)

JUDGE HUNT: The prisoner will stand up. (Here Miss Anthony arose again.) The sentence of the Court is that you pay a fine of one hundred dollars and the costs of the prosecution.

MISS ANTHONY: May it please your honor, I shall never pay a dollar of your unjust penalty. All the stock in trade I possess is a $10,000 debt, incurred by publishing my paper—*The Revolution*—four years ago, the sole object of which was to educate all women to do precisely as I have done, rebel against your man-made, unjust, unconstitutional forms of law, that tax, fine, imprison, and hang women, while they deny them the right of representation in the Government; and I shall work on with might and main to pay every dollar of that honest debt, but not a penny shall go to this unjust claim. And I shall earnestly and persistently continue to urge all women to the practical recognition of the old revolutionary maxim, that "Resistance to tyranny is obedience to God."

JUDGE HUNT: Madam, the Court will not order you committed until the fine is paid.

ON THE SUBJECT OF...

SUSAN B. ANTHONY (1820-1906)

Susan B. Anthony was one of the most influential figures in the early campaign for women's rights in the United States. Active in the temperance movement through the early 1850s, she campaigned against slavery until 1863, when her outrage at finding that the women at a world temperance convention were refused the right to serve as delegates inspired her to the take up the cause of women's rights. Anthony was introduced to Elizabeth Cady Stanton by Amelia Bloomer, the editor of the temperance journal *Lily,* and the women forged a lifelong professional partnership and friendship.

Anthony began her women's rights work by campaigning for several years for women's property rights in the state of New York; in 1860 a law was passed ensuring property rights for married women. In 1868 Anthony founded with Stanton and Parker Pillsbury the *Revolution,* a feminist newspaper, and in 1871 Anthony and Stanton founded the National Women's Loyal League. In 1872 she was arrested for voting in Rochester, New York, in the national election, found guilty, and fined. Anthony ignored the judge's demand that she remain silent and delivered a spontaneous speech in which she refused to recognize all laws in the country that did not grant her basic rights of citizenship.

In the 1880s Anthony toured Europe and began to organize what would become the International Council of Women, and along with Stanton, Matilda Joslyn Gage, and Ida Husted Harper, coauthored the first four volumes of *History of Woman Suffrage,* a written legacy detailing their work for future generations of feminists. In 1889 Anthony helped found the National American Woman Suffrage Association, and served as its president from 1892 to 1900. The nineteenth constitutional amendment granting American women the right to vote is known as the "Susan B. Anthony Amendment."

SUSAN B. ANTHONY AND ELIZABETH CADY STANTON (ESSAY DATE 1882)

SOURCE: Anthony, Susan B. and Elizabeth Cady Stanton. "Political Lessons." In *Early American Women: A Documentary History, 1600-1900,* edited by Nancy Woloch, pp. 509-11. Belmont, Calif.: Wadsworth Publishing Company, 1992.

In the following excerpt, originally published in History of Woman Suffrage, Vol. 2 *in 1882, Stanton and Anthony argue that the rejection of their movement by liberal male abolitionists over issues concerning the Fifteenth Amendment turned out to be a blessing in disguise, freeing women to fight for their rights without the need to compromise with the interests of men.*

So utterly had the women been deserted in the Kansas campaign by those they had the strongest reason to look to for help, that at times all effort seemed hopeless. The editors of the New York *Tribune* and the *Independent* can never know how wistfully, from day to day, their papers were searched for some inspiring editorials on the woman's amendment, but naught was there; there were no words of hope and encouragement, no eloquent letters from an Eastern man that could be read to the people; all were silent. Yet these two papers, extensively taken all over Kansas, had they been as true to woman as to the negro, could have revolutionized the State. But with arms folded, Greeley, Curtis, Tilton, Beecher, Higginson, Phillips, Garrison, Frederick Douglass, all calmly watched the struggle from afar, and when defeat came to both propositions, no consoling words were offered for woman's loss, but the women who spoke in the campaign were reproached for having "killed negro suffrage."

We wondered then at the general indifference to that first opportunity of realizing what all those gentlemen had advocated so long; and, in looking back over the many intervening years, we still wonder at the stolid incapacity of all men to understand that woman feels the invidious distinctions of sex exactly as the black man does those of color, or the white man the more transient distinctions of wealth, family, position, place, and power; that she feels as keenly as man the injustice of disfranchisement. Of the old abolitionists who stood true to woman's cause in this crisis, Robert Purvis, Parker Pillsbury, and Rev. Samuel J. May were the only Eastern men. Through all the hot debates during the period of reconstruction, again and again, Mr. Purvis arose and declared, that he would rather his son should never be enfranchised, unless his daughter could be also, that, as she bore the double curse of sex and color, on every principle of justice she should first be protected. These were the only men who felt and understood as women themselves do the degradation of disfranchisement. . . .

And here is the secret of the infinite sadness of women of genius; of their dissatisfaction with life, in exact proportion to their development. A woman who occupies the same realm of thought with man, who can explore with him the depths of science, comprehend the steps of progress through the long past and prophesy those of the momentous future, must ever be surprised and aggravated with his assumptions of headship and superiority, a superiority she never concedes, an authority she utterly repudiates. Words can not describe the indignation, the humiliation a proud woman feels for her sex in disfranchisement.

In a republic where all are declared equal an ostracised class of one half of the people, on the ground of a distinction founded in nature, is an anomalous position, as harassing to its victims as it is unjust, and as contradictory as it is unsafe to the fundamental principles of a free government. When we remember that out of this degraded political status, spring all the special wrongs that have blocked woman's success in the world of work, and degraded her labor everywhere to one half its value; closed to her the college doors and all opportunities for higher education, forbade her to practice in the professions, made her a cipher in the church, and her sex, her motherhood a curse in all religions; her subjection a text for bibles, a target for the priesthood; seeing all this, we wonder now as then at the indifference and injustice of our best men when the first opportunity offered in which the women of any State might have secured their enfranchisement.

It was not from ignorance of the unequal laws, and false public sentiment against woman, that our best men stood silent in this Kansas campaign; it was not from lack of chivalry that they thundered forth no protests, when they saw noble women, who had been foremost in every reform, hounded through the State by foul mouthed politicians; it was not from lack of money and power, of eloquence of pen and tongue, nor of an intellectual conviction that our cause was just, that they came not to the rescue, but because in their heart of hearts they did not grasp the imperative necessity of woman's demand for that protection which the ballot alone can give; they did not feel for *her* the degradation of disfranchisement.

The fact of their silence deeply grieved us, but the philosophy of their indifference we thoroughly comprehended for the first time and saw as never before, that only from woman's standpoint could the battle be successfully fought, and victory secured. "It is wonderful," says Swift, "with what patience some folks can endure the sufferings of others." Our liberal men counseled us to silence during the war, and we were silent on our own wrongs; they counseled us again to silence in Kansas and New York, lest we should defeat "negro suffrage," and threatened if we were not, we might fight the battle alone. We chose the latter, and were defeated. But standing alone we learned our power; we repudiated man's counsels forevermore; and solemnly vowed that there should never be another season of silence until woman had the same rights everywhere on this green earth, as man.

While we hold in loving reverence the names of such men as Charles Sumner, Horace Greeley, William Lloyd Garrison, Gerrit Smith, Wendell Phillips and Frederick Douglass, and would urge the rising generation of young men to emulate their virtues, we would warn the young women of the coming generation against man's advice as to their best interests, their highest development. We would point for them the moral of our experiences: that woman must lead the way to her own enfranchisement, and work out her own salvation with a hopeful courage and determination that knows no fear nor trembling. She must not put her trust in man in this transition period, since, while regarded as his subject, his inferior, his slave, their interests must be antagonistic.

But when at last woman stands on an even platform with man, his acknowledged equal everywhere, with the same freedom to express herself in the religion and government of the country, then, and not till then, can she safely take counsel with him in regard to her most sacred rights, privileges, and immunities; for not till then will he be able to legislate as wisely and generously for her as for himself.

THE NATIONAL WOMAN SUFFRAGE ASSOCIATION (DOCUMENT DATE 1883)

SOURCE: The National Woman Suffrage Association. Library of Congress. Gift of the National American Woman Association (1 November 1938).

In the following document, originally created in 1883, the members of the National Woman Suffrage Association detail the mission and structure of the organization.

The National Woman Suffrage Association

ARTICLE 1.—This organization shall be called the NATIONAL WOMAN SUFFRAGE ASSOCIATION.

ARTICLE 2.—The object of this Association shall be to secure NATIONAL protection for women citizens in the exercise of their right to vote.

ARTICLE 3.—All citizens of the United States subscribing to this Constitution, and contributing not less than one dollar annually, shall be considered members of the Association, with the right to participate in its deliberations.

ARTICLE 4.—The officers of this Association shall be a President, a Vice-President from each of the States and Territories, Corresponding and Recording Secretaries, a Treasurer and an Executive Committee of not less than five.

ARTICLE 5.—A quorum of the Executive Committee shall consist of nine, and all the Officers of this Association shall be *ex-officio* members of such Committee, with power to vote.

ARTICLE 6.—All Women Suffrage Societies throughout the country shall be welcomed as auxiliaries; and their accredited officers or duly appointed representatives shall be recognized as members of the National Association.

Those desiring to join can do so by sending one dollar with name and address to MRS. JANE H. SPOFFARD, Treasurer, RIGGS HOUSE, Washington, D.C.

OVERVIEWS

ELLEN CAROL DUBOIS (ESSAY DATE 1978)

SOURCE: DuBois, Ellen Carol. Introduction to *Feminism and Suffrage: The Emergence of An Independent Women's Movement in America, 1848-1869,* pp. 15-20. Ithaca, N.Y.: Cornell University Press, 1978.

In the following excerpt, DuBois argues that suffragism is best understood as a social movement that developed its core ideology in reaction to changes brought about by the Industrial Revolution, the Civil War, and Reconstruction.

This book is a study of the origins of the first feminist movement in the United States, the nineteenth-century woman suffrage movement. For three-quarters of a century, beginning in 1848, American women centered their aspirations for freedom and power on the demand for the vote. At its height, the movement involved hundreds of thousands of women. Along with the black liberation and labor movements, woman suffrage is one of the three great reform efforts in American history.[1]

To appreciate the historic significance of the woman suffrage movement, it is necessary to understand the degree to which women expected the vote to lead to a total transformation of their lives. This expectation had to do with changes taking place in the family, its relation to society, and women's role within it. Historically, woman's role has been shaped by her position in the family. Because the traditional family was the site of production and closely integrated with all forms of community life, women were recognized as participants in the larger world of the society. However, the family's central importance in social organization meant that the patriarchal relations between men and women which characterized family life were carried into all other aspects of society as well.

With the growth of industrial capitalism, production began to move outside the home. Yet woman's place, her "sphere," remained within the family. Outside it there arose a public life that was considered man's sphere. Although public life was based on the growing organization of production outside the home, its essence was understood not as economic experience, but as political activity. Beginning in the 1820's and 1830's, an enormous upsurge of popular political energies took place—among working men, in the antislavery societies, and in almost every other aspect of antebellum life. The woman suffrage movement was women's response to these developments. Driven by their relegation to a separate, domestic sphere, which had always been marked by inequality, especially their own, women were also drawn, like the men of their time, by the promise that political activity held for the creation of a truly democratic society.

Until the development of women's rights and woman suffrage politics, the major approach to improving women's status came from domestic reformers, such as Catharine Beecher. To retrieve some of the social recognition that women were losing as production and other aspects of social life moved away from the home, domestic reformers called for an elevation of women's status in the family, and for increased recognition of the contribution that domestic relations made to community life in general. They did not challenge the relegation of women to the domestic sphere, but only the relationship between that sphere and the rest of society. The demand for suffrage represented a much more advanced program for improving women's position. Suffragists recognized that the locus of community life had shifted away from the family and that women's aspirations for a greater voice in the conduct of community affairs could be satisfied only by their moving into the public realm. Moreover, the demand for woman suffrage raised the prospect of sex equality in a way that proposals for domestic reform never could. Notwithstanding domestic reformers' assertions that the influence women wielded as wives and mothers was great, the fact remained that women in the family were dependent on men. Domestic reformers could aspire merely to modify women's subordinate status, never to eliminate it. Women hoped, however, that in the public realm men would be forced to face them as equals. In the mid-nineteenth century, enfranchisement offered women a route to social power, as well as the clearest possible vision of equality with men.

Suffragism has not been accorded the historic recognition it deserves, largely because woman suffrage has too frequently been regarded as an isolated institutional reform. Its character as a social movement, reflecting women's aspirations for and progress toward radical change in their lives, has been overlooked. Abstracting the demand for the vote from its social context, feminists and historians alike have seriously underestimated its relevance for contemporary women. It is certainly true that the Nineteenth Amendment did not emancipate women, and that rediscovering the revolutionary hopes that feminists had for the ballot has a bitter edge for us today. However, it is a mistake to conclude that the woman suffrage movement was a useless detour in women's struggle for liberation because the vote did not solve the problem of women's oppression.[2] The vote did not have the inherent capacity to emancipate women as individuals, isolated from the collective struggles of their sex. Like all institutional reforms, it required an active social movement to give it meaning and make it real. Approached as a social movement, rather than as a particular reform, suffragism has enormous contemporary relevance. It was the first independent movement of women for their own liberation. Its growth—the mobilization of women around the demand for the vote, their collective activity, their commitment to gaining increased power over their own lives—was itself a major change in the condition of those lives. My concern is less with how women won the vote than with how the vote generated a movement of increasing strength and vitality. In other words, this book is intended as a contribution, not to the history of woman suffrage, but to the history of the feminist movement.[3]

The word "movement" should, I think, be taken seriously as a description of the emergence of suffragism and similar historical processes. It suggests an accelerating transformation of consciousness among a group of oppressed people and a growing sense of collective power. The overwhelming majority of challenges to established power are stillborn, but a few generate movements. Prior to a movement's emergence its coming into being is difficult to imagine, but once it begins the initial problem of radical social change is solved and how people could have ever accepted their own powerlessness becomes increasingly difficult to imagine. The early history of woman suffrage vividly demonstrates this phenomenon. The movement started with a handful of mid-nineteenth-century women—scattered, isolated, and handicapped by the limited sphere of their sex—who began to demand political parity with men. Within a generation, they had organized their demand for enfranchisement into a powerful political force that was able not only to sustain itself over a half-century, but to challenge the structures of American political and social life until its goals were met. "We solemnly vowed," Elizabeth Cady Stanton declared on behalf of the first generation of suffragists, "that there should never be another season of silence until woman had the same rights everywhere on this green earth, as man."

Because my concern is to trace the development of the suffrage movement, I have chosen to focus on its earliest period, and to uncover the process by which women's discontent crystallized into the political demand for women's emancipation. The beginnings of this process lie in the dozen years before the Civil War, primarily among women associated with the antislavery movement. They laid the groundwork for a feminist movement by articulating a set of demands for women's rights and by acquiring the skills and self-confidence necessary to offer political leadership to other women. However, the development of feminism before the war was restrained by the organizational connection of its leaders with the antislavery movement, which kept them from concentrating on the mobilization of women around a primary commitment to their own rights.

Postwar politics provided the setting within which feminists came to recognize that the only force capable of bringing about radical change in the condition of women's lives was the organized power of women themselves. From the perspective of feminists, postwar politics had two important aspects. One was the general flowering of radical ambitions for social change that accompanied the defeat of slavery and encompassed demands for racial equality, sexual equality, and labor reform. The other was the process by which the power of the Republican party was marshaled in behalf of only one of these reforms, the demand for black suffrage.[4] Stimulated by the former and thwarted by the latter, feminists came to realize that they needed an independent political base if they were to demand women's enfranchisement with any real force. The particular historical conditions under which they came to this realization shaped the nature of the movement they began to build in response to it.

At the center of the postwar development of the woman suffrage movement—and therefore the central characters in this book—were Elizabeth Cady Stanton and Susan B. Anthony. It was they who realized most clearly the limitations that political dependence on abolitionism imposed on feminism, and who took the lead in finding a new political context for woman suffrage. Their decision to end their twenty-year alliance with abolitionism led to a break with many other leading advocates of woman suffrage, prominent among them Lucy Stone. After the failure of efforts to convince abolitionists to support a Reconstruction program that included woman suffrage as well as black suffrage, Stanton and Anthony attempted to forge an alliance with labor reformers and to build a new reform coalition on that basis. From political cooperation with labor reformers they moved quite naturally into efforts to organize a feminist movement among working women. The failure of these efforts set the stage for their decision to form an organization of women dedicated first and foremost to securing political equality with men. That decision marks the emergence of woman suffrage as an independent feminist movement, and it is with the events surrounding it that the book concludes. While suffragism went through many changes over the next fifty years, reflecting the variety of its political contexts, its basic characteristics were set in the Reconstruction period: it was an independent reform movement, composed primarily of white, middle-class women, which defined women's emancipation and equality largely, although not exclusively, in terms of the franchise.

Notes

1. The major histories of the movement are: Eleanor Flexner, *A Century of Struggle: The Women's Rights Movement in the United States* (New York, 1968); Alan Grimes, *The Puritan Ethic and Woman Suffrage* (New York, 1967); Aileen S. Kraditor, *Ideas of the Woman Suffrage Movement, 1890-1920* (New York, 1965); William O'Neill, *Everyone Was Brave: The Rise and Fall of Feminism in America* (New York, 1969); Ross Evans Paulson, *Women's Suffrage and Prohibition: A Comparative Study of Equality and Social Control* (Glenview, Ill., 1973); and Anne F. Scott and Andrew M. Scott, *One Half the People: The Fight for Woman Suffrage* (Philadelphia, 1975). Also of great importance are two histories generated within the movement itself: Carrie Chapman Catt and Nettie Rogers Shuler, *Woman Suffrage and Politics* (New York, 1923); and the monumental, six-volume *History of Woman Suffrage*, ed. Elizabeth Cady Stanton, Susan B. Anthony, Matilda Joslyn Gage, et al.; the first three volumes were published and distributed by Anthony herself (Rochester, 1881-1886). The *History of Woman Suffrage* is evidence of the extraordinary commitment of these feminists to documenting and preserving the records of their political efforts and passing them on to future generations of women. It embodies their unusually acute sense of their place in and responsibility to history.
2. O'Neill, for instance (pp. 55-64), occasionally slips into an appreciation of the political foresight of antisuffragists for anticipating his own analysis that the vote accomplished very little. The most recent example of this tendency to dismiss suffragism is Carroll Smith Rosenberg's comment that "women's suffrage has proved of little importance either to American politics or American women" ("The New Woman and the New History," *Feminist Studies* 3 (1975), 186).
3. Linda Gordon makes the same distinction about birth control in her brilliant study, *Woman's Body, Woman's Right: A Social History of Birth Control in America* (New York, 1976).
4. In developing this analytical framework, I learned a great deal from David Montgomery's history of Reconstruction politics from the perspective of the labor reform movement, *Beyond Equality: Labor and the Radical Republicans, 1862-1872* (New York, 1967).

MARJORIE SPRUILL WHEELER (ESSAY DATE 1995)

SOURCE: Wheeler, Marjorie Spruill. "Introduction: A Short History of the Woman Suffrage Movement in America." In *One Woman, One Vote: Rediscovering the Woman Suffrage Movement*, edited by Marjorie Spruill Wheeler, pp. 9-20. Troutdale, Oreg.: New Sage Press, 1995.

In the following excerpt, Wheeler traces the origins, strategies, divisions, and state victories of the woman's suffrage movement from 1848 to the end of the nineteenth century.

ON THE SUBJECT OF...

LUCRETIA COFFIN MOTT (1793-1880)

Lucretia Coffin Mott was a pioneer feminist leader and radical abolitionist. She was born on the island of Nantucket, Massachusetts; her family became Quakers and in 1804 moved to the mainland. She was educated in Boston and New York, and after working briefly as a schoolteacher, married James Mott in 1811. At the age of twenty-eight, Mott became a Quaker minister, and when the denomination divided over matters of doctrine she supported the liberal, or Hicksite, faction. The Motts were abolitionists, and their home became a station on the Underground Railroad, by which Southern slaves escaped to the North. Mott helped found the first antislavery society for women in 1837, and later, with other militant abolitionist women, helped William Lloyd Garrison take over the American Antislavery Society.

In 1840 Mott was one of a group of women who accompanied Garrison to London for a world antislavery convention; Garrison sat with Mott and other women in the gallery when they were refused seating in the main area, and denied official recognition as delegates from the United States. At the convention Mott met the young Elizabeth Cady Stanton. Their friendship developed, and Mott inspired Stanton, who in time grew more radical than her mentor. The two eventually organized the first Woman's Rights Convention in Seneca Falls, New York in 1848. During the Civil War, Mott was a vocal supporter of the 13th Amendment to the Constitution. She was deeply distressed by the split in the women's rights movement that developed in the late 1860s, and worked to heal it until her death in 1880.

Origins: 1848-1869

The woman suffrage movement, which began in the northeastern United States, developed in the context of antebellum reform. Many women including Sarah and Angelina Grimké, Abby Kelley Foster, Lucretia Mott, Maria Stewart, Antoinette Brown Blackwell, Lucy Stone, Susan B. Anthony, and Elizabeth Cady Stanton, began speaking out for woman's rights when their efforts to participate fully in the great reform movements of the day—including antislavery and temperance—were rebuffed. These early feminists demanded a wide range of changes in woman's social, moral, legal, educational, and economic status; the right to vote was not their initial focus. Indeed, those present at the Seneca Falls Convention in upstate New York regarded the resolution demanding the vote as the most extreme of all their demands, and adopted it by a narrow margin at the insistence of Elizabeth Cady Stanton and Frederick Douglass.

After the Civil War, women's rights leaders saw enfranchisement as one of the most important, perhaps *the* most important of their goals. Enfranchisement, they believed, was essential both as a symbol of women's equality and individuality and a means of improving women's legal and social condition. They were extremely disappointed when the Fourteenth and Fifteenth Amendments did not provide universal suffrage for *all* Americans, but extended the franchise only to black men. In fact, women's rights advocates divided acrimoniously in 1869 largely over the issue of whether or not to support ratification of the Fifteenth Amendment.

Suffrage Strategies During "The Schism": 1869-1890

Two woman suffrage organizations were founded in 1869, with different positions on the Fifteenth Amendment and different ideas about how best to promote woman suffrage. The National Woman Suffrage Association (NWSA) headed by Elizabeth Cady Stanton and Susan B. Anthony opposed the Fifteenth Amendment, but called for a Sixteenth Amendment that would enfranchise women. Led exclusively by women, the New York-based NWSA focused upon the enfranchisement of women through federal action, and adopted a more radical tone in promoting a wide variety of feminist reforms in its short-lived journal, *The Revolution.*

The other organization, the American Woman Suffrage Association (AWSA) with headquarters in Boston, was led by Lucy Stone with the aid of her husband Henry Blackwell, Mary Livermore, Julia Ward Howe, Henry Ward Beecher, Antoinette Brown Blackwell, Thomas Wentworth Higginson and others. It supported ratification of the Fifteenth Amendment while working for woman suffrage as well. While endorsing a federal amendment for female enfranchisement, this organization concentrated on developing grassroots support for woman suffrage. Employing agents who traveled all over the nation, establishing local and state suffrage organizations, speaking and circulating literature, and working through its newspaper, *The Woman's Journal,* the AWSA engaged in a massive educational campaign designed to make woman suffrage and other feminist reforms seem less radical and consistent with widely shared American values. AWSA members promoted state suffrage amendments and various forms of "partial suffrage" legislation, including bills giving women the right to vote on school or municipal issues or in presidential elections; they believed that these measures were desirable in themselves and a means to the eventual end—full suffrage for all American women.

Meanwhile, suffragists associated with the NWSA, disheartened by the response to the proposed federal amendment, and disdaining the state-by-state approach, tried to win their rights by other approaches, known collectively as the "New Departure." These suffragists challenged their exclusion from voting on the grounds that, as citizens, they could not be deprived of their rights as protected by the Constitution. Victoria Woodhull, a radical, iconoclastic, and beautiful figure who briefly gained the support of Stanton and Anthony in the 1870s (before her scandalous personal life and advocacy of free love were revealed at great cost to the movement), made this argument before Congress in 1871.

In 1872, Susan B. Anthony attempted to vote, hoping to be arrested and to have the opportunity to test this strategy in the courts; she was arrested and indicted for "knowingly, wrongfully and unlawfully vot[ing] for a representative to the Congress of the United States." Found guilty and fined, she insisted she would never pay a dollar of it. Virginia Minor, a suffrage leader in St. Louis, succeeded in getting the issue before the United States Supreme Court, but in 1875 the court ruled unanimously that citizenship did not automatically confer the right to vote and that the issue of female enfranchisement should be decided within the states.

The West Pioneers in Woman Suffrage

Even as the NWSA and the AWSA competed for support and tried several strategies for winning female enfranchisement to no avail, woman suffrage was making headway in the West. While most eastern politicians were dead set against woman suffrage, politicians and voters in several

Illustration of members of the National Women's Suffrage Association speaking at a political convention in Chicago, Illinois, in 1880.

western states enfranchised women and, at times, battled Congress for the right to do so. In 1869 Wyoming led the nation in the adoption of woman suffrage while still a territory; in 1890, when it appeared that Congress would not approve its application for statehood as long as Wyoming allowed woman suffrage, the legislature declared "we will remain out of the Union a hundred years rather than come in without the women." Even the Mormon stronghold of Utah enacted woman suffrage as a territory in 1870 and came into the Union with woman suffrage in 1896. Colorado (1893) and Idaho (1896) were the other "pioneering" suffrage states.

Historians differ as to the reason why the West was so precocious in its adoption of woman suffrage. One theory was that frontier conditions undermined traditional gender roles and that women, having proven their ability to conquer difficult conditions and do "men's work," were rewarded with the vote. Another theory was that the politicians hoped that women voters would help to "civilize" the West. Most historians stress practical politics as opposed to advanced ideology as the explanation, arguing that western politicians found it expedient to enfranchise women for a variety of reasons. In Utah, for example, Mormons were confident that the votes of women would help preserve Mormon traditions—including polygamy—and that enfranchising women would help to dispel the idea widely accepted in the East that Mormon women were an oppressed lot.

For whatever reasons, these four western states were the *only* states to adopt woman suffrage in the nineteenth century. The next round of state victories did not come until 1910, and these were also in the West (Washington, 1910; California, 1911; Oregon, 1912; Kansas, 1912; and Arizona, 1912).

Woman Suffrage and Temperance

Meanwhile, the suffrage movement won a valuable ally when Frances Willard, as president of the Woman's Christian Temperance Union (WCTU), led thousands of otherwise quite traditional women to "convert" to the cause of woman suffrage as a way of protecting the home, women, and children. Following its official endorsement in 1880, the WCTU created a Department of Franchise under Zerelda Wallace and Dr. Anna Howard Shaw (later president of the NAWSA), which encouraged state WCTU chapters to endorse suffrage and distributed suffrage literature. Though Willard was a member of the AWSA and invited Susan B. Anthony to speak before the WCTU, the temperance organization's work for woman suffrage was particularly valuable in creating support for suffrage among women who might have considered the existing suffrage organizations and their leaders eccentric or radical.

The WCTU endorsement, however, gained for the suffrage movement a powerful opponent when the liquor industry concluded that woman suffrage was a threat to be stopped at all costs. Indeed, NAWSA President Carrie Chapman Catt later referred to the liquor industry as "the Invisible Enemy" and believed that its corrupt manipulation of American politics long delayed the coming of woman suffrage.

Unity Restored Through the NAWSA: 1890

One of the most important turning points in the history of the woman suffrage movement came in 1890 as the two national suffrage organizations reunited in one major organization. At the instigation of younger suffragists, the movement's aging pioneers put aside their differences sufficiently to merge their rival organizations into the National American Woman Suffrage Association (NAWSA). Elizabeth Cady Stanton was elected president; Lucy Stone, head of the executive committee; and Susan B. Anthony, vice president; but it was Anthony who actually took command of the new organization. (She became president officially in 1892 and remained in office until 1900.) While continuing to demand a federal amendment, NAWSA leaders concluded that they must first build support within the states, winning enough state suffrage amendments that Congress would approve a federal amendment and three-fourths of the states would be sure to ratify.

Though Stanton continued to address a wide range of feminist issues, many of them quite radical (including an indictment of Christianity in her 1895 *The Woman's Bible*), most NAWSA leaders including Anthony thought it imperative that the movement focus almost exclusively on winning the vote. In keeping with this new approach and influenced by the conservatism of new recruits, the suffragists went to great lengths to avoid association with radical causes.

Woman Suffrage and the Race Issue

This new approach included shedding the traditional association of women's rights with the rights of blacks. Although the NAWSA never stopped using natural rights arguments for woman suffrage, white suffragists—still indignant that black men were enfranchised ahead of them and angry at the ease with which immigrant men were enfranchised—drifted away from insistence upon universal suffrage and increasingly employed racist and nativist rhetoric and tactics.

The new NAWSA strategy included building support in the South. There the historic connection between the woman's movement and antislavery made suffrage anathema to the white conservatives who once again controlled the region and made advocacy of woman suffrage quite difficult for the influential white women the NAWSA wished to recruit. In the 1890s, however, with Laura Clay of Kentucky as intermediary, NAWSA leaders went to great lengths to, in Clay's words, "bring in the South."

Using a strategy first suggested by Henry Blackwell, northern and southern leaders began to argue that woman suffrage—far from endangering white supremacy in the South—could be a means of restoring it. In fact, they suggested that the adoption of woman suffrage with educational or property qualifications that would disqualify most black women, would allow the South to restore white supremacy in politics without "having to" disfranchise black men and risk Congressional repercussions.

The NAWSA spent considerable time and resources developing this "southern strategy," sending Catt and Anthony on speaking tours through the region, and holding the 1895 NAWSA convention in Atlanta. Eager to avoid offending their southern hosts they even asked their aging hero Frederick Douglass—who was an honored participant in women's rights conventions elsewhere in the nation—to stay away from the Atlanta meeting. By 1903, however, it was becoming clear that this southern strategy had failed; the region's politicians refused (in the words of one Mississippi politician) to "cower behind petticoats" and "use lovely women" to maintain white supremacy. Instead, they found other means to do so that did not involve the "destruction" of woman's traditional role.

White suffragists largely turned their backs on African American women in the late nineteenth and early twentieth centuries, and, in the South, excluded them totally from white suffrage organizations. Nevertheless, a growing number of African American women actively supported woman suffrage during this period. Following a path blazed by former slave Sojourner Truth and free blacks Harriet Forten Purvis and Margaretta Forten who spoke at antebellum women's rights conventions, and Massachusetts reformers Caroline Remond Putman and Josephine St. Pierre Ruffin who were active in the AWSA in the 1870s, black women persevered in their advocacy of woman suffrage even in these difficult times. Prominent African American suffragists included Ida B. Wells-Barnett of Chicago, famous as a leading crusader against lynching; Mary Church Terrell, educator and first president of the National Association of Colored Women (NACW); and Adella Hunt Logan, Tuskegee faculty member, who, in articles in *The Crisis,* insisted that if white women needed the vote to protect their rights, then black women—victims of racism as well as sexism—needed the ballot even more.

Still, white suffrage leaders, who either shared the nativism or racism endemic to turn-of-the century America or were convinced they must cater to it in order to succeed, continued in their attempts to shed the movement's radical image and enlarge their constituency.

ELLEN CAROL DUBOIS (ESSAY DATE 1998)

SOURCE: DuBois, Ellen Carol. "What Made Seneca Falls Possible?" In *Remembering Seneca Falls: Honoring the Women Who Paved the Way: An Essay,* pp. 4-16.: Boston: The Schlesinger Library for the History of Women, Radcliffe College, 1998.

In the following excerpt, DuBois compares and contrasts the revolutionary nature of the 1848 Seneca Falls convention calling for women's rights with popular democratic revolutions in Europe that same year.

For both the champions and the denigrators of women's rights, the Seneca Falls Woman's Rights Convention of 1848 was of a piece with the revolutionary upheavals of the age. The year 1848 was of wide historical significance, with revolutions in Europe and major social changes, or demands for change, in the United States, not only by women.

In 1848 Elizabeth Blackwell became the first American woman to earn a regular medical degree, and the organized working women of Lowell petitioned the Massachusetts legislature for a ten-hour day; in 1847 Lucy Stone had been the first woman in American history to earn a Bachelor of Arts degree. In such an atmosphere, the announcement of a public convention dedicated solely to the rights of women, a development for which there was no precedent in this country or any other, was less startling than it might have been in a year in which history was moving at a less breakneck speed.

The Seneca Falls Woman's Rights Convention can be situated in this broader historical context at three levels. First, the international: 1848 was a year of democratic revolution, particularly in Europe. Second, the national: in 1848, the United States defeated Mexico in a controversial war that would accelerate the struggle over slavery and inaugurate a new era of aggressive American nationalism. The third context is that of New York State, which, earlier in 1848, had passed one of the most advanced married women's property acts of any state. Each of these levels helps us to understand the forces behind and the significance of the Seneca Falls convention.

When historians speak of "the revolutions of 1848," they are referring to popular democratic movements in Germany, France, Italy and Austria. In Germany the revolutions of 1848 led Karl Marx and Friedrich Engels to write the *Communist Manifesto.* The revolutionary movements of 1848 were intent on establishing modern constitutional governments, based on a broad popular franchise that would ensure genuine democracy. The *Communist Manifesto* captures for us the degree to which these universal democratic hopes were identified with the political ambitions of a particular class, the wage-earning "proletariat." But it was not only workers whose activism fueled the era's grand political dreams.

Women too saw themselves as a revolutionary class, an oppressed group whose political empowerment would lead to social transformation of the most profound sort. In Germany and France especially, groups of women joined the revolutionary ferment and called simultaneously for national democratic revolution and women's rights. Indeed, in the eyes of female revolutionaries, the two were identical: women's rights were not a single issue, a special interest, counterpoised to "men's" revolution. Lucretia Mott, the senior feminist at the Seneca Falls convention, reflecting on the links among the European revolutions, the demand for women's rights, and democratic rumblings among the upstate New York Seneca Indians whom she visited that summer, said

> All these subjects of reform are kindred in their nature; and giving to each its proper consideration will tend to strengthen and serve the mind for all. . . . [The abolitionist] will not love the slave less in loving universal humanity more.[1]

Americans in general, and women's rights pioneers in particular, were perfectly aware of the revolutionary winds stirring in Europe, and saw their own efforts as a part. "This is the age of revolutions," began the *New York Herald*'s coverage of the Woman's Rights Convention in Seneca Falls. "To whatever part of the world the attention is directed, the political and social fabric is crumbling to pieces; and changes which far exceed the wildest dreams of the enthusiastic Utopians of the last generation, are now pursued with ardor and perseverance."[2]

In taking their historic initiative, American women's rights pioneers appealed to "the upward tending spirit of the age, busy in an hundred forms of effort for the world's redemption." This was the language used at the first national women's rights convention, held two years after Seneca Falls in Worcester, Massachusetts.[3] There, Paulina Wright Davis invoked the unity of women's rights and the era's revolutionary spirit. "The reformation we propose in its utmost scope is radical and universal . . . ," she declared. "It is an epochal movement—the emancipation of a class, the redemption of half the world, and a conforming reorganization of all social, political, and industrial interests and institutions."[4]

At the Seneca Falls convention, Elizabeth Cady Stanton expressed this same historic sensibility.

> A new era is dawning upon the world, . . . when the millions now under the iron heel of the tyrant will assert their manhood, when woman yielding to the voice of the spirit within her will demand the recognition of her humanity, when her soul, grown too large for her chains, will burst the bands around her set and stand redeemed, regenerated and disenthralled.[5]

In this challenge to women to burst their chains we hear distinct echoes of Karl Marx's 1848 call to the workers of the world to unite and rise, as they have "nothing to lose but [their] chains." The *Communist Manifesto* was not available in the United States until 1871, but the similarity is there and reflects the more general influences at work, the spirit of the age and the widespread revolutionary metaphors used in different places by different sorts of visionaries to express it.

In her Seneca Falls speech, Stanton virtually soars on the wings of revolutionary optimism, determined as she is that her sex not only be part of, but indeed help realize, the world historic transformation she feels coming.

> While the globe resounds with the tramping of legions who roused from their lethargy are resolved to be free or perish, while old earth reels under the crashing of thrones and the destruction of despotisms, . . . while the flashing sunlight that breaks over us makes dark so much that men have before revered and shows that to be good that had scarcely been dreamed of . . . ,

she proclaims, and goes on to ask: "shall we the women of this age be content to remain inactive and to move in but a narrow and circumscribed sphere, a sphere which man shall assign us?"[6] Not until the abolition of slavery in 1865, when at least one "scarcely dreamed of" aspiration was realized, did Stanton again take to such revolutionary rhetoric.

For all the similarity, there was also a fundamental difference between what began at Seneca Falls and these other revolutions of 1848: steady growth and development for American women, but reaction and repression in Europe, with particularly brutal consequences for women. In France the Provisional Legislature, elected in 1848 without the votes of women, turned in a radically reactionary direction; one of its first acts (passed just two weeks after the Seneca Falls convention) was a law prohibiting women from participating in any political clubs. Pauline Roland and Jeanne Deroin, two of the leading women of the revolution, were soon imprisoned under this law's provisions. In 1851 they wrote from their jail cells in Paris to the Woman's Rights Convention in Worcester that their American sisters'

> courageous declaration of Woman's Rights has resounded even to our prison, and has filled our souls with inexpressible joy.[7]

Undoubtedly American women were favored in their feminist ambitions by the fact that our national democratic upheaval was safely in the past. Indeed, Stanton and her Seneca Falls compatriots were able to rely on the structure and authority of the American Declaration of Independence as the framework for their feminist manifesto, and thus to confer legitimacy on the radical new direction they were taking. Like the thirteen colonies in revolt against the British throne, their declaration proclaimed, women aspired to overthrow another, domestic tyranny, that of their husbands, fathers and brothers. As radical a framework as this was for American feminism, the spirit of revolutionary nationalism that the Seneca Falls women shared with other '48 radicals did not draw upon them, as it did upon their European sisters, the wrath of existing power structures, threatened in their very existence.

Instead of resulting in outright government repression, the Woman's Rights Convention at Seneca Falls inaugurated an orderly and determined process of movement building, limited only by the limits of women's own aspirations and energy. Seneca Falls was followed two weeks later by a second Woman's Rights Convention in Rochester, New York, where the links among democracy, women's rights and the revolutionary labor movement were even clearer; and then by an accelerating flow of local and national conventions, of traveling women's rights agitators and ambitious women's rights newspapers throughout the 1850s. Indeed, the repressions in Europe even benefited the American women's rights movement. European '48ers escaped to the United States, bringing with them their revolutionary élan, their political experience, and such feminists as the German Mathilde Anneke, who spoke on women's rights around the United States throughout the 1850s.

All of this is not to say that American politics were peaceful and harmonious in 1848; they were not, and the tumultuous national political context is fundamental for understanding the when, why and what of the Seneca Falls convention. Five months earlier, in February 1848, the United States won its year-and-a-half long war against Mexico, fought to acquire Mexico's northern territories. The Mexican war was the first American war in which popular passions were aroused on both sides. Pro-war sentiments in the south and west were strong enough to elect Democrat James Polk to the presidency in 1844, and after him a series of soldier/politicians, all sporting their military credentials.

In the northeast, however, sentiment ran against the war. Most memorably, Henry David Thoreau refused to pay his taxes and wrote the essay "Civil Disobedience" to explain his antiwar stance. The women of Seneca Falls, most of them Quakers, were undoubtedly in the same camp. In their article published in the *Seneca County Courier* soon after the convention, Stanton and her friend Elizabeth McClintock referred several times to "the unjust and cruel war" against Mexico as an example of the unchristian, sinful conduct into which slavery was leading the nation and which the entry of women into politics might help to reverse.[8]

The consequences of the Mexican war for American politics cannot be overstated. The lands brought into the nation by the war, equal to roughly seventy percent of the territory of the United States at that point, carried with them the inescapable question of the status of slavery there and of the role of the national government in controlling its growth or containment in federally administered lands. In turn, the question of slavery in the territories spurred on efforts to form an effective national antislavery party that could stop the expansion of the "peculiar institution."

The first of these aspiring antislavery parties had been formed in 1840, when abolitionists in the Whig Party withdrew to form the Liberty Party. Elizabeth Cady Stanton was part and parcel of this development. Her cousin Gerrit Smith, the man most influential in turning her into a reformer, was one of the Liberty Party's founders. Henry Stanton was deeply involved in the schism of the antislavery movement from which the Liberty Party emerged. Indeed, he and Elizabeth made the snap decision to marry in May 1840, immediately after the new party was formed. Sailing to London for their impromptu honeymoon, a fellow passenger was James Birney, who had just been chosen to run for president on the Liberty Party ticket that November.

> "I like him very much," Elizabeth wrote Gerrit Smith from England, "though he lectures me occasionally through Henry for my want of discretion."[9]

Four years later, a second antislavery party was formed, this one split from the Democratic Party. The Free Soil Party was much more powerful than the Liberty Party, garnering ten percent of the popular vote in 1848 and draining enough support from the Democrats to elect a Whig president, Zachary Taylor. Here Stanton's link was even more intimate: her husband Henry was one of the founders of the Free Soil Party and indeed was off speaking on its behalf in late July. The town of Seneca Falls was a Free Soil hotbed, and throughout the spring and summer of 1848 Free Soil conventions were held in upstate New York from Utica to Buffalo, involving some of the same people who attended the Woman's Rights Convention. One historian of Seneca Falls calculates that, of the twenty-six local families with members attending the Woman's Rights Convention, eighteen were actively involved in the Free Soil movement.[10]

What is the significance of all this political activity for the women of Seneca Falls, who after all could not vote? But of course their disfranchisement was becoming exactly the point. Throughout the 1830s, the abolitionist movement had steered clear of party politics, resting all its faith on "moral suasion." Deeply religious and untainted by male politics, abolitionism in this period was very inviting to women. Foremost among these women were the passionate Christian abolitionist feminists Sarah and Angelina

Grimké. Sexual equality as the Grimkés perceived and preached it in the 1830s was fundamentally a matter of morality: as they put it,

> Whatsoever is right for a man to do, it right for a woman to do.

The authors of *History of Woman Suffrage* wrote that "above all other causes of the 'Woman Suffrage Movement,' was the Anti-Slavery struggle in this country . . . so clearly taught, that the women who crowded to listen, readily learned the lesson of freedom for themselves" and so "the double battle to fight against the tyranny of sex and color" was launched.[11]

When the abolitionists began to turn from moral suasion to political action, however, women's participation was thrown into crisis. Party politics was a male environment, where women were not welcome and few wished to go, and where the franchise was fiercely guarded as the ultimate symbol of American manhood. If women were to continue to play a major battle against slavery, they would have to take an even more dramatic step out of their foreordained sphere than the Grimkés had in 1838 when they became public lecturers "to promiscuous assemblies"[12] and spoke on subjects "about which ladies should not know." Women would have to demand "the sacred right of the elective franchise," the cornerstone of American democratic claims. Few women were willing to enter this particular territory.

Elizabeth Cady Stanton, student and protégé of female abolitionists Lucretia Mott and the Grimkés, wife of one political abolitionist, Henry Stanton, and kinswoman of another, Gerrit Smith, took this step of extending the vision of sexual equality to the political realm.

> So long as we are to be governed by human laws, I should be unwilling to have the making and administering of those laws left entirely to the selfish and unprincipled part of the community,

she had written in 1842.[13] The Woman's Rights Convention of 1848 and the Declaration of Sentiments that it passed, including the much debated ninth resolution in favor of woman suffrage, were the result of her conviction that social change must ultimately be won through politics and that women committed to making social change need political equality.

Notes

1. *A word for the poor Indians. The few hundreds left of the Seneca Nation at the Cataraugus reservation are improving in their mode of living, cultivating their land, and educating their children. They, too, are learning somewhat from the political agitations abroad: and, as man is wont, are imitating the movements of France and all Europe in seeking larger liberty—more independence. Their Chieftainship is therefore a subject of discussion in their councils, and important changes are demanded and expected, as to the election of their chief, many being prepared for a yearly appointment. "Letter from Lucretia Mott,"* Liberator, *6 October 1848.*
2. *Quoted in Elizabeth Cady Stanton, Susan B. Anthony, and Matilda Joslyn Gage, eds.,* History of Woman Suffrage, *vol. 1 (Rochester, N.Y.: Susan B. Anthony, 1881), 805.*
3. Ibid., *221.*
4. Ibid., *222.*
5. *Address by ECS on woman's rights [September 1848],* The Selected Papers of Elizabeth Cady Stanton and Susan B. Anthony, *ed. Ann D. Gordon (New Brunswick, N.J.: Rutgers University Press, 1997), 115*
6. Ibid., *116.*
7. HWS [History of Woman Suffrage], vol. 1, 234
8. *ECS and Elizabeth W. McClintock to the editors,* Seneca County Courier, *[after 23 July 1848],* The Selected Papers . . . , *88-94.*
9. *ECS to Gerrit Smith, 3 August [1840],* The Selected Papers . . . , *16.*
10. Judith Wellman, "The Seneca Falls Women's Rights Convention: A Study of Social Network," *Journal of Women's History* 3, no. 1 (1991):23.
11. HWS, vol. 1, 52 and 53.
12. Ibid., 52 and 53.
13. ECS to Elizabeth Pease, The Selected Papers . . . , 30. (Elizabeth Cady Stanton)

THE CIVIL WAR AND ITS EFFECT ON SUFFRAGE

ELLEN CAROL DUBOIS (ESSAY DATE 1995)

SOURCE: DuBois, Ellen Carol. "Taking the Law Into Our Own Hands: *Bradwell, Minor* and Suffrage Militance in the 1870s." In *One Woman, One Vote: Rediscovering the Woman Suffrage Movement,* edited by Marjorie Spruill Wheeler, pp. 81-98. Troutdale, Oreg.: NewSage Press, 1995.

In the following excerpt, DuBois describes the increasingly militant strategies pursued by women in courts of law during the 1870s in reaction to their exclusion from enfranchisement in both the Fourteenth and Fifteenth Amendments.

Introduction to the New Departure

. . . Most histories of women's rights—my own included—have emphasized the initial rage of women's rights leaders at the Radical Republican authors of the Fourteenth and Fifteenth

Amendments. In 1865 Elizabeth Cady Stanton was horrified to discover what she called "the word male" in proposals for a Fourteenth Amendment. The second section of the amendment defines the basis of congressional representation as "male persons over the age of twenty-one" and in doing so makes the first reference to sex anywhere in the Constitution. The passage of the Fifteenth Amendment in 1869, a much more powerful constitutional defense of political equality, only deepened the anger of women's rights advocates because it did not include sex among its prohibited disfranchisements.[1]

In 1869 the crisis split suffragists into two camps—the National Woman Suffrage Association, which protested the omission of women from the Reconstruction amendments, and the American Woman Suffrage Association, which accepted the deferral of their claims. This part of the story is well known to students of woman suffrage, as is the National Association's concentration, through most of its twenty-one-year life (in 1890 it amalgamated with the American Association), on securing a separate amendment enfranchising women. Inasmuch as the form that federal woman suffrage ultimately took was precisely a separate constitutional amendment—the Nineteenth, ratified in 1920—this strategy is taken as the entirety of woman suffragists' constitutional claims. Yet, in the first few years after the passage of the Fourteenth and Fifteenth Amendments, suffragists in the National Association camp energetically pursued another constitutional approach. They proposed a broad and inclusive construction of the Fourteenth and Fifteenth Amendments, under which, they claimed, women were already enfranchised. This constitutional strategy, known at the time as the New Departure, laid the basis for the subsequent focus on a separate woman suffrage amendment, even as it embodied a radical democratic vision that the latter approach did not have.

The Fourteenth and Fifteenth Amendments

While the Fourteenth Amendment was in the process of being ratified, woman suffragists concentrated on its second clause, because of the offensive reference to "male persons." This phrase was included by the amendment's framers because in 1867 there was an active movement demanding the franchise for women, and it would no longer do to use such gender neutral terms as "person" to mean only men.[2] Yet such explicit exclusions of particular groups from the universal blessings of American democracy were not at all in the egalitarian spirit of the age. Perhaps it was for this reason that in writing the first section of the Fourteenth Amendment, which defines federal citizenship, the framers could not bring themselves to speak of races or sexes but instead relied on the abstractions of "persons" and "citizens." In other words, the universalities of the first section of the Fourteenth Amendment, where federal citizenship is established, run headlong into the sex-based restrictions of the second section, where voting rights are limited. Those Reconstruction Era feminists angered at the restrictive clause quickly recognized these contradictions and became determined to get women's rights demands included in the broadest possible construction of the terms "persons" and "citizens" in the first section, to use, in other words, the first section to defeat the second.

After the Fifteenth Amendment was finally ratified, the suffragists of the National Association therefore shifted from the claim that the Reconstruction amendments excluded women and began to argue instead that they were broad enough to include women's rights along with those of the freedmen. This strategic turn, the New Departure,[3] was first outlined in October 1869 by a husband and wife team of Missouri suffragists, Francis and Virginia Minor. They offered an elaborate and elegant interpretation of the Constitution to demonstrate that women already had the right to vote. Their construction rested on a consistent perspective on the whole Constitution, but especially on a broad interpretation of the Fourteenth Amendment.[4]

The Minors' first premise was that popular sovereignty preceded and underlay constitutional authority. In exchange for creating government, the people expected protection of their preeminent and natural rights. This is a familiar element of revolutionary ideology. Their second premise was to equate the power of the *federal* government with the defense of individual rights, to regard federal power as positive.[5] Historically, the federal government had been regarded as the enemy of rights; the Bill of Rights protects individual rights by enjoining the federal government from infringing on them. In the wake of the devastating experience of secession, the Fourteenth Amendment reversed the order, relying on federal power to protect its citizens against the tyrannical action of the states. The Minors thus argued in good Radical Reconstruction fashion that national citizenship had finally been established as supreme by the first section of the Fourteenth Amendment:

"the immunities and privileges of American citizenship, however defined, are national in character and paramount to all state authority."

A third element in the Minors' case was that the benefits of national citizenship were equally the rights of all. This too bore the mark of the Reconstruction Era. In the words of the amendment, "all persons born or naturalized in the United States" were equally entitled to the privileges and protections of national citizenship; there were no additional qualifications. In the battle for the rights of the black man, the rights of all had been secured. The war had expanded the rights of "proud white man" to all those who had historically been deprived of them, or so these radical reconstructionists believed.[6] In other words, the historic claim of asserting *individual* rights was becoming the modern one of realizing *equal* rights, especially for the lowly.

Finally, the Minors argued that the right to vote was one of the basic privileges and immunities of national citizenship. This was both the most controversial and the most important part of the New Departure constitutional construction. Popular sovereignty had always included an implicit theory of political power. The Minors' New Departure argument took this article of popular faith, reinterpreted it in light of Reconstruction Era egalitarianism, and gave it constitutional expression to produce a theory of universal rights to the suffrage. The New Departure case for universal suffrage brought together the Fourteenth Amendment, which nationalized citizenship and linked it to federal power, and the Fifteenth Amendment, which shifted the responsibility for the suffrage from the state to the national government.[7] This theory of the suffrage underlay much of the case for black suffrage as well, but because the drive for black suffrage was so intertwined with Republican partisan interest, it was woman suffrage, which had no such political thrust behind it, that generated the most formal constitutional expression of this Reconstruction Era faith in political equality.

Women Take the Vote

The New Departure was not simply a lawyer's exercise in constitutional exegesis. Reconstruction was an age of popular constitutionalism. Although presented in formal, constitutional terms, what the Minors had to say had much support among the rank and file of the women's rights movement. The underlying spirit of the Minors' constitutional arguments was militant and activist. The basic message was that the vote was already women's right; they merely had to take it. The New Departure took on meaning precisely because of this direct action element. Many women took the argument to heart and went to the polls, determined to vote. By 1871 hundreds of women were trying to register and vote in dozens of towns all over the country.[8] In 1871 in Philadelphia, to take one of many examples, Carrie Burnham, an unmarried tax-paying woman, got as far as having her name registered on the voting rolls. When her vote was refused, she formed the Citizens Suffrage Association of Philadelphia, dedicated not only to the defense of women's political rights but also to the greater truth that the right to vote was inherent, not bestowed. If the contrary were true, if the right to vote were a gift, this "implied a right lodged somewhere in society, which society had never acquired by any direct concession from the people." Such a theory of political power was patently tyrannical.[9]

That the first examples of women's direct action voting occurred in 1868 and 1869, before the Minors made their formal constitutional argument, suggests that the New Departure grew out of a genuinely popular political faith. In 1868 in the radical, spiritualist town of Vineland, New Jersey, almost two hundred women cast their votes into a separate ballot box and then tried to get them counted along with the men's. "The platform was crowded with earnest refined intellectual women, who feel it was good for them to be there," *The Revolution* reported. "One beautiful girl said 'I feel so much stronger for having voted.'"[10] The Vineland women repeated the effort for several years, and the ballot box eventually became an icon, which the local historical society still owns. From Vineland, the idea of women's voting spread to nearby towns, including Roseville, where, despite the American Association's official disinterest in the New Departure, Lucy Stone and her mother tried—but failed—to register their votes.

On the other side of the continent, Mary Olney Brown also decided she had the right to vote because the legislature of Washington Territory had passed an act giving "all white American citizens above the age of twenty-one years the right to vote." She wrote to other "prominent women urging them to go out and vote at the coming election . . . [but] I was looked upon as a fanatic and the idea of woman voting was regarded as an absurdity." "Many [women] wished to vote . . . ," she decided, "[but] had not the courage to go to the polls in defiance of custom." Finally, in 1869, she went to the polls with her husband, daughter, and son-in-law. Election officials threatened that she would not be "treated as a lady."

> Summoning all my strength, I walked up to the desk behind which sat the august officers of election, and presented my vote. . . . I was pompously met with the assertion, "You are not an American citizen; hence not entitled to vote." . . . I said . . . "I claim to be an American citizen, and a native-born citizen at that; and I wish to show you from the fourteenth amendment to the constitution of the United States, that women are not only citizens having the constitutional right to vote, but also that our territorial election law gives women the privilege of exercising that right." . . . I went on to show them that the . . . emancipation of the Southern slaves threw upon the country a class of people, who, like the women of the nation, owed allegiance to the government, but whose citizenship was not recognized. To settle this question, the fourteenth amendment was adopted.

Whereupon, the local election official, "with great dignity of manner and an immense display of ignorance," insisted "that the laws of congress don't extend over Washington territory" and refused her vote. When Brown was refused again, two years later, she concluded, "It amounts to this: the law gives women the right to vote in this territory, and you three men who have been appointed to receive our votes, sit here and arbitrarily refuse to take them, giving no reason why, only that you have decided not to take the women's votes. There is no law to sustain you in this usurpation of power."[11]

News of the efforts of women to register and vote spread through formal and informal means. Women's rights and mainstream journals reported on them, but information also might have been passed by word of mouth through networks of activists. Many sisters and friends, often in different states, turn up in the stories of New Departure voting women. In her account, Mary Olney Brown tells of her sister, who was inspired by her efforts to try to vote in a nearby town. Brown's sister took a different approach and was more successful. Eager to vote in a school election, she and her friends prepared a special dinner for election officials. "When the voting was resumed, the women, my sister being the first, handed in their ballots as if they had always been accustomed to voting. One lady, Mrs. Sargent, seventy-two years old, said she thanked the Lord that he had let her live until she could vote."[12]

The voting women of the 1870s often went to the polls in groups. They believed in the suffrage as an individual right but an individual right that would be achieved and experienced collectively. The most famous of these voting groups was the nearly fifty local activists, friends, and relatives who joined Susan B. Anthony in attempting to vote in Rochester, New York, in 1872. Virginia Minor herself was swept up in this collective activism. When she and some of her friends, all suffrage activists and Republican partisans, tried to register in St. Louis and were refused, she sued.

The congressional passage of the Enforcement Act in May 1870 to strengthen the Fifteenth Amendment greatly accelerated women's direct action voting. The Enforcement Act was meant to enforce the freedmen's political rights by providing recourse to the federal courts and penalties against local election officials who refused the lawful votes of citizens. Women who wanted to vote saw the act as a way to use the power of the federal government for their own benefit. Benjamin Quarles reports that freedwomen in South Carolina were encouraged by Freedmen's Bureau officials to attempt to vote by appealing to the Enforcement Act.[13] Some election officials responded to the Enforcement Act by accepting women's votes. When Nanette Gardner went to vote in Detroit in 1871, the ward official in her district was sympathetic to her protest and accepted her vote. The same man accepted Gardner's vote again in 1872, and she presented him with "a beautiful banner of white satin, trimmed with gold fringe on which was inscribed . . . 'To Peter Hill, Alderman of the Ninth Ward, Detroit. . . . By recognizing civil liberty and equality for woman, he has placed the last and brightest jewel on the brow of Michigan.'"[14]

Most local officials, however, refused to accept women's votes. While Nanette Gardner voted successfully in Detroit, her friend Catherine Stebbins (the daughter of one of the Rochester voters) was turned away in the next ward. When Mary Brown's vote was refused in Olympia, she concluded that politicians more powerful than the local committeemen had decided to resist women's direct action efforts to vote and that "money was pledged in case of prosecution." In Santa Cruz, California, when Ellen Van Valkenberg was similarly turned back at the polls, she became the first woman to sue an election official under the Enforcement Act for refusing her vote.[15] By 1871 numerous New Departure woman suffrage cases were making their way through the federal courts.

Victoria Woodhull and the New Departure

Meanwhile, the New Departure gained an advocate who moved it from the local level into national politics: Victoria Woodhull. In January of 1871 Woodhull appeared before the House Judiciary Committee to make the constitutional case for women's right to vote. No woman had ever before been invited to address a committee of the United States Congress. Her appearance was sponsored by Massachusetts Republican Benjamin Butler, who may have helped her outline her constitutional case. The deeply felt conviction about women's rights underlying her argument was undoubtedly her own, however. Her memorial asked Congress to pass legislation clarifying the right of all women to vote under the new Reconstruction amendments.[16] The major difference between Woodhull and the Minors was tactical; she urged women to turn to Congress to resolve the question, while they relied on the courts.

Like all New Departure advocates, Woodhull embraced the premise that popular sovereignty was absolute: "the sovereign power of this country is perpetual in the politically-organized people of the United States, and can neither be relinquished nor abandoned by any portion of them." Her case for woman suffrage was simple and, from a radical Reconstruction perspective, virtually unassailable: inasmuch as the first section of the Fourteenth Amendment made no reference to sex, women along with men were citizens of the United States, and foremost among the "privileges and immunities" of national citizenship was the right to vote.[17] Like the Minors, Woodhull argued that the Fourteenth Amendment established the supremacy of national over state citizenship and the obligation of the federal government to protect the rights of all citizens equally.

Woodhull also argued from the Fifteenth Amendment, which she interpreted broadly, that voting is "a Right, not a privilege of citizens of the United States."[18] She directly confronted the most obvious objection to this interpretation, that the Fifteenth Amendment specifically prohibits only disfranchisements by race, color, and previous condition. First, she argued, the amendment's wording does not bestow the right to vote but assumes it to be preexisting. Although it explicitly prohibited certain disfranchisements, Woodhull argued that it could not be read to implicitly permit others. Second, the Fifteenth Amendment forbids disfranchisement "under three distinct conditions, in all of which," Woodhull argued, "woman is distinctly embraced." In other words, "a race comprises all the people, male and female." Woodhull here seems to grasp what many modern white feminists are still struggling to understand, that counterpoising the discriminations of race and sex obscures the experience of those who suffer both, that is, black women. Finally, Woodhull argued for her broad construction of the right of suffrage on the grounds of what she called "the blending of [the Constitution's] various parts," that is, the relation between the Fourteenth Amendment, which nationalizes citizenship and links it to the power of the federal government, and the Fifteenth Amendment, which shifts the responsibility for the suffrage from the state to the national government.[19]

The first official reaction to the New Departure came in response to Woodhull's memorial. The House Judiciary Committee issued two conflicting reports on the constitutional issues she raised.[20] Here we begin to see that debate over the feminists' particular constitutional arguments was inseparable from questions of the larger meaning of the Reconstruction amendments. The Majority Report rejected Woodhull's claims. Its author was John Bingham, one of the framers of the Fourteenth Amendment. Although Bingham conceded that women enjoyed the privileges of United States citizenship along with men, he disagreed that the Fourteenth Amendment added anything new to the content of national citizenship or altered the relationship between national and state citizenship. The Minority Report, signed by William Loughridge of Iowa and Benjamin Butler of Massachusetts, supported Woodhull's memorial and the generous and radical interpretation of the amendments on which it relied. The Minority Report interpreted the Fourteenth Amendment broadly, arguing that it was intended "to secure the natural rights of citizens as well as their equal capacities before the law." The Majority Report rejected Woodhull's argument that the Fifteenth Amendment shifted responsibility for the suffrage from the state to the national level, while the Minority Report agreed that the Fifteenth Amendment "clearly recognizes the right to vote, as one of the rights of a citizen of the United States."[21] "Thus it can be seen," Woodhull observed archly, "that equally able men differ upon a simple point of Constitutional Law."[22]

The mere fact of a congressional hearing was a victory for woman suffrage leaders, and the language of constitutional principle was an im-

Victoria Woodhulll reads her argument in favor of woman's suffrage to the Judiciary Committee of the House of Representatives, January 11, 1871.

provement over the semi-sexual innuendo with which their claims were often met.[23] The favorable Minority Report meant that some of the leaders of the Republican Party supported women's rights claims on the Constitution. In 1871 two committee rooms in the Capitol were put at the disposal of the suffragists to facilitate their lobbying efforts.[24] "Could you feel the atmosphere of . . . Congress, to-day, you would not doubt what the end must be, nor that it will be very soon," Isabella Beecher Hooker wrote.[25] The National Woman Suffrage Association urged women to put pressure on their congressmen to support the Butler Report, as well as to continue trying to vote and to work through the courts.[26]

The Bradwell Case

In late 1871 . . . the first New Departure cases began to reach the dockets of the federal courts. One was the case of Sara Spencer and seventy other women from the District of Columbia, who sued election officials under the Enforcement Act for refusing to permit them to vote. The District of Columbia was a deliberate choice for testing the New Departure argument. There, as advocates of black suffrage had first realized in 1867, the power of the federal government over the suffrage was not complicated by questions of dual sovereignty and states' rights.[27]

In October Judge Cartter of the Supreme Court of the District of Columbia ruled against Spencer. Cartter conceded that the Fourteenth Amendment included women along with men in the privileges and immunities of national citizenship; however, he rejected the democratic theory of suffrage on which the case rested. To concede that voting was a right was, in his opinion, to open the door to anarchy and would "involve the destruction of civil government." "The right of all men to vote is as fully recognized in the population of our large centres and cities as can well be done," wrote Cartter. "The result . . . is political profligacy and violence verging upon anarchy."[28] The larger context of the opinion, therefore, was anxiety about democratic politics, and Cartter's concern for the proper position of women in society was secondary. This was true of the entire New Departure debate (and perhaps of judicial disposition of women's rights claims more generally); it was conducted primarily in terms of "rights," not woman's sphere. What was claimed or denied for women was claimed or denied for all citizens, especially those previously excluded from rights due them. Whether this was because the question of women's place was subsumed in a more general struggle for political democracy or because sex-prejudice was still unspeakable in constitutional terms, the consequence was the same: denying women the rights they claimed under general provisions weakened those provisions in general.

The observation that general questions of constitutional rights had overtaken the specific discourse on woman's place is even clearer in the next major New Departure decision, the *Myra Bradwell* case. *Bradwell* was the first case touching on the New Departure to reach the Supreme Court. In 1869 Myra Bradwell, a Chicago feminist and pioneering woman lawyer, was refused admission to the Illinois bar. The grounds on which the state supreme court refused her application, along with the initial brief that Bradwell submitted in response, were concerned entirely with coverture, that is, with the question of the disabilities of married women before the law. By the time Bradwell brought her case before the United States Supreme Court in October 1871, she had changed the terms radically. Her case was no longer about coverture but had been reformulated in entirely New Departure terms. Her brief argued that her right to practice law was a citizen's right and that Illinois's action in refusing her was prohibited by the Fourteenth Amendment. As for coverture, she asserted that "the great innovation of the XIV Amendment . . . sweeps away the principles of the common law," so that even reforms of married women's property rights were no longer necessary. The *Bradwell* case is one of the few concerning women's rights commonly included in the history of constitutional law, but in my opinion it is not correctly situated, since it is usually cited to illustrate judicial assumptions about woman's place rather than the constitutional issues of citizenship on which it was actually argued and decided.[29]

Bradwell's case was closely watched by suffragists as an indication of how much support to expect from the Republican Party. Bradwell was represented before the Supreme Court by Senator Matthew Carpenter, one of the major second-generation leaders of the Republican Party. While Carpenter took up Bradwell's case and argued it in strong Fourteenth Amendment terms, he prefaced his case with an equally strong argument about why the right to vote was not covered by the Reconstruction amendments. He insisted, in other words, on a distinction between civil and political rights. While the federal government protected civil rights, women's as well as men's, Carpenter argued, the suffrage remained under the control of the states, beyond the lawful interference of federal power.[30]

Suffragists were understandably confused by the way Carpenter argued Bradwell's case. Was it an indication that Republican leaders were in favor of the New Departure or against it? Stanton allowed herself to be encouraged; if women were covered along with men under the Fourteenth Amendment, wasn't the fundamental point of equal rights won?[31] Victoria Woodhull, however, saw it differently; she argued that women might be admitted to the benefits of the postwar amendments only to find those amendments so narrowed that they bestowed virtually nothing at all, certainly not political rights. She charged that Republicans, "frightened by the grandeur and the extent" of the amendments they had enacted, had retreated to the enemies' doctrine of states' rights, where their own greatest achievements would ultimately be undone.[32]

The Supreme Court held back its decision on *Bradwell* until after the election. To trace the final judicial disposition of the suffragists' constitutional arguments, we have to understand what was at stake in this election and what a Republican victory would mean. The election of 1872 was a crisis for the Republicans.[33] In June 1872 an important group of reformers split off from regular Republicans to run an independent presidential campaign. These political rebels, the Liberal Republicans, based their revolt on the old opposition between central government and individual rights. From the perspective of feminists, who were also looking for a political alternative to the regular Republicans, the terms of the bolt were particularly disappointing. Feminists had learned from freedmen to see the federal government not as a threat to their rights but as the agency for winning them.

To add insult to injury, the Liberal Republicans picked as their candidate Horace Greeley, a man who had made his opposition to woman suffrage clear many years before. Infuriated by the nomination of Greeley, many New Departure suffragists campaigned actively for Ulysses Grant in 1872.[34] The regular Republicans cultivated their support, sending them about the country on official speaking tours and inserting a timid little reference to "additional rights" for women in their platform, a plank so insignificant that suffragists called it a "splinter." Holding off a decision on *Bradwell* was consistent with this temporary friendliness. Anthony expected that if Republicans won, they would reward women with the suffrage by recognizing the New Departure claims. She was so sure that when she came home from her last speaking tour on election day, she gathered together friends and relatives and went down to her local polling place to submit her vote for Grant. Although the local Republican official accepted the votes of fifteen of the demonstrators, including Anthony,[35] a few weeks later a United States marshall came to her house and arrested her for violation of federal law—the Enforcement Act.

Anthony's arrest was a signal that the Republicans were ready to dispose of the New Departure. Because she was the most famous woman suffragist in the nation, there is good reason to suspect her arrest had been authorized at the highest level of government. The conduct of her trial several months later reinforces this suspicion. The trial was moved from her home county, where she had lectured extensively to educate potential jurors, to another venue. The judge, Ward Hunt, was no small-town jurist but a recent appointee to the United States Supreme Court. He refused to submit the case to the jury, instead directing a guilty verdict from the bench, a practice that was later found unconstitutional. Years later, Anthony's lawyer observed, "There never was a trial in the country with one half the importance of Miss Anthony's. . . . If Anthony had won her case on the merit it would have revolutionized the suffrage of the country. . . . There was a prearranged determination to convict her. A jury trial was dangerous and so the Constitution was deliberately and openly violated." Anthony was not even permitted to appeal.[36]

In general, the outcome of the election cleared the way for the Republican Party to retreat from the radical implications of the postwar amendments. There is a link between the judicial dismissal of the feminists' New Departure and the larger repudiation of the postwar amendments. It is embodied in the fact that the Supreme Court's opinions on *Bradwell* and on the *Slaughterhouse* cases were delivered on the same day in 1873. *Slaughterhouse* is generally considered the fundamental Fourteenth Amendment Supreme Court decision. The case involved a group of Louisiana butchers who challenged a state law regulating their occupation on the grounds that it violated their rights as federal citizens (to practice their vocation—the same issue as *Bradwell*) and that the Fourteenth Amendment established the supremacy of national over state citizenship.[37]

Six months after the election, the Court delivered negative opinions in both cases, interpreting the Fourteenth Amendment very narrowly and finding it inapplicable in both cases. The case that the Court lingered over was *Slaughterhouse*.[38] By a bare majority, it ruled that the amendment's intent was only to ensure "the freedom of the slave race" and that it did not transfer the jurisdiction over fundamental civil rights from state to federal government. The opinion in *Bradwell* covered much less territory but did so by a larger majority. The Court merely rejected the claim that the right to practice law was one of the privileges and immunities of federal citizenship protected by the amendment. Beyond that, the Court simply commented that "the opinion just delivered in the *Slaughterhouse* Cases . . . renders elaborate argument in the present case unnecessary."[39] We should not be misled by this preemptory dismissal, however. The very interpretation under which the *Slaughterhouse* cases had been decided, that the Fourteenth Amendment was limited to matters of race and did not elevate national over state citizenship, had first been articulated in 1871 in the Majority Report of the House Judiciary Committee, rejecting Victoria Woodhull's claim that the Fourteenth Amendment guaranteed her right to vote.

The Minor Case

The Supreme Court ruled conclusively against the New Departure two years later, in 1875. The case in which it did so was *Minor v. Happersett,* brought, appropriately enough, by Virginia Minor, the woman who had first argued that as a citizen of the United States, she was constitutionally protected in her right to vote. Like Anthony, Minor had tried to vote in the 1872 election, but when her vote was refused, she brought suit under the Enforcement Act. The Missouri courts ruled against her, and she appealed to the United States Supreme Court on the grounds that constitutional protections of the citizen's right to vote invalidated any state regulations to the contrary. The Court ruled unanimously against her. Since the *Slaughterhouse* and *Bradwell* cases had disposed of the first element of the New Departure, that the Fourteenth Amendment established the supremacy of national citizenship, the decision in *Minor* concentrated on the second assertion, that suffrage was a right of citizenship. On this, the Court ruled starkly that "the Constitution of the United States does not confer the right of suffrage upon any one."[40]

Here, too, there was an intimate link between the fate of woman suffragists' constitutional claims and that of the Reconstruction amendments in general. The day after the Court delivered its opinion in *Minor,* it heard arguments in *United States v. Cruikshank.* In this case and in the *United States v. Reese,* black men for the first time brought suit under the Enforcement Act for protection of their political rights under the Fourteenth and Fifteenth Amendments, and the Court ruled against them. In the process of ruling against the plaintiffs, the Court found the Enforcement Act, under which both feminists and freedmen had sought protection, unconstitutional. Citing the recent decision in *Minor,* the Court ruled that inasmuch as the Constitution did not bestow the suffrage on anyone, the federal courts were outside their jurisdiction in protecting the freedmen's political rights.

The rejection of woman suffrage arguments on the grounds that the Fifteenth Amendment was only intended to forbid disfranchisement by race paved the way for a reading of the Fifteenth Amendment that was so narrow it did not even protect the freedmen themselves. In its decision in *United States v. Reese,* the Court argued that the plaintiff, although a black man, had not proved that his vote was denied on the grounds of race and so was not covered by constitutional protections. Eventually, of course, the freedmen were effectively disfranchised on grounds of income, residence, and education, all surrogates for race. Anthony had anticipated this connection. At her own trial, she predicted that the general narrowing of the Reconstruction amendments would follow on the heels of the repudiation of women's claims of equal rights under them. "If we once establish the false principle, that United States citizenship does not carry with it the right to vote in every state in this Union," she said, "there is no end to the petty freaks and cunning devices that will be resorted to exclude one and another class of citizens from the right of suffrage."[41]

Three years after the *Minor* defeat, suffragists began their pursuit of a separate constitutional amendment to prohibit disfranchisement on account of sex. At many levels, this was a less radical strategy. With the defeat of the New Departure, winning the vote for women was no longer tied to an overall democratic interpretation of the Constitution. To the degree that the struggle for women's votes was not strategically linked to the general defense of political democracy, that its goal was "woman suffrage" not "universal suffrage," elitist and racist tendencies faced fewer barriers, had freer reign, and imparted a more conservative character to suffragism over the next half-century.

Yet, despite this very important strategic shift, the New Departure period left a deep mark on the history of feminism. From time to time, some suffragist would see possibilities in the existing propositions of the Constitution and propose some clever legal mechanism for exploiting them.[42] Even direct action voting never completely died away. Twenty years after the *Minor* decision, Elizabeth Grannis of New York City made her eighth attempt to register to vote.[43] Certainly the larger spirit of militant direct action resurfaced in a spectacular way in the last decade of the American suffrage movement. The deepest mark of the New Departure, however, was to make women's rights and political equality indelibly constitutional issues. As Susan B. Anthony wrote, she "had learned . . . through the passage of the Fourteenth and Fifteenth amendments that it had been possible to amend [the Constitution] in such a way as to enfranchise an entire new class of voters."[44] The *Minor* case, the historian Norma Basch has observed, "drew the inferiority of women's status out of the grooves of common law assumptions and state provisions and thrust it into the maelstrom of constitutional conflict. The demand for woman suffrage . . . acquired a contentious national life."[45]

Notes

1. Ellen Carol DuBois, *Feminism and Suffrage: The Emergence of an Independent Women's Movement in America, 1848-1869,* (Ithaca, N.Y., 1978); Elizabeth Cady Stanton, *Eighty Years and More: Reminiscences, 1815-1897,* ed. Ellen Carol DuBois (1898; Boston, 1993), 242.
2. Stanton, *Eighty Years and More,* 242.
3. Elizabeth Cady Stanton, Susan B. Anthony, and Matilda J. Gage, eds., *History of Woman Suffrage,* Vol. 2 (Rochester, N.Y., 1881), 407-520; Ida Husted Harper, ed., *Life and Work of Susan B. Anthony,* (Indianapolis, 1899), 1: 409-48.
4. *HWS* 2: 407-10; on the Minors, see Louise R. Noun, *Strong Minded Women: The Emergence of the Woman Suffrage Movement in Iowa* (Ames, 1986), 168-69.
5. David Montgomery notes the importance of this Reconstruction Era shift in attitude to the positive state in *Beyond Equality: Labor and the Radical Republicans* (New York, 1967), 80-81.
6. On this aspect of Reconstruction Era constitutional thought, see Judith A. Baer, *Equality Under the Constitution: Reclaiming the Fourteenth Amendment* (Ithaca, N.Y., 1983).
7. While the Fifteenth Amendment was still pending, the Minors found an alternative constitutional basis for their claim that suffrage was a natural right in the frequently cited 1820 case *Corfield v. Coryell,* which included the franchise as one of the privileges and immunities protected in Article 4.
8. In New Hampshire in 1870, Matilda Ricker tried to vote (*HWS* 2: 586-87). In New York in 1871, Matilda

Joslyn Cage tried to vote in Fayetteville, and a group of women, led by Louise Mansfield, tried to vote in Nyack (Elizabeth Cady Stanton, Susan B. Anthony, and Matilda Joslyn Gage, eds., *History of Woman Suffrage,* [Rochester, N.Y., 1887], 3: 406; Isabelle K. Savelle, *Ladies' Lib: How Rockland Women Got the Vote* (New York, 1979), 13-16; in New York City, Victoria Woodhull and Tennessee Claflin tried to vote (Johanna Johnston, *Mrs. Satan* [New York, 1967], 110).

9. *HWS* 3: 461-62, and *HWS* 2: 600-601.

10. Eleanor Flexner, *Century of Struggle: The Women's Rights Movement in the United States* (Cambridge, Mass., 1959), 168, citing *The Revolution,* November 19, 1868, 307.

11. *HWS* 3: 780-86.

12. Ibid., 784.

13. Benjamin Quarles, "Frederick Douglass and the Woman's Rights Movement," *Journal of Negro History* 25 (June 1940): 35.

14. *HWS* 3: 523-24.

15. Ibid., 766.

16. Ibid., 2: 443-48.

17. Ibid., 445.

18. Victoria C. Woodhull, *Constitutional Equality: A Lecture Delivered at Lincoln Hall, Washington, D.C., February 16, 1871* (New York, 1871).

19. *HWS* 2: 445-46. The comment on "blending" was made in Woodhull's arguments in support of her congressional memorial. These are available in Victoria Woodhull, *The Argument for Woman's Electoral Rights under Amendment XIV and XV of the Constitution of the United States* (London, 1887), 44.

20. Both reports can be found in *HWS* 2: 461-82.

21. Ibid., 469, 478. In support of their interpretation, they cited the federal district court's decision in what was called the *Crescent City* case, later renamed the *Slaughterhouse* cases.

22. Woodhull, *Constitutional Equality,* 4.

23. Martha Wright complained to Elizabeth Stanton about a congressman who "said rudely to Mrs. Davis & Mrs. Griffing, 'You just call on us because you like to,'" to which Mrs. Griffing answered "'We call on you, because it is the only way known to us, to present our appeal to you,' & Mrs. Davis said 'You must remember that we are your constituents.'" Wright to Stanton, December 29, 1870, Garrison Family Collection, Smith College, Northampton, Mass.

24. *HWS* 2: 489.

25. Isabella Beecher Hooker to the Editor, *Independent,* February 11, 1871, reprinted in *Woodhull and Claflin's Weekly,* March 4, 1871, 10.

26. Ibid.; *An Appeal to the Women of the United States by the National Woman Suffrage and Educational Committee* (Hartford, Conn., April 19, 1871).

27. *HWS* 2: 587-99.

28. Ibid., 598.

29. Ibid., 622. The opinion in Bradwell that is usually cited is not the terse dismissal of the Fourteenth Amendment argument that settled the case, but an individual concurring opinion by Justice Bradley that addressed the coverture issues that Bradwell had removed from her argument.

30. *HWS* 2: 618.

31. Elizabeth Cady Stanton, "Argument before the Senate Judiciary Committee," January 11, 1872, reprinted in *Woodhull and Claflin's Weekly,* January 27, 1872, 7; see also Stanton to Woodhull, December 29, [1872], Stanton Miscellaneous Papers, New York Public Library, New York.

32. Victoria Woodhull, *Carpenter and Cartter Reviewed: A Speech before the National Suffrage Association at Lincoln Hall, Washington, D.C., January 10, 1872* (New York, 1872), 20.

33. Montgomery, *Beyond Equality,* 379-86.

34. Anthony to Stanton, July 10, 1872, box 38, NAWSA Papers, Library of Congress.

35. Nancy A. Hewitt, *Women's Activism and Social Change: Rochester, New York, 1822-1872* (Ithaca, N.Y., 1984), 211. Anthony to Stanton, November 5, 1872, Harper Papers, Huntington Library, San Marino, California.

36. Harper, ed., *The Life and Work of Susan B. Anthony,* 1: 423-53; Charles Fairman, *History of the Supreme Court,* (New York, 1987), 7: 224.

37. Fairman, *History of the Supreme Court,* 285. Carpenter's argument in *Slaughterhouse* can be found in 21 Court Reporters Lawyers Edition, 399-401 (1872).

38. 16 Wall. 36 (1873).

39. 16 Wall. 130 (1873).

40. *HWS* 2: 734-42.

41. Ibid., 641.

42. The most important of these was Catherine McCullough's successful argument that the Constitution permitted states legislatively to enfranchise voters for presidential electors. In 1914 Illinois passed a "presidential suffrage" law, giving women votes in the 1916 presidential election. See Steven W. Buechler, *The Transformation of the Woman Suffrage Movement: The Case of Illinois, 1850-1920* (New Brunswick, N.J., 1986), 174-76.

43. Unidentified clipping, v. 12, 75, Susan B. Anthony Memorial Library Collection, Huntington Library, San Marino, Calif.

44. Susan B. Anthony and Ida Husted Harper, eds., *History of Woman Suffrage,* (Rochester, N.Y., 1902), 4: 10.

45. Norma Basch, "Reconstructing Female Citizenship" (Paper delivered at Women and the Constitution Conference, American University and the Smithsonian, October 1987).

HARRIET SIGERMAN (ESSAY DATE 2000)

SOURCE: Sigerman, Harriet. "Laborers for Liberty: 1865-1890." In *No Small Courage: A History of Women in the United States,* edited by Nancy F. Cott, pp. 303-10. Oxford, England: Oxford University Press, 2000.

In the following excerpt, Sigerman discusses the setbacks and conflicts that plagued the suffrage movement follow-

ing the Civil War and describes how the western states and territories proved most progressive in granting women the right to vote.

After the Civil War ended, American women had battles to wage on other fronts—for the right to vote, to attend college, and to gain greater control over their lives. As Ernestine Rose, a leader in the women's rights movement, once proclaimed, "Freedom, my friends, does not come from the clouds, like a meteor. . . . It does not come without great efforts and great sacrifices; all who love liberty have to labor for it." In the afterglow of victory for the Union and peace for the entire nation, she and other champions of women's rights forged ahead, ready to labor for their freedom. From their battles emerged many new ideas for achieving social and political equality for women.

During the war, leaders of the women's rights movement, such as Elizabeth Cady Stanton and Susan B. Anthony, had shifted their efforts from fighting for women's political and economic rights to campaigning for the abolition of slavery. Now that slavery had been abolished, they confidently expected fellow abolitionists to work for women's right to vote. But they would be sadly disillusioned—a long, hard struggle for woman suffrage lay ahead. Their disillusionment was even more keen because the origins of the postwar women's rights movement lay in the prewar abolition movement, and the two movements had been closely linked for thirty years.

After the Civil War, leaders of the women's rights movement looked to a new source for inspiration: the United States Constitution. They adopted the very same rationale for female suffrage used by proponents of suffrage for African Americans—that the right to vote was the individual's right as a citizen and provided the foundation for democratic government, which the North had just fought to protect in the Civil War. In the immediate post-Civil War years, women's rights leaders maintained that voting was a basic right shared by all citizens, men and women, white and black. Ernestine Rose declared, "Human beings are men and women, possessed of human faculties, and understanding, which we call mind; and mind recognizes no sex, therefore the term 'male,' as applied to human beings—to citizens—ought to be expunged from the Constitution and laws as a last remnant of barbarism."

To achieve this goal, Stanton, Anthony, Antoinette Brown Blackwell, Lucy Stone, and other suffrage fighters established the American Equal Rights Association in 1865 to campaign for both

ON THE SUBJECT OF...

SARAH MOORE GRIMKÉ (1792-1873) AND ANGELINA EMILY GRIMKÉ (1805-1879)

Sarah Moore and Angelina Emily Grimké were the daughters of wealthy, South Carolina plantation and slave owners. In the early 1820s, Sarah moved to Philadelphia and joined the Quaker Society of Friends. Angelina followed her in 1829. Both women devoted their lives first to the antislavery crusade and then to women's rights when they found that their gender hampered their pursuit of reformist goals. Abolitionist William Lloyd Garrison published an antislavery letter by Angelina in *The Liberator* in 1835, the same year Angelina joined the Philadelphia Female Anti-Slavery Society. The sisters left the Society of Friends and moved to New York, where they joined the Anti-Slavery Society, and Angelina wrote the popular pamphlet *An Appeal to the Christian Women of the South* (1836).

The sisters began speaking to small groups of women, urging them to influence their husbands, fathers, and brothers to vote against slavery, and further encouraging any women who owned slaves to free them and pay them wages for their labor. Sarah produced *Address to Free Colored Americans* and Angelina wrote *Appeal to the Women of the Nominally Free States* (1837). Angelina married fellow abolitionist Theodore Weld in 1838. Sarah moved with the couple to New Jersey, where all three continued to be active in the antislavery movement, operated a school, and published works on women's rights. Several major figures in the women's rights movement, including Elizabeth Cady Stanton, Lucy Stone, and Susan B. Anthony, acknowledged their debt to the Grimké sisters. Late in life, the sisters learned that their brother Henry had fathered three sons with one of the family's slaves. The sisters embraced the young men as their nephews, and supported their educational endeavors. One of their nephews, Archibald Grimké, was the father of well-known Harlem Renaissance poet, Angelina Weld Grimké (1880-1958).

Lucretia Coffin Mott (bottom, second from right) and members of the Pennsylvania Abolition Society.

black and female suffrage. Lucretia Mott was elected president, Stanton served as first vice president, and Anthony became corresponding secretary. The creation of this organization was a milestone in the struggle for female equality; it was the first organization formed by American women and men to fight for the right to vote.

Divisions soon emerged within the American Equal Rights Association over the best way to achieve suffrage for all Americans. Some members were willing to support the Republican party's strategy of working first to enfranchise black men—that is, grant them the right to vote—while postponing efforts to enfranchise women until they had achieved their first goal. In contrast, other members continued to support efforts to enfranchise both African-American men and all women. The first major conflict between proponents of black male suffrage and proponents of suffrage for all Americans erupted in 1867 in Kansas. There, two proposals—one that granted female suffrage and one that provided for black male suffrage—came to a vote. Stanton and Anthony campaigned for both, but two of their political partners—Lucy Stone and Henry Blackwell, prominent activists in the prewar abolition movement—supported Republican abolitionists whose first priority was black male suffrage.

Stanton and Anthony were astonished that their fellow reformers would abandon the fight for female suffrage. For their part, Stone and Blackwell were unwilling to divert popular support for black male suffrage. They feared that supporting female enfranchisement would undermine any public support for black male suffrage. As it turned out, both proposals were defeated.

The fight for suffrage for all Americans suffered another blow with the ratification of the 14th Amendment to the Constitution on July 9, 1868. This amendment shattered the common basis of female and black suffrage—natural rights—by affirming black men's status and rights as American citizens while remaining silent about the citizenship rights of women. It did this by introducing into the Constitution the distinction of gender and penalizing states for denying to any of their "male inhabitants" the right to vote. It was the "Negro's hour," insisted former abolitionists—the freedman needed the ballot to protect him from physical harm and political injustice. When women were "dragged from their houses and hung upon lamp-posts" like black men, declared the great orator and former slave Frederick Douglass, then they, too, would need the ballot's protection as much as black men did.

On February 3, 1870, nearly three years after the 14th Amendment was passed, the 15th Amendment was ratified, making women's political invisibility complete. It prohibited states from denying to citizens the right to vote "on account of race, color, or previous condition of servitude" but remained silent about gender prohibitions. In effect, both the 14th and 15th Amendments excluded women from the fundamental right of citizenship—voting.

But the growing division within the women's rights movement and the blow dealt to woman suffrage by the 14th and 15th Amendments did not discourage African-American women from supporting female equality. Sojourner Truth pointedly reminded audiences of black women's need for equal political rights. She claimed that slavery had been only partly abolished because black women did not share the same rights as black men. But she wanted slavery destroyed "root and branch. Then we will all be free indeed."

Other prominent African-American women shared Truth's views. Mary Ann Shadd Cary, a teacher and one of the first women lawyers in the United States, joined the Universal Franchise Association, a suffrage organization composed of both black and white members in Washington, D.C., and represented it at conventions of African-American organizations. Along with other members of the Universal Franchise Association, she addressed the House Judiciary Committee of the U.S. Congress on behalf of woman suffrage. She also helped to organize the Colored Woman's Progressive Franchise Association, a group that set out to challenge the assumption that "men only may conduct industrial and other things." The association hoped to establish newspapers, banks, cooperative stores, and a printing press, all owned and operated by women.

Frances Ellen Watkins Harper was also an outspoken supporter of women's rights. In the following excerpt from her poem "Dialogue on Woman's Rights," she explained why black men should support woman suffrage:

> Some thought that it would never do
> For us in Southern lands,
> To change the fetters on our wrists
> For the ballot in our hands.
> Now if you don't believe 'twas right
> To crowd us from the track
> How can you push your wife aside
> And try to hold her back?

By the late 1860s, Elizabeth Cady Stanton had adopted a new strategy in fighting for female suffrage. Like Sojourner Truth, she no longer emphasized women's common humanity with men and therefore women's common right to suffrage. Instead, she drew on the decades-old arguments that celebrated women's unique intellectual, emotional, and moral qualities to argue that women were *different* from men, and for that reason they were particularly worthy and needful of having the right to vote. In an address to a women's rights convention, she proclaimed, "There is sex in the spiritual as well as the physical and what we need today in government, in the world of morals and thought, is the recognition of the feminine element, as it is this alone that can hold the masculine in check."

Throughout American history, this celebration of women's unique qualities has helped to expand women's influence beyond the home and into the community. Although women were prohibited from voting, serving as legislators, and fighting for the defense of liberty because of their sex, they were obligated to raise liberty-loving sons who dutifully discharged these tasks of citizenship.

In the antebellum years of the 1830s, women had used the same argument to create more visible roles for themselves: As pious, virtuous, and kindly maternal figures, they were obligated not only to raise patriotic sons but to devote themselves to the public good—to extend a helping hand to widows, orphans, "fallen women," and others in need of their excellent influence. Middle-class women had organized or joined charitable societies to spread the moral standards of the home throughout the community. Now, in the post-Civil War era, Stanton and others once again elevated women's "feminine element" into a virtue that would protect the nation's moral life.

Stanton claimed that voting was both a basic right and the most effective way for women to exert their moral influence. In 1868 she and Susan B. Anthony established their own newspaper, the *Revolution,* to promote their campaign for women's rights. In a letter to Anthony, Stanton explained the significance of the newspaper's name and offered her vision of the struggle ahead: "The establishing of woman on her rightful throne is the greatest revolution the world has ever known or will know," she declared. "A journal called the *Rosebud* might answer for those who come with kid gloves and perfumes to lay immortal wreaths on the monuments which in sweat and tears others have hewn and built; but for us . . . there is no name like the *Revolution.*" The motto on the *Revolution*'s masthead read: "Men, their rights and nothing more; women, their rights and nothing less." Anthony managed the office, handled the bookkeeping and bills, and hired the typesetters and printers, while Stanton served as senior editor and primary writer.

Although it lasted for only two and a half years, the weekly newspaper became a mouthpiece for some of the most prominent, creative, and uncompromising members of the women's rights movement. Matilda Joslyn Gage, Paulina Wright Davis, and Ernestine Rose—all highly dedicated and visionary leaders for women's rights—were regular correspondents. More important, the paper, under Stanton's direction, dealt with controversial issues that other papers and forums only touched upon gingerly. Abortion, regulation of prostitution, divorce, and prison reform—all were discussed openly in the *Revolution*'s pages as reasons why women needed political power.

Nor did the paper shrink from condemning the "degrading" legal position of married women and disputing the traditional view of marriage as sacred and indissoluble. Stanton advocated more liberal divorce laws and better legal protection for married women and concluded that giving women the vote would help to rectify married women's legal inequities. The *Revolution* steadily focused the women's rights movement on the need for female suffrage, especially at a time when other reformers supported suffrage only for black men. The newspaper also linked female suffrage to dramatic and controversial reforms for women—reforms that more conservative factions of the movement were unwilling to champion.

The *Revolution* broke other new ground by reaching out to working-class women, whom the women's rights movement had previously ignored. Anthony, in particular, set out to capture working-class women's support. In September 1868, she helped to organize the Working Woman's Association "for the purpose of doing everything possible to elevate women, and raise the value of their labor." The *Revolution* reported on all proceedings of the Working Woman's Association, and Stanton and Anthony established a column entitled "The Working Woman" to highlight issues and events of concern to working-class women. They did not shy away from advocating policies that were highly unpopular, including equal pay for equal work and access to jobs traditionally reserved for men—goals that today's working women are still struggling to achieve.

Meanwhile, the conflict between those who supported women's immediate enfranchisement and those who chose to work for black male suffrage first and woman suffrage later on turned into a bitter schism. By 1869 two organizations had emerged with differing visions and strategies. In May 1869 Stanton and Anthony founded the National Woman Suffrage Association (NWSA). This group refused to support the 15th Amendment—the amendment granting black male suffrage—unless it also enfranchised all women. NWSA members lobbied on a national level for a constitutional amendment to enfranchise women in all states.

In contrast, the American Woman Suffrage Association (AWSA), which was founded by Lucy Stone and Henry Blackwell in November 1869, supported passage of the 15th Amendment. Rather than seek a constitutional amendment to give women the ballot, members of AWSA appealed to individual state legislatures to pass state laws granting female enfranchisement. Members of AWSA published their views in their own newspaper, the *Woman's Journal*. Like its parent organization, the *Woman's Journal* spoke to a more conservative and narrow vision of women's rights. It tried to cultivate the support of conservative middle-class readers by linking suffrage to middle-class benefits, such as higher education for women, professional advancement, and protection of married women's earnings and property from their husbands.

The *Woman's Journal* also avoided discussion of controversial issues, such as abortion and prostitution. It took a chattier, more compromising tone than the *Revolution* and focused strictly on suffrage news—debates, speeches, conventions, and political platforms favoring suffrage. Despite financial reverses and frequent staff changes, the *Woman's Journal* outlasted its rival, the *Revolution,* and eventually became the main organ of the women's rights movement. Lucy Stone was its chief editor, and former abolitionists William Lloyd Garrison, Henry Blackwell, T. H. Higginson, and Julia Ward Howe served as assistant editors.

For twenty years, NWSA and AWSA pursued their separate goals, holding conventions, sponsoring debates, and sending speakers out on the lecture circuit. In 1887 Alice Stone Blackwell, daughter of Lucy Stone and Henry Blackwell, launched a campaign to merge the two organizations. Three years later, in February 1890, the two associations joined hands to become the National American Woman Suffrage Association (NAWSA). Elizabeth Cady Stanton served as the first president of NAWSA until 1892, when she withdrew from active involvement in organized suffrage efforts. When Stanton died in 1902, the women's rights movement lost one of its most original and uncompromising voices. Anthony followed her into the presidency of the National American Woman Suffrage Association and remained at its helm until 1904. She died two years later. Although she was more cautious than Stanton in her thinking, Anthony was a courageous and tireless fighter for female equality.

American women had not yet received the constitutional right to vote, but in the two decades between the founding of the National Woman Suffrage Association and the American Woman Suffrage Association in 1869 and their merger into the National American Woman Suffrage Association in 1890, the cause of female suffrage achieved important successes, especially in the West. The first victory for woman suffrage in the United States occurred in the Wyoming Territory, a sparsely settled region with few political traditions in place. The conditions of this region—the absence of long-standing political traditions and greater frontier opportunities for women—proved fertile ground for voting rights for women. In 1870 the tiny legislature in Wyoming passed a female enfranchisement bill, and the governor, John A. Campbell, who some years earlier had watched women conduct a women's rights convention in Salem, Oregon, signed it.

The neighboring territory of Utah followed suit in 1870. Most of Utah's settlers were Mormon. Although women held no important positions in the church hierarchy, they played an active role in community and church life. Church leaders encouraged women to serve as nurses and midwives, and some women even went to medical school. Mormon women also attended church meetings and voted on church matters, taught the younger children in their settlements, raised money for the church, and educated themselves about government, history, and parliamentary law. The Mormon community's acceptance of women's public responsibilities no doubt contributed to winning female suffrage in Utah.

In the Northwest—the region now comprising Oregon and Washington—Abigail Scott Duniway, a brave and feisty woman, led the fight for woman suffrage. In 1852, at the age of seventeen, she journeyed with her family by wagon train to the Oregon Territory. There she married and raised five children and discovered firsthand what it meant to toil long hours for no wages. She also discovered that even though wives had no legal rights, a wife was responsible for any financial obligations undertaken by her husband. When Duniway's husband became disabled in an accident, she was forced to pay his debts.

By the age of thirty-six, Duniway was ready to dedicate her life to woman suffrage. She established her own newspaper, the *New Northwest,* to convey her ideas and provide a forum for suffrage events out West. She also wrote and published vivid accounts of her travels throughout the Northwest. Duniway crisscrossed the region to give speeches and help organize suffrage events.

Duniway also clashed with East Coast suffrage leaders. She staunchly rejected their strategy of portraying women as morally superior to men in order to win public approval for female suffrage. She argued that this strategy perpetuated women's unequal political and economic status by sentimentalizing them. Instead, she urged, suffrage was the way to end the sexual and economic exploitation of women and give women a measure of control over their lives. Like Stanton, Abigail Scott Duniway was a clear-eyed, tough-minded, and dedicated suffrage leader whose unorthodox views did not always sit well with her more conservative suffrage sisters.

Southerners were even more resistant to women's rights. Because many early suffrage advocates had also been abolitionists, some Southerners regarded the movement as "a heresy that has a real devil in it," according to one suffrage worker traveling in Mississippi. Still, there were pockets of support for female suffrage throughout the South. Some Southern women joined the American Equal Rights Association, and in 1869 suffrage resolutions were offered at constitutional conventions in Texas and Arkansas, two former Confederate states applying for readmission into the Union. Although the resolutions did not pass, suffrage leaders were heartened that they had at least been introduced.

SUFFRAGE: ISSUES AND INDIVIDUALS

SUZANNE M. MARILLEY (ESSAY DATE 1996)

SOURCE: Marilley, Suzanne M. "Airs of Respectability: Racism and Nativism in the Woman Suffrage Movement." In *Woman Suffrage and the Origins of Liberal Feminism in the United States, 1820-1920,* pp. 159-86. Cambridge, Mass.: Harvard University Press, 1996.

In the following excerpt, Marilley describes how suffragists shed their radical image between 1885 and 1900, using a variety of practical strategies, many of them play-

ing on nativist and racist sympathies in order to build greater support for the right of women to vote.

Between 1885 and 1900 the American woman suffrage movement changed from the radical cause of former Garrisonians into a quest for citizenship by diverse groups of women. Although elite white leaders succumbed to racist and nativist sentiments, such sentiments never fully eclipsed their egalitarian aims. Muted egalitarian themes emerged because (1) suffragists were ambivalent about their racism and nativism, (2) feminisms of personal development cropped up that encouraged white elites to exploit their privileged education and wealth but also stimulated positive self-conceptions among oppressed black and working-class women, (3) victims of the reformers' racism and nativism informed elite leaders that such views were hypocritical and unjust, and (4) those who opposed votes for women continued to portray the measure as radically egalitarian.

In the United States during the late nineteenth century, "intellectually respectable" social Darwinism and racialist theories overshadowed egalitarianism. As many scholars have observed, these inegalitarian theories oriented suffragists toward portraying their cause as traditional.[1] The quiet alliances fashioned by Anthony, Stone, and Blackwell with Willard and the WCTU [Women's Christian Temperance Union]; the merger of the radical NWSA [National Woman Suffrage Association] with the conservative AWSA [American Woman Suffrage Association]; the adoption of nonpartisanship; the treatment of votes for women as a single issue; the assertion that women's moral superiority entitled them to the vote; and numerous appeals to nativist and racist sentiments obscured the egalitarian nature and potential of woman suffrage.[2] At the same time, radical themes in Willard's feminism of fear suggest that by 1890 a number of "respectable" women had decided to buck tradition. Egalitarian-minded suffragists faced a dilemma: how, if at all, should white women—many of whom were southern, from Christian evangelical denominations, and ambivalent about equality—be incorporated as suffragists?

The turn toward toleration and away from a primary allegiance to equality for women was a change that Anthony struggled for, even against Stanton. In the mid-1880s, Stanton urged Anthony to avoid making the movement more respectable lest it disintegrate the movement's commitment to overthrow male domination in the home, church, workplace, and government.[3] Anthony disagreed, arguing that the traditional women Willard mobilized should be welcomed and would help in the pursuit of a federal constitutional amendment.

To address Stanton's worries about losing commitment to equality, Anthony urged that the movement become open to all potential members. Anthony correctly anticipated that refusing to accept members who were southern, Christian, temperance reformers, Catholic, atheist, or agnostic would have been foolhardy. Stanton eventually conceded, but without entirely relinquishing her egalitarianism.[4] Putting toleration first encouraged "respectable" prosuffrage women from the WCTU or women's clubs to join. Courting these "respectable" members led suffragists to use nativist and racist themes that denounced the easy political inclusion of new male immigrants, supported educational qualifications for the vote, and defended southern white supremacy. In short, the decision to welcome respectable white women was accompanied by disdain for growing numbers of black and working-class suffragists.

The new generation of leaders also fostered the "feminism of personal development" that had emerged during Reconstruction. Young leaders defined the vote less as a symbol of political equality and more as a political benefit for each woman to exercise as she pleased. Judith Shklar accurately depicts this major change:

> Social Darwinism, health and hygiene-oriented reform, and the Social Gospel were notably undemocratic paths to progress, and the women's movement became a part of this intellectual mainstream. Liberalism had also altered, moving from civic freedom to a concern for self-development and the nurture of the individual personality. For women interested in the suffrage, voting increasingly was just one step toward the fulfillment of these immensely personal ends.[5]

Although some scholars might dispute Shklar's depiction of "health and hygiene-oriented reform, and the Social Gospel" as "notably *undemocratic* paths to progress," her portrayal of the aims of late-nineteenth and early twentieth century suffragists as highly personalized captures their distinctive emphases. As progressive reformers, the mostly native-born Protestants decided that their Anglo-Saxon ancestry and education provided the best qualifications for political inclusion. Following the lead of powerful men, they became less tolerant of the lack of preparedness for political participation by immigrants and newly freed blacks.

Despite cold responses from white leaders, currents of support for suffrage strengthened among black and working women who cultivated egalitarian principles and kept sight of possibilities for radical change. As second-generation white reform leaders showed "respect" for personal choice and varied aims by their nativistic appeals and willingness to include southern white supremacist suffragists in their organization, black women pointed out the contradictions in such policies and called for a more integrated movement. Black female reformers such as Ida B. Wells, Anna Julia Cooper, and Mary Church Terrell kept egalitarian principles alive in their speeches by occasionally embarrassing white leaders with requests for inclusion and by defying their efforts to segregate members.[6] Black suffragists refused to bow to white supremacist attitudes; instead, they envisioned how they would use the vote to foster personal development for blacks. The strides black women made while white women united across region and class were truly exceptional acts of courage.[7]

From the late 1880s until the ratification of the Nineteenth Amendment, suffragists made many racist and nativist arguments for the vote. Adopting Henry Blackwell's "statistical argument," they promised that women's votes would reduce the influence of the black male voters in the South. In an 1867 letter entitled "What the South Can Do," Blackwell proposed that the southern legislatures make reunification possible by accepting the Reconstruction amendments on their face, but then moving immediately to enfranchise women in order to ensure white supremacy. In the early 1890s, native-born white male legislators in Arkansas and Mississippi introduced the idea that the votes of educated, property-holding women could buttress the exclusive system of white supremacy.[8] Although the legislatures in these states rejected votes for women, suffragists often invoked white supremacy and Blackwell's strategy to recruit support in the South. The leading southern white suffragists "believed that in their time white political supremacy was a necessity."[9]

While campaigning in the Midwest and Plains states, Carrie Chapman Catt established common ground with her audiences through nativist remarks about Native American Indians and immigrants. Elizabeth Cady Stanton metamorphosed from the most consistent and daring of liberal thinkers into an outraged Americanist decrying the rights of men she considered less educated, less prepared to think through political problems, and less qualified to assure responsible government than she.[10] In 1909 the WCTU "passed a resolution that the right to vote should be based upon intelligence, not upon sex."[11] Eschewing equality as moral reason for enfranchisement, they concentrated instead on promoting their own reference group's standards as evidence both for their inclusion and for the establishment of these standards for all Americans.

Henry Brown Blackwell's Statistical Argument

Woman suffragists assumed that blacks and most new immigrants were inferior. They also aimed to secure the domination of native-born, white, Protestant ideas and habits in American culture. It would be wrong, however, to consider the reformers' racism and nativism as thematically unambiguous. Their speeches and open letters display both strong convictions and an uncomfortable ambivalence about what they were saying. Instead of bald racism and nativism, these tracts usually show a complex set of conflicting ideas and dispositions, especially over the meaning of racial and ethnic inferiority. As they appealed to racist and nativist views, suffragists often added that not all blacks and immigrants were either inherently inferior or likely to remain unqualified if the state supplied them with adequate education.

In "What the South Can Do," Blackwell used rhetoric to distance his own more egalitarian views from those he proposed. In his letter, Blackwell assessed the "southern problem" *as if* he were making decisions as a southern legislator: "Consider the result from the Southern standpoint. *Your* 4,000,000 of Southern white women will counter balance *your* 4,000,000 of Negro men and women, thus the political supremacy of *your* white race will remain unchanged."[12]

Blackwell's separation of his views from his conception of how southern legislators would think suggests that he may have concocted this argument as much to put woman suffrage on the political agenda as to promote black disenfranchisement. As Marjorie Spruill Wheeler points out, Blackwell did not think about the distribution of the black population in the South. He overlooked the fact that in the black belts there were more blacks than whites; this strategy would never have made black men a minority in these districts.[13]

That Blackwell, a participant in Garrisonian abolitionism, could have written this letter reveals how desires for rapid reunification fed a growing racism. Early in the letter, Blackwell warned white southerners that the "problem of the negro" caused the anguish of war, and he encouraged them to see that they could no longer fight the North: "Wise men try to see things as they are, uncolored by opinion or preference. The interest of both North and South, since they must live together, is peace, harmony, and real fraternity. No adjustment can fully succeed unless it is acceptable to both sections. Therefore the statesman and patriot must find a common ground as a basis of permanent reconciliation."[14] His invocation of "peace, harmony, and real fraternity" suggests that Blackwell so wanted to promote nonviolent reconstruction that he adopted a racist argument. At the time, the southern white founders of the Ku Klux Klan and Knights of the White Camellia had initiated the terror against the freedmen that played a central role in the creation of southern white supremacy.[15]

Blackwell thought he had discovered a way to persuade the southern legislatures to accept the principle of political inclusion for both newly free African Americans and women. If southerners perceived the Reconstruction amendments as principles only—principles that actual patterns of political participation would prevent from leading to the political domination of blacks over whites—then they would be willing to abolish the legalized exclusion of ascriptive groups. He thus painted a vision that would insulate white control: "If you are to share the future government of your States with a race you deem naturally and hopelessly inferior, avert the social chaos, which seems to you so imminent, by utilizing the intelligence and patriotism of the wives and daughters of the South." He even encouraged the South to lead on the question of inclusion so that "the negro question would be forever removed from the political arena." According to Blackwell, full political inclusion would restore the agenda to issues of interest to all citizens; sectional conflict would diminish; and the civic bonds of the nation would be restored. "Capital and population would flow, like the Mississippi, toward the Gulf. The black race would gravitate by the law of nature toward the tropics."[16]

Blackwell's strategy backfired: southern legislatures designed elaborate means to disenfranchise all black and many poor white men. But by the mid-1880s he had hardly modified his appeal in urging southern suffragists to seek the vote for educated women. His rationale, however misguided, appealed to them, perhaps because elite southern women tended to oppose outright political exclusion and extreme violence against blacks, such as lynching.[17] In any case, by the early 1890s white southern woman suffragists were exploring whether white supremacy would be gender inclusive.

After the emergence of, first, a southern suffrage movement whose leaders advocated the enfranchisement of only white women, and second, criticism of "lily-white" suffragists by black intellectuals, Blackwell clarified his principles. Although he admitted supporting an educational suffrage, he emphatically opposed restrictions based on ascriptive characteristics. In December 1904, Blackwell applauded the news that the New Orleans *Times-Democrat* would endorse the proposal to extend "the right to vote in municipal elections to unmarried property-owning women." But he refused to support restrictions that would exclude voters on the basis of race or sex: "One thing is certain—insurmountable qualifications of property, nativity, celibacy, race, sex, or religious opinions are wrong in principle and unjust in practice." Blackwell appealed instead for strong educational qualifications: "The mere ability to read and write seems insufficient. We have that qualification here in Boston now, yet two-thirds of our legal voters are poll-tax defaulters, and two convicts actually serving their time in prison have just been elected as Alderman and Representative."[18]

By supporting educational qualifications for suffrage, elite white leaders such as Blackwell, Stanton, and Carrie Chapman Catt pursued political inequality and equality simultaneously. Literacy tests and other "merit" examinations masked the reconstitution of repressive white domination. But like John Stuart Mill and other suffrage reformers in England, these elites desired measures that would nurture an intelligent, informed, and independently minded electorate.[19] Beginning with educational qualifications, many white reform leaders invoked the relatively egalitarian principle that all educated citizens could eventually become voters regardless of their race, ethnicity, or gender, although they preferred government controlled by educated, native-born white Protestants. Ideas such as Blackwell's "Southern strategy" reduced egalitarian principles to rights of simple inclusion—rights that conveyed no power.

Carrie Chapman Catt

After the turn of the century, Catt became the most ubiquitous and shrewd entrepreneurial leader of the woman suffrage movement. Catt joined the Iowa WCTU during the late 1880s and edited "the temperance column in the *Charles City*

Intelligencer."[20] Although she admired Willard as a leader, by 1890 Catt had left the WCTU because she insisted suffrage be separated from prohibition. Participating in the 1893 Colorado suffrage victory made her the national leader most experienced in carrying out a successful state campaign. NAWSA adopted her suggestions for organizational innovations in the mid-1890s, selected her as its president from 1900 to 1904, and chose her again in 1915. In addition to representing NAWSA in the Colorado victory, Catt helped to establish the International Woman Suffrage Alliance in 1902; this international experience prepared her for interactions with many different people and organizations.[21] She is best known for a "winning plan" that secured the passage and ratification of the federal amendment between 1915 and 1920.[22]

Long celebrated for her organizational genius, Catt also contributed an ideology for mobilizing traditional women that began as nativist feminism but evolved into a more tolerant feminism of personal development. Originally, she isolated educated, middle-class, native-born white women and addressed them as an independent, ill-treated, but qualified constituency of potential citizens. To deny the vote to intelligent, loyal American women, she argued, was an insult.[23]

Discouraged by an 1892 congressional committee's inattention to this "natural rights" argument, Catt decided to design appeals that powerful men would take seriously.[24] Arguments that relied on the grand ideals of equality and justice, she decided, only allowed other issues to take precedence in the minds of male voters. Similarly, during the 1890 South Dakota referendum she had spied local party machine leaders paying voters to defeat woman suffrage. Jacqueline Van Voris argues that after such incidents Catt "always kept her broad vision of equal rights" but focused on building a stronger national organization and winning increased attention for the cause. Her strategic motto became: "In matters of principle go against the current, but in matters of custom go with it."[25]

Catt's motto manifests the turn toward pragmatic tactics that distinguishes second-generation woman suffragists. She decided that mobilizing only wealthy elite women could put the suffrage effort on a more solid footing. To this end, Catt marshaled her argument for female moral superiority and Americanist race superiority.

In two early unpublished speeches, "Subject and Sovereign" and "The American Sovereign," Catt portrays as a major injustice extending political rights to Negroes, Native American Indians, and new immigrants while denying these rights to native-born white women. In "Subject and Sovereign," Catt argued that by offering the vote (as well as "government blankets" and other goods) to Sioux Indians west of the Missouri River in the Dakotas, the national government created "new sovereigns" and left disfranchised American women as "subjects." To intensify feelings of unfairness in her audience, Catt presented a litany of cruelties including tortures and brutal murders that she alleged the Sioux perpetrated against Americans. She also asserted that whereas women had demanded the vote, the Indians had neither asked for nor wanted it. "Gentlemen, I ask you," she declared dramatically, "where is there a principle of government, of economics, of common sense or justice which should have established that inconsistency?"[26]

In "The American Sovereign," Catt forged a similar nativistic argument about both ethnic-led urban political machines and new immigrants from southern and eastern Europe. Making majority rule sovereign, she posited, was the "underlying principle of the far-famed American liberties . . . Take away that sovereign and what kind of government do we possess? Only usurpations of power, despotism, or anarchy." Americans' liberties were endangered, Catt said, because "the political boss has donned the imperial robe." Also threatening liberty were the new immigrant groups that bolstered the party machines and their bosses: "Today there has arisen in America a class of men not intelligent, not patriotic, not moral, nor yet not pedigreed. In caucuses and conventions, it is they who nominate officials, at the polls through corrupt means, it is they who elect them and by bribery, it is they who secure the passage of many a legislative measure."

Catt especially discredited newly arriving immigrants from southern and eastern Europe as less wealthy, less intelligent, and less resourceful than those born in central and northern Europe. There are, she observed, "fewer Germans and Englishmen and more Hungarians and Italians. Fewer Swedes and Danes and more Russian and Polish Jews." She barely qualified her nativist sentiments on this score: these were "men and women whom America gladly welcomes. She still has need of every honest brain and honest muscle; but the fact remains that every year we are receiving fewer good people and more of the slum element." Catt also suggested that rule by party machines exacerbated associated problems: "Does ignorance and poverty cause political corruption, or does political dishonesty cause poverty and crime?"

Women's enfranchisement, Catt argued, would "purify politics" and enable the "perpetuation of the American republic." She unequivocally supported imposing native-born American standards for evaluating personal behavior in school, the workplace, and social life, and Catt depicted American women as the potential voters who could achieve this end. "It is plain," she asserted, "that the ballot in the hands of women means an element a much greater proportion of which has been born upon our soil, educated in our public schools, familiar with our institutions."

Finally, Catt insisted that the new immigrants were the "gravest problem ever presented to the American people." She predicted, as Blackwell had, that adding the votes of loyal native-born American women could outnumber the votes of these immigrants. The "census of 1890 proves that women hold the solution in their hands . . . Expediency demands it as the policy which alone can lift our nation from disgrace. I do not ask the ballot for women as a privilege, nor a favor. I ask it as the highest duty which citizens owe to the nation whose best interests they are pledged to defend."[27] Although we have no evidence on this subject, Catt may have used these very speeches in the victorious Colorado campaign of 1893.

In her two early speeches, Catt was thoroughly nativistic. But she also wrote two Fourth of July speeches, one as early as 1889, that celebrated freedom for all in the inclusive language of an assimilationist. Here Catt stated, "We have met today in commemoration of that victory [of the forefathers]. We have come not as Catholics or Protestants, not as Jews or Gentiles, not as Democrats or Republicans, not as friends or enemies, but simply and solely as American citizens, rejoicing that the victories of Bunker Hill, Valley Forge, and Provincetown rendered it possible for us to enjoy the protection of so liberal a government and the possession of such beneficent institutions."[28]

Although Blackwell and Catt were willing to exploit nativistic and racist sentiments, they avoided endorsing these ideas as principles. Most white southern suffragists concurred with this judgment.

Woman Suffrage and White Supremacy in the South, 1890-1904

As Anthony became firmly committed to winning the vote by federal amendment, she must have realized that it would require two-thirds support in both the House and the Senate. Because woman's vote needed ratification by three-quarters of the states, or thirty-six of forty-eight, national woman suffrage leaders could not avoid organizing southern campaigns.[29] As members of the WCTU, many southern women had already converted to suffrage. By 1890, wealthy, educated, and prominent women such as Laura Clay of Kentucky, Caroline Merrick of New Orleans, and Belle Kearney of Mississippi had persuasively appealed for national attention and support of their interest in woman suffrage.[30]

As Wheeler explains, southern white women of the planter classes who wanted the vote initially thought that white supremacy—and after 1896, the one-party system—offered them better opportunities for political inclusion than had the two-party system imposed during Reconstruction. This assessment may have been partly correct. According to historian William A. Link, poor and illiterate white and black men in the South particularly opposed woman suffrage.[31] Their disenfranchisement probably signaled to politically interested elite white women, most of whom lived in cities, that a strong source of opposition had been removed.[32] Unable to see the formidable opposition that men of their class (as well as many women) would present to their demands, these women organized suffrage campaigns throughout the South.

White southern suffragists' campaigns emerged just as educated African Americans were forming lasting national organizations and articulating a vision of civil rights reform. To avoid overt clashes between the two groups, NAWSA leaders refused to admit that they excluded African-American women from membership in NAWSA. Although national leaders stopped short of approving campaigns that would enfranchise only white women, they never seriously considered subverting the informal rules that sustained segregated cultures. Infrequently, white leaders developed cordial friendships with prominent black women, which facilitated communication across racial divides.[33] But these personal relationships paled against the NAWSA's official approval of white southerners' preference for winning the vote as a states' rights issue. Both Shaw and Catt made every effort to prevent black woman suffragists from attending national conventions or joining white reformers as equals in major public events. African-American suffragists were even asked to march separately as "the colored delegation" in the 1913 parade that greeted Woodrow Wilson.

Although some white leaders protested the appropriateness of white supremacy, all agreed at the outset that southern white women would strengthen and reinforce the white supremacist system "without taking the vote away from those already enfranchised."[34] In 1891, the year NAWSA decided to "do suffrage work in the South,"[35] the Populist movement still had momentum, and white supremacy lacked formal legal supports. Stanton-minded egalitarians could easily have seen a southern woman suffrage movement as a militating force against the most violent defenders of "the lost cause." In her 1891 NAWSA convention speech, "The Degradation of Disfranchisement," Stanton invoked skeletal memories of the struggle for equal rights: "We can not make men see that women feel the humiliation of their petty distinctions of sex precisely as the black man feels those of color. It is no palliation of our wrongs to say that we are not socially ostracized as he is, so long as we are politically ostracized as he is not. That all orders of foreigners also rank politically above the most intelligent, highly-educated women—native-born American—is indeed the most bitter drop in the cup of our grief."[36]

Reconciled to incorporating traditional women, Stanton asserted, "Let us henceforth meet conservatives on their own ground and admit that suffrage for woman does mean political, religious, industrial and social freedom—a new and a higher civilization."[37] White national leaders applauded the formation of southern woman suffrage associations as well as the headway that states such as Louisiana made in winning women taxpayers the right to vote on tax matters. By 1894 northern suffragists felt the southern women's efforts had created some of the best opportunities for winning state campaigns; their 1895 convention was set for Atlanta.

Southern woman suffragists justified their political inclusion with reasons that were little different from those of reformers in other regions. In January and February 1895, just before the Atlanta convention, the *Woman's Journal* published a two-week column entitled "Why Southern Women Desire the Ballot" that included answers from forty-two southern women. The reasons published ranged from principles of equal rights and natural rights to means of protecting and improving oneself, overcoming dominance by foreigners, winning child custody, raising the age of consent, and establishing cooperation between the sexes. Only one writer admitted support for white supremacy, which she equated with "intelligent supremacy." Another called for "a 16th Amendment which will set the female slaves free and give them the ballot to protect themselves, as it has protected the male slaves in their pursuit of life, liberty, and happiness."[38] Written just before the political realignment of 1896 and the subsequent legalization of white supremacy, these letters confirm that southern white women cared most about winning political rights for themselves. In fact, these women's distrust of white men's monopoly of power strongly suggests that southern white men would have perceived such criticisms as radical and threatening. In this context, the advent of legalized white supremacy during the years immediately after the open mobilization for female enfranchisement—the "reactionary revolution"—appears as a backlash against ideas such as woman suffrage as well as against improvements for black middle-class and skilled laborers.[39]

In their own states, white southern suffragists were usually thought of as a respectable group making radical demands. They also brought traditionalism into NAWSA, which was mostly welcomed. Before their 1895 convention in Atlanta, Susan B. Anthony and Carrie Chapman Catt campaigned for six weeks throughout the South, displaying their support for a well-developed regional movement led by white women. At the Atlanta convention, NAWSA created an organizational committee chaired by Catt to formulate a national reform strategy. Drawing on her experience in the 1893 Colorado campaign and victory, Catt argued that

> the suffrage association had been agitating for forty years but had failed to organize the sentiment it created. Three things should be provided at once: correlation of national, state and local branches; a program of concrete aims; a finance committee that would finance. The plan called for a standing committee on organization, to map out the national work and put organizers in the field. The organizers were to travel in pairs, a speaker and a business manager, to raise money . . . for the account of the Organization Committee. It recommended four regional conferences of states, North, South, East and West, midway between national conventions . . . Investigation of laws affecting women and children was recommended with support of improved legislation.[40]

National political parties continued to rely on decentralized power structures—coalitions of city, county, and state bosses united by their vote-getting and job-distributing machines. Woman suffragists could not hope to win without a plan that put similar sustained pressure on local officials throughout the nation.[41] Catt's singular focus on organization also deflected conflicts among suffragists over ideology, party identification, racism, nativisim, and appropriate priorities for women.

In 1895, NAWSA's organization committee, on which Catt served with southerner Laura Clay and Populist Annie L. Diggs, also drafted a carefully guarded "plan of work." The committee recommended that demands for state constitutional amendments be avoided until after party endorsements were obtained, that local unions lead in campaigning for school and municipal suffrage, and that NAWSA mobilize nationally but invest extra resources in the West and South where there were few suffragists. Their emphasis on building strong local organizations, making incremental gains, and obtaining party endorsements helped leaders establish the grassroots base for a federal amendment campaign as well as for state efforts.

Amending state constitutions required overcoming different ratification procedures in each state. For example, in Massachusetts, a state constitutional amendment needed two-thirds of the vote of two successive legislatures plus approval by a voter referendum. As Sharon Hartman Strom contends, such rules gave suffragists little hope that the state-by-state path alone would win women the vote.[42] Accordingly, once they had enough state victories and had established enough organizations in every state to garner a base of support in Congress, the reformers shifted their attention to winning a Constitutional amendment. In 1895 no one knew which states would pass the measure or where suffrage organizations would grow. Led by "respectable women" who would gain a hearing for their views no matter how radical, southern women appeared as likely as most others to win favor for the reform. And mobilization of a southern base could help dampen opposition to a federal amendment.[43]

Initiating campaigns for woman suffrage in the South was tactically both daring and damaging. It took courage to challenge the authority of men responsible for terror and laws such as Jim Crow, poll taxes, and literacy tests.[44] Southern chivalry protected respectable white women from retribution by physical violence, but not from threats by innuendo or ridicule. White suffragists presented white southern Democratic men with an unanticipated but serious challenge from within. To counter this threat, elected male officials in the South accused the suffragists of "unfeminine behavior." Although reformers quickly responded that such accusations were "unchivalrous," they found themselves repeatedly treated as radical privileged white women who did not appreciate the protections of men. The suffragists won less popular support in the South than in any other part of the nation. Indeed, most southern WCTU locals initially evaded pressures to endorse votes for women, and many southern women opposed the measure.[45] Southern suffragists' toleration of white supremacy gave NAWSA conservative members, but in their home states these women were perceived as threatening the southern way of life.

During slavery most native-born, white southern women had religiously dedicated themselves to developing strong families and maintaining stable ties between masters and slaves. These women, whose diaries often reveal profound piety and self-effacement, were less preoccupied than their male relatives with subordinating free blacks.[46]

According to historian Anne Firor Scott, by 1870 a few white southern women had asserted their support for woman suffrage and even joined one of the national suffrage associations. During the 1880s, southern white women's participation in both social justice issues and the suffrage cause escalated after Frances Willard's WCTU recruitment efforts.[47] The white southern women who endorsed suffrage at any time between 1870 and the ratification of the federal amendment in 1920, however, were considered by most white southerners as supporters of a "radical cause."[48]

As they began their reform efforts in the 1890s, most of these suffragists accepted white supremacy as part of what had nationally become segregated cultures. But southern white supremacy was multifaceted, not monolithic. The southern suffragists whom Wheeler studied range from the "Negrophobic" Gordon sisters in Louisiana to Mary Johnston of Virginia, whose private communications reveal her opposition to white supremacy and hopes for social democracy in the United States. Southern suffragists opposed using violence to enforce white domination and aligned themselves with male southern progressives who committed themselves to rule by law. In the 1890s, southern white women suffragists argued that women's moral influence would ensure that law and persuasion, rather than terror and violence, would be used to shore up white supremacy.[49] Most also subscribed to the idea that education and fair treatment would "elevate" African Americans and prepare them for full citizenship. . . .

. . . The suffragists' racist and nativist appeals left a legacy of injustice, deepened stereotypes, and divided political action that ironically undermined their own project of generating solidarity among women *as women*. In struggling to win political inclusion for all women, these elite women presented themselves as not only respectable, but also culturally dominant leaders of foreign women. Representing themselves to black and immigrant women as potential protectors who would be more trustworthy than any men, they simultaneously asserted their dominance as white, native-born women in a racist and xenophobic society.

Notes

1. Aileen Kraditor, *The Ideas of the Woman Suffrage Movement, 1890-1920* (Garden City, N.Y.: Anchor, 1971), pp. 43-45, 51-55, 86-91; William O'Neill, *Everyone Was Brave: A History of Feminism in America* (Garden City, N.Y.: Quadrangle, 1971), pp. 49-76; Judith Shklar, *American Citizenship: The Quest for Inclusion* (Cambridge, Mass.: Harvard University Press, 1991), pp. 57-62; Nancie Caraway, *Segregated Sisterhood: Racism and the Politics of American Feminism* (Knoxville: University of Tennessee Press, 1991), pp. 142-157; Rogers M. Smith, "'One United People': Second Class Female Citizenship and the American Quest for Community," *Yale Journal of Law and the Humanities* 1 (1989): 229-293.

2. *HWS* [*History of Women's Suffrage*], 4:14-30, 4:56-84, 4:112-123; Ruth Bordin, *Frances Willard: A Biography* (Chapel Hill: University of North Carolina Press, 1986), pp. 97-111.

3. Elisabeth Griffith, *In Her Own Right: The Life of Elizabeth Cady Stanton* (New York: Oxford University Press, 1984), p. 178. For a fuller account of the conflicts over reunification of the AWSA with the NWSA, see Kathleen Barry, *Susan B. Anthony: A Biography of a Singular Feminist* (New York: Ballantine, 1988), pp. 283-300.

4. Barry, *Susan B. Anthony*, pp. 297-299. The full text of Stanton's speech is published in Ellen Carol DuBois, ed., *Elizabeth Cady Stanton/Susan B. Anthony: Correspondence, Writings, Speeches* (New York: Schocken, 1981), pp. 222-227.

5. Judith Shklar, *American Citizenship: The Quest for Inclusion* (Cambridge, Mass.: Harvard University Press, 1991), p. 60.

6. Caraway, *Segregated Sisterhood*, pp. 148-163; Anna Julia Cooper, "Woman versus the Indian," in Anna Julia Cooper, ed.; *A Voice from the South* (1892; New York: Oxford University Press, 1988), pp. 80-127; and Rosalyn Terborg-Penn, "Discontented Black Feminists: Prelude and Postscript to the Passage of the Nineteenth Amendment," in Darlene Clark Hine, ed., *Black Women in United States History*, vol. 4, bk. 8 (Brooklyn, N.Y.: Carlson Publishing, 1990), pp. 1159-76.

7. Caraway, *Segregated Sisterhood*, pp. 157-167; Glenda Elizabeth Gilmore, "Gender and Jim Crow: Women and the Politics of White Supremacy in North Carolina, 1896-1920" (Ph.D. diss., University of North Carolina, 1992), pp. 438-480; Paula Giddings, *When and Where I Enter: The Impact of Black Women on Race and Sex in America* (New York: William Morrow, 1984), pp. 119-131; and Evelyn Brooks Higginbotham, *Righteous Discontent: The Women's Movement in the Black Baptist Church, 1880-1920* (Cambridge, Mass.: Harvard University Press, 1993), pp. 88-119.

8. In 1891 J. P. H. Russ introduced the idea of votes for white women in Arkansas. The measure received three readings but only four affirmative votes (*HWS*, 4:476). In 1890 several measures were introduced in the Mississippi legislature to give property-owning married white women the vote. All were defeated (*HWS*, 4:786).

9. Marjorie Spruill Wheeler, *New Women of the New South: The Leaders of the Woman Suffrage Movement in the Southern States* (New York: Oxford University Press, 1993), p. 108.

10. Ellen Carol DuBois, "Working Women, Class Relations, and Suffrage Militance: Harriot Stanton Blatch and the New York Woman Suffrage Movement, 1894-1909," in Ellen Carol DuBois and Vicki L. Ruiz, eds., *Unequal Sisters: A Multi-Cultural Reader in U.S. Women's History* (New York: Routledge, 1990), p. 180.

11. "Editorial Notes," *WJ* [*Women's Journal*], 20 November 1909, p. 185.

12. Henry B. Blackwell, "What the South Can Do (1867)" in Aileen S. Kraditor, ed., *Up from the Pedestal: Selected Writings in the History of American Feminism* (New York: Quadrangle, 1968), p. 255. Emphasis added.

13. Wheeler, *New Women*, pp. 113-116.

14. Blackwell, "What the South Can Do," pp. 254-255.

15. C. Van Woodward, *Origins of the New South, 1877-1913* (Baton Rouge: Louisiana State University Press, 1971), pp. 51-74; Jacqueline Jones, *Labor of Love, Labor of Sorrow: Black Women, Work, and the Family from Slavery to the Present* (New York: Basic, 1985), pp. 44-151. J. Morgan Kousser argues that electoral laws shrunk the electorate and altered the political system in ways white violence did not in *The Shaping of Southern Politics: Suffrage, Restriction and the Establishment of the One-Party South, 1880-1910* (New Haven, Conn.: Yale University Press, 1974), pp. 1-9, 18-21.

16. Blackwell, "What the South Can Do," p. 256.

17. Wheeler, *New Women*, pp. 89, 108. Jacqueline Dowd Hall explains how Jesse Daniel Ames, a southern white woman, led a women's movement against lynching in Hall's *Revolt against Chivalry: Jesse Daniel Ames and the Women's Campaign against Lynching* (New York: Columbia University Press, 1993). Although Glenda Gilmore observes that most white women tacitly accepted lynching against blacks as well as whites' armed siege of city governments (such as that of Wilmington, North Carolina, in 1898), she also argues that by competing to achieve high voter turnouts, southern white voters and black women voters in North Carolina deflected threats of violence. See Gilmore, "Gender and Jim Crow," pp. 215-226, 445-447.

18. Henry Brown Blackwell, "Woman Suffrage Proposed in Louisiana," *WJ*, 3 December 1904, p. 388. One of the "convicts elected to office" was James Michael Cur-

ley, future mayor of Boston. He was put in prison for taking a civil service test under a false name. See Jack Beatty, *The Rascal King: The Life and Times of James Michael Curley, 1874-1958* (Reading, Mass.: Addison-Wesley, 1992), pp. 77-82.

19. John Stuart Mill, *Considerations on Representative Government* (Indianapolis, Ind.: Bobbs-Merrill, 1958), pp. 154-171, esp. pp. 161-164.

20. Jacqueline Van Voris, *Carrie Chapman Catt: A Public Life* (New York: Feminist Press, 1987), pp. 16-17.

21. Ibid., pp. 55-113.

22. Eleanor Flexner, *Century of Struggle: The Woman's Rights Movement in the United States,* rev. ed. (Cambridge, Mass.: Harvard University Press, 1975), pp. 287-292.

23. Robert Booth Fowler, *Carrie Catt: Feminist Politician* (Boston: Northeastern University Press, 1986), pp. 71-76.

24. Van Voris, *Carrie Chapman Catt,* pp. 30-31.

25. Ibid., pp. 29-32, quotation on p. 32.

26. "Subject and Sovereign," Catt MSS, c. 1888. Catt exaggerated the benefits given to Native American Indians, including the franchise. See Sharon L. O'Brien, *American Indian Tribal Governments* (Norman: University of Oklahoma Press, 1989), pp. 68-70, 80, 146-151.

27. "The American Sovereign," Catt MSS, c. 1896. This speech was mistakenly dated as written in or around 1888. Parts of it could not have been written until after the first part of the 1890 census was published in 1895.

28. "4th of July, 1889, Rockford, Illinois," Catt MSS. Unpublished speech.

29. Sinclair, *Emancipation of American Woman,* pp. 293-298.

30. Wheeler, *New Women,* pp. 115-118.

31. William A. Link, *The Paradox of Southern Progressivism, 1880-1930* (Chapel Hill: University of North Carolina Press, 1992), pp. 301-304.

32. J. Morgan Kousser argues that the introduction of the Australian ballot into the southern states added fuel to the disenfranchisement process because it swept away the mode of voting that many illiterate white southern male voters knew and had favored. Educated elite southern women, however, probably perceived this reform as an opportunity to demand the vote. See Kousser, *Shaping of Southern Politics,* pp. 52-60.

33. For the story of how Charlotte Hawkins Brown financed The Palmer School by appealing for white support, see Gilmore, "Gender and Jim Crow," pp. 379-400; and Hall, *Revolt against Chivalry,* pp. 59-128.

34. Wheeler, *New Women of the New South,* p. 114.

35. *HWS,* 4:184.

36. Ibid., p. 177.

37. Ibid., p. 178.

38. "Why Southern Women Desire the Ballot," *WJ,* 26 January 1895, pp. 26-32, and 2 February 1895, p. 34.

39. Gilmore, "Gender and Jim Crow," pp. 188-195.

40. Mary Gray Peck, *Carrie Chapman Catt* (New York: H. W. Wilson, 1944), p. 83.

41. Sinclair, *Emancipation of American Woman,* p. 225.

42. Sharon Hartman Strom, "Leadership and Tactics in the American Woman Suffrage Movement: A New Perspective from Massachusetts," *Journal of American History,* vol. 62, no. 2 (1975): 298.

43. Maud Wood Park, *The Front Door Lobby* (Boston: Beacon, 1960), pp. 26-28.

44. Kousser, *Shaping of Southern Politics,* pp. 39-62, 257-265.

45. Link, *Paradox of Southern Progressivism,* p. 299.

46. Anne F. Scott, "Women, Religion, and Social Change in the South, 1830-1930," in Samuel S. Hill, Jr., ed., *Religion and the Solid South* (Nashville: Abingdon, 1972), pp. 92-121.

47. Anne F. Scott, *The Southern Lady: From Pedestal to Politics, 1830-1930* (Chicago: University of Chicago Press, 1970), pp. 144-150.

48. Ibid., pp. 164-184.

49. Wheeler, *New Women,* pp. 40-45, 74-75. Anne Firor Scott observes that the son of Elizabeth Avery Meriwether reported "that shortly after the war when her husband was engaged in organizing a local Ku Klux Klan, Mrs. Meriwether had suggested giving the vote to white women as an alternative to terrorizing Negro men." See Scott, *Southern Lady,* p. 173.

ROSALYN TERBORG-PENN (ESSAY DATE 1998)

SOURCE: Terborg-Penn, Rosalyn. "African American Woman Suffragists Finding Their Own Voices: 1870s and 1880s." In *African American Women in the Struggle for the Vote, 1850-1920,* pp. 36-53. Bloomington, Ind.: Indiana University Press, 1998.

In the following essay, Terborg-Penn argues that one positive effect of the racial polarization which increasingly divided black and white suffragists during the late nineteenth century was that black women began to emerge as leaders, giving voice to the particular concerns of the nation's most disenfranchised group—women of color.

In the period following the collapse of the American Equal Rights Association, African American women's voices became more evident as their views about woman suffrage began to differ from those of white women. Even the watersheds in the movement differed for the two groups. For white women, the schism that had resulted with the birth of two rival national woman suffrage associations ended in 1890, when the two organizations reunited to achieve votes for women. For Black women the turning point began in the 1870s and 1880s, as their suffrage arguments took on new meaning, more closely identified with their unique status as women of color. They never abandoned the universal suffrage cause, as did many mainstream suffragists. As a result, African American woman suffrage strategies combined demands for Black women's right to vote and civil rights for all Black people. Even when African American women adopted the strategies of the larger woman suffrage movement—demanding suffrage based on the citizenship clause of the Fourteenth Amendment, or calling for a federal amendment to enfranchise women—they included caveats specifically designed for the needs of Black women. The present discussion, in seeking to identify authentic Black women's voices, looks at the differences in how Black women and white women perceived suffrage goals in the 1870s and 1880s.

The New Departure

Following the split that caused the demise of the AERA [American Equal Rights Association], the woman-suffrage-first faction became more militant in its strategy to obtain the vote for women. During the first five years after the split, from 1869 to 1874, the strategy this faction adopted aimed to reinterpret the Fourteenth Amendment, which had introduced the word "male" into the Constitution, yet had guaranteed the right to vote to all citizens of the United States. Missouri suffragists Virginia Minor and her husband Francis took the lead in developing a controversial strategy, the "new departure," which was an attempt to use the Constitution and its definition of citizenship to enfranchise women. Elisabeth Griffith notes how Elizabeth Cady Stanton remained in the midst of this controversy, stimulating women-centered awareness, yet alienating former friends and allies with her offensive statements. Nonetheless, militant suffragists, both Black and white, mobilized to implement the new ideas fostered by Stanton and others.[1]

Harriet Tubman was an active abolitionist and advocate for women's rights who saw an inextricable link between the two causes.

Even before the implementation of the new plan, suffragists had used a modified strategy, which can be described more as a mock political exercise to dramatize women's desires to vote as citizens of the United States. In 1868, the women suffragists of Vineland, New Jersey, set up voting tables across from the platform where the election officials were accepting male ballots. The women had tried unsuccessfully to cast their votes, and when rejected decided on a unique strategy to indicate their protest against disfranchisement. On that election day, 172 women cast mock ballots. Of this group, four were Blacks.[2]

The 1868 New Jersey case appears to have been an isolated event; however, by 1870 Stanton testified that women should challenge the Fourteenth Amendment. She urged women to register, to vote, and if necessary, to go to court and to jail in defense of their right to the ballot. Significantly, Stanton was unable actually to practice this confrontational strategy. It took a charismatic person like Victoria Woodhull to restate the Stanton argument at the 1871 NWSA [National Women's Suffrage Association] convention in the District of Columbia, and to incite Black and white suffragists to implement the strategy. Woodhull also called the tactic the "new departure."[3]

Like the NWSA leaders, several African American women were impressed with the new strategy. At least three Blacks can be identified by name, Mary Ann Shadd Cary of the District of Columbia, Sojourner Truth of Battle Creek, Michigan, and Mrs. Beatty of Portland, Oregon.

Veteran suffragist Mary Ann Shadd Cary had many talents as a journalist, teacher, politician, and law student. In 1869, at the age of forty-six, she had decided to study law and became the first woman student at the newly founded Howard University Law School. She studied in the evenings and taught in the District of Columbia school system in the daytime. During the early 1870s, Cary earned additional income as an agent for *The New National Era,* Frederick Douglass's Black newspaper in the District of Columbia. On summer trips sponsored by the *Era* throughout the South and the East, Cary carried the news about reform and Republican Party politics. Her articles offered feminist strategies aimed to educate public opinion, and feminist commentary upon the economic and the political conditions of African Americans in the District of Columbia. Her speeches, and the items about her in the local Black press, revealed her ideas about woman suffrage.[4]

Although listed in the Howard University law class of 1871-72, Cary was not permitted to graduate because the District legal code limited admission to the bar to men only. Charging sex discrimination, she temporarily ended her law school study. In the meantime, Charlotte E. Ray of New York City completed the law course at Howard. Fortunately for her, the District code struck the word "male" as a qualification for bar admission by the time of her graduation. Yet to be on the safe side, when her name was submitted by Howard University officials to the bar for acceptance, the school, remembering the problems Cary had with sex discrimination, recommended "C. E. Ray," instead of listing her full first name. Bar officials did not realize that Ray was female until after accepting her name. In the meantime, Cary, after suffering for a decade with financial problems, finally returned to Howard University and graduated with her law degree at the age of sixty.[5]

Invoking the ideas of the "new departure," but with a race-specific twist, Cary's unpublished testimony before the House Judiciary Committee contains her views on woman suffrage. In arguing for the right to vote in 1872, Cary clearly applied the Fourteenth and Fifteenth Amendments to Black women, as well as to Black men. She believed that with emancipation, Black men and women realized the same responsibilities needed for survival. Although Cary felt the amendments were "otherwise grand in conception," they left the women of her race only nominally free because they were denied the right to vote. In this nationalist context, Cary's woman suffrage ideology related specifically to African American women. However, she shrewdly redirected her argument in keeping with the mainstream suffragists by noting how all women were discriminated against as long as the word "male" remained in the two amendments. Consequently, Cary called for an amendment to strike the word "male" from the Constitution.[6]

Cary's speech had the sound of a legal argument, reflecting her professional training. Her testimony spoke specifically about why Black women in the District of Columbia needed the vote. Using herself as an example, Cary noted that she was a taxpayer with the same obligations as the male taxpayers of the city. Therefore, she felt suffrage should be her right just as it was theirs. Cary noted that many women of her race in the nation's capital supported woman suffrage and that they too called for the striking of the word "male" from the Constitution.[7] Her position was definitely an NWSA stand against the interpretation of the Fourteenth Amendment. Cary's reference to other Black women who supported her position, however, is an important clue to the fact that more than the three identifiable African American women had welcomed the "new departure."

Other NWSA women challenged the Fourteenth Amendment by attempting to register to vote. The most celebrated case occurred in 1872, when Susan B. Anthony and several Rochester, New York, women registered and attempted to vote. Anthony and her colleagues were all arrested for registering "illegally," found guilty, and fined. The same year Sojourner Truth went to the Battle Creek, Michigan, polls on election day to assert her right to vote; however, she did not succeed in her effort to cast a ballot. Truth and her grandson had managed to acquire enough money to purchase a small house in Battle Creek, where they lived when not touring the country. In addition to Truth in Michigan, Abigail Scott Duniway and two other white suffragists joined Mrs. Beatty (referred to by the chroniclers as a "colored" woman) in their unsuccessful attempt to register. Like Truth and Beatty, Cary was unsuccessful in her attempt to register to vote in 1871. However, Cary and sixty-three other Washington, D.C., women prevailed upon the elections officials to sign affidavits indicating that the women had tried to vote. Unlike the Rochester women, the Washington women were not arrested for asserting their right to the ballot, and the elections officials gave them the requested affidavits.[8]

Several reasons may account for the differences in how the Rochester and Washington women were treated. First, Susan B. Anthony was a nationally known figure, who publicized her attempt to register to vote. The white men in political power felt the need to set an example by her imprisonment and conviction. On the other hand, by 1871 the District of Columbia had obtained home rule; large numbers of Black men voted, and several of them served on the city council, including Frederick Douglass. Perhaps the election officials were sympathetic to the women and their cause. Indeed, in 1870, the Black election officials in certain districts in South Carolina had encouraged Black women to register to vote.[9] Black District of Columbia election officials may have been influenced by these events.

One strategy used by Blacks as well as whites to obtain the ballot for women was an appeal for female enfranchisement based on the Fifteenth Amendment. In 1872, white suffragist Mary Olney Brown of Washington state wrote a letter to Frederick Douglass, editor of the *Era*. Offering an emotional plea for African American male support of the vote for Black women, Brown argued that the Fifteenth Amendment, which had enfranchised Black men in 1870, should be applied to the enfranchisement of women because it did not exclude them in the definition of citizenship. Douglass printed the letter, wherein Brown encouraged voting Black men to support her strategy. This appears to be the first of many efforts by white suffragists to reestablish the political coalition they had severed with African American men. The rarity of their attempts at rapprochement with African American women reveals the degree to which white woman suffragists believed Black men to be more influential than Black women.[10]

Brown's strategy to demand suffrage as woman's legal right, a strategy frequently employed in the 1870s, could very well have come from journalist Mary Ann Cary. She was an example of the women Ellen DuBois calls radical feminists, who emerged in the 1870s as independent suffragists.[11]

Radical suffragists abandoned the "new departure" strategy with the losses of the Anthony case and, more important, the Minor voting rights case. Virginia Minor, president of the Missouri Woman Suffrage Association, and her husband, Francis, sued the St. Louis registrar for refusing to allow Virginia to vote in 1872. The couple took their case to the United States Supreme Court, but lost the suit in 1874. Afterwards the NWSA suffragists realized they needed another strategy. By 1877 they had returned to seeking a new constitutional amendment to prohibit disfranchisement based on sex. This time, it was a call for the Sixteenth Amendment to enfranchise all women. The goal was a woman suffrage amendment, not a universal suffrage amendment, which in itself should have been troubling to African Americans and others who were committed to this broader amendment. Ellen DuBois analyzes the new goal and its implementation to be "elitist and racist."[12] Indeed, the strategy elicited less resistance from the body politic as a whole because of its more conservative character.

Continuing her fight for woman suffrage, Mary Ann Shadd Cary wrote the NWSA in 1876 on behalf of ninety-four Black women from the District of Columbia. Her letter requested that their names be enrolled in the July 4th centennial autograph book as signers of the Woman's Declaration of Sentiments, which called for the immediate enfranchisement of American women. Although the editors of the *History of Woman Suffrage* made note of the letter, the names of the Black women were not included. Hence they remain anonymous. Yet there appeared to be growing political awareness among African American women, at least in the nation's capital. By the 1878 NWSA convention, Cary announced that African American women were determined to obtain the right to vote and that they "would support whatever party would allow them their rights, be it Republican or Democratic." Cary, who had been a staunch Republican since after the Civil War, reflected the disillusionment of African Americans, rather than the disillusionment of white suffragists. The Hayes Compromise of 1877 brought Reconstruction to a final end and signaled the laissez-faire policy toward the South, which ended the growing political influence of African Americans nationwide. Cary continued to develop a Black nationalist feminist perspective, using her own voice—one that reflected the interests of her people, especially the women.[13]

African American Woman Suffragists in the Postschism Era

Little remains of any published data about the views of Black female suffragists during the postbellum period. Nonetheless, several new names can be added to the growing list of African American feminists from throughout the nation. From 1865 to 1875, African American women—both veteran suffragists and new recruits—affiliated with the two rival national associations. Despite the assumptions modern-day writers have about Black women's participation in the two groups, a larger known number selected the AWSA than the NWSA.[14] Of the known African American women who participated in the two national organizations during the 1870s, nine selected the AWSA and six selected the NWSA:

AWSA:
Charlotte Forten
Frances Ellen Watkins Harper
Mrs. K. Harris*
Caroline Remond Putnam*
Charlotta (Lottie) Rollin*
Louisa Rollin*
Josephine St. Pierre Ruffin*
Sojourner Truth
Frances Rollin Whipper*

NWSA:
Naomi Talbert Anderson*
Mrs. Beatty
Mary Ann Shadd Cary
Harriet Purvis
Hattie Purvis
Charlotte E. Ray*

*Women new to the woman suffrage movement.

Whether even more Black women affiliated is not clear, since the trend among white suffrage leaders to write-out the views of Black female suffragists continued. For the most part, African American women's opinions were not recorded, and some women remain anonymous. Of the new names, two came from Massachusetts, where Blacks as well as whites campaigned for woman suffrage. In Massachusetts, unlike many other northern states, notably New York and Pennsylvania, Black men retained the right to vote throughout the antebellum years. During the 1860s and 1870s, six African American men served in the Massachusetts House of Representatives. All of them represented predominantly Black districts, and all supported the various woman suffrage bills that came through the legislature, but failed.[15] It appears that there was a politically motivated Black community living in Boston in particular, and that woman suffrage was an issue consistently supported by the African Americans living in the respective voting districts. Although Black women, as all women, could not vote in Massachusetts, it is safe to say that by the postbellum period they were more politically aware than those in other areas of the nation, because their men could vote. For this reason, it is surprising that more names of African American suffragists were not found for Massachusetts during this period. Perhaps unknown Black women attended meetings without official positions in the woman suffrage organizations. Nonetheless, the two who participated in leadership positions in the state woman suffrage movement were Caroline Remond Putnam and Josephine St. Pierre Ruffin, both educated, affluent women from prominent African American families.

Putnam was a sister of Charles and Sarah Remond. A successful businesswoman, she operated a ladies' hair salon and wig factory in Salem, where most of the clients were white. As a delegate from Salem, Putnam attended the founding meeting of the Massachusetts Woman Suffrage Association, an affiliate organization of the AWSA. This group was organized in January 1870, under the auspices of the AWSA, with Julia Ward Howe, a white abolitionist, as president. Putnam was elected a member of the executive committee of the first board; however, her views about suffrage were not recorded. Presumably she continued her activities in this suffrage association until 1885, when like her sister Sarah, she became an expatriate in Italy.[16]

The Remond sisters' departure from the United States suggests the hopelessness they must have felt about African American women ever achieving equity in their homeland. Unlike most Black women, the Remonds could afford to leave America, as could their brother Charles. However, he remained with his family in the United States and died in Salem in 1874.

Ruffin began her association with the Massachusetts Woman Suffrage Association in 1875. The wife of George L. Ruffin, one of the pro-woman suffrage representatives from Boston in the state legislature, Josephine had been noted as an abolitionist before the Civil War, and would later become a journalist and a Black women's club leader. In later years, she explained that she affiliated with the Massachusetts suffragists because of the warm welcome she received from Lucy Stone, Julia Ward Howe and other movement leaders. Ruffin noted that these white women were wise enough to "include no distinction because of race with no distinction because of sex," as prerequisites for membership in their suffrage organization.[17] These words, spoken in Ruffin's own voice, indicate in a subtle way that African American women were reluctant to seek membership in white women's organizations, fearing rejection. There should be no question about whose was the authentic voice in this case when an African American woman contemporary to the times raised the issue of racism among some persons in the organized woman suffrage movement.

Unlike Massachusetts, South Carolina was not a traditional feeding ground for abolitionists and woman suffragists. Nonetheless, once Reconstruction enabled Blacks to participate effectively in government, several men and women championed woman suffrage. As in Massachusetts, by 1868 Black men could vote in the state; they retained that right until disfranchised in the 1890s. Not surprising, the first South Carolina delegate to a national woman suffrage convention was a Black woman. She was Charlotte Rollin, known as Lottie, of Charleston, who along with her sisters, Frances and Louisa, influenced Reconstruction politics in the South Carolina state capital of Columbia during the late 1860s and 1870s. Frances married William J. Whipper, who as a delegate to the South Carolina Constitutional Convention of 1868, pleaded for the enfranchisement of women as well as Black men. Louisa Rollin spoke on the floor of the South Carolina House of Representatives in 1869 to urge support of universal suffrage. By 1870 Lottie Rollin had been elected secretary of the newly organized South Carolina Woman's Rights Association, and in 1871 she led a meeting at the state capital to promote woman suffrage. The following year she represented South Carolina as an ex officio member of the executive committee of the AWSA.[18]

The South Carolina suffrage group's affiliation with the AWSA was predictable because the political strategy and the membership of the two groups were similar. Like the AWSA, the South Carolina Woman's Rights Association was Republican in party affiliation and included male as well as female members and officers. Of the fifteen delegates cited as either speakers or elected officials, at least three were Black men and four were Black women. In addition to Lottie Rollin, Mrs. Alonzo J. Ransier and Mrs. Robert C. Delarge, the wives of African American Congressmen from South Carolina, were elected vice presidents. Mrs. K. Harris, the wife of a Black Charleston minister, was elected treasurer.[19]

The coalition among African American men and women suffragists in South Carolina is not surprising. The African American men of the state had been enfranchised before the ratification of the Fifteenth Amendment; hence the final goal of this universal suffrage organization remained the enfranchisement of women.[20] With this goal in mind, Lottie Rollin addressed the chair of the 1870 convention, held in Charleston. Her words became the first from an African American woman, other than Sojourner Truth, to be preserved in writing by the chroniclers of the national woman suffrage movement leaders. Rollin exhorted,

> We ask suffrage not as a favor, not as a privilege, but as a right based on the ground that we are human beings, and as such entitled to all human rights. While we concede that woman's ennobling influence should be confined chiefly to home and society, we claim that public opinion has had a tendency to limit woman's sphere to too small a circle, and until woman has the right of representation this will last and other rights will be held by an insecure tenure.[21]

Rollin's words reflected the traditional African American rationale that women were second-class citizens who needed the vote to improve their status in society. It also revealed a significant recurring theme among the voices of Black feminists—the concern with human rights, or in this case universal suffrage, rather than identification with women's rights exclusively.

The goals of the South Carolina Woman's Rights Association exemplified the model Bettina Aptheker used for examining how effective a universal suffrage coalition of men and women could be if gender primacy was not the suffrage goal. Although the Black men in the South Carolina organization had achieved the right to vote with the writing of the new state constitution and women had not, their focus was then directed to enabling their women to obtain that right. When women did not obtain the right to vote in 1868, they did not reject the men who had the ballot, but combined to work for it with those sympathetic to their plight. Nonetheless, the existence of a woman suffrage association in one of the reconstructed former confederate states was unique for the period. An association of men and women with Black female leadership was also quite significant for the times. However, when considering that Louisiana and South Carolina were the two most progressive southern states with sizable Black leadership, it is not surprising that delegates from these states would be among the first to attend AWSA meetings in the 1870s. Whether Laura L. D. Jacobs, the Louisiana delegate to the AWSA Convention in Cleveland was Black or white, I do not know.[22] Nonetheless, no female delegates from reconstructed states appear to have attended NWSA meetings immediately following the founding of the rival woman suffrage organizations. The fact that the AWSA had supported the Fifteenth Amendment may have been one reason why Republican suffragists in the former confederate South were more attracted to the

AWSA than to the NWSA, for the Fifteenth Amendment had been the brainchild of the Republican Party. Besides, during this period, the AWSA leadership seemed more interested than the NWSA in recruiting suffrage associations from the South.

However, affiliating with one of the national woman suffrage organizations was not the only strategy used by African American woman suffragists living in the South. Independent suffragists used traditional strategies such as petitioning the federal government in coalition with their men. A good example of this strategy is found in a petition in the National Archives, circa 1870. The document holds several clues to the ways in which the African American elite in the District of Columbia identified themselves and exerted political influence. The petition was addressed "To the Senate and House of Representatives" on a form with spaces to be filled in by the group of individuals who signed the petition. This format indicated that several of the documents, "Petition for Woman Suffrage," had been reproduced and circulated. The petition read:

> The undersigned, Citizens of the United States, Residents of the *Dist. of Col.*, Country of _____, Town of *Union Town* earnestly pray your Honorable Body to adopt measures for so amending the Constitution as to prohibit the several States from Disfranchising United States Citizens on account of Sex.[23]

The petition form divided the signatories by gender, a customary practice of the times. However, the signers wished to identify themselves by adding the word "Colored" to the categories for "men" and "women." Frederick Douglass, Jr. and his wife, who signed her name "Mrs. Frederick Douglass, Jr.," headed the lists. Only one other woman used her husband's name, and she was Mrs. Nathan Sprague, Frederick Douglass's daughter Rosetta Douglass Sprague. However, seven additional women used the titles "Mrs." or "Miss" before signing both their first and last names. There were no "x" marks in either column, indicating that all of the signatories were literate, probably elite African Americans who lived in the affluent Anacostia suburb of the city. There were eighteen names of women signers. All were new to my list of African Americans, and appeared to be independent woman suffragists. In keeping with the characteristics of earlier Black woman suffragists, several of these women were relatives of other petition signers. This rare find revealed how elusive are the records of Black women suffragists of this era; however, it confirmed my suspicion that there were many more of these women to find in southern cities like Washington:

> Mrs. Frederick Douglass, Jr.
>
> Mrs. Julia Dorsey
>
> Mrs. Sarrah A. Jones
>
> Harriette H. Lee
>
> Jane Lawson
>
> Rozie Harris
>
> Miss Elizabeth Chase
>
> Mrs. Nathan Sprague
>
> Mrs. Eliza A. Spencer
>
> Mrs. Mary V. Berry
>
> Caroline Burnett
>
> Alice Scott
>
> Miss Celia Gray
>
> Mrs. Caroline Chase

I can only speculate about these women's feminist and political sentiments. However, they appeared to be in the Frederick Douglass family network, where there was strong support for the Republican Party, the ratification of the Fifteenth Amendment, and universal suffrage.

Support for the Fifteenth Amendment and interest in southern women probably convinced Frances Ellen Watkins Harper to affiliate with the AWSA. In 1873, after returning from a tour of freedmen's communities in the reconstructed states of the South, she delivered the closing speech at the AWSA convention held in New York City. Harper declared that as "much as white women need the ballot, colored women need it more." Hence, she initiated a rationale that African American women would use in future arguments, distinguishing themselves from suffragists who were white. In addition, Harper indicted what she called the "ignorant and often degraded men" who subjected Black women in the South to arbitrary legal authority. Unlike the white women who used this term, Harper was referring to white authority for the most part. Acknowledging the progress already made by women of her race, Harper pleaded for equal rights and equal access to education for the African American women of the nation. Although there is no written record of Harper's address at the 1873 AWSA convention, she did attend, seated on the platform with the honored guests as a delegate from her state of birth—Maryland.[24]

Harper's call for equal rights and equal access to educational opportunities for Black women may appear to be a conservative matter, but for the AWSA's one-issue politics—woman suffrage—adding Black women's economic and social plight must have seemed radical or inappropriate to some of the membership. Because Harper presented her case at the close of the 1873 convention, there may not have been time for discussion. Nonetheless, the AWSA records show no further discussion about this issue during subsequent conventions. Yet Harper and other Black women spokespersons considered the points important to the survival of their people. Theirs was a nationalist position, a Black survival issue.

The postbellum years had uprooted many Americans, especially the freed people, whose lives were often characterized by social disabilities. As a result, Harper was not alone in her concerns for her race. Sojourner Truth revived many of the old political remedies for new social ills as she observed the plight of the poor freed people who lived in the District of Columbia. Truth reasoned that instead of the District government spending money to imprison vagrants, officials could use the funds to provide adequate housing and education for them. Reportedly, in her narrative, she regretted that women had no political rights, for she believed that if "the voice of maternity" could be heard, "the welfare not only of the present generation, but of future ones, would be assured."[25] While in Topeka, Kansas, she spoke against the evils of intemperance, because like many Black women reformers of the times, Truth connected alcohol abuse to the political corruption of her people. Her strategy for solving this problem included politically empowering Black women. She asserted that they needed the suffrage and equal rights in order to succeed in correcting the evils of government. In this case, temperance laws would discourage politicians from using alcohol to buy votes. By 1871 Truth was in Battle Creek with other African Americans who celebrated the anniversary of the emancipation of the slaves of the British West Indies. On that occasion, she called for the enfranchisement of women. Her continuous connection of women's rights and Black rights was characteristic of African American women of the times, although it was not the goal of the major woman suffrage organizations with which Truth affiliated.[26]

Perhaps for this reason, not all Black female suffragists of the times identified with the AWSA, whose single goal was woman suffrage. Others who focused more on broader feminist issues and women's adversities remained independent or participated in the NWSA as the leadership directed the campaign and recruiting into the Midwest and the Far West. For example, in 1869 the NWSA called a convention in Chicago, where Naomi Talbert (later to become Naomi Anderson) was recruited from among the Black women and spoke from the platform. Anthony and Stanton published excerpts from her speech in *The Revolution,* but, true to tradition, identified her merely as a "colored woman." Talbert, who spoke in the classic Black oratorical style, addressed the convention:

> And gentlemen, I warn you no longer to stand out in refusing the right for which we contend; in trying to withhold from these noble ladies here and their darker sisters the franchise they now demand. Miss Anthony and Mrs. Stanton, with their high moral and intellectual power, have shaken the states of New England, and the shock is felt here today. . . . Woman has a power within herself, and the God that reigns above, who commanded Moses to lead the children of Israel from out the land of Egypt, from out the house of bondage, who walled the waters of the Red Sea, who endowed Samson with power to slay his enemies with the jawbone of an ass, who furnished Abraham Lincoln with knowledge to write the emancipation proclamation, whereby four millions of Blacks were free—that God, our God, is with and for us, and will hear the call of woman, and her rights will be granted, and she shall be permitted to vote.[27]

Talbert's identification with Stanton and Anthony, at a time when they severely criticized Blacks and the pending Fifteenth Amendment, offended many of the African Americans of Chicago. Talbert's biographer, Monroe Majors, noted in the 1890s that she was severely censured as a result. In an attempt to vindicate herself, Talbert wrote an article on woman suffrage that was published in the *Chicago Tribune.* Ironically, the article was quite similar to her speech at the convention, which probably did not endear her to her critics. Her position was radical for Blacks at the time, revealing her identification with white feminists on one hand, yet using words reminiscent of Sojourner Truth's religious exhortations on the other. Talbert seemed caught in her attempts to deal with the problems of racism and sexism at the same time. Nonetheless, both her speech and her newspaper article reflected nineteenth-century African American oratory and writing, in which religious symbolism was often connected to political issues.[28]

Characteristic of several Black feminists of the times, Talbert struggled throughout the 1870s to support her ailing husband and her family. She moved from Chicago to Portsmouth, Ohio, and learned the hairdressing trade. Carrying on another long nationalist tradition among African

American women, she combined work and service to Black communities. In Portsmouth she organized a home for orphaned Black children and continued to write and speak about the merits of temperance as well as woman suffrage. Widowed before the end of the decade, by 1879 Talbert had moved to Columbus, Ohio, where she met and married Lewis Anderson and continued to lobby for women's rights.[29]

Similar to Talbert's growing awareness about the plight of Black women, Mary Ann Shadd Cary continued an even more militant attack on the oppressive system of racism and sexism. Unlike Harper, after the demise of the American Equal Rights Association, Cary affiliated with the NWSA and attended all the national conventions held in Washington during the 1870s. While a law student, she met Charlotte E. Ray, daughter of abolitionists Charlotte B. and Charles B. Ray of New York City. During the 1860s, the elder Rays had been members of the AERA. It was perhaps Cary's influence that stimulated their daughter to affiliate with the NWSA rather than the AWSA, for Mr. and Mrs. Ray's names disappeared from the national suffrage scene with the collapse of the AERA. Regrettably, few details of the younger Ray's participation as a suffragist have survived. She was reported to have participated in the NWSA discussions during the 1876 convention held in New York City, to which she returned after a failing law career in the District of Columbia. Cary by this time had been an active suffragist for twenty years. She was respected by the leadership and appointed to the business committee in 1877.[30] Within a few years, however, Cary's name no longer appeared among NWSA leadership.

In the meantime, NWSA affiliations began to spread among suffragists in the Pacific Northwest, as Susan B. Anthony traveled west to recruit. In 1873 Mrs. Beatty attended the first annual convention of the Oregon State Woman Suffrage Association. The convention met in Portland, and Beatty was among the platform guests who addressed the body as woman suffrage advocates. Her speech was not recorded; nonetheless, her presence indicated the involvement and presence of Black women on the western woman suffrage frontier during the formative period.[31] The question remains about why Beatty's first name has not been found in any of the extant woman suffrage reports. Two possible reasons come to mind. First, the invisibility of Black women in general may have contributed to informants' inability to remember her full name. Second, during the postbellum period and the emancipation of all the enslaved, African American women sought the respectability that mainstream society had denied them. Many, like the women of Union Town outside of the District of Columbia, were reluctant to use their first names, preferring to simply use the title Miss or Mrs., or their first initials, with their last names, or to add Mrs. to their husband's name. In this manner, white people in particular could not casually use the women's first names as was the custom. I suspect Mrs. Beatty herself protected her first name by not making it known publicly. Certainly she was not an anomaly among African American suffragists in the West. However, nearly twenty years passed before additional written sources emerged that told of Black women suffragists west of the Mississippi River.

As the woman suffrage movement progressed into the 1880s, independent African American woman suffragists emerged, such as Mary A. McCurdy and Gertrude Bustill Mossell. McCurdy, like Sojourner Truth and Frances Harper a decade before, viewed intemperance as a major barrier to the uplift of her people. McCurdy edited a temperance newspaper while she lived in Richmond, Indiana, in 1884. A firm believer in woman suffrage, she saw the franchise as the means to prohibit the liquor traffic.[32] Unlike white women who joined the temperance movement in the 1880s and supported woman suffrage as a means to prohibition, McCurdy, like Black women before her, specifically viewed intemperance as a government ploy to keep Black people powerless. Nonetheless, her rhetoric was in keeping with the reform strategies mainstream suffragists developed during the times.

Another journalist, Gertrude Mossell, was consistent with other married African American women of her era and often wrote using her husband's initials—Mrs. N. F. Mossell. In 1885 she used traditional woman suffrage arguments when she initiated a woman's column in T. Thomas Fortune's Black newspaper the *New York Freeman.* Fortune, who was born a slave in Florida, had migrated to New York City after the Civil War. Like Frederick Douglass, he supported woman's rights activities by writing editorials that complimented his women columnist's ideas. Mossell was from a prominent Philadelphia antebellum, free Black family and was married to a physician. She can be characterized as among the Black elite. Her first article for the *Freeman* was entitled "Woman Suffrage," and in it she encouraged Blacks to read the *History of Woman Suffrage* (which had been published for the first time in 1881), the "New Era," the essays of British woman suffragist John

Stuart Mill, and other works about woman's rights that would familiarize Blacks with the woman suffrage movement. Mossell praised Senator Henry W. Blaire of New Hampshire, who had sponsored a bill in the United States Senate calling for an amendment to enfranchise all citizens, regardless of sex. Consequently, Mossell was in step with other woman suffragists of her race who were calling for a federal amendment. In addition, Mossell encouraged other men to join Blair, and noted that most housewives had already embraced woman suffrage.[33]

Although Mossell's frame of reference was taken from the mainstream views in the woman suffrage movement, like McCurdy, she directed her argument to the Black community, via the Black press. Gertrude Mossell was born into the same circle as was Hattie Purvis, who was a teenager when Gertrude was an infant. In addition, Mossell was a cousin of Sarah Douglass, an African American who had been a member of the Philadelphia Female Anti-Slavery society along with the Forten-Purvis women. Although younger than the abolitionist women, Mossell had traveled in similar arenas among white reformers. Hence her frame of reference initiated in their world. As an affluent mother of two, as well as a professional writer, like Stanton, she could relate to the middle-class views of housewives who were feminists. Nonetheless, by the 1880s, Mossell directed her argument to the African American women readers of the *Freeman.* It seems as though some of her words could have been spoken by Hattie Purvis, whose experience in the woman suffrage movement would have been extensive by the 1880s. Purvis was a member of the executive committee of the Pennsylvania Woman Suffrage Association in 1884, and between 1883 and 1900 she served as a delegate to the NWSA, and after the merger of the NWSA and the AWSA in 1890, to the NAWSA.[34] Unlike Mossell, who made her voice heard through the Black press, Purvis apparently did not. As a result, her views about woman suffrage remain unheard.

Conclusion

As the end of the 1880s approached, so did the formative years of the woman suffrage movement and a generation of Black women's involvement in the struggle. As the pioneers were joined by new recruits, at least thirty-five known Black women had petitioned for suffrage or participated actively in the movement during the first generation, with another 100 or more whose names remain unknown. By the mid-1880s, Nancy Prince, Margaretta Forten, Harriet Forten Purvis, and Sojourner Truth were dead. Sarah Remond had emigrated to Europe, with her sister Caroline Remond Putnam soon to follow. Other aging suffragists, such as Charlotte B. Ray, seemed to disappear from woman suffrage activities with the demise of the AERA. As the first generation of Black woman suffragists began to decline, however, a new more militant few began to emerge.

Nonetheless, during the last few years of the formative period, the names of African American women who were once prominent in the woman suffrage movement on a national level started to disappear from the national reports of the woman suffrage leadership. Several possible factors could have caused this trend. Either the white female leadership began not to need the support once sought from early black suffragists, and leaders refrained from recruiting Blacks; or the African American women suffragists saw less benefit from affiliating with white suffragists whose political priorities differed from their own; or there was a combination of both factors at work, provoked by the growing racial polarization in the United States during the late nineteenth century. This polarization stimulated separate political directions among the woman suffragists of the two races. Despite the ideological split in the woman suffrage movement that divided even Black women in the early 1870s, before the 1880s the realities of racism and sexism brought African American women who were feminists to a new political awareness that was more nationalistic in character. As this politicization occurred, Black women remained woman suffrage activists, working with the mainstream suffragists on some levels, but also organizing on local and national levels among themselves. These organizations also brought their leaders into public view on local and national levels. What made the 1870s and 1880s significant, nonetheless, was the emergence of verifiably authentic Black women's voices, which reflect the growing Black nationalist feminism of the era.

Notes

1. Ellen Carol DuBois, "Taking the Law into Our Own Hands," in Wheeler, *One Woman One Vote,* 84-86; Griffith, 119.
2. *Revolution,* vol. 2, no. 20, 19 November 1868, 307.
3. Griffith, 148.
4. *(Washington) New National Era,* 10 August 1871, 23 April 1874.
5. Bearden and Butler, 211-14.

6. Mary Ann Shadd Cary Speech to Judiciary Committee, folder 6, box 2, Mary Ann Shadd Cary Papers, Moorland-Spingarn Research Center, Howard University, Washington, DC, hereinafter cited as MASC Papers.

7. Cary Speech to Judiciary Committee, MASC Papers. In her biography of Oregon suffragist Abigail Scott Duniway, Ruth Barnes Moynihan quotes from the Oregon Herald, "Mrs. A. J. Duniway, a colored, and two white women" tried to vote in Portland. Moynihan notes that Duniway's grandson, David, a retired state archivist, identified the "colored" woman as Mrs. Beatty. Apparently no sources on this woman reveal her first name. Ruth Barnes Moynihan, *Rebel for Rights: Abigail Scott Duniway* (New Haven: Yale University Press, 1983), 85, 238 n. 4.

8. *HWS* 2: 626-27, 689. (History of Woman Suffrage ed. Stanton, Cady etal.)

9. Quarles, "Frederick Douglass," 35.

10. Terborg-Penn, "Nineteenth Century," 17.

11. DuBois, *Feminism and Suffrage,* 201-202.

12. DuBois, "Taking the Law into Our Own Hands," 97.

13. *HWS* 3: 31, 72-73, 955.

14. Both Dorothy Sterling, *We Too Are Your Sisters,* 411, 416, and Dorothy Salem, *To Better Our World: Black Women in Organized Reform, 1890-1920* (Brooklyn: Carlson Publishing, 1990), 38, state that more Black women, including Sojourner Truth, affiliated with the NWSA than the AWSA. On the other hand, Nell Painter says that Truth tried to straddle the two organizations, but "came finally to rest with the AWSA." Painter, *Sojourner Truth: A Life, A Symbol,* 232. Similarly, Adele Logan Alexander concludes that more African Americans supported the AWSA than the NWSA. Alexander, "Adella Hunt Logan, the Tuskegee Woman's Club, and African Americans in the Suffrage Movement," in *Votes for Women: The Woman Suffrage Movement in Tennessee, the South and the Nation,* ed. Marjorie Spruill Wheeler (Knoxville: University of Tennessee Press, 1995), 75. My research findings disagree with both Sterling and Salem.

15. Terborg-Penn, "Afro-Americans in the Struggle for Woman Suffrage," 46-49.

16. *HWS* 3: 268-69; Sterling, 96, 180.

17. *Crisis* vol. 10 (August 1915); 188.

18. Terborg-Penn, "Nineteenth Century Black Women," 16; *HWS* 3: 821, 827-28; for a history of the Rollin family women, see Carole Ione, *Pride of Family: Four Generations of American Women of Color* (New York: Summit Books, 1991).

19. *HWS* 3: 827-28.

20. *HWS* 3: 827-28.

21. Ibid., 828.

22. *HWS* 2: 803.

23. Petition for Woman Suffrage, House of Representatives, RG 233, HR 45th Congress, 1877-79, 45A. H11, folder 14, National Archives, Washington, DC.

24. *HWS* 3: 828; *HWS* 2: 833-34, 842.

25. Truth, *Narrative,* 151.

26. Ibid; 176, 177, 189.

27. *Revolution,* vol. 3 (4 March 1869): 139.

28. Monroe A. Majors, *Noted Negro Women: Their Triumphs and Activities* (Chicago: Donohue and Henneberry, 1893), 84; *(Chicago) Tribune,* 6 March 1869.

29. Majors, 84-85.

30. Scope Notes, MASC Papers; *HWS* 3: 19, 61, 72-73.

31. *HWS* 3: 773.

32. M. A. McCurdy, "Duty of the State to the Negro," *Afro-American Encyclopedia,* edited by James T. Haley (Nashville: Haley and Florida, 1895), 137-41, 144-45.

33. *(New York) Freeman,* 26 December 1885.

34. *HWS* 4: 898, 1104.

Works Cited

Manuscript Collections

Mary Ann Shadd Cary Papers, Moorland-Spingarn Research Center, Howard University, Washington, DC.

Newspapers, Magazines and Journals

Crisis

New National Era

Revolution

Published Sources

Bearden, Jim, and Linda Jean Butler. *Shadd: The Life and Times of Mary Shadd Cary.* Toronto: NC Press, 1977.

DuBois, Ellen Carol. *Feminism and Suffrage: The Emergence of an Independent Women's Movement in America, 1848-1869.* Ithaca, NY: Cornell University Press, 1978.

Painter, Nell Irvin. *Sojourner Truth: A Life, a Symbol.* New York: W. W. Norton, 1996.

Quarles, Benjamin. "Frederick Douglass and the Woman's Rights Movement." *Journal of Negro History* vol. 25 (January 1940): 35-44.

Stanton, Elizabeth Cady, et al., eds. *The History of Woman Suffrage, 1848-1920,* 6 vols. New York: Arno Press and the New York Times, 1969.

Terborg-Penn, Rosalyn. "Nineteenth Century Black Women and Woman Suffrage." *Potomac Review* vol. 7 (Spring-Summer 1977).

Wheeler, Marjorie Spruill, ed. *One Woman, One Vote: Rediscovering the Woman Suffrage Movement.* Troutdale, OR: NewSage Press, 1995.

DORIS WEATHERFORD (ESSAY DATE 1998)

SOURCE: Weatherford, Doris. "The Hour Not Yet, 1871 to 1888." In *A History of the American Suffragist Movement,* pp. 127-54. Santa Barbara, Calif.: ABC-CLIO, Inc., 1998.

In the following essay, Weatherford combines a detailed overview of how suffragists worked at the statewide level in the 1870s and 1880s to secure the right for women to vote, along with a discussion of how the movement began to unite with European organizations in order to gain global acceptance.

At their Chestnut Street headquarters for the Philadelphia centennial, the National Woman Suffrage Association kept "an immense autograph book" for visitors. Greetings "from the old world and the new" in it showed that the women's movement increasingly was going global. Some international links had been part of the movement from the beginning: Scottish Francis Wright had set the example in the 1840s, while German Mathilde Anneke and French Jeanne de Hericourt followed up by speaking to women's rights conventions in the 1850s and 1860s. After the Civil War, two feminist pioneers, Dr. Elizabeth Blackwell and Ernestine Rose, returned to their family roots in Britain and helped to spread the equal rights gospel there. For different reasons, African-American Sarah Remond returned to the United States only briefly after the Civil War; disappointed with the reality of black life in the United States, she lived out the rest of her life in Italy.

The first attempt at globalizing the women's movement came in 1871, when Julia Ward Howe and Caroline Severance, both officials of the American Woman Suffrage Association, called a women's conference on international understanding and peace. Although most people did not know it, Howe had a long list of literary credentials before she became famous for the Civil War's "Battle Hymn of the Republic." That militaristic song, however, clashed with her own liberal views,[1] and this fame motivated Howe to work for peace. Along with Severance, she helped organize a Woman's Peace Conference in London, and she assumed the American presidency of the new Woman's International Peace Association. Some of the foreign women who signed the 1876 autograph book in Philadelphia probably had read Howe's *Appeal to Womanhood Throughout the World* (1870) and were part of her loose network, but no one properly followed-up on this in the 1870s.

Another organization that began in the 1870s also would become international, but the Women's Christian Temperance Union had its greatest effect in the United States. Its beginnings were less consciously planned than most organizations: in the winter of 1873-1874, women in small midwestern towns began singing and praying outside of saloons, hoping to embarrass their men into spending less time and money there. The next year, Annie Wittenmyer, an Iowan who learned organizing skills in the Civil War's Sanitary Commission, linked these gentle protesters together into the Women's Christian Temperance Union (WCTU). They met for the first time in Cleveland, and within a few years, the WCTU—which, unlike the women's rights movement, was endorsed by most ministers—would have 25,000 members, far exceeding the older suffrage associations.

The link between the temperance and suffrage movements, of course, was long and close. Although Amelia Bloomer's *The Lily* became known as the first feminist journal, she had founded it to advocate temperance (and her association with dress reform was accidental). Susan B. Anthony also initially worked as a temperance lecturer, and the refusal of men in the movement to allow her to speak at conventions was an important factor in her decision to prioritize women's rights. Countless other women who were involved in the temperance movement back in the 1830s and 1840s saw this goal coming to fruition in the post-Civil War years, and the move from temperance work to suffrage work was a natural evolution for tens of thousands.

The increase in the social and political activity of women meant an expansion of organizations. Until this time, the average woman belonged to virtually no groups; even church-based ones often were considered unacceptable if they were run by female officers. The endless round of meetings that seemed so commonplace for the women's rights leadership was still an unknown activity for most women—but finally, 30 or 40 years after the travel and speaking taboos had been broken by the exceptional, mainstream women began to emulate them. The 1870s and 1880s saw an explosion of organization-building, especially in the North, which came to be called the club movement.

This movement's best-known pioneers were the Boston-based New England Woman's Club and New York City's Sorosis, both of which began in 1868. Loosely defined, these groups were either "study clubs" that aimed to give women educational and literary access or they were "civic clubs" that aimed to improve their communities with libraries, kindergartens, parks, and playgrounds. Most clubs were stepping stones toward full emancipation and usually did not endorse suffrage, but suffragists almost invariably found them to be helpful campaign tools. Someone within, say, the Peoria Woman's Club or the Portland Woman's Club would step forward to assist Lucy Stone or Susan B. Anthony when they came to Illinois or Oregon.

Julia Ward Howe, the first president of the American Woman Suffrage Association, was particularly active in the club movement. This cross-fertilization of groups was more typical of the American association, which tended to meet women where they were intellectually and only gently prod them into greater politicization. That was not the style of the National, whose leaders were more impatient with the temporizers. To a fairly large extent during the 1870s and 1880s, the American association reached out to mainstream women and men across the country through its *Woman's Journal* and its popular writers and lecturers—Howe, Stone, Livermore, Stowe, and others. Meanwhile, the National concentrated on political action, especially in Washington, where they became adept at lobbying the nation's most powerful men.

Susan B. Anthony headquartered herself at the Riggs Hotel in Washington, D.C., where the owners hosted her without charge partly because they believed in her cause and partly because she attracted other guests. In 1878, at the request of the National association, Senator A. A. Sargent of California introduced a slightly reworded version of the Sixteenth Amendment: "The right of citizens of the United States to vote shall not be denied or abridged by the United States or by any State on account of sex." This would be the lobbying target until its language finally was adopted by Congress in 1919. It came to be known as the "Susan B. Anthony Amendment," as other topics used up numbers 16, 17, and 18 before the "Sixteenth Amendment" finally passed. Senator Sargent became a hero to the women as year after year, he unsuccessfully pushed for adoption.

Literally millions of petitions would support the amendment—but at the same time, women also spoke against it from the beginning. In the same 1878 congressional session that Isabella Beecher Hooker and Dr. Clemence Lozier[2] led the lobbying for the National Woman Suffrage Association, Madeleine Vinton Dahlgren, the well-pensioned recent widow of a Navy admiral and leader of the Anti-Suffrage Association, testified against the Sixteenth Amendment. Her objections, she said:

> are based upon that which in all Christian nations must be recognized as the higher law, the fundamental law upon which Christian society . . . must rest. . . . When women ask for a distinct political life, a separate vote, they forget or willingly ignore the higher law, whose logic may be condensed: Marriage is a sacred unity. . . . Each family is represented through its head. . . . The new doctrine . . . may be defined: Marriage is a mere compact, and means diversity. Each family, therefore, must have a separate individual representation, out of which arises . . . division and discord.

Dahlgren's supporters, although privileged enough that they were permitted unusual access to congressional chambers, remained few. Many more testified in favor of the Sixteenth Amendment, and they came year after year. This amendment and the city of Washington became the focus of the National association: its annual meetings were held there in January because, as Anthony said, "Congress is then in session, the Supreme Court sitting, and . . . [it is] the season for official receptions, where one meets foreign diplomats. . . . Washington is the modern Rome to which all roads lead."

In 1880, however, the National emulated the American and took its show on the road. The suffragists held mass meetings in Indiana, Wisconsin, Michigan, and Illinois—where they met in Chicago during the Republican Party's convention. It was an excellent networking opportunity, and the women even had an unusual rallying point when the Arkansas delegation to the Republican convention came prepared with this resolution: "Resolved, That we pledge ourselves to secure to women the exercise of their right to vote." It was a happy surprise, for not only was this resolution proposed by southern men, but also its wording assumed the applicability of the Fifteenth Amendment—women had a right to vote, and the party merely was asked to enforce it. Not surprisingly, however, the resolution was referred to a convention committee, where arguments by Belva Lockwood and Susan B. Anthony failed to move it forward.

The National also sent representation to the convention of the Greenback Party, a party aimed at improving the economy by ending the gold standard, which limited the circulation of paper dollars. Although a suffrage resolution was presented by a female delegate, it was not even spoken to in committee. "Women were better treated by the Democrats at Cincinnati," according to Anthony, "than by the Republicans at Chicago." The Democrats gave the suffragists seats "just to the back of the regular delegates" and even a room "was placed at their disposal." Although the final outcome was the same, Anthony was pleased that the resolution committee placed no time limit on the women's appeals, even though adjournment waited until two in the morning.

Not surprisingly, the new Prohibition Party, which was formed in 1872, was the most welcoming to women. Even if they did not grant women the sort of full participation that Rev. Antoinette Brown and others had desired so long ago, the party's founders had old and strong philosophical links to the suffrage movement. In adopting the word "prohibition," the new party exhibited greater candor about their old goal, for their objective actually was the same as the "temperance" of the Women's Christian Temperance Union and other, older groups. None of the so-called temperance organizations had ever truly promoted the temperate use of alcohol and other addictives; instead, they wanted to enact legal bans or "prohibition" of alcohol.

The fledgling party in Massachusetts reached out to women when it first began by inviting them to participate in the 1876 party caucuses and, most surprisingly, its primary. Although it proved to be a one-time experiment and made little long-term difference, this unusual opportunity to vote in a party election did give some women a taste of political action. One recalled a decade later, in the 1886 volume of the *History of Woman Suffrage,* the "terror" of casting her first vote:

> It was thought to be a rash act for a woman to appear at the polls in company with men. Some attempt was made to deter them from their purpose, and stories of pipes and tobacco and probable insults were told. . . .
>
> The women learned several things during this campaign. One was that weak parties are no more to be trusted than strong ones; and another, that men grant but little until the ballot is placed in the hands of those who make the demand. They learned also how political caucuses and conventions are managed.

Like the official suffrage organizations, the Prohibition Party would never grow very large compared with other parties, but unlike the suffragists, its men could vote—and they would provide a bloc just large enough to force the major parties to pay heed to them. In the presidential election of 1884, for instance, the Democratic nominee received approximately 4,875,000 votes, while the Republican won 4,852,000. Had even a portion of the 150,000 that went to the Prohibition candidate gone to the Republican instead, he would have won. The party demonstrated that, although it was small, it could be crucial—and women were assumed to be a part of it, for the era's politicos took it as a given that if women could vote, they would vote for Prohibitionist candidates.

The result was that some Prohibitionist men encouraged female political participation—as in the Massachusetts experiment—but only tentatively and for limited purposes. Most male Prohibitionists were so fundamentally conservative that they could not bring themselves to wholeheartedly support this change in the status quo, even if it would mean at least a doubling of their political power. Generally unwilling to concede the injustice of excluding women from voting, they were more likely to push for the "half-loaf" (or more accurately, a slice or two), allowing women to vote in municipal elections on liquor questions only. Elizabeth Cady Stanton, better-traveled and more sophisticated than many suffragists, did not completely share the usual temperance views—but even she was so accustomed to this political alliance that she never straightforwardly challenged her sisters on it. Instead, she was scornful of male Prohibitionists who opposed suffrage: "What people might drink," she said, seemed to them "a subject of greater importance than a fundamental principle of human rights."

Ultimately, whatever slim support for suffrage that male Prohibitionists offered was infinitely less important to women than was the opposition of the liquor industry and all of its powerful allies. Over and over again, women would lose suffrage elections because men were convinced that if women voted, the saloons would dry up. Especially in the West, this belief was devastating to the suffrage movement: already in the Kansas and Colorado referenda—long before the existence of a formal Prohibition Party—suffragists could see the negative effect when men went from the saloon to the polls and back again.

Even in the East, the prohibitionist views that many women held hurt the suffrage cause, and again the problem would grow worse instead of better with time. This was because the movement came of age at the same time that millions of immigrants began changing the national demographics. Prior to the 1840s, when the women's movement began, the United States had been almost wholly filled with Protestant descendants of British colonists. The Irish potato famine and revolutions in Europe began to change all that in the 1840s, as increasing numbers of foreigners began to arrive—many of them Catholic and most of them accustomed to the daily use of alcohol.

The Civil War and its aftermath slowed down immigration briefly, but by the 1880s and 1890s, millions were arriving every year. They came from southern and eastern Europe, from cultures very different from the British, Scandinavian, and German immigrants of the past. Few were Protestant; most were Catholic or Jewish. Virtually all considered a glass of wine to be a routine part of a meal. They were absolutely perplexed by prohibition, and as soon as they could obtain citizenship, their men would vote against it. Add to this the fact that most immigrant men were deeply conservative in their view of women,[3] and a continual clash between these men and the suffragists becomes a foregone conclusion.

The clash was apparent long before the major wave of immigration and far from the cities usually associated with immigrants. Already in the 1867 Kansas campaign, the immigrant/prohibition factor hurt women. "The Germans in their Conventions," reported *The History of Woman Suffrage,* passed a resolution against liquor restrictions, which they linked directly to women: "In suffrage for women they saw rigid Sunday laws and the suppression of their beer gardens."[4] The Irish to whom George Train had appealed in that campaign also were fearful that if American women could vote they would force an end to their ancient pub habits, and so these men, too, voted against suffrage.

The innate conservatism of both Irish and German Catholics on women's roles was reinforced by church officials. During their 1877 campaign, for example, Colorado leaders Mary G. Campbell and Katherine G. Patterson wrote that the Denver bishop "preached a series of sermons . . . in which he fulminated all the thunders of apostolic and papal revelation against women who wanted to vote." Like other clergy, he predicted that female political participation would lead directly to the destruction of marriages and homes. Campbell and Patterson, who like most suffragists were happily married, took particular offense at this attack by an unmarried man whose understanding of women and of family relationships was clearly limited:

> The class of women wanting suffrage are battalions of old maids disappointed in love—women separated from their husbands or divorced by men from their sacred obligations. . . . Who will take charge of those young children (if they consent to have any) while mothers as surgeons are operating. . . . No kind husband will refuse to nurse the baby on Sunday . . . in order to let his wife attend church; but even then, as it is not his natural duty, he will soon be tired of it and perhaps get impatient waiting for the mother, chiefly when the baby is crying.

Suffragists returned the antipathy they felt from most foreign-born men with language that would embarrass most Americans today. For instance, while presiding over meetings dedicated to civil rights, Elizabeth Cady Stanton used "ignorant" as an axiomatic adjective for foreigner, and she unabashedly told a story denigrating Irishmen whose only consolation for their wretched lives was that they could vote while educated women could not. She joined Susan B. Anthony in recording without embarrassment that, in their last meeting with Horace Greeley, they had referred to foreign-born men as "Patrick, Hans, and Yung Fung." This kind of language was not limited to women of the National association: Julia Ward Howe, the first president of the American, had complained in an 1869 article on suffrage that "the Irish or German savage, after three years' cleansing, is admitted" to the voter rolls. Male liberals were capable of the same language and of even worse reasoning. The literary giant Oliver Wendell Holmes, for example, refused to support suffrage because enfranchising women would include the Irish women who invariably worked as servants in middle-class Boston homes—and Hannah, he said, already had enough power at the breakfast table.

Eastern urbanites were not the only xenophobes. In the 1870 debate on enfranchising women in the Colorado territory, women there had lamented—but nevertheless accepted—legislative objections that if "our intelligent women" were allowed to vote, then the government would be forced to extend the same right to "the poor, degraded Chinese women who might reach our shores[5]—and what then would become of our proud, Caucasian civilization?" That most of these immigrants were men who might already vote seemed unnoteworthy—to say nothing of the fact that xenophobic American women could join their men to easily outvote foreigners of both genders. As in the case of black women and the Fifteenth Amendment, the burden of ethnicity was apparently so great that Anglo-Saxon suffragists were unable even to consider an alliance with immigrant women. Instead of joining with these most oppressed groups, most suffragists preferred to blame their own delay on the public's association of them with these minorities. They allowed decades to pass while politicians used black women in the South and immigrant women in the North as their excuse for the disenfranchisement of all women.

In 1871, two years after she formed the National Woman Suffrage Association, Susan B. Anthony traveled to the still-wild country of Oregon. Abigail Scott Duniway organized Anthony's West Coast lecture tour in return for "one-half the gross proceeds," which she needed to support her disabled husband and six children.

Duniway, who also published the increasingly successful *New Northwest,* founded the Oregon Equal Rights Society in 1870—the same year in which her Wyoming and Utah neighbors first voted and the same year in which the first legislative effort for suffrage began in Colorado.

Mary G. Campbell and Katherine G. Patterson, sisters who wrote Colorado's 1886 report for the *History of Woman Suffrage,* did a beautiful job of describing their land's early history:

> In 1848, while those immortal women . . . [met] in Seneca Falls . . . Colorado, unnamed and unthought of, was still asleep with her head above the clouds. . . . In 1858, when the Ninth National Convention of Women . . . was in session in New York, there were only three white women in the now rich and beautiful city of Denver. Still another ten years of wild border life . . . and Colorado was organized into a territory with a population of 5,000 women and 25,000 men.

Campbell and Patterson astutely pointed out that women's best opportunity to obtain legal rights was in the territorial stage, for life during such a regency-type government gave men some experience with living in a woman's world. Men chafed at their loss of democratic rights in territories, where governors were appointed instead of elected and Washington second-guessed every action of the embryonic government. Men who felt they knew best what should be done in their home area instead had to wait for federal approval, and a taxpaying man "could no more enforce his opinion . . . by a vote than could the most intelligent woman." All of a sudden, these men understood what women were talking about.

Thus, at Colorado's fifth territorial legislative assembly in 1870, frontier men again showed more openness than those in the ossified East. Prompted by his "beautiful, accomplished, and gracefully aggressive wife," Gov. Edward McCook sent the assembly a message:

> It has been said that no great reform was ever made without passing through three stages ridicule, argument, and adoption. It rests with you to say whether Colorado will accept this reform in its first stage, as our sister territory of Wyoming has done, or in the last; whether she will be a leader or a follower; for the logic of a progressive civilization leads to the inevitable result of universal suffrage.

Colorado's legislative majority that year was "unexpectedly Democratic, and almost as unexpected was the favor shown by the Democratic members." This partisan picture was so much the opposite of what had been expected that the vote for women came to be "characterized by the opposing Republicans as 'the great Democratic reform.'" But not quite enough Democrats fell into the column, and the proposal lost by one vote in the upper chamber. The House rushed to reinforce the loss with a two-thirds margin.

As they had elsewhere, women regrouped and carried on. Talk turned to achieving statehood during the centennial year of 1876, and that became the next target. On what turned out to be a bitterly cold January night in 1876, "a large and eager audience" filled Denver's spacious Unity Church long before the scheduled time. "The Rev. Mrs. Wilkes" of Colorado Springs, who opened the meeting, pointed out that women owned a third of the taxable property in that city, but had no voice in a recent election when men turned down a water system—despite pollution that endangered public health. Lucy Stone sent an encouraging letter to the group, as did Wyoming's Gov. John M. Thayer, who declared "woman suffrage in that territory to have been beneficial."[6]

The women once again gathered thousands of petitions, and the next month the constitutional convention for the new state took up the question. With a large number of women watching, "some of the gentlemen celebrated the occasion by an unusual spruceness of attire, and others by being sober enough to attend to business." After voting down both full suffrage and partial suffrage for school elections, the men[7] put the question on the fall ballot and—ten years after the suffragists' defeat in Kansas—another referendum attracted national attention.

Apparently unaware of the strain between them, Dr. Alida C. Avery, who led the Colorado effort, invited both Lucy Stone and Susan B. Anthony; both came, along with Henry Blackwell. Colorado women, however, deemed two Pennsylvanians, Philadelphia's Leila Patridge and Pittsburgh's Matilda Hindman, as their most effective campaigners. None were good enough, however, and women were soundly rebuffed in the fall: about 10,000 of the male electorate voted for suffrage, while 20,000 opposed it. Mrs. H. S. Mendenhall wrote an excellent analysis of her experience canvassing at the polls:

> The day led me to several general conclusions. . . . (1) Married men will vote for suffrage if their wives appreciate its importance. (2) Men without family ties, and especially if they have associated with a bad class of women, will vote against it. (3) Boys who have just reached [adulthood] will vote against it more uniformly than any other class of men. We were treated with the utmost respect by all except [young men] . . . destitute of experience, and big with their own

> importance. . . . I have been to-day tempted to believe that no one is fitted to exercise the American franchise under twenty-five years of age. . . .
>
> The main objection which I heard repeatedly . . . was women do not want to vote. . . . Men were continually saying that their wives told them not to vote for woman suffrage.

That no one would drag these conservative wives to the polls and force them to vote against their will, of course, was rarely pointed out. The movement might have met with greater success if it had stressed this point: that it was neither just nor logical to deprive all women of the vote because some professed not to want it. Instead, the leadership concentrated on convincing all women that they *should* want political rights—heedless of the fact that most women (like most men) were simply too absorbed with their personal lives and problems to care very much about remote issues or candidacies. Given the burdens of most women's lives, it was not surprising that they found it easier to say they did not want to vote.

In 1874 a referendum was held in Michigan, where it was again the governor's wife who inspired him and the legislature to place the question on the ballot. Once more, Susan B. Anthony and Elizabeth Cady Stanton went out to campaign. Michigan's report in the *History of Woman Suffrage* replicated the hopefulness of the Kansas referendum, with the same sad result:

> Everything that could be done . . . was done; meetings held and tracts . . . scattered in the most obscure settlements; inspiring songs sung, earnest prayers offered, the press vigilant in its appeals, and on election day women everywhere at the polls, persuading voters to cast their ballots for temperance, moral purity, and good order, to be secured by giving the right of suffrage to their mothers, wives, and daughters. But the sun went down, the polls were closed, and in the early dawn of the next morning the women of Michigan learned that their status . . . had not been advanced by one iota.

The next big state referendum was Colorado's disappointing 1877 campaign. Nebraska followed five years later. The American association held its 1882 convention in Omaha early in September; perhaps because the monthly *Woman's Journal* announced the American's plans, the National also held a convention there later in the month. According to Nebraska's report in the *History of Woman Suffrage,* Lucy Stone, Henry Blackwell, and Hannah Tracy Cutler "remained for some weeks . . . and were warmly received." Perhaps the most diligent worker of all was Margaret W. Campbell of Massachusetts: although she never developed the publicity-seeking personality that creates fame, by the time that the third volume of the *History of Woman Suffrage* was published in 1886, Campbell had represented the American association in 20 different states and territories. Well-experienced in midwestern statewide referenda by now, the women went through the same campaign trails and trials as before, and with the same result:

> As the canvass progressed, it was comical to note how shy the politicians [became] to those they had promised assistance. . . . Towards the close of the campaign, it became evident that the saloon element was determined to defeat the amendment. The Brewers Association sent out its orders to every saloon; bills posted in conspicuous places by friends of the amendment mysteriously disappeared; . . . and the greatest pain was taken to excite the antagonism of foreigners by representing to them that woman suffrage meant prohibition.[8] On the other hand, temperance advocates were by no means a unit for support.

They lost 50,693 to 25,756, although few believed that was the true count. Elections then were unlike modern ones in that voters—many of whom were illiterate or only semiliterate—did not actually mark their ballots, but instead deposited preprinted "tickets" with slates of party-endorsed candidates.[9] In this election, the Nebraska women said, "many tickets were fraudulently printed . . . tickets that contained no mention of the [women's] amendment were counted against it" and even those that used "the abbreviated form, 'For the Amendment' were counted against it." Worse, this would be just one of many future elections controlled by the liquor industry.

Although Indiana had formed one of the first suffrage associations and although Amanda Way addressed its legislature back in 1860, it, too, defeated the suffragists in 1882. Women had lost a legislative vote (51 to 22) in 1877, and they decided to try a different approach in 1882: they worked to influence men to elect candidates to the legislature who were pledged to suffrage. They campaigned for a year; the leaders, who worked with both the National and the American associations, were May Wright Sewall and Helen M. Gougar.

"Large numbers of societies were organized and many meetings held," according to Sewall. The women "sought every opportunity to reach the ears of the people," even including the campgrounds of religious revivalists. They went to "Sunday-school conventions, teacher associations, agricultural fairs, picnics and assemblies of every name." Even some politicians noticed their unusual ability and, "for the first time in the history of Indiana, women were employed by party managers to address political meetings and advocate the election of candidates." Meanwhile, however, "the animosity of the liquor league was aroused, and this powerful association threw itself against" the women's candidates. Another election, and another innovative political strategy, went down to defeat.

After so much disappointment, the next year brought hope. In the first victory since 1870, women in the Washington territory won full voting rights in 1883. Abigail Scott Duniway went up from Oregon on the big day and with "trembling hands," recorded each legislator's vote. When the victory was clear, she rushed to the telegraph office, "my feet seeming to tread the air," and notified her "jubilant and faithful" sons, who took the front page of her Portland-based *New Northwest* off the press to add the news. "A bloodless battle had been fought and won," she said, "and the enemy, asleep in carnal security, had surrendered unaware."

When the "freed women of Washington" began to vote and serve on juries, "the lawbreaking elements," according to Duniway, "speedily escaped to Oregon." Although Oregon women "had carefully districted and organized the State, sparing neither labor nor money in providing 'Yes' tickets for all parties and all candidates," it was clear as soon as the polls opened that the opposition was equally well organized. "Multitudes of legal voters who are rarely seen in daylight" turned up at the polls, while "railroad gangs were driven to the polls like sheep and voted against us in battalions."[10] Not surprisingly, the women lost 28,176 to 11,223.

Even the Washington victory turned out to be a heartbreaker. Just four years later, the Supreme Court struck down the territorial law that enfranchised them, and from 1887 to 1910, Washington women, too, would languish without the vote. The case once again demonstrated that the era's courts were much harsher to women than was its average man. While the Supreme Court ruled against women on the Fifteenth Amendment and again in this Washington case, ordinary men in several western states voted to fully enfranchise women. Even in certain eastern elections, women were winning some limited voting rights, but the nation's highest court repeatedly ruled against half of its citizens.

Nor would Washington women be the only ones to have the vote and then lose it. Utah's

ON THE SUBJECT OF...

VICTORIA WOODHULL (1838-1927)

Victoria Claflin Woodhull was the first woman to run for president in the United States—in 1872, when women did not even have the right to vote. Woodhull's family, the Claflins, ran a traveling medicine show, complete with miracle cures and fortune tellers. Victoria and her sister, Tennessee, forged a partnership and claimed to be clairvoyant. At age fifteen Victoria's father married her to a kind but alcoholic doctor, Canning Woodhull. They had two children and divorced in 1866, though Victoria supported him and their children financially throughout her life. She married Colonel James Harvey Blood in 1868, the same year that she and her sister moved to New York City and charmed railroad promoter Cornelius Vanderbilt. Though Tennessee refused his marriage proposal, the sisters did accept his financial advice and funds to open their own stock brokerage house, and soon enjoyed wealth and a lively social life. With their good looks, spirited personalities and unusual talents, the sisters attracted publicity and many admirers and supporters. They entertained radical intellectuals in their salon and founded a newspaper, *Woodhull and Claflin's Weekly,* in 1870. Through the paper they and their friends championed free love, equal rights for women, birth control, and socialism. The *Weekly* also engaged in muckraking, exposing injustices and hypocrisies.

Woodhull also enjoyed fame as a popular lecturer, demonstrator and public speaker. She contributed enthusiastically to the women's suffrage movement, but many of the movement's other supporters were uncomfortable with the support of such a controversial woman. Woodhull announced her bid for the United States Presidency in a letter to the *New York Herald.* She was thirty-two, and her running mate was Frederick Douglass. Woodhull was defeated, but her speeches in favor of women's suffrage before the House Judiciary Committee in 1871 helped sway many adversaries to her cause.

enfranchisement of women continued to be controversial, even with suffragists, because of polygamy. Despite the favorable attitudes of many in the Women's Christian Temperance Union toward suffrage, the WCTU gathered 250,000 petition signatures requesting Congress to rescind the voting rights of Utah women.[11] Their object was to help nonMormons outvote Mormons by eliminating the women's votes. The petitions had their effect and in 1887, at the same time that it outlawed polygamy, Congress rescinded the right of Utah women to vote.

Emmeline B. Wells, a Utah lobbyist who had successfully defended both polygamy and suffrage, was not present when Congress did this and she immediately organized a state suffrage association to regain the vote. Through their mutual lobbying, Wells had become good friends with Susan B. Anthony and other leaders; in 1874 she was already a vice-president of the National Woman Suffrage Association. It was another case in which the National and American associations differed: although the American would not go so far as to oppose Utah women the way the WCTU did, their leaders did not maintain friendships with Mormons either. Even the National did not rally in Wells's absence, for most suffragists feared that public association of polygamy with their cause would be harmful. Thus, when Congress rescinded Utah women's votes, no one spoke in opposition.

The WCTU also displayed its political muscle in Kansas that year: in addition to the school suffrage they had enjoyed since 1861, Kansas women also won the right to vote in municipal elections in 1887. This was much more significant that it may appear, for a community's decision to be "wet" or "dry"—to allow alcohol sales or ban them—is usually made in a municipal election. The WCTU even was active in municipal elections in the South, where suffrage organizations remained unwelcome. In this same year, a Tampa election on alcohol sales was strongly influenced by WCTU women. They served free food and lemonade at the polls and of more than a thousand ballots cast, the nonvoting women lost by just 25 votes. Foreigners were a factor in this election, too, for the alcohol issue was raised after large numbers of Spanish, Italian, and Cuban immigrants were recruited to work in the city's cigar factories. These men were not about to forego their daily wine and beer, and many Anglo men voted with them out of fear of losing their labor.

So many campaigns of such diverse natures—from municipal and state elections to efforts targeting Congress, the courts, the parties, constitutional conventions, and state legislatures—were taking place in so many areas of the country, with so many people involved, that simply keeping track of them began to be nearly impossible. In 1884 women were defeated in the first of several referenda in Oregon; this election also marked the first national visibility of antisuffrage women. About 20 wealthy Massachusetts women, not satisfied with sending "remonstrances" against suffrage to their own legislature, also sent money to oppose their Oregon sisters.

Just south of Oregon, women in California were akin to eastern women in that they supported national organizations while dawdling at home. Although they had the West's oldest suffrage association, formed in 1869, and although Susan B. Anthony and Elizabeth Cady Stanton visited in 1871, progress there was exceptionally slow in comparison with other western states. Ellen Clarke Sargent, who was married to U.S. Senator A. A. Sargent, saw that her husband remained the chief sponsor of the Sixteenth Amendment, but the Sargents' leadership was in their Washington context, not in California. In 1873, women became eligible to hold school offices, but not to vote in them, and unlike other midwestern and western states, California had little to report in the 1886 volume of the *History of Woman Suffrage*.

The only exception was something that most suffragists did not want to acknowledge, for few supported the 1884 presidential campaign of attorney Belva Lockwood. Although she was an easterner, most of Lockwood's support for her National Equal Rights Party came from the West, and its vice-presidential nominee was Marietta L. B. Stowe of San Francisco. Like Victoria Woodhull in 1872, Lockwood did not expect to be a credible candidate, but she had a method to her madness: her Equal Rights Party hoped to elect one member of the electoral college that formally chooses the president and thereby "become the entering wedge." Even that modest goal was not achieved, however, as she won some 4,000 votes in five states—out of 10 million cast. Not deterred, Lockwood repeated her campaign in 1884. This time the Equal Rights Party met in Iowa, but the midwestern attention made no difference in the fall, when the results were even more disappointing than in 1880. As they had with Woodhull, the leadership of both national associations lamented Lockwood's ambition and audacity, but her response was reasonable enough. She pointed out that Queen Victoria was successfully reigning over a vast empire and responded to critics of her 1884 presidential campaign: "We shall never have equal rights until we take them, nor respect until we command it."

The American association celebrated the thirtieth anniversary of the first National Woman's Rights Convention with great fanfare, meeting again in Worcester as they had in 1850. They featured speeches by women who had spoken then, among them 70-year-old Abby Kelly Foster. She refused to spend her time reminiscing, but instead used the occasion to denounce the concept of partial suffrage. New Hampshire, New York, and other states recently had granted women the vote for school elections, and in Foster's own state of Massachusetts, "school suffrage" was also a hot issue. She deemed "half a vote" worse than none, but most women disagreed: indeed, according to the *History of Woman Suffrage,* Massachusetts's enactment of school suffrage was plotted "in the parlors of the New England Women's Club." It was motivated by the male electorate's failure to reelect Abby May and other women to the Boston school committee, and its legislative sponsors seemed to believe that women would prevent future losses of such public-spirited officeholders.

For whatever reason, Massachusetts women gained school suffrage in 1880—sort of. Partial suffrage, as Abby Kelly Foster foresaw, made the potential voter subject to the whim of local officials who empowered themselves to decide whether or not to grant ballots in these special cases. "The law," according to state suffrage official Harriet H. Robinson, "was very elastic and capable of many interpretations." Six years after the act passed, she counted at least 20 variants, as tax collectors and voter registrars "interpreted the law according to their individual opinion on the woman suffrage question." Some officials required that women pay the state and local poll taxes,[12] ignoring the fact that women could not vote in those races. "In some towns," Robinson reported, women who tried to cast their legitimate school-election ballots were "treated with great indignity, as if they were doing an unlawful act."

Incidentally, while American versions of partial suffrage were defined by the type of election—school or municipal or, very rarely, party primary—partial suffrage overseas was more likely to vary by the type of voter. Defining voters by property ownership or by age or (in the case of women) by marital status was an effective way of keeping the vote securely in the hands of the upper class. In America, however, such blatant class distinction was not a political possibility. After politicians had allowed all men over 21 to vote regardless of taxpaying status or literacy, they could not expect to define women this way. Partial suffrage in America, therefore, was determined not by the status of the voter but by the type of election.[13]

School suffrage continued to be the measure of American progress through the next years. In 1874 Illinois gave a slight boost to women by allowing them to be elected without becoming electors: Illinois followed Boston's example and granted women the right to hold school offices—but not to vote for themselves. Michigan was more enlightened: although it had turned down full suffrage in 1874, it adopted the school version in 1875. Minnesota did the same in the same year—and, significantly, the new law was passed as a constitutional amendment voted on by the entire male electorate, rather than merely the legislature. Moreover, Minnesota men proved more enlightened than its women expected, for the measure passed by a wide margin: 24,340 to 19,468. The state suffrage association's carefully planned and successful strategy was to appear indifferent. Except for contacting the editor of St. Paul's *Pioneer Press*—who "had quite forgotten such an amendment had been proposed"—to write a few favorable pieces at the last minute, the women made "no effort to agitate the question, lest arousing opposition."

Suffragists were becoming astute politicians, but not quite astute enough for the Dakota Territory. In 1872 and another heartbreaker, the territorial legislature failed to enfranchise women by one vote—that of a man, W. W. Moody, who later changed his mind and became one of the suffragists' best supporters. The territory's position on school suffrage showed a similar change of mind: granted in 1879, it was repealed in 1883—except in 15 of the oldest and largest counties, which demonstrated once again the complex and whimsical nature of partial suffrage. But full suffrage was the object, so in this same year, Matilda Joslyn Gage went out to Dakota to work for inclusion of women in the new constitutions when the territory was divided into North Dakota and South Dakota.

Marietta Bones, who was the leader of the small movement in this sparsely populated area, addressed South Dakota's constitutional convention in Sioux Falls and initially was successful. She went to every meeting of the elections committee, and at the last, the men peppered her with questions—most of which revealed their fear of prohibition—for three hours. When the committee turned out to be tied on the suffrage question, the chairman voted yes. "After weeks of hard work I had reached the goal!" Bones wrote. "With eyes brim full of tears," she thanked the committee and left to spread the good news. The next morning, to her "utter surprise," the committee recommended to the full convention only that "women may vote at school elections." Bones was both humiliated and angry. "After all our work and pleading," she summarized, "they turned a deaf ear—worse they were dishonest!" Two years later, the legislature did better: both houses voted for full suffrage by healthy margins, but the governor vetoed the bill. Like so many others, Dakota women were discovering that their hour was not yet.

The hour would be even longer in coming to the South. Not surprisingly, its most western state, Texas, was the most activist. In an 1868 constitutional convention[14] there, a committee of five men proposed granting the vote to "every person, without distinction of sex." Although the full convention did not go along with the committee on suffrage, Texas law was far more liberal than that of most other states. Sarah W. Hiatt, reporting to the National association in 1886, said that she had "never lived in a community where the women are more nearly abreast of men in all the activities of life." The 1885 legislature even passed a law "making it compulsory on the heads of all departments to give at least one-half of the clerical positions in their respective offices to women," something that was considered "a victory for the woman's rights party."

Texas's neighbor to the east, Arkansas, also considered enfranchising women at its 1868 constitutional convention, but only briefly. The proposal caused so much tumult that the meeting adjourned; the next day, the sponsor of the suffrage clause insisted on speaking. Miles L. Langley was from the state's delta country where slavery had prevailed, and yet he declared: "I have been robbed, shot, and imprisoned for advocating the rights of the slaves, and I [will] speak for the rights of women if I have to fight!" His speech, of course, met only "ridicule, sarcasm, and insult," and he concluded sadly, "the Democrats are my enemies because I assisted in emancipating the slaves. The Republicans have now become my opponents because . . . [of] women. And even the women themselves fail to sympathize with me."

Arkansas's neighbor to the south, Louisiana, also addressed the subject in a constitutional convention. In 1879, over 400 "influential" people signed a petition to allow taxpaying women to vote. They pointed to the favorable influence of women on male behavior at Wyoming's polls, and carefully presented a conservative image. A woman testifying before the convention was quick to "assure you we are not cherishing any ambitious ideas of political honors or emoluments for women." The petition's language was similarly couched: "Surely the convention would not ask these quiet house-mothers, who are not even remotely akin to professional agitators, to do such violence to their old-time precedents if the prospect of some reward were not encouraging and immediate." The only reward, however, was very limited: the convention allowed Louisiana women to hold school offices, but not to vote in these or any other elections.

In Georgia, Florida, Mississippi, North Carolina, and Virginia, the era saw no legislative action at all. South Carolina was more successful: members of the American association managed to get a favorable committee report in 1872 for a constitutional amendment enfranchising "every person, male or female," but it never went beyond the committee. Kentucky women, led by women of the state's prominent Clay[15] family, actually held their suffrage meetings "in the legislative hall" at Frankfort. Although members of the legislature were in the audience along with "the best classes of people," they took no genuine political action. Women in the border states of Tennessee and Maryland were even less active, while an 1881 constitutional amendment proposed to a legislative committee in Delaware was shot down with just two favorable votes. Susan B. Anthony, Elizabeth Cady Stanton, Phoebe Couzins, and Belva Lockwood all had appeared before the Delaware legislature, and the two supportive votes they received made it clear that conservatism and prejudice were not traits confined to the Deep South.

Because partial suffrage was a question of state jurisdiction, and because the National association was dedicated to full suffrage, no half-measure for school or municipal suffrage was ever proposed to Congress. Instead, women concentrated on an amendment to the federal Constitution that would overturn the Supreme Court's 1874 *Minor v. Happersett* ruling on the Fifteenth Amendment. They met their first successes in the winter of 1881-1882, when Congress created a special joint committee "to look after the interests of women." It was not without debate, for some congressmen objected to creating any committee beyond the standing ones, while others objected to doing anything at all, but the measure passed 115 to 84 in the House and 35 to 23 in the Senate.

The National association, meeting as usual in Washington in January, went to testify to the new committee, but this time with an updated strategy: "Miss Anthony . . . in making the selection for the first hearing . . . [chose] some who were young, and all attractive . . . in order to disprove the allegation that 'it was always the same old set.'" Despite their inexperience, these women acquitted themselves well. One unnamed woman made a particular point of responding to southern congressmen who said their women did not wish to vote, and perhaps because of Anthony's "attractive" strategy, she succeeded well enough that "the member from Mississippi showed a great deal of interest and really became quite waked up." Senator Morgan from Alabama alleged that no woman from his state had "ever sent a petition . . . or letter to either house of Congress on this question"—but after the hearing, three wives of southern congressmen thanked the suffragists for saying what their husbands simply failed to hear when they said it.

This committee marked the movement's greatest congressional success thus far. A House committee had reported favorably on suffrage in 1871 and a Senate committee in 1879, but 1882 was the first time that the women received a favorable majority report in both houses. Senator Lapham proposed to the full Senate "an amendment to the Constitution of the United States to secure the right of suffrage to all citizens without regard to sex" on 5 June 1882.[16] The Senate ordered a thousand extra copies because of the unusual interest, but summer drifted on and no floor vote was taken. In the fall, both congressmen and suffragists again hit the campaign trail for state elections, and the precedent was set for drift. Although committees continued to issue favorable reports, never in the nineteenth century did the full House cast a vote on the proposal to amend the Constitution.

The Senate did so just once. On 25 January 1887, for the first and only time, senators cast a roll call vote on amending the Constitution to enfranchise all American women. After "a long and earnest discussion" the women got just 16 affirmative votes; there were 34 votes against and 25 sentators who effectively voted against suffrage by failing to vote at all. They hypocritically abstained, hoping that because they had not voted against either side, they could appeal to both.

America led the world in questions of women's rights, but the European continent looked north to Britain as its model. English Harriet Hardy Taylor, publishing under the name of her companion, philosopher John Stuart Mill, had explicated the ideas of the first National Woman's Rights Convention in 1850, and the British suffrage movement thus predated that of other European countries. When Mill was elected to Parliament in 1865, English suffragists began to make their first political moves. The very next year, they experienced a quick victory: the great prime minister Benjamin Disraeli said in Parliament: "In a country governed by [Queen Victoria] . . . I do not see . . . on what reasons she [woman] has not a right to vote."

Disraeli stuck with his quirkily announced position and, according to English suffragist Caroline Ashurst Biggs, "backed it up with his vote and personal influence for many succeeding years." Two petitions with more than 3,000 names on each followed-up this encouraging news, and the next year, suffrage associations were formed in London, Manchester, and the Scottish center of Edinburgh. In 1870 the *Woman's Suffrage Journal* was established in Manchester, the industrial city where the very first suffrage meeting had been held in 1868.

Things began to move much faster in the relatively homogeneous climate of Britain than they did in America, for it had none of the complexities—like prohibition, immigrants, former slaves, or tensions between territories and states—that American women faced. British Parliament first voted on suffrage two decades before the American Congress. Mills's 1867 proposal to substitute "person" for "man" in British voting law lost by 81 to 194, but he did not view this as a defeat: "We are all delighted," he wrote, for the vote was "far greater than anybody expected the first time."

After Mills was no longer in Parliament, the women's champion became Jacob Bright. He refused to let the issue die, bringing it up for a vote an amazing four times before 1874, when famous women such as Florence Nightingale and writer Harriet Martineau were among the 18,000 petitioners. Each new Parliament brought another test vote, and each time the margin was closer. Meanwhile, women won various forms of partial suffrage, including the right to vote in school elections and to hold school offices in 1870. Suffragists then targeted municipal elections: every time the men of a town or village went to the polls, they held a meeting and explained to women the local issues and candidates on which they had no voice. That this clever strategy was never emulated in the United States probably is explained by its quick, and therefore unnoticed, success: British

Susan B. Anthony, Frances Willard, and other members of the International Council of Women.

women won the vote in municipal elections in 1882. Scottish women voted for the first time, since the earlier partial suffrage victories had applied only to English women.

Partial suffrage in its many complexities was clearly inadequate, and in the 1880s women began holding rallies and demonstrations for full enfranchisement. The first was in a Manchester union hall, as British suffragists—unlike their U.S. sisters—understood that working-class women were key to political success. This hall held 5,000 and, according to Biggs, on 3 February 1880 it was packed with "factory women, shop-keepers and hard toilers of every station [who] sat on the steps of the platform and stood in dense masses in every aisle and corner." The strategy was repeated in London and elsewhere, and by 1886, the British electorate had been expanded from 3 million men to 5 million men and women.

Although women's rights languished on the Continent, even there hope began to spring. The French writer known as George Sand[17] had a tremendously liberating midcentury influence of France and the world, and the first international meeting on women's rights took place just two years after her 1876 death. Just as people flocked to Philadelphia for the American centennial fair in 1876, they came to Paris for a trade exposition in 1878, and the first International Woman's Rights Congress met there during July and August. It included representatives from Switzerland, Italy, Holland, Russia, and the United States; the French delegation included two senators and several other officeholders. Sixteen organizations sent delegations; from the United States, Julia Ward Howe and Mary Livermore represented the American suffrage association, while Chicago's Jane Graham Jones and Theodore Stanton spoke for the National association.

Like its Seneca Falls progenitor, the new "organization" did not bother with bylaws and similar formality, but instead plunged straight into the motivating issues. Those present divided their work load into the five categories of women's history, education, economics, moral issues, and legislative interests. The loose structure called for two permanent presidents, one of each gender; Frenchman Antide Martin, a Paris city council member, and Julia Ward Howe were chosen. By the last session of the congress, more representatives had come: the permanent committee that would carry on between meetings included not only the six nations listed above, but also Alsace-Lorraine, England, Germany, Holland, Poland, Rumania, and Sweden. Importantly for internal unity back home, the National association's Elizabeth Cady Stanton and Susan B. Anthony joined the American's Julia Ward Howe and Lucy Stone for the final banquet, and 200 people from at least 12 nations sat down together.

Five years later, on 16 November 1883, the women's movement made its first permanent move toward globalization. Women from France, Ireland, Scotland, and England met in Liverpool and honored Elizabeth Cady Stanton and Susan B. Anthony, who came to share their organizing experience. Like every other good meeting, they began by adopting a resolution: "Recognizing that union is strength and that the time has come when women all over the world should unite." They created committees and decided to follow up five years later, in 1888, when women would be celebrating the fortieth anniversary of the Seneca Falls convention.

They did as planned, and five years later, their efforts paid off better than anyone could have ever expected: the women who gathered in Washington in 1888 represented 49 nations! Many of them were recruited by the Women's Christian Temperance Union and its amazingly successful feminist president, Frances Willard. The previous year, a call had gone out from a committee of seven headed by Susan B. Anthony and Elizabeth Cady Stanton, advocating the formation of an International Council of Women. "It is impossible to overestimate the far-reaching influence of such a Council," they said. "An interchange of opinions on the great questions now agitating the world will rouse women to new thought . . . and give them a realizing sense of the power of combination." They mailed 4,000 calls and spent $12,000 on planning for the council, much of it on printing. The 16-page program for the event was duplicated so often that a "low estimate" was 672,000 pages of printing.

The eight-day meeting, which involved far more speeches and resolutions than can be detailed, was an impressive beginning for a permanent body poised to deal with the widely varied status of women around the world. President and Mrs. Grover Cleveland visited the conference, and the speakers included women of color. The women decided that each nation would hold a national assembly every three years; and they would join together for international follow-up every five years. The platform that was adopted spoke to the range of educational and economic barriers women faced, as well as to the burdens of marital and family law. Unlike Seneca Falls, however, this platform stopped short of demanding the vote. Such an encompassing idea of equality was still too radical for most of the delegates.

They came from countries in which the very idea of democracy was still new: after all, only a little more than a century had passed since America created a model for governing without a monarch or other supreme authority. That model grew out of the ideas of the Enlightenment, and the words of two of its French philosophers helped prepare for feminist theory as an expansion of democratic theory. Montesquieu, on whose ideas much of the American constitution was based, presumably would not have approved of the exclusion of women from that constitution. "The powers of the sexes," he said in 1748, "would be equal if their education were too. Test women in the talents that have not been enfeebled by the way they have been educated, and we will then see if we are so strong." Voltaire, whose 1778 death occurred just after the American Revolution began, had even stronger words for his fellow men: "Women are capable of doing everything we do, with this single difference between them and us, that they are more amiable than we are."

Notes

1. Howe had even considered divorce back when that was an almost impossible idea. Her husband, Dr. Samuel Gridley Howe, was famous as an innovative educator of the deaf; although they shared abolitionist and other liberal views, Dr. Howe resented both his wife's early literary work and her late-in-life success.

2. The current president of the National association, she graduated from Syracuse Medical College in 1852, just a year after Lydia Fowler did. During the Civil War, Dr. Lozier began New York Medical College for Women, a successful institution that eventually trained hundreds of female physicians.

3. For much more detail, see Doris Weatherford, *Foreign and Female: Immigrant Women in America, 1840-1930*, rev. ed. (New York: Facts On File, 1995).

4. Many midwestern Germans had come up the Mississippi from New Orleans in the pre-Civil War years. St. Louis was considered the headquarters of both Lutheran and Catholic Germans, and these Kansans were likely to have gone west from Missouri.

5. Although the argument, of course, was specious, there were more Chinese in Colorado and other Rocky Mountain states than might be expected. Relatively few were women, however; the vast majority were men imported to do dangerous mining and railroad

construction in the mountains. Prejudice against them was so real that, in 1887, at least 40 Chinese were killed and some 600 driven from their homes in Rock Springs, Wyoming.

6. One man who attended this meeting was "Rev. Mr. Wright, who preferred to be introduced as the nephew of Dr. Harriot K. Hunt of Boston."

7. One of the convention delegates who supported the women was Agapita Vigil, a Mexican-American legislator from southern Colorado, who—like many of his constituents—spoke only Spanish. The legislature employed a translator for him and other lawmakers who did not speak English.

8. Nebraska's foreign-born population was largely German, especially from the east (Prussia) and south (Bohemia).

9. In Mary Olney Brown's 1870 test of women's right to vote in the Washington Territory, for example, the role of "tickets" as a way to manage votes was clear. While she attempted to vote, "a cart rattled up bearing a male citizen who was . . . drunk. This disgusting, drunken idiot was picked up out of the cart by two men, who put a ticket in his hand [and] carried him [to the polls]. . . . His vote received, he was tumbled back into the cart."

10. Men who worked on railroad construction were likely to be foreign born. Crews coming from the East frequently were Irish, while those based in the West were Chinese.

11. The WCTU's lobbyist on this was Angela F. Newman of Nebraska. She also succeeded in getting Congress to appropriate tens of thousands of dollars during the next several years for a Salt Lake City rehabilitative center for women who wished to leave polygamous marriages. It probably was the first taxpayer funding for what was essentially a displaced homemaker program.

12. Poll taxes existed in many states and localities as a way of excluding poor voters. In some places, those who owned property on which they paid taxes did not have to pay an additional poll tax; in other places, people had to pay both. In Massachusetts at this time, the poll tax averaged two dollars; later it was lowered to 50 cents. These taxes persisted especially in the South, as a way of excluding black voters, until an amendment to the federal Constitution finally banned them in 1964.

13. One rare exception was in early twentieth-century Alabama, where an aristocratic governing class often behaved like Europeans. Kate Gordon of New Orleans reported at the 1902 National Suffrage Convention: "The clause which lived twenty-four hours in the Alabama Constitution, granting to tax-paying women owning $500 worth of property the suffrage on questions of bondage indebtedness, was killed by a disease particular to the genus homo known as chivalry."

14. All Southern states rewrote their constitutions in the Reconstruction era.

15. Henry Clay was a powerful U.S. senator and presidential candidate in the prewar era; Cassius Clay was an abolitionist founder of the Republican Party and ambassador to Russia.

16. See appendix.

17. That this was a pseudonym became well known during her lifetime. Her maiden name was Amandine Lucie Aurore Dupin; called Aurore by her family, she was officially Baroness Dudevant after a disastrous marriage at 18. Divorce, of course, was impossible in France in 1831, when they permanently separated. Sand frequently dressed like a man, but also had numerous heterosexual relationships, including a long affair with composer Frederic Chopin.

LEILA R. BRAMMER (ESSAY DATE 2000)

SOURCE: Brammer, Leila R. "Matilda Joslyn Gage and Woman Suffrage." In *Excluded from Suffrage History: Matilda Joslyn Gage, Nineteenth-Century American Feminist,* pp. 55-65. Westport, Conn.: Greenwood Press, 2000.

In the following essay, Brammer describes the unwavering principle of natural rights underlying the suffrage work of Matilda Joslyn Gage, who, the critic argues, deserves to be remembered along with Susan B. Anthony and Elizabeth Cady Stanton as one of the preeminent nineteenth-century advocates for women's rights.

Matilda Joslyn Gage's unwavering belief in liberty for all persons was grounded in her commitment to the United States Constitution. Based in natural rights, the Constitution upholds equality and liberty for all. The natural rights foundation is clearly illustrated in the memorable passage, "We hold these truths to be self-evident, that all men are created equal; that they are endowed by their Creator with certain inalienable rights; that among these are life, liberty, and the pursuit of happiness." Joslyn Gage's arguments concerning woman's rights and woman suffrage are firmly rooted in this ideal. She believed and argued vehemently that all persons, including women, had been endowed with inalienable rights that the government was obligated to protect. As a result, underlying Matilda Joslyn Gage's arguments for woman's rights was the basic assumption that women have rights because they are persons and that the government's only function is the protection of those rights. As early as 1852, she argued:

> We claim, as a natural right, the same privilege of acting as we think best, which is accorded the other half of mankind. . . . Although our country makes great profession in regard to general liberty, yet the right to particular liberty, natural equality, and personal independence, of two great portions of this country, is treated, from custom, with the greatest contempt; and color in one instance and sex in the other, are brought as reason why they should be so derided; and the mere mention of such natural rights is frowned upon, as tending to promote sedition and anarchy.
>
> (p. 5)

This natural rights argument for woman's equal treatment extended logically to the ballot as a natural right and as a means of protecting other rights. The grounding of her suffrage arguments in natural rights is significant. Joslyn Gage did not argue out of need, out of benefit, nor out of deserving the vote; to her, the matter was clear-cut. Women were born, as were all people, with inalienable rights, including the right of self-government. However, Joslyn Gage also saw suffrage as a means for women to obtain equality and protect their rights.

Joslyn Gage's extension of woman's rights to the ballot is an argument that dates to the beginning of the woman's rights movement. The initial resolution crafted by Elizabeth Cady Stanton and presented at the Seneca Falls Woman's Rights Convention in 1848 was based in natural rights. Advocates saw suffrage at the time as the key to the advancement of women. However, women were more interested in other issues. In 1870 Cady Stanton observed, "Women respond to my divorce speech as they never did to suffrage. Oh how they flock to me with their sorrows" (Stanton & Blatch, 1922, p. 127). Later, as the demand for suffrage became more acceptable, women began to connect suffrage with other issues and argue that woman suffrage was necessary to secure protection for women, children, and the country. As Alice Kraditor (1965) wrote, "The woman suffrage movement had no official ideology. Its members and leaders held every conceivable view of current events and represented every philosophical position. Although they all agreed that women should have the right to vote, they disagreed on why they ought to have that right" (p. vii). Kraditor identifies two types of suffrage arguments: natural rights arguments based on women as equal to men as persons, and expediency arguments grounded in suffrage as a means for women to enact laws reflecting their unique nature (p. 44). Karlyn Kohrs Campbell (1983) contends that the conflicting views of women, which served as the foundations of these two different arguments for suffrage, resulted in a critical tension. Expediency arguments that claimed women's moral voice was needed in the political arena were directly opposed to natural rights arguments of women's equality. Further, Campbell indicates that the later subjugation of natural rights arguments by morality claims hindered the women's movement and made a second wave of feminism necessary (p. 103).

Although differing views on suffrage arguments were not the cause of the split between early suffrage workers into two organizations, each organization held its own distinct view. Kraditor classifies Lucy Stone's arguments as expedient because she did not argue from a natural rights perspective; rather, she saw the ballot as a means of self-protection for women, particularly as a way of strengthening rape laws and raising the age of consent (Kraditor, 1965, pp. 54-55). Cady Stanton, Susan B. Anthony, Joslyn Gage, and other members of the National did not disagree with using suffrage for political protection, but their arguments for suffrage were grounded in natural rights.

Slowly, natural rights became the less prominent argument for women in the movement as expediency arguments grew. New expediency arguments were the result of natural rights being questioned in the wake of the influx of immigrants into the country. As suffrage workers became more conservative, even less emphasis was placed on common humanity and more emphasis was placed on woman's unique capacity to provide a moral foundation for society (Kraditor, 1965, p. 44). They claimed women, particularly those in the middle class, were suited for suffrage because of their innate morality. Organizations such as the Women's Christian Temperance Union (WCTU) grounded their suffrage arguments in expediency and morality. The spread of these arguments based on claims that women were distinct from men hurt natural rights claims that women and men were created equal. In addition, expediency arguments increased attacks on the suffrage of other groups, such as blacks, immigrants, and the poor.

Joslyn Gage was uncompromising in the consistency of her natural rights stance. Although she supported suffrage as a means of self-protection and linked it to specific changes, the basis of her argument always remained natural rights, and she never strayed from her firm conviction that all persons, regardless of sex, race, or class, shared the same natural rights. While Joslyn Gage unwaveringly saw natural rights as the grounds for suffrage, she did conceive that woman suffrage, once attained, could be used as a means to change the world.

Political Uses for Woman Suffrage

Joslyn Gage's view of suffrage as a means for women to demand and protect their rights was unlike expediency claims for suffrage. There were others who believed as she did, such as Cady Stanton, who argued that suffrage was the means to develop woman's full potential (Kraditor, 1965, p. 10). However, most who argued for suffrage as a

ON THE SUBJECT OF...

MATILDA JOSLYN GAGE (1826-1898)

Speaking before the National Woman's Rights Convention held in Syracuse, New York, in September of 1852, twenty-six-year-old Matilda Joslyn Gage let her strong feelings be known regarding the obsequious acceptance of male authority expected of women. An ardent advocate of reforms to gain women both educational and political equality, Gage dedicated much of her life to writing, editing, and speaking out on suffrage and other feminist issues. A founding member of the National Woman Suffrage Association (NWSA) in 1869, Gage contributed numerous articles to the pages of its journal, the *Revolution.* She joined NWSA's first advisory council and was elected secretary and vice president, becoming president in 1875. A year later, on Independence Day, she and Susan B. Anthony presented the "Declaration of Rights of the Women of the United States" to the nation's vice president. Gage left the NWSA shortly thereafter but remained active in the organization as editor of its newsletter, *National Citizen and Ballot Box,* as well as serving as president of a local branch, the New York State Woman Suffrage Association.

Working with Elizabeth Cady Stanton and Anthony, Gage produced the first three parts of the four-volume *History of Woman Suffrage,* which was published from 1881 to 1886. Gage's contributions include the chapter "Woman, Church and State," the subject of the which informed Gage's later work arguing that the religious indoctrination received by women via organized Christianity perpetuated the social inferiority of women. Therefore, Gage declared, the teachings of the Church were a key obstacle to female equality. Gage founded the Woman's National Liberal Union in 1890 to further promote the dissolution of the socially accepted interrelationship between church and government. In 1893 she published an expansion of her work for *History of Woman Suffrage* entitled *Woman, Church and State.*

means were aligned with the WCTU and other causes seeking to enfranchise women so they could vote for morality. Joslyn Gage and Cady Stanton shared an entirely different conception of the uses of suffrage. They did not see suffrage as a means to advance general moral or political issues but rather as a means for women to advance themselves. The underlying assumptions and the framing of the arguments differed as well. The potential use of suffrage was not a primary argument for Cady Stanton and Joslyn Gage but rather an added advantage of women gaining their natural rights. Joslyn Gage's work attempted to establish woman's natural right to suffrage and, then once gained, to use it to improve the condition of women. In all cases, her arguments based in the uses for suffrage were aimed at audiences of women; in fact, when arguing to Congress or other groups of men, Joslyn Gage made only natural rights arguments. Her focus on the uses of suffrage served as part of her consciousness-raising efforts in *The National Citizen and Ballot Box.*

Joslyn Gage saw political rights as the most important rights, arguing that women "not possessing their political rights . . . are oppressed by society, by the church, by the laws, because political rights underlie all other rights" (Duty, December 1878, p. 2). Men professed to be representatives of the people, when fully one-half of the people did not have a vote. Joslyn Gage argued that this system could not continue because men could not be trusted to protect women. She contended: "Women are frequently asked if they cannot trust their interests in the hands of their husbands and fathers and brothers and sons. At first glance, woman would say yes, . . . but in the light of bitter experience, we emphatically answer No. There is no protection quite like self-protection; there is no power quite like the power a woman holds in her own hands" (1852-1880 [November 9, 1871]). Joslyn Gage was well aware of the injustices that had occurred at the hands of the government and which were not abated by men holding the ballot. Her entire woman's rights argument was built from that perspective. She saw a fundamental problem with assuming that men would protect women, stating that "woman, now, is the being who has no rights man is bound to respect" (His property, August 1878, p. 4). Certainly, if one is thought to have no rights, they cannot be protected. She pointed out that "[m]en make the laws not women. Men make all the child-stealing-fugitive-wife laws; those men who 'protect women;' those men who 'love, honor and respect' women; those men who 'take care' of women. Away with such protection. . . . Put a ballot in her hands and such laws will no longer be enacted" (Notes, December 1878, p. 3). Moreover, she asserted that those who voted were not interested in such protection or were incapable of making such judgments. She observed that, during an election, "[w]e shall once again see ignorant, degraded and drunken men exercise the rights of self-government at the ballot box . . . [while women look on] seeing the grave questions of importance to every individual in the community decided without their consent . . . defeated by masculine voters whose brains are muddled with rum" (The duty, October 1878, p. 1).

With the hope of relief from male voters eliminated, Joslyn Gage knew the only hope was woman suffrage, allowing women to protect themselves from unjust laws and customs. Her research into the oppression of women led her to exclaim, "She must be able to protect herself and she can only do this by having the ballot in her own hands" (Wadleigh's report, July 1878, p. 2). Joslyn Gage also believed that women would vote to protect other women, not just themselves, and, thus, exact protection for all women (From him, May 1878, p. 1). She saw numerous instances in which women could and, she believed, would make a difference for other women. Like Stone, Joslyn Gage argued that one case would be rape laws: "The practice of non-conviction or of pardoning such wretches if convicted, deserves the severest censure. . . . Could women but protect themselves by the ballot, we should see a very different state of affairs" (Drift, August 1878, p. 1). To Joslyn Gage, woman suffrage would not just correct a base injustice but would be the means to punish and prevent many, if not all, of the crimes against women, if the ballot was used by women to protect women. Although she hoped that protection and change for women would result from woman suffrage, she never crossed over to expediency claims of morality. Without exception, her arguments in support of woman suffrage were based entirely in natural rights.

Natural Rights Arguments

In her consistent support for natural rights, Joslyn Gage was unmatched. Unlike some of her colleagues, Joslyn Gage universally applied her natural rights arguments to all segments of society and never denied these rights to any group. Cady Stanton and Anthony had questioned the fitness of suffrage for blacks, immigrants, and the uneducated. In the Kansas Campaign in 1867, both made derogatory references to blacks and campaigned against granting them suffrage. In 1895, Cady Stanton wrote,

> A rapidly increasing class of educated women demand the right of suffrage for their own protection, as well as for the best interests of the State; and they have a right to call a halt on any further enfranchisement of the ignorant classes, until the better element in society is fully recognized in the Government. Our rulers have no excuse for their fears of the ignorant and vicious classes of women. The have it in their power to extent the suffrage to the best class, on an educational qualification.
>
> (p. 2)

Later in the same article, Stanton made a clear moral expediency claim for the ballot when she wrote, "And where can he look for this new, moral force, but in the education, elevation and emancipation of women—the mothers of the race?" (p. 2). These arguments against universal suffrage based in the morality of women became even more prominent in suffrage rhetoric after the merger of the National American, but Joslyn Gage always held firm to the egalitarian nature of rights. Of all those prominent in the suffrage movement, only the Reverend Anna Howard Shaw came close to matching Joslyn Gage's consistency, yet even she advanced arguments critical of suffrage for immigrants (Kraditor, 1965, pp. 52, 126).

Further, Joslyn Gage never argued that women deserved the ballot, that women could use it to support special causes, such as temperance, or that the states were the battleground. In this, she defined and never wavered from the principles of natural rights and the National Woman Suffrage Association. To her, the ballot was a national issue because it was the responsibility of the national government to protect the rights of all persons, including woman's natural right to the ballot. She delivered some of the most important speeches on natural rights, and it is in these speeches, where her arguments stemmed from constitutional law, that Joslyn Gage shows her most effective use of rhetorical strategies. Her fundamental belief in natural rights is clear from her *Woman's Rights Catechism,* published in 1871, and her first known woman's rights speech in 1852.

In a speech delivered for the first time at the National's Washington convention in 1873, Joslyn Gage articulated the basis for her arguments for suffrage on the national level. Her thesis was: "'State rights' has from the very commencement of the Government been the rock on which the ship of the nation has many times nearly foundered, and from which it is to-day in great danger. The one question of the hour is, Is the United

States a Nation with full and complete National powers, or is it a mere thread upon which States are strung as are the beads upon a necklace?" (Stanton et al., 1985/1882, pp. 523-24). She traced the history of the federal government from the founding of the country and praised each step toward strengthening the federal government as a step toward a true nation and the true guarantee of rights. She observed, "State centralization is tyranny; National centralization is freedom. State centralization means special laws; National centralization means general laws. The continued habit of States to make laws for every part of their own boundaries brought to the surface the 'States rights' theory which precipitated upon us our civil war" (p. 528). Joslyn Gage argued that only the national government could protect the rights of its citizens and that it was its duty to do so. She emphasized that national citizenship was central to all rights and privileges. She said, "We are not first citizens of Rhode Island, or South Carolina, but if we belong to the nation at all, we are first parts of that Nation. . . . That every person born or naturalized in the Nation, must be borne in mind, for upon that depend the liberties of every man, woman and child in the Nation, black or white, native or foreign" (p. 526).

As the rights of citizenship in a representative democracy outlined in the Constitution fundamentally include the right to elect representatives, Joslyn Gage connected national citizenship directly to the vote. She stated, "This government does not stand to-day [*sic*] on free trade, or tariff, or the war-power, or its right to manage post-offices, or to coin money, or to make treaties. Not one of these singly, nor all collectively, form the governing power; it stands upon the right of every person governed by the Nation to share in the election of its rulers" (pp. 530-31). Further, Joslyn Gage saw the denial of rights to citizens as a significant issue that affected everyone. She observed, "The question of citizen suffrage is not a woman question alone, but it is a question of the rights of citizenship affecting every man in this wide land" (p. 532). She noted the implications, "If a S[t]ate has a right to deprive one class of citizens of its vote for one cause, it has a right to deprive any other class of its vote for any reason" (p. 530). In support of that claim, she offered evidence of Rhode Island's denial of suffrage to 10,000 naturalized citizens. In that case, Congress reported unfavorably on a petition to restore their rights. Joslyn Gage quickly pointed to the double standard, on one hand, not getting involved in suffrage in this case, and on the other, prosecuting Anthony for voting.

These inconsistencies in practice and the refusal of the federal government to become involved in securing a guaranteed right fundamental to citizenship, particularly refusing to protect the vital principle behind the Republic, greatly disturbed Joslyn Gage. Her commitment to the national government was not a strategy for obtaining the vote; she was committed to a strong, centralized government and believed it was the only security for all rights. She supported the direct election of the president, term limitation, limitations on official patronage, and apportioning senators based on population (p. 533). In every case, liberty was her central concern, and the federal government upholding the Constitution was the only protection.

She further developed this argument in her speeches in support of Anthony before her trial in 1873. In these speeches, she did not concern herself with centralization or the power of the states; instead, she argued completely from the Constitution. Her thesis, drawn directly from the Declaration of Independence, was that governments do not create rights but rather are created to protect rights. Underlying this argument and her attitude toward the powers of government were five principles. These principles were extremely important to her conception of government and, later, they were included in the National's Declaration of Woman's Rights. Joslyn Gage asserted these five original principles as:

> First. The natural right of each individual to self-government.
>
> Second. The exact equality of these rights.
>
> Third. That these rights when not delegated by the individual, are retained by the individual.
>
> Fourth. That no person can exercise these rights of others without delegated authority.
>
> Fifth. That the non-use of these rights does not destroy them.
>
> (1974/1873, p. 181)

Joslyn Gage believed that the idea of representative government was fundamental. She stated, "The great foundation and key stone alike of our Republican ideas, of our Constitution, is individual, personal representation" (p. 188). She then applied this fundamental principle of representative government to citizenship. She observed that, "In the United States, representation is based upon individual, personal rights—therefore, every person born in the United States—every person,—not every white person, not every male person, but every person is born with political rights" (p. 193). Women, of course, were people; they had been part of "the people" from the inception of the United States. Joslyn Gage stated: "At the time of framing this government women existed as well as men, women are part of the people; the people created the government" (p. 189). Indeed, women were governed. If the government derived its "just power from the consent of the governed," then the governed should vote. She then argued that women, most certainly, were among the governed—"they pay taxes, they are held amenable to laws, they are tried for crimes; they are fined, imprisoned, hung" (p. 180). She then turned to the idea behind the Revolution, taxation without representation, and argued that women were still living under an unjust government. The Constitution established that those governed must be represented; those who are taxed must have the right to vote.

Further, the prosecution of Anthony for illegal voting under a federal law proved that women were treated as citizens and that the general government had power over suffrage. "By its prosecution of Miss Anthony, the general government acknowledged her as a citizen of the United States, and what is much more, it acknowledged its own jurisdiction over the ballot—over the chief— . . . over the only political right of its citizens. This prosecution is an admission of the United States jurisdiction, instead of State jurisdiction" (p. 196). Although this argument alone is compelling, Joslyn Gage continued to build her case for women as citizens.

She advanced the inclusion of women in the Constitution. She pointed out that the Constitution itself, while not referring to women specifically, did not refer directly to men either. Women were entitled to and received the same rights as men to worship, speak, assemble, and so forth; therefore, women were included "equally with men in the intentions of the framers" (p. 192). She noted that originally only the Sixth amendment included the words "him" and "his" in referring to the right to a speedy, public trial by a jury of peers; however, "no one can be found wild enough to say women were not intended to be included in its benefits" (p. 192). Joslyn Gage reminded the audience that Anthony had already received protection under the amendment. The argument was effectively based in constitutional law, but carried with it a threat of a reversal possibly to deny women those rights that they had been guaranteed. Interestingly, during the trial when the judge directed the jury to find her guilty, Anthony was denied the right to a trial by a jury of her peers.

Despite the directed verdict and other legal maneuvers, Joslyn Gage had clearly established Anthony's citizenship. She summed up her argument:

> The question brought up by this trial is not a woman's rights question, but a citizen's rights question. It is not denied that women are citizens,—it is not denied that Susan B. Anthony was born in the United States, and therefore a citizen of the United States. . . . It cannot be denied that she is a person,—one of the people,—there is not a word in the Constitution of the United States which militates against the recognition of woman as a person, as one of the people, as a citizen.
>
> (p. 201)

Joslyn Gage's argument eliminated other options. Anthony's citizenship could not be denied and that she was governed and taxed could not be denied; therefore, she must be allowed to vote if the nation abided by its Constitution. The argument also performed another important task of redefining the issue. Joslyn Gage argued repeatedly that the issue was not about women, but about the rights of all citizens. If one could be denied, all were in jeopardy. In this way, Joslyn Gage made Anthony a representative, a test of liberty. She stated: "Miss Anthony is to-day [*sic*] the representative of liberty. In all ages of the world, and during all times, there have been epochs in which some one person took upon their own shoulders the hopes and the sorrows of the world, and in their own person, through many struggles bore them onward. . . . Such an epoch exists now, and such a person is Susan B. Anthony" (p. 205). Presenting Anthony as the enactment of liberty as provided in the Constitution was a very effective strategy, giving the public only one choice if they wanted to reaffirm republican principles. She argued, "If your decision is favorable to the defendant, you will sustain the constitution; if adverse, if you are blinded by prejudice; you will not decide against women alone, but against the United States as well" (p. 205). Her argument from constitutional law was compelling, but it is most effective in the way it provided the background for her to link Anthony and liberty.

At least partially, the judge's direction of the verdict was in response to the strength of the arguments advanced by Joslyn Gage and Anthony. In the courts, natural rights arguments were met with many questionable legal maneuvers and inconsistencies in argument. For example, in 1873, the federal government prosecuted Anthony for voting, but, in the 1874 *Minor v. Happersett* ruling, the Supreme Court found that voting was not the responsibility of the federal government. In the Supreme Court decision, Chief Justice Morrison Remick Waite granted that women were persons and citizens, but argued that voting was not one of the privileges of citizenship and that the United States had "no voters in the States of its own creation" (Stanton et al., 1985/1882, p. 738). As such, Virginia Minor fell under Missouri state law, which allowed only male suffrage. The inconsistencies in Waite's decision were an easy target for Joslyn Gage.

Anthony referred to Joslyn Gage's argument on the Minor Decision as her "most brilliant"; indeed, it was very thorough and cogent. Her main contention was that the United States had created at least eight classes of voters, and in great detail, she showed how each class had gained its vote and how the United States protected it. She summed up her argument as follows:

> Thus at the time of Chief-Justice Waite's decision asserting National want of power over the ballot, and declaring the United States possessed no voters in the States (where else would it have them?), the country already possessed eight classes of voters, or persons whose right to the ballot was in some form under the control or sanction of the United States. The black man, the amnestied man, the naturalized man, the foreigner honorably discharged from the Union army, voters for the lower House of Congress, voters for Presidential electors, pardoned civil and military criminals. Further research may bring still other classes to light.
>
> (Stanton et al., 1985/1882, p. 744)

She also argued that it was the United States that had prosecuted Anthony not the State; if, indeed, it was not a question for the United States, her trial was void, and her vote should be counted. Joslyn Gage had thoroughly declared the decision of the Supreme Court invalid in that it was based on an interpretation of the Constitution and an interpretation of the laws that she, a woman, had proven false. She concluded, "She [Anthony] asks for nothing outside the power of the United States, she ask for nothing outside the duty of the United States to secure. Politicians may as well look this fact squarely in the face . . . for in just so far as they ignore and forget the women of the country, in just so far will they themselves be ignored and forgotten by future generations" (p. 748). Her argument and appeal for justice was powerful, but she also included some other important arguments concerning woman suffrage.

She took up the issue that Congress was trying to take away woman suffrage in Utah and Wyoming, arguing that, according to Waite, it was not a question of the national government. But, she went further to argue that women in Wyoming had used the ballot well. First, she answered charges that women in Wyoming did not deserve the ballot because they were not using it. She responded: "I care very little . . . one way or the other, as long as her right to vote is not interfered with. It will be time to require all women to vote when we have such a law for men; until then let each voter refrain from voting at his or her own option; it is not the vital question" (p. 745). From there, she detailed the impact women voters had on the territory, including the equalization of salaries for men and women teachers. She noted, "[P]olitical power always benefits the parties holding it" (p. 746). Voting also allowed women to sit on juries, and Joslyn Gage contended that juries including women frightened criminals so much that they left the territory (p. 745). But the right to sit on juries had been taken away by the U.S. Marshall, which Joslyn Gage condemned for denying woman's political rights and her industrial rights. She argued: "It is a well-known fact that some women earned their first industrial dollar by sitting in the jury box. And whatever interferes with woman's industrial rights helps to send her down to those depths where want of bread has forced so many women; into the gutters of shame. . . . Every infringement of a person's political rights, touches a hundred other rights adversely" (p. 746). As always for Joslyn Gage, these issues came back to personal liberty and attainment of equal rights for women in every sphere. She made similar arguments regarding woman suffrage to the Joint Congressional Committee on the District of Columbia in 1876.

At the Joint Congressional Committee hearing, Joslyn Gage argued from her usual basis of natural rights and the principles of government, but, in response to claims that women did not desire suffrage, she advanced a rather strong statement showing that women did want to vote. She noted that 7,000 women in the District of Columbia had signed a petition indicating their desire to vote, and they were supported in their efforts by thousands of women across the country. Indeed, claimed Joslyn Gage, men of the District had not demanded the ballot. She concluded, "The men of this District who quietly remain disenfranchised have the spirit of slaves, and if asking for the ballot is any proof of fitness for its use, then the women who do ask for it here prove themselves in this respect superior to men, more alive to the interests of this District, and better fitted to administer the Government" (1876, p. 3). Although she argued from the desires of women, her argument was based in natural rights. She stated: "The freedom of this country is only half won. The women of today have less freedom than our fathers of the Revolution, for they were permitted local self-government, . . . while women have no share in local, state, or general government. All the arguments ever used against extending suffrage to women have been used against granting rights to common men" (p. 5). Again, Joslyn Gage developed the link between sex and class and argued that natural rights had no preferences; they extended to all people.

Joslyn Gage continued her arguments for suffrage monthly in *The National Citizen and Ballot Box*. As the name makes clear, the prime concern of the paper was woman suffrage, but to Joslyn Gage, suffrage was inextricably linked to woman's rights. Her arguments for suffrage in the paper continued to be based in natural rights. She stated in the prospectus, "Suffrage is a citizen's right and should be protected by National law, and that while States may recognize suffrage, they should have no power to abolish it" (May 1878, p. 1). In 1878, before the Joint Congressional Committee on Privileges and Elections, she argued, "But as proud as is this name of American citizen; it brings with it only shame and humiliation to one-half the nation. Woman has no part nor lot in the matter. The pride of citizenship is not for her, for woman is still a political slave. . . . Woman equally with man has natural rights; woman equally with man is a responsible being" (Stanton et al., 1985/1886, p. 93).

Without the ballot, the only power women possessed was the right to protest. Joslyn Gage encouraged women to continue to use that right in the effort to have their other rights recognized. She wrote to the women of Dakota Territory, "Every injustice under which she suffers, as wife, mother, woman, child, in property and in person, is due to the fact that she is not recognized as man's political equal—and her only power is that of protest" (Stanton et al., 1985/1886, p. 664). To that end, she instructed and advocated women's use of petitions as their only recognized political right contending that "men will not be convinced women desire their rights unless they thus demand them. Petition! Petition!! Petition!!!" (Petition!, December 1878, p. 2). Despite their petitions, numbering tens of thousands in many instances, all their efforts were denied. Joslyn Gage argued that the petitions showed women's desire to vote and proved time and time again that, when given the opportunity, women voted, and in greater numbers than men. She gave an example of women in the Dakota Territory who traveled miles through a blizzard to cast their ballots, yet in Massachusetts during a governor's election, only one-third of the men voted (Stanton et al., 1985/1886, p. 668).

In her arguments on suffrage, Joslyn Gage remained consistent in her focus on women's natural rights as people. Her arguments were well researched, detailed, and cogent for her audiences of Congressmen and the public; however, in each case, these arguments were ignored. At one point late in her life, Cady Stanton speaks of how angered she was to have her arguments for suffrage rejected by a group of smug young men (1971/1898, p. 309). Later, she said, "I cannot work in the old ruts any longer. I have said all I have to say on the subject of suffrage" (Gurko, 1974, p. 282). There is some evidence that Joslyn Gage shared this sentiment.

Throughout her life, Joslyn Gage continued to argue actively for suffrage, but, by 1878, she had turned her thoughts to the larger, underlying issues. That judges, lawyers, and other men ignored fine legal arguments while making inconsistent arguments of their own pointed to a larger problem. She began to investigate and theorize about the roots of woman's oppression. She determined that it was not just the law, that it was not just the state, but the church as well, and that collusion between the church and state was at the center of all woman's oppression. She concluded that woman's oppression was a function of patriarchy, a system that was particularly vicious because it induced women to participate in their own oppression.

Although she never denied the importance of suffrage, Joslyn Gage's work turned to educating women about this system of oppression. She realized that while women were controlled by this system, the ballot would make little difference. Women would continue as they were, participating in their own oppression. These were the reasons that she feared Frances Willard and the WCTU so much and was so upset by the merger of the National with the American. Perhaps she had determined that if women received the ballot under those conditions, nothing would change. Thus, exposing patriarchy and educating people to the dangers of it became central to her plan of freeing women from this system of controls, and at the heart of her argument was the institution of the church.

Works Cited

Campbell, K. K. (1983). Femininity and feminism: To be or not to be a woman. *Communication Quarterly, 31,* 101-108.

Gage, M. J. (1852-1880). Scrapbook of writings. In the Matilda Joslyn Gage Papers (MC 377, File 46), Schlesinger Library, Radcliffe Institute, Harvard University, Cambridge, MA.

Gage, M. E. J. (1852). Speech of Mrs. M. E. J. Gage at the woman's rights convention, held at Syracuse, Sept. 1852. *Women's rights tracts,* (No. 7). In *History of Women Microfilm Collection* (1975), 942. New Haven, CT: Research Publications.

Gage, M. J. (1871). *Woman's rights catechism.* In the Matilda Joslyn Gage Papers (MC 377, File 46), Schlesinger Library, Radcliffe Institute, Harvard University, Cambridge, MA.

Gage, M. J. (1876). Arguments before the Committee on the District of Columbia of the U.S. House of Representatives upon the Centennial Woman Suffrage Memorial of the women citizens of this nation. Washington, D.C.: Gibson Brothers. In *History of Women Microfilm Collection* (1975), 946. New Haven, CT: Research Publications.

Gage, M. J. (1878, May). Drift of thought. *The National Citizen and Ballot Box,* p. 1.

Gage, M. J. (1878, May). From him that hath not, shall be taken away that which he hath. *The National Citizen and Ballot Box,* p. 1.

Gage, M. J. (1878, July). Wadleigh's report. *The National Citizen and Ballot Box,* p. 2.

Gage, M. J. (1878, August). His property. *The National Citizen and Ballot Box,* p. 4.

Gage, M. J. (1878, October). The duty of the hour. *The National Citizen and Ballot Box,* p. 1.

Gage, M. J. (1878, December). Duty of the minority. *The National Citizen and Ballot Box,* p. 2.

Gage, M. J. (1878, December). Notes and items. *The National Citizen and Ballot Box,* p. 3.

Gage, M. J. (1878, December). Petition! Petition!! Petition!!! *The National Citizen and Ballot Box,* p. 2.

Gage, M. J. (1974). The United States on trial; *not* Susan B. Anthony. In *An account of the proceeding on the trial of Susan B. Anthony, on the charge of illegal voting, at the Presidential election in November 1872.* New York: Arno Press. (Original work published 1873.)

Gurko, M. (1974). *The Ladies of Seneca Falls: The birth of the woman's rights movement.* New York: Macmillan.

Kraditor, A. S. (1965). *The ideas of the woman suffrage movement, 1890-1920.* New York: Columbia University Press.

Stanton, E. C. (1895, February 14). Educated suffrage. *The Independent,* pp. 1-2.

Stanton, E. C. (1971). *Eighty years and more: Reminiscences 1815-1897.* New York: Schocken Books. (Original work published 1898.)

Stanton, E. C., Anthony, S. B., & Gage, M. J. (Eds.). (1985). *History of woman suffrage* (Vol. 2). Salem, NH: Ayer Company. (Original work published 1882.)

Stanton, E. C., Anthony, S. B., & Gage, M. J. (Eds.). (1985). *History of woman suffrage* (Vol. 3). Salem, NH: Ayer Company. (Original work published 1886.)

Stanton, T., & Blatch, H. S. (Eds.). (1922). *Elizabeth Cady Stanton as revealed in her letters, diary, and reminiscences* (Vol. 2). New York: Harper.

FURTHER READING

Buhle, Mari Jo and Paul Buhle. *The Concise History of Woman Suffrage: Selections from the Classic Work of Stanton, Gage, and Harper,* edited by Mari Jo and Paul Buhle. Urbana, Ill.: University of Illinois Press, 1978, 468 p.

Provides selections of suffrage writings from Elizabeth Cady Stanton, Susan B. Anthony, Matilda Joslyn Gage, and Frances Harper's six-volume collection of speeches and writings from 1848 to 1920.

Catt, Carrie Chapman and Rogers Schuler. *Woman Suffrage and Politics.* New York: Charles Scribner's Sons, 1923, 504 p.

Offers a full-length study of the American woman's suffrage movement.

Cowley, Joyce. *Pioneers of Women's Liberation.* New York: Pathfinder Press, Inc., 1969, 504 p.

Article that first appeared in 1955 in the Fourth International *seeking to place the American woman's suffrage movement within its historical context, concentrating on how black and white suffrage leaders overcame ridicule and internal divisions to secure the right to vote.*

Cullen-Dupont, Kathryn, ed. *Pioneers of Women's Liberation.* New York: Cooper Square Press, 2002, 613 p.

Offers an anthology of works by American women activists that includes speeches and writings by suffrage leaders Elizabeth Cady Stanton, Lucretia Mott, Lucy Stone, Susan B. Anthony, and Victoria Woodhull.

Flexner, Eleanor. *Century of Struggle: The Woman's Rights Movement in the United States.* New York: Atheneum, 1970, 385 p.

Studies of the struggle for equal rights by American women in the nineteenth and early twentieth centuries, concentrating on women's organizing efforts to achieve educational, workplace, and political reforms.

Frost, Elizabeth and Kathryn Cullen-Dupont. *Women's Suffrage in America: An Eyewitness History,* New York: Facts on File, 1995, 464 p.

Provides an overview of the century-long struggle of women suffragists, each chapter including numerous primary sources from the period highlighting women's demands for political inclusion and social equality.

Hall, Florence Howe. *Julia Ward Howe and the Woman Suffrage Movement.* New York: Arno and The New York Times, 1969, 241 p.

Offers a biography of suffragist leader Julia Ward Howe written by her daughter.

Keetley, Dawn and John Pettegrew. *Public Women, Public Words: A Documentary History of American Feminism,* edited by Dawn Keetley and John Pettegrew. Madison, Wisconsin: Madison House, 1997, 193 p.

Anthology of speeches and writings by proto- and early-American feminists, including numerous appeals for women's suffrage.

Kerr, Andrea Moore. *Lucy Stone: Speaking Out for Equality.* New Brunswick, N.J.: Rutgers University Press, 1991, 320 p.

Biography of suffragist leader Lucy Stone, whom the author argues has not been adequately recognized because of her split with Elizabeth Cady Stanton and Susan B. Anthony over whether to campaign against the constitutional amendment giving black men the right to vote.

Kraditor, Aileen S. *The Ideas of the Woman Suffrage Movement, 1890-1920.* New York: Columbia University Press, 1965, 320 p.

Includes discussions of the ideology of the new generation of suffragist leaders who emerged in the 1890s.

Million, Joelle. *Woman's Voice, Woman's Place: Lucy Stone and the Birth of the Woman's Rights Movement.* Westport, Conn.: Praeger Publishers, 2003, 360 p.

Biography of Lucy Stone, concentrating on her leadership in movements against slavery and for temperance as well as for the right of American women to vote.

The National American Woman Suffrage Association. *Victory: How Women Won It: A Centennial Symposium.* New York: The H. W. Wilson Company, 1940, 174 p.

Studies the local and national campaigns suffragists led in the nineteenth century through 1920.

Passet, Joanne E. "We Are Cowards and She Is Not." In *Sex Radicals and the Quest for Women's Equality,* pp. 91-111. Urbana, Ill.: University of Illinois Press, 2003.

Examines the links between the sexual radicalism of Victorian Woodhull and her support for woman's suffrage.

Porter, Kirk H. *The History of Suffrage in the United States.* Chicago, Ill.: The University of Chicago Press, 1918, 260 p.

Provides an overview of suffrage movements in the United States, with several chapters devoted to the efforts of women before and after the Civil War to gain voting rights.

Spongberg, Mary. "Women's History and the 'Woman Question'." In *Writing Women's History since the Renaissance,* pp. 130-49. Basingstoke, England: Palgrave Macmillan, 2002.

Recounts nineteenth-century feminist historiography and includes background on early suffrage efforts in Britain, France, and the United States.

Stern, Madeline B., ed. *The Victoria Woodhull Reader.* Weston, Mass.: M & S Press, 1974, 640 p.

Offers a selection of speeches and writings by Woodhull, including sections of her late-nineteenth-century works on advocacy for woman's suffrage.

LOUISA MAY ALCOTT

(1832 - 1888)

(Also wrote under the pseudonyms Flora Fairfield, A. M. Barnard, Cousin Tribulation, Oranthy Bluggage, Minerva Moody, and Aunt Weedy) American novelist, short story writer, and playwright.

Alcott's stories of nineteenth-century domestic life include what is widely known as the quintessential women's novel: *Little Women; or, Meg, Jo, Beth, and Amy* (1868). Her novels detailing the lives of Jo, Meg, Amy, Beth, their children, and their careers have remained popular for over a century, though many observers consider them the exclusive province of female readers. During her lifetime, Alcott spoke publicly on feminist causes, including suffrage, equal pay, and women's right to education. As a prolific professional author she also set an important precedent, demonstrating the viability of fiction writing as a career for women.

BIOGRAPHICAL INFORMATION

The second of four daughters, Alcott was born November 29, 1832 in Germantown, Pennsylvania, and lived most of her life in Concord, Massachusetts. Both of her parents strongly influenced her education and the development of her social and political views. Her father, Amos Bronson Alcott, was a Transcendentalist philosopher and an educational reformer whose idealistic projects tended to take precedence over his familial and financial responsibilities. Her mother, Abigail May Alcott, shared her husband's Transcendental ideals but sometimes objected to the failure of this way of life to provide for her family's practical needs. Amos was frequently absent as he traveled the world spreading his philosophical precepts, leaving the family severely impoverished. Abigail Alcott assumed the role of family financial manager, and she and her daughters pursued practical employment. Louisa, for example, taught school, took in sewing, and worked briefly as a domestic servant; her early experience of poverty and her observation of her father's financial instability may have contributed to her strong desire to achieve a steady income through her writing. She began writing at age sixteen, and in 1851 her first poem was published in *Peterson's Magazine* under the pseudonym Flora Fairfield. She subsequently published a number of serial stories under the pseudonym A. M. Barnard, providing her family with a relatively steady and significant source of income. In 1862, Alcott traveled to Washington, D. C., to serve as a nurse to soldiers wounded in the American Civil War. Although she was forced to return home after she contracted typhoid fever—the treatment for which resulted in mercury poisoning and permanent damage to her health—the brief experience provided material for the book that would become her first major literary success, *Hospital Sketches* (1863). This Civil War memoir was followed by her first novel, *Moods* (1864), which sold well despite charges that it was immoral. Encouraged by the prospect of financial stability, Alcott agreed to assume the editorship of a girls' magazine titled *Merry's Museum,* for which she composed satires, poems, and advice columns. At the request of her publishers, she also agreed to write a novel for girls, and the publication of her semi-autobiographical novel *Little Women* proved to be the defining moment of her career. The success of the novel made Alcott famous, and she was able to support her family with her earnings. Biographers have noted, however, that this success proved to be a mixed blessing for Alcott, who felt restricted by demands for more books written in a similarly domestic style. She nevertheless accommodated the interests of her readers with three sequels to *Little Women*: *Good Wives* (1869; volume two of *Little Women*), *Little Men: Life at Plumfield with Jo's Boys* (1871), and *Jo's Boys and How They Turned Out* (1886). Alcott was a staunch supporter of both abolition and women's suffrage. Although her frail health kept her from being as active as she would have liked, she consistently supported and encouraged others' efforts, corresponding and meeting regularly with prominent suffragists and abolitionists, and by directly addressing the issues in her fiction and nonfiction. Alcott continued to write juvenile fiction during her later years, although her productivity sharply declined as a result of her failing health. In addition to writing, she devoted her last years to the care of her father and her young niece Lulu, whose mother (Alcott's sister May) had died as a result of complications in childbirth. Alcott died on March 6, 1888, just two days after her father's death. They were buried in the Alcott family plot in Sleepy Hollow Cemetery in Concord, Massachusetts.

MAJOR WORKS

Alcott's literary career can be divided into three periods. The first phase, spanning the 1840s to the late 1860s, is characterized by the lurid, sensational short stories which were published anonymously and pseudonymously in various New England periodicals. Many of these tales feature a mysterious, vengeful woman bent on manipulation and destruction. Whether this motif reflects Alcott's suppressed rage at the restrictions of her life or simply her talent for writing to please a mass audience remains a topic of scholarly debate. The publication of *Moods* inaugurated Alcott's most profitable and popular period. The story of a young woman who makes significant errors in life choices by following the whims of her moods rather than using informed judgment, *Moods* is unique among novels of the period for its discussion of divorce as a real option for unhappy couples. During this period Alcott began the chronicles of the March family, for which she is best known. The first of these, *Little Women,* is the work that still defines Alcott's career. The *Little Women* books, which were the most successful series of their time, illustrate the struggles between adolescence and maturity, but they also represent a prominent theme in much of Alcott's fiction: the conflict experienced by women who must choose between individuality and the bonds of family responsibilities and social traditions. Jo, the heroine of *Little Women,* for example, is an unconventional young woman who strives for independence and personal achievement as a writer, but ultimately modifies her dreams when she gets married. From 1875 onward, as her health deteriorated, Alcott primarily produced popular juvenile literature. Two exceptions are the adult novels *A Modern Mephistopheles* (1877) and *A Whisper in the Dark* (1880). Many of her later works, particularly *Work: A Story of Experience* (1873) and *Rose in Bloom* (1876), depict heroines who have acquired inner strength through personal hardship and achieve personal satisfaction through careers rather than marriage. *Work* is generally considered the most overtly feminist of Alcott's works; the novel details its heroine Christie Devon's search for economic independence. As in *Little Women,* however, Devon's quest for freedom includes a traditional marriage and domestic life. Similarly, in *Jo's Boys,* Nan pursues a career in medicine and chooses not to marry, but Bess and Josie give up their careers as an artist and actress, respectively, in order to marry. Alcott's apparent denial of complete feminine independence for many of her characters has made her final position on women's roles ambiguous at best.

CRITICAL RECEPTION

During Alcott's lifetime, her stories for children were widely regarded as American classics. The early twentieth century, however, witnessed a decline in the critical assessment of Alcott's works, with some critics denouncing the moralizing tone of her fiction. What had once been interpreted as the charm and innocence of the March girls in particular was later seen as overly sentimental. For several decades into the twentieth century, the sentimentality of Alcott's work was assessed by critics as her support for the prevailing ideology of separate spheres of social activity for men and women. With the rise of feminist criticism and women's studies, however, Alcott's works for both children and adults have been the subject of critical reexamination, with much discussion surrounding the nature of her views on the role of women in the family and society. Critics who have identified a feminist champion in Alcott emphasize Alcott's alignment with feminist causes throughout her life, her nonfiction writing in support of women's suffrage and women's work, and her adult fiction as evidence of Alcott's general feminist sensibility. Sarah Elbert emphasizes Alcott's personal involvement in women's social issues, including women's education, the vote, and equal pay for equal work, but she also notes that Alcott considered women's civilizing influence on men to be a peculiar duty of womanhood. Part of the challenge of interpreting *Little Women* and other stories in Alcott's oeuvre is their status as childhood classics; several critics have attempted to analyze the stories' enduring popularity and resonance. Scholars have argued that *Little Women* affects critics emotionally because of their adolescent connection to the story, thus coloring scholarly interpretations of the work. In exploring the depth and nature of Alcott's feminist views, critics have turned to her early thrillers, which were not collected until 1975. For years, critics assumed that the thrillers, published pseudonymously, were written solely for financial gain and represented Alcott's compromising of her artistic principles. More recently, however, some feminist scholars have suggested that the thrillers reveal a repressed rage and possibly a truer representation of Alcott's strong feelings about the unjust status of women than may be present in her other works.

PRINCIPAL WORKS

Flower Fables (fairy tales) 1855

Hospital Sketches (letters and sketches) 1863

Moods (novel) 1864; revised edition, 1882

Little Women; or, Meg. Jo, Beth, and Amy. 2 vols. (novel) 1868-69; published as *Little Women and Good Wives,* 1871

An Old-Fashioned Girl (novel) 1870

Little Men: Life at Plumfield with Jo's Boys (novel) 1871

Aunt Jo's Scrap Bag. 6 vols. (short stories) 1872-82

Work: A Story of Experience (novel) 1873

Eight Cousins; or, The Aunt-Hill (novel) 1875

Rose in Bloom (novel) 1876

A Modern Mephistopheles (novel) 1877

Under the Lilacs (novel) 1878

Jack and Jill: A Village Story (novel) 1880

Jo's Boys and How They Turned Out (novel) 1886

Louisa May Alcott: Her Life, Letters, and Journals (letters and journals) 1889

Comic Tragedies (plays) 1893

Behind a Mask: The Unknown Thrillers of Louisa May Alcott (short stories) 1975

Plots and Counterplots: More Unknown Thrillers of Louisa May Alcott (short stories) 1976

PRIMARY SOURCES

LOUISA MAY ALCOTT (ESSAY DATE 1875)

SOURCE: Alcott, Louisa May. "Woman's Part in the Concord Celebration." In *L. M. Alcott: Signature of Reform,* edited by Madeleine B. Stern, pp. 198-99. Boston: Northeastern University Press, 2002.

In the following essay, originally printed in the Woman's Journal *in 1875, Alcott describes her efforts, as part of a group of women, to break into the traditionally male activities of the Concord Centennial celebration.*

Being frequently asked "what part the women took in the Concord Centennial celebration?" I give herewith a brief account of our share on that occasion.

Having set our houses in order, stored our larders, and filled our rooms with guests, we girded up our weary souls and bodies for the great day, feeling that we must do or die for the honor of old Concord.

We had no place in the procession, but such women as wished to hear the oration were directed to meet in the town hall at half past nine, and there wait till certain persons, detailed for the service, should come to lead them to the tent, where a limited number of seats had been provided for the weaker vessels.

This seemed a sensible plan, and as a large proportion of ladies chose the intellectual part of the feast the hall was filled with a goodly crowd at the appointed hour. No one seemed to know what to do except wait, and that we did with the patience born of long practice. But it was very trying to the women of Concord to see invited guests wandering forlornly about or sitting in chilly corners meekly wondering why the hospitalities of the town were not extended to them as well as to their "men folks" who were absorbed into the pageant in one way or another.

For an hour we women waited, but no one came, and the sound of martial music so excited the patient party that with one accord we moved down to the steps below, where a glimpse of the approaching procession might cheer our eyes. Here we stood, with the north wind chilling us to the marrow of our bones, a flock of feminine Casabiancas with the slight difference of freezing instead of burning at our posts.

Some wise virgins, who put not their trust in men, departed to shift for themselves, but fifty or more obeyed orders and stood fast till, just as the procession appeared, an agitated gentleman with a rosette at his buttonhole gave the brief command,

"Ladies cross the common and wait for your escort:"

Then he vanished and was seen no more.

Over we went, like a flock of sheep, leaving the show behind us, but comforting ourselves with the thought of the seats "saving up" for us and of the treat to come. A cheerful crowd, in spite of the bitter wind, the rude comments of the men swarming by, and the sad certainty which slowly dawned upon us that we were entirely forgotten. The gay and gallant presence of a granddaughter of the Dr. Ripley who watched the fight from the Old Manse, kept up our spirits; for this indomitable lady circulated among us like sunshine, inspiring us with such confidence that we rallied round the little flag she bore, and followed where it led.

Patience has its limits, and there came a moment when the revolutionary spirit of '76 blazed up in the bosoms of these long suffering women; for, when some impetuous soul cried out "Come on and let us take care of ourselves!" there was a general movement; the flag fluttered to the front, veils were close reefed, skirts kilted up, arms locked, and with one accord the Light Brigade charged over the red bridge, up the hill, into the tented field, rosy and red-nosed, disheveled but dauntless.

The tent was closely packed, and no place appeared but a corner of the platform. Anxious to seat certain grey-haired ladies weary with long waiting, and emboldened by a smile from Senator Wilson, a nod from Representative May, and a pensive stare from Orator Curtis, I asked the President of the day if a few ladies could occupy that corner till seats could be found for them?

"They can sit or stand anywhere in the town except on this platform; and the quicker they get down the better, for gentlemen are coming in to take these places."

This gracious reply made me very glad to descend into the crowd again, for there at least good-nature reigned; and there we stood, placidly surveyed by the men (who occupied the seats set apart for us,) not one of whom stirred, though the grandmother of Boston waited in the ranks.

My idea of hospitality may be old-fashioned, but I must say I felt ashamed of Concord that day, when all I could offer my guests, admiring pilgrims to this "Mecca of the mind," was the extreme edge of an unplaned board; for, when the gods were settled, leave was given us to sit on the rim of the platform.

Perched there, like a flock of tempest tossed pigeons, we had the privilege of reposing among the sacred boots of the Gamalials at whose feet we sat, and of listening to the remarks of the reporters, who evidently felt that the elbow room of the almighty press should not be encroached upon even by a hair's breadth.

"No place for women," growled one.

"Never was a fitter," answered a strong-minded lady standing on one foot.

"Ought to have come earlier, if they come at all."

"So they would, if they had not obeyed orders. Never will again."

"Don't see why they couldn't be contented with seeing the procession."

"Because they preferred poetry and patriotism to fuss and feathers."

"Better have it all their own way, next time."

"No doubt they will, and I hope we shall all be there to see."

So the dialogue ended in a laugh, and the women resigned themselves to cold shoulders all around. But as I looked about me, it was impossible to help thinking that there should have been a place for the great granddaughters of Prescott, William Emerson, John Hancock and Dr. Ripley, as well as for Isaac Davis's old sword, the scissors that cut the immortal cartridges, and the ancient flag some woman's fingers made. It seemed to me that their presence on that platform would have had a deeper significance than the gold lace which adorned one side, or the senatorial ponderosity under which it broke down on the other; and that the men of Concord had missed a grand opportunity of imitating those whose memory they had met to honor.

The papers have told the tale of that day's exploits and experiences, but the papers did not get all the little items, and some of them were rather funny. Just before the services began, a distracted usher struggled in to inform Judge Hoar that the wives of several potentates had been left out in the cold, and must be accommodated. Great was the commotion then, for these ladies being bobs to political kites, could not be neglected; so a part of the seats reserved for women were with much difficulty cleared, and the "elect precious" set thereon. Dear ladies! how very cold and wretched they were when they got there, and how willingly the "free and independent citizenesses" of Concord forgave them for reducing their limited quarters to the point of suffocation, as they spread their cloaks over the velvet of their guests, still trying to be hospitable under difficulties.

When order was restored, what might be called "the Centennial Break Down" began. The President went first—was it an omen? and took refuge among the women, who I am happy to say received him kindly and tried to temper the wind to His Imperturbability, as he sat among them looking so bored that I longed to offer him a cigar.

The other gentleman stood by the ship, which greatly diversified the performances by slowly sinking with all on board but the captain. Even the orator tottered on the brink of ruin more than once, and his table would have gone over if a woman had not held up one leg of it for an hour or so. No light task, she told me afterward, for when the inspired gentleman gave an impressive thump, it took both hands to sustain the weight of his eloquence. Another lady was pinned down by the beams falling on her skirts, but cheerfully sacrificed them, and sat still, till the departure of the presidential party allowed us to set her free.

Finding us bound to hear it out, several weary gentlemen offered us their seats, after a time; but we had the laugh on our side now, and sweetly declined, telling them their platform was not strong enough to hold us.

It was over at last, and such of us as had strength enough left went to the dinner, and enjoyed another dish of patriotism "cold without;" others went home to dispense hot comforts, and thaw the congealed visitors who wandered to our doors.

Then came the ball, and there all went well, for Woman was in her sphere, her "only duty was to please," and the more there were, the merrier; so the deserted damsels of the morning found themselves the queens of the evening, and, forgetting and forgiving, bore their part as gaily as if they had put on the vigor of their grandmothers with the old brocades that became them so well.

Plenty of escorts, ushers and marshals at last, and six chairs apiece if we wanted them. Gentlemen who had been as grim as griffins a few hours before were all devotion now, and spectacles that had flashed awful lightning on the women who dared prefer poetry to polkas now beamed upon us benignly, and hoped we were enjoying ourselves, as we sat nodding along the walls while our guests danced.

That was the end of it, and by four A.M., peace fell upon the exhausted town, and from many a welcome pillow went up the grateful sigh:

"Thank heaven we shall not have to go through this again!"

No, not quite the end; for by and by there will come a day of reckoning, and then the tax-paying women of Concord will not be forgotten I think, will not be left to wait uncalled upon, or be considered in the way; and *then,* I devoutly wish that those who so bravely bore their share of that day's burden without its honor, will rally round their own flag again, and, following in the footsteps of their forefathers, will utter another protest that shall be "heard round the world."

GENERAL COMMENTARY

SETH CURTIS BEACH (ESSAY DATE 1905)

SOURCE: Beach, Seth Curtis. "Louisa May Alcott." In *Daughters of the Puritans: A Group of Biographies,* pp. 251-86. Boston: American Unitarian Association, 1905.

In the following essay, Beach emphasizes Alcott's life as the source of her work and her father as a dominant influence in her development and identity.

Miss Alcott has been called, perhaps truly, the most popular story-teller for children, in her generation. Like those elect souls whom the apostle saw arrayed in white robes, she came up

FROM THE AUTHOR

A LETTER TO THE EDITOR OF *WOMAN'S JOURNAL* ON THE CHALLENGES FOR WOMEN IN HAVING AN ACTIVE PUBLIC AND DOMESTIC LIFE

There is very little to report about the woman's vote at Concord Town Meeting, as only eight were there in time to do the one thing permitted them.

With the want of forethought and promptness which show how much our sex have yet to learn in the way of business habits, some dozen delayed coming till the vote for school committee was over. It came third on the warrant, and a little care in discovering this fact would have spared us much disappointment. It probably made no difference in the choice of officers, as there is seldom any trouble about the matter, but it is to be regretted that the women do not give more attention to the duty which they really care for, yet fail, as yet, to realize the importance of, small as it is at present.

Their delay shows, however, that home affairs are *not* neglected, for the good ladies remained doubtless to give the men a comfortable dinner and set their houses in order before going to vote.

Next time I hope they will leave the dishes till they get home, as they do when in a hurry to go to the sewing-society, Bible-class, or picnic. A hasty meal once a year will not harm the digestion of the lords of creation, and the women need all the drill they can get in the new duties that are surely coming to widen their sphere, sharpen their wits, and strengthen their wills, teaching them the courage, intelligence and independence all should have, and many sorely need in a world of vicissitudes.

Alcott, Louisa May. Excerpt from a letter to the editor of *Woman's Journal,* May 8, 1884. In *L. M. Alcott: Signature of Reform.* Edited by Madeleine B. Stern, pp. 218-19. Boston: Northeastern University Press, 2002.

through great tribulation, paying dearly in labor and privation for her successes, but one must pronounce her life happy and fortunate, since she lived to enjoy her fame and fortune twenty years, to witness the sale of a million volumes of her writings, to receive more than two hundred thousand dollars from her publishers, and thereby to accomplish the great purpose upon which as a girl she had set her heart, which was, to see her father and mother comfortable in their declining years.

Successful as Miss Alcott was as a writer, she was greater as a woman, and the story of her life is as interesting,—as full of tragedy and comedy,—as the careers of her heroes and heroines. In fact, we have reason to believe that the adventures of her characters are often not so much invented as remembered, the pranks and frolics of her boys and girls being episodes from her own youthful experience. In the preface to ***Little Women,*** the most charming of her books, she tells us herself that the most improbable incidents are the least imaginary. The happy girlhood which she portrays was her own, in spite of forbidding conditions. The struggle in which her cheerful nature extorted happiness from unwilling fortune, gives a dramatic interest to her youthful experiences, as her literary disappointments and successes do to the years of her maturity.

Miss Alcott inherited a name which her father's genius had made known on both sides of the sea, before her own made it famous in a hundred thousand households. Alcott is a derivative from Alcocke, the name by which Mr. Alcott himself was known in his boyhood. John Alcocke, born in New Haven, Ct., married Mary, daughter of Rev. Abraham Pierson, first president of Yale College. He was a man of considerable fortune and left 1,200 acres of land to his six children, one of whom was Capt. John Alcocke, a man of some distinction in the colonial service. Joseph Chatfield Alcocke, son of Capt. John, married Anna, sister of Rev. Tillotson Bronson, D. D. Of this marriage, Amos Bronson Alcott, father of Louisa, was born, Nov. 29, 1799. The fortunes of Joseph Chatfield Alcocke were those of other small farmers of the period, but Mrs. Alcocke could not forget that she was the sister of a college graduate, and it was worth something to her son to know that he was descended from the president of a college. The mother and son early settled it that the boy should be a scholar, and the father loyally furthered their ambitions, borrowing of his acquaintances such books as he discovered and bringing them home for the delectation of his studious son. At the age of thirteen, Bronson became a pupil in a private school kept by his uncle, Dr. Bronson, and at eighteen, he set out for

Virginia with the secret purpose of teaching if opportunity offered, at the same time taking along a peddler's trunk out of which to turn an honest penny and pay the expenses of his journey. Circumstances did not favor his becoming a Virginia teacher, but between his eighteenth and twenty-third years, he made several expeditions into the Southern States as a Yankee peddler, with rather negative financial results, but with much enlargement of his information and improvement of his rustic manners. Mr. Alcott was rather distinguished for his high-bred manners and, on a visit to England, there is an amusing incident of his having been mistaken for some member of the titled aristocracy.

At the age of twenty-five, Mr. Alcott began his career as a teacher in an Episcopal Academy at Cheshire, Ct. His family were Episcopalians, and he had been confirmed at sixteen. Since the age of eighteen when he started for Virginia as a candidate for a school, he had been theorizing upon the art of teaching and had thought out many of the principles of what, a century later, began to be called the "New Education." He undertook, perhaps too rapidly, to apply his theories in the conduct of the Cheshire Academy. His experiments occasioned a vast amount of controversy, in which Connecticut conservatism gained a victory, and Mr. Alcott retired from the school at the end of two years' service. His results however had been sufficient to convince him of the soundness of his principles, and to launch him upon the troubled career of educational reform.

Among a few intelligent friends and sympathizers who rallied to Mr. Alcott's side in this controversy, was Rev. Samuel J. May, a Unitarian minister then of Brooklyn, Ct., at whose house, in 1827, Mr. Alcott met Mr. May's sister Abbie, who shared fully her brother's enthusiasm for the new education and its persecuted apostle. Miss May began her relations with Mr. Alcott as his admirer and champion, a dangerous part for an enthusiastic young lady to play, as the sequel proved when, three years later, she became Mrs. Alcott.

Mrs. Alcott was the daughter of a Boston merchant, Col. Joseph May, and his wife, Dorothy Sewall, daughter of Samuel Sewall and his wife, Elizabeth Quincy, sister of Dorothy Quincy, wife of John Hancock. By the marriage of Joseph May and Dorothy Sewall, two very distinguished lines of ancestry had been united. Under her father's roof, Mrs. Alcott had enjoyed every comfort and the best of social advantages. She was tall, had a fine physique, good intellect, warm affections, and generous sympathies, but it would have astonished her to have been told that she was bringing to the marriage altar more than she received; and however much it may have cost her to be the wife of an unworldly idealist, it was precisely his unworldly idealism that first won her admiration and then gained her heart.

Life may have been harder for Mrs. Alcott than she anticipated, but she knew very well that she was abjuring riches. Two years before her marriage, her brother had written her: "Mr. Alcott's mind and heart are so much occupied with other things that poverty and riches do not seem to concern him much." She had known Mr. Alcott three years and had enjoyed ample opportunity to make this observation herself. Indeed, two months after her marriage, she wrote her brother, "My husband is the perfect personification of modesty and moderation. I am not sure that we shall not blush into obscurity and contemplate into starvation." That she had not repented of her choice a year later, may be judged from a letter to her brother on the first anniversary of her marriage: "It has been an eventful year,—a year of trial, of happiness, of improvement. I can wish no better fate to any sister of my sex than has attended me since my entrance into the conjugal state."

That Mr. Alcott, then in his young manhood, had qualities which, for a young lady of refinement and culture, would compensate for many privations is evident. Whether he was one of the great men of his generation or not, there is no doubt he seemed so. When, in 1837, Dr. Bartol came to Boston, Mr. Emerson asked him whom he knew in the city, and said: "There is but one man, Mr. Alcott." Dr. Bartol seems to have come to much the same opinion. He says: "Alcott belonged to the Christ class: his manners were the most gentle and gracious, under all fair or unfair provocation, I ever beheld; he had a rare inborn piety and a god-like incapacity in the purity of his eyes to behold iniquity."

These qualities were not visible to the public and have no commercial value, but that Mr. Alcott had them is confirmed by the beautiful domestic life of the Alcotts, by the unabated love and devotion of Mrs. Alcott to her husband in all trials, and the always high and always loyal appreciation with which Louisa speaks of her father, even when perhaps smiling at his innocent illusions. The character of Mr. Alcott is an important element in the life of Louisa because she was his daughter, and because, being unmarried, her life and fortunes were his, or those of the Alcott family. She had no individual existence.

Two years after the marriage of Mr. and Mrs. Alcott, Louisa, their second daughter was born in Germantown, Pa., where Mr. Alcott was in charge of a school belonging to the Society of Friends, or Quakers. The date was November 29, 1832, also Mr. Alcott's birthday, always observed as a double festival in the family. In 1834, Mr. Alcott opened his celebrated school in Masonic Temple in Boston, Mass., under the auspices of Dr. Channing and with the assured patronage of some of the most cultivated and influential families in the city. As assistants in this school, he had first Miss Sophia Peabody afterward Mrs. Hawthorne, her sister Miss Elizabeth Peabody, and finally Margaret Fuller.

The school opened prosperously and achieved remarkable success until, in 1837, the publication of Mr. Alcott's "Conversations on the Gospels" shocked the piety of Boston newspapers, whose persistent and virulent attacks frightened the public and caused the withdrawal of two-thirds of the pupils. Mr. Emerson came to Mr. Alcott's defence, saying: "He is making an experiment in which all the friends of education are interested," and asking, "whether it be wise or just to add to the anxieties of this enterprise a public clamor against some detached sentences of a book which, on the whole, is pervaded by original thought and sincere piety." In a private note, Mr. Emerson urged Mr. Alcott to give up his school, as the people of Boston were not worthy of him. Mr. Alcott had spent more than the income of the school in its equipment, creating debts which Louisa afterward paid; all his educational ideals were at stake, and he could not accept defeat easily. However, in 1839, a colored girl was admitted to the school, and all his pupils were withdrawn, except the little negress and four whites, three of whom were his own daughters. So ended the Temple school. The event was very fateful for the Alcott family, but, much as it concerned Mrs. Alcott, there can be no doubt she much preferred that the school should end thus, than that Mr. Alcott should yield to public clamor on either of the issues which wrecked the enterprise.

Louisa was seven years old when this misfortune occurred which shaped the rest of her life, fixing the straitened circumstances in which she was to pass her youth and preparing the burdens which ultimately were to be lifted by her facile pen. Happily the little Alcotts, of whom there were three, were too young to feel the perplexities that harassed their parents and their early years could hardly have been passed more pleasantly or profitably if they had been the daughters of millionaires. The family lived very comfortably amidst a fine circle of relatives and friends in Boston, preached and practised a vegetarian gospel,—rice without sugar and graham meal without butter or molasses,—monotonous but wholesome, spent their summers with friends at Scituate and, in town or country, partly owing to the principles of the new education, partly to the preoccupation of the parents, the children of the family were left in large measure to the teaching of nature and their own experience.

Very abundant moral instruction there was in this apostolic family, both by example and precept, but the young disciples were expected to make their own application of the principles. The result, in the case of Louisa, was to develop a girl of very enterprising and adventurous character, who might have been mistaken for a boy from her sun-burned face, vigorous health, and abounding animal spirits. It was her pride to drive her hoop around the Common before breakfast and she tells us that she admitted to her social circle no girl who could not climb a tree and no boy whom she had not beaten in a race. Her autobiography of this period, she has given us, very thinly disguised, in **"Poppy's Pranks."**

Meanwhile, her mental faculties were not neglected. Mr. Alcott began the education of his children, in a kindergarten way, almost in their infancy, and before his Boston school closed, Louisa had two or three years in it as a pupil. What his method of education could do with a child of eight years is shown by a poem written by Louisa at that age. The family were then living in Concord, in the house which, in ***Little Women,*** is celebrated as "Meg's first home." One early Spring day, Louisa found in the garden a robin, chilled and famished, and wrote these lines:

"Welcome, welcome, little stranger,
Fear no harm, and fear no danger;
We are glad to see you here,
For you sing, Sweet Spring is near.

Now the white snow melts away;
Now the flowers blossom gay:
Come, dear bird, and build your nest,
For we love our robin best."

It will be remembered that this literary faculty, unusual at the age of eight, had been attained by a girl in the physical condition of an athlete, who could climb a tree like a squirrel.

Readers of ***Little Women*** will remember what a child's paradise "Meg's first home" was, with its garden full of fruit-trees and shade, and its old empty barn which the children alternately turned into a drawing-room for company, a gymnasium for romps, and a theatre for dramatic performances. "There," says Louisa, "we dramatized the fairy tales in great style," Jack the Giant-killer and Cinderella being favorites, the passion for the stage which came near making Louisa an actress, as also her sister Anna, getting early development.

The fun and frolic of these days were the more enjoyed because they alternated with regular duties, with lessons in housework with the mother and language lessons with the father, for which he now had abundant leisure. As he had no other pupils, he could try all his educational experiments in his own family. Among other exercises, the children were required to keep a journal, to write in it regularly, and to submit it to the examination and criticism of the parents. Facility in writing thus became an early acquisition. It was furthered by a pretty habit which Mrs. Alcott had of keeping up a little correspondence with her children, writing little notes to them when she had anything to say in the way of reproof, correction, or instruction, receiving their confessions, repentance, and good resolutions by the next mail.

Some of these maternal letters are very tender and beautiful. One to Louisa at the age of eleven, enclosed a picture of a frail mother cared for by a faithful daughter, and says, "I have always liked it very much, for I imagined that you might be just such an industrious daughter and I such a feeble and loving mother, looking to your labor for my daily bread." There was prophecy in this and there was more prophecy in the lines with which Louisa replied:

"I hope that soon, dear mother,
  You and I may be
In the quiet room my fancy
  Has so often made for thee,—

The pleasant, sunny chamber,
  The cushioned easy-chair,
The book laid for your reading,
  The vase of flowers fair;

The desk beside the window
  When the sun shines warm and bright,
And there in ease and quiet,
  The promised book you write.

While I sit close beside you,
  Content at last to see
That you can rest, dear mother,
  And I can cherish thee."

The versification is still juvenile, but there is no fault in the sentiment, and Miss Alcott, in a later note, says, "The dream came true, and for the last ten years of her life, Marmee sat in peace with every wish granted."

Evidently Louisa had begun to feel the pinch of the family circumstances. The income was of the slenderest. Sometimes Mr. Alcott gave a lecture or "conversation" and received a few dollars; sometimes he did a day's farm work for a neighbor; now and then Mr. Emerson called and clandestinely left a bank note, and many valuable packages came out from relatives in Boston; but frugal housekeeping was the chief asset of the family. Discouraging as the outlook was, some bitter experience might have been escaped if the Alcotts had remained in Concord, pursuing their unambitious career. It was, however, the era of social experiments in New England. The famous Brook Farm community was then in the third year of its existence, and it was impossible that Mr. Alcott should not sympathize with this effort to ease the burden of life, and wish to try his own experiment. Therefore, in 1843, being joined by several English socialists, one of whom financed the undertaking, Mr. Alcott started a small community on a worn-out not to say abandoned farm, which was hopefully christened "Fruitlands."

Visiting the community five or six weeks after its inception, Mr. Emerson wrote: "The sun and the evening sky do not look calmer than Alcott and his family at Fruitlands. They seem to have arrived at the fact,—to have got rid of the show, and so to be serene. They look well in July; we will see them in December." An inhospitable December came upon the promising experiment, as it generally has upon all similar enterprises. Under the title Transcendental Wild Oats, in ***Silver Pitchers,*** Miss Alcott gives a lively account of the varying humors of this disastrous adventure.

Whatever disappointments and privations the enterprise had in store for their parents, the situation, with its little daily bustle, its limitless range of fields and woods, its flower hunting and berry picking, was full of interest and charm for four healthy children all under the age of twelve years. The fateful December, to which Mr. Emerson postponed his judgment, had not come before the elders were debating a dissolution of the community. "Father asked us if we saw any reason for us to separate," writes Louisa in her journal. "Mother wanted to, she is so tired. I like it." Of course she did; but "not the school part," she adds, "nor Mr. L.", who was one of her teachers. The inevitable lessons interfered with her proper business.

"Fruitlands" continued for three years with declining fortunes, its lack of promise being perhaps a benefit to the family in saving for other purposes a small legacy which Mrs. Alcott received from her father's estate. With this and a loan of $500 from Mr. Emerson, she bought "The Hillside" in Concord, an estate which, after the Alcotts, was occupied by Mr. Hawthorne. Thither Mrs. Alcott removed with her family in 1846, and the two years that followed is the period which Louisa looked back upon as the happiest of her life, "for we had," she says, "charming playmates in the little Emersons, Channings, Hawthornes, and Goodwins, with the illustrious parents and their friends to enjoy our pranks and share our excursions." Here the happy girlish life was passed which is so charmingly depicted in ***Little Women,*** and here at the age of sixteen, Louisa wrote, for the entertainment of the little Alcotts and Emersons, a series of pretty fairy tales, still to be read in the second volume of Lulu's Library.

Much as there was to enjoy in these surroundings, the problem of subsistence had not been solved and, with the growth of her daughters toward womanhood, it became more difficult for Mrs. Alcott. The world had, apparently, no use for Mr. Alcott; there were six persons to be fed and clothed, and no bread-winner in the family. The story is that one day, a friend found her in tears and demanded an explanation. "Abby Alcott, what does this mean?" asked the visitor, and when Mrs. Alcott had made her confessions, her friend said, "Come to Boston and I will find you employment."

Accepting the proposition, the family removed to Boston in 1848, and Mrs. Alcott became the agent of certain benevolent societies. Mr. Alcott taught private classes, or held "conversations"; the older daughters, Anna and Louisa, found employment; and we may think of the family as fairly comfortable during the seven or eight years of its life in Boston. "Our poor little home," says Miss Alcott, "had much love and happiness in it, and was a shelter for lost girls, abused wives, friendless children, and weak and wicked men. Father and mother had no money to give but they gave time, sympathy, help; and if blessings would make them rich, they would be millionaires." Fugitive slaves were among the homeless who found shelter, one of whom Mrs. Alcott concealed in an unused brick oven.

In Miss Alcott's journal of this period, we find the burden of existence weighing very heavily upon her, a state of mind apparently induced by her first expereince in teaching. "School is hard work," she says, "and I feel as though I should like to run away from it. But my children get on; so I travel up every day and do my best. I get very little time to write or think, for my working days have begun." Later, she seems to have seen the value of this experience. "At sixteen," she writes, "I began to teach twenty pupils and, for ten years, I learned to know and love children."

Amateur theatricals were still the recreation of the Alcott girls, as they had been almost from infancy, and the stage presented a fascinating alternative to the school-room. "Anna wants to be an actress and so do I," writes Louisa at seventeen. "We could make plenty of money perhaps, and it is a very gay life. Mother says we are too young and must wait. Anna acts splendidly. I like tragic plays and shall be a Siddons if I can. We get up harps, dresses, water-falls, and thunder, and have great fun." Both of the sisters wrote many exciting dramas at this period, and one of Louisa's, **"The Rival Prima Donnas,"** was accepted by the manager of the Boston Theatre, who "thought it would have a fine run" and sent the author a free pass to the theatre, which partly compensated for the non-appearance of the play. Some years later, a farce written by Louisa, **"Nat Bachelor's Pleasure Trip, or the Trials of a Good-Natured Man,"** was produced at the Howard Athenæum, and was favorably received. Christie's experience as an actress, in Miss Alcott's novel entitled, ***Work,*** is imaginary in its incidents, but autobiographical in its spirit.

All these experiments in dramatic literature, from Jack the Giant-Killer on, were training the future story-teller. Miss Alcott's first story to see the light was printed in a newspaper at the age of twenty, in 1852, though it had been written at sixteen. She received $5.00 for it, and the event is interesting as the beginning of her fortune. This little encouragement came at a period of considerable trial for the family. The following is from her journal of 1853: "In January, I started a little school of about a dozen in our parlor. In May, my school closed and I went to L. as second girl. I needed the change, could do the wash, and was glad to earn my $2.00 a week." Notice that this is her summer vacation. "Home in October with $34.00 for my wages. After two days' rest, began school again with ten children." The family distributed themselves as follows: "Anna went to Syracuse to teach; father to the west to try his luck,—so poor, so hopeful, so serene. God be with him. Mother had several boarders. School for me, month after month. I earned a good deal by sewing in the evening when my day's work was done."

Mr. Alcott returned from the west, and the account of his adventures is very touching: "In February father came home. Paid his way, but no more. A dramatic scene when he arrived in the night. We were awakened by the bell. Mother flew down crying, My Husband. We rushed after and five white figures embraced the half-frozen wanderer who came in, hungry, tired, cold, and disappointed, but smiling bravely and as serene as ever. We fed and warmed and brooded over him, longing to ask if he had made any money; but no one did till little May said, after he had told us all the pleasant things, 'Well, did people pay you?' Then with a queer look he opened his pocket book, and showed one dollar, saying with a smile, 'Only that. My overcoat was stolen, and I had to buy a shawl. Many promises were not kept, and traveling is costly; but I have opened the way, and another year shall do better.' I shall never forget how beautifully mother answered him, though the dear, hopeful soul had built much on his success: but with a beaming face she kissed him, saying, 'I call that doing very well. Since you are safely home, dear, we don't ask anything else.'"

One of Miss Alcott's unfulfilled purposes was to write a story entitled "The Pathetic Family." This passage would have found a place in it. It deserves to be said that Mr. Alcott's faith that he had "opened a way and another year should do better," was justified. Fifteen years later, from one of his western tours, he brought home $700, but, thanks to Louisa's pen, the family were no longer in such desperate need of money.

More than once Miss Alcott declares that no one ever assisted her in her struggles, but that was far from true, as appears from many favors acknowledged in her journal. It was by the kindness of a lady who bought the manuscripts and assumed the risk of publication, that her first book, ***Flower Fables,*** was brought out in 1854. It consisted of the fairy tales written six years before for the little Emersons. She received $32.00, a sum which would have seemed insignificant thirty years later when, in 1886, the sale of her books for six months brought her $8,000; but she says, "I was prouder over the $32.00 than over the $8,000."

The picture of Jo in a garret in ***Little Women,*** planning and writing stories, is drawn from Louisa's experiences of the following winter. A frequent entry in her journal for this period is "$5.00 for a story" and her winter's earnings are summed up, "school, one quarter, $50, sewing $50, stories, $20." In December we read, "Got five dollars for a tale and twelve for sewing." Teaching, writing, and sewing alternate in her life for the next five years, and, for a year or two yet, the needle is mightier than the pen; but in 1856, she began to be paid $10 for a story, and, in 1859, the *Atlantic* accepted a story and paid her $50.

A friend for whose encouragement during these hard years, she acknowledges great indebtedness and who appears as one of the characters in her story, entitled ***Work,*** was Rev. Theodore Parker, a man as helpful, loving, and gentle as she depicts him, but then much hated by those called orthodox and hardly in good standing among his Unitarian brethren. Miss Alcott, then as ever, had the courage of her convictions, was a member of his Music Hall congregation, and a regular attendant at his Sunday evening receptions, finding him "very friendly to the large, bashful girl who adorns his parlor regularly." She "fought for him," she says, when some one said Mr. Parker "was not a Christian. He is my sort; for though he may lack reverence for other people's God, he works bravely for his own, and turns his back on no one who needs help, as some of the pious do." After Mr. Parker's death, Miss Alcott, when in Boston, attended the church of Dr. C. A. Bartol, who buried her mother, her father and herself.

In 1857, the Alcotts returned to Concord, buying and occupying the Orchard House, which thenceforth became their home. Other family events of the period were, the death of Miss Alcott's sister Elizabeth, Beth in ***Little Women,*** the marriage of Anna, Meg in ***Little Women,*** and a proposal of marriage to Louisa, serious enough for her to hold a consultation over it with her mother. Miss Alcott is said to have been averse to entangling alliances for herself, to have married off the heroines in her novels reluctantly at the demand of her readers, and never to have enjoyed writing the necessary love-passages.

The year 1860, when Miss Alcott is twenty-seven, has the distinction of being marked in the heading of her journal as "A Year of Good Luck." Her family had attained a comfortable, settled home in Concord; Mr. Alcott had been appointed superintendent of public schools, an office for which he was peculiarly well qualified and in which he was both happy and admirably successful; Anna, the eldest sister, was happily married; May, the youngest, was making a reputation as an artist; and Louisa, in perfect health, having in May before, "walked to Boston, twenty miles, in five hours, and attended an evening party," was becoming a regular contributor to the *Atlantic,* and receiving $50, $75, and sometimes $100 for her stories.

In these happy conditions, Miss Alcott sat down to a more ambitious attempt at authorship and wrote the first rough draft of ***Moods,*** a "problem novel" that provoked much discussion and, though it caused her more trouble than any other of her books, was always dearest to her heart. It was written in a kind of frenzy of poetic enthusiasm. "Genius burned so fiercely," she says, "that for four weeks, I wrote all day and planned nearly all night, being quite possessed by my work. I was perfectly happy, and seemed to have no wants. Finished the book, or a rough draft of it, and put it away to settle." It was not published till four years later. Even in this year of good luck, there seem to have been some privations, as she records being invited to attend a John Brown meeting and declining because she "had no good gown." She sends a poem instead.

The breaking out of the Civil War stirred Miss Alcott's soul to its depths, and we have numerous references to its progress in her journal. "I like the stir in the air," she writes, "and long for battle like a war-horse when he smells powder." Not being permitted to enlist as a soldier, she went into a hospital in Washington as a nurse. Her experiences are graphically and dramatically told in ***Hospital Sketches.*** That book, chiefly made from her private letters, met the demand of the public, eager for any information about the great war; it was widely read and, besides putting $200 in her purse, gave her a reputation with readers and publishers. Many applications for manuscript came in and she was told that "any publisher this side of Baltimore would be glad to get a book" from her. "There is a sudden hoist," she says, "for a meek and lowly scribbler. Fifteen years of hard grubbing may come to something yet." Her receipts for the year 1863, amounted to $600 and she takes comfort in saying that she had spent less than one hundred on herself.

The following year, after having been twice rewritten, ***Moods*** was brought out and, thanks to the ***Hospital Sketches,*** had a ready sale. Wherever she went, she says, she "found people laughing or crying over it, and was continually told how well it was going, how much it was liked, how fine a thing I had done." The first edition was exhausted in a week. An entire edition was ordered by London publishers. She was very well satisfied with the reception of ***Moods*** at the time, though in after years when fifty thousand copies of a book would be printed as a first edition, the sale of ***Moods*** seemed to her inconsiderable.

The present day reader wonders neither at the eagerness of the public for the book, nor at the criticisms that were freely made upon it. It is interesting from cover to cover and as a study of "a life affected by moods, not a discussion of marriage," it is effective. In spite, however, of the warning of the author, everyone read it as "a discussion of marriage," and few were satisfied. The interest centres in the fortunes of a girl who has married the wrong lover, the man to whom, by preference, she would have given her heart being supposedly dead. Would that he had been, for then, to all appearance, she would have been contented and happy. Unfortunately he returns a year too late, finds the girl married and, though endowed with every virtue which a novelist can bestow upon her hero, he does not know enough to leave the poor woman in peace. On the contrary, he settles down to a deliberate siege to find out how she feels, wrings from her the confession that she is miserable, as by that time no doubt she was, and then convinces her that since she does not love her husband, it is altogether wrong to live under the same roof with him. Surely this was nobly done. Poor Sylvia loves this villain, Miss Alcott evidently loves him, but the bloody-minded reader would like to thrust a knife into him. However, he is not a name or a type, but a real man, or one could not get so angry with him. All the characters live and breathe in these pages, and no criticism was less to the purpose than that the situations were unnatural. Miss Alcott says "The relations of Warwick, Moor, and Sylvia are pronounced impossible; yet a case of the sort exists, and a woman came and asked me how I knew it. I did not know or guess, but perhaps felt it, without any other guide, and unconsciously put the thing into my book."

Everyone will agree that Miss Alcott had earned a vacation, and it came in 1865, in a trip to Europe, where she spent a year, from July to July, as the companion of an invalid lady, going abroad for health. The necessity of modulating her pace to the movements of a nervous invalid involved some discomforts for a person of Miss Alcott's pedestrian abilities, but who would not accept some discomforts for a year of European travel? She had a reading knowledge of German and French, and in the abundant leisure which the long rests of her invalid friend forced upon her, she learned to speak French with facility.

On her return from Europe, she found her circumstances much improved. She had established her position as a regular contributor to the *Atlantic* whose editor, she says, "takes all I'll send." In 1868, she was offered and accepted the editorship of *Merry's Museum* at a salary of $500, and, more important, she was asked by Roberts Brothers to "write a girl's book." Her response to this proposition was ***Little Women,*** which she calls "the first golden egg of the ugly duckling, for the copyright made her fortune." Two editions were exhausted in six weeks and the book was translated into French, German and Dutch.

Little Men was written, a chapter a day, in November of the same year, and ***An Old-fashioned Girl,*** a popular favorite, the year following. ***Hospital Sketches*** had not yet outlived its welcome, was republished, with some additions, in 1869, and two thousand copies were sold the first week. She is able to say, "Paid up all debts, thank the Lord, every penny that money can pay,—and now I feel as if I could die in peace." Besides, she has invested "$1,200 for a rainy day," and is annoyed because "people come and stare at the Alcotts. Reporters haunt the place to look at the authoress, who dodges into the woods."

The severe application which her achievement had cost had impaired Miss Alcott's fine constitution and, in 1870, taking May, her artist sister, she made a second trip to Europe, spending the summer in France and Switzerland and the winter in Rome. A charming account of the adventures of this expedition is given in **"Shawl-Straps."** A pleasant incident of the journey was the receipt of a statement from her publisher giving her credit for $6,212, and she is able to say that she has "$10,000 well invested and more coming in all the time," and that she thinks "we may venture to enjoy ourselves, after the hard times we have had."

In 1872, she published ***Work: a story of Experience,*** and it is for the most part, a story of her own experience. "Christie's adventures," she says, "are many of them my own: Mr. Power is Mr. Parker: Mrs. Wilkins is imaginary, and all the rest. This was begun at eighteen, and never finished till H. W. Beecher wrote me for a serial for the *Christian Union* and paid $3,000 for it." It is one of the most deservedly popular of her books.

In 1877, for Roberts Brothers' "No Name Series," Miss Alcott wrote ***A Modern Mephistopheles,*** her least agreeable book, but original, imaginative, and powerful. The moral of the story is that, in our modern life, the devil does not appear with a cloven foot, but as a cultivated man of the world. Miss Alcott's Mephistopheles is even capable of generous impulses. With the kindness of a Good Samaritan, he saves a poor wretch from suicide and then destroys him morally. The devil is apparently a mixed character with a decided preponderance of sinfulness.

Miss Alcott had now reached her forty-fifth year, had placed her family in independent circumstances, thus achieving her early ambition, and the effort began to tell upon her health. A succession of rapid changes soon came upon her. Mrs. Alcott, having attained her seventy-seventh year, was very comfortable for her age. "Mother is cosy with her sewing, letters, and the success of her 'girls,'" writes Miss Alcott in January; but in June, "Marmee grows more and more feeble," and in November the end came. "She fell asleep in my arms," writes Louisa; "My duty is done, and now I shall be glad to follow her."

May, the talented artist sister, whom Louisa had educated, had once taken to Europe and twice sent abroad for study, was married in London in 1878, to a Swiss gentleman of good family and some fortune, Mr. Nieriker. The marriage was a very happy one but the joy of the young wife was brief. She died the year following, leaving an infant daughter as a legacy to Louisa.

Mr. Emerson's death in 1882, was, to her, much like taking a member of her own family: "The nearest and dearest friend father ever had and the man who helped me most by his life, his books, his society. I can never tell all he has been to me,—from the time I sang Mignon's song under his window (a little girl) and wrote letters *a la Bettine* to him, my Goethe, at fifteen, up through my hard years, when his essays on Self-Reliance, Character, Compensation, Love, and Friendship helped me to understand myself and life, and God and Nature."

Mr. Alcott is still with her, vigorous for his years. In 1879, at the age of eighty, he inaugurated the Concord School of Philosophy, "with thirty students. Father the dean. He has his dream realized at last, and is in glory, with plenty of talk to swim in." The school was, for Miss Alcott, an expensive toy with which she was glad to be able to indulge her father. Personally she cared little for it. On one of her rare visits to it, she was asked her definition of a philosopher, and responded instantly: "My definition is of a man up in a balloon, with his family and friends holding the ropes which confine him to earth and trying to haul him down." For her father's sake, she rejoiced in the success of the enterprise. Of the second season, she writes, "The new craze flourishes. The

FROM THE AUTHOR

ALCOTT ASKS WOMEN NOT TO MARRY FOR ANYTHING LESS THAN LOVE, AND NOT TO FEAR THE UNMARRIED LIFE

My sisters, don't be afraid of the words, "old maid," for it is in your power to make this a term of honor, not reproach. It is not necessary to be a sour, spiteful spinster, with nothing to do but brew tea, talk scandal and tend a pocket-handkerchief. No, the world is full of work, needing all the heads, hearts, and hands we can bring to do it. Never was there so splendid an opportunity for women to enjoy their liberty and prove that they deserve it by using it wisely. If love comes as it should come, accept it in God's name and be worthy of His best blessing. If it never comes, then in God's name reject the shadow of it, for that can never satisfy a hungry heart. Do not be ashamed to own the truth—do not be daunted by the fear of ridicule and loneliness, nor saddened by the loss of a woman's tenderest ties. Be true to yourselves; cherish whatever talent you possess, and in using it faithfully for the good of others you will most assuredly find happiness for yourself, and make of life no failure, but a beautiful success.

Alcott, Louisa May. Excerpt from "Happy Women," originally published in the *New York Ledger,* April 11, 1868. In *L. M. Alcott: Signature of Reform.* Edited by Madeleine B. Stern, pp. 146-49. Boston: Northeastern University Press, 2002.

first year, Concord people stood aloof; now the school is pronounced a success, because it brings money to the town. Father asked why we never went, and Anna showed him a long list of four hundred names of callers, and he said no more."

In addition to the labors which the school laid upon Mr. Alcott, he prepared for the press a volume of sonnets, some of which are excellent, especially one to Louisa:

> "Ne'er from thyself by Fame's loud trump beguiled,
> Sounding in this and the farther hemisphere,—
> I press thee to my heart as Duty's faithful child."

Mr. Alcott seemed to be renewing his youth but, in November, he was prostrated by paralysis. "Forty sonnets last winter," writes Louisa, "and fifty lectures at the school last summer, were too much for a man of eighty-three." He recovered sufficiently to enjoy his friends and his books and lingered six years, every want supplied by his devoted daughter.

With Miss Alcott the years go on at a slower pace, the writing of books alternating with sleepless nights and attacks of vertigo. ***Jo's Boys*** was written in 1884, fifty thousand copies being printed for the first edition. In 1886, her physician forbids her beginning anything that will need much thought. Life was closing in upon her, and she did not wish to live if she could not be of use. In March, 1888, Mr. Alcott failed rapidly, and died on the sixth of the month. Miss Alcott visited him and, in the excitement of leave-taking, neglected to wrap herself properly, took a fatal cold, and two days after, on the day of his burial, she followed him, in the fifty-sixth year of her age. Dr. C. A. Bartol, who had just buried her father, said tenderly at her funeral: "The two were so wont to be together, God saw they could not well live apart."

If Miss Alcott, by the pressure of circumstances, had not been a writer of children's books, she might have been a poet, and would, from choice, have been a philanthropist and reformer. Having worked her own way with much difficulty, it was impossible that she should not be interested in lightening the burdens which lay upon women, in the race of life, and though never a prominent worker in the cause, she was a zealous believer in the right of women to the ballot. She attended the Woman's Congress in Syracuse, in 1875, "drove about and drummed up women to my suffrage meeting" in Concord, she says, in 1879, and writes in a letter of 1881, "I for one don't want to be ranked among idiots, felons, and minors any longer, for I am none of them."

To say that she might have been a poet does her scant justice. She wrote two or three fine lyrics which would justify giving her a high place among the verse-writers of her generation. **"Thoreau's Flute,"** printed in the *Atlantic,* has been called the most perfect of her poems, with a possible exception of a tender tribute to her mother. Personally, I consider the lines in memory of her mother one of the finest elegiac poems within my knowledge:

> "Mysterious death: who in a single hour
> Life's gold can so refine,

And by thy art divine,
Change mortal weakness to immortal power."

There are twelve stanzas of equal strength and beauty. The closing lines of this fine eulogy we may apply to Miss Alcott, for both lives have the same lesson:

"Teaching us how to seek the highest goal,
To earn the true success,—
To live, to love, to bless,—
And make death proud to take a royal soul."

SARAH ELBERT (ESSAY DATE 1984)

SOURCE: Elbert, Sarah. "The Social Influence." In *A Hunger for Home: Louisa May Alcott and* Little Women, pp. 205-35. Philadelphia: Temple University Press, 1984.

In the following excerpt, Elbert places Alcott's work in the context of contemporary beliefs about gender and the burgeoning women's movement and connects Alcott's concerns about other social issues to her particular brand of domestic feminism.

The 1870s and 1880s witnessed a challenge to woman's rights in the name of science. The notion of woman's limited mental ability, supposedly the product of her specialized reproductive capacity, was never "more fervently held or more highly elaborated than it was in America after the Civil War."[1] Alcott impatiently took up this challenge in the pages of ***Eight Cousins, Rose in Bloom,*** and ***Jo's Boys.*** Women's minds, she insisted, were every bit as curious as men's; female anatomy, however biologically suited for procreation, presented no impediment to serious mental work.

Motives for the renewed differentiation between the sexes were complex, but clear enough to Alcott and her liberal contemporaries. Women were working outside their homes in even greater numbers, and they were often played out against men in the labor market. Middle-class women, both conservative and liberal, were uniting in serious campaigns to reform public life and public policy in the name of family welfare. Each new role played by women seemed to spur their sex on to greater demands for education, suffrage, and even equal pay for equal work.

As a consequence, "Many Americans believed the need to draw a clear line between appropriately male and female activities had become acute."[2] Dr. Edward Clarke drew that line on Louisa's homeground, speaking at the New England Woman's Club of Boston in 1872.[3] He cited Darwin and Spencer, arguing that it was not so much that one sex was superior, but that the sexes were widely different. His arguments were embellished in his book, *Sex in Education: or A Fair Chance for the Girls.*[4] Men, he claimed, had evolved with a higher metabolic rate than women and a greater tendency to vary; hence they grew progressively stronger and more intelligent than women over the long *Descent of Man.*[5] Because of their biological specificity (and consequently diminished capacity for variance) women were dependent upon men for protection. Motherhood therefore granted women a gentle immunity from the struggle of natural selection, but that same immunity also rendered woman biologically unfit for the mental exertions that stimulated and developed man.

Yours for Reform of All Kinds

Feminists replied to Clarke in *The Woman's Journal,* and Julia Ward Howe eventually assembled a brilliant array of essays under the title *Sex and Education: A Reply to Dr. Clarke's "Sex in Education."*[6] Louisa May Alcott began her own refutation of Clarke's theses with the novel ***Eight Cousins.*** She wrote the first chapters on a farm in Conway, Massachusetts during a summer holiday in 1874. Anna and her sons had accompanied her, and Louisa drew heavily on the boys' adventures and also upon her own childhood recollections. At first she seems intent on creating another version of ***Little Men*** for *St. Nicholas,* the most successful and prestigious magazine for children in late nineteenth-century America.[7] But unlike ***Little Men*** the new serial focussed on one particular heroine. Attacking the presumption of woman's innate fragility, it demonstrates that mental and physical strength are products of environment and education.

Rose Campbell, the sheltered rich orphan in Alcott's tale, joins an array of strong-minded girls depicted in *St. Nicholas* from the 1870s through the early twentieth century. Its editor, Mary Mapes Dodge, set a remarkable standard for young people's literature. She published the fiction of Rebecca Harding Davis, Sarah Orne Jewett, Helen Hunt Jackson, and Helen Stuart Campbell, among others, as well as impressive nonfiction works. ***Eight Cousins*** appeared for twelve months in 1874 and 1875 alongside reports of a gassiz Club's naturalist projects and reports of children's temperance union meetings.[8] All of these offerings were aimed directly at a middle-class audience, but though the tone was uniformly patriotic and genteel, the pervading message was that character is environmentally rather than biologically formed. This conviction enabled Alcott to claim woman's rights as a benefit both for girls' health and America's social welfare.

Rose arrives at the refined home of her Aunt Peace and Aunt Plenty, who cosset and spoil her. The seven male Campbell cousins assume that Rose is a "delicate little creter," which indeed she is at the start of the book.[9] To the proud and prosperous Campbells, Rose's delicacy seems no more than the price of a good breeding. Her first friend is Phoebe, the household's maid and an orphan, like Rose. Phoebe, however, has survived because she is sturdy and self-sufficient. Like Dickens' Charley, she announces, "I'm fifteen now, and old enough to earn my own living."[10] Part of Rose's education involves learning (through Phoebe) how the other half lives. Her schooling also includes learning to make "bread and button holes," because her remarkable Uncle Alec, physician and guardian, believes that all men and women should be self-reliant. The good Doctor, once a sailor, has his own work bag "out of which he produced a thimble without a top, and, having threaded his needle, he proceeded to sew on the buttons so handily that Rose was much impressed and amused."[11]

Doctor Alec Campbell must battle his fashionable sisters-in-law and his own spinster sisters to provide a sensible wardrobe of warm, loose clothing, and a healthy diet of milk and gingerbread instead of hot bread, coffee, and patent medicines for his niece. He wins out, and with the aid of shiny ice-skates and plenty of outdoor exercise, Rose's character, intelligence, and physical strength bloom harmoniously during the year-long educational experiment.[12]

Phoebe does not need lessons in domestic science, nor is her life lacking in physical exertion. Rose finds her "maid, friend, teacher" in silent tears, however, frustrated in an attempt to teach herself to read and write. A "broken slate that had blown off the roof, and inch or two of pencil, an old almanac for a reader, several bits of brown or yellow paper ironed smoothly and sewed together for a copy-book, and the copies of sundry receipts . . . these, with a small bottle of ink and a rusty pen" make up Phoebe's school supplies.[13] In contrast, Rose possesses one of the most delightful chambers imaginable. Her bath, toilet table, curio cabinet, and desk are all arranged to facilitate a young lady's love of both reading and primping. At this point Rose realizes that her own well-stocked library and her leisure for reading are unusual privileges, and she sets out to share her knowledge and supplies with Phoebe. Greek and Latin, courtesy of the Campbell cousins, follow literacy, and finally Uncle Alec takes a hand, agreeing to send Phoebe to school. Fortunately, a new cook and maid are being hired, so Phoebe's work may be taken over by others.

Phoebe, however, is not the only person who needs help. Rose is subsequently sent on monthly sojourns to her cousins' homes as a missionary. The indulgent, well-meaning efforts of the boys' mothers are unable to offset problem fathers and powerful male peer groups. The adolescent male Campbells reenforce one another in smoking, drinking, fighting, betting, and a general lack of old-fashioned deference to elders. Rose's missionary efforts not only benefit her cousins, they improve her own character and physical health. Alcott's message is clear: true womanhood involves setting a civilized example to rude male savages; in turn, such cares strengthen and improve little women. Rose announces that she has learned what little girls are made for—"to take care of boys."[14]

Rose in Bloom

Even in Concord Alcott found that "young American gentlemen, as well as farmers and mill hands" did a great deal of drinking. She expected it, she said, "among the Irish," but such dissolution among native-born Yankee men testified to the need for a wider social influence on the part of reformers. At Franklin and Louisa Sanborn's home she met regularly with Mrs. Julia Ward Howe and William Torrey Harris, and at least once partook of tea with Walt Whitman.[15] Her network of intergenerational reformers stretched from Whitman, with his professed love of cold water baths and plain carpenter's dress, to the Woman's Congress at Syracuse, New York, where Julia Ward Howe led the "Battle Hymn of the Republic," and even to elegant New York City drawing rooms, where an international coterie of free religionists, actresses, writers, and charity organizers met regularly.

Between the publication of ***Eight Cousins*** and ***Rose in Bloom,*** Lousia Alcott travelled the full range of this reformers' network. At Vassar College she listed her duties: "talk with four hundred girls, write in stacks of albums and schoolbooks, and kiss every one who asks me." Vassar students even formed a Little Women Club.[16] Their famous teacher, the astronomer Maria Mitchell, refused to give grades; she acknowledged her ties to Emerson and the Transcendental Circle: "You cannot mark a human mind because there is no intellectual unit."[17] Vice-president of the American Social Science Association, mature both intellectually and emotionally, Mitchell embodied Alcott's ideal of true womanhood.

In 1875, Mitchell offered an opening prayer from the platform of the Woman's Congress at Syracuse, New York.[18] Louisa, who hated making speeches, attended this conference and signed numerous autographs while listening carefully to the full range of woman's issues. Temperance, coeducation, domestic science, suffrage, and the wrongs of poorly-paid working women were all represented and eloquently described. ***Rose in Bloom*** and ***Jo's Boys*** put these issues before a sympathetic middle-class audience.

Later she visited New York City, where she found the contrasts between rich and poor described at the woman's congress all too visible. Dressed in silks, she attended the opera, the theater, and found herself the honored guest of Sorosis, the most advanced and liberal women's club in the city. At Mrs. Croly's reception she found herself sharing guest-of-honor status with the young poet, Oscar Wilde. Twenty-seven years old, he had just won the Newdigate Prize for English verse.[19] Louisa met socially prominent people at the Frothinghams' and the Botta's, and also sampled the water cure and spartan diet of the Bath Hotel in lower New York. Thanksgiving Day found her sharing a carriage ride with her friend Sallie Holley, teacher and missionary to freedmen and women.[20]

On Christmas Day during the same trip to New York, Louisa visited the Tombs, a well-known home for newsboys, and Randalls Island Hospital. She helped give out toys and sweets to poor babies "born of want and sin" who suffered "every sort of deformity, disease, and pain." In letters to Concord she described "one mite so eaten up with sores that his whole face was painted with some white salve—its head covered with an oilskin cap; one eye gone, and the other half filmed over." This babe, she said, could only "moan and move its feet till I put a gay red dolly in one hand and a pink candy in the other; then the dim eye brightened, the hoarse voice said feebly, 'tanky lady' and I left it contentedly sucking the sweetie and trying to see its dear new toy."[21]

The vivid contrast between fashionable drawing rooms and Randalls Island became the focus for ***Rose in Bloom***.[22] Alcott has her heroine, Rose Campbell, take up the causes of poor children, ill-paid working women, and temperance. Alcott also portrays (through Rose and Phoebe) the growing gap between reform-minded middle-class women and their working-class sisters. Rose and Phoebe, can no longer overlook the material and social distances between mistress and maid. After several years abroad with Uncle Alec, the two young women return sharing a belief that "it is as much a right and a duty for women to do something with their lives as for men."[23] Phoebe's imperative is clear: she must support herself. However, Prince Charlie, the most dashing of Rose's Campbell cousins, reminds Rose that a well-to-do girl's proper career is marriage and motherhood. Rose angrily asks him, "Would you be contented to be told to enjoy yourself for a little while then marry and do nothing more til you die?"[24] The fact that women possess minds, souls, hearts, ambition, and talent does not preclude marriage and motherhood, but Rose vows to prove that she is something beside "a housekeeper and a baby tender" before yielding to love.[25]

Phoebe's natural gift for music is cultivated by professional training, and she launches a career as a choir singer and music teacher. A brilliant concert appearance on behalf of an orphan home eventually leads Archie Campbell, Rose's eldest cousin, to propose marriage to Phoebe. Although love is unquestionably his only motive, and although Phoebe returns his affection, Alcott plays out their courtship for the entire length of the novel because Phoebe must overcome the objections of snobbish Campbell mothers and aunts. Not surprisingly, it is Phoebe who feels obliged to prove her worth, and Rose who cannot understand why the young couple should not marry at once. Rose naively tries to minimize the differences between Phoebe and herself by wearing simple gowns and fresh flowers when the two young women attend the same dances. Phoebe, however, continues to call her patroness, "little mistress." Working in the city is Phoebe's only escape from social inferiority.

Left to her own devices, with only lazy cousin Charlie to "play with Rose," the young heiress falls prey to his charming attentions. She mistakes romance for love, and in the fashionable social season she also finds that gift-giving is a sentimental mask for ordinary greed. Charlie himself is gradually revealed as an alcoholic, lured by fast male chums to overindulgences he cannot control. The temperance message is strong in ***Rose in Bloom;*** liquor is the downfall not only of working men who abuse their families, but of gentlemen who cannot observe the old-fashioned moderation exemplified in domestic holiday toasts. Alcott draws a clear line between domestic abundance and a secretive popping of corks behind the closed doors of all-male smoking-rooms. In fact, it hardly matters if the drinking environment is private library or public saloon; the effect is disastrously the same. Similarly, contra dancing represents an old-fashioned intergenerational amusement, while "round" dancing at fashionable balls leads to a romantic intensity that is perilously separate from the safe circle of kin and friends. With the exception of Uncle Alec, all the adult men in the Campbell clan desert domesticity, bent on making money or escaping an imperfect homelife. Fashionable women, Alcott argues here as in earlier novels, are somewhat to blame, failing to create happy homes for husbands and children. Happy homes, in turn, are part of a dense social network which protects and sustains the individual.

Louisa Alcott's own background included her father's enjoyment of New England hard cider, and the author herself admitted she liked a glass of champagne at fashionable New York suppers. Her temperance advocacy is nonetheless genuine; it was immoderate indulgence in members of their own class that led many liberal, sophisticated reformers to support temperance. A founder of the Concord Women's Temperance Society, Louisa linked that cause to woman's suffrage. She wrote her publisher, "We are going to meet the Governor, council and legislature at Mrs. Tudor's next Wednesday and have a grand-set-to. I hope he will come out of the struggle alive."[26]

Conservative church women, previously aloof to woman's rights activities, often became public activists in the Women's Crusade, the temperance organization which soon became the Women's Christian Temperance Union. Frances Willard, subsequently president of the W. C. T. U., regarded the issue of alcohol as the single most important vehicle in persuading women of the helplessness of their sex to defend self and family. If women were dependent upon men as a natural consequence of biology, they were also helpless before the ruin visited upon them by intemperate men. Historian Barbara Epstein concludes further that "in the context of discussing mens' drinking, it was possible for women to talk about their own isolation and loneliness." Moreover, "Women could hardly object to their husbands' involvement in their work, since women's livelihood depended on it, but they could object to their husbands' socializing with other men in their free time. The saloon thus became a symbol for the larger issues of the exclusion of women and children from men's lives."[27]

Charlie Campbell takes the pledge in ***Rose in Bloom*** on the eve of sailing to India with his mother. He does so, however, in order to prove he is dependable enough to join the family mercantile business. Predictably, he is lured by friends for a farewell round of drinks in a saloon. Later that cold, snowy night, he is thrown from his horse in a drunken stupor. Eventually discovered and taken home, Charlie develops pneumonia and dies repentent. Rose is thereby saved from marriage to the wrong man, and soon finds herself happily involved in philanthropic work with her bookish cousin, Mac, now a physician and poet.

Rose's true partner for life, Mac, is interesting to Alcott's readers because he so closely resembles Jo March. Like the heroine of ***Little Women,*** Mac Campbell is shy, honest, and bookish, but occasionally sarcastic when provoked by too many conventional restrictions. He accompanies Rose to a ball, properly garbed in borrowed broadcloth and white gloves, but before the last German can be danced, "His tie was under one ear, his posy hung upside down, his gloves were rolled into a ball, which he absently squeezed and pounded as he talked, and his hair looked as if a whirlwind had passed over it."[28] Mac becomes a physician because he enjoys science as an alternative to fashionable banter and because he wishes to serve the poor. That is not enough to win Rose, however. In the end he achieves her love by proving himself tenderhearted and poetic, an admirer of Emerson's *Essays* and Thoreau's "Week on the Concord and Merrimac Rivers."[29] Mac, we are told, admired, "Heroism" and "Self-Reliance," while Rose preferred "Love" and "Friendship," as they discuss Emerson's *Essays.* Friendly arguments over Concord's distinguished ante-bellum literature proves a proper basis for true love, especially if the reader recalls that Charlie Campbell had admired Jane Eyre's Rochester as a hero.

Drawing upon her Christmas visit to Randalls Island and the Newsboys Home, Alcott uses Mac's work in a charity hospital to impress a middle-class audience with the enormity of the social problems around them. After Charlie's death, Rose takes up the cause of poor children who have no chance of fresh air or decent food; she establishes the Campbells' summer farmhouse as a vacation asylum for slum children. This asylum, in addition to the refurbishing of two old tenements as cooperative, low-cost homes for working women, constitutes the philanthropic career Rose chooses as an alternative to fashionable life. Mac, however, is in daily contact with the worst social inequities. One day while on his hospital rounds he comes across a destitute, dying woman who begs him to take care of her baby. He locates the infant in "a miserable place, left in the care of an old hag, who had shut her up alone to keep her out of the way, and there this mite was, huddled in a corner, crying, 'Marmar,' 'marmar' fit to touch a heart of stone."[30] The baby has been beaten and starved. Mac's own mother refuses to have an unlovely, dirty orphan baby in her house, and none of the "overcrowded institutions" can give the child the care and love she needs. Rose adopts the child, naming her Dulcinea, and a few months of kindness, food, and fresh air restore the little girl. Her new mother admits, however, that she will never really be a "gay, attractive child," having been born "in sorrow and brought up in misery."[31]

The point Alcott makes with this incident is that woman's rights and motherhood go hand in hand; Clarke's books, in fact, help feminists to unite the two. Frances Willard, for example, used the slogan of the Canadian temperance women, "Home Protection ballot," in the 1870s.[32] Women, she argued, needed suffrage in order to protect their homes from demon liquor. Certainly there was opposition within the woman's temperance movement itself to Willard's firm linkage of woman's suffrage and temperance, but she and her allies persevered in making the connection. In 1879 Willard was elected president of the WCTU and remained in that office until her death. Alcott, who was committed somewhat contradictorily both to woman's special virtue and woman's natural rights, corresponded with President Willard. She notes a letter written to her (in 1880) by a reformed convict; the man had heard Louisa read a story at Concord Prison, and wished to explain that drink had led him to steal in the first place. Alcott kept track of him, after checking his story with the prison warden, and she kept up correspondence until he left for work in South America. Alcott's letter of reference and the interest of Frances Willard in the case helped his cause, and Louisa wrote proudly, "Glad to have said a word to help the poor boy."[33]

Rose must marry because a spinster heroine might prove Clarke's charge that education and full-time public service made women unfit for motherhood. Alcott's fictional couples, however, reflect the demographic transformation in her own lifetime; she limits the March women's progeny to three children for Meg, two for Jo, and only one for Amy. ***Jo's Boys*** also offers the full range of demographic changes: each of the March women lives out a genuinely representative mid-nineteenth-century woman's life cycle.[34] Although Alcott marries her heroine, Rose, to young Doctor Alec Campbell in a final chapter appropriately entitled "Short and Sweet," Alcott acknowledges spinsterhood as a real choice in ***Jo's Boys.*** In any case, Rose and Mac are a reformist couple, pledged to "work together and try to make the world better by the music and the love we leave behind us when we go." Rose admittedly has no special talents; she does possess inherited money, which Alcott darkly intimates could only leave her prey to unscrupulous fortune hunters in the absence of a watchful, temperate mate and philanthropic endowments. . . .

Domesticity and Feminism

Only one young man in Alcott's later fiction actually cooks. He is a foundry watchman, "a young and pleasant-looking fellow, with a merry eye, an honest brown face and a hearty voice."[35] A poor orphaned sewing girl finds a friend in him, and **"Letty's Tramp"** (who is not a tramp at all) offers her shelter from a snowstorm, a pallet by his fire, a sandwich and hot coffee. The author knows that a working girl needs the stimulant that only overexcites a lady of leisure. Letty and her friend Joe fall in love because he "tried to express his sympathy in deeds as well as words."[36] Not only does he cook her supper and share his breakfast next morning, he also finds work for her after learning that the putting-out system pays Letty only six cents, "sometimes only four," for each shirt she sews. Joe decides to reject the products of this sweat labor: "Hanged if I buy another."[37] Instead, he orders a bale of red flannel and stakes Letty to a small shirtmaking business, the finished products to be sold to his fellow foundrymen. Joe and Letty marry eventually, but we never learn if he continues to make the coffee and sandwiches.

Moods presented a large class of women identified as a "sad sisterhood," forced by unfortunate circumstances into the world. ***Work*** expanded on their trials and sufferings in a hostile world. ***Little Women,*** in turn, gave domestic reformers an opportunity to demonstrate the possibilities for women in democratic households. Alcott later reached towards enlarged institutions to reproduce the March family's mutual sacrifice. ***Little Men*** began a coeducational experiment in cooperative democracy. Then, in the uncompleted ***Diana and Persis,*** Alcott expresses her suspicion that a private domestic solution to the woman problem is not possible. Even at Lawrence University, in ***Jo's Boys,*** the true union of domesticity and feminism is incomplete. Jo herself is free to write and supervise community morality, but her domestic freedom depends upon the excellent money she earns; moreover; Fritz never challenges her household authority. Even earning a living and having an agreeable, almost invisible spouse is not enough; Jo's liberty also depends upon Daisy's migratory cooking, Meg's baby-sitting, and her own paid household staff.

The March sisters and their progeny at Laurence University never really yield control of their lives to anyone. It is not even clear that children of the March family attend classes there. The college really exists for those who lack family, wealth, or social influence to place them comfortably in the world. The March sons and daughters find their way in that world through a network of family and friends, with only vague references to college educations. Laurence, then, is a vehicle for presenting the feminist demand for coeducation in a pleasing, comfortable way. It is also Alcott's means of reassuring her public about new reformist institutions. Like ***Little Women, Little Men*** and ***An Old Fashioned Girl,*** the final March novel tries to make social change seem like old, familiar history.

Little Women has a timeless resonance which reflects Alcott's grasp of her historical framework in the 1860s. The novel's ideas do not intrude themselves upon the reader because the author wholly controls the implications of her imaginative structure. Sexual equality is the salvation of marriage and the family; democratic relationships make happy endings. This is the unifying imaginative frame of ***Little Women*** which then expands into ***Little Men*** and bravely attempts to work itself out as historical law in ***Jo's Boys.***

The last effort fails, but Alcott is in good company. The progressive social imagination embodied in the utopian works of Twain, Howells, and Gilman (only a few years after ***Jo's Boys***) accepted human nature as constant, but posited history as advancing toward ideal freedom. The inherent contradictions of this position troubled all utopian writers, perhaps Alcott the most of all. She made her choice after the Civil War in favor of the progressive framework, but its concepts never fully live in the fictional worlds she created. Also, despite her debt to the Romantic belief in conflict as the source of creativity, she feared the radical implications of conflict after the war.

It was not enthusiasm which frightened her. Alcott was on the side of Anne Hutchinson and Hester Prynne; it was time to realize the brave new relationship between the sexes prophesized in *The Scarlet Letter.* By the 1880s, that new relationship was as contradictory in her own work as it was in the woman's rights movement itself. She insisted on the full human status of her heroines while also claiming that women must play a major role in society because of their capacity for nurturance. Daisy exercised that gift traditionally by caring for her extended family, while Nan demonstrated her womanly nature by becoming a woman's physician and healing the members of her own sex. Both heroines, of course, deserve suffrage, and therefore the right-minded heroes in ***Jo's Boys*** support their claim. The best of Jo's boys, in fact, learn to expand their nurturing capacities, and in becoming more like women they become more fully human as well.

Sexual segregation permitted Harvard's President Eliot to claim that "the world knows next to nothing about the natural mental capacities of the female sex."[38] Alcott therefore insisted that coeducation was the best method of teaching one sex about the capacities of the other. To that end, Josie competes almost rudely with visiting Harvard students in tennis matches and debates about woman's suffrage. Such competitions, incidentally, separate the real men from the boys; weaker members of the male sex give up quickly in the face of feminist challenge. Defeated men, Alcott says, seek feminine balm for their wounded vanity; they marry girls who are willing to mother them. Having made a strong case for women's natural rights, Alcott then admits a fear that girls, overly protected in youth, might lack the aggressiveness necessary in traditionally masculine territory. She recognized that intellectual and physical skills alone were not enough, and notes in ***Rose in Bloom*** that "we do our duty better by the boys . . . the poor little women are seldom provided with any armor worth having; and, sooner or later, they are sure to need it, for every one must fight her own battle, and only the brave and strong can win."[39] Young women needed the experience of a male-dominated society, she thought, in order to prepare themselves for the "ups and downs of life."

At the same time, the author of ***Little Women*** suspected that democratic domesticity was itself a product of women's segregation from the power struggles of the larger world. In order to reform society, women must have some means of maintaining their own sense of idealism and mutual sacrifice in a coeducational world. The March sisters therefore re-create the old sewing circle, passing on the little women's spirit of egalitarian domesticity to a new generation of coeds who might otherwise succumb totally to male values—and consequently reject the domestic habits that link them to ordinary women outside the university community. Women, Alcott argues, will not remake the world by becoming just like men. Both sexes are united in the old familiar way at the close of ***Jo's Boys*** when Nat plays "the street melody he gave them the first night he came to Plumfield." All of the others remember it and join in singing.

Oh, my heart is sad and weary
Everywhere I roam, still
Longing for the old plantation
And for the old folks at home.[40]

Ancestors and Immigrants

Next to civil war, the conflict Alcott and her friends feared most was brewing in the struggles of immigrants, freedmen, women, industrial workers, and angry small farmers. These groups constituted a growing numerical majority in the United States. True, progressivism at its most rigorous argued that "The Law is Progress: The Result Democracy."[41] But for Alcott a popular victory was cause for celebration only when the victors were familiar native stock whose leaders were of unquestioned good breeding and reputation (such as her friends).

When late nineteenth-century American society expanded beyond the communal myth of the March cottage, Louisa Alcott shifted her perspective uneasily. The primacy of biology over culture, an idea which had never really been defeated by ante-bellum reformers, made a strong come-back in reaction to the woman's rights movement. Combatting this resurgence strengthened Alcott's conviction that no inherent differences existed between races and ethnic groups either. If environment actually shaped human behavior, then Alcott and her set were more determined than ever to provide a single national culture fashioned in their own image. They generally assumed that their own dominance was the result of social laws beyond individual control, thereby absolving themselves from responsibility for institutionalizing poverty, racial and sexual discrimination, and the virtual annihilation of American Indian tribal life. Much of the injustice seemed a regrettable by-product of progress; ultimately there would be abundance for all. They counted upon social influence to blend Americans within a balanced society. In ***Jo's Boys,*** for instance, Alcott tries to accept the social structure around her as given.

She never questioned its historical origins. Believing that her beloved band of reformers had fought for progress, she found it hard to question their achievement. Indeed, there had been great changes: the emancipation of slaves was the greatest of all victories. Louisa deliberately used the old antislavery language as proof of her women's rights allegiance; in 1885 she told Lucy Stone, "After a fifty year acquaintance with the noble men and women of the anti-slavery cause, the sight of the glorious end to their faithful work, I should be a traitor to all I most love, honor and desire to imitate, if I did not covet a place among those who are giving their lives to the emancipation of the white slaves of America."[42]

Although they defend social stability, Alcott's last works also attempt to persuade readers to accept and advance social change. That there were contradictions between democratic ideals and social reality, Alcott never denied. She had lived through a period of extraordinary social ferment. Like many of her circle, including Harris, Sanborn, Cheney, Croly, Abba May and Julia Ward Howe, she was less fearful of destroying the individual than she was of civil war. In any case, molding society into line with the values already held by her set seemed more or less the natural working out of Providence—with a little help from the "best people." It must be said as an explanation, if not an excuse, that Alcott never forgot the examples of David Thoreau, Frank Sanborn, and John Brown. Once she had fiercely supported the effort to arm slaves against their masters, knowing that ownership of human beings is the worst example of property rights. Similarly, she thought that good people would refuse to accept the degradation and exploitation of their fellow human beings after emancipation.

Social roles now seemed to have some intrinsic merit. In Alcott's earlier fiction, stepping out of a role allowed her heroines to see society more truly—as Jo does when she stomps aound in unlaced boots uttering rather mild boyish slang. But Jo's role-swapping did not change society. In ***Jo's Boys,*** her namesake, Josie, does not need to pretend at being a boy. A modern girl, never outside her role, she plays tennis in comfortable clothes, swims and dives like a porpoise, and insists on acting as a profession, not as a mere vent for pent-up feelings. Woman's social role had indeed changed between 1868 and 1885, and the "great changes" are evident in the hope Alcott holds out to a generation of coeds at Laurence University.

From a nineteenth-century feminist perspective, women needed a social structure to replace the code of laissez faire individualism. They could not desert society and light out to the territories as Dan does in ***Jo's Boys.*** Alcott, moreover, does not set her utopia backwards, as Twain does in *A Connecticut Yankee in King Arthur's Court* (1889), or forward, as Bellamy does in *Looking Backward* (1888). Although her society at Laurence University somewhat resembles Charlotte Perkins Gilman's *Herland* (1915), Alcott does not remove men from utopia to achieve social harmony and rational planning.

Jo's Boys is set in Alcott's last historical moment. It chronicles the gains made in her lifetime, but gathers them up into one great cornucopia at Plumfield. There her readers may observe the scattered gains already integrated into a social system. Young men and women have a free, open relationship with one another. They eat healthily, exercise, and work hard in anticipation of happy useful lives. Their educated talent is dedicated to social welfare. Only indolent, dull sons of wealth loll at Harvard with no important plans for the future; Alcott intimates that they will be superfluous in the new order.

For all her energy in depicting a brave new world, Alcott cannot make its inhabitants compelling. Josie at fourteen is a "pretty little lass" with "curly dark hair, bright eyes, and a very expressive face." But she does not capture our hearts as Jo did with her wonderful mixture of self-will and self-sacrifice. Josie has talent but little imagination; she is all common sense. Moreover, she has no apparent ties to her sister Daisy, and unlike Jo, who resented her sisters' marriages, Josie willingly serves as John's go-between in his courtship of Alice Healey. The earlier little women had clung to their childhood and their siblings, but Josie cannot wait to grow up. Young womanhood, Alcott argues, is now glorious independence for those with talent, discipline, and a college education.

There are moments of nostalgia in ***Jo's Boys,*** but they are all for former days of adversity. Moreover, the poor young people at Laurence acquiesce too easily to advice about patience, hard work, and dressmaking. Alcott has not lost her feeling for youth—Dan's plight is evocative of brave John Sulie in ***Hospital Sketches***—but somehow the new little women seem a tame group. It is as if life lies outside the gates of utopia. The ragged children who wander in and out of stories in *St. Nicholas* and the collected tales of ***Aunt Jo's Scrap Bag,*** for example, have the warm spark of Alcott's earliest heroes and heroines. Her later feminist men and women have benefitted greatly from the earlier band's efforts and they do care about the ragged children and working men and women. Alcott never quite saw the world she imagined in ***Jo's Boys*** and she could not portray it as reality. To the end, a "cry for bread and hunger for home" was the woman problem as she knew it.

Notes

1. Rosalind Rosenberg, *Beyond Separate Spheres: Intellectual Roots of Modern Feminism* (New Haven, 1982), xv.
2. Ibid. Rosenberg's chapter, "In the Shadow of Dr. Clarke," graphically details the predicament of Alcott's set.
3. *The Woman's Journal* reported Dr. Clarke's speech in its Dec. 21, 1872 edition. Julia Ward Howe, an editor, then followed with several months coverage of the ensuing debates.
4. Edward Clarke, *Sex in Education: or A Fair Chance for the Girls* (Boston, 1873).
5. Charles Darwin, *The Descent of Man* and *Selection in Relation to Sex,* 2 vols. (London, 1871). For the popular depiction of the Darwinian controversy see issues of *Popular Science Monthly* from the mid-1870s through the 1880s. The social significance of woman's biological specialization is discussed in Charles Rosenberg, *No Other Gods: On Science and American Social Thought* (Baltimore, 1976).
6. Julia Ward Howe, ed., *Sex and Education: A Reply to Dr. Clarke's "Sex in Education"* (Cambridge, Mass., 1874). See also Anna C. Brackett, *The Education of American Girls* (New York, 1874) and Eliza B. Duffey, *No Sex in Education: or An Equal Chance for both Girls and Boys* (Philadelphia, 1874). The latter two books are recommended in Louisa May Alcott *Jo's Boys* (Boston, 1886), Chapter 17, "Among the Maids."
7. Madeleine B. Stern, *Louisa May Alcott* (London, New York, 1957), pp. 236-45. For an excellent description of *St. Nicholas* and the importance of juvenile magazines see Jane Benardette and Phyllis Moe, *Companions of Our Youth: Stories by Women for Young People's Magazines, 1865-1900* (New York, 1980).
8. Ibid. Louisa May Alcott continued to publish in juvenile magazines until the end of her career. Letters to Mary Mapes Dodge, in particular, appear throughout Ednah Cheney, ed., *Louisa May Alcott: Life, Letters and Journals* (Boston, 1928), chapter 11, "Last Years."
9. Louisa May Alcott *Eight Cousins; or, The Aunt-Hill* (Boston, 1890), chapter 2, "The Clan," p. 18.
10. Ibid., chapter 1, "Two Girls," p. 5.
11. Ibid. chapter 16, "Bread and Button-Holes," p. 190.
12. Ibid., chapter 28, "Fashion and Physiology," p. 211.
13. Ibid. chapter 22, "Something to Do," p. 255.
14. Ibid. chapter 24, "Which?" p. 279.
15. Stern, *Louisa May Alcott,* p. 295. In 1862 Frank Sanborn married his cousin, Louisa Augusta Leavitt, after the death of his first wife, Ariana Walker. Ariana, a

close friend of Ednah Dow Cheney, was consumptive, dying eight days after her wedding in 1854. Frank and Louisa Sanborn had three sons. Louisa May Alcott maintained close ties with the Sanborns, and included a poem by one of the Sanborn boys in *Under the Lilacs*.

16. Cheney, ed., *Louisa May Alcott*, chapter 10 (Feb. 1875).
17. Helen Wright, "Biographical sketch of Maria Mitchell," ed. E. James *Notable American Women* (Cambridge, Mass., 1971), II, p. 555.
18. Ibid. See also Cheney, ed., *Louisa May Alcott*, chapter 10 (Sept. and Oct. 1875).
19. See Stern, *Louisa May Alcott*, pp. 297-98. Anna Charlotte Lynch Botta was a notable hostess, admired by Emerson, among others, who called her home, "the house of expanding doors." Botta also contributed poetry to *The Democratic Review* and wrote *A Hardbook of Universal Literature* in 1860. She taught for a time at the Brooklyn Academy for Women.
20. Cheney, ed., *Louisa May Alcott*, chapter 10.
21. Louisa May Alcott to Alcott Family, Dec. 25, 1875, in Ibid., pp. 235-39.
22. Louisa May Alcott, *Rose in Bloom* [(Boston, 1876), page references are to 1934 ed.], chapter 1, "Coming Home." This chapter deals with Rose Campbell's adoption of a poor child.
23. Ibid., p. 10.
24. Ibid., p. 11.
25. Ibid.
26. Cheney, ed., *Louisa May Alcott*, p. 284 (Letter to Thomas Niles, Feb. 18, 1881).
27. Barbara Leslie Epstein, *The Politics of Domesticity*, Women Evangelism and Temperance in Nineteenth Century America (Conn., 1981), p. 106.
28. Louisa May Alcott, *Rose in Bloom*, chapter 6, "Polishing Mac," p. 100. Mac is carrying a volume of Thoreau and reading Emerson.
29. Ibid., chapter 18, "Which Was It?," p. 283.
30. Ibid., chapter 16, "Good Works," p. 260.
31. Ibid., chapter 17, "Among the Hay-Cocks," p. 267.
32. See Epstein, *The Politics of Domesticity*, and Ruth Bordin, *Woman and Temperance, The Quest for Power and Liberty*, 1873-1900 (Philadelphia, 1981).
33. Cheney, ed., *Louisa May Alcott*, p. 283.
34. For discussions of the fact that the mean number of children born to a hypothetical woman dropped in Louisa's lifetime from 6.21 to 3.87, see the following: Peter Uhlenberg, "Changing Configurations of the Life Course," ed. Tamara K. Hareven, *Transitions: The Family and the Life Course in Historical Perspective* (New York, 1978); Robert V. Wells, "Family History and Demographic Transition," *Journal of Social History* (Fall 1975), p. 1-19; and Linda Gordon, *Woman's Body, Woman's Right: A Social History of Birth Control Movement and American Society Since 1830* (New York, 1978).
35. Louisa May Alcott, "Letty's Tramp," *The Independent* 27, no. 1412 (Dec. 23, 1875); rpt. in *The Women's Journal* 3, no. 5 (Jan. 29, 1876).
36. Ibid.
37. Ibid. Louisa May Alcott, *Rose in Bloom* has Rose investing her wealth in cooperative homes for working women.
38. Quoted in Hugh Hawkins, *Between Havard and America: The Educational Leadership of Charles W. Eliot* (New York, 1972), p. 198.
39. Louisa May Alcott, *Rose in Bloom*, Chapter 1, "Coming Home," p. 9.
40. Louisa May Alcott, *Jo's Boys*, chapter 22, "Positively Last Appearance," p. 284.
41. John Lathrop Motley, *Historic Progress and American Democracy* (New York, 1869), p. 6.
42. Louisa May Alcott, letter to *The Woman's Journal* 14 (Jan. 20, 1883).

TITLE COMMENTARY

Little Women

JILL P. MAY (ESSAY DATE SPRING-SUMMER 1994)

SOURCE: May, Jill P. "Feminism and Children's Literature: Fitting *Little Women* into the American Literary Canon." *CEA Critic* 56, no. 3 (spring-summer 1994): 19-27.

In the following essay, May contends that Little Women *has been neglected by critics because it has been seen as a work solely for women and children. May suggests that the dismissive response to* Little Women *fails to consider either Alcott's literary craftsmanship or the book's commentary on contemporary gender roles.*

Louisa May Alcott's ***Little Women*** is an American book that has been reviewed favorably by experts in children's literature throughout the twentieth century. In fact, ***Little Women*** has remained highly visible throughout American society: Textbooks written for undergraduate children's literature classes mention the book's continued popularity with children; new paperback editions are available in the bookstore chains; library lists of popular children's classics almost always include it as a recommended title; and television and theatre renditions are still being produced. Generally, educated people regard ***Little Women*** as a staple in American literature. And as a university professor who teaches children's literature, I, too, thought of ***Little Women*** as a widely read and popular book that has held its place in the American literary canon. However, recent experiences have changed my mind.

When I was asked to give a public library program about Alcott's ***Little Women***, I decided I would briefly address the issue of readership with modern audiences. In previous years, I had used the book in my undergraduate children's literature classes, and many of the students had claimed to have read ***Little Women*** as children. I felt sure that the book was still being read, but I decided to do a reality check before I discussed the book. One day, I asked the twenty-five students attending my undergraduate children's literature class—composed of young people in their twenties—to finish one of the following statements: "I remember that when I read ***Little Women*** as a youngster . . ." or "I never read ***Little Women*** as a child, but from what I heard about the book. . . ."

As I collected their papers, I asked those who had read the book to raise their hands and saw three young women's hands shoot up. Once I started reading their writing, I realized that not all of these students were readers of the entire book, that some were "almost readers" of the book or else had seen a media version of the story. Only one student commented on finishing the book. The one young woman who had read the entire book wrote apologetically,

> I read ***Little Women*** when I was a child, and I thought it was good at the time. You are probably asking us this question because it is a total sexist and stereotypical book about the woman's role in the home. I remember reading it and liking it. It was considered a "classic" when I read it.

Little Women has always been considered a book "for girls," so I was not surprised when the young man in my class commented:

> I never read ***Little Women,*** and . . . I have never heard of it. I guess I never read it, in part, because I am a guy and no one told me about it. However, if someone had told me about it, I probably still would not have read it since it does not interest me too much as a guy.

However, I was offended that he felt a book about females need not be read by males. I wondered if all men looked at "women's lives" in the same way.

Since ***Little Women*** was written during the American Civil War, I asked my husband, Bob—a university professor—to poll the students in his Civil War and Reconstruction course. Most of Bob's students were men, and they were interested in the Civil War from a "male" perspective. Many were Civil War battle buffs. Four of the thirty students in his class claimed they had read the book. One was a male. Three of the four were top students in the class.

I finished off my "survey" in my graduate children's literature course. Eleven of the students were female, and one was male. Some were already teachers in the public schools; they had taken children's literature courses in the past. Of the twelve students, seven at first said they had read ***Little Women.*** However, when we began talking about the book, three of the students began to reflect and reconsider. One of them said, "I don't think I ever finished it." Another added, "I think I saw it as a film or something." And one other student confessed that she had read only the first half because her book ended there. "I think I always knew there was more, but I never looked for the rest." The one male simply looked bored after he admitted that he had not read the book.

Although the book is no longer a part of popular culture's repertoire, I believe that ***Little Women*** is a piece of women's history or, perhaps more important, a piece of women's autobiography that depicts female aspirations, family life, and women's career choices. Furthermore, ***Little Women*** has had an evolving effect upon the women who read and study it as a literary archetype of American female writing. I have read the book several times, seeing it differently each time. As a preteen, I considered Jo the most interesting character. As a college student, I found Jo's relationship with Professor Bhaer intriguing. By the time my article "Spirited Females of the Nineteenth Century: Liberated Moods in Louisa May Alcott's ***Little Women***" was published, I viewed Amy as my favorite sister. For me, ***Little Women*** has taken on the mythic sense that Patricia Meyer Spacks is addressing when she says that adults reminisce about youthful adventures to rediscover "what we were, might have been, hoped to be" (3). Women's autobiographical fiction continues to work for each new generation when realistic characters solve their problems in ways the reader understands. This is probably what keeps ***Little Women*** alive for female critics. The book has remained true to women's lives, but its meaning has shifted through time. Twentieth-century views of Alcott's book often are very different from those of past generations.

Reading the criticism available on ***Little Women*** and the edited journals of Bronson Alcott and Louisa Alcott leaves little doubt that this was an autobiographical book for Alcott. Her father's school, her sisters and their play, and the family habit of journal writing all made their way into the story. Yet ***Little Women*** is more than simple autobiography. Each girl is part of a subplot that reveals a personal story. None of the stories is typical; these girls look beyond the values of their contemporary society. Perhaps one of the reasons

Illustration of Louisa May Alcott dancing with her family.

the book has continued to be read by critics is that the story was also prophetic.

Sarah Elbert points out that Alcott's own reluctance to choose between the images of feminism and domestic life led to her development of complex female characters. Influenced by the political speeches she had heard and the contemporary books she had read, Alcott wanted her main characters to take stances within their families and to expand beyond the constraints of their familial home (144-50).

At the time of publication, the story did not reflect the average American family. Alcott's own life was far from typical, and she could not have written a "typical girls' story." Although contemporary book reviewers labeled the book appealing and realistic, it was not the depiction of a typical American family. The "little women" in Alcott's book choose their destinies. When they are young and first describe what they dream for themselves as adults, Meg chooses marriage and children; Beth describes a life at home with her parents; Amy chooses to be "the best artist in the whole world" (116); and Jo claims, "I'd have a stable full of Arabian steeds, rooms piled with books, and I'd write out of a magic inkstand, so that my works should be as famous as Laurie's music" (115).

Throughout this story, the "little women" remain true to themselves. For instance, Jo refuses to marry a man she likes as a friend. And once married, the two artistic sisters resolve to work beyond the four walls of their homes. Jo notes:

> "I haven't given up the hope that I may write a book yet, but I can wait, and I'm sure it will be all the better for such experiences and illustrations as these;" and Jo pointed from the lively lads in the distance to her father, leaning on the professor's arm . . . and then to her mother, sitting enthroned among her daughters, with their children in her lap and at her feet.
>
> (442)

Amy adds,

> "My castle is very different from what I planned, but I would not alter it, though, like Jo, I don't relinquish all my artistic hopes, or confine myself to helping others fulfill their dreams of beauty. I've begun to model a figure of baby, and Laurie says it is the best thing I've ever done."
>
> (442)

These women do not choose to forsake their artistic plans when they marry, but they alter their purposes and their "training" to fit within the family circle. In other words, Alcott's characters realign their place within society to their artistic endeavors. They replace their childhood goals with goals that fit into contemporary cultural interpretations of family obligations.

Alcott's story does extend beyond the then-traditional boundaries of romance novels about women who use feminine wiles to entrap men into marriage. She introduced her youthful audience to major social (and feminist) issues of the 1860s: Jo will not give up her boyish ways, even when her sisters try to "civilize her"; Jo continually competes with the men she meets; Jo and Amy travel away from home without their immediate families and learn to spend time on their own; Meg, Jo, and Amy learn that love is not simply a romantic flirtation that results in children and a perfect home. Furthermore, all of the sisters are true to themselves, and they set their sights on perfecting the talents that please them, whether or not these talents are valued by society. The sisters represent a dynamic world, one that continually changes for these sisters as they grow up, try their hands at artistic careers, and marry.

When discussing the autobiographies that were being written and published just after the American Civil War, Susanna Egan writes,

> Again and again we find that the self is important essentially in the context of change . . . as an active intelligence through which current events are perceived and understood . . . [and this creates] history in the making, with the self, in varying degrees of objectivity, as participant.
>
> (71)

Little Women shows women adjusting to changing times. It is important as children's literature and as women's history. As archetypal "autobiography" written for contemporary adolescent readers, ***Little Women*** fills a void in the American canon. It shows how nineteenth-century American females could evolve into writers, artists, critics of society, mothers, and teachers.

Anne Hollander has suggested that Amy shows the reader a picture of a woman's total growth from childhood to adulthood, and she argues that Amy is a more ideal model than Jo because she wants to be the best possible artist rather than the most famous artist. Thus, Hollander links feminine self-awareness with the arts:

> Amy's creative talent can be seen as more authentic than Jo's, because Amy does recognize and accept and even enjoy her sexuality, which is the core of the creative self. Alcott demonstrates this through the mature Amy's straightforward, uncoy ease in attracting men and her effortless skill at self-presentation, which are emblems of her commitment to the combined truths of sex and art.
>
> (33)

Still, Hollander's interpretation of Alcott's story is not definitive. The debate about the significance of ***Little Women*** continues to rage among the many female critics who have turned to Alcott's classic and "rewritten" the book to fit their life experiences. Often, the criticism fits a personal stance about women and history. In her essay on the book, Ruth K. MacDonald suggests that women keep the book alive because Alcott deals with the issues that still concern them:

> how to combine marriage and career, how to be a professional in a world which may judge women's efforts to be inferior, how to assert one's principles and rights without so offending the powers that be that the granting of those rights is jeopardized. . . . [T]he tension that results from this struggle keeps academic readers interested, and they in turn help to keep Alcott's reputation alive.
>
> (13)

This is what makes Alcott's view of female adolescence archetypal. The experiences of her characters place the realities of female existence in print for young women and affirm that women continually face a significant personal obligation to affirm their interests and plans while learning to exist within the confines of society. With the exception of Beth, Alcott's young females are active youngsters who determine what they want to be as adults and end up in positions that fit their dreams. Like many other females, they learn that American society has certain expectations for women—including looking good and pampering men—and they determine how to adjust to those expectations. Knowing what they do about their world, they are actively involved in determining their fates.

The pattern of autobiographical interpretation helps the book remain alive for female literary critics. Because it has interested so many scholars, it should be shared in contemporary literature classes. However, a glance at syllabi will show Alcott's absence. Indeed, neither the author nor the book has made any impact on the canon debate within the Modern Language Association. Elaine Showalter has suggested that ***Little Women*** is largely ignored in college American literature classes because men have never really read it, that as a work it has had "enormous . . . critical impact on half the reading population, and so minuscule a place in the libraries or criticism of the other" (42). As I looked back at what other scholars have written, I began to notice that Showalter was right. Lavinia Russ recalls meeting with Hemingway in Paris and hearing him say, "You're so full of sweetness and light you ought to be carrying ***Little Women.***" His conversation with her led her to believe that Hemingway never read the book, and she writes, "If he had read ***Little Women,*** he would have realized that it is not 'sweetness and light'; it is stalwart proof of his definition of courage: grace under pressure" (pamphlet, unpaged).

In fact, there is often no assurance that the men writing about Alcott in the early twentieth century ever read ***Little Women.*** Seth Curtis Beach selected Alcott for his final biography in *Daughters of the Puritans,* but it is never clear whether he read ***Little Women*** and admired Alcott for writing "girls' stories." Throughout his piece, little is said about her children's books. Beach's discussion does reveal another problem for Alcott within academe: She chose to write for girls. Beach suggests that writing "children's books" is a lesser achievement than writing a few lines of adult poetry or working as a speaker addressing issues concerning the needs of others. He concludes, "If Miss Alcott, by pressure of circumstances, had not been a writer of children's books, she might have been a poet, and would, from choice, have been a philanthropist and reformer" (284-85).

It is intriguing that such males have looked at Alcott's life as significant "biography" to be explored and discussed and that they have attested to the book's autobiographical stance while they have dismissed the work as literature, declaring it simple, wholesome, and sweet entertainment for young girls. Rarely have they looked at the structure of Alcott's story or her implied social messages. Yet Alcott's ***Little Women*** contains characters and social situations that make it both children's literature and feminine history.

In his insightful discussion of feminist criticism and children's literature, Perry Nodelman suggests that feminist criticism has revealed a subversive subtext in American literary tradition. He argues that children's literature fits within this pattern—that while it produces a conventional story structure, it contains a response to society that conflicts with society's expectations. He concludes that if men dismiss feminist criticism and children's literature, they are refusing to acknowledge an important literariness and, therefore, cannot enter into the timely debate about "a literature whose specific sort of femininity depends upon the existence of a powerful and autocratic masculinist hegemony" (33).

The subtext about women's life after marriage, to which I alluded earlier, is what makes ***Little Women*** such an intriguing book for many women scholars. This subtext carries the bite of realism. In the end, the sisters are a reflection of Alcott's own society's constraints. Their artistic talents must fit within their married lives, and in order to be considered successful, they must have children of their own. Jo has always wished to become a writer, but when she leaves home, she works as a teacher, an acceptable occupation for unmarried young women at that time. In the end, she settles for life as a "school-mother." Her role at the famous Plumfield School is as mother. Alcott writes,

> It was never a fashionable school, and the Professor did not lay up a fortune; but it was just what Jo intended it to be—"a happy, homelike place for boys, who needed care and kindness." . . . Yes; Jo was a very happy woman there, in spite of the hard work, much anxiety, and a perpetual racket. She enjoyed it heartily, and found the applause of her boys more satisfying than any praise of the world; for now she told no stories except to her flock of enthusiastic believers and admirers. As the years went on, two lads of her own came to increase her happiness.
>
> (438)

Meg works as a governess prior to getting married. Unlike Jo, Meg never really enjoys teaching, but she turns to it as an acceptable position for an unmarried woman. When Meg discusses teaching with John Brooke, she says, "I don't like my work, but I get a great deal of satisfaction out of it after all, so I won't complain; I only wish I liked teaching as you do" (109). When Amy is young, she believes that she will die, and so she makes a will, leaving her art work to her father and Laurie. Once Amy is married, her own daughter is a sickly child, and she returns to art in order to make a marble likeness of her child "so that, whatever happens, I may at least keep the image of my little angel" (396). Amy's use and distribution of her art suggest that approval must come from males if she is to continue to have support for her endeavors. Furthermore, her art has been shaped to fit the ideals of the male patrons who provide the roof over her head. In the end, her artistic talent becomes a way of keeping her family together, even after death. While this seems romantic, it is also disquieting.

Running counter to the romantic story of girls growing up, finding husbands, and living happily-ever-after is the story of women's angst over adjusting their personal desires and lifestyles to society's expectations and demands. Beverly Lyon Clark calls this part of the story's structure double-edged and says that Jo's need to write both frees and conditions her. Jo's fiction, Clark argues, allows her to come to terms with domesticity. In the end, Jo gives up writing fiction. Clark concludes that, as a writer, "Alcott remains ambivalent—about writing, about self-expression and about gender roles" (87). Thus, the subtext contradicts the romantic story, and the book becomes a complex interpretation of women and American family values. According to Nodelman, this is what links feminist criticism to children's literature.

Nodelman argues that personal angst is a significant element in children's literature, whether written by men or by women, because children's literature focuses on how those at the bottom of a hierarchy learn to cope and succeed within the rules of the hierarchy. Pointing out that weak children usually encounter powerful antagonists, he says, "this implies that children's literature, like women's literature is merely a response to repression—a literature whose specific sort of femininity depends on . . . an alternative way of describing reality" (33). These stories contain subtexts that contradict cultural ideals because they question the meanings of play and imagination.

Both children's literature and women's literature contain a literary structure at odds with the established American literary canon, and they reflect a cultural struggle for power. Yet because they are rarely discussed as literature in American education and are not considered for their subtexts and implicit contradictions to traditional values, children's literature is usually taught only as texts that help youngsters fit within the traditional values of their everyday world.

Adults who do not possess the analytical skills derived from feminist theory use literature to show children how to read for instruction, and children learn to trust the simple morals pointed out by the adults who share their reading materials. Literature becomes a tool for talking about the past, and classics become "old-fashioned." Elementary school teachers prefer new titles that depict the past according to present-day historical standards, and classical stories in children's literature are left on the shelves in the children's library. In turn, college literature classes have ignored classical stories about adolescent girls, both in the context of children's literature and in the context of the American literary canon.

None of the students in my class had read ***Little Women*** in a class. Few of the young women in my class remembered sharing ***Little Women*** in a school setting. One of my students wrote that when it was described in the fifth grade, it sounded like "a typical story of women learning their roles." The students' reflections show me that books about women and children are not considered important literature.

A program of literary studies that includes children's and women's literature will create a better American literary canon. It will help all students understand that language not only reflects our world but also shapes our ideas about that world. It will demonstrate that all writers use language to instill attitudes and will encourage debate. And finally, it will encourage readers to think of women authors as writers who create images of their contemporary society that are opaque enough in design and style to encourage change while recording current societal attitudes.

Works Cited

Alcott, Louisa May. *Little Women, or Meg, Jo, Beth and Amy.* Boston: Little, 1968.

Beach, Seth Curtis. *Daughters of the Puritans: A Group of Brief Biographies.* Freeport, NY: Books for Libraries, 1905.

Clark, Beverly Lyon. "A Portrait of the Artist as a Little Woman." *Children's Literature* 17 (1989): 81-97.

Egan, Susanna. "Self-Conscious History: American Autobiography after the Civil War." *American Autobiography: Retrospect and Prospect.* Ed. Paul John Eakin. Madison: U of Wisconsin P, 1991.

Elbert, Sarah. *A Hunger for Home: Louisa May Alcott and* Little Women. Philadelphia: Temple UP, 1984.

Hollander, Anne. "Reflection on *Little Women.*" *Children's Literature* 9 (1981): 28-39.

MacDonald, Ruth K. "Louisa May Alcott's *Little Women*: Who Is Still Reading Miss Alcott and Why." *Touchstones: Reflections on the Best in Children's Literature, Volume One.* Ed. Perry Nodelman. West Lafayette, IN: ChLA, 1985. 13-20.

May, Jill P. "Spirited Females of the Nineteenth Century: Liberated Moods in Louisa May Alcott's *Little Women.*" *Children's Literature in Education* 11 (1980): 10-20.

Nodelman, Perry. "Children's Literature as Women's Literature." *Children's Literature Association Quarterly* 13 (1988): 31-34.

Russ, Lavinia. *Not to Be Read on Sunday!*: Little Women *1868-1968.* Boston: Little, 1968.

Showalter, Elaine. *Sister's Choice: Tradition and Change in American Women's Writing.* Oxford: Oxford UP, 1991.

Spacks, Patricia Meyer. *The Adolescent Idea: Myths of Youth and the Adult Imagination.* NY: Basic, 1981.

Stockton, Frank B. "Miss Alcott: The Friend of Little Women and Little Men." *St. Nicholas Magazine* Dec. 1877: 129-31.

FROM THE AUTHOR

ALCOTT WRITES TO HER FRIEND MARIA S. PORTER ON THE SUBJECT OF WOMEN'S WORK

I rejoice greatly therat, and hope that the first thing that you and Mrs. Sewall propose in your first meeting will be to reduce the salary of the head master of the High School, and increase the salary of the first woman assistant, whose work is quite as good as his, and even harder, to make the pay equal. I believe in the same pay for the same good work. Don't you? In future let woman do whatever she can do; let men place no more impediments in the way; above all things let's have fair play,—let *simple justice* be done, say I. Let us hear no more of "woman's sphere" either from our wise (?) legislators beneath the State House dome, or from our clergymen in their pulpits. I am tired, year after year, of hearing such twaddle about sturdy oaks and clinging vines and man's chivalric protection of woman. Let woman find her own limitations, and if, as is so confidently asserted, nature has defined her sphere, she will be guided accordingly, but in heaven's name give her a chance! Let the professions be open to her; let fifty years of college education be hers, and then we shall see what we shall see. Then, and not until then, shall we be able to say what woman can and what she cannot do, and coming generations will know and be able to define more clearly what is a "woman's sphere" than these benighted men who now try to do it.

Alcott, Louisa May. Letter to Maria S. Porter of 1874. In *L. M. Alcott: Signature of Reform.* Edited by Madeleine B. Stern, p. 152. Boston: Northeastern University Press, 2002.

KAZUKO WATANABE (ESSAY DATE FALL 1999)

SOURCE: Watanabe, Kazuko. "Reading *Little Women,* Reading Motherhood in Japan." *Feminist Studies* 25, no. 3 (fall 1999): 699-709.

In the following essay, Watanabe discusses reader responses to Little Women *in Japan.*

Japan has been acknowledged as a traditionally maternal country, with motherly values sanctified and often mythologized.[1] The term for motherhood, *bosei* (which in literal translation means "nature of motherliness"), was first introduced to Japan by poet Akiko Yosano (1878-1942) in her essay "Abolishing Distorted Images of Motherhood" as the translation of the Western concept.[2] Motherhood is a discourse often characterized as motherly consciousness and gender-defined functions related to reproduction and domesticity. Thus, it provides images and symbols which are often used as an ideological entity.

In discussing how motherhood as a discourse and as a discursive practice affects Japanese women's consciousness, I suggest that many Japanese perceive motherhood as a positive experience in spite of its negative and oppressive aspects. Thus, motherhood has become a lofty and sublime regulator not only of children's behavior but that of society as well. Motherhood is also an agency of domesticity, love, and high morality. Through these characteristics of motherhood, which I call "maternalism," the Japanese concept of self is formulated, with motherhood inhibiting individualism.[3]

The discourse of motherhood allows for immaturity and dependence of both male and female children as well as for grown men who are ready to be cared for and protected by mother. Japanese men seldom reject their mother as do Western men in their process of growth. Given this situation, the Japanese self is enveloped by the mother so that it avoids facing others.

To examine diverse realities and possible choices presented by motherhood, I apply the readership response method to Louisa May Alcott's ***Little Women,*** published in 1868. The way ***Little Women,*** a novel that addresses motherhood as a central theme, is read in Japan reflects motherhood as it is deeply rooted in Japanese cultural consciousness. ***Little Women*** is a classic American text that has remained perennially popular with Japanese women of all ages and social backgrounds since it first appeared in Japanese translation in 1891. The title "Little Women" was translated into "A Story of Young Grass," which signifies a narrative of adolescent girls. In present-day Japan, ***Little Women*** is the second most popular children's book for young female readers, following Lucy Maude Montgomery's *Anne of Green Gables.*[4] Its readers are mainly women, but there are also some men who favor ***Little Women.*** Its popularity makes it a convenient bridge between the discourse of motherhood that we find among general readers in contemporary Japan and the cult of domesticity in the Victorian period as a

Western discourse. ***Little Women*** also can help us understand motherhood as Japanese women's issues in their twentieth-century social context. The novel is set in an era of transition, when the modern family emerged in the nineteenth-century United States. In terms of modernization, urbanization, and consumerism, a comparable period in Japan would be the 1920s. Besides, the discourse of motherhood in this period seems to remain unchanged up to the current postmodern era.

For over a decade, I used ***Little Women*** as a text in university English classes, for which both sexes register. In addition, I supervised students' theses on Alcott; sixteen graduating theses were written by female students in the past ten years. I also used the Japanese translation of this novel several times in municipally sponsored women writers' courses at women's centers, offered as a part of the continuing education program. The students in the women's centers were mostly middle-aged, middle-class urban housewives with school age children. The college female and male students, aged eighteen to twenty, were in the first or second year class of compulsory basic English reading, while the thesis students, aged twenty-two and twenty-three, all were female in their senior year. In terms of generations and experience, women's center students, most of whom are mothers, are distinguished from the college students who are daughters and sons. My aim is not to study the generation or gender gap between these different categories of students. Moreover, my own critiques of motherhood and my feminist expectations might have influenced these original responses produced by both young and adult students in the form of term papers, theses, and class discussions. However, these responses provide valuable materials that demonstrate the respondents' conservatism regarding the values of motherhood and at the same time illuminate the ways that a feminist pedagogy can change some of their cultural consciousness.

The students' most popular reading of ***Little Women*** applauds motherhood as the embodiment of moral virtue for women and men, which is closely related to family values. Almost all students believe that an ideal family is demonstrated by the maternal power and love exhibited by Marmee, the sisters' mother, during the authoritarian father's absence. Most students easily associated this family structure of nurturing mother and absent father with a typical middle-class family pattern in contemporary Japan. These students like the passage in which the mother-centered family in ***Little Women*** is depicted as "the most beautiful thing in the world."[5] Similarly, some of the university students, both female and male, praise Marmee as respectable and powerful and perceive her inexhaustible motherly love to be both valuable and beautiful.

However, these students also interpret Marmee as a self-sacrificing and self-denying mother. One student writes: "Marmee is a role model for her daughters. Based on her own experiences, she gives her daughters lessons on obligations, self-abnegation, and other duties. Marmee tells her daughters that they must learn to sacrifice themselves for others, which she believes is required of a respectable woman and which, in turn, will guarantee their happiness." Marmee encourages her daughters to develop in accordance with the expectations of society as expressed by their mother. Following her lessons, her daughters acquire a motherly consciousness, to which housewife readers positively respond. They see socialization of the children, often called "the lesson for a good wife and wise mother" in the Japanese context, as the chief role of a mother.

Some of the adult students also identify themselves with Marmee's perspective. Through her, they attempt to justify their own status as housewives. One adult student notes that she feels sympathy with Marmee's confession to her daughter Jo and praises her efforts to control herself. One thesis student especially appreciates Marmee's confession addressed to Jo: "I've been trying to cure it [my temper] for forty years, and have only succeeded in controlling it. I am angry nearly every day of my life, Jo; but I have learned not to show it. I still hope to learn not to feel it [anger], though it may take me another forty years to do so."[6] The student interprets Jo's suppression of anger as an essential part of gender socialization, taught by the mother. She also writes that Marmee is a person who needs children for her own identity and for whom she becomes the source of motivation, support, and protection.

Focusing on the daughters' perspective, I pointed out to my students that the term "little women" first appears in the father's letter sent from the battlefield, signifying females in the first process of socialization to develop a sense of themselves as women. Many college students responded that "little women" evokes for them the image of ideal womanhood and potential motherhood, both of which they believe should be the ultimate aspiration of young women as well as their goal.

Paradoxically, however, the favorite character for almost all students across gender and age is Jo, who is very different from the Marmee figure. Such responses are probably based on the structure of the text, for Jo is the author's double and the central character with whom most readers can immediately identify. However, Jo seems to attract both college and adult readers for an additional reason. Even though her nature is different from a typical "little woman," a domestic motherly figure, these students like the way Jo is portrayed in the earlier part of the book as one who is "rude, unladylike," acting like a man, "the man of the family now that Papa is away."[7] These characteristics are also signified by her androgynous name, "Jo." Most female readers of different ages find in Jo's active, boylike actions something of their own lost girlhood. Nevertheless, a kind of self-censorship leads these students to admit that these actions have to be well controlled during a young girl's maturation. College students especially glorify Jo's efforts to assume motherly sensitivity in spite of her nature. One female college student writes that by learning to fight against her extreme, self-conscious "bosom enemies"[8]—such as her temper and anger—Jo comes to control herself through patience, submission, and "loyalty to duty," as Marmee's lessons instruct.

Some college students feel relieved that Jo becomes motherly, although it takes her a long time and requires tremendous effort. Both female and male college readers say that the most moving scene is the one in which Jo has her hair cut for her father, reading it as symbolic of Jo's acceptance of her mother's lessons of self-sacrifice. One thesis student points out that Marmee becomes the agency not only for Jo's self-sacrifice but also for the sacrifice of her own creativity. These students praise Jo's giving up even the autonomous claim to her own work. In ***Good Wives,***[9] the second part of ***Little Women*** published in serial form half a year after the appearance of ***Little Women,*** part 1, Jo's creative self is developed toward the more domestic direction so that she can write a simple but beautiful *little* story by dedicating it to her parents. As the students read in the following passage: "If there is anything good or true in what I write, it isn't mine; I owe it all to you [father] and mother and to Beth."[10]

Moreover, several college readers are relieved by the ending of the story when Jo succeeds in becoming a mother figure to the boys in her school. These students agree that Jo appropriately accepts conformity and "women's mission" within the domestic sphere when she becomes engaged to Bhaer. As Jo herself admits: "I may be strong-minded, but no one can say I'm out of my sphere now, for woman's special mission is supposed to be drying tears and bearing burdens. I'm to carry my share, Frederich, and help to earn the home."[11] These readers are also gratified that Jo contents herself as a mother, referring to the passage where Jo says, "the life I wanted then seems selfish, lonely, and cold to me now" and "I'm far happier than I deserve."[12]

Beth is another favorite of Japanese readers. By virtue of her self-sacrifice, she most fully succeeds in assimilating a motherly consciousness, with which both Japanese college and adult students are ready to sympathize. A typical response can be found in an essay by the Japanese writer and artist Chizuru Miyasako who writes that "when I reread ***Little Women,*** I discovered Beth. . . . She, like Jo, functions as my conscience because of her love for others, however old-fashioned and pale it sounds! However, because of this love for others, I am attracted to Beth."[13] Some college students, like Miyasako, celebrate Beth's unconditional love for others, which seems to the students that Beth practices maternal love.

Many housewives, but few young readers, acknowledge Meg's role as a mother within the domestic sphere. These students frequently quote the passage where Alcott depicts Meg's "home": "A woman's happiest kingdom is home, her highest honor the art of ruling it not as a queen, but as a wise wife and mother."[14] Some mature readers use the quotation to suggest that by becoming mothers, women can assume a greater domestic power and raise their status in society as well as in the private sphere of their homes. As one mature student writes, "Meg and John appreciate the sexual division of labor as a couple, which makes their lives harmonious and happy in the hetero-sexual relationship. Meg shows how women's happiness depends upon their efforts to acquire true womanhood and motherhood."

In ***Little Women,*** most Japanese readers, spanning two generations, find the fulfillment of motherhood as the measure of women's happiness and praise the March sisters for successfully assuming motherly sensitivity. Here I introduce "domestic feminism'; this positive view of motherhood and maternalism has been conceptualized by Daniel Scott Smith to describe women's seizing of power within the family in the nineteenth-century United States.[15]

Similarly, in contemporary Japanese society, women are expected to accept willingly the role of mother as their most important vocation. Many Japanese readers aspire to an idealized concept of motherhood in which a woman's role is to motivate, support, and create "family." This idealized motherhood has also encouraged Japanese housewives, as archetypal mothers, to have a positive picture of their social position and to create emotional bonds among members of the family. However, in a sense their role as a wife in the heterosexual relationship with their husbands seems less important. Likewise, her role of reproductivity and sexuality are seldom discussed in this context. Japanese readers across gender and age lines are ready to accept that self-denial as the brave act depicted in ***Little Women*** is synonymous with and validating maternalism. This appreciation of the novel's "domestic feminism" may be the main reason for its popularity in Japan.

In contrast to the celebration of motherhood, students, especially those who are informed and convinced by feminist thought, arrive at responses that are critical of internalized maternalism. They try to see a feminist critique in the portrait of motherhood in ***Little Women.*** The critique of such motherhood by both thesis students and adult students becomes more pronounced when I introduce Alcott's autobiographical novel, ***Work,*** and her Gothic thriller, "**Behind a Mask or, A Woman's Power.**"[16] I explain to them how these newly recognized works do not celebrate traditional motherly roles but are palpably critical of them. For example, ***Work*** glorifies women's ethics of labor and friendship, while motherhood is only one of the female roles portrayed by the central character. Moreover, in "**Behind a Mask,**" the female protagonist rejects traditional conceptions of motherhood. On the one hand, she uses them as a mask for an ideal woman and performs such motherly roles only to enchant men who are supposed to give her social status.[17] On the other hand, the mothers in these stories are trivialized and degraded.

Several mature students who understand these other works relate their own lives to Marmee's and her daughters' and feel manipulated by the maternal role thrust upon them by social conventions. Such a discourse, they say, discourages women's autonomous development. These readers find in ***Little Women*** a picture of the negative sides of motherhood; the happier the fictional mother is portrayed, the more threatening she is to these students. That is, they realize how such a depiction of motherhood functions to suppress both the self and others. Housewife readers in particular become critical of the celebration of motherhood. In Marmee's confessions and lessons to her daughters, they point to the suppression of Jo's anger as the oppression of her individualism. They also observe that as a little woman, Beth goes to the extreme of self-sacrifice, self-denial, and physical collapse, which eventually lead her to death. One thesis student writes that Beth's death is the outcome of her total conformity to society guided by motherhood because she suffocates within a restricted home life, without any resources to develop her individualism.

Furthermore, the students who are exposed to feminist criticism or those who have innate feminist consciousness seem disturbed by the changes in women's lives between ***Little Women,*** part 1 and part 2. ***Little Women,*** part 1 focuses on the pre-Oedipal homoerotic utopian relationship between mother and daughters with the mother in the center; in part 2 (***Good Wives***) this theme gradually shifts until the heterosexual relationship becomes central. The thesis students who carefully compare the two parts note that women are taught to perform a gender-defined role and suppress their individuality throughout both books. Thus, from a critical perspective, they ironically see it appropriate that the first part was titled ***Little Women,*** and the second, ***Good Wives***; both mythologize and institutionalize stereotyped women's roles.

Students become particularly disappointed with or upset by Jo's metamorphoses. The thesis students argue that Jo learns how to suppress her self-determination as her "motherly consciousness" develops, and begins to criticize her own aspirations to be a writer and to take over Beth's role as a good daughter, a real "little woman." These students are even more dismayed by the fact that Jo avoids a mother-son relationship with Laurie and chooses Bhaer, a patriarchal father-teacher figure. One adult student is quite distressed by Jo's succumbing to his advice, neglecting her potential as a creative writer and ending up playing the traditional role of a housewife—an unpaid female domestic laborer in a patriarchal family. Similar to Japanese patriarchal families, the father figure Bhaer rather psychologically depends on his wife. One thesis student shares Jo's regret and suggests that in the newly established sisters' families, motherly women are expected to sacrifice themselves for their families rather than to develop their individual selves. These students notice that the Marmee-centered family turns into an empty nest when Jo comes to practice the cult of domesticity.

Moreover, after reading feminist criticism, some adult readers readily identified with Meg's feelings of suffocation—"as if they were all nerve and no muscle"—and her entrapment within the domestic realm, depicted as she goes "into a seclusion almost as close as a French nunnery."[18] From this perspective, these readers come to realize that ***Little Women*** clearly depicts how motherhood 'handicaps" women and constricts their world view; the adolescent women do not grow up but grow down. Many adult and some college students began to view the term "little women" as indicating the trivialization and entrapment of women within what Betty Friedan calls a domestic "concentration camp" in *The Feminine Mystique*[19] and to see that the March daughters illustrate what Nina Auerbach calls a "collective death of sisters."[20]

Some of both the mature and young students gradually find that the novel accurately reminds them of the life of typical Japanese women. Some relate the negative aspects of motherhood in ***Little Women*** to Japanese women's low status in public life. These women argue that the modern family has allocated full-time mothering to women and, as a result, created compulsory motherhood and maternal love, which are expected to be innate and instinctive. Japanese housewife students admit that their identity is with their husband's work or their children's lives so that they feel that they have lost their own identity and only stereotyped gender roles are offered to women. The men are supposed to sacrifice their family for companies and the women, themselves for families, and economic power is considered primary. Thus, these readers see that Japanese people are trapped within the capitalistic value system—the opposite of maternal values—and the Japanese work ethic, as well as the institution of an engendered nuclear family.

Moreover, in analyzing the representations of motherhood in ***Little Women,*** those students in both the college and the women's centers learn that the reception of ***Little Women*** among Japanese readers reflects the idealization of motherhood which relates causally to the lack of self-development in Japan. They recognize how motherhood can be responsible for suppression of the self. Those who perceive the necessity for developing their own identities find that compulsory concepts of motherhood which embody self-denial and self-sacrifice threaten their potentiality. They then identify the suppression of self as the main feminist issue in Japan.

Japanese readers' responses to ***Little Women***—either to celebrate motherhood or to reject it—reflect their empirical understanding of motherhood. Japanese motherhood is similarly characterized as a powerful creative image of women and an institutionalized one that causes discrimination against women. This dichotomized view is a pattern that Adrienne Rich has attacked in the earlier stage of Second Wave U. S. feminism.[21] On the one hand, some of these mature students agree that women are endowed with maternal power, and can be agents of a moral value system to change an androcentric and capitalistic contemporary Japanese society and to save the world damaged by male-centered technologies and consumerism. On the other hand, detractors of motherhood conclude that maternalism constitutes the primary edifice suppressing women's lives, particularly their self-development.

The middle-class mature students in women's centers who have become critical of the maternal world represented in ***Little Women*** and who are aware of the destructive function of motherhood are the ones who are, in a sense, in the better position to change Japanese society. These women have tried partly to discard their roles of mothering husbands and children and, in opposition to a maternal value system, have raised a critical voice against patriarchal and capitalist social structures. They would still be able to shake the patriarchal and capitalist social structures which are male-dominant in contemporary Japanese society. Thus, they seek alternative values, which enable them to deconstruct such a rigid nuclear family system. However, they do so in a limited way because they would not totally give up their secure position in the patriarchal society.

Furthermore, female college students who come to an alternative reading of maternalism try to find a means of challenging traditional motherhood. In the last five years, for example, this challenge has been reflected in reproduction rates, called women's strike against motherhood; Japan has witnessed a dramatically declining birth rate, down to 1.43 in 1996, 1.42 in 1997 and 1.36 in 1998. Women have begun to be aware of the disadvantage of performing mother's roles in Japan's capitalist and sexist society. Reading ***Little Women*** as a challenge to maternalism is part of this emerging feminist consciousness.

Notes

1. Masami Ohinata, "The Mystique of Motherhood: A Key to Understanding of Social Change and Family Problems in Japan," in *Japanese Women: New Feminist Perspectives on the Past, Present, and Future,* ed. Kumiko Fujimura-Fanselow and Asuko Kameda (New York: Feminist Press, 1995), 199-211.

2. Mikiyo Kanoh, "History of Motherhood," in *Bosei o Kaidokusuru* (*Interpreting motherhood*), ed. Motherhood Study Group (Tokyo: Yuhikaku, 1991), 70.

3. For example, Ogoshi Aiko emphasizes the suppression and oppression of motherhood over the development of self. See Aiko Ogoshi, "Questioning the Cultural Paradigm of Buddhism," in *Seisabetsusuru Bukkyo* (*Sexual discrimination in Buddhism*) (Kyoto: Hozokan, 1990), 3-86.

4. Annual research of reading in Japan is conducted by Mainichi Daily News Company. See "Why Is *Anne of Green Gables* Popular Now?" *Japanese Children's Literature,* no. 297 (February 1980): 12-27.

5. Louisa May Alcott, *Little Women* (1868; reprint, Boston: Little, Brown & Co., 1994), 495.

6. Ibid., 82.

7. Ibid., 7.

8. Ibid., 11.

9. Louisa May Alcott, *Good Wives* (London: Aldine Press, 1869). This was called *Little Women,* part 2, and was soon added to the original book; but in England it was given a separate title, *Good Wives,* and always appeared as such. There were two further sequels, *Little Men* (1871) and *Jo's Boys* (1886).

10. Alcott, *Little Women,* 446.

11. Ibid., 491.

12. Ibid., 500, 502.

13. Chizuru Miyasako, "Jo Says that Beth Is Her Conscience," *Cho Shojo he* (*To Super-Girl*) (Tokyo: Hokueisha, 1984), 107.

14. Alcott, *Little Women,* 409.

15. Daniel Scott Smith, "Family Limitation, Sexual Control, and Domestic Feminism in Victorian America," in *A Heritage of Her Own: Toward a New Social History of American Women,* ed. Nancy F. Cott and Elizabeth H. Pleck (New York: Simon & Schuster, 1979), 222-45.

16. Louisa May Alcott, *Behind a Mask* (New York: William Morrow, 1975).

17. Kazuko Watanabe, "Louisa May Alcott's Literary Faces: Focusing on *Work* and *Behind a Mask,*" *Kansai American Literature* 24 (November 1987): 22-36.

18. Alcott, *Little Women,* 398.

19. Betty Friedan, *The Feminine Mystique* (1963; reprint, New York: W. W. Norton, 1984), 37.

20. Nina Auerbach, *Communities of Women: An Idea in Fiction* (Cambridge: Harvard University Press, 1978), 53.

21. Adrienne Rich, *Of Woman Born: Motherhood as Experience and Institution* (New York: W. W. Norton, 1976).

FURTHER READING

Bibliography

Payne, Alma J. *Louisa May Alcott: A Reference Guide.* Boston: G. K. Hall, 1980, 87 p.

Offers a comprehensive bibliography of secondary sources on Alcott.

Biographies

Anthony, Katharine. *Louisa May Alcott.* New York: Alfred A. Knopf, 1938, 315 p.

Questions the morality and upbringing of the Alcott family. Anthony's book has been criticized by later biographers for lack of solid evidence.

Cheney, Edna D. *Louisa May Alcott: Her Life, Letters, and Journals.* Boston: Little, Brown, and Co., 1907, 404 p.

Relies heavily on Alcott's journal entries and letters; includes excerpts from previously unpublished poetry. This biography was sanctioned by Alcott's sister.

Saxton, Martha. *Louisa May: A Modern Biography of Louisa May Alcott.* New York: Houghton Mifflin, 428 p.

Presents a psychoanalytical interpretation of Alcott's life, work, and family relations; observes in Alcott's career a regressive movement away from conflict and self-assertion and towards sacrifice and conventional morality.

Stern, Madeleine B. *Louisa May Alcott.* Norman, Okla.: University of Oklahoma Press, 1950, 424 p.

Respected biography that has been influential in generating further research into Alcott's life and works.

Criticism

Auerbach, Nina. "Little Women." In *Communities of Women: An Idea in Fiction,* pp. 55-73. Cambridge: Harvard University Press, 1978.

Compares the social world of Little Women *with that of Jane Austen's* Pride and Prejudice.

Clark, Beverly Lyon. "A Portrait of the Artist as a Little Woman." *Children's Literature* 17 (1989): 81-97.

Discusses Alcott's ambivalence toward fiction writing, particularly as a form of self expression.

———, ed. Little Women. New York: Garland Publishing, 1998, 450 p.

Contains eleven new essays and six seminal essays addressing themes of gender, sexuality, race, culture, and intellectual history in Alcott's novel.

Doyle, Christine. *Louisa May Alcott and Charlotte Brontë: Transatlantic Translations.* Knoxville: University of Tennessee Press, 2000, 203 p.

Compares the family life, careers, spirituality of Alcott and Brontë as well as their treatment of gender relations in their works..

Foster, Shirley, and Judy Simons. "Louisa May Alcott: *Little Women.*" In *What Katy Read: Feminist Re-Readings of "Classic" Stories for Girls,* pp. 85-106. Iowa City: University of Iowa Press, 1995.

Contends that critics tend to be emotionally engaged with Little Women *because its theme, female development, is universal.*

Gay, Carol. "The Philosopher and His Daughter: Amos Bronson Alcott and Louisa." *Essays in Literature* 2, no. 2 (fall 1975): 181-91.

Reexamines Alcott's relationship with her father and Amos Alcott's reputation as an irresponsible dreamer.

Halttunen, Karen. "The Domestic Drama of Louisa May Alcott." *Feminist Studies* 10, no. 2 (summer 1984): 233-54.

Looks at the meaning of Alcott's depiction the theater in her novels.

Heilbrun, Carolyn G. "Louisa May Alcott: The Influence of *Little Women.*" In *Women, the Arts, and the 1920s in Paris and New York,* edited by Kenneth W. Wheeler and Virginia Lee Lussier, pp. 20-6. New Brunswick, N. J.: Transaction Books, 1982.

Argues that Little Women*'s Jo has been a model of female autonomy for twentieth-century women artists.*

MacDonald, Ruth K. *Louisa May Alcott.* Boston: Twayne, 1983, 111 p.

Offers critical discussion of Alcott's major works and considers her place in the history of American children's literature.

Murphy, Ann B. "The Borders of Ethical, Erotic, and Artistic Possibilities in *Little Women.*" *Signs* 15, no. 3 (spring 1990): 562-85.

Examines the debate surrounding Little Women*'s feminism.*

Paulin, Diana R. "'Let Me Play Desdemona': White Heroines and Interracial Desire in Louisa May Alcott's 'My Contraband' and 'M. L.'" In *White Women in Racialized Spaces: Imaginative Transformation and Ethical Action in Literature,* edited by Samina Najmi and Rajini Srikanth, pp. 119-30. Albany: State University of New York Press, 2002.

Examines Alcott's treatment of interracial love in her short fiction.

Rigsby, Mary. "'So Like Women!' Louisa May Alcott's *Work* and the Ideology of Relations." In *Redefining the Political Novel: American Women Writers, 1797-1901,* edited by Sharon M. Harris, pp. 109-27. Knoxville: University of Tennessee Press, 1995.

Emphasizes the political significance of Work *and notes Alcott's affiliation with a feminist form of American Transcendentalism.*

Russ, Lavinia. "Not to Be Read on Sunday." *Horn Book* 44, no. 5 (October 1968): 521-26.

Examines the widespread appeal of Little Women *one hundred years after its original publication.*

Showalter, Elaine. "*Little Women*: The American Female Myth." In *Sister's Choice: Tradition and Change in American Women's Writing,* pp. 42-64. Oxford: Clarendon Press, 1991.

Considers the reasons for the sustained popularity of Little Women *among American female readers of diverse backgrounds.*

Stern, Madeleine B. "Louisa Alcott's Feminist Letters." *Studies in the American Renaissance* (1978): 429-52.

Argues that Alcott's letters reveal a moderate feminism rooted in her humanist beliefs.

Strickland, Charles. *Victorian Domesticity: Families in the Life and Art of Louisa May Alcott.* Tuscaloosa: University of Alabama Press, 1985, 198 p.

Examines Alcott's life and works in terms of conflicts between the ideals and the realities of nineteenth-century family life.

Yellin, Jean Fagan. "From *Success* to *Experience*: Louisa May Alcott's *Work.*" *Massachusetts Review* 21, no. 3 (fall 1980): 527-39.

Argues that Work *is unique among nineteenth-century novels for proposing that women extend their actions into the public sphere.*

OTHER SOURCES FROM GALE:

Additional coverage of Alcott's life and career is contained in the following sources published by the Gale Group: *American Writer's Supplement,* Vol. 1; *Authors and Artists for Young Adults,* Vol. 20; *Beacham's Encyclopedia of Popular Fiction: Biography and Resources,* Vol. 1; *Beacham's Guide to Literature for Young Adults,* Vol. 2; *Children's Literature Review,* Vols. 1, 38; *Concise Dictionary of American Literary Biography, 1865-1917*; *Dictionary of Literary Biography,* Vols. 1, 42, 79, 223, 239, 242; *Dictionary of Literary Biography Documentary Series,* Vol. 14; *DISCovering Authors*; *DISCovering Authors: British Edition*; *DISCovering Authors: Canadian Edition*; *DISCovering Authors Modules*: *Most-studied Authors* and *Novelists*; *DISCovering Authors 3.0*; *Feminist Writers*; *Junior DISCovering Authors*; *Literature and Its Times,* Vol. 2; *Literature Resource Center*; *Major Authors and Illustrators for Children and Young Adults,* Eds. 1, 2; *Nineteenth-Century Literature Criticism,* Vols. 6, 58, 83; *Novels for Students,* Vol. 12; *Reference Guide to American Literature,* Ed. 4; *Short Story Criticism,* Vol. 27; *Something about the Author,* Vol. 100; *St. James Guide to Young Adult Writers*; *Twayne's United States Authors*; *World Literature Criticism*; *Writers for Children*; *Writers for Young Adults*; and *Yesterday's Authors of Books for Children.*

JANE AUSTEN

(1775 - 1817)

English novelist.

Austen is best known as a consummate novelist of manners. The author of six novels, Austen depicted a small slice of English life during the Regency period, a time marked by the Napoleonic Wars, the early growth of the English Empire, and an economic and industrial revolution that was countered by a cultural emphasis on all things proper, elegant, genteel, and truly "English." Austen captured this moment in great detail, focusing narrowly on the lives of the landed gentry in rural England and—more particularly—the little triumphs and defeats faced by the young women attempting to secure their future survival through respectable marriage. In such works as *Pride and Prejudice* (1813), *Emma* (1816), and *Mansfield Park* (1814), Austen employed wit, irony, and shrewd observation to advance the literary status of the women's novel and to address the social and political concerns of nineteenth-century men and women.

BIOGRAPHICAL INFORMATION

The daughter of the Reverend George Austen and Cassandra Leigh Austen, Jane Austen was born December 16, 1775. She was the seventh of eight children and the youngest of two daughters in the middle-class family, then living at Steventon Rectory in Hampshire, England. As the parson's daughter, Austen mixed frequently and easily with the landed gentry of rural England. Among the Austens's neighbors was Madam Lefroy, wife to a parson and sister to an aristocratic squire fond of books. Lefroy, who wrote and published poetry, took a special interest in Austen's education, and encouraged her intellectual development. At home, Reverend Austen entertained the family by reading literature aloud and guided Austen in choosing books from his large library and local circulating libraries, while James Austen, Austen's eldest brother, directed the family in amateur theatricals. Between 1783 and 1786, Austen received formal schooling, first at a boarding school at Oxford, then at the Abbey School in Reading. Around the age of twelve, Austen began writing children's stories. She stayed at Steventon until 1801, reading, writing, and participating in the Hampshire social rounds of balls, visits, and trips to Bath. Austen never married, but in 1795 fell in love with Thomas Langlois Lefroy, the nephew of her mentor Madam Lefroy. Madam Lefroy, however, disapproved of the match, thinking Thomas would lose his inheritance if he married the penniless daughter of a clergyman, and sent her nephew away. During these last years at Steventon, Austen began several early drafts of her mature works. She wrote her first novel in 1796 and 1797; "First Impressions" was sufficiently polished that her father attempted to publish it, but it was turned down. She would eventually revise it as *Pride and Prejudice.* Her next attempt was a novel she titled "Susan," and though she was able to sell it to a publisher in 1803, it was never published in its initial form. She eventually revised it further, and the book was published posthumously as *Northanger Abbey* (1818). Austen's authorial efforts were interrupted by a series of tragedies: in 1804 Madam Lefroy, who had remained her close friend, died in a riding accident, and in 1805 her father died, leaving Austen, her sister, and her mother with no means of support. They became dependent on her brothers, who jointly maintained the women in Bath until 1806, when Frank, a naval officer, invited them to live at his home in Southampton. In 1809, they moved to Chawton Cottage, on her brother Edward's estate in Kent. There, Austen worked on *Sense and Sensibility,* finally succeeding in getting her first novel published in 1811. As with all her works, *Sense and Sensibility* was published anonymously, "By a Lady." That year, she also worked on the final version of *Pride and Prejudice* and began *Mansfield Park.* She was unusually secretive about her writing for some time, even insisting that the door to the chamber she used for writing not be repaired, so that the squeak of the hinges would alert her to intruders. *Sense and Sensibility* and *Pride and Prejudice* both sold out their first printings and went into second editions and *Mansfield Park* sold out its first printing as well. Now a literary success, Austen began work on *Emma* in 1814. The Prince Regent (later George IV) invited Austen to meet with him in November 1815, expressing his admiration for her work and asking her to dedicate her next novel to him. She reluctantly agreed, and *Emma* was released with a dedication to the prince just over a month later. During that year, Austen also began work on *Persuasion* (1818), the last novel she would complete. She began the novel *Sanditon* in 1817 but was forced to leave it unfinished due to illness. In May of that year, she moved with her sister Cassandra to Winchester to obtain medical care but died on July 18. The obituary in the Hampshire newspaper contained one of the first public acknowledgements of her authorship.

MAJOR WORKS

Austen's novels are peopled with characters drawn from her sphere of life: ladies and gentlemen of the landed gentry. The plots of her novels revolve around the intricacies of courtship and marriage between members of the upper class. Austen's novels consider a narrow scope, using wit and irony to develop and further her plots. In many of her novels, women suffer, at least temporarily, for the joint distinctions of sex and class. Jane and Elizabeth Bennett, in *Pride and Prejudice,* are nearly prevented from marrying their wealthy suitors because of social codes forbidding it. Elinor and Marianne Dashwood, in *Sense and Sensibility,* similarly find themselves prohibited from marrying men for lack of adequate resources and social standing to make the connections respectable. As Austen's heroines painfully recognize, being female puts them in a precarious position: the Bennett family's estate will pass into the possession of a male cousin, and the Dashwood sisters and their mother are at the mercy of a half-brother's beneficence after the death of Mr. Dashwood. *Mansfield Park* and *Persuasion* are more complex works and have been considered less accessible to readers. The satirical aspect of *Mansfield Park* is less clear than in other novels; in particular, critics have found the heroine Fanny difficult to sympathize with, and it is not clear if her unusually moralistic thought and behavior is meant as a model to be emulated or one to be avoided. The heroine of *Persuasion,* Anne Elliot, has been characterized as a departure from Austen's usual characters. *Persuasion*'s tone is more subdued and poetic than Austen's earlier work, possibly a reflection of the author's increasing interest in Romanticism and an indication of her greater attention to the pain inflicted by the social mores she examined in her earlier works.

CRITICAL RECEPTION

During the first several decades after Austen published her novels, her work received little commentary. After the 1870 publication of her nephew's *Memoir of Jane Austen,* however, interest in her works increased. James Austen-Leigh's *Memoir* inaugurated a worshipful, nostalgic brand of Austen criticism. Adoring critics praised Austen's characteristic authorial traits, especially the elegance of her prose, but offered no thorough critical analysis of her works. Subsequent studies of Austen therefore reacted strongly to counter this tendency, emphasizing the technical flaws in the novels and dismissing what scholars considered the narrow, trivial world about which she wrote. A pronounced move toward a more balanced, objective mode of criticism came in 1939 with Mary Lascelles's focused attention on the technical and thematic aspects of Austen's work. With the advent of feminist criticism, critics again reexamined Austen's novels. Margaret Kirkham portrays Austen as a proto-feminist who purposefully argued in her novels against the social, political, and economic limitations placed on women by patriarchal English society. Susan Fraiman differs in her assessment of Austen's treatment of women's issues. She notes that although Austen's heroines are often witty and independent, offering an observer's perspective on women's inferior position in society, by the end of the works the heroines are reincorporated back into patriarchal society, no longer free agents and independent thinkers but wives subsumed by their husbands' households. Political and feminist scholarship on Austen's novels was further invigorated by the rise of postcolonial criticism. Moira Ferguson contends that Austen's novels offer a reformist critique of imperialism and finds a close link between the reformist impulse and women's status in English society.

PRINCIPAL WORKS

Sense and Sensibility (novel) 1811

Pride and Prejudice (novel) 1813

Mansfield Park (novel) 1814

Emma (novel) 1816

Northanger Abbey: And Persuasion (novels) 1818

Lady Susan (novel) 1871

The Watsons (unfinished novel) 1871

Love & Freindship, and Other Early Works (juvenilia) 1922

The Novels of Jane Austen. 5 vols. (novels) 1923; republished with revisions to notes and appendices, 1965-66

[Sanditon] Fragments of a Novel (unfinished novel) 1925

Jane Austen's Letters to Her Sister Cassandra and Others (letters) 1932

Volume the First (juvenilia) 1933

Volume the Third (juvenilia) 1951

Volume the Second (juvenilia) 1963

PRIMARY SOURCES

JANE AUSTEN (LETTER DATE 18 NOVEMBER 1814)

SOURCE: Austen, Jane. "Letter to Fanny Knight, November 18, 1814." In *Jane Austen's Letters,* 2nd ed., edited by R. W. Chapman, pp. 407-12. Oxford: Oxford University Press, 1952.

In the following excerpt from a letter to her niece dated November 18, 1814, Austen expresses in detail her opinions on love and marriage.

I feel quite as doubtful as you could be my dearest Fanny as to *when* my Letter may be finished, for I can command very little quiet time at present, but yet I must begin, for I know you will be glad to hear as soon as possible, & I really am impatient myself to be writing something on so very interesting a subject, though I have no hope of writing anything to the purpose. I shall do very little more I dare say than say over again, what you have said before.—I was certainly a good deal surprised *at first*—as I had no suspicion of any change in your feelings, and I have no scruple in saying that you cannot be in Love. My dear Fanny, I am ready to laugh at the idea—and yet it is no laughing matter to have had you so mistaken as to your own feelings—And with all my heart I wish I had cautioned you on that point when first you spoke to me;—but tho' I did not think you then so *much* in love as you thought yourself, I did consider you as being attached in a degree—quite sufficiently for happiness, as I had no doubt it would increase with opportunity.—And from the time of our being in London together, I thought you really very much in love—But you certainly are not at all—there is no concealing it.—What strange creatures we are!—It seems as if your being secure of him (as you say yourself) had made you Indifferent.—There was a little disgust I suspect, at the Races—& I do not wonder at it. His expressions there would not do for one who had rather more Acuteness, Penetration & Taste, than Love, which was your case. And yet, after all, I *am* surprised that the change in your feelings should be so great.—He is, just what he ever was, only more evidently & uniformly devoted to *you.* This is all the difference.—How shall we account for it?—My dearest Fanny, I am writing what will not be of the smallest use to you. I am feeling differently every moment, & shall not be able to suggest a single thing that can assist your Mind.—I could lament in one sentence & laugh in the next, but as to Opinion or Counsel I am sure none will ‹be› extracted worth having from this Letter.—I read yours through the very even[g] I received it—getting away by myself—I could not bear to leave off, when I had once begun.—I was full of curiosity & concern. Luckily your Aunt C. dined at the other house, therefore I had not to manœuvre away from *her*;—& as to anybody else, I do not care.—Poor dear Mr. J. P.!—Oh! dear Fanny, your mistake has been one that thousands of women fall into. He was the *first* young Man who attached himself to you. That was the charm, & most powerful it is.—Among the multitudes however that make the same mistake with yourself, there can be few indeed who have so little reason to regret it;—*his* Character and *his* attachment leave you nothing to be ashamed of.—Upon the whole, what is to be done? You certainly *have* encouraged him to such a point as to make him feel almost secure of you—you have no inclination for any other person—His situation in life, family, friends, & above all his character—his uncommonly amiable mind, strict principles, just notions, good habits—*all* that *you* know so well how to value, *All* that really is of the first importance—everything of this nature pleads his cause most strongly.—You have no doubt of his having superior Abilities—he has proved it at the University—he is I dare say such a scholar as your agreable, idle Brothers would ill bear a comparison with.—Oh! my dear Fanny, the more I write about him, the warmer my feelings become, the more strongly I feel the sterling worth of such a young Man & the desirableness of your growing in love with him again. I recommend this most thoroughly.—There *are* such beings in the World perhaps, one in a Thousand, as the Creature You and I should think perfection, Where Grace & Spirit are united to Worth, where the Manners are equal to the Heart & Understanding, but such a person may not come in your way, or if he does, he may not be the eldest son of a Man of Fortune, the Brother of your particular friend, & belonging to your own County.—Think of all this Fanny. Mr. J. P.—has advantages which do not often meet in one person. His only fault indeed seems Modesty. If he were less modest. he would be more agreable, speak louder & look Impudenter;—and is not it a fine Character of which Modesty is the only defect?—I have no doubt that he will get more lively & more like yourselves as he is more with you;—he will catch your ways if he belongs to you. And as to there being any objection from his *Goodness,* from the danger of his becoming even Evangelical, I cannot admit *that.* I am by no means convinced that we ought not all to be Evangelicals, & am at least persuaded that they who are so from Reason and Feeling, must be happiest & safest.—Do not be frightened from the connection by your Brothers having most wit. Wisdom is better than Wit, & in the long run will certainly have the laugh on her side; & don't be frightened by the idea of his acting more strictly up to the precepts of the New Testament than others.—And now, my dear Fanny, having written so much on one side of the question, I shall turn round & entreat you not to commit yourself farther, & not to think of accepting him unless you really do like him. Anything is to be preferred or endured rather than marrying without Affection; and if his deficiencies of Manner & c & c strike you more than all his good qualities, if you continue to think strongly of them, give him up at once.—Things are now in such a state, that you must resolve upon one or the other, either to allow him to go on as he has done, or whenever you are together behave with a coldness which may convince him that he has been deceiving himself.—I have no doubt of his suffering a good deal for a time, a great deal, when he feels that he must give you up;—but it is no creed of mine, as you must be well aware, that such sort of Disappointments kill anybody.—Your sending the Music was an admirable Device, it made everything easy, & I do not know how I could have accounted for the parcel otherwise; for tho' your dear Papa most conscientiously hunted about till he found me alone in the Din[g]-parlour, your Aunt C. had seen that he *had* a parcel to deliver.—As it was however, I do not think anything was suspected.—We have heard nothing fresh from Anna. I trust she is very comfortable in her new home. Her Letters have been very sensible & satisfactory, with no *parade* of happiness, which I liked them the better for.—I have often known young married Women write in a way I did not like, in that respect.

You will be glad to hear that the first Edit: of ***M. P.*** [***Mansfield Park***] is all sold.—Your Uncle Henry is rather wanting me to come to Town, to settle about a 2[d] Edit:—but as I could not very conveniently leave home now, I have written him my Will and pleasure, & unless he still urges it, shall not go.—I am very greedy & want to make the most of it;—but as you are much above caring about money, I shall not plague you with any particulars.—The pleasures of Vanity are more within your comprehension, & you will enter into

FROM THE AUTHOR

AUSTEN'S IRONIC RESPONSE TO WRITING ADVICE FROM JAMES STANIER CLARKE, LIBRARIAN TO THE PRINCE REGENT, REGARDING THE LIMITATIONS OF HER EXPERIENCE AS A WOMAN

I am quite honoured by your thinking me capable of drawing such a clergyman as you gave the sketch of in your note of Nov. 16th. But I assure you I am *not.* The comic part of the character I might be equal to, but not the good, the enthusiastic, the literary. Such a man's conversation must at times be on subjects of science and philosophy, of which I know nothing; or at least be occasionally abundant in quotations and allusions which a woman who, like me, knows only her own mother tongue, and has read very little in that, would be totally without the power of giving. A classical education, or at any rate a very extensive acquaintance with English literature, ancient and modern, appears to me quite indispensable for the person who would do any justice to your clergyman; and I think I may boast myself to be, with all possible vanity, the most unlearned and uninformed female who ever dared to be an authoress.

Austen, Jane. Letter to James Stanier Clarke of December 11, 1815. In *Jane Austen's Letters to Her Sister Cassandra and Others,* 2nd ed. Edited by R. W. Chapman, pp. 442-43. Oxford: Oxford University Press, 1932.

mine, at receiving the *praise* which every now & then comes to me, through some channel or other.

JANE AUSTEN (NOVEL DATE 1817)

SOURCE: Austen, Jane. "Chapter 8." In *Fragment of a Novel,* pp. 102-112. Oxford: Clarendon Press, 1925.

In the following excerpt from her unfinished novel Sanditon, *written in 1817, Austen directs her satire towards the type of novel popularized by Samuel Richardson—who was nonetheless among her stylistic influences.*

The two Ladies continued walking together till rejoined by the others, who as they issued from the Library were followed by a young Whitby running off with 5 vols. under his arm to Sir Edward's Gig—and Sir Edw: approaching Charlotte, said "You may perceive what has been our Occupation. My Sister wanted my Counsel in the selection of some books.—We have many leisure hours, & read a great deal.—I am no indiscriminate Novel-Reader. The mere Trash of the common Circulating Library, I hold in the highest contempt. You will never hear me advocating those puerile Emanations which detail nothing but discordant Principles incapable of Amalgamation, or those vapid tissues of ordinary Occurrences from which no useful Deductions can be drawn.—In vain may we put them into a literary Alembic;—we distil nothing which can add to Science.—You understand me I am sure?" "I am not quite certain that I do.—But if you will describe the sort of Novels which you *do* approve, I dare say it will give me a clearer idea." "Most willingly, Fair Questioner.—The Novels which I approve are such as display Human Nature with Grandeur—such as shew her in the Sublimities of intense Feeling—such as exhibit the progress of strong Passion from the first Germ of incipient Susceptibility to the utmost Energies of Reason half-dethroned,—where we see the strong spark of Woman's Captivations elicit such Fire in the Soul of Man as leads him—(though at the risk of some Aberration from the strict line of Primitive Obligations)—to hazard all, dare all, achieve all, to obtain her.—Such are the Works which I peruse with delight, & I hope I may say, with amelioration. They hold forth the most splendid Portraitures of high Conceptions, Unbounded Views, illimitable Ardour, indomptible Decision—and even when the Event is mainly anti-prosperous to the high-toned Machinations of the prime Character, the potent, pervading Hero of the Story, it leaves us full of Generous Emotions for him;—our Hearts are paralized—. T'were Pseudo-Philosophy to assert that we do not feel more enwraped by the brilliancy of his Career, than by the tranquil & morbid Virtues of any opposing Character. Our approbation of the Latter is but Eleemosynary.—These are the Novels which enlarge the primitive Capabilities of the Heart, & which it cannot impugn the Sense or be any Dereliction of the character, of the most anti-puerile Man, to be conversant with."—"If I understand you aright—said Charlotte—our taste in Novels is not at all the same." And here they were obliged to part—Miss D. being too much tired of them all, to stay any longer.—The truth was that Sir Edw: whom circumstances had confined very much to one spot had read more sentimental Novels than agreed with him. His fancy had been early caught by all the impassioned, & most exceptionable parts of Richardsons; & such Authors as have since appeared to tread in Richardson's steps, so far as Man's determined pursuit of Woman in defiance of every opposition of feeling & convenience is concerned, had since occupied the greater part of his literary hours, & formed his Character.—With a perversity of Judgement, which must be attributed to his not having by Nature a very strong head, the Graces, the Spirit, the Sagacity, & the Perseverance, of the Villain of the Story outweighed all his absurdities & all his Atrocities with Sir Edward. With him, such Conduct was Genius, Fire & Feeling.—It interested & inflamed him; & he was always more anxious for its Success & mourned over its Discomfitures with more Tenderness than c[d] ever have been contemplated by the Authors.—Though he owed many of his ideas to this sort of reading, it were unjust to say that he read nothing else, or that his Language were not formed on a more general Knowledge of modern Literature.—He read all the Essays, Letters, Tours & Criticisms of the day—& with the same ill-luck which made him derive only false Principles from Lessons of Morality, & incentives to Vice from the History of it's Overthrow, he gathered only hard words & involved sentences from the style of our most approved Writers.

GENERAL COMMENTARY

MARY LASCELLES (ESSAY DATE 1939)

SOURCE: Lascelles, Mary. "Style." In *Jane Austen and Her Art,* pp. 87-116. Oxford: Oxford University Press, 1939.

In the following excerpt, Lascelles discusses the origins and development of Austen's style.

[Austen] did not look to the novelists for direction as to style; and this was well, for the great novels of the mid-eighteenth century had too strong individuality, and their successor, the novel of sentiment, did not know its own business. It wanted, not merely a grand style for its more ambitious passages, but also an unaffected, level style for plain relation of fact and circumstance. This is Fanny Burney's notion of a matter-of-fact introductory statement:

> 'In the bosom of her respectable family resided Camilla. Nature, with a bounty the most profuse, had been lavish to her of attractions; Fortune, with a moderation yet kinder, had placed her between luxury and indigence. Her abode was the parsonage-house of Etherington. . . . The living, though not considerable, enabled its incumbent to attain every rational object of his modest and circumscribed wishes; to bestow upon a deserving wife whatever her own forbearance declined not; and to educate a lovely race of one son and three daughters, with that liberal propriety, which unites improvement for the future with present enjoyment.'[1]

Fanny Burney takes pains to be ridiculous. Her followers are often merely slovenly. Jane Austen neither strains after grandiloquence[2] nor slips into slovenliness. She practises but one grammatical irregularity which is uncomfortable to the ear now—what may be called the dislocated clause.[3] Of this I have found instances in the prose of every one of those writers who seem likely to have influenced her—as a slip; it is occasional, and usually to be found in casual writing—in Goldsmith's task-work, in Gibbon's letters. Jane Austen, however, uses it as freely as though she had never heard it condemned; and Beckford parodies it savagely as an habitual fault of style in women's novels.[4] Was it a licence which had been tacitly permitted to them? Did James and Henry Austen regard it as a fault which they would not have allowed to stand had they noticed it in their own writings, but which might be passed over in their sister's with the apology that Fielding had offered for faults of style in *David Simple*?—'. . . some small Errors, which Want of Habit in Writing chiefly occasioned, and which no Man of Learning would think worth his Censure in a Romance; nor any gentleman, in the writings of a young Woman'.[5] At all events, it may fairly be said that Jane Austen's sentences are rarely if ever ambiguous; a pronoun may sometimes go astray, but the drift of the paragraph always makes the writer's intention clear. Beckford's general satire of the novelists' style does not in fact apply to her.

To the essayists and historians, on the other hand (to adopt Henry Austen's division), his sister seems to have apprenticed herself, even in childhood. Already in ***Love and Freindship*** echoes of Goldsmith's voice are heard—echoes, at least, of some of those tones of his voice that belong to his task-work for booksellers. This summary account of Edward IV—'His best qualities were courage and beauty; his bad, a combination of all the vices'[6]—might equally well come from his *History of England* or from the pert little burlesque version of it in ***Love and Freindship,*** in which I seem to hear a tinkling echo of this very phrase: 'This Monarch [Edward IV] was famous only for his Beauty and his Courage, of which the Picture we have here given of him,[7] and his undaunted Behaviour in marrying one Woman while he was engaged to another, are sufficient proofs.'[8]

This tone of sly simplicity is not, however, audible to me in Jane Austen's later writing. The simplicity of her novels, with that other quality, slyness or shrewdness, which gives this simplicity its value, seems to belong to another tradition and, even so, to belong with a difference. The essayists of the eighteenth century had been kindly masters to the young Jane Austen; the turn of wit, the phrasing, of their lighter moods had come easily to her—and this may perhaps account for that precocious assurance in style which has half hidden her later development. Even in her childish burlesque pieces every sentence is almost as deliberately and neatly turned (on its small scale) as are those of her masters. From the lightest piece of nonsense—'Our neighbourhood was small, for it consisted only of your Mother'[9]—to the sharpest prick of satire—'I expect nothing more in my wife than my wife will find in me—Perfection'[10]—each stands firmly, its weight exactly poised. Here already is the sharp definition of ***Lady Susan,*** and here the promise which ***Pride and Prejudice*** was to fulfil. 'Next to being married,' Mr. Bennet says to Elizabeth, when he hears of Jane's cross fortunes, 'a girl likes to be crossed in love a little now and then. It is something to think of, and gives her a sort of distinction among her companions. When is your turn to come? You will hardly bear to be long outdone by Jane. Now is your time. Here are officers enough at Meryton to disappoint all the young ladies in the country. Let Wickham be *your* man. He is a pleasant fellow, and would jilt you creditably.'

'Thank you, Sir, but a less agreeable man would satisfy me. We must not all expect Jane's good fortune.'[11] This, like many other passages in Jane Austen's novels, tingles with a rhythm which stage comedy[12] could never quite forget, though it might sound but faintly for a generation at a time—rhythm which is justified (as prose rhythm needs to be) by excitement. Instant perception of the absurd charges word and phrase with all the forces which in ordinary talk are dissipated, giving an impression of speed and simplicity not alien from the temper of verse. Such an impression must be elusive; no reader can vouch for more than his own experience. To me this rhythm seems audible in every one of Jane Austen's novels—even where I should least expect it, where no pulse of bodily well-being keeps time with it, in ***Sanditon.*** For it is appropriated by no one kind of comic dialogue. It tingles in the wit of Mr. Bennet—'Wickham's a fool, if he takes her with a farthing less than ten thousand pounds. I should be sorry to think so ill of him, in the very beginning of our relationship.'[13] It is perceptible in the shrewd or droll saying that may be occasionally allowed to 'plain matter-of-fact people, who seldom aim at wit of any kind'—'And very nice young ladies they both are; I hardly know one from the other.'[14] And yet it is not out of place in the merely absurd talk of fools. '*We*', Mr. Parker assures his wife, when she envies their more sheltered neighbours, 'have all the Grandeur of the Storm, with less real danger, because the Wind meeting with nothing to oppose or confine it around our House, simply rages & passes on.'[15] For it is their creator's delight in absurdity that vibrates in their talk. But if Jane Austen learnt from the dramatists the turn of phrase proper to comedy she learnt also, in writing ***Pride and Prejudice,*** how to differentiate her dialogue from that sort she would associate with the stage; how to make it more reflective on the one hand, more inconsequent on the other, according to the bent of the speaker. And what she learnt from the essayists she likewise transmuted to her own use; that, indeed, is the way in which they were good masters, and she an apt pupil—they taught her to make something of her own. Lady Middleton and Mrs. Dashwood 'sympathised with each other in an insipid propriety of demeanour, and a general want of understanding'.[16] That might come from one of the early periodical essays. It has the formality, the preponderance of general and abstract terms, which seems to have repelled Mrs. Meynell[17]—but which we are less likely to take amiss. To us Jane Austen appears like one who inherits a prosperous and well-ordered estate—the heritage of a prose style in which neither generalization nor abstraction need signify vagueness, because there was close enough agreement as to the scope and significance of such terms.[18] Character and motive, for example, might be presented in them—a practice best illustrated, and very likely familiar to Jane Austen herself, in the *Lives of the Poets.* 'His mind was not very comprehensive, nor his curiosity active; he had no value for those parts of knowledge which he had not himself cultivated.'[19] This, surely, and countless passages like it, represent the school in which she trained herself. Lady Russell forms and expresses her judgement on Mr. Elliot in these terms: 'Every thing united in him; good understanding, correct opinions, knowledge of the world, and a warm heart . . . He was steady, observant, moderate, candid'; he possessed 'sensibility', and 'a value for all the felicities of domestic life'[20]—and so on. Here, of course, the ear catches an inflexion of irony in the use of such exact and emphatic terms for a misapprehension; but that implies no dissatisfaction with the terms themselves. They are used to express the opinions on their fellow characters of all the *reflective* heroines (Catherine being a child, and Emma, as she calls herself, an 'imaginist'): for Elizabeth Bennet's criticism of her father's 'ill-judged . . . direction of talents . . . which rightly used, might at least have preserved the respectability of his daughters, even if incapable of enlarging the mind of his wife';[21] for the shrewd observations of Elinor Dashwood and Charlotte Heywood; even for Anne Elliot's gentler judgements. But, more and more freely, they are combined with other kinds of expression in that interplay of formal and colloquial, abstract and concrete, general and particular, to whose interaction are due the firmness and suppleness of the style in which the great prose writers of the eighteenth century could address the Common Reader. Fanny Price, eager to find in her own shortcomings the reason for her mother's early neglect of her, supposed that 'she had probably alienated Love by the helplessness and fretfulness of a fearful temper, or been unreasonable in wanting a larger share than any one among so many could deserve'.[22] Sometimes there is a humorous purpose in the juxtaposition: 'They had a very fine day for Box Hill; and all the other outward circumstances of arrangement, accommodation, and punctuality, were in favour of a pleasant party. . . . Nothing was wanting but to be happy when they got there.'[23] Sometimes it marks the centre of a comic episode—as in Sir Thomas's attempt to give 'Mr. Rushworth's opinion in better words than he could find himself'—and his author's comment: 'Mr. Rushworth hardly knew what to do with so much meaning.'[24] That commonplace turn of expression—the neutral verb mobilized by the preposition—goes with the grain of the language, would not be out of place in dialogue, yet is wholly in keeping with the narrative passage to which it belongs. Scott, the only one of Jane Austen's contemporaries who has a lively appreciation of the prose tradition they inherited, is at a drawback here: the language of his narrative passages must always remain distinct from the dialogue of his Scots-speaking characters, and from the Ossianic drone by which he distinguishes his Gaelic speakers.

If Jane Austen trained herself in Johnson's school, that was not, I think, the limit of her debt to him; something more personal remains—some tones of his voice seem to be echoed in her style. An echo is too elusive to be certainly identified; but conjecture may be worth offering. I think I see in her familiarity with, and love of, his work the explanation of her aptitude for coining pregnant abstractions—such phrases as Miss Bates's *desultory good-will,* of which the sounds pursued her visitors as they mounted her stairs;[25] Mrs. Elton's *apparatus of happiness,* her large bonnet and basket;[26] and Sir Walter's advance towards his grand cousins 'with all the eagerness compatible with anxious elegance';[27] these, surely, may be called Johnsonian phrases and may fairly remind us of such passages in *The Rambler* as the description of the leisurely travellers who 'missed . . . the Pleasure of alarming Villages with the Tumult of our Passage, and of disguising our Insignificancy by the Dignity of Hurry'.[28] From Johnson she may have learnt also a liking for antithetic phrasing, coming to perceive his antitheses closing on his subject as large hands may close on a creature which must be held before it can be set free; coming to distinguish this formality as one congenial to English idiom. Anne Elliot, advising Captain Benwick, 'ventured to hope that he did not always read only poetry; and to say, that she thought it was the misfortune of poetry, to be seldom safely enjoyed by those who enjoyed it completely; and that the strong feelings which alone could estimate it truly, were the very feelings which ought to taste it but sparingly'.[29] I will suggest another small accomplishment which Jane Austen may possibly owe to 'her dear Dr. Johnson': while he has been criticized for making all the fictitious correspondents in his periodical essays address him in his own stately language, his lively mimicry of idiom in *oblique oration* has passed unnoticed. Thus Anthea, who thought nothing so elegant as a display of timidity, 'saw some Sheep, and heard the Weather clink his Bell, which she was certain was not hung upon him for nothing, and therefore no Assurances nor Intreaties should prevail upon her to go a Step farther; she was sorry to disappoint the Company, but her Life was dearer to her than Ceremony'.[30] Now Jane Austen has an aptitude, not very common among the earlier novelists, for these satirically reported conversations: Mrs. Elton on strawberries, and Lady Bertram on the ball, are probably the best-remembered; but these merely confirm impressions already made; her slighter essays in this kind are quite as shrewd, and, within small compass, create the impression in our minds of the talk of some minor character who would otherwise be silent—of Mrs. Philips with her promise of 'a little bit of hot supper',[31] or Mr. Shepherd, with his account of his chosen tenant—'quite the gentleman'.[32]

Among these elusive echoes of the tones of voice of her favourites I seem to detect one that may be worth a moment's notice. The train of possibilities begins with Richardson's realization that a parenthetical phrase, most often built upon a present participle, if introduced abruptly into the midst of a speech—that is, not qualifying the introductory 'he said' or its equivalent, but indicating change of tone or gesture as a stage-direction might do—gives the air of eyewitness to any one who reports the speech; and since, in his novels, the narrator is always, for the moment, autobiographer, that reporter is always supposed to be an eyewitness, and therefore needs this illusion. (Thus, conversations reported by Miss Harriet Byron are not seldom interrupted by the parenthesis 'Snatching my hand'.) Fanny Burney appears to perceive this advantage and follow Richardson, so long as she also lets one of the characters tell the story—that is, in Evelina's letters. (Need it be said that here, too, 'Snatching my hand' is a not infrequent parenthesis?) But it seems to be Boswell who, in his own double character of author and eyewitness reporting an affair, introduces this device into direct narration, in his *Tour to the Hebrides* and, still oftener, in his *Life of Johnson*. Thus, in Johnson's speeches occur such parenthetical phrases as: '(looking to his Lordship with an arch smile)'. Whether or no Jane Austen's ear really caught from one of these three among her favourite authors the impression of immediacy which this device is able to lend to dialogue, her frequent and apt use of it is worth remarking. Nancy Steele's tale of her sister is brought within earshot by such parentheses as '(Laughing affectedly)' and '(giggling as she spoke)',[33] and poor Miss Bates's of her niece by '(twinkling away a tear or two)';[34] while we seem indeed to see Captain Harville's attention divided between Anne and Captain Wentworth: 'There is no hurry on my side', he tells Wentworth. '"I am only ready whenever you are.—I am in very good anchorage here," (smiling at Anne) "well supplied, and want for nothing.—No hurry for a signal at all.—Well, Miss Elliot," (lowering his voice) "as I was saying, we shall never agree I suppose upon this point."'[35]

Evidence as to Jane Austen's *dislikes* in word or phrase is less elusive, for it consists not only in her avoidance of such habits of expression but also in her ridicule of them in her burlesque writings, and in her warnings to Anna against them. Any close observer of her ways must have noticed that she is, so to speak, *shy* of figurative language, using it as little as possible, and least of all in her gravest passages. I do not think it extravagant to find some suggestion of the amusement and discomfort which idle use of figurative expressions caused her in this small quip to Cassandra: 'He . . . poor man! is so totally deaf that they say he could not hear a cannon, were it fired close to him; having no cannon at hand to make the experiment, I took it for granted, and talked to him a little with my fingers. . . .'[36] For this use of stale, unmeaning figures of speech is a common mark of insincerity in her disagreeable people—in Mrs. Elton, with her borrowed plume of poetic image, her chatter of 'Hymen's saffron robe';[37] in General Tilney, whose imagery belongs to the conventions of a heartless gallantry: '"I have many pamphlets to finish," said he to Catherine, "before I can close my eyes; and perhaps may be poring over the affairs of the nation for hours after you are asleep. Can either of us be more meetly employed? *My* eyes will be blinding for the good of others; and *yours* preparing by rest for future mischief"'[38]—a manner of speech that almost seems to excuse Catherine's suspicions; above all, in Mrs. Norris: 'Is not she a sister's child?' she asks, rhetorically, of Fanny Price; 'and could I bear to see her want, while I had a bit of bread to give her?'[39] And one sees a grotesque vision of those two—the child and the woman—confronting one another across the shining expanse of the parsonage dining-table, with a 'bit of bread' between them. But Mrs. Norris did not see that vision; she saw nothing—metaphor was to her a screen for the meaninglessness of her generous words.

I suspect that it was Jane Austen's practice of denying herself the aid of figurative language which, as much as any other of her habits of expression, repelled Charlotte Brontë, and has alienated other readers, conscious of a dissatisfaction with her style that they have not cared to analyse. What prompted her to such a denial? Did she distrust all figurative language because she was sharply aware of the aptitude of the most languid figurative expressions for persisting as a mere habit of speech, after they have lost even the feeble life they had for the imagination?—a not unreasonable distrust, so large is the element of figurative idiom in our tongue. And was she further aware that, since such language commonly carries in the first using some emotional suggestion, it cannot *fossilize* without turning into a lie? Even if this should seem a rashly conjectural explanation of her apparent distrust of all figures of speech, her evident dislike of all that are *ready made,* it is certainly worth while to notice her quick ear for all those ready-made phrases, whether figurative or no, which creep so insidiously into our habitual speech. She had always held aloof from slang:[40] 'Miss Fletcher and I were very thick', she writes to Cassandra in Steventon days, 'but I am the thinnest of the two.'[41] She makes fossil phrases the staple of Lady Bertram's accustomed style of letter-writing—'a very creditable, commonplace, amplifying style':[42] 'We shall greatly miss Edmund in our small circle', she writes to Fanny when he has gone to fetch his sick brother; 'but I trust and hope he will find the poor invalid in a less alarming state than might be apprehended . . .'[43]—a style that breaks up and dissolves under the influence of real feeling: 'He is just come, my dear Fanny, and is taken up stairs; and I am so shocked to see him, that I do not know what to do.'[44] They are a mark also of the talk of Mr. Parker—who was not 'a man of strong understanding':[45] 'Here were we, pent down in this little contracted Nook, without Air or View, only one mile and 3 q^{rs} from the noblest expanse of Ocean between the South foreland & the Land's end, & without the smallest advantage from it. You will not think I have made a bad exchange, when we reach Trafalgar House—which by the bye, I almost wish I had not named Trafalgar—for Waterloo is more the thing now.'[46] And she is at pains to emphasize this habit: 'The Growth of my Plantations is a general astonishment'[47]—*that* was substituted in revision for 'My Plantations astonish everybody by their Growth'.

What it is that disgusts in Mrs. Elton's speech is not so obvious. It is not merely the idle figurative expressions—the recluse torn reluctant from her instrument and crayons, and the rest, though they are many; nor the slang, with its uneasy pretensions, nor the wilful use of concrete and particular expressions where there is no occasion for them: 'A most pitiful business!—Selina would stare when she heard of it.'[48] It is rather a general and insidious misuse of language in the interests of an ugly smartness, which produces much the same sort of unpleasant sensation as seeing a tool misused.

Jane Austen's sharpest critical satire is aimed, however, at the contemporary novelists' peculiar phraseology—commonly a rank weed in the aftermath of a great age of fiction. Miss Clavering, who was to have collaborated with her friend Miss Ferrier, noticed it. 'I don't like those high life conversations', she says shrewdly; 'they are a sort of thing by consent handed down from generation to generation in novels, but have little or no groundwork in truth . . . [they] could at best amuse by putting one in mind of other novels not by recalling to anybody what they ever saw or heard in real life. . . .' And she is pretty severe on her friend's more ambitious writing in this kind, 'which is the style of conversation of duchesses only in novels'.[49] A conversational style handed down from one generation of novelists to another—that is a pitfall, as Jane Austen gently reminds Anna: 'I do not like a Lover's speaking in the 3^{d} person;—it is too much like the formal part of Lord Orville, & I think is not natural.'[50] She had made fun of fossilized phraseology in her earliest pieces, sometimes tilting a fragment of it gently to let the light fall on it: 'his Mother had been many years no more'.[51] Even more unobtrusively it makes its way into her early novels: 'the lenient hand of time did much for [Catherine] by insensible gradations in the course of another day.'[52] Beckford had parodied these stock phrases; but his hand had been heavy: '. . . the finer feelings of the celestial Arabella suffered a new and more terrible shock, which the lenient hand of time could alone hope to mollify. The original breaking of his collar bone, by the fall from his famous hunter, which had once so cruelly alarmed the ladies in the park, was no longer an object of material magnitude, but . . . the innumerable difficulties he might labour under, was indeed a stroke which required the utmost fortitude, and every religious consideration to combat and sustain.'[53] Where he makes nonsense, Jane Austen with a lighter touch makes something that is *almost sense*. She sees where exaggeration is not needed, where demure imitation will serve. She allows Henry Tilney to hit off the style of Mrs. Radcliffe's descriptive passages in his mock forecast of Catherine's arrival at the Abbey,[54] and of the novel of sentiment in his pretended investigation of Catherine's feelings upon the arrival of Isabella's letter.[55] She never lost her taste for mimicry, but her later novels gave her less scope for it. Her consciousness of this particular pitfall is most forcibly expressed in her watchful avoidance of it, most pointedly in that stricture on Anna's novel in which she comes nearest to severity: 'Devereux Forester's being ruined by his Vanity is extremely good; but I wish you would not let him plunge into a "vortex of Dissipation". I do not object to the Thing, but I cannot bear the expression;—it is such thorough novel slang—and so old, that I dare say Adam met with it in the first novel he opened.'[56]

Behind this explicit expression of aversion we can perceive her steady rejection of 'novel slang', and behind this consistent practice her sensitiveness to the entity of the word. Her corrections show her mind moving among words, arranging and rearranging them, until she gets them phrased to her liking; and so every one of them remains exquisitely whole, like a falling drop of water, and no two or three are allowed to run together and settle into stagnant pools.

Delicate precision, resulting from control of the tools chosen—one could almost be content to claim no more than this for Jane Austen's style, surmising that she would hardly claim as much. She might have been willing to accept Richardson's compliment to Lady Bradshaigh: 'The pen is almost as pretty an implement in a woman's fingers as a needle.'[57] She would probably have been puzzled by John Bailey's tribute: 'She wrote . . . well, because she could write well and liked it, and all the better because she did not know how well she wrote.'[58] For I think that she would have been satisfied to transfer to her style her playful boast of her own manual dexterity: 'An artist cannot do anything slovenly.'[59]

Notes

1. *Camilla,* ch. i.
2. Her rare inversions sound to me Johnsonian; that is, an unconscious reflection of her reading.
3. e.g. Lady Catherine, speaking of her daughter and Darcy, says: 'While in their cradles, we planned the union' (*Pride and Prejudice,* p. 355, ch. lvi).
4. *Modern Novel Writing* (under the pseudonym of Lady Harriet Marlow), 1796.
5. Sarah Fielding, *David Simple,* 1744 (2nd edit.)—with a preface by Henry Fielding, in which he mentions his correction of these errors. (They are seldom worse than colloquialisms or awkwardnesses.)
6. Goldsmith, *History of England* (1771), ii. 250.
7. i.e. one of Cassandra's medallions, made, perhaps, in playful imitation of those in the 1771 *History.*
8. *Love and Freindship,* p. 86; *Minor Works,* pp. 140, 141.
9. Ibid., p. 7; *Minor Works,* p. 78.
10. *Volume the First,* p. 46; *Minor Works,* p. 26.
11. *Pride and Prejudice,* pp. 137, 138, ch. xxiv.
12. J. A. was probably an habitual reader of plays.
13. *Pride and Prejudice,* p. 304, ch. xlix.
14. *Persuasion,* p. 92, ch. x.
15. *Sanditon,* p. 48; *Minor Works,* p. 381.
16. *Sense and Sensibility,* p. 229, ch. xxxiv.
17. Alice Meynell, 'The Classic Novelist' in *The Second Person Singular* (1921).
18. It is, I believe, want of realization of this element in Jane Austen's style that has made critics such as Mr. Forster find a reflection of her point of view in the thoughts of all her heroines; see *Abinger Harvest* (1936), p. 149.
19. *Life of Shenstone.*
20. *Persuasion,* pp. 146, 147, ch. xvi.
21. *Pride and Prejudice,* p. 237, ch. xlii.
22. *Mansfield Park,* p. 371, ch. xxxvii.
23. *Emma,* p. 367, ch. xliii.
24. *Mansfield Park,* p. 186, ch. xix.
25. *Emma,* p. 239, ch. xxvii. I think this is not a very common idiom in women's writings, though Mrs. Thrale learnt it from the same master.
26. Ibid., p. 358, ch. xlii.
27. *Persuasion,* p. 184, ch. xx.
28. *The Rambler,* number 142.
29. *Persuasion,* pp. 100, 101, ch. xi.
30. *The Rambler,* number 34.
31. *Pride and Prejudice,* p. 74, ch. xv.
32. *Persuasion,* p. 22, ch. iii.
33. *Sense and Sensibility,* pp. 274, 275, ch. xxxviii.
34. *Emma,* p. 378, ch. xliv.
35. *Persuasion,* p. 234, ch. xxiii.
36. *Letters,* p. 242.
37. *Emma,* p. 308, ch. xxxvi.
38. *Northanger Abbey,* p. 187, ch. xxiii.
39. *Mansfield Park,* p. 7, ch. i.
40. It is Mary Crawford's slang that persuades me she was never meant to be very agreeable.
41. *Letters,* p. 14.
42. *Mansfield Park,* p. 425, ch. xliv.
43. Ibid., p. 426, ch. xliv.
44. Ibid., p. 427, ch. xliv.
45. *Sanditon,* p. 23; *Minor Works,* p. 372.
46. Ibid., p. 44; *Minor Works,* p. 380.
47. Ibid., p. 46; *Minor Works,* p. 381.
48. *Emma,* p. 484, ch. lv. I think that Jane Austen positively disliked this idiosyncrasy—of which she gives variants to Sir Edward Denham and John Thorpe.
49. *Memoir and Correspondence of Susan Ferrier,* ed. J. A. Doyle, pp. 114-118 (letter of 10 May 1813).
50. *Letters,* pp. 387, 388. Charlotte Brontë slipped back into this awkward practice.
51. *Love and Freindship,* p. 10; *Minor Works,* p. 80.
52. *Northanger Abbey,* p. 201, ch. xxv.
53. *Modern Novel Writing,* ch. i.
54. *Northanger Abbey,* ch. xx.
55. Ibid., p. 207, ch. xxv.

56. *Letters,* p. 404.

57. *Correspondence,* ed. Barbauld (1804), vi. 120 (no date).

58. *Introductions to Jane Austen,* 1931, p. 25.

59. *Letters,* p. 30.

References

In referring to Jane Austen's six novels, I give the number of the page as it appears in Dr. Chapman's edition, followed by the number of the chapter as it would appear in any other modern edition. For her letters and other unpublished writings, I refer likewise to his editions. References to the letters are simple; those to the other writings require a little explanation. When I completed my book, Dr. Chapman had already edited (in separate volumes) practically all of Jane Austen's unpublished work other than those three note-books of juvenilia entitled *Volume the First, Second,* and *Third;* but of these we had only the *First* from his hand. *Volume the Second* had appeared (with a preface by G. K. Chesterton) under the title of its principal content, *Love and Freindship,* and it was by this name, therefore, that I referred to it, and to all that it contained. *Volume the Third* had not been printed, nor was it accessible to me in manuscript; it had therefore to be left out of my account. This latter note-book had since been edited by Dr. Chapman, who has moreover now gathered all these and some smaller pieces into a single volume of *Minor Works.* Thus, for Jane Austen's tales, fragments, and drafts, except the contents of *Volume the Second,* we have two earlier editions from his hand; differing in that the earlier records the traces of revision discernible in her manuscripts. Mindful of the diverse needs of readers possessing these different editions, I have retained my original page-reference for every passage quoted, but added another, to the *Minor Works—except* where the subject under discussion was Jane Austen's practice in revision.

For her brother's *Biographical Notice* and her nephew's *Memoir* also I refer to Dr. Chapman's editions, except in those instances where it was necessary to use the first edition of the *Memoir,* or a passage from that part of the second which his edition does not reproduce.

For other books I have, of course, referred to the first editions, except where an authoritative collected edition of the author's works seemed preferable. In references to novels, mindful of the difficulty of getting access to a first edition of many of those I cited, I have given the number not of the page but of the chapter.

In my necessarily brief account of Jane Austen's life (intended only as a foundation to the critical part of this book) I have, I hope methodically, preferred the earliest source of information, except where a later source of equal authority gave fuller detail—for example, where the *Life* was fuller that the *Memoir.*

Full Titles of References

H. Austen, *A Biographical Notice of the Author* prefixed to *Northanger Abbey and Persuasion,* 1818 (reprinted with slight alteration in Bentley's collected edition of J. A.'s novels; the version of 1818 reprinted in R. W. C.'s edition of *Northanger Abbey and Persuasion*).

J. E. Austen-Leigh, *A Memoir of Jane Austen,* 1870 (reprinted with parts of J. A.'s unfinished works, 1871; the second edition, with some of the additions, reprinted, R. W. C., 1926).

M. A. Austen-Leigh, *Personal Aspects of Jane Austen,* 1920.

R. A. Austen-Leigh and W. Austen-Leigh, *Jane Austen: Her Life and Letters,* 1913.

A. C. Bradley, 'Jane Austen,' in *Essays and Studies by Members of the English Association,* 1911.

E. M. Forster, *Aspects of the Novel,* 1927.

H. W. Garrod. 'Jane Austen: A Depreciation,' in *Essays by Divers Hands* (*Transactions of the Royal Society for Literature*), 1928.

C. Hill, *Jane Austen: Her Homes and Friends,* 1902.

P. Lubbock, *The Craft of Fiction,* 1921.

W. Scott, review of *Emma* in the *Quarterly Review,* vol. xiv (for 1815; appeared 1816).

Virginia Woolf, *The Common Reader,* 1925.

MARGARET KIRKHAM (ESSAY DATE 1983)

SOURCE: Kirkham, Margaret. "Allusion, Irony and Feminism in the Austen Novel." In *Jane Austen, Feminism, and Fiction,* pp. 81-98. Brighton, England: Harvester Press Limited, 1983.

In the following essay, Kirkham asserts that Austen's novels are both comic and feminist.

Comedy and the Austen Heroines: The Early Novels

F. R. Leavis placed Jane Austen as the inaugurator of the 'great tradition' of English nineteenth-century fiction. But she is unlike the later novelists of this tradition in that she writes *comedies,* that is, her novels preserve, and call attention to, certain formal features proper to comedy in its theatrical sense, and this is used to distance what is represented from life itself, even though character and events are made, for the most part, to look natural and probable. In George Eliot, Henry James and Joseph Conrad, the distinction between comedy and tragedy is no longer of importance, for their form of realism attempts to embrace the whole of life under a single vision. Auerbach speaks of the *comédie larmoyante* and *Sturm und Drang* as opening the way to the realism of Balzac and the naturalism of Zola, in which 'random individuals from daily life in their dependence upon historical circumstances' are made the subject of 'serious, problematic and even tragic representation'.[1] But the Austen heroine is not realistic in quite this way, for what is 'serious, problematic and dependent upon historical circumstances' about her is subsumed under the formal, comic role which she is required to play. In the Austen novels the narrator, at crucial moments, when everything has been made to look natural and probable, draws the reader's attention to the way in which character and action also fulfil the formal requirements of comedy and, in this way, directs us *not* to mistake what is represented for a straightforward imitation of life itself. Sometimes the conventions adhered to are mocked and this, as Lloyd W. Brown has shown, is especially true of the 'happy endings'.[2]

Some critics with a social conscience, including feminist ones, have found the Austen novels complacent in their optimism, but Jane Austen's vision does not seem complacent or superficial if we take the formal comic features of her novels seriously, as part of their total meaning. The comic vision is partial, but it need not be untruthful provided it is not mistaken for more than it is. Jane Austen puts pressure on the limits of comedy, but she does not seek to break down the distinction between tragedy and comedy, only to enlarge the scope of comedy in prose fiction, by making it capable of embodying a serious criticism of contemporary manners and morals *and of contemporary literature*. As a feminist moralist, Jane Austen criticises sexist pride and prejudice as embedded in the laws and customs of her age, but she was also a critic of the same faults in literature itself. Her interest in the conventions of art is not a means of escaping from her central moral interest, but a way of showing, through drawing attention to them, that they must be questioned critically if true understanding is to be achieved. As her work developed she became more, not less, aware of literary form as in need of the conscious critical attention of the discerning reader. In her later novels she relies upon a greater awareness of contemporary conventions and their accustomed meanings than the modern reader always possesses, and this has led to the belief that she became more conservative in her outlook, whereas she became more radical and more subtle, demanding more in the way of intelligent, critical co-operation in the reader.

The full strength of Austen's feminist criticism of life and literature, and the consistency with which she went on developing new ways of making it, does not appear unless one takes account of literary and theatrical irony as controlling the total meaning of the major late novels, ***Mansfield Park*** and ***Emma***, as well as of the earlier ones. Part Three of this study is mainly about allusion, irony and feminism in these two novels but, before discussing that, a little more needs to be said about the character of the Austen comedy, and the way in which it accommodates both an ideal vision—the *idyllic* element which Lionel Trilling[3] saw in it—together with forceful and sometimes *subversive* (to use D. W. Harding's[4] word) criticism of life and letters as they actually were.

FROM THE AUTHOR

AUSTEN GIVES THE OUTLINE FOR A NOVEL PARODYING THE UNREALISTIC CONVENTIONS OF THE POPULAR ROMANCES OF THE TIME

Early in her career, in the progress of her first removal, heroine must meet with the hero—all perfection, of course, and only prevented from paying his addresses to her by some excess of refinement. Wherever she goes somebody falls in love with her, and she receives repeated offers of marriage, which she always refers wholly to her father, exceedingly angry that *he* should not be first applied to. Often carried away by the anti-hero, but rescued either by her father or the hero. Often reduced to support herself and her father by her talents, and work for her bread; continually cheated and defrauded of her hire; worn down to a skeleton, and now and then starved to death. At last, hunted out of civilized society, denied the poor shelter of the humblest cottage, they are compelled to retreat into Kamschatka, where the poor father, quite worn down, finding his end approaching, throws himself on the ground, and, after four or five hours of tender advice and parental admonition to his miserable child, expires in a fine burst of literary enthusiasm, intermingled with invectives against holders of tithes. Heroine inconsolable for some time, but afterwards crawls back towards her former country, having at least twenty narrow escapes of falling into the hands of anti-hero; and at last, in the very nick of time, turning a corner to avoid him, runs into the arms of the hero himself, who, having just shaken off the scruples which fettered him before, was at the very moment setting off in pursuit of her. The tenderest and completest *éclaircissement* takes place, and they are happily united.

Austen, Jane. Excerpt from *Plan of a Novel*. In *Sanditon, The Watsons, Lady Susan, and Other Miscellanea*, p. 5. London: Dent, 1934, 1979.

Jane Austen is the major comic artist in English of the age we call 'Romantic', her scepticism about Romanticism being largely a product of her feminism, but, in her confidence that the comic vision remained capable of bringing enlightenment, and of reaching towards the ideal, she is the representative of that true comic spirit which the Romantics admired in Shakespeare, and which Shelley thought lost in a corrupt age, like that in which he and Jane Austen lived. Where 'the calculating principle' predominates, he tells us, in *A Defence of Poetry,*

> Comedy loses its ideal universality: wit succeeds to humour; we laugh from self-complacency and triumph, instead of pleasure; malignity, sarcasm and contempt succeed to sympathetic merriment; we hardly laugh, but we smile.

There is, in the Austen comedy, a great deal of wit, some sarcasm and a trace of malignity here and there (for example, in the portrayal of Aunt Norris and Sir Walter Elliot) but there is more sympathetic merriment than sarcasm, and the wit is tempered by humour. Jane Austen's comic vision includes a glimpse of something ideal and universal, together with a sharp, ironic awareness of how far short we mostly are of it, especially when 'dressed in a little brief authority'. The feminism is in the laughter, sometimes rather harsh laughter, but it is also in the visionary ideal, for Austen manages to create a few brief oases where men and women experience equal relationships with one another, and where it would appear that the idea of their being otherwise, at least for those of such superior mind as her heroes and heroines, has never been heard of.

This is not to say that the Austen heroines lead extraordinary lives, or are endowed with extraordinary genius. The difficulties they experience are not, in many instances, the same as those experienced by men, but the way they learn to solve them is what matters. Mary Wollstonecraft, arguing that 'for man and woman . . . truth must be the same', says:

> Women, I allow, may have different duties to fulfil; but they are *human* duties, and the principles that should regulate the discharge of them, I sturdily maintain, must be the same.[5]

That is the central moral principle developed in the Austen novels and, though it goes against Rousseau and Richardson, it does not go against the author's Butlerian, secularised Christianity. Gilbert Ryle, observing that Jane Austen's

> heroines face their moral difficulties and solve their moral problems without recourse to religious faith or theological doctrines. Nor does it ever occur to them to seek the counsels of a clergyman,

suggests that Austen 'draws a curtain between her Sunday thoughts, whatever they were, and her creative imagination'.[6] Perhaps she did think more about revealed religion on Sundays than other days, but even so there would have been no reason for her Sunday thoughts to come into conflict with her weekday ones. The Austen heroines act as independent moral agents because that is the way in which the Creator intended those with powers of reason to act. Since the novelist wishes to show us heroines capable of learning morals through experience and the exercise of their own judgement, she does not send them off to get the advice of the few rational clergymen available in her fiction, for to do so would prevent her showing that, while the Church of England ordains such moral teachers as Mr Collins, Mr Elton and Dr Grant, the natural moral order of things allows Miss Bennet, Miss Woodhouse and Miss Price (under Providence) to do very well without them, having within themselves, as Miss Price puts it, 'a better guide . . . than any other person can be' (***Mansfield Park,*** p. 412).

Jane Austen's heroines are not self-conscious feminists, yet they are all exemplary of the first claim of Enlightenment feminism: that women share the same moral nature as men, ought to share the same moral status, and exercise the same responsibility for their own conduct. As Austen's understanding of the problem of presenting heroines fit to take the place of central moral intelligence in her novels increased, so did their moral stature. It is all done, apparently without effort, as though it were perfectly natural for young women to think, to learn through what passes under their own observation, and to draw conclusions the author thinks valid from it. It looks natural, but it is done by playing with the mirror of art and producing an illusion. The illusion is both visionary and salutary, for it suggests how we might live, and criticises the way we actually live, in a world where women, however marked their abilities, are not thought of (except by a few, mostly *heroes*) as equals and 'partners in life'.

E. H. Gombrich, in his study of *Art and Illusion,* takes John Constable's *Wivenhoe Park,* painted in 1816, as an illuminating example of how what appears an unpremeditated representation of natural landscape is the outcome of lengthy testing of the painter's fresh vision against models of landscape painting in his immediate tradition. Gombrich speaks of Rousseau's assertion that Emile must copy nature and never other men's work as 'one of those programmes charged with explosive ignorance', since a greater appearance of fidelity to Nature is achieved through adaptation and adjustment of earlier models or, as he summarises it, through '*schema* and correction'. *Wivenhoe Park*

> looks so effortless and natural that we accept it as an unquestioning and unproblematic response to the beauty of the English countryside. But, for the historian there is an added attraction to this painting, he knows that this freshness of vision was won in a hard struggle.[7]

These remarks are apposite to Jane Austen as well as to Constable, for her fresh vision of how things might be in a more natural social order was arrived at in a comparable way, and her art is no more an 'unquestioning and unproblematic response' to English society than Constable's was to the English landscape. There is, however, an important difference between the painter and the novelist: Constable wished it to be thought that he drew directly from Nature and played down his debt to Cozens.[8] Austen, being less disturbed than Constable by awareness of how 'the tradition' of any art impinges upon 'the individual talent', and sometimes has to be consciously resisted, draws attention to the models or schemas employed in the formation of her distinctive, feminist vision, expecting the reader better than a 'dull elf' to see their point.

In her earlier work, Jane Austen came up against a major difficulty: the literary models which she needed to use could not, even when adjusted and corrected, be easily freed of anti-feminist bias. It came naturally to her, as her earliest writings show, to write burlesque, and two of her early novels—***Northanger Abbey*** and ***Pride and Prejudice***—develop out of well established burlesque plots. But such burlesque plots, which turn on the early folly of the heroine, make it difficult to establish her as the central moral intelligence of the novel in which she appears. An alternative model, taken from the moralistic tradition of female writing in which contrasting sister-heroines are portrayed, and utilised in ***Sense and Sensibility,*** also proved to have intractable difficulties. Austen's earlier attempts at the adjustment and correction of such schemas must be considered before going on to ***Mansfield Park*** and ***Emma.***

Sense and Sensibility

The schema used in ***Sense and Sensibility***—that of contrasted heroines, one representing female good sense and prudence, the other led into error and difficulty by impulsiveness and excesses of feeling and conduct—was to be found in many women novelists, especially those of an 'improving' tendency. In Maria Edgeworth's *Letters of Julia and Caroline* (1795) and Jane West's *A Gossip's Story* (1796) this schema is used in a straightforward, didactic way. The sensible sister judges aright all the time and eventually, partly as a result of the homilies she delivers, the imprudent sister is brought to acknowledge her faults and amend her ways. The purpose is simply to recommend prudence and self-control without emphasis upon the abilities of the heroines, which make them the proper judges of what is prudent and how self control should be exercised.

Sense and Sensibility is an early work, probably less drastically revised than ***Northanger Abbey*** or ***Pride and Prejudice,*** and Jane Austen shows some uncertainty about her own purposes in employing the schema, but she modifies it in two important ways, both of which increase the stature of her pair of heroines. She shows that both sisters have superior abilities, neither being totally lacking in either sense or sensibility, and she introduces a range of other characters against whose defects Elinor and Marianne shine.

In the first chapter, we are told that Elinor 'possessed a strength of understanding and coolness of judgement', and that 'she had an excellent heart; her disposition was affectionate, and her feelings were strong, but she knew how to govern them'. Marianne, although over-eager and immoderate, is not represented as lacking more solid powers of mind: 'She was sensible and clever.'

As the novel develops, Marianne and Elinor each begin to take on the rounded character of a single, central heroine. Elinor's response to the contrite Willoughby goes beyond what is quite appropriate in a representative of Sense. Marianne's critical self-analysis after her illness, which is induced by her own reflections and not the moralising of her sister, is too intelligent to fit a representative of Sensibility. Austen may have started off with the intention of using this type of schematic plot and characterisation much as it had been used before, merely pruning it of its tendency to encourage moralising and solemnity. But, because she creates heroines fully representative of human nature in a larger sense than the schema allows, she discovers its inadequacies. They become particularly clear in the final chapters, where Marianne's marriage to Colonel Brandon fulfils the requirements of the schematic design, but is felt as a betrayal of the developed character she has become. The schema entailed the showing up of one sister against the other, rather than the endorsements of their superior judgement in the face of prejudice and error in less sensitive and sensible people. It did not therefore permit the adequate representation of a single heroine with a good head and a sound heart.

Northanger Abbey

Northanger Abbey is developed from a schema used by Charlotte Lennox in *The Female Quixote* (1752), by Beckford in *The Elegant Enthusiast* (1796), and by Eaton Stannard Barrett in *The Heroine* (1813), which Austen was later to enjoy, and by a number of other eighteenth- and early nineteenth-century writers of burlesque. It presented particular difficulties for a feminist since, although it turned on the condemnation of romantic illusions inspired by literature, it characteristically made a heroine the victim of such delusions, and called on a hero of sense, perhaps aided by a sensible clergyman, to dispel them. ***Northanger Abbey*** follows the schema in making its heroine the subject of absurd delusions following on the reading of romantic novels, but it corrects the schema in several important ways. First, the heroine, although young and naïve, is always shown as possessing sound, healthy affections and a good deal of native common sense. Her errors, it is pretty plain, are not likely to be long-lasting, for her own abilities, with a little experience, are bound to correct them. Second, the hero, although he is also a clergyman, is not shown as always superior in his judgements. He has the sense to value novels, saying—in reply to Catherine's suggestion that 'gentlemen read better books'—'"The person, be it gentleman or lady, who had not pleasure in a good novel, must be intolerably stupid."' He knows how to admire and how to read Ann Radcliffe:

> 'I have read all Mrs. Radcliffe's works, and most of them with great pleasure. *The Mysteries of Udolpho,* when I had once begun it, I could not lay down again;—I remember finishing it in two days—my hair standing on end the whole time.'
>
> (p. 106)

And he learns to see in Catherine's unaffected character qualities which inspire true affection. But he is not without some of the affections of a clever young man as is shown in his strictures on Catherine's use of 'nice', and in his expounding of the fashionable doctrines of the 'picturesque' in chapter XIV. In both instances he is clever, rather than sensible. Third, although the heroine's delusions about General Tilney and the 'forbidden gallery' at Northanger are exposed as absurd, they lead the reader to something more substantial. Austen's handling of this episode amounts to a major criticism of assumptions associated with the schema of the burlesque novel in which a heroine learns that her romantic notions are all mistaken, and that the world of the everyday is better ordered than that of imagination. Catherine accepts the truth of things as Henry Tilney puts them to her, and is bitterly ashamed of herself for having indulged in wild fantasies about the General's conduct to his late wife but, as events show, she was not so far out as might at first appear.

Henry Tilney's account of his mother's life and death makes it clear that she did suffer greatly during her years as the General's wife and his abstract arguments, in support of the idea that English wives in the Midland counties of England are protected by better laws and more humane customs than those to be found in Mrs Radcliffe's Alps and Pyrenees, ought to raise doubts in the intelligent reader's mind, though they satisfy Catherine. Dismissing her dreadful suspicions, he says:

> 'What have you been judging from? Remember the country and the age in which we live. Remember that we are English, that we are Christians. Consult your own understanding, your own observation of what is passing around you—Does our education prepare us for such atrocities? Do our laws connive at them? Could they be perpetrated without being known, in a country where social and literary intercourse is on such a footing; where every man is surrounded by a neighbourhood of voluntary spies, and where roads and newspapers lay everything open?'
>
> (pp. 197-8)

This is a powerful rejection of the gothic fantasy of the wicked husband who secretly murders his wife, or locks her up for years on end in a turret, and Catherine, on reflection, accepts it. However things might be in Italy, Switzerland and France,

> in the central part of England there was surely some security for the existence of a wife not beloved, in the laws of the land, and the manners of the age. Murder was not tolerated, servants were not slaves, and neither poison nor sleeping potions to be procured, like rhubarb, from every druggist.
>
> (p. 200)

This can be read as a complete dismissal of Catherine's nonsense, yet there is something really evil about the General, and his wife had, in a sense, been imprisoned by her marriage to him, perhaps even brought to an early grave through unhappiness; for General Tilney is allowed by the laws of England and the manners of the age to exert near absolute power over his wife and daughter, and he does so as an irrational tyrant. What must a more experienced Catherine see in observing what passes around her? What do our marriage laws connive at? What does our education prepare us for? A wife not beloved cannot easily be murdered, but perhaps the 'laws of the land and the manners of the age' do little to protect her as an equal citizen. Servants are not slaves, but how does a wife's status differ from that of a slave? Is she not her husband's property?

In view of the General's subsequent conduct, it is clear that the correct answers to these questions are not quite so straightforward as Henry Tilney thinks. As to the matter of sleeping potions, as Austen was to show through Lady Bertram, these are scarcely needed in a country where a woman, if 'well married', may pass away thirty years half asleep on a sofa, with a lap-dog, and a tangled, useless bit of needlework, and still be reckoned a respectable wife of a respected public man.

Northanger Abbey includes some of Austen's strongest criticism of the society in which she lived, but the schema does not permit her to make the heroine herself sufficiently aware of its real defects. Ann Radcliffe's novels, which ought, according to the schema, to be exposed as foolish, are here made into something more complex: a test of the literary intelligence of the hero and heroine. Henry Tilney shows his superiority by responding to Radcliffe's powers of invention and imagination without supposing that *The Mysteries of Udolpho* is an imitation of life. Catherine also shows her responsiveness, but is required to make a childish confusion of life and art. Austen then, through her own more realistic invention, shows that there is a further truth which neither of them has quite seen. This modifies and correct the schema, but at risk of confusing readers.

15 Pride and Prejudice

Under its earlier title of *First Impressions* what was to become ***Pride and Prejudice*** was thought ready for publication as early as 1797. As its first title suggests, it must have been at that stage fairly close to a burlesque schema similar to that of ***Northanger Abbey***—a novel in which the heroine's romantic confidence in first impressions (a common article of faith in such heroines) was corrected by experience. ***Pride and Prejudice,*** as it eventually appeared in 1813, had been extensively and recently revised by the author who had already published ***Sense and Sensibility,*** and had begun to think about ***Mansfield Park.*** In its final form, therefore, it comes closer to the later work than either of the other early novels and the schema is very drastically modified. Elizabeth Bennet's role, as the heroine who puts too high a value on first impressions, can still be seen in her infatuation with Mr Wickham, and in her initial dislike of Mr Darcy, but it becomes unimportant as the novel develops. Half way through the second volume Elizabeth receives the letter from Mr Darcy in which a true account of past events is made plain to her. Once she has read it and reflected upon its contents, which she does with speed and a remarkable display of judicious critical acumen, taking due note of the interest of the writer and the quality of his language, as well as of events and conduct which she had previously misunderstood, she becomes the best informed, as well as the most intelligent character in the entire novel. Quicker and cleverer than the hero, she soon sees that he has solid virtues of head and heart which largely outweigh his tendency to solemnity and self-importance—qualities which his education and upbringing, as well as his wealth, have imposed upon a naturally affectionate heart and a critical mind. From this point onwards Elizabeth Bennet takes on the character of the later Austen heroine; she becomes the central intelligence through whose eyes and understanding events and character are mediated to the reader. Through the use of the 'indirect free style' of narration, Elizabeth's powers of rational reflection, as well as her personal point of view, are made plain.

None of the Austen heroines is more attractive than Elizabeth Bennet, none more clearly possessed of intelligence and warm affections, but as she develops she effectively destroys the role she is supposed to play. The result is that she begins to look too much like a heroine without a part, a real-life character, not a creature in print, and this will not do, for her extreme, and improbable, good luck in marriage is acceptable only if it is properly distanced from life by the formal requirements of plot and part. That is why Jane Austen spoke of ***Pride and Prejudice*** as 'too light and bright and sparkling', and why she developed new ways of dealing with the heroine's role, so that the plot should no longer turn on a major reversal of her beliefs or judgment. The later heroines may make mistakes, sometimes serious ones like Emma's, and their author continues to mock their absurdities, but they are conceived, from the start, as the central and most enlightened minds of the novels in which they appear. They no longer (except incidentally) miscast themselves, their difficulties arise from a miscasting imposed upon them by the society in which they live, where intelligent young women of the middle class have no role appropriate to their abilities.

In the three late novels, the main thrust of irony is against the errors of law, manners and customs, in failing to recognise women as the accountable beings they are, or ought to be; and against those forms of contemporary literature which render them 'objects of pity, bordering on contempt', by sentimentalising their weaknesses and making attractive what ought to be exposed as in need of correction. Austen's adherence to the central convictions of Enlightenment feminism becomes more marked and more forceful, and the scope of her comedy is enlarged, not by taking in a wider social spectrum, but by widening and deepening the range of allusive irony. The catalyst was the popular German dramatist, August von Kotzebue.

Kotzebue and Theatrical Allusion in Mansfield Park and Emma

> I am sure that though none of my plays will be staged in fifty years yet the poets of posterity will use my plots and more often my situations . . . Turn the play into a story and if it still grips it will live.
>
> (August von Kotzebue)[9]

Had Jane Austen not made Kotzebue's *Das Kind Der Liebe* (*Lovers' Vows*) the play-within-the-novel in ***Mansfield Park*** it is unlikely that his name would be familiar to many English readers. His importance to her later work is, however, not confined to this one novel, but plays a part in the plot of ***Emma*** and is still, though more weakly, felt in ***Persuasion.*** In the first two, Austen used his plots and situations and turned the plays into stories which still grip and still live, but perhaps not quite in the way Kotzebue hoped. Kotzebue becomes the grit which irritates Austen into the production of pearls, but her obvious scorn for his plays has not been fully understood as in line with her views as a feminist moralist to whom Kotzebue was the latest and most influential of those disciples of Rousseau, castigated by Wollstonecraft.

Kotzebue's plays enjoyed an enormous success in England from 1798 to about 1810. L. F. Thompson says that, at this time, his 'name was a household word from John O'Groats to Land's End', and his plays, 'especially *The Stranger, Pizzaro, The Birthday* and *The Natural Son [Lovers' Vows],* were represented not only in London season after season but on the boards of every market town that could boast such an ornament'.[10]

Kotzebue's great popularity, however, did not make him admired among the intelligentsia. He became a figure of controversy and was condemned by a good many writers, including Wordsworth, de Quincey, Coleridge and Scott. The chief complaint against him was that he pandered to the public love of sensational plots, created characters who did not resemble human beings as we know them to be, and, through excesses of sentimentality, aroused disgust rather than compassion. Since Kotzebue was also attacked in some right-wing periodicals on account of his revolutionary political sympathies, the view that all hostility to him was on this account has gained ground, especially in studies of Jane Austen which discover in her novels the point of view of an anti-Jacobin. But this is simplistic and hides differences which ought to be considered.

A review of *Lovers' Vows,* which appeared in Cobbett's *Porcupine and Anti-Gallican Monitor* in 1801, has been much quoted in support of the belief that Austen's contempt for this play is a mark of her political conservatism. In it, the reviewer says:

> It is the universal aim of German authors of the present day to exhibit the brightest examples of virtue among the lower classes of society; while the higher orders, by their folly and profligacy, are held up to contempt and detestation. This is fully exemplified in *Lovers' Vows.* The Cottager and his Wife are benevolent and charitable; Frederick, the hero of the piece, a common soldier, the offspring of cupidity, presents an amiable pattern of filial love; while Count Cassel, a travelled nobleman, is a caricature of every odious and contemptible vice.[11]

This view of *Lovers' Vows* is further discussed below in connection with ***Mansfield Park,*** but it ought also to be considered together with what Wordsworth had to say in the following year. In the Preface to *Lyrical Ballads,* in which he sets out his purposes in representing such examples of virtue as appear in men like Michael, Simon Lee the Huntsman, and the Leech-Gatherer, he says that such portraits as these are especially needed at a time when

> a multitude of causes, unknown to former times, are now acting with a combined force to blunt the discriminating powers of the mind, and unfitting it for all voluntary exertion to reduce it to a state of savage torpor.

Among the causes named is the 'craving for extraordinary incident' which is encouraged not only by the press, but the corruption of contemporary literature:

> The invaluable works of our elder writers, I had almost said the works of Shakespeare and Milton, are driven into neglect by frantic novels, sickly and stupid German tragedies, and deluges of idle and extravagant stories in verse.

There can be little doubt that Kotzebue was high on Wordsworth's list of those German dramatists who thus corrupted the ability of the public to think or feel adequately.

It might, of course, be said that Wordsworth, even in 1802, had strong conservative impulses and that therefore to quote him, in arguing that an objection to Kotzebue was not necessarily the mark of a reactionary, carries little weight. But even if there are signs in the Preface of the conflict between Wordsworth's 'levelling muse' and his conservatism, it must surely be difficult to deny that part of his purpose in *Lyrical Ballads* comes close to what the *Porcupine* reviewer complains of in Kotzebue. If it must be allowed that the great poet of 'humble and rustic life', in the 1802 edition of *Lyrical Ballads,* objected to Kotzebue as corrupt, we ought not to convict Jane Austen of a reactionary political motive in making him the target of her scorn, unless we can be sure that she had no other interest more obviously germane to her subject-matter and consistent with the whole development of her work.

Jane Austen must have thought little of Kotzebue and less perhaps of the public taste which clamoured for his works, on account of the extreme silliness of his plays, but she had also a feminist motive in satirising him. Here it is important to insist that, whatever later readers and critics may think of Kotzebue's sentimentalising of innocent adulteresses, or pathetic victims of 'noble' seducers, as revolutionary and liberationist, this view is not in accord with that of Enlightenment feminism. We can see why if we consider L. F. Thompson's remarks, bearing in mind what Wollstonecraft had to say about Rousseauist attitudes to women:

> Kotzebue's plays were excellently suited for a female audience. He is never guilty of an expression to which one can take exception. . . . One of Shakespeare's plays held the stage only a night or two because the cast was too exclusively male. Kotzebue gave almost undue prominence to the other sex and catered especially for their taste with his humanitarianism, his happy endings, his introduction of children and his appeal rather to the heart than to the head.[12]

This explanation of why 'Kotzebue found favour with the ladies' is surely a sufficient explanation of why he did not find favour with the Lady who first appeared in print with ***Sense and Sensibility,*** and who may have wondered, as she watched Bath audiences lapping him up (they can't have included many revolutionaries), whether men or women were really much guided by Reason or Nature, at least in their buying of theatre tickets.

Jane Austen's ability to use the most depressing evidence of folly to advantage came to the rescue. We know that she saw the first performance in Bath of Thomas Dibdin's *The Birthday* (a version of Kotzebue's *Die Versöhnung*) in 1799. It may have been the first time she had seen a Kotzebue play in the theatre at all. It must have stirred her a good deal, for fifteen years later it provided the schema against which *Emma* was constructed. We may assume that she did not share the view of the *Bath Herald and Register* (surely not a journal controlled from Paris by Jacobins) reviewer, who said:

> The pleasing spectacle of *Bluebeard* . . . was again brought forward Saturday evening last . . . preceded by Kotzebue's admirable drama of *The Birthday.* If the German author has justly drawn down censure for the immorality of his productions for the stage—this may be accepted as his *amende honorable*—it is certainly throughout unexceptionably calculated to promote the best interests of virtue and the purest principles of benevolence and, though written much in the style of Sterne, it possesses humour without a single broad Shandyism.[13]

The Birthday is about two brothers who have quarrelled over 'a garden', and been at daggers drawn about it for fifteen years. They are eventually reconciled by the heroine, Emma, the daughter of one of them, who believes (falsely as it turns out) that she can never marry because of her duty to devote herself to her irascible and stupid father. How Jane Austen used this schema in ***Emma*** is discussed below; all that I wish to establish here is that she became acquainted with Kotzebue's work almost as soon as his success in England came about, and that her opinion of it was not in accord with that of the reviewer of a respectable Bath newspaper whose circulation was maintained by its bourgeois (or better) readership, in a city never much associated with revolutionary sympathies. Her use of ironic allusion to Kotzebue in two of the new novels begun after 1812 shows how strongly she reacted to him, and also suggests, as is confirmed by other evidence, that, although the writing of ***Mansfield Park*** did not begin until 1813, the working on ideas that eventually came to fruition in the later work began much earlier under the stimulus of influences away from Steventon.

In developing her later comedy as a criticism of contemporary literature and theatre as well as life, Jane Austen made use of Shakespeare, the touchstone of truth and nature in art not only for Dr Johnson, but for the major poets of her own generation. Johnson says, in the 1765 Preface to his edition of Shakespeare:

> Other dramatists can only gain attention by hyperbolical or aggravated characters, by fabulous and unexampled excellence or depravity, as the writers of barbarous romances invigorated the reader by a giant and a dwarf; and he that should form his expectations of human affairs from the play, or from the tale, would be equally deceived. *Shakespeare* has no heroes; his scenes are occupied only by men, who act and speak as the reader thinks that he should himself have spoken or acted on the same occasion. Even where the agency is supernatural the dialogue is level with life.

Jane Austen's references to Shakespeare in ***Mansfield Park*** (chapter III of the third volume) show that she is here invoking him in such a light to contrast with Kotzebue. Coleridge also contrasts the two. In Shakespeare there is a 'signal adherence to the great law of nature, that all opposites tend to attract and temper each other'. This adherence prevents him from exaggeration of vice and virtue and from the sentimentalising of morals, in the interest of particular classes or groups:

> Keeping at all times in the high road of life, Shakespeare has no innocent adulteries, no interesting incests, no virtuous vice: he never renders that amiable which religion and reason alike teach us to detest, or clothes impurity in the garb of virtue, like Beaumont and Fletcher, the Kotzebues of the day . . . Let the morality of Shakespeare be contrasted with that of the writers of his own, or the succeeding, age, or of the present day, who boast their superiority in this respect. No one can dispute that the result of such a comparison is altogether in favour of Shakespeare . . . he inverts not the order of nature and propriety,—does not make every magistrate a drunkard or glutton, nor every poor man meek, humane, and temperate; he has no benevolent butchers, nor any sentimental rat-catchers.
>
> (*Lectures,* 1818)

Jane Austen's view, as shown in her later novels, is partly in accord with this, for she too sees Shakespeare as upholding what 'religion and reason alike' teach us about Nature and morals, and Kotzebue as distorting it by the sentimental treatment of a particular class of characters. But the class which concerns her is not that of the poor contrasted with the rich, but of women contrasted with men. What she thought about benevolent butchers and sentimental rat-catchers, the figures who, in Coleridge's rhetoric, become the representatives of 'the poor', we can only guess for she avoids dealing with them, but we can see, from her treatment of schemas derived from Kotzebue, that she thought his treatment of women, whether village girls or aristocrats, objectionable, because he does not depict them as full human beings accountable for their own actions, but as relative creatures whose highest moral function is to excite compassion in men.

Austen's criticism of Kotzebue is, above all, that he does not draw women as 'mixed characters', whereas Shakespeare, 'who has no heroes' and no heroines either, if by these we mean 'pictures of perfection', does. Kotzebue's innocent female victims may not be guilty of broad Shandyisms, but their language ought to excite disgust, for it was not fit for Englishwomen of sense. Beside it, the languages of a Portia or a Rosalind (allowing for a little coarseness, common in a less polished age) was from a pure and undefiled well, fit for Englishwomen who valued their liberty under the law of reason and nature.

Some of the most perceptive nineteenth-century critics of Austen—Whately, G. H. Lewes, Richard Simpson—found themselves comparing her with Shakespeare as a humourist and as a faithful portrayer of human nature. And it was her greatest achievement that she brought the central argument and subject matter of English feminists from Astell to Wollstonecraft under the humane influence of Shakespearian comedy, seeing in the poet of Nature an enlarged understanding of men and women which might guide her own age towards something better than Kotzebue. Of course, she also rejoiced, like Shakespeare, in human folly, and relished her own role of female-philosopher-turned-Puck—never more so, perhaps, than when she associated Mansfield Park with the truths of the woods near Athens. For ***Mansfield Park,*** in which the domestic government of an English estate is exposed as based on false principles, makes the education of Sir Thomas Bertram, Bart, MP, rather than of Miss Fanny Price, one of its central ironic themes. The benevolent, but mistaken, Patriarch lives to profit by such 'a contrast . . . as time is for ever producing between the plans and decisions of *mortals,* for their own instruction, and their neighbours' entertainment' (p. 472; my italics). The sparkle of confident, feminist intelligence was never more boldly displayed than in Austen's invocation of Puck's 'Lord what fools these mortals be', in her presentation of the august and formidable Sir Thomas, whose Northamptonshire seat cannot have been many miles distant from that of Sir Charles Grandison.

Notes

Page references to the novels of Jane Austen are to R. W. Chapman's *The Novels of Jane Austen,* Oxford, 1926, and to his *Minor Works,* Oxford, 1954. Page references to the letters are to *Jane Austen's Letters,* ed. R. W. Chapman, Oxford, 1952. Page references to Mary Wollstonecraft's *A Vindication of the Rights of Woman* are to the Penguin edition, ed. Miriam Kramnick, 1975.

1. Eric Auerbach, *Mimesis,* Princeton, 1953, p. 489.
2. Lloyd W. Brown, 'The Comic Conclusions of Jane Austen's Novels', *PMLA.,* no. 84, 1969, *passim.*
3. '*Emma* and the Legend of Jane Austen', Introduction to the Riverside edn of *Emma,* reprinted in *Emma: A Casebook,* ed. David Lodge, London, 1968, p. 154.
4. 'Regulated Hatred: An Aspect of the Work of Jane Austen', *Scrutiny,* VIII, 1940.
5. Wollstonecraft, *Vindication,* p. 139.
6. 'Jane Austen and the Moralists', *Critical Essays* [*Critical Essays on Jane Austen,* ed. B. C. Southam, London, 1968], p. 117.
7. E. H. Gombrich, *Art and Illusion,* London, 1960, p. 29.
8. ibid., p. 155.
9. Introduction to *Neue Schauspiele,* quoted by L. F. Thompson, *Kotzebue, A Survey of His Progress in England and France,* Paris, 1928, p. 47.
10. ibid., p. 55.
11. Quoted by William Reitzel, '*Mansfield Park* and *Lovers' Vows*', *R.E.S.* [*Review of English Studies*], vol. 9, no. 36, October 1933, p. 453.
12. Thompson, op. cit., p. 103.
13. *Bath Herald and Register,* 29 June 1799, quoted by Jean Freeman, *Jane Austen in Bath,* 1969, p. 15.

TITLE COMMENTARY

Emma

LIONEL TRILLING (ESSAY DATE 1965)

SOURCE: Trilling, Lionel. "Emma and the Legend of Jane Austen." In *Beyond Culture: Essays on Literature and Learning,* pp. 28-49. New York: Harcourt Brace Jovanovich, 1965.

In the following essay, Trilling argues that Emma *is the greatest of Austen's novels.*

I

It is possible to say of Jane Austen, as perhaps we can say of no other writer, that the opinions which are held of her work are almost as interesting, and almost as important to think about, as the work itself. This statement, even with the qualifying "almost," ought to be, on its face, an illegitimate one. We all know that the reader should come to the writer with no preconceptions, taking no account of any previous opinion. But this, of course, he cannot do. Every established writer exists in the aura of his legend—the accumulated opinion that we cannot help being aware of, the image of his personality that has been derived, correctly or incorrectly, from what he has written. In the case of Jane Austen, the legend is of an unusually compelling kind. Her very name is a charged one. The homely quaintness of the Christian name, the cool elegance of the surname, seem inevitably to force upon us the awareness of her sex, her celibacy, and her social class. "Charlotte Brontë" rumbles like thunder and drowns out any such special considerations. But "Jane Austen" can by now scarcely fail to imply femininity, and, at that, femininity of a particular kind and in a particular social setting. It dismays many new readers that certain of her admirers call her Jane, others Miss Austen. Either appellation suggests an unusual, and questionable, relation with this writer, a relation that does not consort with the literary emotions we respect. The new reader perceives from the first that he is not to be permitted to proceed in simple literary innocence. Jane Austen is to be for him not only a writer but an issue. There are those who love her; there are those—no doubt they are fewer but they are no less passionate—who detest her; and the new reader understands that he is being solicited to a fierce partisanship, that he is required to make no mere literary judgment but a decision about his own character and personality, and about his relation to society and all of life.

And indeed the nature of the partisanship is most intensely personal and social. The matter at issue is: What kind of people like Jane Austen? What kind of people dislike her? Sooner or later the characterization is made or implied by one side or the other, and with extreme invidiousness. It was inevitable that there should arise a third body of opinion, which holds that it is not Jane Austen herself who is to be held responsible for the faults that are attributed to her by her detractors, but rather the people who admire her for the wrong reasons and in the wrong language and thus create a false image of her. As far back as 1905

Henry James was repelled by what a more recent critic, Professor Marvin Mudrick, calls "gentle-Janeism" and he spoke of it with great acerbity. James admired Jane Austen; his artistic affinity with her is clear, and he may be thought to have shared her social preferences and preoccupations. Yet James could say of her reputation that it had risen higher than her intrinsic interest warranted: the responsibility for this, he said, lay with "the body of publishers, editors, illustrators, producers of magazines, which have found their 'dear,' our dear, everybody's dear Jane so infinitely to their material purpose."[1] In our own day, Dr. Leavis's admiration for Jane Austen is matched in intensity by his impatience with her admirers. Mr. D. W. Harding in a well-known essay[2] has told us how the accepted form of admiration of Jane Austen kept him for a long time from reading her novels, and how he was able to be at ease with them only when he discovered that they were charged with scorn of the very people who set the common tone of admiration. And Professor Mudrick, in the preface to his book on Jane Austen,[3] speaks of the bulk of the criticism of her work as being "a mere mass of cozy family adulation, self-glorif[ication] . . . and nostalgic latterday enshrinements of the gentle-hearted chronicler of Regency order." It is the intention of Professor Mudrick's book to rescue Jane Austen from coziness and nostalgia by representing her as a writer who may be admired for her literary achievement, but who is not to be loved, and of whom it is to be said that certain deficiencies of temperament account for certain deficiencies of her literary practice.

The impatience with the common admiring view of Jane Austen is not hard to understand and sympathize with, the less so because (as Mr. Harding and Professor Mudrick say) admiration seems to stimulate self-congratulation in those who give it, and to carry a reproof of the deficient sensitivity, reasonableness, and even courtesy, of those who withhold their praise. One may refuse to like almost any author and incur no other blame from his admirers than that of being wanting in taste in that one respect. But not to like Jane Austen is to put oneself under suspicion of a general personal inadequacy and even—let us face it—of a want of breeding.

This is absurd and distasteful. And yet we cannot deal with this unusual—this extravagantly personal—response to a writer simply in the way of condemnation. No doubt every myth of a literary person obscures something of the truth. But it may also express some part of the truth as well. If Jane Austen is carried outside the proper confines of literature, if she has been loved in a fashion that some temperaments must find objectionable and that a strict criticism must call illicit, the reason is perhaps to be found not only in the human weakness of her admirers, in their impulse to self-flattery, or in whatever other fault produces their deplorable tone. Perhaps a reason is also to be found in the work itself, in some unusual promise that it seems to make, in some hope that it holds out.

II

Of Jane Austen's six great novels ***Emma*** is surely the one that is most fully representative of its author. ***Pride and Prejudice*** is of course more popular. It is the one novel in the canon that "everybody" reads, the one that is most often reprinted. ***Pride and Prejudice*** deserves its popularity, but it is not a mere snobbery, an affected aversion from the general suffrage, that makes thoughtful readers of Jane Austen judge ***Emma*** to be the greater book—not the more delightful but the greater. It cannot boast the brilliant, unimpeded energy of ***Pride and Prejudice,*** but that is because the energy which it does indeed have is committed to dealing with a more resistant matter. In this it is characteristic of all three novels of Jane Austen's mature period, of which it is the second. ***Persuasion,*** the third and last, has a charm that is traditionally, and accurately, called "autumnal," and it is beyond question a beautiful book. But ***Persuasion,*** which was published posthumously and which may not have been revised to meet the author's full intention, does not have the richness and substantiality of ***Emma.*** As for ***Mansfield Park,*** the first work of the mature period, it quite matches ***Emma*** in point of substantiality, but it makes a special and disturbing case. Greatly admired in its own day—far more than ***Emma—Mansfield Park*** is now disliked by many readers who like everything else that Jane Austen wrote. They are repelled by its heroine and by all that she seems to imply of the author's moral and religious preferences at this moment of her life, for Fanny Price consciously devotes herself to virtue and piety, which she achieves by a willing submissiveness that goes against the modern grain. What is more, the author seems to be speaking out against wit and spiritedness (while not abating her ability to represent these qualities), and virtually in praise of dullness and acquiescence, and thus to be condemning her own peculiar talents. ***Mansfield Park*** is an extraordinary novel, and only Jane Austen could have achieved its profound and curious interest, but its moral tone is antipathetic to contemporary taste, and no essay I have ever written has met with so much resistance as the one in which I tried to say that it was not really a perverse and wicked book. But ***Emma,*** as richly complex as ***Mansfield Park,*** arouses no such antagonism, and the opinion that holds it to be the greatest of all Jane Austen's novels is, I believe, correct.

Professor Mudrick says that everyone has misunderstood ***Emma,*** and he may well be right, for ***Emma*** is a very difficult novel. We in our time are used to difficult books and like them. But ***Emma*** is more difficult than any of the hard books we admire. The difficulty of Proust arises from the sheer amount and complexity of his thought, the difficulty of Joyce from the brilliantly contrived devices of representation, the difficulty of Kafka from a combination of doctrine and mode of communication. With all, the difficulty is largely literal; it lessens in the degree that we attend closely to what the books say; after each sympathetic reading we are the less puzzled. But the difficulty of ***Emma*** is never overcome. We never know where to have it. If we finish it at night and think we know what it is up to, we wake the next morning to believe it is up to something quite else; it has become a different book. Reginald Farrer speaks at length of the difficulty of ***Emma*** and then goes on to compare its effect with that of ***Pride and Prejudice.*** "While twelve readings of ***Pride and Prejudice*** give you twelve periods of pleasure repeated, as many readings of ***Emma*** give you that pleasure, not repeated only, but squared and squared again with each perusal, till at every fresh reading you feel anew that you never understood anything like the widening sum of its delights."[4] This is so, and for the reason that none of the twelve readings permits us to flatter ourselves that we have fully understood what the novel is doing. The effect is extraordinary, perhaps unique. The book is like a person—not to be comprehended fully and finally by any other person. It is perhaps to the point that it is the only one of Jane Austen's novels that has for its title a person's name.

For most people who recognize the difficulty of the book, the trouble begins with Emma herself. Jane Austen was surely aware of what a complexity she was creating in Emma, and no doubt that is why she spoke of her as "a heroine whom no one will like except myself." Yet this puts it in a minimal way—the question of whether we will like or not like Emma does not encompass the actuality of the challenge her character offers. John Henry Newman stated the matter more accurately, and very charmingly, in a letter of 1837. He says that Emma is the most interesting of Jane Austen's heroines, and that he likes her. But what is striking in his remark is this sentence: "I feel kind to her whenever I think of her." This does indeed suggest the real question about Emma, whether or not we will find it in our hearts to be kind to her.

Inevitably we are attracted to her, we are drawn by her energy and style, and by the intelligence they generate. Here are some samples of her characteristic tone:

> "Never mind, Harriet, I shall not be a poor old maid; it is poverty only which makes celibacy contemptible to a generous public!"
>
> Emma was sorry; to have to pay civilities to a person she did not like through three long months!—to be always doing more than she wished and less than she ought!
>
> "I do not know whether it ought to be so, but certainly silly things do cease to be silly if they are done by sensible people in an impudent way. Wickedness is always wickedness, but folly is not always folly."
>
> "Oh! I always deserve the best treatment, because I never put up with any other. . . ."
>
> [On an occasion when Mr. Knightley comes to a dinner party in his carriage, as Emma thinks he should, and not on foot:] ". . . There is always a look of consciousness or bustle when people come in a way which they know to be beneath them. You think you carry it off very well, I dare say, but with you it is a sort of bravado, an air of affected unconcern; I always observe it whenever I meet you under these circumstances. *Now* you have nothing to try for. You are not afraid of being supposed ashamed. You are not striving to look taller than any body else. *Now* I shall really be happy to walk into the same room with you."

We cannot be slow to see what is the basis of this energy and style and intelligence. It is self-love. There is a great power of charm in self-love, although, to be sure, the charm is an ambiguous one. We resent it and resist it, yet we are drawn by it, if only it goes with a little grace or creative power. Nothing is easier to pardon than the mistakes and excesses of self-love: if we are quick to condemn them, we take pleasure in forgiving them. And with good reason, for they are the extravagance of the first of virtues, the most basic and biological of the virtues, that of self-preservation.

But we distinguish between our response to the self-love of men and the self-love of women. No woman could have won the forgiveness that has been so willingly given (after due condemnation) to the self-regard of, say, Yeats and Shaw. We understand self-love to be part of the moral life of all men; in men of genius we expect it to appear in unusual intensity and we take it to be an essential element of their power. The extraordinary thing about Emma is that she has a moral life as a man has a moral life. And she doesn't have it as a special instance, as an example of a new kind of woman, which is the way George Eliot's Dorothea Brooke has her moral life, but quite as a matter of course, as a given quality of her nature.

And perhaps that is what Jane Austen meant when she said that no one would like her heroine—and what Newman meant when he said that he felt kind to Emma whenever he thought of her. She needs kindness if she is to be accepted in all her exceptional actuality. Women in fiction only rarely have the peculiar reality of the moral life that self-love bestows. Most commonly they exist in a moonlike way, shining by the reflected moral light of men. They are "convincing" or "real" and sometimes "delightful," but they seldom exist as men exist—as genuine moral destinies. We do not take note of this; we are so used to the reflected quality that we do not observe it. It is only on the rare occasions when a female character like Emma confronts us that the difference makes us aware of the usual practice. Nor can we say that novels are deficient in realism when they present women as they do: it is the presumption of our society that women's moral life is not as men's. No change in the modern theory of the sexes, no advance in status that women have made, has yet contradicted this. The self-love that we do countenance in women is of a limited and passive kind, and we are troubled if it is as assertive as the self-love of men is permitted, and expected, to be. Not men alone, but women as well, insist on this limitation, imposing the requirement the more effectually because they are not conscious of it.

But there is Emma, given over to self-love, wholly aware of it and quite cherishing it. Mr. Knightley rebukes her for heedless conduct and says, "I leave you to your own reflections." And Emma wonderfully replies: "Can you trust me with such flatterers? Does my vain spirit ever tell me I am wrong?" She is 'Emma, never loth to be first," loving pre-eminence and praise, loving power and frank to say so.

Inevitably we are drawn to Emma. But inevitably we hold her to be deeply at fault. Her self-love leads her to be a self-deceiver. She can be unkind. She is a dreadful snob.

Her snobbery is of the first importance in her character, and it is of a special sort. The worst instance of it is very carefully chosen to put her thoroughly in the wrong. We are on her side when she mocks Mrs. Elton's vulgarity, even though we feel that so young a woman (Emma is twenty) ought not set so much store by manners and tone—Mrs. Elton, with her everlasting barouche-landau and her *"caro sposo"* and her talk of her spiritual "resources," is herself a snob in the old sense of the word, which meant a vulgar person aspiring to an inappropriate social standing. But when Emma presumes to look down on the young farmer, Robert Martin, and undertakes to keep little Harriet Smith from marrying him, she makes a truly serious mistake, a mistake of nothing less than national import.

Here it is to be observed that *Emma* is a novel that is touched—lightly but indubitably—by national feeling. Perhaps this is the result of the Prince Regent's having expressed his admiration for ***Mansfield Park*** and his willingness to have the author dedicate her next book to him: it is a circumstance which allows us to suppose that Jane Austen thought of herself, at this point in her career, as having, by reason of the success of her art, a relation to the national ethic. At any rate, there appears in ***Emma*** a tendency to conceive of a specifically English ideal of life. Knightley speaks of Frank Churchill as falling short of the demands of this ideal: "No, Emma, your amiable young man can be amiable only in French, not in English. He may be very 'aimable,' have very good manners, and be very agreeable; but he can have no English delicacy towards the feelings of other people: nothing really amiable about him." Again, in a curiously impressive moment in the book, we are given a detailed description of the countryside as seen by the party at Donwell Abbey, and this comment follows: "It was a sweet view—sweet to the eye and the mind. English verdure, English culture [agriculture, of course, is meant], English comfort, seen under a sun bright without being oppressive." This is a larger consideration than the occasion would appear to require; there seems no reason to expect this vision of "England's green and pleasant land." Or none until we note that the description of the view closes thus: ". . . and at the bottom of this bank, favourably placed and sheltered, rose the Abbey-Mill Farm, with meadows in front, and the river making a close and handsome curve around it." Abbey-Mill Farm is the property of young Robert Martin, for whom Emma has expressed a principled social contempt, and the little burst of strong feeling has the effect, among others, of pointing up the extremity of Emma's mistake.

It is often said, sometimes by way of reproach, that Jane Austen took no account in her novels of the great political events of her lifetime, nor of the great social changes that were going on in England. ". . . In Jane Austen's novels," says Arnold Hauser in his *Social History of Art,* "social reality was the soil in which characters were rooted but in no sense a problem which the novelist made any attempt to solve or interpret." The statement, true in some degree, goes too far. There is in *some* sense an interpretation of social problems in Jane Austen's contrivance of the situation of Emma and Robert Martin. The yeoman class had always held a strong position in English class feeling, and, at this time especially, only stupid or ignorant people felt privileged to look down upon it. Mr. Knightley, whose social position is one of the certainties of the book, as is his freedom from any trace of snobbery, speaks of young Martin, who is his friend, as a "gentleman farmer," and it is clear that he is on his way to being a gentleman pure and simple. And nothing was of greater importance to the English system at the time of the French Revolution that the relatively easy recruitment to the class of gentlemen. It made England unique among European nations. Here is Tocqueville's view of the matter as set forth in the course of his explanation of why England was not susceptible to revolution as France was:

> It was not merely parliamentary government, freedom of speech, and the jury system that made England so different from the rest of contemporary Europe. There was something still more distinctive and more far-reaching in its effects. England was the only country in which the caste system had been totally abolished, not merely modified. Nobility and commoners joined forces in business enterprises, entered the same professions, and—what is still more significant—intermarried. The daughter of the greatest lord in the land could marry a "new" man without the least compunction. . . .
>
> Though this curious revolution (for such in fact it was) is hidden in the mists of time, we can detect traces of it in the English language. For several centuries the word "gentleman" has had in England a quite different application from what it had when it originated. . . . A study of the connection between the history of language and history proper would certainly be revealing. Thus if we follow the mutation in time and place of the English word "gentleman" (a derivative of our *gentilhomme*), we find its connotation being steadily widened in England as the classes draw nearer to each other and intermingle. In each successive century we find it being applied to men a little lower in the social scale. Next, with the English, it crosses to America. And now in America, it is applicable to all male citizens, indiscriminately. Thus its history is the history of democracy itself.[5]

Emma's snobbery, then, is nothing less than a contravention of the best—and safest—tendency of English social life. And to make matters worse, it is a principled snobbery. "A young farmer . . . is the very last sort of person to raise my curiosity. The yeomanry are precisely the order of people with whom I feel that I can have nothing to do. A degree or two lower, and a creditable appearance might interest me; I might hope to be useful to their families in some way or other. But a farmer can need none of my help, and is therefore in one sense as much above my notice as in every other he is below it." This is carefully contrived by the author to seem as dreadful as possible; it quite staggers us, and some readers will even feel that the author goes too far in permitting Emma to make this speech.

Snobbery is the grossest fault that arises from Emma's self-love, but it is not the only fault. We must also take account of her capacity for unkindness. This can be impulsive and brutal, as in the witticism directed to Miss Bates at the picnic, which makes one of the most memorable scenes in the whole range of English fiction; or extended and systematic, as in her conspiracy with Frank Churchill to quiz Jane Fairfax. Then we know her to be a gossip, at least when she is tempted by Frank Churchill. She finds pleasure in dominating and has no compunctions about taking over the rule of Harriet Smith's life. She has been accused, on the ground of her own estimate of herself, of a want of tenderness, and she has even been said to be without sexual responsiveness.

Why, then, should anyone be kind to Emma? There are several reasons, of which one is that we come into an unusual intimacy with her. We see her in all the elaborateness of her mistakes, in all the details of her wrong conduct. The narrative technique of the novel brings us very close to her and makes us aware of each misstep she will make. The relation that develops between ourselves and her becomes a strange one—it is the relation that exists between our ideal self and our ordinary fallible self. We become Emma's helpless conscience, her unavailing guide. Her fault is the classic one of *hubris,* excessive pride, and it yields the classic result of blindness, of an inability to interpret experience to the end of perceiving reality, and we are aware of each false step, each wrong conclusion, that she will make. Our hand goes out to hold her back and set her straight, and we are distressed that it cannot reach her.

There is an intimacy anterior to this. We come close to Emma because, in a strange way, she permits us to—even invites us to—by being close to herself. When we have said that her fault is *hubris* or self-love, we must make an immediate modification, for her self-love, though it involves her in self-deception, does not lead her to the ultimate self-deception—she believes she is clever, she insists she is right, but she never says she is good. A consciousness is always at work in her, a sense of what she ought to be and do. It is not an infallible sense, anything but that, yet she does not need us, or the author, or Mr. Knightley, to tell her, for example, that she is jealous of Jane Fairfax and acts badly to her; indeed, "she never saw [Jane Fairfax] without feeling that she had injured her." She is never offended—she never takes the high self-defensive line—when once her bad conduct is made apparent to her. Her sense of her superiority leads her to the "insufferable vanity" of believing "herself in the secret of everybody's feelings" and to the "unpardonable arrogance" of "proposing to arrange everybody's destiny," yet it is an innocent vanity and an innocent arrogance which, when frustrated and exposed, do not make her bitter but only ashamed. That is why, bad as her behavior may be, we are willing to be implicated in it. It has been thought that in the portrait of Emma there is "an air of confession," that Jane Austen was taking account of "something offensive" that she and others had observed in her own earlier manner and conduct, and whether or not this is so, it suggests the quality of intimacy which the author contrives that we shall feel with the heroine.

Then, when we try to explain our feeling of kindness to Emma, we ought to remember that many of her wrong judgments and actions are directed to a very engaging end, a very right purpose. She believes in her own distinction and vividness and she wants all around her to be distinguished and vivid. It is indeed unpardonable arrogance, as she comes to see, that she should undertake to arrange Harriet Smith's destiny, that she plans to "form" Harriet, making her, as it were, the mere material or stuff of a creative act. Yet the destiny is not meanly conceived, the act is meant to be truly creative—she wants Harriet to be a distinguished and not a commonplace person, she wants nothing to be commonplace, she requires of life that it be well shaped and impressive, and alive. It is out of her insistence that the members of the picnic shall cease being dull and begin to be witty that there comes her famous insult to Miss Bates. Her requirement that life be vivid is too often expressed in terms of social deportment—she sometimes talks like a governess or a dowager—but it is, in its essence, a poet's demand.

She herself says that she lacks tenderness, although she makes the self-accusation in her odd belief that Harriet possesses this quality; Harriet is soft and "feminine," but she is not tender. Professor Mudrick associates the deficiency with Emma's being not susceptible to men. This is perhaps so; but if it is, there may be found in her apparent sexual coolness something that is impressive and right. She makes great play about the feelings and about the fineness of the feelings that one ought to have; she sets great store by literature (although she does not read the books she prescribes for herself) and makes it a condemnation of Robert Martin that he does not read novels. Yet although, like Don Quixote and Emma Bovary, her mind is shaped and deceived by fiction, she is remarkable for the actuality and truth of her sexual feelings. Inevitably she expects that Frank Churchill will fall in love with her and she with him, but others are more deceived in the outcome of this expectation than she is—it takes but little time for her to see that she does not really respond to Churchill, that her feeling for him is no more than the lively notice that an attractive and vivacious girl takes of an attractive and vivacious young man. Sentimental sexuality is not part of her nature, however much she feels it ought to be part of Harriet Smith's nature. When the right time comes, she chooses her husband wisely and seriously and eagerly.

There is, then, sufficient reason to be kind to Emma, and perhaps for nothing so much as the hope she expresses when she begins to understand her mistakes, that she will become "more acquainted with herself." And, indeed, all through the novel she has sought better acquaintance with herself, not wisely, not adequately, but assiduously. How modern a quest it is, and how thoroughy it confirms Dr. Leavis's judgment that Jane Austen is the first truly modern novelist of England. "In art," a critic has said, "the decision to be revolutionary usually counts for very little. The most radical changes have come from personalities who were conservative and even conventional . . ."[6] Jane Austen, conservative and even conventional as she was, perceived the nature of the deep psychological change which accompanied the establishment of democratic society—she was aware of the increase of the psychological burden of the individual, she understood the new necessity of conscious self-definition and self-criticism, the need to make private judgments of reality.[7] And there is no reality about which the modern person is more uncertain and more anxious than the reality of himself.

III

But the character of Emma is not the only reason for the difficulty of the novel. We must also take into account the particular genre to which the novel in some degree belongs—the pastoral idyll. It is an archaic genre which has the effect of emphasizing by contrast the brilliant modernity of Emma, and its nature may be understood through the characters of Mr. Woodhouse and Miss Bates.

These two people proved a stumbling-block to one of Jane Austen's most distinguished and devoted admirers, Sir Walter Scott. In his review of ***Emma*** in *The Quarterly Review,* Scott said that "characters of folly and simplicity, such as old Woodhouse and Miss Bates" are "apt to become tiresome in fiction as in real society." But Scott is wrong. Mr. Woodhouse and Miss Bates are remarkably interesting, even though they have been created on a system of character portrayal that is no longer supposed to have validity—they exist by reason of a single trait which they display whenever they appear. Miss Bates is possessed of continuous speech and of a perfectly free association of ideas which is quite beyond her control; once launched into utterance, it is impossible for her to stop. Mr. Woodhouse, Emma's father, has no other purpose in life than to preserve his health and equanimity, and no other subject of conversation than the means of doing so. The commonest circumstances of life present themselves to him as dangerous—to walk or to drive is to incur unwarrantable risk, to eat an egg not coddled in the prescribed way is to invite misery; nothing must ever change in his familial situation; he is appalled by the propensity of young people to marry, and to marry *strangers* at that.

Of the two "characters of folly and simplicity," Mr. Woodhouse is the more remarkable because he so entirely, so extravagantly, embodies a principle—of perfect stasis, of entire inertia. Almost in the degree that Jane Austen was interested in the ideal of personal energy, she was amused and attracted by persons capable of extreme inertness. She does not judge them harshly, as we incline to do—we who scarcely recall how important a part in Christian feeling the dream of *rest* once had. Mr. Woodhouse is a more extreme representation of inertness than Lady Bertram of ***Mansfield Park.*** To say that he represents a denial of life would not be correct. Indeed, by his fear and his movelessness, he affirms life and announces his naked unadorned wish to avoid death and harm. To life, to mere life, he sacrifices almost everything.

But if Mr. Woodhouse has a more speculative interest than Miss Bates, there is not much to choose between their achieved actuality as fictional characters. They are, as I have said, created on a system of character portrayal that we regard as primitive, but the reality of existence which fictional characters may claim does not depend only upon what they do, but also upon what others do to or about them, upon the way they are regarded and responded to. And in the community of Highbury, Miss Bates and Mr. Woodhouse are sacred. They are fools, to be sure, as everyone knows. But they are fools of a special and transcendent kind. They are innocents—of such is the kingdom of heaven. They are children, who have learned nothing of the guile of the world. And their mode of existence is the key to the nature of the world of Highbury, which is the world of the pastoral idyll. London is but sixteen miles away—Frank Churchill can ride there and back for a haircut—but the proximity of the life of London serves but to emphasize the spiritual geography of Highbury. The weather plays a great part in ***Emma***; in no other novel of Jane Austen's is the succession of the seasons, and cold and heat, of such consequence, as if to make the point which the pastoral idyll characteristically makes, that the only hardships that man ought to have to endure are meteorological. In the Forest of Arden we suffer only "the penalty of Adam, / The seasons' difference," and Amiens' song echoes the Duke's words:

> Here shall he see
> No enemy
> But winter and rough weather.

Some explicit thought of the pastoral idyll is in Jane Austen's mind, and with all the ambivalence that marks the attitude of *As You Like It* toward the dream of man's life in nature and simplicity. Mrs. Elton wants to make the strawberry party at Donwell Abbey into a *fête champêtre:* "It is to be a morning scheme, you know, Knightley; quite a simple thing. I shall wear a large bonnet, and bring one of my little baskets hanging on my arm. Here,—probably this basket with pink ribbon. Nothing can be more simple, you see. And Jane will have such another. There is to be no form or parade—a sort of gipsy party.—We are to walk about your gardens, and gather the strawberries ourselves, and sit under trees;—and whatever else you may like to provide, it is to be all out of doors—a table spread in the shade, you know. Every thing as natural and simple as possible. Is not that your idea?" To which Knightley replies: "Not quite. My idea of the simple and natural will be to have the table spread in the dining-room. The nature and the simplicity of gentlemen and ladies, with their servants and furniture, I think is best observed by meals within doors. When you are tired of eating strawberries in the garden, there will be cold meat in the house."

That the pastoral idyll should be mocked as a sentimentality by its association with Mrs. Elton, whose vulgarity in large part consists in flaunting the cheapened version of high and delicate ideals, and that Knightley should answer her as he does—this is quite in accordance with our expectation of Jane Austen's judgment. Yet it is only a few pages later that the members of the party walk out to see the view and we get that curious passage about the sweetness of the view, "sweet to the eye and to the mind." And we cannot help feeling that "English verdure, English culture, English comfort, seen under a sun bright without being oppressive" make an England seen—if but for the moment—as an idyll.

The idyll is not a genre which nowadays we are likely to understand. Or at least not in fiction, the art which we believe must always address itself to actuality. The imagination of felicity is difficult for us to exercise. We feel that it is a betrayal of our awareness of our world of pain, that it is politically inappropriate. And yet one considerable critic of literature thought otherwise. Schiller is not exactly of our time, yet he is remarkably close to us in many ways and he inhabited a world scarcely less painful than ours, and he thought that the genre of the idyll had an important bearing upon social and political ideas. As Schiller defines it, the idyll is the literary genre that "presents the idea and description of an innocent and happy humanity."[8] This implies remoteness from the "artificial refinements of fashionable society"; and to achieve this remoteness poets have commonly set their idylls in actually pastoral surroundings and in the infancy of humanity. But the limitation is merely accidental—these circumstances "do not form the object of the idyll, but are only to be regarded as the most natural means to attain this end. The end is essentially to portray man in a state of innocence, which means a state of harmony and peace with himself and the external world." And Schiller goes on to assert the political importance of the genre: "A state such as this is not merely met with before the dawn of civilization; it is also the state to which civilization aspires, as to its last end, if only it obeys a determined tendency in its progress. The idea of a similar state, and the belief in the possible reality of this state, is the only thing that can reconcile man with all the evils to which he is exposed in the path of civilization. . . ."

It is the poet's function—Schiller makes it virtually the poet's political duty—to represent the idea of innocence in a "sensuous" way, that is, to make it seem real. This he does by gathering up the elements of actual life that do partake of innocence, and that the predominant pain of life leads us to forget, and forming them into a coherent representation of the ideal.[9]

But the idyll as traditionally conceived has an aesthetic deficiency of which Schiller is quite aware. Works in this genre, he says, appeal to the heart but not to the mind. ". . . We can only seek them and love them in moments in which we need calm, and not when our faculties aspire after movement and exercise. A morbid mind will find its *cure* in them, a sound soul will not find its *food* in them. They cannot vivify, they can only soften." For the idyll excludes the idea of activity, which alone can satisfy the mind—or at least the idyll as it has been traditionally conceived makes this exclusion, but Schiller goes on to imagine a transmutation of the genre in which the characteristic calm of the idyll shall be "the calm that follows accomplishment, not the calm of indolence—the calm that comes from the equilibrium reestablished between the faculties and not from the suspending of their exercise. . . ."

It is strange that Schiller, as he projects this new and as yet unrealized idea, does not recur to what he has previously said about comedy. To the soul of the writer of tragedy he assigns the adjective "sublime," which for him implies reaching greatness by intense effort and strength of will; to the soul of the writer of comedy he assigns the adjective "beautiful," which implies the achievement of freedom by an activity which is easy and natural. "The noble task of comedy," he says, "is to produce and keep up in us this freedom of mind." Comedy and the idyll, then, would seem to have a natural affinity with each other. Schiller does not observe this, but Shakespeare knew it—the curious power and charm of *As You Like It* consists of bringing the idyll and comedy together, of making the idyll the subject of comedy, even of satire, yet without negating it. The mind teases the heart, but does not mock it. The unconditioned freedom that the idyll hypothecates is shown to be impossible, yet in the demonstration a measure of freedom is gained.

So in ***Emma*** Jane Austen contrives an idyllic world, or the closest approximation of an idyllic world that the genre of the novel will permit, and brings into contrast with it the actualities of the social world, of the modern self. In the precincts of Highbury there are no bad people, and no adverse judgments to be made. Only a modern critic, Professor Mudrick, would think to call Mr. Woodhouse an idiot and an old woman: in the novel he is called "the kind-hearted, polite old gentleman." Only Emma, with her modern consciousness, comes out with it that Miss Bates is a bore, and only Emma can give herself to the thought that Mr. Weston is *too* simple and openhearted, that he would be a "higher character" if he were not quite so friendly with everyone. It is from outside Highbury that the peculiarly modern traits of insincerity and vulgarity come, in the person of Frank Churchill and Mrs. Elton. With the exception of Emma herself, every person in Highbury lives in harmony and peace—even Mr. Elton would have been all right if Emma had let him alone!—and not merely because they are simple and undeveloped: Mr. Knightley and Mrs. Weston are no less innocent than Mr. Woodhouse and Miss Bates. If they please us and do not bore us by a perfection of manner and feeling which is at once lofty and homely, it is because we accept the assumptions of the idyllic world which they inhabit—we have been led to believe that man may actually live "in harmony and peace with himself and the external world."

The quiet of Highbury, the unperturbed spirits of Mr. Woodhouse and Miss Bates, the instructive perfection of Mr. Knightley and Mrs. Weston, constitute much of the charm of ***Emma.*** Yet the idyllic stillness of the scene and the loving celebration of what, for better or worse, is fully formed and changeless, is of course not what is decisive in the success of the novel. On the contrary, indeed: it is the idea of activity and development that is decisive. No one has put better and more eloquently what part this idea plays in Jane Austen's work than an anonymous critic writing in *The North British Review* in 1870:[10]

> Even as a unit, man is only known to [Jane Austen] in the process of his formation by social influences. She broods over his history, not over his individual soul and its secret workings, nor over the analysis of its faculties and organs. She sees him, not as a solitary being completed in himself, but only as completed in society. Again, she contemplates virtues, not as fixed quantities, or as definable qualities, but as continual struggles and conquests, as progressive states of mind, advancing by repulsing their contraries, or losing ground by being overcome. Hence again the individual mind can only be represented by her as a battlefield where contending hosts are marshalled, and where victory inclines now to one side and now to another. A character therefore unfolded itself to her, not in statuesque repose, not as a model without motion, but as a dramatic sketch, a living history, a composite force, which could only exhibit what it was by exhibiting what it did. Her favourite poet Cowper taught her,
>
> "By ceaseless action all that is subsists."

The mind as a battlefield: it does not consort with some of the views of Jane Austen that are commonly held. Yet this is indeed how she understood the mind. And her representation of battle is the truer because she could imagine the possibility of victory—she did not shrink from the idea of victory—and because she could represent harmony and peace.

The anonymous critic of *The North British Review* goes on to say a strange and startling thing—he says that the mind of Jane Austen was "saturated" with a "Platonic idea." In speaking of her ideal of "intelligent love"—the phrase is perfect—he says that it is based on the "Platonic idea that the giving and receiving of knowledge, the active formation of another's character, or the more passive growth under another's guidance, is the truest and strongest foundation of love."[11] It is an ideal that not all of us will think possible of realization and that some of us will not want to give even a theoretical assent to. Yet most of us will consent to think of it as one of the most attractive of the idyllic elements of the novel. It proposes to us the hope of victory in the battle that the mind must wage, and it speaks of the expectation of allies in the fight, of the possibility of community—not in actuality, not now, but perhaps again in the future, for do we not believe, or almost believe, that there was community in the past?

The impulse to believe that the world of Jane Austen really did exist leads to notable error. "Jane Austen's England" is the thoughtless phrase which is often made to stand for the England of the years in which our author lived, although any serious history will make it sufficiently clear that the England of her novels was not the real England, except as it gave her the license to imagine the England which we call hers. This England, especially as it is represented in ***Emma,*** is an idyll. The error of identifying it with the actual England ought always to be remarked. Yet the same sense of actuality that corrects the error should not fail to recognize the remarkable force of the ideal that leads many to make the error. To represent the possibility of controlling the personal life, of becoming acquainted with ourselves, of creating a community of "intelligent love"—this is indeed to make an extraordinary promise and hold out a rare hope. We ought not be shocked and repelled if some among us think there really was a time when such promises and hopes were realized. Nor ought we be entirely surprised if, when they speak of the person who makes such promises and holds out such hopes, they represent her as not merely a novelist, if they find it natural to deal with her as a figure of legend and myth.

Notes

1. *The Question of Our Speech; The Lesson of Balzac: Two Lectures,* 1905.
2. "Regulated Hatred: An Aspect of the Work of Jane Austen," *Scrutiny* VIII, March 1940.
3. *Jane Austen: Irony as Defense and Discovery,* 1952.
4. "Jane Austen," *Quarterly Review* 228, July 1917.
5. Alexis de Tocqueville, *The Old Regime and the French Revolution,* Anchor edition, pp. 82-83. Tocqueville should not be understood as saying that there was no class system in England but only that there was no caste system, caste differing from class in its far greater rigidity. In his sense of the great advantage that England enjoyed, as compared with France, in having no caste system, Tocqueville inclines to represent the class feelings of the English as being considerably more lenient than in fact they were. Still, the difference between caste and class and the social and political importance of the "gentleman" are as great as Tocqueville says.
6. Harold Rosenberg, "Revolution and the Idea of Beauty," *Encounter,* December 1953.
7. See Abram Kardiner, *The Psychological Frontiers of Society,* 1945, page 410. In commenting on the relatively simple society which is described in James West's *Plainville, U.S.A.,* Dr. Kardiner touches on a matter which is dear, and all too dear, to Emma's heart—speaking of social mobility in a democratic, but not classless, society, he says that the most important criterion of class is "manners," that "knowing how to behave" is the surest means of rising in the class hierarchy. Nothing is more indicative of Jane Austen's accurate awareness of the mobility of her society than her concern not so much with manners themselves as with her characters' concern with manners.
8. "On Simple and Sentimental Poetry" in *Essays Aesthetical and Philosophical,* 1875.
9. Schiller, in speaking of the effectiveness that the idyll should have, does not refer to the pastoral-idyllic element of Christianity which represents Christ as an actual shepherd.
10. Volume LXXII, April, pp. 129-152. I am grateful to Professor Joseph Duffy for having told me of this admirable study.
11. Emma's attempt to form the character of Harriet is thus a perversion of the relation of Mrs. Weston and Mr. Knightley to herself—it is a perversion, says the *North British* critic, adducing Dante's *"amoroso uso de sapienza,"* because it is without love.

Pride and Prejudice

SUSAN FRAIMAN (ESSAY DATE 1989)

SOURCE: Fraiman, Susan. "The Humiliation of Elizabeth Bennett." In *Refiguring the Father: New Feminist Readings of Patriarchy,* edited by Patricia Yaeger and Beth Kowaleski-Wallace, pp. 168-87. Carbondale: Southern Illinois University Press, 1989.

In the following essay, Fraiman views Mr. Darcy of Pride and Prejudice *as a father figure for Elizabeth Bennett and therefore reads the novel as transferring patriarchal power from one generation to the next as Elizabeth passes from her father's care to Darcy's.*

I belong to a generation of American feminist critics taught to read by Sandra Gilbert and Susan Gubar. *The Madwoman in the Attic* (1979) both focused our regard on women writers of the nineteenth century and formed in us invaluable habits of attention. It alerted us to eccentric characters, figures off to the side, to the lunatic fringe. We learned to see certain transients—required by the plot to move on before things can work out—as feminist doubles for the author as well as heroine. Bertha Mason in *Jane Eyre* and Lady Catherine de Bourgh in ***Pride and Prejudice,*** unexemplary as they are expendable, register nonetheless the screams and tantrums of Charlotte Brontë's and Jane Austen's own rage. These marginal women voice anger and defiance that split open ostensibly decorous texts.

I want, in keeping with this tradition, to stress the accents of defiance in ***Pride and Prejudice,*** but I locate these less at the edges than at the very center of the book; my argument concerns the much-admired Elizabeth Bennet and the two major men in her life, Mr. Bennet and Mr. Darcy. I read ***Pride and Prejudice*** as the ceding of Mr. Bennet's paternity to Mr. Darcy, with a consequent loss of clout for Elizabeth. Austen's novel documents the collapse of an initially enabling father into a father figure who, in keeping with his excessive social authority, tends to be rather disabling. As Elizabeth passes from Bennet to Darcy, her authorial powers wane: she goes from shaping judgments to being shaped by them. I want to look at Elizabeth's gradual devaluation, her humiliation, in terms of this double father.[1] Austen, I believe, stands back from her decline, ironizing both the onset of marriage and the father-daughter relation. She shows us a form of violence against women that is not hidden away in the attic, displaced onto some secondary figure, but downstairs in the drawing room involving the heroine herself.

Elizabeth's first father is a reclusive man and seemingly ineffectual; beside the rigid figure of ***Northanger Abbey***'s General Tilney, Mr. Bennet may well appear flimsy. But the general (his love of new gadgets notwithstanding) is an old-fashioned father whose authoritarian style was all but outmoded by the end of the eighteenth century.[2] Mr. Bennet is not really a bad father—just a modern one, in the manner of Locke's influential text on education. Smoothbrowed advocate of instruction over discipline and reason over force, he typifies the Lockean father. As Jay Fliegelman points out, however, Locke's concern "is not with circumscribing paternal authority, but with rendering it more effective by making it noncoercive."[3] Mr. Bennet, apparently benign to the point of irresponsibility, may seem to wield nothing sharper than his sarcasm. But what he actually wields is the covert power of the Lockean patriarch, all the more effective for its subtlety.

This aloof, unseen power of Mr. Bennet's suggests to me, for several reasons, the peculiar power of an author. His disposition is emphatically literary. Taking refuge from the world in his library, Mr. Bennet prefers the inner to the outer life, books to people. He asks two things only: the free use of his understanding and his room—precisely those things Virginia Woolf associates with the privilege of the male writer, the privation of the female. Most important, among women whose solace is news, he keeps the upper hand by withholding information. Mr. Bennet is a creator of suspense. In the opening scene, for example, he refuses to visit the new bachelor in town, deliberately frustrating Mrs. Bennet's expectation and desire. Actually, "he had always intended to visit him, though to the last always assuring his wife that he should not go; and till the evening after the visit was paid, she had no knowledge of it."[4] Mr. Bennet relishes the power to contain her pleasure and finally, with his dénouement, to relieve and enrapture her.

But the suspense is not over. Elizabeth's father is, even then, as stingy with physical description as some fathers are with pocket money. He controls his family by being not tight-fisted but tight-lipped, and in this he resembles Austen herself. George Lewes first noted the remarkable paucity of concrete details in Austen, her reluctance to tell us what people, their clothes, their houses or gardens look like.[5] If female readers flocked to Richardson for Pamela's meticulous descriptions of what she packed in her trunk, they must surely have been frustrated by Austen's reticence here.[6] So Mr. Bennet only follows Austen when, secretive about Bingley's person and estate, he keeps the ladies in the dark. Their curiosity is finally gratified by another, less plain-styled father, Sir William Lucas, whose report they receive "second-hand" from Lady Lucas. Much as women talk in this novel, the flow of important words (of "intelligence") is regulated largely by men. In this verbal economy, women get the trickle-down of news.

When Mr. Collins proposes to Elizabeth, Mr. Bennet again contrives to keep his audience hanging. Pretending to support his wife, he hides until the last moment his real intention of contradict-

FROM THE AUTHOR

AUSTEN EXPLAINS HER REASONS FOR KEEPING TO THE NARROW SUBJECT OF ENGLISH COUNTRY LIFE

You are very very kind in your hints as to the sort of composition which might recommend me at present, and I am fully sensible that an historical romance, founded on the House of Saxe Cobourg, might be much more to the purpose of profit or popularity than such pictures of domestic life in country villages as I deal in. But I could no more write a romance than an epic poem. I could not sit seriously down to write a serious romance under any other motive than to save my life; and if it were indispensable for me to keep it up and never relax into laughing at myself or other people, I am sure I should be hung before I had finished the first chapter. No, I must keep to my own style and go on in my own way; and though I may never succeed again in that, I am convinced that I should totally fail in any other.

Austen, Jane. Letter to James Stanier Clarke of April 1, 1816. In *Jane Austen's Letters to Her Sister Cassandra and Others,* 2nd ed. Edited by R. W. Chapman, pp. 452-58. Oxford: Oxford University Press, 1932.

ing her. After a stern prologue he continues: "An unhappy alternative is before you, Elizabeth. From this day you must be a stranger to one of your parents.—Your mother will never see you again if you do *not* marry Mr. Collins, and I will never see you again if you *do*" (112). Not only this particular manipulation but indeed the entire scene goes to show the efficacy of paternal words. Throughout his proposal, to Elizabeth's distress and our amusement, Mr. Collins completely ignores her many impassioned refusals. He discounts what she says as "merely words of course" (108); even his dim, self-mired mind perceives that a lady's word carries no definitive weight. Mr. Collins accuses Elizabeth of wishing to increase his love "by suspense, according to the usual practice of elegant females" (108). Yet creating suspense is exactly what Elizabeth, rhetorically unreliable, cannot do. She has no choice but "to apply to her father, whose negative might be uttered in such a manner as must be decisive" (109). Mr. Bennet's power resides, as I say, in his authorial prerogative: his right to have the last word.

Though Mr. Bennet uses this right to disparage and disappoint his wife, regarding his daughter he uses it rather to praise, protect, apparently to enable her. Like many heroines in women's fiction (think of Emma Woodhouse or Maggie Tulliver) Elizabeth has a special relationship to her father. She is immediately distinguished as a family member and as a character by his preference for her and hers for him. The entail notwithstanding, she is in many respects his heir. To her he bequeaths his ironic distance from the world, the habit of studying and appraising those around him, the role of social critic. In this role, father and daughter together scan Mr. Collins's letter, dismissing man and letter with a few, skeptical words. Mr. Bennet enables Elizabeth by sharing with her his authorial mandate, which is Austen's own: to frame a moral discourse and judge characters accordingly. Through her father, Elizabeth gains provisional access to certain authorial powers.

But Mr. Bennet also shares with her, illogically enough, his disdain for women; he respects Elizabeth only because she is unlike other girls. This puts his exceptional daughter in an awkward position—bonding with her father means breaking with her mother, even reneging on femaleness altogether. Elizabeth is less a daughter than a surrogate son. Like a son, by giving up the mother and giving in to the father, she reaps the spoils of maleness. We can understand her, alternatively, in terms of Freud's scheme for girls. Freud contends that girls first turn to the father because they want a penis like his. They envy, as Karen Horney explained, the social power this organ signifies under patriarchy.[7] To complete their oedipal task, however, girls must shift from wanting a penis for themselves to wanting a man who has one; ceasing to identify with the powerful father, they must accept instead their own "castration."[8] In these terms the cocky Elizabeth we first encounter is charmingly arrested in the early phase of male-identification. We can see her, then, in one of two ways: as an honorary boy who has completed his oedipal task, or as a backward, wayward girl who refuses to complete hers.

The point is, first, that whatever discursive acuity Elizabeth has derives from an alliance and identification with her father. As the Mr. Collins scene demonstrates, the force of her words is highly contingent. Elizabeth's authority is vicarious, second-hand; like a woman writing under a male pseudonym, her credibility depends on the father's signature. In addition, however enabling, Mr. Bennet is essentially ambivalent toward Elizabeth. "They have none of them much to recommend them," he says of his daughters in chapter I. "They are all silly and ignorant like other girls; but Lizzy has something more of quickness than her sisters" (5). Insisting that all of his daughters are silly and ignorant, that none of them have much to recommend them, Mr. Bennet blithely classes Elizabeth with "other girls," even as he appears to distinguish her from them. So we find, already in the opening scene, a tension between Elizabeth's "masculine" alacrity and the slow-witted "femininity" threatening to claim her. Mr. Bennet's double vision of her suggests right away the basic ambiguity of Austen's father-daughter relationship, coded not only diachronically in the Mr. Bennet-Mr. Darcy sequence, but also synchronically in Mr. Bennet's duplicity regarding Elizabeth.

For in Austen the male-bonding between father and daughter is set up to collapse. Eventually the economic reality asserts itself, the axiom of the famous first line held up to a mirror and read backward: a single woman not in possession of a good fortune must be in want of a husband. Sooner or later what Adrienne Rich calls "compulsory heterosexuality" (conspiracy of economic need and the ideology of romance) forces Elizabeth out of the library, into the ballroom, and finally up to the altar.[9] The father's business in this ritual is to give the daughter away. If Mr. Bennet is enabling up to a point, the marriage ceremony requires him to objectify his daughter and hand her over. He not only withdraws his protection and empowerment, but also gives away (reveals) her true "castrated" gender, her incapacity for action in a phallocentric society. This ceremony—posing father as giver, daughter as gift—underlies and ultimately belies the father-daughter relationship in ***Pride and Prejudice.***

So Elizabeth's gradual falling out with her father, which means forfeiting her authorial status, is built into the institution of marriage. Austen makes it quite clear that Mr. Bennet neglects Lydia, failing to protect her from ruinous male designs. Yet, is not the father's letting go of the daughter precisely what the wedding ritual requires?[10] Mr. Bennet's profligacy with Lydia is simply a starker form of his cheerful readiness to give away any and all of his daughters. "I will send a few lines by you," he tells his wife, "to assure [Bingley] of my hearty consent to his marrying which ever he chuses of the girls" (4). Exposing a pattern intrinsic to the nuptial plot, Mr. Bennet's abandonment of Lydia provides a crude paradigm for Elizabeth's milder estrangement from her father and for the literal distance between father and heroine in ***Northanger Abbey*** and ***Mansfield Park.***[11] Bennet, by retiring as Elizabeth's champion, is not ineffectual as a father, but correct.

In his discussion of marriage and the incest taboo, Lévi-Strauss proposes that the exchange of women among kin groups serves, like the exchange of money or words, to negotiate relationships among men. Women are, in effect, a kind of currency whose circulation binds and organizes male society.[12] It seems to me that ***Pride and Prejudice*** offers a similar anthropology. Here, too, marriage betrays the tie between father and daughter in favor of ties among men. I have the idea that Elizabeth's economic imperative is not the only motive for her marriage, that the fathers have an agenda of their own, involving considerations of class.

Mr. Bennet's class interest in a Bennet-Darcy match is fairly obvious and similar to Elizabeth's own. He may laugh at Mrs. Bennet's schemes, but the fact remains that a liaison to aristocracy will benefit him significantly. And in spite of his philosophic detachment, Mr. Bennet is not without a streak of pragmatism—after all, he has always intended to visit Mr. Bingley. Nor is he unimpressed by wealth and rank. He is frankly delighted that Darcy has used his money and influence to straighten out the Lydia-Wickham affair. "So much the better," he exults. "It will save me a world of trouble and economy" (377). Sounding even, for a moment, strangely like Mr. Collins, he consents to Elizabeth's marriage with little of his habitual irony. "I have given him my consent," he tells her. "He is the kind of man, indeed, to whom I should never dare refuse any thing, which he condescended to ask" (376).

Though Mr. Darcy's class interests may seem to rule against a connection to the Bennets, they too are subtly at work here. In her remarks on eighteenth-century marriage, Mary Poovey notes that Cinderella matches frequently allayed not only middle-class status anxiety, but also the financial anxiety increasingly rife among the well-born.[13] Cinderella's family may be obscure, but her share in merchant profits is attractive to a prince who is poor. Austen does not fully represent, until ***Persuasion***'s Sir Walter Elliot, the material as well as moral impoverishment of the landed class in her day. Yet as early as ***Sense and Sensibility*** (1811) she gives us Willoughby who, unsure of his aristocratic heritage, leaves Marianne for a certain Miss Grey with fifty thousand pounds. Of course in ***Pride and Prejudice*** cash flows the other way: Darcy has it and Elizabeth needs it. But a decline in aristocratic welfare is nevertheless suggested by the sickly Miss De Bourgh. It may well be the enfeeblement of his own class that encourages Darcy to look below him for a wife with greater stamina. As a figure for the ambitious bourgeoisie, Elizabeth pumps richer, more robust blood into the collapsing veins of the nobility, even as she boosts the social standing of her relatives in trade. Most important, however—to the patriarchs of both classes—she eases tensions between them. By neutralizing class antagonism, she promotes the political stability on which industrial prosperity depends.[14]

I turn, now, to the handing of Elizabeth from Bennet to Darcy, which is prefigured by a scene on the Lucas dance floor. Here Sir William Lucas stands in for Mr. Bennet, jockeying for power with Mr. Darcy, who has the upper hand. Sir William begins to despair, when suddenly he is "struck with the notion of doing a very gallant thing" (26). Laying claim to Elizabeth, he offers her up to Darcy as "a very desirable partner." Sir William understands that gift-giving can be an "idiom of competition." As anthropologist Gayle Rubin explains, there is power in creating indebtedness.[15] We imagine the three of them: Elizabeth between the two men, her hand held aloft by Lucas, Lucas eager to deposit it, Darcy "not unwilling to receive it" (26). The fathers' device here is synecdoche. Elizabeth is reduced to a *hand,* extended in friendship or hostility, the means of fraternal intercourse. Suddenly, however, Elizabeth pulls back. With startling resolution she withdraws herself from the debt nexus. Indeed, throughout much of the novel Elizabeth resists the conventional grammar of exchange. She would not only extract herself as object but, contesting the fathers' right to control the action, insert herself as subject. Saboteur, Elizabeth threatens to wreck the marriage syntax. Needless to say, this makes for one of the stormier courtships in nineteenth-century fiction.

It was, as I have noted, Lévi-Strauss who first saw marriage as a triangulated moment, a woman exchanged between two (groups of) men. Gayle Rubin went on to identify this kind of traffic, its organization of a sex-gender system, as the basis for female subordination. But the immediate model for my placing such an exchange at the heart of ***Pride and Prejudice*** is provided by Eve Sedgwick; her recent book, *Between Men,* examines the way men bond across the bodies of women in a range of English texts.[16] Her mapping of "male homosocial desire" posits, however, an essentially passive female term. It imagines a triangle that is stable and uncontested; even women who begin active and ambitious, once drawn into the space between two men, fall automatically still. What I have tried to suggest above is that Elizabeth does not readily accept a merely pivotal role. The book stretches out because she puts up a fight before acceding (and never entirely) to the fathers' homosocial plot. The site of her resistance, as well as her compromise, is language.

This brings us to Mr. Darcy—a father by virtue of his age, class, and a paternalism extending to friends and dependents alike. A man given to long letters and polysyllables, a man with an excellent library and even hand, Darcy may also be seen as an aspiring authorial figure. If Bennet sets out to create suspense, Darcy hankers to resolve it. Their relation is one of literary rivals, with Elizabeth the prize. The complication is Elizabeth's own formidable way with words. As surrogate son, father's heir, Elizabeth is herself a contender for the authorial position. Instead of rewarding Darcy for his accession, she competes with him for it. In these terms, Elizabeth's and Darcy's matching of wits is more than flirtation—it is a struggle for control of the text. There are two heated and definitive moments in this struggle: Elizabeth's refusal of Darcy's first proposal and the day after, when he delivers his letter.

Chapter II of the second volume finds Elizabeth alone at the Collins's house in Kent. Concerned sister and conscientious reader, she is studying Jane's letters. Suddenly Darcy bursts in and blurts out a proposal, more an admission of weakness than a confession of love. The chapter closes by resuming Elizabeth's internal dialogue, "the tumult of her mind" (193) after Darcy's departure. But have we, throughout this chapter, been anywhere *but* in Elizabeth's mind? By all rights this should be Darcy's scene, his say. In fact, we get relatively few of his actual words. His amatory discourse is quickly taken over by a narrator who represents the scene, renders Darcy's language, from Elizabeth's point of view: "His sense of her inferiority . . . [was] dwelt on with a warmth which . . . was very unlikely to recommend his suit" (189). The text of Darcy's proposal is completely glossed, and glossed over, by her interpretation of it. Of Elizabeth's refusal, by contrast, Austen gives us every unmediated word, a direct quotation four times as long as that permitted Darcy. This sets the pattern for what follows. Every time Darcy opens his mouth, he is superseded by a speech of greater length and vehemence. She answers his question—Why is he so rudely rejected?—with a tougher question of her own: "I might as well enquire . . . why with so evident a design of offending and insulting me, you chose to tell me that you liked me against your will, against your reason, and even against your character? Was not this some excuse for incivility, if I *was* uncivil?" (190). Conceding nothing, she accuses him at some length of everything: of breaking Jane's heart and unmaking Wickham's fortune, of earning and continually confirming her own dislike. She betters his scorn for her family by scorning him. "I have every reason in the world to think ill of you" (191), she asserts. Her language, her feelings, her judgments overwhelm his and put them to shame. They drive him to platitude, apology, and hasty retreat. This rhetorical round leaves Elizabeth clear victor.

The following day, however, she is obsessed by Darcy: "It was impossible to think of any thing else" (195). She receives his letter. As the man has crowded out all other thoughts, so now his letter crowds out all other words, monopolizing the narrative for the next seven pages. Longer than the entire preceding chapter, it completely dispels Elizabeth's inspired performance of the day before. If Darcy was not "master enough" of himself then, he regains his mastery now. He takes back his story and, in a play for literary hegemony (to be author and critic both), tells us how to read him. The letter is a defense of his judgment, its impartiality and authority. About Jane he insists: "My investigations and decisions are not usually influenced by my hopes or fears.—I did not believe her to be indifferent because I wished it;—I believed it on impartial conviction" (197). As for Wickham, the letter documents Darcy's early suspicions and the events that proved him right. It further demonstrates the power of Darcy's moral discourse over others. Bingley has "a stronger dependence on [Darcy's] judgment than on his own" (199). Georgiana, fearing her brother's disapproval, decides not to elope after all.[17]

Only after Darcy's unabridged epistle do we get Elizabeth's response to it. She reads "with an eagerness which hardly left her power of comprehension, and from impatience of knowing what the next sentence might bring, was incapable of attending to the sense of the one before her eyes" (204). Darcy's letter saps her power to comprehend, disables her attention. It addresses her as reader only to *indispose* her as reader. At first Elizabeth protests: "This must be false! This cannot be! This must be the grossest falsehood!" (204). She rushes through the letter and puts it away forever. But the text, unrelenting, demands to be taken out, read and reread. Against the broad chest of Darcy's logic, Elizabeth beats the ineffectual fists of her own. Putting down the paper, she "weighed every circumstance with what she meant to be impartiality . . . but with little success" (205). Her interruptions, procrastinations, do nothing to stop the inexorable drive of Darcy's narrative to its foregone conclusion. In what Roland Barthes might call its "processive haste," it sweeps away Elizabeth's objections and has its way with her.[18]

In its second sentence, the letter disclaims "any intention of paining" (196). It apologizes for wounding, yet proceeds all too knowingly to wound. There is indeed a disturbing insistence on its hurtfulness, a certain pleasurable recurrence to the violence of its effect. "Here again I shall give you pain" (200), the writer unhesitatingly announces. But now Darcy's determination to inflict seems matched by Elizabeth's to be afflicted. They coincide in their enthusiasm for her humiliation: "'How despicably have I acted!' she cried.—'I, who have prided myself on my discernment!—I, who have valued myself on my abilities! who have often disdained the generous candour of my sister, and gratified my vanity, in useless or blameable distrust.—How humiliating is this discovery!—Yet, how just a humiliation!'" (208). Vindicating Darcy's judgment and debasing Elizabeth's, disqualifying her interpretation of things in favor of his, the letter leaves her "depressed beyond any thing she had ever known before" (209).

This is the point, the dead center, on which the whole book turns. Darcy's botched proposal marks the nadir of his career, after which, launched by his letter, he rises up from infamy in an arc that approaches apotheosis. In the ensuing chapters he turns deus ex machina, exerting an implausible power to set everything straight—a power Mr. Bennet conspicuously lacks. It is Darcy who arranges for three lucky couples to be, each, the happiest couple in the world. Like the authorial persona of ***Northanger Abbey,*** Darcy herds us all to "perfect felicity." The nature of his unseen influence is precisely authorial. Darcy's letter proves his textual prowess. At this point he succeeds Mr. Bennet as controlling literary figure and displaces Elizabeth as her father's scion. From now on the pen, as ***Persuasion's*** Anne Elliot might say, is in his hands.

Soon after receiving Darcy's letter, Elizabeth meets up with Kitty and Lydia. Officer-crazy as ever, Lydia gushes on about Brighton and her plans to join the regiment there for its summer encampment. This first reference to Brighton unfolds into an unexpectedly earnest seduction plot that might seem more at home in a novel by Richardson or Burney. It is latent, however, in Lydia's very character, throwback to those too sentimental heroines so mercilessly parodied by Austen's juvenilia. That such a plot should surface now, seize center page and, brash as its heroine, hold the spotlight for more than seven chapters, is by no means accidental. The Lydia-Wickham imbroglio creates, for one thing, a situation before which Mr. Bennet will prove inadequate, Mr. Darcy heroic. Elizabeth first doubts her father regarding his decision to let Lydia go to Brighton, and she blames her father bitterly for the subsequent scandal. For Mr. Darcy, by contrast, the calamity is a chance to prove his nobility both of heart and of purse, his desire to rectify and his power to do so. The Lydia plot therefore accomplishes Elizabeth's separation from her father and her reattachment to another. It works a changing of the paternal guard.

By showcasing Darcy, the upstart plot that seems to delay and even briefly to replace Elizabeth's and Darcy's courtship serves actually to advance it. Yet there is another reason that Lydia's story, a classic case of seduction, moves into the foreground at this moment. It fills the curious gap between Elizabeth's first, private softening and her final, public surrender. I would argue that, at this juncture, Elizabeth's narrative is displaced onto that of her sister. Lydia's seduction registers an emotional drama—of coercion, capitulation, and lamentation—missing from but underlying Elizabeth's story proper. Of course Elizabeth is a foil for Lydia, one sister's wisdom held up to the other's folly. Yet there remains a sense in which their positions are scandalously similar. At one point, in response to Lydia's rudeness, Elizabeth admits, "However incapable of such coarseness of *expression* herself, the coarseness of the *sentiment* was little other than her own breast had formerly harbored" (220). And perhaps this is more generally the case: that Elizabeth and Lydia differ more in *style* than in substance. In other words, far from being an alternative plot, Lydia's is, albeit in cruder terms, a parallel one. Like the interpolated tales in that protonovel *Don Quixote,* Lydia's tale works less to distract from the central narrative than to distill its meaning. It does not defer Elizabeth's progress toward marriage so much as code the seduction and surrender on which her marriage relies.

We leave Elizabeth at the end of volume 2, chapter 13, completely, under Darcy's influence. "She could think only of her letter" (209). As the next chapter explains, "Mr. Darcy's letter, she was in a fair way of soon knowing by heart" (212). The unusual syntax here is succinct indication of the new order—Mr. Darcy and his text come pointedly before Elizabeth, would-be subject. The narrator continues, "When she remembered the style of his address, she was still full of indignation; but when she considered how unjustly she had condemned and upbraided him, her anger was turned against herself" (212). Elizabeth's reversal here, the introversion of her anger, is again revealing. Her initial judgment of Darcy is now recanted as unjust, its accusation redirected against herself.

When we first meet Elizabeth, daughter of a social critic resembling Austen herself, she is proud of her ability to know things deeply and to judge them knowingly. Yet by the end of the novel she claims only to be high-spirited. Sorry to have refused Darcy, she longs to be schooled by his better judgment: "By her ease and liveliness, his mind might have been softened, his manners improved, and from his judgment, information, and knowledge of the world, she must have received benefit of greater importance" (312). It should not surprise us to find, in an Austen novel, that judgment, information, and knowledge rate higher than ease and liveliness. While these are all Austen's professional virtues, the former are fundamental to her moral lexicon.[19] (Thus her impatience with Jane's dumb neutrality.) What may surprise and sadden us, however, is that a heroine who began so competent to judge should end up so critically disabled, so reliant for judgment on somebody else. Not that Elizabeth lapses into sheer Lydiacy. Just that by the closing chapters her eye is less bold, her tongue less sharp, the angularity—distinguishing her from the rest of her more comfortably curvaceous sex—less acute.

According to one critical truism, ***Pride and Prejudice*** achieves a kind of bilateral disarmament: Elizabeth gives up her prejudice, while Darcy relinquishes his pride.[20] I am arguing, however, that Darcy woos away not Elizabeth's "prejudice," but her judgment entire. While Darcy defends the impartiality of his opinion, Elizabeth confesses the partiality and thus worthlessness of hers. His representation of the world is taken to be objective, raised to the level of universality; hers is taken to be subjective—*prejudiced*—and dismissed. True, Elizabeth was wrong about Wickham. But was she really that wrong about Darcy? He may warm up a bit, and his integrity is rightly affirmed, yet the fact remains that he is hardly less arrogant than Elizabeth at first supposed. Her comment to Fitzwilliam can stand: "I do not know any body who seems more to enjoy the power of doing what he likes than Mr. Darcy" (183).

And is Darcy's own record of accuracy much better? His judgment of Jane is just as mistaken, and as partial, as Elizabeth's of Wickham. Yet his credibility remains intact. Finally admitting to having misinterpreted Jane, Darcy explains that he was corrected not by Elizabeth, but by his own subsequent observations (371). On the basis of his new appraisal he readvises the ever-pliant Bingley. His error, far from disqualifying him to judge, only qualifies him to judge again. Elizabeth's error, on the other hand, is irreparably discrediting. What happens in ***Pride and Prejudice*** is not that an essentially prejudiced character finally sees the error of her ways. Rather, a character initially presented as reliable, who gains our and Austen's respect precisely for her clear-sightedness, is ultimately represented as prejudiced. The real drama lies not in the heroine's "awakening" to her true identity, but in the text's reidentification of her.

If Elizabeth does not overcome her "prejudice," neither does Darcy abandon his pride. Early in the book Elizabeth declares, "I could easily forgive *his* pride, if he had not mortified *mine*" (20). Yet by the last volume her feelings have changed considerably: "They owed the restoration of Lydia, her character, every thing to him. Oh! how heartily did she grieve over every ungracious sensation she had ever encouraged, every saucy speech she had ever directed towards him. For herself she was humbled; but she was proud of him" (326-27). Elizabeth and Darcy begin skeptical of each other, proud of themselves, and they reach a connubial consensus that is altogether different: at last both are skeptical of her, both proud of him.

But wait. Does not Darcy make a pretty speech to his bride confessing, "By you, I was properly humbled" (369)? Here it is useful to see how the text itself defines "pride," and how this definition relates to Mr. Darcy. The bookish Mary—another figure for Austen, if a self-mocking one—distinguishes "pride" from "vanity": "Pride relates more to our opinion of ourselves, vanity to what we would have others think of us" (20). As for Darcy, Charlotte Lucas suggests that his pride is excusable: "One cannot wonder that so very fine a young man, with family, fortune, every thing in his favor, should think highly of himself. If I may so express it, he has a *right* to be proud" (20). A younger Lucas puts it more bluntly: "If I were as rich as Mr. Darcy . . . I should not care how proud I was. I would keep a pack of foxhounds, and drink a bottle of wine every day" (20). The practical Lucases have a point. Darcy's richness gives him if not a "right," then a careless readiness to be proud. A man in his social position need not consider any opinion but his own. Darcy is proud because he does not have to be vain—others' opinions do not affect him. His pride, we might say, comes with the territory. It is less a psychological attribute than a social one, and as such it is only heightened by Darcy's enhanced status—as husband, hero, and authorial figure—in ***Pride and Prejudice***'s last act.

Of course we continue to admire Elizabeth. She may care for Darcy's regard, but she is not so utterly enslaved by it as Miss Bingley. She may hesitate to laugh at Darcy, but she does show Georgiana that a wife may take (some) liberties. We admire her because she is not Charlotte, because she is not Lydia. I am insisting, however, that Elizabeth is a better friend to Charlotte, a closer sister to Lydia—that her story runs more parallel to theirs—than previous readings have indicated. The three women live in the same town, share the same gossip, attend the same balls—why, as some critics have claimed, should Elizabeth alone be above the social decree?[21] There are, in Elizabeth's marriage, elements both of crass practicality and of coercion. Elizabeth is appalled by Charlotte's pragmatism, and yet, choosing Darcy over Wickham, she is herself beguiled by the entrepreneurial marriage plot.[22] If she is embarrassed by her personal connection to Lydia, she is also implicated by the formal intersection of their plots: in the course of the novel she loses not her virginity but her authority.

Elizabeth marries a decent man and a large estate, but at a certain cost. Though she may stretch the marriage contract, it binds her nonetheless to a paternalistic noble whose extensive power is explicitly ambiguous: "How much of pleasure *or pain* it was in his power to bestow!—How much of good *or evil* must be done by him!" (250-51, emphasis added). If Mr. Bennet embodies the post-Enlightenment, modified patriarch, Mr. Darcy harks back to an earlier type—before fathers were curbed by Lockean principles, before aristocrats began to feel the crunch. Darcy disempowers Elizabeth if only because of the positions they each occupy in the social schema: because he is a Darcy and she is a Bennet, because he is a man and she is his wife. If Mr. Bennet permits Elizabeth to fill the role of "son," she marries another father figure only to revert, in terms of privilege, to "daughter."

In ***Pride and Prejudice,*** Austen shows us an intelligent girl largely in the grasp of a complex mechanism whose interests are not hers. She does this, I think, less in resignation than in protest; here, as in ***Northanger Abbey,*** Austen is concerned to ironize girls and novels that hasten to the altar for conclusive happiness.[23] I should stress, however, that my purpose in outlining a trajectory of humiliation has been not to displace but to complexify the reading that takes for granted connubial bliss. We can experience the ending as euphoric (most readers do) and still recognize those aspects of the novel working strenuously against this. I want, as Gilbert and Gubar suggest, to appreciate the doubleness that characterizes the work of nineteenth-century women writers, the tension between conventionality and subversion. This tension is, on the one hand, produced by an author who knows what she is doing, whose art is a deliberate shaping, whose ironic tendencies were manifest at fifteen. To ignore any such intentionality is to slight Austen's mastery. But the ideological slipperiness of ***Pride and Prejudice*** is, on the other hand, finally a matter of the text's own logic, its own legibility. Beyond any fully conscious intention on Austen's part, a pattern of duplicity is at work in the narrative itself, with a consistency amounting to design.

As I have argued, part of this novel's design is to reveal a system of homosocial relations underlying the institution of heterosexuality. Anticipating Claude Lévi-Strauss, Gayle Rubin, and Eve Sedgwick, it recognizes in marriage a displacement of the father-daughter bond by a bond between fathers. Elizabeth's humiliation has everything to do with transactions between various fathers that take place behind her back, over her head, and apart from, if not against, her will. I want to close by offering some further support for this view.

By the end of the book, Mr. Bennet's paternal role has been assumed by his brother-in-law, Mr. Gardiner. Mr. Gardiner, though "gentleman*like,*" is not technically a gentleman. Living by trade "and within view of his own warehouses" (139), he represents, more than Mr. Bennet, the rising middle class. No wonder Elizabeth fears that Darcy will rebuff him, unkind as Darcy has been toward her bourgeois relations. She is quite unprepared for Darcy's civility to Gardiner, and for the apparent power of fishing to overcome class differences. Perhaps their shared fondness for Elizabeth, their lengthy haggle over Lydia, as well as their equal passion for trout, serve to reinforce the social/economic advantages of a Darcy-Gardiner alliance. They become, in any case, suggestively close. The very last paragraph of the novel informs us that: "With the Gardiners, they were always on the most intimate terms. Darcy, as well as Elizabeth, really loved them; and they were both ever sensible of the warmest gratitude towards the persons who, by bringing her into Derbyshire, had been the means of uniting them" (388).

At first this seems a peculiarly insignificant note on which to end. On second glance it appears to confirm the notion I have had: that just as the Gardiners have been the means of uniting Darcy and Elizabeth, so Elizabeth has been the means of uniting Mr. Darcy and Mr. Gardiner. ***Pride and Prejudice*** attains a satisfying unity not only between a man and a woman, but also between two men. Austen's novel accomplishes an intercourse not merely personal, but social—as much a marriage of two classes as a marriage of true minds.

Notes

1. My title and my argument are a turn on Mark Schorer's "The Humiliation of Emma Woodhouse" (1959), in *Jane Austen: A Collection of Critical Essays,* ed. Ian Watt (Englewood Cliffs, N.J.: Prentice-Hall, 1963), 98-111. Here he remarks: "The diminution of Emma in the social scene, her reduction to her proper place . . . is very beautiful" (102).
2. See Lawrence Stone, *The Family, Sex and Marriage in England: 1500-1800* (New York: Harper and Row, 1977), 239-58.
3. Jay Fliegelman, *Prodigals and Pilgrims: The American Revolution Against Patriarchal Authority* (Cambridge: Cambridge University Press, 1982), 13. See Beth Kowaleski-Wallace's discussion of the Lockean father in "Milton's Daughters: The Education of Eighteenth-Century Women Writers," *Feminist Studies* 12, no. 2 (1986): 275-95.
4. Jane Austen, *Pride and Prejudice* (1813), ed. R. W. Chapman, 3rd edition (Oxford: Oxford University Press, 1932), 6. Future references are to this edition.
5. Lewes's observation is cited by Judith O'Neill in her introduction to *Critics on Jane Austen: Readings in Literary Criticism,* ed. Judith O'Neill (London: George Allen, 1970), 8.
6. See Ian Watt, *The Rise of the Novel* (Berkeley: University of California Press, 1957), 153.
7. Karen Horney, "The Flight from Womanhood: The Masculinity Complex in Women as Viewed by Men and by Women" (1926), in *Psychoanalysis and Women,* ed. Jean Baker Miller (New York: Penguin Books, 1973), 19.
8. For a useful recapitulation of Freud on fathers and daughters, see Nancy Chodorow, *The Reproduction of Mothering: Psychoanalysis and the Sociology of Gender* (Berkeley: University of California Press, 1978), 94, 114-16.
9. Adrienne Rich, "Compulsory Heterosexuality and Lesbian Existence" (1980), in *Powers of Desire: The Politics of Sexuality,* eds. Ann Snitow, Christine Stansell, and Sharon Thompson (New York: Monthly Review, 1983), 177-205.
10. See, for example, Lynda E. Boose, "The Father and the Bride in Shakespeare," *PMLA* 97, no. 3 (1982): 325-47. According to Boose, King Lear's faux pas is his unwillingness to release Cordelia—he "casts her away not to let her go but to prevent her from going" (333)—thereby obstructing the ritual process of her marriage to France.
11. In these terms, Emma's conclusion may have certain advantages for its heroine. It is true that Emma defers to Knightley's worldview much as Elizabeth does to Darcy's. But remaining under her father's roof may preserve some of the authority she has had, in his household and the community, as Mr. Woodhouse's daughter.
12. Claude Lévi-Strauss, *The Elementary Structures of Kinship* (1949) (Boston: Beacon, 1969), 61.
13. Mary Poovey, *The Proper Lady and the Woman Writer: Ideology as Style in the Works of Mary Wollstonecraft, Mary Shelley, and Jane Austen* (Chicago: University of Chicago Press, 1984), 11.
14. See Terry Eagleton, *The Rape of Clarissa: Writing, Sexuality and Class Struggle in Samuel Richardson* (Minneapolis: University of Minnesota Press, 1982), 15.
15. Gayle Rubin, "The Traffic in Women: Notes on the 'Political Economy' of Sex," in *Toward an Anthropology of Women,* ed. Rayna R. Reiter (New York: Monthly Review, 1975), 172.
16. Eve Kosofsky Sedgwick, *Between Men: English Literature and Male Homosocial Desire* (New York: Columbia University Press, 1985).
17. Georgiana's position as "daughter" in relation to Darcy contributes to our sense of him as "paternal," as does his fatherly advice to Bingley.
18. Roland Barthes, *The Pleasure of the Text,* trans. Richard Miller (New York: Hill and Wang, 1975), 12.

19. See Austen's famous defense of the novel as a "work in which the greatest powers of the mind are displayed . . . the most thorough knowledge of human nature . . . the liveliest effusions of wit and humour" (*Northanger Abbey,* 1818, ed. R. W. Chapman, 3rd edition [Oxford: Oxford University Press, 1933], 38).

20. John Halperin's recent biography, *The Life of Jane Austen* (Baltimore: Johns Hopkins University Press, 1984) is notably complacent toward this formulation: "It is unnecessary to rehearse again the process by which Darcy's pride is humbled and Elizabeth's prejudice exposed—'*your* defect is a propensity to hate every body,' she tells him early in the novel; 'And I yours . . . is wilfully to misunderstand them,' he replies" (70).

21. I have in mind D. W. Harding and Marvin Mudrick, old guard of Austen criticism's "subversive school" (as opposed to Alistair Duckworth, Marilyn Butler, et al., who see Austen as a social conservative): D. W. Harding, "Regulated Hatred: An Aspect of the Work of Jane Austen," *Scrutiny* 8 (1940): 346-62; Marvin Mudrick, *Jane Austen: Irony as Defense and Discovery* (Princeton: Princeton University Press, 1952); Alistair M. Duckworth, *The Improvement of the Estate: A Study of Jane Austen's Novels* (Baltimore: Johns Hopkins University Press, 1971); Marilyn Butler, *Jane Austen and the War of Ideas* (Oxford: Clarendon Press, 1975). While I am taking Harding's and Mudrick's side, I disagree with their view that Austen challenges her society by allowing Elizabeth somehow to transcend it, that Elizabeth represents the "free individual." *Pride and Prejudice* is not, in my opinion, about the heroine's independence of the social context; it is about her inextricability from it.

22. See Karen Newman, "Can This Marriage Be Saved: Jane Austen Makes Sense of an Ending," *ELH* 50, no. 4 (1983): 693-710. Newman points out that critics as early as Sir Walter Scott have noticed Elizabeth's fascination with Pemberly: "Austen is at pains from early in the novel to show us Elizabeth's response to Darcy's wealth" (698). It is interesting that Hollywood, of venal habits and puritanical tastes, should recognize and be uneasy with Elizabeth's suspicious position as Austen wrote it. In the 1940 film version of *Pride and Prejudice,* Lady Catherine threatens to cut Darcy out of her will if he goes ahead and marries a Bennet. Elizabeth proves her romantic integrity by vowing to marry him anyway. Needless to say, Austen conspicuously chose *not* to test Elizabeth in such a manner.

23. In *The Madwoman in the Attic: The Woman Writer and the Nineteenth-Century Literary Imagination* (New Haven: Yale University Press, 1979), Gilbert and Gubar refer us to Lloyd W. Brown (*Bits of Ivory: Narrative Techniques in Jane Austen's Fiction* [Baton Rouge: Louisiana State Press, 1973]) for "the most sustained discussion of Austen's ironic undercutting of her own endings" (667). Karen Newman also sees the happy ending in Austen as parodic: despite its comic effect, there remain "unresolved contradictions between romantic and materialistic notions of marriage" (695). The idea of a fairy-tale union is falsified by Austen's clairvoyance about why women need to marry. My reading accords a good deal with Newman's, though I am less confident than she that Austen's heroines manage nevertheless to "live powerfully within the limits imposed by ideology" (705).

Mansfield Park

MOIRA FERGUSON (ESSAY DATE 1991)

SOURCE: Ferguson, Moira. "*Mansfield Park*: Slavery, Colonialism, and Gender." *Oxford Literary Review* 13, nos. 1-2 (1991): 118-39.

In the following essay, Ferguson explores the connection between the restrictions on Mansfield Park*'s Fanny Price and the slave trade also discussed in the novel.*

Mansfield Park (1814) is a eurocentric, post-abolition narrative that intertwines with a critique of gender relations and posits a world of humanitarian interactions between slave-owners and slaves. As such, following the successful passage of the Abolition Bill in 1807, ***Mansfield Park*** initiates a new chapter in colonialist fiction. Nonetheless, although the novel works against the idea of the traditionally closed and brutal world of plantocratic relations, it entertains the option of emancipation—as opposed to abolition—only through the sound of muffled rebel voices. In order to stage a future society peaceably perpetuating British rule, Jane Austen transforms Sir Thomas Bertram of Mansfield Park—who is also a plantation-owner in Antigua—from a characteristically imperious 'West Indian' planter—stock figure of ridicule in contemporary drama, poetry and novels—into a benevolent, reforming land-owner.[1]

Given the state of agitation in the Caribbean in the early 1800s, the unreality of this scenario forces textual contradictions and eruptions. No African-Caribbean people speak, no mention is ever made of slave plots or insurrections, and even slaves' white counterparts—Anglo-Saxon women in rebellion in one form or another—are assimilated or banished.[2] Thus gender relations at home parallel and echo traditional relationships of power between the colonialists and colonized peoples: European women visibly signify the most egregiously and invisibly repressed of the text—African-Caribbeans themselves. They mark silent African-Caribbean rebels as well as their own disenfranchisement, class and gender victimization.

Let me contextualize these remarks by noting that ***Mansfield Park*** was begun by Jane Austen in early 1811 and published in 1814, with its novelistic chronology extending from 1808 through 1809. As a result of the energetic abolition movement and parliamentary compromise with the

MANSFIELD PARK:

A NOVEL.

BY JANE AUSTEN,

AUTHOR OF
"SENSE AND SENSIBILITY," "EMMA," &c.

LONDON:
RICHARD BENTLEY, NEW BURLINGTON STREET,
(SUCCESSOR TO HENRY COLBURN):
BELL AND BRADFUTE, EDINBURGH;
CUMMING, DUBLIN; AND
GALIGNANI, PARIS.
1833.

Title page of *Mansfield Park* (1833).

West India lobby in 1792, slaveowners' efforts to resist legal abolition, let alone emancipation, were notorious.[3]

A transatlantic land-owner, Sir Thomas Bertram is fictionally characterized as one of those members of parliament who defended plantocratic interests.[4] He belonged to the 'outer ring' of absentee planters and merchants who never, or rarely, visited the colonies, although their connections remained solid.[5] In Raymond Williams' words:

> Important parts of the country-house system, from the sixteenth to the eighteenth centuries, were built on the profits of . . . trade [with the colonies]. Spices, sugar, tea, coffee, tobacco, gold and silver: these fed, as mercantile profits, into an English social order, over and above the profits on English stock and crops. . . . The country-houses which were the apex of a local system of exploitation then had many connections to these distant lands. . . . [Moreover], the new rural economy of the tropical plantations—sugar, coffee, cotton—was built by [the] trade in flesh, and once again the profits fed back into the country-house system: not only the profits on the commodities but . . . the profits on slaves.[6]

After a brief, quiescent period following the passage of the Bill, however, fierce contestations over slavery began anew at home and abroad. As the British press reported news of increasing atrocities in 1809, 1810, and 1811, it became obvious that the abolitionists' utopian vision of a Caribbean plantocracy committed to ameliorating the conditions of their only remaining slaves was palpably false.[7] This rise in atrocities, in addition to vigorous illicit trading, spurred parliamentary proposals that all Caribbean slaves be registered.[8] Old colonial legislatures that included Antigua opposed slave registries on constitutional grounds because such a procedure violated their right of internal taxation; not until 1820 did colonialists assent.

In fact, the time during which ***Mansfield Park*** was written marked a turning point in the fortunes of the gentry, to which social class Sir Thomas, as a baronet, arguably belonged.[9] In England the Luddite riots fomented unrest, the prime minister was assassinated, war was declared against the United States, and the gentry endured a general economic crisis. Mrs Norris, Sir Thomas' sister-in-law, informs us that Sir Thomas' financial stability depends on maintaining his Caribbean property:[10] his 'means will be rather straitened if the Antiguan estate is to make such poor returns.[11] Sir Thomas needs his Caribbean profits to stay financially afloat in England; colonialism underwrites his social and cultural position.

Thus, ongoing news of Caribbean economic crises exacerbates Sir Thomas' already straitened circumstances. Sugar prices had plummeted as a result of a major depression after 1807. The ensuing urgency to diversify the imperiled sugar monoculture made the physical presence of customarily absentee landlords expedient, and so Sir Thomas was obliged 'to go to Antigua himself, for the better arrangement of his affairs.[12] The task at hand was to maintain his estates at a profit and in the process, since trading was now illegal, to ensure the survival of his slaves as steady, well-nourished workers. Sadistic overseers, with whom Sir Thomas may have been content in the past, provided returns were satisfactory, would no longer do. His appearance when he returns to England suggests not only an exhausting engagement with his overseers and a severe reaction to noisome conditions, but through metonym it also emphasizes his affiliation with the Creole class. He 'had the burnt, fagged, worn look of fatigue and a hot climate' (178).

The society to which Sir Thomas traveled was dominated by aggressive oppositional relations between colonialists and colonized people, although absentee landlordism was unusual on Antigua compared to its frequency on neighboring islands. As a near-noble landowner, Sir Thomas would socialize with the commander-in-chief of the Leeward Islands, the Right Honorable Ralph, Lord Lavington, who, in 'real life', chose to set a constant pointed public example of desirable relations between colonizers and colonized:

> His Christmas balls and routs were upon the highest scale of magnificence; but he was a great stickler for etiquette, and a firm upholder of difference of rank and *colour* [Flanders' underlining]. . . . He would not upon any occasion, receive a letter or parcel from the fingers of a black or coloured man, and in order to guard against such *horrible* defilement, he had a golden instrument wrought something like a pair of sugar tongs, with which he was accustomed to hold the presented article.[13]

Back home, abolitionists contested the condoned maltreatment of slaves encapsulated in Lord Lavington's insidious public behaviour; they decried the atrocities that his cultural practice validated: violations of the Abolition Act, as well as individual cases of heinous maltreatment and murders of slaves by planters in 1810 and 1811.[14] Since the powerful proslavery lobby indefatigably suppressed these events as far as their power allowed, only those with access to ongoing revelations in the press and through rumor could stay abreast of daily developments. The centuries-long ideological battle over the humanity of Africans constantly and variously manifested itself.

Plantocratic Paradigms in Mansfield Park

Power relations within the community of Mansfield Park reenact and refashion plantocratic paradigms; those who work for Sir Thomas and his entourage both at home and abroad are locked into hierarchical and abusive patterns of behaviour, though under widely different circumstances. The cruel officiousness of protagonist Fanny Price's aunt, Mrs Norris, who is effectively Sir Thomas' overseer and lives in the suggestively named white house 'across the park' from the Great House underlines his plantocratic style of administration.

Mrs Norris' surname recalls John Norris, one of the most vile proslaveryites of the day. Austen was well aware of Norris' notoriety, having read Thomas Clarkson's celebrated *History of the Abolition of the Slave Trade* in which Norris is categorically condemned. Clarkson's text was published in 1808 and read by Jane Austen while she was working out the plot of ***Mansfield Park***.[15] Not only had Clarkson's history astounded her but she admitted to her sister Cassandra that she had once been 'in love' with the famous abolitionist whose devotion, industry, and total lack of regard for his own life in the cause was legend.[16] Clarkson chronicles how Norris represented himself to Clarkson in Liverpool as an opponent of the slave trade, then arrived in London as a pro-slavery delegate representing Liverpool.[17] After contacting Norris for an explanation, Clarkson notes Norris' unctuously self-serving response:

> After having paid high compliments to the general force of my arguments, and the general justice and humanity of my sentiments on this great question, which had made a deep impression upon his mind, he had found occasion to differ from me, since we had last parted, on particular points, and that he had therefore less reluctantly yielded to the call of becoming a delegate,—though notwithstanding he would gladly have declined the office if he could have done it with propriety.[18]

Underscoring the intertextual designation of Mrs Norris as sadistic overseer, Sir Thomas himself is centerstaged as 'master', especially in his treatment of niece Fanny Price. With very little ceremony and offering Fanny Price's family no say in the matter, Sir Thomas and Mrs Norris engineer the transference of this ten-year-old poor relation from her home in Portsmouth to Mansfield Park. A marginalized, near-despised family, the Prices lose one of their own to accommodate Mrs Norris' need to appear charitable; Sir Thomas eventually concurs in her decision although he reserves his judgment to return Fanny Price if she threatens domestic stability. Portsmouth, by this account, is the uncivilized other; its members overflow with energies that menace the security of Mansfield Park. Epitomizing the clash of epistemologies in the text, Portsmouth signifies a way of living that negates the tightly controlled social order and challenges the sovereign law embodied in Sir Thomas by ignoring it altogether. On the other hand, in a different way, since Portsmouth as a naval town serves to uphold Sir Thomas' position by enforcing British control of the West Indies, what might be more important is that in the domestic arena of England, the link between the two must be separated. The expropriated Fanny Price hails from the milieu of transgressors who always signify the target of their activities: kidnapped and captive slaves.

Young Fanny Price's removal from her family is described in terms often reserved for epiphanic moments in the narrative of slavery:

> The remembrance . . . of what she had suffered in being torn from them, came over her with renewed strength, and it seemed as if to be at home again, would heal every pain that had since grown out of the separation.
>
> (370)

This mercantilist attitude toward human relationships, represented as disinterested benevolence toward Fanny Price, invokes traditionally conservative rationales for the 'trade-in-flesh'. Family feeling or unity never becomes an issue, since proslaveryites do not recognize African and slave families as social formations. On the contrary, the West Indian lobby argued that bringing slaves to the Caribbean was a good deed, a way of civilizing those whose environment provided them with nothing but barbarism—precisely the same basis for the justification of bringing Fanny Price to Mansfield Park.

So, when Fanny arrives at Mansfield Park, she is closely watched for evidence of her uncouth otherness. She must accept Sir Thomas' authority unconditionally or she will be removed. Sir Thomas scrutinizes her 'disposition', anticipating 'gross ignorance, some meanness of opinions, and very distressing vulgarity of manner' (10-11). Eventually he decides she has a 'tractable disposition, and seemed likely to give them little trouble' (18). She will acclimatize well. Nonetheless, his children 'cannot be equals [with Fanny Price]. Their rank, fortune, rights, and expectations will always be different' (11).

Fanny herself begins to adapt to the value system at Mansfield, learning 'to know their ways, and to catch the best manner of conforming to them'. Fanny thinks 'too lowly of her own claims' and 'too lowly of her own situation' to challenge values that keep her low.[19] Underscoring class difference and alluding to the colonial-sexual nexus, profligate elder son Tom, the heir apparent to Sir Thomas' colonial enterprise, assures Fanny Price that she can be a 'creepmouse' all she wants as long as she obeys his commands.

Just as markedly, when Fanny Price years later is deciding what to wear at the ball, the point of contention is whose chain (or necklace) she will wear. The lurking question is to whom will she subject herself or belong. To what extent has Mansfield Park and its values begun to construct her subjectivity? Gladly, she decides on the chain of her future husband, Sir Thomas' younger son, Edmund. Moreover, when Sir Thomas leaves for Antigua, she steps into his moral shoes; she opposes Mrs Norris' opportunism and informally assumes the role of the 'good' overseer, her aunt's alter ego. Mimicking Sir Thomas, willingly cooperating in her own assimilation, she speaks for and through him. Fanny Price helps to foreshadow and map a new colonialist landscape that upholds the moral status quo but draws the line at arbitrary judgment and excessive indulgence. In the chapel scene at Sotherton, for instance, Fanny Price identifies herself as an opponent of change.[20] Edmund, on the other hand, underscores Fanny's complicity in her own assimilation when he confides—to her delight—as she leaves for Portsmouth that she will 'belong to [them] almost as much as ever' (26-7).

Yet Fanny Price is still the daughter of Portsmouth—Mansfield Park's relegated other, reared to succeed pluckily against the odds. Her master-slave relationship with Sir Thomas operates on the register of two opposing discourses: complicity and rebellion. Her stalwart refusal to marry Henry Crawford and the punishment of summary banishment she incurs identifies Mansfield Park ideologically as an institution that rallies to disempower anyone who jeopardizes Sir Thomas' feudal reign. This is especially true in the case of the déclassé Fanny Price, to whom Mansfield Park has opened its portals. In return she opposes its patriarchal demands on females as property by claiming one form of autonomy, thereby rendering herself an unregenerate ingrate in ruling class eyes. Sir Thomas even describes her in language reserved for slave insurrectionaries:

> I had thought you peculiarly free from wilfulness of temper, self-conceit, and every tendency to that independence of spirit, which prevails so much in modern days, even in young women, and which in young women is offensive and disgusting beyond all common offence. But you have now shewn me that you can be wilful and perverse.
>
> (318)

To Sir Thomas, Fanny Price's feelings are as irrelevant as slaves' feelings; she is his object. In Tzvetan Todorov's words, 'those who are not subjects have no desires.[21]

Fanny Price responds to her natal family almost exclusively as an other, after Sir Thomas banishes her to Portsmouth. Such is the enormity of his ideological power. His risk in sending her to resist Portsmouth and embrace Mansfield Park values pays off. Her home is nothing but 'noise, disorder, impropriety', her overworked impecunious mother pronounced 'a dawdler and a slattern' (388, 390). Portsmouth reconstitutes Fanny Price as Sir Thomas' transformed daughter, no longer the exiled object; while at Portsmouth she barricades herself ideologically, as it were, inside Mansfield Park, functioning as its representative. Her mother's features that she has not seen in over a decade endear themselves to her—not because she has missed seeing them—but because they remind Fanny Price of Lady Bertram's, her mother's sister and Sir Thomas' wife: 'they brought her Aunt Bertram's before her' (377). Fanny Price has come to resemble the eurocentrically conceived 'grateful negro' in pre-abolition tales who collaborated with kind owners and discouraged disobedience among rebel slaves.[22] Her embrace of Mansfield Park's values dissolves any binding association with her family and her old life.

After leaving Portsmouth for the second time, Fanny 'was beloved' by her adopted family in Mansfield Park, the passive tense affirming her surrender of agency. When Edmund decides she will make him an appropriate wife, her parents' response is not mentioned. We assume they are neither told nor invited to the wedding. The only Portsmouth members who textually reappear are the conformists: sister Susan, coded as a second Fanny, ready to satisfy Lady Bertram's need for a round-the-clock assistant, and impeccable sailor-brother William, who exercised 'continued good conduct' (462).

Sir Thomas' commercial approach to Fanny Price reformulates the treatment he previously accorded her mother, Frances Price, who 'disoblig[ed]' her family when she married a lieutenant of marines 'without education, fortune, or connections'; as a result, the Mansfield Park inner circle acts almost as if Frances Price senior did not exist; certainly she has no rights as a parent, so her children can be more or less removed at will. The text hints, too, that having ten babies in nine years is tantamount to a reprehensible lack of restraint. Neither Mrs Price's continuing independence in not seeking help nor her maintenance of a large family on a pittance elicit textual approbation. Rather, she is lucky, in the text's terms, to be the recipient of Sir Thomas' charity. With almost all immediate family ties severed, her status, mutatis mutandi, parallels that of her sister Lady Bertram, whose dowry has doomed her to the borders in a different sense. Within a phallocratic economy, their lives elicit contempt and condescension.

Lady Bertram, Mrs Norris, and Frances Price make up the trio of sisters who collectively display the degradation of colonial-gender relations. In the opening sentence of ***Mansfield Park,*** which highlights Sir Thomas' hegemonic order, the trope of capture and control that infuses the text first appears:

> About thirty years ago Miss Maria Ward of Huntingdon, with only seven thousand pounds, had the good luck to captivate Sir Thomas Bertram, of Mansfield Park, in the county of Northampton, and to be thereby raised to the rank of a baronet's lady, with all the comforts and consequences of an handsome house and large income.

The text thus describes her alleged initial conquest of Sir Thomas in arrestingly ironic tones and in doing so, as in the famous opening assertion in ***Pride and Prejudice, Mansfield Park***'s first sentence also celebrates its opposite: Sir Thomas' acquisition of a desirable social object. Maria Ward instantly drops out of sight, both in nomenclature and in self-led behaviour. Occupying the role of a slatternly plantation mistress—'she never thought of being useful' (179), Lady Bertram's prominent class status through marriage collides with the posture of an undermined female. The lap dog upon which she lavishes attention—'no one is to tease my poor pug'—emblematizes her pathetically protected status.[23] When Sir Thomas has to break news to her, he approaches her as he would a child. During his absence, she rather tellingly works on 'yards of fringe'—appropriate for a marginalized wife—and when he returns, in recognition of her imposed vacuity, she waits to have 'her whole comprehension' filled by his narrative (196). She epitomizes emptiness, a vacant object-status, a slave or constructed subject who commits spiritual suicide. Only once does a hint of spunky self-respect surface. On Sir Thomas' departure for Antigua when she comments that she does not fear for his safety, a momentary ambiguity nags the text. Is she overly confident he will be safe because she is oblivious to maritime danger due to the Napoleonic wars? Or does she not care? Does her comment speak unconsciously about her recognition of powerlessness? Does it quietly express repressed anger?

Sir Thomas' behaviour on both sides of the Atlantic signals a plantocratic mode of behaviour. Through the trope of his journey to Antigua, his long absence, and his sparing commentary about his experiences when he returns, Austen stresses his planter-like detachment from humanity, or his playing down of the facts, or both. One of the few things he did in Antigua—we learn—is attend a ball in the company of creoles—as white planters were mockingly termed in the eighteenth and nineteenth centuries; culturally and economically, Sir Thomas is inextricably linked to his Antiguan counterparts. And given certain much-touted facts about planters, contemporaries could have amplified Sir Thomas' character in a way that would expressively inflect Lady Bertram's remark about not being concerned about his safety. Planters were infamous for taking slave mistresses and fathering children.

Edward Long, who wrote the immensely popular *History of Jamaica* (1774), describes Creole activities as follows:

> Creole men . . . are in general sensible, of quick apprehension, brave, good-natured, affable, generous, temperate, and sober; unsuspicious, lovers of freedom, fond of social enjoyments, tender fathers, humane and indulgent masters; firm and sincere friends, where they once repose a confidence; their tables are covered with plenty of good cheer . . . ; their hospitality is unlimited . . . ; they affect gaiety and diversions, which in general are cards, billiards, backgammon, chess, horse-racing, hog-hunting, shooting, fishing, dancing, and music. . . . With a strong natural propensity to the other sex, they are not always the most chaste and faithful of husbands.[24]

Lowell Joseph Ragatz points out, furthermore, that from the mid-eighteenth century:

> private acts enabling white fathers to make generous provision for their illegitimate half-breed children, despite existing laws prohibiting the transmission of extensive properties to blacks, were passed in all the island legislatures with painfully increasing regularity. The number of free persons of color in Barbados, largely recruited through illicit relations with white men and negresses, rose from 448 to 2,229 between 1768 and 1802, while the number in Dominica soared from 600 in 1773 to more than 2,800 in 1804. This rapid growth of a mixed blood element in the British West Indies after 1750 arose chiefly from the Anglo-Saxon's now merely transitory residence there and the small number of white women remaining in the islands. Concubinage became well-nigh universal in the second half of the eighteenth century and the system pervaded all ranks of society. During the administration of Governor Ricketts in Barbados in the 1790s, a comely negress even reigned at government house, enjoying all a wife's privileges save presiding publicly at his table.[25]

According to August Kotzebue's well-known play that the characters in ***Mansfield Park*** choose to rehearse for their recreation, *Lovers' Vows,* no love/lust exists in England, only 'in all barbarous countries'.[26] Austen uses this play to intertextualize the characters' motives and interactions. A remark from the play's philandering Count Cassel that comments on sexual exploitation in the Caribbean matches contemporary accounts and illumines the character of Sir Thomas.[27]

Jane Austen was well aware of these infamous activities. She knew about the estate of the Nibbs family in Antigua because the Reverend George Austen, Jane Austen's father, was a trustee; she also knew of the Nibbs' 'mulatto' relative.[28] As one critic concretely contends: 'Jane Austen would certainly have been aware of the likelihood of a family such as her fictional Bertrams having numerous mulatto relatives in Antigua'. Sir Thomas' condemnation of Mrs Price marrying low and his anger at Fanny Price's refusal to accommodate him by marrying Henry Crawford mocks planters' infamous, quotidian practices.

A question then crops up: Does Sir Thomas banish his daughter, Maria, and censure Henry Crawford because their sexual indulgences mirror his Antiguan conduct? Is one dimension of his behaviour a form of self-projection, an unconscious denial of his dual and contradictory realities in the Caribbean and Britain?

Another victim of Sir Thomas' mercantilist attitudes, elder daughter Maria refuses to be Lady Bertram's clone. Instead she stands with her exiled Aunt Frances and cousin Fanny in claiming sexual independence. Her actions are even more morally outré since she has already been manipulated into marriage with Rushworth, a man whom her father financially desires. For example in the gate scene at Sotherton, Maria symbolically and literally refuses to be imprisoned. Maria, that is, falls for the ideological trap that is set for her and is punished for trying to release herself.[29] Mary Crawford, who also disregards Sir Thomas' authority and is coded as a predator of sorts, similarly contests for personal autonomy and is configured as more evil because she disregards Sir Thomas' values. Linked by their given names, they are different versions of a gendered bid for identity.[30]

In the text's terms, none of these spirited acts by women in multiple postures of subjection can be vindicated except that of the conflicted Fanny Price. The Crawfords are reduced to the social margins, Henry for visible rakishness, Mary for 'evil' and bold collaboration in her brother's escapades. The possibility smoulders that Sir Thomas cannot contain an English reflection of his Antiguan self. He represents men who control the general slave population and the female slave population in particular through varieties of abuse. When women like Frances and Fanny Price, Maria Bertram, and Mary Crawford articulate a counterdiscourse against their objectification, Sir Thomas stands firm. Insurgent women become deleted subjects, objects of his wrath who must be appropriately punished, usually for keeps. At the conscious and unconscious level, the text continually inscribes challenges to the assumed inferiority of women and the right of a hegemonic patriarch to use women as he pleases.

Most systematically of all, however, *Lovers' Vows* intertextualizes property-owning attitudes that characterize planter-slave relations, including Sir Thomas' flagrant neglect of female welfare.[31] At the same time, the dramatic resolution of these corrupt interrelationships appears to exonerate Sir Thomas and validate patriarchal rule. Clearly coded as Sir Thomas, the Baron is multiply conflicted. In former days, he had abandoned naive and pregnant Agnes, who bore Frederick. Like the 'deserted and neglected negroes' of Antigua who will become a later focus of national concern, Agnes is now starving to death and homeless. Eventually, however, the Baron's callous desertion is mitigated by information that he has hired helpers to search constantly till they find her. In the end the Baron decides to marry Agnes though he fails to consult her about his plan. Like Maria Ward, she is assumed to desire such a splendid match.

In like manner, the Baron's efforts to marry off his daughter Amelia to silly Count Cassel are soon revealed as nonbinding. When he learns that Amelia loves Pastor Anhalt, the Baron readily consents, a scenario that comments on the marital imbroglio of Fanny Price, Henry Crawford, and Edmund Bertram. The case of Frederick, who strikes the Baron in the course of trying to save his mother's life, allusively invokes the nature of Sir Thomas' power: the Baron orders Frederick killed even though 'a child might have overpowered him', for 'to save him would set a bad example'.[32] Only when the Baron discovers that Frederick is his son, does parental feeling induce him to relent. In doing so, the Baron earns permission to be readmitted to the human community. Feudal laws and relations in *Lovers' Vows* sign those of the plantocracy.

Conclusion

Mansfield Park initiated a new chapter in colonialist fiction as old and new abolitionists came to terms with the fact that the Abolition Bill did not fulfil its minimum requirement—amelioration of inhuman conditions. Jane Austen's repugnance toward the slave trade, moreover, is well documented—her brother Francis was a vigorous abolitionist—and by the time she writes ***Emma*** in 1816 her condemnation is forthright.[33] Hence Sir Thomas' chastening is one way of prescribing this letting-up process among a seemingly unregenerate plantocracy. He reconstitutes himself as a moral rather than a profit-oriented planter, a condition inveterately resisted among the colonial ruling class. Recent experience in the House of Commons as well as the Caribbean have persuaded Sir Thomas, Jane Austen subtly argues, that the old order may be doomed and disappearing. As a Parliamentary member, Sir Thomas would have been witnessing at first hand the efforts of Wilberforce and his supporters to initiate corrective legislation. In admitting his errors and curbing his selfishness, Sir Thomas comes to represent the liberal-conservative ideal of humanitarian plantation ownership at a time when outright manumission is effectively a non-issue.

It hardly seems to be a coincidence that ***Mansfield Park*** echoes the name of Lord Chief Justice Mansfield, who wrote the legal decision for the James Somerset case in 1772, stipulating that no slaves could be forcibly returned from Britain to the Caribbean, which was widely interpreted to mean that slavery in Britain had been legally abolished.[34] Austen's invocation of Lord Mansfield's name suggests the novel's intrinsic engagement with slavery and a view of Sir Thomas' plantations as a place where feudal relations are beginning to dissolve.[35] To underscore that point, the word 'plantation' is frequently used to denote Sir Thomas' property on both sides of the Atlantic.

At another level, the intertextualizing of Lord Mansfield's ruling warns and censures all those who try to further impose their will on the already subjugated, in Sir Thomas' case, Fanny Price and by extension his Antiguan slaves. The choice of Mans field for the title underscores the idea of property in the hands of a patriarch—one man's plantations—and in its compression of several frames of meaning and reference, it connects the Caribbean plantation system and its master-slave relationships to tyrannical gender relations at home and abroad.

Jane Austen's recommendations for a kinder, gentler plantocracy, however, do anything but confront that institution head on. Not to put too fine a point on it, the opposite is virtually true. En route to the new dispensation, Sir Thomas' change of heart is accompanied and contradicted by his challenge to the heterogenous utterances of those who flout his power. Hence paradoxically, his moral reformation reconfirms his control. With unruly elements purged or contained and his unitary discourse intact though refashioned, the same power relations persist in slightly different guise between the ruling class elite and dominated people, between male and female. Thus to read ***Mansfield Park*** as a text with closures that favour more benevolent socio-political relationships only serves to mask textual undercurrents that threaten to explode its tightly controlled bourgeois framework.

Let me briefly recite some of these closures that purport to foretell future felicity and a more uniform culture groping toward harmony. First, *Lovers' Vows* is intended to demonstrate how well the Baron (Sir Thomas) suppresses anarchic expression and restores peace after learning his lesson. Second, protagonist Fanny Price, despite announcing her right to autonomy, attains the status of an insider because she mirrors Sir Thomas' values and rather coldly rejects her origins. She embraces an imposed identity as a bona fide member of the Mansfield Park community. Sir Thomas, in turn, offers himself as a father: 'Fanny was indeed the daughter that he wanted. His charitable kindness had been rearing a prime comfort for himself' (472). Third, the Price family in Portsmouth is exposed as decisively inferior except for those who agreeably adapt. Disobedience and heady self-determination are penalized by lifetime expulsion from the old order: Maria Bertram and Mary Crawford are excluded from the ruling class coterie while younger daughter Julia's repentance and her more accommodating disposition gain her a second chance.

Also to the point is Lady Bertram's languid life, which is criticized yet accepted as a familiar though inconsequential existence while the mettlesome spirit of the Price survivors goes unapplauded. That is, although Lady Bertram may draw sympathetic attention as a witless figure, the necessity for a social appendage in female form to round out plantocratic control is never gainsaid. But perhaps the most morally ambiguous textual judgment concerns Mrs Norris herself whose downfall is treated as her just deserts. Former overseer and exposed renegade, she is banished for good, like her sister Frances, from the family circle. That she encourages Maria Bertram to claim a certain kind of freedom is sweepingly condemned. The text obliterates the fact that she represents Sir Thomas' interests, but in excess of how the text wants him portrayed.[36] She is his avatar, Sir Thomas at his most acquisitive and self-indulgent. He cannot countenance the reflection of himself in Mrs Norris, who represents his displaced tacit approval of heinous cruelties and ensuing reduced profits. When he rejects her, he rejects part of his former self and life; he becomes part of the new order that seeks more wholesome relations at home and abroad. Since his regeneration cannot mean that he continues to treat people unfeelingly, Mrs Norris has to be reconstructed as a villain, tidily demolished, and eliminated as a speaking subject.

These methodical but artificial closures, however, in their blanket effort to smother opposition, only highlight ideological antagonisms that decentre Sir Thomas' power and question its validity. They elicit an insistent counterdiscourse. His posture also underwrites a certain anxiety about outsiders, regardless of former familial or friendly relationships. Human connections count for naught compared to the obsession with control.

Most ironically, textual imbeddings surface in the person of Sir Thomas' major vindicator, the Baron, who turns out in one sense to be his most damning accuser. As Sir Thomas' autocratic counterpart, the medieval Baron has no compunction about killing an innocent man who defies his authority. Similarly, Sir Thomas himself can order severe punishment, if not death, against slaves he arbitrarily deems insubordinate. Such was the authority of planters. And not uncoincidentally, the Baron is execrating Frederick in *Lovers' Vows* while that other Baron, Sir Thomas, administers the Antiguan plantations, by implication in the same way. The Baron denies Frederick's humanity as planters deny the humanity of slaves, relenting only when he discovers Frederick is his son. In a remarkably unconscious self-projection, the Baron commands Frederick in words that would make more sense in reverse: 'Desist—barbarian, savage, stop!!' (526). Moreover, by summarily terminating the theatricals, Sir Thomas reestablishes his authority over a symbolically uncontrollable situation.[37]

Most materially, the sparse counterdiscourse concerning slaves pinpoints a fundamental textual repression. Having affirmed her pleasure in Sir Thomas' stories of his Caribbean visit, Fanny inquires about the slave trade. After absorbing her uncle's answer—significantly unreported—she expresses amazement to Edmund about the ensuing 'dead silence' (198), a phrase that requires careful unpacking. Let me back up for a moment.

In this transitional post-abolitionist period that features a shaky British-Caribbean economy and multiple slave insurrections, no safe space, from a eurocentric perspective, is available for colonized others as speaking subjects, let alone as self-determining agents. Put baldly, slave subjectivity has to be effaced. As the oppressed daughter of an exigent family, Fanny Price becomes the appropriate mediator or representative of slaves' silenced existence and constant insurrectionary potential. In her role as a marginalized other (though in a vastly different cultural context), Fanny Price can project and displace personal-political anxieties and mimic her servile subject position.

As a brief for plantocratic gradual reform, the text disintegrates at 'dead silence', a phrase that ironically speaks important debarred and smothered voices. As Mansfield Park's unofficial spokesman for Antiguan society, the beleaguered Sir Thomas has cut slaves off from representation. *Lovers' Vows,* besides, has already voiced and even accentuated the major *topoi* of a muzzled colonialist discourse: brutality, fractured families, and the violated bodies and psyches of innocent people. Thus the conceptualizations of 'dead' and 'silence' that parallel the play's metonyms of bondage further indict the gaps in Sir Thomas' discourse. Beyond that, these loaded inscriptions of death and muteness accost the taboo enforced on dissent in the colonies. 'Dead silence' affirms Sir Thomas' seeming pretence that power relations are stable in Antigua. For what other than dissimulation of some sort—most likely an obfuscation or omission—could explain Fanny Price's ready acceptance of his lengthy speech on the slave trade. 'Dead' and 'silence', in other words, forswear the reality of ubiquitous slave insurrections. For example, plots were organized and carried out in Jamaica, Tobago, and especially in Dominica, where the second maroon war was led by Quashie, Apollo, Jacko, and others.[38] Uncontainable conflicts are further unmasked by textual allusions to several issues of the *Quarterly Review,* which carried many troublesome facts about slavery in 1811:[39] for one, the periodical reported that the progressive diminution in slave population levels persisted, despite abolition of the trade, a fact that threw doubt on promises made by planters and colonial legislatures to ameliorate conditions. Old planters in Jamaica and Antigua were in the news, too, as zealous competitors of the 'new' planters. The *Quarterly Review* also confirmed that the bottom had dropped out of the sugar market by 1808, that estates were in disrepair, and growers could not be indemnified.[40] What's more, the seemingly univocal colonial discourse of ***Mansfield Park*** that upholds a singular view of slavery as 'working', belies domestic agitation inside and outside Parliament for improved conditions.[41]

Antigua, then, tropes an anxiety-creating unknown venue, falsely coded as a run-down locale in need of an individual planter's semi-altruistic, definitively ethnocentric intervention. Profits are down, but workers and administrators suffer too. Antigua also correlates with Portsmouth, both being symbolic sites of indeterminacy near water and places where the allegedly uncivilized cluster. As a port and an island intimately involved with slavery, Portsmouth and Antigua witness slave ships arriving and departing; scenes involving the sale of people and naval engagements are in constant view. Sir Thomas may subsume Antigua within his monocular vision and Fanny Price may fail to see (or evade) Portsmouth's obvious immersion in the slave trade as she gazes at the sights of the town, but their buried knowledge and realities intertextually circulate nonetheless. Like the Orient in Edward Said's formulation, Antigua and Portsmouth are Mansfield Park's wild, colonized others, signs of potential disruption and sexual conflict.[42] They signal that the women of Mansfield Park are ideologically absorbed or unceremoniously expelled—or even obliterated (as the slavewomen of Antigua are) as autonomous beings.

In this space as Mansfield Park's other, Antigua satirizes Sir Thomas' authority. He may conduct his relationships in a recognizably plantocratic mode that solidifies his power, but both vocal and mute suppressions are evident. Sir Thomas' return assumes that he leaves behind a certain order, even harmony, on his plantations. He controls superficially obedient slaves, but that illusion will soon be fractured. By implication, other apparent fixtures might also turn out to be less enduring.

This is not to argue that the possibility of slave emancipation in ***Mansfield Park*** parallels a potential liberation for Anglo-Saxon women. But it is to posit that challenges to ossified thought and the received cultural representation of women are at least conceivable. Lady Bertram is comatose, but can that state last? The condition of indolent plantocratic wives is certainly coming to an end. Besides, the self-determining duo of Maria-Mary will not tolerate permanent disappearance. Their independent natures will soon reassert themselves, the text having forced them into a closure, demonstrably false. Fanny Price, however, the obedient daughter who replaces the ungovernable overseer, is pinioned in a conflict of searing and unresolvable tensions. So little room is available for repudiation of her place in Mansfield Park's social situation that it threatens to bind and fix her.[43] Ultimately the rebellious acts of Fanny Price and her ideological companions, Maria, Frances Price, and Frederick are paradigmatic of slave resistance: Fanny Price signifies a bartered slave and the sign of the absent female slave. The deported Maria, in turn, is a variant of the marginalized Portsmouth family.

By contrast, Sir Thomas' authority is scarcely denied by the men of the text who fare somewhat differently. Each of them projects a part of that complex Sir Thomas, even the sybaritic Bishop Grant, symbolically linked to his malignant niece and nephew as Sir Thomas is linked to Mrs Norris. Despite debauchery, elder son Tom will take up his inheritance, as does the foolish Rushworth, whose wealth and aristocratic status enable him to transcend a temporary setback. Henry Crawford continues to seduce women and Edmund settles down into married life.

Mansfield Park, then, I am arguing, is a post-abolition narrative that intertwines with a critique, conscious or unconscious, of gender relations. Although the text superficially presents itself at the end as an agreeable synthesis that has incorporated its contradictions—the hermeneutics of an attempted restoration of power—the text's relationship to emancipationist ideology creates irrepressible contradictions and signals incompletion. As a colonialist script, it features epistemological ethnocentrisms, blanks, ellipses, substitutions, and the homogenizing of silent slaves, occupying a space between old and new modes of discourse and agitation. It projects the end of an uncompromising proslavery lobby by fusing commentary on slaves and Anglo-Saxon women who are concurrently exhibiting forms of autonomy and powerlessness. Thus the reformed planter's voice in itself becomes a nullified force. His contradictory positions cancel themselves out. The indirectness of the commentary, moreover, indicates Jane Austen's temporary reluctance to sound the controversy over slavery into recognizable audibility. Not until ***Emma*** does she do so unmistakably.

As a quasi-allegory of colonial-gender relations, ***Mansfield Park*** offers itself as a blueprint for a new society of manners. Relationships in the colonies will match those at home, for domestic manners have been transformed for the better. But as we have seen, Sir Thomas' brand of euro-centric benevolence is dubious at best and the socio-political recommendations are decidedly and perhaps necessarily constrained. Nonetheless, the attempt to show the positive consequences of a kinder, gentler world in action, together with many potent silences and irruptions of nuanced subaltern voices, signifies the desirable, though possibly not attainable, transition to a new colonialist dispensation of gradualist politics at home and abroad. Despite this slow but positive evolution, however, emancipation still cannot be named.

Notes

1. Wylie Sypher, 'The West-Indian as a 'Character' in the Eighteenth Century', in *Studies in Philology* vol. 36 (Chapel Hill: University of North Carolina Press, 1939), 504-5, 509.

2. Michael Craton, *Testing the Chains. Resistance to Slavery in the British West Indies* (Ithaca: Cornell University Press, 1982).

3. Elsa V. Goveia, *Slave Society in the British Leeward Islands at the End of the Eighteenth Century* (New Haven: Yale University Press, 1965). See also D. J. Murray, *The West Indies and the Development of Colonial Government 1801-1834* (Oxford: Clarendon Press, 1965); Dale Herbert Porter, *The Defense of the British Slave Trade, 1784-1807,* Dissertation University of Oregon, June 1967, 25-166.

4. Mary Millard points out that Northampton squires were rarely sugar-planters and speculates that 'an earlier Bertram married a lady who brought an estate in Antigua, as her dowry'. Mary Millard, '1807 and All That', *Persuasions,* 50-1. I thank Professor Kenneth Moler for invaluable discussions on the question of Sir Thomas's slave-owning status.

5. Sir Thomas probably belonged to the 'outer ring' of absentee planters and merchants who had never visited the colonies. Between 1807 and 1833 forty-nine planters and twenty merchants belonged to this group. B. W. Higman, 'The West India 'Interest' in Parliament 1807-1833', *Historical Studies* 13 (1967-69) 4, 1-19. See also Lowell Joseph Ragatz, *Absentee Landlordism in the British Caribbean, 1750-1833* (London: Bryan Edwards Press, n.d.), 1-19).

6. Raymond Williams, *The Country and the City* (New York: Oxford University Press, 1973), 279-80.

7. Sir George Stephen, *Anti-Slavery Recollections: in a Series of Letters Addressed to Mrs. Beecher Stowe, written by Sir George Stephen, at Her Request* (London: Frank Cass, 1971), 36-7. Note also that as a result of information about ongoing inhumane treatment, British abolitionists were shortly to publicize the condition of slaves in Antigua even more decisively in forming a committee for the 'Neglected and Deserted Negroes' of that island. See John Rylands Memorial Library 'The Case of the Neglected and Deserted Negroes in the Island of Antigua', pamphlet 21.5, pt. 8.

8. Frank J. Klingberg, *The Anti-Slavery Movement in England. A Study in English Humanitarianism* (New Haven: Yale University Press, 1926), 131, 171-2. B. W. Higman, *Slave Populations of the British Caribbean, 1807-1834* (Baltimore: The Johns Hopkins University Press, 1984). See also James Walvin, 'The rise of British popular sentiment for abolition 1787-1832', *Anti-Slavery, Religion, and Reform: Essays in Memory of Roger Anstey,* eds Christine Bolt and Seymour Drescher (Folkestone: Dawson, 1980), 154 and *passim*; Sir George Stephen, *Anti-Slavery Recollections,* 25-27 and *passim.*

9. Avrom Fleishman, *A Reading of Mansfield Park. An Essay in Critical Synthesis* (Minneapolis: University of Minnesota Press, 1967), 40-2.

10. Fleishman, *A Reading of Mansfield Park,* 35-6.

11. R. W. Chapman, *The Novels of Jane Austen. The Text based on Collation of the Early Editions,* vol. 3 (London: Oxford University Press, 1923), 30. Further references to *Mansfield Park* will be given in the text. The enormous chain of expenses that emanated from the Great House included a host of people from servants and overseers to waiters, 'brownskin gals' of no official function, and the estate's managing attorney who received 60% of the gross. Michael Craton, *Sinews of Empire. A Short History of British Slavery* (New York: Anchor Books, 1974), 132-9).

12. Fleishman, *A Reading of Mansfield Park,* 37. William B. Willcox touches briefly on the turmoil that would have precipitated Sir Thomas's decision, in *The Age of Aristocracy 1688-1830* (Lexington, MS: D. C. Heath and Company, 1971), 174-179. Willcox also points out that: 'Though Miss Austen's two brothers were in the navy throughout the war, her world is untouched by anything outside itself; it is tranquil and timeless' 168. See also *Mansfield Park,* 65.

13. With respect to Sir Thomas's 'near-noble' status, Fleishman argues that 'only some four hundred families could qualify for the higher class, and despite an economic fluidity which enabled some baronets and even commoners to enter it, this was an aristocracy composed mainly of noblemen' (40). Mrs. Flanders, *Antigua and the Antiguans: A Full Account of the Colony and its Inhabitants From the Time of the Caribs to the Present Day, Interspersed with Anecdotes and Legends. Also, an Impartial View of Slavery and the Free Labour Systems; the Statistics of the Island, and Biographical Notices of the Principal Families,* vol. 2 (London, 1844), 136.

14. Sir George Stephen, *Anti-Slavery Recollections,* 8-19; Frank J. Klingberg, *The Anti-Slavery Movement in England,* 176-81.

15. Chapman, *The Novels of Jane Austen,* 553-6.

16. Frank Gibbon, 'The Antiguan Connection: Some New Light on *Mansfield Park*', in *The Cambridge Quarterly,* 11 (1982), 303.

17. Thomas Clarkson, *The History of the Rise, Progress, and Accomplishment of the Abolition of the African Slave-Trade by the British Parliament,* vol. 1 (London: 1808; rpt. Frank Cass, 1968), 378ff; 477ff. In reading Clarkson, Jane Austen would have been abreast of fierce abolitionist and pro-slavery infighting both inside and outside Parliament and of the literature on the subject of the slave trade.

18. Clarkson, *History,* vol. 1, 479.

19. Johanna M. Smith, '"My only sister now": Incest in *Mansfield Park*', *Studies in the Novel* 19:1 (1987), 1-15.

20. Ruth Bernard Yeazell, 'The Boundaries of Mansfield Park', in *Representations,* 6 (1984), 133-152.

21. Tzvetan Todorov, *The Conquest of America. The Question of the Other,* trans. Richard Howard (New York: Harper & Row, 1982), 130.

22. In *Popular Tales* (1804) Maria Edgeworth, for example, has a story entitled 'The Grateful Negro', that exemplifies exactly this familiar binary opposition. It is possible, given Jane Austen's admiration for Maria Edgeworth (Chapman, vol. 5, 299), that she had read some of Edgeworth's tales as well as her novels. Given the popularity of *The Farmer of Inglewood Forest* (1796) by Elizabeth Helme that also features a 'grateful negro', Austen may well have read that novel or others featuring that motif.

23. *Mansfield Park,* 217. The connection of indolent housemistresses despised by their authors frequently appears. Two examples are Lady Ellison in Sarah Robinson Scott's novel, *The History of George Ellison* (1766) and Mary Wollstonecraft's polemical attack on such practices in *A Vindication of the Rights of Woman* (1792).

24. Sypher, 'The West Indian', 503, 506.

25. Ragatz, *Absentee Landlordism,* 1-21. Note also how Sir Thomas's 'burnt, fagged, worn look' (178) matches signs of the contemporary West Indian in fiction. 'A yellowish complexion, lassitude of body and mind, fitful spells of passion or energy, generosity bordering on improvidence, sentimentality combined with a streak of naughtiness and cruelty to subdeviates'; see also Sypher, *The West Indian,* 504.

26. *Lovers' Vows. A Play, in five acts. Performed at the Theatre Royal Covent-Garden. From the German of Kotzebue. by Mrs. Inchbald* (London, 1798) in Chapman, *The Novels of Jane Austen,* 475-538.

27. *Lovers' Vows,* 534.

28. Gibbon, 'The Antiguan Connection', 298-305.

29. Gerald L. Gould, 'The Gate Scene at Sotherton in *Mansfield Park*', in *Literature and Psychology,* 20:1 (1970), 75-8.

30. For the discussions of subjectivity and interpellation in ideology here and elsewhere in the essay, I am indebted to Michel Pêcheux, *Language, Semantics, and Ideology* (New York: St. Martin's Press, 1975).

31. I am assuming here and elsewhere in the text the reader's conversancy with *Lovers' Vows,* an assumption I think Jane Austen makes.

32. In *Discipline and Punish. The Birth of the Prison* (New York: Vintage Books, 1979), Michel Foucault argues that feudal torture of the criminal's body and subsequent death 'made everyone aware . . . of the unrestrained presence [and power] of the sovereign' 'The ceremony of the public torture and execution displayed for all to see the power relation that gave his force to the law . . .'. 'We must regard the public execution, as it was still ritualized in the eighteenth century, as a political operation' 49-53.

33. Jane Austen, *Emma* (first published 1816) (Boston: The Riverside Press, 1933), 233.

34. See F. O. Shyllon, *Black Slaves in Britain* (London: Oxford University Press, 1974), especially 77-124 and 237-43. See also James Walvin, *The Black Presence. A documentary history of the Negro in England, 1555-1860* (New York: Schocken Books, 1972), 95-114.

35. Margaret Kirkham, *Jane Austen, Feminism and Fiction* (New York: Methuen, 1986), 116-119.

36. I am indebted for the argument about the text's excess and unconsciousness to Pierre Macherey's *A Theory of Literary Production,* trans. Geoffrey Wall (London: Routledge & Kegan Paul, 1978), 75-97 and *passim.*

37. Yeazell, 'The Boundaries of *Mansfield Park*', 133.

38. Craton, *Testing the Chains*, 337-8.

39. *Mansfield Park*, 104. I would add data from the *Quarterly Review* to Chapman's list of sources for *Mansfield Park* and refashion his chronology of the novel from 1800-1809 accordingly.

40. See *Quarterly Review*, 164.

41. Pêcheux, *Language, Semantics and Ideology*, 13.

42. I am thinking here of Edward Said's conceptualization of orientalizing in Chapter One, 'The Scope of Orientalism', in *Orientalism* (New York: Vintage Books, 1979), and *passim*.

43. Pêcheux, *Language, Semantics and Ideology*, 156-7.

FURTHER READING

Bibliographies

Handley, Graham. *Jane Austen: A Guide Through the Critical Maze*. New York: St. Martin's Press, 1992, 139 p.

Provides a guide to Austen criticism from early reviews through the 1980s.

Roth, Barry. *An Annotated Bibliography of Jane Austen Studies, 1984-94*, Athens: Ohio University Press, 1996, 438 p.

Offers a bibliography of studies on Jane Austen.

Biographies

Austen-Leigh, James. *A Memoir of Jane Austen*. London: R. Bentley, 1870, 364 p.

Presents an affectionate biography of Austen by her nephew.

Chapman, R. W. *Jane Austen: Facts and Problems*. Oxford: Oxford University Press, 1948, 224 p.

Provides an early biography by one of Austen's twentieth-century critics.

Halperin, John. *The Life of Jane Austen*. Baltimore: Johns Hopkins University Press, 1984, 399 p.

Links Austen's life to her works.

Jenkins, Elizabeth. *Jane Austen: A Biography*. New York: Grosset and Dunlap, 1948, 286 p.

Offers a detailed treatment of Austen's life and works.

Nokes, David. *Jane Austen: A Life*. New York: Farrar, Straus & Giroux, 1997, 512 p.

Attempts to correct the portrait of the sweet maiden aunt painted by Austen's family; considered by critics to be somewhat speculative in its alternative interpretation of Austen's life.

Tomalin, Claire. *Jane Austen: A Life*. New York: Knopf, 1997, 352 p.

Offers a popular biography focusing on Austen's family.

Criticism

Auerbach, Nina. "Jane Austen's Dangerous Charm: Feeling as One Ought About Fanny Price." *Women and Literature* 3 (1983): 11-28.

Considers the character Fanny Price from Mansfield Park *as a version of the "Romantic monster."*

Benedict, Barbara M. "Jane Austen and the Culture of Circulating Libraries: The Construction of Female Literacy." In *Revising Women: Eighteenth-Century 'Women's Fiction' and Social Engagement*, pp. 147-99. Baltimore: Johns Hopkins University Press, 2000.

Links Austen's treatment of women as readers to the rise of consumer society in the late eighteenth and early nineteenth centuries.

Butler, Marilyn. *Jane Austen and the War of Ideas*. Oxford: Clarendon Press, 1975, 310 p.

Contends that Austen's novels are a conservative reaction to the more liberal novels that preceded them but that she is innovative in narrative style and technique.

Craik, W. A. *Jane Austen: The Six Novels*. London: Methuen, 1965, 210 p.

Sees in Austen's novels a harmonic combination of the artist and the moralist; emphasizes the economy of Austen's style and plotting and the serious intent of the novels.

Devlin, D. D. *Jane Austen and Education*. New York: Barnes and Noble, 1975, 140 p.

Interprets Austen's novels as delineating the educative process of their protagonists.

Duane, Anna Mae. "Confusions of Guilt and Complications of Evil: Hysteria and the High Price of Love at Mansfield Park." *Studies in the Novel* 33, no. 4 (winter 2001): 402-15.

Discusses the treatment of feminine desire with respect to the ending of Mansfield Park.

Duckworth, Alistair. *The Improvement of the Estate: A Study of Jane Austen's Novels*. Baltimore: Johns Hopkins University Press, 1971, 239 p.

Focuses on the settings of Austen's novels and their social context.

Gilbert, Sandra M., and Susan Gubar. "Inside the House of Fiction: Jane Austen's Tenants of Possibilities." In *The Madwoman in the Attic: The Woman Writer and the Nineteenth-Century Literary Imagination*, pp. 107-86. New Haven: Yale University Press, 1979.

Comprises two essays, the first on gender and genre in Austen's juvenilia, the second on the novels; discusses Austen's representation of the social and political history of women in her works.

Harding, D. W. "Regulated Hatred." *Scrutiny* 8, no. 4 (March 1940): 346-62.

Focuses on Austen's satire and caricature and reads her novels as variations on the Cinderella tale.

Harris, Jocelyn. "Silent Women, Shrews, and Bluestockings: Women and Speaking in Jane Austen." In *The Talk in Jane Austen*, edited by Bruce Stovel and Lynn Weinlos Gregg, pp. 3-22. Edmonton: University of Alberta Press, 2002.

Examines the treatment of female speech and female silence in Austen's novels.

Johnson, Claudia. *Jane Austen: Women, Politics, and the Novel*. Chicago: University of Chicago Press, 1988, 186 p.

Asserts that Austen's novels contain a political element.

Michaelson, Patricia Howell. *Speaking Volumes: Women, Reading, and Speech in the Age of Austen*. Stanford, Calif.: Stanford University Press, 2002, 261 p.

Applies a sociolinguistic approach to issues of gender, performance, and authority in Austen's novels.

Mudrick, Marvin. *Jane Austen: Irony as Defense and Discovery.* Princeton: Princeton University Press, 1952, 267 p.

Examines Austen's use of irony throughout her novels as well as in her letters and juvenilia.

Poovey, Mary. "Ideological Contradictions and the Consolations of Form: The Case of Jane Austen; True English Style." In *The Proper Lady and the Woman Writer: Ideology as Style in the Works of Mary Wollstonecraft, Mary Shelley, and Jane Austen,* pp. 172-207. Chicago: University of Chicago Press, 1984.

Compares Austen's style to that of Wollstonecraft and Shelley, placing her between Wollstonecraft's direct manner of expression and Shelley's self-effacing style, and connects narrative mode to the authors' ideology of femininity.

Said, Edward. "Jane Austen and Empire." In *Raymond Williams: Critical Perspectives,* edited by Terry Eagleton, pp. 150-64. Boston: Northeastern University Press, 1989.

Interprets Austen's personal ideology as conservative, focusing on Mansfield Park.

Sulloway, Alison. "Emma Woodhouse and *A Vindication of the Rights of Woman.*" *Wordsworth Circle* 7 (autumn 1976): 320-32.

Examines Austen's portrayal of women within the context of Mary Wollstonecraft's work, calling Emma *a subversive and Romantic text.*

Tanner, Tony. *Jane Austen.* Cambridge: Harvard University Press, 1986, 291 p.

Acknowledges Austen's conservatism but nonetheless views her as a social critic; observes the close connection between Austen's controlled and precise prose and her morality.

Todd, Janet. "Who's Afraid of Jane Austen." *Women and Literature* 3 (1983): 107-27.

Considers Virginia Woolf's response to Jane Austen as intimidated; a comparative study of the novelists as women authors.

———. "Jane Austen, Politics, and Sensibility." In *Feminist Criticism: Theory and Practice,* edited by Susan Sellers, Linda Hutcheon, and Paul Perron, pp. 71-87. Toronto: University of Toronto Press, 1991.

Analyzes Sense and Sensibility *in the context of the eighteenth- and nineteenth-century cult of sensibility and its implications for women's sexuality.*

Weldon, Faye. *Letters to Alice on First Reading Jane Austen.* London: Michael Joseph, 1984, 127 p.

Fictional letters from Weldon's persona Aunt Faye to her niece, a "punk" college student, attempting to convince her of Austen's merits; humorous but also scholarly.

Woolf, Virginia. "Jane Austen at Sixty." *Athenaeum* (15 December 1923): 433.

A speculative essay on the paths Austen's career might have taken after Persuasion.

OTHER SOURCES FROM GALE:

Additional coverage of Austen's life and career is contained in the following sources published by the Gale Group: *Authors and Artists for Young Adults,* Vol. 19; *Beacham's Guide to Literature for Young Adults,* Vol. 3; *British Writers,* Vol. 4; *British Writers: The Classics,* Vol. 1; *British Writers Retrospective Supplement,* Vol. 2; *Concise Dictionary of British Literary Biography, 1789-1832*; *Dictionary of Literary Biography,* Vol. 116; *DISCovering Authors*; *DISCovering Authors: British Edition*; *DISCovering Authors: Canadian Edition*; *DISCovering Authors Modules: Most-studied Authors* and *Novelists*; *DISCovering Authors 3.0*; *Exploring Novels*; *Literary Movements for Students,* Vol. 1; *Literature and Its Times,* Vol. 2; *Literature and Its Times Supplement,* Ed. 1; *Nineteenth-Century Literature Criticism,* Vols. 1, 13, 19, 33, 51, 81, 95, 119; *Novels for Students,* Vols. 1, 14, 18; *Twayne's English Authors*; *World Literature and Its Times,* Vol. 3; *World Literature Criticism*; and *Writers for Young Adults Supplement,* Vol. 1.

CHARLOTTE BRONTË

(1816 - 1855)

(Also wrote under the pseudonym of Currer Bell) English novelist and poet.

As the author of vivid, intensely written novels, Brontë broke the traditional nineteenth-century fictional stereotype of a woman as submissive, dependent, beautiful, and ignorant. Her first novel, *Jane Eyre* (1847), was immediately recognized for its originality and power, though it was some time before its author was universally accepted to be a woman, rather than Currer Bell, the masculine pseudonym she consistently employed. Since then, Brontë has been considered by critics as one of the foremost authors of the nineteenth century, an important precursor to feminist novelists, and the creator of intelligent, independent heroines who asserted their rights as women long before those rights were recognized by society.

BIOGRAPHICAL INFORMATION

Brontë was born April 21, 1816 in Thornton, Yorkshire. The eldest surviving daughter in a family of six, she assisted her aunt and her father in raising the three younger children, including her brother Branwell and sisters Emily and Anne. Her mother, Maria Branwell of Cornwall, died from cancer in 1821, at the age of thirty-eight. Two older sisters, Maria and Elizabeth, died of consumption in 1825. Her father, Patrick Brontë, was a strict Yorkshire clergymen who forbade his offspring from socializing with other children in the village of Haworth, where he had been appointed perpetual curate. Instead, he promoted self-education and encouraged his children to read the Bible and the works of William Shakespeare, William Wordsworth, Lord Byron, and Sir Walter Scott, as well as newspapers and monthly magazines. Brontë attended a school near Mirfield, Roe Head, for a year before returning home to tutor her younger siblings. She and Branwell began writing their own stories and poems together, set in the imaginary world of Angria; a volume of Brontë's juvenilia in this vein was published posthumously as *Legends of Angria* (1933). In 1835, Brontë returned to Roe Head as a teacher, while first Emily and then Anne attended the school, though she continued working with Branwell on their Angrian stories. After Anne completed school, Brontë also returned to Haworth, taking occasional positions as a governess. Her interest in writing continued, and she corresponded with established authors of the day, seeking their advice. The poet laureate Robert Southey told her that "literature cannot be the business of a woman's life, and it ought not to be. The more she is engaged in her proper duties, the less leisure she will have for it." Meanwhile, the family developed a plan to open a school run by Charlotte, Emily, and Anne; Charlotte and Emily traveled to Brussels to further their education, but the school never came to fruition. While in Brussels, Charlotte did develop a relationship with her married instructor, Constantin Heger; Heger was supportive of her writing, but their closeness eventually angered his wife, who put a stop to the friendship. Some critics believe Heger to be a model for the character of Rochester in *Jane Eyre.* Back in Haworth, Brontë became alienated from her former writing partner Branwell, as his alcoholism and immoral conduct became increasingly disturbing to her. She drew closer to her sisters following the discovery of Emily's secret manuscript of poems. Anne, too, expressed an interest in writing, and the three collectively published their poems as *Poems by Currer, Ellis, and Acton Bell* (1846), using male pseudonyms to make publication easier. The book sold two copies. Undeterred, Brontë wrote her first novel, *The Professor* (1857), but could not find a publisher. Her second novel, *Jane Eyre,* was more successful: the work was accepted for publication immediately and was praised by such diverse readers as Queen Victoria and George Eliot. The popularity of *Jane Eyre* brought Brontë into the society of authors such as William Makepeace Thackeray, Elizabeth Gaskell, Matthew Arnold, and Harriet Martineau. She began work on the ambitious novel *Shirley* (1849), a love story set in the context of an early Yorkshire labor movement, but the loss of her siblings intervened. Branwell died in September 1848, then Emily became ill and died in December of the same year. Brontë had just begun writing again when Anne also became ill, dying in May 1849. Biographers speculate that the completion of *Shirley* provided a form of therapeutic release for Brontë. The loss of her siblings, however, represented a loss of her writing partners as well. The sisters had exchanged manuscripts and offered authorial advice to each other; writing in solitude presented a challenge. In 1852, she returned to her first effort, *The Professor,* and attempted to expand it, accepting the guidance of her father in styling the work for publication. She took the general plot of *The Professor,* greatly expanded its themes and characterizations, altered the ending (which Mr. Brontë had found too unhappy), and adapted elements of the popular Gothic style. The resulting work was *Villette* (1853), the final novel Brontë published in her lifetime. In 1854, Brontë married Arthur Bell Nicholls; she died the following year from complications related to pregnancy.

MAJOR WORKS

Brontë's novels constitute her major literary output: *Jane Eyre, Shirley, Villette,* and the posthumously published *The Professor. The Professor,* both her first and last work, is unique among her novels in being written from the point of view of a male narrator. It tells the story of William Crimsworth, who leaves his post as a clerk at his brother's mill in England to start a new life in Brussels, teaching English at a girls school. There he falls in love with a pupil-teacher and does battle with the Catholic headmistress, eventually returning with his Belgian bride to England. The novel's main themes are its strong anti-Catholicism and the exploration of male sexuality as it relates to social status. With her next novel, *Jane Eyre,* Brontë examined the position of women in society. *Jane Eyre* is by far the most popularly and critically successful of Brontë's novels. Her heroine, Jane, was a departure from earlier nineteenth-century female characters: where most heroines were beautiful, ignorant, and dependent, Jane is plain, intelligent, and independent. Jane is an orphaned child who is treated cruelly by her relations. Her education enables her to become a governess for the illegitimate daughter of Fairfax Rochester. The position of governess was one of the few options available to unmarried women not supported by their own families, though one that Brontë well knew was precarious and potentially demeaning. Jane refuses to be demeaned, however, and as she seeks an appropriate marriage partner, she insists on an equal and mutually satisfying relationship, defying both the literary and social conventions of the time. The marriage of Jane and Rochester placed Brontë on the vanguard of women's issues. More directly than *Jane Eyre, Shirley* presents a powerful indictment of the position of women in nineteenth-century England. Shirley Keeldar is an independent woman, a land owner and mill owner, whose love for the poor tutor Louis cannot be realized because of the great difference in their social status. Still, she rejects the advances of Robert Moore, a greedy mill owner who is focused solely on profits. Robert was intended for Shirley's friend Caroline Helstone but prefers Shirley's wealth to Caroline's poverty. Bereft of her own marriage opportunities, and lacking any prospects for employment, Caroline is forced to live with an aloof and indifferent uncle and in her despair begins to sink into ill health. Brontë parallels the plight of women whose survival depends on the generosity of men to that of workers dependent on the mill owners. *Villette* similarly depicts a young woman whose fortunes are securely tied either to the men in her life or to the whims of her benefactors. Like *Jane Eyre* and *The Professor, Villette* is told from the first-person perspective of a young person separated from family. Lucy Snow lives with her godparents in England, where she falls in love with Graham Bretton, their son. She then enters domestic service with Miss Marchmont, whose promise to include Lucy in her will goes unfulfilled. She travels to the French village of Villette, where she develops a friendship with the local physician, Dr. John, that eventually develops into an obsession depicted by Brontë in the high Gothic mode. Critics have seen in Lucy's behavior one of the first nervous breakdowns in literature to be rendered in realistic psychological detail. Lucy then discloses to her readers a bizarre secret: Dr. John is Graham Bretton, an unusual twist in narration that reflects Lucy's irrationality. Dr. John falls in love with another woman, and Lucy forms an attachment with the brilliant professor Paul Emanuel. At the novel's end, however, Lucy implies that Paul has died in a shipwreck, again leaving Lucy alone and friendless.

CRITICAL RECEPTION

Initial response to Brontë's novels invariably noted that they were intensely personal and written in an uncommonly natural style. Whether those attributes were interpreted favorably or unfavorably depended on the reviewer. Though none of her later novels were as popular as her first, they received similar assessments by contemporary readers: Brontë developed a reputation for forceful writing and powerful imagery but also for stilted characterization and a didactic tone. From those first reviews forward, critics have also contended that Brontë wrote too much from her own narrow, even eccentric experience. The relationship between her life and her works has consistently been a theme in Brontë criticism. The 1970s saw strongly feminist studies of Brontë's novels as scholars looked at *Jane Eyre* and also studied other works, especially *Villette,* as explorations of women's difficult position in Victorian society—sometimes interpreting Brontë's work as a feminist critique, and in other instances as an example of the obstacles to full self-expression Brontë faced as a woman writer. An important part of the early feminist studies of Brontë's writing came in Sandra Gilbert and Susan Gubar's landmark work *The Madwoman in the Attic,* published in 1979. In this study, Gilbert and Gubar contend that Brontë's novels came to stand for the self-repression, unsatisfied desire, and anxiety of authorship experienced by women writers in the nineteenth century. Gilbert and Gubar's reading of Brontë's work has provided a foundation for much of the later criticism on her novels. Another groundbreaking study of *Jane Eyre* and the Brontë oeuvre came with the rise of postcolonial criticism. Gayatri Chakravorty Spivak (see Further Reading) was the first critic to contribute to what became a series of several studies considering the relationship between the oppressed women of *Jane Eyre* and the subjugated European colonies. Scholars have since differed on Brontë's own positions on slavery and colonialism, but the themes of Orientalism and imperialism have become closely intertwined with the study of issues of gender and sexuality.

PRINCIPAL WORKS

Poems by Currer, Ellis and Acton Bell [as Currer Bell] (poetry) 1846

Jane Eyre: An Autobiography [as Currer Bell] (novel) 1847

Shirley: A Tale [as Currer Bell] (novel) 1849

Villette [as Currer Bell] (novel) 1853

The Professor: A Tale [as Currer Bell] (novel) 1857

Life and Works of the Sisters Brontë. 7 vols. (novels and poetry) 1899-1903

The Twelve Adventurers and Other Stories (short stories) 1925

The Shakespeare Head Brontë. 19 vols. (novels, poetry, and letters) 1931-38

Legends of Angria: Compiled from the Early Writings of Charlotte Brontë. (juvenilia) 1933

Five Novelettes: Passing Events, Julia, Mina Laury, Henry Hastings, Caroline Vernon (novellas) 1971

PRIMARY SOURCES

CHARLOTTE BRONTË (ESSAY DATE C. 1830-40)

SOURCE: Brontë, Charlotte. "Caroline Vernon." In *Legends of Angria,* edited by Fannie Ratchford, pp. 221-301. Port Washington, N.Y.: Kennikat Press, 1973.

In the following excerpt, written sometime between 1830 and 1840, Brontë depicts a plain and unsophisticated young girl coming of age as her guardian prepares her for the dissolution of fashionable society.

Tomorrow came. The young lover of rebels and regicides awoke as happy as could be. Her father, whom she had so long dreamed about, was at last come. One of her dearest wishes had been realized, and why not others in the course of time?

While Elise Touquet dressed her hair, she sat pondering over a reverie of romance, something so delicious, yet so undefined. I will not say it was love, yet neither will I affirm that love was entirely excluded therefrom. Something there was of a hero, yet a nameless and formless, a mystic being, a dread shadow that crowded upon Miss Vernon's soul, haunted her day and night when she had nothing else useful to occupy her head or her hands. I almost think she gave him the name of Ferdinand Alonzo Fitz Adolphus, but I don't know. The fact was, he frequently changed, his designation being sometimes no more than simple Charles Seymour or Edward Clifford, and at other times soaring to the titles Harold Aurelius Rinaldo, Duke of Montmorency di Caldacella, a very fine name, no doubt, though whether he was to have golden or raven hair or straight or aquiline proboscis, she had not quite decided. However, he was to delve before him in the way of fighting to conquer the world and build himself a city like Babylon, only it was to be a place called the Alhambra, where Mr. Harold Aurelius was to live, taking upon himself the title of Caliph and she, Miss Vernon, the professor of republican principles, was to be his chief lady and to be called the Sultana Zara Esmeralda, with at least a hundred slaves to do her bidding. As for the garden of roses and the halls of marble, and the diamonds and the pearls and the rubies, it would be vanity to attempt a description of such heavenly sights. The reader must task his imagination and try if he can to conceive them.

In the course of that day, Miss Vernon got something better to think of than the crudities of her own overstretched fancy. That day was an era in her life. She was no longer to be a child, she was to be acknowledged a woman. Farewell to captivity where she had been reared like a bird. Her father was come to release her, and she was to be almost mistress there. She was to have servants and wealth; and whatever delighted her eye she was to ask for and receive. She was to enter life, to see society, to live all the winter in a great city, Verdopolis, to be dressed as gaily as the gayest ladies, to have jewels of her own, to vie even with those demi-goddesses, the ladies Castlereagh and Thornton.

It was too much; she could hardly realize it. It may be supposed from her enthusiastic character that she received this intelligence with transport, that as Northangerland unfolded these coming glories to her view she expressed her delight and astonishment and gratitude in terms of ecstasy, but the fact is she sat by the table with her head in her hand listening to it all with a very grave face. Pleased she was, of course, but she made no stir. It was rather too important a matter to clasp her hands about. She took it soberly. When the Earl told her she must get all in readiness to get off early tomorrow, she said, "Tomorrow, Papa?" and looked up with an excited glance.

"Yes, early in the morning."

"Does Mamma know?"

"I shall tell her."

"I hope she will not take it to heart," said Caroline. "Let us take her with us for about a week or so, Papa. It will be so dreary to leave her behind."

"She's not under my control," replied Percy.

"Well," continued Miss Vernon, "if she were not so excessively perverse and bad to manage as she is, I'm sure she might get leave to go, but she makes the Duke of Zamorna think she's out of her wits by her frantic way of going on, and he says she's not fit to let loose on society. Actually, Papa, one day when the Duke was dining with us, she started up without speaking a word, in the middle of the dinner, and flew at him with a knife. He could hardly get the knife from her, and afterward he was obliged to tell Cooper to hold her hands. And another time she brought him a glass of wine, and he had just tasted it and threw the rest at the back of the fire. He looked full at her, and Mamma began to cry and scream as if somebody was killing her. She's always contriving to get laudanum and prussic acid and such trash. She says she'll murder either him or herself and I'm afraid if she's left quite alone she'll really do some harm."

"She'll not hurt herself," replied the Earl, "and, as to Zamorna, I think he's able to mind his own affairs."

"Well," said Miss Vernon, "I must go and tell Elise to pack up," and she jumped up and danced away as if care lay lightly upon her. . . .

Miss Caroline is to leave Hawkscliffe tomorrow. She is drinking in all its beauties tonight. So you suppose, reader, but you're mistaken. If you observe her eyes, she's not gazing, she's watching. She's not contemplating the moon, she's following the motions of that person who for the last half hour has been leisurely pacing up and down that gravel walk at the bottom of the garden.

It's her guardian, and she is considering whether she shall go and join him for the last time, that is, for the last time at Hawkscliffe. She's by no means contemplating anything like [the] solemnity of an eternal separation.

This guardian of hers has a blue frock coat on, with white inexpressibles, and a stiff black stock, consequently he considerably resembles that angelic existence called a military man. You'll suppose Miss Vernon considers him handsome, because other people do. All the ladies in the world, you know, hold the Duke of Zamorna to be matchless, irresistible, but Miss Vernon doesn't think him handsome, in fact the question of his charms has never yet been mooted in her mind. The idea as to whether he is a god of perfection or a demon of defects has not crossed her intellect once. Neither has she once compared him with other men. He is himself, a kind of abstract, isolated being, quite distinct from aught beside under the sun. . . .

It seems, however, that Miss Vernon has at length conquered her timidity, for lo! as the twilight deepens, the garden and all is dim and obscure. She, with her hat on, comes stealing quietly out of the house and through the shrubs, the closed blossoms, and dewy grass, trips like a fairy to meet him. She thought she would surprise him, so she took a circuit and came behind. She touched his hand before he was aware. Cast iron, however, can't be startled, so no more was he.

"Where did you come from?" asked the guardian, gazing down from his supreme altitude upon his ward, who passed her arm through his and hung upon him according to her custom when they walked together.

"I saw you walking by yourself, and so I thought I'd come and keep you company," she replied.

"Perhaps I don't want you," said the Duke.

"Yes, you do. You're smiling, and you've put your book away as if you meant to talk to me instead of reading."

"Well, are you ready to set off tomorrow?" he asked.

"Yes, all packed."

"And the head and heart are in as complete a state of preparation as the trunk, I presume," continued his Grace.

"My heart is sore," said Caroline, "I'm sorry to go, especially this evening. I was not half so sorry in the middle of the day, while I was busy. But now—"

"You're tired and therefore low spirited. Well, you'll wake fresh in the morning and see the matter in a different light. You must mind how you behave, Caroline, when you get out into the world. I shall ask after you sometimes."

"Ask after me! You'll see me. I shall come to Victoria Square almost constantly when you're in Verdopolis."

"You will not be in Verdopolis longer than a few days."

"Where shall I be then?"

"You will be in Paris or Fidena or Breslau."

Caroline was silent.

"You will enter a new sphere," continued her guardian, "and a new circle of society, which will mostly consist of French people. Don't copy the manners of the ladies you see at Paris or Fountainbleau. They are most of them not quite what they should be. They have very poor, obtrusive manners, and will often be talking to you about love and endeavouring to make you their confidante. You should not listen to their notions on the subject, as they are all very vicious and immodest. As to men, those you see will be almost universally gross and polluted. Avoid them."

Caroline spoke not.

"In a year or two, your father will begin to talk of marrying you," continued her guardian, "and I suppose you think it will be the finest thing in the world to be married. It is not impossible that your father may propose a Frenchman for your husband. If he does, decline the honour of such a connection."

Still Miss Vernon was mute.

"Remember always," continued his Grace, "that there is one nation under heaven filthier even than the French, that is the Italian. The women of Italy should be excluded from your presence and the men should be spurned with disgust even from your thoughts."

Silence still. Caroline wondered why his Grace talked in that way. He had never been so stern and didactic before. His allusions to matrimony, etc., confounded her. It was not that the idea was altogether foreign to the young lady's mind. She had most probably studied the subject now and then in those glowing day dreams before hinted at; nor I should not undertake to say how far her speculations concerning it had extended, for she was a daring theorist. But as yet, these thoughts had all been secret and untold. Her guardian was the last person to whom she would have revealed their existence. And now it was with a sense of shame that she heard his grave counsel on the subject. What he said, too, about the French ladies and the Italian men and women made her feel very queer. She could not for the world have answered him, and yet she wished to hear more. She was soon satisfied.

"It is not at all improbable," pursued his Grace, after a brief pause, during which he and Caroline had slowly paced the long terrace walk at the bottom of the garden which skirted the stately aisle of trees; "it is not at all improbable that you may meet occasionally in society a lady of the name of Lelande and another of the name St. James, and it is most likely that these ladies will show you much attention—flatter you, ask you to sing or play, invite you to their houses, introduce you to their particular circles, and offer to accompany you to public places. You must decline it all."

"Why?" asked Miss Vernon.

"Because," replied the Duke, "Madam Lelande and Lady St. James are very easy about their characters. Their ideas on the subject of morality are very loose. They would get you into their boudoirs, as the ladies of Paris call the little rooms where they sit in a morning and read gross novels and talk over their secrets with their intimate friends. You will hear of many love intrigues and of a great deal of amorous manoeuvring. You would get accustomed to imprudent conversation and perhaps, become involved in foolish adventures which would disgrace you."

Zamorna still had all the talk to himself, for Miss Vernon seemed to be too busily engaged in contemplating the white pebbles on which the moon was shining, that lay here and there on the path at her feet, to take much share in the conversation. At last she said in a rather low voice, "I never intended to make friends with any French women. I always thought that when I was a woman I would visit strictly with nice people, as Lady Thornton and Mrs. Warner and the lady who lives about two miles from here, Miss Laury. They are all very well known, are they not?"

Before the Duke answered this question, he took out a red silk handkerchief and blew his nose. He then said, "Mrs. Warner's a remarkably decent woman. Lady Thornton is somewhat too gay and flashy: in other respects, I know no harm in her."

"And what is Miss Laury like?"

"She's rather tall and pale."

"But I mean what is her character? Ought I to visit with her?"

"You will be saved the trouble of deciding on that point, as she will never come in your way. She always resides in the country."

"I thought she was very fashionable," continued Miss Vernon, "for I remember when I was in Adrianopolis, I often saw pictures in the shops of her, and I thought her very nice looking."

The Duke was silent in his turn.

"I wonder why she lives alone," pursued Caroline, "and I wonder she has no relations. Is she rich?"

"Not very."

"Do you know her?"

"Yes."

"Does Papa?"

"No."

"Do you like her?"

"Sometimes."

"Why don't you like her always?"

"I don't always think about her."

"Do you ever go to see her?"

"Now and then."

"Does she ever give parties?"

"No."

"I believe she's rather mysterious and romantic," continued Miss Vernon.

"She's a romantic look in her eyes. I should not wonder if she had adventures."

"I dare say she has," remarked her guardian.

"I should like to have some adventures," added the young lady. "I don't want a dull, droning life."

"You may be gratified," replied the Duke. "Be in no hurry. You are young enough yet. Life is only just opening."

"But I should like something very strange and uncommon. Something that I don't at all expect."

Zamorna whistled.

"I should like to be tried, to see what I had in me," continued his ward. "O, if I were only better looking! Adventures never happen to plain people."

"No, not often."

"I am so sorry that I am not as pretty as your wife, the Duchess. If she had been like me she would never have been married to you."

"Indeed! How do you know that?"

"Because I am sure you would not have asked her. But she's so nice and fair—and I'm dark, like a mulatto, Mamma says."

"Dark, yet comely," muttered the Duke involuntarily, for he had looked down at his ward as she looked up at him, and the moonlight disclosed a clear forehead pencilled with soft, dark curls, dark and touching eyes, and a round youthful cheek, smooth in texture and a fine tint as that of some portrait hung in an Italian palace where you see the raven eyelashes and southern eyes relieving the complexion of pure colourless olive and the rosy lips smiling brighter and warmer for the absence of bloom elsewhere.

Zamorna did not tell Miss Vernon what he thought, at least not in words, but when she would have ceased to look up at him and returned to the contemplation of the scattered pebbles, he retained her face in that raised attitude by a touch of his finger under her little oval chin.

His Grace of Angria is an artist. It is probable that the sweet face, touched with soft Luna's light, struck him as a fine artistical study. No doubt it is terrible to be fixed by a tall powerful man who knits his brows and whose dark hair and whiskers and moustaches combine to shadow the eyes of a hawk and the features of a Roman statue. When such a man puts on an expression you can't understand, stops suddenly as you are walking with him alone in a dim garden, removes your hand from his arm, places his hands on your shoulders, you are justified in getting nervous and uneasy.

"I suppose I have been talking nonsense," said Miss Vernon, colouring and half frightened.

"In what way?"

"I've said something about my sister Mary that I shouldn't have said."

"How?"

"I can't tell you, but you don't like her to be spoken of, perhaps. I remember now you said once that she and I ought to have nothing to do with each other, and you would never take me to see her."

"Little simpleton!" remarked Zamorna.

"No," said Caroline, deprecating the scornful name with a look, and a smile showed her transient alarm was departing, "no, don't call me so."

"Pretty little simpleton! Will that do?" said her guardian.

"No. I'm not pretty."

Zamorna made no reply, whereat, to confess the truth, Miss Vernon was slightly disappointed, for of late she had begun to entertain some latent embryo idea that his Grace did not think her quite ugly. What grounds she had for thinking so, it would not be easy to say. It was an instinctive feeling, and one that gave her little vain female heart too much pleasure not to be encouraged, fostered as a secret prize. Will the reader be exceedingly shocked if I venture to conjecture that all the foregoing lamentations about her plainness were uttered with some half-defined interest of drawing forth a little word or two of cheering praise?

Oh human nature! Human nature! Oh experience! In what an obscure dim unconscious dream Miss [Vernon] was enveloped. How little did she know herself. However, time is advancing and the hours, those "wild-eyed charioteers," as Shelley calls them, are driving on. She will gather knowledge by degrees. She is one of the gleaners of grapes in that vineyard where all women-kind have been plucking fruit since the world began—in the vineyard of experience. At present, though, she rather seems to be a kind of Ruth in a corn field, nor does there want a Boaz to complete the picture, who also is well disposed to scatter handfulls for the damsel's special benefit. In other words she has a mentor who, not satisfied with instilling into her mind the precepts of wisdom by words, will, if not prevented by others, do his best to enforce his verbal admonitions by practical illustrations that will dissipate the mists on her vision at once and show her, and show her in light both gross and burning, the mysteries of humanity now hidden, its passions and sins and sufferings, all its passage of strange error, all its after-scenes of agonized atonement.

A skillful Preceptor is that same one, accustomed to tuition. Caroline has grown up under his care a fine and accomplished girl, unspoilt by flattery, unused to compliments, unhackneyed, untrite fashionable conventionalities, fresh, naïve and romantic, really romantic, throwing her heart and soul into her dreams, longing only for the opportunity to do what she feels she could do, and to die for somebody she loves, that is, not actually to become a subject for the undertaker, but to give up heart, soul, and sensations to one loved hero, to lose independent existence in the perfect adoption of her lover's being. This is all very fine, isn't it, reader, almost as good as the notion of Mr. Rinaldo Aurelius. Caroline has yet to discover that she is as clay in the hands of the potter, that the process of moulding is even now advancing and ere long, she will be turned in the wood a perfect, polished vessel of Grace.

CHARLOTTE BRONTË (ESSAY DATE 1850)

SOURCE: Brontë, Charlotte. "Biographical Notice of Ellis and Acton Bell." In *Works of the Sisters Brontë,* Vol. 5, edited by Mary A. Ward, pp. 43-51. New York: Bigelow, Brown, & Co., 1900.

In the following excerpt, originally published in 1850, Brontë gives some of the history of the sisters' decision to publish and to use pseudonyms; she also writes about her sisters' work and their unusual personalities.

About five years ago, my two sisters and myself, after a somewhat prolonged period of separation, found ourselves reunited, and at home. Resident in a remote district, where education had made little progress, and where, consequently, there was no inducement to seek social intercourse beyond our own domestic circle, we were wholly dependent on ourselves and each other, on books and study, for the enjoyments and occupations of life. The highest stimulus, as well as the liveliest pleasure we had known from childhood upwards, lay in attempts at literary composition; formerly we used to show each other what we wrote, but of late years this habit of communication and consultation had been discontinued; hence it ensued, that we were mutually ignorant of the progress we might respectively have made.

One day, in the autumn of 1845, I accidentally lighted on a MS. volume of verse in my sister Emily's handwriting. Of course, I was not surprised, knowing that she could and did write verse: I looked it over, and something more than surprise seized me—a deep conviction that these were not common effusions, nor at all like the poetry women generally write. I thought them condensed and terse, vigorous and genuine. To my ear they had also a peculiar music—wild, melancholy, and elevating.

My sister Emily was not a person of demonstrative character, nor one on the recesses of whose mind and feelings even those nearest and dearest to her could, with impunity, intrude unlicensed; it took hours to reconcile her to the discovery I had made, and days to persuade her that such poems merited publication. I knew, however, that a mind like hers could not be without some latent spark of honourable ambition, and refused to be discouraged in my attempts to fan that spark to flame.

Meantime, my younger sister quietly produced some of her own compositions, intimating that, since Emily's had given me pleasure, I might like to look at hers. I could not but be a partial judge, yet I thought that these verses, too, had a sweet, sincere pathos of their own.

We had very early cherished the dream of one day becoming authors. This dream, never relinquished even when distance divided and absorbing tasks occupied us, now suddenly acquired strength and consistency: it took the character of a resolve. We agreed to arrange a small selection of our poems, and, if possible, to get them printed. Averse to personal publicity, we veiled our own names under those of Currer, Ellis, and Acton Bell; the ambiguous choice being dictated by a sort of conscientious scruple at assuming Christian names positively masculine, while we did not like to declare ourselves women, because—without at that time suspecting that our mode of writing and thinking was not what is called 'feminine'—we had a vague impression that authoresses are liable to be looked on with prejudice; we had noticed how critics sometimes use for their chastisement the weapon of personality, and for their reward, a flattery, which is not true praise.

The bringing out of our little book was hard work. As was to be expected, neither we nor our poems were at all wanted; but for this we had been prepared at the outset; though inexperienced ourselves, we had read the experience of others. The great puzzle lay in the difficulty of getting answers of any kind from the publishers to whom we applied. Being greatly harassed by this obstacle, I ventured to apply to the Messrs. Chambers, of Edinburgh, for a word of advice; *they* may have forgotten the circumstance, but *I* have not, for from them I received a brief and business-like, but civil and sensible reply, on which we acted, and at last made a way.

The book was printed: it is scarcely known, and all of it that merits to be known are the poems of Ellis Bell. The fixed conviction I held, and hold, of the worth of these poems has not indeed received the confirmation of much favourable criticism; but I must retain it notwithstanding. . . .

What more shall I say about them? I cannot and need not say much more. In externals, they were two unobtrusive women; a perfectly secluded life gave them retiring manners and habits. In Emily's nature the extremes of vigour and simplicity seemed to meet. Under an unsophisticated culture, inartificial tastes, and an unpretending outside, lay a secret power and fire that might have informed the brain and kindled the veins of a hero; but she had no worldly wisdom; her powers were unadapted to the practical business of life; she would fail to defend her most manifest rights, to consult her most legitimate advantage. An interpreter ought always to have stood between her and the world. Her will was not very flexible, and it generally opposed her interest. Her temper was magnanimous, but warm and sudden; her spirit altogether unbending.

Anne's character was milder and more subdued; she wanted the power, the fire, the originality of her sister, but was well endowed with quiet virtues of her own. Long-suffering, self-denying, reflective, and intelligent, a constitutional reserve and taciturnity placed and kept her in the shade, and covered her mind, and especially her feelings, with a sort of nun-like veil, which was rarely lifted. Neither Emily nor Anne was learned; they had no thought of filling their pitchers at the well-spring of other minds; they always wrote from the impulse of nature, the dictates of intuition, and from such stores of observation as their limited experience had enabled them to amass. I may sum up all by saying, that for strangers they were nothing, for superficial observers less than nothing; but for those who had known them all their lives in the intimacy of close relationship, they were genuinely good and truly great.

This notice has been written because I felt it a sacred duty to wipe the dust off their gravestones, and leave their dear names free from soil.

GENERAL COMMENTARY

MARGARET LAWRENCE (ESSAY DATE 1936)

SOURCE: Lawrence, Margaret. "The Brontë Sisters, Who Wrestled With Romance." In *The School of Femininity: A Book For and About Women As They Are Interpreted Through Feminine Writers of Yesterday and Today*, pp. 60-88. New York: Frederick A. Stokes, 1936.

In the following excerpt, Lawrence asserts that Brontë's novels are documents of feminist history, reflecting the unsatisfied passion of women with limited options and without mutual and egalitarian love relationships.

When Charlotte read *Wuthering Heights* she was staggered again. She knew that her own ***Professor*** was a silly tame story beside it. She sat down to begin another story; and some of the fire of *Wuthering Heights* transferred itself to the writing of ***Jane Eyre.***

ABOUT THE AUTHOR

BRONTË'S FRIEND AND BIOGRAPHER ELIZABETH GASKELL ON BRONTË'S WRITING PRACTICES

The sisters retained the old habit, which was begun in their aunt's life-time, of putting away their work at nine o'clock, and beginning their study, pacing up and down the sitting room. At this time, they talked over the stories they were engaged upon, and described their plots. Once or twice a week, each read to the others what she had written, and heard what they had to say about it. Charlotte told me, that the remarks made had seldom any effect in inducing her to alter her work, so possessed was she with the feeling that she had described reality; but the readings were of great and stirring interest to all, taking them out of the gnawing pressure of daily-recurring cares, and setting them in a free place. It was on one of these occasions, that Charlotte determined to make her heroine plain, small, and unattractive, in defiance of the accepted canon.

The writer of the beautiful obituary article on "the death of Currer Bell" most likely learnt from herself what is there stated, and which I will take the liberty of quoting, about Jane Eyre.

"She once told her sisters that they were wrong—even morally wrong—in making their heroines beautiful as a matter of course. They replied that it was impossible to make a heroine interesting on any other terms. Her answer was, 'I will prove to you that you are wrong; I will show you a heroine as plain and as small as myself, who shall be as interesting as any of yours.' Hence *Jane Eyre,* said she in telling the anecdote: 'but she is not myself, any further than that.'"

Gaskell, Elizabeth. Excerpt from *The Life of Charlotte Brontë*, pp. 215-16. First published London, 1857; republished London: Dent, 1971.

And ***Jane Eyre*** was the book of the year in England. Charlotte Brontë had let loose all the pent-up hatreds of her nature. She was no longer afraid. There had been hatred in her sister's book. But Charlotte's was a very concrete hatred and very personal. She went after the school that had killed her two older sisters. She made horrible images of the teachers and of the system. She took for her heroine a small plain-looking orphan girl who was designed by nature to be the butt of sadistic people. She wrote herself into little defenseless, tortured Jane Eyre. The hatred that forced the book out of her made its writing astoundingly vivid. It knocked its readers cold. The style was as tortured as the heroine. Charlotte liked being literary, and she never missed a chance to be literary; except when she was so angry she forgot. It was when she was raging angry that the book blazed with power; when she cooled off and got literary it was lame and pretentious; but fortunately for her ambitions the anger far outweighed the literature in it; so it went over. She was unquestionably influenced by Emily's Heathcliffe when she came to draw the hero, Mr. Rochester. Only, as she no doubt thought herself, she improved on him by giving her man a very Continental experience. He had had a group of mistresses, and liked nothing better than to brag about them; but when he was due, by reason of approaching middle age, to be touched by tender love, it was gentle, plain Jane to whom he turned. Not for him were the lovely ladies of title that were brought into the story. But he amused himself while he was trying to make up his mind what to do by philandering a bit; just enough to make Jane jealous. Jealousy made her lose her head. She came out flatly with her love of him. It was Charlotte's famous innovation. No woman had ever done such a thing in literature—certainly not in ladylike literature. It was a great triumph for Mr. Rochester. It gave him courage to plan his final sin. For all this time the bad man had been hiding in his attic a maniac wife, guarded by a gin-consuming nurse. Jane had sensed the mystery in the house. But that had added to her love. Mr. Rochester arranges a start into bigamy; but he is stopped at the altar. The facts have come out. Jane is horrified; but not nearly so horrified as when her darling makes her a proposition. Then she flees the country, as all good women fled in those days from sin. And she flees with only what she has on, and has many melodramatic accidents. But they are nothing compared to what happened to Rochester. His insane wife sets the house on fire, and jumps from the roof to her death. Rochester is paid by fate for his ways by having a burning brand hit him in the eyes; he is blinded for life. And little Jane comes radiantly back and marries him. Charlotte Brontë hugged herself; she had made a plain little woman come into her own; she had been most sophisticated and had not quailed before mistresses and sins and cases for the asylum. In fact she had treated them all with gusto. All London talked about the book. People got all mixed up about the identities of Currer, Ellis and Acton Bell. She thought it was necessary to go to London and straighten things out. But she was afraid to go by herself. So she took Anne. Emily was angry about the whole business. She was still angrier when Charlotte returned and explained that she had told the publisher they were three sisters. It was all a trap, Emily said. Publicity was vulgar. Besides being a nuisance. She must have had a moment of prevision. Publicity was certainly going to be both vulgar and a nuisance for the Brontë future. Not to mention what it was going to do to Brontë historians. That settled it for Emily. She would never write another novel.

But Charlotte had got going. This at last was living. The little plans for the school now seemed to be childish and forlorn. Here was literary fame. Emily looked at her and went off by herself to walk on the moors. But Anne was more impressed. She wanted to get in on the fame.

Emily puzzled Charlotte. There was no understanding the girl. What was she? She decided that she would put Emily into a book. That certainly was the way to deal with what bothered you. Anne was thinking too. But not about Emily. She took Emily for granted. She had been impressed by the sins in Charlotte's book. Sin paid. Not that Branwell ever made his pay. She decided to put Branwell into a book. She patted her conscience by saying to herself that maybe it would keep others from falling into a like sin. The father was coming out in Anne. She wanted to preach. So she wrote *The Tenant of Wildfell Hall.*

One day when Emily came in from the moors followed by her dog, Keeper, Anne told her what she was doing. Emily looked at her. She said quietly that she was surprised. It was bad taste to use one's relatives for copy; it was cruelty to use the weakness of another for professional material. It was also lazy. What was the imagination for? Anne was hurt. She had not meant any harm. Charlotte blazed at Emily. She should let Anne alone. It was time that some woman had the courage to write about what drink did to men and to the women tied to them. Emily looked at her with disconcerting directness. To make copy out of poor Branwell was wrong. They would pay for it.

She must have had another moment of prevision. Branwell might very profitably have been left alone. But Anne was firm. It was her duty. And Charlotte had encouraged her. Which was to be considered. For of the family Charlotte was the successful author. Surely she should know what would sell. What could Emily say to that? She could not summon enough prevision to know that *Wuthering Heights* would be read and reread when Charlotte's books were only remembered as the books that somehow had got placed on the school's supplementary-reading list because of some vague historical significance.

So the writing went on in that unhappy house. And so did the germ. Branwell began to sink. Emily nursed him. His father grieved over his only son. Charlotte hardened herself. She knew that they had to stand it. But he had brought it on himself. Anne thought to herself that it would not all be in vain. People would know what drink did to men.

On the day of Branwell's funeral in September, Emily collapsed. She never went out again on the moors. But she would not stay in bed. She went about her usual household work. She talked less than ever. Charlotte was frantic. She said she was going to send for a London doctor. Emily said she would not see him if he did come. What would the use be? One morning in December she went to the cage where she kept a wild hawk she had tamed. Charlotte watched her and was frightened. Emily opened the door of the hawk's cage and told him to go free. He hesitated. She lifted him out and poised him on her hand, and sent him with a push out into the air. Emily was Irish; she was dying with a symbolic gesture. Charlotte was terrified. Emily turned; she put her hand to her throat; she struggled with her breath. She knew it had come, and she fought. She hated the publicity of death. Reserve was no armor against it. She struggled; she would not die. It was a horrible thing that would leave her helpless and open. She kept on her feet; she held on to the door until the germ had taken her last breath. It was a shocking pagan death.

It hurried the progress of the germ in little Anne. She sickened immediately. Charlotte called the doctor, only to learn that nothing could save Anne. She was already too far gone. Charlotte, however, tried to save her. She took her to Scarborough by the sea; but it was in vain. Anne died in May, and was buried in Scarborough. Charlotte returned to her father. She read Emily's last poems, among them that magnificent last psalm.

No coward soul is mine,
No trembler in the world's storm-troubled sphere;
I see heaven's glory shine,
And faith shines equal, arming me from afar.

O God within my breast,
Almighty, ever-present Deity!
Life—that in me has rest,
As, undying Life—have power in thee!

Vain are the thousand creeds
That move men's hearts; unutterably vain;
Worthless as withered weeds,
Or idlest froth amid the boundless main.

To waken doubt in one
Holding so fast by Thine infinity;
So surely anchored on
The steadfast rock of immortality.

With wide-embracing love
Thy spirit animates eternal years,
Pervades and broods above,
Changes, sustains, dissolves, creates and rears.

Though earth and man were gone,
And suns and universe ceased to be,
And Thou were left alone,
Every existence would exist in Thee.

There is not room for death,
Nor atom that his might could render void;
Thou—Thou art Being and Breath,
And what Thou art may never be destroyed.

Charlotte walked backward and forward in her lonely house. She thought of Keeper, the dog, sitting in his sorrow on Emily's grave. She thought about the wild hawk. What was Emily?

Charlotte tried to make Emily live in ***Shirley.*** But Charlotte could only portray what she loved or what she hated. Emily was beyond both love and hate. She had been spiritually elusive, and humanly a most puzzling person. The pagan fierce death; the religious faith of the last song. Which was Emily? Animals and birds had known her instinctively, and were drawn as by a magnet. Keeper never recovered from her death. His dog heart was broken. Charlotte tried very hard with ***Shirley.*** It was an interesting characterization she managed; but it was not Emily.

The book rolls up in the end into feminist propaganda. Charlotte saw her sister as one of the new women. She sets her as she would have liked to have seen Emily, with wealth and friends. She did not realize that wealth would have meant nothing more to Emily than poverty. She creates conversations between Shirley and her intimate woman friend, Caroline Helstone, such as she imagined Emily would have conducted, had she ever cared to get into conversation. The conversations read like very learned essays on the freedom of women. Emily would have thought they were funny. Charlotte really had nothing to put into ***Shirley.*** The subject was beyond her emotional grip. Emily's temperamental aloofness had always tortured her sister. Her occasional sweetness had never been given to Charlotte. It had gone out to the weakness of Branwell and the pathos of Anne. Charlotte had utterly no comprehension of the mysticism of Emily; she had had no idea that the strangeness of her eyes had come out of a frustration which was a greater frustration than any of the frustrations in that house. Emily Brontë was a tragedy. She handled her tragedy well. She achieved calm. But she could only maintain it when she was alone on the moors. When she went into the world it was broken. So she took care not to go into the world. Emily had pushed herself so far down into the depths of her nature that she only existed in a dream. She needed a Teacher. She got quite far by herself, but she had missed the wisdom that would have made her able to preserve her poise in the world. That could only have come to her from a teacher whose training was far beyond any of the training of western religions. Emily would have understood the East. She could have sat at the feet of Lao-tse.

But all this was out of Charlotte's understanding. All she knew was that she missed the presence of Emily. It bothered her that she had not loved her enough. She took to lying about it. She assured everybody that Emily and she had been devoted to each other. In private she paced up and down with remorse. She had spent years of her life loving a man who had refused even to write to her. She had closed herself up in that love. And Emily had been dying all the time. Perhaps in great need of love. Charlotte hated the Hegers because they had taken her emotion for so long.

So she went for them in ***Villette.*** Emily had never liked them.

Sitting alone with an old father in that dismal house Charlotte got the Hegers out of her system. This time there was very little disguise. She herself lived in the small plain-looking shy English governess, Lucy Snow. The Heger *ménage* came to life in Madame Beck's school for young ladies. She dealt meticulously with Madame Beck's jealousies. Technically the story flags badly in places. Charlotte obviously got frightened at times and tried to cover herself up. She has to divide her love into two men, and little Lucy has to veer from one to the other without much reason for doing so. It makes it rather unconvincing. But the genuine emotion of the writer does get into scenes. With heart-breaking poignancy little Lucy struggled with her hopeless passion. That is very real. And the actual Monsieur Heger is very real and so is the pussyfooting Madame Beck. It is easy to understand why Charlotte should have been attracted to the man. He is fiery and uncertain with all the temperamental virility that the Brontë girls liked in men. It was easy to understand why she hated Madame. It was not only that she possessed Monsieur. She also possessed the bland and irritating self-containment which Charlotte always had lacked. She had the silent superiority that Emily had had, and in addition a completely worldly estimate of the motivation of other people.

The portrait of Madame Beck was so bitter that it floored Mrs. Gaskell when she came to do the biography. She went over to Brussels to look the woman up. Madame Heger felt it was her duty in the interest of history to show her Charlotte's letters. Mrs. Gaskell interpreted it as her duty to the feminine cause to ignore the letters. It would never do. She thought hers would remain the one absolute authoritative biography. She could be as wary as Madame Heger. She put so much outside controversial matter into her biography that it took all the attention. The school to which the Brontës had gone took action; Branwell's mistress sued her; Mr. Brontë considered having the book banned; she had made him out to be a very eccentric person indeed, and hinted that the girls had all contracted the germ because they were starved in their childhood. Mrs. Gaskell was more astute than Victorian ladies were usually given credit for being. She really did outwit Madame Heger by making so much fuss about other matters that Brussels was left alone by the critics. If Charlotte had been wise she would have taken Mrs. Gaskell completely into her confidence; for then Mrs. Gaskell could have made even a neater job of it. Although it is just possible that she would never have undertaken to write the story of a woman who had loved a man in those circumstances. It was not nice. Brussels must have given her quite a jolt. For she had thought Charlotte was a nice woman. She had become acquainted with her two years before her death. Charlotte had visited her, and she had visited Hawarth. The tragedy of the family had caught her imagination. She knew it would make a gorgeous biography. Besides in her mind Charlotte was a literary pioneer and part of the feminist movement. She made a great heroine of her.

Charlotte Brontë did not exactly enjoy her fame.

It was compensation for the erotic wound. There is an historical rumor that the fame brought Monsieur Heger finally to her; that they met secretly in London. The Hegers admitted that Monsieur took a trip to London, and Charlotte during the years of her literary popularity was there several times every year. She was fêted. She met everybody of literary importance. But she was never able to be at ease among people. The cramped childhood told on her, and no amount of admiration could ever give her absolute self-confidence. She knew she was a small, badly-formed, plain-looking woman. Fame never alleviates that in a woman. She knew that she did not *take* with folk; she felt them looking at her interestedly, but still with appraisal. The least unfriendly criticism of her work brought her instantly back to her sensitive youth, and crushed her spirit. She never gained Emily's poise.

She got to need admiration; and her need of it led her to get married. Her father's curate, Mr. Nicholls, had admired her for a long time. He was a gentle Irishman, and had the racial taste for sad people. Charlotte Brontë was a tragic figure to him in spite of all her fame. Charlotte had never liked curates. They were mild men. She had made them ridiculous in the ***Shirley*** story, and Mr. Nicholls had recognized himself. But that had not stopped him admiring her. He liked her literary nerve, as much as he loved her personal lack of it. She accepted Mr. Nicholls.

Her father made just enough trouble about it to give it the attraction of a cause to her. Mr. Brontë had enjoyed Charlotte's fame. It had given him confidence again in the plan of existence. It justified his life. An operation had been performed upon his eyes, and he was able again to take the pulpit and to read all his daughter's books, and also to cherish her press notices. He thought that Nicholls was decidedly forgetting his place to aspire to the hand of Miss Brontë. In his opinion Charlotte could have any man she wanted. So why fall back upon a curate? Her health was much better. He no longer had to worry when she got her feet wet or sat in a draft. The family germ seemed to have been conquered by the fame.

Charlotte had decided to marry. She did not explain to her father how ill at ease she still felt with the great men she met, or that they only saw her as a queer little woman with an emotional talent for writing. After she was married she assured everybody that she was very happy.

She seems to have been happy. Mr. Nicholls was devoted and gentle. He was not the great fierce man of her temperamental yearning. But maybe she knew by then that such men were hard upon women, and demanded a lot of study. She would have had no time for the study; her career was too important. She would have had no energy either. She was too old, and in addition she was tubercular. So she was well off with her gentle curate, and probably she knew it. Maybe the historical rumor explains why she knew it. She was no longer yearning for Monsieur Heger.

She had only a few months of happiness. The germ crept up quietly all the time, and when she was pregnant in her thirty-ninth year it suddenly started to speed. The doctor who was called said it was hopeless. She died thinking she could not die she was so happy.

It was a mercy that she did die. If she had lived to hold a baby to her breast she would have been frightened about the hatreds she had put into publication. There was no taking them back.

She would have understood the need Madame Heger had felt to protect her family by whatever method would work. She would have understood the maternal emotion Emily had packed into her kindness to Branwell. She might even have felt some glimmering of the twisted psychology which leads people to be cruel to children. She would have known that literary cruelty and literary revenge did not correct it. She would have been ashamed of her books, and being Irish, she might have done something drastic.

It was better that she did not. For her three good books, ***Jane Eyre, Shirley*** and ***Villette,*** for all their awkward technique and their high-driven emotionalism, were valuable records. They were documents in the feminist movement. Mrs. Gaskell was right in her belief. Charlotte Brontë was a type. There were many middle-class women like her, unable to find the man who would have satisfied them, and with no real outlet for their energies.

She drove it home that women had feeling and passionality. She glorified feeling in women. Her characters were all subsidiary to that one main idea. She hated the romantic nonsense that men wrote about women. She also hated the picture Miss Austen drew of them. It was too matter-of-fact.

What she was really saying, though it is not clear that she knew it consciously, was that women needed a wider intellectual arena in order to find a more satisfying erotic life. They had to have a chance to explore. Love was far more important to them than to men; and yet they

FROM THE AUTHOR

BRONTË WRITES TO ELIZABETH GASKELL ABOUT THE POSITION OF WOMEN IN SOCIETY AND THE POTENTIAL FOR CHANGE

I do not know the *Life of Sydney Taylor*; whenever I have the opportunity I will get it. The little French book you mention shall also take its place on the list of books to be procured as soon as possible. It treats a subject interesting to all women—perhaps, more especially to single women; though, indeed, mothers, like you, study it for the sake of their daughters. The *Westminster Review* is not a periodical I see regularly, but some time since I got hold of a number—for last January, I think—in which there was an article entitled 'Woman's Mission' (the phrase is hackneyed), containing a great deal that seemed to me just and sensible. Men begin to regard the position of woman in another light than they used to do; and a few men, whose sympathies are fine and whose sense of justice is strong, think and speak of it with a candour that commands my admiration. They say, however—and, to an extent, truly—that the amelioration of our condition depends on ourselves. Certainly there are evils which our own efforts will best reach; but as certainly there are other evils—deep-rooted in the foundation of the social system—which no efforts of ours can touch: of which we cannot complain; of which it is advisable not too often to think.

Brontë, Charlotte. Excerpt from a letter to Elizabeth Gaskell. Reprinted in Gaskell's *The Life of Charlotte Brontë*, pp. 313. First published London, 1857; republished London: Dent, 1971.

were hemmed in by the assumption men had that women were ordained by nature simply to respond to them.

She had been disillusioned personally, but that did not alter the truth of her work. Emily and Charlotte Brontë knew something more than Miss Austen knew, though they lacked her technical mastery. And at the same time Miss Austen knew something more than they knew—which was that after all the exploring, and all the illusion, it was best to take simply what was to be had, and never mind the longing for something else.

It was all an unending confusing circle.

It would have needed the wise fine mind of George Eliot to have explained the circle. Not that Charlotte Brontë would ever have listened to George Eliot. She would not have approved of her. George Eliot had done what Miss Brontë had not managed to do—to live openly with the man she loved, even though he did happen technically to be married to another woman. Her own bitterness had made Charlotte a puritan. It was the puritan in her that caused her to make such a to-do about passion. It was her puritanism that had led her to make a feminist cause out of little Jane Eyre telling Rochester she loved him. Miss Austen would have read that incident with distaste and some amusement. It was a gaucherie, and it was unnecessary. Mary Wollstonecraft would have cheered. It was her idea of equality. And why not? Miss Austen would have shrugged her beautifully molded shoulders. And Mary would have reminded her perhaps that if she had had the nerve to do it she might have got for herself the dark sardonic man she had obviously wanted. A shadow would have flitted over Miss Austen's bright eyes. And Emily Brontë would look at her strangely. She would be thinking it was all fate. Whether one was a fighting puritan like Charlotte, or a polite skeptic like Miss Austen, or an emotional rebel like Mary Wollstonecraft, it all came to the same thing in the end. There was between men and women a bond that was peculiar to individuals, and a fixation of emotional need. Sometimes you looked through life and did not find it. Sometimes you found it and could not have it. Sometimes when you did have it you also had great sorrow. What did it matter? If only you recognized it and were true to it. Maybe that was all that counted. She would look towards George Eliot coming with pity in her deep-set philosopher's eyes.

George Eliot was the only one among them who knew love in its fulness. Having known it, she could set it to one side in her writing. It was only a part of the need of the experiencing spirit; life was a hard long way. It was not a business of getting this, or holding onto that; nor was it a matter of saying one's say. To understand; and not to judge. But she would never be able to convince Charlotte Brontë of that. Not to judge? What was the intellect for if not to judge? Women had intellects and the right to use them in judgment. What sense was there in suffering for its own sake? "Plenty," Emily would at last answer her. "It is the law of the spirit finding its way to God. Maybe in anguish like yours over Monsieur Heger, or in remorse like Branwell's over himself. It may be in disappointment like Mary's because of Gilbert Imlay, or in temperamental restlessness like Miss Austen's; or in terrible loneliness like mine. It is a law, and the wise submit to it." George Eliot would agree, and add in her husky low voice, "We cannot do anything else but submit, though there are various ways of submitting." It would be just here that Miss Austen would laugh lightly. "Variety." That is what had always taken her fancy; the variety of ways in which women would arrive at the same destiny. She would cock her arched eyebrow at George Eliot and say to her, "Now you be careful not to get too inward in your stories. It is a very tricky concern—the soul—especially the soul in women."

TERRY EAGLETON (ESSAY DATE AUTUMN 1972)

SOURCE: Eagleton, Terry. "Class, Power and Charlotte Brontë." *Critical Quarterly* 14, no. 3 (autumn 1972): 225-35.

In the following essay, Eagleton discusses the habit of moderation in Brontë's novels: subversiveness matched by strict adherence to tradition, rebellion appearing simultaneously with submission, furious passion paired with firm reason.

Helen Burns, the saintly schoolgirl of ***Jane Eyre,*** has an interestingly ambivalent attitude to the execution of Charles the First. Discussing the matter with Jane, she thinks "what a pity it was that, with his integrity and conscientiousness, he could see no farther than the prerogatives of the crown. If he had but been able to look to a distance, and see how what they call the spirit of the age was tending! Still, I like Charles—I respect him—I pity him, poor murdered king! Yes, his enemies were the worst: they shed blood they had no right to shed. How dared they kill him!"

Helen's curious vacillation between a coolly long-headed appreciation of essential reformist change and a spirited Romantic conservatism reflects a recurrent ambiguity in the novels of Charlotte Brontë. It's an ambiguity which shows up to some extent in Helen's own oppressed life at Lowood school: she herself, as a murdered innocent, is partly the martyred Charles, but unlike Charles she is also able to "look to a distance" (although in her case towards heaven rather than future history), and counsel the indignant Jane in the virtues of patience and long-suffering. That patience implies both a "rational" submission to the repressive conventions of Lowood (which she, unlike Jane, does not challenge), and a resigned endurance of life as a burden from which, in the end, will come release.

The problem which the novel faces here is how Helen's kind of self-abnegation is to be distinguished from the patently canting version of it offered by the sadistic Evangelical Brocklehurst, who justifies the eating of burnt porridge by an appeal to the torments of the early Christian martyrs. Submission is good, but only up to a point, and it's that point which Charlotte Brontë's novels explore. Jane's answer to Brocklehurst's enquiry as to how she will avoid hell—"I must keep in good health, and not die"—mixes childish naivety, cheek and seriousness: "*I* had no intention of dying with him," she tells Rochester later. And indeed she doesn't: it is mad Bertha who dies, leaving the way clear for Jane (who has just refused St. John Rivers's offer of premature death in India) to unite with her almost martyred master. Helen Burns is a necessary symbol, but her career is not to be literally followed. When she smiles at the publicly chastised Jane in the Lowood classroom, "It was as if a martyr, a hero, had passed a slave or victim, and imparted strength in the transit." The conjunction of "martyr" and "hero" here is significant: martyrdom is seen as both saintly self-abnegation and heroic self-affirmation, a realization of the self through its surrender, as the name "Burns" can signify both suffering and passion. But Helen, who fails to keep in good health and dies, symbolises in the end only one aspect of this desirable synthesis, that of passive renunciation. Like Jane, she triumphs in the end over tyrannical convention, but unlike Jane that triumph is achieved through her own death, not through someone else's.

Where Charlotte Brontë differs most from Emily is precisely in this impulse to negotiate passionate self-fulfilment on terms which preserve the social and moral conventions intact, and so preserve intact the submissive, enduring, everday self which adheres to them. Her protagonists are an extraordinarily contradictory amalgam of smouldering rebelliousness and prim conventionalism, gushing Romantic fantasy and canny hardheadedness, quivering sensitivity and blunt rationality. It is, in fact, a contradiction closely related to their roles as governesses or private tutors. The governess is a servant, trapped within a rigid social function which demands industriousness, subservience and self-sacrifice; but she is also an "upper" servant, and so (unlike, supposedly, other servants) furnished with an imaginative awareness and cultivated sensibility which are precisely her stock-in-trade as a teacher. She lives at that ambiguous point in the social structure at which two worlds—an interior one of emotional hungering, and an external one of harshly mechanical necessity—meet and collide. At least, they do collide if they aren't wedged deliberately apart, locked into their separate spheres to forestall the disaster of mutual invasion. "I seemed to hold two lives," says Lucy Snowe in ***Villette,*** "the life of thought, and that of reality; and, provided the former was nourished with a sufficiency of the strange necromantic joys of fancy, the privileges of the latter might remain limited to daily bread, hourly work, and a roof of shelter." It is, indeed, with notable reluctance that Lucy is brought to confess the existence of an inner life at all: at the beginning of the novel she tells us, in a suspiciously overemphatic piece of assertion, that "I, Lucy Snowe, plead guiltless of that curse, an overheated and discursive imagination"—and tells us this, moreover, in the context of an awed reference to ghostly haunting. Her response to the "ghost" who flits through Madame Beck's garden is almost comical in its clumsy lurching from romance to realism:

> Her shadow it was that tremblers had feared, through long generations after her poor frame was dust; her black robe and white veil that, for timid eyes, moonlight and shade had mocked, as they fluctuated in the night-wind through the garden-thicket.
>
> Independently of romantic rubbish, however, that old garden had its charms . . .

It is a splitting of the self common in Charlotte's novels: Caroline Helstone in ***Shirley*** feels herself "a dreaming fool," unfitted for "ordinary intercourse with the ordinary world"; and William Crimsworth of ***The Professor,*** slaving away as an under-paid clerk, finds little chance to prove that he is not "a block, or a piece of furniture, but an acting, thinking, sentient man."

To allow passionate imagination premature rein is to be exposed, vulnerable and ultimately self-defeating: it is to be locked in the red room, enticed into bigamous marriage, ensnared like Caroline Helstone in a hopelessly self-consuming love. Passion springs from the very core of the self and yet is hostile, alien, invasive; the world of internal fantasy must therefore be locked away, as the mad Mrs. Rochester stays locked up on an upper floor of Thornfield, slipping out to infiltrate the "real" world only in a few unaware moments of terrible destructiveness. The inner world must yield of necessity to the practical virtues of caution, tact and observation espoused by William Crimsworth—the wary, vigilant virtues by which the self's lonely integrity can be defended in a spying, predatory society, a society on the watch for the weak spot which will surrender you into its hands. The Romantic self must be persistently re-called to its deliberately narrowed and withered definition of rationality. "Order! No snivel!—no sentiment!—no regret! I will endure only sense and resolution," whispers Jane Eyre to herself, fixing her errant thoughts on the hard fact that her relationship with Rochester is of a purely cash-nexus kind.

In the end, of course, it isn't. With the ambiguous exception of ***Villette,*** the strategy of the novels is to allow the turbulent inner life satisfying realization without that self-betraying prematureness which would disrupt the self's principled continuity—a continuity defined by its adherence to a system of social and moral convention. The tactic most commonly employed here is the conversion of submissive conventionalism itself from a mode of self-preservation to a mode of conscious or unconscious self-advancement. Mrs. Reed's remark to Jane in the red room—"It is only on condition of perfect submission and stillness that I shall liberate you"—is triumphantly validated by the novel: it is Jane's stoical Quakerish stillness which captivates Rochester. Her refusal to act prematurely for her own ends both satisfies restrictive convention and leads ultimately to a fulfilling transcendence of it. Rochester would not of course find Jane attractive if she were merely dull, but neither would he love her if, like Blanche Ingram, she were consciously after his money. Jane must therefore reveal enough repressed, Blanche-like "spirit" beneath her puritan exterior to stimulate and cajole him, without any suggestion that she is, in Lucy Snowe's revealing words about herself, "bent on success." Jane manages this difficult situation adroitly during their courtship, blending flashes of flirtatious self-assertion with her habitual meek passivity; she sees shrewdly that "a lamb-like submission and turtle-dove sensibility" would end by boring him. She must demonstrate her quietly self-sufficient independence of Rochester as a way of keeping him tied to her, and so, paradoxically, of staying tied to and safely dependent on him. That this involves a good deal of dexterous calculation—calculation which, if pressed too far, would seriously undermine Jane's credibility as a character—should be obvious enough: it isn't, perhaps, wholly insignificant that Rochester's comment to Jane in the original manuscript—"coin one of your wild, shy, provoking smiles"—is misprinted in the first edition as "wild, *sly,* provoking smiles." If Rochester recognises Jane intuitively as a soul-mate, so after all does St. John Rivers, who tells her that his ambition is unlimited, his desire to rise higher insatiable, and his favoured virtues "endurance, perseverance, industry, talent." Rivers must of course be rejected as reason rather than feeling is his guide, and Jane's career can only culminate successfully when "feeling" can be "rationally" released; feeling without judgement, she muses, is "a washy draught indeed," but judgement without feeling is "too bitter and husky a morsel for human deglutition." Even so, there is more than a superficial relationship between Rivers, a rationalist with feverishly repressed impulses, and Jane's own behaviour: in her case, too, "Reason sits firm and holds the reins, and she will not let the feelings burst away and hurry her to wild chasms." Not prematurely, anyway, and certainly not to early death in India.

Rivers's bourgeois values ("endurance, perseverance, industry, talent"), if sinisterly unfeeling in Jane's eyes, are certainly shared by William Crimsworth, whose motto, suitably, is "Hope smiles on effort." Yet Crimsworth is not a middle-class philistine but a feminine, sensitive soul, too delicately genteel to endure the deadeningly oppressive clerical work to which his manufacturing brother Edward sets him. Crimsworth is despised by his brother and jocularly scorned by the radical, sardonic Whig capitalist Hunsden; yet his progress throughout the novel represents an interesting inversion of his original victimised condition. Crimsworth's mother was an aristocrat and his father a manufacturer; but whereas the philistine Edward has inherited, temperamentally, only from his father, Crimsworth has conveniently inherited qualities from both parents, and the combination proves unbeatable. He is superior in imaginative sensibility to both Edward and Hunsden (who hates poetry), and it is this quality which, as with Jane Eyre and Lucy Snowe, brings him at first to suffer isolated torment at the hands of a crassly dominative society. But it is also the quality which, combined with a quietly industrious knack of amassing a little capital through years of "bustle, action, unslacked endeavour," allows him to prosper as a private teacher in Europe and return to England as a gentleman of leisure. Crimsworth is able to make classic bourgeois progress—not, however, on the crudely materialist terms of his brother, but on terms which utilise rather than negate his "genteel" accomplishments. He reproduces the fusion of aristocratic quality and driving bourgeois effort effected in his parents' marriage, and does so in more propitious conditions: his mother had been disowned by her family for marrying beneath her.

To consolidate this progress requires of Crimsworth both a potentially rebellious independence and a prudently conservative wariness, as is evident enough if he is contrasted with Edward on the one hand and Hunsden on the other. From Edward's conservative standpoint, his brother is a congenital misfit who defiantly throws up a safe job in the name of freedom; from the viewpoint of Hunsden, the Whig reformer and dashing Byronic sceptic, Crimsworth is a pallid, meekly cautious conservative. In fact Crimsworth, like Jane, is both spirited *and* conventional; and like Jane also, although in a considerably more conscious and ruthless way, he learns to turn his protective self-possession to devastating advantage in his relentless power-struggles with Mdlle. Reuter and her unruly girl-pupils. He gains faintly sadistic pleasure from the effects of his own self-defensive impenetrability, enjoying the way Mdlle. Reuter is stung by his coolness, quietly tearing up a pupil's essay before her eyes. Crimsworth the victim becomes Crimsworth the dominator:[1] like Jane, he turns his martyrdom to fruitful profit in this world rather than the next.

Part of what we see happening in these novels, in fact, is a marriage of identifiably bourgeois values with the values of the gentry or aristocracy—a marriage which reflects a real tendency of the "spirit of the age." The Brontës were born at a time when a centuries-old system of clothmaking in the West Riding was coming to an end with the advent of water-power and then steam; they grew up in a context of rapid industrialisation and the growth of a wealthy manufacturing middle-class. It was this phenomenon, as Phyllis Bentley has pointed out, which created the demand for governesses who would give the children of wealthy manufacturers an education equivalent to that of the gentry; and in this sense the sisters were involved in the process of social transition. (As the daughters of an Irish peasant farmer's son who had married into socially superior Cornish stock, they also knew something of social transition in a more direct way). But if the West Riding was undergoing rapid industrialisation, it was also a traditional stronghold of the landed gentry, and among the gentry were men who had gone into manufacturing. Characters like Hunsden, or Yorke in ***Shirley,*** therefore assume a particular symbolic importance within the novels. They are presented as Carlylean "natural aristocrats": cultivated gentlemen sprung from a long Yorkshire lineage who combine a settled paternalist tradition of "blood" and stubborn native pride with a rebellious, independent spirit of anti-aristocratic radicalism. Hunsden, although a "tradesman," is secretly proud of his ancient lineage and is bidding to repair through trade "the partially decayed fortunes of his house"; he is a hard-headed anti-sentimentalist, but has a library well-stocked with European literature and philosophy. Yorke prides himself on being down-to-earth and speaks a broad Yorkshire dialect when he wants to, but he can also choose to speak very pure English and takes a quiet interest in the fine arts. Both men unite a spirit of wilful, free-wheeling bourgeois independence with the culture and status of the traditional gentry. In this sense they have a peculiar attraction for the cast-off, down-trodden character lower in the social scale, who finds in them at once a "higher" expression of his or her own fiercely repressed defiance, and the embodiment of a respected social tradition to admire or aim at.

Yet the relationship isn't without its conflicts and ambiguities. Crimsworth, who is both bourgeois and "blood" aristocrat, finds Hunsden (bourgeois and "natural" aristocrat) both attractive and repelling: he is attractive in his energy, initiative and independence, but unpleasant and rather dangerous in his sardonic, free-thinking Whig reformism. These characteristics of Hunsden offend those aspects of Crimsworth which are externalised in his dutiful Anglo-Swiss wife Frances: her meek piety and Romantic-conservative patriotism provide an essential foil to Hunsden's racy iconoclasm. The bourgeois values of Crimsworth ally themselves in one direction with the bourgeois radicalism of Hunsden, in opposition to the oppressive and venal society which has forced him into exile; but at the same time Crimsworth clearly can't afford to endorse Hunsden's radicalism to the point where he would risk undermining the very social order into which he has so painfully climbed. Insofar as Hunsden's bourgeois hard-headedness allies him with the hated Edward, Frances is needed as a representative of alternative, Romantic-conservative values, including a respect for "blood" aristocracy; but the two positions are saved from pure mutual antagonism by the fact that Hunsden's personal energy and impeccable pedigree render him impressive in Romantic-conservative eyes. For the progressive bourgeois manufacturer, the traditional social order is merely obstructive and superannuated; for the traditional aristocrat turned prosperous non-manufacturing bourgeois, that order still has its value. The final relationship between Crimsworth and Hunsden, then, is one of antagonistic friendship: on their return to England, Crimsworth and Frances settle, significantly, next to Hunsden's estate, but Frances and Hunsden continue to argue over politics.

Shirley is perhaps the best novel to demonstrate this theme, since the historical incidents it deals with do in fact closely concern the relations between Tory squirearchy and Whig manufacturers in the West Riding in the early years of the nineteenth century. The central dramatic action of the novel—the Luddite attack on Robert Moore's mill—re-creates the assault in 1812 on William Cartwright's mill at Rawfolds in the Spen Valley; and Cartwright's ruthless repulsion of the Luddites signalled, in Edward Thompson's words, "a profound emotional reconciliation between the large mill owners and the authorities"[2] at a time when squire and mill-owner were bitterly hostile to one another over the war and the Orders in Council. That the novel's main thrust is to re-create and celebrate that class-consolidation, achieved as it was by the catalyst of working-class militancy, is obvious enough in the figure of Shirley herself. Shirley is a landowner, but half her income comes from owning a mill; and even though her attitudes to the mill are significantly Romantic (she is "tickled with an agreeable complacency" when she thinks of it), she is adamant that trade is to be respected, and determined to defend her property "like a tigress." "If once the poor gather and rise in the form of the mob," she tells Caroline Helstone, "I shall turn against them as an aristocrat." The novel registers a few feeble liberal protests against this position: Caroline ventures to point out the injustice of including all working people under the term "mob," and elsewhere Shirley (with no sense of inconsistency, and conveniently enough for herself in the circumstances) can denounce all crying up of one class against another. But her "spirited" attitude is in general endorsed, not least because it has behind it the weight of her ancient Yorkshire lineage, with its traditions of paternalist care for the poor. Indeed, because she is a conservative paternalist, Shirley's position can accommodate a fair amount of reformism: she objects to the Church's insolence to the poor and servility to the rich, and believes it to be "in the utmost need of reformation." In this sense Shirley differs from Robert Moore, whose neglect of philanthropy as a manufacturer is implicitly connected with his ill-luck in not having been born a Yorkshireman; but although Moore is critically measured against the robust traditions of Yorkshire paternalism, it is, significantly, Shirley herself who finally comes to the defence of his callousness. He is, she points out, a man who entered the district poor and friendless, with nothing but his own energies to back him; and it's unfair to upbraid him for not having been able to "popularize his naturally grave, quiet manners, all at once." (Moore's original, Cartwright, who defended his property with soldiers, spiked barricades and a tub of vitriol, and is reputed to have refused injured Luddites water or a doctor unless they turned informer, seems less easily excusable on the grounds of shyness.) It is, in other words, the representative of the gentry who comes to the moral rescue of the bourgeois manufacturer; and Moore is in any case defended by the novel by a use of the "split self" image which suggests that a sensitive dreamer lurks behind his "hard dog" social exterior.

As a hybrid of progressive capitalist and traditional landowner, then, Shirley provides an important defence of trade; but her charismatic presence in the novel is also needed to defend Romantic conservatism against bourgeois ideology. She is, for instance, notably hard on the radical manufacturer Yorke, whose doctrinaire Whiggism she sees as unfitting him for true reform; and the novel itself underscores this judgement by its emphasis on Yorke's lack of "veneration." Shirley, in other words, stands to Yorke as Frances Crimsworth stands to Hunsden: both radicals are admired for their verve and fighting Yorkshire blood (qualities on which ***Shirley*** in particular places tediously chauvinistic emphasis), but their lack of reverence counts heavily against them. It is left to Mrs. Pryor, Caroline's improbably long-lost mother, to deliver the most explicit statement of that reverence, when she tells Caroline that "Implicit submission to authorities, scrupulous deference to our betters (under which term I, of course, include the higher classes of society) are, in my opinion, indispensable to the wellbeing of every community."

Commerce, in the novel's view, represents a genuine threat to such hierarchial harmony: the mercantile classes, Charlotte Brontë remarks, deny chivalrous feeling, disinterestedness and pride of honour in their narrowly unpatriotic scramble for gain. They deny, in fact, the aristocratic, Romantic-conservative virtues: and part of the point of the novel is to validate those neglected virtues without adopting too obviously the bigoted "Church-and-King" posture of Helstone, Caroline's military-parson guardian. This is simple enough, given the novel's structure, since between the formalist Helstone on the one hand and the free-thinking Yorke on the other stands Shirley, paradigm of the desired union between Romanticism and reform, gentry and capitalist, order and progress. By the end of the novel, indeed, the union is literal as well as symbolic: Moore, having recovered his fortunes by the repeal of the Orders in Council, and having been suitably humanised as an employer by Caroline's influence, will add to the income of Shirley (who has married his brother), double the value of her mill-property and build cottages which Shirley will then let to his own workmen. The bond between squire and mill-owner is indissolubly sealed.

The effective *equality* established between Shirley and Robert Moore at the end of the novel is, in fact, only one of the terms on which Charlotte Brontë handles relationships: the others are dominance and submission. The novels dramatise a society in which almost all human relationships are power-struggles, and because "equality" therefore comes to be defined as equality of power, it is an inevitably complex affair. Crimsworth and Hunsden also end up as effectively equal, but within a formal inequality: Hunsden's house, for instance, is a good deal larger than the Professor's. Even Jane Eyre, when stung to righteous anger, is able to claim a fundamentally human equality with Rochester: "Do you think, because I am poor, obscure, plain, and little, I am soulless and heartless?" There are, in fact, reasons other than simple humanitarian ones why Jane and Rochester are not as socially divided as may at first appear. Rochester, the younger son of an avaricious landed gentleman, was denied his share in the estate and had to marry instead into colonial wealth; Jane's colonial uncle dies and leaves her a sizeable legacy, enough for independence. The colonial trade which signified a decline in status for Rochester signifies an advance in status for Jane, so that although they are of course socially and economically unequal, their fortunes spring from the same root. Jane does not, of course, finally claim equality with Rochester: in the end she serves "both for his prop and guide," which is a rather more complex relationship. It suggests subservience, and so perpetuates their previous relationship; but the subservience is also, of course, a kind of leadership. Rochester's blindness inverts the power-relationship between them: it is now he who is the dependent. Whether she likes it or not (and there is no evidence at all that she does), Jane finally comes to have power over Rochester. Her ultimate relation to him is a complex blend of independence (she comes to him on her own terms, financially self-sufficient), deference, and control.

This complex blend is a recurrent feature of relationships in the novels. Charlotte's characters want independence, but they also desire to dominate, and their desire to dominate is matched only by their impulse to submit to a superior will. The primary form which this ambiguity assumes is a sexual one: the need to venerate and revere, but also to exercise power, expresses itself both in a curious rhythm of sexual attraction and antagonism, and in a series of reversals of sexual roles. The maimed and blinded Rochester, for example, is in an odd way even more "masculine" than he was before (he is "brown," shaggy, "metamorphosed into a lion"), but because he is weak he is also "feminine," and Jane, who adopts a traditionally feminine role towards him ("It is time some one undertook to re-humanize you") is also forced into the masculine role of protectiveness. She finds him both attractive and ugly, as he finds her both plain and fascinating. Blanche Ingram is a "beauty," but she also appears as dominatingly masculine beside Jane's subdued femininity; her masculinity leads her to desire a husband who will be a foil to her and not a rival, but it also prompts her to despise effeminate men and admire strong ones. The same applies to Shirley Keeldar, who is decisively independent and believes in sexual equality, but who is also a "masculine" woman holding "a man's position" as landowner. ("Shirley" was the name her parents intended to give to a son.) Physically she is a superior version of Caroline Helstone, whom she resembles; and she thus becomes for Caroline an ideal self-projection to be revered, in a latently sexual relationship. Despite her claims to sexual equality, however, Shirley would be "thrilled" to meet a man she could venerate: she dominates Caroline spiritually but desires to be dominated herself. William Crimsworth, himself a sort of male Jane Eyre, is dominated by the dashing Hunsden, to whom he plays a "feminine" role, but in turn dominates Frances, whose lamb-like devotion to him he smugly savours. Frances continues to call him "Monsieur" after their marriage, and Crimsworth takes a sadistic delight in reproving her; but he is also glad that she (like Jane) isn't all "monotonous meekness," and is thrilled to discover in her flashes of latent defiance which make him "her subject, if not her slave." The relationship recalls that of Lucy Snowe and the fiery Paul Emanuel: Paul enjoys abusing Lucy and tells her that she needs "checking, regulating and keeping down," but he abuses her mainly in order to delight in her anger.

This simultaneity of attraction and antagonism, reverence and dominance, has a relation to the novels' ambiguous feelings about power in its wider senses. It parallels and embodies the conflicting desires of the oppressed outcast for independence, for passive submission to a secure social order, and for avenging self-assertion over that order. Revenge doesn't, in fact, seem too strong a word for what happens at the end of ***Jane Eyre.*** Jane's repressed indignation at a dominative society, prudently swallowed back throughout the book, is finally released—not by Jane herself, but by the novelist; and the victim is the symbol of that social order, Rochester. Rochester is the novel's sacrificial offering to the social conventions, to Jane's unconscious antagonism and, indeed, to her own puritan guilt; by satisfying all three simultaneously, it allows her to adopt a properly submissive place in society while experiencing a fulfilling love and a taste of power. The outcast bourgeoise achieves more than a humble place at the fireside: she also achieves independence vis-à-vis the upper class, and the right to engage in the process of "taming" it. The worldly Rochester has already been tamed by fire: it is now for Jane to "re-humanize" him.

To put the issue that way is to touch implicitly on the elements of Evangelicalism in ***Jane Eyre,*** and it is worth adding a final brief comment on this other major image of power in the novels. Insofar as Evangelicalism sets out to crush the Romantic spirit, it is a tangible symbol of social oppression and must be resisted. Jane Eyre rebels against Brocklehurst's cruel cant and St. John Rivers's deathly Calvinism; she also scorns Eliza Reed's decision to enter a Roman Catholic convent, viewing this as a falsely ascetic withdrawal from the world. But she is at the same time "Quakerish" herself, grimly disapproving of worldly libertinism; and in this sense she is torn between a respect for and instinctive dislike of stringent religious discipline, between pious submission and Romantic rebellion. Charlotte Brontë's attitudes to Evangelical discipline are, in short, thoroughly ambiguous, as is obvious enough if the detestable Brocklehurst is placed in the balance against the treatment of spoilt children in ***The Professor*** and ***Villette,*** where Evangelical attitudes to childhood strongly emerge. The theme of pampered, perverse children crops up in almost all of the Brontës' novels, and the Evangelical responses involved with it are clearly, in part, class-responses—exasperated reactions to the indolent offspring of the rich as in Lucy Snowe's Nelly Dean-like attitude to Polly Home or Ginevra Fanshawe, or Anne Brontë's talk of the need to crush vicious tendencies in the bud in the Bloomfield family scenes of *Agnes Grey.* Lucy Snowe thinks that Madame Beck's rigid disciplinary system "was by no means bad"; despite the fact that Madame Beck is wholly devoid of feeling, her ruthless efficiency makes her in Lucy's eyes "a very great and very capable woman." It is an Evangelical impulse to avoid the "cowardly indolence" of shrinking from life and sally out instead to put one's soul to the test which motivates Lucy's journey to Villette; it is a similar impulse which brings Caroline Helstone to reject as false, Romish superstition the idea that virtue lies in self-abnegation, and decide instead to become a governess. What Hunsden sees as attractive "spirit" in Crimsworth's son Victor, Crimsworth himself interprets as "the leaven of the offending Adam," and considers that it should be, if not whipped out of him, at least soundly disciplined.

Evangelical discipline, then, is hateful in its sour oppressiveness, but useful in curbing the over-assertive, libertine self; it is to be rejected insofar as, like Rivers's Calvinism, it turns one away from the world, but welcomed as a spur to worldly effort and achievement. The safest solution is a middle way between Dissent and High Church, as in *Agnes Grey,* where the vain, sophisticated Ritualist Hatfield is heavily condemned and the "simple evangelical truth" of the low-church curate Weston deeply admired. The double-edged attitude of ***Shirley*** to the Church ("God save it . . . God also reform it!") is symptomatic of the compromising middle-ground which Charlotte Brontë's novels attempt to occupy: a middle-ground between reverence and rebellion, land and trade, gentry and bougeoisie, the patiently deferential and the actively affirmative self.

Notes

1. It is of some interest in this context, perhaps, that both Charlotte and Emily had been first pupils, and then pupil-governesses, at the Pensionnat Heger in Brussels; like Crimsworth, they knew the power-relationship from both sides.

2. *The Making of the English Working Class,* Harmondsworth, 1970, p. 613.

TITLE COMMENTARY

Jane Eyre

SANDRA M. GILBERT AND SUSAN GUBAR (ESSAY DATE 1979)

SOURCE: Gilbert, Sandra M. and Susan Gubar. "A Dialogue of Self and Soul: Plain Jane's Progress." In *The Madwoman in the Attic: The Woman Writer and the Nineteenth-Century Literary Imagination,* pp. 336-71. New Haven: Yale University Press, 1979.

In the following excerpt, Gilbert and Gubar propose Bertha Mason, Rochester's secret first wife, as a double for the darker side of Jane Eyre. The authors interpret Bertha's moments of lashing out as representative of Jane's suppressed rage as well as Brontë's own anger.

That Rochester's character and life pose in themselves such substantial impediments to his marriage with Jane does not mean, however, that Jane herself generates none. For one thing, "akin" as she is to Rochester, she suspects him of harboring all the secrets we know he does harbor, and raises defenses against them, manipulating her "master" so as to keep him "in reasonable check." In a larger way, moreover, all the charades and masquerades—the secret messages—of patriarchy have had their effect upon her. Though she loves Rochester the man, Jane has doubts about Rochester the husband even before she learns about Bertha. In her world, she senses, even the equality of love between true minds leads to the inequalities and minor despotisms of marriage. "For a little while," she says cynically to Rochester, "you will perhaps be as you are now, [but] . . . I suppose your love will effervesce in six months, or less. I have observed in books written by men, that period assigned as the farthest to which a husband's ardor extends" (chap. 24). He, of course, vigorously repudiates this prediction, but his argument—"Jane: you please me, and you master me [because] you seem to submit"—implies a kind of Lawrentian sexual tension and only makes things worse. For when he asks "Why do you smile [at this], Jane? What does that inexplicable . . . turn of countenance mean?" her peculiar, ironic smile, reminiscent of Bertha's mirthless laugh, signals an "involuntary" and subtly hostile thought "of Hercules and Samson with their charmers." And that hostility becomes overt at the silk warehouse, where Jane notes that "the more he bought me, the more my cheek burned with a sense of annoyance and degradation. . . . I thought his smile was such as a sultan might, in a blissful and fond moment, bestow on a slave his gold and gems had enriched" (chap. 24).

Jane's whole life-pilgrimage has, of course, prepared her to be angry in this way at Rochester's, and society's, concept of marriage. Rochester's loving tyranny recalls John Reed's unloving despotism, and the erratic nature of Rochester's favors ("in my secret soul I knew that his great kindness to me was balanced by unjust severity to many others" [chap. 15]) recalls Brocklehurst's hypocrisy. But even the dreamlike paintings that Jane produced early in her stay at Thornfield—art works which brought her as close to her "master" as

Orson Welles and Joan Fontaine in a scene from the 1944 film adaptation of *Jane Eyre.*

Helen Graham (in *The Tenant of Wildfell Hall*) was to hers—functioned ambiguously, like Helen's, to predict strains in this relationship even while they seemed to be conventional Romantic fantasies. The first represented a drowned female corpse; the second a sort of avenging mother goddess rising (like Bertha Mason Rochester or *Frankenstein*'s monster) in "electric travail" (chap. 13); and the third a terrible paternal specter carefully designed to recall Milton's sinister image of Death. Indeed, this last, says Jane, quoting *Paradise Lost,* delineates "the shape which shape had none," the patriarchal shadow implicit even in the Father-hating gloom of hell.

Given such shadowings and foreshadowings, then, it is no wonder that as Jane's anger and fear about her marriage intensify, she begins to be symbolically drawn back into her own past, and specifically to reexperience the dangerous sense of doubleness that had begun in the red-room. The first sign that this is happening is the powerfully depicted, recurrent dream of a child she begins to have as she drifts into a romance with her master. She tells us that she was awakened "from companionship with this baby-phantom" on the night Bertha attacked Richard Mason, and the next day she is literally called back into the past, back to Gateshead to see the dying Mrs. Reed, who reminds her again of what she once was and potentially still is: "Are you Jane Eyre? . . . I declare she talked to me once like something mad, or like a fiend" (chap. 21). Even more significantly, the phantom-child reappears in two dramatic dreams Jane has on the night before her wedding eve, during which she experiences "a strange regretful consciousness of some barrier dividing" her from Rochester. In the first, "burdened" with the small wailing creature, she is "following the windings of an unknown road" in cold rainy weather, straining to catch up with her future husband but unable to reach him. In the second, she is walking among the ruins of Thornfield, still carrying "the unknown little child" and still following Rochester; as he disappears around "an angle in the road," she tells him, "I bent forward to take a last look; the wall crumbled; I was shaken; the child rolled from my knee, I lost my balance, fell, and woke" (chap. 25).

What are we to make of these strange dreams, or—as Jane would call them—these "presentiments"? To begin with, it seems clear that the wailing child who appears in all of them corresponds to "the poor orphan child" of Bessie's song at Gateshead, and therefore to the child Jane herself, the wailing Cinderella whose pilgrimage began in anger and despair. That child's complaint—"My feet they are sore, and my limbs they are weary; / Long is the way, and the mountains are wild"—is still Jane's, or at least the complaint of that part of her which resists a marriage of inequality. And though consciously Jane wishes to be rid of the heavy problem her orphan self presents, "I might not lay it down anywhere, however tired were my arms, however much its weight impeded my progress." In other words, until she reaches the goal of her pilgrimage—maturity, independence, true equality with Rochester (and therefore in a sense with the rest of the world)—she is doomed to carry her orphaned alter ego everywhere. The burden of the past cannot be sloughed off so easily—not, for instance, by glamorous lovemaking, silk dresses, jewelry, a new name. Jane's "strange regretful consciousness of a barrier" dividing her from Rochester is, thus, a keen though disguised intuition of a problem she herself will pose.

Almost more interesting than the nature of the child image, however, is the *predictive* aspect of the last of the child dreams, the one about the ruin of Thornfield. As Jane correctly foresees, Thornfield *will* within a year become "a dreary ruin, the retreat of bats and owls." Have her own subtle and not-so-subtle hostilities to its master any connection with the catastrophe that is to befall the house? Is her clairvoyant dream in some sense a vision of wish fulfilment? And why, specifically, is she freed from the burden of the wailing child at the moment *she* falls from Thornfield's ruined wall?

The answer to all these questions is closely related to events which follow upon the child dream. For the apparition of a child in these crucial weeks preceding her marriage is only one symptom of a dissolution of personality Jane seems to be experiencing at this time, a fragmentation of the self comparable to her "syncope" in the red-room. Another symptom appears early in the chapter that begins, anxiously, "there was no putting off the day that advanced—the bridal day" (chap. 25). It is her witty but nervous speculation about the nature of "one Jane Rochester, a person whom as yet I knew not," though "in yonder closet . . . garments *said* to be hers had already displaced [mine]: *for not to me appertained that . . . strange wraith-like apparel*" (chap. 25 [ital. ours]). Again, a third symptom appears on the morning of her wedding: she turns toward the mirror and sees "a robed and veiled figure, so unlike my usual self that it seemed almost the image of a stranger" (chap. 26), reminding us of the moment in the red-room when all had "seemed colder and darker in that visionary hollow" of the looking glass "than in reality." In view of this frightening series of separations within the self—Jane Eyre splitting off from Jane Rochester, the child Jane splitting off from the adult Jane, and the image of Jane weirdly separating from the body of Jane—it is not surprising that another and most mysterious specter, a sort of "vampyre," should appear in the middle of the night to rend and trample the wedding veil of that unknown person, Jane Rochester.

Literally, of course, the nighttime specter is none other than Bertha Mason Rochester. But on a figurative and psychological level it seems suspiciously clear that the specter of Bertha is still another—indeed the most threatening—avatar of Jane. What Bertha now *does,* for instance, is what Jane wants to do. Disliking the "vapoury veil" of Jane Rochester, Jane Eyre secretly wants to tear the garments up. Bertha does it for her. Fearing the inexorable "bridal day," Jane would like to put it off. Bertha does that for her too. Resenting the new mastery of Rochester, whom she sees as "*dread* but adored," (ital. ours), she wishes to be his equal in size and strength, so that she can battle him in the contest of their marriage. Bertha, "a big woman, in stature almost equalling her husband," has the necessary "virile force" (chap. 26). Bertha, in other words, is Jane's truest and darkest double: she is the angry aspect of the orphan child, the ferocious secret self Jane has been trying to repress ever since her days at Gateshead. For, as Claire Rosenfeld points out, "the novelist who consciously or unconsciously exploits psychological Doubles" frequently juxtaposes "two characters, the one representing the socially acceptable or conventional personality, the other externalizing the free, uninhibited, often criminal self."[1]

It is only fitting, then, that the existence of this criminal self imprisoned in Thornfield's attic is the ultimate legal impediment to Jane's and Rochester's marriage, and that its existence is, paradoxically, an impediment raised by Jane as well as by Rochester. For it now begins to appear, if it did not earlier, that Bertha has functioned as Jane's dark double *throughout* the governess's stay at Thornfield. Specifically, every one of Bertha's appearances—or, more accurately, her manifestations—has been associated with an experience (or repression) of anger on Jane's part. Jane's feelings of "hunger, rebellion, and rage" on the battlements, for instance, were accompanied by Bertha's "low, slow ha! ha!" and "eccentric murmurs." Jane's apparently secure response to Rochester's apparently egalitarian sexual confidences was followed by Bertha's attempt to incinerate the master in his bed. Jane's unexpressed resentment at Rochester's manipulative gypsy-masquerade found expression in Bertha's terrible shriek and her even more terrible attack on Richard Mason. Jane's anxieties about her marriage, and in particular her fears of her own alien "robed and veiled" bridal image, were objectified by the image of Bertha in a "white and straight" dress, "whether gown, sheet, or shroud I cannot tell." Jane's profound desire to destroy Thornfield, the symbol of Rochester's mastery and of her own servitude, will be acted out by Bertha, who burns down the house and destroys *herself* in the process as if she were an agent of Jane's desire as well as her own. And finally, Jane's disguised hostility to Rochester, summarized in her terrifying prediction to herself that "you shall, yourself, pluck out your right eye; yourself cut off your right hand" (chap. 27) comes strangely true through the intervention of Bertha, whose melodramatic death causes Rochester to lose both eye and hand.

These parallels between Jane and Bertha may at first seem somewhat strained. Jane, after all, is poor, plain, little, pale, neat, and quiet, while Bertha is rich, large, florid, sensual, and extravagant; indeed, she was once even beautiful, somewhat, Rochester notes, "in the style of Blanche Ingram." Is she not, then, as many critics have suggested, a monitory image rather than a double for Jane? As Richard Chase puts it, "May not Bertha, Jane seems to ask herself, be a living example of what happens to the woman who [tries] to be the fleshly vessel of the [masculine] *élan*?"[2] "Just as [Jane's] instinct for self-preservation saves her from earlier temptations," Adrienne Rich remarks, "so it must save her from becoming this woman by curbing her imagination at the limits of what is bearable for a powerless woman in the England of the 1840s."[3] Even Rochester himself provides a similar critical appraisal of the relationship between the two. "That is *my wife*," he says, pointing to mad Bertha,

> And *this* is what I wished to have . . . this young girl who stands so grave and quiet at the mouth of hell, looking collectedly at the gambols of a demon. I wanted her just as a change after that fierce ragout. . . . Compare these clear eyes with the red balls yonder—this face with that mask—this form with that bulk. . . .
>
> [chap. 26]

And of course, in one sense, the relationship between Jane and Bertha is a monitory one: while acting out Jane's secret fantasies, Bertha does (to say the least) provide the governess with an example of how not to act, teaching her a lesson more salutary than any Miss Temple ever taught.

Nevertheless, it is disturbingly clear from recurrent images in the novel that Bertha not only acts *for* Jane, she also acts *like* Jane. The imprisoned Bertha, running "backwards and forwards" on all fours in the attic, for instance, recalls not only Jane the governess, whose only relief from mental pain was to pace "backwards and forwards" in the third story, but also that "bad animal" who was ten-year-old Jane, imprisoned in the red-room, howling and mad. Bertha's "goblin appearance"—"half dream, half reality," says Rochester—recalls the lover's epithets for Jane: "malicious elf," "sprite," "changeling," as well as his playful accusation that she had magically downed his horse at their first meeting. Rochester's description of Bertha as a "monster" ("a fearful voyage I had with such a monster in the vessel" [chap. 27]) ironically echoes Jane's own fear of being a monster ("Am I a monster? . . . is it impossible that Mr. Rochester should have a sincere affection for me?" [chap. 24]). Bertha's fiendish madness recalls Mrs. Reed's remark about Jane ("she talked to me once like something mad or like a fiend") as well as Jane's own estimate of her mental state ("I will hold to the principles received by me when I was sane, and not mad—as I am now [chap. 27]"). And most dramatic of all, Bertha's incendiary tendencies recall Jane's early flaming rages, at Lowood and at Gateshead, as well as that "ridge of lighted heath" which she herself saw as emblematic of her mind in its rebellion against society. It is only fitting, therefore, that, as if to balance the child Jane's terrifying vision of herself as an alien figure in the "visionary hollow" of the red-room looking glass, the adult Jane first clearly perceives her terrible double when Bertha puts on the wedding veil intended for the second Mrs. Rochester, and turns to the mirror. At that moment, Jane sees "the reflection of the visage and features quite distinctly in the dark oblong glass," sees them as if they were her own (chap. 25).

For despite all the habits of harmony she gained in her years at Lowood, we must finally recognize, with Jane herself, that on her arrival at Thornfield she only "*appeared* a disciplined and subdued character" [ital. ours]. Crowned with thorns, finding that she is, in Emily Dickinson's words, "The Wife—without the Sign,"[4] she represses her rage behind a subdued facade, but her soul's impulse to dance "like a Bomb, abroad," to quote Dickinson again,[5] has not been exorcised and will not be exorcised until the literal and symbolic death of Bertha frees her from the furies that torment her and makes possible a marriage of equality—makes possible, that is, wholeness within herself. At that point, significantly, when the Bertha in Jane falls from the ruined wall of Thornfield and is destroyed, the orphan child too, as her dream predicts, will roll from her knee—the burden of her past will be lifted—and she will wake. In the meantime, as Rochester says, "never was anything at once so frail and so indomitable . . . consider the resolute wild free thing looking out of [Jane's] eye. . . . Whatever I do with its cage, I cannot get at it—the savage, beautiful creature" (chap. 27).

* * *

That the pilgrimage of this "savage, beautiful creature" must now necessarily lead her away from Thornfield is signalled, like many other events in the novel, by the rising of the moon, which accompanies a reminiscent dream of the red-room. Unjustly imprisoned now, as she was then, in one of the traps a patriarchal society provides for outcast Cinderellas, Jane realizes that this time she must escape through deliberation rather than through madness. The maternal moon, admonishing her ("My daughter, flee temptation!") appears to be "a white human form . . . inclining a glorious brow," a strengthening image, as Adrienne Rich suggests, of the Great Mother.[6] Yet—"profoundly, imperiously, archetypal"[7]—this figure has its ambiguities, just as Jane's own personality does, for the last night on which Jane watched such a moon rise was the night Bertha attacked Richard Mason, and the juxtaposition of the two events on that occasion was almost shockingly suggestive:

> [The moon's] glorious gaze roused me. Awaking in the dead of night, I opened my eyes on her disk. . . . It was beautiful, but too solemn: I half rose, and stretched my arm to draw the curtain.
>
> Good God! What a cry!
>
> [chap. 20]

Now, as Jane herself recognizes, the moon has elicited from her an act as violent and self-assertive as Bertha's on that night. "What was I?" she thinks, as she steals away from Thornfield. "I had injured—wounded—left my master. I was hateful in my own eyes" (chap. 28). Yet, though her escape may seem as morally ambiguous as the moon's message, it is necessary for her own self-preservation. And soon, like Bertha, she is "crawling forwards on my hands and knees, and then again raised to my feet—as eager and determined as ever to reach the road."

Her wanderings on that road are a symbolic summary of those wanderings of the poor orphan child which constitute her entire life's pilgrimage. For, like Jane's dreams, Bessie's song was an uncannily accurate prediction of things to come. "Why did they send me so far and so lonely, / Up where the moors spread and grey rocks are piled?" Far and lonely indeed Jane wanders, starving, freezing, stumbling, abandoning her few possessions, her name, and even her self-respect in her search for a new home. For "men are hard-hearted, and kind angels only / Watch'd o'er the steps of a poor orphan child." And like the starved wanderings of Hetty Sorel in *Adam Bede,* her terrible journey across the moors suggests the essential homelessness—the nameless, placeless, and contingent status—of women in a patriarchal society. Yet because Jane, unlike Hetty, has an inner strength which her pilgrimage seeks to develop, "kind angels" finally do bring her to what is in a sense her true home, the house significantly called *Marsh End* (or Moor House) which is to represent the end of her march toward selfhood. Here she encounters Diana, Mary, and St. John Rivers, the "good" relatives who will help free her from her angry memories of that wicked stepfamily the Reeds. And that the Rivers prove to be literally her relatives is not, in psychological terms, the strained coincidence some readers have suggested. For having left Rochester, having torn off the crown of thorns he offered and repudiated the unequal charade of marriage he proposed, Jane has now gained the strength to begin to discover her real place in the world. St. John helps her find a job in a school, and once again she reviews the choices she has had: "Is it better, I ask, to be a slave in a fool's paradise at Marseilles . . . or to be a village schoolmistress, free and honest, in a breezy mountain nook in the healthy heart of England?" (chap. 31). Her unequivocal conclusion that "I was right when I adhered to principle and law" is one toward which the whole novel seems to have tended.

The qualifying word *seems* is, however, a necessary one. For though in one sense Jane's discovery of her family at Marsh End does represent the end of her pilgrimage, her progress toward selfhood will not be complete until she learns that "principle and law" in the abstract do not always coincide with the deepest principles and laws of her own being. Her early sense that Miss Temple's teachings had merely been superimposed on her native vitality had already begun to suggest this to her. But it is through her encounter with St. John Rivers that she assimilates this lesson most thoroughly. As a number of critics have noticed, all three members of the Rivers family have resonant, almost allegorical names. The names of Jane's true "sisters," Diana and Mary, notes Adrienne Rich, recall the Great Mother in her dual aspects of Diana the huntress and Mary the virgin mother;[8] in this way, as well as through their independent, learned, benevolent personalities, they suggest the ideal of female strength for which Jane has been searching. St. John, on the other hand, has an almost blatantly patriarchal name, one which recalls both the masculine abstraction of the gospel according to St. John ("in the beginning was the *Word*") and the disguised misogyny of St. John the Baptist, whose patristic and evangelical contempt for the flesh manifested itself most powerfully in a profound contempt for the *female.* Like Salome, whose rebellion against such misogyny Oscar Wilde was later also to associate with the rising moon of female power, Jane must symbolically, if not literally, behead the abstract principles of this man before she can finally achieve her true independence.

At first, however, it seems that St. John is offering Jane a viable alternative to the way of life proposed by Rochester. For where Rochester, like his dissolute namesake, ended up appearing to offer a life of pleasure, a path of roses (albeit with concealed thorns), and a marriage of passion, St. John seems to propose a life of principle, a path of thorns (with no concealed roses), and a marriage of spirituality. His self-abnegating rejection of the worldly beauty Rosamund Oliver—another character with a strikingly resonant name—is disconcerting to the passionate and Byronic part of Jane, but at least it shows that, unlike hypocritical Brocklehurst, he practices what he preaches. And what he preaches is the Carlylean sermon of self-actualization through work: "Work while it is called today, for the night cometh wherein no man can work."[9] If she follows him, Jane realizes, she will substitute a divine Master for the master she served at Thornfield, and replace love with labor—for "you are formed for labour, not for love," St. John tells her. Yet when, long ago at Lowood, she asked for "a new servitude" was not some such solution half in her mind? When, pacing the battlements at Thornfield she insisted that "women [need] a field for their efforts as much as their brothers do" (chap. 12), did she not long for some such practical "exercise"? "Still will my Father with promise and blessing, / Take to his bosom the poor orphaned child," Bessie's song had predicted. Is not Marsh End, then, the promised end, and St. John's way the way to His bosom?

Jane's early repudiation of the spiritual harmonies offered by Helen Burns and Miss Temple is the first hint that, while St. John's way will tempt her, she must resist it. That, like Rochester, he is "akin" to her is clear. But where Rochester represents the fire of her nature, her cousin represents the ice. And while for some women ice may "suffice," for Jane, who has struggled all her life, like a sane version of Bertha, against the polar cold of a loveless world, it clearly will not. As she falls more deeply under St. John's "freezing spell," she realizes increasingly that to please him "I must disown half my nature." And "as his wife," she reflects, she would be "always restrained . . . forced to keep the fire of my nature continually low, . . . though the imprisoned flame consumed vital after vital" (chap. 34). In fact, as St. John's wife and "the sole helpmate [he] can influence efficiently in life, and retain absolutely till death" (chap. 34), she will be entering into a union even more unequal than that proposed by Rochester, a marriage reflecting, once again, her absolute exclusion from the life of wholeness toward which her pilgrimage has been directed. For despite the integrity of principle that distinguishes him from Brocklehurst, despite his likeness to "the warrior Greatheart, who guards his pilgrim convoy from the onslaught of Apollyon" (chap. 38), St. John is finally, as Brocklehurst was, a pillar of patriarchy, "a cold cumbrous column" (chap. 34). But where Brocklehurst had removed Jane from the imprisonment of Gateshead only to immure her in a dank valley of starvation, and even Rochester had tried to make her the "slave of passion," St. John wants to imprison the "resolute wild free thing" that is her soul in the ultimate cell, the "iron shroud" of principle (chap. 34).

* * *

Though in many ways St. John's attempt to "imprison" Jane may seem the most irresistible of all, coming as it does at a time when she is congratulating herself on just that adherence to "principle and law" which he recommends, she escapes from his fetters more easily than she had escaped from either Brocklehurst or Rochester. Figuratively speaking, this is a measure of how far she has traveled in her pilgrimage toward maturity. Literally, however, her escape is facilitated by two events. First, having found what is, despite all its ambiguities, her true family, Jane has at last come into her inheritance. Jane Eyre is now the heir of that uncle in Madeira whose first intervention in her life had been, appropriately, to define the legal impediment to her marriage with Rochester, now literally as well as figuratively an independent woman, free to go her own way and follow her own will. But her freedom is also signaled by a second event: the death of Bertha.

Her first "presentiment" of that event comes, dramatically, as an answer to a prayer for guidance. St. John is pressing her to reach a decision about his proposal of marriage. Believing that "I had now put love out of the question, and thought only of duty," she "entreats Heaven" to "Show me, show me the path." As always at major moments in Jane's life, the room is filled with moonlight, as if to remind her that powerful forces are still at work both without and within her. And now, because such forces are operating, she at last hears—she is receptive to—the bodiless cry of Rochester: "Jane! Jane! Jane!" Her response is an immediate act of self-assertion. "I broke from St. John. . . . It was *my* time to assume ascendancy. *My* powers were in play and in force" (chap. 35). But her sudden forcefulness, like her "presentiment" itself, is the climax of all that has gone before. Her new and apparently telepathic communion with Rochester, which many critics have seen as needlessly melodramatic, has been made possible by her new independence and Rochester's new humility. The plot device of the cry is merely a sign that the relationship for which both lovers had always longed is now possible, a sign that Jane's metaphoric speech of the first betrothal scene has been translated into reality: "my spirit

. . . addresses your spirit, just as if both had passed through the grave, and we stood at God's feet, equal—as we are!" (chap. 23). For to the marriage of Jane's and Rochester's true minds there is now, as Jane unconsciously guesses, no impediment.

* * *

Jane's return to Thornfield, her discovery of Bertha's death and of the ruin her dream had predicted, her reunion at Ferndean with the maimed and blinded Rochester, and their subsequent marriage form an essential epilogue to that pilgrimage toward selfhood which had in other ways concluded at Marsh End, with Jane's realization that she could not marry St. John. At that moment, "the wondrous shock of feeling had come like the earthquake which shook the foundations of Paul and Silas' prison; it had opened the doors of the soul's cell, and loosed its bands—it had wakened it out of its sleep" (chap. 36). For at that moment she had been irrevocably freed from the burden of her past, freed both from the raging specter of Bertha (which had already fallen in fact from the ruined wall of Thornfield) and from the self-pitying specter of the orphan child (which had symbolically, as in her dream, rolled from her knee). And at that moment, again as in her dream, she had *wakened* to her own self, her own needs. Similarly, Rochester, "caged eagle" that he seems (chap. 37), has been freed from what was for him the burden of Thornfield, though at the same time he appears to have been fettered by the injuries he received in attempting to rescue Jane's mad double from the flames devouring his house. That his "fetters" pose no impediment to a new marriage, that he and Jane are now, in reality, equals, is the thesis of the Ferndean section.

Many critics, starting with Richard Chase, have seen Rochester's injuries as "a symbolic castration," a punishment for his early profligacy and a sign that Charlotte Brontë (as well as Jane herself), fearing male sexual power, can only imagine marriage as a union with a diminished Samson. "The tempo and energy of the universe can be quelled, we see, by a patient, practical woman," notes Chase ironically.[10] And there is an element of truth in this idea. The angry Bertha in Jane *had* wanted to punish Rochester, to burn him in his bed, destroy his house, cut off his hand and pluck out his overmastering "full falcon eye." Smiling enigmatically, she had thought of "Hercules and Samson, with their charmers."

It had not been her goal, however, to quell "the tempo and energy of the universe," but simply to strengthen herself, to make herself an equal of the world Rochester represents. And surely another important symbolic point is implied by the lovers' reunion at Ferndean: when both were physically whole they could not, in a sense, *see* each other because of the social disguises—master/servant, prince/Cinderella—blinding them, but now that those disguises have been shed, now that they are equals, they can (though one is blind) see and speak even beyond the medium of the flesh. Apparently sightless, Rochester—in the tradition of blinded Gloucester—now sees more clearly than he did when as a "mole-eyed blockhead" he married Bertha Mason (chap. 27). Apparently mutilated, he is paradoxically stronger than he was when he ruled Thornfield, for now, like Jane, he draws his powers from within himself, rather than from inequity, disguise, deception. Then, at Thornfield, he was "no better than the old lightning-struck chestnut tree in the orchard," whose ruin foreshadowed the catastrophe of his relationship with Jane. Now, as Jane tells him, he is "green and vigorous. Plants will grow about your roots whether you ask them or not" (chap. 37). And now, being equals, he and Jane can afford to depend upon each other with no fear of one exploiting the other.

Nevertheless, despite the optimistic portrait of an egalitarian relationship that Brontë seems to be drawing here, there is "a quiet autumnal quality" about the scenes at Ferndean, as Robert Bernard Martin points out.[11] The house itself, set deep in a dark forest, is old and decaying: Rochester had not even thought it suitable for the loathsome Bertha, and its valley-of-the-shadow quality makes it seem rather like a Lowood, a school of life where Rochester must learn those lessons Jane herself absorbed so early. As a dramatic setting, moreover, Ferndean is notably stripped and asocial, so that the physical isolation of the lovers suggests their spiritual isolation in a world where such egalitarian marriages as theirs are rare, if not impossible. True minds, Charlotte Brontë seems to be saying, must withdraw into a remote forest, a wilderness even, in order to circumvent the strictures of a hierarchal society.

Does Brontë's rebellious feminism—that "irreligious" dissatisfaction with the social order noted by Miss Rigby and ***Jane Eyre***'s other Victorian critics—compromise itself in this withdrawal? Has Jane exorcised the rage of orphanhood only to retreat from the responsibilities her own principles implied? Tentative answers to these questions can be derived more easily from ***The Professor, Shirley,*** and ***Villette*** than from ***Jane Eyre,*** for the qualified and even (as in ***Villette***) indecisive endings of Brontë's other novels suggest that she herself was unable clearly to envision viable solutions to the problem of patriarchal oppression. In all her books, writing (as we have seen) in a sort of trance, she was able to act out that passionate drive toward freedom which offended agents of the status quo, but in none was she able consciously to define the full meaning of achieved freedom—perhaps because no one of her contemporaries, not even a Wollstonecraft or a Mill, could adequately describe a society so drastically altered that the matured Jane and Rochester could really live in it.

What Brontë could not logically define, however, she could embody in tenuous but suggestive imagery and in her last, perhaps most significant redefinitions of Bunyan. Nature in the largest sense seems now to be on the side of Jane and Rochester. *Ferndean,* as its name implies, is without artifice—"no flowers, no garden-beds"—but it is green as Jane tells Rochester he will be, green and ferny and fertilized by soft rains. Here, isolated from society but flourishing in a natural order of their own making, Jane and Rochester will become physically "bone of [each other's] bone, flesh of [each other's] flesh" (chap. 38), and here the healing powers of nature will eventually restore the sight of one of Rochester's eyes. Here, in other words, nature, unleashed from social restrictions, will do "no miracle—but her best" (chap. 35). For not the Celestial City but a natural paradise, the country of Beulah "upon the borders of heaven," where "the contract between bride and bridegroom [is] renewed," has all along been, we now realize, the goal of Jane's pilgrimage.[12]

As for the Celestial City itself, Charlotte Brontë implies here (though she will later have second thoughts) that such a goal is the dream of those who accept inequities on earth, one of the many tools used by patriarchal society to keep, say, governesses in their "place." Because she believes this so deeply, she quite consciously concludes ***Jane Eyre*** with an allusion to *Pilgrim's Progress* and with a half-ironic apostrophe to that apostle of celestial transcendence, that shadow of "the warrior Greatheart," St. John Rivers. "His," she tells us, "is the exaction of the apostle, who speaks but for Christ when he says—'Whosoever will come after me, let him deny himself and take up his cross and follow me'" (chap. 38). For it was, finally, to repudiate such a crucifying denial of the self that Brontë's "hunger, rebellion, and rage" led her to write ***Jane Eyre*** in the first place and to make it an "irreligious" redefinition, almost a parody, of John Bunyan's vision.[13] And the astounding progress toward equality of plain Jane Eyre, whom Miss Rigby correctly saw as "the personification of an unregenerate and undisciplined spirit," answers by its outcome the bitter question Emily Dickinson was to ask fifteen years later: "'My husband'—women say— / Stroking the Melody— / Is *this*—the way?'"[14] No, Jane declares in her flight from Thornfield, *that* is not the way. *This,* she says—this marriage of true minds at Ferndean—this is the way. Qualified and isolated as her way may be, it is at least an emblem of hope. Certainly Charlotte Brontë was never again to indulge in quite such an optimistic imagining.

Notes

1. Claire Rosenfeld, "The Shadow Within: The Conscious and Unconscious Use of the Double," in *Stories of the Double,* ed. Albert J. Guerard (Philadelphia: J. B. Lippincott, 1967), p. 314. Rosenfeld also notes that "When the passionate uninhibited self is a woman, she more often than not is dark." Bertha, of course, is a Creole—swarthy, "livid," etc.
2. Chase, "The Brontës, or Myth Domesticated," p. 467.
3. Rich, "Jane Eyre: The Temptations of a Motherless Woman," p. 72. The question of what was "bearable for a powerless woman in the England of the 1840s" inevitably brings to mind the real story of Isabella Thackeray, who went mad in 1840 and was often (though quite mistakenly) thought to be the original of Rochester's mad wife. Parallels are coincidental, but it is interesting that Isabella was reared by a Bertha Mason-like mother of whom it was said that "wherever she went, 'storms, whirlwinds, cataracts, tornadoes' accompanied her," and equally interesting that Isabella's illness was signalled by mad inappropriate laughter and marked by violent suicide attempts, alternating with Jane Eyre-like docility. That at one point Thackeray tried to guard her by literally *tying* himself to her ("a riband round her waist, & to my waist, and this always woke me if she moved") seems also to recall Rochester's terrible bondage. For more about Isabella Thackeray, see Gordon N. Ray, *Thackeray: The Uses of Adversity, 1811-1846* (New York: McGraw-Hill, 1955), esp. pp. 182-85 (on Isabella's mother) and chap. 10, "A Year of Pain and Hope," pp. 250-77.
4. See Emily Dickinson, *Poems,* J. 1072, "Title divine—is mine! / The Wife—without the Sign!"
5. See Emily Dickinson, *Poems,* J. 512, "The Soul has Bandaged Moments."
6. Rich, "Jane Eyre; The Temptations of a Motherless Woman," p. 106.
7. Ibid.
8. Ibid.
9. *Sartor Resartus,* chap. 9, "The Everlasting Yea."
10. Chase, "The Brontës, or Myth Domesticated," p. 467.
11. Robert Bernard Martin, *The Accents of Persuasion: Charlotte Brontë's Novels* (New York: Norton, 1966), p. 90.

12. *The Pilgrim's Progress* (New York: Airmont Library, 1969), pp. 140-41.

13. It should be noted here that Charlotte Brontë's use of *The Pilgrim's Progress* in *Villette* is much more conventional. Lucy Snowe seems to feel that she will only find true bliss after death, when she hopes to enter the Celestial City.

14. See Emily Dickinson, *Poems*, J. 1072, "Title divine—is mine!"

CAROL A. SENF (ESSAY DATE 1985)

SOURCE: Senf, Carol A. "*Jane Eyre* and the Evolution of A Feminist History.[1]" *Victorians Institute Journal* 13 (1985): 67-81.

In the following essay, Senf interprets Jane Eyre *as an evolutionary history, both in Jane's developing feminist consciousness and in her effort to make an egalitarian marriage.*

Traditional criticism generally regards the Brontës as separate from the mainstream of Victorian literature. For example, in *The Great Tradition*, F. R. Leavis calls *Wuthering Heights* a "kind of sport" which breaks completely "both with the Scott tradition that imposed on the novelist a romantic resolution of his themes" and with the tradition that began in the eighteenth century "that demanded a plane-mirror reflection of the surface of 'real' life."[2] Taking a slightly different approach, Q. D. Leavis focuses on the mythic qualities of Charlotte's novels and says that ***Jane Eyre*** includes a "general confusion of dates, eras, fashions, and facts . . . even more irrational than anything Dickens allowed himself, suggesting the timeless world of the myth and the daydream."[3]

While recent feminist critics, such as Ellen Moers, Elaine Showalter, Sandra Gilbert and Susan Gubar,[4] have linked the Brontës to a different "great tradition" of women's literature, even they have failed to connect the Brontës with the prevailing nineteenth-century preoccupation with history, a preoccupation which links writers as otherwise different as Scott, Carlyle, Marx, Macaulay, Dickens, Thackeray, Trollope, Eliot, and Gaskell. Nonetheless, the Brontë novels are the most persuasive evidence of the sisters' intense interest in history. For example, the first word of *Wuthering Heights* is the date "1801"; and the novel alternates between the history of that year and the distant history of the Earnshaws. Similarly, the beginning of *The Tenant of Wildfell Hall* places that novel within a clear historical perspective by asking the reader to "go back with me to the autumn of 1827."[5] Charlotte's second published novel, ***Shirley***, set in 1811-12, focuses on such historical matters as the British government's Orders in Council, the condition of women question, and the Luddite riots. As a result, it is, as Andrew and Judith Hook state in their introduction to the Penguin edition, as much a "condition of England" novel as "Disraeli's *Sybil*, Mrs. Gaskell's *Mary Barton* and *North and South*, Dickens's *Hard Times*, and Kingsley's *Alton Locke*."[6]

However, instead of focusing on these three novels, which take place in a particular place during a particular historical period, this paper focuses on ***Jane Eyre*** and hopes to demonstrate that this novel, apparently the most personal and least historical of the Brontë novels, deserves to be called an historical novel, one which relates a feminist version of history—"herstory" as it were. In fact, Brontë's novel does exactly what the feminist historian, Gerda Lerner, says is necessary for the development of feminist history:

> History must include an account of the female experience over time and should include the development of feminist consciousness as an essential aspect of women's past. . . . The central question it raises is: What would history be like if it were seen through the eyes of women and ordered by values they define?[7]

Jane Eyre is just such "an account of the female experience over time," and it is ordered by a very feminine set of values, which include greater freedom for women and mutuality instead of mastery—in short, a "softening" of patriarchal values. Moreover, it uses a particularly Victorian concept—historical evolution—to show how a writer of "herstory" develops from a reader of history. Furthermore, the novel compares Jane's individual evolution to humankind's evolution toward a more modern civilization by drawing analogies between Jane's behavior and the actions of people at different historical periods. These analogies are drawn as Jane moves gradually from primitive and occasionally violent reactions to a more rational and civilized response. Eventually, both Jane and the novel evolve to the point that they must transcend what she and her contemporaries knew of history, a history which revolves around the exploitation of the weak by the strong, to something more feminine and egalitarian.

Brontë's interest in history, which began in the Haworth parsonage, was reinforced by her formal education and by the general Victorian interest in history. Winifred Gérin, one of her biographers, explains that Mr. Brontë's library included Homer and Virgil, Milton's works, Johnson's *Lives of the Poets*, Goldsmith's *History of Rome*, Hume's *History of England*, and Scott's *Life of Napoleon Bonaparte*. She adds that the children could also "borrow books from the Heatons' library at Ponden House . . . which accounts for their precocious knowledge of French history and literature."[8] Moreover, the children could also read Mr. Brontë's subscription volumes from the Keighley Mechanics' Institute Library and listen to their elders discuss current events from the Whig and Tory newspapers to which their father subscribed.[9] This early interest in history was reinforced by Brontë's experience at Roe Head, where Miss Wooler "advocated 'Rollin for Ancient history', Mangnall's 'Questions' for History and Biography—followed by the inescapable Hume."[10]

Charlotte and her sisters may have learned about history in other ways as well, for the region around Haworth was being rapidly transformed during their lifetime there. Mrs. Gaskell explains that Keighley, a town four miles from Haworth, was being transformed from an old-fashioned village into a modern town "with villas, great worsted factories, rows of workmen's houses."[11] In addition, if the surrounding area gave the Brontë children a glimpse into England's industrial future, it also helped to reinforce their link to the past. As Gaskell explains, the area around Roe Head was thoroughly steeped with a sense of the past. Remnants of "the old Plantagenet times" are "side by side with the manufacturing interests of the West Riding of to-day. . . . In no other part of England . . . are the centuries brought into such close, strange contact"[12] as the area around Roe Head.

Mrs. Gaskell also explains that most of the inhabitants of the West Riding during the Brontës' lifetime had a strong historical sense. Because their manufacturing had been restricted by the Stuart monarchs, most Yorkshiremen had fought beside Cromwell, and their descendents, who "live on the same lands as their ancestors," remembered those days:

> . . . perhaps there is no part of England where the traditional and fond recollections of the Commonwealth have lingered as long as in that inhabited by the woollen manufacturing population of the West Riding.[13]

Therefore, the Brontë children may have picked up their strong sense of history from the people around them as well as from the books they read.

In addition to these specific influences, there were also the general influences that they might have acquired from living during a period that was acutely conscious of history. For example, Roy Strong links the Victorian interest in history, the historical novel, and painting of historical subjects in *Recreating the Past: British History and the Victorian Painter*; and he explains that the eighteen-thirties, forties, and fifties were "the years of history as best-selling literature." Carlyle's *French Revolution,* which was published in 1837, and Macaulay's *History of England* (1849-61) "sold by the thousand, and the middle classes of Victorian England devoured history with the same kind of hunger as they had for the historical novel."[14] The following excerpt from one of Charlotte Brontë's letters to William Smith Williams (October 25, 1850) reveals her interest in the thought of the day and points directly to her interest in history: "You say I keep no books; pardon me—I am ashamed of my own rapaciousness: I have kept 'Macaulay's History,' and Wordsworth's 'Prelude,' and Taylor's 'Philip Van Artevelde'."[15]

Familiar as she was with the thought of the period, Brontë may have also been familiar with the notions about evolution which were also part of the general consciousness of the age. As William Irvine explains in *Apes, Angels, and Victorians,* a belief in evolution was part of the romantic legacy:

> Meanwhile, the romantic movement—with its wonder at nature, its nostalgic curiosity about origins, its fascination with change, its exultation in plenitude and diversity—had caused students in every field to think in terms of evolution. Kant and Laplace found it in the solar system, Lyell on the surface of the earth, Herder in history, Newman in church doctrine, Hegel in the Divine Mind, and Spencer in nearly everything.[16]

Perhaps as a result of this familiarity, there was little outcry in 1831 when Lyell published *The Principles of Geology.* In fact, Irvine states that ordinary readers responded to the work enthusiastically and cites Harriet Martineau's statement that people from the middle classes "'purchased five copies of an expensive work on geology for one of the most popular novels of the time.'"[17] There is no evidence that Patrick Brontë was such a purchaser or that Charlotte herself ever read the work. However, the following exchange between Jane Eyre and Helen Burns suggests that the author was familiar with the general concept of historical evolution:

> 'I must resist those who punish me unjustly. It is as natural as that I should love those who show me affection, or submit to punishment when I feel it is deserved.'
>
> 'Heathens and savage tribes hold that doctrine; but Christians and civilized nations disown it.'
>
> (p. 50)

Thus Jane is compared to primitive people and told that she can become more civilized. Explaining that Jane should read the New Testament and try to become a better person, Helen adds that she expects one day to evolve into a better life, one beyond history:

> . . . the impalpable principle of life and thought, pure as when it left the Creator to inspire the creature: whence it came it will return; perhaps again to be communicated to some being higher than man—perhaps to pass through gradations of glory, from the pale human soul to brighten to the seraph! Surely it will never, on the contrary, be suffered to degenerate from man to fiend?
>
> (p. 51)

Thus Charlotte Brontë here seems to combine the Victorian belief in historical evolution with an older Christian belief in achieving perfection in an afterlife.

Although ***Jane Eyre*** suggests that Charlotte Brontë accepted the Victorian belief in progress, it also reveals that she knew that women were not progressing at the same rate as men. This awareness was impressed on her whenever she tried to "evolve." For example, in 1837, when she wrote Southey for his advice on becoming a writer, she was told that this desire was wrong and unfeminine. Her reply is dutifully submissive:

> Following my father's advice—who from my childhood has counselled me, just in the wise and friendly tone of your letter—I have endeavored . . . to observe all the duties a woman ought to fulfil. . . . I don't always succeed, for sometimes when I'm teaching or sewing, I would rather be reading or writing; but I try to deny myself; and my father's approbation amply rewarded me for the privation.[18]

Ten years later, however, she creates a heroine who refuses to stay in her place, a heroine whose own approbation is her reward, and a heroine whose autobiography incarnates what is seen today as a feminist approach to women's history.

Acting as her own historian, Jane draws analogies between her progress from dependent, oppressed child to independent woman with the historical evolution of greater dignity and freedom for the average man. Thus her quest for economic freedom and spiritual independence takes her on a metaphorical journey, which begins with the Roman Emperors, continues through the English Civil War, and finally progresses beyond the nineteenth century. For example, the adult historian looks back at her childhood—her origins—and links her oppression and her poverty when she explains that the Reed children sneer at her impoverished state; and she compares their treatment of her to the treatment of slaves in ancient Rome, a metaphor which she had discovered in her reading of history. Unlike John Reed, who could simply bask in his power over her, she had been studying him and learning about historical oppression by reading Goldsmith's *The Roman History*; and she adds that, reading of Nero and Caligula, she had drawn "parallels in silence" (p. 8) which she never intended to vocalize.

Like a good child, Jane silently endures John's oppression until he finally provokes her to rebel violently against him. The adult narrator reinforces the similarity between this violence and the behavior which her contemporaries (like Helen Burns) would have expected of the barbarian people who were enslaved in ancient Rome by referring to herself as a "rebel slave" and by drawing the reader's attention to her cousin's character: "I really saw in him a tyrant: a murderer. I felt a drop or two of blood from my head trickle down my neck, and was sensible of somewhat pungent suffering" (p. 9). Thus, Jane alludes to both her own past history at the Reeds and to history in general, a history which begins with oppression and silence. The silence is ruptured at this point, just as the silences of history are ruptured when oppressed people begin writing their own stories as a step toward controlling their own affairs.

The Gateshead episode focuses on a period in Jane's life that resembles the silences of prehistory and the beginnings of primitive rebellion. However, ***Jane Eyre*** uses the evolution of history as a metaphor of the evolution of Jane's consciousness. Jane's study of history, which begins with the victim's silent recognition of her oppression, continues when she is sent away to school at Lowood. No longer alone, she becomes a member of an entire group, implying that Jane's history is not individual history any longer but an historical treatment of her entire sex. The Lowood section is also a reminder of the complexity of historical oppression. While Jane and her fellow students are victims of both poverty and gender, Jane also suggests that women remain oppressed because their inferior (or at the time the novel takes place, virtually nonexistent) educations prevent them from understanding their condition.[19] Certainly the study of history which Jane describes as part of her education is not likely to lead women to a greater understanding of themselves:

> A chapter having been read through twice, the books were closed and the girls examined. The lesson had comprised part of the reign of Charles

> I., and there were sundry questions about tonnage and poundage, and ship-money, which most of them appeared unable to answer.
>
> (p. 46)

Focusing on the rote memorization of discrete facts about matters totally beyond their experience, the history lesson is alien to most of the students. The result of this kind of education is not "access to knowledge and culture and to the power that goes with them" but something that Jane criticizes as "a narrow catalogue of accomplishments" which includes the "usual branches of a good English education, together with French, Drawing, and Music" (p. 76). It is this "education" which makes women dependent and guarantees that they will remain no more than ineffective governesses. On the roof at Thornfield, Jane reflects on her own situation—the result of her limited education—but she connects her life to the lives of all women:

> Nobody knows how many rebellions besides political rebellions ferment in the masses of life which people earth. Women are supposed to be very calm generally: but women feel just as men feel; they need exercise for their faculties and a field for their efforts as much as their brothers do; they suffer from too rigid a restraint, too absolute a stagnation, precisely as men would suffer; and it is narrow-minded in their more privileged fellow-creatures to say that they ought to confine themselves to making puddings and knitting stockings, to playing on the piano and embroidering bags.
>
> (p. 96)

The reference to piano playing and embroidering links the passage with Jane's comments about her narrow list of accomplishments and with the "women's work" that Southey had recommended for Charlotte Brontë herself.

While Jane links her personal history to the history of all women, her consciousness of history clearly sets her apart. Her references to *The Roman History,* to her history class at Lowood, and to women's education suggest an ability to learn lessons concealed from men and ordinarily lost even on women. In fact, her entire history records her developing awareness of the reasons for women's oppression. One of these reasons is the basic inequality in the sexes, an inequality which places all power in the hands of men. For example, the adult narrator reveals that Jane (and therefore other women as well) is often confronted by those who, because of both gender and class prejudice, believe that she should be submissive and subservient: the Reed family, Brocklehurst, St. John Rivers, and Rochester.[20] Recording her first official meeting with Rochester, Jane seems to encounter an absolute tyrant who warns her, "'Excuse my tone of command; I am used to say "Do this," and it is done: I cannot alter my customary habits for one new inmate'" (p. 109). His tone of command may be justified while he is her employer, but Jane reveals that she finds both it and his paternalistic treatment of her degrading when he becomes her lover. Although she and Rochester declare their spiritual equality, Jane reveals that they remain unequal in terms of sexual roles and social class. Jane, the daughter of a poor clergyman, is a governess while Rochester is both her employer and a member of the landed gentry whose family has owned "almost all the land in this neighborhood, as far as you can see" (p. 91) for generations. Recognizing their inequality, Jane continues to refer to him as a tyrant and to resist his absolute authority over her. Her response to his tyranny, however, is very different from her earlier reaction to John Reed. Thus it reveals her personal evolution:

> I'll be preparing myself to go out as a missionary to preach liberty to them that are enslaved—your harem inmates amongst the rest. I'll get admitted there, and I'll stir up mutiny; and you . . . shall in a trice find yourself fettered amongst our hands: nor will I . . . consent to cut your bonds till you have signed a charter, the most liberal that despot ever yet conferred.
>
> (p. 237)

This passage is full of erotically charged language and subtle political allusions. For example, the reference to Rochester's harem reveals that Jane understands the power that men traditionally had over women. Furthermore, her reference to mutiny and to fetters reveals that she understands the traditional ways people acquire power over others, but her actions reveal that she also understands the extent to which economic power has replaced this brute physical power during the nineteenth century. Hoping to overcome Rochester's power over her, Jane writes to her uncle of her upcoming marriage. However, her real reason for soliciting her uncle's approval is much more pragmatic: ". . . if I had but a prospect of one day bringing Mr. Rochester an accession of fortune, I could better endure to be kept by him now" (p. 236). No longer a rebel slave or "a sort of infantine Guy Fawkes" (p. 21), Jane responds to Rochester calmly and rationally. In fact, recognizing the economic basis of women's oppression and their absolute dependence on men, she asks to continue as Adele's governess after their marriage. This request does not promise equality with Rochester. Nonetheless, her desire for employment seems to be an attempt to replace the master-slave

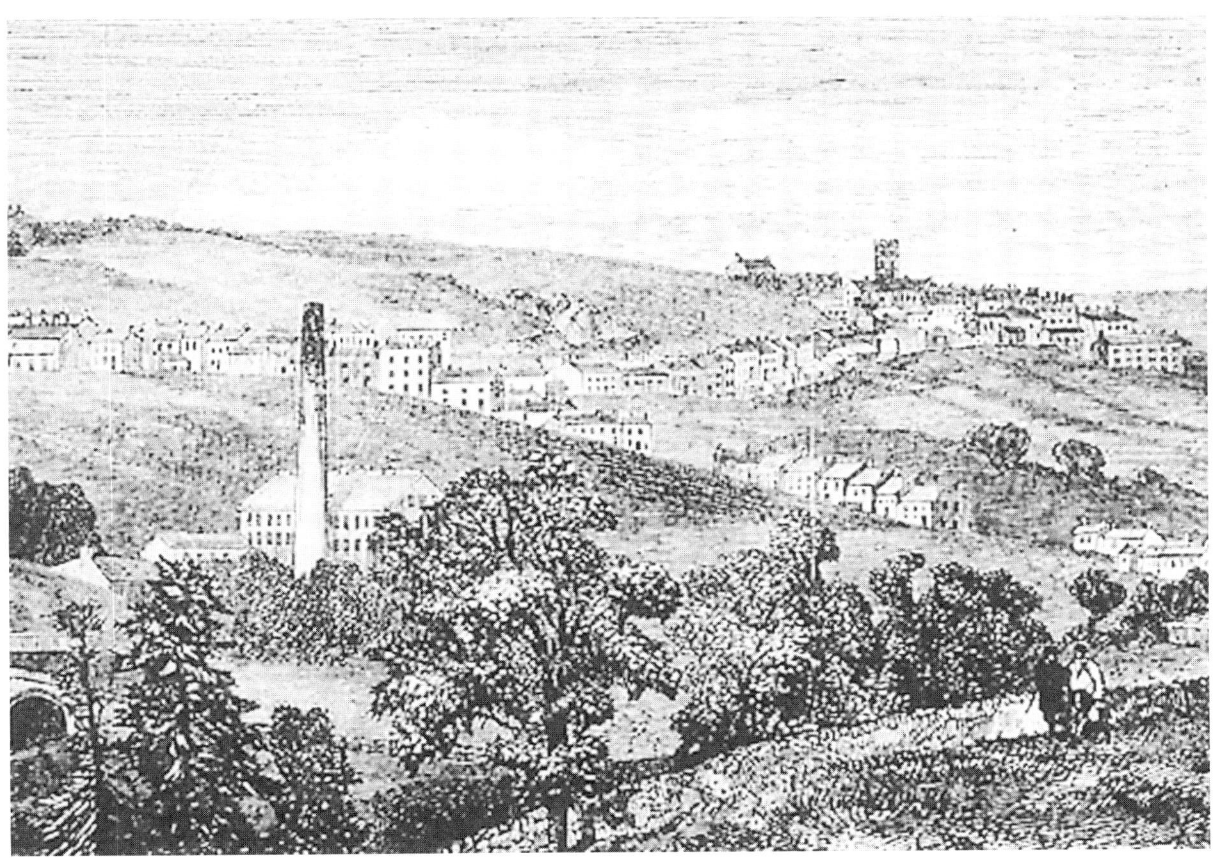

Engraving of Haworth Village, the home of the Brontë family.

relationship, to which she had alluded earlier, with a contract based on mutual responsibility.

Jane's reference to her charter is consistent with her desire for independence (or at least for a less oppressive form of dependence) and also with her development as a liberated Victorian woman. It is also a subtle historical allusion, either to Magna Carta or to the English Civil War or both.[21] Early in the novel, Jane had been impressed by Helen Burns's ability to answer questions about Charles the First, the monarch whose failure to work with Parliament led to his death and to the English Civil War. Although Helen accuses Charles of failing to understand the direction of history, her pity lies with the "poor murdered king" whose "enemies were the worst" because "they shed blood they had no right to shed" (p. 49). Jane drops the discussion at this point, and it is only when she speaks of her charter that the reader realizes how much she had learned from this discussion and from the history lesson which prompted it. The lesson had focused on memorization of discrete facts, but the astute Jane had learned that the social, economic, and political forces that combined to destroy Charles are still important. For example, she appears to recognize the parallels between the Civil War and her own history. The Civil War was precipitated by a variety of forces: by a rising middle class which desired political power commensurate with its economic power and by a religious group which, believing in a convenant between men and God, desired a similar contract between men and their rulers. (The barons who forced King John to sign Magna Carta had demanded much the same thing.) Furthermore, it is clear that Jane's sympathies are, as usual, with the rebels. Like the Parliamentarians who gained political power during the Civil War and lost it again during the Restoration, Jane's money comes from trade. She is thus part of that trend which is individualistic and middle class. Moreover, she is a member of a group which is gaining power during the nineteenth century, not through violence, but through economic strength and through political strategy. In fact, Brontë stresses Jane's right to this power by having St. John learn of her true identity (and makes it possible for her to claim her inheritance) on November 5, a holiday which is both the traditional English Guy Fawkes Day and the anniversary of the landing of William and Mary in 1688, an event which concluded the English Civil War. These veiled historical presences suggest an historic evolution from bloody rebellion to bloodless victory and therefore imply how far Jane herself has evolved from the violent child who had retaliated against John Reed to the maturing woman.

Similarly, Jane's portrait of Rochester, which also uses the English Civil War as an historical metaphor, shows that the modern man is likely to use subtle economic methods to subjugate women rather than the crude physical dominance associated with John Reed. Rochester's background resembles the Royalists.[22] With the exception of the colonial wealth which he acquired when he married Bertha Mason, his wealth comes from land; therefore, he represents a group which was losing its power base during the nineteenth century. Charlotte Brontë further emphasizes this connection by providing the reader with a partial genealogy of Rochester's family. Besides his father and elder brother, she mentions only one of his ancestors, a Damer de Rochester, who was killed at Marston Moor, a battle (July 2, 1644) which gave the Parliamentarians a decisive victory over the Royalists. Although Jane never mentions specifically whether this ancestor was Royalist or Parliamentarian, indications are that he was Royalist. In addition, Rochester's obedience to his father's orders and his later failure to abide by Jane's charter show his reverence for established authority rather than for the rights of the individual. Rochester is not a rebel, and his marriage to Jane is no act of defiance. However, when he and Jane meet again after her long absence, her inheritance has made her a member of the rising Victorian middle class and an independent woman. In fact, Jane responds to Rochester when they first meet: "I told you I am independent, sir, as well as rich: I am my own mistress" (p. 383). Her legacy of five thousand pounds has made her an independent woman who can afford to build a cottage near his door, a woman who is free to meet him on equal economic terms.

Separated initially by class and by historical consciousness, Jane can marry Rochester only after her circumstances have changed dramatically. Thus far, the novel appears to mirror the kind of historical progression which Charlotte Brontë had actually witnessed, for the marriages of members of the gentry to members of the rising middle classes were fairly common, and the rising political and economic power of the middle classes was one of the most important developments in nineteenth-century England. However, Brontë also manages to transcend the history of her own time. By focusing on the spirituality of the supernatural voice and on the married life of Jane and Rochester, she suggests how her story can evolve out of history. Unlike the masterly voice which St. John hears at the end of the novel, a voice which Jane earlier admits that she cannot obey ("But I was no apostle,—I could not behold the herald,—I could not receive his call" [p. 354]), this voice reflects feminine values: it is a request rather than a command. It is also the voice of a fellow human being—"a known, loved, well-remembered voice—that of Edward Fairfax Rochester" (p. 369), which liberates her. "It was *my* time to assume ascendancy. *My* powers were in play and in force" (p. 370). And she reinforces this sense of liberation by comparing it to an episode from ancient history: "The wondrous shock of feeling had come like the earthquake which shook the foundations of Paul and Silas's prison: it had opened the doors of the soul's cell and loosed its bands—it had wakened it out of its sleep, whence it sprang trembling, listening, aghast" (p. 371).

The change in Jane is only one aspect of the conclusion, however. The Rochester she finds at the end of her journey is greatly changed from the proud tyrant he had once been; and his physical changes are, as Elaine Showalter suggests, "symbolic immersions . . . in feminine experience."[23] As a result, he is willing to accept Jane's help and an equal partnership in marriage as he confesses to her: "You know I was proud of my strength; but what is it now, when I must give it over to foreign guidance, as a child does its weakness" (p. 393). This sense of mutual support contrasts to the final view of St. John Rivers whose echo of Revelations reinforces the patriarchal paradigm of mastery instead of mutuality: "My Master . . . has forewarned me . . . 'Surely I come quickly!' . . . Amen; even so come, Lord Jesus!'" (p. 398). Jane and Rochester manage to escape this mastery on both the physical and the spiritual levels.

The evolution from history to herstory, from exploitation of the weak by the strong to a kind of mutuality, works in ***Jane Eyre*** on more than one level. As we have seen, ***Jane Eyre*** includes many of the characteristics which Lerner says are essential to feminist history: "an account of the female experience over time" and the "development of feminist consciousness." Jane grows from victim to independent woman; she achieves mastery over herself without desiring mastery over others. In fact, she shares her wealth with her cousins just as she shares her spiritual strength with Rochester. Charlotte Brontë uses historical metaphors—slavery in ancient Rome, oppression under the Stuart monarchs, and power for the middle classes in the nineteenth century—to show how Jane's thinking evolves toward a more complete feminine consciousness and how history itself can evolve toward herstory. The emphasis on both historical progress and spiritual development thus combines the Victorian belief in historical evolution with the traditional Christian belief in achieving perfection in an afterlife.

On another level, the conclusion is not as optimistic. In fact, there are several problems that Jane ignores. For example, the basis for Jane's and Rochester's happiness—idyllic though it may appear—is the very social situation which Jane previously found so stifling. Their ability to live in seclusion, away from society's corrupting influence, is at least partially the result of their economic status; their happy domestic life is, however, financed with his rents and with the money which she had inherited from her uncle's colonial ventures. The change to mutuality instead of mastery in their personal lives is merely a glimpse into future feminist history, a history which Charlotte Brontë could but foreshadow and a history which remains to be written and experienced.[24]

Faced by the historical changes which they witness and experience, all three Brontë sisters attempted to come to terms with the history of their age and to evaluate the notion of progress in human terms. More optimistic about man's spiritual and economic progress than her sisters, Charlotte subscribed to the progressive notion of history so characteristically Victorian; and she underlines this belief by comparing Jane's individual growth to the historical development of Europe from savagery to civilization. Thus, her concern with history connects ***Jane Eyre*** to novels as otherwise dissimilar as *Vanity Fair, A Tale of Two Cities,* and *Middlemarch.* In addition, a careful look at her symbolic representation of historical events helps dispel the commonly accepted belief that she was a mythic writer who was somehow out of step with her times and connects her more closely to the prevailing intellectual trends of nineteenth-century England.

Notes

1. All references to *Jane Eyre* are included in the text and are to the following edition: Charlotte Brontë, *Jane Eyre,* ed. Richard J. Dunn (New York: W. W. Norton, 1971).
2. F. R. Leavis, *The Great Tradition* (New York: New York University Press, 1973), p. 27.
3. Q. D. Leavis, "Dating *Jane Eyre,*" *Times Literary Supplement,* 27 May 1965, p. 436.
4. Ellen Moers, *Literary Women: The Great Writers* (Garden City, New York: Doubleday, 1976); Elaine Showalter, *A Literature of Their Own: British Women Novelists from Brontë to Lessing* (Princeton, New Jersey; Princeton Univ. Press, 1977); Sandra M. Gilbert and Susan Gubar, *The Madwoman in the Attic: The Woman Writer and the Nineteenth-Century Literary Imagination* (New Haven: Yale Univ. Press, 1979).
5. Anne Brontë, *The Tenant of Wildfell Hall,* ed. G. D. Hargreaves (New York: Penguin Books, 1979), p. 35.
6. Andrew and Judith Hook, Introd., *Shirley* by Charlotte Brontë (New York: Penguin Books, 1974), p. 9. More important, Gaskell's biography reveals that Charlotte strived in *Shirley* for historical accuracy: ". . . and she sent to Leeds for a file of the 'Mercuries' of 1812, '13, and '14; in order to understand the spirit of those eventful times. She was anxious to write of things she had known and seen" (p. 378). Elizabeth Gaskell, *The Life of Charlotte Brontë,* ed. Alan Shelston (New York: Penguin Books, 1975).
7. Gerda Lerner, "The Challenge of Women's History," *The Majority Finds Its Past* (New York, 1981). Cited by Elaine Showalter, "Feminist Criticism in the Wilderness," *Critical Inquiry,* 8 (Winter 1981), p. 198.
8. Winifred Gérin, *Charlotte Brontë: The Evolution of Genius* (New York: Oxford Univ. Press, 1967), p. 24. Gérin also mentions the books that Mr. Brontë used to teach his daughters—the Bible, Mangnall's *Historical Questions,* Lindley Murray's *Grammar,* and Goldsmith's *Geography* (p. 22). Certainly the first two books would have reinforced the children's interest in history.
9. Gaskell cites the Brontës' *History of the Year 1829* on pp. 116-17, which mentions the periodicals they read. She also mentions their interest in current events:

   > Long before Maria Brontë died at the age of eleven, her father used to say he could converse with her on any of the leading topics of the day with as much freedom and pleasure as with any grown-up person.
   >
   > (p. 95)

10. Gérin, p. 65. One wonders exactly how big an impression such study made on Charlotte and why she named Zamorna's childwife, Marian Hume.
11. Gaskell, p. 54.
12. Gaskell, pp. 125-26.
13. Gaskell, p. 63.
14. Roy Strong, *Recreating the Past: British History and the Victorian Painter* (Over Wallop, Hampshire: Thames and Hudson, 1978), p. 32.
15. Gaskell, p. 432.
16. William Irvine, *Apes, Angels, and Victorians: Darwin, Huxley, and Evolution* (New York: Time Inc., 1963), pp. 105-106.
17. Irvine, p. 106.
18. Gérin, p. 111.
19. Mary Jacobus explains that George Eliot is also concerned with women's education, when she states that the "all-important question of women's access to

knowledge and culture and to the power that goes with them . . . is often explicitly thematized in terms of education" (p. 213). "The Question of Language: Men of Maxims and *The Mill on the Floss," Critical Inquiry,* 8 (Winter 1981).

20. John Reed's social background is rather sketchy. All Jane mentions is that Mr. Reed was a magistrate and that Mrs. Reed sneers at John Eyre for being in trade. She is more precise about Rochester's background. Jane refers to Thornfield as "a gentleman's manor house" (p. 86) and provides him with an ancestor who fought in the English Civil War and a father who is unwilling to divide his property between his two sons. However, even Brocklehurst and St. John, who are not wealthy, have the power of patriarchy behind them.

    Karen Mann also refers to the power of the ruling classes:

    > Both [John Reed and Richard Mason] seem to be the expression of a class gone sour: Reed is bloated by the indulgent materialism of the bourgeoise, while Mason is the weak and degenerate issue of the colonial system. In typical Brontean fashion, then, they show two possible results of the power and corruption of money and class consciousness.

    Karen B. Mann, "Bertha Mason and Jane Eyre: The True Mrs. Rochester," *Ball State University Forum,* XIX (Winter 1978), 32.

21. It is more likely to refer to the Civil War, the period in English history which most appealed to the Victorians. Roy Strong explains the reason for this fascination:

    > This concept of conflict between the old establishment and the new classes found its ideal expression in the Civil War. In the person of Charles I . . . was discovered the perfect symbol of the *ancien régime* at its best. . . . In Cromwell the Chartists and other reformers saw their historic sanction for the new self-made man; they presented him as the hero of the common people. . . . Out of this struggle had been born that most prized possession of British people, the Constitution, monarchic yet democratic, the envy of the rest of Europe.
    >
    > (p. 45)

    This fascination, as Strong explains, also resulted in a plethora of paintings about the Civil War: "More works of art were produced depicting scenes connected with Charles I, Oliver Cromwell, Henrietta Maria and the struggle of Cavalier versus Roundhead than for any other period of British history" (p. 137). Brontë, who was extremely interested in the visual arts, may have been familiar with some of these works.

22. Lawrence Stone discusses the gentry prior to and during the Civil War and explains that members of the gentry were more likely to ally their fortunes with the king after 1645. He adds that the most important single factor was religion, however, and this is something to which Brontë provides no clue. *The Causes of the English Revolution: 1529-1642* (New York: Harper and Row, 1972), p. 143.

23. *A Literature of Their Own,* p. 152.

24. Gilbert and Gubar summarize the modern reader's disappointment at the same time they explain why Brontë failed in this way:

    > In all of her books, . . . she was able to act out that passionate drive toward freedom which offended agents of the status quo, but in none was she able consciously to define the full meaning of achieved freedom—perhaps because no one of her contemporaries, not even a Wollstonecraft or a Mill, could adequately describe a society so drastically altered that the matured Jane and Rochester could really live in it.
    >
    > (pp. 369-70)

MARYANNE C. WARD (ESSAY DATE 2002)

SOURCE: Ward, Maryanne C. "The Gospel According to Jane Eyre: The Suttee and the Seraglio." *Journal of the Midwest Modern Language Association* 35, no. 1 (2002): 14-24.

In the following essay, Ward takes a postcolonial and historicist approach to Jane Eyre, *examining the direct and secondary references to slavery and English imperialism in Brontë's novel.*

Much postcolonial scholarship examines the use of colonial language and cultural references by European authors. The cultural transfer is not always successful, too often revealing those authors' acceptance of, or insensitivity to, the destructive force of the colonial project. Over the last ten years, explanations of references to slavery and the emancipation in ***Jane Eyre*** have appeared in places like *Notes and Queries* and *Postscript.* In longer articles two critics, Susan L. Meyer and Gayatri Chakrovorty Spivak, examined ***Jane Eyre*** in a postcolonial context concentrating on the novel's relation to the slave trade (mandated by the West Indian setting) and British imperialism (as St. John Rivers' mission suggests). Meyer concludes that "What begins as an implicit critique of British domination and an identification with the oppressed collapses into merely an appropriation of the metaphor of 'slavery'" (265). Spivak reads ***Jane Eyre*** as a novel which posits "the unquestioned ideology of imperialist axiomatics" (248). While each of these notes and articles focuses attention on some aspect of the novel, none explores or develops a consistent and persuasive pattern incorporating not only the specific but the secondary references to slavery and imperialism in the Lowood/Thornfield and the Marsh End sections of the text. Meyer's treatment of the rhetoric of slavery is the most thorough to date. However, while Meyer acknowledges that the novel was written more than ten years after the full emancipation of the slaves in the British colonies (1833), she analyzes the text as if it were generated early in the century at the presumed date of the story itself. A very different view of

Charlotte Brontë's attitude toward slavery emerges when all the references to slavery are included and placed in a post-emancipation context. With a careful examination of historical background as well as authorial practice, the rhetoric of the novel emerges as more consistent and unified than previously assumed. Brontë uses the rhetoric of abolition and the effects of slavery in post-emancipation Britain as an underlying rhetorical structure for her novel.[1] When read in the appropriate historical context, a consistent use of the abolition rhetoric thematically unites the West Indian (Lowood/Thornfield) and Eastern (Marsh End) elements of the novel into a cohesive and consistent "liberation" theology.

Slavery in the West Indies

Charlotte Brontë's ***Jane Eyre*** (1847) was published the same year that the French freed the slaves in their colonies. The fact that the novel does not speak out for the abolition of slavery is thus quite understandable; the British and French battle for emancipation had already been won. The success of the emancipation movement did not mean, however, that the powerful rhetoric of that struggle disappeared. In her early years Brontë heard the burning political questions of the day, slavery being chief among them, discussed at home. This awareness was deepened through her school experience. Reading back through the Lowood section of the novel, we tend to fuse the fictional and the real and make the author's terrible experience at the Clergy Daughters' School at Cowan Bridge even more "Gothic" than it really was. Once her father realized the true conditions at the school, Charlotte Brontë was, in fact, brought home. Charlotte Brontë was not sent to the school because she was not loved at home. Patrick Brontë would not have intentionally sent his daughters to a school which practiced the kind of Calvinistic approach which he abhorred. While Winifred Gérin in her biography, *Charlotte Brontë: The Evolution of Genius,* rightly emphasizes the negative aspects of the experience, she acknowledges the laudable original goals for the school, which

> had been conceived with vision and daring by its founder, and was enthusiastically supported by most of the progressive educationists of the day. The names of William Wilberforce, Hannah More, and the Rev. Charles Simeon headed the list of its subscribers, next to those of the local members of Parliament and the surrounding clergy, who welcomed the chance of a really comprehensive education for their daughters.
>
> (2)

Charlotte Brontë was acquainted with William Wilberforce's work for emancipation early in her life and later demonstrated a real appreciation for the work of Harriet Beecher Stowe, another force in the emancipation movement. These influences are certainly present in her writing.

In a methodological preamble to her discussion of ***Jane Eyre,*** Spivak asserts that she does not want "to touch Brontë's life" and thus maintains the distinction between "book and author" and "individual and history," but in Brontë's case such a distinction obscures her actual method of composition, which was highly autobiographical (244). Meyer, on the other hand, links the historical and the individual when she notes that Brontë has the young Jane talk about her experiences both at Gateshead and Lowood "appropriating" the language of slavery. These references are neither accidental nor cynical. Brontë was by instinct and because of her education and rather limited experience a highly autobiographical writer. In certain scenes and episodes, such as those depicting Lowood, the author draws heavily upon her own life. The energy behind her texts was emotional rather than cerebral as opposed to the approach of George Eliot, who was a tireless researcher. Brontë's method of composition as well as her deeply felt opposition to slavery and her familiarity with one of the most effectual of all anti-slavery novels are evident in a letter she wrote to her publisher in late October of 1852:

> I cannot write books handling the topics of the day; it is of no use trying. Nor can I write a book for its moral. Nor can I take up a philanthropic scheme, though I honour philanthropy; and voluntarily and sincerely veil my face before such almighty subject as that handled in Mrs. Beecher Stowe's work, *Uncle Tom's Cabin.* To manage these great matters rightly, they must be long and practically studied—their bearing known intimately, and their evils felt genuinely; they must not be taken up as a business matter, and a trading speculation. I doubt not, Mrs. Stowe had felt the iron of slavery enter her heart, from childhood upwards, long before she ever thought of writing books. The feeling throughout her work is sincere, and not got up.
>
> (cited in Gaskell, 364-365)

In fact, Brontë probably learned those terms which Meyer sees as "appropriated" at the school which was the model for Lowood. If not at the time, then certainly later she must have recognized the irony of the name of a great leader for emancipation being linked with an educational experience she felt to be little better than penal servitude. The distance between the ideal and the practice at the school was extreme, and Brontë's

FROM THE AUTHOR

BRONTË WRITES TO REVIEWER G. H. LEWES ABOUT USING A MASCULINE PSEUDONYM AND HER EXPECTATIONS FOR THE RECEPTION OF *SHIRLEY*

MY DEAR SIR,—It is about a year and a half since you wrote to me; but it seems a longer period, because since then it has been my lot to pass some black milestones in the journey of life. Since then there have been intervals when I have ceased to care about literature and critics and fame; when I have lost sight of whatever was prominent in my thoughts at the first publication of *Jane Eyre*; but now I want these things to come back vividly, if possible: consequently, it was a pleasure to receive your note. I wish you did not think me a woman. I wish all reviewers believed 'Currer Bell' to be a man; they would be more just to him. You will, I know, keep measuring me by some standard of what you deem becoming to my sex; where I am not what you consider graceful, you will condemn me. All mouths will be open against that first chapter; and that first chapter is true as the Bible, nor is it exceptionable. Come what will, I cannot, when I write, think always of myself and of what is elegant and charming in femininity; it is not on those terms, or with such ideas, I ever took pen in hand: and if it is only on such terms my writing will be tolerated, I shall pass away from the public and trouble it no more. Out of obscurity I came, to obscurity I can easily return. Standing afar off, I now watch to see what will become of *Shirley*. My expectations are very low, and my anticipations somewhat sad and bitter; still, I earnestly conjure you to say honestly what you think; flattery would be worse than vain; there is no consolation in flattery. As for condemnation I cannot, on reflection, see why I should much fear it; there is no one but myself to suffer therefrom, and both happiness and suffering in this life soon pass away.

Brontë, Charlotte. Letter to G. H. Lewes of November 1, 1849. Reprinted in Gaskell's *The Life of Charlotte Brontë*, pp. 283. London: Dent, 1857.

use of the concept of slavery for the helplessness felt by a child has both pedagogical and psychological bases. Thus Brontë "appropriates" the slave references in the early section of the novel to create Jane's immature (and perhaps insensitive and overwrought) depiction of her experience, not to devaluate the work of the abolitionists or diminish sympathy for the plight of the slaves. In many ways Meyer's fascinating information about Brontë's unfinished novel ***Emma*** (1853), in which the author appears to have decided to explore racial prejudice by having her heroine be of mixed race, emphasizes that Brontë's concern went a great deal deeper than the mere "appropriation" of terms. The fact that Brontë broached the subject at all is telling; she wrote only of those things about which she cared deeply.

Brontë was very familiar with the individuals and institutions in her society which had fought for and won the battle for emancipation and the social and religious rhetoric of that fight. Knowing the movement and its rhetoric well, she naturally, but perhaps subconsciously, returned to it when creating a heroine who would challenge gender inequities and, to a limited extent, the class distinctions which Brontë felt so keenly. The heroine in Brontë's tale of a young woman's struggle for emancipation would be a self-described "plain, Quakerish governess" (225). This description associates Jane with the group which had been so steadfast in support of Wilberforce and emancipation.[2] The references to Quakers are far more powerful and resonant than mere metaphors for Jane's plainness and simplicity of dress. Jane is guided by an inner voice not unlike the Quaker's Inward Light.

David Brion Davis's award-winning study, *The Problem of Slavery in the Age of Revolution 1770-1832,* details the activities of the Society of Friends in the emancipation movement in England and the United States. Davis notes that from the late eighteenth century the one issue on which the Society was completely united and on which it did not follow the individual Inward Light, even in the American South, was the abolition of slavery (202). There could be no deviation from the belief that slavery was wrong and that to support that institution in any way was not permitted by the Society. Our contemporary reading of Quaker pacifism into Jane's character probably differs from nineteenth-century reader response, particularly those with West Indian holdings, who viewed the Society of Friends as non-violent but persistent and threatening troublemakers.

While the lack of explicit cries for emancipation may be explained away by the historical content, Meyer sees racism in the text itself, although it is not unmitigated. She concludes that "The story of Bertha . . . does indict British colonialism in the West Indies and the 'stained' wealth that came from its oppressive rule" (255). Yet, Meyer sees the underlying assertion as basically racist because "the novel persistently displaces the blame for slavery onto the 'dark races' themselves, only alluding to slavery directly as a practice of dark-skinned people" (262). She bases her assertion on the racial background of Bertha Mason and a set of references to characters who are clearly white, although "swarthy," morally "stained," and therefore, by association, black. A coherent analysis of the attitude toward race in the text depends heavily on the actual racial background of Bertha Mason. Meyer describes Bertha's brother as the "yellow-skinned yet socially white Mr. Mason" (252); Meyer argues quite strongly for Bertha being either of mixed parents or at least strongly associated with the slaves by her "swarthy" complexion. At the very least she asserts a symbolic identification.

Brontë's biographer, Winifred Gérin, points out that in Charlotte's class at Cowan Bridge were two orphan girls from the West Indies. Apparently, their brother, who visited regularly, was "sallow looking" (unlike the sisters whose color was unremarkable) and therefore an exotic figure when he came to the school. Gérin speculates that this "direct prototype of Mr. Mason" was "doubtless suffering from the English cold" (333). A more likely explanation for his sallowness would be that after an ocean voyage into the northern Atlantic, the tan gained in the West Indies would have begun to fade leaving a sallow cast, as it does to the skin of those with slightly olive complexions such as the Masons. (The British experience with tanned skin was fairly limited to the army and navy, and the effects of the sun on fair British complexion usually resulted in a burn and not a tan.) There is no indication that Brontë suspected a mixed racial background in her classmates' brother despite his strange coloring, although the fragments of ***Emma*** indicate that Brontë would have befriended such a person without prejudice. Thus I infer the most likely explanation to be true, that Charlotte Brontë did not wish to present the Masons as of mixed racial heritage. The designation "Creole" after the mother's name indicated, as was customary, that she was born in the islands as opposed to her merchant husband, who was an emigré Englishman. Such a reading makes sense of the madness and excess in the mother's family without inviting the contradictory vision of the novel as being anti-slavery, and yet blaming the oppression on the oppressed.

Charlotte Brontë was certainly neither sensitive nor consistent, but rather very conventional in her use of adjectives of color, which could simultaneously have racial and/or moral overtones. Her color polarities come from two different sources: literary and religious. The first set are ambiguous in their moral judgments; the second, not open to debate. Out of the Gothic and the Byronic comes the contrast between the light hero and the dark anti-hero, the latter preferred by the Brontës. From conventional Christian theology and the Bible come references to the works of darkness and the children of light, references which are spiritual judgments. (A case could certainly be made here for institutionalized use of racist language in Christian theology. However, when the abolitionists called slavery a work of darkness, no one would suggest that they were referring to slaves, but rather to the devil and the evil of the institution.)

The dark, brooding Byronic figure of Brontëan juvenilia is Rochester's ancestor. He, like Emily Brontë's Healthcliff, is "colored" by his passion, sexuality, and flawed humanity, and is pitted against the colorless, cold morality of Rivers and Linton. Readers' emotional engagement and, to some extent, sympathy lie with the dark, brooding half-victim, half-villain. Yet, this ambiguous moral darkness of social and economic oppression does not rival the moral horror of slavery. Abolitionists, Anglican evangelicals, and Quakers alike not only stressed the harm done to the person enslaved, but also advertised the moral danger to the slaveholders themselves. When Rochester's secret is revealed and Jane cannot marry him, he asks her to live with him without the sanction of marriage. He pleads that he does not want to go back to his old practice of taking a mistress: "Hiring a mistress is the next worst thing to buying a slave: both are often by nature, and always by position, inferior: and to live familiarly with inferiors is degrading" (274). Jane understands that despite his protestations, she would be, in fact, his mistress and therefore have equal value to him as a slave. His plea reveals his underlying assumption of the existence of an inferiority based in nature, not enforced by social position. Brontë forces us to see that Rochester's belief in Jane's inferiority necessitates more than that she "give up your governessing slavery" (238). Early in the novel Rochester had set himself up as Jane's liberator from the constraints placed on her by her occupation and by her Lowood past which causes her to "fear in the presence of a man and a brother" (122). He puts himself in the position of benevolent benefactor/master and, later, lover. Ironically, as R. J. Dingley reveals in *Notes and Queries,* Rochester's own word choice damns him. The very phrase he uses was taken from the seal of the Slave Emancipation Society. On that widely known and copied medallion, originally modeled by Josiah Wedgwood, the kneeling figure pleads "Am I not a Man and a Brother?" (66). In all these instances, Rochester is both dark and "stained," but in no way could the blame for his attitudes and actions be passed to the oppressed.

Brontë not only puts the words of the inscription of the popular medallion in Rochester's mouth, but she also buries in his abhorrent formulation about his mistresses the argument of the abolitionists, particularly the Quakers, on the cost of owning another human being. To own a slave is not only to harm the captive, but also to degrade oneself. On the one hand, Rochester's characterization of Bertha as not only mad, but also "intemperate and unchaste" is an extravagant description, part of Rochester's self-justification as he seeks to win Jane's sympathy (270). Yet, there is also a link between the unstable and corrupt family Rochester describes and the belief on the part of the abolitionists that owning slaves helped to cheapen all aspects of human life. Davis's study helps to put this section of the novel in an historical context when he asserts that "the godless character of West Indian society made it easy to perceive slavery as a product of irreligion and infidelity, closely linked to the sins of intemperance, profanity, and shameless sexuality" (203). Abolitionists used the planters as examples of how slave ownership was joined to incontinent lives. Charlotte Brontë would have heard those cautionary tales from her school days. Brontë's description of the character of Bertha Mason and her Creole family should be read in light of contemporary beliefs about life on those islands, which according to Davis had more than a little basis in fact. Thus, Bertha's madness is not a result of racial, but of sexual inheritance, the result of being the heiress to a family corrupted by the nature of their livelihood. The swarthy Rochester is tainted by having married into a society where his income is derived from a slave-holding estate and by his acceptance of the institution of slavery. He has owned slaves as well as taken mistresses. He says he wants to avoid the practice of taking a mistress and, although now he is presumably supported by his family's money, he still wants not only to "own" Jane, but to chain her, clearly not the action of a liberator:

> "and when I have fairly seized you, to have and to hold, I'll just—figuratively speaking—attach you to a chain like this" (touching his watchguard). "Yet, bonny wee thing, I'll wear you in my bosom, lest my jewel I should tyne."
>
> (238)

Only when he has been blinded and maimed does Rochester hand over his watch chain to Jane, relinquishing his possession.

Missionaries, Colonialism and Women's Liberation

Susan Meyer is wisely wary about appropriations of the moral and physical horror of slavery to lesser, although certainly unjust, forms of oppression. I do not believe that the novel or Brontë herself is ambiguous on the question of slavery; she simply felt that the battle for emancipation had been won, at least on the British front, and that Mrs. Stowe was doing the work in America. The same cannot be said on the question of missionary work in the East and its link to the expansion of the British Empire. As the daughter of an Anglican minister and a conventional Christian, Brontë approved of the work of the missionaries. Because of the resentment of the planters in the West Indies to missionary work, many believed that the missionaries were very active in the cause of emancipation. Davis maintains that "English missionaries to the West Indies were interested in religious conversion, not revolution, although some of the planters were too blind or bigoted to see the difference" (203). On the other hand, the Quakers were politically active in trying to free the slaves in both the British colonies and the United States, but made few converts. Brontë does affirm the work of St. John Rivers which, as in the case of the work of the Anglican missionaries in the West Indies, is certainly open to question in this post-colonial era. Spivak is correct in her reading of the novel as very Eurocentric. (Given Brontë's lack of affection for Belgian Catholics as evinced in ***Villette,*** I don't doubt that she would have seen that country as in need of Anglican missionary activity as well.) There must not have been many, novelists or otherwise, who would have challenged the "rightness" of Rivers's work.

However, as closely aligned as they often are, Brontë and her character are not one and the same. Only under extreme pressure from Rivers does Jane agree to serve God in the mission field. The coldness and dominance of Rivers's character reveal the dark side of the missionary spirit. His is a mission of dominance, not of liberation, let alone love. In opposition to Rivers's mission, Jane articulates her own gospel of liberation. Jane sees herself both as one to be liberated and as a potential liberator. While St. John Rivers believes that a woman could not go out on her own as an Anglican missionary, the same did not apply to Quakers. Davis points out that Friends of either sex could undertake a traveling mission "and receive the assent of the appropriate meetings." In America one of the tasks of the traveling Friends was "gently rebuking the families they visited for retaining Negro slaves or for displaying worldly vanities" (226). Brontë has Jane doing exactly that to Rochester, rebuking him for his attitude and former practice from the proposal scene on. Revolution is much easier if you actually hate your oppressor; the bondage of care is much more insidious. His patriarchal assumptions are very familiar territory in feminist analyses of ***Jane Eyre.*** My concern is with the particular rhetoric of Jane's struggle and with Jane's deliberate limitation of her role as "missionary" to unemancipated women. Unlike the Anglican missionaries, whose work she rejects for herself, Jane seeks liberty and not salvation for the "slaves" whom she believes herself particularly suited to "convert."

The rhetorical and thematic bridge between the West Indian and the Eastern elements of the novel actually occurs after Jane has accepted Rochester's proposal. Despite the fact that she will not change her habits of dress and prefers to remain "Quakerish" (a sign of her role as free individual), Rochester tells her, in an easy bit of flattery, that he wouldn't exchange her for a harem. She is offended ("bit") by the "Eastern allusion" and tells him he might find better use for his money than buying silks and jewels for her:

> "And what will you do, Janet, while I am bargaining for so many tons of flesh and such an assortment of black eyes?"
>
> "I'll be preparing myself to go out as a missionary to preach liberty to them that are enslaved—your harem inmates amongst the rest. I'll get admitted there, and I'll stir up mutiny; and you, three-tailed bashaw as you are, sir, shall in a trice find yourself fettered amongst our hands: nor will I, for one, consent to cut your bonds till you have signed a charter, the most liberal that despot ever yet conferred."
>
> (237)

Jane will liberate those sexual slaves held in physical bondage in a harem or, as in the case of England, in emotional bondage, linked by love to a man whom she gradually realizes still views her as property. Later in this same pre-marital conversation, she gets the second hint that Rochester has only given lip service to the gospel of natural equality as preached by Jane. He sings her a sentimental ballad ending with the assertion that his love has agreed "With me to live—to die." He is startled when Jane counters that "'I had as good a right to die when my time came as he had: but I should bide that time, and not be hurried away in a suttee'" (240). Thus, in preaching against the seraglio and the suttee (the required death of a widow on her husband's funeral pyre) Jane has limited her missionary activity to those institutions and customs which were based on the presumption of sexual inequality.

Much earlier in the proposal scene in the Thornfield garden, Jane had instinctively questioned Rochester on equality, to which he all too glibly agreed. The nature of Jane's rhetoric, although not her level of mistrust, indicated that she knew that Rochester viewed her, not only "by position" but "by nature," as inferior. Jane's liberation theology for women relies heavily on, and does not casually appropriate, the language of emancipation theology. Davis points out that during the struggle for abolition there were attempts at establishing a theological basis for slavery by "proving" the less than equally human status of the slaves. The abolitionists had to counter Biblically-based arguments that the slaves were doomed as either sons of Ham cursed by Noah to eternal slavery or a separate lesser creation (539-541). Jane asks Rochester if he thinks she is "soulless and heartless," two of the things that the slave-owners wanted to believe about their captives. Thus, slave-owners were unwilling to have their slaves baptized because this act would acknowledge that they had souls. When Jane proclaims that she has "as much soul as you—and full as much heart," she is proclaiming a kind of equality which Rochester has not challenged. Her vulnerability to him comes from her lack of money, family support and the information Rochester is withholding. She asserts her equality in the rhetorical terms of the abolitionists by asking that not merely her station but her body be disregarded, which in her case would disguise gender rather than race: "I am not talking with you now through medium of custom, conventionalities, nor even mortal flesh—it is my spirit which addresses your spirit; just as if both had passed through the grave, and we stood at God's feet, equal,—as we are" (222). God's view of her status is not really the question, but the attitude of

Rochester and men like him who are at ease with the seraglio and the suttee.

A minister's daughter, Charlotte Brontë produced a testament in the form of a fictional autobiography, and like the earliest attempt in this genre, *Moll Flanders,* the life is put before us as an *exemplum.* What are we to learn from this life? While Jane's life and teaching certainly are the basis for an engendered liberation theology, Jane's individual happiness, which Spivak sees as a triumph of individualism, does not point toward the beginning of a women's movement that would struggle against class and gender oppression. In fact, Jane's preaching is not what "converts" Rochester. He is "reformed" through the radical intervention of Bertha, perhaps guided by the Providence which spared him in the refining fire. Whatever Brontë would have us believe about Jane's strength, her missionary effort is unable to claim even a single convert. Jane's state at the end of the novel is not unlike that of the liberated slaves; she has achieved the acknowledgment of her equality, but is given a very narrow sphere within which to exercise her freedom. According to Davis, "Most of the Negroes freed by Quaker masters were quietly dissuaded from trying to join the Society of Friends. Liberation from slavery did not mean freedom to live as one chose, but rather freedom to become a diligent, sober, dependable worker who gratefully accepted his position in society" (254).

Although Charlotte Brontë does not explicitly challenge the missionary/imperialist assumptions of the British activity in the East, a closer examination of the character and to some extent of the work of St. John Rivers allows us a subversive reading. Only the most fanatic religious reader could have wanted Jane to marry and serve Rivers. Rivers achieves martyrdom at the hands of the Eastern climate, not at the hands of those who oppose his mission. If we recall the other interventions of nature in the novel, such as the oak tree split by lightning, Brontë asks nature to say what she could not: that Rivers has made the wrong choice and that he did not belong in the East. Thus, the anti-colonial thrust of the novel and the cry for gender equality signaled by emancipation rhetoric are subtexts, masked by the Gothic romance and heroic Christian missionary plots they subvert.

Are we to read the conclusion as an affirmation of individualism or despair? Jane and Rochester's isolation in the end may either be a new Eden or a sign of the failure of the preaching of this Quakerish governess. Analysis of the issues of emancipation and missionary work has helped to answer this question. Charlotte Brontë, supported by the rhetoric of emancipation, creates her ideal missionary and then, looking at the mission field, loses faith and relegates Jane to Ferndean, where, like Esther Summerson in the new Bleak House, she will be untouched by and unable to touch the society so much in need. We may be looking for affirmation on the social level which Brontë knew was impossible in her society. Perhaps she did not lack courage or imagination, but was merely unwilling to produce a romance ending for a very real problem.

George Levine, commenting on the conclusion of George Eliot's *Daniel Deronda,* sees Daniel's setting off "to create a community, outside the reaches of the society and of the novel whose language can no longer evoke one" as Eliot's "renouncing the possibility of satisfactory life within society" (46). As with the Jews in anti-semitic Britain or the freed slaves in the West Indies, acknowledging equality did not bring with it economic or social inclusion; it merely indicated the escape from legal restrictions. Brontë successfully uses the rhetoric of emancipation to describe Jane's personal struggle, but lacking a model for a truly integrated conclusion for her text and her heroine's life, she produced a conclusion which revealed how far her society had to go to realize and accept the social and economic implications of emancipation.

Notes

1. While the emancipation struggle in the British colonies and *Jane Eyre* certainly did not generate a women's movement in Britain, Charlotte Brontë's use of emancipation rhetoric in the cause of gender equality is paradigmatic of the relationship between the rhetoric of the American emancipation movement and its appropriation for women's suffrage.

2. There are three main references to Quakers. The first occurs early in the novel when Jane describes her black frock, "Quaker-like as it was" (86). Jane describes Grace Poole's warning to her to lock her door at night as being delivered "with the demureness of a Quakeress" (136); she intends the comment ironically, but the irony really is that Mrs. Poole is trying to protect Jane from danger. The third reference is Jane's description of herself as a "plain Quakerish governess" who does not need or want Rochester's jewels (227).

Works Cited

Brontë, Charlotte. *Jane Eyre.* New York: W. W. Norton, 1971.

Davis, David Brion. *The Problem of Slavery in the Age of Revolution 1770-1823.* New York: Cornell UP, 1975.

Dingley, R. J. "Rochester as Slave: An Allusion in *Jane Eyre.*" *Notes and Queries* 31 (1984): 66.

Gaskell, Elizabeth. *The Life of Charlotte Brontë.* New York: E. P. Dutton, 1924.

Gérin, Winifred. *Charlotte Brontë: The Evolution of Genius.* Oxford: Oxford UP, 1967.

Gibson, Mary Ellis. "Seraglio or Suttee: Brontë's *Jane Eyre,*" *Postscript* 4 (1987): 1-8.

Levin, George. *The Realistic Imagination.* Chicago: U of Chicago P, 1981.

Meyer, Susan L. "Colonialism and the Figurative Strategy of Jane Eyre." *Victorian Studies: A Journal of the Humanities, Art and Sciences* 33 (Winter 1990): 247-268.

Spivak, Gayatri Chakrovorty. "Three Women's Texts and a Critique of Imperialism." *Critical Inquiry* 12 (Autumn 1985): 143-161.

Tasch, Peter A. "*Jane Eyre*'s 'Three-tailed Bashaw,'" *Notes and Queries* 29 (1982): 232.

FURTHER READING

Bibliographies

Crump, Rebecca W. *Charlotte and Emily Brontë: A Reference Guide.* 3 vols. Boston: G. K. Hall, 1982-1986, 194 p.

Provides an annotated compilation of secondary sources from 1846 to 1983.

Passel, Anne. *Charlotte and Emily Brontë: An Annotated Bibliography.* New York: Garland Publishing, 1979, 359 p.

Organizes criticism by text.

Biographies

Gaskell, Elizabeth. *The Life of Charlotte Brontë.* London: E. P. Dutton, 1908, 411 p.

Offers a biography by one of Brontë's contemporaries; includes large extracts from Brontë's correspondence.

Gérin, Winifred. *Charlotte Brontë: The Evolution of Genius.* London: Oxford University Press, 1967, 617 p.

Biography focusing on Charlotte Brontë's development as an author.

Gordon, Lyndall. *Charlotte Brontë: A Passionate Life.* New York: W. W. Norton, 1996, 418p.

Provides revisionist insights into Brontë's life.

Miller, Lucasta. *The Brontë Myth.* New York: Knopf, 2004, 351p.

Offers a biography that retraces myth surrounding the Brontë sisters, particularly Charlotte.

Criticism

Adams, Maurianne. "*Jane Eyre*: Woman's Estate." In *The Authority of Experience: Essays in Feminist Criticism,* edited by Arlyn Diamond and Lee R. Edwards, pp. 137-59. Amherst: University of Massachusetts Press, 1977.

Reads Jane Eyre *as a feminist novel despite Jane's initial discomfort with her feminist awareness.*

Argyle, Gisela. "Gender and Generic Mixing in Charlotte Brontë's *Shirley.*" *Studies in English Literature 1500-1900* 35, no. 4 (autumn 1995): 741-56.

Explores the use of the third-person narrator in Shirley *as a departure from Brontë's usual style.*

Baines, Barbara. "*Villette*: A Feminist Novel." *Victorians Institute Journal* (1976): 51-60.

Interprets Villette *as the story of a young woman observing the identities available to her and gradually realizing her personal power.*

Craik, W. A. *The Brontë Novels.* London: Methuen, 1968, 266 p.

Studies the novels by the Brontë sisters.

Eagleton, Terry. *Myths of Power: A Marxist Study of the Brontës.* London: Macmillan, 1975, 148 p.

Takes a Marxist literary approach to interpreting the Brontës' work.

Ewbank, Inga-Stina. "Charlotte Brontë: The Woman Writer As an Author Only." In *Their Proper Sphere: A Study of the Brontë Sisters as Early Victorian Female Novelists,* pp. 156-204. Cambridge: Harvard University Press, 1966.

Analyzes Brontë's work in terms of the novelist's principle of artistic truth.

Federico, Annette R. "The Other Case: Gender and Narration in Charlotte Brontë's *The Professor.*" *Papers on Language and Literature* 30, no. 4 (fall 1994): 323-45.

Discusses Brontë's use of a male narrator in The Professor.

Greene, Sally. "Apocalypse When? *Shirley*'s Vision and the Politics of Reading." *Studies in the Novel* 26, no. 4 (winter 1994): 350-71.

Contends that earlier feminist criticism of Shirley *has failed to consider its context, particularly in its religious themes; argues that anachronistic criticism is unable to recognize the challenges to the limitations placed on women that Brontë's work presents.*

Levine, Caroline. "'Harmless Pleasure': Gender, Suspense, and *Jane Eyre.*" *Victorian Literature and Culture* (2000): 275-86.

Connects Brontë's use of a pseudonym with narrative suspense as pleasurable methods of subversion.

Meyer, Susan. *Imperialism at Home: Race and Victorian Women's Fiction.* Ithaca: Cornell University Press, 1996, 220 p.

Examines the treatment of race and colonialism in Jane Eyre.

Millett, Kate. "The Sexual Revolution, First Phase: 1830-1930." In *Sexual Politics,* pp. 61-156. New York: Doubleday and Company, 1970.

Includes Brontë's works in a discussion of subversive works by women; sees in Villette *a revolutionary sensibility with respect to gender issues.*

Moglen, Helene. *Charlotte Brontë: The Self Conceived.* New York: W. W. Norton, 1976, 256 p.

Explores Brontë's novels as an indication of the development of her personality.

Pell, Nancy. "Resistance, Rebellion, and Marriage: The Economics of 'Jane Eyre.'" *Nineteenth-Century Fiction* 31, no. 4 (March 1977): 397-420.

Interprets Jane Eyre *as a critique of the social and economic strictures on Victorian women.*

Plasa, Carl. "Charlotte Brontë's Foreign Bodies: Slavery and Sexuality in *The Professor.*" *Journal of Narrative Theory* 30, no. 1 (winter 2000): 1-28.

Examines the representation of colonialism found in The Professor.

Poovey, Mary. "The Anathematized Race: The Governess and *Jane Eyre.*" In *Feminism and Psychoanalysis,* edited by Richard Feldstein and Judith Roof, pp. 230-54. Ithaca: Cornell University Press, 1989.

Considers the historical position of the governess and Brontë's treatment of it in her work.

Ratchford, Fannie E. *The Brontës' Web of Childhood.* New York: Columbia University Press, 1941, 293 p.

A pioneering study of the Brontës' childhood works.

Rich, Adrienne. "'Jane Eyre': The Temptations of a Motherless Woman." In *On Lies, Secrets, and Silence: Selected Prose, 1966-1978,* pp. 89-106. New York: W. W. Norton, 1979.

Assesses Jane Eyre *as a novel that depicts alternatives for women.*

Spacks, Patricia Meyer. "Power and Passivity." In *The Female Imagination,* pp. 45-96. New York: Avon, 1975.

Suggests that while Brontë's heroines must accept their dependency on men, they are able to retain at least some power in their relationships.

Spivak, Gayatri Chakravorty. "Three Women's Texts and a Critique of Imperialism." *Critical Inquiry* 12, no. 1 (autumn 1985): 243-61.

Relates Jane Eyre *to Mary Shelley's* Frankenstein *and Jean Rhys's reimagining of Bertha Mason's story in* Wide Sargasso Sea.

Taylor, Irene. "*The Professor, Jane Eyre, Shirley.*" In *Holy Ghosts: The Male Muses of Emily and Charlotte Brontë,* pp. 159-99. New York: Columbia University Press, 1990.

Links Brontë's characters' struggles with gender roles with her own desires for gender equality in society and a deeper sense of balance between the male and female qualities within herself.

Tillotson, Kathleen. "*Jane Eyre.*" In *Novels of the Eighteen-Forties,* pp. 257-313. Oxford: Oxford University Press, 1954.

Describes Jane Eyre *as a novel of the inner life; discusses Brontë's development as a writer through the Angrian chronicles and* The Professor *to the more coherent and insightful* Jane Eyre.

Woolf, Virginia. "Jane Eyre and Wuthering Heights." In *The Common Reader,* pp. 219-27. New York: Harcourt Brace Jovanovich, 1925.

Emphasizes the poetry of Brontë's writing and the intensity of Jane Eyre.

Yaeger, Patricia. "Honey-Mad Women: Charlotte Brontë's Bilingual Heroines." *Browning Institute Studies* 14 (1986): 11-35.

Compares the treatment of bilingualism in Jane Eyre *and* Villette *with Romantic poetry.*

Zonana, Joyce. "The Sultan and the Slave: Feminist Orientalism and the Structures of *Jane Eyre.*" *Signs* 18, no. 3 (spring 1993): 592-617.

Looks at Brontë's use of Orientalist themes and their relationship to feminist issues in Jane Eyre.

OTHER SOURCES FROM GALE:

Additional coverage of Brontë's life and career is contained in the following sources published by the Gale Group: *Authors and Artists for Young Adults,* Vol. 17; *Beacham's Guide to Literature for Young Adults,* Vol. 2; *British Writers,* Vol. 5; *British Writers: The Classics,* Vol. 2; *British Writers Retrospective Supplement,* Vol. 1; *Concise Dictionary of British Literary Biography, 1832-1890; Dictionary of Literary Biography,* Vols. 21, 159, 199; *DISCovering Authors; DISCovering Authors: British Edition; DISCovering Authors: Canadian Edition; DISCovering Authors Modules: Most-studied Authors* and *Novelists; DISCovering Authors, 3.0; Exploring Novels; Literature and Its Times,* Vol. 2; *Literature Resource Center; Nineteenth-Century Literature Criticism,* Vols. 3, 8, 33, 58, 105; *Novels for Students,* Vol. 4; *Twayne's English Authors; World Literature and Its Times,* Vol. 4; and *World Literature Criticism.*

EMILY BRONTË

(1818 - 1848)

(Also wrote under the pseudonym of Ellis Bell) English novelist and poet.

The author of *Wuthering Heights* (1847), Brontë was one of a trio of sisters whose writings introduced some of the most compelling characters in the history of the novel. Though Brontë completed only one novel, hers is often acknowledged as the greatest of the works by the Brontë sisters: the most complete, with the most expansive vision of both men and women. Her reputation as a difficult, temperamental individual has colored the reception and interpretation of her work, and the intensity and violent passions of *Wuthering Heights* and its female characters have made it a difficult work for feminist critics to interpret as a woman's novel. Nonetheless, Brontë's depiction of polarized gender differences and women's desire have led to the assessment of *Wuthering Heights* as an important text in the history of women's writing.

BIOGRAPHICAL INFORMATION

Brontë was born July 30, 1818 in Thornton, Yorkshire, England, the fifth of six children born to Maria Branwell Brontë and the Reverend Patrick Brontë. The family moved to the nearby parsonage at Haworth in 1820, which was her home for her entire life but for intermittent bursts of formal schooling. Her mother died in 1821, leaving Reverend Brontë and Brontë's maternal aunt to raise the children; Brontë was sent to the Clergy Daughter's School at Cowan Bridge in 1825. The dismal conditions at the school led to the death of two of her older sisters, and Brontë returned to Haworth, where her father determined the remaining children—Charlotte, Branwell, Emily, and Anne—should be self-educated and kept apart from the other children of the village. In addition to a diverse reading program, the children spent much time in imaginative play. Emily and her younger sister Anne invented the realm of Gondal, for which they created a romantic legend and history. In 1835, Emily followed Charlotte to Roe Head, a school in East Yorkshire where Charlotte was teaching, but Emily apparently did not thrive there and soon returned home, and Anne was sent to Roe Head in her place. In 1838, Brontë worked as an assistant teacher at the Law Hill School near Halifax, but this too was short-lived. Her time in Halifax likely provided the model for the house of Wuthering Heights, in High Sunderland Hall, and possibly some hints of the story of Heathcliff, in stories about local Halifax legend Jack Sharp. In 1842, she and Charlotte traveled to Brussels to acquire the skills needed to establish a school of their own, but when their aunt died later that year the Brontës returned to Haworth again, and for the rest of Emily's life the parsonage was her residence. In 1845, Charlotte discovered one of Emily's private poetry notebooks, and at Charlotte's urging the three remaining Brontë sisters published a collection titled *Poems by Currer, Ellis, and Acton Bell* (1846). The few notices of the book were generally positive, but it sold only two copies. Meanwhile, Emily had been working on *Wuthering Heights,* which was published in an edition that also included Anne's first novel, *Agnes Grey,* in December 1847. Charlotte's first novel, *Jane Eyre,* had been published just two months earlier. *Wuthering Heights* was not well received, and Brontë began to turn her attention again to poetry. Her work was interrupted by the death of her brother Branwell on September 24, 1848. Branwell had been unhealthy for some time, in part the result of alcoholism, and Brontë had been one of his primary caretakers. By October of the same year, Brontë was ill herself with what appeared to be a cough and cold but was actually tuberculosis. According to popular accounts, Brontë, allegedly strong-willed by nature, refused rest and medical attention. She died on December 19, 1848, and was buried at Haworth.

MAJOR WORKS

Brontë authored 193 poems and verse fragments in her life, but none of her poetry compares in reputation to her novel *Wuthering Heights,* which has become one of the most widely read novels in the English language. The novel chronicles the attachment between Heathcliff, an orphan taken in by the Earnshaw family of Wuthering Heights, and the family's daughter Catherine. The two characters are joined by a spiritual bond of preternatural strength, yet Catherine elects to marry her more refined neighbor, Edgar Linton of Thrushcross Grange. Ultimately, this decision leads to Catherine's madness and death and prompts Heathcliff to take revenge upon both the Lintons and the Earnshaws. Heathcliff eventually dies, consoled by the thought of uniting with Catherine's spirit, and the novel ends with the suggestion that Hareton Earnshaw, the last descendent of the Earnshaw family, will marry Catherine's daughter, Catherine Linton, and abandon Wuthering Heights for Thrushcross Grange. Brontë's narrative style is marked by fierce animal imagery, scenes of raw violence, and supernatural overtones. While Brontë's unique methods of storytelling and artistic craftsmanship have been appreciated by critics, the characters of Heathcliff and Catherine are at the center of the novel's power: ambiguous, sometimes unsympathetic protagonists, they represent not only ill-fated lovers but reflections of the tension between natural and civilized values and between the spiritual and material worlds. The unreliability of the novel's narrators and the uneven morality of its characters render *Wuthering Heights* problematic when interpreting the book's themes and moral sensibility. Critical interest in the paradoxes of *Wuthering Heights* led to a modern increase of interest in Brontë's early poetry, particularly the poems of Gondal, which have been read as a creative forerunner of the book. The passionate characters and violent motifs of the Gondal poems reappear in *Wuthering Heights,* and scholars have begun to connect Brontë's other poetry to her fantasy world of Gondal.

CRITICAL RECEPTION

Immediate critical response to Brontë's work mixed admiration for the power of the storytelling with distaste for the harsher, more shocking elements of the novel. When "Ellis Bell" was discovered to be a woman, that distaste tended toward disapproval. Critics suggested that if such writing was strong for a man, it was unseemly for a woman; some critics took a paternalistic tone in suggesting that Brontë lacked feminine discretion. Others, however, could not believe a woman capable of creating a character like Heathcliff. Several reviewers argued that the brutality of *Wuthering Heights* and the insightful depiction of a male character proved that at least parts of the novel were written by Branwell Brontë. While such gender stereotypes have come to seem obsolete by modern standards, critics have continued to observe that Brontë eludes forms of analysis and interpretation usually applied to women authors. In a 1991 essay, Emma Francis asks, "Is Emily Brontë a Woman?" as a reflection of the challenges in reading Brontë's work from a conventional feminist perspective. Many critics have focused their attention on the circumstances and environment that could have produced such an unusual mind. Mary A. Ward saw the foundations for Brontë's "wildness" of thought in her breeding, in the landscape surrounding her, and in her tendency to withdraw from social life. While some feminist critics have seen in Brontë's self-imposed seclusion an example of the nineteenth-century repression of women's self-expression, Stevie Davies suggests that Brontë led a life of remarkable independence and that the unusual freedom with which she lived allowed her to develop her unique creative vision. But as Carol Senf has observed, the tendency to emphasize Brontë's solitude and interiority has led scholars to miss the author's broader feminist vision. Senf claims that *Wuthering Heights* also examines the evolution of women's roles in a patriarchal society and imagines the possibility of further changes, a view of women's potential empowerment also observed by Drew Lamonica. The mystique of Brontë's unusual personality has also hindered the study of *Wuthering Heights* as serious literature. Not until 1926, with C. P. Sanger's study *The Structure of* Wuthering Heights (see Further Reading), did critics begin to approach the novel as a work of art.

PRINCIPAL WORKS

**Poems by Currer, Ellis, and Acton Bell* [as Ellis Bell] (poetry) 1846

†*Wuthering Heights* [as Ellis Bell] (novel) 1847

**Life and Works of the Sisters Brontë.* 7 vols. (novels and poetry) 1899-1903

**The Shakespeare Head Brontë.* 19 vols. (novels, poetry, and letters) 1931-38

Gondal Poems (poetry) 1938

The Complete Poems of Emily Jane Brontë (poetry) 1941

* This collection includes works by other members of the Brontë family.

† This edition of *Wuthering Heights* also includes the novel *Agnes Grey,* written by Anne Brontë.

PRIMARY SOURCES

EMILY BRONTË (POEM DATE 1846)

SOURCE: Brontë, Emily. "How Clear She Shines." In *The Poems of Emily Brontë,* edited by Clement Shorter, pp. 31-32. London: Hodder and Stoughton, 1910.

In the following poem, originally published in the 1846 collection Poems of Currer, Ellis, and Acton Bell, *Brontë displays some of the passionate motifs that later appear in* Wuthering Heights.

HOW CLEAR SHE SHINES

How clear she shines! How quietly
   I lie beneath her guardian light;
While heaven and earth are whispering me,
   'To-morrow, wake, but dream to-night.'
Yes, Fancy, come, my Fairy love!
   These throbbing temples softly kiss;
And bend my lonely couch above,
   And bring me rest, and bring me bliss.

The world is going; dark world, adieu!
   Grim world, conceal thee till the day;
The heart thou canst not all subdue
   Must still resist, if thou delay!

Thy love I will not, will not share;
   Thy hatred only wakes a smile;
Thy griefs may wound—thy wrongs may tear,
   But, oh, thy lies shall ne'er beguile!
While gazing on the stars that glow
   Above me, in that stormless sea,
I long to hope that all the woe
   Creation knows, is held in thee!

And this shall be my dream to-night;
   I'll think the heaven of glorious spheres
Is rolling on its course of light
   In endless bliss, through endless years;
I'll think, there's not one world above,
   Far as these straining eyes can see,
Where Wisdom ever laughed at Love,
   Or Virtue crouched to Infamy;

Where, writhing 'neath the strokes of Fate,
   The mangled wretch was forced to smile;
To match his patience 'gainst her hate,
   His heart rebellious all the while.
Where Pleasure still will lead to wrong,
   And helpless Reason warn in vain;
And Truth is weak, and Treachery strong;
   And Joy the surest path to Pain;
And Peace, the lethargy of Grief;
   And Hope, a phantom of the soul;
And Life, a labour, void and brief;
   And Death, the despot of the whole!

EMILY BRONTË (ESSAY DATE 1846)

SOURCE: Brontë, Emily. "No Coward Soul is Mine." In *The Poems of Emily Brontë,* edited by Clement Shorter, pp. 81-82. London: Hodder and Stoughton, 1910.

In the following poem, originally published in the 1846 collection Poems of Currer, Ellis, and Acton Bell, *Brontë offers what many commentators have identified as a reflection of her personality and private beliefs. Charlotte Brontë published it with the preface, "The following are the last lines my sister Emily ever wrote." Emily Dickinson selected the poem to be read at her own funeral.*

NO COWARD SOUL IS MINE
      No coward soul is mine,
No trembler in the world's storm-troubled
   sphere:
      I see Heaven's glories shine,
And faith shines equal, arming me from fear.

      O God within my breast,
Almighty, ever-present Deity!
      Life—that in me has rest,
As I—undying Life—have power in Thee!

      Vain are the thousand creeds
That move men's hearts: unutterably vain;
         Worthless as withered weeds,
Or idle froth amid the boundless main,

ABOUT THE AUTHOR

HARRIET MARTINEAU WRITES IN CHARLOTTE BRONTË'S OBITUARY ABOUT THE LIVES OF THE THREE SISTERS AND THE SHOCKING NATURE OF *WUTHERING HEIGHTS*

In her obituary notice of her two sisters 'Currer' reveals something of their process of authorship, and their experience of failure and success. How terrible some of their experience of life was, in the midst of the domestic freedom and indulgence afforded them by their studious father, may be seen by the fearful representatives of masculine nature of character found in the novels and tales of Emily and Anne. They considered it their duty . . . to present life as they knew it, and they gave us *Wuthering Heights* and *The Tenant of Wildfell Hall.* Such an experience as this indicates is really perplexing to English people in general, and all that we have to do with it is to bear it in mind when disposed to pass criticism on the coarseness which to a certain degree pervades the works of all the sisters, and the repulsiveness which makes the tales by Emily and Anne really horrible to people who have not iron nerves.

Martineau, Harriet. Excerpt from an obituary for Charlotte Brontë, *Daily News,* April 1855. In *Emily Brontë* Wuthering Heights*: A Casebook,* edited by Miriam Allott, p. 72. London: Macmillan, 1970.

To waken doubt in one
Holding so fast by Thine infinity;
So surely anchored on
The steadfast rock of immortality.

With wide-embracing love
Thy spirit animates eternal years,
Pervades and broods above,
Changes, sustains, dissolves, creates, and rears.

Though earth and man were gone,
And suns and universes ceased to be,
And Thou were left alone,
Every existence would exist in Thee.

There is not room for Death,
Nor atom that his might could render void:
Thou—THOU art Being and Breath,
And what THOU art may never be destroyed.

GENERAL COMMENTARY

EMMA FRANCIS (ESSAY DATE 1991)

SOURCE: Francis, Emma. "Is Emily Brontë a Woman?: Femininity, Feminism, and the Paranoid Critical Subject." In *Subjectivity and Literature from the Romantics to the Present Day,* edited by Philip Shaw and Peter Stockwell, pp. 28-40. London: Pinter, 1991.

In the following essay, Francis looks at the avant-garde aspects of Brontë's work to consider how her poetry confounds a conventional feminist reading.

The critical history of Emily Brontë's poetry is a history of evasion. The vast body of work which advertises its subject as 'Emily Brontë' is, in fact, almost wholly engaged with ***Wuthering Heights*** (1847) (Brontë 1965). Where her poetry *is* read, the cacophony of other poetic voices almost invariably invoked when speaking of her work—ranging through the canon of male romanticism and its antecedents such as Milton—is at its loudest. That these comparisons function not to elucidate her poetics, but to avoid encountering them, became abundantly clear in 1986 when Robert K. Wallace published *Emily Brontë and Beethoven.* Wallace manages to go one better than the usual account of Brontë as an honorary male romantic a decade or more after the event. His variation of the theme—that Brontë was crucially influenced by her knowledge of the 'Byronic' life and works of Beethoven—is argued out within a structure which alternates discussion of Brontë's work with analysis of three of Beethoven's piano sonatas. This effectively drowns out Brontë for at least half the book, in a grotesque reification of the dynamic more generally at work in readings of her relation to romanticism.

I do not believe that the problem is that critics are incapable of understanding the issues Brontë is exploring in her poetry. For example, J. Hillis Miller's essay on ***Wuthering Heights*** in *Fiction and Repetition* (1982) is a sophisticated discussion of the way the novel frenetically generates more and more signs out of its sparse archetypes which, paradoxically, drives the possibility of establishing a central referent for them all, further and further away. The reader becomes as confused and disoriented in her search for a coherent interpretation of the narrative as Lockwood, when he is tormented by the 'swarms of Catherines' he sees after examining the first Cathy's alternative signatures graffitied on the windowsill at Wuthering Heights, and by the ever multiplying sermons of the Reverend Jabes Branderham he dreams of when he tries to sleep after reading her diary (Brontë 1965: 61-73). As I will argue later, this seems to me to be one of the main dynamics the poetry is engaged with. In a book concerned with narrative, it would not, of course, be necessary for Miller to make reference to the poetry at all. But he does invoke it, not to draw this parallel but to deny it. He claims that

> Brontë's problem, once she had agreed with her sisters to try her hand at a novel was to bend the vision she had been more directly and privately expressing in the Gondal poems to the conventions of nineteenth century fiction . . .
>
> (Miller 1982: 46)

That 'vision' cannot be expressed directly or privately and in the attempt to do so becomes distorted and refracted by the conventions of the medium it unsuccessfully attempts to represent itself in; is a form of stress which is extremely urgent in the poetry. It seems extraordinary that Miller makes his argument for the stress attached to the process of representation in ***Wuthering Heights*** by a comparison which (fallaciously) denies this stress in the poetry, when an affirmation of it would have substantiated his thesis even more effectively.

Similarly, an essay by Lawrence Starzyk, 'The Faith of Emily Brontë's Mortality Creed' (Starzyk 1973: 295-305),[1] which makes a virtue of the contradictions in Brontë's vision and analyses them in terms of her radical theology, chooses to do this by discussion of one of the few poems where identity, representation and argument are comparatively unified—**"No Coward Soul is Mine"** (Brontë 1985). Starzyk's point is much more clearly made in two other poems about religious experience, **"The Prisoner"** and **"The Philosopher"** (Brontë 1985) which I will consider below. Like Miller, he refuses to encounter his own view of Brontë at the point in her texts where the justification for it is being generated.

I have considered these two writers in the same space as the more outrageous instances of critical bad faith in order to give some idea of the force of the readerly paranoia Brontë's poetry seems to generate. I want to investigate why this might be the case in two ways. First, as a test case, I will give an account of the problems I encountered in my own reading of her poetry; my work on Brontë forms part of a project on nineteenth-century women's poetry. In previous work I had managed to identify a poetics of power and transgression in the poetry of women like Felicia Hemans (1793-1835), Letitia Landon (1802-1838) and Christina Rossetti (1830-1894). They were recuperable for a constructive political reading despite having been encumbered by two very unhelpful critical conventions. They have been read by traditional criticism as most charmingly willing to accept a subordinate poetic role, writing conventional and innocuous lyrics about flowers and piety, leaving the struggle with the collapse of teleology and the philosophical quandary of the relation between subject and object to the Big Boys.[2] Latterly, the reading of them produced by certain feminist critics, under the influence of Lacanian theories of women's problematic entry into and hold upon language, surprises itself with the fact that they managed to write at all.[3] In the face of the hugely prolific output of, in particular, Hemans and Landon who managed to support themselves and their families from their poetry, such accounts, for me, became incomprehensible. I also realized that their assiduous accession to aesthetic restraint—in relation to the forms of poetic language it was permissible for nineteenth-century women to use (which I will discuss below) and, thus, the positions it was possible for them to take up in the political and philosophical debates happening within nineteenth-century aesthetics—results in a repetition of the contradictions upon which those limits were based, which throws them into crisis.

This form of poetic (and political) triumph emerges from a writing and a reading which begins and ends firmly inside the gendered constraints of nineteenth-century poetics. But as I turned to Brontë, here at last, I thought, was a woman whose poetry deals with transgression in such an explicit way that I could not help but produce a rousing hymn of celebration to a woman's achievement, taking control of poetic language to articulate a programme of liberation. But it was precisely in terms of Brontë as a *woman* that I encountered problems in my analysis. The readings of her outlined above function around a refusal of Brontë as being what she is. In the readings of her in relation to the male romantics, there is a refusal that she is a Victorian. In the disproportionate emphasis on ***Wuthering Heights*** and the avoidance of her poetics at the point where they are most apparent, there is a refusal that she is a poet. As I began to investigate her poetics I experienced the temptation of a similar refusal—of Emily Brontë as a woman. This was not only because of her differences from the poetics of other nineteenth-century women. The terms of the debate about transgression her work led me into, seemed to contain no room for any account of femininity.[4] I will refer to the terms of Georges Bataille's (1973) discussion of Emily Brontë in *Literature and Evil* as representative of the tradition of theorizing transgression Brontë seems to relate to most, but which excludes some of the most crucial aspects of her poetry. Bataille's account brings to light the problems of Brontë's position as the 'avant-gardist' amongst nineteenth-century women poets and the price attached to the radical respectability she has retained among feminist and non-feminist critics.

Second, I will look in detail at "**The Prisoner**" and "**The Philosopher.**" It is from a stanza of "**The Prisoner**" that Bataille demonstrates his maxim 'Eroticism is the approval of life up until death'. (Bataille 1973: 4):

> Yet I would lose no sting, would wish no torture
> less;
> The more the anguish racks, the earlier it will
> bless;
> And robed in fires of hell or bright with
> heavenly shine,
> If it but herald death, the vision is divine!
>
> (stanza 18)

This account of desire, as the desire for the ultimate expenditure of identity in death certainly has some purchase on the poem. But the way in which this view of ecstasy as a kind of collapse is framed, by the context of political oppression it is situated in within the poem, reproduces the strategy present in many of the poems: the identities and moral categories which have been collapsed are redistinguished and redeployed. "**The Prisoner**" ends with the assertion that the disempowerment of the prisoner's oppressors is the result of (their perception of) an 'overruling' by heaven. This resurrects the recuperative dialectic Bataille celebrates Brontë for refusing. The point of excess, where 'life and death, the real and the imaginary, the past and the future, the communicable and the incommunicable' (Bataille 1973: 15 quoting Breton 1972: 123) and all other oppositional categories spill over into and erase each other, is alongside the reassertion of the power of these oppositions.

When we appreciate the way in which these two accounts of power interact with, and actually depend upon, each other in Brontë's poetics, we are getting close to understanding the issues at stake in the refusal she generates in us.

Is Emily Brontë a Woman?

Contrary to the view unproblematically assumed by traditional twentieth-century criticism and theorized by feminist critics such as Margaret Homans (1980),[5] nineteenth-century women were not under psychic or cultural prohibition against the use of poetic language *per se*. What *was* demanded of them was that they use a particular form of it—the language of the Beautiful. The aesthetic split between the Sublime and the Beautiful was formally theorized by Edmund Burke (1958) in *A Philosophical Enquiry into the Origins of Our Ideas of the Sublime and the Beautiful,* and had a huge purchase on English poetry throughout the nineteenth century. The prohibition nineteenth-century women poets were under was against the use of the language of the Sublime, which the male romantics used. The vast amount of poetry written by women in the nineteenth century exploring this aesthetic of the Beautiful was not just suffered, it was enormously popular and received a good deal of contemporary critical acclaim. For the most part, the only objections raised against the poetry are at the points when it transgresses the boundaries of the Beautiful. An explicitly gendered account of power is inscribed across this aesthetic demarcation. Power is produced in the Sublime (gendered male) and becomes dispersed in the Beautiful (gendered female). It is produced by the Sublime experience of threatened privation or death. The Beautiful cannot comprehend power because it is a structure of plenitude which does not have this threat of lack inscribed within it (Burke 1958: 54-71). Thus Brontë, who consistently refuses to write within the aesthetics of the Beautiful, places herself in a unique, and apparently attractively decisive, relation to the power up for grabs in nineteenth-century poetics.

It is largely on the basis of this ostensible lack of relation to the aesthetic of the Beautiful and her engagement with the Sublime structure of empowerment that Emily Brontë has retained her reputation as one woman who is unfettered by the 'masculinist' poetics which many feminist critics have seen as a force of symbolic prohibition on the production of other nineteenth-century women poets. Paradoxically, this has lead to a discussion of Brontë's transgressiveness in terms of parallels which have been drawn between her work and the male romantics. It is at this intersection that Bataille situates her triumph:

> Reproduction and death condition the immortal renewal of life; they condition the instant which is always new. That is why we can only have a tragic view of the enchantment of life, but that is also why tragedy is the symbol of enchantment. The entire romantic movement may have heralded this, but that late masterpiece, ***Wuthering Heights,*** heralds it most humanely.
>
> (Bataille 1973: 11)

Bataille also reminds us that she 'certainly read Byron' (Bataille 1973: 17). To situate my discussion of Brontë's radicalism within the terms of these poetics of transgression is to enter territory where my specifically feminist engagement with the poems, which attempts to speak about Brontë's radicalism in the same space as that of the other nineteenth-century women I am reading, becomes very difficult. Brontë's 'triumph' identified from this perspective is precisely the strategy refused by the other women who interrogate and redefine the limits of their aesthetic permission from within the confines of the Beautiful. I thus forego the possibility of establishing any kind of relation between Brontë's 'feminist' or even 'feminine' poetics and those of almost all other nineteenth-century women poets who refuse strategies of overt transgression, and who will, in this logic, be rendered negligible. Brontë's radicalism will be seen as a function of her *lack of* or difference from 'femininity'.

The dangers of this are highlighted by the striking similarity between Bataille's portrait of Brontë and that always drawn by traditional criticism of her, which has a large stake in disguising her radicalism. Bataille focuses on her 'courage', 'reserve' and 'devotion' (Bataille 1973: 1):

> She lived in a sort of silence which, it seemed, only literature could disrupt. The morning she died, after a brief lung illness, she got up at the usual time, joining her family without uttering a word and expired before midday, without even going back to bed. She had not wanted to see a doctor.
>
> (Bataille 1973: 1)

This discussion of lack of Victorian womanly vulnerability is accompanied in Bataille, as in traditional criticism, by an emphasis on the extremely sublimated nature of her 'passion':

> For though Emily Brontë, despite her beauty, appears to have had no experience of love she had an anguished knowledge of passion . . . keeping her moral purity intact, she had a profound experience of the abyss of evil.
>
> (Bataille 1973: 3)

It hardly needs to be pointed out that this is in complete contrast with the other writers discussed in Bataille's volume, whose implication in the most violent and transgressive forms of sexual practice is located by Bataille at the same point as the emanation of their transgressive philosophy and textual strategy. It is through an analysis of Brontë that Bataille concludes that 'Evil . . . is not only the dream of the wicked: it is to some extent the dream of the good' (Bataille 1973: 18). This involves him in the alignment of Brontë with Catherine (as against Heathcliff) who he defines as

> absolutely moral. She is so moral that she dies of not being able to detach herself from the man she loved when she was a child. But although she knows that Evil is deep within him, she loves him to the point of saying 'I am Heathcliff'.
>
> (Bataille 1973: 8)

This form of goodness, so overdetermined that it can comprehend evil, Bataille terms 'hypermorality' (Bataille 1973: 10). But it is Heathcliff who craves death in order to repair his attachment to Catherine. In chapter 29 he makes it his business to mutilate Cathy's coffin so that when he is buried next to her their two bodies will mingle in decomposition.

What is at stake in this most uncharacteristic demarcation of identities on Bataille's part is a refusal of femininity and feminine sexuality as nontransgressive. The patriarchal psychic formations implicated in this refusal are too obvious to merit discussion. The point is that she is placed by Bataille in the same isolation from the mass of nineteenth-century women poets as traditional criticism has always placed her, even if he does it for the opposite reason; the wish to recuperate, rather than deny her transgressiveness. It is significant that in this essay Bataille repairs his link with surrealism, which he had broken away from several decades before, in the invocation of Breton's *Second Surrealist Manifesto* (1972). His quarrel with Breton had been that some surrealist accounts imply that transgression comes about for the individual on a psychic level, detached from social reality, rather than, as Bataille was anxious to emphasize, at the point where 'individual' psychic forces break down into the corporate movement of the 'Popular Front in the streets' (Bataille 1985: 161-168). The following passage comes from the same essay Bataille quotes to elucidate Brontë's conceptualization of the 'point . . . where life and death, the real and the imaginary' etc collapse into each other:

> What could those people who are still concerned about the position they occupy *in the world* expect from the Surrealist experiment? (It is) in this mental site, from which one can no longer set forth except for oneself on a dangerous but, we think, a supreme feat of reconnaissance.
>
> (Breton 1972: 124)

I cannot help feeling that by re-establishing the proximity of this text to his own work Bataille is gesturing towards a source of justification for his isolationist strategy. To make Brontë's transgressiveness a function of her uniqueness in this way, is to make it a function of her a-sexualism in both senses. Bataille's approach refuses her transgressiveness at the same point as traditional criticism does: her femininity. The transgressive moments which draw me to Brontë's texts, on closer examination repel me, as seemingly incompatible with identifying her in any meaningful way as a woman.

THE PRISONER

"The Prisoner" (Brontë 1985) is curiously conscious of this dilemma. The woman who experiences what, I would agree with Bataille, is the most intense instance of this ecstasy within the poetry, is a 'marble' (if not plaster) saint, akin to the de-sexualized Emily Brontë thought capable of conceiving her:

> The captive raised her head; it was as soft and
> mild
> As sculptured marble saint or slumbering
> unweaned child.
> It was so soft and mild, it was so sweet and fair
> Pain could not trace a line nor grief a shadow
> there.
>
> (stanza 7)

The contradiction implicit in this description, that she is both 'soft' and 'hard', is multiplied by the fact that this celebration of her inviolacy comes precisely at the point at which she has been violated:

> The captive raised her hand and pressed it to her
> brow:
> 'I have been struck', she said, 'and I am suffering
> now'.
>
> (stanza 8)

Readers of **"The Prisoner,"** from Charlotte Brontë (who separated the first three stanzas from the rest of the poem in its 1850 edition) onwards, have been unable to comprehend the apparent disjuncture between different parts of the poem. I want to consider this phenomenon not as a manifestation of some kind of 'failure' but as central to its strategy. The initial encounter between the speaker and the prisoner establishes the dynamic of his relation to her as one of misrecognition. This lack of encounter occurs throughout the poem. The first three stanzas stand in problematic relation to the rest of the poem. They occur chronologically after, not before the narrative of the prisoner, making it impossible to read the beginning of the poem until we have read the end. The experience it describes seems to bear some relation to the prisoner's ecstasy. It looks to the coming of a 'Wanderer' who is invisible and invulnerable to hostile gazes, as the prisoner's 'messenger of hope' is. But this is not stated explicitly. Disparities in the language used to describe the two experiences throw into doubt whether they are the same. Within stanzas 13-18, the most frequently anthologized because the most seemingly unified section of the poem, are the most acute instances of lack of encounter, this time between experience and its representation. The transition between stanzas 13 and 14 signals that a representation of the ecstatic experience is about to be given: 'visions rise and fall that kill me with desire— / Desire for . . .'. But in stanza 14 the language of the collapse of identity we expect *is* employed, but to describe what the ecstatic experience *is not*. The desire invoked by the 'visions' is 'for nothing known in [the prisoner's] maturer years'. The remaining three lines of the stanza are given over to describing the condition of these 'maturer years', where the prisoner has insisted the experience cannot be situated. But it is at this moment when it is denied that all the elements of ecstasy occur. Time is disrupted and collapsed. Although the 'maturer years' are in the future, what will happen in them is spoken of in terms of history not prophecy: 'when joy *grew* mad with awe'. This reversal is then reversed again as the future, which is expressing itself as the past, doubles itself by looking towards a further future: 'at counting future tears'. The stanza then throws itself back to the (future) past: 'When, if my spirit's sky was full of flashes warm, / I knew not whence they came, from sun or thunder storm'. The breakdown of the boundary between interiority and exteriority of 'spirit's sky', and of demarcations in the natural world in the confusion of 'sun' and 'thunder storm' is made even more significant by the fact that the experience they are thrown into conflict by, the 'flashes warm', is expressed in a form which inverts the conventional order of noun and adjective.

Having (not quite) avoided representing ecstatic experience in this curious way, the prisoner's narrative picks up the description of the prelude to the experience and continues with it for the next two stanzas. The next point of disjuncture comes on the (second) point where the description tries to move into a representation of ecstasy, at the end of stanza 16:

> My outward sense is gone, my inward essence
> feels:
> Its wings are almost free—its home, its harbour
> found;
> Measuring the gulf it stoops and dares the final
> bound.

The battle between the imagery of liberation—'Its wings are almost free', 'it dares'—and that of restriction—'Its harbour found', 'it stoops'—culminates at the end of the stanza, where language is 'bound' inside the stanza, denied entry into the territory of the ecstatic experience which occurs, completely unrepresented, between stanzas 16 and 17. Representation comes back into operation at the point where the recession of ecstasy induces pain.

I do not believe that this avoidance of representing ecstatic experience should be seen as either aesthetic or ethical failure on Brontë's part. **"The Prisoner"** does not avoid encountering ecstasy. What it does is to deploy the experience and its representation separately. This interrogates, in an extraordinary anticipation of the avant-gardist dilemma, the political purchase of ecstatic experience.

Although this moment of ecstasy is situated at the point of the collapse of identity, encountering it in its represented form means that identity and agency are re-activated as we read the experience. The poem throws the act of reading into sharp relief; in both the emphasis on the lack of full encounter between the prisoner and the speaker persona, and in the problematic mis-reading we are forced to employ in order to reconstruct the ecstatic experience. Bataille's reading of Brontë's transgressiveness is achieved at the cost of de-sexualizing her in a way which, I have argued, is indistinguishable from the strategy of the most reactionary accounts of her. This is not the inevitable consequence of reading her accounts of the collapse of identity, but some politically charged consequence *is* inevitable. We can now begin to understand the relation of the first three stanzas to the rest of the poem. They explore, from within the text, what happens when the ecstatic experience is *read*. Affected by the prisoner's account of her liberation, the speaker of the poem attempts to enter into it himself. That he has misread it becomes apparent in his failure to reproduce the terms the prisoner represented it in. The prisoner's 'messenger' 'comes with western winds', 'evening's wandering airs' and 'that clear dusk of heaven that brings the thickest stars' (stanza 13). It is unclear whether it is the determining movement of these elements which brings the 'messenger', or whether his coming is coincidentally simultaneous with their coming. In the first speaker's perception there is none of this indeterminacy: 'The little lamp burns straight; its rays shoot strong and far / I trim it well to be the Wanderer's guiding star' (stanza 2). There is no doubt here that the material will determine the immaterial. The natural has also become transformed into the artificial. The substantiality of the 'thickest stars' has become transformed into 'lamp', the singular mimic of a star. Whereas the prisoner's stars thicken and burn of their own volition—they 'take a tender fire'—this severely edited version of them in the first speaker's narrative is mutilated further as he 'trims' the lamp. The first speaker situates the coming of his 'Wanderer' at the point when 'all (except himself) are laid asleep' despite the fact that the prisoner is identified with sleep by his admission—he calls her a 'slumbering unweaned child' and her own 'mute music soothes my breast, unuttered harmony / That I could never *dream* till earth is lost to me'. The 'Wanderer' is identified in more personified terms than the 'messenger' as the presence of the capital letter in his name implies. The prisoner's 'messenger' is mentioned once and then disappears in favour of the depersonalized 'visions'. The 'Wanderer' is retained in the first speaker's account and by the third stanza he has become an 'angel'. The transformation of the prisoner's experience, from the desire for the 'visions' of stanzas 13-16, to the desire for the 'Death' they will 'herald' in stanza 18, also fails to happen in the first speaker's account. He identifies his encounter with the 'Wanderer' or 'angel' wholly with the 'Cheerful', 'soft', pleasurable, interior he looks to draw him into. Violence and pain are identified with the outside, the 'wildering drifts' and 'groaning trees' tormented by the 'breeze'. The prisoner's account not only destroys the demarcation between inside and outside, but the 'visions' bring with them enough pain to 'kill', seemingly by means of the violence they have taken possession of from the 'winds' and 'stars', which are rendered 'pensive' and 'tender', more passive, by the visions' passage through them.

The political effect this (mis-) reading of the prisoner's ecstatic experience has is to activate an explicit master/slave dialectic. The ending of the poem, which propels us back to its opening, asserts the breakdown of the speaker's power over the prisoner. In the first three stanzas we find the speaker conscious of specific social oppression, paradoxically from those his language identifies as his social inferiors:

> Frown my haughty sire, chide, my angry dame;
> Set yourselves to spy, threaten me with shame;
> But neither sire nor dame, nor prying serf shall know
> What angel nightly tracks that waste of winter snow.
>
> (stanza 3)

The triumph of the prisoner is to construct liberation out of her oppression, to exchange 'short life' for 'eternal liberty'. The experience of her observer demonstrates that the attempt to reproduce the latter half of the equation involves invoking the former: the attempt to transgress involves simultaneously a deeper entry into the economy which resists transgression. At this point where the (inevitable) interaction of identity and its collapse produces paranoia, I will begin my discussion of **"The Philosopher"** (Brontë 1985), which deals with this structure even more explicitly.

THE PHILOSOPHER

> There is indeed, etymologically, a close relationship between paranoia and ecstasy. If ecstasy is to be outside of oneself, then paranoia is to be literally beside oneself: *para* (alongside, beyond) + *noos, nous* (mind). In a sense paranoia can be understood as ecstasy experienced from 'within', ecstasy which still fears the loss of self, which has to be 'beside itself' but also has a desperate need to maintain the boundaries of it self's territories.
>
> (Williams 1989: 14)

If 'ecstasy' signifies the process of going beyond the self and the economy which sustains it, then paranoia is the process of (mis-) recognizing, with distress, that transgression. It is the inability to fully relinquish an identity which is collapsing. It is the disruption brought about within the economy ecstatic experience transcends, generated by the attempt to read that experience from a point of view still within that economy. It is the highly-stressed political articulation of ecstatic experience:

> *O for the time when I shall sleep*
> *Without identity—*
> *And never care how rain may steep*
> *Or snow may cover me.*
>
> (stanza 2)

Before he utters it, the poem has interpreted the philosopher's expression of desire for the ecstatic collapse of identity as the function of his paranoia. Whilst the philosopher is contemplating the physical suffering he could escape by death, the physical reality he separates himself from is wholly benign and pleasurable:

> Enough of Thought, Philosopher;
> Too long hast thou been dreaming
> Unlightened in this chamber drear
> While summer's sun is beaming— . . .
>
> (stanza 1)

This mis-recognition signals that the philosopher is in the same problematic 'paranoid' relation to ecstatic experience as the speaker in **"The Prisoner."** His 'sad refrain' sets up insurmountable barriers to reaching ecstasy. If

> *No promised Heaven these wild Desires*
> *Could all or half fulfil—*
> *No threatened Hell with quenchless fires,*
> *Subdue this quenchless will!*
>
> (stanza 3)

it is impossible to imagine how identity *is* to be extinguished. The philosopher's appeal to a language of transcendence, to express the urgency of his plea, back-fires on him. The categories of Heaven and Hell have failed, but he can find no new language to replace them which could conceptualize a greater power to erase the need for 'fulfilment' and 'subdual'. Neither does he erase their authority. This is not a demonstrable atheism; the 'promise' and 'threat' of Heaven and Hell are not rendered negligible within the logic of the stanza. The literal meaning of these lines is that, due to the lack of any representative proof of the possibility of an economy beyond Heaven and Hell, the subsistence of identity, which is the inevitable consequence of it, will continue. Any other reading which would see this stanza as looking towards (the possibility of) an alternative economy, depends upon a preconception of that economy's existence and constitution. This mismatch between what we and the philosopher feel the stanza should say and what it actually does say is registered by the overdeterminedly or doubly poetic nature of the two stanzas. In **"The Prisoner,"** the problem of how to represent ecstatic experience is dealt with by deploying the experience and its representation in different places. In these two stanzas of **"The Philosopher"** the problem is much more urgent. Not only is there a complete failure to represent ecstasy, but the enormous stress generated by trying to represent it creates the need for language to signal itself as present and pre-eminent, by italicizing itself. Similarly, the first speaker's appeal to the philosopher in stanza 1 'what sad refrain / concludes thy musings once again?' invites and expects the repetition of a pre-existent linguistic pattern. These poems seem to allow no escape from the argument that the attempt to represent the collapse of identity is militated against by the process of representation itself.

But as the poem continues, the possibility of encountering, through representation, even the economy of fixed identities disappears. The philosopher recalls his encounter with 'A Spirit' who seems to suggest some way out of this bleak situation. He appeared in a very specific spatial and temporal position, 'I saw a Spirit standing, man / Where thou dost stand an hour ago', (stanza 7). Yet when the philosopher attempts to search for him within this economy of identifiable time and space he finds that the spirit is no longer there:

> —And even for that Spirit, Seer,
> I've watched and sought my lifetime long;

Sought Him in Heaven, Hell, Earth and Air,
An endless search and always wrong!

(stanza 10)

This desperate searching around definable space and time activates the limitless—'endless' and 'always'. The philosopher appeals to the spirit as an alternative to the need for the erasure of identity:

Had I but seen his glorious eye
Once light the clouds that 'wilder me,
I ne'er had raised this coward cry
To cease to think and cease to be.

(stanza 11)

But the very condition and motivation of the philosopher's appeal is that the spirit is part of the economy where identity collapses, he is both present and absent, reachable and unreachable in the structure of the poem. The philosopher's search within the economy of identity activates the categories of its dissolution. As was the case in **"The Prisoner,"** the (partial) representation the poem makes of the possibility of this collapse is thus dependent on the activity of the economy which refuses it. The philosopher attributes to the spirit the power of a transformatory gaze. In fact the poem argues that in spite of himself, the philosopher's gaze is transformative. Under pressure of it, the spirit shifts from one economy to another. But this power is dependent upon the philosopher at each stage mis-recognizing the economy he is within. He is perpetually 'beside himself', failing to comprehend and encounter where he is.

This 'paranoia' is fundamental to the strategy of the poem as a whole. Unlike **"The Prisoner"** which was split between two voices, **"The Philosopher"** has a triple articulation. We have extremely sparse information about the first speaker. He is identified directly twice by the philosopher, in stanzas 7 and 10, on both occasions immediately after an identification of the spirit. The syntax of the first identification allows for the designation 'Man' to be a qualification of the ontology of the spirit: 'I saw a Spirit standing, Man,' (stanza 7). The fact that he has the closest spatial and temporal contact with the elusive spirit adds to the suggestion that they are identical. The second address identifies him as 'Seer'. Because of the semantic similarity of this category with that of philosopher, a similar collapse occurs between the philosopher and the one to whom he expresses his alienation. So, in a sense, the collapse of identity the philosopher longs for is already happening, and is a symptom of the strength of his despair of it.

Poetics, Politics and Paranoia

The study of transgression happening in these two poems is more complex than Bataille suggests. Alongside an expression of the desire for the collapse of identity, Brontë places an account of the paranoia—the distress registered at this collapse—which is the inevitable consequence of encountering it. In a sense, Brontë is giving us an account of what happens when we try to read her, inside her poems.

In the light of this analysis it becomes possible to see why all readers of Brontë, including me, have experienced such a strong temptation to refuse her poetry. My readerly paranoia, my temptation to make Brontë into a 'special case' because she challenged a category I was determined to invoke in relation to her, arose through trying to place her as a *woman* in the face of her repudiation of the poetics other nineteenth-century women poets unanimously embrace, and (consequently) the undesirably misogynist conceptualizations of transgression I was forced into. These problems seemed to be unique to the particular context of my reading. But uncovering this dynamic of the production of paranoia which is so central to the poems, indicates the link of my specific problems with those of the other readers of Brontë I cited at the beginning of this paper. It seems that the stronger the temptation Brontë produces to try and identify a particular formation her poetry offers us, and the stronger the critical good faith we are prepared to employ in this attempt, the more the poetry confounds us. But looking closely at, in particular, **"The Philosopher"** has made me realize how vital it is that I do not abandon her, that I do not deny that she is a woman. In this poem it is at the point where the process of mis-reading is at its most acute that what is being searched for emerges. The desired collapse of identity is articulated by the philosopher's cry of despair of it ever being possible. Translated back onto my reading of Brontë, this means that I do not need to be haunted by her image as a male Romantic, developing a poetics which repudiates femininity.

From a methodological point of view, I also find this concept of reading as a form of paranoia extremely attractive. It seems to me to be a very productive way to conceive the strategy I, as a feminist critic, want to bring to the texts I am working on. A central problem in feminist readings of texts from previous historical periods is that they either place twentieth-century political problems and structures of thought onto texts to which in various ways they are not appropriate, or, alternatively, they attempt to let the text determine its own terms of discussion, which is impossible; but even if it were not, it removes the focus of the reading from the political urgency which originally stimulated it. If, as a feminist critic, I admit myself as terminally paranoid—that is, in distress at the way in which the political questions and demands I carry are being undermined and reformulated by the texts as I am reading them—I will be simultaneously encountering both my own motivation for entering these texts *and* the way the uniqueness of each text can sustain and enrich this motivation.

This paranoia, this point of crisis in reading which I believe is potential in all texts, but which is inescapable in Brontë's poetry, is an agony which is wholly productive. If Miller, Starzyk, all the other critics of Brontë and my own reading of her would enter into it fully, we would experience fully the power of the political vision we must never be ashamed to own in our relation to the text. But we must also not be afraid to see collapse, in order to have it returned to us in forms we could never imagine without this violence.

Notes

1. This is the only extended discussion of Emily Brontë, in the periodical *Victorian Poetry,* which indicates the strength of the refusal to engage with her as a Victorian, generated by her association with romanticism.
2. See, for example, Elizabeth Jennings' 'Introduction' to *A Choice of Christina Rossetti's Verse,* Faber (1970): 'Christina was the least intellectual of the family of two girls and two boys . . . Her subjects were limited, it is true, but she never made the mistake of writing beyond the limits of her experience' (pp. 11-12).
3. This assumption has been axiomatic since the onset of feminist work on nineteenth-century women's texts. Both Sandra Gilbert and Susan Gubar's *The Madwoman in the Attic,* Yale University Press (1979), and Margaret Homans' *Women Writers and Poetic Identity,* Princeton University Press (1980), take it as read that women are psychically and culturally prohibited from using poetic language. This assumption has remained so inviolate that in 1987 Jan Montefiore could devote her chapter on Christina Rossetti, in *Feminism and Poetry,* to a Lacanian reading of the sonnet sequence *Monna Innominata,* arguing that the text expresses the poet's inability to overcome symbolic prohibition in the structure of poetic language.
4. In *Gender and Genius,* The Women's Press (1989), Christine Battersby has pointed out the problems clustered around the use of the term 'femininity' in nineteenth-century aesthetics. Standing in for a particular condition of consciousness and language the romantics sought to achieve in their poetry, it in fact excludes women (as biological and historical subjects) from itself. I am attempting to reclaim this term, using it to signify not just the biological category of 'woman', but at the point in my argument where I attempt to align this category with an account of language which will represent *and* transgress it.
5. See note 3. above.

ABOUT THE AUTHOR

CRITIC G. H LEWES COMMENTS IN AN 1850 REVIEW ON THE BRILLIANCE OF *WUTHERING HEIGHTS* AND THE GENDER OF THE AUTHOR

Curious enough it is to read *Wuthering Heights* and *The Tenant of Wildfell Hall,* and remember that the writers were two retiring, solitary, consumptive girls! Books, coarse even for men, coarse in language and coarse in conception, the coarseness apparently of violent and uncultivated men—turn out to be the productions of two girls living almost alone, filling their loneliness with quiet studies, and writing these books from a sense of duty, hating the pictures they drew, yet drawing them with austere conscientiousness! There is matter here for the moralist or critic to speculate on.

That it was no caprice of a poor imagination wandering in search of an 'exciting' subject we are most thoroughly convinced. The three sisters have been haunted by the same experience. Currer Bell throws more humanity into her picture; but Rochester belongs to the Earnshaw and Heathcliff family. . . . The power, indeed, is wonderful. Heathcliff, devil though he be, is drawn with a sort of dusky splendour which fascinates, and we feel the truth of his burning and impassioned love for Catherine, and of her inextinguishable love for him. It was a happy thought to make her love the kind, weak, elegant Edgar, and yet without lessening her passion for Heathcliff. Edgar appeals to her love of refinement, and goodness, and culture; Heathcliff clutches her soul in his passionate embrace . . . although she is ashamed of her early playmate she loves him with a passionate abandonment which sets culture, education, the world, at defiance. It is in the treatment of this subject that Ellis Bell shows real mastery, and it shows more genius, in the highest sense of the word, than you will find in a thousand novels. . . .

Lewes, G. H. Excerpt from a review of *Wuthering Heights* and *Agnes Grey* in the *Leader,* December 28, 1850. In *Emily Brontë* Wuthering Heights*: A Casebook,* edited by Miriam Allott, pp. 68-9. London: Macmillan, 1970.

Bibliography

Bataille, G. (1973), 'Emily Brontë', *Literature and Evil,* 3-17, (tr. Hamilton, A.), London, Calder and Boyars.

Bataille, G. (1985), 'The Popular Front in the Streets', *Visions of Excess,* 161-168, (tr. Stoekl, A.), Manchester, Manchester University Press.

Battersby, C. (1989), *Gender and Genius: Towards a Feminist Aesthetic,* London, The Women's Press.

Breton, A. (1972), 'Second Surrealist Manifesto' (1930), *Manifestos of Surrealism,* (tr. Seaver, R. and Lane, H. R.), Ann Arbor, University of Michigan Press.

Brontë, E. J. (1846a), 'No Coward Soul Is Mine', in Brontë (1985): 172-3.

Brontë, E. J. (1846b), 'The Prisoner', in Brontë (1985): 170-2.

Brontë, E. J. (1846c), 'The Philosopher', in Brontë (1985): 161-2.

Brontë, E. J. (1965), *Wuthering Heights* (1847), (ed. Daiches, D.) Harmondsworth, Penguin.

Brontë, E. J. (1985), *Selected Brontë Poems,* (ed. Chitham, E. and Winnifrith, T.), Oxford, Basil Blackwell.

Burke, E. (1958), *A Philosophical Inquiry into the Origins of Our Ideas of the Sublime and the Beautiful* (1757), (ed. Boulton, J. T.), Oxford, Basil Blackwell.

Gilbert, S. and Gubar, S. (1979), *The Madwoman in the Attic: The Woman Writer and the Nineteenth-Century Literary Imagination,* New Haven, University of Yale Press.

Homans, M. (1980), *Women Writers and Poetic Identity: Dorothy Wordsworth, Emily Brontë and Emily Dickinson,* Princeton (N. J.), Princeton University Press.

Jennings, E. (1970), 'Introduction' to *A Choice of Christina Rossetti's Verse,* London, Faber and Faber.

Miller, J. H. (1982), *Fiction and Repetition,* Oxford, Basil Blackwell.

Montefiore, J. (1987), *Feminism and Poetry,* London, Pandora Press.

Starzyk, L. (1973), 'The Faith of Emily Brontë's Mortality Creed', *Victorian Poetry,* 11, 295-305.

Wallace, K. (1986), *Emily Brontë and Beethoven,* Athens, Georgia University Press.

Williams, L. R. (1989), 'Submission and Reading: Feminine Masochism and Feminist Criticism', *New Formations 7: Modernism and Masochism,* 11-17.

TITLE COMMENTARY

Wuthering Heights

MARY A. WARD (ESSAY DATE 1899)

SOURCE: Ward, Mary A. Introduction to *Wuthering Heights* and *Agnes Grey,* pp. xviii-xxxix. London: John Murray, 1899.

In the following excerpt, Ward discusses the genesis of Wuthering Heights *from the influence of German Romanticism to the unique temperament of Brontë herself.*

Emily Brontë, like her sister, inherited Celtic blood, together with a stern and stoical tradition of daily life. She was a wayward, imaginative girl, physically delicate, brought up in loneliness and poverty, amid a harsh yet noble landscape of hill, moor and stream. Owing to the fact that her father had some literary cultivation, and an Irish quickness of intelligence beyond that of his brother-clergy, this child of genius had from the beginning a certain access to good books, and through books and newspapers to the central world of thought and of affairs. In 1827, when Emily was nine, she and her sisters used to amuse themselves in the wintry firelight by choosing imaginary islands to govern, and peopling them with famous men. Emily chose the Isle of Arran, and for inhabitants Sir Walter Scott and the Lockharts; while Charlotte chose the Duke of Wellington and Christopher North. In 1829, Charlotte, in a fragment of journal, describes the newspapers taken by the family in those troubled days of Catholic emancipation and reform, and lets us know that a neighbour lent them 'Blackwood's Magazine,' 'the most able periodical there is.' It was, indeed, by the reading of 'Blackwood' in its days of most influence and vigour, and, later, of 'Fraser' (from 1832 apparently), that the Brontë household was mainly kept in touch with the current literature, the criticism, poetry, and fiction of their day. During their eager, enthusiastic youth the Brontë sisters, then, were readers of Christopher North, Hogg, De Quincey, and Maginn in 'Blackwood,' of Carlyle's early essays and translations in 'Fraser,' of Scott and Lockhart, no less than of Wordsworth, Southey, and Coleridge. Charlotte asked Southey for an opinion on her poems; Branwell did the same with Hartley Coleridge; and no careful reader of Emily Brontë's verse can fail to see in it the fiery and decisive influence of S. T. C.

So much for the influences of youth. There can be no question that they were 'romantic' influences, and it can be easily shown that among them were many kindling sparks from that 'unextinguished hearth' of German poetry and fiction which played so large a part in English imagination during the first half of the century. In 1800, Hannah More, protesting against the Germanising invasion, and scandalised by the news that Schiller's 'Räuber' 'is now acting in England by persons of quality,' sees, 'with indignation and astonishment, the Huns and Vandals once more overpowering the Greeks and Romans,' and English minds 'hurried back to the reign of Chaos and old Night by distorted and unprincipled compositions, which, in spite of strong flashes of

Anne, Emily, and Charlotte Brontë in a 1939 painting by Patrick Branwell.

genius, unite the taste of the Goths' with the morals of the 'road.' In 1830, Carlyle, quoting the passage, and measuring the progress of English knowledge and opinion, reports triumphantly 'a rapidly growing favour for German literature.' 'There is no one of our younger, more vigorous periodicals,' he says, 'but has its German craftsman gleaning what he can'; and for twenty years or more he himself did more than any other single writer to bring the German and English worlds together. During the time that he was writing and translating for the 'Edinburgh,' the 'Foreign Review' and 'Fraser,'—in 'Blackwood' also, through the years when Charlotte and Emily Brontë, then at the most plastic stage of thought and imagination, were delighting in it, one may find a constant series of translations from the German, of articles on German memoirs and German poets, and of literary reflections and estimates, which testify abundantly to the vogue of all things Teutonic, both with men of letters and the public. In 1840, 'Maga,' in the inflated phrase of the time, says, indeed, that the Germans are aspiring 'to wield the literary sceptre, with as lordly a sway as ever graced the dynasty of Voltaire. No one who is even superficially acquainted with the floating literature of the day can fail to have observed how flauntingly long-despised Germanism spreads its phylacteries on every side.' In the year before, (1839) 'Blackwood' published a translation of Tieck's 'Pietro d'Abano,' a wild robber-and-magician story, of the type which spread the love of monster and vampire, witch and werewolf, through a Europe tired for the moment of eighteenth-century common-sense; and, more important still, a long section, excellently rendered, from Goethe's 'Dichtung und Wahrheit.' In that year Emily Brontë was alone with her father and aunt at Haworth, while her two sisters were teaching as governesses. 'Blackwood' came as usual, and one may surely imagine the long, thin girl bending in the firelight over these pages from Goethe, receiving the impress of their lucidity, their charm, their sentiment and 'natural magic,' nourishing from them the vivid and masterly intelligence which eight years later produced ***Wuthering Heights.***

But she was to make a nearer acquaintance with German thought and fancy than could be got from the pages of 'Blackwood' and 'Fraser.' In 1842 she and Charlotte journeyed to Brussels, and there a certain divergence seems to have declared itself between the literary tastes and affinities of the two sisters. While Charlotte, who had already become an eager reader of French books, and was at all times more ready to take the colour of an environment than Emily, was carried, by the teaching of M. Héger acting upon her special qualities and capacities, into that profounder appreciation of the French Romantic spirit and method which shows itself thenceforward in all her books, Emily set herself against Brussels, against M. Héger, and against the French models that he was constantly proposing to the sisters. She was homesick and miserable; her attitude of mind was partly obstinacy, partly, perhaps, a matter of instinctive and passionate preference. She learnt German diligently, and it has always been assumed, though I hardly know on what first authority, that she read a good deal of German fiction, and especially Hoffmann's tales, at Brussels. Certainly, we hear of her in the following year, when she was once more at Haworth, and Charlotte was still at Brussels, as doing her household work 'with a German book open beside her,' though we are not told what the books were; and, as I learn from Mr. Shorter, there are indications that the small library Emily left behind her contained much German literature.

Two years later, Charlotte, in 1845, discovered the poems which, at least since 1834, Emily had been writing. 'It took hours,' says the elder sister, 'to reconcile her to the discovery I had made, and days to persuade her that such poems merited publication.' But Charlotte prevailed, and in 1846 Messrs. Aylott & Jones published the little volume of ***Poems by Currer, Ellis, and Acton Bell.*** It obtained no success; but 'the mere effort to succeed,' says Charlotte, 'had given a wonderful zest to existence; it must be pursued. We each set to work on a prose tale: Ellis Bell produced ***Wuthering Heights,*** Acton Bell "Agnes Grey," and Currer Bell also wrote a narrative in one volume'—'The Professor.' For a year and a half ***Wuthering Heights,*** in common with 'Agnes Grey' and 'The Professor,' travelled wearily from publisher to publisher. At last Messrs. Newby accepted the first two. But they lingered in the press for months, and ***Wuthering Heights*** appeared at last, after the publication of 'Jane Eyre,' and amid the full noise of its fame, only to be received as an earlier and cruder work of Currer Bell's, for which even those who admired 'Jane Eyre' could find little praise and small excuse. Emily seems to have shown not a touch of jealousy or discouragement. She is not known, however, to have written anything more than a few verses—amongst them, indeed, the immortal **"Last Lines"**—later than ***Wuthering Heights,*** and during the last year of her life she seems to have given herself—true heart, and tameless soul!—now to supporting her wretched brother through the final stages of his physical and moral decay, and now to consultation with and sympathy for Charlotte in the writing of 'Shirley.' Branwell died in September, and Emily was already ill on the day of his funeral. By the middle of December, at the age of thirty, she was dead; the struggle of her iron will and passionate vitality with hampering circumstances was over. The story of that marvellous dying has been often told, by Charlotte first of all, then by Mrs. Gaskell, and again by Madame Darmesteter, in the vivid study of Emily Brontë, which represents the homage of a new poetic generation. Let us recall Charlotte's poignant sentences—

> Never in all her life had she lingered over any task that lay before her, and she did not linger now. She sank rapidly. She made haste to leave us. Yet while physically she perished, mentally she grew stronger than we had yet known her. Day by day, when I saw with what a front she met suffering, I looked on her with an anguish of wonder and love. I have seen nothing like it; but indeed I have never seen her parallel in anything. Stronger than a man, simpler than a child, her nature stood alone. The awful point was, that while full of ruth for others, on herself she had no pity; the spirit was inexorable to the flesh; from the trembling hand, the unnerved limbs, the faded eyes, the same service was exacted as in health. . . . She died December 19, 1848.

'Stronger than a man, simpler than a child:'—these words are Emily Brontë's true epitaph, both as an artist and as a human being. Her strength of will and imagination struck those who knew her and those who read her as often inhuman or terrible; and with this was combined a simplicity partly of genius partly of a strange innocence and spirituality, which gives her a place apart in English letters. It is important to realise that of the three books written simultaneously by the three sisters, Emily's alone shows genius already matured and master of its tools. Charlotte had a steady development before her, especially in matters of method and style; the comparative dulness of 'The Professor,' and the crudities of 'Jane Eyre' made way for the accomplished variety and brilliance of 'Villette.' But though Emily, had she lived, might have chosen many happier subjects, treated with a more flowing unity than she achieved in ***Wuthering Heights,*** the full competence of genius is already present in her book. The common, hasty, didactic note that Charlotte often strikes is never heard in ***Wuthering Heights.*** The artist remains hidden and self-contained; the work, however morbid and violent may be the scenes and creatures it presents, has always that distinction which belongs to high talent working solely for its own joy and satisfaction, with no thought of a spectator, or any aim but that of an ideal and imaginative whole. Charlotte stops to think of objectors, to teach and argue, to avenge her own personal grievances, or cheat her own personal longings. For pages together, she often is little more than the clever clergyman's daughter, with a sharp tongue, a dislike to Ritualism and Romanism, a shrewd memory for persecutions and affronts, and a weakness for that masterful lover of whom most young women dream. But Emily is pure mind and passion; no one, from the pages of ***Wuthering Heights*** can guess at the small likes and dislikes, the religious or critical antipathies, the personal weaknesses of the artist who wrote it. She has that highest power—which was typically Shakespeare's power, and which in our day is typically the power of such an artist as Turgueniev—the power which gives life, intensest life, to the creatures of imagination, and, in doing so, endows them with an independence behind which the maker is forgotten. The puppet show is everything; and, till it is over, the manager—nothing. And it is his delight and triumph to have it so.

Yet, at the same time, ***Wuthering Heights*** is a book of the later Romantic movement, betraying the influences of German Romantic imagination, as Charlotte's work betrays the influences of Victor Hugo and George Sand. The Romantic tendency to invent and delight in monsters, the *exaltation du moi,* which has been said to be the secret of the whole Romantic revolt against classical models and restraints; the love of violence in speech and action, the preference for the hideous in character and the abnormal in situation—of all these there are abundant examples in ***Wuthering Heights.*** The dream of Mr. Lockwood in Catherine's box bed, when in the terror of nightmare he pulled the wrist of the little wailing ghost outside on to the broken glass of the window, 'and rubbed it to and fro till the blood ran down and soaked the bed-clothes'—one of the most gruesome fancies of literature!—Heathcliff's long and fiendish revenge on Hindley Earnshaw; the ghastly quarrel between Linton and Heathcliff in Catherine's presence after Heathcliff's return; Catherine's three days' fast, and her delirium when she 'tore the pillow with her teeth;' Heathcliff dashing his head against the trees of her garden, leaving his blood upon their bark, and 'howling, not like a man, but like a savage beast being goaded to death with knives and spears;' the fight between Heathcliff and Earnshaw after Heathcliff's marriage to Isabella; the kidnapping of the younger Catherine, and the horror rather suggested than described of Heathcliff's brutality towards his sickly son:—all these things would not have been written precisely as they were written, but for the 'Germanism' of the thirties and forties, but for the translations of 'Blackwood' and 'Fraser,' and but for those German tales, whether of Hoffmann or others, which there is evidence that Emily Brontë read both at Brussels and after her return.

As to the 'exaltation of the Self,' its claims, sensibilities and passions, in defiance of all social law and duty, there is no more vivid expression of it throughout Romantic literature than is contained in the conversation between the elder Catherine and Nelly Dean before Catherine marries Edgar Linton. And the violent, clashing egotisms of Heathcliff and Catherine in the last scene of passion before Catherine's death, are as it were an epitome of a whole *genre* in literature, and a whole phase of European feeling.

Nevertheless, horror and extravagance are not really the characteristic mark and quality of ***Wuthering Heights.*** If they were, it would have no more claim upon us than a hundred other forgotten books—Lady Caroline Lamb's 'Glenarvon' amongst them—which represent the dregs and refuse of a great literary movement. As in the case of Charlotte Brontë, the peculiar force of Emily's work lies in the fact that it represents the grafting of a European tradition upon a mind already richly stored with English and local reality, possessing at command a style at once strong and simple, capable both of homeliness and magnificence. The form of Romantic imagination which influenced Emily was not the same as that which influenced Charlotte; whether from a secret stubbornness and desire of difference, or no, there is not a mention of the French language, or of French books, in Emily's work, while Charlotte's abounds in a kind of display of French affinities, and French scholarship. The dithyrambs of 'Shirley' and 'Villette,' the 'Vision of Eve' of 'Shirley,' and the description of Rachel in 'Villette,' would have been impossible to Emily; they come to a great extent from the reading of Victor Hugo and George Sand. But in both sisters there is a similar *fonds* of stern and simple realism; a similar faculty of observation at once shrewd, and passionate; and it is by these that they produce their ultimate literary effect. The difference between them is almost wholly in Emily's favour. The uneven, amateurish manner of so many pages in 'Jane Eyre' and 'Shirley;' the lack of literary reticence which is responsible for Charlotte's frequent intrusion of her own personality, and for her occasional temptations to scream and preach, which are not wholly resisted even in her masterpiece 'Villette;' the ugly tawdry sentences which disfigure some of her noblest passages, and make quotation from her so difficult:—you will find none of these things in ***Wuthering Heights.*** Emily is never flurried, never self-conscious; she is master of herself at the most rushing moments of feeling or narrative; her style is simple, sensuous, adequate and varied from first to last; she has fewer purple patches than Charlotte, but at its best, her insight no less than her power of phrase, is of a diviner and more exquisite quality.

* * *

Wuthering Heights then is the product of romantic imagination, working probably under influences from German literature, and marvellously fused with local knowledge and a realistic power which, within its own range, has seldom been surpassed. Its few great faults are soon enumerated. The tendency to extravagance and monstrosity may, as we have seen, be taken to some extent as belonging more to a literary fashion than to the artist. Tieck and Hoffmann are full of raving and lunatic beings who sob, shout, tear out their hair by the roots, and live in a perpetual state of personal violence both towards themselves and their neighbours. Emily Brontë probably received from them an additional impulse towards a certain wildness of manner and conception which was already natural to her Irish blood, to a woman brought up amid the solitudes of the moors and the ruggedness of Yorkshire life fifty years ago, and natural also, alas! to the sister of the opium-eater and drunkard Branwell Brontë.

To this let us add a certain awkwardness and confusion of structure; a strain of ruthless exaggeration in the character of Heathcliff; and some absurdities and contradictions in the character of Nelly Dean. The latter criticism indeed is bound up with the first. Nelly Dean is presented as the faithful and affectionate nurse, the only good angel both of the elder and the younger Catherine. But Nelly Dean does the most treacherous, cruel, and indefensible things, simply that the story may move. She becomes the go-between for Catherine and Heathcliff; she knowingly allows her charge Catherine, on the eve of her confinement, to fast in solitude and delirium for three days and nights, without saying a word to Edgar Linton, Catherine's affectionate husband, and her master, who was in the house all the time. It is her breach of trust which brings about Catherine's dying scene with Heathcliff, just as it is her disobedience and unfaith which really betray Catherine's child into the hands of her enemies. Without these lapses and indiscretions indeed the story could not maintain itself; but the clumsiness or carelessness of them is hardly to be denied. In the case of Heathcliff, the blemish lies rather in a certain deliberate and passionate defiance of the reader's sense of humanity and possibility; partly also in the innocence of the writer, who, in a world of sex and passion, has invented a situation charged with the full forces of both, without any true realisation of what she has done. Heathcliff's murderous language to Catherine about the husband whom she loves with an affection only second to that which she cherishes for his hateful self; his sordid and incredible courtship of Isabella under Catherine's eyes; the long horror of his pursuit and capture of the younger Catherine, his dead love's child; the total incompatibility between his passion for the mother and his mean ruffianism towards the daughter; the utter absence of any touch of kindness even in his love for Catherine, whom he scolds and rates on the very threshold of death; the mingling in him of high passion with the vilest arts of the sharper and the thief:—these things o'erleap themselves, so that again and again the sense of tragedy is lost in mere violence and excess, and what might have been a man becomes a monster. There are speeches and actions of Catherine's, moreover, contained in these central pages which have no relation to any life of men and women that the true world knows. It may be said indeed that the writer's very ignorance of certain facts and relations of life, combined with the force of imaginative passion which she throws into her conceptions, produces a special poetic effect—a strange and bodiless tragedy—unique in literature. And there is much truth in this; but not enough to vindicate these scenes of the book, from radical weakness and falsity, nor to preserve in the reader that illusion, that inner consent, which is the final test of all imaginative effort.

* * *

Nevertheless there are whole sections of the story during which the character of Heathcliff is presented to us with a marvellous and essential truth. The scenes of childhood and youth; the upgrowing of the two desolate children, drawn to each other by some strange primal sympathy, Heathcliff 'the little black thing, harboured by a good man to his bane,' Catherine who 'was never so happy as when we were all scolding her at once, and she defying us with her bold saucy look, and her ready words;' the gradual development of the natural distance between them, he the ill-mannered ruffianly no-man's-child, she the young lady of the house; his pride and jealous pain; her young fondness for Edgar Linton, as inevitable as a girl's yearning for pretty finery, and a new frock with the spring; Heathcliff's boyish vow of vengeance on the brutal Hindley and his race; Cathy's passionate discrimination, in the scene with Nelly Dean which ends as it were the first act of the play, between her affection for Linton and her identity with Heathcliff's life and being:—for the mingling of daring poetry with the easiest and most masterly command of local truth, for sharpness and felicity of phrase, for exuberance of creative force, for invention and freshness of detail, there are few things in English fiction to match it. One might almost say that the first volume of 'Adam Bede' is false and mannered beside it,—the first volumes of 'Waverley' or 'Guy Mannering' flat and diffuse. Certainly, the first volume of 'Jane Eyre,' admirable as it is, can hardly be set on the same level with the careless ease and effortless power of these first nine chapters. There is almost nothing in them but shares in the force and the effect of all true 'vision'—Joseph, 'the wearisomest self-righteous Pharisee that ever ransacked a Bible to rake the promises to himself, and fling the curses to his neighbours;' old Earnshaw himself, stupid, obstinate and kindly; the bullying Hindley with his lackadaisical consumptive wife; the delicate nurture and superior wealth of the Lintons; the very animals of the farm, the very rain- and snow-storms of the moors,—all live, all grow together, like the tangled heather itself, harsh and gnarled and ugly in one aspect, in another beautiful by its mere unfettered life and freedom, capable too of wild moments of colour and blossoming.

And as far as the lesser elements of style, the mere technique of writing are concerned, one may notice the short elastic vigour of the sentences, the rightness of epithet and detail, the absence of any care for effect, and the flashes of beauty which suddenly emerge like the cistus upon the rock.

> 'Nelly, do you never dream queer dreams?' said Catherine suddenly, after some minutes' reflection.
>
> 'Yes, now and then,' I answered.
>
> 'And so do I. I've dreamt in my life dreams that have stayed with me ever after and changed my ideas: they've gone through and through me like wine through water, and altered the colour of my mind. And this one; I'm going to tell it—but take care not to smile at any part of it.'

Nelly Dean tries to avoid the dream, but Catherine persists:—

> 'I dreamt once that I was in heaven.'
>
> 'I tell you I won't hearken to your dreams, Miss Catherine! I'll go to bed,' I interrupted again.
>
> She laughed, and held me down; for I made a motion to leave my chair.
>
> 'This is nothing,' cried she: 'I was only going to say that heaven did not seem to be my home; and I broke my heart with weeping to come back to earth; and the angels were so angry that they flung me out into the middle of the heath on the top of Wuthering Heights; where I woke sobbing for joy! That will do to explain my secret, as well as the other. I've no more business to marry Edgar Linton than I have to be in heaven; and if the wicked man in there had not brought Heatchliff so low, I shouldn't have thought of it. It would degrade me to marry Heathcliff now; so he shall never know how I love him: and that, not because he's handsome, Nelly, but because he's more myself than I am. Whatever our souls are made of, his and mine are the same; and Linton's is as different as a moonbeam from lightning, or frost from fire.'

'The angels flung me out into the middle of the heath—where I woke sobbing for joy'—the wild words have in them the very essence and life-blood not only of Catherine but of her creator!

The inferior central scenes of the book, after Catherine's marriage, for all their teasing faults, have passages of extraordinary poetry. Take the detail of Catherine's fevered dream after she shuts herself into her room, at the close of the frightful scene between her husband and Heathcliff, or the weird realism of her half-delirious talk with Nelly Dean. In her 'feverish bewilderment' she tears her pillow, and then finds

> childish diversion in pulling the feathers from the rents she had just made, and ranging them on the sheet according to their different species: her mind had strayed to other associations.
>
> 'That's a turkey's,' she murmured to herself; 'and this is a wild duck's; and this is a pigeon's. Ah, they put pigeons' feathers in the pillows—no wonder I couldn't die! Let me take care to throw it on the floor when I lie down. And here is a moor-cock's; and this—I should know it among a thousand—it's a lapwing's. Bonny bird; wheeling over our heads in the middle of the moor. It wanted to get to its nest, for the clouds had touched the swells, and it felt rain coming. This feather was picked up from the heath, the bird was not shot: we saw its nest in the winter, full of little skeletons. Heathcliff set a trap over it, and the old ones dared not come. I made him promise he'd never shoot a lapwing after that, and he didn't. Yes, here are more! Did he shoot my lapwings, Nelly? Are they red, any of them? Let me look.'
>
> 'Give over with that baby-work!' I interrupted, dragging the pillow away, and turning the holes towards the mattress, for she was removing its contents by handfuls. 'Lie down, and shut your eyes: you're wandering. There's a mess! The down is flying about like snow.'
>
> I went here and there collecting it.
>
> 'I see in you, Nelly,' she continued, dreamily, 'an aged woman: you have grey hair and bent shoulders. This bed is the fairy cave under Penistone Crags, and you are gathering elf-bolts to hurt our heifers; pretending, while I am near, that they are only locks of wool. That's what you'll come to fifty years hence: I know you are not so now. I'm not wandering: you're mistaken, or else I should believe you really *were* that withered hag, and I should think I *was* under Penistone Crags; and I'm conscious it's night, and there are two candles on the table making the black press shine like jet.'

To these may be added the charming and tender passage describing Catherine's early convalescence, and her yearnings—so true to such a child of nature and feeling—for the first flowers and first mild breathings of the spring; and the later picture of her, the wrecked and doomed Catherine, sitting in 'dreamy and melancholy softness' by the open window, listening for the sounds of the moorland, before the approach of Heathcliff and death:—

> Gimmerton chapel bells were still ringing; and the full mellow flow of the beck in the valley came soothingly on the ear. It was a sweet substitute for the yet absent murmur of the summer foliage,

> which drowned that music about the Grange when the trees were in leaf. At Wuthering Heights it always sounded on quiet days following a great thaw or a season of steady rain.

Lines which, for their 'sharp and eager observation,' may surely be matched with these of Coleridge, her master in poetic magic, her inferior in all that concerns the passionate and dramatic sense of life:—

> All is still,
> A balmy night! and though the stars be dim,
> Yet let us think upon the vernal showers
> That gladden the green earth, and we shall find
> A pleasure in the dimness of the stars.

* * *

Of what we may call the third and last act of ***Wuthering Heights,*** which extends from the childhood of the younger Catherine to the death of Heathcliff, much might be said. It is no less masterly than the first section of the book and much more complex in plan. The key to it lies in two earlier passages—in Heatchliff's boyish vow of vengence on Hindley Earnshaw, and in his fierce appeal to his lost love to haunt him, rather than leave him 'in this abyss where I cannot find her.' The conduct of the whole 'act' is intricate and difficult; the initial awkwardness implied in Nelly Dean's function as narrator is felt now and then; but as a whole, the strength of the intention is no less clear than the deliberate and triumphant power with which the artist achieves it. These chapters are not always easy to read, but they repay the closest attention. Not an incident, not a fragment of conversation is thrown away, and in the end the effect is complete. It is gained by that fusion of terror and beauty, of ugliness and a flying magic—'settling unawares'—which is the characteristic note of the Brontës, and of all that is best in Romantic literature. Never for a moment do you lose hold upon the Yorkshire landscape and the Yorkshire folk—look at the picture of Isabella's wasteful porridge-making and of Joseph's grumbling rage, amid her gruesome experience as a bride; never are you allowed to forget a single sordid element in Heathcliff's ruffianism; and yet through it all the inevitable end developes, the double end which only a master could have conceived. Life and love rebel and reassert themselves in the wild slight love-story of Hareton and Cathy, which break the final darkness like a gleam of dawn upon the moors; and death tames and silences for ever all that remains of Heathcliff's futile cruelties and wasted fury.

But what a death! Heathcliff has tormented and oppressed Catherine's daughter; and it is Catherine's shadow that lures him to his doom, through every stage and degree of haunting feverish ecstasy, of reunion promised and delayed, of joy for ever offered and for ever withdrawn. And yet how simple the method, how true the 'vision' to the end! Around Heathcliff's last hours the farm-life flows on as usual. There is no hurry in the sentences; no blurring of the scene. Catherine's haunting presence closes upon the man who murdered her happiness and youth, interposes between him and all bodily needs, deprives him of food and drink and sleep, till the madman is dead of his 'strange happiness,' straining after the phantom that slays him, dying of the love whereby alone he remains human, through which fate strikes at last—and strikes home.

'Is he a ghoul or vampire?' I mused. 'I had read of such hideous incarnate demons.' So says Nelly Dean just before Heathcliff's death. The remark is not hers in truth, but Emily Brontë's, and where it stands it is of great significance. It points to the world of German horror and romance, to which we know that she had access. That world was congenial to her, as it was congenial to Southey, Scott, and Coleridge; and it has left some ugly and disfiguring traces upon the detail of ***Wuthering Heights.*** But *essentially* her imagination escaped from it and mastered it. As the haunting of Heathcliff is to the coarser horrors of Tieck and Hoffmann, so is her place to theirs. For all her crudity and inexperience, she is in the end with Goethe, rather than with Hoffmann,[1] and thereby with all that is sane, strong, and living in literature. 'A great work requires many-sidedness, and on this rock the young author splits,' said Goethe to Eckermann, praising at the same time the art which starts from the simplest realities and the subject nearest at hand, to reach at last by a natural expansion the loftiest heights of poetry. But this was the art of Emily Brontë. It started from her own heart and life; it was nourished by the sights and sounds of a lonely yet sheltering nature; it was responsive to the art of others, yet always independent; and in the rich and tangled truth of ***Wuthering Heights*** it showed promise at least of a many-sidedness to which only the greatest attain.

Notes

1. For any one who has waded through Hoffmann's *Serapion-brüder*—which has become for our generation all but unreadable,—in spite of the partial explanation which the *physical violence* of these tales may perhaps offer of some of the minor detail of *Wuthering Heights,* there is only one passage which memory will in the end connect with Emily Brontë. The leading idea of the stories which make up the Serapion-collection—if they can be said to have a leading idea—is that all

which the imagination really *sees*—man or goblin, monster or reality—it may lawfully report. 'Let each of us try and examine himself well, as whether he has really *seen* what he is going to describe, before he sets to work to put it in words.' The vividness of the Romantics,—as compared with the measure of the Classicalists; there is here a typical expression of it, and it is one which may well have lingered in Emily Brontë's mind.

CAROL A. SENF (ESSAY DATE FALL 1985)

SOURCE: Senf, Carol A. "Emily Brontë's Version of Feminist History: *Wuthering Heights*." *Essays in Literature* 12, no. 2 (fall 1985): 201-14.

In the following essay, Senf discusses the Victorian interest in the idea of history as a context for Wuthering Heights, *countering the prevailing critical view that Brontë's authorial vision was limited only to her own time and place.*

Perhaps more than the people of any period before or since, the Victorians were acutely aware of history, an awareness fostered by both intellectual developments and political and social events and one that, at mid-century, resulted in university reform and the establishment of history as a legitimate profession. The immediate result for most Victorians, however, was not a systematic approach to either the past or the present but simply a profound interest in anything that might be included under a broad umbrella called "history."

When first confronted with the artifacts of ancient civilizations, which explorers brought home with them, the Victorians began to think about the past; and they were made even more conscious of the changes that take place over time by what Walter L. Reed calls "theories and events in a world . . . beyond history . . . by new scientific theories in biology and geology (Werner, Hutton and Lyell, Lamarack, Cuvier, and Darwin) and of course most profoundly by the political events of the Revolution in France."[1] Immersed in a historical period that was changing before their eyes, they attempted to come to grips with the present and even to predict the future. As a result, the nineteenth century was, as Andrew Sanders states, "an acutely historical age" which "believed in the efficacy of the study of the past . . . avidly collected the relics and the art of the past" and "rejoiced . . . in the idea of being enveloped by Time, past, present, and future."[2]

In addition, James C. Simmons explains that people in the nineteenth century became aware that the past was "profoundly different from the present," a realization "nurtured and encouraged by the profusion of historical romances which provided many Victorian readers with their sense of the historical past."[3] He adds, however, that writers (he cites Dickens, Kingsley, Edwin Abbott, Dean Frederic W. Farrar, and Cardinals Wiseman and Newman as examples) often used the historical romance "as a medium for the discussion of contemporary problems; the past for them would reflect the present."[4] Similarly, Roy Strong, who in *Recreating the Past: British History and the Victorian Painter* links Victorian history painting to the historical novel and to history itself, reinforces the notion of relevance: "History to the Victorians was practical wisdom. It was presented in nationalistic terms as the evolution of a people and their culture."[5] Both Simmons and Strong thus assert that Victorian artists often chose historical subjects that helped them come to terms with their own times.

While many Victorian writers probed the past for subject matter, others revealed their interest in history by focusing on their own time instead of on some remote period. As a result, when one thinks of the great nineteenth-century writers of history, the names Carlyle, Macaulay, Ranke, Michelet, Burckhardt, and Tocqueville come to mind. When one thinks of historical novelists, one is likely to think of Lytton, George Eliot, or Thackeray, but not of Emily Brontë. Sanders, Simmons, and Lukács, for example, don't even mention her in their studies of the historical novel; and Keith Sagar's study of ***Wuthering Heights*** restates the prevailing view that she was uninterested in history: "Emily Brontë had no social life, few relationships outside the household, and neither knew now cared about the world beyond Haworth."[6] However, another view was expressed by Arnold Kettle who thirty years ago reminded readers that ***Wuthering Heights*** takes place "not in a never-never land but in Yorkshire;"[7] and recent studies by Terry Eagleton, Rosemary Jackson, David Musselwhite, and Sandra Gilbert and Susan Gubar also focus on her response to the times in which she lived.[8]

Although ***Wuthering Heights*** will not meet everyone's definition of history, not only because those definitions are both complex and varied, but because history includes so many facets (including the current systematic studies of political and constitutional development, biography, social evolution, and economics), it is, in fact, a profoundly historical work. First, because ***Wuthering Heights*** narrates events that took place during a particular period (in this case, the early nineteenth century, when England experienced rapid industrialization and repercussions from the recent revolution in France)[9] and because it creates vivid representatives of that period, it meets Hayden White's definition of history: "a verbal structure in the form of a narrative prose discourse that purports to be a model, or icon, of past structures and processes in the interest of *explaining what they were by representing them*."[10] More important, ***Wuthering Heights*** also provides a symbolic reading of the movement of history, one that—like those of Brontë's contemporaries, Macaulay, Marx, and Engels—reveals a belief in evolutionary development: that each age evolves from the previous one and that history itself reveals a gradual and progressive movement for the betterment of man, not only materially but intellectually and spiritually as well. However, Brontë in one way surpasses these historians—by writing a novel that, unique among literature of its time, reveals that this evolution towards a greater social good will not be complete until women enter the mainstream of history.

To argue that ***Wuthering Heights*** explores the question of historical evolution is not to argue that Brontë was necessarily influenced by the same thinkers who influenced other Victorians.[11] A highly original writer, Brontë assimilated the history that was taking place around her, material from the past, and her own uniquely personal vision. Although a work of genius, ***Wuthering Heights*** was not created in an intellectual vacuum, for Brontë was familiar with classical historical texts, including Goldsmith's *History of Rome,* Hume's *History of England,* and Scott's *Life of Napoleon Bonaparte;*[12] she was also a pragmatic observer who watched history unfold. An avid newspaper reader like the rest of her family, she had an additional reason for keeping abreast of current events. Because she had taken some of the money that she and her sisters had inherited from their aunt and invested it in the railways, she watched the newspapers carefully and, according to Charlotte, read "'every paragraph and every advertisement in the newspapers that related to railroads. . . .'"[13] Furthermore, as Eagleton explains, she lived during a historical period when the impact of modern industrialism brought far-reaching social consequences to the area where she lived,[14] a period in which the power base shifted from rural areas to large industrialized towns and cities. It was a period of intense and sometimes violent confrontations between individuals and classes, a time that resembled the conclusion of Lockwood's first dream when "Every man's hand was against his neighbour."[15] Such enormous social changes had a profound effect on the lives of individuals.

To construct a feminist history, it is necessary to combine an interest in history with an interest in women as a unique group of people. There are no letters to indicate that Emily shared Charlotte's interest in "the woman question," but evidence other than ***Wuthering Heights*** reveals her interest in women's condition. Gérin, for example, uses Gondal material to suggest Brontë's preoccupation with strong women characters[16] and also alludes to Emily's interest in Queen Victoria. Apparently concerned with the manner in which Victoria would use the immense power given to her, Brontë named one of her Gondal heroines Augusta to assert her "regal status" and to comment on "the known fact that the name had been refused the Princess Victoria at her baptism by her uncle George IV because it had sounded ominously imperious in his ears."[17]

Reading history and newspapers and being interested in Queen Victoria and the condition of women do not make Emily Brontë unique, however, since these interests were shared by other people of her time. The mark of her genius is that she combines so many insights into historical evolution and the condition of women into a highly original work. In ***Wuthering Heights,*** when she writes her version of historical development, she incorporates her awareness that most women do not have Victoria's access to power. Thus she concludes her novel with a vision of what might happen if the relationships between the sexes (relationships that give men power over women and certain men power over other men and make women either passive victims or sly manipulators) so familiar to patriarchal history were replaced by something both more feminine and more egalitarian. Moving away from the mythic world of Gondal to the more realistic world of ***Wuthering Heights,*** she also chooses a realistic heroine, the younger Catherine, to embody her feminist vision, the final stage in her history. No longer a queen, her heroine has power over only her own life.

Brontë reaches this concluding vision by examining three distinct historical stages in the novel, each represented by a particular family or person: the Earnshaws, yeoman farmers, are the remnants of an earlier historical period;[18] the Lintons, landed gentry, are the ruling class at the time the novel was written;[19] and Heathcliff, an odd and seemingly contradictory mixture of primitive nature and modern capitalism, is the power of the future.[20] A natural man at the beginning, Heathcliff later acquires the tools of patriarchy and uses these tools to bring about his revenge. When he returns after his three-year absence, he is no longer merely a representative of nature. The great unknown, Heathcliff is a product of both an urban and a rural environment. Although both Catherine and Mrs. Dean associate him with the unchanging forces of nature, Mr. Earnshaw apparently finds him in Liverpool; and Heathcliff presumably acquires his later sophistication in the city as well. As both a natural force and a representative of modern capitalistic development, however, Heathcliff opposes the gentry, the group in power at the time the events of the novel take place. In both cases, he is a vital force of unpredictable power.

In addition, in the courtship and projected marriage of Cathy and Hareton, Brontë reveals the peaceful merger of capitalistic economic power with the traditional political power of the landed gentry, a merger that would have been familiar to her contemporary readers. She also adds a feminist twist because their mutual acceptance of one another provides a glimpse of a more egalitarian, more feminine future.

Moreover, although ***Wuthering Heights*** suggests that Brontë shares the Victorian belief that history is progressive, it also reveals that, more than many other historians, Brontë realizes that the violence and irrationality of the primitive past have been transformed, not eliminated, in the present.[21] She reveals, for example, that violence, which is an integral part of Hindley's power over others, remains in Edgar Linton, the despicable Linton Heathcliff (who acquires his love of power in the city, not from his father), and the effete Lockwood—described by one critic as Brontë's view of "what is wrong with the present state of society."[22] Early in the novel, she has Lockwood unwittingly reveal his desire for power, his skill at psychological violence, and his ability to manipulate others when he relates his seacoast experience:

> I "never told my love" vocally; still if looks have language, the merest idiot might have guessed I was over head and ears: she understood me at last, and looked a return—the sweetest of all imaginable looks. And what did I do? I confess it with shame—shrunk icily into myself like a snail; at every glance retired colder and farther; till, finally, the poor innocent was led to doubt her own senses. . . . By this curious turn of disposition, I have gained the reputation of deliberate heartlessness, how undeserved, I alone can appreciate.
>
> (p. 15)

Although Lockwood relates this episode as proof that he is unworthy of a "comfortable home," it is evident from the conclusion of the passage that he sees nothing intrinsically wrong in his overt manipulation of the young woman. A complete egotist, Lockwood focuses on his behavior, not on the victim of it. Brontë, however, uses this brief episode both to illustrate a shift in the modern world from physical violence to psychological cruelty and to indicate that men continue to have inordinate power over women. As Gilbert and Gubar comment, "Thus if literary Lockwood makes a woman into a goddess, he can unmake her at whim without suffering himself."[23] Brontë is also aware that, although the sheer physical power that men have over other men is diminishing, men still have power over women. The young woman of Lockwood's choice, like Catherine Earnshaw and most other women during this historical period, had apparently learned to consider herself only in relation to men. Having no strong sense of individual identity, she comes to doubt her sanity as well as her intrinsic value when she sees herself through Lockwood's indifferent eyes.

Lockwood's rejection of the young woman at the seacoast is not as openly violent as the behavior of either Heathcliff or Hindley, but it is Brontë's first indication that supposedly civilized men can be both cruel and perverse. Later in the novel, she uses Lockwood's response to the little ghost girl to reveal that the civilized man can be as openly violent as his primitive ancestors:

> As it spoke, I discerned, obscurely, a child's face looking through the window. Terror made me cruel; and finding it useless to attempt shaking the creature off, I pulled its wrist on to the broken pane, and rubbed it to and fro till the blood ran down and soaked the bed-clothes. . . .
>
> (p. 30)

This is one of the most horrifying scenes in the book precisely because Lockwood's violence is so openly directed against a weaker individual and because only a day's residence in the primitive world of the Heights unleashes the violence masked by Lockwood's urbanity. Similarly, when Heathcliff returns, his civilized veneer serves merely to mask the primitive nature of his passions.

The violence of Lockwood and Heathcliff and the presence of ghosts in the novel are Brontë's ways of suggesting that history—although progressive—does not move in a straight line; shadows from the past continue to exert their influence on the present. The cruelty and exploitiveness of the male characters also provide objective reasons for changing patriarchal history by introducing gentleness and cooperation, virtues generally associated with women—in short, of making history more feminine.

Brontë is aware that history is more than the objective events, that it is also the subjective narration (or interpretation) of these events. Lockwood, the novel's first narrator, is also the novel's chief historian. Therefore, it is significant that the first word in the text is the date "1801,"[24] a date which immediately focuses the reader's attention on Brontë's interest in the recent past. (Had she been interested only in writing a romance, she could have chosen any historical period or even a timeless era, such as those she had used in the Gondal saga. Instead she chooses Yorkshire and a period of significant historical change in England, when the Industrial and French Revolutions made most Englishmen aware of change over time.) Almost immediately thereafter, Lockwood confirms his interest in history by commenting on the antiquity of the house:

> I detected the date '1500,' and the name 'Hareton Earnshaw.' I would have made a few comments, and requested a short history of the place from the surly owner, but . . . I had no desire to aggravate his impatience, previous to inspecting the penetralium.
>
> (p. 14)

Initially more interested in the remote past than in the present and curious about the origins of Wuthering Heights, Lockwood is soon caught up in the history of his own times when he is confronted by the strange behavior of Catherine Heathcliff and the even more enigmatic behavior of Heathcliff himself.

Brontë reveals, however, that the historian must understand the past before he can come to grips with the present; and she emulates one method common to nineteenth-century historians when she confronts Lockwood and the reader with a number of artifacts from the past.[25] The first, of course, is the house itself, which Lockwood attempts to "read" as the remnant of a past civilization.[26] Named for a distant patriarch and therefore literally a relic of the past, the house remains an enigma to Lockwood. More important, however, are the artifacts he discovers at its interior when a snowstorm forces him to spend the night in Catherine Earnshaw's childhood bedroom, the heart of the house.

The first of the artifacts in the bedroom is "nothing but a name repeated in all kinds of characters, large and small—*Catherine Earnshaw,* here and there varied to *Catherine Heathcliff,* and then again to *Catherine Linton*" (p. 25). Nothing but a name! Yet that repetition of names is a key that unlocks the mystery of patriarchal history as well as the history of Wuthering Heights. Although she is not a trained historian, Emily Brontë has insights that surpass those of Hume, Macaulay, and John Richard Green,[27] historical writers who attempted to expand their readers' understanding of historical development by showing that history includes social as well as political development. Brontë's genius is that she also shows how the lives of women and other groups previously ignored even by these historians can influence the course of historical development.

The story of ***Wuthering Heights*** is not the story of Hareton, the patriarch, or even of Heathcliff, the character who initially piques Lockwood's curiosity. It is the almost buried story of Catherine, mother and daughter. Although Lockwood continues to be more interested in Heathcliff and never understands this fact, the reader eventually discovers that decyphering the mystery behind ***Wuthering Heights*** necessitates understanding these three names as well as the name over the door—in short, understanding both patriarchal history and women's hitherto buried history. This revelation—that understanding history includes understanding the victims of patriarchal history as well as the patriarchs themselves—makes Emily Brontë seem so much more modern than most Victorian historians. (The most notable exception to this generalization is another woman novelist, George Eliot.)

The second artifact—the marginalia in her book, which Lockwood describes as "faded hieroglyphics"—records a period of innocence in the first Catherine's history before she was aware of the power that patriarchy has over her. The freedom of the marginalia thus contrasts with the names on the windowsill, names that suggest the limited choices—spinsterhood or marriage—available to Catherine.

Lockwood's curiosity about these artifacts, his confrontation with the little ghost girl, his interest in Heathcliff's response, and his romantic fascination with the younger Catherine combine with his illness to bring him to Ellen Dean, the novel's second historian, who explains the significance of the "faded hieroglyphics."

Unlike Lockwood, Mrs. Dean is an "eyewitness" to most of the events in ***Wuthering Heights.*** However, while Mrs. Dean should be a more reliable historian, Brontë reveals that both she and

Lockwood are to be distrusted because their prejudice in favor of the present makes them ineffectual historians, or at least historians who are guilty of distortion. Lockwood, for example, shows that he is definitely the product of his historical period when he mistakes a brace of dead rabbits for Catherine's house pets. Although, like most gentlemen of his time, he goes hunting—he mentions, for example, his invitation "to devastate the moors of a friend, in the North" (p. 241)—Lockwood is apparently unfamiliar with people who hunt for food instead of sport (or with people who keep game in the front parlor). Accustomed to pampered and protected women with a sentimental attachment to their pets, he is even more uncomfortable with the younger Catherine's recognition that the dogs at the Heights are working animals, retrievers and herding dogs, and with her refusing both his assistance and his offer of companionship. Such behavior (as well as the fact that, while he does not work, he can travel to the seacoast and rent Thrushcross Grange for a year) suggests that he is a member of the landed gentry. (The sons of factory owners and tradesmen at this period were more likely to join their fathers in business.) His overall fastidiousness reveals him as something of a dandy as well.

Ellen Dean, on the other hand, appears to be a simple rustic, but she is actually much more. Characterized by Gilbert and Gubar as "a stereotypically benevolent man's woman,"[28] she is also allied with the forces of the landed gentry. For example, when she first begins to tell her story to Lockwood, she makes a curious slip: "Hareton is the last of them, as our Miss Cathy is of us—I mean, of the Lintons" (p. 37). This statement might be interpreted simply as a servant's identification with the family she serves except that Nelly had been reared at the Heights and is currently employed by Heathcliff. Moreover, she identifies herself with the Lintons when she confesses with pride that she is familiar with books—the way by which history is usually transmitted: "I have read more than you would fancy, Mr. Lockwood. You could not open a book in this library that I have not looked into, and got something out of also . . . it is as much as you can expect of a poor man's daughter" (p. 59). That Nelly is a reader links her conclusively with the bookish Lintons. Furthermore, confessing her familiarity with books may be her way of telling Lockwood and the reader that she is also familiar with the wills and other documents by which patriarchal culture and patriarchal power are transmitted from generation to generation. She certainly knows the law well enough to act for Cathy until the younger woman learns to manage her affairs. A "poor man's daughter" and a servant to the gentry, Mrs. Dean recognizes power when she sees it. More important, being a survivor, she generally sides with that power or, at least, rarely challenges it openly.

Oriented to the present instead of to the past (with Hindley's death Mrs. Dean shifts allegiance from the yeomanry to the gentry) or the future, Lockwood and Mrs. Dean are confused by Heathcliff and Catherine and the primitive forces that they represent. Lockwood initially believes that Healthcliff is simply a man like himself whose "reserve springs from an aversion to showy displays of feeling—to manifestations of mutual kindliness" (p. 15), and Nelly's story does not convince him that the forces of raw nature continue to influence the present. Therefore, believing that these primitive forces have been removed forever, he concludes the novel with the pious assertion that the dead are at rest. Similarly, Ellen Dean admits her preference for Edgar over Heathcliff.[29] She is extremely critical of the adult Catherine's desire to be "a girl again, half savage, and hardy, and free" (p. 107); and she doesn't even try to understand the peculiar love that Heathcliff and Catherine feel for one another. Her response to Heathcliff's suffering at Catherine's death is characteristic of her prejudices:

> He dashed his head against the knotted trunk; and, lifting up his eyes, howled, not like a man, but like a savage beast getting goaded to death with knives and spears.
>
> I observed several splashes of blood about the bark of the tree, and his hand and forehead were both stained; probably the scene I witnessed was a repetition of others acted during the night. It hardly moved my compassion—it appalled me.
>
> (p. 139)

Incapable of understanding this asocial passion, Mrs. Dean prefers the younger Catherine because her "anger was never furious; her love never fierce; it was deep and tender" (p. 155). Because she cannot understand the primitive forces in Catherine and Heathcliff, her rendering of events is bound to be distorted.

While the first half of the novel focuses on the past, the second half, which details Heathcliff's revenge, follows a pattern familiar to Brontë's contemporaries. Heathcliff, who represents primitive, natural forces in the first part of the book, comes to resemble many nineteenth-century capitalists after his return; and he uses the sophisticated strategies by which many of them gained economic and political power during the period. His acquisitions of both Wuthering Heights and Thrushcross Grange is typical of both their using wealth gained through industry or trade to acquire landed property and their marrying into established families to gain respectability or power or both.[30]

Although recognizing this historical pattern is easy, interpreting its significance is much more difficult. Thus it is not surprising that critical responses to the conclusion of ***Wuthering Heights*** have been mixed. Q. D. Leavis, Tom Winnifrith, and John Hewish believe that the old world has yielded to the new while Rosemary Jackson and Gilbert and Gubar believe that the conclusion is the victory of tradition over innovation.[31] However, because the text suggests a slightly different view of history, I want to offer a third interpretation of this conclusion, a period that begins with Lockwood's departure from Thrushcross Grange and his return the following year.

Bored with the misanthropic role he had chosen to play and with his attempts to understand Wuthering Heights, Lockwood leaves the area and vows never to pass another winter there. Before departing, however, he concludes with his version of how that history might have ended: "What a realization of something more romantic than a fairy tale it would have been for Mrs. Linton Heathcliff, had she and I struck up an attachment, as her good nurse desired, and migrated together into the stirring atmosphere of the town!" (pp. 240-41). Had Brontë wished merely to reproduce what was happening in England at the time she wrote, this migration from country to city would have been the logical conclusion. However, because that marriage would ignore both Catherine's needs and Lockwood's desire for power over women, it would merely repeat the other unhappy marriages in the novel—the first Catherine's marriage to Edgar or Isabella's even more disastrous marriage to Heathcliff. Wanting to create a version of history that is both more feminine and more egalitarian, a history in which women are no longer the victims of patriarchal history, Brontë concludes her novel with a different kind of marriage.

When Lockwood returns, the new historical epoch has already begun. Heathcliff is dead, and Cathy stands to inherit his fortune, which includes both the Heights and the Grange. Recognizing that economic independence gives women some freedom from masculine power (the first Catherine, having no money of her own, had been more or less forced to make a "good marriage"), Brontë makes her heroine an heiress like the heroines of her sister Charlotte's novels—Jane Eyre, Shirley Keeldar, and Lucy Snow. However, realizing that true power and identity demand more than wealth, Brontë undercuts the importance of wealth in her heroine's future. Thus, she has Cathy plan to marry her cousin Hareton at a period when her fortune would automatically belong to her husband.

Although the projected marriage might appear to be another version of the conventional happy ending which will produce more unhappiness by giving Hareton absolute power over Cathy, it is not, as Leo Bersani states, "as if Emily Brontë were telling the same story twice, and eliminating its originality the second time."[32] Bersani is correct to focus on the numerous repetitions in the novel. However, he doesn't recognize that the marriage of Cathy and Hareton provides a unique twist to the familiar plot and illustrates a shift in the history of patriarchal power.

To understand that difference fully, the reader must understand that Hareton and the younger Catherine differ from their predecessors in several important ways. When Cathy enters his life, Hareton is what Heathcliff terms "a personification of my youth, not a human being" (p. 255). Hareton is thus in the same state of graceless nature that Heathcliff was when the first Catherine said that it would degrade her to marry him; however, Hareton is apparently without Heathcliff's greed or his desire for power over others. The younger Catherine is similarly different from her mother and from her two aunts. True heir to the Lintons and therefore conscious of rank and power, she initially treats her boorish cousin like a servant and attempts to make both him and the servants subject to her commands. However, disinfranchised from her economic and social heritage, Catherine soon learns to interpret life differently and to recognize Hareton's human equality. The scene in which she makes peace with him is proof of these changes. Instead of responding with the Earnshaw violence or the Linton manipulation, Catherine plants a friendly kiss on Hareton's cheek to make peace. When this gesture fails to elicit the desired response, she wraps a book as a present and asks Mrs. Dean to be her messenger: "And tell him if he'll take it, I'll come and teach him to read it right . . . and, if he refuse it, I'll go upstairs, and never tease him again" (p. 248).

Rather than try to dominate him or seduce him (an attempt to gain power that is typically used by those without power), Cathy leaves Hareton free to choose.

Hareton chooses to accept her offer, and the two become as oblivious to Heathcliff's threats as the first Catherine and Heathcliff had been to the violence of Hindley and Joseph. Despite the apparent similarities, however, the two relationships are quite different. The love between Heathcliff and Catherine had been primitive, violent, elemental, and frequently as cruel as those natural elements. Catherine confesses, "I *am* Heathcliff—he's always, always in my mind—not as a pleasure, any more than I am always a pleasure to myself—but as my own being" (p. 74). The love between Hareton and Cathy, on the other hand, is more conscious and mature, partially because it begins when they are older, partially because it develops over books. However, unlike the other "readers" in the novel, Cathy and Hareton use these written texts (the legacy of patriarchal culture) to establish a relationship that extends far beyond anything they might have learned directly from the texts or from the human models around them. For example, the pragmatic Mrs. Dean reads books to understand the power she sees around her. The romantics, Lockwood and Isabella, attempt to model their lives on the material they find in popular romances and fairy tales; and Gilbert and Gubar demonstrate that these romantic fictions reinforce the traditional sexual roles that give power to men. Thus Lockwood pretends to worship women, but his "phrases, like most of his assumptions, parody the sentimentality of fictions that keep women in their 'place' by defining them as beneficent fairies or amiable ladies."[33] The same works that have taught Lockwood to exert power over women have prepared Isabella to be a passive victim:

> Ironically, Isabella's bookish upbringing has prepared her to fall in love with (of all people) Heathcliff. Precisely because she has been taught to believe in coercive literary conventions, Isabella is victimized by the genre of romance. Mistaking appearance for reality, tall athletic Heathcliff for 'an honourable soul' . . . she runs away from her cultured home in the naive belief that it will simply be replaced by another cultivated setting.[34]

Another reader, Edgar Linton asserts his power over his wife by ignoring her needs for human warmth and escaping to his library; and Joseph uses the printed word to justify his harsh behavior. In a marvelous scene, which briefly hints at the social and economic power given even to a factotum like Joseph and denied to virtually all women, he "solemnly spread his large Bible on the table, and overlaid it with dirty bank-notes from his pocket-book, the produce of the day's transactions" (p. 249). These people, no matter how well they have learned the lessons of partriarchy and the way to gain power over others, are hardly healthy role models for the people who will initiate a new stage in historical development.

Although Brontë is silent about the titles of the books Cathy and Hareton discuss, practically any book would have reinforced the human role models found in their society. Even though they are victims of patriarchal power, Cathy and Hareton reject the role models they saw around them or found in books, refusing to follow them blindly. Therefore, as the first members of a more egalitarian historical stage, they are different from their contemporaries because their relationship is based on cooperation and trust rather than on dominance. Eagleton notices this difference although he seems unaware of its larger significance: "The culture which Catherine imparts to Hareton in teaching him to read promises equality rather than oppression, an unemasculating refinement of physical energy."[35] Thus the younger Catherine and Hareton—strong individuals nonetheless—use their strength to support, not to manipulate, the other. In this way, they are unlike their equally strong ancestors.

By using literal genealogy to symbolize economic and cultural development, Brontë shows how one historical stage evolves naturally into the next. Despite apparent repetitions, the conclusion is unlike the beginning; and it provides a glimpse—merely a glimpse—at a feminist version of history. For example, the Hareton Earnshaw who prepares to leave Wuthering Heights is *not* the same Hareton whose name is carved over the door; and Cathy is his strong and equal partner, *not* his nameless bride. Her history will not be scrawled at the interior of the house—hidden from the world—as her mother's had been: it will *not* be a faded hieroglyphic, but the articulate history of an equal partnership.

Free of oppressive models, Cathy and Hareton represent the next stage of historical development. As a result, Brontë shows that they are not haunted by the past in the same way as Heathcliff and the other characters, including the pragmatic Ellen Dean. Although pretending not to believe that Heathcliff and Catherine walk the moors, she tells Lockwood about the shepherd boy who claimed to see them; and she refuses to stay at the

WUTHERING HEIGHTS.

A Novel.

BY

THE AUTHOR OF "JANE EYRE."

NEW YORK:

HARPER & BROTHERS, PUBLISHERS,

82 CLIFF STREET.

1848.

Title page of *Wuthering Heights* (1848), which erroneously attributes the novel's authorship to Charlotte Brontë, author of *Jane Eyre*.

Heights at night. Having rid themselves of their oppressive past, Cathy and Hareton are, as Lockwood grumbles jealously at the conclusion, "afraid of nothing" (p. 265), including the ghosts of an oppressive past.

Having rid themselves of the burden of the past, Cathy and Hareton must leave Wuthering Heights, the masculine house with its hidden feminine center. The move to Thrushcross Grange is not an entirely satisfactory move in terms of historical theory even though Bersani demonstrates that "the Lintons are somewhat squeezed out" by the union of Cathy and Hareton.[36] Eliminating the Lintons may be Brontë's way of combining the best of the old with the best of the new. It may also be a concession to the direction in which history was moving at the time Brontë wrote. To ask her to do more is to insist that she write the kind of feminist Utopian fiction that was written by Charlotte Perkins Gilman or the kind of science fiction currently being written by feminist writers such as Ursula LeGuin. Such writers have had to leave their society—even their planet—behind. Brontë attempts something much more revolutionary in suggesting that the next stage of historical evolution, the stage of equality, will develop naturally and logically from the old. Having Cathy and Hareton move to Thrushcross Grange is her way of suggesting that they do not have to leave their old world behind.

Having seen too many of the problems associated with traditional marriage, both as symbol and as reality, modern feminists are usually uncomfortable with the anticipated marriage of Cathy and Hareton. However, seeing that it differs from the other marriages in ***Wuthering Heights,*** readers should see it as a softening—a feminizing—of patriarchal history, and therefore, as the first tentative step toward a less oppressive world for both men and women.

Notes

1. Walter L. Reed, "A Defense of History: The Language of Transformation in Romantic Narrative," *Bucknell Review,* 23 (1977), 42.

   Georg Lukács also credits the French Revolution with making people aware of historical progression: "It was the French Revolution, the revolutionary wars and the rise and fall of Napoleon which . . . made history a *mass experience*. . . . During the decades between 1789 and 1814 each nation of Europe underwent more upheavals than they had previously experienced in centuries. And the quick succession of these upheavals gives them a qualitatively distinct character, it makes their historical character far more visible than would be the case in isolated, individual instances: the masses no longer have the impression of a 'natural occurrence.'" Georg Lukács, *The Historical Novel,* trans. Hannah and Stanley Mitchell (Atlantic Highlands, NJ: Humanities Press, 1962), p. 23.

2. Andrew Sanders, *The Victorian Historical Novel 1840-1880* (New York: St. Martin's Press, 1979), p. 1.

   In his study of the Victorian historical novel, James C. Simmons documents the nineteenth-century interest in history: "The volume of historical research swelled to such proportions that . . . for the thirty-five year period between 1816 and 1851 books on history and geography far outstripped fiction, titles in the latter category being a full third fewer than in the former." James C. Simmons, *The Novelist as Historian: Essays on the Victorian Historical Novel,* Studies in English Literature, 88 (The Hague: Mouton, 1973), p. 31.

3. Simmons, p. 27.

4. Simmons, p. 21.

5. Roy Strong, *Recreating the Past: British History and the Victorian Painter* (New York: Thames and Hudson, 1978), p. 32.

   Lukács also connects the interest in history with nationalism when he discusses Scott's historical novels: "He is a patriot, he is proud of the development of his people. This is vital for the creation of a real historical novel, i.e. one which brings the past close to us and allows us to experience its real and true being. Without a felt relationship to the present, a portrayal of history is impossible" (p. 53).

6. Keith Sagar, "The Originality of *Wuthering Heights,*" in *The Art of Emily Brontë,* ed. Anne Smith (New York: Barnes and Noble, 1976), p. 121.

7. Arnold Kettle, "Emily Brontë: *Wuthering Heights,*" in *Twentieth Century Views of Wuthering Heights,* ed. Thomas A. Vogler (Englewood Cliffs, NJ: Prentice-Hall, 1968), p. 28.

8. Terry Eagleton, *Myths of Power: A Marxist Study of the Brontës* (New York: Barnes and Noble, 1975); Rosemary Jackson, "The Silenced Text: Shades of Gothic in Victorian Fiction," *The Minnesota Review,* 13 (1979), 98-112; David Musselwhite, "*Wuthering Heights:* the unacceptable text," in *Literature, Society and the Sociology of Literature* (Proceedings of the conference held at the University of Essex, 1977), pp. 154-60; Sandra M. Gilbert and Susan Gubar, *The Madwoman in the Attic: The Woman Writer and the Nineteenth-Century Literary Imagination* (New Haven: Yale Univ. Press, 1979).

9. John Kenyon, *The History Men: The Historical Profession in England Since the Renaissance* (Pittsburgh: Univ.of Pittsburgh Press, 1983) also links the Victorian interest in history to the French Revolution: "As the careers of men like Macaulay, Carlyle, and Froude show, there was an enormous appetite for history in Victorian England, and a new belief in its importance. The movement for university reform in general at last forced modern history into the degree syllabus. . . . The international reputation of Mommsen and Ranke drew attention to England's comparative backwardness. At the same time the French Revolution was a cataclysmic interruption of the orderly development of human history, calling for an explanation which presumably historians were best equipped to give" (p. 144).

10. Hayden White, *Metahistory: The Historical Imagination in Nineteenth-Century Europe* (Baltimore: Johns Hopkins Univ. Press, 1973), p. 2.

11. Winifred Gérin does make one interesting connection between Macaulay and Brontë: "From his various literary contacts (and Branwell still had some, like Macaulay, Hartley Coleridge, Edward Baines, from his Bradford days) he learnt that fiction was the most profitable form of literary hack work at the time." *Emily Brontë: A Biography* (Oxford: Clarendon Press, 1971), p. 180.

12. Winifred Gérin, *Charlotte Brontë: The Evolution of Genius* (New York: Oxford Univ. Press, 1967), p. 24. Gérin also mentions the books that Mr. Brontë used to teach his daughters: the Bible, Magnall's *Historical Questions,* Lindley Murray's *Grammar,* and Goldsmith's *Geography* (p. 22). Certainly the first two books would have reinforced the children's interest in history.

13. Gérin, *Emily Brontë,* p. 163; she cites Charlotte's letter to Miss Wooler on April 23, 1845.

14. Eagleton notes: "The Brontës' home, Haworth, was close to the centre of the West Riding woollen area; and their lifetime there coincided with some of the fiercest class-struggles in English society. . . . Their childhood witnessed machine-breaking; their adolescence Reform agitation and riots against the New Poor Law; their adulthood saw the Plug strikes and Chartism, struggles against the Corn Laws and for the Ten Hours Bill" (p. 3). One of the first to notice the historical origins of *Wuthering Heights,* which he calls "an expression . . . of the stresses and tensions and conflicts . . . of nineteenth-century capitalist society," (p. 42) Kettle comments on an interesting exhibit in the Haworth museum: "a proclamation of the Queen ordering the reading of the Riot Act against the rebellious workers of the West Riding" (p. 42). Less interested in industrialism, Gérin also comments on contemporary influences: ". . . in August 1845 Branwell was sent to Liverpool in the care of John Brown after his dismissal by the Robinsons. It was the time when the first shiploads of Irish immigrants were landing at Liverpool and dying in the cellars of the warehouses on the quays. Their images, and especially those of the children, were unforgettably depicted in the *Illustrated London News.* . . . The relevance of such happenings within a day's journey of Haworth . . . cannot be overlooked in explaining Emily's choice of Liverpool for the scene of Mr Earnshaw's encounter with Heathcliff" (pp. 225-26).

15. Emily Brontë, *Wuthering Heights,* ed. William M. Sale, Jr. (New York: Norton Critical Editions, 1963), p. 29. All future quotations will be to this edition and will be included in the text.

16. Gérin, *Emily Brontë,* pp. 22-23.

17. Gérin, *Emily Brontë,* p. 23.

18. Gilbert and Gubar observe that Wuthering Heights is "close to being naked or 'raw' in Levi Strauss's sense—its floors uncarpeted, most of its inhabitants barely literate, even the meat on its shelves open to inspection . . ." (pp. 273-74).

19. Following their argument that *Wuthering Heights* is a myth of the war between nature and culture, Gilbert and Gubar explain that Thrushcross Grange is "clothed and 'cooked': carpeted in crimson, bookish, feeding on cakes and tea and negus" (p. 274).

20. Gilbert and Gubar argue that Heathcliff's general aim ". . . is to wreak the revenge of nature upon culture by subverting legitimacy" (p. 296).

21. Leo Bersani comments on the numerous repetitions in the novel: "There are obvious differences between the two situations, but in each case children are tyrannized or neglected (or both) by a man grief-stricken at the loss of a loved woman. And this similarity tends somewhat to dilute Heathcliff's originality. When we look at the novel in this way, certain configurations of characters begin to compete for our attention with the individual characters themselves." *A Future for Astyanax: Character and Desire in Literature* (Boston: Little, Brown and Co., 1969), p. 199.

22. Irving H. Buchen, "Metaphysical and Social Evolution in *Wuthering Heights,*" *The Victorian Newsletter,* 33 (1967), 18.

23. Gilbert and Gubar, p. 289.

24. Charles Percy Sanger states that the date was what first brought him to study the book more closely. Sanger, who also wrote *Rules of Law and Administration relating to Wills and Intestaces,* demonstrates that

Brontë knew the laws of property and inheritance. His article is included in the "Essays in Criticism" section of the Norton Critical Edition of *Wuthering Heights,* pp. 286-97. A more recent article by Barbara Gates shows that Brontë was also familiar with both the law and the lore of suicides. "Suicide and *Wuthering Heights,*" *The Victorian Newsletter,* 50 (1976), 15-19.

25. Kenyon mentions at least two historical methods when he explains that Macaulay's "technique was thus entirely divergent from that of his contemporary Ranke, who forcefully argued that the sources must be allowed to tell their own story. . . . [It] was the historian's function to establish and evaluate these sources, which would then impose their own pattern on his narrative; in fact, the material would construct its own story. This ideal, which was never fully realized, even by Ranke himself, nevertheless dominated the historical thinking of the nineteenth century" (p. 85).

26. A number of critics have focused on "reading" in the novel. Included in this group are Musselwhite and Carol Jacobs, "*Wuthering Heights:* At the Threshold of Interpretation," *Boundary 2,* 7 (1979), 49-71.

27. According to Kenyon, Green was "the first historian of England who tried to give equal weight to social as well as political development, and to include art and literature" (p. 161). Kenyon also refers to the Scottish reaction against narrative or biographical history in the previous century: "John Logan, in his *Elements of the Philosophy of History,* published in 1781, deprecated the current preoccupation with the achievements of great men—'All that legislators, patriots, philosophers, statesmen and kings can do,' he wrote, 'is to give a direction to that stream which is for ever flowing.' The great Adam Ferguson, in his *Essay on the History of Civil Society* (1767) had already sketched out a 'total' history, covering commerce, social habits and the arts as well as politics and war. . . . The brief general chapters on trade and social trends tacked by Hume onto his account of each reign were a hesitant step in the same direction . . ." (pp. 57-58). Such historians were working along the same lines as Brontë.

28. Gilbert and Gubar, p. 291.

29. Gilbert and Gubar call Nelly Dean "patriarchy's paradigmatic housekeeper, the man's woman who has traditionally been hired to keep men's houses in order by straightening out their parlors, their daughters, and their stories . . . and she expresses her preference by acting throughout the novel as a censorious agent of patriarchy" (pp. 291-92).

30. John Hewish relates a true story of a Halifax man on whom Brontë may have modeled Heathcliff. This man was taken into the household as a dependent nephew, but "he was clever and unscrupulous enough to gain control of their business" in much the same way that Heathcliff gained control of the Linton and Earnshaw land. "Heathcliff, to the extent that he is a villain of property melodrama . . . may owe something to this man." *Emily Brontë: A Critical and Biographical Study* (New York: St. Martin's Press, 1969), p. 47.

31. Leavis's article, "A Fresh Approach to *Wuthering Heights*" is found in the "Essays in Criticism" section of the Norton Critical Edition of *Wuthering Heights,* pp. 306-321; Tom Winnifrith, *The Brontës and Their Background: Romance and Reality* (New York: Barnes and Noble, 1973).

32. Bersani, p. 222

33. Gilbert and Gubar, p. 261.

34. Gilbert and Gubar, p. 288.

35. Eagleton, p. 28.

36. Bersani, p. 199.

DREW LAMONICA (ESSAY DATE 2003)

SOURCE: Lamonica, Drew. "*Wuthering Heights*: The Boundless Passion of Catherine Earnshaw." In *"We are three sisters": Self and Family in the Writing of the Brontës,* pp. 95-117. Columbia: University of Missouri Press, 2003.

In the following excerpt, Lamoncia interprets Wuthering Heights *from the perspective of family relations, seeing Catherine's struggle as an attempt to free herself from the role of a token of exchange between two households. Lamonica contends that in Catherine, Brontë offers a feminist commentary on the potential for female selfhood outside of traditional family and social structures.*

Female identity, both in the late-eighteenth-century Yorkshire setting of ***Wuthering Heights*** and in the mid-nineteenth-century culture in which Emily Brontë wrote, was bound to a family. Women were socially recognized in their roles as daughters, sisters, wives, and mothers, leading to the now-popular designation of Victorian women as "relative creatures," a term derived from Sarah Ellis's 1839 conduct book *The Women of England.* Female agency, like female identity, was also bound by family ties. In 1844, Ann Richelieu Lamb observed, "Woman not being permitted by our present social arrangements and conventional rules, to procure a livelihood through her own exertions, *is compelled* to unite herself with some one who can provide for her."[1] Chief of the family man's responsibilities was to provide for daughters, sisters, and wives, thus securing a woman's dependency on, and containment within, a family—her father's or her husband's—throughout her life.

The world of ***Wuthering Heights*** is one of dominant patriarchs who control domestic space and govern kinship structures, seeking to enforce female relativity and limit female activity. All female movement in the novel is regulated between the two families of Wuthering Heights and Thrushcross Grange and is entirely dependent upon marital exchange. Even Nelly Dean's reloca-

ABOUT THE AUTHOR

CHARLOTTE BRONTË WRITES ABOUT ELLIS BELL'S ABILITY TO WRITE REALISTICALLY WITH LIMITED EXPERIENCE OF THE OUTSIDE WORLD

With regard to the rusticity of 'Wuthering Heights,' I admit the charge, for I feel the quality. It is rustic all through. It is moorish, and wild, and knotty as a root of heath. Nor was it natural that it should be otherwise; the author being herself a native and nursling of the moors. Doubtless, had her lot been cast in a town, her writings, if she had written at all, would have possessed another character. Even had chance or taste led her to choose a similar subject, she would have treated it otherwise. Had Ellis Bell been a lady or a gentleman accustomed to what is called 'the world,' her view of a remote and unreclaimed region, as well as of the dwellers therein, would have differed greatly from that actually taken by the home-bred country girl. Doubtless it would have been wider—more comprehensive: whether it would have been more original or more truthful is not so certain. As far as the scenery and locality are concerned, it could scarcely have been so sympathetic: Ellis Bell did not describe as one whose eye and taste alone found pleasure in the prospect; her native hills were far more to her than a spectacle; they were what she lived in, and by, as much as the wild birds, their tenants, or as the heather, their produce. Her descriptions, then, of natural scenery are what they should be, and all they should be.

Brontë, Charlotte. Excerpt from a Preface to *Wuthering Heights,* from first edition of 1847. In *Wuthering Heights,* edited by Mary A. Ward, pp. liv-lv. London: Bigelow, Brown, & Co., 1900.

tion from the Heights to the Grange and back again is dependent upon the marriages of the two Catherines. For Catherine Earnshaw, the journey is a one-way transfer from her brother's house to her husband's—a restriction that she fails in enduring. Like Emily Brontë, Catherine never successfully moves beyond her childhood home.

Following Helene Moglen's view that ***Wuthering Heights*** is fundamentally "Catherine's story," this chapter examines Catherine's story as a historically specific struggle and protest against her relativity and the terms of female exchange from one family to another.[2] Catherine's protest is carried out through her relationship with Heathcliff, which challenges not only the conventional notion of male and female relations, but also the relative nature of female identity. The tragedy of Catherine's story arises from her failure to negotiate the marital exchange: her physical and positional relocation from daughter and sister at Wuthering Heights to "the lady of Thrushcross Grange" (***WH,*** 153) is ultimately foiled by her "unmovable" identification with Heathcliff and her unsatisfied longing in adulthood to return to her childhood home.

"Home" in the novel is figured as a psychological and emotional state, a condition of self-fulfillment that is associated with domestic structures and kinship relations, but never actually realized in them. In seeking to attain this home, Catherine Earnshaw tests various sites and relationships, but the sense of being "at home" is continually deferred, and any domestic enclosure remains imprisoning. Catherine's sense of confinement within domestic spaces is indicative of her position within family structures, first as a daughter/sister at the Heights and later as a wife/expectant mother at the Grange. Her pubescent dissatisfaction with Wuthering Heights compels her relocation to the only available alternative, Thrushcross Grange, which itself becomes dissatisfying, and she longs for a return to the Heights and, finally, for death.

Yet even the vision of an angelic family in heaven cannot sustain or fulfill Catherine's search. In the dream she relates to Nelly, Catherine maintains that "heaven did not seem to be my home" (***WH,*** 99), and she rejects its attempts to contain her as well. Emily Brontë's feminism, unlike Charlotte's, does not foresee a traditional heaven as the ultimate home for her heroine, and ***Wuthering Heights*** significantly lacks an active providential intervener. Rather, Emily stresses female agency in the struggle for a selfhood independent of familial and social constraints, though she acknowledges the limitations of that agency. Catherine is ultimately unable to "go home"—literally unable to return to her childhood home once she is installed at the Grange and figuratively unable to find fulfillment during her lifetime. Insofar as she remains a "relative creature" until her death, Catherine reflects certain nineteenth-century female realities. Her story, therefore, can be considered as Emily Brontë's commentary on the familial positioning of female selfhood, which, for Catherine, proves to be ultimately destructive. . . .

Catherine's delirious return to childhood and Wuthering Heights prefaces her ultimate escape to her home among the dead, a place "without identity." In a moment of "feverish bewilderment" (***WH,*** 149), she believes herself to be back at Wuthering Heights, the mirror in her chamber transformed into the black press in the room that she and Heathcliff shared as children. Terrified of the face she sees in the press/mirror, she does not recognize it as her own, despite Nelly's insistence that "It was *yourself,* Mrs. Linton; you knew it a while since" (***WH,*** 151). But, in her delirium, she dissociates her idea of herself from the image she sees in the glass; her fear arises from seeing "Mrs. Linton," the figure of a woman (and, dreadfully, a pregnant woman), as opposed to Catherine Earnshaw, the child she thinks she is, lying in her chamber at Wuthering Heights. Catherine relinquishes her womanhood, her marriage, and her ties to Thrushcross Grange, telling Nelly that in her vision, "the whole last seven years of my life grew a blank! I did not recall that they had been at all. I was a child; my father was just buried, and my misery arose from the separation that Hindley had ordered between me and Heathcliff—I was laid alone, for the first time" (***WH,*** 153).

Catherine's current state of "frightful isolation," self-exiled to her bedchamber in protest of the separation her husband seeks to impose between her and Heathcliff, recalls the original separation imposed by Hindley—and the separation she herself imposed in exchanging Wuthering Heights for the Grange. Yet, significantly, Catherine reinvents her removal from the Heights to conform with her present feelings of powerlessness: "But supposing at twelve years old I had been wrenched from the Heights, and every early association, and my all in all, as Heathcliff was at that time, and been converted at a stroke into Mrs. Linton, the lady of Thrushcross Grange, and the wife of a stranger; an exile, and outcast, thenceforth, from what had been my world—You may fancy a glimpse of the abyss where I grovelled!" (***WH,*** 153). In this version, Catherine—a twelve-year-old child instead of the eighteen-year-old woman she was when she left the Heights—is "wrenched" from Heathcliff and her home, as opposed to actively desiring and pursuing her escape. Her desired haven, Thrushcross Grange, is converted to a place of exile, and she becomes an outcast from her true home. Catherine is trapped in the exchanges she has made—Earnshaw for Linton, Wuthering Heights for Thrushcross Grange—and she longs to undo the original exchange. "I wish I were a girl again, half savage and hardy, and free. . . . Why am I so changed?" she asks herself (***WH,*** 153). The changes Catherine recognizes—her womanhood and wifehood, of which her pregnancy is the most obvious sign—preclude the longed-for return to childhood.

This return is an attempt to recapture a time when Catherine felt herself to be whole, a feeling inextricably bound to a time when Heathcliff was "my all in all." With Heathcliff, Catherine envisions the "ideal of a nontransforming union,"[3] a vision also advanced in Emily Brontë's poem **"The Death of A. G. A.,"** in which Angelica identifies A. G. A. as

> my all-sufficing light—
> My childhood's mate, my girlhood's guide,
> My only blessing, only pride.[4]

But, similarly, as A. G. A. is transformed from an "all-sufficing light" to Angelica's "mortal foe" in the Gondal saga, a time comes in ***Wuthering Heights*** when Catherine no longer recognizes Heathcliff as her "all in all." She appropriates Edgar in marriage, hoping to regain a lost sense of "all in all." But, while Catherine maintains that Heathcliff will be as much to her as he has always been, her marriage to Edgar transforms and relocates her from a daughter and sister at Wuthering Heights to "the lady of Thrushcross Grange" (***WH,*** 153).

Catherine never fully negotiates the exchange. Stevie Davies has argued that "Catherine Linton never leaves off being Catherine Earnshaw" and that "Emily Brontë authorises an opposite journey: the way home is always potentially open." But the return home is realized only in Catherine's feverish delusions. She never returns to Wuthering Heights once she is installed at the Grange. Her visions of the Heights and Heathcliff as the original lost sites of her self-fulfillment are also feverish delusions. Writing on George Eliot's *The Mill on the Floss* (1860), Mary Jacobus argues that, at the conclusion of the novel, Tom and Maggie Tulliver long for an idyllic childhood past that never truly existed.[5] This assertion is equally applicable to Catherine. The childhood world of Wuthering Heights was one of family conflict, patriarchal oppression, sibling rivalries and jealousies, beatings, punishments, and enforced separation. Catherine formed her bond with Heathcliff in the pursuit of escape from the family, and the two children are never so happy as when they are tucked away together in the oak-paneled bed or out on the moors by themselves. Catherine longs not to return to the reality of her childhood home, but to the dream-place of self-fulfillment where she enjoys undisturbed union with Heathcliff. Imagination provides a temporary return; death promises a permanent one.

Emily Brontë ultimately authorizes Catherine's longed-for return to her childhood home by proxy. The novel concludes with the promise of the younger Cathy's return to the Grange, where she will live out her married life with her cousin, Hareton, whom many critics identify as a brother figure occupying a position in his relationship with Cathy at the Heights similar to that which Heathcliff occupied with Catherine.[6] Cathy is allowed an "opposite journey," reversing the one-way course her mother took from her childhood home to her marital home. For the younger Cathy, fraternal love and married love can cohabit; she is not forced to choose between them. By marrying the brother figure and by returning to her beloved childhood home, Cathy fulfills the domestic desires of her mother. The symbolic incest between Catherine and Heathcliff is actualized by Cathy and Hareton but also licensed, since Hareton is Cathy's cousin. The two are bound by blood ties but spared the taboo of an incestuous bond. Cousins in Brontë fiction occupy a position halfway between siblings and lovers; thus, romance and marriage between cousins is always a viable possibility (e.g., Jane Eyre and St. John Rivers in *Jane Eyre,* and Caroline Helstone and Robert Moore in *Shirley*). In addition to securing a union with the sibling-lover, Cathy also manages the domestic subversions that her mother and her aunt Isabella were not able to negotiate: she successfully returns to inhabit her original home, thereby escaping the irreversible relocation that marriage typically required of a wife.

The names that Lockwood discovers carved into the windowsill at Wuthering Heights can now be interpreted in light of Catherine's protest against female identity exclusively determined by family relationships and irreversibly transferred from father to husband upon marriage. The writing, "a name repeated in all kinds of characters, large and small—*Catherine Earnshaw,* here and there varied to *Catherine Heathcliff,* and then again to *Catherine Linton*" (***WH,*** 23), is not necessarily a young woman's attempt to weigh her choices in marriage against dependent daughterhood or sisterhood, or to question her true identity. Rather, the writing expresses her desire to be all Catherines at once. Catherine tells Nelly that she never means to forsake Heathcliff for Edgar, intending to sustain a relationship with both, and so too Catherine never means to substitute one name for another, as is the usual course for a woman upon marriage. Catherine Earnshaw-Heathcliff-Linton can be read as a single identity encompassing all of its guises, just as a man has one name for all his guises as son, brother, husband, father. This inclusive identity is capable of incorporating all of the names, so expansive that to Lockwood "the air swarmed with Catherines" (***WH,*** 24).

The tragedy of Catherine's story rests on her inability, in the end, to fulfill her desire to be Catherine Earnshaw-Heathcliff-Linton. She cannot escape the exclusive and linear progression from her family name to her married name—a transference that passes over her bond with Heathcliff, never recognizing it. Once she has exchanged the Earnshaw name for Linton, she can never return to it, despite her desperate longing to be a girl again. Even the ghost child that Lockwood encounters announces herself as "Catherine Linton," though she is cast in the form of Catherine Earnshaw and is begging to reenter the home of her youth.

"Earnshaw" and "Linton" are the signifiers of Catherine's dependency on and subordination to her father and her husband and their respective families. The identity of Catherine Heathcliff is expressed in the novel only in its terms of equality and complete identification, "I am Heathcliff." Catherine's bond with Heathcliff is not relational or hierarchical; it does not designate her membership in a family. Rather, "Catherine Heathcliff" is a signifier of her desire to break free of family systems of determination and her relational identity as a female. But the name of Catherine Heathcliff and union with Heathcliff are not realized in Catherine's lifetime, and neither is her desire.

Heathcliff's Revenge: Appropriating Women's Property and Women as Property

While Catherine Earnshaw feels her social reality as a "relative creature" to be psychologically and emotionally imprisoning, Isabella and the younger Cathy Linton experience their relativity in terms of physical bondage. The Linton women play pivotal roles in Heathcliff's successful appropriation of Wuthering Heights and Thrushcross Grange, through which he secures his revenge against the families who worked to separate him from "his heart's darling" (***WH,*** 35). Emily Brontë has been praised for her remarkable knowledge of family succession and property laws, which Heathcliff shrewdly manipulates. But Heathcliff's revenge ultimately succeeds by his ability to exploit the female's role in the inheritance of property—more specifically, by his ability to exploit woman's position *as* property.

Randolph Trumbach has written: "Patriarchy presumed that there was property not only in things but in persons and that ownership lay with the heads of households. It meant that some men were owned by others, and all women and children by their husbands or father."[7] Heathcliff moves from being at the mercy of this patriarchal system to assuming the role of the patriarch himself. ***Wuthering Heights*** traces Heathcliff's evolving relationship to property, from penniless orphan to ardent protocapitalist and master of both the Heights and the Grange. As a boy, he first witnesses the battle for possession in the Linton children's struggle over the exclusive right to hold their dog, in which they nearly tear it in two. Heathcliff scorns them and rejects their world, remarking to Nelly, "When would you catch me wishing to have what Catherine wanted?" (***WH,*** 59).

Part of Heathcliff's introduction to the world at the Heights, and undoubtedly part of his socialization process during his three-year absence, is his realization that possession, whether of houses and lands or women and children, is power.[8] Hindley's power over Heathcliff and Catherine derives from his claim to Wuthering Heights. When Hindley mortgages the land to fund his "mania for gaming" (***WH,*** 231), Heathcliff takes possession of the Heights, thus reversing the dynamics of power and securing his domination over both Hindley's person and property. Likening Catherine to a piece of property, Heathcliff strives to take possession of her, believing that only by treating her as a possession, as Hindley did and Edgar does, can he hope to secure her entirely for himself. Catherine thus becomes the object over which he and Edgar struggle for exclusive possession, a tug-of-war that does eventually split her in two.

Heathcliff's desire to possess Catherine becomes, after her death, a relentless quest to possess all things connected with her. Steven Vine has argued that Heathcliff substitutes property gain for Catherine's loss in a desperate attempt to retain his hold on her.[9] His first act as master of Thrushcross Grange is to appropriate Catherine's portrait and instruct that it be transported to Wuthering Heights—an attempt to substitute the portrait for the departed reality. Catherine thus becomes part of the property he possesses and controls, like his wife, Isabella, and daughter-in-law, Cathy.

Relationships in ***Wuthering Heights*** are repeatedly expressed in the language of ownership. Upon his arrival at the Heights, Lockwood is uncertain whether Heathcliff or Hareton is the "favoured possessor" of the younger Cathy (***WH,*** 16). When he finds Heathcliff without an "owner" in Liverpool, Mr. Earnshaw assumes possession of him and carries him home along with his children's other gifts (***WH,*** 45). Heathcliff ominously refers to Linton as "my property" (***WH,*** 253) and assumes his ownership of Hindley's son, Hareton, upon Hindley's death, despite Nelly's insistence that "There is nothing in the world less yours than he is!" (***WH,*** 230). The head of the household assumed legal custody of children and wives: being in "custody" at Wuthering Heights is tantamount to physical imprisonment and domestic violence with no recourse to the law for protection.

Through ownership of people, specifically women, Heathcliff secures the ownership of property. It is not entirely clear whether Mr. Linton made a will or whether Thrushcross Grange was entailed, though the logical order of inheritance in either case would be first Edgar, then his sons, then Isabella, then her sons. Cathy would inherit the Grange only in the last instance, being passed over in favor of first Isabella and then her son, Linton. Both women are potential property owners, but they maintain a precarious hold. Theorists of property ownership, such as Thomas Hobbes and John Locke, failed to clarify "how women's control of property and their expected subordination within the family could be reconciled."[10]

A woman's property, like her identity, fell under the rule of coverture. Under common law, all of a woman's liquid property (i.e., money, stocks, jewels, clothes, etc.) became her husband's at marriage, and the husband was entitled to the possession and usufruct of his wife's freehold property. Unless a father or male guardian made a particular stipulation in his will or created a trust, "a woman's inheritance passed to the legal control and use of her husband."[11] Marriage, then, as Heathcliff seems fully aware, is the quickest way to usurp a woman's position in the line of inheritance and thereby claim her inherited property. This is his all-but-stated purpose in marrying Isabella, and it is his clear design in arranging the marriage of his and Isabella's son, Linton, to Catherine and Edgar's daughter, Cathy. And Heathcliff clearly informs Linton of his prerogative as Cathy's husband over her body and her property, both of which are legally the objects of male ownership. Linton delights in the prospect of owning Thrushcross Grange upon his marriage and Edgar's death: "I'm glad, for I shall be master of the Grange after him—and Catherine always spoke of it as *her* house. It isn't hers! It's mine—papa says everything she has is mine" (***WH,*** 340).

The Linton order of succession implies, however, that it would not be necessary for Linton to marry the younger Cathy in order to inherit the estate when Edgar dies. Yet Linton's failing health and the possibility of his death preceding Edgar's make the marriage with Cathy urgent to Heathcliff's plan to secure the estate for himself. Nelly argues with him that when Linton dies, Cathy will become the sole heir. But Heathcliff denies this: "There is no clause in the will to secure it so; his property would go to me; but, to prevent disputes, I desire their union, and am resolved to bring it about" (***WH,*** 263). The marriage of the younger Cathy to Linton would necessarily prevent any disputes over rightful ownership of Thrushcross Grange. James H. Kavanagh has argued that "it hardly matters what the inheritance laws say, since Cathy's marriage transfers all the personal wealth she has just inherited to her new husband, who immediately leaves it to Heathcliff."[12]

Edgar likewise desires his daughter's union with his heir, but he envisions their marriage as a means of protecting her from Heathcliff and allowing her to remain in "the house of her ancestors" (***WH,*** 315-16). He resolves to alter his will so that her fortune (i.e., her personal property) is guarded by trustees for use by her and any children she may bear, and thus, is protected against Heathcliff's claim should Linton die. The trust, as Davidoff and Hall explain, recognized the vulnerability of female property and served to protect it after marriage. Heathcliff, however, is able to prevent Edgar from taking this precaution, delaying the lawyer Edgar has summoned. Edgar dies before his will can be changed, leaving his daughter at the mercy of his greatest enemy, who takes control of the Grange. Nelly questions the legality of Heathcliff's claim to ownership: since Linton was a minor when he died, he cannot by law devise real property, but Heathcliff claims the lands "in his wife's right, and his also" (***WH,*** 356), implying his double claim under coverture and the terms of Linton's will.[13] At any rate, there is little that Nelly or Cathy, both penniless, propertyless women, can do to disturb his possession. Cathy nonetheless remains indignantly sensible of the injustice done to her. When Heathcliff berates her for planting flowers at the Heights, she retorts, "You shouldn't grudge a few yards of earth for me to ornament, when you have taken all my land!" (***WH,*** 388).

The appropriation of property marks Heathcliff's quest for fulfillment in Catherine's absence. But, like Catherine's search, it is unsuccessful. The houses and lands that he has worked methodically to acquire give him no pleasure and provide no compensation for his loss. He comes to regard his property only as a burden he must relinquish before he can join Catherine in death: "I have not written my will yet, and how to leave my property, I cannot determine! I wish I could annihilate it from the face of the earth" (***WH,*** 407). Catherine, for whom his earthly possessions are inadequate substitutes, eludes him still. She remains, until Heathcliff's death, "incomparably beyond and above" him (***WH,*** 197), and yet he sees everything in relation to her: "The entire world is a dreadful collection of memoranda that she did exist, and that I have lost her!" (***WH,*** 394). Even Hareton and the younger Cathy, the remaining victims of his revenge, whose persons and properties are his possessions, look at him with the elusive eyes of Catherine Earnshaw, reminding Heathcliff that she remains beyond possession. By depriving the cousins of their rightful land and money, Heathcliff unwittingly makes possible the bond of love that defeats him: there is no threat of degradation to keep them apart, and, in their love, they appear as beyond his power to control as the ghostly Catherine.

Following Heathcliff's death, the novel concludes with the restoration of the "the lawful master and the ancient stock" (***WH,*** 411) in Hareton Earnshaw who, in marriage to Cathy, will assume control of both the Heights and the Grange. Joseph's unbridled joy over Hareton's accession seems to indicate a reassertion of a world of dominant patriarchy, this time with a less-rebellious relative female in the younger Cathy. But the final journeys for the lovers of both generations are ultimately female-directed: Cathy, after leading Hareton through a course in literacy, leads him to the "house of *her* ancestors" (***WH,*** 315-16, my italics), and Catherine calls Heathcliff to her in death with the promise of a shared heaven. Catherine Earnshaw's struggle against female containment within kinship structures is finally realized not in unlimited female agency, but in a male and female relationship that promises to be "enabling and operative, rather than repressive and restrictive."[14] Cathy and Hareton represent a compromise between ultimate possession and unbounded freedom, shaping the excesses of Catherine and Heathcliff into a viable domestic relationship.

Notes

1. Lamb, *Can Woman Regenerate Society?* 122.
2. Helene Moglen, "The Double Vision of *Wuthering Heights*: A Clarifying View of Female Development," 405. Many feminist studies displace Heathcliff as the novel's protagonist in favor of Catherine. Moglen, for example, discusses the entire novel as a linear progression of female maturation, which is only finally completed by the younger Cathy. See also Carol A. Senf, "Emily Brontë's Version of Feminist History: *Wuthering Heights*."
3. Bersani, *Future for Astyanax,* 221.
4. "The Death of A. G. A.," ll. 78-80 (January 1841-May 1844), Roper, *Poems,* 112.
5. Davies, *Emily Brontë,* 74; Mary Jacobus, "The Question of Language: Men of Maxims and *The Mill on the Floss*."
6. Stevie Davies, *Emily Brontë,* 106-7, for example, calls Hareton a "legitimized Heathcliff" and maintains that Hareton and the younger Cathy reassert the brother-sister bond, thereby fulfilling the yearning of the first generation.
7. Trumbach, *Egalitarian Family,* 119-20.
8. For a standard chronology of *WH,* see A. Stuart Daley, "A Revised Chronology of *Wuthering Heights,*" 169-73.
9. Vine, "The Wuther of the Other," 354.
10. C. P. Sanger and James H. Kavanagh have written extensively on the order of inheritance of Thrushcross Grange. See Sanger, *The Structure of Wuthering Heights,* and Kavanagh, *Emily Brontë.* See also "Land Law and Inheritance in *Wuthering Heights,*" in *WH,* appendix 6, 497-99. Davidoff and Hall, *Family Fortunes,* 275-76.
11. Joan Perkin, *Women and Marriage in Nineteenth-Century England,* 10-31, provides a useful outline of Barbara Leigh Smith Bodichon's *Brief Summary, in Plain Language, of the Most Important Laws of England Concerning Women; Together with a Few Observations Thereon.* Perkin notes that when the *Summary* was published, "very little had changed in Common Law since feudal times," so the laws therein are clearly applicable to both the late-eighteenth-century setting of *WH* and the mid-nineteenth century when EB was writing (11). There were no substantial changes in legislation until the Married Women's Property Act of 1870, which entitled a married women her separate earnings, as well as other specified inheritances. Davidoff and Hall, *Family Fortunes,* 276.
12. Kavanagh, *Emily Brontë,* 77.
13. Davidoff and Hall, *Family Fortunes,* 209-10; see "Land Law and Inheritance," *WH,* 499, for a dispute to Heathcliff's claims.
14. Lyn Pykett, *Emily Brontë,* 119.

Bibliography

Works by the Brontës

Brontë, Emily. *The Poems of Emily Brontë.* Edited by Derek Roper with Edward Chitham. Oxford: Clarendon Press, 1995.

———. *Wuthering Heights.* Edited by Hilda Marsden and Ian Jack. Oxford: Clarendon Press, 1976.

Other Primary Works

Bodichon, Barbara Leigh Smith. *A Brief Summary, in Plain Language, of the Most Important Laws Concerning Women; Together with a Few Observations Thereon.* London: John Chapman, 1854.

Lamb, Ann Richelieu. *Can Woman Regenerate Society?* London: John W. Parker, 1844.

Secondary Sources

Bersani, Leo. *A Future for Astyanax: Character and Desire in Literature.* London: Marion Boyars, 1978.

Butler, Judith. *Subjects of Desire: Hegelian Reflections in Twentieth-Century France.* New York: Columbia University Press, 1987.

Cohen, Paula Marantz. *The Daughter's Dilemma: Family Process and the Nineteenth-Century Domestic Novel.* Ann Arbor: University of Michigan Press, 1991.

Daley, A. Stuart. "A Revised Chronology of *Wuthering Heights.*" *Brontë Society Transactions* 21 (1995): 168-73.

Davidoff, Leonore, and Catherine Hall. *Family Fortunes: Men and Women of the English Middle Class, 1780-1850.* London: Hutchinson, 1987.

Davies, Cecil W. "A Reading of *Wuthering Heights.*" *Essays in Criticism* 19 (1969): 254-72.

Davies, Stevie. *Emily Brontë.* Key Women Writers Series. Hemel Hempstead: Harvester Wheatsheaf, 1988.

Elfenbein, Andrew. *Byron and the Victorians.* Cambridge Studies in Nineteenth-Century Literature and Culture, no. 4. Cambridge: Cambridge University Press, 1995.

Gilbert, Sandra M., and Susan Gubar. *The Madwoman in the Attic: The Woman Writer and the Nineteenth-Century Literary Imagination.* New Haven: Yale University Press, 1979.

Jacobus, Mary. "The Question of Language: Men of Maxims and *The Mill on the Floss.*" *Critical Inquiry* 8 (1981): 207-22.

Kavanagh, James H. *Emily Brontë.* Rereading Literature Series. Oxford: Basil Blackwell, 1985.

Kettle, Arnold. *An Introduction to the English Novel.* 2 vols. London: Hutchinson, 1951.

Knoepflmacher, U. C. *Emily Brontë: Wuthering Heights.* Cambridge: Cambridge University Press, 1989.

Leavis, Q. D. "A Fresh Approach to *Wuthering Heights.*" In *Lectures in America,* 83-152. New York: Pantheon Press, 1969.

Moglen, Helene. "The Double Vision of *Wuthering Heights*: A Clarifying View of Female Development." *Centennial Review* 15 (1971): 391-405.

Perkin, Joan. *Women and Marriage in Nineteenth-Century England.* Chicago: Lyceum Press, 1989.

Pykett, Lyn. *Emily Brontë.* Basingstoke: Macmillan, 1989.

Sanger, C. P. *The Structure of Wuthering Heights.* Hogarth Essays, no. 19. London: Hogarth Press, 1926.

Senf, Carol A. "Emily Brontë's Version of Feminist History: *Wuthering Heights.*" *Essays in Literature* 12 (1985): 201-14.

Solomon, Eric. "The Incest Theme in *Wuthering Heights.*" *Nineteenth-Century Fiction* 14 (1959): 80-83.

Stoneman, Patsy. Introduction to *Wuthering Heights.* Oxford: Oxford University Press, 1995.

Trumbach, Randolph. *The Rise of the Egalitarian Family: Aristocratic Kinship and Domestic Relations in Eighteenth-Century England.* New York: Academic Press, 1978.

Vine, Steven. "'When I Am Not': Mourning and Identity in *Wuthering Heights.*" Paper presented at conference, The Legacy of the Brontës, 1847-1997, School of English, University of Leeds, April 1997.

———. "The Wuther of the Other in *Wuthering Heights.*" *Nineteenth-Century Fiction* 49 (1994): 339-59.

Yaeger, Patricia. "Violence in the Sitting Room: *Wuthering Heights* and the Woman's Novel." *Genre* 21 (1988): 203-29.

FURTHER READING

Bibliographies

Barclay, Janet M. *Emily Brontë Criticism 1900-1982: An Annotated Checklist.* Westport, Conn.: Meckler, 1984, 162 p.

Provides an annotated list of writings on Emily Brontë.

Crump, Rebecca W. *Charlotte and Emily Brontë: A Reference Guide.* 3 vols. Boston: G. K. Hall, 1982.

Provides critical sources from 1846-1983.

Stoneman, Patsy. "Feminist Criticism of *Wuthering Heights.*" *Critical Survey* 4, no. 2 (1992): 147-53.

Surveys modern criticism on Wuthering Heights *applying feminist literary theory and addressing gender issues.*

Biography

Grin, Winifred. *Emily Brontë* Oxford: Oxford University Press, 1971, 290 p.

Offers a scholarly biography that attempts to clarify the myths about Brontë's personality.

Criticism

Apter, T. E. "Romanticism and Romantic Love in *Wuthering Heights.*" In *The Art of Emily Brontë,* edited by Anne Smith, pp. 205-22. London: Vision Press, 1976.

Contends that Cathy and Hareton's relationship presents an alternative model to the destructive, Romantic love of Catherine and Heathcliff.

Barreca, Regina. "The Power of Excommunication: Sex and the Feminine Text in *Wuthering Heights.*" In *Sex and Death in Victorian Literature,* pp. 227-40. London: Macmillan Press, 1990.

Argues that the female characters in Wuthering Heights *assert their power over the patriarchal system by creating and shaping the text.*

Davies, Stevie. *Emily Brontë: The Artist as a Free Woman.* Manchester: Carcanet, 1983, 170 p.

Traces Brontë's artistic development as revealed in her life and works; emphasizes her uniquely independent environment as a source for her unusual perspective on love and womanhood.

Eagleton, Terry. *Myths of Power: A Marxist Study of the Brontës.* London: Macmillan, 1975, 148 p.

Takes a Marxist literary approach to interpreting the Brontës' work.

Gilbert, Sandra M. and Susan Gubar. "Looking Oppositely: Emily Brontë's Bible of Hell." In *The Madwoman in the Attic: The Woman Writer and the Nineteenth-Century Literary Imagination,* pp. 248-308. New Haven: Yale University Press, 1979.

Reads Wuthering Heights *as a myth of the origins of Victorian women's culture; from a seminal work of feminist literary criticism.*

Gold, Linda. "Catherine Earnshaw: Mother and Daughter." *English Journal* 74, no. 3 (March 1985): 68-73.

Discusses Catherine Earnshaw's maturation in the novel in terms of Freud's theory of the development of personality.

Gorsky, Susan Rubinow. "'I'll Cry Myself Sick': Illness in *Wuthering Heights.*" *Literature and Medicine* 18, no. 2 (fall 1999): 173-91.

Addresses the theme of illness as it relates to women and gender issues in the novel.

Homans, Margaret. "Emily Brontë." In *Women Writers and Poetic Identity: Dorothy Wordsworth, Emily Brontë, and Emily Dickinson,* pp. 104-61. Princeton: Princeton University Press, 1980.

Investigates the challenges that Brontë faced in establishing her identity as a writer.

Leavis, Q. D. "A Fresh Approach to *Wuthering Heights.*" In *Lectures in America,* pp. 85-138. New York: Random House, 1969.

Points to Brontë's treatment of Catherine Earnshaw as evidence of the realistic nature and moral responsibility of the novel.

Lenta, Margaret. "Capitalism or Patriarchy and Immortal Love: A Study of *Wuthering Heights.*" *Theoria* 42 (May 1984): 63-76.

Examines the social forces that shape the relationship between Heathcliff and Catherine.

Mass, Michelle A. "'He's More Myself Than I Am': Narcissism and Gender in *Wuthering Heights.*" In *Psychoanalyses/Feminisms,* edited by Peter L. Rudnytsky and Andrew M. Gordon, pp. 135-53. Albany: State University of New York Press, 2000.

Discusses the relationship between narcissism and women's agency, applying models of modern literary criticism.

McKinstry, Susan Jaret. "Desire's Dreams: Power and Passion in *Wuthering Heights*." *College Literature* 12, no. 2 (spring 1985): 141-46.

Interprets Wuthering Heights *as a celebration of the power of desire to overthrow the obstacles to love and fulfillment.*

Mermin, Dorothy. "The Damsel, the Knight, and the Victorian Woman Poet." *Critical Inquiry* 13, no. 1 (autumn 1986): 64-80.

Compares poetry by women authors including Brontë, Elizabeth Barrett Browning, Christina Rossetti, and Emily Dickinson.

Meyer, Susan. *Imperialism at Home: Race and Victorian Women's Fiction.* Ithaca: Cornell University Press, 1996, 220 p.

Examines the treatment of race and colonialism in Wuthering Heights.

Moser, Thomas. "What is the Matter with Emily Jane? Conflicting Impulses in *Wuthering Heights*." *Nineteenth-Century Fiction* 17, no. 1 (June 1962): 1-19.

Applies Freudian literary theory to Brontë's novel, focusing on Heathcliff's role as the embodiment of sexual energy that is the driving force of the work.

Parker, Patricia. "The (Self)-Identity of the Literary Text: Property, Propriety, Proper Place, and Proper Name in *Wuthering Heights*." In *Identity of the Literary Text,* edited by Mario J. Valds and Owen Miller, pp. 92-116. Toronto: University of Toronto Press, 1985.

Discusses Brontë's disruption of chronology and the impossibility of a linear reading of Wuthering Heights.

Ratchford, Fannie E. *The Brontës' Web of Childhood.* New York: Columbia University Press, 1941, 293 p.

Examines the Brontës' juvenilia, including Emily Brontë's Gondal poetry; a pioneering study of the Brontë's childhood works.

Sanger, Charles Percy. *The Structure of* Wuthering Heights. London: Hogarth Press, 1926, 23 p.

Contends that Wuthering Heights *contains painstaking execution and prose craftsmanship.*

Van Ghent, Dorothy. "The Window Figure and the Two-Children Figure in 'Wuthering Heights.'" *Nineteenth-Century Fiction* 7, no. 3 (December 1952): 189-97.

Studies two recurring images in Wuthering Heights *as metaphors for doubleness and otherness.*

Visick, Mary. *The Genesis of* Wuthering Heights. Hong Kong: Hong Kong University Press, 1965, 88 p.

Studies the relationship between Wuthering Heights *and the Gondal poems.*

Wion, Philip K. "The Absent Mother in Emily Brontë's *Wuthering Heights*." *American Imago* 42, no. 2 (summer 1985): 143-64.

Employs psychological theories about the mother-child relationship to examine conflicts involving separation and unity in Wuthering Heights.

Yaeger, Patricia. "Wuthering Heights and the Woman's Novel." *Genre* 21, no. 2 (summer 1988): 203-229.

Examines the use of comedy, violence, and narrative and generic styles in nineteenth-century women's novels, using Wuthering Heights *as a representative example.*

OTHER SOURCES FROM GALE:

Additional coverage of Brontë's life and career is contained in the following sources published by the Gale Group: *Authors and Artists for Young Adults,* Vol. 17; *Beacham's Encyclopedia of Popular Fiction: Biography and Resources,* Vol. 1; *Beacham's Guide to Literature for Young Adults,* Vol. 3; *British Writers,* Vol. 5; *British Writers: The Classics,* Vol. 1; *British Writers Retrospective Supplement,* Vol. 1; *Concise Dictionary of British Literary Biography 1832-1890*; *Dictionary of Literary Biography,* Vols. 21, 32, 199; *DISCovering Authors*; *DISCovering Authors: British Edition*; *DISCovering Authors: Canadian Edition*; *Discovering Authors Modules: Most-studied Authors, Novelists* and *Poets*; *DISCovering Authors 3.0*; *Exploring Novels*; *Literature and Its Times,* Vol. 1; *Literature Resource Center*; *Nineteenth-Century Literature Criticism,* Vols. 16, 35; *Poetry Criticism,* Vol. 8; *Twayne's English Authors*; *World Literature and Its Times,* Vol. 3; and *World Literature Criticism.*

ELIZABETH BARRETT BROWNING

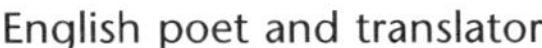

(1806 - 1861)

English poet and translator.

Browning was likely the first woman poet in England to be considered for the post of poet laureate, a reflection of her success in the battle against the marginalized status of "woman writer." Despite popularity and critical acclaim during her lifetime, scholars have tended to remember her as the passionate woman who left home to marry her young poet-lover rather than as the innovative poet who gave voice to women's private and intellectual desires. Browning wrote widely on political and social topics, and she produced some of the world's most famous love poetry in her *Sonnets from the Portuguese* (1850). She also penned the semi-autobiographical story of a female poet striving for literary success and an equal partnership in marriage; her verse novel *Aurora Leigh* (1856) has been hailed by feminist critics as a new model of poetry and of womanhood.

BIOGRAPHICAL INFORMATION

Elizabeth Barrett was born March 6, 1806, into a wealthy family of Herefordshire, England, the oldest of eleven children. In addition to the family estate in Herefordshire, called Hope End, her father owned extensive sugar plantations in Jamaica. She began writing poetry at the age of four, a calling to which her father encouraged her. When she was six, her father paid her for a poem with a note addressed to "the Poet-Laureate of Hope End." In 1820 Mr. Barrett privately published *The Battle of Marathon,* an epic-style poem Browning had written around the age of twelve, though the fifty copies he printed remained within the family. Also about this time, Browning injured her spine in a riding accident, and seven years later she suffered a burst blood vessel in her chest, leaving her permanently weakened. Her family's fortunes also began to suffer. Mrs. Barrett died in 1828, and in 1832 the mismanagement of Mr. Barrett's sugar plantations forced him to sell Hope End at a public auction. The family rented houses in Sidmouth, Devonshire, before settling in London in 1835. By the time Browning arrived in London, she had already developed a reputation as an emerging poetic talent. In 1826 she published *An Essay on Mind, with Other Poems,* and subsequently produced a translation of Aeschylus' *Prometheus Bound* (1833). The publication of *The Seraphim, and Other Poems* in 1838 brought her into the most elite literary society in London, and she was considered one of England's most original and gifted young poets. The atmosphere of London did not agree with her, however; and just as her career began to develop, she was forced to retire to Torquay, another Devonshire coastal town. She spent three miserable years in Torquay in poor health, her misery compounded by the drowning death of a favorite brother. Even upon her return to London, illness and depression kept her confined in a sickroom, where she dedicated her life to literature. She was shy and refused to entertain her friends and admirers, but she did correspond with several literary notables, including Edgar Allen Poe, James Russell Lowell, Thomas Carlyle, and Robert Browning. Browning had appreciated Robert Browning's poetry even before she met him—her room at Wimpole Street contained an engraving of the poet—and she mentioned his name in the poem "Lady Geraldine's Courtship," from her two-volume collection *Poems* of 1844. He responded to the compliment in a letter claiming, "I love your verses with all my heart, dear Miss Barrett," and later in the letter added "I love you, too." Thus the courtship began, with Robert Browning becoming one of the few visitors apart from family whom Browning would admit. Despite her father's objections—Mr. Barrett preferred to keep his children dependent on him—the couple arranged a secret wedding, marrying September 12, 1846, then moved to Florence, Italy. Although she remained somewhat frail, Browning was invigorated by her love for her husband and for her adopted homeland, and began writing with a new passion. In 1849 the Brownings delivered their only child, Robert Weidemann Barrett Browning, whom they nicknamed "Pen." Browning cared deeply for her new home in Italy and closely followed the political tumult of the 1850s. She was excited at the prospect of the unification of the Italian States in 1861, a movement led by Count Cavour. Cavour unexpectedly died in June 1861, a political and personal blow that drove Browning into seclusion. Two weeks later she was confined to her bed with a severe cough and cold, and on the morning of June 29 she died in Browning's arms, at the age of fifty-five.

MAJOR WORKS

Among Browning's poetry collections, *The Seraphim, and Other Poems* was the first to achieve significant notice, and it established her reputation as an important poet. Through the years, interest in many of the Italian poems has waned—they are generally considered overly zealous—but the poems collected in *Sonnets from the Portuguese* continue to be the foundation of her standing as a significant English poet. The poems were written to celebrate the courtship of Browning and Robert Browning, although in their initial publication the Brownings styled them as the story of a young girl's love for the Portuguese poet Luis Vaz de Camoëns. The sonnets begin with Browning's disbelief that a middle-aged invalid could find love with a young man and her hesitation to marry because of her age and infirmity. She then wonders if he can fulfill her needs. When she finally accepts his love for her, and hers for him, she expresses her feelings in the famous "Sonnet XLIII," which begins, "How do I love thee? Let me count the ways." The work of most interest to feminist scholars, however, is the blank-verse novel *Aurora Leigh.* Ignored by scholars for many years, the advent of feminist literary criticism during the 1970s brought the romance back into the canon. The book is part autobiography and part social criticism, chronicling the life of an Englishwoman and poet, Aurora, as she pursues a literary career and a marriage that is a true partnership. An important secondary character is Marian Erle, a poor young woman who is repeatedly victimized by the wealthy and powerful people in her life. In a highly controversial section of the story, Marian is discovered in a Paris brothel—having been forced from London by the unscrupulous Lady Waldemar—where she is sexually assaulted and bears a child. The graphic depiction of the abuse and neglect suffered by impoverished women was the severest expression of *Aurora Leigh*'s overarching critique of Victorian society as sexist and classist. Aurora's love interest, Romney, is a wealthy philanthropist who attempts to correct those wrongs, in part by creating a socialist utopian community, but the community eventually collapses and Romney comes to doubt traditional philanthropy as a means for addressing the systemic injustices of society. At the conclusion of the novel, Aurora finally accepts Romney's proposal of marriage—a proposal she had rejected while establishing herself as a poet—and decides that love and partnership are crucial to creativity and self-realization.

CRITICAL RECEPTION

At the time of her death, Browning was eulogized in the papers as England's greatest woman poet. Through time, however, the romantic legends of her life began to overshadow the appreciation of her work, and attention to her career as a uniquely female poet fostered a critical emphasis on her femininity over her poetic skill and imagination. Kay Moser, along with other scholars, has argued that by praising Browning specifically as a woman poet, her early reviewers made her an oddity rather than a recognized author, and muted any feminist message in her work. In addition, Dorothy Mermin (see Further Reading) has suggested that the passionate female longing voiced in the poet's sonnets may have presented a mystery or an embarrassment to male reviewers. As a result, Browning's poetry was long undervalued both for its artistry and for its strong statements about women's emotional and intellectual power. The work of remaking her reputation had begun with a study by Alethea Hayter in 1962 (see Further Reading); Hayter labored to wrest the trend of Browning criticism away from the myth of the romanticized lady poet of the sickroom and move it toward a scholarly examination of the poet's writing and ideas. Major studies in the 1970s again asserted Browning's place in the tradition of nineteenth-century women authors who were struggling to create a position from which a woman could express herself with authority. Scholars identify Browning as the matriarch of the family of female poets who followed her, both in England and in America. Browning's originality is a common theme in much of the scholarship; in particular, critics have focused on her innovation in *Aurora Leigh,* both its unusual story and its unusual form. Critics have suggested that the blending of genres in *Aurora Leigh* is a reflection of Browning's egalitarian views on gender roles; the poet's creation of a new literary form mirrors her real-life creation of a new kind of marriage and a new status for women in public life. SueAnn Schatz argues that *Aurora Leigh* attempts to free women from the Victorian ideal of domestic womanhood by suggesting that women could be active and successful in domestic and public roles simultaneously. Similarly, Rebecca Stott's interpretation of Browning's love poetry emphasizes the poet's strong belief that a truly equal marriage grounded in mutual affection would benefit not only the marriage partners, but also the society in which both men and women were free to pursue self-fulfillment.

PRINCIPAL WORKS

An Essay on Mind, with Other Poems (poetry) 1826

Prometheus Bound, Translated from the Greek of Aeschylus and Miscellaneous Poems by the Translator [translator] (poetry) 1833

The Seraphim, and Other Poems (poetry) 1838

Poems (poetry) 1844; published in the United States as *A Drama of Exile, and Other Poems,* 1844

**Poems* (poetry) 1850

Casa Guidi Windows (poetry) 1851

Aurora Leigh (poetry) 1856

Poems before Congress (poetry) 1860

Last Poems (poetry) 1862

* This is a new and enlarged edition of the 1844 *Poems,* and contains *Sonnets from the Portuguese.*

PRIMARY SOURCES

ELIZABETH BARRETT BROWNING (ESSAY DATE C. 1820-22)

SOURCE: Browning, Elizabeth Barrett. "Glimpses into My Own Life and Literary Character." In *The Brownings' Correspondence,* Vol. 1, edited by Philip Kelley and Ronald Hudson, pp. 348-56. Winfield, Kans.: Wedgestone, 1984.

In the following excerpt from an unpublished essay, a young Browning discusses her poetic ambitions and her tendency toward sentiment. The essay was likely written during a period of at least two years, beginning when the poet was fourteen and ending sometime after her illness of 1821-22.

I was always of a determined and if thwarted violent disposition—My actions and temper were infinitely more inflexible at three years old than now at fourteen—At that early age I can perfectly remember reigning in the Nursery and being renowned amongst the servants for self love and excessive passion—When reproved I always considered myself as an injured martyr and bitter have been the tears I have shed over my supposed wrongs. At four and a half my great delight was poring over fairy phenomenons and the actions of necromancers—& the seven champions of Christendom in "Popular tales" has beguiled many a weary hour. At five I supposed myself a heroine and in my day dreams of bliss I constantly imaged to myself a forlorn damsel in distress rescued by some noble knight and often have I laid awake hours in darkness, "THINKING," as I expressed myself; but which was nothing more than musing on these fairy castles in the air!

I perfectly remember the delight I felt when I attained my sixth birthday[;] I enjoyed my triumph to a great degree over the inhabitants of the nursery, there being no UPSTART to dispute my authority, as Henrietta was quite an infant and my dearest Bro tho my constant companion and a beloved participator in all my pleasures never allowed the urge for power to injure the endearing sweetness of his temper.

I might, tho perhaps with injustice to myself, impute my never changing affection to this ever dear Brother to his mild and gentle conduct at this period. But he and I have attained an age not merely childish, an age to which infantine pursuits are no longer agreeable, we have attained an age when reason is no longer the subject of childish frivolity!—Still I believe that our affection for each other has become infinitely more enthusiastic and more rivetted—At four I first mounted Pegasus but at six I thought myself priviledged to show off feats of horsemanship—In my sixth year for some lines on virtue which I had pen[n]ed with great care I received from Papa a ten shilling note enclosed in a letter which was addrest to *the Poet Laureat of Hope End*; I mention this because I received much, more pleasure from the word *Poet* than from the ten shilling note—I did not understand the meaning of the word laureat but it being explained to me by my dearest Mama, the idea first presented itself to me of celebrating our birthdays by my verse[.] *"Poet laureat of Hope End"* was too great a tittle [*sic*] to lose—Nothing could contribute so much to my amusement as a novel. A novel at six years old may appear ridiculous, but it was a real desire that I felt,—not to instruct myself, I felt no such wish, but to divert myself and to afford more scope to my nightly meditations.. and it is worthy of remark that in a novel I carefully past over all passages which described CHILDREN—

The Fops love and pursuit of the heroines mother in *"Temper"* delighted me, but the description of the infancy of Emma was past over—At SEVEN I began to think of *"forming my taste"*—perhaps I did not express my thoughts in those refined words but I considered it time *"to see what was best to write about & read about"*! At 7 too I read the History of England and Rome—at 8 I perused the History of Greece and it was at this age that I first found real delight in poetry—"The Minstrel" Popes "Illiad"[,] some parts of the "Odyssey" passages from "Paradise lost" selected by my dearest Mama and some of Shakespeares plays among which were, "The Tempest," "Othello" and a few historical dramatic pieces constituted my Studies!—I was enchanted with all these but I think the story interested me more that [*sic*] the poetry till "The Minstrel" met my sight—I was then too young to feel the loveliness of simple beauty, I required something dazling to strike my mind—The brilliant imagery[,] the fine metaphors and the flowing numbers of "the Minstrel" truly astonished me. Every stanza excited my ardent admiration nor can I now remember the delight which I felt on perusing those pages without enthusiasm—

At nine I felt much pleasure from the effusions of my imagination in the adorned drapery of versification but nothing could compensate for the regret I felt on laying down a book to take up a pen—The subject of my studies was Pope's Illiad some passages from Shakespeare & Novels which I enjoyed to their full extent. At this age works of imagination only afforded me gratification and I trod the delightful fields of fancy without any of those conscientious scruples which now always attends me when wasting time in frivolous pleasures—

At ten my poetry was entirely formed by the style of written authors and I read that I might write—Novels were still my most delightful study combined with the sweet notes of poetic inspiration! At eleven I wished to be considered an authoress. Novels were thrown aside. Poetry and Essays were my studies & I felt the most ardent desire to understand the learned languages—To comprehend even the Greek alphabet was delight inexpressible. Under the tuition of M[r]. M[c].Swiney I attained that which I so fervently desired. For 8 months during this year I never remember having directed my attentions to any other object than the ambition of gaining fame—Literature was the star which in prospect illuminated my future days[;] it was the spur which prompted me.. the aim.. the very soul of my being—I was determined (and as I before stated my determinations were not "airlike dispersable") I was determined to gain the very pinnacle of excellence and even when this childish & foolishly ambitious idea had fled not by the weight of the argument of a more experienced adviser but by my own reflections & conviction I yet looked with regret.. painful regret to the beacon of that distinguished fame I had sighed for so long.. & so ardently!

I never felt more real anguish than when I was undecieved on this point. I am not vain naturally & I have still less of the pedant in my composition than self conceit but I confess that during these eight months I never felt myself of more consequence and never had a better opinion of my own talents—In short I was in infinite danger of being as vain as I was inexperienced! During this dangerous period I was from home & the fever of a heated imagination was perhaps increased by the intoxicating gai[e]ties of a watering place Ramsgate where we then were and where I commenced my poem "The Battle of Marathon" now in print!! When we came home one day after having written a page of poetry which I considered models of beauty I ran down stairs to the library to seek Popes Homer in order to compare them that I might enjoy my OWN SUPERIORITY—I can never think of this instance of the intoxication of vanity without smiling at my childish folly & ridiculous vanity—I brought Homer up in triumph & read first my own Poem & afterwards began to compare—I read fifty lines from the glorious Father of the lyre—It was enough.. I felt the whole extent of my own immense & mortifying inferiority—

My first impulse was to throw with mingled feelings of contempt & anguish my composition on the floor—my next to burst into tears! & I wept for an hour and then returned to reason and humility—Since then I have not felt MANY twitches of vanity and my mind has never since been intoxicated by any ridiculous dreams of greatness!!—From this period for a twelvemonth I could find no pleasure in any book but Homer. I read & longed to read again and tho I nearly had it by heart I still found new beauties & fresh enchantments—

At twelve I enjoyed a literary life in all it's pleasures. Metaphysics were my highest delights and after having read a page from Locke my mind not only felt edified but exalted—At this age I was in great danger of becoming the founder of a religion of my own. I revolted at the idea of an established religion—my faith was sincere but my religion was founded solely on the imagination. It was not the deep persuasion of the mild Christian but the wild visions of an enthusiast. I worshipped God heart and soul but I forgot that my prayers should be pure & simple as the Father I adored[.] They were composed extempore & full of figurative & florid apostrophes.

I shall always look back to this time as the happiest of my life[;] my mind was above the frivolous sorrows of childhood when I trusted with enthusiastic faith to His mercy "who only chasteneth whom he loveth"—. . .

ELIZABETH BARRETT BROWNING (LETTER DATE 18 SEPTEMBER 1846)

SOURCE: Barrett Browning, Elizabeth. "Letter to Mary Russell Mitford, September 18, 1846." In *Women of Letters: Selected Letters of Elizabeth Barrett Browning and Mary Russell Mitford,* edited by Meredith B. Raymond and Mary Rose Sullivan, pp. 195-98. Boston: Twayne, 1987.

In the following letter to her close friend Mary Russell Mitford, Browning discusses her elopement with Robert Browning. The letter reflects her unconventional views of love and marriage.

FROM THE AUTHOR

BROWNING RESPONDS TO AN ARTICLE ON "POETESSES" FROM THE JANUARY 1845 *NEW QUARTERLY REVIEW* IN A LETTER TO THE AUTHOR, HENRY CHORLEY

England has had many learned women, not merely readers but writers of the learned languages, in Elizabeth's time and afterwards—women of deeper acquirements than are common now in the greater diffusion of letters: and yet where were the poetesses? The divine breath which seemed to come and go, and, ere it went, filled the land with that crowd of true poets whom we call the old dramatists—why did it never pass, even in the lyrical form, over the lips of a woman? How strange! And can we deny that it was so? I look everywhere for grandmothers and see none. It is not in the filial spirit I am deficient, I do assure you—witness my reverent love of the grandfathers!

Elizabeth Barrett Browning. Excerpt from a letter to Henry Chorley, January 7, 1845. In *Elizabeth Barrett Browning and Robert Browning: Interviews and Recollections,* edited by Martin Garrett, p. 17. New York: St. Martin's, 2000.

My dearest friend I have your letter & your prophecy,—& the latter meets the event like a sword ringing into its scabbard. My dear dearest friend I would sit down by your feet & kiss your hands with many tears, & beseech you to think gently of me, & love me always, & have faith in me that I have struggled to do the right & the generous & not the selfish thing,—though when you read this letter I shall have given to one of the most gifted & admirable of men, a wife unworthy of him. I shall be the wife of Robert Browning. Against *you,..* in allowing you no confidence,.. I have not certainly sinned, I think—so do not look at me with those reproachful eyes. I have made no confidence to any.. not even to my & his beloved friend M[r]. Kenyon—& this advisedly, & in order to spare him the anxiety & the responsibility. It would have been a wrong against him & against you to have told either of you—we were in peculiar circumstances—& to have made you a party, would have exposed you to the whole dreary rain—without the shelter we had—If I had loved you less—dearest Miss Mitford, I could have told you sooner.

And now.. oh, will you be hard on me? will you say.. "This is not well".?

I tell you solemnly that nothing your thoughts can suggest against this act of mine, has been unsuggested by *me* to *him*—He has loved me for nearly two years, & said so at the beginning. I would not listen—I could not believe even. And he has said since, that almost he began to despair of making me believe in the force & stedfastness of his attachment. Certainly I conceived it to be a mere poet's fancy.. an illusion of a confusion between the woman & the poetry. I have seen a little of the way of men in such respects, and I could not see beyond that with my weary, weeping eyes, for long.

How can I tell you on this paper, even if my hands did not tremble as the writing shows, how he persisted & overcame me with such letters, & such words, that you might tread on me like a stone if I had not given myself to him, heart & soul. When I bade him see that I was bruised & broken.. unfit for active duties, incapable of common pleasures.. that I had lost even the usual advantages of youth & good spirits—his answer was, "that with himself also the early freshness of youth had gone by, & that, throughout his season of youth, he had loved no woman at all, nor had believed himself made for any such affection—that he loved now once & for ever—he, knowing himself———That, for my health,.. he had understood, on first seeing me, that I suffered from an accident on the spine of an incurable nature, & that he never could hope to have me stand up before him. He bade me tell him, what, if that imagination had been true, what there was in that truth, calculated to suppress any pure attachment, such as he professed for me? For his part, the wish of his heart had been *then*—that by consenting to be his wife even so, I would admit him to the simple priviledge of sitting by my side two hours a day, as a brother would: he deliberately preferred the realization of *that dream,* to the brightest, excluding me, in this world or any other."

My dear friend, feel for me. It is to your woman's nature that I repeat these words, that they may commend themselves to you & teach you how *I* must have felt in hearing them—I who loved Flush for not hating to be near me.. I, who by a long sorrowfulness & solitude, had sunk into the very ashes of selfhumiliation—Think how I must have felt to have listened to such words from such a man. A man of genius & of miraculous attainments.. but of a heart & spirit beyond them all!———

He overcame me at last. Whether it was that an unusual alikeness of mind.. (the high & the low may be alike in the general features).. a singular closeness of sympathy on a thousand subjects,.. drew him fast to me—or whether it was *love simple*.. which after all is *love proper*.. an unreasonable instinct, accident.. 'falling', as the idiom says.. the truth became obvious that he would be happier with me than apart from me—and I.. why I am only as any other woman in the world, with a heart belonging to her. He is best, noblest———If you knew him, YOU should be the praiser.

I have seen him only & openly in this house, observe—*never elsewhere,* except in the parish church before the two necessary witnesses. We go to Italy.. to Pisa—cross to Havre from Southampton.. pass quickly along the Seine, & through Paris to Orleans—till we are out of hearing of the dreadful sounds behind. An escape from the winter will keep me well & still strengthen me—& in the summer we come back.. if anyone in the world *will* receive us—We go to live a quiet, simple, rational life—to do work "after the pattern in the mount" which we both see.. to write poems & read books, & try to live not in vain & not for vanities—

In the meanwhile, it is in anguish of heart that I think of leaving this house *so*—Oh—a little thread might have bound my hands, from even working at my own happiness—But all the love came from *that side*! on the other—too still it was—not with intention.. I do not say so—yet too still. I was a woman & shall be a wife when you read this letter. It is finished, the struggle is———

As to marriage.. it never was high up in my ideal, even before my illness brought myself so far down. A happy marriage was the happiest condition, I believed vaguely—but *where were the happy marriages*? *I,* for my part, never could have married a common man—and never did any one man whom I have had the honour of hearing talk love, as men talk, lead me to think a quarter of a minute of the possibility of being married by such an one. Then I thought always that a man whom I could love, would never stoop to love me—That was my way of thinking, years ago, in my best days, as a woman's days are counted—& often & often have I been gently upbraided for such romantic fancies—for expecting the grass underfoot to be sky blue, & for not taking M^{r}. A or B or C for the "best possible" whatever might be.

We shall not be rich—but we shall have enough to live out our views of life—& fly from the winters in Italy.

I write on calmly to you—How little this paper represents what is working within in the intervals of a sort of *stupour.*

Feel for me if not with me my dear dear friend—*He* says that we shall justify by our lives this act,—which may & must appear to many,.. as I *say*.. wilful & rash. People will say that he is mad, & I, *bad*—with my long traditions & associations with all manner of sickness. Yet God judges, who sees the root of things—And I believe that no woman with a heart, could have done otherwise.. much otherwise—You do not know *him*.

May God bless you—I must end. Try to think of me gently—& if you can bear to write to me, let me hear.. at Orleans—Poste Restante.

Here is the truth—I *could not* meet you & part with you now, face to face.

. . . . .

Your most affectionate

EBB

GENERAL COMMENTARY

KAY MOSER (ESSAY DATE 1985)

SOURCE: Moser, Kay. "The Victorian Critics' Dilemma: What to Do With a Talented Poetess?" *Victorians Institute Journal* 13 (1985): 59-66.

In the following essay, Moser surveys the challenges Browning faced in being accepted as a woman and poet in the Victorian era.

And whosoever writes good poetry,
Looks just to art.
He will not suffer the best critic known
To step into his sunshine of free thought
And self-absorbed conception and exact
An inch-long swerving of the Holy lines.[1]

These lines from ***Aurora Leigh*** express Elizabeth Barrett's determination to remain true to a personal vision of her poetic art regardless of the critical response. Yet no author, least of all a poet, could afford to alienate the critics totally, for critics were the shapers of the Victorian audience; they were the gateway to that audience. A poetess was particularly dependent on good reviews, for even a single bad review could damn her work to an undeserved obscurity.

The arrival of Elizabeth Barrett on the poetic scene created special problems, for critics of this age were convinced that full poetic power simply could not exist in a woman. Thomas De Quincey had expressed the attitude of the age when he wrote: "'Woman, sister, there are some things which you do not execute as well as your brother, man; no, nor ever will. Pardon me, if I doubt whether you will ever produce a great poet from your choirs, or a Mozart, or a Phidias, or a Michael Angelo, or a great scholar. If you can create yourselves into any of these great creators, why have you not?'"[2] DeQuincey's charge raised major questions for Victorian critics: could womankind produce a great poet, and had this creation appeared in Elizabeth Barrett? However, in spite of the natural inclination of critics to dispute, all admitted that she was the greatest woman poet who had ever lived, "our single Shakespearean woman."[3] But Elizabeth Barrett refused to be judged by the lower standards habitually applied to women poets. In ***Aurora Leigh*** she makes her dislike of gender-based criticism quite clear as she insists that women[4]

. . . never can be satisfied with praise
Which men give women when they judge a
book
Not as men's work, but as mere woman's work,
Expressing the comparative respect
Which means the absolute scorn. "Oh, excellent!
What grace! what facile turns! what fluent
sweeps!
What delicate discernment—almost thought!
The book does honour to the sex, we hold.
Among our female authors we make room
For this fair writer, and congratulate
The country that produces in these times
Such women, competent to—spell."

Elizabeth Barrett's work was obviously too good and too provocative to be dismissed as merely pretty woman's verse. Thus, the dilemma of the Victorian critics emerged, what is one to do with a talented female poet who refused to be judged as a woman in an age which so clearly relegated women and their creative work to a lesser position on the aesthetic scale of value?

A review of Victorian criticism reveals divergent opinions on this issue. The few times when Elizabeth Barrett is judged by the same standards as a male counterpart, she is often considered the equal of such poets as Wordsworth and Tennyson.[5] However, when her work is blamed, that criticism often takes the form of two accusations, one of which is definitely gender-based. She is frequently denounced for being too masculine because of her masculine subjects. Also she is charged with choosing topics, specifically contemporary social and political topics, that are inappropriate for poetry.

It is difficult for the modern mind to place itself in a Victorian perspective and imagine itself damning a woman poet for "manliness." In fact, it is nonsensical to attempt to evaluate a woman's work *in terms of her male peers* and at the same time demand that she be distinctly feminine. And yet, this is the contradictory standard, often unconscious of its bias, that was applied to Elizabeth Barrett. Readers were told that "she is all that the highest feminine intellect can attain to. Thoughtful, philosophic, vigorous and tender, with a passion and an earnestness that carry her right on to her object and sustain her throughout."[6] However, in the same paragraph she is accused of "the effort to stand, not on a pedestal beside man, but actually to occupy his place" and in so doing commits what the critic judges to be grave errors. He writes, "She is occasionally coarse in expression and unfeminine in thought; and utters what, if they be even truths, are so conveyed that we would hesitate to present them to the eye of the readers of her own sex." And which of Elizabeth Barrett's poems is being described as "almost a closed volume for her own sex"?[7] It is ***Aurora Leigh,*** and the "unfeminine thoughts" include the stories of two women: one, a poetess who commits the unpardonable sin of preferring a profession to marriage, and the second, a woman who is drugged, raped and bears an illegitimate child. The critic warns Elizabeth Barrett and her sex that: "Woman must be ever true to her womanly instincts if she would be the meet helper as well as companion of man."[8]

Aurora Leigh incited still another critic to attempt defining woman's role in the creation of poetry, and his comments are noticeably at odds with Elizabeth Barrett's performance, a performance he claims transgresses "the bounds of delicate feeling" in its "endeavour to show masculine vigour."[9] He admits that women have "the most fundamental qualities required for poetic composition" particularly "the realizing imagination . . . which causes us to pity and to love. . . ."[10] Where women go wrong, he insists, is invading the intellectual realm rather than limiting themselves to the emotional sphere where their talents lie. And further, women poets, and Elizabeth Barrett in particular, have gone wrong "by attempting descriptions of those feelings and passions which their sex is supposed neither to possess or even be acquainted with."[11]

What specifically did Victorian critics deem to be "coarse and indelicate" lines, lines that were too "masculine" to have come from a woman? The critics' favorite choice for indicating the "indelicacy" and "masculine vigor" in Elizabeth Barrett's verse comes again from ***Aurora Leigh***:

> Never flinch,
> But still, unscrupulously epic, catch
> Upon the burning lava of a song,
> The full-veined, heaving, double-breasted Age:
> That, when the next shall come, the men of that
> May touch the impress with reverent hand, and say,
> "Behold,—behold the paps we have all sucked!"[12]

Such a passage would surely escape critical censorship today at least for "indelicacy", but in an age that could not even bring itself to use the word "leg" in polite conversation, such writing was considered shockingly explicit. As one critic writes, "Lines such as these doth ill become a lady to have written, and only excite feelings of disgust when they are read."[13]

The disapproval and even anger of the critics flared when Elizabeth Barrett published ***Poems Before Congress*** in 1860. This time she was accused of being unfeminine not because of her indelicate expressions but because she had written on a political topic. *Blackwood's Edinburgh Magazine* declared, "We are strongly of opinion that, for the peace and welfare of society, it is a good and wholesome rule that women should not interfere with politics."[14] Begging to be defended from "a domestic female partisan," the writer outlines the accepted Victorian view of woman's sphere. Women may write verse as long as "they warble like larks in the firmament . . . or coo like pigeons in spring" or they may write of the finer arts of culinary affairs. When women confine their writing to these spheres, the critics

> listen, read, comment, perpend, and approve without the slightest feeling that they have in any degree overstepped the pale of propriety. And when we see them engaged in deeds of true charity—in visiting the sick, relieving the distressed, providing food for the hungry and clothing for the naked, or praying at the lonely deathbed,—we acknowledge that it is no vain figure of poetry, no fanciful association of thought, that likens women to angels![15]

But from politics women must be banned because "[to] reason they will not listen; to argument they are utterly impervious."[16] Specifically, ***Poems Before Congress*** was criticized for being bad poetry, blind politics, and grossly unfair to England and English feeling. And once again Elizabeth Barrett was accused to being "masculine," this time for writing politically.

Thus, some critics thought political issues too "masculine" a subject for a woman poet. Still others considered all contemporary social and political issues inappropriate for *any* poet—man or woman. And this critical stance Elizabeth Barrett repeatedly violated, most notably in ***Casa Guidi Windows, Aurora Leigh*** and ***Poems Before Congress.*** In fact, in ***Aurora Leigh,*** she writes emphatically that the chief aim of a poet should be to illustrate the age in which s/he lives. She states:

> But poets should
> Exert a double vision; should have eyes
> To see near things as comprehensively
> As if afar they took their point of sight,
> And distant things, as intimately deep,
> As if they touched them. Let us strive for this.
>
> Nay, if there's room for poets in this world
> A little overgrown (I think there is),
> Their sole work is to represent the age,
> Their age, not Charlemagne's,—this live throbbing age,
> That brawls, cheats, maddens, calculates, aspires,
> And spends more passion, more heroic heat,
> Betwixt the mirrors of its drawing-rooms,
> Than Roland with his knights, at Roncesvalles.[17]

Claiming the contemporary as a fit subject for her poetry put Elizabeth Barrett into direct conflict with a number of her major critics. In its review of ***Aurora Leigh,*** *Blackwood's Edinburgh Magazine* chastized her, explaining that her philosophy "would lead to a total sacrifice of the ideal." They continue

> It is not the province of the poet to depict things as they are, but so to refine and purify as to purge out the grosser matter, and this he cannot do if he attempts to give a faithful picture of his own times. For in order to be faithful, he must necessarily include much which is abhorrent to art, and revolting to the taste. . . . All poetical characters, all poetical situations must be idealised. Whilst dealing with a remote subject the poet can easily effect this, but not so when he brings forward characters of his own age.[18]

The *London Quarterly Review* echoed the same criticism four years later in 1861 when reviewing the newly released ***Poems Before Congress.*** They described the poems as "a perfect shriek"[19] when she expresses her opinions about Italian politics. It should be noted that in ***Poems Before Congress,*** Elizabeth Barrett infuriated many critics with the stance she took in favor of Louis Napoleon, and much of the insistence that she stay away from political topics probably resulted from this reaction.

However, not all critics agreed that political and social issues were inappropriate poetic topics. The *Chambers Edinburgh Journal* insisted "that the age we live in is not destitute of themes for the poet when the inspiration of genius comes to mould the modern event into the poetic thought."[20] After reminding its readers that women have been able to write only "poetry of the affections" and that "In the higher walks of poetry—such as the dramatic—few women have won a reputation,"[21] the critic applauds Elizabeth Barrett for her ***Casa Guidi Windows.***

> Apart from the fine poetic fire which burns in many parts of the ***Casa Guidi Windows,*** the views which it gives us of Italian politics are clear and interesting. We do not usually look to poems for such things, least of all do we expect to find them in poetry written by a lady, but as we have said, Mrs. Browning's sympathies are not such as are confined within the sphere of feminine likings and dislikings. She has a great deal of masculine energy, and her writings are often pervaded by a spirit of political zeal not common in those even of the other sex.[22]

In the same complimentary vein, *Fraser's Magazine* applauds ***Casa Guidi Windows*** for being "a most wise and beautiful and noble poem,—a poem with a purpose and that purpose carried out in speech, as few are in these days of purposeless song twittering."[23]

Some critics accepted modern themes in poetry but felt the need to justify their stance. Speaking of ***Casa Guidi Windows,*** the *Athenaeum* explains that it is acceptable for Elizabeth Barrett to write of contemporary themes because "the familiarities of the present have not hid from her the spiritual truth which underlies them."[24] Furthermore, the application of a high intelligence to contemporary events transforms them into appropriate poetic subjects.

> In dealing with these "modern instances," Mrs. Browning has invested them with a tone of ideal grandeur which gives them in point of poetic effect all the remoteness of antiquity. We could cite no better example of the truth that the distance between the common and the ideal is not that between the past and the present, but that between objects as perceived by the senses and objects as interpreted by the mind.[25]

The blame that fell upon ***Aurora Leigh*** is representative of the criticism Elizabeth Barrett was to receive for much of her work. There were critics who damned her for what they deemed "unfeminine ideas" and "indelicate images." Others objected to her honest confrontation of the social issues of the day, issues they considered inappropriate for poetry or women. Specifically, in ***Aurora Leigh*** they objected to the independence and worldliness of Aurora and were appalled at the inclusion of the seduction of Marian Earle. However, other critics applauded Elizabeth for the content of ***Aurora Leigh*** and considered it appropriate poetical material. For example, in commenting on the story of Marian Earle and its depiction of the results of class oppression and class suffering, the *Dublin University Magazine* declared: ". . . the writer who exposes to public view these gangrenes that eat into and corrupt the heart of the social body, discharges a high duty to humanity."[26] Moreover, the New York *Daily Times* describes ***Aurora Leigh*** as a "thoughtful, profound reflection on the problems of society and individual life. In these Mrs. Browning is no visionary, nor is she that terrible thing, a didactic professor in petticoats. She has much to say. . . ."[27] Truly, Victorian critics could not agree on how to receive Elizabeth Barrett's poetry. In several ways she was charting new courses for critics to follow.

The quality of Elizabeth Barrett's poetical works produced difficulties for many Victorian critics because she exploded the received myths they had perpetuated about the poetical abilities of women, and she enlarged the accepted spheres of poetry. Defying Victorian judgements of women's abilities, she refused to limit herself to the superficial, emotional lyrics that were considered women's poetical sphere and instead tackled serious intellectual, social, political, and philosophical issues of the day forthrightly, not as a Lady Poet but as an intelligent, human thinker who asked to be judged as such. De Quincey had asked the question of women, "If you *can* create yourselves into any of these great creators, why have you not?" He expected only embarrassed silence as his answer. When Elizabeth Barrett appeared on the poetic scene, the question became moot.

Notes

1. Elizabeth Barrett Browning, *Aurora Leigh,* in *The Poetical Works of Elizabeth Barrett Browning,* ed. Ruth M. Adams (Boston: Houghton Mifflin Co., 1974), Book V, 11. 251-257.
2. Peter Bayne, "Studies of English Authors," *Literary World,* New Series 19, (June 6, 1879), 360.
3. Bayne, p. 360.
4. *Aurora Leigh,* Book II, 11. 232-243.
5. Bayne, p. 360.
6. *"Aurora Leigh," Dublin University Magazine,* 49 (April 1857), 470.
7. *Dublin University Magazine,* p. 470.
8. *Dublin University Magazine,* p. 470.
9. E. L. Bryans, "Characteristics of Women's Poetry," *Dark Blue,* 2, No. 10 (Dec. 1871), 490.
10. Bryans, p. 484.
11. Bryans, p. 490.
12. *Aurora Leigh,* Book V, 11. 214-219.
13. Bryans, p. 491.
14. "Poetic Aberrations," *Blackwood's Edinburgh Magazine,* 87, No. 534 (April 1860), 490.
15. "Poetic Aberrations," p. 490.
16. "Poetic Aberrations," p. 490.
17. *Aurora Leigh* Book V, 11. 184-188; 200-207.
18. William Aytown, "Mrs. Barrett Browning—*Aurora Leigh," Blackwood's Edinburgh Magazine,* 81, No. 961 (Jan. 1857), 34-35.
19. "Mrs. Browning—*Poems Before Congress," London Quarterly Review* 16, No. 32 (July 1861), 405.
20. "The Poetry of Elizabeth Barrett Browning," *Chamber's Edinburgh Journal,* n.d., found in the Meynell Collection (Item No. 80), Armstrong Browning Library, Baylor University, Waco, Texas, 362.
21. "The Poetry of Elizabeth Barrett Browning," p. 361.
22. "The Poetry of Elizabeth Barrett Browning," p. 361.
23. "This Year's Song-Crop," *Fraser's Magazine.* 44, No. 264 (Dec. 1851), 619.
24. "Reviews; *Casa Guidi Windows," The Athenaeum,* No. 1232 (June 7, 1851), 598.
25. "Reviews: *Casa Guidi Windows,"* p. 597.
26. *"Aurora Leigh," Dublin University Magazine,* 49, No. 292 (April 1857), 464.
27. *"Aurora Leigh.* Mrs. Elizabeth Barrett Browning's New Poems," *New York Daily Times,* 9 Dec. 1856). Meynell Collection (Item No. 287), Armstrong Browning Library, Baylor University.

REBECCA STOTT (ESSAY DATE 2003)

SOURCE: Stott, Rebecca. "'How Do I Love Thee?': Love and Marriage." In *Elizabeth Barrett Browning,* pp. 134-55. London, England: Pearson Education Limited, 2003.

In the following essay, Stott traces Browning's philosophy of love through its important influences and into her poetry, particularly Aurora Leigh *and* Sonnets from the Portuguese.

On January 10, 1845, Robert Browning wrote to Elizabeth Barrett for the first time, after reading her volume of poetry, *Poems.* He was a little-known thirty-two-year-old poet and playwright, she was an internationally renowned poet, an invalid, and a thirty-nine-year-old spinster. 'I love your verses with all my heart, dear Miss Barrett—I do, as I say, love these verses with all my heart,' the letter said. Over the course of the next twenty months, they would write each other close to six hundred letters—one of the greatest literary correspondences of all time. The pair's last letter was exchanged on September 18, 1846, the night before the two left for a trip to Italy, and two weeks after their secret marriage. Their romance,

FROM THE AUTHOR

BROWNING DESCRIBES HER YOUNG SELF, HER AMBITIONS AS A POET, AND HER CONTEMPT FOR STEREOTYPICAL FEMININITY

Beth intended to be very much in love when she was fifteen,—but she did not mean to go so far as to be married, even at sixteen. She meant however to be in love, & she settled that her lover's name sh^{d}. be Henry;—if it were not L^{d}. Byron. Her lover was to be a poet in any case—and Beth was inclined to believe that he w^{d}. be L^{d}. Byron.

But Beth was a poet herself—& there was the reigning thought—No woman was ever before such a poet as she w^{d}. be. As Homer was among men, so w^{d}. she be among women—she w^{d}. be the feminine of Homer. Many persons w^{d}. be obliged to say that she was a little taller than Homer if anything. When she grew up she w^{d}. wear men's clothes, & live in a Greek island, the sea melting into turquoises all around it. She w^{d}. teach the islanders the ancient Greek, & they should all talk there of the old glories in the real Greek sunshine, with the right ais & ois—Or she w^{d}. live in a cave on Parnassus mount, and feed upon cresses & Helicon water, & Beth might have said Grace after the sweet diet of that dream.

Poor Beth had one great misfortune. She was born a woman. Now she despised nearly all the women in the world except Ma^{dme}. de Stael—She could not abide their littlenesses called delicacies, their pretty headaches, & soft mincing voices, their nerves & affectations. She thought to herself that no man was vain of being weaker than another man, but rather ashamed. She thought that a woman's weakness, she sh^{d}. not be vain of therefore, but ashamed. One word Beth hated in her soul.. & the word was "feminine". Beth thanked her gods that she was not & never w^{d}. be feminine.

Elizabeth Barrett Browning. Excerpt from an untitled, unpublished essay. In *The Brownings' Correspondence*, Vol. 1. Edited by Philip Kelley and Ronald Hudson, p. 361. Winfield, Kans.: Wedgestone Press, 1984.

which she would eventually credit with saving her life, lasted for fifteen years and spawned some of the world's most beautiful poetry.

(www.historychannel.com/exhibits/valentine/browningss.html)

This extract comes from an internet site dedicated to the history of Valentine's Day. The story of the Brownings' marriage and Barrett Browning's ***Sonnets from the Portuguese*** have a powerful presence on wedding and romance internet sites, pages usually studded or embossed with cupids, roses and flowers, for the ***Sonnets from the Portuguese*** rank highly in the early twenty-first-century canon of poems-to-be-read-at-weddings. The Brownings' union has become memorialised as one of the nineteenth century's greatest love stories (see Lootens, 1996a: 116-57) and their poetry has become 'exhibit A in almost any discussion of nineteenth-century romance' (Pinch, 1998: 7). Yet both Robert and Elizabeth Barrett Browning were fascinated as poets not only by the beauty, transcendence and pleasure of love itself, but also by the problems of its expression, by its institutionalisation in marriage, by its relationship to 'darker' emotions such as hate, obsession and possession, and by its relationship to power.

In this chapter I will examine Barrett Browning's love poetry, her attempt to express her thoughts about love and her struggle with what we might call the 'epistemology of love' (how do we *know* the loved person; how do we *know* love; how do we feel except through an already mediated set of literary tropes?). I will also explore Barrett Browning's treatment of the ethics of love (what is the role of thinking in love; what conditions justify giving up the self to another?), and the sociology of love (what happens to men and women when their love becomes institutionalised in marriage?). And I will show that, for a woman who has become an icon of romance and of idealised marriage, Barrett Browning was often fiercely critical and political in her analysis of marriage as an institution.

Love as Heaven

In a letter written to her sister soon after the publication of ***Aurora Leigh,*** Barrett Browning mused on the fact that people were talking about the poem as her 'gospel' and explained that the spiritual truths were not her own but were based on the teaching of the eighteenth-century Swedish philosopher and mystic Emmanuel Swedenborg:

> I was helped to it—did not originate it—& was tempted much (by a natural feeling of honesty) to say so in the poem, & was withheld by nothing except a conviction that the naming of the name of Swedenborg, that great seer into the two worlds, would have utterly destroyed any hope of general acceptance & consequent utility . . . most humbly I have used [Swedenborg's 'sublime truths'] as I could. My desire is, that the weakness in me, may not hinder that influence.
>
> (Letter to Arabella Barrett, Dec 10-18, 1856; cited in Reynolds, 1996: 339)

Emmanuel Swedenborg (1688-1772) was the son of a professor of theology at Upsala who was driven to seek a scientific explanation of the universe and of the relation of the soul to the body and the finite to the infinite. He experienced a series of visions in the 1740s upon which he based a series of theosophical and visionary writings. Followers of Swedenborg's theosophical interpretations of the Bible formed the 'New Church' in London in 1778. Swedenborg influenced the works of many nineteenth-century writers, including the poets William Blake and Samuel Taylor Coleridge, the American philosopher and poet Ralph Waldo Emerson and the American feminist Margaret Fuller. His writings would also leave a mark on the writings of Honore Balzac, Charles Baudelaire, William Butler Yeats, August Strindberg and the philosopher William James.

Elizabeth Barrett, always hungry for philosophical and spiritual ideas but also temperamentally wary of dogma, approached Swedenborg's ideas from the earliest reading with some scepticism, as she wrote to Mary Mitford in 1842:

> Do you know anything of Swedenborgianism? Swedenborg was a mad genius—there are beautiful things in his writings, but manifold absurdities,—and more darkness I do assure you though you may scarcely find it creditable, than in mine. Anthropomorphism, universal in application, is the principal doctrine. God is man in form & spirit,—incarnate essentially in Christ, a manifestation of God as He is—only one Person being recognized. Moreover all the angels are men in form & spirit,—and Heaven itself is in the shape of a man—that being the perfect form. The text insisted on is of course 'Let us make man in our image'—and then Scripture is preached away, dreamed away, fancied away into thin air—only, you know, Swedenbourg [sic] was inspired himself, & when a man says that's he's inspired, what can anybody else say?
>
> (*BC* [*The Browning's Correspondence*] 6:128)

Yet she was right to identify the 'gospel' of ***Aurora Leigh*** as having its origins in Swedenborg's writings, for Swedenborg's central claim that 'The joys of heaven and eternal happiness are from love and wisdom and the conjunction of these in usefulness' (Swedenborg, 1995: 10) is the vision expressed by both Aurora and Romney at the end of the verse-novel:

> The world waits
> For help. Beloved, let us love so well,
> Our work shall still be better for our love,
> And still our love be sweeter for our work,
> And both commended, for the sake of each,
> By all true workers and true lovers born.
>
> (***AL*** [***Aurora Leigh***] 9:923-8)

Swedenborg taught that God was infinite love and infinite wisdom and that from the Godhead emanated both the material and the spiritual world. Because the two worlds had a common origin in God, they were connected through a series of 'correspondences'. Spiritual truths are therefore embodied in the material world. He also believed that the original divine order had been perverted by human beings who, using their free will, had gradually severed the connection between the spiritual and material worlds. The intervention of Christ had therefore restored order to the universe by creating a new external pathway through which humans could approach God, and the Second Coming would be accomplished, not in the flesh, but rather through an intellectual and spiritual revolution, which Swedenborg saw as being achieved through his own writings and through his revelation of the hidden truths of the Bible.

In ***Aurora Leigh,*** Aurora comes to a Swedenborgian understanding that love, rather than art, is what 'makes heaven' (***AL*** 9:659). The poem moves towards a full revelation of Swedenborgian principles as Romney and Aurora reconcile their differences in a passionate declaration of the three central Swedenborgian ideas of love, wisdom and use, couched in the vision of a New Jerusalem and in language that borrows heavily from Swedenborg's writings. Thus Barrett Browning casts Romney and Aurora as workers in an intellectual and emotional revolution which will transform society by opening the roads between the material and spiritual worlds. Within Swedenborgian teaching love and wisdom become manifest in *use*; indeed, 'Love and wisdom without use are not anything; they are only ideal entities; nor do they become real until they are in use' (Swedenborg, 1971: 875). 'Use is the doing of good from love by means of wisdom. Use is goodness itself' (Swedenborg, 1995: 183). So Aurora, always dedicated to her art, comes to understand the superior power of love in Book 9, at the point that she declares her love for Romney:

Art symbolises heaven, but Love is God
And makes heaven.

(*AL* 9:658-9)

When she and Romney do embrace finally in Book 9, their embrace, though described in erotically physical terms, is also a spiritual one. Love and wisdom unite. The persistent crossing and bridging of the material and spiritual worlds is both the subject and the mission of the poem for, in Aurora's words, the role of the poet is expressed in Swedenborgian terms: 'to keep up open roads / Betwixt the seen and the unseen,—bursting through / The best of your conventions with his best' (2:468-70). In this scene of union the material and spiritual worlds are fused through their bodies and souls:

Could I see his face,
I wept so? Did I drop against his breast,
Or did his arms constrain me? were my cheeks
Hot, overflooded, with my tears, or his?
And which of our two large explosive hearts
So shook me? That I know not. There were
words
That broke in utterance.. melted, in the fire,—
Embrace, that was convulsion,.. then a kiss
As long and silent as the ecstatic night,
And deep, deep, shuddering breaths, which
meant beyond
Whatever could be told by word or kiss.

(*AL* 9:714-24)

While the communion between Aurora and Romney is said to be beyond understanding and beyond words, communion there is nonetheless:

The intimate presence carrying in itself
Complete communication, as with souls
Who, having put the body off, perceive
Through simply being. Thus,-twas granted me
To know he loved me to the depth and height
Of such large natures . . .

(*AL* 9:749-54)

This is a description of physical and spiritual union much influenced by Swedenborg's ideas on conjugal love:

The Lord's Divine providence is most specific and most universal in connection with marriages and in its operation in marriages, because all delights of heaven flow from the delights of conjugial love, like sweet waters from a gushing spring. It is therefore provided that conjugial pairs be born, and they are raised and continually prepared for their marriages under the Lord's guidance, neither the boy nor the girl being aware of it. Then, after a period of time, the girl—now a marriageable young woman—and the boy—now a young man ready to marry—meet somewhere, as though by fate, and notice each other. And they immediately recognise, as if by a kind of instinct, that they are a match, thinking to themselves as from a kind of inner dictate, the young man, 'she is mine,' and the young woman, 'he is mine.' Later, after this thought has for some time become settled in the minds of each, they deliberately talk about it together and pledge themselves to each other in marriage. We say as though by fate, by instinct and as from a kind of dictate, when we mean by Divine providence, because when one is unaware that it is Divine providence, that is how it appears. For the Lord unveils their inner similarities so that they notice each other.

(Swedenborg, 1995: 20)

The portrayal of the love of Romney and Aurora as a love which is inevitable (preordained) yet postponed until both are spiritually ready for union, is one aspect of the poem that may have had its origin in the ideas of Swedenborg. But while Swedenborg symbolises conjugal union as the sweet waters of a gushing spring, Barrett Browning's metaphor is characteristically more violent. She describes Aurora and Romney's embrace as an overflowing, but it is also a convulsion, a melting and an explosion. The metaphors of sexual desire and spiritual union are geological: it is like an earthquake, a volcano and a flood all at once, part of the geological violence and transformation of the old that will result in the New Jerusalem and new landscape envisaged at the end of the book.

Yet, characteristically for Barrett Browning, the poem also challenges Swedenborgian teachings at the same time as asserting them. Aurora begins to wonder about the implication of believing that love makes heaven—the implication for women in particular. After all, she has loved Romney for some time. Should she have refused him as she did when he proposed all those years ago? In particular, she worries that denying him then meant that she has been in a fallen state since, fallen from the heaven that she might have made:

Art symbolises heaven, but Love is God
And makes heaven. I, Aurora, fell from mine.
I would not be a woman like the rest,
A simple woman who believes in love
And owns the right of love because she loves,
And, hearing she's beloved, is satisfied
With what contents God: I must analyse,
Confront, and question; just as if a fly
Refused to warm itself in any sun
Till such was *in leone* [a constellation of the stars
which signifies late summer]

(*AL* 9:658-67)

As Sandra Gilbert and Susan Gubar point out (1979: 577), the imagery of this passage reveals significant contradictions in Aurora's attitude to love. Aurora claims that her options as a woman are either to make heaven (to love) or to fall from heaven (not to love), yet being in love is also like being a fly basking in sunshine—satisfied, contented, unthinking, drunk with warmth and pleasure. Aurora claims that, in declining Romney's offer of love, she had refused to be 'a woman like the rest, / A simple woman' because instead of just accepting the gift of love at that point, she had insisted on analysing, confronting, questioning it. This refusal had resulted in her fall from heaven but had also ensured that she did not become a fly basking in the sunshine. The implication hangs for a moment that perhaps if she had been less proud when Romney had first proposed, more honest in her own feelings, the two lovers would not have had to suffer. Yet at the same time, the drama of the poem is created by that refusal and by the period of their joint exile from the 'heaven' of requited love, a period in which Aurora fulfils her vocation as a poet. It is also a period in which Romney is transformed; blinded, he comes to see Aurora not as a help-meet on a joint mission of reform, but as a woman and poet with a soul. Aurora's acceptance of love at the end of the poem is made possible precisely because they have both entered this struggle to understand, analyse and confront their feelings about each other.

Thinking Love

Love is idealised in the poem as what makes heaven, but *unthinking* love is disparaged. Earlier in the poem, at the point at which Aurora refuses to marry Romney in Book 2, for instance, she offers an analysis of women who are prepared to settle for any kind of love, unquestioningly:

> Women of a softer mood,
> Surprised by men when scarcely awake to life,
> Will sometimes only hear the first word, love,
> And catch up with it any kind of work,
> Indifferent, so that dear love go with it.
> I do not blame such women, though, for love,
> They pick much oakum . . .
>
> (***AL*** 2:443-9)

Picking oakum refers to the practice of untwisting and unpicking old rope to be mixed with tar and used for ship's caulking. It was tedious and backbreaking work which made the fingers bleed, work often given to convicts and the inmates of workhouses. Barrett Browning claims therefore that where love is acted upon by women in unthinking ways, a life of enforced servitude will often follow. Although the poem endorses the work ethic, it does not endorse the domestic slavery which so often accompanied marriage. Aurora is, after all, refusing not Romney's love, but Romney's offer of marriage as *work*; Romney was, she tells him scornfully, looking for a fellow-worker, not a lover. So Aurora's claims that she had been wrong not to yield to love earlier are undermined by such alternative reflections and knowledge. As she describes the proposal scene, Aurora suddenly assumes a retrospective view of Romney's proposal and her refusal, wondering for a moment what would have happened if she had accepted his offer of love:

> If he had loved,
> Ah, loved me, with that retributive face,..
> I might have been a common woman now
> And happier, less known and less left alone,
> Perhaps a better woman after all,
> With chubby children hanging on my neck
> To keep me low and wise.
>
> (***AL*** 2:511-17)

These tensions between love represented as an entry into servitude and/or unthinking complacency, and love as a Swedenborgian 'heaven' are shown to be tensions between being a 'common woman' and a dissenting independent-minded, *thinking* one, as Aurora is. For love is both a divine condition to be aspired to, as she discovers, and also one that at least potentially represents an obstacle to her own dissenting selfhood and to her ambitions to write. Had she said 'yes' when Romney first proposed, her life plot would have been a different one.

So while Barrett Browning endorses, even preaches, Swedenborgian principles about love as that which 'makes heaven' in ***Aurora Leigh,*** she constantly casts these 'truths' within the social and political contexts that bear on women's lives. **'Sonnet 22'** of ***Sonnets from the Portuguese*** also shows her questioning Swedenborgian doctrines, exploring the relative benefits of the earthly/material and the divine/spiritual worlds as a place 'to love in'. In this poem male and female lovers, perfectly unified in love, transcend the material plane and turn into eroticised angels, their wings on fire. Barrett describes this process of angelic transformation and transcendence and then stops it abruptly with her injunction to the lover to 'think'. This monosyllabic imperative in the middle of the poem forms a 'volta' or turning point (interestingly a volta which arrives half a line earlier than it would be expected within a Petrarchan sonnet and so takes us by surprise). At this point, having raised these two soul/angels in erotic rapture, she brings them sharply down to earth again. At least on earth they will be left alone, she says, and not be pressed upon by other angels, for the 'contrarious moods of men' recoil from pure spirits. At least on earth there will be a secluded place to 'love in' even though (and perhaps *because*) that space is rounded by 'darkness and the death-hour'.

> When our two souls stand up erect and strong,
> Face to face, silent, drawing nigh and nigher,
> Until the lengthening wings break into fire
> At either curvèd point,—what bitter wrong
> Can the earth do to us, that we should not long
> Be here contented? Think. In mounting higher,
> The angels would press on us and aspire
> To drop some golden orb of perfect song
> Into our deep, dear silence. Let us stay
> Rather on earth, Belovèd,—where the unfit
> Contrarious moods of men recoil away
> And isolate pure spirits, and permit
> A place to stand and love in for a day,
> With darkness and the death-hour rounding it.
>
> ('**Sonnet 22**')

Angels, so often disembodied and androgynous in Western art, are given tangible, heavy, erotic bodies here. Barrett describes souls as bodies, seraphic bodies which have their feet on the earth: 'When our two souls *stand up* erect and strong' (emphasis mine). Instead of casting souls as ineffable, insubstantial, shadowy presences, Barrett Browning fully embodies them, beautifully describing, for instance, the delicate curve and lengthening of the angels' wings. By doing so she challenges established binaries between the body and soul and sets up a 'correspondence' between the spiritual and material worlds. So while on the one hand the poem questions the Swedenborgian privileging of the spiritual plane over the material one by reasserting the worth of earthly love, it reconciles that tension by bringing the material and spiritual into correspondence. The romantic sentiments of mutually enjoined bodies and souls, of love as heaven and as a revelation of divine truth may sound clichéd to a contemporary reader, but for Barrett Browning it was part of a philosophical and theological system of considerable rigour and complexity.

The Epistemology of Love

Dorothy Mermin and Angela Leighton have both attended to the problem of reading the ***Sonnets from the Portuguese*** too reductively as direct autobiographical expressions of sincerity (Leighton, 1986; Mermin, 1986). Mermin instead emphasises the sonnet sequence's 'emotional and intellectual complexity, the richness of reference, the elaborate and ingenious conceits, and the subtle ways in which images are used both for their emotional power and to carry an argument' (145). It is this intertwining of emotional and intellectual enquiry, a quest to *understand* as well as *feel* love, that characterises these poems. In this respect the ***Sonnets*** reveal a philosophical concern with the 'epistemology of love'—the relationship between love and knowledge, and the ethics of love—what is the role of thinking and reflection in romantic love: is it inimical to feeling or an integral part of it?

I have already claimed that Barrett Browning in ***Aurora Leigh*** idealises love but not unthinking love. Her love poetry is driven by the same concerns as Aurora's: 'I must analyse, / Confront and question' and the ***Sonnets*** are full of this concern to know, measure and define love. The most famous line, of course, is 'How do I love thee? Let me count the ways'. As Adela Pinch points out (Pinch, 1998: 7), the first verb of '**Sonnet 1**' and therefore of the whole set of poems is 'thought': 'I thought,' the speaker begins, 'once how Theocritus had sung'. The poet/speaker mocks herself here as the contemplative musing poet who while thinking about love, becomes aware of a mystic shape moving behind her who draws her backward by the hair:

> And a voice said in mastery, while I strove,—
> 'Guess now who holds thee?'—'Death,' I said.
> But there,
> The silver answer rang,—'Not Death, but Love'.
>
> ('**Sonnet 1**', ll.12-14)

This concern with the role of thinking in love echoes Aurora's musings in ***Aurora Leigh*** about whether she was right to have refused Romney's love. Barrett seems to be suggesting in this opening sonnet that the overcontemplative poet can risk losing heaven (love), yet the *unthinking* lover risks being turned into the 'common woman' who settles unquestioningly for the first declaration of love. The project of the sequence of sonnets is to work at that paradox—to integrate thinking and feeling.

Secondly, as Pinch points out, the sequence as a whole is obsessed with:

> spatial relations, with questions of scale and size, with measuring which of the two lovers is greater, smaller, higher, lower, nearer, or further than the other [and that this is] a symptom of the poem's meditation, on a more phenomenological level, on what it might mean to have a person, literally, in one's mind. What, Barrett Browning wants to know, does it mean to turn a person into a thought?
>
> (Pinch, 1998: 8)

Pinch argues that the poems question the ethics of such meditations by dramatising the conflicts between thinking, knowing and loving, with these conflicts coming to a head in '**Sonnet 29**,' where the poet is once again struck by self-consciousness about her own thinking:

> I think of thee!—my thoughts do twine and bud
> About thee, as will vines, about a tree,

Put out broad leaves, and soon there's nought to see
Except the straggling green which hides the wood.
Yet, O my palm-tree, be it understood
I will not have my thoughts instead of thee
Who art dearer, better! Rather, instantly
Renew thy presence; as a strong tree should,
Rustle thy boughs and set thy trunk all bare,
And let these bands of greenery which insphere thee
Drop heavily down—burst, shattered, everywhere!
Because, in this deep joy to see and hear thee
And breathe within thy shadow a new air,
I do not think of thee—I am too near thee.

('**Sonnet 29**')

In this extended metaphor, the speaker's thoughts are cast as the vines about the tree that, by an excess of budding and growth, soon conceal the tree itself and threaten to strangle it (there is also an implication that the vines are like restrictive clothes which conceal the true shape of the loved one—for when they are cast off the tree becomes 'all bare'). The kind of thoughts represented here, produced by a dangerous proximity, are cast as destructive and inimical to true knowing. The tree can only renew itself by casting off the insphering thoughts/vines, bursting and shattering them. Again these metaphors of explosion and bursting are part of the violence of love and knowledge, suggesting that, through such epiphanic moments of throwing off, new knowledge is gained. Finally, it is important to note that for Barrett Browning it is the degree of *proximity* in which these thoughts have been produced that is the problem, not thinking in itself: 'I do not think of thee—I am too near thee'. In '**Sonnet 15**,' for instance, which seems to pair with this one, an alternative kind of sight is represented, a vision of love which exceeds the object of love and travels into future time and space and ultimately to oblivion:

But I look on thee—on thee—
Beholding, besides love, the end of love,
Hearing oblivion beyond memory;
As one who sits and gazes from above,
Over the rivers to the bitter sea.

('**Sonnet 15**,' ll.10-14)

And it is also thought and feeling enshrined or forced *into words* which is persistently problematised in these poems, not because Barrett necessarily believes that thought and feeling are possible without words, but rather that the words, phrases, conceits and metaphors that have been used to describe love in literature inhibit freshness of expression because they have been overused. After all, the first words of the sonnet sequence begin 'I thought once how Theocritus had sung'. She is thinking through the words of another as the poem begins, musing on a written text. Barrett persistently draws our attention to the way in which speech and writing, particularly literary writing, not only fashions experience, but also traps it in tropes, conceits and metaphors. She draws our attention to those habits and conventions of thought and representation that falsely or inadequately shape experience. Language—the attempt to fashion feeling into speech—is the paradox of these poems. Putting love into words must be done, particularly by lovers who are also poets, and yet the full expression of love is elusive. Literature and the conventions of writing can 'insphere' (contain, imprison, suffocate) established knowledge or can throw off the 'vines' of old knowledge, allowing us to see the tree as if for the first time. Barrett does not reject thinking about love but she does question our adherence to the old ways of knowing it, ways of knowing that have been controlled by writers and poets.

Nothing Like the Sun: The Literariness of Love

In the chapter on genre I showed how Barrett reused the sonnet form, pushing it to its limits, spilling over its confines in a way that mimicked the cut and thrust of charged, enquiring conversation, demonstrating how closely related these poems are to the love letters written by herself and Robert. The poems both utilise the conventions of courtly love and challenge them so that Barrett, for instance, in speaking as a woman, troubles the long-established gender conventions of the sonnet form of the male speaking-thinking lover-poet and the female silent-listening or absent object of desire. Here in the ***Sonnets from the Portuguese,*** as I said earlier, the poems become a duet or at least the reported half of an on-going conversation.

But there are other important ways in which Barrett recasts the conventions of courtly love in the ***Sonnets.*** They question, for instance, the established epithets and conceits of love established by the Petrarchan form in particular. Barrett was acutely aware in her letters and poetry of the literariness of romantic love, made all the more intense because she and Robert as poets were engaged in a shared quest to define their love for each other and experiencing the weight of literary tradition in doing so. Shakespeare had also wittily rejected established conceits ('false compare') in his famous Sonnet 130, struggling instead to find new ways of expressing feeling:

My mistress' eyes are nothing like the sun;
Coral is far more red than her lips' red;
If snow be white, why then her breasts are dun;
If hairs be wires, black wires grow on her head.
I have seen roses damasked, red and white,
But no such roses see I in her cheeks;
And in some perfumes is there more delight
Than in the breath that from my mistress reeks.
I love to hear her speak, yet well know
That music hath a far more pleasing sound;
I grant I never saw a goddess go;
My mistress, when she walks, treads on the ground.
And yet, by heaven, I think my love as rare
As any she belied with false compare.

Several sonnets in ***Sonnets from the Portuguese*** address this problem of 'false compare'. '**Sonnet 13**,' for instance, begins:

And wilt thou have me fashion into speech
The love I bear thee, finding words enough,
And hold the torch out, while the winds are rough,
Between our faces, to cast light on each?
('**Sonnet 13**,' ll.1-4)

Instead, in this sonnet, the speaker opts for silence as the best form of sincerity:

Nay, let the silence of my womanhood
Commend my woman-love to thy belief,—
Seeing that I stand unwon, however wooed,
And rend the garment of my life, in brief,
By a most dauntless, voiceless fortitude,
Lest one touch of this heart convey its grief.
('**Sonnet 13**' ll.9-14)

This conflict between potentially hollow speech and sincere silence is repeated elsewhere in the sequence. The speaker reminds her lover in '**Sonnet 21**,' for instance, that although she needs him to reiterate his love like the cuckoo he must 'love [her] also in silence with thy soul' (l.14). In the following sonnet in the sequence, Barrett continues to engage with the problems of language and silence explored in '**Sonnet 13**' as the speaker addresses her lover as a *writer,* commanding him to find new ways of expressing his love and not to pre-script and define their love in ways that will not accommodate change:

If thou must love me, let it be for nought
Except for love's sake only. Do not say
'I love her for her smile—her look—her way
Of speaking gently,—for a trick of thought
That falls in well with mine, and certes brought
A sense of pleasant ease on such a day'—
For these things in themselves, Belovèd, may
Be changed, or change for thee,—and love, so wrought,
May be unwrought so. Neither love me for
Thine own dear pity's wiping my cheeks dry,—
A creature might forget to weep, who bore
Thy comfort long, and lose thy love thereby!
But love me for love's sake, that evermore
Thou mayst love on, through love's eternity.
('**Sonnet 14**')

But all the soul-searching about the impossibility of original expression of romantic love is not all in earnest. As Mary Rose Sullivan has shown, the Brownings' habit of echoing each other's words and of 'adapting, reforming, and returning them ever more freighted with meaning' began early in their correspondence and 'inevitably spilled over into their composition of poetry' (Sullivan, 1987: 57). There is much that is self-parodic and witty in Barrett Browning's ***Sonnets.*** In '**Sonnet 37**,' for instance, the speaker laments the difficulty of originality and representation—writing about love, she laments, can be at worst a 'worthless counterfeit':

Pardon, oh, pardon, that my soul should make,
Of all that strong divineness which I know
For thine and thee, an image only so
Formed of the sand, and fit to shift and break.
('**Sonnet 37**,' ll.1-4)

But while the poem strives for originality of expression, it culminates ironically with an image borrowed from one of Robert Browning's most well-known poems, *My Last Duchess,* in which the Duke draws the envoy's attention to a sculpture of 'Neptune . . . / Taming a sea-horse, thought a rarity, / Which Claus of Innsbruck cast in bronze for me' (ll.54-6). In Barrett's sonnet, she ends by claiming that art is sometimes as hopelessly inadequate as commemorating salvation from shipwreck in the form of a sculptured porpoise, repeating Robert's image:

As if a shipwrecked Pagan, safe in port,
His guardian sea-god to commemorate,
Should set a sculptured porpoise, gills a-snort
And vibrant tail, within the temple-gate.
(ll.11-14)

But while literature and the literary expression of love is often a hindrance to direct expression, the sonnets show how useful literary or artistic representation can be in providing tropes to think through. For instance, Barrett alludes to Tennyson's *Mariana in the Moated Grange* in one letter to Robert: 'I am like Mariana in the moated grange & sit listening too often to the mouse in the wainscot' (*BC* 10:254). But in a later letter she clarifies the analogy when she writes 'For have I not felt twenty times the desolate advantage of being insulated here and of not minding anybody when I made my poems? . . . and caring less for suppositious criticism than for the black fly buzzing in the pane?' (*BC* 10:271). The analogy is actually a difference, for unlike Mariana who suffers from an excess of feeling, Barrett's insulation has resulted not in emotional excess but in indifference to criticism. Throughout the sonnet sequences the burdensome legacy of Romantic poetry is used both as the material for new poetry and its adversary.

Love in Text; Love in Context

In *Victorian Women Poets: Writing Against the Heart,* Angela Leighton argues that Elizabeth Barrett Browning 'learned early to distrust the iconic postures of romance in favour of a socialised and contextualised account of desire' (Leighton, 1992: 87). This claim is everywhere confirmed by Barrett Browning's love poetry which relentlessly places love under a sociological microscope. Love does not exist in the abstract—it is always felt and acted upon by people shaped and determined by the ideas of their time, people in the world. For many women in the nineteenth century, love, however pleasurable or transcendent, was especially deterministic, for love was so often the entry point into a much more circumscribed world within the institution of marriage or outside it as a result of betrayal or a fall from respectability:

> It is this sceptical awareness of the sexual politics of sensibility which marks out Barrett Browning's poetry from that of her predecessors. Love, in her work, is not a sacred ideal, removed from the contingencies of the world, but is dragged in the dust of that reality which was itself so hard-won an experience and a theme for her.
>
> (Leighton, 1992: 544)

Barrett's ballads in particular address the danger of untempered feeling, of women who, like the 'women of a softer mood' evoked in ***Aurora Leigh*** (2:443), are consigned to a life of picking oakum because they love too much or too quickly or unwisely. In **'Bertha in the Lane'** and **'A Year's Spinning,'** the two heroines have been betrayed by absent lovers who do not even appear in the poem. In the first poem, the heroine, on her deathbed, confesses to her sister Bertha that she is dying of a broken heart. She had overheard, she says, her lover, Robert, declaring his love to her more beautiful sister in the lane. Still in love with Robert, still listening out for the sound of his footstep at the door like Mariana in Tennyson's poem, she dies self-consumed, yet refusing to blame either Bertha or Robert for their feelings. Instead it is the weakness of her own womanhood that has killed her:

> Do not weep so—Dear,—heart-warm!
> All was best as it befell.
> If I say he did me harm,
> I speak wild,—I am not well.
> All his words were kind and good—
> *He esteemed me*! Only, blood
> Runs so faint in womanhood.
>
> (ll.155-61)

In **'A Year's Spinning'** the betrayed woman, a spinner, has borne her lover's child which has since died. Her lament, like that of the dying sister in **'Bertha in the Lane'**, is not a call of revenge but rather one of despair about the weakness and vulnerability of women raised on a diet of false ideals and romantic love. These are the fragile 'women of a softer mood' resigned to picking oakum or death. Now that 'her spinning is all done' (l.5), her life and hope are extinguished. In **'The Romance of the Swan's Nest'** the danger of self-deluding, self-consuming love is all the more sharply drawn as Barrett tells the story of **'Little Ellie'** who sits beside a river imagining an idealised lover for herself in the language and imagery of romantic and chivalric love, straight out of a formulaic romance. In this fantasy, she imagines herself taking him to see the swan's nest among the reeds. In reality, while she has been dreaming, the swan's nest has been deserted and the eggs gnawed by rats. The dream has been violated.

The act of betrayal always happens offstage in these ballads for it is the consequences of the betrayal on women's lives that interest Barrett. So often the damage affects other women and children in the story: the spinner's shamed mother, the dead baby, Bertha who loses her sister because her beauty stimulated the act of betrayal. In **'A Romance of the Ganges'**, Luti, betrayed by her lover, reveals that betrayal to her rival Nuleeni and demands that Nuleeni become her accomplice in revenge. She demands that Luti whisper Nuleeni's name to her husband on their wedding day and again to their child when he asks about his father's deeds. These ballads show that untempered love is dangerous and often the result of the socialisation of women to expect to fulfil their lives only in a love plot (what we might call the imposition of a 'false consciousness'), a subject also addressed by other women writers of the nineteenth century from Mary Wollstonecraft to Harriet Taylor. In the ballads, Barrett persistently shows love as taking its place within an economy of power and sexual exchange. Indeed as Stone argues:

> In her ballads of the 1830s and 40s, [Barrett] employs the starker power structures of medieval society to foreground the status of women in a male economy of social exchange, and to unmask the subtler preservation of gender inequities in contemporary Victorian ideology.
>
> (Stone, 1995: 108-9)

The Politics of Marriage

Throughout her life Barrett Browning, icon of Victorian marriage and romance, was outspokenly critical of the institution of marriage and of many of the marriages she saw around her. '*Marriage in the abstract* has always seemed to me the most profoundly indecent of all ideas,' she wrote to Mary Mitford during Robert's courtship (*BC* 12:63), continuing:

> & I never could make out how women, mothers & daughters, could talk of it as of setting up in trade,.. as of a thing to be done. That life may go on smoothly upon a marriage of convenience, simply proves to my mind that there is a defect in the sensibility & the delicacy, & an incapacity to the higher happiness of God's sanctifying. Now think & see if this is not near the truth. I have always been called romantic for this way of seeing, but never repented that it was *my* way, nor shall.
>
> (*BC* 12:62-3)

While Barrett Browning valued love as transcendent, even divine, she was no romantic as far as marriage was concerned—she had always been critical of women who believed marriage to be the only fulfilment for a woman; even during her often lonely and reclusive life, she was no **'Little Ellie'** conjuring an imaginary lover out of thin air. A dream recorded in her diary when she was twenty-five shows that here at least marriage was experienced as a nightmare of further incarceration not a release from her present circumstances: 'I dreamt last night that I was married, just married; & in an agony to procure a dissolution of the engagement' (*D* [***Diary by E. B. B.: The Unpublished Diary of Elizabeth Barrett Browning***]; 111). Even when Robert insisted that she consider marriage as the only way they could live together abroad, she procrastinated and deferred committing herself to a final decision (see Forster, 1988: 164-77); the love letters written in the six months before they married show Barrett wrangling and tormented about marriage and its relation to power and money. She shows herself uncertain about how to judge the materialism of wedding preparation (the trousseau) in a letter to Miss Mitford, 'A year for marriages, is it? Well—it seems so—and some marry unfortunately (or fortunately) *without* trousseaus' (*BC* 13:213). Watching the preparations for her cousin Arabella Hedley's wedding, Barrett commented: 'there does enter into the motives of most marriages a good deal of that hankering after the temporary distinction, emotion and pleasure of being for a while a chief person . . .' (*BC* 13:213). The expense of Arabella's wedding seemed grotesque to her: 'six dress pocket handkerchiefs, at four guineas each [. . .] forty guineas of lace trimming on the bridal dress' (*BC* 13:185). She was haunted by her experience and memory of repressive or unhappy marriages, she wrote to Robert:

> To see marriages which are made everyday! Worse than solitudes & more desolate! In the case of the two happiest I ever knew, one of the husbands said in confidence to a brother of mine . . . that he had 'ruined his prospects by marrying,'—& the other said to myself at the very moment of professing an extraordinary happiness, . . . 'But I should have done as well if I had not married her.'
>
> (*BC* 12:259)

And again only a few months before she agreed to marry him, she wrote:

> When I was a child I heard two married women talking. One said to the other 'The most painful part of marriage is the first year, when the lover changes into the husband by slow degrees.' The other woman agreed, as a matter of fact is agreed to. I listened with my eyes & ears, & never forgot it . . . as you observe—It seemed to me, child as I was, a dreadful thing to have a husband by such a process.
>
> (*BC* 13:126)

Barrett was supremely conscious of how divided their experiences were and would be—marriage would establish very different rights and conventions of behaviour for them as men and women. Would they be able to resist the stereotypical male and female behaviour so visible in all the marriages around them?

> Did you ever observe a lord of creation knit his brows together because the cutlets were underdone, shooting enough fire from his eyes to overdo them to cinders[. . .] Did you ever hear of the litany which some women say through the first course.. low to themselves.. Perhaps not! it does not enter into your imagination to conceive of things, which nevertheless *are*.
>
> Not that I ever thought of YOU with reference to SUCH—oh, no, no!
>
> (*BC* 12:221)

The answer was to dissent, of course, to determine not to be a 'common woman' or a 'common man' in life and marriage (a determination which would be given to Aurora Leigh later), but the abuse of power, she felt, seemed to be enshrined in marriage—almost produced by it. She wrote the following letter on the anniversary of American Independence (at a time when she had already significantly begun to write **'A Runaway Slave at Pilgrim's Point'** which so powerfully attacks the institutionalisation of slavery and the abuse of power):

> Oh, I understand perfectly, how as soon as ever a common man is sure of a woman's affections, he takes up the tone of right & might.. & he *will* have

it so.. & he *wont* have it so!—I have heard of the bitterest tears being shed by the victim as soon as ever, by one word of hers, she had placed herself in his power. Of such are 'Lover's quarrels' for the most part. The growth of power on one side.. & the struggle against it, by means legal & illegal, on the other.

(*BC* 13:116)

Her critique of marriage at this point is powerfully and astutely political. One wonders how, with this view of marriage, she could ever agree to marry, but at the same time one wonders how in the 1840s the Brownings might have lived together abroad *without* being married. Barrett Browning's critique of marriage did not decline after her marriage either; indeed she continued to write ever more politically about marriage and the abuse of women's rights. As Margaret Forster points out, 'the happier Elizabeth became with her man, the more furious she became at how men abused women' (Forster, 1998: 204).

The politics of marriage were most powerfully explored in ***Aurora Leigh.*** Romney in the course of the poem makes four proposals—two to Aurora and two to Marian. Three of these proposals are made, Barrett Browning shows us, for the wrong reasons, for Romney is driven by motives which are bound up with money, duty and inheritance. As Angela Leighton points out (1986), Aurora's answer to Romney's first proposal and Marian's answer to his second provide a critique of the system of values that underpin his dubious good intentions: 'Here's a hand shall keep / For ever clean without a marriage-ring', Marian replies to his offer of marriage. She is, she claims, already clean—she does not need his marriage ring to cleanse her. Aurora's rejection of his first proposal is based upon her understanding of what he has actually said which in her words amounts to the following statement:

'Come, sweep my barns and keep my hospitals,
And I will pay these with a current coin
Which men give women'

(***AL*** 2:539-41)

In paraphrasing Romney's proposal this way, Aurora shows her understanding of marriage as a transaction based upon law and money—marriage is the 'current coin' which men pay women in exchange for their labour. This analysis is also extended by Marian when she angrily asserts her rights as a mother:

'Mine, mine,' she said. 'I have as sure a right
As any glad proud mother in the world,
Who sets her darling down to cut his teeth
Upon her church-ring. If she talks of law,
I talk of law! I claim by mother-dues
By law,—the law which now is paramount,—
The common law, by which the poor and weak
Are trodden underfoot by vicious me,
And loathed for ever after by the good'

(***AL*** 6:661-9)

Barrett Browning, dissenter, is audible here in Marian's words, in this fierce analysis of the conflicts between common law and natural law. What is common is not always right. Instead, common law enshrines the rights of men against 'the poor and weak'. In this analysis she places herself in the tradition of Mary Wollstonecraft, Margaret Fuller, George Sand, and Barbara Bodichon who wrote in *A Brief Summary, In Plain Language, Of The Most Important Laws Concerning Women; Together With A Few Observations Thereon* in 1854: 'Women, more than any other members of the community, suffer from over legislation' (Bodichon, 1854: 13).

Marriage was a political issue in 1856 when this poem was published. The Matrimonial Causes Bill was making its way through Parliament and would become an Act in 1857. The Act would allow wives who could prove extreme cruelty or desertion to obtain a divorce and empower courts to force estranged husbands to pay maintenance to their former wives. It would deny the husband rights to the earnings of a wife he had deserted, and returned to a woman divorced or legally separated the property rights of a single woman. Behind this Act was the much-publicised marriage of the poet and novelist Caroline Norton which drew public attention to the severe economic penalties which women suffered when they separated from their husbands. After leaving her abusive husband in 1836, Norton had been prevented from seeing their three sons and had been cut off financially for by law all she had once owned including her inheritance, was her husband's by marriage. After her husband's unsuccessful attempt to prove her guilty of an adulterous affair, Norton filed for divorce on the grounds of cruelty. Her claim was rejected, however, as English law did not recognise cruelty as just cause for divorce. By this point Norton was earning money from her writing, but by law all her earnings belonged to her husband. Determined to use her personal misfortune to gather support for legal reform, she drew attention and support for her cause through the publication of pamphlets and the influence of her friends in Parliament, and in 1855, she published her most important pamphlet, *A Letter to the Queen on Lord Chancellor Cranworth's Marriage and Divorce Bill,* in which she reviewed the position of married women under English law:

1. a married woman has no legal existence whether or not she is living with her husband;

2. her property is his property;

3. she cannot make a will, the law gives what she has to her husband despite her wishes or his behaviour;

4. she may not keep her earnings;

5. he may sue for restitution of conjugal rights and thus force her, as if a slave to return to his home;

6. she is not allowed to defend herself in divorce;

7. she cannot divorce him since the House of Lords in effect will not grant a divorce to her;

8. she cannot sue for libel;

9. she cannot sign a lease or transact business;

10. she cannot claim support from her husband, his only obligation is to make sure she doesn't land in the parish poorhouse if he has means;

11. she cannot bind her husband to any agreement.

> In short, as her husband, he has the right to all that is hers; as his wife she has no right to anything that is his.
>
> (33)

Marriage, and women's rights and ownership of property within it, was the subject of much conversation and writing in the mid-1850s; it preoccupied social reformers, legislators, churchmen, poets and novelists. The Act secured some property rights to wives who were separated from their husbands but it maintained men's legal rights to all marital property. Barrett Browning's commitment to examining the legal injustice of marriage was part of that series of conversations and part of her commitment to exploring the concerns of 'this live, throbbing age' (***AL*** 5:203). 'No longer,' writes Angela Leighton, 'a poetry of "love of love", hers is a poetry which constantly asks about the conventions of power which lie behind love, and which affect the improvised expression of the heart . . . those systems of socialisation represented by sex, class and money, for instance, and the systems of literary meaning, represented by historical and political reference, for instance, everywhere make themselves felt' (Leighton, 1992: 80).

In *The Ring and the Book* published after Elizabeth Barrett Browning's death, Robert Browning memorialised his wife's language and understanding of love and marriage. The passage reads as a homage to her ideas (Swedenborg taught that marriage as a pure union existed in heaven among angels) and part of the on-going conversation between them about marriage as a flawed human institution, a 'conversation' that continued beyond Barrett Browning's death:

> Marriage on earth seems such a counterfeit,
> Mere imitation of the inimitable:
> In heaven we have the real and true and sure.
> 'Tis there they neither marry nor are given in
> Marriage but are as angels: right,
> Oh how right that is, how like Jesus Christ
> To say that! Marriage-making for the earth,
> With gold so much,—birth, power, repute so
> much,
> Or beauty, youth so much, in lack of these!
> Be as the angels rather, who, apart,
> Know themselves into one, are found at length
> Married, but marry never, no, nor give
> In marriage; they are man and wife at once
> When the true time is: here we have to wait
> Not so long neither!
>
> (*The Ring and the Book,* 7:1821-38)

Abbreviations

The following abbreviations are used throughout the text

AL Aurora Leigh, ed. Margaret Reynolds, New York and London: Norton, 1996

BC The Brownings' Correspondence, ed. Philip Kelley, Ronald Hudson and Scott Lewis, 14 vols, Winfield, Kan.: Wedgestone Press, 1984-1998

D Diary by E.B.B.: The Unpublished Diary of Elizabeth Barrett Browning, 1831-1832, ed. Philip Kelley and Ronald Hudson, Athens, Ohio: Ohio University Press, 1969

Bibliography

Bodichon, Barbara (1854), *A Brief Summary, In Plain Language, Of The Most Important Laws Concerning Women; Together With A Few Observations Thereon,* London: John Chapman

Forster, Margaret (1988), *Elizabeth Barrett Browning,* London: Chatto and Windus

Gilbert, Sandra M. and Susan Gubar (1979), *The Madwoman in the Attic: Women Writers and the Nineteenth-Century Literary Imagination,* New Haven and London: Yale University Press

Leighton, Angela (1986), *Elizabeth Barrett Browning,* Brighton: Harvester Press

———(1992), *Victorian Women Poets: Writing Against the Heart,* Hemel Hempstead: Harvester Wheatsheaf

Lootens, Tricia (1996*a*), *Lost Saints: Silence, Gender and Victorian Literary Canonization,* Charlottesville, VA. and London: University Press of Virginia

Mermin, Dorothy (1986), 'The Damsel, the Knight, and the Victorian Woman Poet', *Critical Inquiry* 13:64-80

Pinch, Adela (1998), 'Thinking about the Other in Romantic Love', in Romantic Circle Praxis Series, *http:www.r-c.umd. edu/praxis/passions/pcts.html*

FROM THE AUTHOR

BROWNING TELLS HER CLOSE FRIEND MARY RUSSELL MITFORD ABOUT HER IDEA FOR A NEW KIND OF POEM; HER IDEAS WERE THE GERM OF HER NOVEL-POEM *AURORA LEIGH*

A few characters—a simple story—and plenty of room for passion and thought—that is what I want. . . . [P]eople care for a story—there's the truth! And I who care so much for stories, am not to find fault with them. And now tell me,—where is the obstacle to making as interesting a story of a poem as of a prose work—Echo answers *where.* Conversations and events, why may they not be given as rapidly and passionately and lucidly in verse as in prose—echo answers *why.* You see nobody is offended by my approach to the conventions of vulgar life in 'Lady Geraldine'—and it gives me courage to go on, and touch this real everyday life of our age, and hold it with my two hands. I want to write a poem of a new class, in a measure—a Don Juan, without the mockery and impurity,—under one aspect,—and having unity, as a work of art,—and admitting of as much philosophical dreaming and digression (which is in fact a characteristic of the age) as I like to use. Might it not be done, even if I could not do it? and I think of trying at any rate.

Elizabeth Barrett Browning. Excerpt from a letter to Mary Russell Mitford, December 30, 1844. In *Elizabeth Barrett Browning and Robert Browning: Interviews and Recollections,* edited by Martin Garrett, p. 15-16. New York: St. Martin's, 2000.

Reynolds, Margaret (ed) (1996) *Aurora Leigh,* New York and London: Norton

Stone, Marjorie (1995), *Elizabeth Barrett Browning,* Basingstoke: Macmillan

Sullivan, Mary Rose (1987), '"Some Interchange of Grace": "Saul" and *Sonnets from the Portuguese*', *Browning Institute Studies* 15:55-68

Swedenborg, Emmanuel (1995), *Conjugal Love,* trans. N. Bruce Rogers, New York: Church of the New Jerusalem

TITLE COMMENTARY

Aurora Leigh

SUEANN SCHATZ (ESSAY DATE WINTER 2000)

SOURCE: Schatz, SueAnn. "*Aurora Leigh* as Paradigm of Domestic-Professional Fiction." *Philological Quarterly* 79, no. 1 (winter 2000): 91-117.

In the following essay, Schatz presents Aurora Leigh *as Browning's effort to counter the Victorian idealization of the domestic woman by creating a heroine who could appear in both domestic and professional roles.*

I am waiting for a story, and I won't take one, because I want to make one, and I like to make my own stories, because then I can take liberties with them in the treatment.

—Elizabeth Barrett to Robert Browning; February 27, 1845

If, therefore, I move certain subjects in this work, it is because my conscience was first moved in me not to ignore them.

—Elizabeth Barrett Browning to Julia Martin; February, 1857

1

Through an analysis of ***Aurora Leigh*** as domestic-professional fiction, in this essay I investigate Elizabeth Barrett Browning's evolving feminist and artistic philosophy. I define domestic-professional fiction as possessing several distinctive attributes: a prominent character is a professional woman writer who also occupies the role of caregiver in the home. While fulfilling the role of the ideal Victorian woman, "The Angel in the House," the domestic-professional author also subverts Victorian expectations of women by asserting her right to confront immediate political and moral issues and offer solutions. Domestic-professional texts offer paradigms of the woman/writer whose chosen vocation is that of social critic, a model intended to replace the Victorian ideal of woman precisely by co-opting it. Finally, domestic-professional fiction ultimately challenges its readers to make the decision to effect social change.

Barrett Browning's philosophy of literature, revealed in the content and form of ***Aurora Leigh,*** most definitively envisions a feminine strength and morality that address society's needs, extending the domestic ethics into the public sphere. Barrett Browning also stresses the power of writing as a means of discovering "truth" and as a woman's construction and acceptance of her self. Aurora's growth as a writer and a woman results from her relationships with Romney Leigh and Marian Erle. Thus, since a central thematic principle in domestic-professional fiction is that a woman break free from cultural conventions to cultivate the power that can transform society, Barrett Browning's doctrine of art encompasses the personal and the political, of which Aurora and Romney's marriage is the ultimate symbol; the "New Jerusalem" they anticipate at the end of this epic verse-novel emphasizes the need to work toward a just society. Importantly, while Barrett Browning advocates the construction of a fair society, she does so by critiquing a cherished Victorian ideal, that of the Angel in the House that she believes denigrates both women and society. For Barrett Browning, society will benefit much more from the professional woman than from the woman who has no creative outlet other than her domestic duties.

Aurora Leigh was first published in 1856, two years after another poem whose female figure would increasingly personify the ideal Victorian woman, Coventry Patmore's *The Angel in the House*. Barrett Browning uses a variety of characters familiar to Victorian readers—the lovelorn heroine (Aurora), the "good" woman (Aurora again), the "fallen" woman (Marian), the social idealist (Romney), and the conniving aristocrat (Lady Waldemar), among others, in surprising ways to address her concerns regarding contemporary issues, such as the woman question, individualism and social conditions. One character type that appears only marginally is the Angel in the House, the feminine figure who is becoming increasingly codified into the middle-class norm as the ideal woman.'[1] There are several instances in which the Angel does show up briefly in ***Aurora Leigh,*** only to be exorcised by Barrett Browning, who realizes how damaging this image is to women. She teasingly introduces such a woman in the form of Aurora's mother on the first page of the book:

> But still I catch my mother at her post
> Beside the nursery-door, with finger up,
> 'Hush, hush—here's too much noise!' while her sweet eyes
> Leap forward, taking part against her word
> In the child's riot.[2]

But Barrett Browning immediately destroys such an image by informing the reader that Aurora's mother is already dead. Further, Aurora's study of her mother's portrait conjures up not an idealized version of the woman, but shows the layers of complexity that women truly are (1.149-68). Images range from "abhorrent" to "beautiful," from Muses and Fates, Psyche and Medusa, to Our Lady of Passion and Lamia: "Ghost, fiend, and angel, fairy, witch, and sprite" (1.154). All of these female images, including Aurora's mother, are women of power, specifically women whose power the patriarchal order wants to limit or destroy. In their place the Angel in the House is instituted in order to control female power and influence. From the outset of her poem, Barrett Browning seems to suggest that the Angel in the House is an ideal and only that. Furthermore, it is not necessarily an ideal that should be pursued. Why, after all, seek an unattainable model of a woman when real women contain within them "the burning lava of a song / The full-veined, heaving, double-breasted Age" (5.215-16)?

AURORA LEIGH.

BY

ELIZABETH BARRETT BROWNING.

NEW YORK:
C. S. FRANCIS & CO., 554 BROADWAY.
BOSTON:—53 DEVONSHIRE STREET.
1857.

Title page of *Aurora Leigh* (1857).

Aurora Leigh met with great success, despite some critics' reservations. But even reviewers who found major fault with Barrett Browning's subject matter or style almost unanimously praised some portion of the poem. For example, W. E. Aytoun, in *Blackwood's Edinburgh Magazine,* complained that the story was one "which no admirer of Mrs. Browning's genius ought in prudence to defend. In our opinion it is fantastic, unnatural, exaggerated; and all the worse, because it professes to be a tale of our times." Yet, he ends his review thusly: "Still, with all its faults, this is a remarkable poem; strong in energy, rich in thought, abundant in beauty; and it more than sustains that high reputation, which by her previous efforts, Mrs. Browning has so honourably won."[3] ***Aurora Leigh*** continued to be reprinted and influential through the end of the century, as did Coventry Patmore's *The Angel in the House,* however, with one major difference. While Barrett Browning made corrections but no major revisions to her poem before her death in 1861, Patmore continually revised his, finally settling on a last revision in 1886.[4] It is this edition that has been reprinted and been the standard for twentieth-century scholars.[5]

Recently, though, several critics have returned to Patmore's original versions of the two parts of the poem, "The Betrothal" and "The Espousals," which help highlight Barrett Browning's ideological endeavor in ***Aurora Leigh.*** In particular, Linda K. Hughes argues that Patmore's revisions indicate an alarmist reaction to the social upheaval Britain was facing by the end of the century. Hughes notes that in the 1854 version, "the husband and wife are collaborators, she the critic rather than the passive recipient of his verses."[6] But by the time Patmore finished revising his poem for the standard and approved edition,

> [W]hat increasingly disappeares . . . is a sense of women as living presences. . . . [They become] far more disembodied and reified, far more relegated to the status of symbols manipulated for artistic purposes. Far more in the final than in the first edition, that is, the female becomes entombed, drained of life and vitality and encased in form.[7]

What Hughes is noting in the revision of *The Angel in the House* is a tightening of ranks, so to speak, a retrenching from the idea that British society was progressing toward a more liberated and egalitarian one. Certainly much of this change had to do with the burgeoning industrial and colonial empire that Britain had developed, creating what Karl Beckson calls the "characteristically Victorian assumptions that the age required manliness and determination to sustain Britain's industrial progress, its programs of reform, and the expansion of its empire."[8] Since the definition of "manliness" was changing, so too was the definition of "womanliness." The Angel in the House figure became increasingly codified in a middle-class psyche that was more and more confused about moral integrity. If "being a good man" was about obtaining material goods to offer proof of one's economic status, then "being a good woman" was about offering a certain kind of self-sacrifice to counter such rampant materialism, a balancing of intangible morality with tangible acquisitiveness.

As I will show, Barrett Browning eschews the mere idealization of women in favor of presenting a complex individual who might actually improve society. Through Aurora's maturation process, both as a writer and a woman, Barrett Browning suggests a "real-life" role model, a woman who can successfully combine the professional and domestic spheres. In light of nineteenth-century attitudes towards women, for Barrett Browning to imply that women belonged in the professional as well as the domestic sphere required a layered, sophisticated argument. Accordingly, throughout this article I quote several long passages of Barrett Browning's verse-novel; many of her ideas are complicated and deserve citation in full because, as Margaret Reynolds points out, "[T]here is little chance of economical quotation as clauses accumulate and argument opens into allegory."[9]

2

In the famous garden scene in Book 2 of ***Aurora Leigh,*** Aurora's cousin Romney admonishes her,

> 'There it is!—
> You play beside a death-bed like a child,
> Yet measure to yourself a prophet's place
> To teach the living. None of all these things,
> Can women understand. You generalise
> Oh, nothing—not even grief! Your quick-breathed hearts,
> So sympathetic to the personal pang,
> Close on each separate knife-stroke, yielding up
> A whole life at each wound, incapable
> Of deepening, widening a large lap of life
> To hold the world-full woe. The human race
> To you means, such a child, or such a man,
> You saw one morning waiting in the cold,
> Beside that gate, perhaps. You gather up
> A few such cases, and when strong sometimes
> Will write of factories and of slaves, as if
> Your father were a negro, and your son
> A spinner in the mills. All's yours and you,
> All, coloured with your blood, or otherwise
> Just nothing to you.'
>
> (2.179-98)

There are two delicious ironies in Romney's smug accusation. One is that Romney just previously said that he had not read Aurora's poems, but insinuates he knows what she writes about anyway. Since the apostrophe "you" in this speech changes from the singular "Aurora" to the plural "women," one presumes that Romney has read the work of other poetesses and surmises that they all write about the same things. He faults them for not generalizing, for only caring about an individual's problems. Romney here is guilty of exactly the opposite: he generalizes too much (about women poets) and, moreso, he is uninformed. Further, he does not explain why it is important to generalize rather than to individualize. The second irony is Romney's contention that women will "teach the living" what they know "of factories and of slaves" (2.182, 194) Romney overlooks the fact that "ladies" were not "educated" to concern themselves with such matters as slavery and child-labor laws, and since Aurora and other women do so indicates these writers educated themselves regarding political matters, regardless of societal opinion.

Furthermore, Romney is missing the point when he complains, "'The human race / To you means, such a child, or such a man, / You saw one morning waiting in the cold, / Beside that gate, perhaps'" (2.189-92): he does not understand that the personal is political, that an individual's actions towards other individuals are the basis for social change. Yet, Romney is not altogether wrong here. At age twenty, Aurora has not witnessed such things as workhouses and mills personally and so if she has written about them, it is from second-hand experience or from what she has gathered reading about such. The fact is we are never quite sure what Aurora writes about because ***Aurora Leigh*** is the only piece of her writing that we actually read. Beverly Taylor notes that we never read the poetry that changes Romney's opinion that art cannot induce social good: "Instead the poetry by Aurora that we do read is ***Aurora Leigh*** itself, the poem that relates the social turmoil of the Victorian period to the interior life of individual woman."[10] More importantly, as my discussion will show, what Aurora precisely does need to learn is to care deeply rather than superficially for an individual's problems before she can fulfill her potential of becoming a poet who affects and changes society. That is, Aurora must incorporate the ideology of social change within her own life before she can be a true poet.

Despite her belief in her work, Aurora thinks she needs to make a choice between being a professional writer or a wife, thus prompting her initial rejection of Romney's marriage proposal. She vehemently opposes Romney's conventional argument that women cannot produce great art, but totally accepts the societal convention that she must choose between work and love. Barbara Charlesworth Gelpi asserts that Aurora consistently denies her femininity precisely because it interferes with her chosen vocation as poet, traditionally a male domain.[11] It is only through her interaction with Marian that Aurora comes to realize her true self is a combination of the writer and the wife: she is the poet who will enact social change by calling attention to the wrongs of society, and she is the woman who will influence social change through the model of her personal life, as a partner in an egalitarian marriage. As befitting mirror images, Aurora only achieves her true sense of self when her reflector Marian does.

Thus, one reason why Barrett Browning chooses not to give us examples of Aurora's poetry may be the verse-novel's objective in describing the growth of a poet's mind, specifically a woman poet's mind. Despite the modest fame and critical acclaim she receives for her poetry, Aurora consistently doubts her talent as a force for social change. It is only after she shares in her "sister-mirror" Marian Erle's traumatic experiences that she is truly able to write a poem that she believes is worthy of her genius (and that is ***Aurora Leigh*** itself) and so is also worthy to share with readers. She claims in Book 1 that she "Will write my story for my better self" (1.4), but in actuality she also writes Marian's story. As final proof to Romney that political acts spring from personal experience, Aurora's story tells a writer's story and a woman's story, two narratives that are enmeshed and cannot be divided in Barrett Browning's aesthetic credo of domestic-professional fiction.

In some respects, Aurora Leigh is the conventional heroine of mid-Victorian novels who seeks her hero, for despite her own unwillingness to admit her love for Romney, it is consistently brought to the reader's attention. She regularly listens for and encourages his name to be brought up in conversations, and several times she purposely finds reasons to write to him. After fleetingly seeing a woman in Paris she believes to be the lost Marian, her first inclination is not to follow, but "to write to Romney" (6.333). Even in her disquisitions on art, the focal point is her cousin; for example, Aurora questions her ability to write poetry that will affect people since Romney was not touched. She nearly convinces herself of her inadequacy: "I must fail, / Who fail at the beginning to hold and move / One man,—and he my cousin, and he my friend" (5.30-2).

But what sets her apart from the traditional lovelorn heroine is that she is a writer and that does make all the difference. Aurora thinks about things Victorian women are not necessarily supposed to think or write about and she does things women are not necessarily supposed to do. She defies convention by siding with a "fallen woman" and questioning social injustice towards women. More important, Aurora does so by writing and creating a philosophy of art. As Kathleen K. Hickok notes, Barrett Browning's use of familiar characters makes the poem all the more bold because she uses them unconventionally to address controversial social issues: "The audacity and the achievement of ***Aurora Leigh*** resided in its confrontation all at once of so many social and personal facts of nineteenth-century English life and in its challenges to the validity of the conventions which customarily concealed those facts."[12] Despite the conventional ending of ***Aurora Leigh*** with the impending marriage of Aurora and Romney, the conclusion is achieved through unorthodox means and so holds the promise that the future will challenge or change conventions. More specifically it will be the woman writer who envisions such a society, the "New Jerusalem" that Aurora and Romney anticipate at the end of ***Aurora Leigh.*** Though Aurora concedes that "Art is much, but love is more" (9.656), it is precisely her experiences as a writer that allow her to come to this conclusion because Aurora realizes that "Art symbolises heaven, but Love is God / And makes heaven" (9.658-9). Love is the ultimate artist/creator of a just society and all other art must be created in duty to Love.

Not content with solely utilizing familiar characters in stereotypical ways, Barrett Browning opposes *and* aligns these characters, specifically the "good" woman and the "fallen" woman. Several critics, including Gail Turley Houston and Ellen Chafee, have noted the connotation of a woman's writing in the nineteenth century as a form of prostitution.[13] Aurora's moral integrity, however, is never questioned either by herself or readers of ***Aurora Leigh,*** and so in this way the woman writer is set against the prostitute or fallen woman. Even though Aurora transgresses boundaries by writing professionally and rejecting marriage, she is still seen as morally good; it is her unconventionality that paradoxically emphasizes her integrity. At the same time, Barrett Browning aligns the woman writer with the fallen woman by having Aurora tell Marian's story, thereby vicariously participating in the young woman's disgrace. By giving voice to Marian's story, Aurora allows the reader to see that, despite her circumstances, Marian is also good and should be accorded the same respect as honorable women. However, Barrett Browning makes it clear that Marian is fallen through circumstances not of her own doing and not through caprice. Thus while challenging Victorian standards, Aurora's defense of Marian is acceptable to middle-class readers because of the younger woman's noncomplicity in the situation.

Aurora and Marian are explicitly linked by several comparisons, revealing to the reader that their relationship will address problems that women of both the higher and lower classes faced, and that Marian is necessary to and indivisible from Aurora's self-construction: both were sickly children and both were "parentless," Aurora literally orphaned by her parents' deaths and Marian figuratively by an abusive, alcoholic father and a mother willing to prostitute her daughter. Living in the fashionable district of Kensington in London, the adult Aurora occupies an apartment "up three flights of stairs / Not far from being as steep as some larks climb" (3.158-59), prompting Lady Waldemar to remark on "'the trouble of ascent / To this Olympus'" (3.372-73). Going to visit Marian, now engaged to her cousin, Aurora notes her ascent in a tenement slum of St. Margaret's Court: "Still, up, up! / So high lived Romney's bride!" (3.793-94). Although Aurora's rationale for her top-floor rooms is to conserve money, Marian's similar living situation indicates that Aurora is dangerously close to crossing the boundaries of middle-class respectability. Most important, both women share a misguided (Aurora) or an absent (Marian) sense of self. Aurora must correct this condition by realizing that she must construct a new sense of herself as a writer and a woman before she can accept the laurels of the true poet.

Part of this task is Aurora's learning from and recording Marian's construction of herself. They first meet through Romney's act of putting his social theory of abolishing the class system into action; he has asked Marian to marry him: "'Twixt class and class, opposing rich to poor, / Shall we keep parted? Not so. . . . / . . . joining in a protest 'gainst the wrong / On both sides. / . . . fellow-worker, be my wife?'" (4.124-25, 130-31, 150). He thus performs the same action of which he earlier accused Aurora: using the individual to represent the universal. Marian agrees to marry, but not because she loves him. Her past has destroyed any positive sense of herself and she docilely accepts Romney's proposal on the grounds that she will be his "fellow-worker" (ironically the same grounds on which Aurora refused him). When Aurora asks her, "'So indeed / He loves you, Marian?'" (4.167-68), she replies that he does only in the sense that as one of the masses, she is part of his social idealism, and so he loves her as he loves the cause:

> 'Loves me!' She looked up
> With a child's wonder when you ask him first
> Who made the sun—a puzzled blush, that grew,
> Then broke off in a rapid radiant smile
> Of sure solution. 'Loves me! he loves all,—
> To work with him for ever and be his wife.'
>
> (4.167-75)

Marian cannot, as Aurora at this point in time cannot, conceive of herself as a sexual woman, for similar and differing reasons. Both women are trapped by societal constructions of womanliness from which they cannot presently free themselves. Trained to become only good wives and mothers, Victorian women were consistently reminded of their perceived lack of intellect. Thus, Victorian conventions envisioned women as sexless, spiritual creatures, yet women were constantly made aware that theirs was the inferior sex.

Aurora's inability to form an authentic sense of herself as a woman comes from her belief that she cannot have both a professional and personal life: Victorian culture separated the spheres of domestic and public, and she must live in one or the other. Her identification with the male-dominated arena of poetry writing further denies Aurora the faculty to acknowledge her womanliness, and hence her sexuality.[14] Marian's absence of a strong sense of self develops from a past that denied her dignity. Her mother's intention to sell her to the landlord has so scarred Marian that she rejects her right to pure Victorian womanhood. She defines being Romney's wife as being his co-worker, thus rejecting her sexuality. Marian is also constrained by middle-class definitions of her as a working-class woman: for her to believe herself worthy of Romney would be considered presumptuous and arrogant.

Since both Aurora and Marian see themselves as transgressing the boundaries of nineteenth-century womanhood, they surrender their sexuality so that they cannot be accused of unwomanliness. Barrett Browning, however, utilizes this conventional attitude to expose the unconventional reality of women's sexuality, of which she consistently reminds her readers through her sensual language, Marian's rape and pregnancy, and Aurora and Romney's sensuous kiss in Book 9. Moreso, according to Barrett Browning, women must not only accept but celebrate their sexuality as part of their identity and as part of their poetry. Aurora and Marian will learn to break free of the restraints imposed upon them by society, each defining for herself what role she will play. Aurora's writing of these self-reconstructions is vitally important to Barrett Browning's philosophy of art, which I will discuss presently: through the creation of art itself comes the creation of the individual, which in turn empowers and changes society.

However, Aurora's transformation is often a slow and painful one, revealing the phases Aurora must maneuver through to achieve an authentic sense of self. For example, Aurora's account of a discussion between herself and Romney reveals a condescending attitude toward Marian, troubling to the reader because it is written several years later, after Aurora knows Marian's whole story and has come to realize how worthy she is. Yet, Aurora must offer this scene because it emphasizes Marian's lowly sense of self. Aurora and Romney objectify her as a "thing" and a "gift," speaking as if Marian were not present:

> 'Here's one, at least, who is good,' I sighed, and touched
> Poor Marian's happy head, as doglike she
> Most passionately patient, waited on,
> A-tremble for her turn of greeting words;
> 'I've sate a full hour with your Marian Erle,
> And learnt the thing by heart,—and from my heart
> Am therefore competent to give you thanks
> For such a cousin.
> 'You accept at last
> A gift from me, Aurora, without scorn?
> At last I please you?'
>
> (4.280-89)

But, despite Aurora's condescension, we must also take this telling as an essentially truthful chronicle of the meeting. Aurora describes Marian as "doglike" precisely because Marian's estimation of herself at that time demands that Aurora do so.

However, when she begins to relate Marian's narrative in Book 3, Aurora reveals, "I tell her story and grow passionate. / She, Marian, / did not tell it so, but used / Meek words that made no wonder of herself / For being so sad a creature" (3.847-50). Aurora realizes the power of her writing, that it can bring about change, but only if it is "truthful." She is willing to make herself look patronizing in order for Marian's tale to fully affect the reader. Her recounting of Marian's story is "truthful" then to its essence, rather than to the actual words used, an important point of Aurora's philosophy that art can enact social change:

'The speakable, imaginable best
God bids [the poet] speak, to prove what lies
beyond
Both speech and imagination? . . .
I hold you will not compass your poor ends
Of barley-feeding and material ease,
Without a poet's individualism
To work your universal. It takes a soul,
To move a body: it takes a high-souled man,
To move the masses, even to a cleaner stye:
It takes the ideal, to blow a hair's-breadth off
The dust of the actual.—Ah, your Fouriers failed,
Because not poets enough to understand
That life develops from within. . . .'
(2.471-3, 476-85)

Aurora's command that "It takes a soul, / To move a body" intimates that poets must first know themselves before being able to affect the lives of others. Even though she understands completely "That life develops from within," Aurora does not know her own soul well enough to trust her instincts regarding her feelings toward Romney. She begins to develop her first steps toward wholeness through relating to Marian's degradation.

Marian's dishonor comes at the expense of her chastity and her naive trusting of others. In an attempt to sabotage their wedding, Lady Waldemar convinces Marian that Romney needs a wife of his own class, and implores her to leave for Australia where she can begin a new life. Lady Waldemar's "maid," who is supposed to make the arrangements, instead orchestrates Marian's kidnapping; she is drugged and sent to France, where raped and impregnated, she later gives birth to a son. Finding her in Paris, Aurora persuades Marian to continue on with her to Florence, where she can care for the young mother and child. Here Aurora's growth is again mirrored by Marian's; Aurora's first impression is that Marian is at fault, accusing her of "'tak[ing] / The hand of a seducer'" (6.746-47), until Marian explains what actually happened. As Marian loses her naiveté, Aurora loses her judgmental superiority and learns to be in sympathetic identification—what Keats termed essential for a poet—with the young woman.

Marian's self-identity is conditioned by her role now as "'nothing more / But just a mother'" (6.823-24). Additionally, as she speaks of Romney, "She felt his / For just his uses, not her own at all" (6.906-7). But Marian is realizing who she is and how she became such: "'man's violence, / Not man's seduction, made me what I am'" (6.1226-27). Because of the brutality of her rape, Marian must learn to stand for herself and her child since she knows no one else will do so. She has made sacrifices for her son, but more important, Marian has gained a self-confidence that is essential to her and her child's survival. This insight allows her to reject Romney's second offer of marriage in Florence, despite knowing that marrying him will give her son a name and a place in society: "'a woman, poor or rich, / Despised or honoured, is a human soul, / And what her soul is, that, she is herself'" (9.328-30).

When Marian finally recognizes that her acceptance of Romney's first proposal was wrong precisely because she did not love him as a woman should love a man ("'What was in my thought? / To be your slave, your help, your toy, your tool. / To be your love . . . / Did I love, / Or did I worship?'" [9.369-71, 378-79]), Aurora admits that she does indeed love Romney. Both women fully embrace a definition of womanliness they have constructed, rejecting the Victorian ideology of womanhood. Marian refuses Romney in order to take full responsibility for herself and her son. Even though her pregnancy was not of her own proclivity, Marian realizes that she must be proud of her maternity, confronting society about its prejudicial attitudes towards unmarried mothers. Her rejection of Romney enables Aurora to spiritually, intellectually, and physically accept him. Flaunting Victorian conventions as a writer and a woman, through her poetry, she will address prejudice and injustice. And as she embraces Romney, she will embrace her sexuality. However, these victories have been hard-fought battles.

3

As I will show, Barrett Browning's delineation of Aurora's philosophy of art discloses her philosophy of womanhood, one that integrates the writer's concerns with the woman's. Despite her protestations to Romney that women can write great art, Aurora's philosophy is a complex weaving of newly-emerging feminist and long-embedded patriarchal ideas. As critics have noted, Aurora has inculcated male hereditary conceptions of poetry because she has been educated only by men's ideas.[15] Her father taught her Greek and Latin, thus "wrap[ping] his little daughter in his large / Man's doublet, careless did it fit or not" (1.727-28); and her aunt yields to conventional wisdom concerning a girl's education: to train her to be the Angel in the House. Accordingly, her aunt has Aurora learn French and German "since she liked a range / Of liberal education" (1.401-2); some algebra and science "because / She misliked women who are frivolous" (1.405-6); and makes her read "a score of books on womanhood"

To prove, if women do not think at all,
They may teach thinking, (to a maiden-aunt

Or else the author)—books that boldly assert
Their right of comprehending husband's talk
When not too deep, and even of answering
With pretty 'may it please you,' or 'so it is,'—
Their rapid insight and fine aptitude,
Particular worth and general missionariness,
As long as they keep quiet by the fire
And never say 'no' when the world says 'ay,'
For that is fatal,—their angelic reach
Of virtue, chiefly used to sit and darn,
And fatten household sinners,—their, in brief,
Potential faculty in everything
Of abdicating power in it: she owned
She liked a woman to be womanly,
And English women, she thanked God and
sighed,
(Some people always sigh in thanking God)
Were models to the universe.

(1.427-46)

Reynolds believes that the section dealing with "books on womanhood" refers to conduct books by Sarah Stickney Ellis, while lines 438 and 440, which contain the words *angel*ic and *house*-hold, prompt Paul Turner to argue that ***Aurora Leigh*** was a direct reference and refutation to Patmore's poem.[16] In either case, despite her insistence that Aurora become a "womanly woman" and her perpetuation of the patriarchal system of education, Aunt Leigh herself has rejected this model, and so becomes a different kind of role model for Aurora. Although she seemingly preserves patriarchy through her attitudes, nonetheless, Aunt Leigh remains a single and independent woman.

Amidst the total immersion in patriarchal doctrine but also because of her aunt's example, Aurora finds seeds of feminist thought growing within her. So it is fitting that on the morning of her twentieth birthday, Aurora walks in the garden and crowns herself with a wreath of ivy "In sport, not pride, to learn the feel of it" (2.34), a scene that deftly interweaves these two competing ideologies. She chooses ivy over bay, the traditional crown of the poet, because "The fates deny us if we are overbold" (2.39); but she also refuses bay because it is the crown of the male poet and Aurora, though confident of her writing ability, is less than convinced of her genius. Notwithstanding rebuking Romney for his contention that "'We shall not get a [woman] poet'" (2.225), Aurora has, because of her education, internalized much the same perspective. But she has also found a strength through and in her writing that allows her to struggle against such indoctrination.

Her blossoming philosophy of art is contained within her description of the ivy. While it invokes a pessimistic vision of woman's writing as dead or forgotten since ivy "grow[s] on graves," (2.51), the ivy also resonates with images of power and tradition. Aurora describes the ivy as she envisions her poetry to be: "bold" and "strong," but "pretty too, / (And that's not ill)" (2.50, 51, 52-53). The ivy's ability to grow "as good . . . on graves / As twist about a thyrsus" (2.51-52) invokes the poetic traditions of elegies and epics. Finally, that "not a leaf will grow / But thinking of a wreath" (2.47-48) represents poetry's utilitarian function, what will eventually become Aurora's chosen, and decidedly feminist, position as a poet of social criticism.

Aurora's growing feminism is evident in the reasons for her rejection of Romney's marriage proposal on the grounds that "'What [he] love[s], / Is not a woman, . . . but a cause'" (2.400-1). She will not marry a man who puts social activism before love. Aurora also points out the irony that in order to be good wives, women must embody all the qualities that they have been educated and encouraged not to acquire, specifically strength and individuality of character:

. . . 'am I proved too weak
To stand alone, yet strong enough to bear
Such leaners on my shoulder? poor to think,
Yet rich enough to sympathise with thought?
Incompetent to sing, as blackbirds can,
Yet competent to love, like HIM?'[17]

(2.359-64)

Ironically, Aurora, later living in London pursuing her career, finds similar paradoxes in being a writer:

My critic Belfair wants another book
Entirely different, which will sell, (and live?)
A striking book, yet not a startling book,
The public blames originalities,—. . .
Good things, not subtle, new yet orthodox,
As easy reading as the dog-eared page
That's fingered by said public fifty years,
Since first taught spelling by its grandmother,
And yet a revelation in some sort:
That's hard, my critic Belfair.

(3.68-71, 74-9)

The reading public wants something new, yet something comfortable while the husband wants a wife who is morally strong but dependently weak. While Victorian culture associated a woman's writing with prostitution, Barrett Browning also clearly makes the correlation between prostitution and marriage. Any relationship that relies on an uneven power base ultimately abuses the less powerful.

Aurora recognizes the prostitution involved with writing: "I wrote for cyclopaedias, magazines, / And weekly papers, holding up my name / To keep it from the mud" (3.310-12);[18] but she also realizes that acceptance of Romney's proposal of marriage would be tantamount to "the sanctioned prostitution of marriage":[19] "If I married him, / I should not dare to call my soul my own / Which so he had bought and paid for" (2.785-87). Convinced there is no compromise, the young Aurora chooses the writing because she believes in the God-given right to use her talent for work: "'. . . every creature, female as the male, / Stands single in responsible act and thought / As also in birth and death'" (2.437-39).

Throughout ***Aurora Leigh,*** Barrett Browning reveals Aurora's complex process of finding out who she is as a writer and a woman. As Angela Leighton points out, it is Aurora's (and Barrett Browning's) belief in a poetry that embraces and celebrates everyday life that allows Barrett Browning to "derive a theory of women's writing as contemporary, combative and self-sufficient. However, it is one of the strengths or merits of [***Aurora Leigh***] that it also traces the hidden personal cost of this achievement."[20] At first Aurora holds onto an unflagging belief in the patriarchal conditions of art. She attempts the traditional forms, with varying degrees of success, but certainly without a sense of accomplishment: ballads and pastorals "the worse done, I think, / For being not ill-done" (5.132-33). Aurora shuns dramatic writing because it mostly "Adopts the standard of the public taste / To chalk its height on" (5.270-71). She concedes that there is great drama, Shakespeare's for example, but the distrust of her own genius convinces her that she would "keep it down / To the level of the footlights" (5.318-19). Romney's words that "[Women] miss the abstract when we comprehend. / We miss it most when we aspire,—and fail" (5.57-58) continue to haunt Aurora's conscience until she decides, "I'll have no traffic with the personal thought / In art's pure temple" (5.61-62). Aurora temporarily thinks that Romney is right, that the personal must be disconnected from the political. However, this notion is short-lived as she realizes her own truth: that to be socially responsible, a poet must deal with important current issues, not with the past.

Thus Aurora makes a startling break with tradition, claiming the right for poetry to be concerned with the contemporary age: "All actual heroes are essential men, / And all men possible heroes" (5.151-52). That epic and, more important, socially-beneficial poetry occupies itself with the past is "wrong thinking, to my mind, / And wrong thoughts make poor poems. . . . / I do distrust the poet who discerns / No character or glory in his times" (5.165-66, 189-90). Barrett Browning's most unabashed declaration of her theory of art is Aurora's "womanization," in Gail Turley Houston's term, not only of the age but of its poetry:[21]

> Never flinch,
> But still, unscrupulously epic, catch
> Upon the burning lava of a song
> The full-veined, heaving, double-breasted Age:
> That, when the next shall come, the men of that
> May touch the impress with reverent hand, and
>   say
> 'Behold,—behold the paps we all have sucked!
> This bosom seems to beat still, or at least
> It sets ours beating: this is living art,
> Which thus presents and thus records true life.'
> (5.213-22)

Here Barrett Browning connects the Victorian age with the power of women, a power that transcends time and will affect future generations. More explicitly, the poetry that she endorses, "Which thus presents and thus records true life," is the literature that doesn't "flinch" nor shy from controversy. In fact, it will produce contention (as did the above passage that earned ***Aurora Leigh*** such epithets as "infelicitous," "unnatural," "coarse," "mean, gross, and puerile" from the critics) in order to coerce the public into confronting injustice, another essential doctrine of domestic-professional fiction. The amazonian image that Barrett Browning presents as indicative of true poetry and the true age is Woman, "full-veined" and "heaving," establishing a model for future generations. When Aurora finally decides that "The artist's part is both to be and do, / Transfixing with a special, central power / The flat experience of the common man" (5.367-69), her faith in her genius begins to bloom. But she will go even one step further and "be and do" the experience of the common *woman* in telling Marian's story. Aurora's initial step in the correction of her sense of self is her sharing in Marian's degradation and allowing her a voice to speak to a society that says such women should be silent.

One of Aurora's chief moves that reveals she is coming to terms with the divisions within herself is her decision to confront Lady Waldemar. Agonizing over her rejection of Romney several years earlier and his now impending marriage to Lady Waldemar, for the first time in the poem Aurora upbraids herself for not being the kind of woman that society says a man wants as a wife:

> I thought, 'Now, if I had been a woman, such
> As God made women, to save men by love,—
> By just my love I might have saved this man,
> And made a nobler poem for the world

Than all I have failed in.' But I failed besides
In this; and now he's lost! through me alone!
(7.184-89)

Aurora sees herself falling short as a poet and a woman here because she has not yet been able to reconcile a professional life with a personal one; as Susanna Egan points out, "Failing to recognize her own love for Romney, Aurora has separated head from heart and art from life."[22] But Aurora does not dwell on this defeat for long; she has Marian and her son to look after. In learning to care for them, Aurora ironically must learn what Romney accused her of many years previously: the importance of individualizing a problem rather than generalizing it. Through this devotion, Aurora can then acknowledge her love for Romney and extend to him her empathy.

Her dawning realization that she must be responsible for others leads Aurora to protect Romney by writing Lady Waldemar, letting her know that she knows what part Lady Waldemar played in Marian's tragedy. That the writing of this letter comes immediately after Aurora's denouncement of herself as not womanly enough is significant. Aurora finally is able to put behind her Victorian society's ideal woman because she realizes she has no use for her as a model for herself; however, stripped of its idealization, the ideology reveals hows the image denigrates and suppresses women and their abilities. In this letter, Aurora demands, when they are married that Lady Waldemar be Romney's "faithful and true wife" (7.344). She then invokes the image of the Angel in the House, but not for the usual idealization:

Keep warm his hearth and clean his board, and,
when
He speaks, be quick with your obedience;
Still grind your paltry wants and low desires
To dust beneath his heel; . . .
. . . You shall not vex him,—mark,
You shall not vex him, jar him when he's sad,
Or cross him when he's eager. Understand
To trick him with apparent sympathies,
Nor let him see thee in the face too near
And unlearn thy sweet seeming. Pay the price
Of lies, by being constrained to lie on still:
'Tis easy for thy sort: a million more
Will scarcely damn thee deeper.
(7.345-48, 353-61)

Aurora summons up the ideal figure of Victorian womanhood not as a model for Lady Waldemar, but as a punishment. Lady Waldemar's false mask of concern for Romney and the lower classes forces Aurora not only into the role of Romney's protector, but also of blackmailer. Despite its "unladylike" connotations, Aurora's threat reveals that she has learned that caring for and protecting others is more important than social conventions. She may not be able to stop the marriage, but she can see to it that Romney is treated well. Not even bothering to veil her threat, Aurora's words are clear:

. . . Fail a point,
And show our Romney wounded, ill-content,
Tormented in his home, we open mouth,
And such a noise will follow, the last trump's
Will scarcely seem more dreadful; even to
you; . . .
And so I warn you. I'm . . . Aurora Leigh.
(7.364-68, 374)

It is interesting that Barrett Browning constitutes the Angel of the House image as punishment here, and I think it can be read in two ways. It must first be understood, as Elizabeth Langland has convincingly established, that the Angel in the House was largely a middle-class ideal.[23] So, if seen as representative of the aristocracy's selfishness and indifference to the lower classes, Lady Waldemar can receive no greater chastisement than having to conduct herself as a middle-class woman. But I think Barrett Browning appropriates this image for a much broader purpose. The Angel in the House, as an unattainable ideal for middle-class women, is clearly a punishment, not a goal, for these women also. This image is a lie, forcing women "to lie on still." Barrett Browning instead offers Aurora Leigh, a not-so-perfect woman who is self-asserting rather than self-effacing. This model of woman, because not ideal nor forced into silence or hypocrisy, is the one who will, with hope and work, change society and create a New Jerusalem.

4

After Aurora has formulated her ultimate philosophy of art, a change appears in the narrative in Book 6. No longer written in the past tense from a distanced perspective, Aurora's story is now told in journal- or diary-like form, with "entries written down, as it were, soon after the events described have taken place."[24] Barrett Browning, says Alison Case, presents two kinds of narrative plots—'a female *Kunstlerroman* [Books 1-5] and a feminine love story [Books 6-9]"—and then matches them with appropriate narrative styles.[25] But it is more than just the construction of two different types of stories here. Once Aurora has fulfilled her quest as artist—definitively elucidating her philosophy of art—, she can break free of the male rules of writing, returning to the more conventionally-accepted feminine writing of diaries and letters, comfortably accepting it but also using it for socio-political purposes. Barrett Browning also breaks from the traditional masculine dictates of writing: her combination of writing an epic concerned with the contemporary and utilizing the traditionally feminine epistolary and diary novel genres leads Barrett Browning to invent a new genre of her own: the novel-poem, a form that she seems to specifically designate as woman's writing. This new genre, specifically designed to address contemporary social problems and offer a woman's solutions to them, marks Barrett Browning's poem as the most prominent, if not the first, example of nineteenth-century domestic-professional fiction.[26]

The distinctive form of ***Aurora Leigh*** met with mixed critical reception, many reviewers accusing Barrett Browning of experimenting for experimentation's sake. While R. A. Vaughn of the *British Quarterly Review* enthusiastically applauded the poem's novelty as "original, because natural—for originality is but nature—a genuine spontaneity,"[27] other reviewers censured Barrett Browning's boldness in breaking the rules. W. E. Aytoun, of *Blackwood's,* questioned her presumption in mixing the high aesthetics associated with epic poetry with the low social concerns of reality associated with the novel:

> We may consider it almost as a certainty that every leading principle of art has been weighed and sifted by our predecessors; and that most of the theories, which are paraded as discoveries, were deliberately examined by them, and rejected because they were false or impracticable. . . . All poetical characters, all poetical situations, must be idealised. The language is not that of common life, which belongs essentially to the domain of prose. There lies the distinction between a novel and a poem. . . . We cannot allow fancy to be trammelled in its work by perpetual reference to realities.[28]

And H. F. Chorley of *The Athenæum* concurred:

> This looks not like a poem, but a novel. . . . But what are we to say if we waive purpose—if we do not discuss the wisdom of the form selected . . . if we treat 'Aurora Leigh' as a poetical romance? Simply, that we have no experience of such a mingling of what is precious with what is mean . . . as we find in these nine books of blank verse.[29]

Aytoun and Chorley articulate a familiar theme of nineteenth-century criticism: the hallowing of tradition and maintaining of the status quo. Both reviewers see poetry strictly in aesthetic terms; it is not an arena in which to promote change—either in society or in literature. Barrett Browning, however, postulated that poetry should and must confront immediate social issues and knew that she was threatening long-held, sanctioned views. She anticipated reactions such as Aytoun's and Chorley's.

In a letter to art critic Anna Jameson, Barrett Browning conceded that ***Aurora Leigh*** was an assay into uncharted territory, but it was one that was borne of lengthy contemplation, not of, in Aytoun's words, "a token of morbid craving for originality"[30]: "But 'the form,' in this sense is my experiment, & I dont [*sic*] 'give it up' yet, having considered the subject much & long."[31] Barrett Browning not only expected unfavorable reviews, she also seemed to revel in them; in fact, what appears to have surprised her most of all was the immense amount of commendatory reaction, not only from critics but the reading public. In another letter to Jameson, Barrett Browning laughs at the image of herself as a revolutionary:

> And as for the critics—yes, indeed, I agree with you that I have no reason to complain. More than that, I confess to you that I am entirely astonished at the amount of reception I have met with—I who expected to be put in the stocks and pelted with the eggs of the last twenty years' 'singing birds' as a disorderly woman and freethinking poet![32]

One senses from reading Barrett Browning's letters that she was somewhat disappointed that ***Aurora Leigh*** did not draw as much fire as she had thought it would. No cowering wallflower, Barrett Browning wanted the format of her verse-novel to draw attention to the concerns within it, specifically "the condition of women in our cities": "If a woman ignores these wrongs, then may women as a sex continue to suffer them; there is no help for any of us—let us be dumb and die."[33]

Barrett Browning's anticipation of the predicted reaction from conservative reviewers is reflected in Aurora and Romney's early discordant relationship: Romney is the critic of the woman poet's attempt to transform literature and society. But Barrett Browning makes it clear through their evolving association that it is not so much a confrontational situation as it is a sustaining, nurturing one. From the start, Romney is influential in bringing out the "fight" in Aurora. While all others around her whisper among themselves that she "'Thrives ill in England'" (1.497), but do nothing about it, Romney confronts her "With sudden anger": "'You wish to die and leave the world a-dusk / For others, with your naughty light blown out?'" (1.500, 502-3). Aurora responds by looking "into his face defyingly" (1.504). Men and women, Barrett Browning believes, should not be combative for confrontation's sake, but engage in a communication that debates, challenges, and encourages each other.

Throughout the course of their relationship, each will repeatedly dare the other to achieve his or her highest potential. Romney's assertions that she (nor other women) can write great poetry may be contemptible, but they also challenge Aurora to achieve such greatness. In return, Aurora's contention that Romney's social idealism will not attain its intended ends because it fails to consider the individual will eventually make Romney reconsider his work. After reading one of Aurora's later books of poetry (one that his words dared her to write), Romney concedes that art can affect the political precisely because of its effect on the individual:

> . . . 'We want more quiet in our works,
> More knowledge of the bounds in which we
> work;
> More knowledge that each individual man
> Remains an Adam to the general race,
> Constrained to see, like Adam, that he keep
> His personal state's condition honestly,
> Or vain all thoughts of his to help the world,
> Which still must be developed from its one
> If bettered in its many.'
>
> (8.852-60)

Romney and Aurora's courtship/friendship survives its on-again/off-again condition because each understands, if somewhat unconsciously, that they are encouraging each other to their fullest capability. Aurora realizes the necessity for both men and women to fulfill their potential for the embetterment of society. However, she also recognizes that women, more often than not, are dissuaded or refused from fulfilling that potential. Therefore, a central thematic principle in domestic-professional fiction is that a woman break free from cultural conventions to cultivate the power that can transform society. That power is embodied in Aurora and Romney's vow of love for each other; their passion for their work is matched by their passion for each other:

> There were words
> That broke in utterance . . . melted, in the
> fire,—
> Embrace, that was convulsion, . . . then a kiss
> As long and silent as the ecstatic night,
> And deep, deep, shuddering breaths, which
> meant beyond
> Whatever could be told by word or kiss.
>
> (9.719-24)

Aurora now can fully engage herself with her work as a social poet, to which the writing of ***Aurora Leigh*** will attest, while Romney, blinded in a fire attempting to achieve social idealism by force, understands that his life must actively involve the loving of another, not the cold embracing of a social ideal: "'Shine out for two, Aurora, and fulfil / My falling-short that must be! work for two, / As I, though thus restrained, for two, shall love!'" (9.910-12). His previous figurative blindness now replaced by literal blindness, Romney now "sees" clearly, as does Aurora, that life must be a balance of individualizing and generalizing.

5

At the beginning of Book 2, Aurora labels herself "Woman and artist,—either incomplete, / Both Credulous of completion" (2.4-5). It is through the writing of her story, within which Marian's story is so crucial a part, that the writer is now completed. Her forthcoming marriage to Romney completes the woman. Deirdre David argues that their union signifies that "woman's poetry is created from her sexuality," and that by uniting Aurora and Romney, Barrett Browning's verse-novel is not feminist, but one that ultimately reifies the concept that "woman's art is made the servitor of the male ideal."[34] However, David ignores the revolutionary concept of Barrett Browning's giving Aurora (and ***Aurora Leigh***) a definite sexuality in the first place.[35] Life without love is unbalanced; until she can put her life in balance (and the same can be said of Romney), Aurora cannot fulfill her potential as a poet. Once she does so, the result is ***Aurora Leigh*** and a part in a promising union. As Beverly Taylor notes, "The existence of the poem, ***Aurora Leigh,*** written after the events it records, demonstrates that her projected marriage to Romney does not silence her as a poet or reduce her to the status of dependent and helpmate she had so much feared initially; instead, their union engenders richer, more complex and more satisfying verse."[36] Aurora is now mature enough to realize not only that art and love are compatible, but also mature enough to take on the creation of two "New Jerusalems": the writing of socially-beneficial poetry and partnership in an egalitarian marriage, both embodied within her text.

A new society, based upon "new laws / Admitting freedom" (9.947-8), holds the hope for an equitable community, much as Aurora and Romney's relationship holds the promise of an egalitarian union. Indeed, the entire verse-novel has seemed to be headed in this direction. However, I say "holds the promise" because Aurora writes this ending immediately after the scene where the lovers stand facing the east, toward the rising sun, envisioning a new society that will fuse art and social activism. We are left exactly where Aurora and Romney leave off—looking toward a new dawn, but never entirely confident that this new dawn will be unlike the previous ones. It is an ending of guarded optimism. Barrett Browning would like to believe that a just society is only a sunrise away, yet having Aurora write her story and end it at this moment signifies that she is not certain it will ever be achieved. It is the end of the verse-novel, but only the beginning of social transformation should the readers of ***Aurora Leigh*** take up Barrett Browning's challenge as she intends.

Notes

1. The "Angel in the House" was certainly the ideal long before Patmore's time, but his poem sanctified the image and gave it its celestial epithet.

2. Elizabeth Barrett Browning, *Aurora Leigh,* ed. Margaret Reynolds (New York: W. W. Norton, 1996), 1.15-19. Citations of the text are to this edition.

3. W. E. Aytoun, "Mrs. Barrett Browning—Aurora Leigh," *Blackwood's Edinburgh Magazine* 81 (January 1857): 32, 41.

4. In a letter to Isa Blagden on January 7, 1859, Barrett Browning noted the somewhat tediousness of revising proofs for the third edition of *Aurora Leigh,* claiming she "dizzied myself with the 'ifs' and 'ands,' and done some little good I hope at much cost . . ." *The Letters of Elizabeth Barrett Browning,* ed. Frederic Kenyon (London: Smith, Elder, 1897), 2.302.

5. The most widely-used collection of Patmore's poetry is Frederick Page's 1949 edition, *The Poems of Coventry Patmore,* "complete so far as [Patmore] wished them to be republished and in the text as he finally revised it." (Oxford U. Press), v.

6. Linda K. Hughes, "Entombing the Angel: Patmore's Revision of *Angel in the House,*" in *Victorian Authors and Their Works: Revision Motivations and Modes,* ed. Judith Kennedy (Ohio U. Press, 1991), 143.

7. Hughes, 140-41.

8. Karl Beckson, *London in the 1890s: A Cultural History* (New York: W. W. Norton, 1992), 62.

9. Margaret Reynolds, "*Aurora Leigh*: 'Writing her story for her better self,'" *Browning Society Notes* 17.1-3 (1987-88): 5.

10. Beverly Taylor, "'School-Miss Alfred' and 'Materfamilias': Female Sexuality and Poetic Voice in *The Princess* and *Aurora Leigh,*" in *Gender and Discourse in Victorian Literature and Art,* ed. Antony H. Harrison and Beverly Taylor (Northern Illinois U. Press, 1992), 23-24.

11. Barbara Charlesworth Gelpi, "*Aurora Leigh*: The Vocation of the Woman Poet," *Victorian Poetry,* 19 (1981), 41.

12. Kathleen K. Hickok, "'New Yet Orthodox': The Female Characters in *Aurora Leigh,*" *International Journal of Women's Studies* 3 (1980): 480.

13. Gail Turley Houston, "Gender Construction and the *Kunstlerroman: David Copperfield* and *Aurora Leigh,*" *PQ* 72 (1993): 213-36 and Ellen Chafee, "Conceiving Literary Femininity: Figures of the Woman Writer 1857-1900" (Diss., Rutgers University, 1996), 16.

14. See Gelpi.

15. In addition to Gelpi, see Kathleen Blake, "Elizabeth Barrett Browning and Wordsworth: The Romantic Poet as a Woman," *Victorian Poetry,* 24(1986): 387-98 and Patricia Thomas Srebrnik, "'The Central Truth': Phallogocentrism in *Aurora Leigh,*" *Victorian Newsletter,* 84 (1993): 9-11.

16. Reynolds, *Aurora Leigh*: 18, note 1 and Paul Turner, "Aurora Versus the Angel," *RES* 24 (1948): 227-35.

17. Reynolds glosses this word as "Christ, presumably," *Aurora Leigh,* 49, note 2.

18. Aurora's feelings that she "dirties" herself by writing for periodicals echo the sentiments of Mary Shelley who, after Percy Shelley's death, needed to write on an almost constant basis for various magazines in order to support herself and her young son: "I write bad articles which help to make me miserable—But I am going to plunge into a novel, and hope that its clear water will wash off the mud of the magazines—." From a letter to Leigh Hunt, February 9, 1824, in *The Letters of Mary Wollstonecraft Shelley,* ed. Betty T. Bennett (Johns Hopkins U. Press, 1980), 1.412. Shelley had originally written the word "dirt," but crossed it out in favor of the harsher "mud," indicating how much she detested writing such.

19. Susanna Egan, "Glad Rags for Lady Godiva: Woman's Story as Womanstance in Elizabeth Barrett Browning's *Aurora Leigh,*" *English Studies in Canada* 20 (1994): 290.

20. Angela Leighton, *Elizabeth Barrett Browning* (Sussex: Harvester Press, Ltd., 1986), 115-16.

21. Gail Turley Houston, *Royalties: The Queen and Victorian Writers* (U. Press of Virginia, 1999).

22. Egan, 295.

23. Elizabeth Langland, *Nobody's Angels: Middle-Class Women and Domestic Ideology in Victorian Culture* (Cornell U. Press, 1995), 79.

24. Reynolds, *Aurora Leigh,* 194, note 2.

25. Alison Case, "Gender and Narration in *Aurora Leigh,*" *Victorian Poetry* 29 (1991): 17.

26. This essay is part of a larger project that examines the influence of *Aurora Leigh* on British women's domestic-professional fiction of the 1890s. The major texts of my discussion are Rhoda Broughton's *A Beginner* (1894), Mary Cholmondeley's *Red Pottage* (1899), Marie Corelli's *The Sorrows of Satan* (1895), Ella Hepworth Dixon's *The Story of a Modern Woman* (1894), Sarah Grand's *The Beth Book* (1897), and Annie E. Holdsworth's *The Years That the Locust Hath Eaten* (1895).

27. R. A. Vaughn, "Aurora Leigh. By Elizabeth Barrett Browning," *British Quarterly Review* 25 (January 1857): 263.

28. Aytoun, 34, 34-5, 41.

29. H. F. Chorley, "*Aurora Leigh.* By Elizabeth Barrett Browning," *The Athenæum* no. 1517 (November 22, 1856): 1425.

30. Aytoun, 39.

31. Quoted in Reynolds, *Aurora Leigh,* 341.

32. *Letters,* 2:252.

33. *Letters,* 2:254.

34. Deirdre David, "'Art's A Service': Social Wound, Sexual Politics, and *Aurora Leigh," Browning Institute Studies* 13 (1985): 130, 113.

35. See, for example, Christine Sutphin, "Revising Old Scripts: The Fusion of Independence and Intimacy in *Aurora Leigh," Browning Institute Studies,* 15 (1987): 43-54.

36. Taylor, 23.

FURTHER READING

Bibliography

Donaldson, Sandra. *Elizabeth Barrett Browning: An Annotated Bibliography of the Commentary and Criticism, 1826-1990.* New York: G. K. Hall, 1993, 642 p.

Includes an introduction identifying principal works and dominant themes; criticism is in English, French, and Italian.

Biographies

Forster, Margaret. *Elizabeth Barrett Browning: A Biography.* London: Chatto & Windus, 1988, 416 p.

Offers new primary evidence about Browning's childhood.

Taplin, Gardner B. *The Life of Elizabeth Barrett Browning.* New Haven: Yale University Press, 1957, 482 p.

Provides a definitive biography, with a detailed account of the creation, publication, and critical reception of Browning's poetry.

Criticism

Byrd, Deborah. "Combating an Alien Tyranny: Elizabeth Barrett Browning's Evolution as a Feminist Poet." *Browning Institute Studies* 15 (1987): 23-41.

Examines Browning's place in the history of women writers, including the poet's own reading and influences and the development of her social thought.

Case, Alison. "Gender and Narration in *Aurora Leigh." Victorian Poetry* 29, no. 1 (spring 1991): 17-32.

Contends that in Aurora Leigh *Browning transgressed the conventions of the novel.*

Cooper, Helen. "Working into Light: Elizabeth Barrett Browning." In *Shakespeare's Sisters: Feminist Essays on Women Poets,* edited by Sandra M. Gilbert and Susan Gubar, pp. 65-81. Bloomington: Indiana University Press, 1979.

Considers Browning's portrayal of the patriarchal literary tradition and her criticisms of women's complicity in their own oppression.

———. *Elizabeth Barrett Browning, Woman and Artist.* Chapel Hill: University of North Carolina Press, 1988, 231 p.

Analyzes Browning's work in the context of liberal humanism and at a unique moment in the nineteenth century open to nontraditional authors who represent a middle-class spirit.

David, Deirdre. "Woman's Art as Servant of Patriarchy: The Vision of *Aurora Leigh."* In *Intellectual Women and Victorian Patriarchy: Harriet Martineau, Elizabeth Barrett Browning, George Eliot,* pp. 143-58. Ithaca, N.Y.: Cornell University Press, 1987.

Contends that despite feminist interpretations to the contrary, Aurora Leigh *engages in a traditional and conservative endorsement of patriarchal politics.*

Friewald, Bina. "'The praise which men give women': Elizabeth Barrett Browning's *Aurora Leigh* and the Critics." *Dalhousie Review* 66 (1986): 311-36.

Suggests that Victorian reviewers' praise for Aurora Leigh *weakened its potential force as a radical or subversive text.*

Gelpi, Barbara Charlesworth. *"Aurora Leigh*: The Vocation of the Woman Poet." *Victorian Poetry* 19, no. 1 (spring 1981): 35-48.

Sees Aurora Leigh *as a metaphorical investigation of Browning's changing attitudes toward herself, her profession, and womanhood in general.*

Gilbert, Sandra M. "From *Patria* to *Matria*: Elizabeth Barrett Browning's Risorgimento." *PMLA* 99, no. 2 (1984): 194-211.

Parallels Browning's interest in Italy's nationalization with the poet's own search for a new identity grounded in a feminine tradition; contends that she sees in Italy the potential for a new kind of society separate from patriarchy.

Gilbert, Sandra M. and Susan Gubar. "The Aesthetics of Renunciation." In *The Madwoman in the Attic: The Woman Writer and the Nineteenth-Century Literary Imagination,* pp. 539-80. New Haven: Yale University Press, 1979.

Interprets Aurora Leigh *as a compromise between self-assertion and feminine submission, where the heroine must learn to give up her identity.*

Hayter, Alethea. *Mrs. Browning: A Poet's Work and its Setting.* London: Faber and Faber, 1962, 261 p.

Attempts to shift the course of criticism on Browning by emphasizing poetic craft and originality over personality and "womanly sweetness."

Jones, Christine Kenyon. "'Some World's-Wonder in Chapel or Crypt': Elizabeth Barrett Browning and Disability." *Nineteenth Century Studies* 16 (2002): 21-35.

Looks at the relationships among gender, disability, and identity in Browning's poetry and letters.

Leighton, Angela. *Elizabeth Barrett Browning.* Bloomington: Indiana University Press, 1986, 192 p.

Interprets Browning's work with feminist and psychoanalytic approaches, including an emphasis on the poet's family relationships as reflected in the poems.

———. "'Because men made the laws': The Fallen Woman and the Woman Poet." In *New Feminist Discourses: Critical Essays on Theories and Texts,* edited by Isobel Armstrong, pp. 342-60. New York: Routledge, 1992.

Observes how women poets including Browning, Christina Rossetti, and others ally themselves with the figure of the fallen woman to help create a feminine poetic voice.

Lupton, Mary Jane. "The Printing Woman Who Lost Her Place: Elizabeth Barrett Browning." *Women* 2, no. 1 (1970): 2-5.

Suggests that Browning's work has been undervalued because of misplaced attention to her illness and her femininity; critiques the poet's handling of gender issues in Aurora Leigh.

Mermin, Dorothy. "Genre and Gender in *Aurora Leigh." The Victorian Newsletter* 69 (spring 1986): 7-11.

Contends that Aurora Leigh *transgresses the distinction between poetry and fiction as it does the distinction between males and females.*

———. *Elizabeth Barrett Browning: The Origins of a New Poetry.* Chicago: University of Chicago Press, 1989, 325 p.

Emphasizes Browning's creation of new poetic forms as well as new ways of being a woman in society, particularly in her marriage; notes the influence of both Romantic and Victorian culture.

Moers, Ellen. *Literary Women: The Great Writers.* Garden City, N.Y.: Doubleday, 1976, 336 p.

Includes Browning in the tradition of nineteenth-century women writers, noting common themes, images, and genres.

Schor, Esther. "The Poetics of Politics: Barrett Browning's *Casa Guidi Windows." Tulsa Studies in Women's Literature* 17, no. 2 (fall 1998): 305-24.

Analyzes Browning's political poetry about Italy.

Steinmetz, Virginia. "Images of 'Mother-Want' in Elizabeth Barrett Browning's *Aurora Leigh." Victorian Poetry* 21, no. 4 (1983): 351-67.

Takes a psychoanalytic approach to maternal imagery in Aurora Leigh.

Stephenson, Glennis. *Elizabeth Barrett Browning and the Poetry of Love.* Ann Arbor, Mich.: U.M.I. Research Press, 1989, 153 p.

Asserts that Browning's love poetry uses a female voice employing a male tradition; observes the poet's insistence on an active role for women in relationships and the reality of feminine sexual desire.

Stone, Marjorie. "Cursing as One of the Fine Arts: Elizabeth Barrett Browning's Political Poems." *Dalhousie Review* 66, no. 1-2 (1986): 155-73.

Sees the curses in Browning's poems as expressions of anger for women's oppression.

Straight, Julie. "'Neither Keeping Either Under': Gender and Voice in Elizabeth Barrett's *The Seraphim." Victorian Poetry* 38, no. 2 (summer 2000): 269-88.

Focuses on Browning's treatment of the Crucifixion and its relationship to hierarchy and the female Voice.

Walsh, Susan. "'Doing the Afra Behn': Barrett Browning's Portrait of the Artist." *Victorian Poetry* 36, no. 2 (summer 1998): 163-86.

Links the discourse of Victorian sanitation reform and public health concerns to the treatment of gender roles in Aurora Leigh.

OTHER SOURCES FROM GALE:

Additional coverage of Browning's life and career is contained in the following sources published by the Gale Group: *British Writers,* Vol. 4; *Concise Dictionary of British Literary Biography, 1832-1890; Dictionary of Literary Biography,* Vols. 32, 199; *DISCovering Authors; DISCovering Authors: British Edition; DISCovering Authors: Canadian Edition; DISCovering Authors Modules: Most-studied Authors and Poets; DISCovering Authors 3.0; Exploring Poetry; Literature Resource Center; Nineteenth-Century Literature Criticism,* Vols. 1, 16, 61, 66; *Poetry Criticism,* Vol. 6; *Poetry for Students,* Vols. 2, 16; *Poets: American and British; Twayne's English Authors; World Literature and Its Times; World Literature Criticism; and World Poets.*

FANNY BURNEY

(1752 - 1840)

(Born Frances Burney; later Madame d'Arblay) English novelist, playwright, and diarist.

Burney's best known novel *Evelina; or, A Young Lady's Entrance into the World* (1778), is an early comedy of manners that depicts the coming-of-age of a young woman subject to the whims of irresponsible men and the restrictions of English society. With *Evelina* and three later books, Burney greatly influenced the early development of the novel, incorporating domestic and feminine concerns, and set a successful precedent for aspiring women authors, making way for the novel to become a genre both by and for women.

BIOGRAPHICAL INFORMATION

Burney was born June 13, 1752 in London to Esther Sleepe and Charles Burney. Her mother died when Burney was ten, and she became attached to her father, a prominent musician and England's first musicologist. Although Burney was a shy child and received little formal education, she met a number of artists and intellectuals through her father. She read extensively and, while her father preferred that she devote herself to activities other than writing, she secretly began to compose poems, plays, and fiction. In 1767, however, apparently in response to her father's disapproval of her writing, Burney destroyed all her manuscripts. Among these early manuscripts was the novel "The History of Caroline Evelyn." When Burney began to write again several years later, the novel formed the basis of the first part of *Evelina.* To Burney's surprise, the success of *Evelina* delighted her father; Dr. Burney had read and enjoyed *Evelina,* which had been published anonymously, without knowing that his daughter was the author. He introduced his daughter to such prominent literary figures as Samuel Johnson and Edmund Burke, who warmly welcomed her into London's literary circles and encouraged her to continue writing. However, because Dr. Burney privately pronounced her next work, a drama entitled "The Witlings," a failure, it was never published or produced. Several critics now contend that her father objected to this parody of bluestocking society for its controversial subject. Despite Burney's popularity as an author, her family continued to be concerned about her unmarried status and future financial security. When she was offered a position as second keeper of the robes to Queen Charlotte in 1786, she accepted the prestigious post at her father's urging. However, Burney's estrangement from the society that inspired her novels made her miserable. She recorded her experience in journals and letters, published posthumously in the *Diary and Letters of Madame d'Arblay* (1842-46), that are today considered a telling account of the rigors and restrictions of life at court. Several tragedies that she composed during this period also bear witness to Burney's increasing unhappiness and frustration. Eventually, she became ill and Dr. Burney obtained her release from royal service. She left court in 1791, receiving a pension of one hundred pounds a year. Soon after, Burney married Alexandre d'Arblay, a penniless French exile. In 1794 she gave birth to a son, Alexander. Burney resumed her novel-writing career in 1796 with *Camilla; or, A Picture of Youth,* a satirical examination of the social restrictions of marriage. The work yielded sufficient funds to build the d'Arblays a new home, Camilla Cottage. Burney's days at Camilla Cottage were productive; there she wrote several unpublished comedies before traveling to France with her family in 1802. Though they intended to visit briefly, they were forced to stay until 1812 because of the outbreak of war between France and England. In 1811, Burney underwent a mastectomy—performed before the invention of anesthesia—hiding her ordeal even from her husband, who was away on business. Upon the couple's return to England, Burney wrote her last novel, *The Wanderer; or, Female Difficulties* (1814). In 1815, during Napoleon's Hundred Days, d'Arblay aided the forces against Napoleon while Burney fled to Brussels for the duration of the conflict; they returned to England later that year and settled in Bath. After d'Arblay's death in 1818, Burney moved back to London, where she began to revise her journals to add her experiences in exile during wartime. She died at the age of eighty-eight.

MAJOR WORKS

Burney published *Evelina* anonymously, aided by her brother Charles, who disguised himself when submitting the manuscript. An epistolary novel with a focus on female identity, the book met with immediate acclaim. In Evelina, Burney created a heroine who is considered one of the most vibrant and realistic in English literature, and the novel is the primary source of Burney's modern reputation. Burney next wrote *Cecilia; or, Memoirs of an Heiress* (1782), in which she continued to explore the social mores of her era with wit and satire. It was also her first use of third-person narrative, which she employed in both her subsequent novels. While not as great a success as *Evelina, Cecilia* was generally well received. Critics favorably compared it with the works of Samuel Richardson, Henry Fielding, and Laurence Sterne but argued that it lacked the spontaneity of *Evelina,* a flaw also detected in *Camilla* and *The Wanderer.* Though most commentators fault *Camilla* as a sensational work written purely for financial reasons, it was extremely popular. *The Wanderer,* criticized as dated and awkwardly constructed, was the most poorly received of her novels. The novel's depiction of a nineteenth-century woman struggling to earn her own living, however, has prompted some commentary in recent years, particularly from a feminist standpoint. During the final years of her life, Burney edited her father's memoirs and correspondence, *Memoirs of Dr. Burney, Arranged from His Own Manuscripts, from Family Papers, and from Personal Recollections* (1832). Though she claimed to have carefully edited sections to avoid including any slanderous materials, detractors have charged that Burney chose to incorporate material that illuminates her own life rather than her father's. Her *Diary and Letters,* published by her niece after Burney's death, generated a great deal of public interest and she was remembered more as a diarist than as a novelist well into the twentieth century.

CRITICAL RECEPTION

Many critics have described Burney as occupying a crucial middle position between early novelists, such as Fielding and Richardson, and later novelists, including Jane Austen, who perfected the novel of manners that Burney had innovated. She was also in the vanguard of respectable women authors: whereas the earlier aristocratic writer Mary Wortley Montagu attempted to keep most of her writings private, Burney pursued publishing as a career and consequently encountered opposition from those who believed a woman should not write, even as she enjoyed a considerable degree of celebrity and respect. The challenge of self-expression has been a continuing theme in scholarship on Burney, as both the author and her heroines struggle to establish and legitimize their own authority. Scholars have noted the theme of violence and fear in Burney's novels as a symbol or symptom of the male-dominated culture in which she lived and about which she wrote. Kristina Straub's study of Burney's "feminine strategy" as an authoress contends that even when Burney's novels were generally accepted and acclaimed, Burney herself found it difficult to negotiate her entry into the public sphere. Likewise, Samuel Choi argues that *Evelina* bears the marks of its author's anxiety about approaching a traditionally male form of writing. Other feminist analyses of Burney focus on the figure of the father. Scholars have often read in *Evelina* the quest for paternal validation, and Kay Rogers (see Further Reading) proposes that the critique of patriarchy in *Cecilia* is muted by Burney's worshipful attitude toward her father. Susan Greenfield finds greater ambivalence in Burney's father figures, and proposes that *Evelina* attempts to establish the mother as the source of creativity and authority.

PRINCIPAL WORKS

Evelina; or, A Young Lady's Entrance into the World (novel) 1778

Cecilia; or, Memoirs of an Heiress (novel) 1782

Camilla; or, A Picture of Youth (novel) 1796

Edwy and Elgiva (drama) 1796

The Wanderer; or, Female Difficulties (novel) 1814

Memoirs of Dr. Burney, Arranged from His Own Manuscripts, from Family Papers, and from Personal Recollections [editor] (memoirs) 1832

Diary and Letters of Madame d'Arblay. 7 vols. (diary and letters) 1842-46

The Early Diary of Frances Burney, 1768-1778. 2 vols. (diary) 1889

The Journals and Letters of Fanny Burney (Madame D'Arblay). 12 vols. (diary and letters) 1972-84

PRIMARY SOURCES

FANNY BURNEY (DIARY DATE 3 AUGUST 1778)

SOURCE: Burney, Fanny. "Diary entry for August 3, 1778." In *The Diary and Letters of Madame D'Arblay.* Vol. 1, edited by Charlotte Barrett with notes by Austin Dobson, pp. 50-53. London: Macmillan, 1904.

In the following excerpt from her diary dated August 3, 1778, Burney recounts in detail the revelation of her authorship of Evelina *and the attention she received, including praise from Samuel Johnson.*

Susan has sent me a little note which has really been less pleasant to me, because it has alarmed me for my future concealment. It is from Mrs. Williams, an exceeding pretty poetess, who has the misfortune to be blind, but who has, to make some amends, the honour of residing in the house of Dr. Johnson: for though he lives almost wholly at Streatham, he always keeps his apartments in town, and this lady acts as mistress of his house.

> "*July* 25.
>
> "Mrs. Williams sends compliments to Dr. Burney, and begs he will intercede with Miss Burney to do her the favour to lend her the reading of ***Evelina.***"

[I was quite confounded at this request, which proves that Mrs. Thrale has told Dr. Johnson of my secret, and that he has told Mrs. Williams, and that she has told the person whoever it be, whom she got to write the note.

I instantly scrawled a hasty letter to town to entreat my father would be so good as to write to her, to acquaint her with my earnest and unaffected desire to remain unknown.

[And yet] I am frightened at this affair, I am by no means insensible to the honour which I receive from the certainty that Dr. Johnson must have spoken very well of the book, to have induced Mrs. Williams to send to our house for it. [She has known my father indeed for some years, but not with any intimacy; and I never saw her, though the perusal of her poems has often made me wish to be acquainted with her.]

I now come to last Saturday evening, when my beloved father came to Chessington, in full health, charming spirits, and all kindness, openness, and entertainment.

[I inquired what he had done about Mrs. Williams. He told me he went to her himself at my desire, for if he had written she could not herself have read the note. She apologised very much for the liberty she had taken, and spoke highly of the book, though she had only heard the first volume, as she was dependent upon a lady's good nature and time for hearing any part of it; but she went so far as to say that "his daughter was certainly the first writer, in that way, now living!"]

In his way hither he had stopped at Streatham, and he settled with Mrs. Thrale that he would call on her again in his way to town, and carry me with him! and Mrs. Thrale said, "We all long to know her."

I have been in a kind of twitter ever since, for there seems something very formidable in the idea of appearing as an authoress! I ever dreaded it, as it is a title which must raise more expectations than I have any chance of answering. Yet I am highly flattered by her invitation, and highly delighted in the prospect of being introduced to the Streatham society.

She sent me some very serious advice to write for the theatre, as, she says, I so naturally run into conversations, that ***Evelina*** absolutely and plainly points out that path to me; and she hinted how much she should be pleased to be "honoured with my confidence."

My dear father communicated this intelligence, and a great deal more, with a pleasure that almost surpassed that with which I heard it, and he seems quite eager for me to make another attempt. He desired to take upon himself the communication to my daddy Crisp, and as it is now in so many hands that it is possible accident might discover it to him, I readily consented.

Sunday evening, as I was going into my father's room I heard him say, "The variety of characters—the variety of scenes—and the language—why she has had very little education but what she has given herself,—less than any of the others!" and Mr. Crisp exclaimed, "Wonderful—it's wonderful!"

I now found what was going forward, and therefore deemed it most fitting to decamp.

About an hour after, as I was passing through the hall, I met my daddy (Crisp). His face was all animation and archness; he doubled his fist at me, and would have stopped me, but I ran past him into the parlour.

Before supper, however, I again met him, and he would not suffer me to escape; he caught both my hands, and looked as if he would have looked me through, and then exclaimed, "Why you little hussy,—you young devil!—an't you ashamed to look me in the face, you *Evelina,* you! Why, what a dance have you led me about it! Young friend, indeed! Oh you little hussy, what tricks have you served me!"

I was obliged to allow of his running on with these gentle appellations for I know not how long, ere he could sufficiently compose himself after his great surprise, to ask or hear any particulars; and then, he broke out every three instants with exclamations of astonishment at how I had found time to write so much unsuspected, and how and where I had picked up such various materials; and not a few times did he, with me, as he had with my father, exclaim, "Wonderful!"

He has, since, made me read him all my letters upon this subject. He said Lowndes would have made an estate had he given me £1000 for it, and that he ought not to have given less! "You have nothing to do now," continued he, "but to take your pen in hand, for your fame and reputation are made, and any bookseller will snap at what you write."

I then told him that I could not but really and unaffectedly regret that the affair was spread to Mrs. Williams and her friends.

"Pho," said he, "if those who are proper judges think it right that it should be known, why should you trouble yourself about it? You have not spread it, there can be no imputation of vanity fall to your share, and it cannot come out more to your honour than through such a channel as Mrs. Thrale."

FANNY BURNEY (PLAY DATE 1778-80)

SOURCE: Burney, Fanny. "The Witlings." In *The Witlings; and, The Woman-Hater,* edited by Peter Sabor and Geoffrey Sill, pp. 43-172. Peterborough, Canada: Broadview Press, 2002.

In the following excerpt written between 1778 and 1780 from the unpublished play "The Witlings," Burney lampoons the figure of the Bluestocking in Lady Smatter, who was thought to be modeled on Lady Mary Wortley Montagu. Burney mocks the pretensions of a female author who craves publicity, although Montagu herself avoided taking public credit for her work, considering it inappropriate for a woman of her station, much as Burney herself dreaded being identified as the author of Evelina.

Scene, a Drawing Room at Lady Smatter's

LADY SMATTER. Yes, yes, this song is certainly Mr. Dabler's, I am not to be deceived in his style. What say you, my dear Miss Stanley, don't you think I have found him out.

CECILIA. Indeed I am too little acquainted with his Poems to be able to judge.

LADY SMATTER. Your indifference surprises me! for my part, I am never at rest till I have discovered the authors of every thing that comes out; and, indeed, I commonly hit upon them in a moment. I declare I sometimes wonder at myself, when I think how lucky I am in my guesses.

CECILIA. Your Ladyship devotes so much Time to these researches, that it would be strange if they were unsuccessful.

LADY SMATTER. Yes, I do indeed devote my Time to them; I own it without blushing, for how, as a certain author Says, can Time be better employed than in cultivating intellectual accomplishments? And I am often Surprised, my dear Miss Stanley, that a young lady of your good sense should not be more warmly engaged in the same pursuit.

CECILIA. My pursuits, whatever they may be, are too unimportant to deserve being made public.

LADY SMATTER. Well to be sure, we are all Born with sentiments of our own, as I read in a

Book I can't just now recollect the name of, so I ought not to wonder that yours and mine do not coincide; for, I declare, if my pursuits were not made public, I should not have any at all, for where can be the pleasure of reading Books, and studying authors, if one is not to have the credit of talking of them?

CECILIA. Your Ladyship's desire of celebrity is too well known for your motives to be doubted.

LADY SMATTER. Well but, my dear Miss Stanley, I have been thinking for some Time past of your becoming a member of our Esprit Party: Shall I put up your name?

CECILIA. By no means; my ambition aspires not at an Honour for which I feel myself so little qualified.

LADY SMATTER. Nay, but you are too modest; you can't suppose how much you may profit by coming among us. I'll tell you some of our regulations. The principal persons of our party are Authors and Critics; the authors always bring us something new of their own, and the Critics regale us with manuscript notes upon something old.

CECILIA. And in what class is your Ladyship?

LADY SMATTER. O, I am among the Critics. I love criticism passionately, though it is really laborious Work, for it obliges one to read with a vast deal of attention. I declare I am sometimes so immensely fatigued with the toil of studying for faults and objections, that I am ready to fling all my Books behind the Fire.

CECILIA. And what authors have you chiefly criticised?

LADY SMATTER. Pope and Shakespeare. I have found more errors in those than in any other.

CECILIA. I hope, however, for the sake of readers less fastidious, your Ladyship has also left them some beauties.

LADY SMATTER. O yes, I have not cut them up regularly through; indeed I have not, yet, read above half their Works, so how they will fare as I go on, I can't determine. O, here's Beaufort. *Enter Beaufort.*

BEAUFORT. Your Ladyship's most obedient.

CECILIA. Mr. Beaufort, I am quite ashamed to see You! yet the disappointment I occasioned you was as involuntary on my part, as it could possibly be disagreeable on yours. Your Brother, I hope, prevented your waiting long?

BEAUFORT. That you meant he should is sufficient reparation for my loss of Time; but what must be the disappointment that an apology from you would not soften?

LADY SMATTER. *(reading)* O lovely, charming, beauteous maid,—I wish this Song was not so difficult to get by Heart,—but I am always beginning one Line for another. After all, Study is a most fatiguing thing! O how little does the World suspect, when we are figuring in all the brilliancy of Conversation, the private hardships, and secret labours of a Belle Esprit!

FANNY BURNEY (LETTER DATE C. 13 AUGUST 1779)

SOURCE: Burney, Fanny. "A Letter from Frances Burney to Dr. Charles Burney, c. 13 August 1779." In *The Witlings; and, The Woman-Hater,* edited by Peter Sabor and Geoffrey Sill, pp. 303-04. Peterborough, Canada: Broadview Press, 2002.

In the following letter dated c. August 13, 1779, Burney addresses her father about her disappointment in burying her comedy "The Witlings" after her efforts at playwriting had been so much encouraged by Mrs. Thrale and others of their circle.

The fatal knell then, is knolled! and down among the Dead Men sink the poor Witlings,—for-ever and for-ever and for-ever!—

I give a *sigh* whether I will or not to their memory, for, however worthless, they were *mes Enfans,* and *one must do one's Nature,* as Mr. Crisp will tell you of the Dog.

You, my dearest Sir, who enjoyed, I really think, even more than myself the astonishing success of my first attempt, would, I believe, even more than myself, be hurt at the failure of my second;—and I am sure I speak from the bottom of a very honest Heart when I most solemnly declare that upon *your* Account any disgrace would mortify and afflict me *more* than upon my own,—for what ever appears with your *knowledge,* will be naturally supposed to have met with your *approbation,* and perhaps with your *assistance;*—and therefore, though all *particular* censure would fall where it *ought,* upon *me,*—yet any *general* censure of the *whole,* and the *Plan,* would cruelly, but certainly, involve *you* in its severity.

Of this I have been sensible from the moment my *Authorshipness* was discovered,—and therefore, from that moment, I determined to have no *opinion* of my own in regard to what I should thenceforth part with out of my own Hands. I would, long since, have Burnt the 4th Act, upon your disapprobation of it, but that I waited, and was by Mrs. Thrale so much *encouraged* to wait, for your finishing the Piece.

You *have* finished it, now,—in *every* sense of the Word,—*partial* faults may be corrected, but what I most wished was to know the general effect of the Whole,—and as *that* has so terribly failed, all petty criticisms would be needless. I shall wipe it all from my memory, and endeavour never to recollect that I ever writ it.

You bid me open my Heart to you,—and so, my dearest Sir, I will,—for it is the greatest happi-

ABOUT THE AUTHOR

HESTER LYNCH THRALE, ALSO KNOWN AS MRS. PIOZZI, WRITES IN HER DIARY ABOUT BURNEY'S WRITING TALENT

Our Miss Burney is big with a Comedy for next Season; I have not yet seen the *Ebauche,* but I wish it well: Can I help wishing well to every thing that bears the name of *Burney*? The Doctor is a Man quite after my own Heart, if he has any Fault it is too much Obsequiousness, though *I* should not object to a Quality *my* Friends are so little troubled with.—his following close upon the heels of Johnson or Baretti makes me feel him softer though; like turning the Toothpick after you have rubbed your Gums with the *Brush* & immediately applying the *Spunge* to them. his Daughter is a graceful looking Girl, but 'tis the Grace of an Actress not a Woman of Fashion—how should it? her Conversation would be more pleasing if She thought less of herself; but her early Reputation embarrasses her Talk, & clouds her Mind with scruples about Elegancies which either come uncalled for or will not come at all: I love her more for her Father's sake than for her own, though her Merit cannot as a Writer be controverted. The Play will be a good one too I doubt not—She is a Girl of prodigious Parts—

Thrale, Hester Lynch. Excerpt from *Thraliana: The Diary of Mrs. Hester Lynch Thrale (Later Mrs. Piozzi)*. Vol 1, edited by Katharine C. Balderston, p. 368. Oxford: Clarendon Press, 1951.

ness of my life that I *dare* be sincere to you,—I expected many Objections to be raised, a thousand errors to be pointed out, and a million of alterations to be proposed;—but—the *suppression of the piece* were words I did *not* expect,—indeed, after the warm approbation of Mrs. Thrale, and the repeated commendation and flattery of Mr. Murphy, how could I?—

I do not, therefore, pretend to *wish* you should think the decision for which I was so little prepared has given me no disturbance;—for I must be a far more egregious Witling than any of those I tried to draw to imagine you could ever credit that I writ without some remote hope of success *now,* though I literally did when I composed Evelina. But my mortification is not at throwing away the Characters, or the contrivance;—it is all at throwing away the *Time,*—which I with difficulty stole, and which I have Buried in the mere trouble of *writing.*

What my Daddy Crisp says, "that it would be the best *policy,* but for pecuniary advantages, for me to write no more"—is exactly what I have always thought since ***Evelina*** was published;—but I will not *now* talk of putting it in practice,—for the best way I can take of shewing that have a true and just sense of the *spirit* of your condemnation, is not to sink, sulky and dejected, under it, but to exert myself to the utmost of my power in endeavours to produce something less reprehensible. And this shall be the way I will pursue, as soon as my mind is more at ease about Hetty and Mrs. Thrale,—and as soon as I have *read* myself into a forgetfulness of my old Dramatis persona,—lest I should produce something else as *Witless* as the last.

Adieu, my dearest, kindest, truest, best *Friend,*—I will never proceed so *far* again without your counsel, and then I shall not only save *myself* so much useless trouble, but *you,* who so reluctantly blame, the kind pain which I am sure must attend your disapprobation. The World will not always go well, as Mrs. Sap. might say, and I am sure I have long thought I have had more than my share of success already.

GENERAL COMMENTARY

KRISTINA STRAUB (ESSAY DATE 1987)

SOURCE: Straub, Kristina. "The Receptive Reader and Other Necessary Fictions." In *Divided Fictions: Fanny Burney and Feminine Strategy,* pp. 152-81. Lexington: University Press of Kentucky, 1987.

In the following excerpt, Straub examines Burney's self-awareness as an author as her career developed, particularly after the success of Evelina.

Evelina's fictional situation reflects Burney's own dilemma as a woman who sought solutions to female difficulties among conventional, patriarchal answers. Writing gave her aesthetic and imaginative choices among the options for women in patriarchal society that were not matched by her social and personal powers.[1] Burney could, in other words, easily endow her fictional heroine with the secure, emotionally based power over males that she, herself, could only gain with considerable difficulty, if at all, in life. Fiction is, then, as dangerous, in setting up false expectations, to Fanny Burney as Lord Orville is to Evelina; as Villars says, the age did not encourage women to trust to appearances, particularly when perception is brightened by hopeful illusions about the disinterested generosity of male power. Such illusions are the stuff of novels that end happily for their heroines. Burney seems aware of this danger to personal sanity and safety, and she projects it into her heroine's Cinderella story. The dangers that track Evelina's entrance into the world are ones that Burney knew: disappointment, powerlessness, and regret for lost hopes. Balanced against these dangers is her ability to sustain the fantasy of patriarchal benevolence, the rewards that await female virtue, and, given the grimness of her alternatives, it is not strange that she chose the fantasy.

In a telling passage dated 1768 in ***The Early Diary,*** Burney records her conversation with a "Mr. S." who claims that Richardson's Sir Charles Grandison is "too perfect for human nature." Burney responds that "it quite hurts me to hear anybody declare a really and thoroughly good man never lived. It is so *much* to the disgrace of mankind." When Mr. S. patronizingly admires her "innocence and credulity of heart," however, she worries that such innocence may expose one to danger. Mr. S. answers that since danger cannot be avoided in any case, Burney is better off believing in the possibility of a "really and thoroughly good man" (***ED*** [***The Early Diary of Frances Burney, 1768-1778***] 1:36-37). Three years later, she seems to confirm Mr. S.'s fatalistic endorsement of innocence as the least culpable approach to a no-win situation: "What can one think of the natural disposition of a young person who, with an eye of suspicion, looks around for secret designs in the appearance of kindness, and evil intentions in the profession of friendship? *I* could not think well of such apprehensions and expectations in youth. A bad opinion of the world should be dearly bought to be excusable" (***ED*** 1:110-11). In this passage, Burney presents innocence as a self-consciously formulated strategy for coping with a lack of real options. Accordingly, the "innocence" that allows Evelina and Fanny Burney to believe in Lord Orville as a Grandisonian protector is a considered choice, made with full knowledge of its danger, among the few solutions offered by patriarchal culture, and Burney's presentation of Lord Orville calls attention to the dangers as well as the desirability of believing in such creations.

Hence, ***Evelina***'s happy ending is literary schizophrenia of a particularly calculated nature; it is withdrawal from reality as a coping mechanism or strategy. Yet the text is not, in this sense, totally "insane," but rather a split or doubled embodiment of Burney's self-consciousness, expressive of the dangers and the limits of the very solutions it advocates. This reflexivity—in the form of a sentimental artifice that calls attention to its artificiality—is less a case of literary cleverness than a manifestation of the contradiction inherent in Burney's position as woman writer. In that role, she implicitly claims a public voice that felt awkward and unwieldy to what Mary Poovey has aptly named the Proper Lady in her character, the woman who saw herself in essentially private—not public—terms.[2] The contradictory nature of this ideological position both gave authority and took it away, leaving Burney licensed to use the affective power of eighteenth-century sentimental literary conventions and, at the same time, leaving her inclined to see that power as unauthorized and unreliable unless grounded in the personal affection that justified more fully established uses of feminine power in the domestic sphere. Hence, ***Evelina*** asserts the heroine's power to define herself through others' controlled estimations of her, while suggesting how tenuous this power is, how much it depends on human emotion's proper—and lucky—deployment. The public success of ***Evelina*** disturbed this tenuous, compromised resolution of Burney's contradictory feelings toward authorial power. Instead of feeling that her right to a public voice had been validated, Burney seems to have transposed public acclaim to a personal level: her success either made her all the more personally valued or—devastatingly—exposed her to personal degradation.

Burney's feelings about gaining a public voice remain curiously ill-defined, as if she were masking feelings of invasion with indifference—"I have an exceeding odd sensation, when I consider that it is now in the power of *any* and *every* body to read what I so carefully hoarded even from my best friends, till this last month or two,—and that a work so lately lodged, in all privacy of my bureau, may now be seen by every butcher and baker, cobler and tinker, throughout the three kingdoms, for the small tribute of three pence" (***ED*** 2:214). But whether Burney is, as I suspect, shielding herself from a role that felt untenable to her or whether she actually gave the public nature of her work as little attention as appears from her journals, she shows only slight concern for the reading public at large, and the audience that seems to matter to her was known to her in person or by name: her family (in particular her father), friends, and the literary circle to which her father had access through his relationship with the Thrales.[3] Public success, for Burney, did not mean the anonymity of writing in the privacy of a closet for unknown readers. It meant, rather, being exposed to real, specific individuals who would feel personally let down if she did not live up the success of her novel. She writes, after reading Susan Burney's account of her praises in the mouths of Hester Thrale and Samuel Johnson, "I tremble for what all this will end in. I verily think I had best stop where I am, and never again attempt writing: for after so much honour, so much success—how shall I bear a downfall?" (***DL*** [***Diary and Letters of Madame d'Arblay***] 1:126-27). It is hard to say, however, whether the responses of the famous unknown thrilled and terrified her more than those of her father; both seem to have had equally personal, specific significance to Burney, and both created enormous anxiety—about continuing to please, about whether or not the people who praised the novel would be disappointed by Burney, the woman.[4]

Burney's anxiety was partially and temporarily relieved after she became intimate with Johnson and the Thrales, during the time just previous to writing ***Cecilia.***[5] Her journals express a sense of feeling personally known and valued; she says of Thrale that "had I been the child of this delightful woman, she could not have taken more pains to reconcile me to my situation" (***DL*** 1:98), and somewhat later Burney adds that "I flatter myself that if he [Johnson] were now accused of loving me, he would not deny it, nor as before, insist on waiting longer ere he went so far" (***DL*** 1:181). But her growing personal security with her new literary friends does not seem to have affected her continuing insecurity as a writer. As she worked on a play, **"The Witlings,"** her journals reveal her trepidation at another public display of her art struggling against her brief, tenuous sense of personal security with her new audience. This precariously established balance between contradictory feelings—that her new-found public role both augmented and debased her personal value—was upset by a mild lampoon on "dear little Burney" published in *Warley: a satire*.[6] She had previously expressed her fears that writing might expose her to "the horror irrecoverable of personal abuse" (***DL*** 1:127); given her need for personal approbation, this extreme, almost phobic response seems inevitable rather than prissy. "Personal abuse" denied the efficacy of her writerly control over how she was seen, and when "the worst" happened, and Burney's name was dropped in a lampoon, she was "for more than a week unable to eat, drink, or sleep for vehemence of vexation" (***DL*** 1:161). The soothing effects of Johnson's concern over her distress and the flattering encouragement of her family and Hester Thrale probably helped her to continue writing the play (***DL*** 1:158-60, 182-83), although her conviction that "no success could counter-balance the publishing of my name" (***DL*** 1:166) remained firm after the *Warley* incident. Under continuing encouragement, she went on with **"The Witlings,"** deciding, however, to "keep my own counsel; not to whisper even the name of it; to raise no expectations, which were always prejudicial, and finally, to have it performed while the town knew nothing of whose it was" (***DL*** 1:208). Unfortunately, the protective mask of anonymity proved unnecessary; Dr. Burney and Crisp, apparently concerned that **"The Witlings"** was a too-obvious satire of the bas bleu, advised her to suppress the play.[7]

Burney seems to have seen their advice as "disapprobation" of a personal nature, not as a political strategy for the good of her career. She responded to her father and "Daddy" Crisp like a chastened, slightly resentful child determined not to be caught in the wrong: "I will never proceed so far again without your counsel, and then I shall not only save myself so much useless trouble, but you, who so reluctantly blame, the kind pain which I am sure must attend your disapprobation. . . . I have long thought I have had more than my share of success already" (***DL*** 1:258-59). Burney's next project shows how seriously she meant never to "proceed so far again without your counsel"; with the writing of ***Cecilia,*** Burney turned to her paternal mentors for actual creative direction as well as emotional energy, beginning "hard fagging" at the novel that Crisp and Dr. Burney urged her to write. Resolving to exert herself so as not to appear "sulky" over her mentors' suppression of the play (***DL*** 1:258), she wrote in order to rewin a secure sense of approval from the men who personally mattered most to her.

Burney's attitude toward her work in her later career as a writer shows a chronic need to reaffirm the early relationship with paternal mentors who made her feel safe as a writer. After her return to the Burney household from court, she sees the pleasure, almost the point of her work on a long poem as the gaining of Charles Burney's approval: "This is a delight to my dear Father inexpressibly great: and though I have gone no further than to let him know, from time to time, the species of Matter that occupies me, he is perfectly contented, and patiently waits till something is quite finished, before he insists upon reading a Word. This suits my humour well, as my own industry is all gone, when once its intent is produced" (*JL* [***The Journals and Letters of Frances Burney***] 1:73). With ***Camilla*** as well, Burney placed her father's praise high in her gratifications as a writer: "with the utmost truth I can aver, never, in all their amazing circle of success have procured me any satisfaction I can put on a par with your approbation of them." Charles Burney's approval—"that approbation I *most* prize of all approbations in this lower sphere" (*JL* 3:255-56)—seems to have had more value to Burney than public opinion; the mixed reviews on ***Camilla*** do not seem to have disturbed her greatly, being only what Burney rather expected now that Johnson, Burke, and Reynolds no longer protected her with their praise: "But those immense Men whose single praise was Fame and Security, who established by a Word, the two elder sisters, are now silent" (*JL* 3:205). Burney persists in seeing audience response in specific, personal terms; I suspect that doing so gave her the semblance, at least, of a comforting fusion between the authorial control that her culture gave her reason to mistrust and the more known, more fully reassuring authority of the beloved over the lover.

The journals and letters written in 1813 during Burney's preparation to return to England from France with the manuscript of her last novel, ***The Wanderer,*** reveal how Charles Burney had assumed the psychic function of fusing Burney's public role as writer with her private identity of daughter, wife, mother: "Could I but have had my work for my dearest Father, the certainty of giving him so much pleasure, and of reaping hence ourselves so abundant an harvest, would have made affection, filial affection, and conjugal and maternal interest unite to give me fortitude for bearing my personal regret [at the absence from her husband]" (*JL* 6:675). Burney writes of her "true, heart-dear Joy in making such a presentation to my beloved Father; Joy, there at our meeting, in giving HIM so great a satisfaction, will indubitably take the lead. It will necessarily be one of the most blessed moments of my life, for it is what, I know, beyond all things in the world, he most wishes" (*JL* 6:690). After a ten-year separation from her elderly, failing father and with little notion of what Charles Burney's real interests and condition were at the time, Burney constructs a climactic reunion scene between father and daughter that not only recapitulates ***Evelina***'s dedicatory poem addressed to the "author of my being," but also is a sort of reverse echo of the fictional Mr. Villars' wish to embrace Evelina before his death. The imagined emotional encounters between father and daughter are, in the case of both journal and novel, fictions, projected affirmations of female affective power in the hands of the heroine/writer. This is not to say that Burney could not tell the difference between life and art or the personal and the public. Rather, writing—both of journals and of fiction—gave her a way of imaging the results of affective rhetoric as well as a means of exerting it. And her image of affective control over audience, in both her fiction and her journals, consistently binds together authorship and traditionally feminine modes of cultural empowerment. Burney collapses the distance between writing as a public act and writing as a personal mode of relating—not out of confusion, but in order to extend and consolidate her sense of control.

But while Burney's personal concept of audience probably gave her a useful justification for continuing to write, it does not mask, in her fiction, the ideologically contradictory and divisive nature of female authorial control. The contradictions between public and private, active and passive roles for women reach a tenuous resolution in the reflexivity of ***Evelina.*** In the novels that followed, Burney discloses more fully than in ***Evelina*** the psychic cost of the contradictions inherent in her profession; whereas ***Evelina*** merely calls attention to the artificiality of the power granted to women in the sentimental novel, ***Cecilia*** is far more explicit about what is at risk in the woman writer's work: self-alienation, madness, and mental disintegration haunt the process by which the heroine gains control over her audience and, hence, her own identity.

Cecilia marks a shift in Burney's fiction from a romance plot that points to its source in female creative desire—signalling its own generic limits—to a plot that emphasizes far more painfully the tenuousness of female creative control over audience. Cecilia, like Evelina, finds her best, happiest self in marriage with the man of her choice, and, as in ***Evelina,*** the heroine reaches that goal through the hero's learning to read her character accurately—a painful process, fraught with mishaps and difficulties, by which he comes to appreciate her real worth. While Evelina suffers under Orville's possible and real misreadings of her—as simpleton, bumpkin, or object of sexual jealousy—Cecilia is nearly destroyed by Delvile's inability to see her accurately, an inability that persists even after the lovers are avowed and wed. Each heroine finally brings the hero to a correct reading of her, and they do so in ways that suggest a parallel between their power to control and the author's power to create the hero capable of such a reading—an implied analogy that, by calling attention to the tenuousness of a female control grounded in fictional rather than social convention, points to the enormous risks implicit in female creative power. Whereas this self-referential process in ***Evelina*** is arduous, suggestive of the difficulties inherent in commanding sentimental or authorial control, in ***Cecilia*** it is torturous, suggesting the near-self-destruction risked by the authorial manipulation of audience.

Evelina unconsciously creates Lord Orville—happily, as it turns out. But Cecilia's conscious attempts to see a lover in Delvile reflect a dark side of Burney's self-conscious manipulation of literary romantic love: by creating a false happy ending and by suffering a more intense form of the disillusionment that Evelina momentarily feels and then evades, Cecilia reflects her author's awareness of her own psychic risk in creating sentimental fantasies of female happiness. Like her author, who knows a sentimental hero when she sees one, Cecilia quickly recognizes Delvile's potential as her avowed lover and eventual husband. Furthermore, she believes, like the author of ***Evelina,*** that love will override practicalities, will "make every obstacle to the alliance seem trifling, when put in competition with mutual esteem and affection" (IV, 287). Delvile, however, sets a precedent for subsequent Burney heroes in being far denser than Orville in reading the heroine. Whereas Orville bears out Evelina's unworldly assumption about the power of love over finance and family pride, Delvile is bound into a contradictory line of behavior by the familial and social expectations that Cecilia, in her first sanguine perception of his love, dismisses so lightly. And, even when hero and heroine become first avowed lovers and then husband and wife, Delvile continues to misread Cecilia, interpreting her behavior in the light of circumstances and appearances that link her sexually with other men. His misguided jealousy leads him, at the crisis point in their relationship, to run from Cecilia, apparently intent on violent revenge, an act that finally, as the culmination of misreading upon misreading, drives Cecilia into madness. The emotional control secured to Evelina by the title of "wife" is, in ***Cecilia,*** as unreliable as the created vision of patriarchal benevolence that both heroines weave around their men. Marriage, the relationship that ensures Evelina's self and security, renders Cecilia voiceless and powerless; in a dramatic mad scene, she cries out that "no one will save me now! I am married, and no one will listen to me!" (X, 881). Cecilia's attempts to "make sense" of herself to the hero break down into a state of madness and meaninglessness that has disturbing implications for women's ability to use language as affective control: speech, in Burney's second novel, not only fails to gain the heroine a just interpretation; it turns against her, alienating her from the hero—and herself.

Cecilia's ability to name, to give linguistic form to her sense of herself in relation to Delvile, becomes a mad parody of female creativity. She speaks her husband's name as if it—the name itself, the verbal token of her claim to power over her husband—were a child, a being made as well as known, which has turned treacherously upon its maker: "'Tis a name, . . . I well remember to have heard, and once I loved it, and three times I called upon it in the dead of night. And when I was cold and wretched, I cherished it; and when I was abandoned and left alone, I repeated it and sung to it" (X, 885). In ***Cecilia,*** creative control—betrayed by its object in a biblically resonant triple denial—disintegrates into a mad parody of maternal power over the masculine. Ironically, this act of madness works for Cecilia as her saner attempts to secure affective control over Delvile do not. Although her fantasy loses its grounding in reality, Cecilia unconsciously uses its affective power to regain her control: her madness is the dark, unconscious side of Evelina's fantasy, her power to command the male protection she needs in order to survive. Loss of control over her own mind allows her to shock Delvile into a just interpretation of her integrity, giving her, finally, the control over the hero's mind that she has forfeited over her own.

Burney turned to the literary convention of "running mad" to express female desire, the will to power, through emotional blackmail of the particularly risky sort that walks a fine line between the creation and the immolation of self. ***Cecilia,*** then, stresses the contradictions implicit in acts of female creative power—between the public and private, art and artlessness—that ***Evelina*** precariously resolves through a self-referential assertion of authority. The self-alienation of ***Cecilia*** is a more extreme form of the contradiction implicit in ***Evelina,*** an exaggerated version of Evelina's sexual unselfconsciousness—her "delicate" dissociation from her own sexual impulses. Cecilia's madness suggests Burney's awareness, on some level, of the danger implicit in her heroine's affective power over hero and reader. And Burney's self-consciousness sets her apart from—without denying her implication in—the self-destructive potential of Cecilia's attempts to manipulate audience. Cecilia wins over husband and father-in-law by running mad; Fanny Burney gains patriarchal recognition by writing in a form in which the threat of her own self-alienation is implicit.

Evelina does, however, suggest, in half-submerged form, the dangers that patriarchal discourse can entail for the woman writer—dangers that ***Cecilia*** makes clear. Burney's first novel also culminates in the heroine's envelopment in male authority, a milder, benign version of the self-alienation to which Cecilia is reduced to gain affective control over her male audience. Looked at carefully, Evelina's fairy-tale union with Lord Orville is a sort of love-death in which the record of female consciousness is buried in the text of conventionally defined female "happiness." Evelina's closing account of her marriage brings to a climax Mr. Villars' longings for the almost sexual consummation of reunion with her by blurring, I think deliberately, the line between her sexual union with her husband and her anticipated reunion with her guardian. Evelina's affirmative answer to Villars' desire to die in her arms seems as much her "end" as it is his:

> All is over, my dearest Sir, and the fate of your Evelina is decided! This morning, with fearful joy, and trembling gratitude, she united herself for ever with the object of her dearest, her eternal affection!
>
> I have time for no more; the chaise now waits which is to conduct me to dear Berry Hill, and to the arms of the best of men.
>
> [406]

The arms that enfold Evelina in death are almost indistinguishable from those which embrace her in marriage, and, in a sense, it matters little whose arms hold her with what intent: both afford release from the ambiguities of power used within an ideological context—the public sphere—that assumes her powerlessness. Evelina runs happily (though with "fearful joy" and "trembling gratitude") to her "end," of course, a willing Isolde to the Villars/Orville Tristan, but Cecilia's dash into arms that temporarily betray her has more of auto-da-fé than *liebestod* about it. In ***Cecilia,*** the heroine is not so much enveloped as she is cannibalized by the ostensible protection of masculine authority.

Cecilia's hysteria allows her language to express a gothic side to the novel's fairy tale of romantic love. Her ravings about Delvile, her husband and "prince," reflect the psychic reality of her brutally frustrated attempts to be known and hence protected by him. The prince becomes an agent of blood, the source and center of a terrifyingly vague violence whose lack of a clear object makes it all the more threatening: "Oh, if he is yet to be saved, if already he is not murdered . . . he is only in the next street, I left him there myself, his sword drawn, and covered with human blood!" Delvile's death is the imagined result of his violence, but the visionary "poniard" in "his wounded bosom" reflects Cecilia's "bloodied" vision of her marriage as well: "Oh, it was a work of darkness, unacceptable and offensive! it has been sealed, therefore, with blood, and tomorrow is will be signed with murder!" (X, 880-81). Cecilia refers to her own guilt, of course, in consenting to a clandestine marriage to Delvile after his father had refused consent, but hysteria allows her language to express more than a sense of her own wrongdoing: it also suggests her fears at being trapped in a situation in which male violence aggravates her mistaken action into an ultimate act of destruction. Cecilia is afraid *for* Delvile, but she is also afraid *of* him, a condition that Burney can express by disjointing and decentering her heroine's sense of relationship between self and the other, the patriarchal reality. Failing to recognize Delvile, Cecilia makes explicit the threat that she feels:

> Cecilia now, half rising, and regarding him with mingled terror and anger, eagerly exclaimed, "if you do not mean to mangle and destroy me, begone this instant."
>
> "To mangle you!" repeated Delvile, shuddering, "how horrible!—but I deserve it all!"
>
> [X, 884-85]

The plot contingencies of Cecilia's madness allow her to make this accusation—she thinks Delvile is the villain, Monckton; they also allow her to become again the loving, gentle heroine after the delirium has passed, so that Burney can incorporate in her novel both the expression of female anxiety and the reconciliation that is important to her heroine's happy ending. But insane, Cecilia can state a truth that does not become the lips of a conventional heroine: the psychic and social pressures created by her love for Delvile have indeed "mangled" her, and by his own admission, at that. Madness, then, is both rhetoric—a communicative act that is specifically pointed at gaining the desired effect on men who have power over women's lives—and a way of naming the threat of self-victimization implicit in acts of female power in the context of a male-controlled society—and literature.

In each of Burney's novels written after ***Evelina,*** a moment comes in the course of the heroine's troubled romance when the familial, sexual, and social pressures of her attempts to gain a just "reading" culminate in a crisis of self-alienation. Also at that moment, the hero comes to his own crisis in the course of his feelings for the heroine by observing her pain and debilitation. Delvile discovers Cecilia in her madness; Edgar finds his estranged fiancée, Camilla, teetering at the brink of a self-willed death. Harleigh, of ***The Wanderer; or, Female Difficulties,*** witnesses Juliet's sane but even more chilling abdication of self as she turns herself over to the husband whom political circumstances in France have forced her to marry—this time, a specifically sexual form of alienation from self. At this crisis point in all three of Burney's novels after ***Evelina,*** the heroine's temporary loss of self-control ultimately leads to a right understanding with the man of her desires—and the rhetorical purpose of female self-abdication is fulfilled. But in each case, the actual moment of encounter between the estranged lovers focuses on the emotional distance that the hero must overcome to understand his beloved, and on his weakness and inability to do so, suggesting that the female crisis of self-alienation needs to be read as more than a cry for patriarchal help: it is also Burney's clearest expression of the damages that the articulation of women's feelings—an affective act of power—inflicts on the female ego in a male-dominated world and art.

In ***Cecilia,*** Delvile persists, for a while, in misreading Cecilia's insanity as reproach and rejection; when he finally realizes that she is out of her senses, her madness "turns him to stone," leaving him weak and unable to help her either emotionally or physically: "Delvile now attempted to carry her in his arms; but trembling and unsteady, he had not strength to sustain her; yet not enduring to behold the helplessness he could not assist, he conjured them to be careful and gentle, and, committing her to their trust, ran out himself for a physician" (X, 886). The hero can only help the heroine by running away, a pattern that is repeated in ***Camilla,*** when the sight of the heroine's hand stretched out to him from behind the curtains of a sickbed causes the hero to flee the tormenting presence of his beloved. In both discovery scenes, the man blunders helplessly out of the room, leaving the woman isolated in a psychological darkness which is a type of death, or at least its prelude: "Declining all aid, Camilla continued in the same position, wrapt up, coveting the dark, and stifling sighs that were rising into sobs."[8] "Cecilia resisted them with her utmost power, imploring them not to bury her alive, and averring she had received intelligence they meant to entomb her with Mr. Monckton" (X, 886). Although more rational than Cecilia's ravings, Camilla's stillness is more chilling, since she seems to be "coveting" the living death that Cecilia, however irrationally, thinks she is fighting off. In both novels, the heroine's moment of most extreme alienation from herself and her life is, ironically, the crisis that gains her the patriarchal reward she desires. But Burney also seems to be embedding in this rhetoric of female madness the cost of alienation from one's self and from the patriarchal other that results from attempts to communicate female being in a world that assumes the suspect or insubstantial nature of female acts of power.

In ***The Wanderer,*** the hero is cut off from the heroine in her moment of crisis by the institutions of a society that, in Burney's view, has gone wrong at the core of its moral order. Instead of symbolic curtains or the heroine's own disordered mental state, marriage (ironically) alienates the hero from the heroine: Juliet has been forced to wed a brutal French Republican through the hope of saving those she loves during the Reign of Terror. She flees to England, but when she is discovered by her husband, numbly submits to the obligation of obedience that the institution of marriage entails for women. The discovery scene dramatizes her own self-abdication; it also focuses on the psychological alienation of her lover, Harleigh, who witnesses it: "A sudden sensation, kindred even to hatred, took possession of his feelings. Altered she appeared to him, and delusive. She had always, indeed, discouraged his hope, always forbidding his expectations; yet she must have seen that they subsisted, and were cherished; and could not but have been conscious, that a single word, bitter, but essentially just, might have demolished, have annihilated them in a moment."[9] Harleigh shifts quickly into pity for Juliet's plight and elation at the evidence that, although married to someone else, she still loves him. But Burney seems to have included this moment of near-hatred with a kind of instinct for the gap that separates male from female in the misreadings, revisions, and re-revisions that constitute "communication" between the sexes. In ***The Wanderer,*** a whole social order, rather than personal and familial pressure, is responsible for female alienation from self, her male lover, even sexuality itself—the Revolution serves as a sort of gothic objective correlative for the madness that Burney seems to think is implicit in female attempts to control male response, the madness of trying to merge the female will with an enabling male other.

The connection between the act of control implicit in writing and the heroine's sentimental ability to move the hero becomes, perhaps, clearest in ***Camilla,*** a novel that Burney wrote with the renewed sense of financial urgency that the birth of her son brought in 1794. Burney wrote this novel with a clear practical purpose in mind—the security of her family—and perhaps because of this acceptably feminine motivation seems to have taken a pleasure in writing it that was missing from the composition of ***Cecilia.*** Yet ***Camilla*** is still more explicit than ***Cecilia*** in its symbolic connection of writing with a power that turns back on the woman who wields it. Like Cecilia, Camilla is offered the promise of marriage early in the novel, and, like Cecilia, is put through a purgatory of doubt and loss after a promising beginning. Edgar, like Delvile, misreads Camilla through a too-scrupulous deference to a (patriarchal) moral authority figure. Edgar's caution produces the same results as Delvile's jealousy, and Camilla, ill and desperate, has a nightmare just before her rediscovery by Edgar that parallels Cecilia's waking delirium. This dream sequence, as Julia Epstein wisely points out, is the culmination of a linguistic struggle that occupies Camilla throughout the novel. Whereas Evelina artlessly controls her audience and determines her own "reading," ***Camilla*** dramatizes the debilitating struggle underlying the ostensibly unselfconscious expression of female identity and links that struggle to writing—the heroine's abortive attempts to make herself known on paper. The nightmare sequence in ***Camilla*** writes large the implications of this process, Epstein explains.[10] Camilla falls asleep, wishing herself dead and out of the troubles that her naiveté and Edgar's implacability have led her into; Death comes to her and demands that she write "thy claims, thy merits to mercy." Her hand "involuntarily" grasps "a pen of Iron, and with a velocity uncontrollable" writes out the "guilty characters," which become "illuminated with burning sulpher." Death tells her, "These are thy deserts; write now thy claims," but when she grasps the pen a second time it makes no mark on the page (875). This scene expresses the pain and difficulty of a woman struggling to redeem herself through a medium that she is not fully authorized to control. Burney, probably like other women, found herself writing out of patriarchal assumptions about writing as an act of power in which her oppression and even destruction were implicit. Hence, self-expression is closely allied with self-condemnation: the "iron pen" will write Camilla's guilt, but not her "claims."

Camilla's nightmare also expresses the disintegration of female personality implicit in Cecilia's earlier madness. The act of writing is accompanied, in the heroine's dream, by a cacophany of voices that seem to emanate from within her, most angry and accusatory, others querying or defeated:

> When again she made a feeble effort to rid her oppressed lungs of the dire weight that had fallen upon them, a voice hollow, deep, and distant, dreadfully pierced her ear, calling out: "Thou hast but thy own wish! Rejoice, thou murmurer, for thou diest!" Clearer, shriller, another voice quick vibrated in the air: "Whither goest thou," it cried, "and whence comest thou?"
>
> A voice from within, over which she thought she had no controul, though it seemed issuing from her vitals, low, hoarse, and tremulous, answered, "Whither I go, let me rest!" . . . Quick then another voice assailed her so near, so loud, so terrible . . . she shrieked at its horrible sound.
>
> [874-75]

The voices multiply until she is assailed "by hundreds, by thousands, by millions, from side to side, above, below, around" (876). Camilla is beset with a nightmare chorus of her own feelings, the seemingly alien voices of her overwrought mind; the attempt to write her own self-defense is not only painful, but is accompanied by a splintering of self into dissociated fragments. Camilla's nightmare passes, of course, like Cecilia's madness and Evelina's greensickness: even Juliet's brutal husband conveniently dies so that she can marry Harleigh. Burney repeatedly asserts the power of successful romantic love to banish the female nightmare, at least in novels, but she also asserts, more and more forcefully after ***Evelina,*** that happy endings are created at great risk to the woman who holds a pen in a world that defines public, writerly power as male. For Burney, writing meant a self-division that could either be carried off in reflexivity or painfully expressed in images of self-estrangement; the split between public and private along the lines of gender created internal contradictions in the most "respectable" and successful of eighteenth-century women novelists that her fiction does not fully resolve. I would argue, however, that the dissonances of Burney's fiction reveal not aesthetic failure but an impressive ability to resist false unities and resolutions designed to mask the real difficulty of her historical and personal circumstances. Burney's novels body forth contradiction, allowing her power over her identity as a woman writer and giving her the ability to confront her audience with the often-painful evidence of the difficulty in sustaining that identity. There is nothing easy and a great deal that is courageous in Burney's assimilation and management of the ideological dissonances that assailed her, like Camilla's nightmare voices, when she picked up her pen.

Notes

1. [Judith Lowder] Newton's discussion of *Evelina* in *Women, Power, and Subversion* [U Georgia P, 1981] makes the parallel point that Burney's position as "a genteel unmarried woman could force her to credit and give value to ideologies about her experience which at some level she understood to be untrue" (39).
2. Poovey theorizes that the role of a "proper lady"—the retiring and submissive attitudes appropriate to the female denizens of the domestic and private sphere—cut women off from direct uses of power, reserving their energies for a strictly supportive relationship with the public, male world. *Proper Lady* 3-47 [Mary Poovey, *The Proper Lady and the Woman Writer* (Chicago UP, 1984)].
3. See [Joyce] Hemlow, [The History of Fanny Burney (Clarendon, 1958)], 53-77, for an account of Burney's introduction into the Thrale household by her gregarious father.
4. See *ED* [*The Early Diary of Frances Burney, 1768-1778*] 1: 222-23 for Susan Burney's breathless account to Fanny of their father reading *Evelina*, and *DL* [*Diary and Letters of Madame d'Arblay*] 1: 35-37 for Burney's agitated response to her father's praise. See post it
5. Hemlow, *History*, 105-38.
6. See Hemlow, *History*, 135-36 and *DL* 1: 166-72 for an account of Burney's distress.
7. Hemlow, *History*, 137.
8. Frances Burney, *Camilla; or, a Picture of Youth*, ed. Edward A. Bloom and Lillian D. Bloom (London: Oxford UP, 1972), 877-78. References to *Camilla* are to this edition and are indicated in the text.
9. Frances Burney, *The Wanderer; or, Female Difficulties* (London: Longman, Hurst, Ress, Orme, and Brown, 1814) 5: 47-48.
10. Julia L. Epstein, "Fanny Burney's Epistolary Voices," *The Eighteenth Century: Theory and Interpretation* 27 (1986): 162-79.

FROM THE AUTHOR

BURNEY WRITES IN A LETTER TO HER SISTER ABOUT THE EXCITEMENT AND ANXIETY ATTENDING HER SUCCESS AS A NOVELIST

I often think, when I am counting my laurels, what a pity it would have been had I popped off in my last illness, without knowing what a person of consequence I was!—and I sometimes think that, were I now to have a relapse, I could never go off with so much *éclat*! I am now at the summit of a high hill; my prospects on one side are bright, glowing, and invitingly beautiful; but when I turn round, I perceive, on the other side, sundry caverns, gulphs, pits, and precipices, that, to look at, make my head giddy and my heart sick. I see about me, indeed, many hills of far greater height and sublimity; but I have not the strength to attempt climbing them; if I move, it must be downwards. I have already, I fear, reached the pinnacle of my abilities, and therefore to stand still will be my best policy.

Burney, Fanny. Excerpt from a letter to Suzy Burney, July 5, 1778. In *Diary and Letters of Madame D'Arblay*, Vol 1. Edited by Charlotte Barrett with notes by Austin Dobson, pp. 40-41. London: Macmillan, 1904.

TITLE COMMENTARY

Evelina

SUSAN C. GREENFIELD (ESSAY DATE JULY 1991)

SOURCE: Greenfield, Susan C. "'Oh Dear Resemblance of Thy Murdered Mother': Female Authorship in *Evelina*." *Eighteenth-Century Fiction* 3, no. 4 (July 1991): 301-20.

In the following essay, Greenfield counters the common interpretation of Evelina *as a quest for the validation of the father, instead arguing that Evelina—and Burney—in fact establish their legitimacy through the authority of the mother.*

Frances Burney's first published novel, ***Evelina*** (1778),[1] is a story about an orphan girl's quest for identity and her development as a writer. The novel traces the heroine's search for a parental author who can name her and establish her position in the world; at the same time, since the text is epistolary and most of the letters are written by

Title page of *Evelina* (1824).

Evelina, the heroine herself is an author. In this essay I examine ***Evelina***'s representation of authorship in each sense of the term and argue that identity and literary power are depicted as matrilineal gifts. I also suggest that the book's female-centred family romance parallels both Burney's personal myth about her own writing and her culture's narrative about the origins of the novel as a genre.

Such claims may seem puzzling because, on the surface, ***Evelina*** focuses on the heroine's longing for a patriarchal name. Patricia Spacks correctly points out that the "identity she cares about most is given her from without by husband and father."[2] What studies of ***Evelina*** have not yet revealed, however, is that there is also a subtext that undercuts the patriarch and privileges Evelina's dead mother's authority. Surprising as it may seem, the account of the heroine author's search for her parental author suggests that identity, title, and the power of writing all descend through the maternal line. In the climactic recognition scene, for instance, when Evelina finally meets the father who abandoned her and precipitated her mother's death, she gives him her mother's last letter. After reading the text, he exclaims: "Oh my child, my child! . . . Oh dear resemblance of thy murdered mother! . . . Oh . . . thou representative of my departed wife, speak to me in her name" (pp. 385-86). In part, the moment represents the culmination of Evelina's efforts to gain paternal legitimation, to have her father describe her as "my child." And yet, it is ultimately the dead mother who signs the daughter's body (stamping Evelina with her own physical features) and she who writes the letter that defines kinship relationships. The father must acknowledge his familial history, but the mother's posthumous ability both to name the daughter and enable the daughter to speak in her name eclipses his authorial power.

I am not claiming that ***Evelina*** is a radical text, for every reference to female control is balanced by a contradictory position and the work concludes by glorifying the patriarchy. Indeed, as Kristina Straub points out, the novel is divided between its emphasis on "the autonomy of female consciousness" and its "deference to masculine authority."[3] In terms of the problem of authorship, there is always a tension in the work. Clearly, ***Evelina*** appropriates hegemonic values, but it also subverts these values in its representation of female creativity.

* * *

It is useful to begin by examining Burney's stories about the family dynamics of her own early writing career,[4] for the conflicting representation of patriarchal authority in the novel also surfaces in Burney's accounts of her relationship with her author father, Dr Charles Burney. According to autobiographical sources, Burney felt that in order to write she had to conceal her words from her father as well as distance herself from him and his name. Consider, for instance, the famous story about how Burney celebrated her fifteenth birthday by making a bonfire in the garden and destroying all of the writing she had produced since age ten. Included in the pile was a novel entitled **"The History of Caroline Evelyn,"** the antecedent of ***Evelina.*** In her Dedication of ***The Wanderer*** (1814), addressed to her father, Burney explains how she burned the novel because she knew that the genre was generally held in low esteem. But then she goes on to describe how she had also assumed that her father was contemptuous of novels since he only had one in his library. Speaking to her father directly, Burney says that, even though he never knew she had written **"Caroline Evelyn,"** she burned it in his honour, for "I felt ashamed of appearing to be a votary to a species of writing that by you, Sir . . . I thought condemned."[5] Thus, Burney represents Dr Burney as her censor and as one of the primary sources of the fire.[6] And yet at the same time that she empowers him by emphasizing her respect for his opinions, she also seems to take a certain pleasure in drawing attention to his ignorance of **"Caroline Evelyn"**: "You, dear Sir, knew nothing of its extinction, for you had never known of its existence" (p. xxii).

Her account of the completion of ***Evelina*** more than ten years later repeats the theme. Burney wrote ***Evelina*** in secret and arranged for its anonymous publication. Because she did not want her father to read the novel but also did not want to be disobedient, she told Dr Burney about the text, but then requested permission to withhold its contents:

> When I told my father, I *never* [wished or] intended, [that] . . . he . . . should see my essay, he forbore to ask me its name. . . . He made no sort of objection to my having my own way in total secrecy and silence to all the world. . . . [He] is contented with hearing I shall never have the courage to let him know its name.[7]

Although in this story Burney tells her father about her text's existence, she again conceals her work as she twice points out that her father does not even know her book's name. Burney also announces that she will remove her name from the work. It was then common for novelists (especially women novelists) to claim anonymity, but in the Dedication Burney suggests that at the time of ***Evelina***'s publication, namelessness also had personal significance. She had, she tells her father, always been proud that after the publication of ***Evelina*** both Johnson and Burke "condescended to stand for the champion of my . . . small work . . . ere they knew that I bore, my Father! your honoured name" (p. xviii). Recognizing that, as Gilbert and Gubar explain, a woman's proper name designates "her role as her father's daughter" and is "always in a way *im*proper because it is not . . . her own, either to have or to give,"[8] Burney viewed anonymity as a form of self-promotion.

In the prefatory ode to her father in ***Evelina,*** Burney again wields the power of censorship and treats the name of her father ironically. She honours her parent by dedicating the text to him, but then avoids naming him in the verses. Instead, she addresses the poem to nobody, "To———" and writes: "Concealment is the only boon I claim; / Obscure be still the unsuccessful Muse, / Who cannot raise, but would not sink, your fame" (p. 1). Thus, she paradoxically calls attention to her father and erases him in the same move. Although the omission obviously springs from her desire for anonymity, the effect on her father's name is telling. Burney's gesture at once deprecates her writing, honours the name of the father, and yet—by concealing his name, concealing his power to name her and concealing the name of the text from him—subverts his authority.[9]

Both the novel and the autobiographical accounts reiterate the idea that if a woman wants to own her writing—or indeed herself—she must be nameless, must divorce herself from the father's language. When Burney resumed journal writing after the bonfire, for instance, she addressed her diary to "Nobody." In her opening 1768 entry she explains:

> To Nobody . . . will I write my Journal! since To Nobody can I be wholly unreserved. . . . No secret can I conceal from No-body . . . No-body's self has not power to destroy. . . .

> From this moment, then, my dear Girl—but why, permit me to ask, must a female be made Nobody? Ah! my dear, what were this world good for, were Nobody a female?[10]

The passage is a marvel of wit and confusion. In part, Burney suggests that Nobody stands for what it means—absence. But she also transforms Nobody into an implicitly female figure who exists even though she has no body and no name. In contrast to her father, then, Burney can trust Nobody with her writing because "No-body's self has not power to destroy." Burney also implies that by addressing Nobody she is actually addressing herself. Indeed, in one 1774 entry she announces that she is writing "[to myself, that is to Nobody!]."[11] Apparently, the idea of being and speaking to Nobody freed Burney to construct a journal. In order to design herself in prose, she had to erase all externally determined marks of identity and become a blank slate upon which only she could write.

* * *

Corresponding to Burney's stories about how she had to distance herself from her father and his language in order to become a writer, ***Evelina*** demonstrates that woman's rise to authorship is predicated on the fall of paternal control. We know that the novel must, in part, reflect Burney's feelings about authorship and paternity because she refers to the heroine as "nobody." Evelina is nobody because her father, Sir John Belmont, abandoned her at birth and left her no title and no social identity. Her two names signal her anonymous status: the first is an adaptation of her dead mother's maiden name, Caroline Evelyn, and she has no legal surname, only the fictitious "Anville," invented by her guardian.[12] Often, Evelina's nobodiness is represented as a liability. She is deprecated in public ("really, for a person who is nobody, to give herself such airs," p. 35), ignored in high company ("like a cypher, whom to nobody belonging, by nobody was noticed," p. 340), and continually vulnerable to sexual attack.[13] Because Evelina lacks a patriarchal identity nearly all the men she encounters (except the noble Lord Orville) assume she is public property and should be at their disposal. Most flagrantly, Sir Clement Willoughby wants to seduce but not marry her, because nobody "would recommend to me a connection . . . with a girl of obscure birth, whose only dowry is her beauty" (p. 347).

Despite these liabilities, however, in her novel as in her autobiographical stories, Burney links nobodiness with female literary power. ***Evelina*** depends upon the heroine's being a nobody, for the plot is based on the trials Evelina experiences as a result of her nameless state. Moreover, the epistolary form reinforces the link between the book's structure and the heroine's literary control. After all, it is Evelina who employs nobodiness as her literary subject. In one of his few letters Mr Villars describes her as the "child of a wealthy baronet . . . whose name she is forbidden to claim; entitled as she is to lawfully inherit his fortune and estate, is there any probability that he will *properly* own her?" (p. 19). True, Evelina's namelessness obstructs her right to own property. Yet the hidden implication of Villars's words—which he could not appreciate—is that anonymity is partly an asset, for were Evelina to be acknowledged, she would become property; she would be "owned." It is only because Evelina is not owned that she can go her own way in the world and describe the experience. Were she named, Evelina would be spoken for. Because she is nameless, she has both the opportunity and need to speak for herself.

Paralleling the way Burney presents her father as the suppressor of her writing, ***Evelina*** also suggests that a woman must determinedly produce her own narrative because the father has a tendency to destroy it. Indeed, Belmont erases a woman's story and body. The novel opens with the revelation that, for all practical purposes, Belmont murdered his wife—Evelina's mother—by denying that he was married to her. In addition to having precipitated Caroline Evelyn's death, Belmont's denial destroyed her history by creating the illusion that she had been seduced. The details here are important: Caroline died from shock and sorrow after Belmont "burnt the certificate of their marriage" (p. 15). In a sense, this was not the first time Caroline Evelyn had been burned, for "**Caroline Evelyn**" was set aflame in the bonfire fuelled by Burney's father. Ignited by the patriarch, both the story of "**Caroline Evelyn**" and Caroline Evelyn's true story were destroyed.

In contrast to Belmont, Mr Villars appears to be a benign, trustworthy and helpful parent. "*That man is* ALWAYS *right*" Charles Burney said of him, and readers are apt to agree.[14] But a closer scrutiny of Villars reveals that the old man is not always right. He candidly tells Evelina the accurate details of her past, but withholds this information from the public. "I am," he says "very desirous of guarding her from curiosity and impertinence, by concealing her name, family, and story" (p. 19). The concealment may at first seem wise, but it hurts the heroine. At the end of the novel we learn that Belmont had reformed after Caroline's death, and had wanted to acknowledge and care for his daughter. He had been under the impression that he was doing so, for Evelina's nurse had presented him with a baby she claimed was his daughter, but who was actually her own. Because Villars had so effectively secluded Evelina and buried her history, Belmont failed to discover the fraud. As Evelina explains, the "name by which I was known, the secrecy observed in regard to my family, and the retirement in which I lived, all conspired to render this [the nurse's] scheme . . . by no means impracticable" (pp. 373-74). Evelina does not emphasize the connection, but we should recognize that, since Mr Villars was responsible for the secrecy surrounding the heroine, he unwittingly assisted the nurse's plot to disinherit her.

Caroline had made Villars promise to hide her daughter from Belmont until the latter reformed, but Villars has his own reasons for concealing the heroine from her true parent. He wants Evelina to develop into an ideal domestic woman and believes she must stay home with him and be humble and private for this to happen. Often he echoes popular conduct book writers such as Lord Halifax, who tells his daughter that the "government of your House, Family, and children . . . is the province alloted to your Sex;" it is only the "Husband, whose province is without dores."[15] Similarly, Mr Villars tells Evelina that she is "unfit for the thorny paths of the great and busy world," and that he hopes one day to "see my Evelina the . . . pride and delight of her family" (p. 116). Villars justifies his unwillingness to reunite Evelina with Belmont by claiming that the dissipated father would "expose her to the snares and dangers" of nondomestic life. The feminine virtues she developed in his own home away from the great and busy world—"her artless openness" and "ingenuous simplicity"—would be corrupted (p. 126).

Some studies of Burney have assumed that her texts endorse domestic ideology,[16] but in ***Evelina*** the message is actually ambiguous. Although the novel ends with Evelina's marriage and retirement from public life, it shows no interest in depicting the heroine in her private state. As Burney pointedly says in her Preface, the text is about Evelina's emergence from retirement, an account of her experiences "*after her* Entrance into the World" (p. 8). Thus, as much as the narrative depends upon Evelina's being separated from her natural father, it equally depends on her dissociation from the domestic containment that her surrogate father and his home at Berry Hill represent.

In this respect, the heroine's first letter is especially telling, for in it she requests permission to travel to London, although she knows that Villars does not want her to go the place that for him epitomizes public danger.[17] In effect, Evelina emerges as an author in order to defy her surrogate father and enter the forbidden public world. Indeed, she herself seems to realize that her writing passes beyond the boundaries of passive obedience:

> I believe I am bewitched! I made a resolution when I began, that I would not be urgent; but my pen—or rather my thoughts, will not suffer me to keep it—for I acknowledge, I must acknowledge, I cannot help wishing for your permission. . . . [P]ray forget [this confession] . . . if this journey is displeasing to you. But I will not write any longer; for the more I think of this affair the less indifferent to it I find myself.
>
> (p. 24)

Resembling the stories of the way in which Burney established a distance between her own father and her writing, this passage is suitably ambiguous. Like Burney, Evelina portrays writing as an act against the father: she knows he will disapprove of her request, and is, she claims, "half ashamed of myself for beginning this letter" (p. 23). And yet, as when Burney asked for permission to conceal her published novel, having already decided to withhold it, Evelina asks for permission to see London, but has already decided she must go. Both narratives associate the daughter's writing with filial defiance and public emergence, and both demonstrate how the daughter develops a dutiful rhetoric that masks her ulterior motives.[18]

Evelina's linguistic experiences with other male characters are also telling. She often describes herself as lacking verbal control when she encounters men such as Orville and Willoughby. Of her first meeting with Lord Orville Evelina says "I was seized with such a panic, that I could hardly speak a word" (p. 30). The pattern continues throughout their early encounters and is repeated at the end of the novel when their marriage is arranged. Willoughby presents a similar problem, for his sexual affronts shock her into speechlessness. When he tries to seduce Evelina, she is "so much embarrassed . . . that I could not tell what to answer" (p. 97). Although she avoids the seduction by screaming, Willoughby forces her to offer words of forgiveness: "for he . . . would not let me rest till I gave him my word" (p. 100). Thus even when the heroine speaks, her language is not her own.[19] Given such suppression, Evelina's letters are all the more remarkable for offering her the opportunity to speak freely. Although silenced by Orville and Willoughby when she is with them, Evelina regains linguistic mastery by describing these men in prose. In her letters she does all the talking—she controls the representation of both Orville and Willoughby (as well as everyone else) and even the accounts of her verbal effacement are ironically offset by the fact that she is writing the description.[20]

The heroine's narrative is, in a sense, bound by patriarchal discourse because she directs her prose to Mr Villars. As Julia Epstein points out, "We cannot expect . . . that her letters to this guardian . . . will be straightforward. She has no choice but to edit them carefully."[21] And yet, like Burney, who concealed information from her father, Evelina manipulates and censors Villars's access to her language. "She writes from the angle from which she chooses Villars to view her adventures . . . and he reads ultimately only what she wants him to know."[22] So too, Evelina puts a spin on her words. In her letter about the London trip, she openly flatters Villars but at the same time persuades him to let her leave against his wishes—persuades him, that is, to undermine his own authority.

* * *

Although teleologically ***Evelina*** is designed to reunite the heroine and her father, much of the novel questions paternal authority. Both of Evelina's fathers injure and conceal women and their stories. In order to establish her identity, Evelina must separate from them and emerge in the world alone, and through this independence she becomes an author. Because the other men she meets also demonstrate the fathers' capacity for suppression, it is only by writing that she can consistently evade male control. By contrast, Evelina's dead mother is represented as a source of narrative power and legitimacy. The fathers would deny her access to a history and self; but through her transcendental union with her mother, Evelina gains these very entitlements. Ultimately, the mother becomes the supreme author who acquires the power to name her daughter and herself.

In order to trace this phenomenon we must first recognize that, because Belmont burned the marriage certificate, Evelina and her dead mother suffer the same plight. Both have been denied a name, both have been turned into nobody (the mother literally has no body), and both need to be legitimated: it is necessary to prove that Caroline had been a legal wife and that therefore Evelina was a legitimate daughter. In addition to having parallel problems, Evelina and Caroline reflect each other in a literal way, for the novel repeatedly draws attention to their physical resemblance. Produced at the very moment of Caroline's death, Evelina's body has grown into a seemingly perfect replica of the mother. She is described as "the lovely resemblance of her lovely mother" (p. 132) and "the living image of an injured saint" (p. 130). Indeed, when Belmont finally sees her he cries, "My God! does Caroline Evelyn still live!" (p. 372).

It is in part through her resemblance to her mother that Evelina is able to correct the injustices perpetrated against her parent and herself. When she is preparing to meet Belmont in the hope that he will acknowledge her, Villars reassures her of success and says, "without any other *certificate* of your birth, that which you carry in your countenance, as it could not be effected by artifice, so it cannot admit of a doubt" (p. 337, my emphasis). His language harkens back to the "burnt . . . certificate of . . . marriage" (p. 15) that constituted the father's original offence. The implication is that by reproducing her own features in those of her daughter, Caroline has inscribed the evidence of lawful kinship on her child's body and rewritten the marriage certificate. Evelina's countenance reflects the same information once contained in the legal document. There is no avowal of the tenuousness of this association—no admission that Evelina's resemblance to her mother does not necessarily prove that she is Belmont's legitimate child. It is simply assumed that since Evelina looks just like her mother, who was a virtuous woman, Belmont must be the father. Accordingly, when he sees Evelina for the first time, Belmont senses that she is his real daughter and suspects that the girl he raised is a fraud. Echoing Villars, Evelina explains that "the certainty I carried in my countenance, of my real birth, made him . . . suspect . . . the imposition" (p. 374).

The climactic recognition scene, however—the one in which Belmont definitively acknowledges Evelina as his daughter and Caroline as his wife—is not brought about by Evelina's body alone. Evelina must meet her father twice. During their first encounter, Belmont cries, "I see, I see thou art her child! she lives—she breathes—she is present to my view!" (p. 372). But Belmont does not cry, "I see thou art my child!" Nor does he refer to Caroline as his wife. He is moved by Evelina's appearance, but not moved to offer either woman legal recognition.[23] Between this and the second encounter Mrs Selwyn uncovers the nurse's plot and convinces Belmont that his supposed daughter is not his real one, obviously an important step in the legitimation process.

But more important for our purposes is the fact that, when Evelina meets her father again, she bears new evidence of kinship. This time Evelina carries the letter that Caroline wrote to Belmont on her deathbed. Since she died in giving birth, we know that Caroline produced the text and the daughter at about the same time. Caroline's final acts of creation are conflated and Evelina's body and the letter are presented as simultaneous births. Moreover, like Evelina's countenance, the letter functions as a certificate of birth and a replacement for the burnt marriage certificate. In it Caroline tells her husband: "Thou know'st I am thy wife!—clear, then, to the world the reputation thou hast sullied, and receive as thy lawful successor the child who will present thee this my dying request" (p. 339). Thus the letter and Evelina's face both tell the true story of the heroine's heritage. Correspondingly, Belmont characterizes each in the same way. He tells Evelina that "Ten thousand daggers could not have wounded me like this letter!" (p. 385); then he says: "Evelina! thy countenance is a dagger to my heart!" (p. 386). By virtue of the interactive force of the letter and body, Belmont finally fulfils Caroline's desire. Acknowledging his legal relationship to both child and wife, he pronounces the key words: "Oh my child, my child. . . . Oh dear resemblance of thy murdered mother! . . . Oh then, thou representative of my departed wife, speak to me in her name" (pp. 385-86).

In destroying the marriage certificate, Belmont had erased the mother's story and body. But, because she reproduces herself in the body of her daughter and produces an irrefutable document about the marriage, Caroline replaces the certificate and finally overpowers her husband. Through her dual creation of Evelina and the letter, she generates the definitive text—the indelible mark of familial relationships. The silenced mother speaks again and her "voice of equity" (p. 339) sounds loud and clear. True, Belmont must claim Evelina as "my daughter" and Caroline as "my wife" for all to be resolved. But the novel diminishes his paternal privilege by showing how much Belmont's authority depends on Caroline's word. The father acts in response to the mother's command. It is Caroline who "charges" (p. 385) Belmont to claim ownership, she who "mark[s] the conditions upon which" he will be forgiven for his crime (p. 339). In Evelina and her letter, the mother writes the final version of the familial script. The father exerts no creative control; he merely reads and publishes the mother's printed lines. Thus it is really Caroline who composes the resolution. For all its emphasis on Evelina's need to be united with her paternal author, the novel actually proves that her ultimate author is her mother. It is only because Caroline speaks through Evelina that the heroine's identity is finally established and real history confirmed. Had it been left to either of the fathers, the daughter's story would have remained suppressed.

Reread in this context, Burney's dedicatory ode to her father is even less complimentary. Burney calls Charles Burney the "author of my being," but then undercuts him by refusing to name him, to name the text to him, or to name herself as its author. The novel confirms the poem's irony, suggesting that, although the daughter must appeal to her father, the mother has ultimate authority. The frontispiece to the first volume of the fourth edition of ***Evelina*** (1779)[24] offers a similar message. A woman in classical dress stares at a tombstone engraved with the word "Belmont." Beneath are the lines of the poem: "Oh author of my being." As Caroline Belmont is the only dead Belmont in the story, the tombstone must be hers. The illustration both reinforces the scene in which Evelina's mother proves to be the author of her being and pushes the implications of the poem to their extreme. In the poem the father's name is erased and in the frontispiece he is entirely replaced by the mother who *is* named (as Belmont) and designated the ultimate author.[25]

The novel also invests Evelina with the power to author her parent, for in bearing her mother's features and letter, she disseminates the legitimate words about Caroline's past. Caroline names Evelina, and Evelina finally establishes her mother's name. So too, because she writes the letters that describe Caroline's real story, Evelina produces the definitive manuscript about her mother's life. Through its insistence that Evelina is authored by her mother, who in turn is authored by Evelina, the novel demonstrates that the ability to delegate names and offer a legitimate narrative is a female generative power. The recognition scene challenges traditional familial roles by giving the mother the right to determine the kinship structure and establish identity.

I do not want to suggest that the entire novel should be viewed as a subversive account of maternal creativity. Caroline is dead, after all, and thus hardly an unwavering symbol of empowerment. Even worse, the other major maternal figure, Evelina's grandmother, is depicted as a vulgar woman and dangerous parent. It was because Mme Duval tried to force her daughter into an undesirable marriage that Caroline eloped with Belmont in the first place. Partly responsible for her daughter's death, the grandmother is barely less destructive than the father. Evelina's reunion with Caroline may be positive, but Mme Duval is a frightening fool from whom she must escape. As Margaret Anne Doody says of Evelina's encounter with her, the "discovery of the mother, of the inevitable female descent and fate, is very bad news."[26]

Moreover, the recognition scene itself is double-sided. For although the scene constitutes the novel's most radical moment, it also creates the conditions for a patriarchal conclusion. Once Belmont heeds Caroline's call and owns his relationship to Evelina, he owns her and Evelina can no longer act on her own. As she explains to Orville before travelling to see Belmont, this "journey will deprive me of all right to act for myself" (p. 354). The recognition scene may highlight the mother's ability to designate kinship relationships, but it does so only to give Evelina over to her father and transform her into marriageable property. Like a true hero, Orville proposes to Evelina before her origins are clarified, but she tells him she cannot marry until she finds a father to give her away (p. 370). After Belmont acknowledges her, Orville can both introduce Evelina by her "real name," and look forward to presenting her "by yet another name, and by the most endearing of all titles" (p. 381). Thus, Evelina becomes an item that men can exchange and rename, and the ecstatic Orville finally declares: "You are now . . . all my own!" (p. 404).

The most oppressive effect of this transition is that it deprives Evelina of her literary power. It logically follows that once she is named by the patriarch, the heroine must relinquish her own ability to name, must become a linguistic referent and cease to be a speaking subject. Thus, as soon as marriage plans are arranged, Evelina begins to have difficulty reading and writing. When Orville proposes, she is speechless and she faints. Later she says, "I cannot write the scene that followed, though every word is engraven on my heart" (p. 352). Again Evelina's body becomes a text,[27] but in contrast to the time when she was her mother's text and promoted woman's word, here her body is a language over which she has no control. When Evelina receives Villars's letter of consent to the marriage, she is blinded by tears and cannot read it. Orville asks her about its contents, but she has "no voice to answer the enquiries" and has to "put the letter into his hands," and leave it "to speak" both for her and itself (p. 404). After this she produces only one more, brief letter in the text. Appropriated by the patriarchy, the heroine loses her voice, and the novel she has constructed must come to an end.[28]

Significantly, though, Evelina is permitted a final moment of self-assertion before the novel concludes. She signs her last letter exactly as she had signed her previous ones, with her first name only, making "Evelina" the last word in the text. Although at this point the heroine is married and could use her married name,[29] the novel ends not by celebrating Evelina's changed state, but by valorizing her anonymity. Just as Burney derived power by separating from her father and his name, the final signature (and the title of the novel) erases patriarchal language and suggests that a woman is most herself when most removed from men. Moreover, since Evelina is a derivative of the mother's maiden name, the signature highlights the enduring authority of the matrilineal word.

* * *

The conservative conclusion is conventional, but the novel's subtext—its subversion of the patriarch and insistence that naming and textual production are matrilineal powers—is more perplexing. One could rely on biographical information and argue that here the work reflects Burney's personal need to undermine her author father. Her relationship with her mother, Esther, is also relevant. Autobiographical sources suggest that as a child Burney could barely read or write until age ten when she suddenly "began scribbling, almost incessantly, little works of invention."[30] Significantly, this was the same year that Burney's mother died. Thus, as Doody notes, there "seems to be a connection between Frances's first great spurt of writing and the death of her mother";[31] so too, the novel associates authorship with the dead mother.

But although Burney's psychobiography is revealing, much more can be gained by attending to the larger literary and historical context that produced both the writer and her work. Burney wrote ***Evelina*** at a time when the novel as a genre was beginning to be seen as a female product designed by, for, and about women.[32] Viewed from this perspective, the emphasis on female authorship in ***Evelina*** can be read as a reflection of the genre's feminine status, the mother-daughter account of creation seen as a story about the evolution of the novel form. Current literary theory often defines textual production as a paternal, phallic act, but such a metaphor does not necessarily apply to the history of the late eighteenth-century novel. ***Evelina*** was born into a culture that saw the novel as a representative of female language and subjectivity; correspondingly, the heroine's history suggests that women have a unique capacity to generate words and identity. While it is hard to tell if Burney consciously associated Evelina's family romance with the process of novelistic production, it seems likely that she was influenced by the literary climate; for both Evelina's history and the stories Burney told about ***Evelina***'s creation parallel contemporary attitudes about the origin of the genre.

One obvious connection between the novel form and the heroine is that like Evelina, the novel was seen as an illegitimate child. Because the novel had not clearly descended from any previous literary tradition, its parentage was obscure; it was not part of the family. As Burney puts it in the Preface to ***Evelina,*** authors of novels were like bastard siblings: "In the republic of letters, there is no member of such inferior rank, or who is so much disdained by his brethren of the quill, as the humble Novelist" (p. 7). So too, just as the heroine's parentlessness is associated with the instability of her name, the novel was plagued by name problems. For one thing, the words "romance," "history," and "novel" were, for a long time, used interchangeably.[33] For another, any work identified as a "novel" was liable to be viewed with contempt. Burney was all too aware of this: "The power of prejudice annexed to nomenclature is universal. . . . [I]n nothing is the force of denomination more striking than in the term Novel; a species of writing . . . rigidly excommunicated, from its appellation" (Dedication, p. xxi). Because of her problematic parentage and name, Evelina is marked as an outsider; she is always in danger of being categorized as inferior and always vulnerable to violence. So too, the novel's problematic parentage and name excluded it from the literary community, branded it as inferior, and exposed it to critical attack.

And yet the genre's liabilities were also the very characteristics that made it appealing to female writers. It was because the novel was an illegitimate form, because it did not require a traditional education, that a large group of women could actively participate in its production. On the other hand, the rise of the professional female writer was paralleled by the rising importance of female domesticity; increasingly women were taught to stay home and avoid all forms of public activity—especially wage-earning activity. Thus, at the same time that women had more opportunities to publish than ever before, those who published necessarily subverted feminine rules.

Obviously troubled by this contradiction, Burney was fiercely private about her work before ***Evelina*** was published, And yet she was also thrilled when the novel was printed precisely because it marked her own emergence as a public figure. In her journal she memorably exclaims: "At the latter end of January, the literary world was favoured with the first publication of the ingenious, learned, and most profound Fanny Burney!" And later she describes "this year" as "the first of my appearing in public."[34]

Again, the parallels are striking. In the novel's Preface Burney says that the text is "presented to the public." So too, in language that echoes her discussion of herself, she describes the heroine making "her first appearance upon the great and busy stage of life" (p. 7) and embarking on "her Entrance into the world" (p. 8). Thus, novel, author, and heroine are in analogous positions as all are in the process of crossing the boundaries of private feminine space. The movement is in keeping with the transgressive power of the novel genre itself, for the form allowed women to enter a public literary world for the first time.

For the most persuasive evidence that Burney associated the heroine's history with the history of the novel's production, we must return to the bonfire episode. Burney claimed that her father sparked the fire that destroyed the mother novel, **"Caroline Evelyn,"** and in ***Evelina*** the father sets fire to the marriage document that destroys the mother character, Caroline Evelyn. But in the continuation of the bonfire story, Burney also describes how she could not prevent herself from beginning to write the daughter novel after the sacrifice. Despite her own best attempts to obey the father's censorship, ***Evelina*** rose out of the "ashes of '**Caroline Evelyn**'" and "struggled herself into life" (Dedication, p. xxii). Similarly, in the novel, the daughter Evelina emerges on her mother's ashy grave (the mother is associated with the burnt certificate and more than once referred to as "ashes," pp. 130, 337), overcomes her father's attempts to annihilate her, establishes her identity, and produces the story of her life in her letters.

And yet it must be emphasized that, as much as ***Evelina*** celebrates female creativity, it simultaneously reflects Burney's overwhelming longing for paternal approval—her desire both to earn her father's acceptance and to be welcomed into the literary ranks to which he belonged. Just as

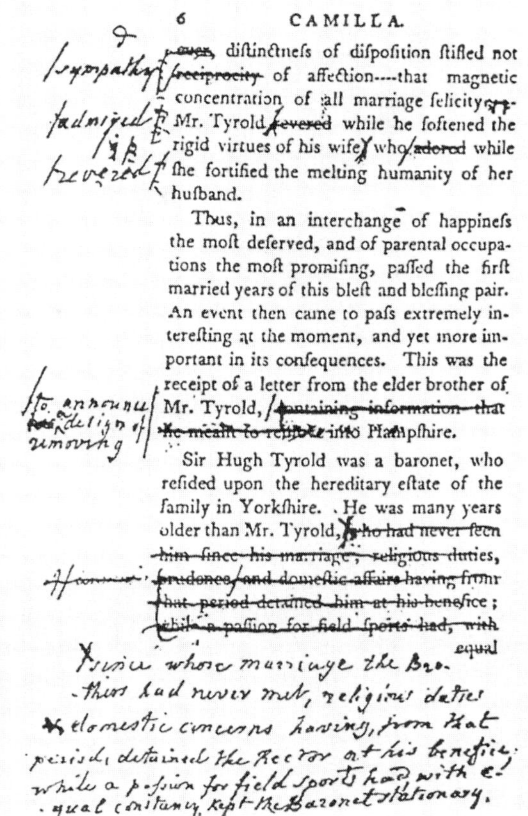

6 CAMILLA.

powers, distinctness of disposition stifled not reciprocity of affection----that magnetic concentration of all marriage felicity. Mr. Tyrold revered while he softened the rigid virtues of his wife, who adored while she fortified the melting humanity of her husband.

Thus, in an interchange of happiness the most deserved, and of parental occupations the most promising, passed the first married years of this blest and blessing pair. An event then came to pass extremely interesting at the moment, and yet more important in its consequences. This was the receipt of a letter from the elder brother of Mr. Tyrold, containing information that he meant to remove into Hampshire.

Sir Hugh Tyrold was a baronet, who resided upon the hereditary estate of the family in Yorkshire. He was many years older than Mr. Tyrold, who had never seen him since his marriage; religious duties, prudence and domestic affairs having from that period detained him at his benefice; while a passion for field sports had, with equal

CAMILLA.

equal constancy, kept his brother stationary upon his own grounds. The baronet began his letter with kind enquiries after the welfare of Mr. Tyrold and his family, and then entered upon the state of his own affairs, briefly narrating, "that he had lost his health, and, not "knowing what to do with himself, had "resolved to change his habitation, and "settle near his relations. The Cleves' "estate, which he heard was just by Etherington, being then upon sale, he desired "his brother to make the purchase for "him out of hand; and then to prepare "Mrs. Tyrold, with whom he was yet unacquainted, though he took it for "granted she was a woman of great learning, to receive a mere poor country "'squire, who knew no more of hic, hæc, "hoc, than the baby unborn. He begged "him to provide a proper apartment for "their niece Indiana Lynmere, whom he "should bring with him, and another for "their nephew Clermont, who was to follow at the next holidays; and not to "forget

Proofed manuscript pages of *Camilla.*

Evelina needs to be read by her father, Burney clearly wanted her father to read and approve of ***Evelina*** (even though she withheld the work). After learning that Dr Burney had finally read and greatly enjoyed the book, Burney wrote, "the approbation of all the world put together would not bear any competition, in my estimation, with that of my beloved father."[35] So too, she was understandably overjoyed when she learned that Dr Johnson liked her novel. Her response to his "approbation" is famous: "it almost crazed me with agreeable surprise—it gave me such a flight of spirits, that I danced a jig."[36]

Like Evelina, who addresses her letters to her "father" Villars and whose countenance is addressed to her father Belmont, ***Evelina*** is addressed to a male audience. Burney dedicates the book to her father, includes an introductory letter directed to "Gentlemen" critics (p. 3), and refers to a series of "great [male] writers" in her Preface. The plot emphasizes Evelina's need for paternal justice: Villars tells Lady Howard he has considered "presenting Evelina to her father, and demanding the justice which is her due" (p. 126); Lady Belmont accuses her husband of being "hardened against every plea of justice" (p. 338); and Mrs Selwyn tells Evelina "justice demands you should appear . . . [as] Sir John Belmont's daughter" (p. 378). Similarly, Burney uses the word "justice" with reference to the novel's reception. In her introductory letter to the "Gentlemen" "Authors of The *Monthly* and *Critical* Reviews," she writes "to your Justice alone I am entitled" (p. 4). And she concludes her Preface by saying "*Whatever may be the fate of these letters, the editor is satisfied they will meet with justice*" (p. 9). As in the case with Evelina, ultimately the most pressing question for ***Evelina*** is: will the text be properly legitimated by its father(s)—will it receive patriarchal justice?

Burney mythologizes female literary creation in ***Evelina,*** but the heroine's search for paternal acknowledgment also symbolizes her own desire to be claimed and named by male authors and readers, accepted as an offspring of the masculine literary lineage. Her longing is understandable. The novel may have revolutionized women's literary possibilities and been seen as a matrilineal product, but a woman's work still could not gain prestige unless it was read, published, and promoted by important men. At least Burney's repeated references to "justice" suggest she believed that, like Evelina, ***Evelina*** warranted such respect because of its intrinsic worth.

But, as the author discovered after ***Evelina*** was treated with more justice than she had ever dared hope, paternal recognition had its disadvantages. Burney wrote ***Evelina*** her "own way in total secrecy and silence to all the world," but once she was publicly named as author (in a pamphlet written by the Reverend George Huddlesford), her father began to control her words. He and "Daddy" Crisp denounced her subsequent production, **"The Witlings,"** and insisted that the play be suppressed. Dr Burney also interfered with the creation of ***Cecilia.*** Eager to advance his daughter's (and thus his own) fame, he supervised Burney's progress, forced her to write the novel too rapidly, and pressed her so much that she became ill. Despite his interference, the novel was a success and the author became an even greater celebrity. As a result, she was offered a position at court and, although she had reservations, Burney accepted the role at her father's urging. In addition to making her ill and depressed, five years of court life left her no time to pursue her literary career. It was not until 1796, fourteen years after ***Cecilia***'s publication, that Burney was able to complete ***Camilla,*** her third novel.[37]

Thus, with uncanny accuracy the resemblance between novel and heroine foreshadowed the author's own future. As soon as ***Evelina*** gained the paternal acknowledgment that Evelina sought and won, Burney experienced the very defeat her heroine's fate had anticipated. She lost her anonymity, gained legitimation, and was subsequently stripped of her literary independence. As with Evelina, paternal acceptance ultimately deprived Burney "of all right to act [and write] for myself."

Notes

1. Frances Burney, *Evelina; or The History of a Young Lady's Entrance into the World,* ed. Edward A. Bloom (London: Oxford University Press, 1968). References are to this edition.

2. Patricia Meyer Spacks, *Imagining a Self: Autobiography and Novel in Eighteenth-Century England* (Cambridge: Harvard University Press, 1976), p. 179.

3. Kristina Straub, *Divided Fictions: Fanny Burney and Feminine Strategy* (Lexington: University Press of Kentucky, 1987), p. 1.

4. I deliberately use the word "story" here. Burney's autobiographical descriptions may be based on "true" events, but she develops a narrative about her history that has become legendary among those interested in her work and bears remarkable similarity to the story told in *Evelina.*

5. Frances Burney, "Dedication to Doctor Burney" in *The Wanderer; or Female Difficulties* (London: Pandora Press, 1988), p. xxii. References are to this edition (cited as Dedication).

6. See Margaret Anne Doody, *Frances Burney: The Life in the Works* (New Brunswick, NJ: Rutgers University Press, 1988) pp. 35-38 for a discussion of the link between the bonfire and this passage in the Dedication. In their respective introductions to Burney's diary and letters, both Charlotte Barrett and Annie Raine Ellis suggest that Burney was reacting to her stepmother's attacks on scribbling girls when she burned "Caroline Evelyn." While this may have been true, in her published Dedication Burney focuses only on her anxiety about her father's role in the destruction. See *Diary and Letters of Madame D'Arblay,* ed. Charlotte Barrett, 7 vols (London: Bickers and Son, 1876), p. xiv; *The Early Diary of Frances Burney, 1768-1778,* ed. Annie Raine Ellis, 2 vols (London: George Bell and Sons, 1907), I, lxv.

7. *The Early Diary,* II, 164.

8. Sandra M. Gilbert and Susan Gubar, *No Man's Land 1: The War of the Words* (New Haven: Yale University Press, 1988), p. 237.

9. In her discussion of the dedicatory ode, Doody points out that, while here "Charles Burney is only '———,'" he is also "the Super-Author, the author of the author." Ultimately, my reading of the poem differs from Doody's, for she de-emphasizes Burney's act of censorship and suggests that the daughter "apologizes for doing something on her own; she apologizes for being an author" (p. 32).

10. *The Early Journals and Letters of Fanny Burney, 1768-1773,* ed. Lars E. Troide (Oxford: Clarendon Press, 1988), I, 2.

11. *The Early Diary,* I, 338. The brackets indicate that Burney probably substituted this passage later in life.

12. See Julia Epstein, *The Iron Pen: Frances Burney and the Politics of Women's Writing* (Madison: University of Wisconsin Press, 1989), p. 96. For an interesting discussion of the "Eve" in "Evelina," see Doody, pp. 40-41, and Gina Campbell, n. 28, below.

13. For Evelina's vulnerability to sexual violence see Susan Staves, "Evelina; or Female Difficulties," *Modern Philology* 73 (1976), 368-69, 376. Cf. Judith Lowder Newton, *Women, Power and Subversion: Social Strategies in British Fiction, 1778-1860* (Athens: University of Georgia Press, 1981), p. 23.

14. *The Early Diary,* II, 242. Six months after the novel's publication Dr Burney learned that *Evelina* was his daughter's work and read the book with great delight.

15. "Advice to a Daughter," in *The Works of George Savile Marquis of Halifax,* ed. Mark N. Brown (Oxford: Clarendon Press, 1989), II. 381, 383.

16. For instance Nancy Armstrong writes that *Evelina* "had the virtue of dramatizing the same principles sketched out in the conduct books." Nancy Armstrong, *Desire and Domestic Fiction: A Political History of the Novel* (New York: Oxford University Press, 1987), p. 97.

17. Villars contrasts London with private country living, associates the city with "the thorny paths of the great and busy world," and calls it the "harbour of fraud and of folly, of duplicity and of impertinence," and the centre of "public and dissipated life" (p. 116).

18. Cf. Julia Epstein's useful discussion of Evelina's first letter, pp. 102-3.

19. For other examples of Evelina's silence with Orville see pp. 61, 71, 78. For evidence of her verbal powerlessness with Willoughby see pp. 198-99. For an analysis of the recurring problem of female expression in all of Burney's novels see Juliet McMaster, "The Silent Angel: Impediments to Female Expression in Frances Burney's Novels," *Studies in the Novel* 21 (1989), 235-52.

20. Other critics have also drawn attention to the narrative power Evelina develops in her letters—especially the power she gains by satirizing the social world. See John Richetti, "Voice and Gender in Eighteenth-Century Fiction: Haywood to Burney," *Studies in the Novel* 19 (1987), 270-71. Also see Newton, pp. 43-44.

21. Epstein, pp. 98-99.

22. Epstein, p. 100.

23. See Irene Fizer, "The Name of the Daughter: Incest and Identity in *Evelina*," in *Refiguring the Father: New Feminist Readings of Patriarchy*, ed. Patricia Yaeger and Beth Kowaleski-Wallace (Carbondale: Southern Illinois University Press, 1989), pp. 91-97.

24. Doody reproduces and discusses this frontispiece in her biography, where I first learned about the illustration.

25. As Doody explains: "if—as makes sense within the context of the story—the tomb is the mother's, at last properly acknowledged with her name on it, then the first two lines of the verse which appear underneath refer not to the idea of father, but to the idea of *mother*" (pp. 32-33).

26. Doody, p. 51. See Straub, pp. 28-33 for a sympathetic reading of Mme Duval and the general problems of female maturity.

27. See Epstein, p. 100.

28. For an excellent discussion of *Evelina*'s representation of the problems of marriage, see Straub, pp. 53-77.

29. In her first letter to Villars, Evelina laments the fact that she can sign no last name. But now that she has one, she avoids using it.

30. Frances Burney, *Memoirs of Doctor Burney, arranged from his own Manuscripts, from Family Papers, and from Personal Recollections*, 3 vols (London: Edward Moxon, 1832) II, 123. Quoted in Doody, p. 21 and Epstein, p. 23.

31. Doody, p. 22.

32. One writer's remarks in the *Monthly Review* (Dec. 1790) are often quoted on this point: "Of the various species of composition that in course come before us, there are none in which *our* writers of the male sex have less excelled, since the days of Richardson and Fielding, than in the arrangement of the novel. Ladies seem to appropriate to themselves an exclusive privilege in this kind of writing."

33. See Michael McKeon, *The Origins of the English Novel 1600-1740* (Baltimore: Johns Hopkins University Press, 1987), p. 25.

34. *Diary and Letters*, I, 1, 3.

35. *Diary and Letters*, I, 7.

36. *Diary and Letters*, I, 18.

37. For a more detailed account of the suppression of *The Witlings* as well as a thorough discussion of how Dr Burney affected his daughter's writing throughout her life see Doody's biography. For a brief description of Burney's difficulties after *Evelina*'s publication see Judy Simons, Introduction in *Cecilia* (New York: Virago Press, 1986), pp. xii-xiii.

SAMUEL CHOI (ESSAY DATE FALL 1999)

SOURCE: Choi, Samuel. "Signing Evelina: Female Self-Inscription in the Discourse of Letters." *Studies in the Novel* 31, no. 3 (fall 1999): 259-78.

In the following essay, Choi examines the motif of naming in Evelina.

The story of Frances Burney's entrance into the literary world could hardly be more complicated if she herself had designed the various deferrals, deceptions, and deflections that problematize any attempt to characterize her authorial status. One would be hard pressed to decide among ***Evelina,*** which appears unsigned, **"The History of Caroline Evelyn,"** which perishes unpublished, and *A General History of Music,* which appears with her hand unacknowledged, as Burney's first literary work. I do not propose to establish, in these or any other works, the moment of Burney's authorial emergence, but, rather, to discuss the ways in which she consciously draws attention to her anonymity and her active deferral of authority in the formal features of ***Evelina.*** Each of the book's abundant introductory apparatuses—the title page, the epigraph, the dedication, the letter "To the Authors of the Monthly and Critical Reviews," and the preface—seems designed to play with the reader's expectation of finding an author—each acting like a drumroll, each calling out "Oh author of my being!" But in each case Burney refuses to reveal her name. In this essay I argue that Evelina's acts of signing her name to her letters are not haphazard but significant and legible events of self-inscription. Each of her signatures represents a conscious self-positioning individually considered and specifically framed within local issues, contingencies, and conventions. These performances reflect, in turn, the way that Burney creates a space for herself, her name, and her work by manipulating the conventions of the literary world from her own position as an unknown and unrecognized outsider.

In general, the suggestions that ***Evelina*** raises the issue of authority, that the story plays on concepts of names and naming, or that the book's publication history allegorically represents Burney's understanding of her place in literary history are not new. For instance, Susan Greenfield asserts that "***Evelina*** demonstrates that woman's rise to authorship is predicated on the fall of paternal control," arguing that Burney links traits considered liabilities under a patriarchal system with female literary agency.[1] Margaret Anne Doody would warn, however, that Burney gains this agency only by facing great difficulties and by overcoming enormous obstacles in writing and publishing ***Evelina.*** Doody rightly points out that because Burney made fair copies of her father's manuscripts, she had to copy ***Evelina*** "in a hand *artificially* assumed for the occasion."[2] In Julia Epstein's reading, Burney most willingly engages with authority in the medium of the letter as "a site of struggle" against cultural norms.[3] These and other writers have already discussed various aspects of Burney's authority with respect to the writing and publishing of ***Evelina.***

They have not specifically commented, however, on Evelina's strategy of using her signatures—and the deferral of them—to insert herself into events, dialogues, and social structures from which she was previously excluded. Amy Pawl does point to Evelina's first signature as a moment of intentionally conspicuous self-definition.[4] Although Pawl analyzes this as a discursively conditioned act of assuming ownership and authority—and rightfully so—she does not explicitly comment on the formal discursive dynamics of this particular signature as opposed to any other signature or any other letter. I argue that Evelina only selectively signs her letters. And I believe that each of these specific occasions serves to distinguish a particular point of discursive disjunction. Evelina's signatures are not simply perfunctory acts randomly distributed throughout the series of letters, but are inflection points at which Evelina attempts to deflect deleterious opinions, positions, or conditions. Although they appear completely conventional at first glance, Evelina's selective and purposeful use of signatures reinstills them with new semantic and symbolic value. When one ignores these signatures because they seem standard structures, one also ignores the code tapped out on their walls through the manipulation of them and silences the alternative voice that must use socially and culturally determined tools to create a position within the "republic of letters."

* * *

At times it is all too easy to figure Evelina merely as a victim of social orders and her acts merely as performances of consent or resistance. But too strong a version of this reading that positions Evelina in simple opposition to social conventions would not fairly allow her to determine the conditions and implications of her own life. For instance, the conclusion of the novel certainly does not seem to convey an overt sense of rebellion against or liberation from her social order, but, at least literally, it rather strongly indicates Evelina has found, established, and successfully legitimated a place within it:

> All is over, my dearest Sir, and the fate of your Evelina is decided . . . I have time for no more; the chaise now waits which is to conduct me to dear Berry Hill, and to the arm of the best of men.
>
> ***Evelina.***[5]

On the other hand, to overstate Evelina's contentment in this seemingly fairy-tale-like ending would be to overlook the complicated way in which Burney treats the institution of marriage, as Kristina Straub writes: "The novel evidences not only the conventional assumptions that marriage is the shortest route to female happiness, but also the equally conventional notion that marriage is one of life's major snares, a trap in which people (especially women) are destroyed or at best given a life sentence of discomfort."[6] Certainly the first sentence of the letter beginning "All is over" does lend itself to sad if not sinister undertones—a young, newly-wedded bride's life described as "over" could easily suggest the sort of marriage "trap" that Straub mentions. And the way in which Evelina yokes seemingly contradictory words to describe her feelings, "with fearful joy and trembling gratitude" (p. 406), might validate the suggestion that she (or Burney) maintains strong apprehensions (or at least some ambivalences), with regard to life in matrimony. The last phrase does seem, however, to discount the strongest version of this thesis, as Evelina willingly signs her letter to go "to the arms of the best of men." To argue too forcefully that this ending is just "an illusion, a fairy-tale drawing down of the curtain on the fair prospect of Evelina's future happiness"[7] would be to displace Evelina, rather antagonistically, from a subject position within a social and authorial order exactly at the moment when she finally reaches out to claim it for herself—to negate its symbolic ramification precisely the instant she is able, finally, without being forced by threat or uncertain circumstance, to sign her name "Evelina."

To imply so much from a simple and possibly perfunctory signature at the close of a letter would seem forced were authorship and the function of signatures not issues the book seems to address. Indeed, if one were to judge the novel by its current critical reception, one might think that these are practically the only issues it addresses. I assign much weight to this signature not only because it represents, as signatures do, subjectivity and authority, but also because Evelina's signatures are, in general, relatively scarce. Of the sixty letters that Evelina writes, she only signs 13 (or arguably 14) of them.[8] That she is merely careless about signing her letters seems implausible considering the very high level of self-consciousness she exhibits when signing; for instance, at the end of her penultimate letter she writes:

> Now then, therefore, for the first time—and probably the last time I shall ever own the name, permit me to sign myself,
>
> Most dear Sir,
>
> Your gratefully affectionate,
>
> Evelina Belmont.
>
> (p. 404)

Such a long and deliberate closing calls a great deal of attention to her act of claiming a name. Doody asserts, "Evelina is unplaced in society, unclassified. Her name is a crucial problem . . . In her novel, Burney explores the universal adolescent experience of making an entrance into the world as 'nobody,' without an established personality or fixed social self."[9] And to this Pawl adds, "Dangerous as names are, however, there is a greater danger in not being named—or owned . . . Being 'owned,' far from turning Evelina into a commodity whose personhood is denied, is actually what allows her to become a person."[10] The two successive letters with signatures, at the end of a collection of letters remarkable for the relative absence of signatures, seem to support a reading that constructs (even if somewhat simplistically) a sort of teleological progression toward assuming a name. As is the case with the final letter, however, the juxtaposition of opposites in this letter, "first" and "last," indicates, at the very least, a sort of ambivalence. Certainly, the postscript of the penultimate letter (of only four postscripts in the entire collection of letters and by far the longest of them) after her signature suggests unfinished business; it suggests that her signature, which follows the anticipatory drumroll of her final paragraph, does not necessarily conclude this story. Perhaps this chain of five abruptly starting and stopping phrases is as much a stuttering as it is a flourish, an attempt to defer the end, the final naming of herself.

Rather than completely undermining the notion of Evelina's coming to a name from anonymity, these remarkable juxtapositions demonstrate Evelina's (or Burney's) grave ambivalences but also dependencies in taking refuge in (and thus participating in) a naming system. All thirteen of the letters that Evelina signs appear in the context of great turmoil in, or threat to, her particular position. Furthermore, these signatures appear in clusters. And though characterizing them entirely in such limited terms would be to ignore a host of other issues and concerns, each of these clusters of letters seems to respond to a particular kind of symbolic assault on Evelina's agency. For just as Evelina encounters numerous persons who, on one level, attempt to insinuate themselves, their lives, their names, and their bodies into hers (to the effacement of hers), so too does she meet with circumstances that threaten to displace or replace her symbolically. Her signatures serve to mark each of these occasions and to reassert herself at fundamental levels.

The opening of Evelina's first letter demonstrates a high level of self-consciousness with respect to the propriety and legitimacy of her writing:

> Well but, my dear Sir, I am desired to make a request to you. I hope you will not think me an incroacher; Lady Howard insists upon my writing!—yet I hardly know how to go on; a petition implies a want,—and have you left me one? No indeed.
>
> I am half ashamed of myself for beginning this letter. But these dear ladies are so pressing—I cannot, for my life, resist wishing for the pleasures they offer me,—provided you do not disapprove them.
>
> (p. 23)

The timidity and hesitancy with which she enters the discussion and the way she displaces the responsibility of her "incroachment" onto others indicate her uncertain place and, more importantly, her understanding of her uncertain place in their discourse. This hesitancy also signals, however, the vital importance of her letter—that despite such misgivings, Evelina feels compelled to enter this discourse. The significance of her letter is not in the textual content, for all she does is but to defer judgment to Villars, saying "Decide for me" (p. 24). Instead, the letter merely, albeit importantly, serves as a vehicle by which to assert the name of this "poor child"—Evelina's understanding of this act figured, perhaps, in the way she describes London: "They tell me that London is now in full splendour. Two playhouses are open,—the Opera-House,—Ranelagh,—the Pantheon.—You see I have learned all their names" (p. 24). Indeed the name "Evelina" never appears in the seven letters exchanged between

Villars and Lady Howard that open the novel. The very first reference to Evelina appears in Lady Howard's letter as "an infant orphan" and immediately afterward as "the child" (p. 12). Villars first refers to Evelina as "her [Duval's] granddaughter" and afterward usually as "her" (p. 13) and "that child" (p. 15). The closest either of these correspondents come to writing "Evelina" is Villars's use of the name "Anville" (p. 19), which, he admits, refers to nothing more than the neighborhood of her father. Of course, some of the contents of these letters deal with events long before Evelina's birth, serving as a brief introduction to the circumstances of the book's main plot. And the comment by Villars, revealing his practice of "concealing her name" (p. 19), does explain, to some extent, its omission in their discourse. This does not change the fact that before Evelina's first letter, Villars and Lady Howard refer to Evelina no fewer than twenty-seven times as "the child," "ward," or in some other anonymous way, not including the several dozen times they use pronouns. And this does not mitigate, in any way, Evelina's strong need to sign her name—to establish her own subject position within the discourse, which supposedly operates around her—to declare "I am Evelina."

Indeed, this is the very structure of each of her three signatures in this cluster: "I am . . . Evelina." But asserting that Evelina's first signatures perform a sort of self-identification, convenient as such a reading may be for discussing issues of representation and naming, may seem a bit naive. After all, the practice of signing a letter "I am" is entirely conventional in the eighteenth century. This does not discount Evelina's acts of self-inscription but, rather, illustrates the strategy of resistance both Burney and Evelina employ. As mentioned, Evelina's language strongly suggests that she recognizes her insinuations into these affairs—her own affairs!—as transgressions against convention. She deftly mitigates her trespass, not only with her humble apologies, but also with her deferences to convention. In the signature, her use of the construction "I am" performs a clever and skillful manipulation of convention. Although it serves an absolutely vital function, it appears in an absolutely conventional form so that casual glances would pass over it without so much as a blink. It is, however, a wink to an inside audience. While the phrase bears the clothing of a banal and meaningless closing, its use, in her context, forces the reader to reinstill the words with real, living semantic significance. After all, there are plenty of other ways in which Evelina could have signed—and, in other places, does sign—her letters while still appearing to employ purely conventional manners. In using the same closing three times in sequence (and then using different ones later), Evelina calls attention to these usages, for as dull as conventions may seem, decisions on whether or not to employ them or on which one to employ can be significant. Indeed, the very assumption that these conventions have no value—the marginalization of these acts—creates the possibility for Evelina's self-inscription and provides discarded material for her to recycle.

One finds the next cluster of signatures in the letters dealing with the confrontation of Belmont—that is, in the attempt by parent figures to affix a certain, other, name to Evelina. Although she can only appreciate the efforts of her benefactors, their cause, particularly in its tenuous nature, only highlights to Evelina her unnamed, unstable, and misfit status. Her ambivalences and apprehensions at the thought of this enterprise are clear enough in her reaction to Duval's announcement, which she introduces: "I now write in the greatest uneasiness" (p. 120). Rather than comforting Evelina with luxury, peace, and a "high style of . . . future grandeur" (p. 121), Duval's efforts make Evelina feel lost and insecure. Once again the issue is Evelina's name, this time not her first name, which operates as a differential signifier to distinguish and individualize persons in a synchronic field, but her family name, which serves to link individuals together in a diachronic chain and to instill them with symbolic value and socioeconomic worth. It is perhaps fitting that Evelina's first signature in this cluster marks a letter that describes men evaluating and, literally, valuing women:

> "They'd need be goddesses with a vengeance," said the Captain, "for they're mortal dear to look at. Howsomever, I should be glad to know what you can see in e'er a face among them that's worth half a guinea for a sight."
>
> "Half a guinea!" exclaimed that same Lord, "I would give half I am worth, for a sight of only *one*, provided I make my own choice."
>
> (p. 107)

Evelina's response to Duval's attempt to "make something of" her and to impose on her "another name than that of Anville" (p. 121) is, once again, more legible in her closing and signature than in her letter:

And now, most honoured Sir, with all the follies and imperfections which I have thus faithfully recounted, can you, and with unabated kindness, suffer to sign myself

Your dutiful

and most affectionate

Evelina?

(p. 115)

This signature expresses her wish to align herself with Villars and, in a way, asks him to claim her. And Villars immediately responds to "Your . . . Evelina" with "My Evelina" (p. 115) in the opening of his next letter. Thus, Evelina, acting as a ventriloquist, performs Villars's claiming of her as his heir. Soon after this exchange, Villars, perhaps because of the seed planted by this manipulation, confides to Lady Howard his intention to claim Evelina (p. 126).

Although she certainly expresses her frustration and anger with the overbearing Duval's handling of her affairs, Evelina's letters do not speak directly to the issue of her authority. Indeed, she weakly admits, "as to *me,*—I know not what to say, nor even what to wish" (p. 122). It is only in her signatures that she expresses her volition:

May Heaven bless you, my dearest Sir! and long, long may it continue you on earth, to bless

Your grateful

Evelina.

(p. 131)

She repeats the form of "your . . . Evelina" that joins her to Villars. And after learning of Belmont's response to Lady Howard's entreaty on her behalf she reaffirms her tie once more:

Adieu, my dearest Sir! Heaven, I trust, will never let me live to be repulsed and derided by *you,* to whom I may now sign myself

Wholly your

Evelina.

(p. 160)

This consistent use of the same form of closing within each cluster of signatures, in my opinion, discounts the simple counterargument that Evelina is merely employing convention and no more. Clearly her signatures conform to standard closings, yet I believe close readings of the closings and the conditions around them reveal that Evelina skillfully manipulates these conventions for her own purposes. In this context, "I am Evelina" is a declaration.

From her first letter at the beginning of the book through the ordeal with Belmont, Evelina uses exclusively her first name in her signatures. In a letter to Miss Mirvan while under the guardianship of Mme. Duval she signs "Evelina Anville" (p. 173). The simple pun on *en ville,* as she writes from London, signifies not only Evelina's assertion of her autonomy from Mme. Duval (one may even describe this as defiance, as it specifically contradicts Duval's ambition to banish the name "Anville" [p. 121]), but also her understanding of herself as a coherent agent. As I assert for each occasion of a signature by Evelina, this one marks her response to a crisis of identity. Immediately after Belmont's refusal to recognize his daughter formally, Mme. Duval forces Villars to permit her to take Evelina to London. By signing "Evelina Anville" she asserts with no uncertainty her independence from Mme. Duval, and that her current circumstance of lodging indicates no acceptance of any other kind of relationship. Interestingly, in this letter that marks her first use of the name Anville, Evelina describes the great *ville* of London: "[It] now seems no longer the same place where I lately enjoyed so much happiness; every thing is new and strange to me; even the town itself has not the same aspect:—my situation so altered! my home so different!—my companions so changed" (p. 172). This description of Evelina's sense of self and place harkens back to a letter in which she writes, "*the work of seventeen years* remains such as it was . . . I am not half so happy here at present, as I was ere I went to town: but the change is in the place, not in me" (p. 117). Evelina Anville is not only not subject to Duval but heir to *Vill*ars, at home in and owned by herself. The name Anville as practically an anagram for Evelina suggests that transient changes in her station and companions cannot displace Evelina from her self, her place that defines her, "Anville."

The only other letter she signs "Evelina Anville" is one to Lord Orville after she discovers the Branghtons' fraudulent use of her name to request his carriage. This embarrassment is an affront to Evelina's agency and propriety. She has to respond to maintain that propriety. This occasions two more signatures. In a letter to Orville, which she closes in the form "I am . . . Evelina Anville" (p. 249), Evelina asserts her identity in a way similar to the manner in her first signatures. In her next letter, to Miss Mirvan, she closes, "So witness in all truth, / Your affectionate / Evelina" (p. 255), asserting her authenticity and propriety. As always,

Evelina presents no argument in the body of her letter, but, instead, speaks in her signature using words "witness" and "truth," indicating that she understands this misuse of her name as a legal as well as a personal issue. That she should write to Orville is unremarkable. That she should sign her letter in such a way is also understandable. This letter and signature appear, however, not as originals, but as transcriptions. That is, the entire letter to Orville appears within a letter that she writes to Villars, and the entire letter, including the signature, appears within quotation marks. And though she carefully transcribes her signature in this letter, she does not sign the actual letter to Villars. In the context of my assertion that each signature and its specific conditions is significant, this unusual displacement makes perfect sense. For the crisis of identity and propriety takes place in London and in the context of her relationship to Orville. Therefore her signature should appear in her letter to Orville, not one to Villars. The remarkable act of transcribing this signature appears in the context of her letter to Villars, to whom she must demonstrate her ability to understand and maintain her agency. This extremely careful situating of her signature only further highlights how consciously and conscientiously Evelina considers each occasion so that she uses her name only in the most important and appropriate moments in the most precise and relevant ways.

* * *

This act of copying her letter and her signature highlights the fact that Evelina is neither the first child whom Villars rears, nor the first Lady Belmont in this story. She is, rather, the second—in a way, a copy. In her, in her life, and in her story there is also the first. For just as her face recalls the "image" (p. 372) of her mother, so too does her life recall her mother's story, as Villars says, "The public appearance of the daughter of Sir John Belmont will revive the remembrance of Miss Evelyn's story to all who have heard it" (p. 337). This clearly carries meta-novelistic import. For just as Evelina's face seems to reflect, indeed, to represent to Belmont, Caroline's, so too does the text of ***Evelina*** represent the destroyed manuscript of **"The History of Caroline Evelyn."**[11] ***Evelina*** performs both the possibility and pitfalls of creating a matrilineal history within the confines of a patriarchal culture.

The two remaining signatures of Evelina, both in letters to Macartney, deal with, once again, a fundamental assault on Evelina's identity, yet in the much larger scope of cultural and historical, rather than individual, representation. For they respond to a letter from Macartney. Once again, the signature reveals the nature of the intrigue:

> I am, Madam, with the most profound respect, and heart-felt gratitude,
>
> Your obedient, and devoted humble servant,
>
> J. Macartney.
>
> (p. 231)

This would seem, in other contexts, an innocent enough closing to a letter except that it uses a form, as discussed earlier, that Evelina uses when asserting her identity, her existence, and her right to self-representation. Furthermore, this signature closes Evelina's letter to Villars. The logical explanation for this is simple enough, for Evelina merely encloses the letter from Macartney for Villars's perusal. Thematically and symbolically, in the context of an epistolary novel in which signatures are so rare and seem to suggest such portentous moments, the fact that a letter from Evelina bears the signature of Macartney, so that he is represented in the nominal position of the author of the letter to Villars, is unusual and quite problematic. Indeed, virtually the entire text sent to Villars consists of Macartney's words, with only a single introductory paragraph from Evelina. In this letter the text and story of Macartney, as well as the signature, threaten to (and temporarily do) displace, replace, and efface Evelina's. The "I am . . . J. Macartney" at the end suggests the possibility of the same sort of claim and ascension to agency and centrality that Evelina enacted at the very beginning of the novel. For just as her letter and signature mark her assertion of self-identity and demonstrate, quite literally, her act of assuming the role of subject and author of her life, implicitly casting the Villars-Howard letters as a mere introduction, so too do Macartney's signature, letter, and narrative seem poised to replace Evelina's, as if the entire first half of the book were merely an extended preamble to his story.

Certainly, in terms of gripping the reader with awe at the fantastic, the incredible events of Macartney's story, related in just a few pages, seem to outstrip by far all those preceding that Evelina narrates. Briefly, Macartney's story mentions an entire gauntlet of intrigues including fatherlessness, melancholy, travel, forbidden romance, sword play, murder, parricide, fugitive flight, orphanage, and roguery. As the reader imagines these amazing adventures of Macartney, and forgets those of Evelina, *his* story threatens to overshadow and to replace *her* story. During the several pages of this elaborate plot, the story of Evelina's life, and presumably all that "History" will ever retain of her life, rests precariously on hold, in danger of being pushed aside to the margins by a more adventurous, titillating, and masculine counterpart. Macartney's narrative threat represents at least as dangerous an intrusion in Evelina's story as the insinuations of the sometimes mischievous and often ungentlemanly bachelors such as Willoughby, Lovel, and Smith. Just as they manipulate her into compromising positions through their intimate knowledge of the rigid codes of social convention, which under the auspices of protecting a young woman from less than honorable suits actually expose her to them,[12] Macartney's story weaves itself into Evelina's, under the pretense of securing protection from her, culminating in this letter, which creates a meta-narrative crisis, threatening to usurp the central plot and to leave Evelina a nameless nobody by the wayside.

The response to this crisis operates on several different levels and is marked, predictably, by her signature:

> Oh Sir, could I, upon this subject, could I write as I feel,—how animated would be the language of
>
> Your devoted
>
> Evelina!
>
> (p. 238)

Not only does this signature mark the locus of her response; it draws attention to her "language"—a language unique in kind, betraying an unusual anxiety of inadequacy as a writer and storyteller, but one that also displays a strong sense of urgency and self-consciousness with respect to the telling of her story. Furthermore, it points to the "animated" language found in the entire letter, beginning from the very opening:

> Holborn, July 1, 5 o'clock in the morn.
>
> O Sir, what an adventure have I to write!—all night it has occupied my thoughts, and I am now risen thus early, to write it to you.
>
> (p. 231)

Including the time, "5 o'clock," in the heading is unique to this letter. Evelina then adds "in the morn," once again unique, to obviate any possible ambiguity. And finally, she points back to the header in her first sentence, declaring "I am now risen thus early."

As the opening suggests with its repeated self-referentiality and the closing points out with the reference to its own language, the words in this letter seem calculated to excite the reader. In this letter she uses the word "adventure" three times, as well as words such as "fireworks," "explosion," "danger," "terror," "fright," "horror," "distress," "violence," "cruelly," "revenged," "melancholy," "persecutions," "mortification," "escape," "release," "liberty," "cavalierly," "titter," and "monstrous," among others. Beyond merely titillating the reader, these extraordinary measures form one aspect of Evelina's crucial response to the narrative challenge of Macartney's letter. These words seem calculated to match those of Macartney's. Evelina transports the narrative "fireworks" and the "danger" of Macartney's story into hers. All the "violence" "cruelly" "revenged" on persons resulting in "melancholy" and "persecutions," thus requiring "escape" to "liberty" . . . all these words and events appear in Evelina's letter. The "language" that her closing signature refers to matches that of Macartney's adventure.

This imitative way in which the frightful events of Evelina's narrative match those of Macartney's story also suggests the second level of response. That is, Macartney's story, which relies so heavily on fantastic and extraordinary events and situations, seems precisely the kind of story Burney denounces in her preface—"Let me therefore, prepare for disappointment" (p. 8)—precisely the novel she announces that she does not intend to write. As the preface suggests, Burney offers, in place of a romance, ***Evelina*** as an alternative model of writing for women. Rather than avoiding every suggestion of this genre, Burney boldly dangles just such a story before her reader's eyes in the most tenuous moment of narrative and meta-narrative crisis. Assuming that this response, the recounting of Evelina's own "adventures," which mimics the emotional energy of Macartney's continental romance without even leaving the presumably drab domesticity of England, succeeds in recapturing the reader's imagination, this exchange serves to validate ***Evelina*** as a formal model and Evelina as a subject of such writing.[13]

That Macartney turns out to be Evelina's brother suggests a convergence in the lineal, literal, and literary threats of obscurity—that is, Macartney's story threatens not only the telling of Evelina's by dominating the narrative space and the legitimacy of the mode of telling it by challenging its genre, but also the space in which to tell it by attempting to assume a place in a patrilineal history. While reading *Plutarch's Lives,* Burney remarks in her journal:

> I have Just finish'd Paulus Amilius, whom I love & honour, most particularly, for his fondness for his Children, which instead of blushing at, he avows

> & glories in: and that at an Age, when almost all the heros & great men thought that to make their Children & Family a secondary concern . . . At such an Age, I say, I think the paternal affection of Paulus Amilius his first & principle [sic] glory.[14]

In reading of the various exploits of these famous men, Burney seems to have felt that History affords only a very limited allotment of space for each name. That is, when History chooses to honor a particular individual by recording his story, the others bearing the same name, whether parent, spouse, child, or sibling, can find very little space to tell their stories. From this perspective, the letters of Macartney and Evelina suggest a confrontation not only between "Romance" and "Nature," not only between man and woman, but also between brother and sister. Macartney's life story, just like Evelina's, begins with a fatherless child and ends in marriage—a marriage occurring on the same day and signified by the same invitation—an invitation whose reference is intentionally and irresolvably ambiguous. As the subtitle implies, Evelina's letters constitute a certain history, which, in a sense, can represent one generation in the history of the Belmont family line. Thus, Macartney's story, which threatens to efface or marginalize Evelina's, also constitutes an alternative history—a story synchronic with Evelina's that, transcribed from historical time to literary space, must either subsume or be subsumed by Evelina's. (One can read the scene in which Evelina declines Branghton's offer of Macartney's stool as a comic enactment of this sibling confrontation that Evelina tries so hard to avoid.) For Burney, Evelina's response and her ability to reassert herself represent a personal victory as well as a victory for English women's stories and English women's writing.

* * *

On the level of literary production and posterity, the threat of Macartney's story may articulate Burney's response to Richardson's *Pamela,* or, rather, her response to Fielding's response.[15] By including Macartney, exposing the story of Evelina to the threat of a sibling's competing story, and resolving this conflict in her own story, Burney preempts the possibility of another *Joseph Andrews.*[16] Whether or not Burney actually believed that a Fielding-like response might actually appear in the wake of any popular success ***Evelina*** might enjoy, the dynamics of this usurpative literary relationship perfectly play into the field of Burney's social, political, and literary concerns. For if the project that Burney outlines in her preface resembles any one previous novel, it is certainly that found in *Pamela.* The issues that Burney mentions in her preface, if made into a list, would repeat, nearly word for word, those of Richardson's. And Richardson's description of *Pamela* might just as easily appear on the title page of ***Evelina***: "A narrative which has its Foundation in Truth and Nature; and at the same time that it agreeably entertains, by a Variety of curious and affecting Incidents, is intirely divested of all those Images which, in too many pieces calculated for Amusement only, tend to inflame the Minds they should instruct."[17]

In seeming opposition to Richardson, Fielding describes in the first sentence of his preface his project as a "Romance"—also the very genre from which Burney sets ***Evelina*** apart. If one takes seriously the way that Fielding seems to construct *Joseph Andrews* out of Richardson's *Pamela,* not only usurping its name, fame, and popularity (and, hence, economic inheritance), one would have to conclude that it threatens, at least literally, to re-close the possibility of a woman's narrative. *Joseph Andrews* begins by mentioning Pamela only to subjugate her, suggesting that her story is merely a small part of his story. Structurally, this is identical to the potential threat of Macartney to Evelina, whose name may replace hers, whose claim to birthright and inheritance may supersede hers, and whose story may replace hers. *The History of Joseph Andrews,* as the archetype of a genre that Fielding defines and defends through his entire lengthy preface, presents a literary challenge to the genre of *Pamela* and, were they contemporaries, ***Evelina.***

The possible effect of this challenge, if taken seriously, is perhaps most clear in the first chapter of *Joseph Andrews.* At the exact moment in which it mentions Pamela, it effaces her and her story. While the chapter describes the great Histories of men, mentioning, "the History of John the Great, who by his brave and heroic Actions against Men of large and athletic Bodies, obtained the glorious Appellation of the Giant-killer; that of an Earl of Warwick, whose Christian Name was Guy,"[18] it then passes Pamela by, commenting, "What the Female Readers are taught by the Memoirs of Mrs. Andrews, is so well set forth in the excellent Essays or Letters prefixed to the second and subsequent Editions of that Work, that it would be here a needless Repetition" (1:4). The agenda seems clear. While the description of each great male story "which deals in Male-Virtue" requires writers to "spread their History" (1:2), such representations of a woman's story would be merely a "needless Repetition." In the first chapter of the third book, titled "Matter prefatory in Praise of Biography," Fielding's narrator dismisses all possibility of doubt that he regards the stories of men superior to those of women, writing, "Truth is only to be found in their Works who celebrate the Lives of Great Men" (2:1), repeating "Men" numerous times in the passage, and then opposing the stories of men to stories of women, asserting,

> Achievements of the renowned Don Quixote, more worthy the Name of a History than even Mariana's; for whereas the latter is confined to a particular Period of Time, and to a particular Nation; the former is the History of the World in general.
>
> (2:4-5)

Interestingly, Burney mentions Fielding in the same breath as Richardson. In fact, Fielding precedes Richardson in her list of "predecessors." It does not seem plausible that Burney might have missed Fielding's challenge to women's stories and that any similarity between the pairings of MacCartney and Evelina with Joseph Andrews and Pamela—not to mention Polly Green (the false Evelina) and Shamela—is mere coincidence. But what were Burney's alternatives? Her strategy, a strategy she employs in practically every aspect of the book and one which practically every character in the book employs, is not open confrontation but insinuation and manipulation. Burney does not respond to Fielding in her prefatory matter but, as discussed, in her narrative. In her prefaces she represses any distinction between Fielding and Richardson. And though she states explicitly that she does not wish to write Romance, she also seems to learn much from Fielding. If *Pamela* is her generic model, then *Joseph Andrews* may serve as her strategic one. If from Richardson Burney learns how to portray her subject, then from Fielding Burney learns how to pose it. The stories of MacCartney and Polly Green merely serve as winks that both acknowledge Fielding's contribution and preempt any attempt to imitate it.

In addition, by declining to vilify Fielding in her prefatory letters, Burney insinuates herself into the company of other renown novelists, whom she calls "our predecessors." Burney's purpose is to address the critics of literature and the custodians of History. This address begins perhaps as early as the insertion of the word "history" in her subtitle, which invokes the notion of legitimacy—to announce, from the outset, the seriousness of her enterprise. In his entry for "history," Samuel Johnson employs a couplet from Pope that bases its definition on the distinction it makes from the fickle, flowery arts, "Justly Caesar scorns the poet's lays; / It is to history he trusts for praise."[19] If Burney intended to renegotiate the margins of "the republic of letters" by introducing the "History of a Young Lady's Entrance into the World," along with the world of a young lady into "History," she had to confront the kind of prejudices that implicitly, yet quite perniciously and obstinately, bind the female sex with frivolity and dissimulation, clearly rendering them poor subjects for the "higher arts"—prejudices arguably best articulated by Mary Wollstonecraft half a generation later:

> [A]nxious to render my sex more respectable members of society, I shall try to avoid that flowery diction which has slided from essays into novels, and from novels into familiar letters and conversation.
>
> These pretty superlatives, dropping glibly from the tongue, vitiate the taste, and create a kind of sickly delicacy that turns away from simple unadorned truth; and a deluge of false sentiments and overstretched feelings, stifling the natural emotions of the heart, render the domestic pleasures insipid, that ought to sweeten the exercise of those severe duties, which educate a rational and immortal being for a nobler field of action.[20]

Burney seems to anticipate some of Wollstonecraft's charges implicitly in her own version of a somewhat aggrandized pontification on the evil effects of the novel on young women:

> Perhaps were it possible to effect the total extirpation of novels, our young ladies in general, and boarding-school damsels in particular, might profit from their annihilation: but since the distemper they have spread seems incurable, since their contagion bids defiance to the medicine of advice or reprehension, and since they are found to baffle all the mental art of physic, save what is prescribed by the slow regimen of Time, and bitter diet of Experience, surely all attempts to contribute to the number of those which may be read, if not with advantage, at least without injury, ought rather to be encouraged than condemned.
>
> (p. 8)

Like Wollstonecraft, Burney seems initially to concede a good deal to popular prejudice, while likewise locating the supposed intellectual and moral weakness of women largely in the lamentable state of their education and upbringing. What seems most striking about this passage is its construction of its audience in voicing these unflattering charges. Whereas Wollstonecraft's diatribe, authorized with her own name, against the inconstant and whimsical sex (as constructed by social presumptions) seems to address an educated and socially preceptorial, if not a bit condescending, community of men, Burney's anonymous voice clearly recognizes at least two quite distinct groups of readers. The first is the same sort of audience—socially prominent men—to whom Wollstonecraft writes and to whom Burney must justify her novel or risk censure. The second, the speaker locates, yet recognizes only in the third person, as the young ladies themselves who presumably comprise the majority of any novel's readership, whom Burney cannot alienate with the kind of unbuffered vitriolic attack Wollstonecraft occasionally voices.

This preface serves as an attempt to appease, while conjoining two distinct interests. And the move in the preface to reinsert the presence of the novel's female audience within a text clearly coded for the perusal of well-educated men reinforces the suggestion in the subtitle that attempts to insert Evelina, her story, into history. These insinuations, and the way in which Frances Burney positions her work with respect to "the republic of letters," invite comparison to the way in which the great "History" of her life positions itself in relation to the great History of her time. The preface of the latter, Gibbon's *The Decline and Fall of the Roman Empire,* quite self-assuredly exhibits no outward expressions of anxiety with respect to the status or merit of its subject: "It is not my intention to detain the reader by expatiating on the variety, or the importance of the subject, which I have undertaken to treat."[21] With only a short gesture of modesty before demarcating the space of his "general plan," seemingly, Gibbon's sense of anxiety arises from the thought that perhaps readers might find the work too lengthy, which he alleviates by assuring, "But it is not my intention to expatiate with the same minuteness on the whole series of the Byzantine history" (p. 27). Gibbon confidently addresses his reading public directly with the full understanding that they recognize the importance, import, and legitimacy of his work's contents and ambition.

In contrast, Charles Burney, in the prefatory letter, "To the Queen," of his *A General History of Music,*[22] which Frances Burney probably transcribed for the publisher, begins very tentatively with regard to the book's claim to legitimacy: "The condescension with which your Majesty has been pleased to permit your name to stand before the following History, may justly reconcile the author to his favorite study, and convince him, that whatever may be said by the professors of severer wisdom, the hours which he has bestowed upon Music have been neither dishonourably, nor unprofitably spent."[23] This deference to and borrowed authority from the Queen, however, permits him practically to mimic Gibbon's stance, writing, "To those who know that Music is among your Majesty's recreations, it is not necessary to display its purity, or assert its dignity" (Burney, p. iv). Charles Burney further assuages his anxiety by constructing his work as his "favorite study," drawing a comparison to Gibbon's description of his project as that "of leisure"[24]—a description Gibbon repeats in the preface to his fourth volume in the context of announcing his retirement from public service: "Yet I consider that the annals of ancient and modern times may afford many rich and interesting subjects; that I am still possessed of health and leisure" (Gibbon, p. 31).

Furthermore, in that same way that Gibbon defines a space for his history, placing it between "the ancient and modern history of the world" (p. 26), Charles Burney excavates a space for his book by describing all the ancient treatises that have been lost. This affords him the opportunity to imitate Gibbon's catalog of ancient writers, which he exploits fully, referring to more than thirty different philosophers, historians, and writers. This allows him, once again, to imitate Gibbon's words, "performance of an indispensable duty" (pp. 27-28), writing, "It was neither with a view to rival others, nor to expose the defects of former attempts, but merely to fill up, as well as I was able, a chasm in English literature."[25]

Frances Burney both imitates her father's strategy of creating a historical space for her project and also positions her work for her audience and critics by manipulating his tactics. She assumes the metaphor that her father employs, writing "I yet presume not to attempt pursuing the same ground which they have tracked," but plants in it the flowers that his male view disregards: "though they may have cleared the weeds, they have also culled the flowers, and though they have rendered the path plain, they have left it barren" (p. 9). For though Burney recognizes that her father anxiously created a literary space for himself within a sometimes intractable discourse, she understands that she cannot presume to address her audience in exactly the same way. And just as Evelina's signatures and closings mark and form her response to circumstances, so too do Frances Burney's—or, in this case, the absence of her signature. Except in two aspects, Frances Burney's closing appears nearly identical to her father's, for as Charles Burney writes,

Madam,
your Majesty's
most obedient
and most devoted Servant
Charles Burney,[26]

Frances Burney writes,

Gentlemen,
your most obedient
humble servant.

(p. 5)

The implications of these differences seem clear. First, whereas her socially prominent father owns a name, a sign that coherently signifies in a social and cultural discourse, she, hardly more than a child, does not. The absence of her name points to her social anonymity. Second, she addresses "Gentlemen" whereas her father addresses, "Madam." Beyond simply marking the difference in gender, which is obviously very significant, Burney also manipulates the relationship between the author and two distinctly different audiences with this change. Charles Burney's letter addresses the Queen on one level, but it invites a readership of literate men. This narrator exploits his relationship with a woman to force men to submit to her authority and, in that process, accept his book. Frances Burney's letter addresses directly a similar group of men, while it points out that although they nominally wield the power to critique or censor, they too must reserve their judgment and defer to another authority, the reading public. That reading public is, however, female. Thus Frances Burney deftly places her male critics into a position similar to that of Charles Burney's critics. This clever manipulation of authoritative structures points both to her anxiety about the male-dominated hegemony of the literary world and to her gendering of her readership. For in both cases, the audience that accepts the new contribution and willingly creates a space in history is a female one. And Frances Burney emphasizes that the censors who criticize and reject are all male. Her careful reinsertion of the female in her preface, as discussed earlier, serves to problematize this male authority. While appearing to conform to every accepted convention, Burney cleverly displaces (or replaces) the authority of the male critics to the female reading audience.

These comparisons with the writings of Richardson, Fielding, Gibbon, and Charles Burney demonstrate as much Frances Burney's models as her contexts. For ***Evelina*** is an orphan attempting to find a place in society and history. Born without direct traditional ties she must struggle to discover her lineage and to establish her legitimacy within patriarchal authority structures. ***Evelina*** represents both the material and the performance of the possibility of a female story and history. The clever narrative ironically describes, in letters, the history of men using social and cultural conventions to insinuate themselves into the life of a young woman, as the very story insinuates itself into the male-dominated realm of history by manipulating the formal and literary conventions of the "republic of letters." ***Evelina,*** in this way, indeed is and is not that "Monster, that the World ne'er saw" (p. 8), for the literary world has both seen and not seen her before.

Notes

1. Susan C. Greenfield, "'Oh Dear Resemblace of Thy Murdered Mother': Female Authorship in *Evelina,*" *Eighteenth Century Fiction* 3 (1991): 303-07.
2. Margaret Anne Doody, "Introduction," *Evelina: or The History of a Young Lady's Entrance into the World,* ed. and intro. Margaret Anne Doody (London: Penguin, 1994), p. xii.
3. Julia Epstein, *The Iron Pen: Frances Burney and the Politics of Women's Writing* (Madison: Univ. of Wisconsin Press, 1989), pp. 29-37.
4. Amy J. Pawl, "'And What Other Name May I Claim?': Names and Their Owners in Frances Burney's *Evelina,*" *Eighteenth Century Fiction* 3 (1991): 284-86, 293.
5. Frances Burney, *Evelina; or The History of A Young Lady's Entrance into the World,* ed. Edward A. Bloom (London: Oxford Univ. Press, 1968), p. 406. Subsequent references are to this edition.
6. Kristina Straub, *Divided Fictions: Fanny Burney and Feminine Strategy* (Lexington: Univ. of Kentucky Press, 1987), p. 55.
7. *Ibid.* p. 54.
8. Formally, eighty-four letters comprise this book: thirty-one in vol. 1, thirty in vol. 2, and twenty-three in vol. 3. These figures do not include, however, letters completely transcribed within letters, such as Macartney's letter to Evelina. These figures also do not account for the sometimes multiple short letters that comprise a single formal letter. Considering all of these as individual letters would raise the grand total to 104 letters, of which Evelina authors seventy-seven. Although Evelina signs only thirteen of her formal letters, she also transcribes her signature, a fourteenth, along with the letter to Orville, appearing within the formal frame of her letter to Villars.
9. Margaret Anne Doody, *Frances Burney: The Life in the Works* (New Brunswick: Rutgers Univ. Press, 1988), pp. 40-41.
10. Pawl, p. 286.
11. Margaret Anne Doody has already discussed the relationship between the lost manuscript of "The History of Caroline Evelyn" and *Evelina* in both the works cited above, and it is beyond the scope of this essay to discuss this issue in greater detail.

12. See Katharine M. Rogers, *Frances Burney: The World of 'Female Difficulties'* (New York: Harvester Wheatsheaf Press, 1990), pp. 26-27.

13. I make no claim that this structure of narrative displacement is unique to *Evelina* or that Burney originates the technique. Indeed, one can locate framed stories in Plato, Chaucer, Shakespeare, or any number of other writers. For instance, in *Don Quixote* the goatherds (1:12-14) consider Quixote's talk of squires and knights errant "gibberish," and offer to entertain him with their pastoral tale, seeming to unseat Quixote from narrative and generic primacy. Cervantes, Miguel, *The Adventures of Don Quixote,* trans. J. M. Cohen (London: Penguin, 1950).

14. *The Early Journals and Letters of Fanny Burney,* ed. Lars E. Troide (Oxford: Clarendon Press, 1988), p. 25.

15. It is beyond the scope of this paper to comment on the literary "debate" between Richardson and Fielding. See Jill Campbell, *Natural Masques: Gender and Identity in Fielding's Plays and Novels* (Stanford: Stanford Univ. Press, 1995), pp. 2-10, for a concise discussion of some of the issues raised.

16. The coincidence of Fielding's preface addressed, "To Fanny," in *Shamela* might also provide the occasion for the subplot of Polly Green, preempting the possibility of a false *Evelina.*

17. Samuel Richardson, *Pamela: or, Virtue Rewarded* (London: C. Rivington and J. Osborn, 1741), title page.

18. Henry Fielding, *The History of the Adventures of Joseph Andrews and His Friend, Mr. Abraham Adams,* 2 vols. (London: A. Miller, 1742), 1:3.

19. Samuel Johnson, *A Dictionary of the English Language* (London: W. Strahan for J & Knapton, 1756).

20. Mary Wollstonecraft, *A Vindication of the Rights of Woman,* ed. Carol H. Poston (New York: Norton, 1988), p. 10.

21. Edward Gibbon, preface to *The Decline and Fall of the Roman Empire,* ed. William Smith (New York: Bigelow, Brown and co., 1845), p. 25.

22. For comparison, Charles Burney, in his introduction to *The Present State of Music in France and Italy* (London: T. Becket, 1771), without the word "History" in the title, exhibits no similar anxiety.

23. Charles Burney, *A General History of Music from the Earliest Ages to the Present Period* (London: printed for the author, 1776-1789), p. iii.

24. Gibbon, p. 26.

25. Burney, preface to *A General History of Music,* p. v.

26. Burney, dedication to *A General History of Music,* p. v.

FURTHER READING

Bibliography

Grau, Joseph A. *Fanny Burney: An Annotated Bibliography.* New York: Garland Publishing, 1981, 210 p.

Provides a detailed primary and secondary bibliography.

Biographies

Dobson, Austin. *Fanny Burney.* London: Macmillan, 1903, 216 p.

Presents an important early biography, the standard until Joyce Hemlow's 1958 study.

Doody, Margaret Anne. *Frances Burney: The Life in the Works.* New Brunswick, N.J.: Rutgers University Press, 1988, 441 p.

Offers an updated biography of Burney by an important scholar in the history of the novel; takes a psychoanalytic approach and emphasizes Burney's relationship with her family.

Hemlow, Joyce. *The History of Fanny Burney.* Oxford: Clarendon Press, 1958, 528 p.

Provides a biography by a foremost Burney scholar.

Criticism

Agress, Lynne. "Wives and Servants: Proper Conduct for One's Proper Place." In *The Feminine Irony: Women on Women in Early-Nineteenth-Century English Literature,* pp. 114-45. Rutherford, N.J.: Fairleigh Dickinson University, 1978.

Contends that Evelina *offers the message that a young woman must marry well to lead a happy life.*

Allen, Emily. "Staging Identity: France Burney's Allegory of Genre." *Eighteenth-Century Studies* 31, no. 4 (summer 1998): 433-51.

Considers theatricality in Evelina *and the creating of female subjectivity.*

Backscheider, Paula. "Woman's Influence." *Studies in the Novel* 11, no. 1 (spring 1979): 3-22.

Analyzes the means by which Evelina learns to influence the men around her.

Bilger, Audrey. *Laughing Feminism: Subversive Comedy in Frances Burney, Maria Edgeworth, and Jane Austen.* Detroit: Wayne State University Press, 1998, 261 p.

Contends that women authors employed humor to inject their writings with a feminist subtext.

Bradbrook, Frank W. "The Feminist Tradition." In *Jane Austen and Her Predecessors,* pp. 90-119. Cambridge: Cambridge University Press, 1966.

Discusses Jane Austen's literary debt to Burney.

Brown, Martha G. "Fanny Burney's 'Feminism': Gender or Genre?" *Fettered or Free? British Women Novelists, 1670-1815,* pp. 29-39. Athens: Ohio University Press, 1986.

Argues that feminist tendencies in Burney's novels are less a reflection of her beliefs than a remnant of the romance tradition that inspired her work.

Campbell, Gina. "How to Read Like a Gentleman: Burney's Instructions to Her Critics in *Evelina.*" *ELH* 57, no. 3 (fall 1990): 557-83.

Evaluates how male characters "read" female characters, making them objectified texts.

Cecil, David. "Fanny Burney." In *Poets and Story-Tellers,* pp. 77-96. London: Constable, 1949.

Surveys Burney's career as having a place in the history of the novel.

Cutting, Rose Marie. "A Wreath for Fanny Burney's Last Novel: *The Wanderer*'s Contribution to Women's Studies." *Illinois Quarterly* 37, no. 3 (spring 1975): 45-64.

Asserts the importance of Burney's least acclaimed novel as a depiction of women's historic poverty.

———. "Defiant Women: the Growth of Feminism in Fanny Burney's Novels." *Studies in English Literature* 17 (1977): 519-30.

Discusses images of women in Burney's novels as heroines and rebels.

Cutting-Gray, Joanne. *Woman as 'Nobody' and the Novels of Fanny Burney.* Gainesville: University Press of Florida, 1992, 169 p.

Critiques the conventional connection between women and nature, or artlessness.

Doody, Margaret Anne. "Deserts, Ruins and Troubled Waters: Female Dreams in Fiction and the Development of the Gothic Novel." *Genre* 10, no. 4 (winter 1977): 529-72.

Discusses the significance of female dreams and madness in novels including Cecilia *and* Camilla.

Epstein, Julia. "Writing the Unspeakable: Fanny Burney's Mastectomy and the Fictive Body." *Representations* 16 (fall 1986): 131-66.

Discusses Burney's letter describing her mastectomy and her secrecy about the procedure.

———. *The Iron Pen: Frances Burney and the Politics of Women's Writing.* Madison: University of Wisconsin Press, 1989, 276 p.

Focuses on themes of violence in Burney's novels, interpreting them as instances of her own suppressed rage and evidence of an obsession with violence.

Fizer, Irene. "The Name of the Daughter: Identity and Incest in *Evelina.*" *Refiguring the Father: New Feminist Readings of Patriarchy* (1989): 78-107.

Interprets the novel as a crisis of the father figure due to the numerous paternal figures it portrays.

Hemlow, Joyce. "Fanny Burney and the Courtesy Books." *PMLA* 65, no. 5 (September 1950): 732-61.

Traces in Burney's novels the influence of contemporary conduct books.

Hilliard, Raymond F. "Laughter Echoing from Mouth to Mouth: Symbolic Cannibalism and Gender in *Evelina.*" *Eighteenth-Century Life* 17, no. 1 (February 1993): 46-61.

Psychoanalytic analysis of symbolic violence and its role in the creation and enforcement of gender identity.

Johnson, Claudia L. "Statues, Idiots, Automatons: *Camilla.*" In *Equivocal Beings: Politics, Gender, and Sentimentality in the 1790s: Wollstonecraft, Radcliffe, Burney, Austen,* pp. 141-64. Chicago: University of Chicago Press, 1995.

Proposes Burney's heroines as the novelist's ideal of feminine propriety.

Kowaleski-Wallace, Beth. "A Night at the Opera: The Body, Class, and Art in *Evelina* and Frances Burney's *Early Diaries.*" In *History, Gender and Eighteenth-Century Literature,* edited by Beth Fowkes Tobin, pp. 141-58. Athens: University of Georgia Press, 1994.

Argues that Evelina attempts to define herself in relation to others' misbehavior, viewing this practice as suggestive of Burney's own social ideology.

McMaster, Juliet. "The Silent Angel: Impediments to Female Expression in Frances Burney's Novels." *Studies in the Novel* 21, no. 3 (fall 1989): 235-52.

Interprets Burney's novels in terms of the difficulty of female self-expression.

Richetti, John. "Voice and Gender in Eighteenth-Century Fiction: Haywood to Burney." *Studies in the Novel* 19 (1987): 263-72.

Examines the narrative power Evelina develops through the satirical voice in her letters.

Rogers, Katharine M. "Fanny Burney: The Private Self and the Published Self." *International Journal of Women's Studies* 7, no. 2 (March-April 1984): 110-17.

Contends that Burney created her heroines to be less independent than Burney herself.

Spacks, Patricia Meyer. "Dynamics of Fear: Fanny Burney." In *Imagining a Self: Autobiography and Novel in Eightieth-Century England,* pp. 158-92. Cambridge: Harvard University Press, 1976.

Uses Burney's letters and diaries to support an autobiographical analysis of her novels, suggesting that the novels allowed Burney freer self-expression.

Staves, Susan. "*Evelina*; or, Female Difficulties." *Modern Philology* 73, no. 4 (May 1976): 368-81.

Contends that the focus of Evelina *is the heroine's powerful anxiety; emphasizes the psychological implications of the novel.*

Straub, Kristina. "Women's Pastimes and the Ambiguity of Female Self-Identification in Fanny Burney's *Evelina.*" *Eighteenth-Century Life* 10, no. 2 (May 1986): 58-72.

Examines Burney's discomfort with the ways women were told to spend their time; finds in Evelina *an attempt to separate female identity from trivial female pursuits.*

OTHER SOURCES FROM GALE:

Additional coverage of Burney's life and career is contained in the following sources published by the Gale Group: *British Writers Supplement,* Vol. 3; *Dictionary of Literary Biography,* Vol. 39; *Literature Resource Center; Nineteenth-Century Literature Criticism,* Vols. 12, 54, 107; *Novels for Students,* Vol. 16; *Reference Guide to English Literature,* Ed. 2; and *Twayne's English Authors.*

INDEXES

The main reference

Austen, Jane 1775-1817 **1:** 122, 125, 220; **2:** 104, 196, **333-384**

lists the featured author's entry in volumes 1, 2, 3, 5, or 6 of Feminism in Literature; *it also lists commentary on the featured author in other volumes of the set, which include topics associated with* Feminism in Literature. *Page references to substantial discussions of the author appear in boldface.*

The cross-references

See also AAYA 19; BRW 4; BRWC 1; BRWR 2; BYA 3; CD-BLB 1789-1832; DA; DA3; DAB; DAC; DAM MST, NOV; DLB 116; EXPN; LAIT 2; LATS 1; LMFS 1; NCLC 1, 13, 19, 33, 51, 81, 95, 119; NFS 1, 14, 18; TEA; WLC; WLIT 3; WYAS 1

list entries on the author in the following Gale biographical and literary sources:

AAL: Asian American Literature
AAYA: Authors & Artists for Young Adults
AFAW: African American Writers
AFW: African Writers
AITN: Authors in the News
AMW: American Writers
AMWR: American Writers Retrospective Supplement
AMWS: American Writers Supplement
ANW: American Nature Writers
AW: Ancient Writers
BEST: Bestsellers (quarterly, citations appear as Year: Issue number)
BG: The Beat Generation: A Gale Critical Companion
BLC: Black Literature Criticism
BLCS: Black Literature Criticism Supplement
BPFB: Beacham's Encyclopedia of Popular Fiction: Biography and Resources
BRW: British Writers
BRWS: British Writers Supplement
BW: Black Writers
BYA: Beacham's Guide to Literature for Young Adults
CA: Contemporary Authors
CAAS: Contemporary Authors Autobiography Series
CABS: Contemporary Authors Bibliographical Series
CAD: Contemporary American Dramatists
CANR: Contemporary Authors New Revision Series
CAP: Contemporary Authors Permanent Series
CBD: Contemporary British Dramatists
CCA: Contemporary Canadian Authors
CD: Contemporary Dramatists
CDALB: Concise Dictionary of American Literary Biography
CDALBS: Concise Dictionary of American Literary Biography Supplement
CDBLB: Concise Dictionary of British Literary Biography
CLC: Contemporary Literary Criticism
CLR: Children's Literature Review
CMLC: Classical and Medieval Literature Criticism
CMW: St. James Guide to Crime & Mystery Writers
CN: Contemporary Novelists
CP: Contemporary Poets
CPW: Contemporary Popular Writers
CSW: Contemporary Southern Writers
CWD: Contemporary Women Dramatists
CWP: Contemporary Women Poets
CWRI: St. James Guide to Children's Writers
CWW: Contemporary World Writers
DA: DISCovering Authors
DA3: DISCovering Authors 3.0
DAB: DISCovering Authors: British Edition
DAC: DISCovering Authors: Canadian Edition
DAM: DISCovering Authors: Modules
DRAM: Dramatists Module; *MST:* Most-Studied Authors Module;
MULT: Multicultural Authors Module; *NOV:* Novelists Module;
POET: Poets Module; *POP:* Popular Fiction and Genre Authors Module
DC: Drama Criticism
DFS: Drama for Students
DLB: Dictionary of Literary Biography
DLBD: Dictionary of Literary Biography Documentary Series
DLBY: Dictionary of Literary Biography Yearbook
DNFS: Literature of Developing Nations for Students
EFS: Epics for Students
EXPN: Exploring Novels
EXPP: Exploring Poetry
EXPS: Exploring Short Stories
EW: European Writers
FANT: St. James Guide to Fantasy Writers
FW: Feminist Writers

GFL: Guide to French Literature, Beginnings to 1789, 1798 to the Present
GLL: Gay and Lesbian Literature
HGG: St. James Guide to Horror, Ghost & Gothic Writers
HLC: Hispanic Literature Criticism
HLCS: Hispanic Literature Criticism Supplement
HR: Harlem Renaissance: A Gale Critical Companion
HW: Hispanic Writers
IDFW: International Dictionary of Films and Filmmakers: Writers and Production Artists
IDTP: International Dictionary of Theatre: Playwrights
LAIT: Literature and Its Times
LAW: Latin American Writers
JRDA: Junior DISCovering Authors
LC: Literature Criticism from 1400 to 1800
MAICYA: Major Authors and Illustrators for Children and Young Adults
MAICYA: Major Authors and Illustrators for Children and Young Adults Supplement
MAWW: Modern American Women Writers
MJW: Modern Japanese Writers
MTCW: Major 20th-Century Writers
NCFS: Nonfiction Classics for Students
NCLC: Nineteenth-Century Literature Criticism
NFS: Novels for Students
NNAL: Native North American Literature
PAB: Poets: American and British
PC: Poetry Criticism
PFS: Poetry for Students
RGAL: Reference Guide to American Literature
RGEL: Reference Guide to English Literature
RGSF: Reference Guide to Short Fiction
RGWL: Reference Guide to World Literature
RHW: Twentieth-Century Romance and Historical Writers
SAAS: Something about the Author Autobiography Series
SATA: Something about the Author
SFW: St. James Guide to Science Fiction Writers
SSC: Short Story Criticism
SSFS: Short Stories for Students
TCLC: Twentieth-Century Literary Criticism
TCWW: Twentieth-Century Western Writers
WCH: Writers for Children
WLC: World Literature Criticism, 1500 to the Present
WLCS: World Literature Criticism Supplement
WLIT: World Literature and Its Times
WP: World Poets
YABC: Yesterday's Authors of Books for Children
YAW: St. James Guide to Young Adult Writers

AUTHOR INDEX

The Author Index lists all of the authors featured in the Feminism in Literature *set. It includes references to the main author entries in volumes 1, 2, 3, 5, and 6; it also lists commentary on the featured author in other author entries and in other volumes of the set, which include topics associated with* Feminism in Literature. *Page references to author entries appear in boldface. The Author Index also includes birth and death dates, cross references between pseudonyms or name variants and actual names, and cross references to other Gale series in which the authors have appeared. A complete list of these sources is found facing the first page of the Author Index.*

A

Akhmatova, Anna 1888-1966 **5: 1–38**
See also CA 19-20; 25-28R; CANR 35; CAP 1; CLC 11, 25, 64, 126; DA3; DAM POET; DLB 295; EW 10; EWL 3; MTCW 1, 2; PC 2, 55; RGWL 2, 3

Alcott, Louisa May 1832-1888 **2:** 78, 147, **297–332**
See also AAYA 20; AMWS 1; BPFB 1; BYA 2; CDALB 1865-1917; CLR 1, 38; DA; DA3; DAB; DAC; DAM MST, NOV; DLB 1, 42, 79, 223, 239, 242; DLBD 14; FW; JRDA; LAIT 2; MAICYA 1, 2; NCLC 6, 58, 83; NFS 12; RGAL 4; SATA 100; SSC 27; TUS; WCH; WLCWYA; YABC 1; YAW

Allende, Isabel 1942- **5: 39–64**
See also AAYA 18; CA 125; 130; CANR 51, 74, 129; CDWLB 3; CLC 39, 57, 97, 170; CWW 2; DA3; DAM MULT, NOV; DLB 145; DNFS 1; EWL 3; FW; HLC 1; HW 1, 2; INT CA-130; LAIT 5; LAWS 1; LMFS 2; MTCW 1, 2; NCFS 1; NFS 6, 18; RGSF 2; RGWL 3; SSC 65; SSFS 11, 16; WLCS; WLIT 1

Angelou, Maya 1928- **5: 65–92**
See also AAYA 7, 20; AMWS 4; BLC 1; BPFB 1; BW 2, 3; BYA 2; CA 65-68; CANR 19, 42, 65, 111; CDALBS; CLC 12, 35, 64, 77, 155; CLR 53; CP 7; CPW; CSW; CWP; DA; DA3; DAB; DAC; DAM MST, MULT, POET, POP; DLB 38; EWL 3; EXPN; EXPP; LAIT 4; MAICYA 2; MAICYAS 1; MAWW; MTCW 1, 2; NCFS 2; NFS 2; PC 32; PFS 2, 3; RGAL 4; SATA 49, 136; WLCS; WYA; YAW

Atwood, Margaret (Eleanor) 1939- **5: 93–124**
See also AAYA 12, 47; AMWS 13; BEST 89:2; BPFB 1; CA 49-52; CANR 3, 24, 33, 59, 95; CLC 2, 3, 4, 8, 13, 15, 25, 44, 84, 135; CN 7; CP 7; CPW; CWP; DA; DA3; DAB; DAC; DAM MST, NOV, POET; DLB 53, 251; EWL 3; EXPN; FW; INT CANR-24; LAIT 5; MTCW 1, 2; NFS 4, 12, 13, 14; PC 8; PFS 7; RGSF 2; SATA 50; SSC 2, 46; SSFS 3, 13; TWA; WLC; WWE 1; YAW

Austen, Jane 1775-1817 **1:** 122, 125, 220; **2:** 104, 196, **333–384**
See also AAYA 19; BRW 4; BRWC 1; BRWR 2; BYA 3; CDBLB 1789-1832; DA; DA3; DAB; DAC; DAM MST, NOV; DLB 116; EXPN; LAIT 2; LATS 1; LMFS 1; NCLC 1, 13, 19, 33, 51, 81, 95, 119; NFS 1, 14, 18; TEA; WLC; WLIT 3; WYAS 1

B

Beauvoir, Simone (Lucie Ernestine Marie Bertrand) de 1908-1986 **5: 125–174**
See also BPFB 1; CA 9-12R; 118; CANR 28, 61; CLC 1, 2, 4, 8,

14, 31, 44, 50, 71, 124; DA; DA3; DAB; DAC; DAM MST, NOV; DLB 72; DLBY 1986; EW 12; EWL 3; FW; GFL 1789 to the Present; LMFS 2; MTCW 1, 2; RGSF 2; RGWL 2, 3; SSC 35; TWA; WLC

Brontë, Charlotte 1816-1855 **1:** 553; **2:** 17, 100, 133, 135, 177, 183–185, 198–202, **385–428**
See also AAYA 17; BRW 5; BRWC 2; BRWR 1; BYA 2; CDBLB 1832-1890; DA; DA3; DAB; DAC; DAM MST, NOV; DLB 21, 159, 199; EXPN; LAIT 2; NCLC 3, 8, 33, 58, 105; NFS 4; TEA; WLC; WLIT 4

Brontë, Emily (Jane) 1818-1848 **2: 429–466**
See also AAYA 17; BPFB 1; BRW 5; BRWC 1; BRWR 1; BYA 3; CDBLB 1832-1890; DA; DA3; DAB; DAC; DAM MST, NOV, POET; DLB 21, 32, 199; EXPN; LAIT 1; NCLC 16, 35; PC 8; TEA; WLC; WLIT 3

Brooks, Gwendolyn (Elizabeth) 1917-2000 **4:** 287–289; **5: 175–210**
See also AAYA 20; AFAW 1, 2; AITN 1; AMWS 3; BLC 1; BW 2, 3; CA 1-4R; 190; CANR 1, 27, 52, 75; CDALB 1941-1968; CLC 1, 2, 4, 5, 15, 49, 125; CLR 27; CP 7; CWP; DA; DA3; DAC; DAM MST, MULT, POET; DLB 5, 76, 165; EWL 3; EXPP; MAWW; MTCW 1, 2; PC 7; PFS 1, 2, 4, 6; RGAL 4; SATA 6; SATA-Obit 123; TUS; WLC; WP

Browning, Elizabeth Barrett 1806-1861 **1:** 429, 432, 439; **2: 467–502**
See also BRW 4; CDBLB 1832-1890; DA; DA3; DAB; DAC; DAM MST, POET; DLB 32, 199; EXPP; NCLC 1, 16, 61, 66; PAB; PC 6; PFS 2, 16; TEA; WLC; WLIT 4; WP

Burney, Fanny 1752-1840 **1:** 115–116, 122, 219, 224; **2: 503–539**
See also BRWS 3; DLB 39; NCLC 12, 54, 107; NFS 16; RGEL 2; TEA

C

Cather, Willa (Sibert) 1873-1947 **5: 211–252**
See also AAYA 24; AMW; AMWC 1; AMWR 1; BPFB 1; CA 104; 128; CDALB 1865-1917; DA; DA3; DAB; DAC; DAM MST, NOV; DLB 9, 54, 78, 256; DLBD 1; EWL 3; EXPN; EXPS; LAIT 3; LATS 1; MAWW; MTCW 1, 2; NFS 2; RGAL 4; RGSF 2; RHW; SATA 30; SSC 2, 50; SSFS 2, 7, 16; TCLC 1, 11, 31, 99, 132; TCWW 2; TUS; WLC

Chopin, Kate 1851-1904 **3: 1–46**
See also AAYA 33; AMWR 2; AMWS 1; BYA 11, 15; CA 104; 122; CDALB 1865-1917; DA; DAB; DA3; DAC; DAM MST, NOV; DLB 12, 78; EXPN; EXPS; FW; LAIT 3; MAWW; NFS 3; RGAL 4; RGSF 2; SSC 8, 68; SSFS 17; TCLC 127; TUS; WLCS

Christine de Pizan 1365(?)-1431(?) **1:** 39–40, 66–68, 84, 86, **281–320**
See also DLB 208; LC 9; RGWL 2, 3

Cisneros, Sandra 1954- **5: 253–284**
See also AAYA 9, 53; AMWS 7; CA 131; CANR 64, 118; CLC 69, 118; CWP; DA3; DAM MULT; DLB 122, 152; EWL 3; EXPN; FW; HLC 1; HW 1, 2; LAIT 5; LATS 1; LLW 1; MAICYA 2; MTCW 2; NFS 2; PC 52; PFS 19; RGAL 4; RGSF 2; SSC 32; SSFS 3, 13; WLIT 1; YAW

Cixous, Hélène 1937- **5: 285–312**
See also CA 126; CANR 55, 123; CLC 92; CWW 2; DLB 83, 242; EWL 3; FW; GLL 2; MTCW 1, 2; TWA

D

Dickinson, Emily (Elizabeth) 1830-1886 **2:** 408, 412; **3: 47–92**
See also AAYA 22; AMW; AMWR 1; CDALB 1865-1917; DA; DA3; DAB; DAC; DAM MST, POET; DLB 1, 243; EXPP; MAWW; NCLC 21, 77; PAB; PC 1; PFS 1, 2, 3, 4, 5, 6, 8, 10, 11, 13, 16; RGAL 4; SATA 29; TUS; WLC; WP; WYA

Doolittle, Hilda (H. D.) 1886-1961 **4:** 271–272, 287, 292–293; **5: 313–358**
See also AMWS 1; CA 97-100; CANR 35; CLC 3, 8, 14, 31, 34, 73; DA; DAC; DAM MST, POET; DLB 4, 45; EWL 3; FW; GLL 1; LMFS 2; MAWW; MTCW 1, 2; PC 5; PFS 6; RGAL 4; WLC

Duras, Marguerite 1914-1996 **5: 359–404**
See Donnadieu, Marguerite
See also BPFB 1; CA 25-28R; 151; CANR 50; CLC 3, 6, 11, 20, 34, 40, 68, 100; CWW 2; DLB 83; EWL 3; GFL 1789 to the Present; IDFW 4; MTCW 1, 2; RGWL 2, 3; SSC 40; TWA

Dworkin, Andrea 1946- **5: 405–416**
See also CA 77-80; CAAS 21; CANR 16, 39, 76, 96; CLC 43, 123; FW; GLL 1; INT CANR-16; MTCW 1, 2

E

Edgeworth, Maria 1768-1849 **3: 93–128**
See also BRWS 3; DLB 116, 159, 163; FW; NCLC 1, 51; RGEL 2; SATA 21; TEA; WLIT 3

Eliot, George 1819-1880 **2:** 100–108, 130, 133, 135–136, 138–139, 177–179, 182–186, 194–203, 398–399, 426; **3: 129–166**
See also BRW 5; BRWC 1, 2; BRWR 2; CDBLB 1832-1890; CN 7; CPW; DA; DA3; DAB; DAC; DAM MST, NOV; DLB 21, 35, 55; LATS 1; LMFS 1; NCLC 4, 13, 23, 41, 49, 89, 118; NFS 17; PC 20; RGEL 2; RGSF 2; SSFS 8; TEA; WLC; WLIT 3

Emecheta, (Florence Onye) Buchi 1944- **5: 417–432**
See also AFW; BLC 2; BW 2, 3; CA 81-84; CANR 27, 81, 126; CDWLB 3; CLC 14, 48, 128; CN 7; CWRI 5; DA3; DAM MULT; DLB 117; EWL 3; FW; MTCW 1, 2; NFS 12, 14; SATA 66; WLIT 2

Erdrich, Louise 1954- **5: 433–468**
See also AAYA 10, 47; AMWS 4; BEST 89:1; BPFB 1; CA 114; CANR 41, 62, 118; CDALBS; CLC 39, 54, 120, 176; CN 7; CP 7; CPW; CWP; DA3; DAM MULT, NOV, POP; DLB 152, 175, 206; EWL 3; EXPP; LAIT 5; LATS 1; MTCW 1; NFS 5; NNAL; PC 52; PFS 14; RGAL 4; SATA 94, 141; SSFS 14; TCWW 2

O

P

R

S

T

W

TITLE INDEX

The Title Index alphabetically lists the titles of works written by the authors featured in volumes 1, 2, 3, 5, and 6 of Feminism in Literature *and provides page numbers or page ranges where commentary on these titles can be found. English translations of foreign titles and variations of titles are cross referenced to the title under which a work was originally published. Titles of novels, dramas, nonfiction books, and poetry, short story, or essay collections are printed in italics; individual poems, short stories, and essays are printed in body type within quotation marks; page references to illustrations appear in italic.*

A

F

G

H

I

M

N

O

P

Q

R

S

T

U

V

W

X

Y

Z

SUBJECT INDEX

The Subject Index includes the authors and titles that appear in the Author Index and the Title Index as well as the names of other authors and figures that are discussed in the Feminism in Literature *set. The Subject Index also lists literary terms and topics covered in the criticism, as well as in sidebars. The index provides page numbers or page ranges where subjects are discussed and is fully cross referenced. Page references to significant discussions of authors, titles, or subjects appear in boldface; page references to illustrations appear in italic.*

A

SUBJECT INDEX

B

SUBJECT INDEX

C

SUBJECT INDEX

D

SUBJECT INDEX

E

F

SUBJECT INDEX

G

I

J

K

L

SUBJECT INDEX

M

SUBJECT INDEX

Q

R

S

SUBJECT INDEX

SUBJECT INDEX

T

U

V

X

Y

Z